THE BETTER PART

A CHRIST-CENTERED RESOURCE
for
PERSONAL PRAYER

BY FR JOHN BARTUNEK, LC

CIRCLE
PRESS

Press
ox 5425
iden, CT 06518-0425
w.circlepress.org

Cover image: iStock_000002399334Large.jpg
http://www.istockphoto.com

Mosaics: taken from the Basilica of St. Paul Outside the Walls, Rome

Cover and interior design by Rule29 Creative | www.rule29.com

Gospel text taken from *The Jerusalem Bible* by Alexander Jones, ed., copyright © 1966 by Darton, Longman & Todd, Ltd. and Doubleday, a division of Random House, Inc. Used by permission of Doubleday, a division of Random House, Inc.

Imprimi Potest:
Francisco Mateos, LC

Nihil Obstat
Imprimatur
† Most Reverend Henry J. Mansell
Archbishop of Hartford
June 14, 2007

ISBN: 1-933271-10-8

Printed in China

10 9 8 7 6 5 4 3

The
BETTER PART

A CHRIST-CENTERED RESOURCE
for
PERSONAL PRAYER

INTRODUCTION

THE IMPORTANCE OF PERSONAL PRAYER

Conscientious Christians pray. Their typical days, weeks, months, and years are seasoned with prayer – traditional prayers, liturgical prayers, spontaneous prayers. They make prayer commitments, giving structure and consistency to their faith journey. Prayer keeps Christians united to the Vine, so their lives can bear the fruit both they and Christ long for.[1]

Among the most basic prayer commitments is one that can have more bearing on your life than any other, because it is more personalized: the daily meditation. Certainly you can't mature as a Christian without the sacramental life, just as crops can't mature without sunlight and soil. And the various devotional and vocal prayers that punctuate your day keep you strong and focused amid the unrelenting blows of the unchristian culture all around you. But, as generations of saints and sinners have found out, that is not enough.

Without the daily renewal and deepening of your personal relationship with Jesus Christ that happens especially through meditation, sooner or later routine sets in. You get into a rut. Your prayers get mechanical, your sacramental life slides into hollow ritualism, and before you know it, your faith gets sidelined and you get dragged back into the rat race in some form or other. The daily meditation keeps your faith, that pearl of great price,[2] lively, supple, and relevant. It irrigates the soil of your soul, making your sacramental life more fruitful, keeping your other prayer commitments meaningful, and continually opening up new vistas along the path to spiritual maturity.

This is why spiritual writers through the ages have so consistently emphasized the importance of meditation, also known as mental prayer, since it is a deeply interior way of praying. Here is what two doctors of the Church have to say about it:

He who neglects mental prayer needs not a devil to carry him to hell, but he brings himself there with his own hands.

- St Theresa of Avila

It is morally impossible for him who neglects meditation to live without sin.

- St Alphonsus Ligouri

---

[1] "I am the vine, and you are the branches. He who dwells in me, as I dwell in him, bears much fruit; for apart from me you can do nothing" (John 15:5).

[2] "Again, the kingdom of Heaven is like a merchant looking for fine pearls; when he finds one of great value he goes and sells everything he owns and buys it" (Matthew 13:45-46).

And by experience we see that many persons who recite a great number of vocal prayers, the Office and the Rosary, fall into sin, and continue to live in sin. But he who attends to mental prayer scarcely ever falls into sin, and should he have the misfortune of falling into it, he will hardly continue to live in so miserable a state; he will either give up mental prayer, or renounce sin. Meditation and sin cannot stand together. However abandoned a soul may be, if she perseveres in meditation, God will bring her to salvation.

- St Alphonsus Ligouri

The daily meditation, in other words, is not an optional extra for super-Christians; it's every Christian's bread and butter. Without it, your Christian identity shrivels. But it's not enough just to do a daily meditation; you need to learn to do it better and better. Maturity in the spiritual life depends to a great extent on constantly going deeper in your personal prayer life. The law of life is growth, so if your capacity for mental prayer isn't growing, your life with Christ is in danger of wasting away.[3]

THE BENEFITS OF THE BETTER PART

The Better Part is meant to foster and accompany growth in mental prayer. It is not primarily instructional (like a "how-to" book on prayer), and not complete in itself (like ready-made meditations). Rather, *The Better Part* is a companion for your daily meditation, providing enough structure and content to serve as a catalyst for you to learn to pray better as you pray, to make your meditation more personal and personalized, to help you learn to follow the Holy Spirit's lead more readily.

Used well, *The Better Part* helps you discover at least three things:

1. HOW YOU PRAY BEST. Prayer is similar to walking. To walk, everyone has to follow the same principles of physics – friction, gravity, muscle propulsion, momentum. And yet, even though the principles are the same, everyone's walk is a little bit different. When babies learn to walk, they start out clumsy and awkward, until they develop the rhythm and style proper to their body type, personality, and environment. Meditation follows a similar pattern: the same principles for all, activated uniquely by each. *The Better Part* can help you wherever you happen to be on the spectrum.

---

[3]*This intensely personal prayer – the Christian meditation – contributes significantly to the communal life of the Church. As our personal friendship with Christ develops, we become more mature and fruitful members of his Body, the Church. Therefore, although this book focuses on the personal encounter with Christ in meditation, it does not mean to belittle the ecclesial nature of the Christian vocation. The two aspects are complementary and intertwined.*

2. **THE DIMENSIONS OF CHRIST** (his characteristics, actions, words, sufferings) that speak most profoundly to your soul. The heart of Christianity is each believer's friendship with Jesus Christ, and friendship is never generic. If you read the lives of the saints, you quickly discover how each one's holiness has its own, unique flavor – St Francis' friendship with Christ was different than St Dominic's, because St Francis and St Dominic were different. Every person has a unique personality, so each person will relate to Christ uniquely. God created you to know him as only you can know him. *The Better Part* is designed to help you uncover and develop the distinctiveness of your friendship with Christ, without which you will always feel more restless and dissatisfied than you need to.

3. **THE INESTIMABLE VALUE OF A DEEP PRAYER LIFE.** Every Christian has a responsibility to become an expert in prayer. Without a mature prayer life, you cannot become a mature Christian, in which case you will never discover the authentic Christian joy, wisdom, and fruitfulness that flow from being fully formed in Christ.[4] This expertise in prayer comes only from the Holy Spirit, who uses two training methods:

First, he instructs you in prayer through the experience of others. Through the ages, the Church and its saints have produced a whole library of accessible, practical, and inspiring books on prayer. You'll want to read them and study them. All Christians who take their friendship with Christ seriously should regularly read good books (and plenty of good articles) on prayer or the spiritual life.[5] *The Better Part* is not one of these treatises on prayer, but Part 1: The Fundamentals of Christian Meditation will serve as a refresher course on the central principles of Christian meditation, something you can refer to in order to keep your meditation in shape.

Second, the Holy Spirit makes you an expert in prayer when you actually pray. You need to dive into the pool and splash around so that your coach can teach you to swim. Here *The Better Part* is a valuable tool. Instead of supplying you with spiritual reflections gleaned from others' experience of God in prayer, as many spiritual books do so well, this is a truly Christ-centered resource, purposely open-ended, but in a strategically structured way. Each

---

[4] *"My dear children, for whom I am again in the pains of childbirth until Christ is formed in you…"* (Galatians 4:19); *"…to build up the Body of Christ, until we all reach unity in faith and knowledge of the Son of God and form the perfect man, fully mature with the fullness of Christ himself. If we live by the truth and in love, we shall grow completely into Christ"* (Ephesians 4: 12-13, 15). Emphasis added.
[5] *See the Appendix for a list of excellent books on prayer and the spiritual life.*

unit in *The Better Part* will thus serve as a springboard for your own praying, a way to aid your docility to the Holy Spirit's coaching (Part I: The Fundamentals of Christian Meditation explains more fully how this works).

And so, if you are just starting out in Christian meditation, *The Better Part* can help you lay a firm foundation. If you are already adept at mental prayer, its open-ended, Christ-centered structure makes it a rich and flexible source of meditation material. It is perhaps most helpful, however, for those who would label themselves neither beginners nor advanced, but somewhere in between.

Many Christians – even committed, well-formed Christians – reach a plateau in their prayer life because their meditation stays at the level of reflective spiritual reading, even when their soul is ready to go higher (this distinction is explained more fully later). *The Better Part*, used rightly, can help foster this move forward.

The rest of this Introduction will explain how *The Better Part* is composed and organized. It will show how to make this book a tool for knowing, loving, and following Christ more wholeheartedly, which is what God is hoping for, your soul is thirsting for, and all prayer is striving for. Then, Part 1: The Fundamentals of Christian Meditation will review in detail the fundamental principles, steps, and difficulties of Christian meditation, and it will equip you to do a check-up on your own prayer life. The rest of the book contains the actual meditation units.

Be forewarned – *The Better Part* is not necessarily the easier part. Christ never promised that following him would be easy. In fact, he promised it wouldn't. The spiritual life is full of mystery. You find yourself on unfamiliar ground when you trust God to lead you to richer pastures. Often it is much more comfortable to keep doing what you already know how to do, like Martha, who busied herself in the kitchen when Jesus and the apostles dropped by for dinner. Her sister Mary put normal activities on hold for a little while instead, and sat at Jesus' feet, drinking in his wisdom, his love, and his beauty. When Martha complained that Mary was being lazy and impractical, Jesus smiled at her and said:

"Martha, Martha. You worry and fret about so many things, and yet few are needed, indeed only one. It is Mary who has chosen the better part, and it is not to be taken from her" (Luke 10:41-42).

HOW TO USE *THE BETTER PART*

No book can pray for you. No book can teach you to pray. At most, a book can be a useful tool. *The Better Part* is designed to help you engage more actively in the quest of Christian meditation so you can reap more fruits of spiritual growth.

The Better Part is divided into units. Each unit consists of five parts: a passage from the Gospels and a four-part commentary based on the same four themes throughout the book: Christ the Lord, Christ the Teacher, Christ the Friend, and Christ in My Life. This structure is substantive, meditative, and flexible.

SUBSTANTIVE: A CHRIST-CENTERED RESOURCE *The Better Part* is substantive because it is eminently Christ-centered. Christ is the "power of God and the wisdom of God" (1 Cor 1:24). The gospel is the good news of the "boundless riches" (Eph 3:8) of Christ. The Christian life consists in knowing, loving, and imitating Christ. He is God made man – "for the sake of our salvation," as the Creed puts it. You will never be able to exhaust the Gospels. They are the heart of the Bible and the privileged place of God's revelation. The Old Testament was a preparation for the revelation of the mystery of Christ, and the rest of the New Testament shows the consequences and flowering of this revelation. The Church has always taught that because Christ is God as well as man, all of his words and actions as recorded in the Gospels are not merely edifying events from the past. Christ spoke and lived them with you in mind, so that they are alive and relevant and addressed to you and the circumstances of your life at every moment: "Jesus Christ is the same yesterday and today and forever" (Heb 13:8).

This eminently Christ-centered approach derives especially from the spirituality characterizing the Legionaries of Christ and the Regnum Christi Movement.[6] This spirituality, one of the many fragrant blossoms in the Church's rich garden of charisms, imbues the entire book.

At times in your spiritual journey you may find other sources more stimulating and helpful for your personal prayer, but after each such sojourn you will feel yourself drawn back to the Gospels, the living Word of God, the life, words, actions, passion, death, and resurrection of our Lord and Savior, the inexhaustible fountain of the Christian life:

---

[6]*For more information on the Legionaries of Christ and the Regnum Christi Movement, visit www. legionariesofchrist.org and www.regnumchristi.org.*

"In the beginning was the Word… Through him all things were made; without him nothing was made that has been made. In him was life, and that life was the light of men… grace and truth came through Jesus Christ. No one has ever seen God. It is God the only Son, who is close to the Father's heart, who has made him known" (John 1:1, 3-4, 17-18).

MEDITATIVE: A PRAYER-INDUCING COMMENTARY ON THE GOSPELS *The Better Part* is meditative because the commentaries are drawn from the Gospel passages themselves and point back to them. They do not develop an instructional treatise on the spiritual life, nor do they focus on biblical exegesis or catechetical apologetics. Those themes are addressed only to help the magnificent figure of Christ emerge more clearly.

The four-part commentaries on each Gospel passage follow the same structure, which is based on the faculties of the human soul. Thus, each unit helps bring the whole person into contact with Christ.

The "Christ the Lord" commentary points out how a particular passage illuminates Christ's mission and qualities as Savior, Redeemer, and Eternal King. It appeals most directly to the will, the faculty by which you make the decisions that direct your life. As you contemplate more and more the grandeur and splendor of Christ the Savior and King, your decision to follow him unconditionally grows firmer and firmer.

The "Christ the Teacher" commentary draws out the lessons that Christ teaches by word and example, appealing more directly to the intellect. You cannot live out your desire and decision to follow Christ if you don't know the standards and criteria of thought, speech, and behavior that Christ asks of his disciples.

The "Christ the Friend" commentary brings out the intimate and personal love of Christ's heart. Jesus doesn't want to be a distant Savior and Leader; he longs to be your companion and most intimate friend, and he shows this longing over and over again in the Gospels. This commentary appeals to your heart, so that your discipleship grows in passion, intimacy, and warmth as well as determination and wisdom.[7]

The "Christ in My Life" commentary (mostly written in the first person) consists of observations and questions in the form of prayers that help you evaluate how you should follow Christ in light of the passage you are meditating on.

---

[7]*Sometimes this commentary includes paragraphs written in such a way that Jesus or others are speaking in the first person. This literary technique is designed to stimulate fresh encounters with familiar passages, not to revise Catholic doctrine.*

This is a safety net: if for some reason your reflections up to that point have stayed too abstract, this section will bring Christ's light to bear on your own life, behavior, and attitudes, provoking a fresh conversion and recommitment to Christ. This commentary will also help ensure that your spiritual life goes beyond mere feelings and good dispositions to become truly transforming.

The quotations from saints and popes that introduce each chapter of the Gospels and each meditation unit can also spark reflection. They add spice to the commentaries by giving glimpses into the deep experience of Christ had by your older brothers and sisters in the faith.

Each unit in *The Better Part*, then, facilitates bringing your will, mind, heart, and life into contact with Christ, helping you bathe your soul in his truth and his grace. The entire series has only one aim: to help you know, love, and follow Christ more closely by encountering him more deeply and personally in prayer.

FLEXIBLE: THEMES AND VARIATIONS *The Better Part* is flexible because it can be used in so many ways – it is not a book of meditations, but a resource for personal prayer.

At the end of the book you will find two detailed indexes. The first index lists the units in the order in which their Gospel passages appear throughout the liturgical cycle. The second lists them in relation to some pivotal virtues of the spiritual life. Thus this resource can be used in numerous ways, depending on your personal needs and preferences.

You may want to have your meditations follow the liturgical cycle, in which case you can bookmark that index, and use the ribbon to mark each day's unit. In this plan, it will be useful to include in your Consider stage (the second step of your meditation) some reflections on how the passage ties in to the spirit of the liturgical season.

You may prefer to coordinate your meditations with the needs of your own spiritual life, in accord with your program of spiritual work. For a Christian, growth in virtue never occurs simply through one's own effort; you become more like Christ by contemplating Christ, opening your heart to his grace, loving him more, and being moved to imitate him within the circumstances of your own life. In this case, you can keep the ribbon on the thematic index and bookmark whichever unit you happen to be meditating on.

You may choose to take a chronological approach and meditate on one of the

Gospels, from start to finish, simply seeking to know, love, and follow Christ more closely. This is an excellent way to organize your meditations during Ordinary Time, for example.

You can also combine *The Better Part* with other meditation material, alternating between Gospel passages and spiritual books, or using a Gospel passage and one of its commentaries from *The Better Part* as the first point of consideration, a paragraph from another source as the second point, and so on.

The Better Part is also a good resource if you have a commitment to do a daily Gospel reflection in addition to a morning meditation.

MEDITATING WITH *THE BETTER PART* However you choose to arrange your meditation themes (and this is a good topic to discuss with a confessor or spiritual director), always keep in mind the difference between spiritual reading and meditation.

If you were to use *The Better Part* for spiritual reading or a daily Gospel reflection, you would simply read an entire unit or two straight through each day – a helpful and beneficial spiritual exercise.

Meditating on a unit, however, requires a different approach. In this case, each part of the unit is treated separately, like five connected rooms in an art gallery. During the Consider and Converse stages of your meditation, you spend plenty of time in one room before moving on to the next.

Start with the Gospel passage itself. You take enough time to enter into the scene with your imagination, with your mind, searching for whatever God has to say to you in that passage. You may find a word or phrase or characteristic in the Gospel passage itself that is sufficient material for consideration and conversation for the entire meditation. The next day, you begin there again, and you may find that the Holy Spirit wants you to stay with the same point and continue to savor it. This is ideal, because it means that your prayer is intensely personal – direct contact between you and the Gospels, with the Holy Spirit setting the pace.

When you are ready, either in the same meditation or the next day, you move on to the first commentary. You read it and consider it calmly, inquiringly. The main point of the commentary may strike you and become the matter of further conversation and consideration, or a tangential point may pop out at you. The commentary may bring you right back into the Gospel passage, showing you something that you hadn't noticed before. Here again, your search for what

13

Christ has to tell you proceeds at a more meditative pace than spiritual reading – there is no rush; you take your time and seek out what the Holy Spirit has to say to you.

Just one of the commentaries may occupy an entire meditation, or even two or three meditations, or on the other hand, it may take only a minute or two. Whenever you are ready, you move on to the next commentary, into the next room of the gallery, continuing to search for whatever nourishment God has ready for your soul.

If you find yourself regularly spending more than one day with the same unit, try going back to the Gospel passage each day at the start of your meditation, before moving on to the next commentary. Thus, your first point each day is the Gospel passage, then you move on to the first commentary; the next day you start again with the Gospel passage, then move right to the second commentary, and so on. God's Word really is the privileged place for your encounter with him.

Feel free to write in the margins and mark certain passages or units that speak to you in a special way. All Christians should have their favorite Gospel passages, the ones they go back to again and again to feed their souls. In fact, since *The Better Part* is built on the Gospels themselves, it is a resource that can be used over and over again, through the years.

As a resource for meditation, then, *The Better Part* affords you both substantive structure (Gospel commentaries directed to your will, intellect, and heart) and flexibility. You should feel no pressure to go at any particular pace. One unit a day is more than enough material for a twenty-minute meditation done well, or even for thirty or sixty minutes. You may find yourself drawn to stay with the same unit for a few days, working through it slowly. Try your best to follow along, however the Holy Spirit guides you. What matters is that your prayer life deepen and your friendship with Christ grow – not that you finish this book in record time.

The Meditation Guide found on the front and back flaps of the cover will remind you of the different steps in your meditation, arming you to fight against distractions, tiredness, and inertia as you take up and engage in the battle of prayer each day.

SMALL GROUP USE *The Better Part,* though primarily a resource for personal prayer, also can be adapted for use in small groups. It is more spiritual than instructional, but its Christ-centered character can make it rewarding as a change of pace from typical Bible study guides or Catechism studies.

A prayer group that meets each week, for instance, may use *The Better Part* throughout a liturgical season (following the liturgical index), or for a few weeks before a particular event (a pilgrimage, convention, or local Feast Day), or when they want to get a Christ-centered perspective on a particular aspect of the spiritual or moral life (following the thematic index), or as the regular material for their first meeting of every month. It can also be used in this way for breakout activities during retreats or weekend conferences.

In any of these instances, the small group can read through the Gospel passage and commentaries together, a different member reading each paragraph out loud. Then the members of the group can reflect on the passage together, discussing what strikes them and what applications it has to their own lives. To facilitate this type of use, suggested questions for small group discussion and references to the Catechism finish off each unit. These can be skipped when the book is being used by individuals.

Now that you understand the approach and usefulness of *The Better Part*, you can start using the meditation units (Part 2) immediately. Eventually, however, you may want to take some time to read over Part 1: The Fundamentals of Christian Meditation. If you feel called to go deeper in your personal prayer life, a review of Part 1, with its explanation of the fundamentals of Christian prayer and meditation, could be just the kick-start you need.

PART 1:
THE FUNDAMENTALS
OF CHRISTIAN MEDITATION

GOD'S IDEA OF PRAYER

What do you picture yourself doing when you start to pray? What image, conscious or not, do you have in mind? Maybe you see yourself merely fulfilling a duty, as when you mechanically recited the Pledge of Allegiance at the start of homeroom in elementary school. Maybe you see prayer as an exercise in self-mastery and self-help, an activity – like yoga, aerobics, or weightlifting – that keeps you fit. Whatever you *think* you are doing when you pray affects the *way* in which you do it. So the more your idea of prayer matches God's, the better.

Prayer at its most basic level is conversation with God. This seems obvious, but it harbors an awesome reality. To converse with someone implies that that someone wants to pay attention to you, otherwise you have a monologue, not a conversation. The mere existence of prayer, then, implies that God is paying attention, that he is interested in spending time with you. Christian prayer is an invitation from God to the one who prays – it starts with God, not with you.

The whole Christian edifice is built on this simple but awe-inspiring reality. The Catechism highlights it in its very first numbers: "At every time and in every place, God draws close to man... God never ceases to draw man to himself" (1, 27). God is always drawing close to you, and he is always drawing you closer to him. That means he is always thinking of you, just like the Good Shepherd who is always thinking of and watching over his sheep. Prayer starts here.

You are the lost and hungry sheep; God is the shepherd who knows what you desire and need and is guiding you to the lush fields and cool, refreshing waters of his Truth and Love. The shepherd sees the big picture, the whole landscape, the weather, the seasons, the dangers and the opportunities; the sheep can only focus on this little patch of grass here, and then that one over there. Prayer is the Good Shepherd, wise and loving, guiding the hungry, shortsighted, and needy sheep.

God is the real protagonist of Christian prayer. Prayer is the soul's response to God's initiative. The essence of Christian prayer is relationship. As the Catechism puts it:

> "Great is the mystery of the faith!"... This mystery, then, requires that the faithful believe in it, that they celebrate it, and that they live from it in a vital and personal relationship with the living and true God. *This relationship is prayer* (2558, emphasis added).

Prayer, then, is more than just a dry religious duty, more than self-centered and self-sufficient self-help techniques; Christian prayer is a friendship with God in Christ. It's being led by the Good Shepherd to ever richer pastures in the Father's Kingdom.[1]

CHRISTIAN PRAYER: EMINENTLY CHRIST-CENTERED What matters most in prayer, then, is docility to that Good Shepherd, listening honestly, and responding honestly. God is already at work; you have only to hear and heed his voice. So how does he speak to you?

> At various times in the past and in various different ways, God spoke to our ancestors through the prophets; but in our own time, the last days, he has spoken to us through his Son, the Son that he has appointed to inherit everything and through whom he made everything there is. He is the radiant light of God's glory and the perfect copy of his nature, sustaining the universe by his powerful command… That is why all you who are holy brothers and have had the same heavenly call should *turn your minds to Jesus,* the apostle and the high priest of our religion (Heb 1:1-3, 3:1, emphasis added).

Christian prayer consists of that "turning your minds to Jesus," the Jesus who comes to us through the revelation of the Gospels, the good news of the "boundless riches" (Eph 3:8) of Christ.

The riches of Christ are boundless because Christ is God-revealing-himself-to-man, and God is infinite. If you want to get to know someone, it is not enough to learn *about* him from the outside; he has to open his mind and heart to you so that you can really get to know *him*, his thoughts and desires, his yearnings, his way of seeing things, his concerns. Interpersonal knowledge, the knowledge of friendship, can only come through personal revelation. Christ is God-revealing-himself-to-you, offering you his friendship.

Only Christianity is so bold as to claim that in Christ we can become God's friends, because only Christianity offers a God who becomes man, a Good Shepherd who becomes a lamb in order to win the hearts of his sheep:

> I shall not call you servants any more, because a servant does not know his master's business; I call you friends, because I have made known to you everything I have learnt from my Father (John 15:15).

True Christian prayer, therefore, is Christ-centered prayer. Above all, it consists

---

1.This definition of prayer – as an ongoing relationship – doesn't eliminate the need for particular times dedicated to conversing exclusively with God. There's no better way to make a relationship grow cold than by not spending quality time together. As the Catechism puts it, "… we cannot pray 'at all times' if we do not pray at specific times, consciously willing it." (2697)

in contemplating and conversing with Christ, the "one Mediator" between man and God (1 Tim 2:5). In prayer you sit at the feet of the Master, listening, learning, and loving. Prayer comes before action; the active life, for a Christian, overflows from the contemplative life. Christ taught this clearly when he gently reprimanded the busy and active Martha for resenting her sister Mary's preference for *the better part*.[2]

CHRISTIAN PRAYER: INTENSELY PERSONAL But Christian prayer is also intensely personal. This friendship that God has struck up with you is unique, because you are unique. Christ is not an abstract concept; he is a real person. Your friendship with him will be different than mine, because your life experience, your personality, your problems and talents and worries and dreams are different from mine, and all those things go into a friendship.

In prayer, the Good Shepherd calls his sheep individually: "… one by one he calls his own sheep and leads them out. When he has brought out his flock, he goes ahead of them, and the sheep follow because they know his voice" (John 10:3-4).

Prayer is Christ speaking to you in your heart, revealing himself to you in accordance with what he knows you need to discover, to know, to see. At the same time, prayer is your attentive listening to that revelation, your response to what he reveals, and the trusting, reciprocal revelation of your heart – your needs, your hopes, your desires – to him.

In this mysterious, beautiful exchange, the Holy Spirit is the bridge between Christ's heart and yours: "Now instead of the spirit of the world, we have received the Spirit that comes from God, to teach us to understand the gifts that he has given us" (1 Cor 2:12). The Holy Spirit guides you from within, into the arms of Christ, the Good Shepherd of your soul.

If you want to continue to discover and follow God's path for your life, this intensely personal prayer is a necessary element in your spiritual life. While you are here on earth, God always has more he wants to reveal to you and teach you; he has more he wants to do in your soul, making it the masterpiece that he envisioned from the moment of your creation. He also has more work he wants you to do, work that will bear eternal fruit to his glory and to your temporal and everlasting happiness. All of this, however, requires that you grow closer to him, and without a deep, personal prayer life, you simply can't.

---

[2] *"Martha, Martha, you worry and fret about so many things, and yet few are needed, indeed only one. It is Mary who has chosen **the better part**; it is not to be taken from her"* (Luke 10:42, emphasis added).

TYPES OF PRAYER

The Catechism points out three basic types of personal (as distinct from liturgical) prayer: vocal, meditative, and contemplative, all of which have a place in the life of every Christian.

VOCAL PRAYER Vocal prayer consists in reciting ready-made prayers, either silently or aloud, uniting the intention of your heart to the meaning of the words. This is the kind of prayer recited together before a meal, or the prayers often used each morning to offer the day to God. The words of these prayers help you express your faith, and that conscious expression in turn reinforces and exercises your faith. All Christians should have their favorite vocal prayers, the ones that resonate best with their own experience of Christ, the ones they can go back to in moments of dryness, sickness, or difficulty.

MEDITATIVE PRAYER Meditative prayer is less formulaic. It consists in lifting the heart and mind to God through focused reflection on some truth of God's revelation. It involves the intellect, the imagination, the memory, the emotions – the whole person.

In meditation, as you turn your gaze to God's self-revelation in Christ, you are moved to respond to what you discover there, and you converse with God in the silence of your own heart, using words that flow naturally from your reflection.

Reflecting on the beauty of God's creation, for example, may move your heart to expressions of gratitude, wonder, and praise. Reflecting on the sufferings of Christ during his crucifixion may move your heart to expressions of humility, repentance, or sorrow. The essence of Christian meditation is this exchange between God and the soul, this intimate conversation that can take an infinite variety of forms.

Whatever form it takes, however, meditation puts the soul in contact with the eternal truths, with the love and goodness of God in its myriad manifestations, and thus it *nourishes* the soul. Just as the body needs food and water, the soul feeds on truth and love. This reality is categorically ignored by today's secularized, materialistic culture, which denies the existence of moral and spiritual truth and reduces love to mere feelings. Meditative prayer, however, only makes sense in light of this reality. Your soul, your intellect, and your will yearn for the true and the good as much as your body yearns for solid food and fresh drink. "Happy those who hunger and thirst for what is right: they shall be satisfied" (Matthew 5:6).

Meditation's loving dialogue between God and you praying in Christ opens your soul to experience the highest, most nourishing truth of all: the total, transforming, unconditional love with which God himself regards you. This experience literally feeds the soul, enlivening its own capacity for love, energizing it, and inspiring it.

Meditative prayer, then, exercises the great Christian virtues of faith, hope, and love, helping the soul that has been wounded by sin, both original and personal, to rehabilitate its capacity to discover, experience, and communicate God's own truth, goodness, and beauty.

Christian meditation differs essentially from transcendental meditation and other New Age centering techniques.[3] Christian meditation is Christ-centered, a loving dialogue between Christ and the soul that deepens your friendship with Christ. It starts with the Holy Spirit urging you to pursue a greater knowledge and love of Christ, and ends with your renewed commitment to follow and imitate Christ in the unique circumstances of your daily life.

Transcendental meditation, on the other hand, is self-centered. Instead of a dialogue with God, an opening of the soul to God, it consists primarily in calming the many passions of the soul, creating a self-induced interior tranquility and focus that overflows in certain types of feelings. The goal of transcendental meditation is to withdraw from the complexities of life in order to experience emotional tranquility; the goal of Christian meditation is to know, love, and follow Jesus Christ more completely, to discover and embrace God's will for you more and more each day.

CONTEMPLATIVE PRAYER Contemplative prayer consists of a more passive (and more sublime) experience of God. If meditation is the soul's inspired quest to discover God, contemplation is God's lifting of the soul into himself, so that it effortlessly basks in the divine light. It is the soul's silent gazing upon the grandeur of God.

---

[3]*Some Christian spiritualities have tried to adopt so-called centering prayer techniques from non-Christian sources. Although some of these techniques can be incorporated into the first stage of the meditation (Concentrate), they are unnecessary and can often be harmful. They frequently result in becoming ends in themselves; the one praying uses them to create certain higher emotional states, as if those states were the goal of prayer. Christian prayer is interpersonal; centering prayer is really no more than a technique for calming oneself. It originated in the context of eastern transcendental asceticism, and these techniques are ill-suited for Christian prayer. For a more complete discussion of this issue, see the Pontifical Council for Interreligious Dialogue's document from 3 February 2003, "Jesus Christ: The Bearer of the Water of Life," available on the Vatican Web site, www.vatican.va.*

Often meditation leads to contemplation – the line of demarcation is hazy. When you find yourself lifted into silent contemplation during your meditation, there is no need to fear. The practice of Christian meditation gradually purifies the heart and familiarizes it with the voice and the ways of God, so that little by little the soul is made more docile to the promptings of God, and God can reveal himself more and more completely.

All three types of prayer – vocal, meditative, and contemplative – put the Christian in contact with the grassy pastures and refreshing waters of God's grace. They are the sure paths along which the Good Shepherd faithfully leads his sheep.

MEDITATION VS. SPIRITUAL READING

The Better Part is not a book of meditations. Sometimes following ready-made meditations[4] is an excellent way to pray. The structure helps you stay focused, the content is sure to be healthy, and the easy access motivates you to keep up a regular prayer life. But ready-made meditations also have a disadvantage. They can become nothing more than spiritual reading.

Spiritual reading refers to reading texts – books, articles, homilies, essays – that teach you about the spiritual life; it's like taking a class from whoever wrote the book. It enlightens your conscience by helping you see yourself and the world around you from a Christian perspective. As such, it is an essential ingredient for growth as a Christian. Just as historians are always reading about history, and teachers are always informing themselves about developments in pedagogy, so Christians should constantly be refining and expanding their understanding of how to be a follower of Christ.[5]

Christian meditation also involves an effort to better understand Christ and the Christian life, and so it often yields results similar to those of spiritual reading, especially for beginners in the spiritual life. Primarily, though, meditation is a matter of the heart more than the intellect; it's like taking a leisurely walk with Christ, your friend.

The focused reflection at the core of meditation opens the soul to hear not an abstract truth about the Christian life, but a particular word that God, the

---

[4] *Like those published daily through the Regnum Christi Web site, www.regnumchristi.org*
[5] *Regnum Christi members' daily Gospel Reflection falls into this category of spiritual reading. It keeps you constantly in touch with Christ's criteria and example, so that throughout the day you can keep aligning your thoughts, attitudes, and actions with Christ's. It's like rebooting your computer – it clears away the interior clutter that accumulates during the day.*

Good Shepherd, wishes to speak to you in the unique *here and now* of your life. When you tune into this word, this truth, this message from the Holy Spirit, your heart is drawn to stay with it, to consider it, to savor it. Savoring it in turn stirs your heart to express itself and give voice to your most intimate, personal yearnings, hopes, affections, or needs. In this conversation, you are actually *exercising* the Christian virtues of faith, hope, and love; you are exercising your friendship. In spiritual reading, you are learning, you are gaining knowledge. Both spiritual reading and meditation are useful – indeed, both are necessary for a healthy spiritual life – but it's important not to confuse them.

Although ready-made meditations have many advantages, they also have the disadvantage of easily morphing into spiritual reading. You lead a busy life with little time to prepare your daily meditation. You have committed to doing it, though, so you faithfully gather the daily meditation from the Web site and read it over in between errands or before speeding off to work. It keeps you in touch with spiritual things, and gives you new insights or renews old ones, but because it's a complete, self-contained meditation, you easily slip into the spiritual reading mode: instead of using the points of reflection as springboards for focused personal reflection, attentive listening to the Holy Spirit, and intimate, heart-to-heart conversation with Christ, you simply read, understand, agree, and move on.

Spiritual reading is valuable; it will help you grow closer to Christ. The Lord is happy that you make time for him. And yet, unless you learn to go deeper, to personalize your prayer more, you will limit your growth in virtue. God wants to make you into the saint he created you to be, but that requires a more personal, heart-to-heart prayer life. He wants to give you that grace, but he needs you to give him the chance.

The Better Part is a resource designed to help your personal prayer time become more personalized, increasingly deeper, and more transforming. Instead of offering ready-made meditations, it provides a structure for meditation along with Christ-centered commentaries that are more open-ended, more flexible, more personalized than complete meditations.

THE 4-STEP STRUCTURE OF YOUR MEDITATION

AN OVERVIEW Perhaps you are already familiar with the general meditation structure recommended in *The Better Part*. Drawn from the long-lasting and fruitful traditions of Ignatian and Carmelite spirituality, it follows four steps: *Concentrate, Consider, Converse, and Commit.*

Sometimes a meditation flows easily, following these steps one after another without a hitch. Other times tiredness, distractions, or temptations plague you so persistently that each step demands a heroic effort. Still other times, the steps blend together and your conversation with God happens almost spontaneously. This shows that the four-step method of meditation is not an end in itself, nor is it an arbitrary concoction. Rather, this method sets out the basic elements of any heart-to-heart conversation with God, as gleaned from experience and theology. In so doing, it provides a dependable framework for your personal encounter with God in spite of the persistent and sometimes almost overwhelming obstacles to prayer that surface.

At first you may find it awkward to follow the steps. You may feel tempted to fall back into the less demanding pattern of spiritual reading, but as your prayer life deepens, this simple structure becomes second nature. When kids first learn to play basketball, they have to master the basic skills – dribbling, shooting, passing – one at a time. As they improve, they develop the ability to combine these fundamentals into a smooth, seamless whole. Eventually they are free to really play. Assimilating the structure of your meditation happens a lot like that.

MAKING PROGRESS Keep in mind that growth in the spiritual life and in prayer takes time and consistent effort. Sometimes you may feel that you are making great progress; then suddenly you seem to have a relapse. Other times you may feel that you are making no progress at all, and then unexpectedly spring forward.

This isn't because God whimsically comes and goes. Rather, he is mysteriously guiding you through a gradual purification of the selfish tendencies deeply embedded in your soul. Points of view, emotional patterns, mental landscapes – all of these, because of original and personal sin, are shot through with myriad forms of self-centeredness that clog the flow of God's grace. Thus, learning to pray better is like turning a wild, overgrown plot of rocky ground into an ordered, fragrant, beautiful garden – God supplies the sunshine, the water, and the soil, but you still have to dig and plant and prune, and then keep on digging and planting and pruning…. Think of the four steps of the meditation as your gardening tools.

Understanding the reasons behind each step will help you follow them more peacefully and fruitfully. These steps can also be useful reference points as you discuss your prayer life during spiritual direction. A clear idea of these elements will make your ongoing reading about prayer more fruitful as well. Remember, every Christian should steadily strive to become an expert in prayer, since prayer is that "vital and personal relationship with the living and true God"[6] – the relationship which gives life itself and all of life's components their deepest, most authentic, and most satisfying meaning. Below is an explanation of each step. After the explanation you will find the full text of a real, sample meditation with all the steps identified.

STEP 1: CONCENTRATE

1. This involves drawing your attention away from the exterior activities and practical concerns that tend to monopolize your thoughts, and turning your attention to God, who is already paying full attention to you. You refresh your awareness of God's presence, which tends to be drowned out by the din of the daily grind.

2. Useful in this step are the traditional preparatory acts of faith, hope, and love, wherein you lift your heart and mind to God, tuning your attention to God's wavelength. You can use ready-made texts for your preparatory acts, compose your own, voice them spontaneously, or combine all three methods. *The Better Part* provides some sample preparatory acts. The morning prayers from your prayer book can make for good preparatory acts as well.

3. The most important part of this step is not the actual words you use. Rather, you need to remind yourself of the truths that underlie your relationship with God, reviving your most basic Christian attitudes. The goal of this step is fourfold:

    • *Recall that God is truly present*, listening to you, paying attention. Remember that God is all-powerful, all-wise, all-loving, and that he knows you intimately and cares for you more than you care for yourself. He deserves your praise, your attention, and your time.

    • *Recall that God has something he wants to say to you.* He has a word for you today. He knows what you are struggling with, in the short term and the long; he knows what the day will have in store for you; he knows the path he has marked out for your growth in happiness and holiness. He is going to work in your soul while you pray, whether you feel anything or not. Remember, your daily meditation isn't just your idea, it is a prayer commitment linked with your particular vocation in the Church, and your vocation

---

[6]*Catechism of the Catholic Church*, 2558

comes from God. You know without a doubt that God has something to say to you during this time, because he made the appointment.

- *Recall that you need to hear that word.* You are dependent on God for everything, starting with your existence. You have failed and sinned many times; the duties and mission you have in life are beyond your own natural capabilities; you are surrounded by morally and spiritually corrupting influences, by a variety of temptations… In short, you are a dependent, created being damaged by sin: you need God's grace.

- *Renew your desire to hear that word.* You want to follow him. You believe that he is the Lord, your Savior, your Friend, and your Guide. You have committed your life to him; you have put your trust in him.

4. In this context, part of your concentration will consist in asking God for the grace you feel you most need, in accordance with your program of spiritual work. Sometimes this is called the petition or the fruit of the meditation. Asking God for this grace brings all those basic attitudes into play. At the same time, however, you leave the reins in his hands, knowing that he will guide you in hidden ways to the rich pastures he has in store for you.

5. Whether you use your favorite traditional acts of faith, hope, and love to achieve this concentration matters less than simply achieving it. Sometimes it is enough to call to mind your favorite verse or Psalm from the Bible to activate all these sentiments; sometimes it's enough to remember the beauties of nature or one of your most powerful experiences of God.

6. As the weeks and months pass by, you may need to vary the way you concentrate, in order to avoid falling into a dry routine where you say all the right words, but in fact fail to turn your heart and mind to God. Without that, without concentrating on God, it will be nearly impossible for you to really enter into conversation with him and hear what he wants to tell you – your prayer will turn into a self-centered monologue or an empty, wordy shell.

7. At times these preparatory acts may launch you directly into a heart-to-heart conversation with the Lord, bypassing Step 2, *Consider*. When this happens, don't feel obliged to backtrack; the material of your preparatory acts has provided the Holy Spirit with all he needed to lift you right into Step 3, *Converse*.

8. Concentrating on God doesn't mean ignoring the realities of your life. Your worries and concerns and yearnings and dreams and challenges should all enter into your meditation. But they come into play within the context of your heart-to-heart conversation with the God who loves you. This is the difference between simply worrying and actually praying about something. When you sit down to have a cup of coffee with a close friend, your worries and dreams don't disappear, but they fall into line behind the attention you give to your friend, and the attention your friend gives to you.

9. Related to Step 1 is your choice of time and place for your daily meditation. These factors affect your ability to *Concentrate*.

   • *The time.* Most spiritual writers agree that doing your meditation in the morning helps imbue your coming day's activities with their true Christian meaning. Your mind is fresh, so it's easier to focus. And a morning meditation can give unity and direction to your daily duties by reminding you of your life's mission (to know, love, and follow Christ) and preparing you to meet the day's unexpected (or expected) challenges. With a little effort and creativity, you can usually make room for the morning meditation, whether it's ten, fifteen, twenty minutes, or even half an hour. (If you have any doubts about the proper length of your daily meditation, you should discuss them with a confessor or spiritual director.) If the morning is simply impossible, try to find some space in your day when you know you won't be interrupted – a time when you will be able to give your best to your prayer. Use the same time slot each day as much as possible. Try not to just squeeze it in; give your best time to God.

   • *The place.* Where you do your meditation should be out of range of interruptions and conducive to your conversation with God. Some people prefer their church or a chapel with the Blessed Sacrament; others prefer a particular room at home. Here again creativity and practical convenience come into play. A businessman in Boston stops at a cemetery on his way to work and does his meditation walking among the tombs and monuments (during the summer) – it's the only place where he can consistently dodge interruptions. Avoid changing places frequently in a vain search for the perfect atmosphere; the place doesn't make the prayer, it is only a means to help.

- *On special days or during certain periods* (e.g., vacation, Holy Week), you may find it helpful to change your normal place and time of prayer. Temporary, planned changes can keep you from falling into a dull routine.

10. If you habitually find it hard to concentrate at the start of your meditation, check on the status of your *remote* and *proximate* preparation. These terms refer to what you do outside of your meditation that affects what happens during your meditation.

   - *Remote preparation.* You don't meditate in a vacuum. The more you live in God's presence during the rest of day, seeking his will and finding other times here and there to pray (vocal prayers, the Rosary, examination of conscience), the easier it will be for you to turn your heart and soul to God at the start of the meditation. This is your remote preparation.

   - *Proximate preparation.* You will also avoid a plethora of distractions if you get your meditation materials (the book you will be using, your notebook or journal for writing down thoughts) ready the night before. You can even briefly look over the passage you will be meditating on before you go to bed; this too primes the prayer-pump. This is your proximate preparation.

11. Jesus himself explained the step of concentrating simply and vividly: "When you pray, go to your private room and, when you have shut your door, pray to your Father who is in that secret place, and your Father who sees all that is done in secret will reward you" (Mt 6:6). The prophet Elijah discovered this truth when the Lord spoke to him on the mountain:

   Then the Lord himself went by. There came a mighty wind, so strong it tore the mountains and shattered the rocks before the Lord. But the Lord was not in the wind. After the wind came an earthquake. But the Lord was not in the earthquake. After the earthquake came a fire. But the Lord was not in the fire. And after the fire there came the sound of a gentle breeze (1 Kings 19:11-12).

12. *Concentrate*, the first step of your meditation, involves shutting the door on the storms and tumult of daily life for a time, so that you can hear the Lord's still, small voice that whispers in your heart like a gentle breeze.

STEP 2: CONSIDER

1. With life's hustle and bustle in its proper place, you are ready to listen to

God's message for you today. Here you take time for focused reflection on God's words, usually as they are found in Scripture – although you can also turn to other spiritual writings, the works of the saints, Church documents, and even sacred art as texts for consideration. For members of Regnum Christi or other Movements, the documents and writings of the Founder, through whom God enriched the Church with a new charism, also provide rich meditation material. Gradually, with the help of your confessor or spiritual director, you will find the kind of material that helps you most, in accordance with your program of spiritual work.

2. During this stage, you slowly and thoughtfully read the text you will be meditating on. You reflect on it, you examine it, you dig into it. You read it again, searching to discover what God is saying to you through it in the *here and now* of your life. You exercise your whole mind: intellect, imagination, and memory. You involve your emotions, relating the passage to your own life experience.

3. This type of meditative consideration differs from study. The goal of meditation is not necessarily to learn new truths, but to give God a chance to make the truths you need most sink deeper into your mind and heart. Considering a truth involves understanding it more clearly, more deeply. But it also involves savoring it, gazing upon it, basking in it.

4. This step poses a challenge for victims of the media age. The human mind is capable of wonder, contemplation, and reflection, but when the principle source of information is mass media, these capacities can atrophy. Mass media stimulates the surface of the mind, but the constant, rapid flow of images and information militates against going deep. Meditation provides a respite from frenzied mental stimulation and gives the soul a chance to simply love and be loved in the intimacy of a spiritual embrace.

5. Just as it takes the body time to digest food and benefit from its nutrients, so the soul needs time to take in and assimilate the healing, enlightening, and strengthening truths God has revealed through Christ's Gospel. Just as it takes long hours in the sun for plants to photosynthesize so they can grow and flourish, so the soul needs extended exposure to the light of Christ in order for God's grace to purify, enliven, and heal it.

6. God knows which truths you need to dwell on; part of the *Consider* stage is searching for them. God speaks most often in whispers, not storms, and so you have to move forward in your meditation calmly, gently, hunting for the

insight God wishes to give you. This is one of the most mysterious aspects of meditation. Christ the Good Shepherd guides you towards the rich pastures and refreshing waters of his truth and grace, sometimes along an easy path and other times along a steep and difficult path. For each day when it is easy to find and savor God's word for you, there is another day when your meditation seems to entail nothing but work.

7. This exercise of seeking out where God is speaking to your soul turns Christian meditation into a quest: "Meditation is a prayerful quest engaging thought, imagination, emotion, and desire."[7] Usually, as you read and reflect on the subject of your meditation, you can detect where the Holy Spirit wants you to stop and consider simply by the reaction of your heart.

8. In a garden full of beautiful flowers and plants, you stay longer in front of one because you find that its beauty resonates more deeply with you. In a gallery of magnificent works of art, you are drawn to one or two of them more powerfully, because they have something to say to you, in the here and now of your life, that the others don't. Likewise with meditation. If you have done your best to focus the powers of your soul on God in the *Concentrate* step, as you begin to *Consider* the material for your meditation, one or two things will catch your attention; they will jump out at you, as if they were highlighted. It may be a phrase in the actual text, or an idea that comes to your mind. That highlight is the guiding hand of the Good Shepherd. Thus the Holy Spirit gently leads you to the spiritual food your soul needs most.

9. If nothing strikes you right away, you can intensify your consideration by asking questions.

   • For instance, if you are considering a passage from the Gospel, you can enter into the scene by asking basic, journalistic questions: *Who is here? What are they feeling, doing and saying? When is this event taking place? Where is it happening and what does everything look like? Why is it happening in this way? How is each person reacting?* As you enter more deeply into the living Word of God, the Holy Spirit will guide your mind and heart to the point he wants you to consider. When you find it, savor it.

   • Another approach uses less imagination and more reason. You can begin to consider the material of your meditation by asking analytical questions: *What strikes me about this passage? What does*

---

[7]*Catechism of the Catholic Church, 2723*

this mean? What does it tell me about Christ, the Church, the meaning of life? And after having looked at it in the abstract, make it personal – *What does it mean for me? What is Christ saying to me in the here and now of my life? How is this truth relevant to my own struggles, my own mission, and vocation, my own program of spiritual work, my own friendship with Christ and my own journey of faith?*

10. It may take almost the whole time you have set aside for meditation to discover the point God wants you to consider. This is not a cause for discouragement or frustration: during the search, the quest, you are exercising all of the Christian virtues – faith in God, hope in his goodness, love for him, humility, and trust. The more difficult the search, the more these virtues are being exercised; the Holy Spirit is giving you a vigorous spiritual workout. God knows just what you need and how to guide you; he is the Good Shepherd.

11. Sometimes you never seem to find the highlights at all. In these cases too, God is at work. Never doubt his active presence. When the material you have set aside for consideration doesn't yield any insights worth savoring, you can feel free to turn to your favorite biblical images, your favorite vocal prayers, or your favorite verses – go back to the waters and pastures that have nourished you in the past. All mature Christians gradually discover certain truths of the Gospel that can always provide food for their souls.

12. At times you may find so many highlights that you feel overwhelmed. Stay calm. Don't rush. Take one flower, one painting, one highlight at a time and exhaust it, delight in it until your heart is saturated. Only then move on to the next highlight. As long as your consideration continues to move your heart, stay with that point, like a bee extracting nectar from a blossom. Never move on just because you feel like you're supposed to. Prayer is a personal conversation, not a generic connect-the-dots operation.

STEP 3: CONVERSE

1. Precisely because Christian prayer is interpersonal, your consideration of the truths of Christ, your basking in his light, is never only passive. In an embrace, both people receive and both people give. In the embrace of prayer, you receive the truth and grace of God's revelation, and you give your personal response. As soon as the truth you are considering touches your heart, it will stir a response. This is the heart of your meditation.

2. If you are considering the wonders of God's creation, you may be moved to respond with words or sentiments of praise: *How great you are, my God! How beautiful you must be if your creation is this awe-inspiring….*

3. If you are considering God's mercy, you may be moved to respond with contrition, remorse, and sorrow for your sins: *You are so good and generous, so patient; why, Lord, am I so slow to trust you, why am I so selfish? Forgive me, Lord, a thousand times, please forgive me; I know you have, you do, and you will, but still I ask you to forgive me, I am sorry….*

4. If you are considering some of the many gifts he has given you, like your faith, your family, or the Eucharist, you may be moved to express gratitude: *Thank you, Father, from the bottom of my heart, I really mean it, thank you. Thank you for giving me life, and for showing me the meaning of life, and for saving me from so many dangers, so many sins….*

5. Whatever you may be considering, sooner or later, like a child in the presence of his benevolent and powerful father, you will probably find yourself asking for good things from God: *O my Lord, how I want to love as you love! How I need your grace to be patient, to see the good side of others and not just the negative. Please teach me to do your will, to be your true disciple….* This asking can also take the form of confusion and complaint, as happens so often in the Book of Psalms: *Why, my God, have you forsaken me? Why do you let these things happen? Lord, I don't understand, teach me, enlighten me. Help me to go where you want me to go, because right now I don't feel like going there….*

6. As your consideration gives rise to these responses, the response will naturally come to a close and give way to a new consideration, and you will find yourself turning back to the meditation material. You may look again at the same highlight you just considered, or you may move on to something else, until a new consideration sparks a new response and a new topic of conversation. This exchange – this ongoing conversation in which you reflect on God's revelation and respond in your heart, with your own words – is the essence of Christian meditation. This is usually where the soul comes into its most intimate contact with Christ through the action of the Holy Spirit. Consideration is never enough; it must stir the heart to *Converse* with God.

7. During your meditation, then, you may often find yourself going back and forth between Steps 2 and 3, *Consider* and *Converse*. Just because you have considered one point and conversed with Christ about it doesn't mean you can't go back and consider it again from another angle, or consider another

point, and then converse about that. The conversation is two-way; you move back and forth between considering (listening) and responding, as much or as little as the Holy Spirit leads you.

8. Sometimes your response will be a torrent of words – so many that they tumble over each other as you struggle to express all that's in your heart. Other times you may find yourself simply repeating a short phrase, or even one word, and it says everything: *Lord... Jesus...* Sometimes, like the famous peasant of Ars, you will simply find yourself held by God's gaze and gazing back, and words, even in the silence of your heart, will be unnecessary. Whatever its specific form, this third step of your meditation, *Converse*, consists in letting down the guard around your heart, so that God's word for you today penetrates, regenerates, and inflames the most secret depths of who you are.

9. In this step of the meditation, you may also feel moved to converse with the saints and angels or the Blessed Virgin Mary, speaking with them about Christ, whom they know much better than you do, contemplating their example of fidelity to Christ, and asking for their intercession.

STEP 4: COMMIT

1. Towards the end of your meditation, it will be time for you to draw this heart-to-heart conversation to a close. There is a need to bring all the senti- ments together, to wrap things up. Before you step back into life's hectic activity, you need to renew your commitment to the mission God has given you. In your prayer he has renewed his call, and now you renew your answer, accepting once again the life-project that gives meaning to your ex- istence – that of following him, of imitating Christ by your fidelity to God's will in the big things as well as the small.

2. Usually this desire to renew your adherence to God's will flows naturally and easily out of the consideration and conversation stages. The renewal and deepening of your commitment to Christ and his Kingdom, whether or not it is accompanied by intense feelings, is actually a prayer of adoration, wor- ship, and love: *You know how weak I am, my Lord, but you also know how much I want to follow you. You have planted that desire in my heart: I am yours, Lord. Wherever I go, whatever happens, I belong to you. I never want to be separated from you. As hard as it is, I want to do your will, because you are God, my Creator and Redeemer, my Father and my faithful Friend. Thy will be done in my life today, Lord; thy Kingdom come.*

3. You may even find yourself responding to your considerations with acts of adoration similar to those during the *Converse* stage of the meditation – this is fine. It doesn't mean you have to end your meditation right then. If you have time, you can go back and continue the consideration, or converse with other responses, like praise and gratitude. Then, at the end of the time you have set aside to meditate, you can return to this adoration, to this *Commit* step.[8]

4. If you can link this recommitment to the concrete tasks of your day, all the better. Most often, the daily meditation has followed themes connected to your program of spiritual work. In that case, you can recommit to following your program, or one particular point of your program, as a specific way of expressing your love for Christ. Sometimes, however, the Holy Spirit will nudge you towards a specific act of charity (i.e., visit your colleague who's in the hospital), or of self-governance (i.e., call your brother and apologize) – this too can give substance to your recommitment.

5. The meditation itself has glorified God and nourished your soul, regardless of any specific resolution you make in Step 4. The lifeblood of the meditation is your heart-to-heart conversation with the Lord, a conversation that puts you in contact with God and his grace, gradually transforming you into a mature Christian. You have deepened your friendship with Christ through spending this time with him. A new specific resolution may be an appropriate way to express this friendship at the end of the conversation, but often its most sincere expression is simply a renewal of your commitment to Christ and his Kingdom, to the points of spiritual and apostolic work already on your agenda, and to the everyday tasks that are his will for you.

6. This fourth step is the bridge between prayer and action. If you are working on being more courageous about sharing your faith with your coworkers, you may finish your meditation by a commitment to put forth in a natural way the Christian point of view in today's conversations around the water cooler. If God has been leading you towards being a better spouse, you may renew your commitment to Christ by promising to avoid today that particular thing that you know really bothers your wife or husband. If you have been neglecting your prayer life, you may commit to giving your best attention to your daily Rosary in the evening. The specific form your recommitment takes will depend on the overall direction of your spiritual life. It

---

[8] *In both the* Converse *and the* Commit *steps, then, you find the traditional types, the traditional goals of prayer: Praise, Adoration, Sorrow, Thanksgiving, and Asking – P.A.S.T.A.*

doesn't have to be anything new (although it may be); it just has to be true.

7. Finish up your meditation by renewing your commitment to Christ in your own words. Then take a few moments to write down the lights God sent you during the meditation and thank him for them. Briefly go over how the meditation went. Did you follow the steps? Did anything in particular help you? Was there anything that hindered you? This brief analysis will help you get to know better each day what kind of pray-er you are, so that you can apply this knowledge in subsequent meditations, gradually learning to pray as God created you to pray.

8. It often helps to conclude your meditation with a short vocal prayer like the Our Father, the Hail Mary, the Anima Christi, or another favorite prayer of your own. *The Better Part* provides some possibilities at the end of Part I.

Concentrate, Consider, Converse, and *Commit.* These are the four elements of a Christian meditation. The many books and manuals of prayer that enrich our Christian heritage offer numerous aids to meditation, and you should familiarize yourself with them and take advantage of them, but in the end, the methods and aids all tie in to these four steps of prayer. This tried and true structure will give God more room to work in your soul than he would have if you only dedicated yourself to vocal prayer and spiritual reading.

DIFFICULTIES IN PRAYER

You will always face difficulties in prayer. Just accept it. The saints all experienced it, the Catechism teaches it, and theology confirms it. The difficulties stem from two sources – two unique qualities of your friendship with Christ.

1. First, this friendship is mediated by faith. You can't just call Jesus on the phone, as you can with your other friends. He is always with you, but your awareness of and access to his presence passes through faith. Faith is a virtue, which means that it can be more or less developed. The less developed it is, the more effort it takes to activate your awareness of God's presence. Many modern Christians have an underdeveloped faith. They have been unwittingly contaminated by the consumer culture's veneration for quantifiable evidence ("I won't believe it unless a scientific study proves it") and its elevation of feelings over reason ("I don't feel in love anymore, so why should I stay married?") – both of which weaken faith.

A scrawny faith often makes Jesus look fuzzy and seem distant, just as the sun seems weak and irrelevant when you're wearing dark glasses. Your ability to pray will suffer the consequences. Have you ever noticed how hard it is to be distracted when you watch a good movie? Effortlessly you pay perfect attention to a complex story for two hours. Contrast that with what typically happens during your fifteen minutes of meditation. What's the difference? Contact with God takes faith, "going as we do by faith and not by sight" (2 Cor 5:7). It takes the effort of "all your heart, soul, mind, and strength" (Mark 12:30) to align your fallen nature (which tends to seek fulfillment in the things of this earth) with the sublime truths that God has revealed through the teachings of the Church.

2. Your friendship with Christ is unique not only by its mediation through faith, but also because the two friends are not equals. Christ is not just your friend; he is also your Creator, your Redeemer, and your Lord; he is all-wise and all-loving, and he's trying to lead you along the steep and narrow path of Christian maturity. So, on your part, your relationship with him requires docility. But docility demands self-denial, which rubs your concupiscence the wrong way. Remember, baptism gave you back God's grace, but it didn't take away your deep-seated tendencies to selfishness (arrogance, independence, vanity, laziness, anger, lust, greed, etc.) that you inherited from original sin. Because of them, docility chafes. Sometimes the Good Shepherd leads you where you would rather not go, or pushes you farther along when you would prefer to sit back and relax, or doesn't let you drink from a stream that looks fine to you. This divergence of wills makes prayer a constant battle.

SLOTH AND DISTRACTIONS The difficulties flowing from this need for faith and docility come in two basic varieties: *sloth* and *distractions*.

Sloth is spiritual laziness, distaste, and sluggishness in cultivating your relationship with God: *I can't pray before I go to work, because I need that extra few minutes of sleep; I can't go on a retreat, since the playoffs start this weekend and I really want to watch them; I know I committed to begin praying the Rosary again, but I just don't feel like it, I have so much else to do....* Anything but spend time attending to the most important thing: your "vital and personal relationship with the living and true God,"[9] i.e., your life of prayer. That's sloth.

In the meditation itself, sloth can tempt you in numerous ways: procrastinating (*I'll do it later; I'll start meditating tomorrow*), not getting your material ready ahead of time, giving in to tiredness, rushing through your preparatory acts

---

[9]*Catechism of the Catholic Church, 2558*

instead of really concentrating, simply reading for most of the time instead of really engaging in the quest to consider and converse, or finishing with a vague and half-hearted commitment that really has no practical effect at all in your daily life or the pursuit of spiritual maturity. In these and many other ways, sloth slyly undermines the life of prayer.

Sloth *drains* energy from your spiritual life; distractions, on the other hand, *steer* that energy away from God. You go to Mass and sincerely want to worship God, but can't take your eyes off that family in the front pew that's making such a ruckus (or maybe you're part of that family); you pray the Rosary every day, but halfway through you realize that you have no idea which decade you're on because you're thinking about the budget presentation you have to make on Tuesday; you desperately try to spend some time every day in personal prayer, in Christian meditation, but you end up thinking about everything *except* God – family worries, upcoming engagements, temptations, pending bills and phone calls, job interviews, billboards, news stories…. They all violently and unremit-tingly claw at your attention as soon as you try to quiet your soul and attend to the Lord (more often than not, the devil has a hand in this). And sometimes when you pray, you're just plain bored. Welcome to the world of distractions.

SOLVING THE DIFFICULTIES The best defense against sloth and distractions is a good offense. Following a sound and simple meditation method like the one outlined above both flushes these temptations out of hiding – since you know clearly what you *should* be doing during your meditation, you catch yourself more easily as soon as you stop doing that – and also gives you a rudder and a lighthouse to navigate through their ambushes. But the method won't resolve the difficulties all by itself. You still have to steer the rudder and look to the lighthouse.

Temptations to sloth or distractions don't damage your prayer life – only *giving in* to temptations does that. In fact, each temptation is permitted by God because it gives you a chance for spiritual growth.

Take for example a temptation to slothfulness. The alarm clock goes off. Bleary-eyed, I wake up, and the last thing I feel like doing is getting up to pray. If I cut out my fifteen-minute meditation, I can have fifteen minutes more sleep. How sweet that sounds! But wait a minute, why did I set my alarm to get up fifteen minutes earlier than I actually need to? Because I made a commitment; I resolved to start out my day with God because he is the purpose of my life and deserves my praise and because I need his grace. A crisis of the heart has arisen:

my feelings and habits of self-indulgence (egged on by the devil) tell me to hit the snooze button, roll over, and doze off again; my faith (animated by my guardian angel) tells me to turn off the alarm, throw back those cozy covers, touch my bare feet down on that cold tile floor, and keep my appointment with God.

If God wanted to, he could resolve the crisis for me: he could push me out of bed, or make the bed disappear, or give me good feelings about prayer and bad feelings about staying in bed. But he doesn't, at least not usually. Rather, he leaves it up to me, nudging my conscience perhaps, but not forcing me either way. Here is where I can exercise the virtues of faith and docility, and in exercising them, strengthen them.

Distractions work the same way. I'm in the Blessed Sacrament chapel doing my daily meditation. Someone else comes through the door and enters the silent, sacred space. He takes a seat not too far away. I can't help noticing that he's wearing brand new tennis shoes. Are they Nikes or Reeboks? That reminds me about the marketing presentation I have to give this afternoon. My boss will be there. It's a critical account for the company…. Suddenly I realize that my mind is wandering. Up to this point, I haven't been responsible for the distraction, because I wasn't even aware of it, but now I have three options: 1) I keep thinking about the presentation. After all, a lot is hanging on it, and my meditation is a bit dry anyway; 2) I get distracted by my distraction: "There I go again. Why can't I stay focused? I always get distracted. I am such an idiotic Christian, such a hypocrite. I'm so frustrated with myself…." 3) I calmly steer my attention back to my meditation, renewing my conviction that God and his action here matter far more than fruitless worrying about my presentation (which I have already prepared anyway), and that my tendency to get distracted affords me a new opportunity to exercise my faith and docility and turn back once again to my Lord.

Will I choose 1, 2, or 3? If I choose 3, then that distraction, which the devil wants to use to distance me from God, will actually have become an instrument of God's grace, drawing me closer to him and giving him glory. God allows temptations against my communion with God in order to afford me opportunities to deepen that communion.

The more closely you try to follow the 4-step method of meditation outlined above, the more you will get to know how these ubiquitous temptations try to derail your personal prayer life in particular, and the better equipped you will be to stay on track, using them to build up the virtues of faith and docility and become the pray-er God wants you to be.

HOW DO I KNOW IF I'M PRAYING WELL? We all tend to measure our prayer by our feelings: I prayed well if I *felt* God's presence, if I *felt* an emotional thrill. That's not the way to evaluate your prayer. Your relationship with Christ is a deep friendship built on faith and love. It goes much deeper than feelings. Feelings and emotions change with the weather, with our biorhythms, with our circumstances – they are often unpredictable and always undependable. Any friendship built on feelings, therefore, is doomed to frustration and failure. Mature Christians don't seek feelings or emotional states in their prayer. If God provides good feelings too, great, but the sincere Christian is after Christ: praising him, knowing him better, discovering what he wants, and renewing and deepening the decision to imitate him and follow him in the nitty-gritty of daily life, no matter the cost. Feelings are frills, but Christ is the core.

The fruit of a healthy prayer life takes time to grow and mature. Ultimately, it shows itself by growth in virtue, as you become more like Christ. Gradually, you grow in self-governance (controlling and channeling your instincts, passions, and basic human desires), prudence (seeing clearly what ought to be done in any particular situation and doing it), love (seeing others as Christ sees them and being able to sacrifice your own preferences for their sake), fortitude (taking on challenging tasks or projects for the sake of Christ's Kingdom, and persevering through difficulties, obstacles, and opposition), and wisdom (detecting and relishing God's presence in all things and circumstances). Growth in these virtues takes place gradually, almost imperceptibly, on a day-to-day basis, just as a child slowly but surely grows into adulthood, or as plants mature in a garden. Meditation supplies much of the spiritual nutrients that cause these virtues to grow.

On any given day, then, measuring whether your meditation went well or badly is not so easy. Your meditation may have been quite pleasing to God and full of grace for your soul even when it was unpleasant and difficult from a strictly emotional perspective. An athlete may have a great practice session even though it was painful and frustrating – likewise with a daily meditation.

You'll find some helpful indicators below. The most important thing, though, is simply to keep striving to pray better. Speak about your prayer life in spiritual direction and confession, and trust that if you are sincerely doing your best, the Holy Spirit will do the rest.

MY MEDITATION WENT BADLY WHEN I...

- Didn't plan ahead regarding what material I would use, when and where I would meditate, making sure to turn off my cell phone, etc.

- Simply gave in to the many distractions that vied for my attention

- Let myself fall asleep

- Skipped over the first step, *Concentrate*, or did it sloppily; how can my prayer go well if I am not keenly aware of God's presence?

- Didn't humbly ask God to help me and to give me whatever graces I need to continue growing in my spiritual life

- Spent the whole time reading, thinking, or daydreaming, and didn't stop to ask what God was saying *to me* and then respond from my heart

- Tried to stir up warm, fuzzy feelings and intense emotions instead of conversing heart-to-heart on the level of faith

- Didn't renew my commitment to Christ and his Kingdom at the end of the meditation

- Shortened the time I had committed to without a really important reason

MY MEDITATION WENT WELL WHEN I...

- Actually fulfilled the commitment I made to spend a certain amount of time in meditation every day

- Faithfully followed the methodology in spite of tiredness, distractions, dryness, or any other difficulty (or if it was impossible to follow the four-step method, did my best to give praise to God in whatever way I could throughout my meditation time)

- Stayed with the points of consideration that struck me most as long as I found material there for reflection and conversation

- Sought only to know and love Christ better, so as to be able to follow him better

- Made sure to speak to Christ from my heart about whatever I was meditating on (or whatever was most on my heart), even when it was hard to find the words

- Was completely honest in my conversation – I didn't say things to God just out of routine or because I wanted to impress him with my eloquence; I told him what was really in my heart

- Made a sincere effort to listen to what God was saying to me throughout the time of prayer, seeking applications for my own life, circumstances, needs, and challenges

- Finished the meditation more firmly convinced of God's goodness and more firmly committed to doing my best to follow him faithfully

A SAMPLE MEDITATION

The paragraphs below are adapted from a meditation directed by Father Anthony Bannon, LC, and taken with permission from www.vocation.com. Although everyone prays a little bit differently from everyone else, reading through a real meditation from start to finish can help these ideas come into focus. Comments are included in italics.

STEP 1: CONCENTRATE *I come into the place where I will be meditating. I remind myself that God is truly present, here and everywhere, that he is watching over me and listening to me, eager to spend this time together; he sees into the depths of my heart. Then I kneel or sit, make the sign of the cross, and address him.*

I thank you, Father, for the immense love you showed me in creating me and redeeming me, giving me this time with you, spending this time with me, intervening in my life. I know you have something to say to me today. I want hear it; I need to hear it. I want to love you in a real way, not abstractly or in theory only. I want to love you today, and not tomorrow. I want to love you here where you have placed me and not somewhere else in my dreams. I want to love you in your Church. I want to love you in the people that you place in my path.

STEP 2: CONSIDER *First, I read the Gospel passage, then I read it again, more slowly, picturing it, paying attention to whichever words jump out at me. Maybe something strikes me right away, and I stay with that, considering it and letting it lead me into a conversation with Christ.*

Gospel Passage: Matthew 13:47-50

"The Kingdom of Heaven is like a dragnet that is cast into the sea and brings in a haul of all kinds of fish. When it is full, the fishermen haul it ashore. And then sitting down they collect the good ones in baskets and throw away those that are no use. This is how it will be at the end of time. The Angels will appear and separate the wicked from the upright, to throw them into the blazing furnace where there will be weeping and grinding of teeth."

Maybe one thing that strikes you after reading the passage is a consideration like the following:

Unlike the previous parables in this chapter, which described the Kingdom as already present, this one describes the Kingdom as something still to come. Jesus speaks about the relationship between this Kingdom of God and the future life at the end of time. And Jesus seems to want to get across to us one particular message. "The kingdom is like a dragnet that is cast into the sea and brings in a haul of all kinds of fish." The end of time is just as unexpected for us as a net that drops into the water and is pulled along behind the boat is for the fish it catches. Just as sudden as that…

STEP 3: CONVERSE *After making that reflection, you may naturally find yourself wanting to converse with Christ about it, simply and sincerely, as follows, for example:*

I know and I believe that the end of the world will come, that you will judge me and everyone. And yet, I really don't think about it very much. You thought about it a lot. You often spoke about it. Lord, you know all things; you are Wisdom itself. I thank you for this reminder that the end will come. You want me to be ready. You want me to keep the end in mind. I want to too. I don't want to live like an animal, interested only in satisfying my momentary desires. No, I want to live in the light of your truth. I believe in the power of your truth. Lord Jesus, enlighten me, guide me, never stop teaching me how you want me to live.

STEP 2 AGAIN: CONSIDER *After I have had my say and spoken what is in my heart, I turn my attention back to the Lord's word to see what else he has to say to me. I have already sought material for reflection and conversation in the passage itself, and I don't seem to find any more. So now I move on to the commentary. I read one section of the commentary, which points out something I may have overlooked. It sparks another personal reflection, so I pause and consider it – what it means, what it tells me about Christ, what it means for me, how it applies to my hopes and struggles:*

Prewritten Commentary

When it is full, the fishermen haul the net ashore. Then they do the all-important thing: they sit down and start sorting out their catch. They keep the good fish and throw away the useless ones. And Jesus said, "This is the way it is going to be at the end of time. The Angels will appear and separate the wicked from the upright." At the end of time, the angels won't simply check and see how God has made us, and separate us according to the qualities that God has given us. Instead, their criteria will be our own wickedness and uprightness. In other words, we will be judged according to what we have done with those things that God has given us, whether we have used them wickedly (selfishly) or uprightly.

A personal reflection sparked by that commentary could be something like this:

PERSONAL CONSIDERATION OF THE COMMENTARY What do the angels recognize in each one of those people? They recognize which ones are members of Christ's Kingdom; they see signs of that in each person's heart, each person's character, which was formed by the choices they made throughout their lifetime.

I will be one of those fish, one of those people. Will the angels recognize in me the signs of the Kingdom that Jesus has talked about in the previous parables? Will they see in me someone who searched for the fine pearl, recognized its value and beauty, and had the good sense to sell everything else in order to possess it? Will they see me as someone who recognized the treasure in the field, and sold everything else in order to buy it? When the angels find me, will they recognize in me the leaven that uplifted the people around me? Will they see in me someone who spent his whole life transforming the world around him, transforming himself as he served those around him, or will they find me no different from those I should have changed? Will they find just the flat dough of the world in my life, unrisen?

STEP 3 AGAIN: CONVERSE *At some point while you consider whatever struck you in the commentary, you may find yourself wanting to respond directly to the Lord, to say something in response to what the Holy Spirit has been saying to you through your consideration. If nothing comes spontaneously, as your time for meditation draws to its close, you will need to purposely transition into a conversation. Remember, consideration only matters insofar as it draws you into a heart-to-heart conversation with God. Your response to God that emerges out of the above consideration may look something like this:*

Lord Jesus, I thank you for speaking this parable, because so often I get too caught up with the urgent cares of today and the apparent difficulty of following you. I forget that all of this will come to an end, and that you have a bigger plan in mind.

You invite me to look at what is coming in the future life, to be ready for the dragnet. You ask me to look at heaven, which is awaiting me. Lord, I can only live as your faithful disciple, as a member of your Kingdom, with the help of your grace. I can only persevere with your help. Please never let me lose sight of the hopes and expectations that you have for me – you really do have a dream for my life; this parable reminds me that you do. The greatest thing that I can do, the greatest thing I will ever see will be the joy on your face if you can one day say to me, "Well done, good and faithful servant." Then you will be able to receive me as you want to receive me, among the upright, and bring me into the true Kingdom of Heaven.

STEP 4: COMMIT *As your meditation time comes to an end, you need to recommit yourself to Christ in light of what the Holy Spirit has been showing you through your considerations and conversation. Most importantly, you want to refocus your most basic attitudes: you are a follower of Christ, and God's will is the path of your life. You can also translate that focused attitude into a concrete commitment; e.g., in accordance with your program of spiritual work, or in accordance with a particular circumstance you will be facing today. You also wrap up the meditation itself, thanking God for the graces you have received, and asking forgiveness for your distractions and shortcomings. For this meditation, your recommitment may look something like this:*

Jesus, you know that I want to live as a true Christian, with my sights set on your Kingdom. Whatever you ask me today, I will do, if you give me the strength I need to do it. I know I will need your strength to be patient with my coworkers, and to give myself eagerly to this tedious project at work. If I stay faithful to your will, to my conscience and to these normal duties of my state in life, and if I live your will with love and gratitude in my heart, then I will be ready for the last day, whenever you decide to bring it along. And don't let me hide my faith in my conversation at lunch today. Jesus, they need to know you as much as I do; make me a good messenger. Thy will be done, Lord, not mine.

Thank you, Lord, for being with me in this meditation. Thank you for the good thoughts, the good affections, and the beginnings of good resolutions that you have placed in my heart. I am sorry for the moments I have been distracted, gone off on tangents, been less attentive to your presence. Grant me in some other way any graces that I might have missed. And I also pray for each one of my brothers and sisters: I pray for each one who wants to follow you. Our Father…

SOME POSSIBLE PREPARATORY AND CONCLUDING PRAYERS

PREPARATORY PRAYERS These are provided as examples and helps. Sometimes you may need help during Step 1 of your meditation, *Concentrate*. These small prayers express the attitudes that you need to stir up at the start of your meditation. They can also sometimes serve as material for *Consider* and *Converse* as well.

1. ENTERING INTO GOD'S PRESENCE

My Lord and my God, I firmly believe that you are present here and everywhere, that you are looking upon me and listening to me, and that you see into the very depths of my soul. You are my Creator, my Redeemer, and my Father. I believe in your love for me. You never take your eyes off me. You have something to say to me today. Your love for me never grows weary. You never stop drawing close to me, and drawing me closer to you.

Lord, who am I to place myself in your presence? I am a poor creature unworthy of appearing before you, and yet amid all my misery I adore you devoutly. I ask you to forgive my many sins.

Jesus, teach me to pray. Direct my prayer, so that it may rise to your throne like fragrant incense. Let all the thoughts of my spirit and my heart's inmost sentiments be directed towards serving and praising God in a perfect way. I need to hear your Word for me today, and I long to hear it. You know how much I need you, how much I want to follow you. Grant me in this prayer the grace of knowing you better, loving you more, and becoming more like you. Grant me the grace I most need.

My loving Mother Mary, my holy guardian angel, angels and saints in heaven: intercede for me so that this prayer will help me and all the other people connected to my life.

2. TRADITIONAL ACTS OF FAITH, HOPE, AND LOVE

Act of Faith

My God, I firmly believe all that you have revealed and that the Holy Church puts before us to be believed, for you are the infallible truth, who does not deceive and cannot be deceived. I expressly believe in you, the only true God in three equal and distinct persons, the Father, Son, and Holy Spirit. And I believe in Jesus Christ, Son of God, who took flesh and died for us, and who will give to each one, according to his merits, eternal reward or punishment. I always want to live in accordance with this faith. Lord, increase my faith.

Act of Hope

My God, by virtue of your promises and the merits of Jesus Christ, our Savior, I hope to receive from your goodness eternal life and the necessary grace to merit it with the good deeds I am required and propose to do. Lord, may I be able to delight in you forever.

Act of Love

My God, I love you with all my heart and above all things, because you are infinitely good and our eternal happiness; for your sake I love my neighbor as I love myself, and I forgive the offenses I have received. Lord, grant that I will love you more and more.

Petition

My God, here present now, hear and guide my prayer, and lead me to the verdant pastures and refreshing waters of your Truth and your Love.

3. ENTERING INTO GOD'S PRESENCE THROUGH ACTS OF GRATITUDE AND HUMILITY

My Lord and my God, you are infinitely kind and merciful. I thank you with all my heart for the countless gifts you have given me, especially for creating and redeeming me, for calling me to the Catholic faith and to my vocation, and for freeing me from so many dangers of soul and body.

You have shown me the door that leads to heaven, to being one with you forever. What am I? Mere sand. And so, why have you sought me out, why have you loved me, why have you shown me that door? Why did you become flesh and leave me your Gospel? Because you love me. I want to thank you for everything you did for me, and all that you do for me. In this prayer I want to praise and glorify you.

How I need your grace! Please guide me now. Teach me to know, love, and do your will for me. I am nothing without you; I am no one without you, but I know that with you all things are possible.

4. IN THE CONTEXT OF SEEKING GOD'S WILL

My Lord and my God, you are Love itself, and the source of all love and goodness. Out of love you created me to know you, love you, and serve you in a unique way, as no one else can. I believe that you have a plan for my life, that you have a task in your Kingdom reserved just for me. Your plan and your task are far better than any other I might choose: they will glorify you, fulfill the desires of my heart, and save those souls who are depending on my generous response.

Lord, grant me the light I need to see the next step in that plan; grant me the generosity I need to set aside my own plans in favor of yours; and grant me the strength I need to put my hands to your plough and never turn back. You know me better than I know myself, so you know that I am sinful and weak. All the more reason that I need your grace to uphold the good desires you have planted in my heart, O Lord!

Make my prayer today pleasing to you. Show me your will for me, O gentle and eternal God, and help me to say with Mary, "I am the servant of the Lord; let it be done to me according to your word," and to say with Jesus, "Let not my will be done, but yours."

5. RECALLING CHRIST'S PERSONAL LOVE FOR ME

Lord, you wished to create me. I would not exist were it not for your almighty power. You created me because you love me, and I want to love you the way you have loved me. Lord, two thousand years ago mankind walked the earth in darkness, lost by the sin of our first parents. And you, in obedience to the Father and out of love for me, decided to become flesh in the Virgin's womb. You became a man so as to suffer for me, redeem me from my sins, and open the gates of heaven for me. Thank you for your love, Jesus; thank you for being born of the Blessed Virgin. Thank you, dear Mother, for saying yes to God and allowing the Second Person of the Blessed Trinity, Jesus Christ, to become man.

Lord Jesus, you are here with me now. You came into the world to teach me. You left me the path I must take to reach you and possess you forever in the Gospel. Thank you, Jesus, for such love. You truly are almighty God. I am a poor and miserable creature; and yet you loved me and continue to love me, not only in words, but with real love: love shown in works. That is why I know that you are with me now, in my heart, watching over me. Guide my prayer, Lord, cleanse my soul of all my sins and selfishness, and fill it with your light and your love. Grant me the grace I need most, because without you, I can do nothing.

6. FROM THE CHURCH'S RICH LITURGICAL TRADITION

THE TE DEUM

You are God: we praise you; you are the Lord: we acclaim you; you are the eternal Father: all creation worships you. To you all angels, all the powers of heaven, Cherubim and Seraphim, sing in endless praise: Holy, holy, holy, Lord, God of power and might, heaven and earth are full of your glory. The glorious company of apostles praises you, the noble fellowship of prophets praises you, the white-robed army of martyrs praises you. Throughout the world the holy Church acclaims you: Father, of majesty unbounded, your true and only Son, worthy of all worship, and the Holy Spirit, advocate and guide. You, Christ, are the King of glory, the eternal Son of the Father. When you became man to set us free, you did not spurn the Virgin's womb. You overcame the sting of death, and opened the Kingdom of heaven to all believers. You are seated at God's right hand in glory. We believe that you will come, and be our judge. Come then, Lord, and help your people, bought with the price of your own blood, and bring us with your saints to glory everlasting. Save your people, Lord, and bless your inheritance. Govern and uphold them now and always. Day by day we bless you. We praise your name forever. Keep us today, Lord, from all sin. Have mercy on us, Lord, have mercy. Lord, show us your love and mercy, for we put our trust in you. In you, Lord is our hope: and we shall never hope in vain. Lord, hear my prayer, and let my cry reach you.

PREFACES TO THE EUCHARISTIC PRAYER, SUNDAYS IN ORDINARY TIME I

Father, all-powerful and ever-living God, we do well always and everywhere to give you thanks through Jesus Christ our Lord. Through his cross and resurrection he freed us from sin and death and called us to the glory that has made us a chosen race, a royal priesthood, a holy nation, a people set apart. Everywhere we proclaim your mighty works, for you have called us out of darkness into your own wonderful light.

PREFACE TO THE FOURTH EUCHARIST PRAYER

Father in heaven, it is right that we should give you thanks and glory: you are the one God, living and true. Through all eternity you live in unapproach-able light. Source of life and goodness, you have created all things, to fill your creatures with every blessing and lead all men to the joyful vision of your light. Countless hosts of angels stand before you to do your will; they look upon your splendor and praise you night and day.

[You may want to include other prayers that you find particularly helpful for the first step of your meditation.]

CONCLUDING PRAYERS Once you have renewed your commitment to follow Christ and expressed that in your own words and in a concrete resolution, briefly reviewed how your meditation went, and jotted down the insights God gave you (Step 4, *Commit*), it often helps to wrap up your meditation with a short, ready-made prayer that sums things up. St Ignatius of Loyola used to finish with the Our Father, the Hail Mary, and the Glory Be. Here are some other options, in case you still haven't found your personal favorites. It is customary to end the meditation with the Sign of the Cross.

PRAYER OF DEDICATION

Lord Jesus,
I give you my hands to do your work.
I give you my feet to follow your way.
I give you my eyes to see as you do.
I give you my tongue to speak your words.
I give you my mind so you can think in me.
I give you my spirit so you can pray in me.
Above all, I give you my heart
So in me you can love your Father and all people.
I give you my whole self so you can grow in me,
Till it is you, Lord Jesus,
Who lives and works and prays in me. Amen.

PRAYER TO THE HOLY SPIRIT

Holy Spirit,
Inspire in me
What I should think,
What I should say,
What I should leave unsaid,
What I should write,
What I should do
And how I should act
To bring about the good of souls,
The fulfillment of my mission,
And the triumph of the Kingdom of Christ. Amen.

LEAD KINDLY LIGHT

Lead, kindly Light, amid the encircling gloom,
Lead thou me on;
The night is dark, and I am far from home,
Lead thou me on.
Keep thou my feet; I do not ask to see
The distant scene; one step enough for me.

I was not ever thus, nor prayed that thou
Shouldst lead me on;
I loved to choose and see my path; but now
Lead thou me on.
I loved the garish day, and, spite of fears,
Pride ruled my will: remember not past years.

So long thy power hath blest me, sure it still
Will lead me on.
O'er moor and fen, o'er crag and torrent, till
The night is gone,
And with the morn those Angel faces smile,
Which I have loved long since, and lost awhile.

- Venerable J.H. Newman (1801-1890)

FROM ST PATRICK'S BREASTPLATE

I bind unto myself today
The strong name of the Trinity:
By invocation of the same,
The Three in One and One in Three

Christ be with me, Christ within me,
Christ behind me, Christ before me,
Christ beside me, Christ to win me,
Christ to comfort and restore me.
Christ beneath me, Christ above me,
Christ in quiet, Christ in danger,
Christ in hearts of all that love me,
Christ in mouth of friend and stranger.

Praise to the Lord of my salvation –
Salvation is of Christ the Lord!

- Ascribed to St Patrick of Ireland (circa 450 A.D.)

PRAYER OF SELF-DEDICATION TO JESUS CHRIST

Take, Lord, and receive
all my liberty, my understanding, my whole will,
all I have and all I possess.
You gave it all to me;
To you, Lord, I return it all.
It is all yours: Do with me entirely as you will.
Give me your love and your grace:
This is enough for me. Amen.

- St Ignatius of Loyola (1491-1556)

PRAYER OF ST FRANCIS

Lord, make me an instrument of Your peace.
Where there is hatred, let me sow love;
where there is injury, pardon;
where there is doubt, faith;
where there is despair, hope;
where there is darkness, light;
and where there is sadness, joy.

O, Divine Master,
grant that I may not so much seek
to be consoled as to console;
to be understood as to understand;
to be loved as to love;
for it is in giving that we receive;
it is in pardoning that we are pardoned;
and it is in dying that we are born to eternal life. Amen.

- St Francis of Assisi (1181-1226)

LITANY OF HUMILITY

This prayer renews one's commitment to follow Christ's summary for Christian living: "Set your hearts on his kingdom first, and on his righteousness, and all these other things will be given you as well" (Mt 6:33). It should be prayed from that perspective.

Jesus, meek and humble of heart, hear me!
From the desire of being esteemed, *Lord Jesus, free me!*

From the desire of being loved…
From the desire of being acclaimed…
From the desire of being honored…
From the desire of being praised…
From the desire of being preferred…
From the desire of being consulted…
From the desire of being approved…
From the desire of being valued…

From the fear of being humbled, *Lord Jesus, free me!*
From the fear of being despised…
From the fear of being dismissed…
From the fear of being rejected…
From the fear of being defamed…
From the fear of being forgotten…
From the fear of being ridiculed…
From the fear of being wronged…
From the fear of being suspected…
From resenting that my opinion is not followed…

That others will be more loved than I, *Lord Jesus, make this my prayer!*
That others will be esteemed more than I…
That others will increase in the opinion of the world while I diminish…
That others will be chosen while I am set aside…
That others will be praised while I am overlooked…
That others will be preferred to me in everything…

Lord Jesus, though you were God, you humbled yourself to the extreme of dying on a cross, to set an enduring example to the shame of my arrogance and vanity. Help me to learn your example and put it into practice so that, by humbling myself in accordance with my lowliness here on earth, you can lift me up to rejoice in you forever in heaven. Amen.
- *Cardinal Merry del Val, Secretary of State under Pope St Pius X (1865-1930)*

MISSION PRAYER

Lord, you have created me to do you some definite service; you have committed some work to me which you have not committed to another. I have my mission—I never may know it in this life, but I shall be told it in the next. Somehow I am necessary for your purposes, as necessary in my place as an Archangel in his—if, indeed, I fail, you can raise another, as you could make the stones children of Abraham. Yet I have a part in this great work; I am a link in a chain, a bond of connection between persons. You have not created me for naught. I shall do good, I shall do your work; I shall be an angel of peace, a preacher of truth in my own place, while not intending it, if I do but your commandments and serve you in my calling.

Therefore I will trust you. Whatever, wherever I am, I can never be thrown away. If I am in sickness, my sickness may serve you; in perplexity, my perplexity may serve you; if I am in sorrow, my sorrow may serve you. My sickness, or perplexity, or sorrow may be necessary causes of some great end, which is quite beyond me. You do nothing in vain; you may prolong my life, you may shorten it; you know what you are about; you may take away my friends, you may throw me among strangers, you may make me feel desolate, make my spirits sink, hide the future from me—still you know what you are about.

- Adapted from a reflection composed by
Venerable J.H. Newman (1801-1890)

MORE FROM THE CHURCH'S RICH LITURGICAL TRADITION

THE GLORIA

Glory to God in the highest and peace to his people on earth.
Lord God, heavenly King, almighty God, and Father,
  we worship you, we give you thanks, we praise you for your glory.
Lord Jesus Christ, only Son of the Father,
Lord God, Lamb of God,
You take away the sin of the world: have mercy on us;
You are seated at the right hand of the Father: receive our prayer.
For you alone are the Holy One, you alone are the Lord,
You alone are the Most High, Jesus Christ, with the Holy Spirit,
In the Glory of God the Father. Amen.

THE APOSTLES' CREED

I believe in God, the Father almighty, creator of heaven and earth. I believe in Jesus Christ, his only Son, our Lord. He was conceived by the power of the Holy Spirit and born of the Virgin Mary. He suffered under Pontius Pilate, was crucified, died, and was buried. He descended to the dead. On the third day he rose again. He ascended into heaven, and is seated at the right hand of the Father. He will come again to judge the living and the dead. I believe in the

Holy Spirit, the holy catholic Church, the communion of saints, the forgiveness of sins, the resurrection of the body, and the life everlasting. Amen.

Here is some space where you can write in other prayers that you personally find helpful for wrapping up your meditation and returning to your other daily activities...

PART 2:
MEDITATION UNITS

THE GOSPEL ACCORDING TO
ST. MATTHEW

THE GOSPEL OF MATTHEW CHAPTER 1

"The Father sent his Son out of his immeasurable love for us sinners. He sent him to free us from the tyrannical power of the devil, to invite us to heaven and lead us into its innermost sanctuary. He was sent to show us truth itself, to teach us how we should live, to share with us the source of all goodness, to enrich us with the treasures of his grace. Finally, he was sent to make us sons of the Father and heirs to eternal life… The Church wants us to understand that as he came once into the world in the flesh, so now, if we remove all barriers, he is ready to come to us again at any minute or hour, to make his home spiritually within us in all his grace."

- St Charles Borromeo, Pastoral Letters

1. THE WAIT IS OVER (MT 1:1-17)

"He who enriches others becomes poor. He took to himself the poverty of my flesh so that I might obtain the riches of his godhead."

- St Gregory Nazienzen

Matthew 1:1-17

A genealogy of Jesus Christ, son of David, son of Abraham: Abraham was the father of Isaac, Isaac the father of Jacob, Jacob the father of Judah and his brothers, Judah was the father of Perez and Zerah, Tamar being their mother, Perez was the father of Hezron, Hezron the father of Ram, Ram was the father of Amminadab, Amminadab the father of Nahshon, Nahshon the father of Salmon, Salmon was the father of Boaz, Rahab being his mother, Boaz was the father of Obed, Ruth being his mother, Obed was the father of Jesse; and Jesse was the father of King David.

David was the father of Solomon, whose mother had been Uriah's wife, Solomon was the father of Rehoboam, Rehoboam the father of Abijah, Abijah the father of Asa, Asa was the father of Jehoshaphat, Jehoshaphat the father of Joram, Joram the father of Azariah, Azariah was the father of Jotham, Jotham the father of Ahaz, Ahaz the father of Hezekiah, Hezekiah was the father of Manasseh, Manasseh the father of Amon, Amon the father of Josiah; and Josiah was the father of Jechoniah and his brothers. Then the deportation to Babylon took place.

After the deportation to Babylon: Jechoniah was the father of Shealtiel, Shealtiel the father of Zerubbabel, Zerubbabel was the father of Abiud, Abiud the father of Eliakim, Eliakim father of Azor, Azor was the father of Zadok, Zadok the father of Achim, Achim the father of Eliud, Eliud was the father of Eleazar, Eleazar the father of Matthan, Matthan the father of Jacob; and Jacob was the father of Joseph the husband of Mary; of her was born Jesus who is called Christ. The sum of generations is therefore: fourteen from Abraham to David; fourteen from David to the Babylonian deportation; and fourteen from the Babylonian deportation to Christ.

CHRIST THE LORD Hidden in this passage, so familiar and seemingly so insignificant, is one of Christianity's key ingredients.

Almost all pre-Christian world religions (with the obvious exception of Judaism) divided the universe into two completely separate camps: the mythic and the human. In this view, human time was the arena of all human deeds, our own and those of our ancestors – the noble and the despicable, the memorable and the mundane. Mythic time, on the other hand, embraced the events outside of history that had given birth to the universe and the milieu of the gods. And so, no pagan god could (or would) ever claim a human genealogy.

But that's exactly the claim Jesus makes. In Jesus, the one true God doesn't just dip into history for a lark (as some of the mythic characters used to do), but he actually enters fully into the human reality – like an artist painting himself into his picture. In Christ, the originator of history becomes historical. He redeems the human family from sin and divinizes it. He forges a real, not merely ritualistic or legendary, communion between God and man.

Jesus' genealogy, then, beams with theological significance. It links him to the gritty reality of every epoch – and every person – in the human timeline, all the way back to the beginning. It bridges the mysterious gap, so impenetrable to other religions, between myth and history. Through Christ, God gets involved in our lives. Christianity is no myth or fairy tale; those were just warm-ups for the Story of the Lord.

CHRIST THE TEACHER St Matthew's arrangement of the genealogy emphasizes the connection between Abraham, David, the Babylonian exile, and Jesus. It starts with Abraham, the forefather of the Chosen People of Israel. It then divides up the list of names into groups of fourteen. The groups take shape around the references to David "the King" (the only name linked to a title, besides Christ's) and to the exile from Jerusalem (this occurred in 586 when the Babylonian King Nebuchadnezzar deported the Jews into Babylon). It culminates in Jesus. It's almost like a rosary in which the big beads are Abraham, David, the exile, and Jesus.

This emphasis brings God's Providence onto center stage. It drives home a simple message: the Lord really does govern human history. God promised Abraham (probably around the year 1900 B.C.) that he would become the father of kings. That promise was realized most magnificently in Israel's most revered leader, King David (who reigned around the year 1000 B.C.). God promised David that his royal line would never die out. Then David's Kingdom sank into division, corruption and idolatry, resulting in the exile to Babylon. At that point, through the Prophets, God promised to send a descendent of David as a Savior, a royal Messiah who would reestablish the Kingdom on a scale hitherto unimagined – that was Jesus Christ. (For this reason the Gospels often use the title "Son of David" to refer to Jesus.)

Two thousand years of turbulent historical change, the brilliant rises and crashing falls of human empires, the harrowing upheavals and transformations of entire civilizations – none of it could hinder God from guiding the course of history exactly as he in his wisdom desired. If he did it with the human story, he can certainly do it with each of our stories. That's the Providence of our God.

CHRIST THE FRIEND Genealogies were common among the Jews of Jesus' time. The Jewish people were keenly aware of their special status as God's Chosen People, so they closely guarded their racial purity and recorded their family trees in detail. Most genealogies, however, only contained the male ancestors. In Jesus' genealogy, St Matthew makes a point of mentioning four women (not including Mary). None of them were Jewish (Tamar and Rahab were Canaanite, Ruth was Moabite, and the wife of Uriah – Bathsheba – was Hittite), and three of them had been involved in dishonorable escapades. Why would St Matthew break with custom in order to include these names in his list?

Certainly one of the reasons was to emphasize that Christ never held himself aloof from sinners. Later in his Gospel, St Matthew narrates how Jesus described himself as being sent "for sinners, not the righteous." Jesus never keeps his distance from us when we fail, fall, or falter. Precisely then he runs to our side; it is the lost sheep he longs to embrace and carry home to his flock.

CHRIST IN MY LIFE The greatness of your mystery, Lord, stirs my soul. You are the Lord of the entire universe, and you decide to come and walk among us, speak with us, and teach us. Let the wonder of this active love of yours penetrate my heart and clear away all the petty, selfish ideas that cloud my understanding. Help me to live in the light of your glory…

If you in your Providence can guide the entire course of human history without violating human freedom, you can certainly guide the events of my life. If you brought salvation out of annihilation, surely you can bring joy out of my sorrows and success out of my failures. I believe in your goodness and your power. Jesus, I trust in you…

You love without exception. Sinners and the despised are on the top of your list. You smile on the despicable and save them. Why is it so hard for me to follow your example? Why do I play favorites, criticize, and judge others? Jesus, meek and humble of heart, make my heart more like yours…

QUESTIONS FOR SMALL GROUP DISCUSSION

1. What struck you most about this passage? What did you notice that you hadn't noticed before?

2. Do you think there is any significance in St Matthew's division of the genealogy into groups of fourteen? St Jerome pointed out that the total number of generations in this arrangement, forty-two, corresponds to the number of encampments the Israelites made on their Exodus from Egypt into the Promised Land. Could there be any spiritual meaning to that coincidence?

3. Why do you think God chose to prepare for the coming of Christ by setting aside a Chosen People, guiding them for hundreds of years, and then letting them be taken into exile?

4. Do you see any similarity between personal spiritual growth and the history of Israel's relationship with God?

Cf. Catechism of the Catholic Church, 522-524 on the preparations for Christ's coming; 464-469 on Jesus as true God and true man

2. SALVATION IS BORN (MT 1:18-25)

"What is this wealth of goodness? What is this mystery that touches me? I received the divine image and I did not keep it. He receives my flesh to save the image and grant immortality to the flesh. This, his second communion with us, is far more marvellous than the first."

- St Gregory Nazienzen

Matthew 1:18-25

This is how Jesus Christ came to be born. His mother Mary was betrothed to Joseph; but before they came to live together she was found to be with child through the Holy Spirit. Her husband Joseph; being a man of honour and wanting to spare her publicity, decided to divorce her informally. He had made up his mind to do this when the angel of the Lord appeared to him in a dream and said, 'Joseph son of David, do not be afraid to take Mary home as your wife, because she has conceived what is in her by the Holy Spirit. She will give birth to a son and you must name him Jesus, because he is the one who is to save his people from their sins.'

Now all this took place to fulfil the words spoken by the Lord through the prophet:

'The virgin will conceive and give birth to a son and they will call him Emmanuel, a name which means 'God-is-with-us'. When Joseph woke up he did what the angel of the Lord had told him to do: he took his wife to his home and, though he had not had intercourse with her, she gave birth to a son; and he named him Jesus.

CHRIST THE LORD God is all-powerful, and he could have saved us in any number of ways. He chose the Incarnation: becoming one of us. Such an uncomfortable choice – at least, it certainly upset Joseph's plans. But God is not obliged to act within the parameters of our personal comfort zones. He has said as much himself: "As high as the heavens are above the earth, so high are my ways above your ways and my thoughts above your thoughts" (Isaiah 55:9).

Joseph finds his fiancée pregnant. He knows her virtue and can't imagine what happened. It seems she is not free to tell him, or if she does tell him, he finds it hard to accept, so Mary has to trust that God will work it out. After a period of anxiety and confusion, the angel appears, only to give Joseph some short-term instructions. Why didn't God simply explain it all beforehand, send a letter with the whole plan mapped out step-by-step? Why did the ancient prophecies leave so much room for interpretation?

God is the Lord; he acts according to his own wisdom and love, and we follow him "by faith, not by sight" (1 Corinthians 5:7). If at times following the Lord was uncomfortable even for Joseph and Mary, we can expect nothing less for ourselves.

CHRIST THE TEACHER God's becoming a man to save us from sin – just that simple fact – contains an inexhaustible storehouse of teachings for every follower of Christ. One particularly relevant lesson emerges from the name the angel gives to the Lord: "Jesus [God saves], because he is the one who is to save his people from their sins."

For the Jewish mentality at the time of Christ, names corresponded to real characteristics of the one being named. In Jesus, this correspondence reaches its culmination: "his name is the only one that contains the presence it signifies" (Catechism of the Catholic Church #2666). Jesus is God who comes to save us; he is the Savior God. This implies that *we need a Savior;* otherwise, God would have given him a different name.

That's the lesson – so basic, but so vital. Unfortunately, even practicing, believing Catholics often live as if Christ were merely an add-on. We can easily treat religion like one more thing on our to-do list – an important one, certainly, but just one among a bunch of important things. We forget that if Jesus is the Savior God, then we for whom he came *need* him to save us. We really need him in our lives, in every sector of our lives, in every corner. When we live as if we do not, we fall into the swelling crowd of practical atheists: those who profess to believe in God, but live as if God were only remotely relevant. That's building a life on undependable sand – but Jesus wants to be our rock.

CHRIST THE FRIEND Friends come to friends in need. Jesus came to be our truest friend, because he came to bring us what we need most: himself, his love, and his grace.

Jesus: I created you to desire fulfillment in life, and I created you to find it only in one place: an intimate relationship with me. I know your heart, and I know that it will be restless until it rests in me. But original sin took away the possibility for that intimate relationship. It ruptured your communion with God; the human race had forsaken my friendship. I didn't give up on you. I came to earth to renew that communion, to reestablish that friendship. In my perfectly but painfully obedient incarnation, life, death, and resurrection, I reversed on your behalf the human family's sinful rebellion. I did it because I wanted you once again to be able to call God "Father"; I wanted you to come home.

But even that wasn't enough. I couldn't wait until heaven to be with you. I wanted to stay with you, intimately, individually. So, I founded my Church, and I left you my ever-living presence in the Eucharist – thus I fulfilled the promise I had made through my prophets, to bear the name Emmanuel: "God is with us." I came to save you and give you the hope of heaven, and I stay with you to keep that hope alive. How I looked forward to that first Christmas, the door into your life!

CHRIST IN MY LIFE Many times I resent when my plans are foiled and my hopes left unfulfilled. When you throw me curve balls, I get nervous, or angry, or doubtful. And yet, I know that you are always guiding me with your infinite wisdom. Teach me to discover your will in the midst of life's ups and downs, and to be docile, like Joseph and Mary. Thy Kingdom come, Lord – not mine…

So often I depend almost entirely on my own talents and strength to succeed. And yet, here you are, teaching me by your quiet coming to earth, that when it comes to the only success that really matters, success as a human being, as a child of God, I am helpless! I need you, Lord, to be my Savior. I need your love and your grace to give meaning and direction to my life. Grant me success, Lord, the kind that lasts forever…

 It amazes me that you want to stay so close to me. Thank you for giving me the gift of faith, for bringing me into your family, the Church. Never let me be separated from you, Lord…

QUESTIONS FOR SMALL GROUP DISCUSSION

1. What struck you most in this passage? What did you notice that you hadn't noticed before?

2. Why do you think God made Joseph wait before sending an angel to tell him what was going on with Mary?

3. What difficulties must Mary have faced as her pregnancy became evident? How might she have reacted?

4. Some traditions of spirituality give a special place to simple prayers that consist of lovingly repeating the titles and names of Christ (or just one of them) over and over again. What value do you see in that kind of prayer? Could it be useful in your life situation?

Cf. Catechism of the Catholic Church, 456-478 on the Incarnation – why, what, and how; 430-451 on the names of Jesus; 2123-2126 on atheism and practical atheism; 27-30 on our innate need for God; 396-409 on original sin and its consequences; 410-412 on God's response to original sin

ᴛʜᴇ ɢᴏsᴘᴇʟ ᴏf ᴍᴀᴛᴛʜᴇw CHAPTER 2

"God, who creates and maintains all things by his Word, provides men with constant evidence of himself in created realities. And furthermore, wishing to open up the way to heavenly salvation, he manifested himself to our first parents from the very beginning. After the fall, he buoyed them up with the hope of salvation, by promising redemption; and he has never ceased to take care of the human race. For he wishes to give eternal life to all those who seek salvation by patience in well-doing. In his own time God called Abraham, and made him into a great nation. After the era of the patriarchs he taught this nation, by Moses and the prophets, to recognize him as the only living and true God, as a provident Father and just judge. He taught them, too, to look for the promised Saviour. And so, throughout the ages, he prepared the way for the Gospel."

- Second Vatican Council, Constitution on Divine Revelation

3. THE KING IS COMING (MT 2:1-6)

"Christ abode for nine months in the tent of Mary's womb; he abides until the consummation of the ages in the tent of the Church's faith; he will abide for ever and ever in the knowledge and love of the faithful soul."

- Blessed Isaac of Stella

Matthew 2:1-6

After Jesus had been born at Bethlehem in Judaea during the reign of King Herod, some wise men came to Jerusalem from the east. 'Where is the infant king of the Jews?' they asked. 'We saw his star as it rose and have come to do him homage.' When King Herod heard this he was perturbed, and so was the whole of Jerusalem. He called together all the chief priests and the scribes of the people, and enquired of them where the Christ was to be born. 'At Bethlehem in Judaea,' they told him 'for this is what the prophet wrote: And you, Bethlehem, in the land of Judah, you are by no means least among the leaders of Judah, for out of you will come a leader who will shepherd my people Israel'.

CHRIST THE LORD In ancient times Christians celebrated the mystery of Christmas for twelve consecutive days. They let loose their joy in a crescendo culminating on the solemnity of Epiphany, the manifestation (that's what epiphany means) of the Lord to the Gentiles – the non-Jewish peoples represented by these wise men. The Jews always knew that their Messiah would be a mighty King, but they did not clearly know that his Kingship would extend to every nation, to all people. The moving scene of these wise men coming to pay Christ homage focuses our attention on God's plan for his New Covenant. This Covenant would bring all people into the ranks of his Chosen People, creating a new Israel bounded neither by geography nor by race, but only by the generosity of each individual human heart. With the coming of the wise men, the age of the Catholic – meaning "universal" – Church begins.

But the universality of his reign has some uncomfortable consequences. Christ is the Lord – not merely one among many, but the One. The universe is not a democracy, but a monarchy with only one rightful King, a King who is all-wise and all-good and who will never die. Herod recognized this; he immediately felt his own authority threatened by Christ's arrival – here was one who had divine authority, whose right to rule was absolute, which meant that Herod would have to take second place (at best). Second place was repugnant to his enormous pride. So even though he recognized Christ's lordship, he resisted it, he tried to do away with it.

Every human heart has a Herod lurking inside it. We are children of Adam and Eve, heirs of their disobedience, and part of us detests the idea of having to submit to a higher authority. For some, the revulsion is so strong that they convince themselves there is no God, or that the universe is a democracy, so they can be their own gods. They do violence to their conscience just as Herod was soon to do violence to the infants of Bethlehem. They massacre part of their own rational nature, which longs to recognize a creator and offer him homage (as the wise men did), just as Herod was to massacre a portion of his own people. Each human heart is a battlefield where Herod and the wise men vie for predominance. Will we kneel before the Lord and worship him, or will we vainly strike out to destroy him?

CHRIST THE TEACHER Most of the time, God doesn't work in weird, inscrutable ways. He actually wants us to find him, to know him, to discover the full and vibrant life that he created us to live. He spent the whole Old Testament preparing Israel to welcome the Messiah; they even knew the city where the Messiah would be born! And when the moment came, God sent a sign to the Gentiles as well; he gave them a star to guide them to the very dwelling where the Savior could be found. And just to make sure that neither the Gentiles nor the Israelites would have any doubts, he arranged for them to confer together at the very time of the Messiah's coming. What more could God have done to announce the Savior's arrival? And yet, only a few believed.

He repeats this methodology with each one of us. He bombards us with signs of his love, of his presence, of his will – through the Scriptures, through the examples of thousands of saints, through volumes of instruction and explanation propagated by his Church, through the symbols and forms of the liturgy, through the living words of popes and pastors…. How easy he makes it for us to know him, to find him, to know how he would have us live! And yet, still, how few of us really believe, how often we doubt and disobey, how fervently we demand more and more signs. We are fortunate that this divine Teacher has infinite patience; without it, he would long ago have given up on such slow pupils.

CHRIST THE FRIEND St Matthew points out exactly where and when Christ was born, the actual place and the actual period of time: "at Bethlehem in Judea, during the reign of King Herod." We can find the place on maps today, and also on ancient maps; we can travel there. We can find Herod's name in today's reference books, as well as in documents written two thousand years ago.

Christianity is not a mythic religion. The saving deeds of Jesus Christ do not take place in some prehistorical epoch that we mimic by empty reenactments. Our God came into the world and "dwelt among us," and he continues to do the same today. His Church and his sacraments are extensions of his desire to meet each one of us in the here-and-now of our lives, to befriend us as we are and where we are, and to walk with us along our earthly journey. Is that how we think of him? Is that how we live our faith? He is certainly hoping so, and he will help us – if we let him.

CHRIST IN MY LIFE You are the one Lord. I believe in you, and I want to follow you. You have every right over me, and I renew my commitment to obey you in all things. What a great gift you have given me! I know you, I am close to you, and I live through your grace. Dear Lord, never let me be separated from you, and help me to bring many others into your friendship…

You have always reached out to all peoples through your Church. Only because of that did the faith make its way to my people, to my nation, and into my life. Thank you for coming to me; thank you for the Church. Guide and protect your Church, Lord, and make me an energetic, faithful, active member within her ranks…

Why do I prefer extraordinary manifestations of your presence in my life and ignore so regularly the normal ways you speak to me – the Church's teaching, the everyday circumstances of my life, the Scriptures, the sacraments? You have given me so much, and you just keep on giving. Open my eyes, Lord, so that I can see you in all your gifts, and thank you in them, and respond to your love with love…

QUESTIONS FOR SMALL GROUP DISCUSSION

1. What struck you most about this passage? What did you notice that you hadn't noticed before?

2. Why do you think that the "all Jerusalem" was so greatly affected by the wise men's arrival?

3. Can you see any parallels between the wise men coming to Jerusalem and a Christian going to Sunday Mass?

4. The chief priests and scribes knew where the Messiah was to be born, and yet none of them accompanied the wise men to look for him in Bethlehem. Why not? If you had been one of them, would you have gone?

Cf. Catechism of the Catholic Church, 528 on the meaning of Epiphany; 1-3, 781, 1066-1068 on God's plan of salvation; 2258-2265 on prayer as an intimate relationship with God

4. THE START OF CHRISTIAN WORSHIP (MT 2:7-12)

"You alone are the Lord. To be ruled by you is for us salvation. For us to serve you is nothing else but to be saved by you!"

- William of St-Thierry

Matthew 2:7-12

Then Herod summoned the wise men to see him privately. He asked them the exact date on which the star had appeared, and sent them on to Bethlehem. 'Go and find out all about the child,' he said 'and when you have found him, let me know, so that I too may go and do him homage.' Having listened to what the king had to say, they set out. And there in front of them was the star they had seen rising; it went forward, and halted over the place where the child was. The sight of the star filled them with delight, and going into the house they saw the child with his mother Mary, and falling to their knees they did him homage. Then, opening their treasures, they offered him gifts of gold and frankincense and myrrh. But they were warned in a dream not to go back to Herod, and returned to their own country by a different way.

CHRIST THE LORD   Christ deserved the gift of gold. Gold has always indicated royalty, and the visiting Magi knew that this child was the newborn King of the Jews. That the Magi themselves were not Jews and still did him homage shows that in Christ all the Old Testament prophecies have reached their fulfillment: the time has come for Israel (through Jesus) to become a blessing to all peoples.

Gold is a precious metal not only because it is beautiful, but also because it is rare. To make an offering of gold is to make an offering of what we count most valuable; even to this day gold is the preferred metal for the sacred vessels used in the Mass, to symbolize that Christ's Body and Blood are the most precious gifts we have to offer. Because he is our King, Christ deserves our very best. We should follow the Magi's lead and do him homage by putting all of our talents and gifts at his service, resolving never to use them except in ways that will please him the most.

This offering, however, takes faith. God only explained part of the story to the three wise men. They had to follow a mysterious star in order to make their way to Jesus. The star drifted in and out of sight: when they saw it, they were filled with delight, when clouds obscured it, they had to journey by faith. To follow the Lord and give him our all means learning to trust him, to keep his star shining in our hearts, no matter the weather.

CHRIST THE TEACHER   Even before Jesus can talk, he teaches us a precious truth about ourselves. In our hearts there dwell two potential responses to the coming of such a King: Herod's or the Magi's. Herod had spent his life murdering and extorting and building a personal kingdom ruled by his whim and for his personal glory. Christ enters the scene, a King with authority from on high. Herod immediately feels the threat: if Christ is not destroyed or discredited, it could spell the end of all his labors.

The Magi detect the arrival of the long-awaited King of the Jews in natural signs, which God surely used as a way to communicate with them in a language they would understand. Far from fearing the demands that this new King might make on their personal lives, they rejoice to know that God's Savior is finally coming. Instead of hoarding their treasures, the fruits of their life's labors, they generously offer them to Christ as gestures of honor and respect, of homage due to the one come to rule over an everlasting Kingdom.

When Christ enters our lives, which he does every day through the voice of conscience, the teachings of his Church, and the designs of Providence, we must choose in whose steps we will follow, Herod's or the Magi's.

CHRIST THE FRIEND The Magi's journey had not been an easy one. Traveling in ancient times involved risks and hardships almost unknown to us; the Magi had to traverse deserts and mountains on foot, braving harsh weather, outlaws, and wild animals at every turn. They undertook the journey because they believed in Jesus Christ, even though they had seen none of his miracles, knew not the full meaning of Israel's prophecies, and lacked the ultimate testimony of his love on the cross. Christ rewarded their determined faith with profound joy: "The sight of the star filled them with delight." When we, who have many more reasons to believe, sincerely pursue friendship with Christ the King, he is glad to give it, along with all the joy it affords.

But our friendship also gives *him* joy. Frankincense (incense) was burned in houses of worship for the pleasure of God. The Old Testament speaks of sweet smelling burnt offerings that pleased the Lord, and the Book of Revelation mentions incense (which stands for the prayers of God's people) being offered ceaselessly to the Lamb (Christ). The incense itself is powerless to warm the heart of God; only the attitude that moves us to offer it can do that. God longs for us to come to him, to trust him, to seek answers and help from him – just as a father rejoices when his children bring him all their troubles and triumphs. Our humble, confident, and sincere prayers fill the heavenly courts with the pleasing aroma of spiritual frankincense; let us not deprive our Lord of such delights, which he relishes so much.

CHRIST IN MY LIFE You deserve my worship, my allegiance, my adoration – you deserve the very best I can give you in all things. How negligent I am in giving it! I don't know how you put up with my pettiness and self-absorption. Thank you for giving me the gift of faith; teach me to live that faith to the hilt. With the love of your heart, inflame my heart…

Part of me is just like Herod: when my will or wishes are contradicted, I go ballistic. You know that. It doesn't surprise you. I want to take advantage of those moments, Lord. In them I can glorify you, offer you the precious incense of self-mastery out of love for you. Teach me to kneel before you and offer you my most prized possession: my own will…

So many times you have let me see the star! You have given me so many blessings, so many experiences of your love. Thank you, Lord. Keep filling me heart with your joy, so that I can overflow with it to everyone around me, and they too can lift their gaze to the heavens and see the light of your love, even if that star disappears behind a cloud…

QUESTIONS FOR SMALL GROUP DISCUSSION

1. What struck you most about this passage? What did you notice that you hadn't noticed before?

2. Myrrh was an expensive spice, usually found in the form of ointment, used to embalm corpses for burial. Why would Providence have moved the Magi to offer this as a gift to Jesus?

3. Jesus wasn't alone when the Magi finally found him; St Matthew points out that he was with his mother, Mary. What is the significance of this detail?

4. What do you think Mary's sentiments were when the Magi offered their valuable gifts to Jesus, who had been born into such humble circumstances?

Cf. Catechism of the Catholic Church, 528 on the meaning of Epiphany; 1-3, 781, 1066-1068 on God's plan of salvation; 1776-1794 on the role of our conscience

5. THE SUFFERING BEGINS (MT 2:13-23)

"We needed an incarnate God who would die that we might live."

- St Gregory Nazianzen

Matthew 2:13-23

After they had left, the angel of the Lord appeared to Joseph in a dream and said, 'Get up, take the child and his mother with you, and escape into Egypt, and stay there until I tell you, because Herod intends to search for the child and do away with him'. So Joseph got up and, taking the child and his mother with him, left that night for Egypt, where he stayed until Herod was dead. This was to fulfil what the Lord had spoken through the prophet: 'I called my son out of Egypt.'

Herod was furious when he realised that he had been outwitted by the wise men, and in Bethlehem and its surrounding district he had all the male children killed who were two years old or under, reckoning by the date he had been careful to ask the wise men. It was then that the words spoken through the prophet Jeremiah were fulfilled: 'A voice was heard in Ramah, sobbing and loudly lamenting: it was Rachel weeping for her children, refusing to be comforted because they were no more.'

After Herod's death, the angel of the Lord appeared in a dream to Joseph in Egypt and said, 'Get up, take the child and his mother with you and go back to the land of Israel, for those who wanted to kill the child are dead'. So Joseph got up and, taking the child and his mother with him, went back to the land of Israel. But when he learnt that Archelaus had succeeded his father Herod as ruler of Judaea he was afraid to go there, and being warned in a dream he left for the region of Galilee. There he settled in a town called Nazareth. In this way the words spoken through the prophets were to be fulfilled: 'He will be called a Nazarene.'

CHRIST THE LORD Christ is God, and God can do whatever he pleases; his authority and power are unlimited. He could have chosen to form a body for the Incarnation out of the dust of the earth, just as he had done with Adam. Instead he chose to take on human life in all its dimensions, entering into a family and giving real people crucial roles in the plan of salvation. After all, it wasn't as if Mary and Joseph received a detailed business plan outlining what to do so as not to mess up God's design. Rather, God entrusted them with caring for the child Jesus, helping them here and there with divine interventions, but leaving most of the work up to them. The Holy Family is not holy because Mary and Joseph never struggled, never wondered what to do, or never had problems; the Holy Family was holy because in the face of all their challenges they never let their trust in God waver. They did their best, trusting that God would take care of the rest, and he did.

This is still his policy. God has chosen to administer the salvation won by Christ through the action of the Church. He guarantees the guidance of the Holy Spirit, but the Lord has given the keys of his Kingdom into Peter's hands. In union with Christ's vicar and Peter's successor, the pope, every Catholic is called to carry out a particular, unrepeatable role in the plan of salvation. As St Augustine put it, "God created us without us, but he did not will to save us without us." Christ is a King, but knows how to delegate like a good CEO.

CHRIST THE TEACHER One of the gifts the wise men brought to Jesus was myrrh, a spice most often found in the form of ointment, used to embalm dead bodies before burial. In Herod's massacre of these innocent children, we learn why such a gift was fitting for this King, who was going to save the human family from sin precisely through his suffering and death, though he too was innocent. In this way, he begins to reveal the meaning of suffering.

On the feast of the Holy Innocents, the liturgy contains this prayer, "Father, the Holy Innocents offered you praise by the death they suffered for Christ."

What does that mean? An evil man (Herod) commits a horrendous deed, and according to the Church this echoes the glory of God. At first glance, it seems hard to believe. But in truth, it's quite simple. These innocent children suffered for Christ; in other words, the evil was directed at Christ, but it fell upon them. Because of this, God will certainly give them a share in his heavenly glory.

All evil, ultimately, is directed against Christ – its original source is the devil, and the devil is in rebellion against God. Therefore, when innocent people suffer because of the forces of evil (and evil is always, some way or another, at the source of suffering), they too are taking upon themselves blows meant for Christ. And so we entrust them to God's mercy. In other words, God's answer to the question of why he permits the innocent to suffer is Christ. He sent Christ, and Christ, in his own flesh, redeemed suffering. He made it a path to salvation, by taking it upon himself. That's why saints don't respond to injustice with violence; they respond with charity, with love – they share the burden of their suffering neighbor, just as Christ shared ours.

These ideas and explanations, as true as they are, don't take away the pain from our suffering, but they do wrap it up in a bigger package, a package full of meaning and destined for heaven. Even so, the Church teaches us that the only way to understand it completely is to love Christ and our neighbors more intensely.

CHRIST THE FRIEND Real friendship demands and thrives on loyalty. No one is more loyal than Jesus Christ. St Matthew makes this particularly clear in his Gospel by frequently pointing out how Jesus fulfilled throughout his earthly life the many prophecies that the Old Testament made about him – he mentions three of them in this passage. As the testimony of the saints – the men and women who have banked completely on God's loyalty – ceaselessly reminds us, God can never be outdone in generosity.

God the Father: I promised to send a Savior; I promised to establish an everlasting covenant; I promised to pour my Spirit into your heart; I promised to inaugurate a Kingdom that will never end. All these promises I fulfilled by sending you my Son, Jesus Christ. In him you no longer have to be alone, you no longer have to wonder if you can trust me, you no longer have to be afraid. In him, you have the most loyal of friends. In him you can see that I am pure goodness and mercy. All you have to do is trust in him by following his commands. He will never let you down; he will lead you home.

CHRIST IN MY LIFE Lord, I believe that you choose to work out my salvation by making use of my cooperation, but at times I wonder why. Sometimes I would prefer that you leave it all up to me, and other times I want you to do everything and just let me kick back and relax. Life is so unsteady, Lord. Be my anchor. Don't let the storms and temptations throw me off course. Teach me to do your will…

You came to earth to suffer, to take upon yourself our sufferings, the ones our sins have generated. I have to admit that I don't understand fully why you haven't just eliminated suffering, but I know that your wise plan is better than anything I could ever concoct. Teach me to suffer with faith, with love, as you did…

You have never let me down. You are my faithful friend. You are as faithful as the mountains, the snowcapped mountains that never change. I can depend on you. And I want you to be able to depend on me. I want to live close to you, just as you want to live close to me. Lord Jesus, let me know your love…

QUESTIONS FOR SMALL GROUP DISCUSSION

1. What struck you most in this passage? What did you notice that you hadn't noticed before?

2. What are the best ways to comfort someone who is suffering from a tragic loss?

3. Why didn't Jesus just eliminate suffering instead of choosing to use it to teach us faith, hope, and love?

4. How would Joseph and Mary have felt towards God while they were fleeing to Egypt?

Cf. Catechism of the Catholic Church, 309-324 on Providence and the problem of evil

THE GOSPEL OF MATTHEW CHAPTER 3

"After God had spoken many times and in various ways through the prophets, in these last days he has spoken to us by a Son. For he sent his Son, the eternal Word who enlightens all men, to dwell among men and to tell them about the inner life of God. Hence, Jesus Christ, sent as a man among men, speaks the words of God, and accomplishes the saving work which the Father gave him to do. As a result, he himself – to see whom is to see the Father – completed and perfected Revelation and confirmed it with divine guarantees. He did this by the total fact of his presence and self-manifestation – by words and works, signs and miracles, but above all by his death and glorious resurrection from the dead, and finally by sending the Spirit of truth. He revealed that God was with us, to deliver us from the darkness of sin and death, and to raise us up to eternal life. The Christian economy, therefore, since it is the new and definitive covenant, will never pass away; and no new public revelation is to be expected before the glorious manifestation of our Lord, Jesus Christ."

- *Second Vatican Council, Constitution on Divine Revelation, #4*

6. WAKE-UP CALL (MT 3:1-12)

"The brightest of all lights follows the lamp that goes before him. The Word follows the voice in the wilderness. The bridegroom follows the friend of the bridegroom who is making ready for God a special people, cleansing them with water in anticipation of the Spirit."

- St Gregory Nazianzen

Matthew 3: 1-12

In due course John the Baptist appeared; he preached in the wilderness of Judaea and this was his message: 'Repent, for the kingdom of heaven is close at hand'. This was the man the prophet Isaiah spoke of when he said: 'A voice cries in the wilderness: Prepare a way for the Lord, make his paths straight.' This man John wore a garment made of camel hair with a leather belt round his waist, and his food was locusts and wild honey. Then Jerusalem and all Judaea and the whole Jordan district made their way to him, and as they were baptised by him in the river Jordan they confessed their sins.

But when he saw a number of Pharisees and Sadducees coming for baptism he said to them, 'Brood of vipers, who warned you to fly from the retribution that is coming? But if you are repentant, produce the appropriate fruit, and do not presume to tell yourselves, We have Abraham for our father, because, I tell you, God can raise children for Abraham from these stones. Even now the axe is laid to the roots of the trees, so that any tree which fails to produce good fruit will be cut down and thrown on the fire. I baptise you in water for repentance, but the one who follows me is more powerful than I am, and I am not fit to carry his sandals; he will baptise you with the Holy Spirit and fire. His winnowing-fan is in his hand; he will clear his threshing-floor and gather his wheat into the barn; but the chaff he will burn in a fire that will never go out.'

CHRIST THE LORD No prominent figure makes an official visit unannounced. Long before the pope sets foot in a country, the people there begin their preparations, so as to give him a fitting reception. Presidents announce ahead of time when they will make a public appearance, so that proper arrangements can be made.

Jesus Christ is no less gracious. Before he began his public ministry, the Holy Spirit sent John to make the preparations, to remind the people of Israel of their long-standing covenant with the God of heaven and earth, to inform them that the eagerly awaited Messiah was soon to arrive, and to instruct them about how to get ready. John himself was such a powerful figure – Israel's only prophet in more than two centuries, described by Christ as the greatest of all prophets – that many Jews thought he was the Messiah. But the Messiah, John assured them, would be much greater; he would be a true King (for whose travels in ancient times roads were built and repaired, explaining the phrase "make straight his paths") coming to inaugurate his rule – as he still does today and every day, when he comes to his people in the Eucharist.

CHRIST THE TEACHER Christ's messenger offers an invaluable lesson. He teaches us how to prepare for the Lord's coming (thus this passage's prominence in the liturgy of Advent, when the Church focuses its attention on the three comings of Christ: Bethlehem, history's end, and the "today" of the liturgy). Clearing the road for Christ to enter our lives means first of all repenting, turning from our selfish ways, and secondly bearing good fruit (actions of self-giving and self-forgetful love) to show that our repentance is real. It begins with acknowledging our sins, because how can we have room in our hearts for a Savior when we do not think we need to be saved? It concludes with a decision to leave sin behind and concrete actions to carry out that decision. Only then, after repenting and reforming, will we be able to really experience the joys of the coming Kingdom.

CHRIST THE FRIEND A powerful Lord demands loyalty from his subjects; a wise teacher explains the ways to be loyal; but a friend goes one step further, offering forgiveness for disloyalties committed, and providing strength to start over again. Jesus Christ is our Lord, and he is our Teacher, but no matter how small or large our infidelities may be, he is above all our Friend, reaching out his hand again and again to strengthen and forgive, especially through the sacrament of reconciliation. What greater gift can we offer the heart of Christ than the gift of taking that hand in our own? If the pope were coming to our house, we would be sure to have everything in order. Christ wants to come anew into our hearts each day, each season, each time we receive Holy Communion – bringing new graces to help us meet all the challenges we face and all those still to come; should we not prepare our hearts well?

CHRIST IN MY LIFE Lord, help me to know myself. If I were to meet John the Baptist, what warning would he have for me? Which of my habits or attitudes are constricting your action in my life, limiting the intimacy of our friendship? I really do want to follow you. I believe that you are the King of kings, my Lord and Savior. Dear Jesus, come and cleanse my heart from all desires except the desire to follow wherever you lead…

You are eager to come into my life, to be my Savior. You are eager to come into everyone's life, to lead all people to the fullness of human happiness here on this earth and forever in heaven. I know some people who need to hear this good news. Show me how to be like John the Baptist for them. I am your ambassador; please keep me faithful…

You never get tired of forgiving me. Why is it often so hard for me to forgive those around me? My heart is resentful. I take offense… Jesus, I put my anger at your feet. Maybe I can't help feeling those emotions, but I offer them to you so that you can make sure my words and actions stay true to yours: "Father, forgive them…"

QUESTIONS FOR SMALL GROUP DISCUSSION

1. What struck you most in this passage? What did you notice that you hadn't noticed before?

2. John reprimands the Pharisees and Sadducees (religious and political leaders of Israel) for being hypocrites, for coming to be baptized but not changing their lives. In what ways is it especially easy for Christ's followers to be hypocritical in today's society? In your particular life situation?

3. St Matthew uses the phrase "Kingdom of heaven" thirty-two times in his Gospel. What does this term tell you about the nature of Christ's Kingdom?

Cf. Catechism of the Catholic Church, 717-720 on the role of John the Baptist in the mystery of salvation; 1430-1433 on interior penance; 678 on Jesus taking up John's theme of judgment; 541, 669, 671 on the Kingdom of Heaven

7. CHRIST TAKES OUR PART (MT 3:13-17)

"He took the nature of a servant without stain of sin, enlarging our humanity without diminishing his divinity. He emptied himself; though invisible he made himself visible, though Creator and Lord of all things he chose to be one of us mortal men."

- Pope St Leo the Great

Matthew 3:13-17

Then Jesus appeared: he came from Galilee to the Jordan to be baptised by John. John tried to dissuade him. 'It is I who need baptism from you' he said 'and yet you come to me!' But Jesus replied, 'Leave it like this for the time being; it is fitting that we should, in this way, do all that righteousness demands.' At this, John gave in to him. As soon as Jesus was baptised he came up from the water, and suddenly the heavens opened and he saw the Spirit of God descending like a dove and coming down on him. And a voice spoke from heaven, 'This is my Son, the Beloved; my favour rests on him.'

CHRIST THE LORD   There are very few times in the Bible that God speaks "from heaven" for all to hear. On the threshold of Jesus' public ministry, however, the Father feels compelled to make clear who Christ is and why he has come.

Jesus Christ was God's Son, even before he became Mary's son. Though the nature of Christ's eternal sonship remains cloaked in the unfathomable mystery of the Holy Trinity, the Church gives us an inkling of what it means through the words we use in praying the Creed: "The only son of God, eternally begotten of the Father, God from God, Light from Light, true God from true God, begotten, not made, one in being with the Father." Somehow, while being a distinct person from God the Father, Jesus Christ shares fully in the God-ness of the Father. Jesus Christ, then, is God, the second person of the Trinity: "This is my Son, the Beloved."

At Christmas, we celebrate Christ's coming to earth as a man. This he did in order to reestablish communion between mankind and God, a communion broken when the human family displeased God and rebelled against him through committing original sin. In Christ's baptismal theophany (a manifestation of God perceivable by the senses – in this case, the descent of the Holy Spirit in the form of a dove and the voice of God coming from the heavens), God the Father reiterates this fundamental mission of his incarnate Son, and explains why we should pay attention to Christ: "…my favor rests on him." Christ restores friendship between God and man by being a man who thoroughly pleases God; if we want to enter into that renewed friendship, we only need to follow Christ.

CHRIST THE TEACHER   The term "Christ" comes from a Greek translation of the Hebrew word, "Messiah," which literally means "the anointed one," the one set aside for a special mission. The Messiah was the one anointed and sent by God to bring about complete redemption from sin and suffering. Christ's baptism illustrates the fulfillment of the Old Testament prophecies about what kind of anointing the Messiah would receive: an anointing with the Holy Spirit.

We each receive that same anointing in the sacrament of confirmation, where the perfumed oil (or "chrism") applied to our forehead symbolizes the beginning of our own public ministry, the time when, in fulfillment of our baptismal commitment, we take on the task of publicly spreading the sweet aroma of Christ through our words and deeds. When Christ took our part by being baptized just like one of us, he did so in order to enable us to share his part in the work of redemption.

CHRIST THE FRIEND Christ's puzzling response to John the Baptist's hesitancy reveals the heart of a trustworthy friend. John offered baptism in order to help his fellow Jews repent, but Christ, who was sinless, did not need to repent. Rather, Jesus' submission to baptism foreshadows his work on the cross, where although he had no sin of his own, he "made himself sin" (2 Corinthians 5:21) in order to wipe away our sins.

As St Paul put it, Christ "loved me and sacrificed himself for my sake" (Galatians 2:20). Notice how personal Paul's experience of Christ's love is – he loved me; he sacrificed himself for me. That's what comes across in this account of Jesus' baptism: it's all about Jesus taking my part, coming down to my level in order to lift me up to his level. What more could he have done to prove himself our friend?

CHRIST IN MY LIFE Lord, the day of my confirmation was no empty ceremony – you were the one who confirmed me, through the bishop's hands. And you did it in order to recruit me into the ranks of your army. And you equipped my soul with the gifts of the Holy Spirit, so I would be ready to spread your light and truth wherever I go. Why do I forget about my mission? Lord, I say again what I said that day: I believe in you…

When I was baptized, you took up residence in my soul. I am your tabernacle. You are always with me. How much you must love me! I can barely put up with myself, yet you, who are perfect in every way, have desired to be my constant companion. Thank you, Lord. Never let me be separated from you. I want to be worthy of this gift, and I want to share it with everyone around me. Lord Jesus, make me holy…

Increase my faith, Lord. Teach me to see all things as you see them, to find your goodness and love in them. You are my brother; we share the same life, the life of grace. Make that life grow and spread in me, and grow and spread through me…

QUESTIONS FOR SMALL GROUP DISCUSSION

1. What struck you most in this passage? What did you notice that you hadn't noticed before?

2. Why do you think the Holy Spirit descended in the form of a dove? Does the dove appear elsewhere in Scripture? What does this tell us about how the Holy Spirit acts in our lives?

3. Why did St John baptize with water from the Jordan River? Why does the Church use water as baptism even now? What role has water played in the history of salvation?

4. Why did God the Father say that his favor rests with Christ even before Christ had begun to preach, perform miracles, and offer himself on the cross? What does it teach us about how to please God?

Cf. Catechism of the Catholic Church: 436-440 on the meaning of the word "Christ"; 441-445 on the meaning of the title "Son of God"; 535-537 on the baptism of Jesus; 1285-1314 on the sacrament of confirmation

THE GOSPEL OF MATTHEW CHAPTER 4

"No reason, then, for despair when we find ourselves exposed to temptation; it only means that we must pray to God more earnestly than ever, asking for his gracious help in all our trials. Has not St Paul told us that God, with the temptation itself, will ordain the issue of it, and enable us to hold our own? Humbly, then, let us submit to God's dealings with us, when any temptation or trial comes; it is the humble soul he will set free, and lift up to greatness. No such test as these of a man's spiritual progress, no such occasion of merit, no such area to show his fighting qualities. After all, when a man is not conscious of any difficulties in his path, is it any special credit to him to be devout and zealous? But let him carry himself patiently when everything goes against him – then there is good promise of spiritual advancement. Why is it that some people are preserved from grave temptation, yet fight a losing battle all the time against their petty, day-to-day faults? Surely it is to keep them humble; with such proof of their frailty in things of little moment, they are not likely to err throughout self-confidence where great issues are at stake."

- The Imitation of Christ, Book I, Chapter 13

8. DESERT STORM (MT 4:1-11)

"Lord of the universe, he hid his infinite glory and took the nature of a servant. Incapable of suffering as God, he did not refuse to be a man, capable of suffering."

- Pope St Leo the Great

Matthew 4:1-11

Then Jesus was led by the Spirit out into the wilderness to be tempted by the devil. He fasted for forty days and forty nights, after which he was very hungry, and the tempter came and said to him, 'If you are the Son of God, tell these stones to turn into loaves'. But he replied, 'Scripture says: Man does not live on bread alone but on every word that comes from the mouth of God'. The devil then took him to the holy city and made him stand on the parapet of the Temple. 'If you are the Son of God' he said 'throw yourself down; for scripture says: He will put you in his angels' charge, and they will support you on their hands in case you hurt your foot against a stone'. Jesus said to him, 'Scripture also says: You must not put the Lord your God to the test'. Next, taking him to a very high mountain, the devil showed him all the kingdoms of the world and their splendour. 'I will give you all these' he said, 'if you fall at my feet and worship me.' Then Jesus replied, 'Be off, Satan! For scripture says: You must worship the Lord your God, and serve him alone.' Then the devil left him, and angels appeared and looked after him.

CHRIST THE LORD The King of Light does battle with the Prince of Darkness and comes out victorious, reversing Adam's original defeat. No one else before or after has so soundly trounced the devil. We may think it is because Christ had special powers, but the Scriptures don't present it that way. According to them, the source of Christ's victory is his humility.

The devil tries to trick him into being selfish, but each time, Jesus appeals to a higher law – he refuses to do things any way but his Father's way. Christ is the humblest man who ever lived. Having received everything from his Father, he claimed nothing as his own. And it was the strength of such absolute humility that crushed the devil's kingdom, not only in this desert temptation, but also later, in his final temptation. While he agonized in the Garden of Gethsemane on the eve of his Passion, he resisted the devil's onslaught with the prayer to his Father: "Yet not as I will, but as you will" (Matthew 26:39). Christ is the Lord, and humility is his scepter.

CHRIST THE TEACHER The first lesson in this passage is easy to overlook: *temptation is not sin*. Christ himself was the "spotless lamb" foreshadowed by the Old Testament sacrifices, the new Adam who had no sin. And yet, he experienced temptation. He was invited to disobey God's will. As his followers, then, we should expect nothing less. We too will experience temptation; we should neither be surprised nor perturbed by feeling the attraction of sin. In fact, by battling against temptation we grow in our love for God, showing we love him and giving him glory.

The second lesson is even easier to overlook: *the devil is real*. St Matthew leaves no room for doubt on this point. The reason the Spirit led Christ into the desert in the first place, he tells us, was "to be tempted by the devil." (The forty days of Lent correspond to this forty-day sojourn of Christ in the desert.) We don't fully understand the nuts and bolts of *how* the devil influences things, but the Church has always taught that his influence is *real*. The devil is dead-set against Christ and his Kingdom. Therefore, we should expect him and his minions to do all they can to disrupt Christians who try to build that Kingdom: stirring up opposition, multiplying difficulties, and putting up plenty of roadblocks.

The third lesson is the most important one. By his all-out attack on Christ, the devil shows his hand. Jesus' three temptations expose *the devil's three favorite ploys*. In order to divert us from God's path, the devil will appeal to our desire for comfort and pleasure ("Turn those stones into jelly donuts"), our desire for recognition ("Do a swan dive off the top of the temple; that will impress them"), or our desire for greatness ("Just do it – it'll make you rich and powerful"). Of course, merely knowing the devil's tactics won't neutralize them completely. Our desires for comfort, recognition, and influence run deep. To be able to resist them, we have to desire something else even more, just as Christ did: we have to "set our hearts on his Kingdom first" (Matthew 6:33), and then everything else will fall into place.

CHRIST THE FRIEND Jesus Christ knows what it means to suffer temptation. He is truly human, just like us in all things except sin. Therefore, we can appeal to him when temptations beset us – he knows what we are going through. He did not want to leave us alone in our struggles; he wishes to walk by our side every step along the way. That's why he came to earth in the first place. In Christ we have a friend like no other: his patience is boundless, his empathy is complete, and his concern for us is as personal as it is pure.

Jesus: Do not be afraid – even when you are weak and you fall, I will be there to pick you up. Trust in the strength of prayer and sacrifice, and no temptations will drag you away from me. To be tempted doesn't mean to deny me – just turn your gaze back to me and I will be there to strengthen you against the wiles of the devil. In the desert, the thought of you spurred me on. I wanted to suffer in the wilderness to convince you that I can be there to hold you and guide you in the dark nights of your soul. I am with you until the end of time.

CHRIST IN MY LIFE Lord, your motto was so simple: "Thy will be done." I want to live by the same motto. But I often follow other mottos, other desires. Teach me how to close the gap between what I want to be (your faithful follower), and what I too often am (self-seeking, self-absorbed, self-indulgent). With the Kingdom of your heart, reign in my heart…

I have fallen victim to all three of the devil's favorite ploys, but you know the one that plagues me most. It comforts me to know that you faced temptation too. You will never let me be tempted more than I can resist. Be my strength, Lord, because I am so weak; always guide me along your true, sure path. Help me not to give in to the tricks of the devil…

You have done so much for me, Lord. And I forget so easily. You suffered for me – just for me. You were tempted, you fasted, you were hungry – all for me, to save me, to redeem me. Thank you, Lord. What would you have me do?...

QUESTIONS FOR SMALL GROUP DISCUSSION

1. What struck you most in this passage? What did you notice that you hadn't noticed before?

2. Which of the devil's three favorite ploys seem to be most popular in today's world? In the environment where you live?

3. In what ways does Christ's reaction to the devil's temptations differ from Adam and Eve's reaction in the Garden of Eden?

4. Jesus uses verses from the Bible to parry the devil's thrusts. Is that a practical tactic for all Christians? Why or why not? Think of some examples.

Cf. Catechism of the Catholic Church: 538-540 on Jesus' temptations; 407-409 on the hard battle that we must wage against temptation; 377 on the three ploys of the devil, or the "triple concupiscence"

9. JESUS GOES PUBLIC (MT 4:12-17)

"God is faithful: he made himself our debtor not by accepting anything from us, but by promising us such great blessings."

- St Augustine

Matthew 4:12-17

Hearing that John had been arrested he went back to Galilee, and leaving Nazareth he went and settled in Capernaum, a lakeside town on the borders of Zebulun and Naphtali. In this way the prophecy of Isaiah was to be fulfilled: 'Land of Zebulun! Land of Naphtali! Way of the sea on the far side of Jordan, Galilee of the nations! The people that lived in darkness has seen a great light; on those who dwell in the land and shadow of death a light has dawned.' From that moment Jesus began his preaching with the message, 'Repent, for the kingdom of heaven is close at hand.'

CHRIST THE LORD The arrest of John the Baptist marks the beginning of what the Church has traditionally called Jesus' "public life." This period of two or three years between his hidden life (when he grew up under the tutelage of Mary and Joseph and worked as a carpenter in Nazareth) and his Passion (when he was arrested, condemned, and crucified) fills the bulk of the four Gospels (the first four books of the New Testament, written by Saints Matthew, Mark, Luke, and John).

During this time, Jesus explained his mission and his message, both by the words he spoke and by the deeds he performed. He also chose and trained his twelve closest disciples, later known as the Apostles, who would be the foundation stones of the Church and the first Christian missionaries.

In a Bible of 1400 pages, the Gospels take up only 126: a remarkably brief account of God's thirty-three-year sojourn on earth. And yet, every word of those 126 pages counts. Nothing in the Gospels is recorded by chance; from the smallest detail to the longest speech, it was all included (under the inspiration of the Holy Spirit) for the sole purpose of bringing us into real, personal, intimate contact with our Lord and Savior – or rather, of bringing him into contact with us.

CHRIST THE TEACHER When John the Baptist was arrested, Jesus knew that the time had come to inaugurate the New Covenant. He decides to leave his home and family in Nazareth, and take up residence in the more cosmopolitan lakeside city of Capernaum. He knew that he had a limited time in which to fulfill a demanding mission; moving to Capernaum was one way of cutting all ties so as to be completely free to do what he had come to do. In our lives too, there are times when we need to make definitive decisions, as hard as they may be.

Jesus could have set up his headquarters anywhere in Palestine. He chose Galilee, Palestine's most populous province, located at the intersection of the two great roads that linked the Near East and the Mediterranean. He also began his work by teaching in the synagogues, which were the religious, social, and educational centers of Jewish culture. Jesus was a spiritual man, but that didn't hinder him from being practical and commonsensical; he had a mission to accomplish, and he used his wits to choose the most effective ways to go about it.

In this way, Christ teaches us that our mission field is the environment around us. This means not only spreading the good news in our homes, work, and social circles, but venturing out into the towns and cities where people gather, everywhere the message needs to be heard. It means courageously trusting that Christ is with us, speaking and acting through our prayers, words, and example.

CHRIST THE FRIEND In fulfilling the Old Testament prophecies about where the Messiah would live and work, Christ shows once again that God is faithful, that he keeps his promises, and that he is dependable. In summing up Christ's mission as bringing a "great light" to a people "that lived in darkness" and "dwell in the land and shadow of death," St Matthew reminds us that fallen humanity desperately needs a Savior. Sin leads people and societies into depression and destruction; Christ can lead them back to joy and prosperity. Whenever Christ asks something of us – whether through our consciences or through the teaching of the Church – he is motivated solely by what's best for us. He wasn't frowning when he called out "Repent, for the kingdom of heaven is near"; he was gladly bringing us good news – in fact, the best news of all.

CHRIST IN MY LIFE I don't think I have come to appreciate the Gospels the way I should. They are so familiar, Lord. And yet, what a treasure! The inspired record of your own words and deeds, the words and deeds of God-made-man. How I should cherish them! How I should study and enjoy and meditate on them! Make me a truly gospel person, Lord. But even more – make my life a bright reflection of the Gospels…

Is there perhaps something holding me back from following you as closely as you want me to – some unhealthy relationship, a vain ambition, or a selfish fear? If there is, Lord, please root it out. Show me how I can use my natural talents (the ones you gave me) more intelligently to build up the Church and bring others closer to you…

Many around me don't have the gift of faith. They suffer the consequences of sin and selfishness even more than I do. Use me to bring them your light, Lord! Don't let your people keep groping around in the darkness. Raise up apostles, send out missionaries – send me, Lord…

QUESTIONS FOR SMALL GROUP DISCUSSION

1. What struck you most in this passage? What did you notice that you hadn't noticed before?

2. What can we do to make better use of the great gift of the Gospels? During Mass, how does the Church treat the Gospel differently from the rest of Sacred Scripture, and what meaning do you see in those symbolic gestures?

3. Why do you think Jesus waited for John the Baptist to be arrested before beginning his own public ministry?

4. Try to rephrase "Repent, for the Kingdom of heaven is near" to make it more understandable for your typical nonbelieving acquaintance.

Cf. Catechism of the Catholic Church, 541-542 on the beginning of Jesus' public life

10. YOU CALL OUT MY NAME (MT 4:18-25)

"It was not enough for God to give us his Son merely to point out the way. He made the Son himself the way, so that you might journey with him as guide, as he walks in his own way."

- St Augustine

Matthew 4:18-25

As he was walking by the Sea of Galilee he saw two brothers, Simon, who was called Peter, and his brother Andrew; they were making a cast in the lake with their net, for they were fishermen. And he said to them, 'Follow me and I will make you fishers of men'. And they left their nets at once and followed him. Going on from there he saw another pair of brothers, James son of Zebedee and his brother John; they were in their boat with their father Zebedee, mending their nets, and he called them. At once, leaving the boat and their father, they followed him. He went round the whole of Galilee teaching in their synagogues, proclaiming the Good News of the kingdom and curing all kinds of diseases and sickness among the people. His fame spread throughout Syria, and those who were suffering from diseases and painful complaints of one kind or another, the possessed, epileptics, the paralysed, were all brought to him, and he cured them. Large crowds followed him, coming from Galilee, the Decapolis, Jerusalem, Judaea and Transjordania.

CHRIST THE LORD This passage immediately precedes the Sermon on the Mount. In the Sermon, St Matthew will bring together a summary of Jesus' moral and spiritual teaching. Before he does, however, he gives another summary, one that shows how Jesus spent his time (he followed a very busy schedule, it seems) and the impact he had on people's lives. With his teaching, Christ enlightens minds darkened by sin; with his proclamation of the Kingdom, he gives his listeners something worth living for, a mission, a destination, a purpose; with his healings and exorcisms, he gives them new hope and a fresh start. And all of this he did for immense crowds of Jews and non-Jews (many non-Jews lived in Transjordania and the Decapolis), irresistibly attracted by his wisdom, his love, and his power.

Today, that same Lord continues to make the same staggering impact, working just as tirelessly as ever through the preaching, sacraments, and apostolate of his Church, the extension through time of his presence and mission. We should let ourselves be amazed at the Christ of the Gospel, and we should rejoice to be a confirmed ambassador of such a King. And this amazement and joy should overflow into a desire to win over as many people as possible to Christ's Kingdom, letting his call, "Follow me," continue to resound through us to everyone he puts in our path.

CHRIST THE TEACHER Jesus didn't want to establish his Kingdom all by himself – he chose coworkers (his disciples) to work with him. And he trained his disciples by living side-by-side with them for three years. He invited them to follow him and live with him (as St Matthew narrates in this passage), and then he involved them in his work. He is not a King who stands aloof and sends orders from afar; he calls us personally, teaches us personally, and sends us out personally.

And that's why being his disciple is so demanding. Jesus doesn't follow our timetable or comply with our convenience. He could have called Peter and the others on their day off, when they weren't in the middle of work and in the presence of family members, but he chose to interrupt, to make them uncomfortable. Christianity is neither a philosophy nor an ideology: it is a personal encounter and a community endeavor, one that demands decision, action, trust, and sacrifice. To let Christ make us into fishers of men, we have to leave behind some things that look very appealing. It's always worth it in the end, because the Lord knows what he's doing, but it's still a hard lesson to learn. Maybe that's why Christ gives us so many chances to learn it.

CHRIST THE FRIEND Peter, Andrew, James, and John had all met Jesus before, when they were baptizing with John the Baptist (cf. John 1). Now he calls them to leave everything and follow him. And how does he issue this invitation? By coming into their own environment, by entering into their everyday lives – the same way he does with us, constantly inviting us to follow him more closely.

Jesus: I am always walking along the shore of your life. I am always thinking of you, watching you, and calling out to you. I want you to follow me more closely today than yesterday, more passionately tomorrow than today. I am at work in all the normal events and encounters of your day. Listen for my voice. How it thrills me whenever I see you listening, whenever you hear and heed my call! Just as it thrilled me when my first disciples showed their love, their trust, and their faith in me by leaving all that they knew and cared for in order to come and work in my Kingdom.

CHRIST IN MY LIFE You know me personally, better than my mother knows me, better than I know myself. You have called me to follow you. Why do I forget that so easily? The Creator of the universe asks me to give him a hand building up his everlasting Kingdom! Jesus, thank you for coming into my life. Thank you for making me your disciple. Thank you for calling my name. You are my Lord: Thy Kingdom come…

What is holding me back from being the disciple you created me to be? Am I trying to hang on to my boat, my nets, my father? You are my Creator; you deserve my complete obedience. Let it be done to me according to your word…

Surely you are calling many others to follow you. Don't you want everyone in your Kingdom? I am sorry for the times I resist sharing my faith, for the times I let my selfishness interfere with the mission you have entrusted to me of bringing all those around me into your friendship. With the zeal of your heart, Lord, set my heart on fire…

QUESTIONS FOR SMALL GROUP DISCUSSION

1. What struck you most in this passage? What did you notice that you hadn't noticed before?

2. Jesus could have chosen anyone to be his Apostles. Why do you think he chose these fishermen from Galilee?

3. Neither Peter nor the others knew what the future held when they decided to follow him – probably they couldn't have even imagined it. So why did they accept the call?

4. How do you think Jesus sounded when he called these first disciples? Serious, joyful, mysterious... What expression do you think he had on his face?

Cf. Catechism of the Catholic Church: 547-550 on the signs of the Kingdom; 551-553 on Jesus' call of the Twelve Apostles

THE GOSPEL OF MATTHEW CHAPTER 5

"If you are caught in the river of time and are drifting down the rapids, you have a choice. Either you may drown in the water, or you can catch hold of a tree by the stream and save your life. Similarly, you have a choice in the world. Either you may love the world that passes away with time, or you may hold on to Christ and live eternally with God… The sun is greater than the stars because only the sun provides daylight. Moreover, Christ is greater than all the saints and wise men. But there is a difference in the comparison. For there is a certain distance between the sun and the stars. But far greater is the distance between Christ and all the saints and wise men."

- St Augustine

11. A PATH AND A GOAL (MT 5:1-12)

"Waiting and patience are necessary if we are to fulfill what we have begun to be, and to receive, through God's unfailing help, what we hope for and believe."

- St Cyprian

Matthew 5:1-12

Seeing the crowds, he went up the hill. There he sat down and was joined by his disciples. Then he began to speak. This is what he taught them: 'How happy are the poor in spirit; theirs is the kingdom of heaven. Happy the gentle: they shall have the earth for their heritage. Happy those who mourn: they shall be comforted. Happy those who hunger and thirst for what is right: they shall be satisfied. Happy the merciful: they shall have mercy shown them. Happy the pure in heart: they shall see God. Happy the peacemakers: they shall be called sons of God. Happy those who are persecuted in the cause of right: theirs is the kingdom of heaven. Happy are you when people abuse you and persecute you and speak all kinds of calumny against you on my account. Rejoice and be glad, for your reward will be great in heaven; this is how they persecuted the prophets before you.'

CHRIST THE LORD When Jesus teaches, he takes an authoritative posture: he is not just giving advice, he is unveiling Truth. St Matthew illustrates this with two details prefacing Chapters 5-7 of his Gospel, the chapters that present in summary form Christ's idea of how we ought to live, commonly called the Sermon on the Mount.

First, Jesus sat down before he began to teach. When rabbis in Israel sat down to teach, it indicated that they were presenting their official doctrine. Second, the Greek used for "Then he began to speak…" contains a phrase that, literally translated, would read: "he opened his mouth." In the ancient world, this phrase indicated an official declaration or a setting forth of the speaker's most deeply held convictions. When St Matthew depicts Jesus as sitting down and opening his mouth, it is as if he were saying: "What follows is the soul of Christ's doctrine, his very heart expressed in the most important words spoken by the Word of God."

When Christ teaches, he claims to have authority; we can either accept it or reject it, but we cannot write it off, nor can we treat it like one opinion among many. Our attitude towards Jesus' teaching is our attitude toward the Lord himself.

CHRIST THE TEACHER At the end of the Beatitudes (the name given to these eight sentences outlining the characteristics of Christian living), we encounter Jesus' first indication that his teaching is intrinsically linked to his person. He makes an odd claim: "Happy are you when people abuse you and persecute you… *on my account.*" Instead of only pointing to his teaching, as most of history's great religions leaders did, he links his teaching to *himself*. Buddha, Mohammad, Confucius, and even Moses all said, "Look at this teaching!" Christ, on the other hand, says, "Look at *me*, follow *me*." Many times throughout the Gospels he will make similar claims: "I am the vine… I am the living bread… I am the way, the truth, the life… I am the light…"

Christ is a teacher who must either be accepted completely or rejected completely; to claim that he was merely one insightful religious leader and philosopher among history's many is to falsify his doctrine and miss the point. With Jesus Christ, it's all or nothing.

This link between his teaching and his person is also part of our vocation as his followers. Because Christ's claims go beyond mere philosophical logic, our own efforts to spread his teaching must do so as well. As Pope Paul VI put it, "Modern man listens more willingly to witnesses than to teachers, and if he does listen to teachers, it is because they are witnesses."

CHRIST THE FRIEND Entire books can be (and have been) written on the meaning of the Beatitudes – and they are worth studying. Each one identifies a fundamental Christian virtue, the very virtues that Christ exemplified throughout his life: humility, gentleness, mercy, purity, fortitude, justice, and sorrow for sin. The best way to develop these virtues in our own lives is to study and imitate them as lived out by Christ. Something that often goes unnoticed in this passage, however, is *why* Christ wants us to practice these virtues.

In the Greek texts of St Matthew's Gospel, these sentences actually don't contain any verbs, and the word translated as "happy" (or sometimes "blessed") refers to a kind of happiness independent of circumstances, complete in itself, and unshakable. As one scholar puts it, it is as if Christ were saying: "Oh, the bliss of…" instead of "Blessed are…" Christ teaches us not only how to get to heaven, but also how to find true and lasting joy on earth. He knows the secret to true happiness, and, like the friend that he is, he does his best to share it with us.

CHRIST IN MY LIFE The authority of your teaching astonished your audiences back in the days of your public life. And you continue to teach with the exact same divine authority today – through the Magisterium. Too often I give little attention to those teachings. Help me, Lord, to hear your voice resounding through the teachings of the Church, so that I will hearken to you in them, love you there, and follow you faithfully…

You want my happiness. This is why you created me, why you redeemed me. Lord, I have had moments of happiness, but you want me to have something more – a life completely fulfilled, truly and eternally fruitful. You look at me and you see your dream for my life… Thank you, Lord; all my hope is in you…

If I followed you more closely, I might experience more of the persecution and abuse you talk about. I wonder if fear of that is holding me back. Why am I afraid of what you consider to be a blessing? O Lord, with the knowledge of your heart make my heart wise, and with the courage of your heart free me from my fears…

QUESTIONS FOR SMALL GROUP DISCUSSION

1. What struck you most in this passage? What did you notice that you hadn't noticed before?

2. St Thomas Aquinas interprets the Beatitudes as types of actions that correspond to virtuous, Christian living in a fallen world. Go through them again and try to come up with real life examples of actions – choices – for each beatitude.

3. If an advertising firm were to make a list of three or four beatitudes describing where the society around you thinks happiness can be found, what might they come up with?

4. Why do you think God built into human nature the desire for a kind of happiness that can only be fulfilled supernaturally, that is, through our friendship with God?

Cf. Catechism of the Catholic Church, 1716-1729 on the Beatitudes; 581-582 on Jesus as someone who teaches with authority

12. A MISSION IN LIFE (MT 5:13-16)

"Of all divine things, the most godlike is to cooperate with God in the conversion of sinners."
- St Denis the Areopagite

Matthew 5:13-16

'You are the salt of the earth. But if salt becomes tasteless, what can make it salty again? It is good for nothing, and can only be thrown out to be trampled underfoot by men. You are the light of the world. A city built on a hill-top cannot be hidden. No one lights a lamp to put it under a tub; they put it on the lamp-stand where it shines for everyone in the house. In the same way your light must shine in the sight of men, so that, seeing your good works, they may give the praise to your Father in heaven.'

CHRIST THE LORD We are the salt "of the *earth*" and the light "of the *world*"; the entire globe and all of mankind are included in the mission Christ gives us. Here again Jesus Christ claims to be much more than an eloquent rabbi, a wise philosopher, or a pious prophet. Christ is the King of all people; his Kingdom extends over the whole of time and space. This universal King has made us his ambassadors; he has sent us to announce his Kingship everywhere, and to invite all people to enter into the Kingdom. Therefore, if we are to be his faithful followers, faithful to Christ's all-encompassing and everlasting mission, we must never put limits on what we will do for him, or on what we will let him do with us.

CHRIST THE TEACHER Christ is not a "lone ranger." He chooses to depend on Christians to carry forward his mission of salvation, to be the world's "salt" and "light." Through baptism and the Eucharist he gives us his own divine life;

through the teaching of the Church he fills us with his truth; and he is counting on us not to hoard these treasures, nor let them go to waste.

He is the only Savior. His name is "the only one by which we can be saved" (Acts 4:12). But he reaches out to those who need him *through* us. Our Christian witness and charity can save those whose lives are wasting away because of ignorance and sin, just as salt was used to preserve food from going bad before the invention of refrigerators. Our efforts to radiate Christian truth into society can enlighten those who are floundering in the darkness of mistaken philosophies and blind ideologies. Christ is teaching us that in him, by vocation, we have already become builders of an eternal Kingdom, but it is still up to us to get to work.

CHRIST THE FRIEND Friends do things together. Christ's main activity on this earth is salvation, being salt and light for souls dying and blinded because of sin. By bringing us into the Church – the "city on a hill" – he has invited us to work side by side with him. He wants to include us in his most engaging task – glorifying God the Father by working for the salvation of our brothers and sisters. He has offered his hand in friendship by offering us a share in his invaluable, incomparable work. Will we accept the offer?

Jesus: My child, I know that you want your life to matter. I created you with that desire, and I want to work with you to fulfill it. Nothing you can do will truly matter if it is disconnected from my Kingdom, because only my Kingdom will last forever. Even if you build magnificent buildings, climb to the top of the social ladder, or rule over thousands of people, what will you gain without linking your efforts and achievements to the most important mission of all, that of being salt and light for this dying and darkened world? If you only help one other person come into my Kingdom, to enter into my friendship, it will be worth more than even the richest reward this world can offer you. Come, follow me. Be my ambassador. Make all you do part of this privileged mission; let us work together; let me show you how meaningful life can really be.

CHRIST IN MY LIFE When I look into the depths of my heart, Lord, I am not sure if I have really accepted my vocation to be a saint. Sometimes I think it's good enough just to be pretty good. It's not that I doubt your ability to make me into a saint, it's just that I doubt myself. Such idle fears! You created me for this, for this great mission, for this great love. And it's the only thing that matters. Lord Jesus, make me holy!...

Why am I not more eager to bring others into your friendship? My heart is still tangled up in so many concerns and desires. Purify my heart and my mind, Lord. Right now, you are looking into my eyes and saying: "You are the salt of the earth, the light of the world." I want to follow you. I want to love you and make you loved. Lord Jesus, help me…

When I consider my Christian responsibility to build up the Church, some aspects of that responsibility make me enthusiastic, as with any project that friends take on together, and some leave me cold, as with duties impersonally imposed from the outside. Why is this?…

QUESTIONS FOR SMALL GROUP DISCUSSION

1. What struck you most in this passage? What did you notice that you hadn't noticed before?

2. As Christians, we are members of a worldwide, divinely established organization: the Catholic Church. How should that fact affect how we live our normal, everyday lives?

3. In what ways have other Christians been salt and light for you in your personal faith journey?

4. How can you be better salt and light for those around you – those you know personally, or those who live in the same environment (work, neighborhood, school, parish…)?

Cf. Catechism of the Catholic Church, 849-856 on the mission of the Church; 846-848 on the necessity of the Church for salvation; 900 on the necessity of every Christian to give witness and engage in apostolic action; 897-913 on the role of the laity in the mission of the Church

13. THE HEART OF THE MATTER (MT 5:17-37)

"The Christian life is the continuation and completion of the life of Christ in us. We should be so many Christs here on earth, continuing his life and his works, laboring and suffering…"

- St John Eudes

Matthew 5:17-37

'Do not imagine that I have come to abolish the Law or the Prophets. I have come not to abolish but to complete them. I tell you solemnly, till heaven and earth disappear, not one dot, not one little stroke, shall disappear from the Law until its purpose is achieved. Therefore, the man who infringes even one of the least of these commandments and teaches others to do the same will be considered the least in the kingdom of heaven; but the man who keeps them and teaches them will be considered great in the kingdom of heaven. For I tell you, if your virtue goes no deeper than that of the scribes and Pharisees, you will never get into the kingdom of heaven.

'You have learnt how it was said to our ancestors: You must not kill; and if anyone does kill he must answer for it before the court. But I say this to you: anyone who is angry with his brother will answer for it before the court; if a man calls his brother Fool he will answer for it before the Sanhedrin; and if a man calls him Renegade he will answer for it in hell fire. So then, if you are bringing your offering to the altar and there remember that your brother has something against you, leave your offering there before the altar, go and be reconciled with your brother first, and then come back and present your offering. Come to terms with your opponent in good time while you are still on the way to the court with him, or he may hand you over to the judge and the judge to the officer, and you will be thrown into prison. I tell you solemnly, you will not get out till you have paid the last penny.

'You have learnt how it was said: You must not commit adultery. But I say this to you: if a man looks at a woman lustfully, he has already committed adultery with her in his heart. If your right eye should cause you to sin, tear it out and throw it away; for it will do you less harm to lose one part of you than to have your whole body thrown into hell. And if your right hand should cause you to sin, cut it off and throw it away; for it will do you less harm to lose one part of you than to have your whole body go to hell. It has also been said: Anyone who divorces his wife must give her a writ of dismissal. But I say this to you: everyone who divorces his wife, except for the case of fornication, makes her an adulteress; and anyone who marries a divorced woman commits adultery.

'Again, you have learnt how it was said to our ancestors: You must not break your oath, but must fulfil your oaths to the Lord. But I say this to you: do not swear at all, either by heaven, since that is God's throne; or by the earth, since that is his footstool; or by Jerusalem, since that is the city of the great king. Do not swear by your own head either, since you cannot turn a single hair white or black. All you need say is Yes if you mean yes, No if you mean no; anything more than this comes from the evil one.'

CHRIST THE LORD   If any of Christ's other claims to ultimate authority leave room for doubt, the one he makes here removes it completely.

The Jews are aware that they are God's chosen people. Their individual and national identities stem from this acute awareness. They trace the origin of their uniqueness to the covenant God made with Moses: when God freed the ancient Hebrews from slavery in Egypt, he established them as the Chosen People, and through Moses he gave them the Law as a kind of identification card. The Law of Moses, then, was the mark of God's unique relationship with the Jewish people. In this Sermon on the Mount, Jesus claims to bring that Law to its fulfillment. In other words, he asserts himself to be higher than the Law, and therefore able to explain the full meaning behind it – a meaning that the Jewish people had previously failed to apprehend.

If Christ puts himself above the Law, and the Law is God's own message to

Israel, then clearly Jesus Christ is claiming to have divine authority. Anyone who says otherwise has not understood the Gospel, or is trying to falsify it. Our Lord is also our God.

CHRIST THE TEACHER   Each of the lessons taught in this passage could be expanded into an entire book. The core of them all, however, is in the heart. Our exterior behavior must follow God's will ("Do not think I have come to abolish the law…"), but that is not enough. For a citizen of Christ's Kingdom, the attitudes and desires of the heart must also be pleasing to God ("I have come… to *fulfill*…").

Friendship with God (which is what Jesus offers) requires a union of hearts. If God "wills all men to be saved" (1 Timothy 2:4), how can my friendship with him be complete when I harbor resentment against some people, or hold them in contempt, or tarnish their good name by spreading rumors about them or speaking ill of them? Christ is explaining the Law from this perspective when he explains the true meaning of sinful anger, lust, and lying. How can I live in intimacy with a God who loves every man and woman as a father loves his children, when in my heart I desire to use some of them only as objects for my pleasure and self-indulgence? How can I be a true friend of God, when I make promises that I don't intend to keep? (Some Jews had developed the habit of swearing oaths in the name of God if they meant to keep them, and swearing on something else if they meant to break them.) Other people may be satisfied with exterior success, with a hefty "bottom line"; Christ is interested in *every* line.

CHRIST THE FRIEND   The Greek word Jesus uses for "hell" is "Gehenna." Gehenna was Jerusalem's garbage dump. It had been the valley where unfaithful Jews in past centuries offered human sacrifices to foreign gods. When the nation reformed and such practices were stopped, they decided to use Gehenna as an open-air incinerator. Thus, the ever-smoldering and worm-infested valley became a symbol for the place where people who reject friendship with God suffer eternal frustration: hell.

Christ's frequent mention of hell in the Gospels has caused some critics to accuse Christianity of manipulating weak and superstitious people by instilling fear. Nothing could be less accurate. Christ's warnings are those of a friend. If you were in the car with a friend and saw that he was about to collide with an oncoming eighteen-wheeler, you would try to get him to turn out of the way. Jesus knows that we can only reach lasting happiness through friendship with God, and he wants us to be happy, so he warns us about everything that could damage or destroy that friendship. The truth is that eternity spent without God will be indescribably painful, because the human person was created to live in union with God. Since Christ loves us, he tells us the truth - even the tough truth.

CHRIST IN MY LIFE   You care about what happens in my mind and my heart – where only you and I can see. Help me look there now; show me what is pleasing to you and what is not, and then change what is not. Please, Lord – you know I can't do it on my own. You know how self-centered and wounded I am. If you don't change my heart, it will never change. Jesus, meek and humble of heart, make my heart more like yours...

Why do you give so much importance to such little things? A false promise here, a lustful fantasy there, an angry or spiteful word now and then... Lord, why don't you teach us about political systems and economic justice – the big picture? Somehow, the little picture of each soul matters more to you. Make me wise, Lord; teach me to follow you...

Some aspects of your will are harder for me to follow than others. Some of the Church's teachings I understand easily – others not so much. It doesn't matter, Lord. What matters is that I know it comes from you, my Creator and Redeemer. I want to do your will, no matter how hard. Increase my weak faith; Jesus, I trust in you...

QUESTIONS FOR SMALL GROUP REFLECTION

1. What struck you most in this passage? What did you notice that you hadn't noticed before?

2. What helps does the Church offer us to grow in our friendship with Christ, to make sure that our faith doesn't get reduced to a superficial, empty routine?

3. What has helped you most to grow in your friendship with Christ?

4. Christ links the action of murder with the attitude of anger and condemns them both as sinful. He does the same with the action of adultery and the attitude of lust. What does this teach us about human behavior?

Cf. Catechism of the Catholic Church, 1033-1037 on the reality and nature of hell; 577-582 on Jesus and the Law

14. GIVING LIKE GOD (MT 5:38-48)

"Finally, may Christ inflame the desires of all men to break through the barriers which divide them, to strengthen the bonds of mutual love, to learn to understand one another, and to pardon those who have done them wrong."

- Pope John XXIII, Pacem in terris

Mathew 5:38-48

'You have learnt how it was said: Eye for eye and tooth for tooth. But I say this to you: offer the wicked man no resistance. On the contrary, if anyone hits you on the right cheek, offer him the other as well; if a man takes you to law and would have your tunic, let him have your cloak as well. And if anyone orders you to go one mile, go two miles with him. Give to anyone who asks, and if anyone wants to borrow, do not turn away. You have learnt how it was said: You must love your neighbour and hate your enemy. But I say this to you: love your enemies and pray for those who persecute you; in this way you will be sons of your Father in heaven, for he causes his sun to rise on bad men as well as good, and his rain to fall on honest and dishonest men alike. For if you love those who love you, what right have you to claim any credit? Even the tax collectors do as much, do they not? And if you save your greetings for your brothers, are you doing anything exceptional? Even the pagans do as much, do they not? You must therefore be perfect just as your heavenly Father is perfect.'

CHRIST THE LORD   When Jesus says, "You have learnt how it was said," he is referring to the Old Covenant, the Law of Moses. That Law gave the Jewish people their unique standing among all the nations of the world, because God himself had given it to them. For 1500 years Israel's prophets and rabbis had interpreted it, applied it to changing circumstances, and exhorted the people to live it out, but never had a faithful Israelite ever claimed authority over it. Therefore, when Jesus says, "… but I say to you…" – implying an addition to the Law – his listeners are faced with something entirely new: someone who claims authority over the Law of Moses. Jesus is requiring of them a new allegiance and making way for a New Covenant. The Sermon on the Mount was revolutionary not only in its ideas, but in the claims of the Lord who gave it.

Jesus' claim to have authority means that his commands demand obedience. In the ancient world, obedience to a ruler was a familiar concept. In today's world, dominated by political democracies, it has become less so. In fact, the critical, self-sufficient, democratic mindset (so useful for politics) can even seep into the Church (where it's much less useful). But the truth of Christ doesn't change with trends and referendums. In our relationship with Jesus and his Church, humble obedience to legitimate authority is a virtue, not a vice.

CHRIST THE TEACHER   In St Matthew's Gospel, the Sermon on the Mount brings together into one discourse the substance of what Jesus taught on many different occasions. This particular passage illustrates the idea Christ's followers ought to have of themselves, and the idea they ought to have of others.

According to Jewish custom, as Biblical scholars point out, slapping someone on the face with the back of one's hand was twice as insulting as slapping him with the *palm* of one's hand. A right-handed person slapping someone else on the right cheek (the case Jesus implicitly refers to) implies just such a back-handed blow. This shows that Jesus is interested here in how we react to insults and humiliations. We should not cave in to feelings of resentment when we are insulted, slighted, and humiliated. If we do, it shows that we have yet to learn Christ's precious lesson of meekness and humility of heart.

By law, a Jew could be forced to hand over a tunic as a payment of legal rec-ompense (even poor men of the time would have owned two tunics), but not his cloak. Most often a person had only one cloak, and it was used not only as a coat during the day, but also as a blanket at night. By urging us to give our cloak as well as our tunic, Christ shows how the Christian heart reaches beyond the letter of the law and takes no personal umbrage even when treated unfairly.

Palestine during the time of Jesus was under direct Roman control. The oc-cupying forces were permitted to enlist the natives as guides or pack-bearers for a mile of any journey they may be taking. By admonishing us to go along for a second mile, Jesus teaches us that the Christian heart fulfills every duty, even the humiliating and inconvenient ones, not with stern resentment and grumbling, but with generosity and enthusiasm.

Because followers of Christ depend on God's unfailing love and generous forgive-ness for their self-esteem, they can live out these shocking ethical norms, main-taining interior peace when most people would seethe with resentment. Likewise, because they know that Christ offers the gift of God's love and forgiveness to every man and woman, his followers can rise above merely natural feelings of antipathy and sincerely strive to help others (even their enemies) find what they themselves have found. This universal Christian charity is the distinguish-ing mark of Christ's followers, because it's the distinguishing mark of God, who is, in his very being, Love.

CHRIST THE FRIEND   God makes the sun shine and the rain come down on both his faithful children and the rebellious ones. His love is, in the truest sense of the word, unconditional. This means that the friendship he offers us in Christ is also unconditional. Christ is the true friend, whose love and devotion to you doesn't depend on looks, popularity, intelligence, success, money, or anything else: he loves you simply because you are you. He can't love you any more than he already does. There is no pressure here, only peace.

A lot of good it would do if Christ gave these impossible instructions (to love as he loves) and then left us alone to try and carry them out. But he doesn't. He walks this narrow and steep path in front of us and beside us. That was the lesson of Good Friday, when he was betrayed and abandoned by his closest friends, cruelly tortured, slandered, publicly humiliated, unjustly condemned, and put to death. Throughout the ordeal, he never once resented, hated, or retaliated. The love in his heart and his trust in the Father buoyed him up, to the point where his dying words included, "Father, forgive them, they know not what they do" (Luke 23:34). That also is the lesson of the Eucharist, the supernatural food of our Christian souls; he gives it to us to supplement our weak efforts and to keep us strong as we follow his difficult path.

CHRIST IN MY LIFE   Sometimes, Lord (and you know which times I'm talking about) it's hard for me to turn the other cheek, hand over my cloak, and go the extra mile. It is not natural to love one's enemies, Lord, so if you want me to do this, I am going to need a lot of help. But I want to. I know that only truly Christian love will bring peace to my heart, and to the world. Lord Jesus, give me strength…

You have forgiven me so many times. You have practiced everything you preached in relation to me. Somehow, you really do love me. You really are interested in my life. How can that be? I don't understand, but I believe, and I thank you with all my heart, Lord – you know how much I need your love. Teach me to love as you do…

There are so many things I want to do for you and your Church, Lord. My mind and heart are full of desires to change this world and bring everyone around me into your friendship. Yet I can barely control my own temper. Help me focus on the most important thing: loving my neighbor as you have loved me…

QUESTIONS FOR SMALL GROUP DISCUSSION

1. What struck you most in this passage? What did you notice that you hadn't noticed before?

2. What examples might Christ pick to teach this lesson in modern terms?

3. Will following these teachings make Christians into weaklings?

4. How can we reconcile personal meekness and humility with our duty to defend the innocent, promote justice, and help those who are being oppressed?

Cf. Catechism of the Catholic Church, 1961-1974 on the Old and the New Law; 1812-1832 on the theological virtues; 2302-2306 on safeguarding peace in the world

THE GOSPEL OF MATTHEW CHAPTER 6

"The founder of no other religion is absolutely essential for that religion in the same way that Christ is essential for Christianity. It is true that the founder was necessary for the founding, but the believer in a particular religion does not enter into the same kind of an encounter that a Christian enters into with Christ. It is the personal relationship to him which is decisive. Christ therefore occupies a different place in Christianity than Buddha does in Buddhism, than Confucius in Confucianism, Mohammed in Islam, and even Moses in Judaism. When you come to Christ, Christianity demands the personal, intimate bond. We have to be one with him, one with him in such a way that we cannot in any way claim to be Christian unless we reflect the person, the mind, the will, the heart, and the humanity of Christ."

- Archbishop Fulton Sheen

15. THE SECRET RENDEZVOUS (MT 6:1-6, 16-18)

"But there is another and interior way of praying without ceasing, and that is the way of desire. Whatever else you are doing, if you long for that Sabbath, you are not ceasing to pray. If you do not want to cease praying, do not cease longing. Your unceasing desire is your unceasing voice."

- St Augustine

Matthew 6:1-6, 16-18

'Be careful not to parade your good deeds before men to attract their notice; by doing this you will lose all reward from your Father in heaven. So when you give alms, do not have it trumpeted before you; this is what the hypocrites do in the synagogues and in the streets to win men's admiration. I tell you solemnly, they have had their reward. But when you give alms, your left hand must not know what your right is doing; your almsgiving must be secret, and your Father who sees all that is done in secret will reward you. And when you pray, do not imitate the hypocrites: they love to say their prayers standing up in the synagogues and at the street corners for people to see them; I tell you solemnly, they have had their reward. But when you pray, go to your private room and, when you have shut your door, pray to your Father who is in that secret place, and your Father who sees all that is done in secret will reward you… When you fast do not put on a gloomy look as the hypocrites do: they pull long faces to let men know they are fasting. I tell you solemnly, they have had their reward. But when you fast, put oil on your head and wash your face, so that no one will know you are fasting except your Father who sees all that is done in secret; and your Father who sees all that is done in secret will reward you.'

CHRIST THE LORD   Of all the great leaders, kings, and emperors throughout human history, only one has been omniscient: Jesus Christ. As the second Person of the Holy Trinity, our Lord shares God's complete knowledge, which includes knowledge of every human heart. And unlike leaders of this world, who have to worry about material stability and citizens' obedience to exterior laws, the Lord plants the standard of his Kingdom precisely there, in the spiritual soil of the human heart. Jesus is a Lord who loves his subjects to the point of dying for them, and all he asks in return is their love for him – the decision of the heart to seek and heed the will of God. That love plugs sinners' souls into eternal communion with God, which is exactly what they were made for. This Lord strives to conquer his followers' hearts, so he can sweep them into his arms and carry them to his heavenly mansion. He is a Lord who loves, and who longs for love.

CHRIST THE TEACHER   Jesus teaches two lessons with these exhortations: *what* following Christ involves, and *how* to carry that out.

Following Christ – the Christian religion – is not one sector of life; it is the very center of everything, like the hub from which a wheel's spokes radiate. Following Christ affects your relationships with other people, thus the reference to almsgiving, (which includes all good deeds done to neighbors in need); it includes your direct relationship with God, thus the instructions on prayer; and it includes your relationship with yourself, your efforts to discipline yourself and mature both as a human being and as a disciple of Christ – thus the comments on fasting, which comprises all the many forms of self-governance and abnegation needed to grow in virtue. What a simple yet complete vision of human life! Relationship with God, with others, and with oneself: the threefold path of life – Christ invites us to travel this path as he did, by following in his footsteps and thereby achieving the purpose for which we were created.

And the key to staying on track in that journey is equally simple: live in the sight of God. God sees everything, because he is God. It is useless to try and put up a façade in order to deceive God. The word "hypocrite" comes from the Greek word for actor. When we try to put on an act for other people around us instead of living in close friendship with God, we end up throwing ourselves at the mercy of the fickle and cruel opinions of our sinful fellow travelers. Christ is pleading with us in this passage to build our lives on firmer stuff, on his stable and unconditional love, which alone can give us true meaning and lasting peace.

CHRIST THE FRIEND   Hidden behind this sobering lesson against the temptation of hypocrisy is a beautiful revelation of the heart of Christ. He points out that he sees "what is done in secret." He repeats this three times. He has seen all of the most selfish, vitriolic, and morose chapters of each of our ongoing interior monologues... everything. He knows it all. And yet, he still loves us with the tender love of the perfect Father, the perfect friend. If this doesn't prove what unconditional love really is, nothing does.

But it doesn't stop there. He actually wants us to let him into that monologue, to turn it into an ongoing dialogue, a conversation with him. He wants to take part in everything we do; he wants to be our closest companion, our most intimate friend. And why? Because he has some psychological need that we can pacify for him? No. Just the opposite. Because he has more he wants to give us. He has a reward to give each one of us, the reward of our true name (cf Rev 2:17), our fulfillment, the satisfaction of our deepest yearnings – most of all, he wants to give us himself, now and for all eternity.

CHRIST IN MY LIFE You see all my motives and intentions, but I think sometimes I try to hide from them. Show them to me, Lord. I don't want anything to get in the way of our friendship. I don't want to fall into hypocrisy. I want to do all things out of a humble, sincere love for you. With the humility of your heart, Lord, shape my heart...

At times life seems so complicated... but you simplify it. Stay with me, Lord, walk with me; teach me how to love you, to love my neighbor, and to master my own selfish tendencies. With the silence of your heart, speak to my heart...

Teach me to fast, Lord. Teach me to govern my urges and instincts, to be the master of my passions and not their slave. Teach me to be free to give myself to you and to my neighbors. Show me how to make loving sacrifice as much a part of my life as it was a part of yours...

QUESTIONS FOR SMALL GROUP DISCUSSION

1. What struck you most in this passage? What did you notice that you hadn't noticed before?

2. What are some common ways we can fall into hypocrisy in our day and age?

3. Jesus lists three activities as the essential aspects of religion (i.e., righteous living): almsgiving, prayer, and fasting. Which of the three do you think is most important, and why? How do they fit together?

4. We read this passage usually at the beginning of Lent. How can we improve the way we live during this season that the Church gives us to prepare for the drama of Holy Week? How can we live more deeply every liturgical season?

Cf. Catechism of the Catholic Church, 1436-1439 on the many forms of penance in a Christian's life; 1969-1974 on the New Law and the practices of religion

16. PRAY LIKE A CHRISTIAN (MT 6:7-15)

"Mindful then of our condition, that we are essentially limited and absolutely dependent on the Supreme Being, before everything else let us have recourse to prayer. We know through faith how great is the power of humble, trustful, persevering prayer."

- *Pope Pius XI, Caritate Christi compulsi*

Matthew 6:7-15

'In your prayers do not babble as the pagans do, for they think that by using many words they will make themselves heard. Do not be like them; your Father knows what you need before you ask him. So you should pray like this: Our Father in heaven, may your name be held holy, your kingdom come, your will be done, on earth as in heaven. Give us today our daily bread. And forgive us our debts, as we have forgiven those who are in debt to us. And do not put us to the test, but save us from the evil one.

'Yes, if you forgive others their failings, your heavenly Father will forgive you yours; but if you do not forgive others, your Father will not forgive your failings either.'

CHRIST THE LORD   Jesus contrasts the babbling prayer of the pagans with the heartfelt, simple prayer of the Christian. By giving us a glimpse of what kind of Lord Christ really is, he shows us what kind he is not.

The false gods of pagan religions were conceived of as unpredictable, irresponsible, self-seeking, aloof, fickle, vain, and powerful. Religious activity for the pagans, therefore, was bent on keeping those gods placated, so that their power would not be used against the believers. This usually involved performing certain rituals flawlessly (for instance, if the priest hiccoughed or coughed in the middle of it, he might have to start it all again), or saying certain prayers according to the rules. It was all about going through the right motions. If you had a particularly important need, you could increase the number of rituals and prayers, and the gods would supposedly pay you back proportionately.

The Christian Lord is different. He is close, caring, generous, kind, forgiving, and attentive – he is our Father. Prayer in this context takes on an entirely new dimension – that of love, sincerity, and heartfelt exchange; it's the kind of secure, confident interaction that takes place between trusting children and faithful parents. The Kingdom of Christ isn't a tyranny; it's a family.

CHRIST THE TEACHER The crux of the Our Father is forgiveness. Jesus realizes that linking God's forgiveness of our own sins with our forgiveness of those who offend us is a hard doctrine. That's why he reemphasizes it after he's finished teaching the words of the prayer. Why does he put this difficult condition on our forgiveness? Simply put, because unless we forgive those who offend us, God *can't* forgive us.

Forgiveness requires humility – from both directions. Basically, humility means recognizing that you are not God, and when we refuse to forgive someone, we are forgetting precisely that. A refusal to forgive involves passing judgment on the offender. But to pass judgment on another person is to put oneself in God's place. Only God can see the whole interior world of a human being; only God can see into the secret recesses of the human heart. And so, only God has the right to pass judgment. (This same reasoning applies to forgiving yourself; a refusal to forgive yourself comes, ultimately, from arrogance. We find it hard to forgive ourselves if we think we are so perfect that we, unlike normal human beings, are beyond the possibility of falling short, failing, or sinning – it indicates a shortage of healthy humility.)

So those who refuse to forgive are acting like God, elevating themselves above their offender. But acting like God inhibits them from recognizing their true dependence on God and their own need for his forgiveness – the throne of judgment only has enough room for one judge at a time, either oneself or God. This attitude, then, simply ousts God, shutting the door on him. And so the merciful, forgiving God is left standing outside in the cold, unable to bring us his forgiveness.

The tragedy of this dilemma is that every human soul *needs* to experience God's forgiveness in order to be at peace. And so, the unforgiving person ends up destroying himself in his self-righteous attempt to destroy his neighbor.

CHRIST THE FRIEND Friends share what they have with each other. Good friends freely share their most valuable possessions. By this standard, Christ's friendship is in a class all by itself. He didn't just share things, or knowledge, or companionship; he shared his nature as God's Son – *his divine nature*.

In this prayer, he teaches us to call God "Father." And to make sure we don't think that's just some pretty poetry, he also describes God as "our Father [who] knows what we need…" In Christ, we have become not just citizens of God's Kingdom, but members of God's own family. We have Christ's blood flowing

105

in our veins. We have an eternal inheritance, we have our own room in the heavenly mansion, our own family servant (our guardian angel), and the rest of the family is eagerly awaiting our arrival.

This is the core message of the entire New Testament: through our incorporation into Christ and through our friendship with him, we have become full members of God's household, along with everything that entails. Doesn't it make you want to pray the Our Father in a whole new way?

CHRIST IN MY LIFE Thank you for the gift of prayer. I can always raise my mind and heart to you, no matter where I am or what I'm doing. Thank you for the prayers and prayer commitments that you have brought into my life. I want to pray them well. I want to seek and find you in prayer, not just go through the motions. Stir my heart, Lord; remind me that you are my loving Father. Lord, teach me to pray...

Thank you for your priceless gift of forgiveness, and for letting me experience that forgiveness so many times. I want to forgive as you forgive. You know who and what offends and hurts me most – and you permit those offenses and hurts. They give me opportunities to become more like you. Who do I need to forgive right now? Have mercy on me, Lord, and make me merciful...

At times it is hard for me to call you Father. Jesus, you won this intimacy with God for me and offer it to me, but I think I still have some false ideas and fears that impede me from claiming it in my life. Purify my mind, cleanse my heart, and free me to experience and accept the strong, flowing, unconditional love that you have for me. With the love of your heart, inflame my own...

QUESTIONS FOR SMALL GROUP DISCUSSION

1. What struck you most in this passage? What did you notice that you never noticed before?
2. Why do you think Jesus taught his disciples to pray "Our Father" instead of "My Father"?
3. If God already knows our needs before we ask him, why does Christ still want us to ask for things?
4. The Our Father contains seven petitions in just a few sentences. Why do you think it is so pleasing to God to hear us ask for things from him? Isn't that selfish of us?

Cf. Catechism of the Catholic Church, 2761-2776 on the Lord's Prayer as the summary of the whole Gospel, and the subsequent numbers analyzing each phrase

17. LASTING TREASURE (MT 6:19-23)

"But to merit this happiness let's not tire of fighting during this exile. Let's despise the

world and its false gods. Let's despise its honors. In vain would we seek our happiness in them. It will benefit us greatly to receive nothing from the world but ingratitude and opposition. This will detach us from it and attach us closely to God alone."

- St Joan Antide-Thouret

Matthew 6:19-23

'Do not store up treasures for yourselves on earth, where moths and woodworms destroy them and thieves can break in and steal. But store up treasures for yourselves in heaven, where neither moth nor woodworms destroy them and thieves cannot break in and steal. For where your treasure is, there will your heart be also. The lamp of the body is the eye. It follows that if your eye is sound, your whole body will be filled with light. But if your eye is diseased, your whole body will be all darkness. If then, the light inside you is darkness, what darkness that will be!'

CHRIST THE LORD Jesus' tone throughout the Sermon on the Mount is hardly diplomatic. Instead of making suggestions and reflections, he issues unambiguous commands: Do this and don't do that. He is trying to convince his listeners to follow him and thus embrace what he knows is the right thing, the fruitful thing, and the wise thing (as the Church continues to do now). He knows what his listeners don't know – the true path to a meaningful life. He speaks not in conjectures, but in rock solid convictions.

This is hardly a popular communication style in our self-centered world, which tries to drown out the cry of violated consciences with the soothing lies of ambiguity, mediocrity, and sophisticated tolerance. It's one reason why Jesus isn't so popular.

But popularity can't change the way things really are, and that's what our Lord has: the truth. In fact, he is the Truth. When we follow him, we live in the truth, we walk in light, and we shine as a much-needed testimony against the dark backdrop of the world.

CHRIST THE TEACHER The lesson of the lamp and the eye is simpler than it seems. In Christ's metaphor, the eye stands for our desires (our eyes show us good things, which we can then desire). These desires are meant to bring light (joy, meaning, goodness) to our souls, just as a lamp gives light to a dark room.

In other words, we were created with a healthy yearning for happiness. Happiness consists in a life well lived, a life lived pursuing good things in the right way – a virtuous life that gradually puts our whole mind and heart in fuller and fuller communion with God, the source of all good things. That is what we were created to do. In God's original plan, this *desire* for happiness through do-ing good things well is the *lamp* that gives the light of hope, joy, and meaning to the soul as it journeys towards God.

But when sin entered the picture, it disrupted the inner harmony of the human person. We still yearn for happiness, but we have a tendency to seek it in the wrong places – to desire wrongly, to seek the good through self-indulgence in-stead of through self-forgetful love. That wrong desire darkens the soul, filling it with frustration, anger, depression, and anxiety.

Jesus gives this lesson in the context of teaching us what we ought to desire, what treasures we ought to set our hearts on: not the passing material fancies of self-centered indulgence, but the everlasting satisfaction that comes from a life of generosity and self-forgetfulness. He came to relight the lamp that sin had maliciously extinguished.

CHRIST THE FRIEND   Friends love giving good news to friends. In this passage, Jesus gives some of the greatest news ever given: he assures us that heaven is real – not only that life after death exists, but that an indescribably beautiful and satisfying life after death exists, one completely void of the pains and trag-edies of earthly life (i.e., loss of every kind, conflict, crime, death, the passing of joy, etc.) and full to overflowing with everything that is good, everything we truly desire. He assures us that heaven exists, and invites us to place our hopes on it by placing our hopes in him and his teaching. And he does it all so simply, dismissing with a smile and a wave of his hand what has been one of the most ponderous anxieties of the human predicament since the very dawn of civilization.

Jesus: Come with me to heaven. It will be better there. Place your heart where the REAL treasure lies – in the friendship that we forge here on earth. I am your true happiness, joy, and meaning. It is through me that you will be able to bask in the light of heaven, and it is through me that you will be able to start shining with that light here on earth, thereby inviting everyone you meet to set their hearts on eternity, too.

CHRIST IN MY LIFE   Thank you for teaching me the truth. Thank you for your Church, which continues to teach the truth with authority and clarity. Increase in my heart an eager desire to know the truth, to study your saving doctrines, and to spread them. I want to be hungry to know your will, and hungry to help others know it too. With the zeal of your heart, Lord, set my heart on fire…

Are you pleased with my hopes? Are my hopes and desires giving light to my soul? I am not always sure what my deepest desires are. Enlighten me, Lord. If someone were to watch my exterior actions for a week, without being able to look into my heart, what would they think was my highest priority, the treasure I have set my heart on? O Lord, make my heart and my actions strive after you in all things and above all…

Lord, be my light, my strength, my inspiration. Make me more like you. I want my words and actions to reflect your light. I want my life to be a lighthouse guiding others through life's storms to the safe harbor of your love…

QUESTIONS FOR SMALL GROUP DISCUSSION

1. What struck you most in this passage? What did you notice that you hadn't noticed before?

2. What desires does our culture try to stir up and keep stirred up? Why?

3. How would society change if everyone believed firmly in heaven?

4. What should Christians do when they find it difficult to understand something that the Church asks or commands them to do?

Cf. Catechism of the Catholic Church, 978-980 on the battle against evil desires; 1023-1029 on heaven; 1718-1724 on the desire for happiness

18. WORRY RIGHT (MT 6:24-34)

"Keep the word of God… Let it pierce deep into your inmost soul and penetrate your feelings and actions. Eat well and your soul will delight and grow. Do not forget to eat your bread or your heart will wither, but let your soul feast richly."

- St Bernard of Clairvaux

Matthew 6:24-34

'No one can be the slave of two masters: he will either hate the first and love the second, or treat the first with respect and the second with scorn. You cannot be the slave both of God and of money. That is why I am telling you not to worry about your life and what you are to eat, nor about your body and how you are to clothe it. Surely life means more than food, and the body more than clothing! Look at the birds in the sky. They do not sow or reap or gather into barns; yet your heavenly Father feeds them. Are we not worth much more than they are? Can any of you, for all his worrying, add one single cubit to his span of life? And why worry about clothing? Think of the flowers growing in the fields; they never have to work or spin; yet I assure you that not even Solomon in all his regalia was robed like one of these. Now if that is how God clothes the grass in the field which is there today and thrown into the furnace tomorrow, will he not much more look after you, you men of little faith?

'So do not worry; do not say, What are we to eat? What are we to drink? How are

109

we to be clothed? It is the pagans who set their hearts on all these things. Your heavenly Father knows you need them all. Set your hearts on his kingdom first, and on his righteousness, and all these other things will be given you as well. So do not worry about tomorrow: tomorrow will take care of itself. Each day has enough trouble of its own.'

CHRIST THE LORD Jesus points out that we can either serve God or serve money. (The Greek word *mamona*, sometimes translated "mammon," refers more generally to material goods and possessions, the things money can buy.) We can put our trust either in God, or in the things of this world. Since there is only one God, and everything else is part of this created world, we really do have no other options. Jesus describes what life is like when we put our trust in the things of this world: full of worry and anxiety (aka stress): worries about our bank account, our career, our health, our grades, our future, the needs of our family – when we trust in material things we put ourselves at their mercy, and they are intrinsically unstable. Then Jesus describes what life is like when we put our trust in God: free from worry and anxiety, peaceful, joyful, fruitful. If God is God, then he is Lord of all things; and if he is also our Father, then his Lordship is at our service, and all we have to do is put more trust in him than in ourselves and all our stuff.

CHRIST THE TEACHER We would all like to be free from worry and anxiety. But Christ's words seem too good to be true. How can we extricate our trust from the visible things of this world and plant it in the fertile soil of God's love? How can we leave behind our worldly servitude and experience the freedom of serving God? Jesus tells us how: "Set your hearts on his kingdom first, and on his righteousness, and all these other things will be given you as well." It's all about setting our hearts on the right thing, wanting the right thing, seeking it wholeheartedly. Seeking Christ will set us free from the shackles of this world. We are all seeking something; human nature spurs us on to look for meaning, happiness, and fulfillment. If we can activate our faith and direct this natural search towards knowing, loving, and following Jesus Christ, then we will be seeking God's Kingdom (for Christ is the King). The only variable in this equation is us: how energetically will we "set our hearts on his Kingdom first"? The more we do, the sooner our stress will dissipate, and the sooner "all these other things" will fall into place as well.

CHRIST THE FRIEND Friendship is built on trust. The friendship with God enjoyed by Adam and Eve was lost for lack of trust: "Man, tempted by the devil, let his trust in his Creator die in his heart" (Catechism of the Catholic Church, 397). Christ came to win back that trust. His words, his miracles, his example, and above all his passion and death are all huge billboards that God puts up saying, "Trust me! I only want to give you the deep meaning you long for!" Just as Adam and Eve exhibited their lack of trust by *disobedience* to God (they thought they knew more than God about the best way to live), we exhibit and grow in our trust by our *obedience* to God – through following the dictates of our conscience and the teachings of the Church. The fundamental message of the gospel is that Christ, God-become-man, is a friend worthy of our trust; all that remains is for us to heed that message… God hopes we will.

Jesus: Do you trust me? I rule the universe. I created all things. I watch over your life. Nothing happens to you without my permission. Do you trust that when you encounter difficulties, sorrows, and suffering I am there with you, wanting you to exercise your trust? Each time you exercise your trust in me, that trust grows. And each time it grows, your soul comes nearer to the fulfillment and fruitfulness I created you to experience. When worries assail you, rejoice in the chance to repel them with acts of trust: I am your shield.

CHRIST IN MY LIFE I wonder what my greatest worries look like from your perspective, Lord. Jesus, purify my heart. Teach me, please, to seek your Kingdom above all things, and to trust in you so completely that every worry that shows up turns into a prayer and that nothing ever disturbs the peace of my heart, which is set firmly on you…

So many people are seeking peace and stability in all the wrong places. I know your heart goes out to them. Mine does too, Lord. I want to help them find you and follow you. I know I am far from being your perfect disciple, but can't I still help? Send me, Lord – balance out my shortcomings with your grace and make me an instrument of your peace…

It's often a mystery to me why I don't trust you more completely. Do I think that you would ever abuse my trust – you who are all-good, all-powerful, all-knowing, and all-loving? And what's more, you have given me so many personal experiences of your goodness! Thank you for them, Lord; remind me of them right now, and never let me forget them. I want to trust in you as I ought…

QUESTIONS FOR SMALL GROUP DISCUSSION

1. What struck you most in this passage? What did you notice that you hadn't noticed before?

2. What are most people around us really seeking?

3. What are some concrete actions or activities that we can do individually and as a group to "seek first the Kingdom"?

4. How can the importance of our learning to trust God help explain why God permits suffering in our lives?

Cf. Catechism of the Catholic Church, 396-401 on the role of trust in original sin; 222-231 on the implications of having "faith in one God"; 2544-2550 on the secret to happiness

THE GOSPEL OF MATTHEW CHAPTER 7

"Come now, insignificant man, fly for a moment from your affairs, escape for a little while from the tumult of your thoughts. Put aside now your weighty cares and leave your wearisome toils. Abandon yourself for a little to God and rest for a little while in him. Enter into the inner chamber of your soul, shut out everything save God and what can be of help in your quest for him and having locked the door seek him out. Speak now, my whole heart, speak now to God: 'I seek your countenance, O Lord, your countenance I seek.' Come then, Lord my God, teach my heart where and how to seek you, where and how to find you."

- St Anselm, Proslogion

19. A CRITICAL EYE (MT 7:1-6)

"Today we must translate the words of Scripture into deeds, and instead of speaking saintly words, we must act them."

- St Jerome

Matthew 7:1-5

'Do not judge, and you will not be judged; because the judgements you give are the judgements you will get, and the amount you measure out is the amount you will be given. Why do you observe the splinter in your brother's eye and never notice the plank in your own? How dare you say to your brother, Let me take the splinter out of your eye, when all the time there is a plank in your own? Hypocrite! Take the plank out of your own eye first, and then you will see clearly enough to take the splinter out of your brother's eye. Do not give dogs what is holy; and do not throw your pearls in front of pigs, or they may trample them and then turn on you and tear you to pieces.'

CHRIST THE LORD Jesus rules his Kingdom through charity, through self-forgetful love. In profiling how his disciples ought to think of and treat one another, Jesus gives us a glimpse of his leadership style. Christ has nothing stuck in his eye. He sees clearly all the sins, faults, and offenses of his subjects. And yet, he doesn't condemn them. He constantly holds out his forgiveness, invites them to start fresh, helps them along the way, and hopes in their capacity for reform. He who could judge with perfect justice has mercifully delayed the judgment.

How self-contradicting we become when we rail against the delay! By condemning our brothers and sisters in thought and word, whether or not they deserve the condemnation, we despise the very mercy from which we have benefited so greatly. In thus separating ourselves from Christ's standard instead of seconding his patience, we end up exposing ourselves as well to the sharp sword of justice: God has no choice but to measure us with the measure we have used to judge others, because we have scorned the only other measure – his mercy.

CHRIST THE TEACHER Jesus seems to contradict himself. On the one hand, he commands his disciples not to judge others, while on the other hand, he commands them precisely to judge whether someone is worthy to be given the pearl of the gospel (in the early Church, this pearl, this "what is holy" was understood primarily as the sacrament of the Eucharist, which was – and still is – reserved to those who share completely the Catholic faith). The concept of discernment resolves the paradox: Christ is teaching his disciples to be men and women of reflection and discernment.

The Greek verb used for "judge" connotes "to judge harshly and condemn," not merely to form an opinion (how can we avoid forming opinions?). Therefore, Jesus is really warning his disciples against thinking and speaking badly of others. Since only God can see the heart, only God can pass sentence on someone's moral conduct. Certainly an objective action can be identified as good or bad, in accordance or not with the gospel and the natural law, but only God can see into the conscience of the culprit – we are blinded to this level of reality by the beam of ignorance and self-centeredness. Think of it this way: how easy it is for us to make excuses for our own faults and failings, yet how quickly we condemn the failings of others. Jesus is simply teaching us to be as generous in our thoughts and words about other people (family members, friends, superiors, strangers, celebrities, politicians, etc.) as we are with ourselves.

At the same time, Jesus calls for prudence. It is naïve to pretend that everyone is a saint (though it is true that everyone is called to be a saint). We are to avoid thoughtlessly exposing our lives, our faith, and the Church's patrimony to the destructive malice of the enemies of Christ. You pray for and work to reform a criminal, but you don't hire him as your babysitter. If we are to love the sinner yet hate the sin, we have to be honest about both.

CHRIST THE FRIEND Following Christ's standard of mercy, the standard by which he deals with us, involves forming the habit of reflection. Each of us has natural tendencies, some to be harsh and judgmental and others to be perhaps too trusting and unsuspecting. The mature Christian learns to balance these natural tendencies by taking time to reflect before speaking and acting, and by constantly examining his own conduct in the light of Christ's wisdom.

Jesus: How I long to give you my love and wisdom! Yet I can only do so if you are open to receive them. Strive to love as I love. The more your heart is open to your neighbors, the more my grace and love will be able to flow into your soul. Think well of others, excuse their faults, speak kindly and generously about them, and you will see your heart expand. Then I will be able to pour into your soul the light and truth that will set you free.

CHRIST IN MY LIFE Lord, why is it so easy for me to fall into the trap of useless criticism? In some circumstances and relationships especially I am always seeing faults and failings, and condemning them as if I were the perfect one. Jesus, have mercy on me. Be more merciful with me than I am with my neighbors. Give me the strength to be humble, to judge as you judge, with the light of your love…

Thank you for your unquenchable mercy. You are merciful because you are all-loving and all-powerful. Mercy is the strength of your love. Lord, I believe in you! I believe in your love! I believe in the power of your love to enliven the deadest hearts, just as you have enlivened mine. I want to be a walking advertisement for your goodness and mercy. Speak to me, Lord, and speak through me…

Lord, when I take time to reflect on your words and your example, I feel my heart engaged. I want so much to follow your path! It is time for me to change, Lord. Teach me to turn these good desires you have given me into actions. Teach me to be an effective ambassador of your Kingdom…

QUESTIONS FOR SMALL GROUP DISCUSSION

1. What struck you most in this passage? What did you notice that you hadn't noticed before?

2. How would the social atmosphere where you live change if no one ever had to worry about being criticized behind their backs?

3. What aspects of the media culture foster the generous, forgiving attitude that Christ commands us to have? What aspects of the media culture encourage the opposite?

4. What tactics can help you condemn the sin and not the sinner in your conversations about current events and other people's actions and decisions?

Cf. The Catechism of the Catholic Church, 2475-2487 on rash judgment, detraction, and calumny; 2196 on loving one's neighbor

20. IMAGING GOD'S GOODNESS (MT 7:7-14)

"Teach me to seek you, and reveal yourself to me as I seek, because I can neither seek you if you do not teach me how, nor find you unless you reveal yourself."

- St Anselm

Mathew 7:7-14

'Ask, and it will be given to you; search, and you will find; knock, and the door will be opened to you. For the one who asks always receives; the one who searches always finds; the one who knocks will always have the door opened to him. Is there a man among you who would hand his son a stone when he asked for bread? Or would hand him a snake when he asked for a fish? If you, then, who are evil, know how to give your children what is good, how much more will your Father in heaven give good things to those who ask him! So always treat others as you would like them to treat you; that is the meaning of the Law and the Prophets. Enter by the narrow gate, since the road that leads to perdition is wide and spacious, and many take it; but it is a narrow gate and a hard road that leads to life, and only a few find it.'

CHRIST THE LORD Because we are wounded by sin, we are continually tempted to perceive God in a distorted way. Every person we encounter in this fallen world, even a truly loving parent or an exceptionally devoted spouse, is flawed. No one is exempt from selfish, hurtful tantrums or ignorant, erroneous points of view. These encounters sometimes damage our own attitudes and emotions, making us suspicious and self-protective. Trust becomes hard. Self-sufficiency becomes more comfortable – both in our relationships with other people, and also in our relationship with God. How much of a hold the world can have on us!

Even so, we still experience flashes of goodness and generosity – more frequently the more closely we follow Christ. These small triumphs of virtue resonate in our soul, because our souls were created for that. In this passage, Jesus latches on to this limited but real experience of goodness (for example, the image of a father giving good gifts to his children) to help correct our suspicious perception of God. God is perfect goodness—goodness without the slightest shadow of selfishness, weakness, or fault. He is eager goodness, ready and waiting to give us what we most need. Our Lord is like an overflowing, rushing river of pure goodness. How he longs for us to dive in and allow him to refresh our souls!

CHRIST THE TEACHER Jesus presents us with another apparent contradiction. He says that the entire law and the prophets (all of God's revelation about how to live a fulfilling life) can be summed up in the simple command to do to others whatever we would have them do to us. Then, in the very next sentence, he tells us that the path to this fulfilling life is narrow and hard and that few people actually find it. Why is loving your neighbor as yourself so easy to say and yet so hard to do?

We have to go back to original sin to resolve the paradox. The human family was created in the image and likeness of God. But God is a community of Persons – Father, Son, and Holy Spirit. Thus, the human person is created for community, created to achieve fulfillment through coming to know and be known by others, through coming to love and be loved by them. When our first parents, influenced by the devil, freely decided to rebel against their Creator, the harmony with which their relationship was originally endowed disintegrated. Adam was alienated from Eve, Eve from Adam, and the human family no longer reflected the image of God. Instead, it began reflecting the image of the rebel against God (the devil) whom they had obeyed rather than God.

The human vocation is to love and to be loved, because the life of God in whose likeness we are made is love. That's why the law and the prophets (again, God's revelation about how to lead a fulfilling life) can be summed up so easily: treat others as another self, give them the same unconditional acceptance you give yourself, seek what is good for them just as you seek what is good for yourself; this is how we image God. But sin attacked that image of God within us, and so what should be most natural for us has become most burdensome – it is a difficult path and a narrow gate.

CHRIST THE FRIEND Friendship cannot be forced, not even friendship with God. Since Christ wants us to relate to him as friends, not as zombies, he refuses to force us to follow him. He lets us seek happiness in the world's many empty wells and false promises, if we so choose. And yet, he *wants* us to look for it in him. Imagine how eagerly and energetically he pronounced this threefold command: "Ask! Seek! Knock!" It's as if he is pleading for us to turn to him, to let him be our guide and coach and Savior and friend. It's all his heart wants. Why do so many refuse the invitation?

CHRIST IN MY LIFE Certain things always remind me of your goodness: the beauties of nature, the crucifix, the love of my family… How many there are! Right now I want to contemplate them, to remember them… Strengthen my conviction, Lord, that you are the perfect Father who loves me even more than I love myself. Always remind me of your goodness, so I will never, ever walk away from you…

I believe in you, Lord, and so I believe you when you say that the meaning of life and the quality of my discipleship corresponds to the way I treat my neighbor in thought, word, and deed. And isn't that how you lived? Your whole life was one continuous act of self-giving that reached its climax on the cross. Teach me to give my whole self to you. Jesus, meek and humble of heart, make my heart more like yours...

Whenever I have really asked/sought/knocked, you have always rewarded me with a new experience of your goodness. Why don't I ask more? Is it because I think I can give meaning and fruitfulness to my life all by myself? That is foolish, I know. But I am a fool, Lord. I need your wisdom and grace to transform me…

QUESTIONS FOR SMALL GROUP DISCUSSION

1. What struck you most in this passage? What did you notice that you hadn't noticed before?

2. Christ promises that if we ask, we will receive. So how can we explain the seemingly contradictory reality of unanswered prayer?

3. Christ's Golden Rule is to treat others as you would have them treat you. What is the Golden Rule of the society where we live? What would happen to us and to those around us if we started living Christ's standard more authentically?

4. What are some practical ways in which we can ask, seek, and knock?

Cf. The Catechism of the Catholic Church, 153-165 on the characteristics of faith; 2012-2016 on Christian holiness

21. WISE SURVIVORS (MT 7:15-29)

"The hope of truth and of freedom is already ours, dearly beloved, but if we are to attain truth and freedom in reality we must endure and persevere."

- St Cyprian

Matthew 7:15-29

'Beware of false prophets who come to you disguised as sheep but underneath are ravenous wolves. You will be able to tell them by their fruits. Can people pick grapes from thorns, or figs from thistles? In the same way, a sound tree produces good fruit but a rotten tree bad fruit. A sound tree cannot bear bad fruit, nor a rotten tree bear good fruit. Any tree that does not produce good fruit is cut down and thrown on the fire. I repeat, you will be able to tell them by their fruits.

'It is not those who say to me, Lord, Lord, who will enter the kingdom of heaven, but the person who does the will of my Father in heaven. When the day comes many will say to me, Lord, Lord, did we not prophesy in your name, cast out demons in your name, work many miracles in your name? Then I shall tell them to their faces: I have never known you; away from me, you evil men!

'Therefore, everyone who listens to these words of mine and acts on them will be like a sensible man who built his house on rock. Rain came down, floods rose, gales blew and hurled themselves against that house, and it did not fall: it was founded on rock. But everyone who listens to these words of mine and does not act on them will be like a stupid man who built his house on sand. Rain came down, floods rose, gales blew and struck that house, and it fell; and what a fall it had!' Jesus had now finished what he wanted to say, and his teaching made a deep impression on the people because he taught them with authority and not like their own scribes.

CHRIST THE LORD God wants us to have the life we truly long for, one full of meaning and fulfillment. Indeed, God was the one who planted the desire for happiness in our hearts in the first place: it's like a homing device that, no matter how many wrong turns we take along the way, keeps drawing us back to him, because only a vital and personal relationship with him will satisfy that indelible yearning. In Christ, God came among us to take each of us by the hand and lead us into that relationship, meaning, and fulfillment. On every page of the Gospels, this divine Savior is given to us.

In this particular passage, Jesus is just completing the Sermon on the Mount – St Matthew's summary of all his teaching – and here he explains how that teaching should be received. Are the words of Jesus just like any other? Did he consider himself one rabbi among many? Hardly. Christ claims yet again that his teachings point out the sure path to eternal life, that they are the door to the Kingdom of heaven, and that they communicate perfectly the will of his Father, the will of God himself. Those who follow his teachings will stand firm forever and never collapse. Jesus was either a megalomaniac or the incarnate Son of God. He certainly did not see himself as just another great religious teacher or a particularly wise philosopher – it was either follow him or collapse and be completely ruined. This is worth reflecting on again and again. He leaves no doubt here about the authority he claims, the identity he asserts: Christ is the Lord.

CHRIST THE TEACHER Christ teaches about his hopes for our lives. He wants us to enter the Kingdom of heaven. He wants us to stand strong when the gales of this world swirl around our fragile lives. He wants us to "have life and have it more abundantly" (John 10:10) – this is the sole reason he came.

He gives two stern warnings in this passage. The first is to beware of false prophets, leaders, or teachers who claim to guide you to the rich pastures of truth, but in fact only want to manipulate you for their own vanity or greed, heedless of the damage they cause. Christ wouldn't issue the warning unless it was a real possibility. We can be deceived. We can be led astray. We can err – all the most destructive heretics started out as zealous, faithful members of the Church and ended up sowing division and destruction in their own souls and among their followers.

The secret to staying on track is to look for the evident fruit. This doesn't consist in dramatic or impressive signs and miracles – these don't necessarily indicate the presence of Christ. Rather, the authentic Christian teacher and follower is the one who stays firmly attached to the one foundation even through the most terrible of storms. Those who cling to Peter, Christ's chosen Vicar on earth, the solid foundation, the "rock on whom I will build my Church" (Mt 16:18), show by their good fruit of persevering fidelity – of real virtue, not dramatic demonstrations – that they are good, dependable shepherds, not wolves in sheep's clothing.

The second warning – that not all who say "Lord, Lord" will be saved, but only those who obey God's will – shocks us. Is this not the God of compassion and mercy? And yet on his lips we hear, "Depart from me you evildoers." Imagine his eyes as he gave this warning. He gazed at his listeners, who were hanging on every syllable; his eyes were full of eager determination, piercing the very depths of their souls with his fierce love, passionately hoping that they – *that we* – will be wise; he was hoping that his followers would learn to measure their discipleship not by feelings, not by other people's opinions, not by their achievements, but by authentic virtue, by obedience to God's will as manifest in the Ten Commandments, the teaching of the Church, and their consciences. He is still hoping for that, longing for his words to find fertile soil in our fickle hearts: "Let him who has ears to hear, hear!"

CHRIST THE FRIEND There are only two requirements for friendship with Christ: to listen with faith and to act accordingly. We are to listen to Christ, the Savior, the only one "who has words of eternal life" (John 6:68). And we are to heed what we hear, to act according to the word of God. This is the New Covenant: "If you keep my commandments you will remain in my love" (John 15:10). That we remain in his love is Christ's burning desire, but whether such remaining actually happens is up to us.

Jesus: Remain in my love, and your house will be firmly rooted in the rock of the Church. Remain in me through prayer, remain in me through the sacraments, remain in me through fidelity to my Father's will. I do not promise an easy life, with perfect weather and tasks that are always pleasing. I promise that storms and struggles will batter the foundations of your faith; they are part of my plan. Never turn from me – remain in my Church – remain in my love. And let me remain in you.

CHRIST IN MY LIFE Only you have the authority to teach with absolute certainty, and to demand absolute acceptance and loyalty, because you are God. You have shared this authority with your Church – or rather, you exercise it through your Church. Thank you for caring enough about me to come and teach me the truth. And thank you for the gift of faith. Lord, don't let me squander either of these great gifts...

I tend to be impressed by showy things, but your standard goes straight to the heart. You are interested in virtue. This is how you lived as well. By normal standards, your life ended in a failure, but the truth is just the opposite! Greatness is in fidelity, Lord, in persevering love. Change my mind, so I too make that the standard of greatness in all I think and do...

Those around me (family members, coworkers, teachers, friends, teammates) should easily be able to tell by my everyday actions (not just by my words and my church attendance) that friendship with you is my highest priority. Can they? What do you want me to change, Lord? Help me to grow closer to you every day so I can be your faithful ambassador...

QUESTIONS FOR SMALL GROUP DISCUSSION

1. What struck you most in this passage? What did you notice that you hadn't noticed before?

2. It is not always easy to accept or understand the claims of Christ and his Church to be the one true vehicle of salvation for all people. What is a healthy reaction when a difficulty pops up in one's own life, or in conversations with others? What is an unhealthy reaction?

3. Christ is more interested in us doing "the will of my Father in heaven" than he is in our keeping up the right appearances (simply saying "Lord, Lord"). What is the Father's will?

4. Why does obedience to God matter more than eloquent words and even great achievements made outside of obedience?

Cf. Catechism of the Catholic Church 430-460 on the person and mission of Jesus Christ; 1691-1698 on life in Christ; 2558 on Christianity as a "vital and personal relationship" with God; 144-149 on the obedience of faith

THE GOSPEL OF MATTHEW CHAPTER 8

"Man does not see God by his own powers; but God of his own will appears to men, to whom he wills, and when he wills, and as he wills. For God can do all things: he was seen in former times prophetically through the Spirit, he is seen in the Son by adoption, and he will be seen in the kingdom of heaven as Father. The Spirit prepares man for the Son of God, the Son brings him to the Father, and the Father bestows on him incorruptibility for eternal life, which comes to everyone from his beholding God. As those who see the light are in the light, and partake of its splendor, so those who see God are in God, partaking of his splendor. But God's splendor gives life; those therefore who see God will partake of life."

- St Irenaeus, Against the Heresies

22. HUMILITY AND HEALTH (MT 8:1-17)

"I desire that priests proclaim this great mercy of mine towards souls of sinners. Let the sinner not be afraid to approach me. The flames of mercy are burning me – clamoring to be spent; I want to pour them out upon these souls. Distrust on the part of souls is tearing at my insides."

- Words of Jesus to St Faustina Kowalska

Matthew 8:1-17

After he had come down from the mountain large crowds followed him. A leper now came up and bowed low in front of him. 'Sir,' he said 'if you want to, you can cure me.' Jesus stretched out his hand, touched him and said, 'Of course I want to! Be cured!' And his leprosy was cured at once. Then Jesus said to him, 'Mind you do not tell anyone, but go and show yourself to the priest and make the offering prescribed by Moses, as evidence for them..

When he went into Capernaum a centurion came up and pleaded with him. 'Sir,' he said 'my servant is lying at home paralysed, and in great pain.' 'I will come myself and cure him' said Jesus. The centurion replied, 'Sir, I am not worthy to have you under my roof; just give the word and my servant will be cured. For I am under authority myself, and have soldiers under me; and I say to one man: Go, and he goes; to another: Come here, and he comes; to my servant: Do this, and he does it.' When Jesus heard this he was astonished and

121

said to those following him, 'I tell you solemnly, nowhere in Israel have I found faith like this. And I tell you that many will come from east and west to take their places with Abraham and Isaac and Jacob at the feast in the kingdom of heaven; but the subjects of the kingdom will be turned out into the dark, where there will be weeping and grinding of teeth.' And to the centurion Jesus said, 'Go back, then; you have believed, so let this be done for you'. And the servant was cured at that moment.

And going into Peter's house Jesus found Peter's mother-in-law in bed with fever. He touched her hand and the fever left her, and she got up and began to wait on him. That evening they brought him many who were possessed by devils. He cast out the spirits with a word and cured all who were sick. This was to fulfil the prophecy of Isaiah: He took our sicknesses away and carried our diseases for us.

CHRIST THE LORD Jesus has power over sickness, one of the most visible results of the evil introduced into the world by original sin. These three miracles show that this power, which Christ wields in love, extends to every strata of sickness.

Leprosy was one of the most feared (and most frequently encountered) diseases in ancient times. This bacterial skin infection started small, almost imperceptibly, but it soon spread, rotting the victim's extremities (fingers, nose, lips, etc.) and issuing a thoroughly repugnant odor. Lepers were excluded from society and left to die a slow, painful, humiliating death. The gradual but incurable descent into death was an eloquent symbol of sin's effect on a person's soul.

The Centurion's servant suffered from some kind of paralysis, a sickness that went deeper than leprosy's skin-deep infection. Peter's mother-in-law suffered from a fever, a sickness that went deeper yet, its cause frequently unknown, often inciting the invalid to slip into delirium, or even to lose consciousness altogether.

Citizens of the third millennium, so familiar with advanced medicine, can still identify with the desperate feeling of helplessness in the face of illness that comes across so clearly in these encounters. And yet, Jesus cures them all. Not everyone is helpless in the face of evil, sickness, and impending death. The One who just finished teaching us the path to true happiness now proves that he isn't helpless at all; rather, he is worthy of our trust – he is the Lord.

CHRIST THE TEACHER The Centurion's faith impresses Christ so much that it inspires him to give an impromptu sermon, a sermon with a sobering lesson. In order to take our seats at the Messianic banquet (the biblical image for heaven – a huge banquet, a massive wedding reception), we must have faith in Jesus Christ, a faith as vibrant as the Centurion's. But the Centurion only came to such a strong faith by traveling the uncomfortable path of humility – a path that those who are more familiar with Christ (the Centurion was a foreigner, remember, not part of the Jewish family) often try to bypass.

The Centurion was stationed in Galilee and obviously had become familiar with Jewish doctrine – that the Israelites were a people chosen by the one, true God, and that the Gentiles would receive salvation only through them, not because the Gentiles deserved it, but solely because of God's mercy. He was in charge of a division of 100 soldiers, an officer in the world's most powerful army, and a Roman ruler of a conquered people – yet in spite of so many reasons to be arrogant, he says to this poor carpenter from Nazareth: "I am not worthy to have you enter under my roof." No wonder Christ was amazed.

The leper expressed this same humility and faith. He approached Jesus, did him homage, and then simply laid his need at Jesus' feet: "Lord, if you wish, you can make me clean."

Entrance into Christ's Kingdom passes through one door only, that of humble faith in Jesus Christ. Without stooping to admit our need for God, and our basic unworthiness to receive his grace, we simply can't make it across the threshold.

CHRIST THE FRIEND Lepers were forced by Jewish law to live completely separate from the rest of the community, primarily because of the highly contagious nature of the disease, but also because leprosy was commonly viewed to be a punishment inflicted by God for some hidden sin. They weren't allowed to come within 100 yards of healthy people. And yet, this leper approached Jesus; he came right up to him. There must have been something about Christ that inspired confidence.

The leper sensed that Jesus would not be repulsed by his disgusting disease. And he was right. Jesus not only smiled and healed him, but he reached out and touched him – not for publicity's sake (he urged the man to keep the miracle under wraps), but just to be close to him. Jesus wants to be close to us, to "take our sicknesses away" by walking by our side. He touches the mother-in-law's hand; he offers to come to the Centurion's house – the heart of Christ is the heart of a faithful, close, unconditional Friend.

CHRIST IN MY LIFE Sometimes I wish I could see your miracles firsthand. But many saw them and still didn't believe. I believe in you. I don't need to see any miracles. You have given me so much and shown me so much. One sunset is enough for me, Lord. You are goodness itself and the source of all that is good. I want to follow you, through sickness or health, and I want to help many others to follow you too...

Lord, at times I wish you would simply resolve all my problems right away. But in your wisdom you don't. You know how necessary it is for me to learn how much I need you. Humility is so hard for me! How much peace there must be in a humble soul! You were humble, Lord; all that mattered to you was doing the Father's will. Make me like you; Thy will be done...

You know all my hidden sins and infirmities. And yet you still reach out to touch me. This love dazzles and disorients me. Thank you, Jesus. Lord Jesus, strengthen and enlighten my heart that is so weak and dark...

QUESTIONS FOR SMALL GROUP DISCUSSION

1. What struck you most in this passage? What did you notice that you hadn't noticed before?
2. Who are the lepers of the communities where we live and work? How can we be more Christlike in their regard?
3. If we believed more deeply in the power of prayer to heal people in need, how would that affect our prayer habits?
4. The Church has taught us to pray the Centurion's prayer right before receiving Holy Communion: "Lord, I am not worthy...." Why do you think this phrase is placed precisely there in the liturgy? How can this Bible passage help you pray it more fervently?

Cf. The Catechism of the Catholic Church, 547-550 on the signs of the Kingdom; 2546, 2713, and 2777-2778 on humility in prayer

23. THE COST OF CALM (MT 8:18-27)

"Man is created to praise, reverence, and serve God our Lord, and by this means to save his soul. All other things on the face of the earth are created for man to help him fulfill the end for which he is created."

- St Ignatius of Loyola

Matthew 8:18-27

When Jesus saw the great crowds all about him he gave orders to leave for the other side. One of the scribes then came up and said to him, 'Master, I will follow you wherever you go'. Jesus replied, 'Foxes have holes and the birds of the air have nests, but the Son of Man has nowhere to lay his head'. Another man, one of his disciples, said to him, 'Sir, let me go and bury my father first'. But Jesus replied, 'Follow me, and leave the dead to bury their dead'. Then he got into the boat followed by his disciples. Without warning a storm broke over the lake, so violent that the waves were breaking right over the boat. But he was asleep. So they went to him and woke him saying, 'Save us, Lord, we are going down!' And he said to them, 'Why are you so frightened, you men of little faith?' And with that he stood up and rebuked the winds and the sea; and all was calm again. The men were astounded and said, 'Whatever kind of man is this? Even the winds and the sea obey him.'

CHRIST THE LORD St Matthew is still showing us Jesus' credentials. Not only does he heal the sick, but he also has power over the elements of nature. Storms were frequent in the Sea of Galilee, situated like a bowl surrounded by mountains, whence strong winds came sweeping across the water; violent storms would brew suddenly and then just as quickly play themselves out. At least some of the disciples present were fishermen, so they knew the weather patterns well, and they knew how to navigate a boat to ride out a storm. For them to panic means that the situation was truly perilous – the waves were high enough and the wind strong enough that they feared shipwreck. And yet, for Jesus, all it takes is a word to rein in the violent primal forces.

The passage is reminiscent of the Book of Jonah. Jonah too was asleep in the hold while the ship's crew panicked. In that case as well, God calmed the sea in an instant – as soon as they threw the disobedient prophet into the water. But there is a difference. In Jesus, St Matthew shows us, the very God who acted from on high to bring Jonah to Nineveh has come to dwell among men. No wonder the disciples were "amazed" – they were just starting to get the picture: Jesus is the Lord.

CHRIST THE TEACHER The Church has long seen in this passage an analogy for the life of every Christian. The storm rages and threatens and batters the boat – just as temptations, sufferings, persecutions, and difficulties unceasingly beat against the mind and will of the Christian. Sometimes it seems that they are too much – the journey of doing God's will is simply too difficult. Panic sets in. But the Holy Trinity has been in the Christian's soul the entire time, ever since the day of baptism. And when human efforts fail to calm the storm, the Christian remembers the Lord, turns to him, and asks for help. Soon Jesus restores the "great calm" that comes from confiding in the power and the promises of God instead of in the dim knowledge and withered strength of self.

St Therese of Lisieux used to meditate on this passage in times of inner turmoil or darkness. But she wouldn't wake up the Lord. For her, it was enough to go over and sit beside him as he slept. Let the tempest rage; stay close to Christ and all will be well.

CHRIST THE FRIEND At this point in St Matthew's Gospel Jesus has not yet called apart his Twelve Apostles. A larger group of disciples, including the future Twelve, is following him. As he prepares to get away from the crowds and spend some time with them across the Sea of Galilee, a couple of newcomers approach him and ask to be let into the group. They have been watching and listening, and Jesus has moved their hearts. But the Lord doesn't exactly welcome them with open arms.

He doesn't send them away, but he does point out that following him will not be easy. They will have to forego some of the comforts and stability enjoyed by their peers and neighbors ("the Son of Man has nowhere to rest his head"); they will have to make their relationship with him their highest priority – even higher than good and natural family ties (the disciple who requests that Jesus let him "bury his father" is expressing his willingness to follow Christ in the future, after his father dies, when it would be more convenient). Christ is a friend who loves too intensely not to demand the very best for his friends. Whenever he makes demands, it's only because he loves.

CHRIST IN MY LIFE You are so patient with me, and you stay so close to me, that sometimes I forget about your greatness. You inspired awe in your disciples. There have been moments when I too have experienced profound reverence in your presence. Jesus, don't let me take you for granted. Remind me of your greatness; make me worthy to serve such a Lord; make me follow you as you deserved to be followed…

Are you pleased with how I react to the storms that come into my life? They are precious moments, when things come into focus, when you remind me of my fragility and weakness. I want to stay close to you; I want to lean on you; I want to work hard for your Kingdom and even suffer for it, but always with a joyful heart, because you are always in the boat of my soul…

What are you asking of me right now, at this specific point in my life, that makes me uncomfortable? Is our friendship worth that kind of sacrifice? All I have to do is look at the crucifix and you give me the answer: of course it is. I want to follow you, Lord, and I want to help many others follow you as well. You are my life and my salvation – what could I possibly fear?…

QUESTIONS FOR SMALL GROUP DISCUSSION

1. What struck you most in this passage? What did you notice that you hadn't noticed before?

2. Why does following Jesus have to be so demanding? Why doesn't God make it easier?

3. Why didn't Jesus prevent the storm from happening in the first place instead of making his disciples suffer the fear of shipwreck?

4. Jesus falls asleep on the boat. What does this tell you about him?

Cf. The Catechism of the Catholic Church, 222-227 on the implications of faith in one God; 407-409 on the hard battle of life

24. EVIL AT BAY (MT 8:28-34)

"And therefore the Word of God, God, the Son of God, who in the beginning was with God and through whom all things were made and without whom was not anything made, became man to liberate man from eternal death."

- Pope St Leo the Great

Matthew 8:28-34

When he reached the country of the Gadarenes on the other side, two demoniacs came towards him out of the tombs – creatures so fierce that no one could pass that way. They stood there shouting, 'What do you want with us, Son of God? Have you come here to torture us before the time?' Now some distance away there was a large herd of pigs feeding, and the devils pleaded with Jesus, 'If you cast us out, send us into the herd of pigs'. And he said to them, 'Go then', and they came out and made for the pigs; and at that the whole herd charged down the cliff into the lake and perished in the water. The swineherds ran off and made for the town, where they told the whole story, including what had happened to the demoniacs. At this the whole town set out to meet Jesus; and as soon as they saw him they implored him to leave the neighbourhood.

CHRIST THE LORD St Matthew's presentation of Christ's credentials continues. He has shown his mastery over sickness of every kind and over the powerful forces of the natural world, so antagonistic to mankind after original sin. Now Jesus unfurls his lordship over the very source of evil in the world, the devil and his minions.

The demons recognize Jesus as the Messiah and even try to reproach him for interfering with their evil conquests. Their comment about "before the time" refers to the final judgment, when history's ongoing battle between good and evil will come to its definitive end. But their hideous and violent outbursts, so fearsome that no one even dared to travel that road, failed to daunt Jesus in the least. His mere presence tortures them. They grovel before him and beg for a smattering of clemency. He grants it, and at the same time, with merely a word, he releases these two men from their seemingly hopeless slavery.

This show of spiritual force sends shock waves through the entire town. The whole population recognizes the superior power of Jesus, but they don't know what to make of it. Gadara was a Gentile town; its inhabitants didn't have the benefit of the Jewish faith. They only realize that this man's continued presence will disrupt their usual routine, even more than the demons' presence did. They fear the disruption and ask Jesus to leave them in peace. Knowing that they are not ready for his message, Jesus complies.

Nothing escapes the lordship of Christ, not sickness, not storms, not demons. But he won't force his way into anyone's life – he is the Lord, but he is not a tyrant.

CHRIST THE TEACHER One of the major players in the Gospels is the devil. In this encounter, Jesus teaches us two things about the devil.

First, he shows unambiguously that the devil and his fellow demons really do exist. Every few decades, it becomes fashionable to reinterpret Christ's exorcisms as merely his condescension to the superstitions of the time, in spite of the Church's clear doctrine to the contrary. Those reinterpreters get flustered by this passage. If Jesus had simply sent the demons right back to hell, it would allow such theorists to speculate that maybe these two supposedly possessed men were just insane, and Jesus simply cured their psyches. (And while healing of their troubled psyches was indeed significant, that alone doesn't explain how they could recognize Christ as the Son of God, but we'll ignore that for now). But Christ sends the demons into a herd of pigs, and the demons drive the pigs over the cliff into the sea. And so, it's much more difficult to interpret this frightening event as a mere psychological malfunction. No, the devil indeed exists.

The second lesson teaches us what the devil wants: destruction. He wants to destroy our happiness, our health, our prosperity (he threw the poor pig farmers into the red, let alone the damage he did to the two possessed men), and most of all our relationship with God. This is the single motivation behind every temptation, no matter how tempting. This seems like an obvious lesson, and yet, every time we give into temptation, we seem to forget it.

CHRIST THE FRIEND Without Christ, we would all still be floundering in ignorance and helplessness in the face of evil. He has come to bring us light and strength, to lead us back to full spiritual, intellectual, and moral health – and eventually, to have our very bodies share in the glory of his Resurrection. All of his words, miracles, and deeds were performed for us – for our benefit, for our salvation, and for our health in body, mind, and spirit. Jesus looks into our eyes today, just as he looked into the faces of these two demoniacs two thousand years ago; he wants to set us free. Will we let him?

The Demoniacs: Lord, we will never forget that first moment after you freed us from the power of those demons. It was too good to be true. Thank you, Lord, for setting us free. You gave us a new life, a new chance to live. Now we can see clearly that every day is a gift. Every day we can choose to live in your presence, to glorify you by loving you and loving our neighbor, by bringing the good news of your salvation to everyone around us. We were helpless before. Evil had put our minds in chains. You know what it was like, because you know all things. Still, so many of our brothers and sisters are in chains – they are looking for freedom and happiness in all the wrong places, striving for success by sin and selfishness, and getting tangled up in frustration and depression. Are you not the same Lord today that you were that day when you freed us? Come, Lord, make us channels of your saving grace, never let us forget what you did for us, never let us take this life, this new chance, this day, for granted.

CHRIST IN MY LIFE Sometimes I am like the inhabitants of Gadara: I don't want you to disrupt my usual routines. But in my heart I know that anything you ask of me, through my conscience, through the Church's teachings, through circumstances – anything you ask flows directly from your infinite wisdom. Flood my life with your wisdom and your truth; cleanse my selfishness; make me shine with true virtue. Come, Lord Jesus…

When you made me your disciple, you shared your mission with me. You want to work through me to help set free people who are trapped in sin and error. Help me to keep this as a priority! I think of how much you have done for me – and you want to do that and more for everyone I encounter, especially the ones suffering most. Lord, make me a channel of your peace…

Thank you, Lord, for all your gifts to me – life, faith, hope, knowledge, forgiveness, and those special graces only you and I know about. You know I trust in you. I really do, though I am weak and careless. Lord Jesus, with you all things are possible…

QUESTIONS FOR SMALL GROUP DISCUSSION

1. What struck you most in the passage? What did you notice that you hadn't noticed before?

2. What do people you know generally think about evil and the devil?

3. Why is the devil interested in tempting human beings and making them suffer?

4. What do you think the Gadarenes said to Jesus in order to convince him to leave their town? How do you think Jesus felt when they said that to him?

Cf. The Catechism of the Catholic Church, 2850-2854 on deliverance from the devil; 407 and 409 on our struggle against the powers of evil

THE GOSPEL OF MATTHEW CHAPTER 9

"My son, says our Lord, there are still a good many things you need to learn, things that up to now you have not learned properly. What things do you mean, Lord? These: to make your desires wholly in accordance with my good pleasure, to stop being a lover of yourself, and to become instead a zealous doer of my will. Often you feel within you the flame of desire, urging you insistently forward; but you ought to consider which motive spurs you the more – my honor, or your own advantage. If it is on my account that you act, you will be perfectly happy, however I make things turn out; if, on the other hand, there is a certain amount of self-interest concealed among your motives, you have something there which you will find a bar and a drag."

- The Imitation of Christ, Book III, Chapter 11

25. FORGIVING FOR REAL (MT 9:1-8)

"We ought to pity and love our enemies rather than hate and detest them, for they heap up evils on themselves but deserve well of us; they provoke God's anger against themselves, but adorn us with the crown of eternal glory. We ought to pray for them; we should not be overcome by evil."

- St Antony Mary Zaccaria

Matthew 9:1-8

He got back in the boat, crossed the water and came to his own town. Then some people appeared, bringing him a paralytic stretched out on a bed. Seeing their faith, Jesus said to the paralytic, 'Courage, my child, your sins are forgiven'. And at this some scribes said to themselves, 'This man is blaspheming'. Knowing what was in their minds Jesus said, 'Why do you have such wicked thoughts in your hearts? Now, which of these is easier to say, Your sins are forgiven, or to say, Get up and walk? But to prove to you that the Son of Man has authority on earth to forgive sins,' – he said to the paralytic – 'get up, and pick up your bed and go off home'. And the man got up and went home. A feeling of awe came over the crowd when they saw this, and they praised God for giving such power to men.

CHRIST THE LORD Jesus has just exhibited his power over the effects of sin (sickness, natural adversity) and the instigator of evil (the devil). Now St Matthew completes the grand slam by showing how Jesus absolves us from sin itself.

The other miracles could be taken as signs that Jesus is merely a great prophet, but by forgiving sins Christ leaves no room to doubt that he claims to be much more. In the Old Covenant, only God could forgive sins, because every sin was a rebellion against God, a conscious refusal to adhere to the truth of life's purpose as established by God. Furthermore, in the Old Covenant, this forgiveness could only be obtained through the ritual sacrifices in the Temple stipulated by the Mosaic Law.

When the paralytic comes before Jesus to be healed, the Lord goes to the root of the man's true need and assures him that his sins are forgiven. The Jewish scholars observing the encounter are immediately suspicious of such a divine claim being made so unceremoniously by an upstart rabbi. Jesus acknowledges (but doesn't validate) their suspicion, and then performs the miracle to show that instead of being blasphemous, his claim is true. He can't make the actual forgiveness of sins visible, but he can make the paralytic walk, which certainly shows that he can do what he says – more than enough proof to allay their doubts.

Once again, Christ shows that he is much more than a wise philosopher; he is Emmanuel, God among us - the Lord of life and history.

CHRIST THE TEACHER St Matthew points out that Jesus saw the faith of the people who brought the sick man to Jesus, not the paralyzed man's faith, and *this* triggered Christ's saving action. The paralyzed man was unable to come to Jesus on his own power. Others brought him to the Lord, and the Lord honored their selfless, faith-filled deed. How many people whose souls are paralyzed by sin and doubt need the prayers and charity of faith-filled Christians to bring them into contact with Christ's saving grace!

St Matthew also subtly explains why the Jewish leaders didn't recognize Christ as the Messiah (notice that it is precisely here, at the crescendo of the series of miracles, where the opposition between those leaders and Jesus begins). They had already formed an idea of what the Messiah would be, and they left no room for God to outdo their expectations by coming himself. They had closed their minds; they were attached to their own ideas, their own standards, their own limited understanding – they thought they had God all figured out. It is a common failure among people who seem to be experts in religion. They think they know it all, and they end up missing God's most wonderful surprises. But the humble folk who recognized their own limitations and God's greatness were open to the awe-inspiring glory of Christ. The arrogant scribes went home angry and unhappy; the humble crowed went home rejoicing.

CHRIST THE FRIEND Jesus calls the sick man "my child," and then happily and generously relieves the greatest burden of his life – the gnawing guilt of his violated conscience.

How glad Christ is to welcome us into his family! How eager he is to forgive us, to renew us, to enlighten and strengthen our anxious and tired souls! All we have to do is come to him with faith and admit our needs, our helplessness, our sins. The Tabernacle, an ongoing appointment that Christ never misses; the confessional, a failsafe loving embrace and perpetual fresh start; the Gospels, a fountain of truth and grace that flows without respite – a Christian can find peace of heart wherever he turns, if only he doesn't turn away from Christ.

Jesus: Come to me and I will heal you, I will set you free. Come to me in the Tabernacle, in all my sacraments, in the inspired word of the Bible! Come to me when you are filled with joy, as well as when you are crushed with troubles! When you turn to me in your weakness and acknowledge in all humility your need, then my mercy can make you walk once more, can make your heart resound with true peace and joy. Let me reach into the deepest recesses of your soul, bringing light to the hidden crevices carved by sin.

CHRIST IN MY LIFE The world is full of so many promises, Lord. So many gurus and life coaches and therapists promise to show the way to peace and wholeness. But can they forgive sins? Only you can reach into the depths of my soul; only you can see even deeper than I can; only you can heal me and cleanse me and give me a new start. Thank you, Lord, for coming to forgive my sins and for giving me a new start, as often as I need one…

Certainly you have more that you want to do in me and through me. I don't want to hinder you by stubbornly sticking to my own desires and plans if you are leading me along new paths. Your will, Lord, is beyond my comprehension; your plan is greater than I can imagine. Guide me, as you have promised to do, in spite of my selfishness and arrogance. Teach me to be humble, so I can be filled with awe and joy in the face of your wonderful deeds…

What do I enjoy most and value most about being a Christian and a member of your Church? So many things, Lord. Let me savor them… Thank you for those gifts, Lord. I know that your love for me is as vast as the heavens, though at times it's hard for me to accept. I want to use your gifts and rejoice in them. Teach me, Lord, to do your will…

QUESTIONS FOR SMALL GROUP DISCUSSION

1. What struck you most in the passage? What did you notice that you hadn't noticed before?

2. It seems impossible that the scribes would miss the significance of such a remarkable miracle performed right before their eyes, and yet they did. In what ways can we fall into the same trap, missing Christ's message because of our own pet peeves and preconceived notions?

3. Jesus has the authority to forgive sins. Later in this Gospel he will share that authority with the Apostles, giving rise to the sacrament of confession. Why do you think he chose to establish this sacrament, instead of just letting individual sinners turn directly to God, without any intermediaries? What about the sacrament of anointing of the sick?

4. Do you see any parallel between the sequence of events in this miracle and the doctrine of the future resurrection of the body?

Cf. Catechism of the Catholic Church, 1440-1449 on the sacramental forgiveness of sins; 452-455 on Jesus' names in the Gospels, which show his divinity

26. GETTING UP TO GO (MT 9:9-13)

"We open the door at the sound of his voice to receive him, when we freely assent to his promptings, whether secret or open, and when we do what we know we should do. He enters, then, to eat with us and we with him, since he lives in the hearts of his elect by the gift of love."

- St Bede the Venerable

Matthew 9:9-13

As Jesus was walking on from there he saw a man named Matthew sitting by the customs house, and he said to him, 'Follow me.' And he got up and followed him. While he was at dinner in the house it happened that a number of tax collectors and sinners came to sit at the table with Jesus and his disciples. When the Pharisees saw this, they said to his disciples, 'Why does your master eat with tax collectors and sinners?' When he heard this he replied, 'It is not the healthy who need the doctor, but the sick. Go and learn the meaning of the words: What I want is mercy, not sacrifice. And indeed I did not come to call the virtuous, but sinners.'

CHRIST THE LORD Jesus Christ makes more "I" statements than any other of the world's great religious figures, and we shouldn't overlook this. Buddha pointed to the Four Noble Truths, Mohammad to the words he received from Allah, and even Moses drew his people's attention to their covenant with God and the Ten Commandments, but Jesus Christ never tires of calling men to *himself*: "I am the way, the truth and the life" (John 14:6); "I am the vine" (John

15:5); "I am the light of the world" (John 8:12); and in this passage: "Follow me… I came to call sinners." Jesus Christ himself is the cornerstone (cf. Acts 4:11), the one foundation upon which the house of our salvation is built (cf. 1 Corinthians 3:11).

CHRIST THE TEACHER We do not know the background to this dramatic encounter between St Matthew and Jesus Christ. Perhaps Matthew had been following Christ at a distance for some time; perhaps they had known each other for years and only now did Christ call him to closer discipleship; perhaps they had never met before and Christ simply knew at first sight that this man was meant to be one of the Twelve. We do know, however, that Christ really knew Matthew, and that the innocuous phrase "and he got up and followed him" implies a full-scale revolution in Matthew's life. Leaving behind his lucrative and secure (albeit unpopular) position of collecting taxes for Palestine's foreign oppressors required taking a risk, to say the least. It required putting more faith in an itinerant carpenter from Galilee than in money, power, and all the pleasures they can offer. Why did Matthew do it? What gave him the courage to forsake the wide and smooth road of the world for the narrow and steep way of Christ?

Christ tells us – he wants us to know so that we can do the same: Matthew recognized and admitted his need for God. "Those who are well do not need a physician… I came to call sinners…" In Christ, God "never ceases to call every man to seek him, so as to find life and happiness" (Catechism of the Catholic Church, 30), but only those who admit their need can hear his voice. The Pharisees rejected Christ, because they did not believe they needed him; the Law and their own efforts were sufficient, they thought. Matthew (and his fellow sinners) followed him, because Matthew knew that something was missing from his life, and the look of love and power that he saw in Christ's eyes while he sat tallying coins in the market square gave him hope that in Christ he would find it.

CHRIST THE FRIEND Christ never let Matthew down in their friendship, and Matthew followed him to the point of giving his life in the name of Jesus. By leaving everything, Matthew experienced what all true Christians experience, over and over again: in letting Christ into our lives, we lose nothing, because he takes nothing away and gives everything.

When Christ calls someone to follow him, it is a dramatic event, a real encounter, face-to-face, eye-to-eye, heart-to-heart. Christianity is no abstract philosophy or aloof ideology, but a drama, a "covenant drama," as the Church calls it (Catechism of the Catholic Church, 2567), which addresses every man and woman at the core of their existence as a living, thinking, searching human being. Christianity is communion with God through friendship with Christ – nothing more, but nothing less.

CHRIST IN MY LIFE I have heard your call in my life; I have recognized you looking me in the eye and inviting me. Let me relive these experiences and thank you for them... Jesus, you call me to follow you because you know me and love me. Only in heaven will I find out how much. I still want to follow you. Keep calling me; you know how hard it is for me to hear your voice amid the jingle of coins...

I sometimes take you for granted. I forget that in the Eucharist, in the priest, and in the Church, you, the very God who created the universe, the only Savior from sin, the perfectly wise and infinitely good Lord are always with me and reaching out to me. Remind me, Lord. Never let me forget. Use me to bring this good news to those around me. I believe in you; help my weak faith…

Jesus, never let me be ashamed to admit my sin. You know me better than I know myself. You invite me to open my heart to you through the channels you have given me, through confession, through the guidance you wish to give me in your representatives. I trust in you, Lord. Nothing can stop you from loving me…

QUESTIONS FOR SMALL GROUP DISCUSSION

1. What struck you most in the passage? What did you notice that you hadn't noticed before?

2. What are some common ways in which Christ continues to make his call heard in the world? Does everyone have a vocation in life, or only priests and consecrated men and women? Do you know of any particularly dramatic vocation stories?

3. The Pharisees are perturbed because Jesus associates with disreputable people. Why? What does Jesus mean when he tells them to go and learn the saying "I desire mercy, not sacrifice" (from Hosea 6:6) – what is he really saying?

4. Is there any relationship between this encounter and the cure of the paralytic, which St Matthew puts just before this scene?

Cf. Catechism of the Catholic Church, 1996-2005 on grace and our need for God; 27-49 on our innate need for God

27. NEW WINE AT THE WEDDING (MT 9:14-17)

"God's splendor is the source of life, those who see him share his life. Because he was beyond the reach of man's mind, incomprehensible and invisible, he made himself visible, intelligible and knowable so that those who see and accept him may possess life."

- St Irenaeus

Matthew 9:14-17

Then John's disciples came to him and said, 'Why is it that we and the Pharisees fast, but your disciples do not?' Jesus replied, 'Surely the bridegroom's attendants would never think of mourning as long as the bridegroom is still with them? But the time will come for the bridegroom to be taken away from them, and then they will fast. No one puts a piece of unshrunken cloth on to an old cloak, because the patch pulls away from the cloak and the tear gets worse. Nor do people put new wine into old wineskins; if they do, the skins burst, the wine runs out, and the skins are lost. No; they put new wine into fresh skins and both are preserved.'

CHRIST THE LORD Jesus refers to himself as the bridegroom, a title that reveals two things.

First, it reiterates the Messiah's divinity. In the Old Testament, especially in the sayings of the prophets, God frequently uses the image of betrothal to describe and comment on his relationship with the Chosen People of Israel. The covenant bond God makes, renews, and deepens with his Chosen People has the same unifying, fructifying, and enduring quality of a marriage bond. When Jesus identifies himself as the bridegroom, therefore, he is asserting that the betrothal has come to an end, and the marriage is now, in him, imminent – language reminiscent of his first preaching: "The Kingdom of heaven is at hand!" If he were merely a prophet or an anointed earthly king (like David) such claims would be out of place. He must be more. He must be the eternal God himself come to wed his beloved spouse, the new Chosen People, the Church.

Second, the bridegroom image reveals the sort of love this Lord has for his people – a passionate, personal, determined love, the love that a young man in the prime of his life bears towards his beautiful young fiancée in the prime of her life. This is no philosophical God, no distant, cold watchmaker in the sky, no abstract, Aristotelian unmoved mover. The God of Abraham, Isaac, and Judah loves not less than the greatest human love, but even more.

CHRIST THE TEACHER The lesson of the new wine and the new cloth becomes clear only in its carefully chosen context.

John the Baptist's disciples are still committed to John, even though John himself had explained unambiguously that he was simply the messenger, while Christ was the Messiah, the Lamb of God. These disciples hadn't been able to accept John's message, or at least they didn't get it. They were perplexed, and now that their leader was in prison, they were closely watching Jesus to try and figure things out. They noticed that Christ and his disciples didn't fast (fasting was a ubiquitous penitential practice among religious folks of the time), and this seemed to prove definitively that Jesus couldn't be the real thing.

Jesus sets them straight, not by giving excuses for his behavior, but by trying to get them to see that the promise around which the Old Covenant pivoted has been fulfilled in him; it has reached completion; the building is finished, so the inelegant scaffolding can be removed.

The New Covenant is the final, everlasting Covenant; it will not change. And yet, even so, we in the Church can still fall into this same error. In every age, the Holy Spirit raises up new saints and new apostolates to keep building up the Church and equip it to meet new onslaughts of evil. In each Christian's life he does the same. Life is growth, and growth means change; let's keep a stash of new wineskins close at hand.

CHRIST THE FRIEND Jesus wants to come into your life because he wants you to share his joy. He calls his disciples his "wedding guests." The Greek term literally means "children of the bridal chamber," a phrase that referred to those special guests who were the bridegroom's best friends, the ones who spent the weeklong wedding reception (the ancient Palestinian alternative to modern-day honeymoons) at his side, sharing his joy and celebrating with him. Jesus wants your friendship, and he wants it to deepen, so that the indescribable joy that overflows from his love can spill into your life and the lives of those around you. He only needs you say one thing to make it happen – but he needs you to say it over and over: "Jesus, thy will be done."

CHRIST IN MY LIFE I know, Lord, that a sad saint is a bad saint. You are a God of joy. I long for true joy, the kind that lasts even in the midst of suffering, because it is grounded in your love, a love that never tires. I believe in your love, Jesus, but I still need you to teach me how to live in its light. You are the bridegroom of my heart. Teach me the way to go; show me the path to follow...

Sometimes I am afraid of what you may ask me. I hesitate to follow you, like John the Baptist's disciples. Why, Lord? Enlighten me. Your will is full of wisdom. Give me the courage to be wise...

You guide all of history – you prepared the world for the Incarnation, and now you spread your grace slowly but surely through the work of your Church. Thank you for your presence, your forgiveness, and your grace. I want to build your Church, to be a healthy cell in the Body of Christ. Make use of me, Lord. With you I can do all things…

QUESTIONS FOR SMALL GROUP DISCUSSION

1. What struck you most in the passage? What did you notice that you hadn't noticed before?

2. Why is it often so hard to accept God's will when it demands changes in our lives?

3. What new initiatives of the Holy Spirit have you seen in the Church (local and universal) recently?

4. How can a faithful Catholic distinguish between new ideas and apostolates that are authentic inspirations of the Holy Spirit and those that aren't?

Cf. The Catechism of the Catholic Church, 702-716 on the Holy Spirit in the time of the promises; 717-730 on the Spirit at the fullness of time; 731-741 on the work of the Holy Spirit in the age of the Church

28. THE HEALING TOUCH (MT 9:18-26)

"Nothing can come but that which God wills. And I make myself very sure that whatever that be, seem it never so bad in sight, it shall in deed be best."

- St Thomas More

Matthew 9:18-26

While he was speaking to them, up came one of the officials, who bowed low in front of him and said, 'My daughter has just died, but come and lay your hand on her and her life will be saved'. Jesus rose and, with his disciples, followed him. Then from behind him came a woman, who had suffered from a haemorrhage for twelve years, and she touched the fringe of his cloak, for she said to herself, 'If I can only touch his cloak I shall be well again'. Jesus turned round and saw her; and he said to her, 'Courage, my daughter, your faith has restored you to health'. And from that moment the woman was well again. When Jesus reached the official's house and saw the flute-players, with the crowd making a commotion he said, 'Get out of here; the little girl is not dead, she is asleep'. And they laughed at him. But when the people had been turned out he went inside and took the little girl by the hand; and she stood up. And the news spread all round the countryside.

CHRIST THE LORD Each of us puts our faith in someone. It may be a great teacher you once had, or your boss, or an effective leader, or it may simply be yourself. Human life is fragile, confusing, and brief – we naturally seek stability, which comes from putting one's faith in someone. St Matthew shows once again in this passage that Jesus alone is worthy of total faith.

We have already seen him heal a conscience by forgiving sins, calm a raging storm at sea, cure the sick and cast out devils… As if that weren't enough, now he heals a disease that has persisted for twelve years to show that his power has no limits, and then raises a girl from the sleep of death to show that he is the Lord of life. This is the God who created you and knows your name, the Lord who gives his body and blood to be your saving food and drink. How worthy he is to receive the trust we all need to give!

CHRIST THE TEACHER St Matthew emphasizes the role of faith in these miracles. The official kneels in front of Jesus – an act of homage and self-deprecation, an acknowledgment of his need and Jesus' superiority and power. When the suffering woman touches him, it is her faith that reveals her presence to Jesus, and her faith that activates the cure.

Faith – belief in Jesus as Savior, trust in his goodness and omnipotence – unleashes the transforming power of God's grace in our lives. God is not a Coke machine – we don't pay the price of a few rote prayers and rituals, press a button, and get divine grace in exchange. God is a person; faith is our relationship with that person. We are created to know and love him and to share in his knowledge and love, but to do that we have to trust in him. We have to take him at his word, just as we have to do with anyone else we want to let into our lives.

CHRIST THE FRIEND St Matthew shows us a Jesus who is utterly approachable. A sick woman is unafraid to fight through the crowds so she can reach out and touch the tassel on his cloak, and her confidence is rewarded with a miracle, a smile, and a tender, intimate word of encouragement. A synagogue official feels perfectly comfortable inviting Jesus into his house to resolve a tragic family crisis, and Jesus gladly complies, taking the little girl's hand in his own and restoring her to life. This illustrates the message of the Incarnation. God is close to us; he is with us. He wants us to approach him – he wants us to open our hearts to him. If we are willing to accept the friendship of Christ, we never have to be alone.

CHRIST IN MY LIFE Have I unwittingly put any limits on what I think you can do in my life? This sick woman had been suffering for twelve years. It must have seemed like an eternity for her. But she didn't give up hope. Have I? You are my hope, Lord. I place my sufferings at your feet. Let me hear your words of encouragement; let me feel your saving power. With the joy of your heart, expand my heart…

I believe in You, Lord. I believe in your Catholic Church. I believe in love; I believe in your love. I trust in you – you know I do. But I want to trust more. I want to be as close and hope-giving to others as you are to me. Give me what I ask of you, Lord, and then ask what you will...

Lord, I know that no matter how bad things look, you are still at my side. I know that even when I can see only darkness with my reason, your light shines through my faith. Yet, in times of trouble, it is so hard to see your light. Lord Jesus, increase my faith. Teach me to see all things as you see them, and to see you in all things...

QUESTIONS FOR SMALL GROUP DISCUSSION

1. What struck you most in the passage? What did you notice that you hadn't noticed before?

2. Why did this woman have to touch Jesus' cloak to be healed? Why did the official require Jesus to come and lay his hands on his daughter to restore her? Do you see any connection between these miracles and Christ's choice to distribute his grace through the Church's sacraments?

3. Why did the official show such deference to Jesus, while the professional mourners in the house ridiculed him? Does the ridicule of those people tell us anything about what the physical presence of Jesus was or wasn't like?

4. St Matthew points out that news of these deeds spread throughout the land. How? What can we do to make the good news of Jesus spread more widely and deeply throughout our own land?

Cf. The Catechism of the Catholic Church, 1114-1121 on the sacraments; 1122-1126 on the role of faith in receiving God's grace

29. BELIEVING LEADS TO SEEING (MT 9:27-35)

"Therefore, that shining light of which has been lit for our salvation must always shine in us."

- St Chromatius

Matthew 9:27-35

As Jesus went on his way two blind men followed him shouting, 'Take pity on us, Son of David'. And when Jesus reached the house the blind men came up with him and he said to them, 'Do you believe I can do this?' They said, 'Sir, we do'. Then he touched their eyes saying, 'Your faith deserves it, so let this be done for you'. And their sight returned. Then Jesus sternly warned them, 'Take care that no one learns about this'. But when they had gone, they talked about him all over the countryside. They had only just left when a man was brought to him, a dumb demoniac. And when the devil was cast out, the dumb man spoke and the people were amazed. 'Nothing like this has ever been seen in Israel' they said. But the Pharisees said, 'It is through the prince of devils that he casts out devils'. Jesus made a tour through all the towns and villages, teaching in their synagogues, proclaiming the Good News of the kingdom and curing all kinds of diseases and sickness.

CHRIST THE LORD With this passage, St Matthew finishes his narration of ten miracles performed in the aftermath of the Sermon on the Mount, in confirmation of the trustworthiness of what was said in that sermon, as it were. These last two miracles mark the final flourish on this section of the Gospel, showing that nothing, absolutely nothing, is excluded from Christ's saving mission.

Jesus doesn't come to rescue bits and pieces of broken humanity; he comes to gather it all into a new, everlasting Kingdom. His redemption actually brings good out of evil. If evil – whether on a grand scale of human history or on the smaller scale of individual human lives – were able to damage our humanity beyond the possibility of restoration, we would have no reason to hope. Jesus, however, shows that God's loving goodness is far superior to evil. Those who let him into their lives discover not only forgiveness, security, and relief, but a profound renewal that gradually extends to every corner of their being. The Lord is Savior, but he is also *Redeemer*.

CHRIST THE TEACHER Jesus works in our lives according to a plan. He knows what he is doing, just as he knew what he was doing during the days of his public life.

He orders the two blind men to keep the miracle under wraps. This is a frequent injunction, especially in the Gospel of Mark. He knew that the Israelites' hearts had been hardened and confused through the centuries, so he was gradually revealing his full identity and the full extent of his mission. He wanted time to train his closest disciples, and he wanted freedom of action – all of which could be compromised if news of his miracles sparked precipitous action from the authorities or spawned too quickly a suffocating wave of wonder-loving crowds. Although his heart couldn't resist the desperate, faith-filled appeals of the suffering people he came to save, he was nevertheless following a clear strategy.

Just so, he works in our lives intelligently, gradually, strategically. But we can't see the whole plan – it's too big and bright for our mortal gaze. And so we have to learn to simply travel along by his side like the disciples, listening, obeying, and trusting, carrying out one piece of the plan at a time.

CHRIST THE FRIEND The Pharisees were unbelieving. They didn't want to believe in a Messiah that didn't fit their preconceived ideas, so they found ways to justify their resistance – if Jesus drives out demons, he must be possessed by a stronger demon, that's all. Imagine how Christ's heart reacted to those accusations, such stubborn resistance to his grace. Imagine how he reacts to the disbelief of so many people who refuse to see the signs of his love and truth in our world today.

When a friend is in pain, you do whatever you can to comfort him. Christians can comfort Christ by keeping their own faith fresh and, above all, by living a real, practical, and universal Christian charity. That's the only way to lay a successful siege against the world's many barricaded hearts – breaching their walls with love, so the gift of faith can come streaming in.

CHRIST IN MY LIFE You have let me see some miracles, Lord. You have given me experiences that can have no other explanation than yourself. Don't let me forget them, Lord; let them nourish my faith. I believe in your saving power and your continued presence. Thank you for the amazing things you have done in my life. Pray for me, Holy Mother of God, that I may be made worthy of the love of Christ…

Lord, there are people in my life who are blind, who are mute, who are trapped in the darkness of sin. Jesus, I pray for them now. Free them, enlighten them, as you have done with me. Free me, too; keep enlightening me. I want to comfort you, Lord, with my faith and charity. Teach me to bear the torch of your love. Sacred Heart of Jesus, I trust in you…

These two blind men prayed so simply, so faithfully, and so directly! "Son of David, take pity on us!" Lord, have pity on me. You know my misery and my blindness. I believe that you can heal me. I believe that you can make me into a saint. You can do all things, Lord…

QUESTIONS FOR SMALL GROUP DISCUSSION

1. What struck you most in the passage? What did you notice that you hadn't noticed before?

2. Why do you think Jesus questioned the two blind men before healing them?

3. Some critics of the Bible claim that the demon possessions narrated in the Gospels were just natural diseases that people in ancient times didn't know how to diagnose. Can you find any evidence in this passage against such a view? Can you think of any reasons why demon possession might be manifested in symptoms similar to natural or psychological disorders?

4. Think of some people you know who don't believe in God or Christ. Why don't they believe? What single thing would do most to help them believe?

Cf. The Catechism of the Catholic Church, 897-913 on how Catholics should spread the faith; 2118-212 on different forms of disbelief

THE GOSPEL OF MATTHEW CHAPTER 10

"The Church's fundamental function in every age and particularly in ours is to direct man's gaze, to point the awareness and experience of the whole of humanity towards the mystery of God, to help all men to be familiar with the profundity of the Redemption taking place in Christ Jesus. At the same time man's deepest sphere is involved – we mean the sphere of human hearts, consciences and events… Jesus Christ is the stable principle and fixed center of the mission that God Himself has entrusted to man. We must all share in this mission and concentrate all our forces on it, since it is more necessary than ever for modern mankind. If this mission seems to encounter greater opposition nowadays than ever before, this shows that today it is more necessary than ever and, in spite of the opposition, more awaited than ever."

- Pope John Paul II, Redemptor hominis

30. THE CHURCH GETS GOING (MT 9:36 – 10:8)

"The apostles have preached the Gospel to us from the Lord Jesus Christ; Jesus Christ has done so from God. Christ therefore was sent forth by God, and the apostles by Christ. Both these appointments, then, were made in an orderly way, according to the will of God."

- Pope St Clement of Rome

Matthew 9:36-10:8

And when he saw the crowds he felt sorry for them because they were harassed and dejected, like sheep without a shepherd. Then he said to his disciples, 'The harvest is rich but the labourers are few, so ask the Lord of the harvest to send labourers to his harvest'. He summoned his twelve disciples, and gave them authority over unclean spirits with power to cast them out and to cure all kinds of diseases and sickness. These are the names of the twelve apostles: first, Simon who is called Peter, and his brother Andrew; James the son of Zebedee, and his brother John; Philip and Bartholomew; Thomas, and Matthew the tax collector; James the son of Alphaeus, and Thaddaeus; Simon the Zealot and Judas Iscariot, the one who was to betray him. These twelve Jesus sent out, instructing them as follows: 'Do not turn your steps to pagan territory, and do not enter any Samaritan town; go rather to the lost sheep of the House of Israel. And as you go, proclaim that the kingdom of heaven is close at hand. Cure the sick, raise the dead, cleanse the lepers, cast out devils. You received without charge, give without charge.'

CHRIST THE LORD Jesus Christ is a man for others. His heart was moved by the needs of those around him. His heart is moved by our need for him. The whole project of his life, from Bethlehem to Calvary, consisted in winning back for us what we had lost by sin: hope, eternal life, meaning, friendship with God, lasting joy, enduring peace. All he wants is to reap a harvest of souls for his Father's house. His teaching shows us the way; his miracles convince us of this teaching; his suffering, death, and resurrection plant the new Tree of Life, whose fruit we receive in the Eucharist. Not one word, not one deed, not one thought of Christ's earthly journey was for himself: he lived to please his Father (cf. John 8:29) and to "save sinners" (1 Timothy 1:15). Even at the peak of his atrocious suffering, as he hung writhing with excruciating pain on the cross, his lifeblood trickling away, his heart did not turn in on himself, but continued to love others – even his own crucifiers: "Forgive them Father, for they know not what they do" (Luke 23:34). What more could he have done for us? What greater love could he have shown? What more glorious Lord could we serve? We can serve him in no better way than by sharing his concern for the "sheep without a shepherd."

CHRIST THE TEACHER Jesus Christ always works according to objectives. Oftentimes we think that our faith and our relationship with God in his Church do not require us to use our heads. When we want to build a business, engage in research, or achieve any success in earthly matters, we put our minds to work and come up with a strategy. We set goals; we troubleshoot and problem-solve and multitask and evaluate and report; we often get very demanding with ourselves and our coworkers. But when it comes to building up the Kingdom of Christ in our hearts and in those around us, we leave it up to feelings, impressions, and vague, so-called inspirations. Christ didn't. He sends his missionaries to accomplish a particular goal: preaching and healing in the Jewish towns first (not the pagan ones), knowing that he must guide the growth of his Church by logical stages. He formed his team of Twelve Apostles, painstakingly prepared them, and commissioned and equipped them to carry the Gospel throughout the world… He had a vision, he had clear idea of where he was going, and he made a specific plan. He would have been a great CEO.

CHRIST THE FRIEND Jesus Christ is a team player. As God, he could have chosen to fulfill the mission of salvation all alone, to come to earth and stay here bodily forever, continuing his Galilean-style ministry for all time, until he had made his way to all the peoples throughout the world. And yet, he chose not to. Rather, when his heart was moved he summoned his Twelve Apostles and began preparations for establishing his Church, which would be the extension of his incarnation and mission throughout all ages and in every land. Christ chose to administer his salvation through the cooperation of missionaries, of disciples, of men and women who would roll up their sleeves and bring in the abundant harvest. He chose to involve the very sinners he came to save in the project of their salvation, and in that way to give meaning and purpose to their lives. He asks us now to contemplate the injured world around us and respond generously by working with him to bring life to all.

Philip: I was scared when Jesus sent me out. I have to admit that I don't think I would have gone if he had sent me alone. When he gave us these instructions and sent us as his ambassadors for the first time, the look in his eyes was, well, hard to describe. It flashed with a conqueror's fire, but it also glowed with a tinge of sadness, as if he were pleading with us, as if he were afraid we would start making excuses. I was afraid to go, but some of his fire stirred me, and I wanted to show him that I was on his side. And soon after we set out, all my fears vanished, because we saw right away that his own Spirit was with us.

CHRIST IN MY LIFE Jesus, I am your disciple, but I am a weak and needy one. In my weakness, your strength can shine through. Teach me to depend on you; make my heart like yours: compassionate, concerned, courageous. Help me to see the needs of those around me and not be blinded by my selfishness. You have given me so much; help me to share it all with those around me…

You are all-powerful, Lord, and all-wise. In your wisdom and power, you founded your Church on Peter and the other Apostles. Its endurance and growth and fruitfulness through the ages, in spite of unremitting persecution from within and without, prove your constant presence within it. Thank you for the Church. Protect your Church. Use my life for the good of your Church. Continue to call men and women to serve your Church. We are one body in Christ; blest be the name of the Lord!....

I remember when I first heard your voice in my heart. I knew you were speaking to me, calling to me, inviting me. Thank you for looking into my eyes and speaking my name. Thank you for giving my life a purpose. Thank you for giving me a mission, for sharing your mission with me. I want to be your faithful follower until the day I die. Your Kingdom come…

QUESTIONS FOR SMALL GROUP DISCUSSION

1. What struck you most in the passage? What did you notice that you hadn't noticed before?

2. What does this passage teach us about the *origin* and *mission* of the Church?

3. What does Jesus mean when he says "the harvest is abundant but the laborers are few"? Why are there so few laborers? Why does God want us to pray for more vocations? Why doesn't he just give them automatically?

4. What are the greatest needs right now in our local Church? What more can we do to help meet those needs?

Cf. Catechism of the Catholic Church, 1, 737-740 on the essential role of the Church in the plan of salvation; 620 on God's love for us; 606-618 on Jesus' self-offering out of love for us

31. READING THE INSTRUCTIONS (MT 10:5-15)

"It may be said in all truth that the Church, like Christ, goes through the centuries doing good to all."

- Pope Pius XI, Divini redemptoris

Matthew 10:5-15

These twelve Jesus sent out, instructing them as follows: 'Do not turn your steps to pagan territory, and do not enter any Samaritan town; go rather to the lost sheep of the House of Israel. And as you go, proclaim that the kingdom of heaven is close at hand. Cure the sick, raise the dead, cleanse the lepers, cast out devils. You received without charge, give without charge. Provide yourselves with no gold or silver, not even with a few coppers for your purses, with no haversack for the journey or spare tunic or footwear or a staff, for the workman deserves his keep. Whatever town or village you go into, ask for someone trustworthy and stay with him until you leave. As you enter his house, salute it, and if the house deserves it, let your peace descend upon it; if it does not, let your peace come back to you. And if anyone does not welcome you or listen to what you have to say, as you walk out of the house or town shake the dust from your feet. I tell you solemnly, on the day of Judgement it will not go as hard with the land of Sodom and Gomorrah as with that town.'

CHRIST THE LORD In ancient times, when Jewish travelers would return to the Holy Land from Gentile territory, they would shake the Gentile dust from their feet. Thus they reaffirmed their faith in the one true God, a faith not shared by the pagans. The gesture also reaffirmed their assurance that God's promised redemption would come to them, the Chosen People.

God fulfilled his promise in Christ, who gives "first dibs" for salvation to the "lost sheep of the house of Israel" – the non-Jews would have to wait until after the Resurrection to hear the Good News. And by instructing his Apostles to shake the dust from their feet whenever they leave a town that doesn't accept faith in Christ, Jesus shows clearly that he is fulfilling the promises of old by erecting a new Israel – a new Chosen People based not on race, but on their adherence to him and his doctrine. The new Holy Land is not limited by geography, but by the heart: a town that rejects the gospel has set itself outside the confines of Christ's Kingdom, so the King's disciples shake its dust from their feet.

With this first mission of the Apostles, the Lord is beginning his conquest of the world, a conquest that will offer freedom and everlasting prosperity to those who submit, but for those who don't...well, not even Jesus cares to go into details.

CHRIST THE TEACHER In these instructions to his twelve chosen Apostles, Jesus reveals his own idea of the Church. The tasks he specifies correspond exactly to the tasks he has just performed in the last five chapters of St Matthew's Gospel. His first preaching consisted in proclaiming the imminence of the Kingdom of heaven – these were his very first words after the arrest of John the Baptist and the beginning of his public ministry – and the ten miracles following his Sermon on the Mount displayed precisely the items on his list of commands: curing of the sick, raising of the dead, cleansing of lepers, and driving out demons. In Christ's mind, what is the Apostles' task, and what is the task of the Church? *The very same as Jesus' own task.*

The Church is the extension of Christ's own incarnation throughout the long stretch of human history before the end of time. All that Christ did in Galilee and Judea for the few years before his Ascension into heaven, he will continue to do in every corner of the earth and in every human heart, through the ministry of the Church. In this first commission to the Twelve Apostles, Jesus reveals the amazing doctrine that the Church is, quite really, "the Body of Christ" (Cf. Colossians 1:24).

Are we taking part fully in this mission? It is not enough to contemplate and pray – we need to act, extending Christ's own actions of love throughout the world. Today Christ is sending us out on a mission no less important than that of the Apostles. No one is exempt. As the Catechism puts it: "Service of and witness to the faith are necessary for salvation" (1816).

CHRIST THE FRIEND The first word Christ's messengers are to speak is "peace." The history of salvation, the moral conduct of a Christian, the demands of living in God's grace – these other topics can wait. First and foremost, suffering and searching sinners must be shown the sheer goodness of God, the source of interior and exterior peace. Only then, convinced of his goodness, will they be open to hearing the demands of his discipleship.

To be able to communicate this peace, Christ's collaborators have to first experience it themselves. He has shown it to them already, in many ways, but now

147

they need to deepen their conviction. And so Jesus gives them instructions that will prove his friendship even more dramatically. In carrying out their mission, they are to depend entirely upon his Providence. They aren't to bring money, or extra clothes, or supplies – nothing of their own. God will take care of them completely. They are not preaching their own message; they are not going on their own initiative; they are ambassadors for Christ, and Christ will be everything for them, just as he wants to be everything for each of us.

Jesus: The Kingdom of God is at hand… You have experienced it; I have given you a taste of it. Now I send you to bring the good news to others. In doing so, you will experience it even more, just as teachers really start to learn once they begin giving their knowledge to others. All of my followers are my ambassadors: your words and your example will carry my grace into many hearts. You don't need to be perfect before you start – I have called you just as you are. Trust in my saving word, and I will work miracles through you. Go only in my name; you need nothing else.

CHRIST IN MY LIFE Jesus, my hands, words, and feet are yours. I give them to you. Reach out through them to the people I encounter who don't yet know your light and love. How can I be a better apostle, Lord? You have chosen me and sent me out; you will be my guide, my coach. I depend on you. I am just a rusty pipe, but the clear cool water of your grace can flow through rusty pipes as well as any. Count on me, Jesus; never leave me alone…

The law of your Kingdom is love and self-giving. Only love will break down the defensive barriers that are keeping you out of people's hearts. I want to love you more, and I know that loving you means loving my neighbor, bringing them peace. You know how hard this can be for me, but you ask almost nothing else. Jesus, meek and humble of heart, make my heart more like yours…

I know that I can only give to others what I myself have received. So please, Lord, grant me a deep experience of the peace you wish to spread into every heart. Help me to think more of others than of myself. Never let me be separated from you, so that I can keep on building your Kingdom…

QUESTIONS FOR SMALL GROUP DISCUSSION

1. What struck you most in the passage? What did you notice that you hadn't noticed before?

2. How do these instructions still apply today to our lives as Christ's disciples?

3. Jesus implies that as we try to spread his Kingdom we will sometimes experience rejection and failure. Why does he allow that to happen? What is a disciple's proper response?

4. Jesus tells the Twelve to give without demanding payment, and then he tells them to bring

no food, because the laborer deserves his keep. How can you reconcile this apparent contradiction?

Cf. The Catechism of the Catholic Church, 787-796 on the Church as the Body of Christ; 857-865 on the apostolic nature of the Church

32. THE MARKS OF AN APOSTLE (MT 10:16-25)

"It is by his power and not by the wisdom of men that the world is converted, and to prove this he has chosen unlearned men to be his preachers and has sent them into the world."

- Pope St Gregory the Great

Matthew 10:16-25

'Remember, I am sending you out like sheep among wolves; so be cunning as serpents and yet as harmless as doves. Beware of men: they will hand you over to sanhedrins and scourge you in their synagogues. You will be dragged before governors and kings for my sake, to bear witness before them and the pagans. But when they hand you over, do not worry about how to speak or what to say; what you are to say will be given to you when the time comes; because it is not you who will be speaking; the Spirit of your Father will be speaking in you. Brother will betray brother to death, and the father his child; children will rise against their parents and have them put to death. You will be hated by all men on account of my name; but the man who stands firm to the end will be saved. If they persecute you in one town, take refuge in the next; and if they persecute you in that, take refuge in another. I tell you solemnly, you will not have gone the round of the towns of Israel before the Son of Man comes. The disciple is not superior to his teacher, nor the slave to his master. It is enough for the disciple that he should grow to be like his teacher, and the slave like his master. If they have called the master of the house Beelzebul, what will they not say of his household?'

CHRIST THE LORD We are used to this passage, since we have heard it so many times. But it is actually quite strange. Here we have the Lord of the universe, the eternal King, giving instructions to his disciples. He is telling them what they can look forward to if they follow him: hardship, pain, and suffering – not exactly an attractive job description. And yet, his Apostles were not deterred; neither was the first generation of Christians, nor the second, nor the third… Something about Christ, about his person, his authority, his wisdom, the almost irresistible force of his intense and overflowing goodness, wins out over all prospective problems. He is worth it. His Kingdom is worth it. He alone is the Lord of lords.

CHRIST THE TEACHER Two lessons shine through in this harrowing discourse. First, the faithful disciple of Christ will suffer because of his fidelity. St Matthew puts these instructions in the context of Jesus' conversation with the Twelve Apostles, but they apply to all Christians – by the sacraments of baptism and confirmation, we all share in the Apostolic mission. Every Christian, then, should expect to face opposition, misunderstanding, hatred, and even violence. Jesus speaks of his followers being scourged, maligned, falsely accused, torn apart, and even killed. This wasn't just empty rhetoric. The history of the Church is the fulfillment – over and over again – of this warning. It continues today, and it will continue "until the end." We should not be surprised by it; we should expect it, even from the unlikeliest sources ("children will put their parents to death"!). In fact, if we don't run into problems, something is probably wrong; after all, a Christian is supposed to follow in the footsteps of Christ.

The second lesson is what to do when we experience persecution. We should not give in to fear. Instead, we are to trust that God will use our suffering and witness to advance his Kingdom, save souls, and glorify his name. We should not abort our efforts to build up the Church – Jesus will be reaching kings and governors through us. We should put all our talent and intelligence at the service of our mission without ever adopting the methods of sin and evil (shrewd as serpents, but innocent as doves). And above all, we should never give up on Christ: "The man who stands firm to the end will be saved." If Jesus gave this assurance, it's because we need it; there will be times so tough that we are tempted to abandon our allegiance to Christ. Jesus wants us to be ready ahead of time, to decide now that we will stay faithful then.

CHRIST THE FRIEND In an offhand way, Jesus here makes our hearts rejoice – he links us to himself in an unconditional, intensely intimate way. We are no longer outsiders; we are his close collaborators, his coworkers, his brothers and sisters. If his enemies calumniate "the master of the house," he says, "what will they not say of his household!" He's talking about us. We are now even closer than friends; we are members of his household, members of his family. If we have taken his part and are willing to suffer the consequences, how much more will he take our part and give us a share in his joys! When we have to struggle and suffer to fulfill our Christian mission, we unite ourselves even more intimately to the cross of Christ. When we allow our struggles to bind us more tightly to the heart of Christ, we begin to understand the beauty of suffering; instead of fearing it, we embrace it.

CHRIST IN MY LIFE In your eyes, Lord, I can see the ardent, eager love with which you issue these warnings. You know that following you is worth it, no matter what. Convince me of that, Lord. I never want to abandon you. Your saints longed to share your suffering, so that they could love you more. I am weak and fearful, but I will walk with you wherever you send me. Be my strength, O Christ; be my joy; be my all...

Nothing matters more to you than the advance of your Kingdom, the progress of your Church. Are my priorities the same as yours, Lord? What do I care about, think about, and value most? Am I your authentic follower? Why do I still fear the world's rejection, when I know that the world needs the very authenticity that makes it uncomfortable? I want to think as you think, to will as you will, to love as you love. Come into my heart, Lord; teach and transform me. Mary, make me like him...

Thank you for making me a member of your household. Thank you for wanting to spend all eternity with me. Thank you for not giving up on me. Teach me to be as good to those around me as you have been to me. I want to radiate your goodness, your meekness, and your strength...

QUESTIONS FOR SMALL GROUP DISCUSSION

1. What struck you most in the passage? What did you notice that you hadn't noticed before?

2. Have you ever experienced persecution or opposition in your efforts to be faithful to Christ and spread his Kingdom?

3. What examples of perseverance in the face of difficulty have inspired you most in your life up to now?

4. Why do you think Christ permits his followers to suffer persecution and violence? Is it a sign that he doesn't really love them, or that he is not the Lord of history?

Cf. The Catechism of the Catholic Church, 675, 769, 1816 on persecution of the Church; 162 and 2016 on perseverance

33. ETERNAL REASSURANCE (MT 10:26-33)

"All my nothingness is drowned in the sea of your mercy. With the confidence of a child, I throw myself into your arms, O Father of mercy, to make up for the unbelief of so many souls who are afraid to trust in you."

- St Faustina Kowalska

Matthew 10:26-33

'Do not be afraid of them [your persecutors] therefore. For everything that is now

151

covered will be uncovered, and everything now hidden will be made clear. What I say to you in the dark, tell in the daylight; what you hear in whispers, proclaim from the housetops. Do not be afraid of those who kill the body but cannot kill the soul; fear him rather who can destroy both body and soul in hell. Can you not buy two sparrows for a penny? And yet not one falls to the ground without your Father knowing. Why, every hair on your head has been counted. So there is no need to be afraid; you are worth more than hundreds of sparrows. So if anyone declares himself for me in the presence of men, I will declare myself for him in the presence of my Father in heaven. But the one who disowns me in the presence of men, I will disown in the presence of my Father in heaven.'

CHRIST THE LORD We enter this scene midstream: Christ has just chosen his Twelve Apostles and is giving them instructions for their first missionary journey. He warns them that they will face persecution and hardship, just as he himself has faced, that their mission will demand courage, perseverance, and fidelity in the face of suffering, humiliation, and opposition. We can imagine the faces of his rookie disciples as he speaks of such things. Initially elated and excited at having been set apart as his personal emissaries, maybe Christ glimpsed in their eyes a flash or two of apprehension and concern: "It's not going to be quite so glorious as we thought. Persecution, hardship, suffering, humiliation... Why is the Master speaking of such things? Can he not preserve us from them?" Christ recognizes their trepidation, and in these few lines St Matthew shows how Christ comforted and encouraged his little band of future martyrs and pillars of the Church – and how he wants to comfort us.

CHRIST THE TEACHER Christ longs for us to accept an antidote to our fears: to see life and all its hazards from the perspective of eternity. All that is now hidden will be uncovered; those who kill the body cannot kill the soul; if we are faithful to him during our earthly life, he will faithfully award us everlasting life. Christ speaks frequently about the Kingdom of heaven, about what comes after this life. Perhaps he really does mean what he says; perhaps he really wants us to "set our hearts on his Kingdom first" (Matthew 6:33); perhaps he really knows what he is talking about.

We do not spend our lives only for the few years of our earthly existence, but also for the fullness of the life to come. Catholics through the ages have administered this antidote to worry and fear by keeping always in the back of their minds the potent little Latin phrase: "Quid est hoc ad aeternitatem?" What is this in the light of eternity?

CHRIST THE FRIEND In this passage Christ commands us not to be afraid – three times! He commands us – he doesn't advise or cajole or recommend, he *commands* us – to courageously fulfill our mission as his followers. He commands us to trust in him without reserve, for we are under the loving and powerful care of the Father, who even knows the number of hairs on our heads.

Jesus: I know even better than you do how difficult this earthly pilgrimage is. But take courage. Be faithful. Let your true Christian self shine. Let my call resonate deep within you so that just the thought of me and of my immense love for you will propel you through every difficulty and opposition. Am I not always by your side? Suffer in faith, bear my cross with patience and trust, stay faithful to your baptismal commitment, and go through this world boldly bearing the touch of faith. Believe me, the prize is worth the fight. If anyone declares himself for me in the presence of men, I will declare myself for him in the presence of my Father. Be not afraid – courageously fulfill the mission I have given you. Trust in me without reserve, for you are in my loving and powerful care.

CHRIST IN MY LIFE You know my fears, Lord. When I hesitate to be your witness in word, deed, and example, it's because I'm thinking that happiness will come from something else besides my friendship with you. But what more could I desire than to be your companion? The whole universe belongs to you. You created me and have invited me to your heavenly banquet. Lord, what more could I desire than to walk by your side...

You want me to trust in you, Lord. You allow hardships because you want to give me chances to exercise that trust. You know that nothing but intimate communion with you will fill the desires of my heart. Thank you for your love, Lord, and for the troubles you send me...

Many of those around me live lives of fear and instability, even if they seem to have it all together. They don't know you, Lord. They don't have you. Come to them, show them, give yourself to them. Make me your messenger. I don't care what happens to me; I already have you. Reach them through me. Jesus, I trust in you...

QUESTIONS FOR SMALL GROUP DISCUSSION

1. What struck you most in the passage? What did you notice that you hadn't noticed before?

2. What impact should belief in everlasting life have on everyday life?

3. Jesus says, "Don't be afraid" three times in this passage. He must know that fears are common. What are some of the most common fears people experience these days? What would Christ say about them?

4. Can you think of anyone you know who has suffered persecution for their fidelity to Christ? What were the long-term results, for them and for others around them?

Cf. Catechism of the Catholic Church, 1818, 1723, and 222-227 on living in the light of eternity; 268-274 on God's omnipotence love

34. COSTS AND BENEFITS (MT 10:34-11:1)

"But in order that faith and hope may attain their full fruit, there is need of patience."

- St Cyprian

Matthew 10:34-42

'Do not suppose that I have come to bring peace to the earth: it is not peace I have come to bring, but a sword. For I have come to set a man against his father, a daughter against her mother, a daughter-in-law against her mother-in-law. A man's enemies will be those of his own household. Anyone who prefers father or mother to me is not worthy of me. Anyone who prefers son or daughter to me is not worthy of me. Anyone who does not take his cross and follow in my footsteps is not worthy of me. Anyone who finds his life will lose it; anyone who loses his life for my sake will find it. Anyone who welcomes you welcomes me; and those who welcome me welcome the one who sent me. Anyone who welcomes a prophet will have a prophet's reward; and anyone who welcomes a holy man will have a holy man's reward. If anyone gives so much as a cup of cold water to one of these little ones because he is a disciple, then I tell you solemnly, he will most certainly not lose his reward.' When Jesus had finished instructing his twelve disciples he moved on from there to teach and preach in their towns.

CHRIST THE LORD Jesus Christ is either a madman or the Son of God. Who else would demand such an absolute allegiance? He calls us to put our friendship with him ahead of every other human relationship. Not even the deepest human ties are to go before him, not even the deepest human desires, not even our own success and happiness in this world can compare to a life lived for and with this rabbi from Nazareth – so he says. How can he make such a claim?

Only out of love. He is God. He came to earth to save us from eternal frustration and reestablish friendship between our Creator and us. We faced the prospect of eternal frustration because in the sin of Adam and Eve the human race rebelled against God, attempting to find in themselves the fulfillment that only God can give. God created us with a built-in desire for happiness so profound that only intimacy with God himself could produce it. He then freely gave us that intimacy in the Garden of Eden. But, deceived by the devil, mankind "let his trust in his Creator die in his heart, and, abusing his freedom, disobeyed God's command" (Catechism of the Catholic Church, 397).

God looked upon us who had rejected his friendship, and instead of rejecting us in turn, he concocted a plan to win us back. Christ is the fulfillment of that plan. Christ is God come to earth to win back for the Father the friendship of men, and for men the friendship of the Father. He knows that only in God will we find what we seek. He knows that he is the Savior, our only bridge back to God, and therefore he can make such drastic claims. Only because he loves us with such unshakable determination does he demand that we love him with all our heart, soul, mind, and strength, and love our neighbor as ourselves (Cf. Mark 12:30-31). Christ the Lord demands a lot from his followers, but only because he gives them even more.

CHRIST THE TEACHER At the end of this long discourse of instructions to his Apostles, Jesus identifies the motivation that should be at the core of every Christian's efforts to bring others to Christ. This motivation is so deep, so strong, and so overriding that it will enable Christians to face up to and endure all the hardships and sufferings that Jesus promises will come.

Bringing others closer to Christ gives them what they need most, what they can get nowhere else. When they encounter a Christian, they are actually encountering Christ himself. When they welcome and listen to and show hospitality to one of Christ's disciples, they are already making deposits in their heavenly bank account. The disciple shouldn't be nervous or hesitant; he should be proud of the gospel and eager to share it – those whom he approaches will receive benefits that far outweigh any inconveniences the encounter affords. If the Christian apostle focuses on this basic truth, he will be able to weather any reception at all, even the most irredeemably unpleasant.

CHRIST THE FRIEND Christ is demanding. To follow Christ means to deny one's many deep-seated tendencies toward self-sufficiency and self-indulgence in favor of obedience and self-governance. And yet, Jesus never asks us to give more than he has already given. He says we must take up our cross, true, but we must do so in order to follow where he has already gone. We must even be willing to break from family members in order to stay faithful to his will, but he too had to watch his own mother suffer unspeakably at the foot of his cross. We must be ready to face the sword of persecution and opposition, but his very heart has already been pierced by a spear. In short, though here on earth it is hard for us to understand how God permits our lives to run into so many

155

difficulties, we know for certain that he has his reasons, because he has trodden the path before us and promises to walk it again by our side.

CHRIST IN MY LIFE You talk of crosses, Lord, but also of rewards. You want me to keep both in mind. You are a doctor who knows that wholeness can only emerge through painful operations and rehabilitation. You took up your cross for my sake, when I was still a sinner, and when you didn't have to. Teach me to take up my cross for you...

There is no task in my life more important than helping others find and follow you. I believe in you. I want my life to reflect your goodness and truth. Please strengthen my faith. I want to follow you, even on the way of the cross...

Help me to know myself through and through, Lord. What are the preferences in my life that keep me from living closer to you? What am I holding back from you? I want to be your faithful friend, just as you have been faithful to me. Help me, Lord; show me the way to go...

QUESTIONS FOR SMALL GROUP DISCUSSION

1. What struck you most in the passage? What did you notice that you hadn't noticed before?

2. When Jesus was born, the angels declared that he had brought peace on earth, and the prophets called him the "prince of peace." Yet in this passage Jesus says he did not come to bring peace, but the sword. How can you reconcile this apparent contradiction?

3. Why does Jesus promise a "prophet's reward" to anyone who welcomes a prophet because he is a prophet? Is that fair?

4. How much of these predictions of suffering do you think the Apostles understood? Do you think you understand more than they did?

Cf. The Catechism of the Catholic Church, 1435, 1460, 1615, 1642, 2029, 2427 on taking up and bearing one's own cross; 555, 1816, 2015 on the cross as the way to follow Christ

THE GOSPEL OF MATTHEW CHAPTER 11

"When a field is burned and weeded, the dry and useless brambles and thorns are consumed. When the sun rises and its rays drive away the darkness, thieves, wanderers by night, and burglars hide themselves. Similarly, when Paul preached to the people it was like a great clap of thunder or a fire blazing up with greater force or the sun rising more brilliantly than ever: unfaithfulness was destroyed, falsity disappeared, truth shone forth as when wax liquefies before a blazing fire. For he carried the name of Jesus around by his words, his letters,

his miracles, and his example. He praised Jesus' name without ceasing, and gave glory to it with thanksgiving."

- St Bernardino of Siena

35. INCONTROVERTIBLE EVIDENCE (MT 11:2-11)

"The redeemer of man, Jesus Christ, is the center of the universe and of history."

- Pope John Paul II, Redemptor hominis

Matthew 11:2-11

Now John in his prison had heard what Christ was doing and he sent his disciples to ask him, 'Are you the one who is to come, or have we got to wait for someone else?' Jesus answered, 'Go back and tell John what you hear and see; the blind see again, and the lame walk, lepers are cleansed, and the deaf hear, and the dead are raised to life and the Good News is proclaimed to the poor; and happy is the man who does not lose faith in me'. As the messengers were leaving, Jesus began to talk to the people about John: 'What did you go out into the wilderness to see? A reed swaying in the breeze? No? Then what did you go out to see? A man wearing fine clothes? Oh no, those who wear fine clothes are to be found in palaces. Then what did you go out for? To see a prophet? Yes, I tell you, and much more than a prophet: he is the one of whom Scripture says: Look, I am going to send my messenger before you; he will prepare your way before you. I tell you solemnly, of all the children born of women, a greater than John the Baptist has never been seen; yet the least in the kingdom of heaven is greater than he is.'

CHRIST THE LORD John was in prison because he vociferously denounced King Herod for licentious behavior and public scandal. (On a trip to Rome, Herod had seduced his brother's wife, and when he returned to Palestine he dismissed his own wife and married that sister-in-law.) Perhaps during his cruel imprisonment, John began to have difficulties about Jesus, whom he had earlier pointed out as the "Lamb of God," another title for the long-awaited Messiah. More likely, John's disciples still doubted what John was telling them of Jesus and were reluctant to leave John in order to follow Christ. So John sends them to Christ himself, in order to resolve all doubts. Jesus' response does not disappoint. He doesn't just say, "Oh yes, I am the Messiah," which could so easily be construed as the kind of empty claim typical of any vain public figure. Rather, he points to his irrefutable deeds, and applies the Messianic prophecies to them (cf. Isaiah 35:5, 61:1). No matter what others may say of him, Christ himself claims to be nothing less than the very Son of God, the Savior, the Messiah.

CHRIST THE TEACHER Christ makes a curious statement at the end of this encounter. He begins a rhetorical buildup of praise for John, only to conclude it with a paradoxical reverse: John is the greatest of prophets, but the humblest of Jesus' followers is greater than John. Jesus Christ wants his listeners to realize that his Kingdom differs from all others not only in degree, but in essence. He has brought to mankind not just a better earthly life, but something entirely new: a share in the very life of God. Saints aren't just especially good and nice people; they are new creations. They defy usual categories, and they turn the standards of this world upside down. When we first begin to follow Christ, and all along our journey to sainthood, we have to jettison our own expectations and make room for a supernatural revolution that begins with our baptismal commitment to holiness and apostolate.

CHRIST THE FRIEND Friends accept us as we are, but encourage us to change for the better. Christ came among sinners, but he did so in order to save them. He met the blind and gave them sight; the poor and gave them hope; the lame and gave them strength. He is still a friend like that to each one of us: we are blinded by ignorance and selfishness, and he offers us light in the teachings of his Church; we are poor in virtue and generosity, and he fills us with the gifts of the Holy Spirit; we are lame, unable to pray as we ought, to bear witness as we ought, to love as we ought, and he heals us and strengthens by feeding us with bread from heaven, nourishing us with his very self in the Eucharist. He is always encouraging us to grow, because he loves us too much to leave us the way we are.

CHRIST IN MY LIFE I thank you, Lord, for the example given by these disciples of John the Baptist. They had doubts, they didn't understand your plans, and so they came to you to find the answers. I always want to do the same. I have had times of doubt and difficulty, and you have always been faithful. I want to stay close to you always, no matter what. Guide my steps, Jesus; I trust in you...

The standard by which I should evaluate my life is yours, not the world's. You are truth itself. You are my Lord and Teacher. Cleanse my mind from false and selfish ideas. Open my eyes to see myself and those around me as you do...

Thank you for your many gifts. You are always watching over me. I have no need to fret or worry; all I need to do is seek your will. Teach me to trust in you more and more, and give me the courage to be as generous with others as you have been with me...

QUESTIONS FOR SMALL GROUP DISCUSSION

1. What struck you most in the passage? What did you notice that you hadn't noticed before?

2. If God really wanted people to recognize Jesus as the Messiah, couldn't he have made it more obvious? Many of Jesus' contemporaries didn't believe in him. Could God have done anything more to convince them?

3. Today's Christian can see many more signs than John the Baptist's disciples could, especially the endurance and growth of the Catholic Church and the lives of thousands of saints. Why do Christians still struggle to obey God's will? Why do nonbelievers resist all these signs?

4. How can we be better signs of Christ's truth for those around us?

Cf. Catechism of the Catholic Church, 410, 436-445, 453, 547 on the meaning of Christ as the "Messiah"; 524 on John the Baptist as model for Advent living; 1716-1729 on the newness of life Christ's Kingdom

36. A TINGE OF SADNESS (MT 11:12-24)

"Consequently, anyone who today would want to ask God questions or desire some vision or revelation, would not only be acting foolishly but would commit an offense against God by not fixing his eyes entirely on Christ, without wanting something new or something besides him."

- St John of the Cross

Matthew 11:12-24

'Since John the Baptist came, up to this present time, the kingdom of heaven has been subjected to violence and the violent are taking it by storm. Because it was towards John that all the prophecies of the prophets and of the Law were leading; and he, if you will believe me, is the Elijah who was to return. If anyone has ears to hear, let him listen! 'What description can I find for this generation? It is like children shouting to each other as they sit in the market place: We played the pipes for you, and you wouldn't dance; we sang dirges, and you wouldn't be mourners. For John came, neither eating nor drinking, and they say, He is possessed. The Son of Man came, eating and drinking, and they say, Look, a glutton and a drunkard, a friend of tax collectors and sinners. Yet wisdom has been proved right by her actions.'

Then he began to reproach the towns in which most of his miracles had been worked, because they refused to repent. 'Alas for you, Chorazin! Alas for you, Bethsaida! For if the miracles done in you had been done in Tyre and Sidon, they would have repented long ago in sackcloth and ashes. And still, I tell you that it will not go as hard on Judgement day with Tyre and Sidon as with you. And as for you, Capernaum, did you want to be exalted as high as heaven? You shall be thrown down to hell. For if the miracles done in you had been done in Sodom, it would have been standing yet. And still, I tell you that it will not go as hard with the land of Sodom on Judgement day as with you.'

CHRIST THE LORD Jesus continues reflecting out loud about the most important moment of human history – the time of his coming, the hour of redemption. He puts John's prophetic mission in historical context: it is the culmination of the age of prophecy, its fulfillment and its conclusion. All Jews at the time were familiar with Malachi's prophecy that in the days of the Messiah the prophet Elijah would return (Malachi 4:5). Jesus gives the definitive interpretation of this prophecy, declaring that John the Baptist was the new Elijah and at the same time leaving no doubt about his own claims to be the Messiah.

Yet this history lesson is tinged with regret. In thinking of John, and John's arrest at the hands of King Herod, the egoist, Jesus can't avoid facing the hard fact that his saving message is being rejected and opposed. John is suffering because of it, we have already seen the beginning of the Pharisees' antagonism to Jesus, and Christ knows what is in store for him at the end of his earthly mission: agony and death. His Kingdom is already suffering violence, and he knows that it will continue to do so. In these reflections we get a further glimpse of what he meant when he said that he came not to bring peace, but a sword: the Lord came to conquer a Kingdom, and the victory can only be obtained through spiritual and moral battle.

CHRIST THE TEACHER Jesus' parable about the moody children playing in the town square teaches us a hard lesson about the human heart. No rhyme or reason governs the children's decisions. They don't feel like playing weddings, and they don't feel like playing funerals – they are completely at the mercy of their whims. This is okay for children, but adults should be wiser. They should recognize the truth of things – the actions of John the Baptist, the miracles and wonders performed by Jesus – and adjust their decisions and behavior accordingly, instead of letting their moody decisions cloud their view of the truth. Simple human maturity involves being able to master selfish tendencies and emotional tantrums in order to act in accordance with true principles and real circumstances (the "deeds of wisdom" that Christ mentions).

That's exactly what the inhabitants of the towns around the Sea of Galilee refused to do. Their selfishness blinded them to Christ's truth – a truth brighter and more eloquent than anything that had ever come before. As we look into our own hearts, and as we see the lives of those around us, it's clear that little has changed in two thousand years.

CHRIST THE FRIEND Throughout this discourse, we detect a note of anger. But it isn't the anger of wounded vanity; it's the anger of a broken heart. The Greek word translated "woe" could just as easily be translated "alas"! Jesus doesn't condemn the towns who haven't responded to his preaching and miracles – they have condemned themselves. No pain is more intense than that which comes from unrequited love, which is exactly what Jesus experiences. He came from heaven to extend God's offer of reconciliation to sinners. They need that grace, but they don't deserve it. And what is their reaction? Scorn, rejection, ingratitude…. They crucify their Savior. No wonder a hint of sadness taints Christ's words; he is a friend who has been doubly betrayed. Where can he find comfort? In hearts that trust him – in hearts that teach others to trust in him too.

Jesus: It was a risk to create you. I knew that in making you capable of knowing me and loving me, you would also be capable of rejecting me. Why did I take the risk? Because you're worth it. The universe is better with you than without you. I want you to discover all the wonders and joys that I have in store for you. I will never lead you astray – I created you for glory, for life, for joy. Come, follow me.

CHRIST IN MY LIFE You have shown me that this world is a spiritual battle-ground. Through the ages, your followers have suffered for their fidelity to you. They have undergone hardships whenever they tried to be faithful to your mission for them – just like John the Baptist. Give me courage, Lord, to fight for your kingdom of justice and love…

I too, Lord, am a player in this mysterious drama where the creatures disdain their Creator. At times, I have said no to you; I have turned away from your will. I am an enigma to myself, Lord. I kneel before you and ask once again for mercy. Forgive me my sins. Don't let me say no to you anymore – especially in those things where you know I struggle…

I have experienced rejection in my life, Lord. But I have never loved as much as you loved, and so your pain at being rejected must be much greater than I know. If you show me how, I will bring others to your friendship – I will help those who have rejected you come back to you. Be comforted. I love you; I believe in you; I thank you…

QUESTIONS FOR SMALL GROUP DISCUSSION

1. What struck you most in the passage? What did you notice that you hadn't noticed before?
2. Christ views history from the perspective of the history of salvation. If we shared that viewpoint more, how would it affect our attitudes, actions, and opinions?

3. St Matthew implies that Jesus did many other miracles in Chorazin and Bethsaida that aren't recorded in the Gospels. Why do you think the evangelists didn't record them?

4. Which does popular culture encourage more: immaturity (living by whims, moods, and emotions) or maturity (living by principles and truths)? How?

Cf. Catechism of the Catholic Church, 1731-1738 on freedom and responsibility; 1767-1770 on the morality of passions and emotions

37. A FLASH OF JOY (MT 11:25-30)

"This Spirit, the dispenser of the treasures that are in the Father and keeper of the counsels that are between the Father and the Son, pours himself so sweetly into the soul that he is not perceived, and his greatness is understood by few."

- St Mary Magdalene of Pazzi

Matthew 11:25-30

At that time Jesus exclaimed, 'I bless you, Father, Lord of heaven and of earth, for hiding these things from the learned and the clever and revealing them to mere children. Yes, Father, for that is what it pleased you to do. Everything has been entrusted to me by my Father; and no one knows the Son except the Father, just as no one knows the Father except the Son and those to whom the Son chooses to reveal him. Come to me, all you who labour and are overburdened, and I will give you rest. Shoulder my yoke and learn from me, for I am gentle and humble in heart, and you will find rest for your souls. Yes, my yoke is easy and my burden light.'

CHRIST THE LORD After reflecting on those who reject him and his message, Jesus now takes comfort in thinking of those who accept him. In his prayer of thanksgiving, he gives us yet another glimpse of his utter uniqueness.

He alone among men "knows the Father," because he alone is the Son. Therefore, no one can reveal God to us as he can. If we want to know God, as every human heart does (consciously or not), we have only one recourse: Jesus Christ. Christ's Lordship derives from his very identity as God, not from some extrinsic privilege. And so, if we go to him, look to him, study him, speak with him, follow him, delve into his teachings, and query those who have come to know him better than we have, we will be discovering God himself. If we lift our minds up to him, we will begin to think and see as he does, and if we give him our hearts, we will allow him to take the reins of our lives. God wants to be known and loved, and so he sent us Jesus Christ to be his self-revelation.

CHRIST THE TEACHER Since every heart innately yearns for God, this Gospel passage ought to be prized above all others, for it teaches us the secret for satisfying that yearning. To encounter God requires only one thing. Not intellectual prowess, worldly excellence, or sophisticated achievements, but *simplicity*. God gives himself to those who are "mere children" – to those who are childlike. The mark of children is not innocence; most often they are quite mischievous. It is not ignorance, for they often surprise us with their insights and thoughtful questions. Nor is it helplessness, for many of them are streetwise survivors, as often seen in situations of poverty and war.

The mark of the child is *trust*. Children readily put their trust in those given charge over them (until that trust is violated). It is natural for children to depend on their parents, to follow unquestioningly their older siblings. They have not yet developed the average adult's haughty air of self-sufficiency. By word and example (as for example in the Garden of Gethsemane) Jesus teaches us that intimacy with God requires trust above all. *Faith* is trusting that what God reveals is true; *hope* is trusting that what he promises will come about; *love* is trusting that what he asks us to do is what we should do. If we put our trust in God, and not in ourselves, we will find God.

CHRIST THE FRIEND Pulling weeds for a whole day all by oneself is a wearisome thing. But working side-by-side with a good friend considerably lessens the weariness. Life lays upon us many burdens, which our own selfish tendencies make doubly hard. Jesus Christ wants to bear them with us, softening them with his wise humility, walking by our side as the best of friends. Those who have accepted his invitation and hitched their life to his under the same yoke, like two oxen pulling a plough together, have discovered the difference. They are called saints, and their joy never wanes, not in this life and not in the next.

CHRIST IN MY LIFE I want to know you, Lord. I want to know what you care about, what you think about, what's on your mind and in your heart. I want to know what makes you smile, what makes you frown. I want to discover the God who created me – who created all things. Jesus, your face reveals God's face. Open my eyes, Lord, let me see you...

Lord, I know you don't judge me, because you promise that you are meek and lowly of heart. How hard it is for me not to judge! How much grief I cause myself and others by my outbursts of vanity, arrogance, and anger! I want to learn from you, Lord, and I know you want to teach me. Jesus, meek and humble of heart, make my heart more like yours...

Lord, why do I think I can do everything by myself? You designed me to need other people, to help other people, and to depend upon God for everything. This is the law of your universe. Like a little child in its mother's arms, so I keep myself in you, O Lord. Teach me to trust you and to obey your will. Thy Kingdom come…

QUESTIONS FOR SMALL GROUP DISCUSSION

1) What struck you most in the passage? What did you notice that you hadn't noticed before?

2) Why would Christ thank the Father for revealing himself to the humble and not to the proud? What does Jesus really mean?

3) Jesus invites us to learn from him how to be "meek and humble of heart." Why?

4) In practical terms, how can we take Christ's yoke upon ourselves in the current circumstances of our lives?

Cf. Catechism of the Catholic Church, 456-460 on the reasons that Jesus became man; 232-260 on the Trinitarian relation between the Father and the Son; 464-469 on Jesus as both God and man; 441-445 on what it means for Christ to be the "Son of God"

THE GOSPEL OF MATTHEW CHAPTER 12

"Lord, it is good for me to suffer, so long as you are with me, better than to reign without you, to feast without you, to boast without you. Lord, it is better for me to embrace you in tribulation, to have you with me in the furnace, than to be without you, even in heaven. What is there for me in heaven, and what have I desired save you on the earth? Gold is tried in the furnace, and just men in the test of tribulation. Lord, there you are, there with them: there you stand in the midst of those who are gathered in your name, as you stood once with the three young men. Why are we afraid, why do we delay, why do we flee from this furnace? The fire rages, but the Lord is with us in tribulation. If God is with us, who can be against us? Furthermore, if he rescues us, who can snatch us out of his hand? Who can take us from his grasp? Finally, if he glorifies us, who can make us inglorious? If he glorifies us, who can humiliate us?"

- St Bernard of Clairvaux

38. GREATER THAN THE TEMPLE (MT 12:1-8)

"There are many people whose spirits are in their bodies like corpses in their tombs. And, just as God will, at the end of time, raise up dead bodies by his word, so he now gives life to dead spirits by the power of his word."

- St Humbert of Romans

Matthew 12:1-8

At that time Jesus took a walk one sabbath day through the cornfields. His disciples were hungry and began to pick ears of corn and eat them. The Pharisees noticed it and said to him, 'Look, your disciples are doing something that is forbidden on the sabbath.' But he said to them, 'Have you not read what David did when he and his followers were hungry – how he went into the house of God and how they ate the loaves of offering which neither he nor his followers were allowed to eat, but which were for the priests alone? Or again, have you not read in the Law that on the sabbath day the Temple priests break the sabbath without being blamed for it? Now here, I tell you, is something greater than the Temple. And if you had understood the meaning of the words: What I want is mercy, not sacrifice, you would not have condemned the blameless. For the Son of Man is master of the sabbath.'

CHRIST THE LORD Opposition between Jesus and the Pharisees is increasing. In this episode, they clash about one of the most sacred duties of all, honoring God on the Lord's Day. Jesus defends his Apostles and uses the clash as a chance to try and win over the Pharisees by meeting them on their favorite ground: argumentation.

Jesus' argument has three parts. First, he shows that King David's men violated the rules of the Temple by eating the bread of offering (reserved for the priests) when they were on the run and in need. Nowhere do the Scriptures condemn David for this. Clearly, then, the needs of the king and his companions take precedence over the Temple laws. Second, Jesus shows that the Temple laws take precedence over Sabbath rules, since the priests in charge of the Temple were permitted to work on the Sabbath, replacing the bread of offering and performing sacrifices. Finally, he repeats a Scripture passage he has already used in conversation with the Pharisees, Hosea 6:6, to reiterate the most important premise of his argument: that God prefers mercy – deeds of goodness, generosity, and kindness – to Temple sacrifices. The logical conclusion, then, is that since mercy trumps Temple sacrifices and Temple sacrifices trump the Sabbath, mercy (in this case, feeding the hungry) also trumps the Sabbath.

This is a language the Pharisees would understand well; they prided themselves on multilayered arguments and intellectual dexterity. By couching his own identity as the messianic heir of David in such a ploy (and by prefacing the whole thing with the rhetorical question "Have you not read?" – which certainly would have pricked the Pharisees' smugness about their superior knowledge of Sacred Scripture), Jesus gives them yet another chance to see the truth of his claim to be the Messiah and Lord – even Lord of the Sabbath, even greater than the Temple, two institutions that came from and belonged exclusively to God.

CHRIST THE TEACHER From Christ's point of view, religion is primarily a relationship. Mercy – which involves communication, affection, and give-and-take between persons – ranks higher in his book than other outward forms of devotion. This crucial lesson was hard for many in Christ's time to accept, and its relevance hasn't dimmed with the passing of the centuries.

As human beings, we naturally express our faith, our respect, our love – all of the spiritual realities that give meaning to our lives – through physical symbols. A kiss, a present, a handshake, a song: these and similar gestures serve as vehicles to show what's in our hearts. But, again because we are human beings, these outward forms of expression can gradually lose their significance. We can fall into routine, doing meaningful things but forgetting about the meaning. It can happen in human relationships, and it can happen in our relationship with God. Religion can sink into empty ritualism.

That's what happened to the Pharisees. They became so enamored of their own perfection in performing pious practices that they lost sight of the reasons behind them. They were so blinded by self-righteousness, in fact, that they didn't even recognize the very face of God when he looked into their eyes. We are not exempt from the same danger.

CHRIST THE FRIEND St Hilary interprets this passage with a beautiful allegory. The field is the world. Christ's presence walking through it is his incarnation. The crop is the many souls ready to be harvested for the Kingdom. The disciples picking grain is the eager desire and efficacious action of Christians bringing more souls into the bosom of the Church. Walking with our Lord through the field of the world, hungry for the spread of his Kingdom – what a simple but poignant way to conceive of what it means to live in friendship with Christ!

Jesus: It is enough for you to stay with me, to walk with me. I will teach you what to do. I will protect you and guide you. I have chosen you to spread my message and my grace to others, and so I will help you to understand that message and experience that grace. Never leave my side. Am I not enough for you – I who created and redeemed you? Today, follow my example of patience and hard work, of faithfulness and self-sacrifice. This is the path to wisdom, and wisdom brings peace, both to you and to those around you.

CHRIST IN MY LIFE I never want to forget that religion is about a personal relationship with God. Show me, Lord, where I am falling into routine. Keep my faith fresh, my love aflame. Stir up in my heart a hunger to bring others into your Church…

Sometimes I take Sunday, the Christian "Sabbath," for granted and forget that it is the day in which you wish to renew our covenant. Teach me to live it well, refreshing my love for you and for my neighbor, and taking time to rest and put things back into your perspective. Lord, never let Sunday Mass turn into a mere ritual, but help me to offer myself freely to you every week…

Why am I not more eager to do your will? Why am I less patient than you are with the "pharisees" I encounter? Show me, Lord, how to be your true disciple: enlighten my mind, strengthen my will, and protect me from temptation…

QUESTIONS FOR SMALL GROUP DISCUSSION

1. What struck me most about this passage? What did I notice this time that I hadn't noticed before?

2. Jesus claims to be greater than the Temple – he claims to be Lord of the Sabbath. Considering the significance of those two institutions, what are some theological implications of this claim?

3. Why is mercy more pleasing to God than Temple sacrifices?

4. Jesus often links himself to King David. What are some reasons for that connection?

39. DOING GOOD WELL (MT 12:9-21)

"Our divine Savior brought to ignorant and weak man his truth and his grace: truth to point out the road leading to his goal; grace to give him the strength to reach that goal. To travel on that road means, in practice, to accept the will and the commandments of Christ, to conform one's life to them."

- Pope Pius XII

Matthew 12:9-21

He moved on from there and went to their synagogue, and a man was there at the time who had a withered hand. They asked him, 'Is it against the law to cure a man on the sabbath day?' hoping for something to use against him. But he said to them, 'If any one of you here had only one sheep and it fell down a hole on the sabbath day, would he not get hold of it and lift it out? Now a man is far more important than a sheep, so it follows that it is permitted to do good on the sabbath day.' Then he said to the man, 'Stretch out your hand.' He stretched it out and his hand was better, as sound as the other one. At this the Pharisees went out and began to plot against him, discussing how to destroy him. Jesus knew this and withdrew from the district. Many followed him and he cured them all, but warned them not to make him known.

This was to fulfil the prophecy of Isaiah: Here is my servant whom I have chosen, my beloved, the favourite of my soul. I will endow him with my spirit, and he will proclaim the true faith to the nations. He will not brawl or shout, nor will anyone hear his voice in the streets. He will not break the crushed reed, nor put out the smouldering wick till he has led the truth to victory: in his name the nations will put their hope."

CHRIST THE LORD If Jesus had merely been a good talker, the Pharisees' persistent resistance would have been understandable. But Christ backs up his flawless arguments with undeniable deeds. A man with a withered hand (picture that – a tragic deformity, an arm without a hand; how much suffering this man must have undergone!) comes to Jesus, full of hope that this famous, wonder-working rabbi from Nazareth might pour out some healing power on him. And Jesus, full of the surpassing love that God bears towards his children, obliges. The whole synagogue is witness to the miracle. Before their very eyes, the withered hand is made whole.

Yet the Pharisees react not with humble awe, not even with humble inquiry, to find out how a man so clearly sent by God can at the same time scorn what they consider to be God's commands. Rather, they become more firmly fixed in jealous anger and begin plotting their Savior's death.

There is only one explanation: their pride. Their self-sufficiency and arrogance had grown to colossal proportions, and no matter how brilliant, eloquent, powerful, and good this upstart Nazarene rabbi may be, they refuse to do the one thing required to become his follower: humble themselves and obey. They cannot say, "Thy will be done" – the only proper response to the coming of the King. Instead, they echo the ancient serpent's refrain, "I will not serve" (Jeremiah 2:20). With Christ, it's either one or the other, because there really is only one Lord.

CHRIST THE TEACHER Jesus has just defeated the Pharisees in an argument about picking grain on the Sabbath. He deigned to discuss their accusations on their own terms, hoping that stooping to their level would open their minds. But instead, they renew the dispute from another angle. Jesus successfully argued that one doesn't have to go hungry on the Sabbath in order to respect the spirit of God's law. Now he is faced with a different case: is it acceptable to heal someone on the Lord's Day?

The Pharisees had made a distinction in this regard. It was lawful, they taught, to heal someone who couldn't wait to be healed, but if the injury wasn't urgent, the Lord's day should be honored by refraining from this type of work. Jesus points out the hypocrisy of this position, since those same Pharisees permitted the tending of needy livestock on the Sabbath – not only when those animals were in danger of death. The Pharisees have tangled themselves up in their own arrogance. In leaning so confidently on their education and intelligence, they have unwittingly begun to idolize their self-made rules. Jesus has to remind them that the Sabbath, as all of God's commands, is for the benefit of God's children. These commands are not ends in themselves, but means to an end: loving God above all things and loving one's neighbor as oneself.

If St Matthew decided to include this episode, it's because the Holy Spirit knows we too can use the reminder.

CHRIST THE FRIEND As soon as his enemies begin plotting his death, Jesus retires from the public eye. He was unable to convince them of the truth, and so he retreats. He knows that little time remains in which to prepare his Apostles. How accurately the quotation from Isaiah (42:1-4) describes the Savior's heart! A vain, power-hungry political leader would have continued to look for public clashes with his opposition once he had put them on the run. But Jesus is thinking first of all of them, his enemies – they are the bruised reeds and the smoldering wicks. He will not browbeat them. He will continue to heal and preach and gently instruct his disciples about his Kingdom. There will be other opportunities to try again to reach out to the Pharisees, but in the meantime, Jesus is focused on the bigger picture: preparing the ground for the foundation of the Church, which will bring his hope, his forgiveness, and the light of his truth far beyond the boundaries of the Holy Land to the lands of the Gentiles throughout the world.

CHRIST IN MY LIFE Parts of me are just like the Pharisees. I throw tantrums in my heart when I don't get what I want. How many times I have unknowingly been on the verge of falling into spiritual disaster, but you secretly protected me? Thank you, Lord, for putting up with me. Forgive my bursts of selfishness. Lead me along the path of spiritual maturity, the path of self-forgetful love – your path…

Sometimes I wonder why my growth as a Christian seems to happen so slowly, but it is no mystery. The habits of my heart are focused on myself. Let me always remember that pride and God can never coexist; like oil and water, like night and day, if my heart is full of arrogance, it can't be full of you. With the humility of your heart, Lord, shape my heart to be more like yours…

In your wisdom and love, you take care of me. You don't let the feeble flame of my weak faith die out; you don't aggravate my weak spots. You are patient with me. Thank you. Make me like you. Teach me…

QUESTIONS FOR SMALL GROUP DISCUSSION

1. What struck you most about this passage? What did you notice that you hadn't noticed before?

2. How do you think Jesus' disciples reacted to this miracle? How do you think the man who was cured reacted?

3. Jesus exclaims in this passage that a person is of infinitely more value, in God's eyes, than a sheep. What is the Christian concept of human dignity? Does this concept belittle the value of the rest of creation?

4. What does the Church teach us about observing the Lord's Day, Sunday? Why? Is this commandment (the Third Commandment, to keep holy the Lord's Day) really still relevant? How can we observe it better?

Cf. Catechism of the Catholic Church, 356-361 and 1701-1709 on human dignity; 2174-2188 on Sunday as the fulfillment of the Sabbath

40. DEVILISH TALK (MT: 12:22-37)

"You do not yet see God, but by loving your neighbor you gain the sight of God; by loving your neighbor you purify your eye for seeing God…"

- *St Augustine*

Matthew 12:22-37

Then they brought to him a blind and dumb demoniac; and he cured him, so that the dumb man could speak and see. All the people were astounded and said, 'Can this be the Son of David?' But when the Pharisees heard this they said, 'The man casts out devils only through Beelzebul, the prince of devils'. Knowing what was in their minds he said to them, 'Every kingdom divided against itself is heading for ruin; and no town, no household divided against itself can stand. Now if Satan casts out Satan, he is divided against himself; so how can his kingdom stand? And if it is through Beelzebul that I cast out devils, through whom do your own experts cast them out? Let them be your judges, then. But if it is through the Spirit of God that I cast devils out, then know that the kingdom of God has overtaken you. Or again, how can anyone make his way into a strong man's house and burgle his property unless he has tied up the strong man first? Only then can he burgle his house. He who is not with me is against me, and he who does not gather with me scatters. And so I tell you, every one of men's sins and blasphemies will be forgiven, but blasphemy against the Spirit will not be forgiven. And anyone who says a word against the Son of Man will be forgiven; but let anyone speak against the Holy Spirit and he will not be forgiven either in this world or in the next.

'Make a tree sound and its fruit will be sound; make a tree rotten and its fruit will be rotten. For the tree can be told by its fruit. Brood of vipers, how can your speech be good when you are evil? For a man's words flow out of what fills his heart. A good man draws good things from his store of goodness; a bad man draws bad things from his store of badness. So I tell you this, that for every unfounded word men utter they will answer on Judgement day, since it is by your words you will be acquitted, and by your words condemned.'

CHRIST THE LORD Many modern scholars have questioned the existence of the devil. Jesus never did. The devil exists. In fact, it is to "destroy the works of the devil" (1 John 3:8) that Jesus came among us. And destroy them he does. With a mere command (in contrast to the elaborate rituals used by ancient magicians and Jewish exorcists) Christ sets countless souls free from their satanic slavery. In the face of Jesus' divine prerogative, the "strong man" who had bound God's children and taken over God's house is rendered completely powerless.

Christ's mastery over these evil forces astounds the crowd, but it infuriates his jealous rivals. In fact, their absurd accusation that Jesus is a common magician in league with the very devils he casts out rebounds on their own heads. They are the ones who have taken Satan's part, by closing their hearts to the Lord. History really is a battle between good and evil, and much to the consternation of sophisticated academics and modern Pharisees, good wins out in the end.

This battle is won or lost in the depths of each of our hearts. When we conquer our temptations and inclinations to sin, we are conquering more of the world for Christ. To whom does your heart pay allegiance?

CHRIST THE TEACHER Here Jesus exposes the true nature of every sin: worship of self. The Pharisees have become so self-centered, so confident in their own understanding, so attached to getting their own way, that they identify as evil whatever contradicts their desires.

Jesus invites them to leave their comfortable and self-glorifying ways behind, repent, and enter the Kingdom of heaven. They react furiously; since Jesus

171

doesn't accept their ideas and acknowledge their superiority, he must be an agent of the devil. Here we get a glimpse of the terrifying perversion worked by sin: placing myself on God's throne, I mistake God himself (Jesus) as Satan's accomplice. Sin (a love of self to the point of despising God) has grown to full maturity in the hearts of these Pharisees. No longer can they be forgiven, because they can no longer even recognize their need for forgiveness in the first place. Whenever we choose our own will in opposition to God's will, we are taking a step down the Pharisee's calamitous path.

CHRIST THE FRIEND The worst damage a friend can do to a friend is often done with spiteful words. Gossip, lies, backbiting, criticism – they wound more deeply than swords and bullets. in fact, they give rise to violence and war. They destroy families, friendships, communities, and nations. On the other hand, words of encouragement, praise, forgiveness, and truth (or sometimes simply keeping quiet) open hearts, spread hope, comfort the troubled, and reconcile even bitter and enduring enemies.

No one knew the power of words better than Jesus, the Word of God. In this passage he even seems to reduce the material by which we will be judged to words alone, because our words are the product of our hearts, and it is in our hearts that we decide for Christ or against him. Jesus wants to give us an undistorted glimpse into our own hearts. We may not like what we see, but we need to see it if we are going to grow in friendship with Christ. What do your words tell you about your heart?

CHRIST IN MY LIFE The sacrament of confession is the surest weapon against the tragic and subtle growth of diabolical pride. Frequent confession assures me I am not worshipping myself, since I'm asking for your forgiveness. It keeps open the flow of your grace in me and through me. Thank you for this gift, Lord! Why do I not profit more from it? Why do I not promote it more? Jesus, never let me be separated from you. Grant saintly priests to the world, to bring us your presence and love...

I want to say with my life as well as my words, "Thy will be done." Do I ponder your will for my life? Do I seek your will concerning my normal responsibilities, my vocation, my commitments, the Church's teachings, and my conscience? Mary, teach me always to say with you, "Let it be done unto me according to your word..."

You will judge me by my words. Teach me to use them only to build up my neighbors and never, in any circumstances, to tear them down. Give me good-ness of heart that overflows in everything I say…

QUESTIONS FOR SMALL GROUP DISCUSSION

1. What struck you most about this passage? What did you notice that you hadn't noticed before?

2. Think of examples from your own experience of the positive and negative effect of words. Why do our words matter so much in God's eyes?

3. Why is it so hard to control our speech?

4. The Pharisees didn't even recognize their own sinfulness anymore, and yet Jesus says they are responsible for having come to that point. What tools does the Church give us to avoid falling into such a deplorable spiritual situation?

Cf. Catechism of the Catholic Church, 409 on the world being in the devil's power; 385-387, 2852, 1854 on the reality of sin and the sin against the Holy Spirit

41. MISSING THE SIGNS (MT 12:38-50)

"It is necessary that each person freely accept the truth of the love of God. He is Love and Truth, and love as well as truth never impose themselves: They knock on the door of the heart and mind and, where they enter, bring peace and joy. This is the way God reigns; this is his plan of salvation."

- Pope Benedict XVI

Matthew 12:38-50

Then some of the scribes and Pharisees spoke up. 'Master,' they said 'we should like to see a sign from you.' He replied, 'It is an evil and unfaithful generation that asks for a sign! The only sign it will be given is the sign of the prophet Jonah. For as Jonah was in the belly of the sea-monster for three days and three nights, so will the Son of Man be in the heart of the earth for three days and three nights. On Judge-ment day the men of Nineveh will stand up with this generation and condemn it, because when Jonah preached they repented; and there is something greater than Jonah here. On Judgement day the Queen of the South will rise up with this generation and condemn it, because she came from the ends of the earth to hear the wisdom of Solomon; and there is something greater than Solomon here. When an unclean spirit goes out of a man it wanders through waterless country looking for a place to rest, and cannot find one. Then it says, I will return to the home I came from. But on arrival, finding it unoccupied, swept and tidied, it then goes off and collects seven other spirits more evil than itself, and they go in and set up house there, so that the man ends up by being worse than he was before. That is what will happen to this evil generation.'

He was still speaking to the crowds when his mother and his brothers appeared; they were standing outside and were anxious to have a word with him. But to the man who told him this Jesus replied, 'Who is my mother? Who are my brothers?' And stretching out his hand towards his disciples he said, 'Here are my mother and my brothers. Anyone who does the will of my Father in heaven, he is my brother and sister and mother.'

CHRIST THE LORD Jonah and Solomon both prefigured Christ. They were "shadows of things to come" (Colossians 2:17), as St Paul puts it. Solomon was David's son; he built the Temple and extended the Kingdom of ancient Israel over Gentile nations. Jesus was the definitive promised descendent of David, the Messiah; he erected the everlasting Temple (the Church) and extended the privilege of grace to the Gentiles. Jonah rose again after spending three days in the belly of a great fish (Christ was going to rise after three days in the tomb) and successfully preached repentance to a Gentile city (the Church would take root all throughout the Roman – and Gentile – Empire). The parallels are uncanny, and yet they don't do justice to the reality. Christ is "greater" than both: they were only God's instruments; he is the Lord himself.

CHRIST THE TEACHER Jesus shows in this encounter a wonderful and terrible truth. In order to give us the possibility to know and love God and share in his everlasting life, he has chosen to limit, in a sense, his omnipotence.

The Pharisees have clearly understood Christ's claims. But they don't want to accept him. So they ask for a sign. For the crowds and the disciples, Jesus' miracles are signs enough. For the Pharisees, though, they want a sign that leaves no room for doubt. But no such sign exists; since faith in God necessarily involves trusting in his word, no sign can impose it (otherwise you wouldn't need to trust). God won't force us.

This is why Jesus calls these skeptics an evil and adulterous generation: they don't want to believe, because they are no longer seeking to please God. They have betrayed their true vocation and fallen in love with their own glory and honor. The Lord used the same phrase – "evil generation" – to refer to the Israelites who were freed from Egypt by the parting of the Red Sea. Even after the plagues on the Egyptians, the parting of the Red Sea, the giving of the Ten Commandments, the manna, and numerous other awe-inspiring miracles, they still doubted God's power and goodness and wavered in their obedience. And so they were not permitted to enter the Promised Land. They didn't want to believe (the requirements of faith ruffled their selfish feathers), and therefore no matter what God did to prove his love, it simply wasn't enough – it just made them more stubborn, and more vulnerable to temptation. When we accept God's benefits but refuse to obey him, we leave more and more room for sin to spread – one devil becomes seven.

More than a little of the Pharisee lurks in each of us. When God's will makes us uncomfortable, we often sidestep it by asking for clearer signs. It's not that we don't *know* what God wants of us, it's just that we don't always trust him enough to want it with him. We should be slow to criticize the Pharisees too harshly, since we so often do what they did, even though we have already seen the sign of Jonah, which *they* were still waiting for.

CHRIST THE FRIEND In this passage, Jesus opens wide his heart, showing us how we can please him, and how we can vex him. The people of Nineveh pleased God, because they heeded his call to repentance. The Queen of Sheba pleased God, because she eagerly went to God's anointed King to seek out true wisdom. Mary his mother pleased him most of all, because she surrendered herself completely to the Father's will. At first, Jesus' response to his mother's message seems harsh, but in fact he is complimenting her, pointing out that her real greatness lay in the spiritual docility that enabled her to fulfill her vocation, not in the mere fact of physical motherhood.

Jesus: It is simple to sustain our friendship: just follow the path of those who have traveled before you – always be attentive to my voice, echoing in the interior of your conscience; seek always true wisdom, following my vicar on earth, the pope, so that my loving will can govern your life. Then you will be closer to my heart than you could ever imagine, closer even than genetic ties, and I will fulfill you beyond anything you could hope for.

CHRIST IN MY LIFE No one compares to you, Lord, not history's great kings, like Solomon, and not history's great prophets, like Jonah. You are far above the greatest of history's champions. Why do I forget this? Why do I get so used to having you so close, you who are my Creator, the source of life and wisdom? Teach me to love you more…

I think of all the signs you have given me in my life. So many gifts, so many assurances of your presence. I thank you for making yourself known to me, Lord. Never let me give in to doubt. Never let me prefer my will to yours, even when yours is demanding and uncomfortable. Your love and your grace are enough for me; just show me your will and give me the strength to do it…

The same Lord of life and history, greater than Jonah and Solomon and all the others who came before and after them, is present in my soul and in the Eucharist.

What more could I desire in life than to have you so close? So many people don't know you. They desperately look for Solomons and Jonahs. Send me to tell them about you. Help me to show you to everyone in my life by living just like you…

QUESTIONS FOR SMALL GROUP DISCUSSION[1]

1. What struck me most about this passage? What did I see this time that I didn't see before?

2. Can you think of any other Old Testament heroes who prefigured Christ? What light do they shed on Christ's mission?

3. Jesus sets the Father's will as the standard for Christian behavior. Does this mean we are supposed to practice blind, mindless obedience? From the Church's perspective, what does God's will include and how do we discover it?

4. The Pharisees were some of ancient Palestine's most powerful and popular leaders. Why wasn't Jesus afraid to contradict them?

Cf. Catechism of the Catholic Church, 487-507 on Mary's role in Christ's mission; 150-152 on the uniqueness of faith in the triune God

THE GOSPEL OF MATTHEW CHAPTER 13

"Because we cannot endure perpetually the hardships of life, we seek rest in some earthly thing. It may be our house, our family, our children, a little farm, an orchard, or a book we have published. God allows us to suffer tribulations even in these innocent delights in order that we may love only life eternal. Otherwise, as travelers going to their country, we might choose the inn – this world – instead of our true home: eternal life."

- St Augustine

42. SEEKING A FERTILE HEART (MT 13:1-23)

"While the Lord was calling me, all the world's pleasures stood nearby. As though holding deliberations with a friend, my mind pondered what course to take, which to abandon. Thanks be to you, good Jesus, who, moved by the holy entreaties of your servant, broke my bonds and cast upon me the bonds of your love."

- St Hilary of Arles

---

[1] *St Matthew mentions Jesus' "brothers" in this passage. They do not refer to other children had by Mary – she remained a virgin even after giving birth to Christ. Exegetes have provided many proofs of this. One of the simplest is the use in the Greek translation of the Old Testament of the same Greek word used for brothers here to refer to cousins, uncles, and other relations (cf. 1 Chronicles 23:21-22, Deuteronomy 23:7-8, 2Kings 10:13-14, Gen 13:8, etc.).*

Matthew 13:1-23

That same day, Jesus left the house and sat by the lakeside, but such large crowds gathered round him that he got into a boat and sat there. The people all stood on the beach, and he told them many things in parables. As he sowed, some seeds fell on the edge of the path, and the birds came and ate them up. Others fell on patches of rock where they found little soil and sprang up straight away, because there was no depth of earth; but as soon as the sun came up they were scorched and, not having any roots, they withered away. Others fell among thorns, and the thorns grew up and choked them. Others fell on rich soil and produced their crop, some a hundredfold, some sixty, some thirty. Listen, anyone who has ears!'

Then the disciples went up to him and asked, 'Why do you talk to them in parables?' 'Because' he replied 'the mysteries of the kingdom of heaven are revealed to you, but they are not revealed to them. For anyone who has will be given more, and he will have more than enough; but from anyone who has not, even what he has will be taken away. The reason I talk to them in parables is that they look without seeing and listen without hearing or understanding. So in their case this prophecy of Isaiah is being fulfilled: You will listen and listen again, but not understand, see and see again, but not perceive. For the heart of this nation has grown coarse, their ears are dull of hearing, and they have shut their eyes, for fear they should see with their eyes, hear with their ears, understand with their heart, and be converted and be healed by me. But happy are your eyes because they see, your ears because they hear! I tell you solemnly, many prophets and holy men longed to see what you see, and never saw it; to hear what you hear, and never heard it.

'You, therefore, are to hear the parable of the sower. When anyone hears the word of the kingdom without understanding, the evil one comes and carries off what was sown in his heart: this is the man who received the seed on the edge of the path. The one who received it on patches of rock is the man who hears the word and welcomes it at once with joy. But he has no root in him, he does not last; let some trial come, or some persecution on account of the word, and he falls away at once. The one who received the seed in thorns is the man who hears the word, but the worries of this world and the lure of riches choke the word and so he produces nothing. And the one who received the seed in rich soil is the man who hears the word and understands it; he is the one who yields a harvest and produces now a hundredfold, now sixty, now thirty.'

CHRIST THE LORD There is power in the words of Christ. Immense crowds press upon him. Christ was attractive to so many. Clearly, if he roused them to a revolution, they would follow; if he led them to storm a city, they would rally; but instead he invites them to change their hearts, and they do not understand him. Christ's Lordship is real ("many prophets and righteous people longed to see what you see…" – i.e., Jesus himself, the Lord), but he wields it gently; he refuses to bully us into following him. He was the "sower" of the parable, and he remains thus until today. His Church continues to plant the seed of truth, but never forces hearts to welcome it.

This combination of eagerness to win over disciples but respect for his listeners' freedom is especially evident in Jesus' use of parables. Some interpret this tactic and his quotation from Isaiah to mean that he uses these stories and comparisons to conceal his meaning from his opponents, but there is also another way to look at it. When someone refuses to accept the plain truth, you sometimes have to take a roundabout way to convince them. In his parables, Jesus offers his listeners a chance to accept certain truths in the abstract, before perceiving how those truths apply to them personally (this is what the prophet Nathan did with King David after his sin with Bathsheba – see 2 Samuel 12). It's a way of sneaking uncomfortable truths through his listener's mental defense mechanisms. In this way, he may be able to penetrate indirectly minds that have closed themselves to direct proclamations. Even his parables show how wise and loving is the Lord.

CHRIST THE TEACHER We are free, but we are not alone – numerous factors compete for our freedom's attention.

We are free to hear and heed God's saving word. He offers it to us (he sows the seed), gives us plenty of chances to listen to it and put it into practice, but he respects the freedom that he has endowed us with, and leaves the response up to us. Nevertheless, we do not exercise that freedom in a vacuum. The devil (again, Jesus affirms the devil's existence and continues to warn us about him), our own selfishness, and the world's attractions contend with one another to seduce our freedom. When we welcome Christ, our lives bear abundant fruit – meaning, purpose, joy; when we hearken to other voices, our lives are barren, perhaps filled with pretty briars and brambles, but empty of any lasting achievement or value. As Jesus says later on, "I am the vine, you are the branches. Whoever remains in me and I in him will bear much fruit, because without me you can do nothing" (John 15:5). He wasn't exaggerating.

CHRIST THE FRIEND Jesus does not leave us by ourselves to fight against the devil, the world, and our own selfishness. He wants us to hear him, so he explains his parables – to his Apostles. Jesus comes to us through the many ministries of his Church, built on the foundation stones of the Apostles (cf.

Ephesians 2:20, Revelation 21:14) and their successors, the bishops in union with the bishop of Rome. And he assures us that when we are willing to receive his truth and grace, he will give us more and more ("for anyone who has will be given more"). Here again the Church instructs us, through the example of the saints, the ones who have received that "more." Still, despite the Church's endurance and growth through the centuries, which proves her divine origin, so many "ears do not hear, and eyes do not see." How it must pain his heart to watch his seed wither away! Let us, at least, keep rich and ready the soil of our hearts.

CHRIST IN MY LIFE Do you know how much I long to share in your wisdom, Lord? My mind is full of so many questions, my heart is so restless – I want to be closer to you, to live in your presence, to discover you and your loving, saving action in every event of my life, in every person I know. Open my ears to hear your voice, Lord; open my eyes to see you…

Jesus, you compare my soul to a garden, or to a farmer's field. Your word has taken root there, but that doesn't mean that I can coast along. Gardens need tending. Weeds crop up every day, every hour. The soil, the birds, the elements… Jesus, help me know myself better. Show me what is choking your grace. Give me the strength to root it out. And give me constancy to continually tend the soil of my soul. I want my life to bear fruit that will last…

You didn't give up when they refused to understand you. You kept teaching, you kept trying to win them over, to save them, to convince them, to love them into your Kingdom. Make my heart like that. I believe that you are the Savior, the Light, and the Way. Only you have words of eternal life. Teach me to be your faithful ambassador. Never let me give up on the souls you have entrusted to my care. Reach out through me to save many souls…

QUESTIONS FOR SMALL GROUP DISCUSSION

1. What struck you most in this passage? What did you notice that you hadn't noticed before?

2. Which of the three enemies of God's Word (the devil, the attractions of this world, our own selfishness – especially in fearing persecution and self-sacrifice) is most present in today's popular culture?

3. How can we better help till and fertilize the soil in the hearts of those around us, so that they will more readily welcome God's word when they hear it?

4. Why are Christ's parables so memorable?

Cf. Catechism of the Catholic Church, 142-175 on the nature and necessity of man's response of faith to God's revelation; 29 on reasons for atheism; 51-67 on God's gradual self-revelation

43. QUALITIES OF THE KINGDOM (MT 13:24-43)

"In prayer I always find light and strength of spirit although there are moments so trying and hurtful, that it is sometimes difficult to imagine that these things can happen in a convent. Strangely, God sometimes allows them, but always in order to manifest or develop virtue in a soul. That is the reason for trials."

- St Faustina Kowalska

Matthew 13:24-43

He put another parable before them, 'The kingdom of heaven may be compared to a man who sowed good seed in his field. While everybody was asleep his enemy came, sowed darnel all among the wheat, and made off. When the new wheat sprouted and ripened, the darnel appeared as well. The owner's servants went to him and said, Sir, was it not good seed that you sowed in your field? If so, where does the darnel come from? Some enemy has done this he answered. And the servants said, Do you want us to go and weed it out? But he said, No, because when you weed out the darnel you might pull up the wheat with it. Let them both grow till the harvest; and at harvest time I shall say to the reapers: First collect the darnel and tie it in bundles to be burnt, then gather the wheat into my barn.'

He put another parable before them, 'The kingdom of heaven is like a mustard seed which a man took and sowed in his field. It is the smallest of all the seeds, but when it has grown it is the biggest shrub of all and becomes a tree so that the birds of the air come and shelter in its branches.' He told them another parable, 'The kingdom of heaven is like the yeast a woman took and mixed in with three measures of flour till it was leavened all through'. In all this Jesus spoke to the crowds in parables; indeed, he would never speak to them except in parables. This was to fulfil the prophecy: I will speak to you in parables and expound things hidden since the foundation of the world.

Then, leaving the crowds, he went to the house; and his disciples came to him and said, 'Explain the parable about the darnel in the field to us'. He said in reply, 'The sower of the good seed is the Son of Man. The field is the world; the good seed is the subjects of the kingdom; the darnel, the subjects of the evil one; the enemy who sowed them, the devil; the harvest is the end of the world; the reapers are the angels. Well then, just as the darnel is gathered up and burnt in the fire, so it will be at the end of time. The Son of Man will send his angels and they will gather out of his kingdom all things that provoke offences and all who do evil, and throw them into the blazing furnace, where there will be weeping and grinding of teeth. Then the virtuous will shine like the sun in the kingdom of their Father. Listen, anyone who has ears!'

CHRIST THE LORD Jesus Christ knows why he has come: to establish a Kingdom. His confidence in this Kingdom is absolute: the Kingdom will endure and grow to fruition. Enemies will act against it, but they cannot stop it. To be with Christ is to be with the King who reigns forever; to follow him is to tread the surest path; to fight for his Kingdom is to win an eternal victory, no matter the vagaries of this or that battle.

His Kingdom, in its seminal form of the Church, has already outlasted empires, wars, invasions, heresies, disasters, and every imaginable happenstance and hiccup of history. Not only is it still intact after twenty centuries – still recognizable and identifiable by its enduring doctrine and structure – but it continues to play a major role in millions of lives and in world affairs, and it continues to pump into human society generation after generation of saints, men and women who renew what is best in humanity and purify what is worst. How many earthly kingdoms and empires and achievements has the Church witnessed come and go, like so many arrows whizzing through the air or so many pebbles tossed into the sea? They are innumerable. But Christ's Kingdom remains and grows and spreads. This is the Kingdom we love and serve, because its King is the everlasting and loving Lord.

CHRIST THE TEACHER The Kingdom that Jesus came to establish, the one we entered by our baptism, has certain characteristics that he wants us to recognize.

First, the Kingdom is always growing. It started small when Christ established it, and it starts small whenever it takes root anew, but it is always growing. This growth takes place on all levels: the individual soul, a particular community, and the Church as a whole. Critics of the Catholic Church often claim that its current appearance differs so much from its initial appearance of a small group of fishermen gathered around their rabbi that it simply couldn't be the authentic Christian Church. They have not learned the lesson of this parable. When you plant a mustard seed you expect it to grow into a bush (mustard shrubs grow to about ten feet in height). This bush will not resemble the mustard seed at all, but even so it will produce more seeds, and more bushes, and even attract birds to come and nest in it (this detail is a reference to Daniel 4, one of a few Old Testament passages that compared kingdoms to trees, and conquered foreign peoples to birds nesting in the tree – an allusion, perhaps, to the eventual extension of the Church beyond the borders of the Holy Land). Christ's Kingdom is alive; it's always growing.

Second, opposition and contradiction will always beset the Kingdom. The weeds and the wheat grow up together, side by side. In our own souls, evil, sinful tendencies do not disappear as our Christian identity matures, and the Church itself never lacks for scandals within and assaults from without. Critics often point out sins committed by Catholics as a sign that it is not Christ's true Church, but did Judas' betrayal invalidate Peter's repentant perseverance?

Third, the Kingdom's impact will always be out of proportion to its dimensions. A little leaven makes the whole loaf rise; a little holiness sends ripples throughout the world. How odd, for instance, that Blessed Mother Teresa of Calcutta was as famous as the world's great kings and queens (and business tycoons and movie stars); that she, a consecrated virgin from Albania, was guest speaker at Harvard's graduation and at the United States' National Prayer Breakfast. Similarly, the faithful mothers, lawyers, and teachers who fill their souls with Christ's love are spreading the grace of God far and wide; their impact will only be known at the end of the age, when mere appearances give way to universal knowledge of the truth. In our own apostolic work, let us always sow with the hope of future fruits for the Kingdom of Christ.

CHRIST THE FRIEND Some people prefer to dodge the thought of hell. Jesus was not one of them. The two ultimate destinations – heaven and hell – were among the most common themes of his preaching: if you know that one road leads to bliss and the other to misery, you will do your best to inform your friends about which is which, so that they take the better road. Christ, our truest friend, informs us that rejecting him leads to torment and following him leads to glory. "Thrown into the fiery furnace... will shine like the sun in the kingdom..." Surely he spoke these words with eagerness for his listeners to opt more fully for him. He, at least, knows what is really at stake in the choices we make during this brief earthly journey. He wants us to know as well. Let's listen, so that the blood he shed for us on the cross will not have been shed in vain.

CHRIST IN MY LIFE Your wisdom, Lord, is total, life-giving, and beautiful, and you have given it to me in the teachings of your Church. And yet, I still see things and think of things from an earthly perspective. I want my priorities to be your priorities. I want to be a channel for your grace to reach into the hearts of those around me and spread, transforming them and taking deep root. Make me a channel of your peace...

You have taught me to expect weeds among the wheat. Why am I surprised and scandalized at evil? In your wisdom, you permit the wheat and the weeds to grow up together. Help me to accept your will, to seek and promote the good, and never to be discouraged, surprised, or thrown off track by the evil I encounter, wherever it may be. Jesus, I trust in you...

You are so patient. Mustard seeds, leaven, slow-growing crops – this is your Kingdom. I am a product of the fast-food culture that wants everything right away. Patience... teach me patience, Lord. Blessed are the patient, for they will inherit the earth. You are in control, and all I need to worry about is your will right now...

QUESTIONS FOR SMALL GROUP DISCUSSION

1. What struck me most about this passage? What did I notice that I hadn't noticed before?

2. Jesus explains why he permits evil to crop up, even in his Church. How would you explain that to someone who claimed that Church scandals disprove the Christian faith?

3. How should our awareness of the reality of an eternal destiny affect our daily lives and priorities?

4. Jesus made his doctrine accessible by explaining it using everyday examples. What are some every-day examples that would be effective in explaining the gospel to the people around us today?

Cf. Catechism of the Catholic Church, 543-547 on the nature of the Kingdom and the genius of Christ's parables; 1033-1037 on hell; 1023-1028 on heaven

44. INVESTING WISELY (MT 13:44-52)

"Let me seek you in desiring you; let me desire you in seeking you; let me find you in loving you; let me love you in finding you."

- St Anselm

Matthew 13:44-52

"The kingdom of heaven is like treasure hidden in a field which someone has found; he hides it again, goes off happy, sells everything he owns and buys the field. Again, the kingdom of heaven is like a merchant looking for fine pearls; when he finds one of great value he goes and sells everything he owns and buys it. Again, the kingdom of heaven is like a dragnet cast into the sea that brings in a haul of all kinds. When it is full, the fishermen haul it ashore; then, sitting down, they collect the good ones in a basket and throw away those that are no use. This is how it will be at the end of time: the angels will appear and separate the wicked from the just to throw them into the blazing furnace where there will be weeping and grinding of teeth. Have you understood all this?' They said, 'Yes.' And he said to them, 'Well then, every scribe who becomes a disciple of the kingdom of heaven is like a householder who brings out from his storeroom things both new and old.'

CHRIST THE LORD Great leadership requires clear vision. Christ's vision could not have been clearer. His parables fill the Gospels with brilliant snap-shots of the Kingdom, taken from every angle. He speaks of something he knows vividly and completely, wanting to infect his hearers with his own volca-nic enthusiasm. His descriptions of the Kingdom flow from his lips like water over a waterfall – his vision is so rich and vibrant that language itself can barely contain it. The same characteristic marks the words of the Church's saints throughout the ages; their sayings always seem ready to explode, bursting with more meaning than they can hold. Such is the vision of our Leader; such can be our vision too, if we follow him well.

CHRIST THE TEACHER Two characteristics of the Kingdom shine through these parables. First, its incomparable value. Accepting the message of Christ (which means accepting Christ himself – he is the pearl and the treasure), entering the community of his Church, and living faithfully the Church's life is worth more than anything else. The treasure will give the farmer more satisfac-tion than the most bountiful of harvests; the pearl will give the merchant the success he has long been toiling for; the Kingdom will give us the peace and purpose we so energetically seek everywhere else. Therefore, it is worth enter-ing the Kingdom even if we must forsake everything to do so. The steady flow of martyrs through the last twenty centuries bears witness to this; they found in Jesus Christ a cause worth living for, and a Kingdom worth dying for.

The parable of the fishing net gives us yet another reason for the Kingdom's incomparable value. In the end, if we are found living a vital and personal rela-tionship with Christ (this is the key – it's not enough just to have the externals in place; not all the fish in the net – the Church – will be kept), we will enter into his glory. If not, we will suffer eternal frustration. Jesus Christ mentions no other alternative.

CHRIST THE FRIEND Jesus' wisdom surpassed the old wisdom of the Law and the Prophets, but it did not nullify it. If we have understood his teaching, we have not lost all we knew before, but only added to it – now we have both the "new and the old." This applies not only to religious knowledge, but to all knowledge. The Christian doctor is a better doctor for being a Christian; his faith infuses his profession with deeper motivations and ennobling virtues. The Christian statesman is a better leader for being a Christian, because his faith and God's grace enable him to serve with less thought for himself and more thought for his fellow men and women. The Christian student excels because his thirst for knowledge is coupled with a thirst to discover more about the wisdom and beauty of God hidden in the world he created. The same goes for the Christian athlete, the Christian artist, the Christian journalist…. Christ takes our hand and leads us into a fuller, more intense life in every way, as no other friend can do.

CHRIST IN MY LIFE I am amazed at how easily I forget how great you are. You, Lord, are a volcano of love, a torrent of wisdom, a constellation of hope. And here I am, your disciple, so close to you, yet so easily tangled up by little things. Why is my faith so weak? I believe in you. You are my Lord. I long for your joy and peace. I believe, Lord, increase my little faith...

My treasure is your friendship. It gives life and meaning to everything else – my relationships, my responsibilities, my dreams, and my battles. You have so much you want to give me, and so much you want to give others through me. All you need is for me to say yes to you each day, to follow your example of fidelity, to do your will, and love my neighbor as myself. It's so simple, yet so hard. Be my strength, Lord…

Lord, you have made me for heaven. If I could only set my eyes on that goal and realize that this life is just a journey, so much peace would flow into my soul. Imbue me with the hope of the Resurrection, with an eagerness for the day when I will finally see you face-to-face. With the power of your love, set my heart on you…

QUESTIONS FOR SMALL GROUP DISCUSSION

1. What struck you most about this passage? What did you notice that you hadn't noticed before?

2. Why do you think Christ spoke so directly and frequently about heaven and hell?

3. Do you think the merchant's friends were able to notice that he had found "the pearl of great price"? Should those around us be able to notice that we have found Christ? How?

Cf. Catechism of the Catholic Church, 871-933 on the different states in which we can live out our Christian vocation; 543-547 on the nature of the Kingdom and the genius of Christ's parables; 1033-1037 on hell, 1023-1028 on heaven

THE GOSPEL OF MATTHEW CHAPTER 14

"You will say, perhaps, 'this is ordinary bread.' But this bread which is no more than bread before the sacramental words, becomes the Body of Christ from the moment of the consecration. Let us prove it. How can bread become Christ's Body? By what

words is the consecration achieved, and whose words are they? They are the words of Jesus. Indeed, all that is said before them is said by the priest: he praises God, prays for the people, for kings, for all men. But when he comes to make present the venerable sacrament, he no longer uses his own words, but uses those of Christ. It is the word of Christ, then, that produces this sacrament. But what word of Christ? That word by which all things were made. God spoke, and the heavens were made. God spoke, and the earth was made. God spoke, and the sea was made. God spoke, and all creatures were made. Does not this show you how powerful is the Word of Christ?"

- St Ambrose

45. HOME COURT DISADVANTAGE (MT 13:53-14:12)

"Do not be afraid to be holy! Have the courage and humility to present yourselves to the world determined to be holy, since full, true freedom is born from holiness. This aspiration will help you discover genuine love."

- Pope John Paul II

Matthew 13:53-14:12

When Jesus had finished these parables he left the district; and, coming to his home town, he taught the people in their synagogue in such a way that they were astonished and said, 'Where did the man get this wisdom and these miraculous powers? This is the carpenter's son, surely? Is not his mother the woman called Mary, and his brothers James and Joseph and Simon and Jude? His sisters, too, are they not all here with us? So where did the man get it all?' And they would not accept him. But Jesus said to them, 'A prophet is only despised in his own country and in his own house,' and he did not work many miracles there because of their lack of faith.

At that time Herod the tetrarch heard about the reputation of Jesus, and said to his court, 'This is John the Baptist himself; he has risen from the dead, and that is why miraculous powers are at work in him.' Now it was Herod who had arrested John, chained him up and put him in prison because of Herodias, his brother Philip's wife. For John had told him, 'It is against the Law for you to have her.' He had wanted to kill him but was afraid of the people, who regarded John as a prophet. Then, during the celebrations for Herod's birthday, the daughter of Herodias danced before the company, and so delighted Herod that he promised on oath to give her anything she asked. Prompted by her mother she said, 'Give me John the Baptist's head, here, on a dish.' The king was distressed but, thinking of the oaths he had sworn and of his guests, he ordered it to be given her, and sent and had John beheaded in the prison. The head was brought in on a dish and given to the girl who took it to her mother. John's disciples came and took the body and buried it; then they went off to tell Jesus.

CHRIST THE LORD In one sense, the consternation of Jesus' listeners is justified. His wisdom and his eloquence surpassed mere human capabilities; Jesus wasn't just an especially gifted motivational speaker. Something else entirely is going on here. His listeners recognized that. But then they went awry. They could have concluded that this extraordinary teaching deserved to be listened to and explored and delved into. They could have asked Jesus to keep teaching them and to explain himself at greater length. But they didn't. Instead, they let their selfishness get in the way. *Jesus is just one of us,* they thought, *so all this wonder-working and wise teaching must be some kind of a sham. He's no better than us, and we could never rise to such a level, so there must be some other explanation...* How often human vanity and arrogance shackle progress: when we don't feel capable of being lordly, we pettily resent the Lord.

CHRIST THE TEACHER In this passage, St Matthew shows two common obstacles to spiritual growth. First, familiarity. When we are used to things, we can be blinded to their true worth. Nazareth was a little village; everyone knew everything about everyone. Jesus' fellow townspeople were so familiar with him, they had so firmly pigeonholed him, that even his astounding wisdom failed to breach their preconceptions. As Christians, Christ is as present in our lives as he was in that synagogue, and yet we are often just as blind as those townspeople, because we have let ourselves get used to God's gifts. The Eucharist, confession, the papacy, the Bible, baptism, vocations to the priesthood and consecrated life, conversions... God is right here among us, working wonders, saving souls, and making saints, and we shake our heads and say, "Nahhh, that's just Betty being pious again." And then we have the gall to wonder why Jesus doesn't do more of his "mighty deeds" in us and through us.

The second obstacle is what spiritual writers call human respect. This refers to a form of vanity in which you care so much about making sure other people respect you that you betray your own conscience. This is what happened to Herod. In a moment of passion he made an imprudent commitment (sound familiar?), and when it came back to haunt him, he ended up perpetrating a despicable crime (executing a man he knew was innocent) just to avoid being ridiculed by his courtiers. Every day the Christian is tempted to do the exact same thing. In conversations, in behavior, in entertainments, the pressure to conform and the fear of being disdained or rejected strive against the persistent, but gentle, voice of God's will in the conscience. It only takes a little string to keep an eagle tied to the ground; until we are willing to sacrifice the opinions of fickle people in order to please the dependable Lord of the universe, there's no way we'll really learn to fly.

CHRIST THE FRIEND Jesus had praised John the Baptist more than anyone else. He had started his ministry with some of John's disciples. He had received his own baptism at John's hands. And when John is in trouble, does Jesus come to the rescue? No, he lets him suffer unjust imprisonment and violent execution. Was Jesus helpless to set John free? Not at all – we have seen his miracles. So why did he let someone he respected and loved so dearly perish so horribly? Somehow, the martyrdom of John the Baptist, which the Church still celebrates as a liturgical feast, was part of the plan. The last and greatest prophet had to announce the Messiah not only by his words, but even by pointing to Christ's future Passion with his own self-sacrifice.

Only in heaven will we see how all the pieces of history fit together, especially pieces that involve the suffering of innocents, but we know that they will fit: "For the Lamb who is in the center of the throne will shepherd them and lead them to springs of life-giving water, and God will wipe away every tear from their eyes" (Revelation 7:17). In the meantime, however, we have to trust that since Christ himself trod the path of rejection, suffering, and death, it's okay when he leads his friends along it too.

CHRIST IN MY LIFE It scares me to think of your own townspeople not recognizing you, Lord. What if you are speaking to me in simple, direct ways, and I am not listening? Jesus, you know how much I need your help to hear and heed your call in my life. Teach me to do your will. Keep me humble, so I will always be ready to find you, however you wish to come to me…

You are the Lord of the universe. You are my Creator, my Redeemer, the eternal Word of God. You became man just because you love me. If I were the only person in the world who needed salvation – the one lost sheep – you still would have come for me, and taught me, and suffered to save me. Your love overwhelms me. Let it sink deep into my heart. Teach me to love like that. With the love of your heart, Lord, inflame my heart…

Do you know how weak I am? I am so concerned about what others think of me. This is an unhealthy habit of my heart. I don't want to live at the mercy of fickle opinions. I want to live in light of your truth, to seek your will, to build your Kingdom, and to give you free rein to make me a saint. First, with your help, I will stop judging others, and then I will stop being afraid of their judging me…

QUESTIONS FOR SMALL GROUP DISCUSSION

1. What struck you most about this passage? What did you notice that you hadn't noticed before?

2. Why is it often so hard to do what's right when we know that people will make fun of us because of it?

3. God is always acting in our lives – the saints are able to detect this. How can we begin forming the habit of more readily recognizing his action and his presence?

4. Jesus promised that his followers would all have to carry their own crosses. What can we do to get ready for the suffering we will have to endure in order to stay faithful to Christ?

Cf. Catechism of the Catholic Church, 1783-1785, 1798, and 1802 on the formation of the conscience; 162 and 2016 on persevering in the faith; 2473-2474 on the significance of martyrdom

46. SELF-FORGETTING LOVE (MT 14:13-21)

"I love because I love; I love by loving."

- St Bernard of Clairveaux

Matthew 14:13-21

When Jesus received this news he withdrew by boat to a lonely place where they could be by themselves. But the people heard of this and, leaving the towns, went after him on foot. So as he stepped ashore he saw a large crowd; and he took pity on them and healed their sick. When evening came, the disciples went to him and said, 'This is a lonely place, and the time has slipped by; so send the people away, and they can go to the villages to buy themselves some food'. Jesus replied, 'There is no need for them to go: give them something to eat yourselves'. But they answered 'All we have with us is five loaves and two fish'. 'Bring them here to me' he said. He gave orders that the people were to sit down on the grass; then he took the five loaves and the two fish, raised his eyes to heaven and said the blessing. And breaking the loaves handed them to his disciples who gave them to the crowds. They all ate as much as they wanted, and they collected the scraps remaining; twelve baskets full. Those who ate numbered about five thousand men, to say nothing of women and children.

CHRIST THE LORD John the Baptist's death moves Jesus deeply. Not only had they been cousins, and men who shared a deep common bond of dedication to God's Kingdom, but John's death was for Christ a signal that his own ministry was to rise to another level: the Precursor had finished his mission; the King was now to arrive. Christ's heart was heavy with sorrow for John's tragic death, and his mind was full of its consequences. He goes away to be alone, to have time to reflect and to pray as he begins a new stage of his mission.

But the crowds won't leave him alone; they give him no space. They flock around him, begging and pleading for him to heal them and teach them and save them from all their troubles. Christ cannot resist their pleas. He sits down and begins to give audience to the throngs of people; his disciples bring each plaintiff into his presence, he hears them, and he heals their diseases. All day he is there, listening, teaching, and healing – all day he pours out his love on these needy crowds, when what he had planned to do was go off on his own to reflect and pray. Our Lord truly is a man for others.

CHRIST THE TEACHER Finally, his exhausted and exasperated disciples try to get him to send away the hungry throng, as much for the sake of the people (who need to eat) as for their own sake, so they can have a break. But Christ wants to teach them a lesson: just as the Son of Man (Jesus) has come to serve, to give and not to count the cost, so his followers must do the same. "Feed them yourselves," he quips. Imagine the look on the disciples' faces! Five thousand men, with another few thousand women and children, and the Master tells the Apostles to give them a meal. They point out that they really have barely enough food even for themselves, let alone to feed thousands of hungry hangers-on. But however little they have, when they put it into the hands of the Lord it becomes more than enough.

St Matthew emphasizes Christ's example of self-forgetting love in this episode by drawing a parallel between it and the culmination of Jesus' self-giving, the Eucharist. The four verbs that describe what Jesus does with the five loaves in this scene are the same four verbs that describe what Jesus does with the bread that becomes his body during the Last Supper – the same ones every priest still uses today in the sacrifice of the Mass: took... blessed... broke... gave. It is a summary of Christian theology. Jesus did that with human nature: taking flesh, praying to his Father, suffering his passion, and spreading the Good News. He does it with each of his disciples: he calls them, pours out his grace on them, gives them a share in the cross, and sends them into the world to make more disciples. The Eucharist is Christ's ongoing love affair with the souls for whom he died, and it makes what it teaches (self-forgetting love) actually happen in those who receive it with faith.

CHRIST THE FRIEND Jesus: My heart thirsts for those who are thirsty. I hunger for those who hunger. I want to feed those who are hungry; I want to heal those who are sick; I want to teach those who are confused. This is why I came, to put my omnipotence, my goodness, and my wisdom at the service of others. But I don't want to do everything myself. I choose apostles to work with me, because I want to bring all people together into my Kingdom, to make all people full, active citizens. In wisdom and love I choose to need the generosity of those whom I call to follow me: the successors of the apostles (the Pope and the bishops in union with him) and through them priests, consecrated men and women, and all Christians. If each of my followers will give me what little they have, I will multiply it, I will make it feed the starving masses, with both food for their bodies and for their souls. No matter how little it seems you can do, I want you to do it, and I will take care of making it overflow into eternity.

CHRIST IN MY LIFE I have benefited from your self-forgetting love, your pity, and your generosity. Even when I was too self-absorbed to look for help, you have come to my aid. Thank you, Lord. Now teach me to do the same with those around me. Teach me to forget myself, to put all my talents and treasure and time at the service of your Kingdom, out of love for you and for my neighbor. Nothing else will last...

If you have left us the great gift of the Eucharist, it's because we need it. Do I live as if I need it? Why do I take it for granted so much? Why don't I visit you more often? Why don't I speak about this gift with those who are searching for you? Increase my faith, Lord. Teach me the lessons you have hidden in the Eucharist – the ones that are there just for me. I believe in your love; make me love like you...

You have given me so much, Lord, and I have been so stingy in giving myself to you. I have a few loaves and a few fish – right now I put them into your hands. You want me to work with you to build up your Kingdom; it seems too tall a task for someone so small as myself. If anyone else were asking it of me, I would have no hope, but I believe in the power of my nothingness united to your omnipotence...

QUESTIONS FOR SMALL GROUP DISCUSSION

1. What struck you most about this passage? What did you notice that you hadn't noticed before?

2. Why did Jesus go through the trouble of having his apostles distribute the loaves and fish instead of just having food appear in front of each group of people?

3. Do you think there is any symbolic meaning in there being precisely twelve baskets of leftovers?

4. What can we do to appreciate better the gift of the Eucharist, and to promote it among others?

Cf. Catechism of the Catholic Church, 1335 on this miracle as prefiguring the Eucharist; 547-553 on "The signs of the Kingdom of God" and Jesus' methodology of choosing apostles to carry on his ministry; 897-913 on the laity's role in the life of the Church

47. WHY DO WE DOUBT? (MT 14:22-36)

"If I try by myself to swim across the ocean of this world, the waves will certainly engulf me. In order to survive I must climb aboard a ship made of wood; this wood is the Cross of Christ. Of course, even on board ship there will be dangerous tempests and perils from the sea of this world. But God will help me remain on board the ship and arrive safely at the harbor of eternal life."

- St Augustine

Matthew 14: 22-33

Directly after this he made the disciples get into the boat and go on ahead to the other side while he would send the crowds away. After sending the crowds away he went up into the hills by himself to pray. When evening came, he was there alone, while the boat, by now far out on the lake, was battling with a heavy sea, for there was a head-wind. In the fourth watch of the night he went towards them, walking on the lake, and when the disciples saw him walking on the lake they were terrified. 'It is a ghost' they said, and cried out in fear. But at once Jesus called out to them, saying, 'Courage! It is I! Do not be afraid.' It was Peter who answered. 'Lord,' he said 'if it is you, tell me to come to you across the water.' 'Come' said Jesus. Then Peter got out of the boat and started walking towards Jesus across the water, but as soon as he felt the force of the wind, he took fright and began to sink. 'Lord! Save me!' he cried. Jesus put out his hand at once and held him. 'Man of little faith,' he said, 'why did you doubt?' And as they got into the boat the wind dropped. The men in the boat bowed down before him and said, 'Truly, you are the Son of God.'

Having made the crossing, they came to land at Gennesaret. When the local people recognised him they spread the news through the whole neighbourhood and took all that were sick to him, begging him just to let them touch the fringe of his cloak. And all those who touched it were completely cured.

CHRIST THE LORD A few hours earlier, Jesus had demonstrated his divine power by the miraculous multiplication of the loaves. As his disciples struggle to keep afloat in the midst of one of the Sea of Galilee's characteristic storms, which arise suddenly and progress violently due to the peculiar geography of the region, Jesus gives them more signs of his divinity: walking on the water, enabling Peter to walk on the water, and calming the gale as suddenly as nature had stirred it up. The reaction of the astonished Apostles leaves no room to doubt the extraordinary quality of this encounter: they "bowed down before him" and acknowledged him as the Messiah. If we take enough time to contemplate the episode, we will find ourselves doing the same.

CHRIST THE TEACHER The incident overflows with lessons for the attentive Christian. First of all, the Church has long viewed the back-to-back miracles having to do with bread (multiplication of the loaves) and with Christ's body (walking on the water) as a preface to the mystery of the Eucharist, the ongoing miracle involving bread and Christ's body. Just as the Apostles share in these two miracles – they distributed the miraculously multiplying loaves, and Peter walks on the water – so through the Eucharist all Christians will come to share in the transforming power of divine grace. Christ proves he has power over elemental objects and material forces; why could he not have that same power to turn bread and wine into his own body through the hands of his Apostles?

Secondly, Christ teaches us by example the importance of spending time in prayer. St Matthew notes how Jesus went up into the hills by himself to pray. Before the miracle of the loaves, Christ had received news of John the Baptist's martyrdom and had attempted to go off by himself to reflect and pray in its aftermath, but the needs of the crowds deterred him. Nevertheless, here we see that although he delayed his time alone with his Father, he did not let his busy schedule crowd it out altogether. As soon as he could, he retreated into the quiet of prayer. Jesus teaches us to keep first things first; if he who is the Son of God needed time alone in prayer, how much more do we!

Thirdly, Christ uses Peter's impulsiveness to teach us the secret of navigating through the winds and waves of life. As long as Peter kept his eyes on Christ he was able to walk unhindered through the stormy sea; as soon as he let his eyes wander away from Christ to examine the intimidating waves, he began to sink. Just so, as we strive to make our way to Christ through the stormy temptations and challenges of life in a fallen world, focusing on Christ is the only way to keep afloat.

CHRIST THE FRIEND Christ never abandons us in our need; he only asks us to believe in him. In his words to Peter, tinged perhaps with disappointment, we catch a glimpse of his heart, longing so deeply for us to trust him without limits: "Why did you doubt?" And when he steps into the boat, the storm dies away and peace resumes. Christ wants to be our peace, our strength, and our solution to all of life's troubles. As the continued healings St Matthew mentions at the end of the chapter attest, he wants to accompany us on each stage of our life's journey. St Peter learned this lesson well; in his first Letter he put it like this: "cast all your anxieties on him, for he cares about you" (1 Peter 5:7).

Peter: How could I ever forget that night? We were terrified. Have you ever seen someone walking across the stormy waters right next to your boat? When we heard his voice telling us to take courage, I felt a surge of recognition and confidence, but when I looked into the others' faces, I could tell they didn't know what to think. That's when I got the idea to have him call me to walk on the waters with him, to put everyone's fears to rest. And I did! I walked on the stormy sea. Who had ever heard of such a thing? After a few steps, as the boat retreated farther behind me, I began to notice how great the storm really was. That's when I took my eyes off the Lord. Whenever I took my eyes off him, I always got in trouble. I started to sink. The whole world was caving in on me. I could barely even cry out for help. But he was there. He was always there. He never gave up on me. He believed in me even when I didn't believe in him, or in myself.

CHRIST IN MY LIFE   Why did you need to pray, Lord? You were God! But you did need to pray. Do I feel such a need to pray? Am I willing to sacrifice other things in order to make sure I spend time with you? Why am I not more concerned about learning to pray better? Jesus, you want me to pray. I want to pray better, so that I can love you better. Teach me, Lord, to pray. Thy will be done...

That boat was the infant Church, with Peter at the helm. It struggled then, and your Church still struggles today. Lord, give strength and prudence to our Pope, to the bishops, to the priests and consecrated men and women, and to the laity. Grant saintly priests to the world. Take us by the hand, save us, increase our faith, calm the storms. Never let me be separated from you...

You always saw the needs of others and went out to meet them. Why I am so slow to do good, especially with those who are near to me? My heart goes in slow motion sometimes, weighed down by my immense selfishness. Your grace can change me. Jesus, meek and humble of heart, with the zeal of your heart inflame my heart...

QUESTIONS FOR SMALL GROUP DISCUSSION

1. What struck you most about this passage? What did you notice that you hadn't noticed before?

2. What are some of the common storms and winds that hinder our progress as Christians here and now? Why does Jesus permit them?

3. Peter disappointed Jesus by not trusting fully in him. In what areas of life is it common for today's Christians to disappoint Christ by not trusting him enough?

4. What has helped you most to grow in your prayer life?

Cf. Catechism of the Catholic Church, 1373-1381 on Christ's presence in the Eucharist; 2567, 2725-2745 on the importance and battle of prayer; 305, 322 on trusting in God's care

THE GOSPEL OF MATTHEW CHAPTER 15

"The chief reason why it was permissible under the Old Law to ask God questions and quite in order for the prophets and priests to seek revelations and visions from him was that, in those times, the faith was not yet firmly founded, nor was the Law of the Gospel established. Hence, it was necessary for them to question God and for him to reply. This he did sometimes in words, sometimes by visions and revelations, or in figures and types, and then again by many other ways that expressed his meaning. Everything he replied and spoke and revealed was about the mysteries of our faith or matters related to it or leading to it. But now that the faith is founded in Christ and the Law of the Gospel made known in this age of grace, there is no longer any reason to question him in that way. Nor need he speak and answer as he did then. When he gave us, as he did, his Son, who is his one Word, he spoke everything to us, once and for all in that one Word. There is nothing further for him to say."

- St John of the Cross, The Ascent of Mt Carmel

48. HYPOCRITICAL HEARTS (MT 15:1-20)

"The humble resemble a rock. Even though the rock lies downward, it is nevertheless firm. The proud are like smoke. Even though the smoke is lofty, eventually it disappears."

- St Augustine

Matthew 15:1-20

Pharisees and scribes from Jerusalem then came to Jesus and said, 'Why do your disciples break away from the tradition of the elders? They do not wash their hands when they eat food.' 'And why do you' he answered 'break away from the commandment of God for the sake of your tradition? For God said: Do your duty to your father and mother and: Anyone who curses father or mother must be put to death. But you say, If anyone says to his father or mother: Anything I have that I might have used to help you is dedicated to God, he is rid of his duty to father or mother. In this way you have made God's word null and void by means of your tradition. Hypocrites! It was you Isaiah meant when he so rightly prophesied: This people honours me only with lip-service, while their hearts are far from me. The worship they offer me is worthless; the doctrines they teach are only human regulations.' He called the people to him and said, 'Listen, and understand. What goes into the mouth does not make a man unclean; it is what comes out of the mouth that makes him unclean.'

Then the disciples came to him and said, 'Do you know that the Pharisees were shocked when they heard what you said?' He replied, 'Any plant my heavenly Father has not planted will be pulled up by the roots. Leave them alone. They are blind men leading blind men; and if one blind man leads another, both will fall into a pit.' At this, Peter said to him, 'Explain the parable for us'. Jesus replied, 'Do even you not yet understand? Can you not see that whatever goes into the mouth passes through the stomach and is discharged into the sewer? But the things that come out of the mouth come from the heart, and it is these that make a man unclean. For from the heart come evil intentions: murder, adultery, fornication, theft, perjury, slander. These are the things that make a man unclean. But to eat with unwashed hands does not make a man unclean.'

CHRIST THE LORD Jesus shows once again that he is a merciful Lord. Instead of ignoring his Pharisaic interlocutors, he instructs them, hoping that maybe this time some light will penetrate their self-imposed, self-righteous blindness.

In the first place, he does for them what they can no longer do on their own: an examination of conscience. He points out that in their pursuit of legalistic and ritualistic exactitude, they have let selfishness run wild. Many religious leaders at the time had taken to dedicating their property and their wealth to the Temple, supposedly as sign of devotion. This gave them continued use of their possessions for the time being (until death, when it would revert to the Temple treasurers). It also meant that they had a good excuse not to use their wealth to support their aging parents – that would be an illicit profanation of sacred property. It was a convenient loophole that saved them a lot of trouble and inconvenience, while looking to all the world like a pious and commend- able sacrifice. Jesus exposes their hypocrisy: they have preferred their own rab- binical practices (human tradition) to a clear precept of the Mosaic Law (divine revelation) purely out of self-interest.

Jesus always exposes our hypocrisy. We may ignore or dim or try to drown out the voice of conscience, but as long as we walk this earth, God continues to speak to our hearts in one way or another. It is the voice of the Lord, who knows us through and through, and longs for us to submit to his wise and redeeming lordship now, so we can enjoy eternal life in his Kingdom later.

CHRIST THE TEACHER For the ancient Jews, there were two types of realities, the sacred and the profane. The Chosen People, because of the special privi- leges granted them by the one true God, had unique access to the sacred, that which belonged to God, the Holy One of Israel. They had his sacred Temple, a sacred priesthood, the sacred scriptures, and the Law, which governed both worship and behavior. At the same time, they lived in the midst of a fallen, profane world. As a result, they were constantly moving back and forth between the sacred and the profane. To help keep the proper attitudes amid this transit, the rabbinical schools had developed thousands of small traditions, related to but not stipulated by the divinely revealed Mosaic Law. Palestine's religious leaders at the time of Jesus followed all of these traditions minutely, and were therefore called Pharisees, or "the perfect." Among these traditions were many that had to do with ritual washings before eating. These were the ones the Pharisees accuse Jesus and his disciples of neglecting.

Jesus' response elevates the argument. He points out, once again, that the Pharisees have inverted real religion. Religion is not about rituals, it's about a relationship with God – friendship with and fidelity to the Lord and Creator lived out through obedience to his will. External, physical realities don't determine whether someone is in communion with the sacred – rather, the attitude and decisions of the heart do. The Pharisees don't love God; they love themselves and their pious prowess. Jesus invites them to take care of their souls by loving God and deciding to do what is right and pleasing to him, not by worrying over empty, man-made traditions.

CHRIST THE FRIEND Jesus seeks our hearts. What pains him about the Pharisees is that their hearts are far from him. The heart – the place where we decide if we will be self-indulgent or self-giving, where we decide to accept or reject Christ's offer of friendship – the heart is the stage of the human drama. When Christ looks at us, he looks with love, but also with a smattering of anxiety: will we opt for him? Will we let his saving love guide us through life? It's a decision he cares about more than any other, and it's the only one that he can never make.

Jesus: The Pharisees were one of my heaviest crosses. They shut out my love no matter how much I did to prove it to them. Every generation has its Pharisees; every soul has its pharisaic moments. Whenever you find yourself judging others, looking down on them, criticizing them from the heights of a self-erected pedestal, you are following in their footsteps. I know how hard it is for you to avoid falling into this attitude, but remember, I am changing you, I am making your heart more like mine, more able to love the sinner while hating the sin. Stay close to me, protect that interior chamber of your soul where you listen to my voice, so that I can keep teaching you. I haven't given up on you; don't give up on me.

CHRIST IN MY LIFE The Pharisees always challenge and resist you... just like me. How many times I give in to little, unhealthy indulgences, making all kinds of pharisaical excuses! Why do I do that? Why is it so hard to be faithful to your will in obeying my conscience, in little things as well as big ones? What good is winning, earning, being popular, getting all these passing things if selfishness keeps stifling my heart? Save me, Lord!...

You are so patient with me. How do you put up with me? Bring me to the next level. I know what mission you have given me in life; now teach me to focus on it, as you focused on yours. No distractions! I give you my heart; please give me yours in return...

Am I more worried about appearing to be your faithful follower than really following you? Please enlighten me, Lord. I don't want to be a hypocrite. Help me to live my faith from the inside out, authentically, showing it in generosity, kindness, and charity, not in judging, condemning, and criticizing. With the knowledge of your heart, make my heart wise...

QUESTIONS FOR SMALL GROUP DISCUSSION

1. What struck you most about this passage? What did you notice that you hadn't noticed before?

2. Why do you think the apostles pointed out to Jesus that his comment had offended the Pharisees?

3. In what ways can we be tempted to fall into pharisaic ritualism nowadays? For example, would a nonbeliever be edified by the sincerity with which you make the sign of the cross, or amused by its superficiality?

4. Do the sacraments and moral teaching of the Church fall into the category of merely human traditions or commandments of God?

Cf. Catechism of the Catholic Church, 874-896 on Christ's establishment of the Church's hierarchy; 1776-1802 on the conscience; 576, 579, and 595 on the Pharisees

49. FORCED BY FAITH (MT 15:21-28)

"Thanks be to you, my Lord Jesus Christ, for all the blessings and benefits which you have given me, for all the pains and insults you have borne for me. O most merciful friend, my brother and redeemer, grant that I may know you more clearly, love you more dearly, and follow you more nearly, day by day, day by day. Amen."

- *St Richard of Chichester*

Matthew 15:21-28

Jesus left that place and withdrew to the region of Tyre and Sidon. Then out came a Canaanite woman from that district and started shouting, 'Sir, Son of David, take pity on me. My daughter is tormented by a devil.' But he answered her not a word.

And his disciples went and pleaded with him. 'Give her what she wants,' they said 'because she is shouting after us.' He said in reply, 'I was sent only to the lost sheep of the House of Israel.' But the woman had come up and was kneeling at his feet. 'Lord,' she said 'help me.' He replied, 'It is not fair to take the children's food and throw it to the house-dogs.' She retorted, 'Ah yes, sir; but even house-dogs can eat the scraps that fall from their master's table.' Then Jesus answered her, 'Woman, you have great faith. Let your wish be granted.' And from that moment her daughter was well again.

CHRIST THE LORD Christ takes his small band of twelve Apostles away from Jewish lands into the Phoenician territory around the cities of Tyre and Sidon in order to put the final touches on their training before making his way back to Jerusalem to suffer his Passion. There he once again shows forth his power as he casts out a demon with merely a word.

The miracles of Christ are referred to in Scripture as "signs and wonders," the same kind of signs and wonders that manifested God's presence in the Old Testament. They show that Christ is of God, that God is at work in Christ, and they are meant to stir up faith in him. Someone who demonstrates such power, and who wields it with such self-restraint, must either be accepted as God's messenger or rejected as the devil's lackey, but he should not be ignored. All three reactions appear in the Gospels; which corresponds to our own?

CHRIST THE TEACHER The heart of God can be moved. Jesus had a particular mission to accomplish; the age of the universal Church was still waiting in the wings while he worked among the Jews. The parameters of this mission did not include Canaanites (ancestral enemies of the Israelites). But the woman had what Christ's heart yearns for: love, faith, and humility.

She was seeking a miracle not for herself, but for the sake of her beloved daughter and at her own expense (imagine how humiliating it would be to tag along behind a Jewish rabbi in public screaming to get his attention). And she believed in Christ. It is hard to imagine how she had come to believe in him. Perhaps her initial faith was quite small (she calls him "Son of David," which could be a merely political title), but contact with him increased it – at last she came, "kneeling at his feet," as to a divinity. In any case, she knew that he could do it. She also knew that he would not do it because she deserved it, but simply because he cared. She was not angry with God for sending this trial; she did not come to Jesus furiously demanding justice. She accepted the trial and recognized that the miracle would be no less a gift than existence itself. This enabled her to take the rebuff and come right back with another petition to the Lord.

Love, faith, and humility: these are the secret ingredients for prayer that moves the heart of God – even a prayer as simple as, "Lord, help me."

CHRIST THE FRIEND The dialogue between Jesus and the Canaanite woman shows how eager Christ is to fill us with the joy of his Kingdom. His objection to the woman's first petition must not have been too strenuous; at least, she saw something in his eyes or heard something in his voice that encouraged her to persevere. Even the harsh insult he levels against her seems designed to elicit an even greater act of faith than she had already made. (We should note that it is possible to say harsh things in a gentle way, which may have been the case here.) The bottom line is that Christ was willing to be convinced; he allowed her faith to change his agenda, something even friends are rarely able to do. This flexibility shows the readiness of his love.

The Canaanite Woman: I had almost given up hope, but then he smiled at me and told me that my prayer was answered. He did it so simply. I was silenced. I looked up at him, hardly believing what he had said. In fact, I didn't really believe it. While I was hurrying home I was wondering, hoping that my daughter was saved, but still wondering. I guess I thought he would perform the miracle with some drama, or that he would come to my home. But it was enough for him to will to do it. When I finally reached my little house, I hesitated to go in. Could it really be true? I pulled aside the curtain and looked at my little daughter lying on the mat. She was sleeping peacefully, her face relaxed, her breathing regular. She was healed. I knelt down and embraced her. Through my tears I prayed in thanksgiving to Jesus.

CHRIST IN MY LIFE How different this woman is from the Pharisees! How it must have gladdened your heart to find someone so humble, someone so trusting in you, after those long and fruitless discussions with the self-righteous Pharisees. Lord Jesus, teach me to be humble. Teach me to pray from my heart. Show me how to let your grace enlighten my mind and enliven my will…

You always hear my prayers. Why don't I pray more? I don't deserve your mercy and grace, but I do need them, and I know you want to give them. Help me to want the right things, to implore your help for the people I love. I can't give them everything they need, but you can. Here me now as I pray for these people. Make me a channel of your peace…

A Christian is supposed to follow in your footsteps. I wonder if there is some-one in my life who is insistently crying out to me for help, and I simply don't realize it. You have given me so much. Give me one more thing: an eagerness to share all I have received with others who need it. With the love of your heart, Lord, inflame my heart…

QUESTIONS FOR SMALL GROUP DISCUSSION

1. What struck you most about this passage? What did you notice that you hadn't noticed before?

2. Considering the fact that we have the testimony of Christ's resurrection and of 2000 years of the life of the Church, our faith ought to be at least as strong as the Canaanite woman's. Why is it often so weak?

3. What do you think the disciples would have learned from this encounter? How would they have reacted?

4. How can we insure that our prayer is filled with love, faith, and humility, and not simply empty words?

Cf. Catechism of the Catholic Church, 547-550 on the meaning of Christ's miracles; 2734-2745 on trust and perseverance in prayer

50. LOVE WITHOUT BORDERS (MT 15:29-39)

"It was the Lord who saved men, because they were incapable of saving themselves."

- *St Irenaeus*

Matthew 15:29-39

Jesus went on from there and reached the shores of the Sea of Galilee, and he went up into the hills. He sat there, and large crowds came to him bringing the lame, the crippled, the blind, the dumb and many others; these they put down at his feet, and he cured them. The crowds were astonished to see the dumb speaking, the cripples whole again, the lame walking and the blind with their sight, and they praised the God of Israel. But Jesus called his disciples to him and said, 'I feel sorry for all these people; they have been with me for three days now and have nothing to eat. I do not want to send them off hungry, they might collapse on the way.' The disciples said to him, 'Where could we get enough bread in this deserted place to feed such a crowd?' Jesus said to them, 'How many loaves have you?' 'Seven' they said 'and a few small fish.' Then he instructed the crowd to sit down on the ground, and he took the seven loaves and the fish, and he gave thanks and broke them and handed them to the disciples who gave them to the crowds. They all ate as much as they wanted, and they collected what was left of the scraps, seven baskets full. Now four thousand men had eaten, to say nothing of women and children. And when he had sent the crowds away he got into the boat and went to the district of Magadan.

CHRIST THE LORD Picture this scene. Jesus goes up on a mountainside – just as he did back in Chapter 5 at the beginning of the Sermon on the Mount. Throngs of people gather around him. This time, however, instead of teaching in words, he teaches in actions. One by one, families bring forward their suffering members, full of anxious hope that he will heal them. And Jesus cures them all; he sets them free from the evil that had enslaved them, and they believe in him. It's as if this particular group of people wouldn't have understood the Sermon on the Mount; they understand only their suffering, and Jesus communicates the truth of God's love by relieving that suffering.

St Matthew is presenting once again a contrast between the unbelieving Pharisees and the vibrant, powerful faith of the uneducated masses. What was the difference? These suffering crowds came to Jesus aware of their needs; the Pharisees came wanting only to discredit him. The more we acknowledge Christ as Lord, the more room we give him to work in our lives, the more we too will go away joyfully, giving glory to God.

CHRIST THE TEACHER Some commentators accuse Matthew of making a mistake by including this passage. They say that the similarities between it and the other multiplication scene in the previous chapter show that the event must have happened only once. They forget that Matthew was actually there. If it had happened only once, he would have included it only once. In fact, the differences between them make clear the importance of this second miracle of the loaves.

That the crowds responded to Christ's healing miracles by praising "the God of Israel" is the first clue. That the town of Magadan is mentioned only in this passage, and still today is unidentifiable by scholars, is the second. We also note that Jesus had just encountered a Canaanite woman in the district of Tyre and Sidon, and in the next chapter he will be making his way to Caesarea Philippi – two Gentile regions bordering Jewish provinces. It seems safe to say that this second multiplication, then, was performed for the benefit of the Gentiles. Jesus' condescension to cure the Canaanite woman's daughter is extended here to other non-Jews. The prefiguring of the Eucharist is now given to them as well, providing a glimpse of the sacrament that will some day unite the entire human family around one altar. Even the seven leftover baskets have this connotation. The previous episode had twelve leftover baskets, signifying the twelve Tribes of Israel. Now there are seven – the number of completion and ending, the number of times the Gentile army commander, Naaman the Syrian, had to wash in the Jordan River to be cured of his leprosy (cf. 2 Kings

5). St Matthew wants to drive the lesson home: the love of Christ doesn't play favorites.

CHRIST THE FRIEND When we hear Jesus tell his disciples that his heart goes out to the crowd, not wanting to send them away hungry lest they faint along their journey, we should hear him speaking those words to us. We are the hungry, poor, needy crowd. Jesus reaches out to us with his truth and love and wisdom, feeding our souls through the ministry of the Church. The Church is the incontrovertible sign of his continued concern for each one of us. It has no other purpose than to give us the strength and guidance we so desperately need to make it safely through this journey on earth to our eternal home in heaven.

But he is also speaking to us in the way he spoke to his disciples. He tells us to look out at the crowds, to open our eyes and our hearts to those around us, and to share with them what he has given to us. We are not, in his eyes, merely objects of his beneficence; we are his companions, collaborators, ambassadors, and friends.

CHRIST IN MY LIFE I am so used to this miracle, but it must have amazed the disciples and the crowds. You fed thousands of people with just a few loaves of bread and a few fish. Take my loaves and fish; take my talents and hopes. Do miracles with them, Lord. Turn my life into a garden blooming with your own virtues and goodness…

You never get tired of giving yourself to others. Yet I get tired so easily. I need your strength. I know you will never fail me; I just have to decide once again to follow you, today. The cross looks heavy from afar, but if I pick it up, if I deny myself and live for others, it will be light and easy, because I won't be carrying it alone. Who do you want me to give myself to today, Lord? Thy will be done…

I'm thinking about the Eucharist. You are present in tabernacles all over the world. You are feeding immense crowds with your body and blood, the bread of eternal life, on every continent, on little islands, in tiny villages, and in the largest cities. You are bringing the whole human family together in your heart. Thank you for this great gift. Increase my faith. With the humility of your heart, shape my heart…

QUESTIONS FOR SMALL GROUP DISCUSSION

1. What struck me most about this passage? What did I notice that I hadn't noticed before?
2. Why do you think Jesus chose bread and wine to transform into the Eucharist, instead of something else?

3. The crowds reacted with wonder and amazement at Jesus' miracles. Why don't we typically react that way to the miracles of the Eucharist and confession?

4. What amazing deeds of Christ have I witnessed in my lifetime?

5. Who are the needy crowds around us today, and how can we better bring them Christ's saving grace?

Cf. Catechism of the Catholic Church, 1397 on the Eucharist and the poor; 1212, 1275, and 1436 on the Eucharist as spiritual food; 1323 and 1394-1395 on the Eucharist as the sacrament of charity; 1935-1938 on the unity of the human race

The Gospel of Matthew CHAPTER 16

"This Sacred Council… teaches and declares that Jesus Christ, the eternal Shepherd, established his holy Church, having sent forth the apostles as he himself had been sent by the Father; and he willed that their successors, namely the bishops, should be shepherds in his Church even to the consummation of the world. And in order that the episcopate itself might be one and undivided, he placed Blessed Peter over the other apostles, and instituted in him a permanent and visible source and foundation of unity of faith and communion."

- Second Vatican Council, Dogmatic Constitution on the Church, Lumen gentium #18

51. SIGN LANGUAGE (MT 16:1-12)

"Trust Christ; listen attentively to his teachings, fix your eyes on his face, persevere in listening to his Word. Allow him to focus your search and your aspirations, all your ideals and the desires of your heart."

- Pope John Paul II

Matthew 16:1-12

The Pharisees and Sadducees came, and to test him they asked if he would show them a sign from heaven. He replied, 'In the evening you say, It will be fine; there is a red sky, and in the morning, Stormy weather today; the sky is red and overcast. You know how to read the face of the sky, but you cannot read the signs of the times. It is an evil and unfaithful generation that asks for a sign! The only sign it will be given is the sign of Jonah.' And leaving them standing there, he went away. The disciples, having crossed to the other shore, had forgotten to take any food. Jesus said to them, 'Keep your eyes open, and be on your guard against the yeast of the Pharisees and Sadducees'. And they said to themselves, 'It is because we have not brought any bread'. Jesus knew it, and he said, 'Men of little faith, why are you talking among yourselves about having no bread? Do you not yet understand? Do you not remember the five loaves for the five thousand and the number of baskets you collected? Or the seven loaves for the four thousand and the number of baskets you collected? How could you fail to understand that I was not talking about bread? What I said was: Beware of the yeast of the Pharisees and Sadducees.' Then they understood that he was telling them to be on their guard, not against the yeast for making bread, but against the teaching of the Pharisees and Sadducees.

CHRIST THE LORD This conversation with the Pharisees illustrates once again their unwillingness to believe. They had already had this conversation once, back in Chapter 12. They had asked for the same thing – some kind of definitive, undeniable sign. And this time Jesus gives them the same answer: only the sign of Jonah will be given them (the Resurrection), and even that will not be enough for hearts that don't want to believe.

This is still a common request of unbelievers. They want mathematical, scientific proof that God exists – something as predictable and indisputable as meteorological data. Brilliant intellectuals and scientists scoff at believers who accept Christ without such a proof. They are sadly mistaken. It's as if they were to demand mathematical proof that their fiancée loves them before they agree to get married. Man's relationship with God is interpersonal, not mathematical. God can show that he is worthy of our trust (e.g., Jesus' many healings, his passion and resurrection), but our faith in him still must spring from a free decision of the heart. We don't need to trust anyone to accept the truth that two plus two equals four; it is self-evident, we can accept it by depending only on ourselves. But love reaches beyond mathematics, just as it reaches beyond oneself. The Lord refuses to have slaves. He wants his subjects to be his friends.

CHRIST THE TEACHER Often we are just like the disciples: in spite of the many times God acts in our lives, we continue to misunderstand, to doubt, and to fear. How absurd it seems to us that the disciples are worried about forgetting bread, so soon after the miracles of the multiplication of the loaves! And yet, we fall into the same types of worries, too easily forgetting how eager and capable God is to take care of all our needs.

The only antidote to this forgetfulness, which pains Christ, is a better life of prayer. We have to form the habit of reflecting serenely and deeply on God's action in history, in the Church, and in our own lives. We must treasure and ponder in our hearts the wonderful things God has done. This is how St Luke describes Mary's interior life. It characterizes the interior lives of the saints as well. And Jesus is hoping that we too will opt out of the flashy superficiality of a media- and information-crazed culture in favor of the lasting wisdom that comes from reflection and prayer.

CHRIST THE FRIEND Picture Jesus in the boat with his disciples. They are talking away, engaged in normal conversation, basically small talk. Jesus is separated from the group, lost in his own thoughts. Then suddenly he makes his remark about the yeast of the Pharisees and Sadducees, Palestine's religious and social leaders. It's almost as if his thoughts had been lingering on those truculent adversaries, mulling over in his mind the mysterious stubbornness of these Jewish leaders in not accepting his teaching and the many signs (the healings) that corroborated it. It bothers Jesus. It pains him and preoccupies him. He warns his disciples to watch out for that kind of self-satisfied attitude. His warning may even be directed to one of them in particular – Jesus already knows that Judas' heart is turning away from him.

St Matthew puts this exchange in his Gospel because the warning applies to us as well, and to Christians of every era. We can all fall prey at any time, even when we are near to Christ, as Judas was, to the persistent temptation of exaggerated self-reliance: "I want to do it my way, my way is God's way, and I'll have it no other way." This is the deadly leaven of the Pharisees. Nothing afflicts the Savior's heart more sorely.

CHRIST IN MY LIFE Jesus, I too have been with you for a long time, and I too still misunderstand many of the things you do in my life. Open my eyes, Lord. I want to know you better, to see you in all things. Be patient with me, as you were with your apostles. Stay with me, don't give up on me, tell me what you mean, give me understanding and love…

I know so many people who resist your truth and goodness, just like the Pharisees. And I know that the world is full of many, many more. How it must pain your heart, you who are so eager to pour out your mercy. I will pray for them. I will believe and trust in their place. Have mercy on them. Open their hearts. Use me to reach them. Teach me, guide me, and make me a channel of your grace…

I don't want to live superficially. I long to be wise with your true wisdom, the kind that comes from spending time with you, from reflecting deeply on your goodness, on your revelation. I want my life to be like a clear, fresh, flowing fountain, where everyone around me can find your truth and love in all my words and actions. Jesus, meek and humble of heart, make my heart more like yours...

QUESTIONS FOR SMALL GROUP DISCUSSION

1. What struck you most in this passage? What did you notice that you hadn't noticed before?

2. Why do you think the Apostles were still worried about having forgotten to pack bread, even after Jesus' two miracles of multiplying the loaves?

3. If someone you know asked you to show them a "sign" that Christ really is God to prove to them that they should become a Christian, how would you respond?

4. Practically speaking, how can we avoid being swept away by the superficiality of popular culture while still taking advantage of its benefits?

Cf. Catechism of the Catholic Church, 2496, 2498, and 2523 on the right use of mass media; 31-35 on ways of coming to know God; 39-43 on how we can speak about God

52. CHRISTIAN ROCK (MT 16:13-20)

"Love for the Roman Pontiff must be in us a delightful passion, for in him we see Christ."

- St José María Escrivá

Matthew 16:13-20

When Jesus came to the region of Caesarea Philippi he put this question to his disciples, 'Who do people say the Son of Man is?' And they said, 'Some say he is John the Baptist, some Elijah, and others Jeremiah or one of the prophets'. 'But you,' he said 'who do you say I am?' Then Simon Peter spoke up, 'You are the Christ,' he said 'the Son of the living God'. Jesus replied, 'Simon son of Jonah, you are a happy man! Because it was not flesh and blood that revealed this to you but my Father in heaven. So I now say to you: You are Peter and on this rock I will build my Church. And the gates of the underworld can never hold out against it. I will give you the keys of the kingdom of heaven: whatever you bind on earth shall be considered bound in heaven; whatever you loose on earth shall be considered loosed in heaven.' Then he gave the disciples strict orders not to tell anyone that he was the Christ.

CHRIST THE LORD The Lord announces his plans to build a Church, a community of believers that will overthrow the rule of evil, which has dominated the world since the fall of Adam and Eve.

The city of Caesarea Philippi was constructed on the top of a huge hill, one side of which was a bare rock cliff. It gave the town an appearance of invincibility and magnificence. Here Jesus explains that his Church will be invincible, because it too will be founded on rock, the rock of Peter, whose special role is guaranteed by "my heavenly Father." Peter will receive the authority to rule that Church in Christ's name. This authority is symbolized by the keys and the "binding and loosing": the former refers to authority held in ancient Israel by the King's master of the palace (cf. Is 22:22]; the latter refers to the authority of the Jewish synagogue leader to expel and reinstate people from the synagogue community, in order to preserve the community's religious and moral integrity. This authority has remained intact through twenty centuries of popes (the successors of St Peter as Vicars of Christ on earth), giving the Catholic Church unity of faith, worship, and governance in spite of its members' many failings. Christ had the authority; he demonstrated it over and over again. He gave it to Peter – he didn't have to, but he wanted to spread his Kingdom through a Church that was both human and divine, just as he wanted to redeem us through the two natures (human and divine) of the Incarnation. We may find God's strategy hard to understand (why didn't Christ himself just stick around after his resurrection to rule the Church?) but we cannot deny it.

Critics twist this passage into nonsensical knots by pointing out that the Greek word for rock (Peter) is of the feminine gender (in Greek all nouns are gender-specific). They conclude, therefore, that Christ wasn't really applying the term to Simon (even though he changed it into a masculine form when he made it into a name) but only to Simon's faith. Or else they claim that Christ said these words while pointing to himself. Such objections make complicated a text that is actually quite simple. They also ignore the many other passages in the New Testament that illustrate Peter's primacy among the Twelve. For example: Christ originally renamed him "Peter" in Chapter 1 of John's Gospel, when he first met him – and renaming people in the Bible is much more than handing out nicknames; it signifies receiving a new role in salvation history. During the Last Supper Christ prayed in a special way for Peter and gave him a special commission to "confirm your brethren in the faith" (Luke 22:32); Christ gave him a unique commission after his resurrection (John 21); Peter's name always appears first on the lists of the Twelve Apostles…

There is one Lord: Jesus Christ. And he founded one Church to wage his definitive war against sin and evil: that Church's keys are in Peter's hands.

CHRIST THE TEACHER Good teachers know when their students are ready for a new lesson. Christ knew that this was the time to give his Twelve their first quiz. They passed. But the rest of the people were not ready. Their idea of a Messiah was still too worldly, too focused on hopes for a mere earthly kingdom, too limited by images of past prophets. They needed more preparation, especially the instruction of Good Friday and Easter Sunday. Therefore, the Master tells his disciples to keep this lesson to themselves for now. We also need to know when to speak with words and when to speak with actions; the more in tune we are with the Holy Spirit, the fewer times we'll flub.

At the same time, we still need to relearn how to see things from God's perspective. Sometimes the trials of life and the strong currents of anti-Christian culture make us forget that Christ's Kingdom is truly present in the Church. Instead of embracing and honoring the papacy, the guarantee of Christ's guiding presence among his people, we become impatient for the Church to adapt itself more to the world. Christ's idea of a Messiah, however, is not the world's idea. It includes the cross; it wins victory through the cross. We should regularly check up on ourselves, to see if we are seeing the world and the Church with Christ's eyes, or with the world's.

CHRIST THE FRIEND Friends are people you can count on. We can count on Christ. He promises that the gates of the underworld (the gates of hell, the powers of the devil) will not prevail against the ferocious assaults of his Church. In other words, his team will win; his Kingdom will stand – both in our hearts and in the world. If we follow Christ, if we stay faithful to him, we will share in his victory; we can count on it. The history of the Church confirms it. Scandals, heresies, wars, slander, and seduction have all tried to halt her advance – to no avail. In every age her voice rings out in defense of human freedom and the truth of Jesus Christ. In every epoch she renews the human race with saints whose divine love sets the world ablaze. In every era she widens the scope of her saving action. We can count on Christ, but can he count on us?

Jesus: I knew that you would need a firm point of reference as you travel through life. I knew that you would need a rock to hang on to when fashionable trends and apparently reasonable cultural options tried to sweep you away. This is why I left you my vicar on earth, the pope. Follow his teaching, because it is my teaching. Listen to him, because I want to guide you through him. If I hadn't left you a guide, you would be at the mercy of flippant fads. I want you to grow in wisdom and grace steadily, without interruptions, without going down dead-end detours, without suffering the damage inflicted by false philosophies and distorted theologies. Stay close to me, stay close to my vicar; I won't lead you astray…

CHRIST IN MY LIFE I believe that you are the Son of God, the Savior. I believe that you were sent by the Father to redeem me. You were sent to rescue me, to bring me into your Kingdom, your family, your heart. I believe in you, Lord; increase my faith. Never let me be separated from you and from your Church…

I get so used to your Church. I take so many of your gifts for granted. Help me to live less superficially. Enlighten my mind. I want to appreciate the teaching and guidance you offer me through the pope and the bishops, through your saints, and through the rich doctrine of the Church. I want to do my part to build up your Church. I love you, Lord, so how can I not love your Bride, for whom you died?…

I am no genius, Lord, but I want to be able to defend the truths of your doctrine, to be able to explain them. You are the one Lord, the one Savior. And so many people just don't know you! So many lies, so much misinformation and misunderstanding deceive them. Instruct me, teach me – help me do my homework, so that I can bear the torch of your transforming truth with elegance, respect, and gusto…

QUESTIONS FOR SMALL GROUP DISCUSSION

1. What struck you most in this passage? What did you notice that you hadn't noticed before?

2. How can we promote and pay better attention to what the pope is teaching, to the priorities he is setting for the Church?

3. What effect should the knowledge of Christ's assured victory have on our daily actions and attitudes? What can we do to increase that effect?

4. If someone you know were to ask you why Catholics have to "go through the pope to get to God," how would you answer?

Cf. Catechism of the Catholic Church, 874-896 and 934-937 on the hierarchy and governing authority of the Church; 551-553 on the meaning of the "keys of the Kingdom"

53. GOD'S WILD IDEA (MT 16:21-28)

"Offer him your sufferings according to all the intentions for which he continually offers himself on the altars of our churches. Your sacrifice, united to the sacrifice of Jesus, will bring many sinners back to the Father; many without faith will find the true faith; many weak Christians will receive the strength to live fully the teaching and the law of Christ."

- Pope Pius XII

Matthew 16:21-28

From that time Jesus began to make it clear to his disciples that he was destined to go to Jerusalem and suffer grievously at the hands of the elders and chief priests and scribes, to be put to death and to be raised up on the third day. Then, taking him aside, Peter started to remonstrate with him. 'Heaven preserve you, Lord;' he said 'this must not happen to you'. But he turned and said to Peter, 'Get behind me, Satan! You are an obstacle in my path, because the way you think is not God's way but man's.' Then Jesus said to his disciples, 'If anyone wants to be a follower of mine, let him renounce himself and take up his cross and follow me. For anyone who wants to save his life will lose it; but anyone who loses his life for my sake will find it. What, then, will a man gain if he wins the whole world and ruins his life? Or what has a man to offer in exchange for his life? 'For the Son of Man is going to come in the glory of his Father with his angels, and, when he does, he will reward each one according to his behaviour. I tell you solemnly, there are some of these standing here who will not taste death before they see the Son of Man coming with his kingdom.'

CHRIST THE LORD We have reached a definitive moment in Jesus' career. "From this time" he intensely prepares his disciples for his passion, death, and resurrection. The drama of Christ's mission is approaching its climax, and he knows it. How many men know what the future holds for them? How many would be able to endure such knowledge? Christ knows what awaits him and walks squarely towards it, confident in the Father's plan. Even the loving dissuasions of his closest friends fail to divert him. Not only is Christ Lord of history, he is also master of himself. For those who know the unruliness of the human heart, this second mastery may be even more impressive than the first. We have to be open to him teaching us lessons we would rather not accept.

CHRIST THE TEACHER The Church has decreed that above each of her altars there should be a crucifix. When we enter a Catholic Church, therefore, the crucifix will be the focus of our field of vision. The crucifix: a depiction of ignominy, torture, pain, and death. The crucifix: not just an empty cross, clean and elegant, but a cross being used to crucify the one man who never sinned, the one man who didn't deserve to die. Why such pride of place for such a cruel reality? Why not put scenes of Christ's birth above every altar, or his resurrection or ascension? Because, "If anyone wants to be a follower of mine, let him renounce himself and take up his cross and follow me."

Christ dying on the cross was the perfect sacrifice offered to God in loving atonement for our sins. Christ dying on the cross was the perfect, loving act of obedience that reversed the vile disobedience of Eden. With his arms stretched wide and raised between heaven and earth, Christ reconciled us to God and bridged the gulf opened by sin. If we want to go over that bridge, we too must pass through the cross. We must follow the footsteps of our Lord: suffering, self-denial, opposition, humiliation, and difficulty – perhaps losing the "whole world," but winning "life." There is no other path. Uninterrupted joy is reserved for heaven; however, the road to heaven is paved with crosses – rather, with crucifixes, for the cross of a Christian is always borne together with Christ, so that we who die with him will also rise with him.

CHRIST THE FRIEND Jesus Christ loves us enough to tell us the truth about ourselves. Those who use other people instead of seeking their authentic good rarely tell them hard truths. It's too risky; pointing out their failings may result in offense and rejection – like parents who are afraid to discipline their child. But love will take the risk, because love always goes after what is best for the beloved. A true friend will tell you when you're wrong, so that you can straighten out. Christ is a true friend. He just finished elevating Peter to a position of prominence in the coming Kingdom (this scene follows immediately the one where Christ dubs him the "rock" upon which he will build his Church), but when Peter lets his judgment be skewed by faithless, human prudence, Christ vehemently reproaches him.

Often the Church and its ministers insist on the hard truths (no contraception, no divorce, no in vitro fertilization, no cloning; the necessity of weekly Mass, confession, self-control, daily prayer…). Often we complain, whine, or even rebel. But if Christ loved Peter enough to admonish him so clearly, how can the Church do anything less? It was a risk for Christ (Peter might have taken offense and abandoned him), and it is a risk for the Church. If we take our medicine as Peter took his, however, we won't regret it; Christ is coming again, and he wants to be able to give us a bounteous reward.

CHRIST IN MY LIFE Jesus, nothing could deter you from your mission. The Father's plan for your life was always on your mind; it was your guiding star. Make me like that, Lord. Make me care only about living as you want me to live. Detach my heart from every other desire: I want to live the life you created me for, a faithful and fruitful life. Lord Jesus, give me light and strength…

I am your disciple. You have promised that I will have crosses in my life. You love me too much not to let me share in your passion. In some ways I am already sharing in it. Am I ready for my cross? Convince my weak and fearful heart that you are enough for me. I look at your crucifix, Lord. I am so used to it. Help me get past the routine; let me know and imitate your love…

You were willing to risk losing Peter's esteem for the sake of the truth. You had his priorities straight. Why am I so worried about what others think of me? What matters is following you! What matters is what you think of me! Free me from these old selfish desires for the esteem of others. I hate them, Lord, because they keep me from you. Free me to love as you love. Thy Kingdom come in my heart…

QUESTIONS FOR SMALL GROUP DISCUSSION

1. What struck me most in this passage? What did I notice that I hadn't noticed before?

2. Why did Peter rebuke Christ for saying he was going to have to suffer and die? Why was Peter's idea "not as God thinks, but as men think"?

3. What might Christ's tone of voice have been when he explained this core teaching about the centrality of the cross and self-sacrifice in the life of every Christian? How might the disciples have responded?

4. How does the society around me say I should react to the crosses I encounter, to the difficulties, challenges, and suffering that life and fidelity to my Christian identity bring on? What can I do to react more like Christ?

Cf. Catechism of the Catholic Church, 556, 1435, 2015 on the role of the cross in the life of Christians; 599-618 on the meaning of Christ's suffering and death

THE GOSPEL OF MATTHEW CHAPTER 17

"What greater proof could he have given of his mercy than by taking upon himself that which needed mercy? Where is there such fullness of loving-kindness as in the fact that the Word of God became perishable like the grass for our sakes? … Let man infer from this how much God cares for him. Let him know from this what God thinks of him, what he feels about him. Man, do not ask about your own sufferings; but about what he suffered. Learn from what he was made for you, how much he makes of you, so that his kindness may show itself to you from his humanity. The lesser he has made himself in his humanity, the greater has he shown himself in kindness. The more he humbles himself on my account, the more powerfully he engages my love… The humanity of God shows the greatness of his kindness, and he who added humanity to the name of God gave great proof of this kindness."

- St Bernard of Clairveaux

54. MOUNTAINTOP MEETINGS (MT 17:1-13)

"If he were not of the same nature as ourselves, his command to imitate him as a master would be a futile one."

- St Hippolytus

Matthew 17:1-13

Six days later, Jesus took with him Peter and James and his brother John and led them up a high mountain where they could be alone. There in their presence he was transfigured: his face shone like the sun and his clothes became as white as the light. Suddenly Moses and Elijah appeared to them; they were talking with him. Then Peter spoke to Jesus. 'Lord,' he said 'it is wonderful for us to be here; if you wish, I will make three tents here, one for you, one for Moses and one for Elijah.' He was still speaking when suddenly a bright cloud covered them with shadow, and from the cloud there came a voice which said, 'This is my Son, the Beloved; he enjoys my favour. Listen to him.' When they heard this the disciples fell on their faces overcome with fear. But Jesus came up and touched them. 'Stand up,' he said 'do not be afraid.' And when they raised their eyes they saw no one but only Jesus. As they came down from the mountain Jesus gave them this order, 'Tell no one about the vision until the Son of Man has risen from the dead'. And the disciples put this question to him, 'Why do the scribes say then that Elijah has to come first?' 'True;' he replied 'Elijah is to come to see that everything is once more as it should be; however, I tell you that Elijah has come already and they did not recognise him but treated him as they pleased; and the Son of Man will suffer similarly at their hands.' The disciples understood then that he had been speaking of John the Baptist.

CHRIST THE LORD This scene, known as the Transfiguration, directly reveals Christ's Lordship. For a moment, Jesus removes the humble veil of his earthly attire to reveal his true glory as Son of God and King of Kings. He converses with the two greatest figures of the Old Testament: Moses, the lawgiver, the one through whom God established the covenant; and Elijah, the holiest of prophets, so holy that he did not die, but was assumed into heaven. Jesus Christ has come to establish a new covenant and to fulfill all the ancient prophecies – he is Lord not only of the present and the future, but even of the past.

The Church's liturgy presents this passage to the faithful during Lent (and also on August 6th, the annual Feast of the Transfiguration), as we prepare to celebrate the passion, death, and resurrection of Christ during Holy Week. Both the brilliance of Christ's future glory and God's wise preparation through the first covenant, each evident in the Transfiguration, thus remind us that the pivotal events of Holy Week, the highpoint of God's self-revelation in Christ the Lord, are the culmination of his marvelous plan of salvation, begun so long ago and destined to last for all eternity. There is simply no limit to Christ's glory: "The Lord is the goal of human history, the focal point of the longings of history and of civilization, the center of the human race, the joy of every heart and the answer to all its yearnings" (*Gaudium et Spes,* 45).

CHRIST THE TEACHER The Church has always recognized the Transfigura-tion as a theophany, a visible manifestation of God. Christ himself is the Second Person of the Trinity; the cloud represents the Holy Spirit, the Third Person (who "hovered over the waters" before creation, cf. Genesis 1:2); and the voice is God the Father, the First Person, speaking as plainly as we could ever ask for, in order to teach us the one necessary lesson: "Listen to him [Christ]." It is the same lesson that came at the theophany during Jesus' baptism at the hands of John the Baptist, the new Elijah who was to usher in the age of the Messiah. In St Matthew's Gospel, God the Father speaks only twice from heaven, and says essentially the same thing both times. It behooves us to consider deeply what that saying really means.

Listening to Christ means getting to know him, understanding his heart, and heeding his call in our lives. Jesus Christ is God's own Son, sent by the Father to be our guide to fulfillment, to the meaning and happiness we all long for. There is "no other name under heaven given to the human race by which we are to be saved" (Acts 4:12). Christ alone is the answer, the secret to a life lived to the full. All we need to do is listen to him, to turn our gaze to him. How? By spending time in heartfelt prayer, by delving into the marvelous teachings of the Church, by steeping ourselves in the priceless living waters of the Gospels and the rest of Holy Scripture, by experiencing Christ himself truly present in the Eucharist, and most of all by doing his will each day with faith, hope, and love, no matter what the cost.

CHRIST THE FRIEND A detail of this passage shows us what a sensitive friend we have in Christ. This event took place just a little while before his crucifixion. He knew that his passion and death would be a blow to the faith of his disciples, so he gave them this glimpse of his glory before-hand, to help them persevere during the upcoming trial. He often does the same with us. The cross is a necessary element in our Christian lives – we cannot reach Easter Sunday without going through Good Friday. But in order to support us in the dark moments, he gives us moments of light and grace, mountaintop experiences of his love and power that can serve as reference points in times of turbulence – if we keep them fresh in our minds.

His admonition to the disciples not to mention this event until after his resur-rection also shows something of his sensitivity. He knows what we need and when we need it. Our life of faith is a journey, a pilgrimage to our eternal homeland; it is a gradual growth in knowledge, love, and imitation of Christ.

Sometimes we become impatient, but Christ knows what he is doing, and we need to trust in his timetable, even if we don't always understand it.

CHRIST IN MY LIFE You are the Lord of life and history. I believe in you, Lord. I believe that you are the focal point of all human history. I put my life in your hands. I want to serve you, to walk with you, to help build your kingdom. I want to follow you, Lord, today, tomorrow, and every day of my life, no matter what you may ask of me...

Sometimes I wish that you would show yourself to me as marvelously as you did to these three Apostles. Wouldn't that make it easier to follow you? But you know exactly what I need. All of your life, your doctrine, and your love are mine. I have the Gospels, the Church, the Eucharist, my spirituality. I have your forgiveness, guaranteed. Lord, the time has come for me to stop complaining. Christ, be my life...

The cross still frightens me. I want things to go smoothly; I want to stay on the mountaintop. But you didn't. How much rejection, envy, and betrayal you suffered! And you did it to teach me what love really is: self-giving and self-forgetting. You love me with a personal, determined love. Teach me to love like that, with fidelity in tough times, with sincere deeds, no matter what the cost. Jesus, I trust in you...

QUESTIONS FOR SMALL GROUP DISCUSSION

1. What struck me most about this passage? What did I notice that I hadn't noticed before?
2. How can we fulfill the Father's command to listen to Christ in the here and now of our lives?
3. Why do you think Jesus only took these three disciples (the three who would be next to him in Gethsemane as well) up the mountain? Why not take all the disciples?
4. What mountaintop experiences has God given me? How does he want me to make use of them?

Cf. Catechism of the Catholic Church, 444,459, 554-556 on the meaning of the Transfiguration

55. THE FISHERMAN CATCHES A FISH (MT 17:14-27)

"God might give him this answer... 'Fix your eyes on him alone, because in him I have spoken and revealed all. Moreover, in him you will find more than you ask or desire.'"

- St John of the Cross

Matthew 17:14-27

As they were rejoining the crowd a man came up to him and went down on his knees before him. 'Lord,' he said 'take pity on my son: he is a lunatic and in a wretched state; he is always falling into the fire or into the water. I took him to your disciples and they were unable to cure him.' 'Faithless and perverse generation!' Jesus said in reply 'How much longer must I be with you? How much longer must I put up with you? Bring him here to me.' And when Jesus rebuked it the devil came out of the boy who was cured from that moment. Then the disciples came privately to Jesus. 'Why were we unable to cast it out? they asked. He answered, 'Because you have little faith. I tell you solemnly, if your faith were the size of a mustard seed you could say to this mountain, Move from here to there, and it would move; nothing would be impossible for you.' [2]

One day when they were together in Galilee, Jesus said to them, 'The Son of Man is going to be handed over into the power of men; they will put him to death, and on the third day he will be raised to life again'. And a great sadness came over them. When they reached Capernaum, the collectors of the half shekel came to Peter and said, 'Does your master not pay the half-shekel?' 'Oh yes' he replied, and went into the house. But before he could speak, Jesus said, 'Simon, what is your opinion? From whom do the kings of the earth take toll or tribute? From their sons or from foreigners?' And when he replied, 'From foreigners', Jesus said, 'Well then, the sons are exempt. However, so as not to offend these people, go to the lake and cast a hook; take the first fish that bites, open its mouth and there you will find a shekel; take it and give it to them for me and for you.'

CHRIST THE LORD   Peter clearly doesn't want Jesus to get into more trouble with the authorities than he is in already. So he commits Jesus to paying the Temple tax (all Jewish males older than nineteen were required to pay the annual tax) without first consulting him. Peter's intentions are wholesome, but Jesus doesn't let the moment go by without taking advantage of it to reiterate the constant refrain of these last few chapters: Jesus is greater than the Temple; he has come to establish a New Covenant; he is not merely a mighty rabbi or a powerful human king or even a wise prophet – he is the Messiah, the Son of God. Taxes are for subjects who aren't of the King's family, not for the King. Jesus' dialogue with Peter points out once again that he is the Lord of lords, to whom everyone else owes allegiance and obedience, even the fish of the sea.

---

[2] *Some manuscripts add a line to this sentence: "But this kind never comes out except by prayer and fasting." The official Catholic Bible (the New Vulgate) does not include this line here, though some other translations do.*

CHRIST THE TEACHER In the last few chapters of St Matthew's Gospel, Peter has been emerging more and more clearly as the leader of the apostles. Here the Temple guards come up to him, acknowledging him as the group's spokesman. When Jesus has Peter pay the tax for both of them, he is identifying him in a special way with his mission; Christ's future vicar shares his royal authority (thus the fish coughs up only one coin and its value covers both payments). Jesus has traveled all over Palestine healing and teaching, but his most important work up to now has been preparing the apostles, laying the foundations for his Church, the new Israel, the sacrament of salvation for all the world. The Church wasn't a post-Christ invention; it was the Lord's plan from the very beginning.

CHRIST THE FRIEND As soon as Jesus and his three closest disciples come down from the mountain after the Transfiguration, they are met with a crisis: a seething demonic possession that the disciples couldn't resolve. How familiar this experience is for every Christian! A beautiful weekend retreat, an inspiring meditation – and then life's hustle and bustle come mercilessly roaring back. Jesus isn't fazed. What bothers him isn't the desperate man pleading for his son to be healed; rather it is the disciples' lack of faith. For some reason, they were not able to expel the demon, and Jesus says point blank it's because they still don't believe enough. A robust faith is sufficient for all the disciple's needs and crises; that's the lesson of the comparison between the mustard seed (something so small as to be almost invisible) and the mountain, a radical disproportion between appearances and effects. The apostles' lack of this faith is also the reason Jesus has to describe yet again his coming passion – and they still can't understand it; they just grow sad at the thought of it.

In a sense, this sadness is a good sign. It shows that the apostles are listening to Jesus; his comments about having to suffer have registered in their minds. Nevertheless, in these encounters, St Matthew highlights Jesus' frustration at the weak faith of his disciples, still so frail even after all they have seen. The thought of Jesus having to suffer upsets them; they still doubt his lordship, and that makes Christ's cross even heavier. Nothing hurts a friend more than lack of trust from his friends.

Peter: In these days, Jesus was preoccupied, and we didn't understand why. How little we understood him! And yet he never stopped instructing us, walking with us, and encouraging us. How our blindness and slowness must have pained him! But his love went deeper than his suffering. He put up with my impetuosity, and he did so with the warm smile of a friend, of a brother, or even of a father. He always stays by the side of his followers. He always finds a way to speak the truth without crushing the needy soul. In later years, remembering his example of tireless patience and merciful love became my daily sustenance…

CHRIST IN MY LIFE Often following you seems to be such a chore, Lord, and I forget who you really are. You are the creator of the universe, the all-knowing God, the Savior and Redeemer. And you have deigned to look at me, to invite me to follow you, to serve you and work for your Kingdom, just as you invited your first apostles. You want to walk with me, to share my life, to lead me to the fullness of life. Thank you, Lord; never let me be separated from you…

Bless the pope, Lord. Bless the bishops. I believe in you, and I believe in your promise to be with your Church until the end of time. I want to build up the Church. Teach me love it as you do. Grant saintly priests to the world. Give wisdom and fortitude to everyone in the Church. Help me to see all things with the eyes of faith. We are weak, but you are strong; when we are weak, then we are strong in you…

Sometimes I have such shortsighted vision. You are the Lord of life and history. You are guiding all human lives and all human events. Nothing escapes your omniscience and omnipotence. And you have given me a job to do in this grand plan of salvation. I want to do it. And with you, I can. Increase my faith, and nothing will be impossible for me…

QUESTIONS FOR SMALL GROUP DISCUSSION

1. What struck me most about this passage? What did I notice that I hadn't noticed before?

2. How do you think Peter felt after this conversation with Jesus?

3. How do Christians today express their faith in Christ? What are some practical things we can do to increase our faith?

4. What aspects of today's popular culture encourage and support our faith? What aspects threaten and weaken it?

Cf. Catechism of the Catholic Church, 65-67 on Jesus as mediator and fullness of all revelation; 599-605 on Jesus' death in God's redemptive plan; 2828, 2836, and 2861 on our trust in God

THE GOSPEL OF MATTHEW CHAPTER 18

"Sick, our nature demanded to be healed; fallen, to be raised up; dead, to rise again. We had lost the possession of the good; it was necessary for it to be given back to us. Closed in the darkness, it was necessary to bring us the light; captives, we awaited a Savior; prisoners, help; slaves, a liberator. Are these things minor or insignificant? Did

they not move God to descend to human nature and visit it, since humanity was in so miserable and unhappy a state?"

- St Gregory of Nyssa

56. GREAT AND LITTLE (MT 18:1-14)

"As God sees the world tottering to ruin because of fear, he acts unceasingly to bring it back by love, to invite it by grace, to hold it by charity and clasp it firmly with affection."
- St Peter Chrysologus

Matthew 18:1-14

At this time the disciples came to Jesus and said, 'Who is the greatest in the kingdom of heaven?' So he called a little child to him and set the child in front of them. Then he said, 'I tell you solemnly, unless you change and become like little children you will never enter the kingdom of heaven. And so, the one who makes himself as little as this little child is the greatest in the kingdom of heaven.

'Anyone who welcomes a little child like this in my name welcomes me. But anyone who is an obstacle to bring down one of these little ones who have faith in me would be better drowned in the depths of the sea with a great millstone round his neck. Alas for the world that there should be such obstacles! Obstacles indeed there must be, but alas for the man who provides them! 'If your hand or your foot should cause you to sin, cut it off and throw it away: it is better for you to enter into life crippled or lame, than to have two hands or two feet and be thrown into eternal fire. And if your eye should cause you to sin, tear it out and throw it away: it is better for you to enter into life with one eye, than to have two eyes and be thrown into the hell of fire. 'See that you never despise any of these little ones, for I tell you that their angels in heaven are continually in the presence of my Father in heaven.[3]

'Tell me. Suppose a man has a hundred sheep and one of them strays; will he not leave the ninety-nine on the hillside and go in search of the stray? I tell you solemnly, if he finds it, it gives him more joy than do the ninety-nine that did not stray at all. Similarly, it is never the will of your Father in heaven that one of these little ones should be lost.'

CHRIST THE LORD Great leaders look for great lieutenants. Every Charlemagne has his Alcuin, every Alexander the Great his Lysimachus; what King doesn't want to surround himself with the most intelligent, intrepid, imposing, good-looking, and powerful assistants? This one! Christ doesn't look for what the world looks for. His Kingdom is built on stronger stuff. The saints don't

---

[3] *Some ancient manuscripts here add, "For the Son of Man came to save the lost."*

become saints because they are eloquent, gorgeous, bright, or athletic. They become saints because they discover God's love and let it conquer their hearts. Jesus taught this lesson before, back in Chapter 11; now he drives it home. To find the true meaning of life and unleash your true potential requires trusting in God more than in yourself, letting God's grace flow through and maximize your natural talents.

As the Lord continues preparing his first lieutenants, then, he wants to be as clear as possible: the Church is the family of God, not a political party; the leaders of the Church must be like Christ, meek and humble of heart, so they can in turn teach others the true path to self-fulfillment now and in eternity: forgetting oneself.

CHRIST THE TEACHER Jesus uses some powerful language in his discussion of sin and temptation. The image of cutting off one's hand or foot, or gouging out one's eye is not meant to be taken literally – although throughout the ages, some overzealous converts have done so. It is never the member or the organ that really causes the sin; these are simply instruments. Sin is a spiritual decision, and it always arises from the heart. The point of the comparison lies elsewhere than literal self-mutilations. It illustrates the damage sin does to the sinner and to society. Sin is so damaging – because it separates the soul from God, its sustainer and goal – that any physical suffering, deformation or deprivation is infinitely preferable to even the slightest moral evil.

Sin is not a popular topic in today's culture. It is much more chic to speak of psychological complexes, childhood trauma, and social conditioning – anything that remits personal responsibility. Although external influences do affect human actions, habits, and personalities, the overwhelmingly clear lesson of this passage is that sin matters. Sin is purposely choosing to do evil, to break the moral law that God built into human nature as a natural guide to happiness and fulfillment. And sin has dire consequences. Especially for those who have been given responsibility to lead in the Church, or in a family, or in a community: Jesus knows that some of these leaders will abuse their privileged position and cause others to fall away from the right path, but he makes no excuses for them. Rather, he warns all of his disciples to decide once and for all to declare sin their archenemy. And as for anything that may lead to sin – get rid of it! Cut it off! Few places in the Gospels does Jesus speak so harshly. Maybe he really meant what he said.

CHRIST THE FRIEND The early Christians had a special affinity for the image of Christ as the Good Shepherd, an affinity which Jesus seems to have shared. It appears in the earliest Christian art, like the catacombs and tombstones. At that time everyone lived closer to the land, and shepherds were familiar figures. It is a comparison worth considering deeply.

Some of the early Church Fathers saw in this image a snapshot of all salvation history. The ninety-nine sheep that never strayed represent the angels who stayed faithful when Satan rebelled (this ties in nicely with this context: in warning his Apostles to respect and protect the innocent and weak, Jesus has just referred to angels – guardian angels, most commentators agree). The one lost sheep stands for the human race, which was led astray by the devil. The hills represent heaven, whence Jesus descended in the Incarnation in order to rescue the one lost sheep and carry it back home to eternal life.

What stands out most in this allegorical interpretation is the gratuitous nature of Christ's saving mission. What good did it do him to come and save us from destruction and sin? None – all the good he does is for us. What the allegory misses, though, is even more important. Jesus wasn't satisfied with merely saving the poor sheep; he decided to befriend them, to lift them even higher than the angels and give them a share in his own divine life, so that they could enjoy a real, everlasting intimacy with him. No longer would it be shepherd-to-sheep, but friend-to-friend: redeemed mankind becomes Christ's brothers and sisters.

CHRIST IN MY LIFE Lord, I want to receive the message you suffered so much to give. I want to live it out. Teach me, Lord. You who are meek and humble of heart, make my heart more and more like yours...

Why do I still flirt with sin? Only you know, Lord. But you also know that I believe in you, and I want to grow in virtue and in grace, not in selfishness. Give me strength to break definitively with every sin, and every habit of self-indulgence that puts me into tempting situations. You know better than I do how much I need your help, especially with this. I know you will never let me down. May your fidelity be my fidelity...

When you saw me lost and in danger from the wolves, you came to rescue me. Thank you for not giving up on me. Never let me be separated from you. But what about all the other sheep that are still lost, stuck in the briars of vice and lies? I know you care about them too. And I know that's why you send me to them. I want to bring them home to you. But how can I without your help?

QUESTIONS FOR SMALL GROUP DISCUSSION

1. What struck me most about this passage? What did I notice that I hadn't noticed before?

2. What is the idea of sin that popular culture communicates? How does it compare to Christ's conception of it?

3. Why are we attracted by temptation? What are the best weapons to resist temptation?

4. In practical terms, how can we be better sheepdogs to help the Good Shepherd round up his beloved lost sheep?

Cf. Catechism of the Catholic Church, 1472-1473 on punishments of sin; 943 on ways to uproot sin; 1853-1854 on distinguishing different types of sin; 1459 on the weakened life of the sinner; 478 on the personal love in Christ's heart

57. UNITED WE STAND (MT 18:15-20)

"He proved that neither unity nor peace could be kept unless the brethren treat one another with mutual forbearance, and preserve the bond of concord through patience."

- St Cyprian

Matthew 18:15-20

'If your brother does something wrong, go and have it out with him alone, between your two selves. If he listens to you, you have won back your brother. If he does not listen, take one or two others along with you: the evidence of two or three witnesses is required to sustain any charge. But if he refuses to listen to these, report it to the community; and if he refuses to listen to the community, treat him like a pagan or a tax collector. I tell you solemnly, whatever you bind on earth shall be considered bound in heaven; whatever you loose on earth shall be considered loosed in heaven. 'I tell you solemnly once again, if two of you on earth agree to ask anything at all, it will be granted to you by my Father in heaven. For where two or three meet in my name, I shall be there with them.'

CHRIST THE LORD We come once again upon Christ instructing his Twelve as the end of his earthly mission draws near. He is preparing them to govern his Church. Critics accuse St Matthew of misquoting Jesus in this passage, since he references a Church organization that would not have existed until well after Jesus' ascension into heaven. But if Christ knew of his coming passion and resurrection, would he not have known of his future Church and be able to refer to it? The context (Jesus instructing his Twelve) and the meaning (that every effort should be made to reconcile recalcitrant Christians with God and with the Church) of the passage, in any case, cohere perfectly with St Matthew's whole series of instructions to the apostles. Likewise, the first generations of Christians never disputed Christ's intention to build the Church upon the "foundation of the apostles" (Ephesians 2:20). Clearly, Jesus knew that the time of his earthly Lordship was ending, and he expressly transferred his authority to those he had chosen. The Church was the willed invention of Christ the Lord, not the other way around.

CHRIST THE TEACHER We must do everything we possibly can to bring one another back when we stray. We must hold each other accountable – not by arrogantly judging our brothers and sisters (we can hardly see the speck in their eyes for the plank in our own, remember), but by reaching out to them when they are in trouble. This passage follows Christ's parable of the good shepherd who leaves his ninety-nine sheep alone in order to seek out the one who has strayed. Christ is insisting here that his ministers have the same selfless and determined attitude.

The leader of the Christian community is traditionally called a pastor, which comes from the Latin word for shepherd. Bishops are pastors of their diocese; priests are pastors of their parishes; all Christians, in a sense, are pastors of those souls entrusted to their spiritual or physical care. With this instruction, Jesus is enjoining each of us (but especially his ordained ministers, those who will carry on the ministry of his Twelve Apostles) to give everyone the attention they need, to go after the wandering sheep, and to do everything possible to bring them back into the safety of his fold.

CHRIST THE FRIEND Friends like to be together. Christ likes to be with us. When we "gather in his name" (especially as a whole community in the Sunday celebration of the Eucharist, but also in less official ways), he gathers with us. When we offer our prayers as members of the one family of God, he joins his own voice to ours, insuring that they will please the Father and win his favor. The Christian community is unique; it is not based merely on common goals, hobbies, or preferences. Instead, it is a real but mystical unity brought about by Christ's own presence among us. For this reason, a Catholic community (especially the parish) will always include all types – young and old, fervent and apathetic, pleasant and crotchety, ignorant and learned, rich and poor. As one reluctant member put it, the Catholic Church can be defined as "Here comes everybody!" That's because Christ is a faithful friend to each of us; he plays no favorites… and neither should we.

CHRIST IN MY LIFE You never envisioned any of your followers going it alone. You chose your first disciples and built them into a community. Now, centuries later, that community still exists; it's still growing and thriving, in spite of continuous attacks. I am glad to be a member of your Church, Lord. I don't want to give into the temptation to be a loner. I want to be a Christian, now and forever, securely incorporated into your mystical body...

I have so many things on my to-do list, Lord, that sometimes I forget the most important thing: fidelity to my Christian mission of being another Christ. Your first priority was bringing people back into communion with God, showing them the Father's love, and teaching them the way to fullness of life. Make me more aware of other's needs – physical, emotional, and spiritual. Love them, Lord, through me...

At times, I can get a little frustrated with the humanity of your Church. But you never do. Teach me rather to see the Church as you see it. Teach me to forgive, make excuses for, and help all my brothers and sisters, not just the ones I naturally get along with. Help me to care for and love my pastors in concrete ways. Teach me to welcome them, as you always welcome me...

QUESTIONS FOR SMALL GROUP DISCUSSION

1. What struck me most about this passage? What did I notice that I hadn't noticed before?

2. How is Christ's vision of unity among his believers being lived out in my local Catholic community? How aware are we that he is present when we gather in his name? What can we do to live this out more fully?

3. Why would Christ say that our prayer is more efficacious when "two or three are gathered in his name" than when we pray alone?

4. What are some concrete ways we encourage our fellow Christians to greater fidelity without putting ourselves on a pedestal or making them feel rejected?

Cf. Catechism of the Catholic Church, 1536-1571 on the sacrament of holy orders and the place of the priesthood in the Church; 1585-1589 on how priests and bishops should perform their ministry; 781-796 on the nature of the Church; 763-765 on Christ's institution of the Church

58. OCEAN OF MERCY (MT 18:21-35)

"O Christian, be aware of your nobility – it is God's own nature that you share; do not then, by an ignoble life, fall back into your former baseness."

- Pope St Leo the Great

Matthew 18:21-35

Then Peter went up to him and said, 'Lord, how often must I forgive my brother if he wrongs me? As often as seven times?' Jesus answered, 'Not seven, I tell you, but seventy-seven times.

'And so the kingdom of heaven may be compared to a king who decided to settle his accounts with his servants. When the reckoning began, they brought him a man who owed ten thousand talents; but he had no means of paying, so his master gave orders that he should be sold, together with his wife and children and all his possessions, to meet the debt. At this, the servant threw himself down at his master's feet. Give me time he said and I will pay the whole sum. And the servant's master felt so sorry for him that he let him go and cancelled the debt. Now as this servant went out, he happened to meet a fellow servant who owed him one hundred denarii; and he seized him by the throat and began to throttle him. Pay what you owe me he said. His fellow servant fell at his feet and implored him, saying, Give me time and I will pay you. But the other would not agree; on the contrary, he had him thrown into prison till he should pay the debt. His fellow servants were deeply distressed when they saw what had happened, and they went to their master and reported the whole affair to him. Then the master sent for him. You wicked servant, he said, I cancelled all that debt of yours when you appealed to me. Were you not bound, then, to have pity on your fellow servant just as I had pity on you? And in his anger the master handed him over to the torturers till he should pay all his debt. And that is how my heavenly Father will deal with you unless you each forgive your brother from your heart.'

CHRIST THE LORD This passage immediately follows Jesus' instructions to his Twelve about being good shepherds. That instruction took place in a small gathering after a full day of ministry. One can imagine the disciples discussing it. Possibly, one of the many quarrels among them arose as their discussion turned upon how many times they should go after the same sheep if it keeps wandering away. Rabbinic teaching at the time placed the limit of forgiveness at three times – a fourth offense was not to be forgiven. Perhaps Peter was proposing a reform of this custom in light of Christ's lesson, while some of the others were sticking to the traditional view, and so he brought it to the Lord to settle the question. That was the right thing to do. The buck stops with Jesus. He is the Lord; he is the final word God has spoken to us. In him we have the answers we need for every dilemma we face. Like Peter, we should bring our questions to the Lord in prayer; we should cast the light of the Church's teachings on our moral and intellectual quandaries. And, also like Peter, we should accept Christ's solution.

CHRIST THE TEACHER In Christ, God offers us forgiveness of a debt we could never pay – the debt of sin. But when we refuse to forgive the little offenses others cause us, we handcuff God's mercy and put ourselves under strict justice. Previously, Christ pointed out, "For as you judge, so will you be judged, and the measure with which you measure will be measured out to you" (Matthew

7:2). This is the way God has found to unfurl his mercy without compromising his justice; he leaves each person free to choose between the two.

But this lesson is hard for us to learn. We tend to resent not only willful of-fenses, but also innocent mistakes. Whenever someone else causes us even a tiny inconvenience, we can easily lash out at the offender. This is especially the case close to home – we often have less patience with our siblings, parents, spouses, children, or roommates than we do with strangers and acquaintances.

In this parable, as in the Our Father, Jesus gives us the secret to forming a patient, forgiving heart. It consists in recognizing the immense evil of our own sin, and thereby perceiving the vastness of God's goodness in forgiving it. Until we see the ugliness of the ingratitude and selfishness that characterize our relationship with God, we will never grasp how generous his forgiveness really is. When we do, however, our shriveled hearts expand, and our joyful patience knows no bounds.

CHRIST THE FRIEND This brilliant parable rightly convicts us of our repul-sive self-righteousness, but we should not therefore overlook its illustration of Christ's magnanimity. Jesus himself is the King who forgives the "huge amount." In the Greek text, this amount is quantified as 10,000 talents – an unimagi-nable, astronomical quantity of money. Likewise, Christ's compassion exceeds even the malice of his own murderers: "Father, forgive them, they know not what they do," he spoke from the cross (Luke 23:34).

Jesus: You can count on my forgiveness. You just need to do what this servant did: kneel down before me and ask for it. I know that sometimes it's hard for you to accept this forgiveness; your pride keeps you from forgiving yourself, so you hold my forgiveness at arm's length, or you doubt it. I don't want you to doubt my forgiveness. I want you to be absolutely sure. This is why I made it tangible in the sacrament of reconciliation. When you come to me through the ministry of my chosen, ordained priest, you actually hear my own words speaking through his voice: "I absolve you from your sins…." I invented this wonderful gift just for you, just so I could flood the depths of your misery with the ocean of my mercy.

CHRIST IN MY LIFE It amazes me to think that I can always come to you; I can always ask you a question; you are always available. You never cease think-ing of me. Like Peter, I can turn to you to resolve my doubts. Why do I turn to you so infrequently? Why do I forget about your presence, your guidance, your passionate interest in my life?

Forgiveness is harder for me in some cases than others. Some people who have wounded me really don't deserve to be forgiven, Lord. And yet, you offer your forgiveness to them. Why, then, do I resist? Free me from this snare of the devil. Teach me to forgive, no matter how I feel. Refresh my embittered heart. You love even those who have offended me terribly, and you can turn them into saints...

Thank you for putting no limits on how much you would forgive me. Thank you for continuing to assure me of your forgiveness through confession. There is no hesitancy in your love for me, no holding back, no tinge of self-seeking. Why don't I trust you more? Jesus, teach me to trust you more...

QUESTIONS FOR SMALL GROUP DISCUSSION

1. What struck me most about this passage? What did I notice that I hadn't noticed before?

2. Why didn't the servant forgive the man who owed him a small debt, even after he himself had been forgiven such a large debt?

3. In what circumstances is it especially hard to forgive or to show patience and understanding to others?

4. Why do many Catholics tend not to make regular use of the sacrament of reconciliation? What can we do to promote this beautiful sacrament in our Catholic community?

Cf. Catechism of the Catholic Church, 2838-2445 on the link between our forgiving and God's forgiving; 1485-1498 on the sacrament of reconciliation

THE GOSPEL OF MATTHEW CHAPTER 19

"Consider that God wants to fill you up with honey, but if you are already full of vinegar where will you put the honey? What was in the vessel must be emptied out; the vessel itself must be washed out and made clean and scoured, hard work though it may be, so that it be made fit for something else, whatever it may be."

- St Augustine

59. MARRIED IN CHRIST (MT 19:1-15)

"Yes: the wife and the mother is the radiant sun of the family. She is this sun by her generosity and gift of self, by her unfailing readiness, by her watchful and prudent delicacy in all matters which can add joy to the lives of her husband and her children. She spreads around her light and warmth."

- Pope Pius XII

Matthew 19:1-15

Jesus had now finished what he wanted to say, and he left Galilee and came into the part of Judaea which is on the far side of the Jordan. Large crowds followed him and he healed them there. Some Pharisees approached him, and to test him they said, 'Is it against the Law for a man to divorce his wife on any pretext whatever?' He answered, 'Have you not read that the creator from the beginning made them male and female and that he said: This is why a man must leave father and mother, and cling to his wife, and the two become one body? They are no longer two, therefore, but one body. So then, what God has united, man must not divide'. They said to him, 'Then why did Moses command that a writ of dismissal should be given in cases of divorce?' 'It was because you were so unteachable' he said 'that Moses allowed you to divorce your wives, but it was not like this from the beginning. Now I say this to you: the man who divorces his wife – I am not speaking of fornication – and marries another, is guilty of adultery.' The disciples said to him, 'If that is how things are between husband and wife, it is not advisable to marry'. But he replied, 'It is not everyone who can accept what I have said, but only those to whom it is granted. There are eunuchs born that way from their mother's womb, there are eunuchs made so by men and there are eunuchs who have made themselves that way for the sake of the kingdom of heaven. Let anyone accept this who can.'

People brought little children to him, for him to lay his hands on them and say a prayer. The disciples turned them away, but Jesus said, 'Let the little children alone, and do not stop them coming to me; for it is to such as these that the kingdom of heaven belongs.' Then he laid his hands on them and went on his way.

CHRIST THE LORD Once again Jesus gives the Pharisees a chance to accept him for who he really is: the Lord, the new Lawgiver, the Son of God. As he makes his way towards Jerusalem and the culmination of his mission, the Pharisees charge forward with yet another attack, another attempt to discredit and ruin him. The trap they set is subtle. If Jesus responds by saying that divorce is permitted in any case, they can accuse him of falsifying the Mosaic Law, which put limiting stipulations on divorce. If he says that divorce is not permitted at all, then he may fall prey to the same Herodian wrath that ended John the Baptist's career (being "on the far side of Jordan," Jesus is now in the territory ruled by Herod, who had divorced his lawful wife to marry his mistress, who also happened to be his sister-in-law). The Pharisees are still not interested in a true answer; they only want to undermine Christ's credibility.

And Jesus responds as he always does, taking their dishonest ploy as a chance to bring them face to face with what they need and fear most, the truth, in hopes that some of them will see at least a glimmer of the light. He answers by appealing to the Scriptures, as every good rabbi and Pharisee would do, but calls on a higher authority than Moses to resolve the dilemma: the Creator himself, and his original plan for the union of man and woman. In doing so, he repeats his refrain from the Sermon on the Mount, "Now I say this to you," setting himself above Moses, the giver of the old law. Jesus brings the Old Covenant to its fullness, restores the fallen human race to its state of grace, like children, and does so with the utmost respect and charity, speaking in a way perfectly suited to win over his unwilling interlocutors. And this is the Lord we follow.

CHRIST THE TEACHER Two of Jesus' most controversial teachings emerge from this conversation: his unqualified prohibition of divorce and remarriage, and his advocacy of freely chosen celibacy.

Jesus' teaching on divorce and remarriage is much discussed. The disciples understood his message clearly: divorce and remarriage is simply not permitted. This is why they reacted with such shock, saying that it's better never to get married in the first place if you don't have the safety valve of divorce and remarriage. Christ's teaching differed from the Jewish tradition, in which Moses had legally circumscribed the ubiquitous practice of divorce in order to safeguard as much dignity and justice as possible. But Jesus reestablishes God's original plan. He explicitly shows that the marriage bond is not man-made; marriage is an institution inscribed in human nature by the Creator's wisdom. Here is the origin of Jesus' elevation of marriage to a sacrament: in order to reestablish the original institution, severely damaged by original sin, he turns it into an efficacious sign of God's New Covenant grace. And so, in Jesus' eyes, and in truth, the marriage bond, established in nature and grace by God himself, cannot be broken. Divorce and remarriage are identical to adultery. Only when the marriage bond itself never took form, due to some impediment, can an apparent marriage be annulled. This has been the invariable teaching of the Church from its inception.[4]

Jesus then takes advantage of the disciples' shock at this strict view of marriage to issue his teaching on celibacy, the state of life that he has chosen for himself. His use of the term "eunuch" elucidates his view. In ancient times, kings and

---

[4] *According to the Ignatius Catholic Study Bible, the phrase that many Protestant churches mistakenly use to justify divorce and remarriage (translated here "I am not speaking of an illicit marriage") is properly understood in one of three ways: 1) recognizing that certain behavior merits the separation of spouses temporarily or permanently; 2) referring to apparent marriages that the Church can legitimately annul; 3) a way for Jesus to sidestep rabbinical squabbles about conditions that justified divorce.*

emperors in the Middle East and the East often had more than one wife, in addition to a harem of concubines. The king's officials in charge of taking care of his wives and harem were frequently eunuchs, men either naturally impotent or physically castrated. This saved the king from suspicion of infidelity. When Jesus refers to celibacy as a freely chosen state of life, then, he creates a new category of followers: ministers of his Kingdom who willingly embrace celibacy, as Christ did, and dedicate themselves to caring for his bride, the Church.

Both these teachings were hard for people of his time to accept, as Jesus recognizes ("let anyone accept this who can"). Even after twenty centuries' worth of evidence for their benefits (both natural and supernatural), they still stand as signs of contradiction.

CHRIST THE FRIEND *Philip: There was such a throng of women with their children, and they were all trying to get close to Jesus – all at the same time. We thought we were doing him a favor by shielding him from their bothersome entreaties. He had more important things to do, or so we thought. He disagreed. He wasn't pleased at all with our bodyguarding. He wanted everyone to come close; he wanted to bless all the children. They were so happy, those mothers, and the children too. They just couldn't get enough of him. It was such a contrast to the Pharisees, who kept their distance. We talked about this meeting a lot later. It gave us such insight into what his kingdom is like. Earthly kingdoms are so often built on vain self-importance and impressive pomp. But his kingdom belongs to those who, like little children, are helpless and long for his healing and strengthening touch.*

CHRIST IN MY LIFE Your doctrine is demanding, Lord, but it is true, because you are Truth. Although I don't always understand the reasons behind what you ask or permit, I trust in you, and so I want to accept and obey. In the end, this brief journey through life is only a tiny point in the midst of eternity. I want to follow you now, and to help others follow you, so we all can be together with you then...

Lord, help me to trust in the vocation that you have called me to. Everyone's vocation is unique and personal, but you call each of us to faithful love, no matter what our state in life is. You want me to give myself purely, to love others always in, through, and with you. With the love of your heart, Lord, inflame my heart, so it will love just as yours does...

Who am I more like – the Pharisees or the children? I am like both. In many ways I assert my self-importance and try to dominate and manipulate. But in my heart, I also recognize that without you I can do nothing. This is the battle still raging in my soul. Come with the weapons of your grace and give this child your victory. Advance your Kingdom in my soul, Lord, so I can help advance it in others...

QUESTIONS FOR SMALL GROUP DISCUSSION

1. What struck you most about this passage? What did you notice that you hadn't noticed before?

2. Why do you think these two Catholic teachings – divorce and remarriage, voluntary celibacy – are so hard to accept in today's society?

3. Jesus' encounter with the children here is seen as the foundation for infant baptism. What does it tell us about the sacrament of baptism?

4. In this passage Jesus speaks about marriage and children. How would you describe God's view of family life? Do you think the teaching on celibacy demeans marriage and family or elevates it? Why?

Cf. Catechism of the Catholic Church, 1579 and 1618-1620 on celibacy and virginity for the sake of the Kingdom; 1602-1617 on marriage in God's plan; 403 and 1250-1252 on the baptism of infants

60. GIVING UP AND GETTING MORE (MT 19:16-30)

"Penance then is, as it were, a salutary weapon placed in the hands of the valiant soldiers of Christ, who wish to fight for the defense and restoration of the moral order in the universe. It is a weapon that strikes right at the root of all evil, that is at the lust of material wealth and the wanton pleasures of life."

- Pope Pius XI

Matthew 19:16-30

And there was a man who came to him and asked, 'Master, what good deed must I do to possess eternal life?' Jesus said to him, 'Why do you ask me about what is good? There is one alone who is good. But if you wish to enter into life, keep the commandments.' He said, 'Which?' 'These:' Jesus replied 'You must not kill. You must not commit adultery. You must not bring false witness. Honour your father and mother, and: you must love your neighbour as yourself.' The young man said to him, 'I have kept all these. What more do I need to do?' Jesus said, 'If you wish to be perfect, go and sell what you own and give the money to the poor, and you will have treasure in heaven; then come, follow me'. But when the young man heard these words he went away sad, for he was a man of great wealth. Then Jesus said to his disciples, 'I tell you solemnly, it will be hard for a rich man to enter the kingdom of heaven. Yes, I tell you again, it is easier for a camel to pass through the eye of a needle than for a rich man to enter the kingdom of heaven.'

When the disciples heard this they were astonished. 'Who can be saved, then?' they said. Jesus gazed at them. 'For men' he told them 'this is impossible; for God everything is possible.' Then Peter spoke. 'What about us?' he said to him 'We have left everything and followed you. What are we to have, then?' Jesus said to him, 'I tell you solemnly, when all is made new and the Son of Man sits on his throne of glory, you will yourselves sit on twelve thrones to judge the twelve tribes of Israel. And everyone who has left houses, brothers, sisters, father, mother, children or land for the sake of my name will be repaid a hundred times over, and also inherit eternal life. 'Many who are first will be last, and the last, first.'

CHRIST THE LORD Who has ever spoken with as much authority as Christ? This man comes to him with the greatest of all questions; he asks about the meaning of life, about how to achieve lasting fulfillment. Jesus doesn't hem and haw; he doesn't present the various hypotheses of the great philosophers; he speaks clearly, simply, powerfully. Jesus knows the answer. And when the young man refuses to accept it, Jesus turns and makes such sweeping statements that he shocks even his faithful apostles. He turns the wisdom of this world on its head by identifying the dangers of earthly success, and then he proclaims his mastery over both this world and the next. He claims to know everything: how to achieve happiness; what the greatest obstacle to happiness is; the limits of human nature and the manner of God's interventions; the past, the present, and the future.... He even paints a picture of eternity itself, with him on the throne of glory and his Twelve Apostles enthroned all around him, ruling together the new heavens and the new earth. Who has ever spoken with such audacity? Only Jesus Christ, the Lord of life and history, the one who knows you and calls you by name.

CHRIST THE TEACHER In this brief encounter, Jesus sums up mankind's entire moral life.

He tacitly acknowledges that the questioner is seeking the right purpose: eternal life, the fullness of life, and authentic happiness. He points out that the minimum requirement for this life is to follow the moral law that God has inscribed in human nature, the foundation for all the rest. And then he reveals what no one else ever has or ever could have revealed: the fullness of human life, for which every human heart yearns without respite, comes only and exclusively from following him – from an intimate, personal friendship with Jesus Christ that leads to the communion with God for which man was created. That's the path to a fulfilled and flourishing life.

But the path is strewn with snares. In order to follow Christ and live in friendship with him, you have to trust in him more than in yourself; you have to be willing to relinquish the reins of your life. This is what the fallen human heart, so wounded by sin and by the sins of others, finds hardest of all to do: trust. That's why money becomes the greatest snare and the source of so many others. Not because money is evil in itself (in fact, for the Jews of Jesus' time, wealth was considered one of God's blessings, which explains the disciples' surprise at Christ's revaluation), but because it gives you the illusion that you can fend for yourself, that you can crack life's mystery on your own. This is a particularly tempting illusion, since it actually holds true for material matters; money really does enable a man to fend for himself – in business and pleasure. Thus money gives the seductive illusion of security, even of omnipotence; money promises to solve every problem and meet every need, because it really does solve *so many* problems and meet *so many* needs.

But not the most important ones. You can have unlimited riches and still be miserable, confused, and unfulfilled. Only Christ, only the truth of God's love and his loving plan of salvation reaches into the heart and the conscience, where man's deepest needs and hardest problems dwell. You can be dirt poor, sick, abandoned, and even dying, but still be at peace, if you have Christ. This is why many that are "first" in the eyes of the world will actually end up "last," and many who are last in the eyes of the world will end up first in Christ's everlasting Kingdom.

Trusting in Christ is harder than trusting in money, because you can't control Christ. But you don't need to control Christ in order to find what your heart desires; you just need to follow him.

CHRIST THE FRIEND Jesus always invites; he never forces. He wants to shower every person with his gifts of fulfillment, meaning, and abundant life (he says those who follow him will receive "a hundred times as much"), but he can't do so if someone refuses his friendship.

St Matthew astutely observes that this young man "went away sad" after he refused Christ's invitation. His was a divided soul. He wanted a deeper, more meaningful life. He wanted the fullness of life that comes from intimacy with God, and yet at the same time he wasn't willing to give up his security, his self-sufficiency, or his hard-earned money that promised him comfort, influence, and respect in this world. And he went away sad, because he had already discovered that money and the things of this world couldn't satisfy his soul; even living an honest and moral life left him wanting more. And now, when he senses a chance at true meaning, he finds himself in chains. The chains are of his own making, but he can't seem to break free of them.

How Jesus' heart must have bled in the face of this young man who *almost* made the right choice. We can hear the righteous anger in his voice as he condemns the ruin that riches so easily cause; we can see the righteous fire in his eyes as he "gazed at" his disciples and then taught them the true path to fulfillment. Christ wants hearts, because he knows that only he can satisfy hearts – in a way that far surpasses our wildest imagining.

CHRIST IN MY LIFE   I think I am a good Christian. But do I really trust you as I ought? Maybe I follow the commandments, do all the right things, even teach catechism, and yet in the secret places of my heart I am still unhealthily unsatisfied. What do I need to give up in order to follow you as you wish and as I need to?...

So many people around me don't know you, Lord. They are searching for fulfillment in all the glitzy but wrong places. How can I tell them about you? What more can I do? What more do you want me to do?...

I know you are calling many young men and women to follow you more closely. First you stir their hearts, then they come to you, and finally you invite them. But how hard it is for them to give up this world's seductions and false promises! How good this passing world looks! They want to follow you, but they need you to give them courage. Please do, Lord. Send more workers to your harvest…

QUESTIONS FOR SMALL GROUP DISCUSSION

1. What struck you most about this passage? What did you see that you hadn't seen before?

2. Why didn't Jesus just tell this inquirer right away to give away his goods and follow him? Why engage in the whole conversation to get to that point?

3. Jesus' image of a camel going through the eye of a needle is a parable of impossibility: the rich can't get to heaven without God's help. How would you explain the reason behind this teaching to someone who questioned you about it? Can the poor get to heaven without God's help? What's the difference?

4. Why is it so hard for those Jesus is calling to the priesthood and consecrated life to follow him? What aspects of popular culture encourage those vocations? What aspects discourage them?

Cf. Catechism of the Catholic Church, 2113, 2172, 2424 and 2526 on the dangers of idolizing money; 1965-1974 on the New Law of the gospel

THE GOSPEL OF MATTHEW CHAPTER 20

"It is necessary that each person freely accept the truth of the love of God. He is Love and Truth, and love as well as truth never impose themselves: They knock on the door of the heart and mind and, where they enter, bring peace and joy. This is the way God reigns; this is his plan of salvation…"

- Pope Benedict XVI

61. GIVE AND TAKE (MT 20:1-19)

"It is not only as past history that we know all that the Son of God did and taught for the reconciliation of the world; here and now we feel the effects of its power."

- Pope St Leo the Great

Matthew 20:1-19

'Now the kingdom of heaven is like a landowner going out at daybreak to hire workers for his vineyard. He made an agreement with the workers for one denarius a day, and sent them to his vineyard. Going out at about the third hour he saw others standing idle in the market place and said to them, You go to my vineyard too and I will give you a fair wage. So they went. At about the sixth hour and again at about the ninth hour, he went out and did the same. Then at about the eleventh hour he went out and found more men standing round, and he said to them, Why have you been standing here idle all day? Because no one has hired us, they answered. He said to them, You go into my vineyard too. In the evening, the owner of the vineyard said to his bailiff, Call the workers and pay them their wages, starting with the last arrivals and ending with the first. So those who were hired at about the eleventh hour came forward and received one denarius each. When the first came, they expected to get more, but they too received one denarius each. They took it, but grumbled at the landowner. The men who came last, they said, have done only one hour, and you have treated them the same as us, though we have done a heavy day's work in all the heat. He answered one of them and said, My friend, I am not being unjust to you; did we not agree on one denarius? Take your earnings and go. I choose to pay the last comer as much as I pay you. Have I no right to do what I like with my own? Why be envious because I am generous? Thus the last will be first, and the first, last.'

Jesus was going up to Jerusalem, and on the way he took the Twelve to one side and said to them, 'Now we are going up to Jerusalem, and the Son of Man is about to be handed over to the chief priests and scribes. They will condemn him to death and will hand him over to the pagans to be mocked and scourged and crucified; and on the third day he will rise again.'

CHRIST THE LORD Christ is the generous landowner. To pay these hired work-ers a full day's wage for only a few hours of work is the epitome of generosity. Palestine's day laborers had no steady work and no steady income; they were hired on a daily basis. The workers still waiting to be given work late in the day were probably resigned to another hungry evening for themselves and their families. Only a man with a generous heart would take the trouble to put them to work when only an hour remained till sundown, and only an extraordinarily generous man would pay them the full day's wage.

Jesus Christ is extraordinarily generous; the history of salvation is the story of his boundless giving. First he gives life, then after the Fall he gives hope, then he gives redemption, and finally he gives everlasting heavenly bliss. Ultimately, we deserve none of those gifts, but his generosity is so great that he even cre-ates a chance for us to "earn" them. Just as the landowner gave the laborers real work to do in his vineyard, Christ has arranged the economy of salvation so that it is administered through his Church, through our own efforts to defend and extend his Kingdom throughout the world. We have a Lord whose infinite wealth is wholly at our service.

CHRIST THE TEACHER If our Lord and Leader is bountifully generous, how can we claim to be his followers if we don't follow suit? The landowner was looking out for the needs of his fellow men. He did not carelessly overcommit himself in order to meet them, and he did not sacrifice justice (he fulfilled his agreement with the first workers) or prudence (he made sure they all worked to gather the harvest, even if only for an hour), but he went beyond the con-fines of mere duty. How rarely we do this! We stand by our "rights" when they are not rights at all, grumbling enviously because someone else is more success-ful or more fortunate than us. What peace we would have if we rejoiced in all of God's gifts, and not only those he gives to us.

CHRIST THE FRIEND "The last will be first, and the first will be last." This is a warning. Christ tells this parable after Peter asks him what the Twelve will get in return for having given up everything to follow him. It most obviously applies to the Jewish people in general, and to the Twelve in particular: the Jews were the Chosen People, but when the eternal Kingdom appears, they may find others honored more than them; the Twelve were chosen to be the visible foundation of the Church, but in the end, others will achieve greatness in Christ's name as well.

Jesus wants us to have interior peace. Nothing disturbs us more than vying for honors and worrying over coveted esteem – and this can occur even within our own Christian communities. If we recognize the abundant generosity of God's love, we will trust him enough to discard such selfish motives, and we will look only to Christ for the unshakable security that only he can give.

Jesus not only teaches that lesson in this parable; he also clears the path with his own actions. At the end of this passage, St Matthew places the third prediction of Christ's passion. This time Jesus gets more specific, indicating the collaboration between Jewish and Gentile leaders, and even listing the different types of mistreatment he will suffer. Instead of honor, he will be scorned; instead of a reward, he will receive punishment; instead of praise, mockery. Accepting unjust humiliation and rejection is an odd recipe for success, but true nonetheless – those who seek first place will end up in last place, but those who humble themselves will be exalted. He treads the path first, so his friends won't fear to follow.

CHRIST IN MY LIFE Why am I resentful when others succeed more than me? Why do I grumble when others are praised and I am overlooked? Is it because I love you above all things and my neighbor as myself? Envy, jealousy, backbiting, criticism: these are the exact opposite of what you lived and what you call your disciples to live. Give me strength to master my emotions; make my heart more like yours…

You knew exactly what awaited you on your last trip to Jerusalem. And you didn't avoid it. You have called me to follow in your footsteps, and that means you will give me a share in your cross as I journey through my vocation. At times it makes me tremble. But all fear subsides when I remember that the cross unites me more to you, and that you never ask me to carry it alone…

You never tire of giving. You only want to give. You are pure love, pure generosity. Thank you, Lord, for all the gifts you have given to me. Thank you, Lord, for giving me a mission in life, and giving me the generosity to accept it. Now please give me the grace to persevere and please you…

QUESTIONS FOR SMALL GROUP DISCUSSION

1. What struck you most about this passage? What did you notice that you hadn't noticed before?

2. Can you think of any other scenes or words from the Gospels that express the generosity of God?

3. What are some practical things we can do to battle ingratitude towards God and our tendency to "grumble" enviously?

4. How would Christ define success? How does popular culture define success?

Cf. Catechism of the Catholic Church, 2534-2550 on envy and its antidotes; 2006-2011 on God's pure generosity and the possibility we have to gain merit because of our good works

62. SERVANTS AND SIGNS (MT 20:20-34)

"He it is whose sufferings are shared by the martyrs with their glorious courage and by all those who believe and are born again at the moment of their regeneration."

- Pope St Leo the Great

Matthew 20:20-34

Then the mother of Zebedee's sons came with her sons to make a request of him, and bowed low; and he said to her, 'What is it you want?' She said to him, 'Promise that these two sons of mine may sit one at your right hand and the other at your left in your kingdom'. 'You do not know what you are asking' Jesus answered. 'Can you drink the cup that I am going to drink?' They replied, 'We can.' 'Very well,' he said 'you shall drink my cup, but as for seats at my right hand and my left, these are not mine to grant; they belong to those to whom they have been allotted by my Father.' When the other ten heard this they were indignant with the two brothers. But Jesus called them to him and said, 'You know that among the pagans the rulers lord it over them, and their great men make their authority felt. This is not to happen among you. No; anyone who wants to be great among you must be your servant, and anyone who wants to be first among you must be your slave, just as the Son of Man came not to be served but to serve, and to give his life as a ransom for many.'

As they left Jericho a large crowd followed him. Now there were two blind men sitting at the side of the road. When they heard that it was Jesus who was passing by, they shouted, 'Lord! Have pity on us, Son of David.' And the crowd scolded them and told them to keep quiet, but they only shouted more loudly, 'Lord! Have pity on us, Son of David.' Jesus stopped, called them over and said, 'What do you want me to do for you?' They said to him, 'Lord, let us have our sight back.' Jesus felt pity for them and touched their eyes, and immediately their sight returned and they followed him.

CHRIST THE LORD The cure of these two blind men immediately precedes Jesus' triumphant entry into Jerusalem. St Matthew places it here for a reason.

The two blind beggars throw the Pharisees into sharp relief. The beggars hear that the crowd has gathered because Jesus of Nazareth is passing through town. They have heard of him – by this time all of Palestine knew of the wonder-working Rabbi from Galilee. They probably thought they would never have a chance to meet him, and now here he is passing right beside them. Immediately they start yelling. They give him the messianic title "Son of David" and ask for his attention and his favor. They want him to come and heal them. They want it so much that even when the crowds try to browbeat them into silence they keep on shouting, even more loudly. They don't care what other people think of them – they are not going to let this moment of grace pass them by. Jesus hears their cries; he senses their faith. He comes over to them. He asks them what they want. They in turn ask him to open their eyes, to let them see again. Jesus touches their eyes, heals them, and they follow him rejoicing.

Ever since the beginning of his public ministry, Jesus has been assailed by Pharisees who actually saw his miracles and heard his teaching, unlike these beggars who had only heard about Jesus from others. The Pharisees never acknowledged his claim to be the Messiah, they never admitted they had any need for God's grace in their lives, and instead of following him, they tried to trip him up again and again. They never sincerely asked Jesus to open their eyes to the truth. As Jesus enters Jerusalem, the Holy Spirit gives us a glimpse of what might have happened if the Holy City's leaders had shown a touch of humility in the presence of Christ the Lord.

CHRIST THE TEACHER Jesus has just finished explaining for the third time that his messianic mission will achieve fruition only through suffering and humiliation, and two of his closest disciples come up to him, vying for power and honor in his court. How little they have understood! In spite of the frequent predictions of his passion, in spite of repeating that greatness in his Kingdom means becoming small, like a child, Jesus has not been able to convince his disciples that Christian glory is hidden in this world and only bears fruit in the next. But the Lord doesn't lose patience. He restates his lesson, more clearly and directly this time. His followers, and therefore even more emphatically the leaders of his Church, must redirect their natural ambition for excellence. They have to seek to serve, not to be served; to praise, not to be praised; to sacrifice themselves for others, not use others for their own self-aggrandizement. They must become not only like children, but lower themselves even to becoming slaves. Then, no longer blinded by their worldly ambitions, they will be kings with the King, and their longing for a worthy life will be fulfilled.

CHRIST THE FRIEND James and John send their mother to make a bold request, one they were probably ashamed to make themselves (as evidenced by the umbrage the other disciples take at hearing about it). Jesus sees through their ploy. He addresses his answer to them and not to her. But he answers without taking offense. He is glad that these two disciples want to be close to him and be great in his Kingdom. If he could give them what they ask for, he would. But since he can't promise them that, he will give them the next best thing: they too will suffer for the Kingdom (thus staying close to him). Here he teaches them the secret to real greatness – serving, giving, forgetting oneself. Is our path any different? Jesus wants us to confide in him, to be honest with him; that's all he needs in order to make us his everlasting friends.

CHRIST IN MY LIFE I too want to see, Lord. I want to see you. I want to see the truth about myself, about the world, and about the meaning of life. I want to see your will for me and the way to fulfill it. I want to see the needs of those around me and how to meet them. I want to see the beauty of your doctrine and of your heart, so that no other ambition will interfere with my striving to be truly great in your Kingdom...

Excellence – how ardently I long to excel! And yet you, the Lord of all, chose for yourself just the opposite: humility, obscurity, humiliation, suffering. You chose this path to prove to me that the only satisfying excellence is the excellence of love, of self-giving. Teach me to follow in your footsteps, Lord. Be my good shepherd...

Lord, I am reluctant to serve. My natural tendency is to want to be served, especially at home, among those I should serve most. So often I think first of myself. But if you call me to follow in your footsteps, to give my life for others, then it must be possible. You never ask the impossible. Through you, with you, and in you, I can be all that you created me to be. Okay, Lord, whatever you want. Thy will be done...

QUESTIONS FOR SMALL GROUP DISCUSSION

1. What struck you most about this passage? What did you notice that you hadn't noticed before?

2. Why doesn't Jesus reprimand John and James for wanting to be great in his Kingdom? Is ambition bad?

3. Why do you think Jesus touched the blind men's eyes in order to cure them? Why didn't he just cure them with a word?

4. Why do you think the crowds following Jesus tried to get the beggars to stop crying out? Is there a lesson in that for us as followers of Christ?

Cf. Catechism of the Catholic Church, 786 on the nature of Christ's (and Christians') vocation to serve; 615 on the nature of Jesus' self-offering as a ransom for many; 1503-1505 on Christ's miracles as a sign of his love

THE GOSPEL OF MATTHEW CHAPTER 21

"Let us offer him our songs of praise, symbolizing palms, before his passion. Let us acclaim him not with olive branches but by honouring one another in charity. Let us strew the desires of our hearts like garments at his feet that he may direct his steps towards us and make his home in us. May he place us wholly in him, and himself wholly in us."

- St Andrew of Crete

63. THE KING COMES HOME (MT 21:1-11)

"He left behind the glory which he had with his Father before the world was made and went forth for the salvation of his people."

- St Anastasius of Antioch

Matthew 21:1-11

When they were near Jerusalem and had come in sight of Bethphage on the Mount of Olives, Jesus sent two disciples, saying to them, 'Go to the village facing you, and you will immediately find a tethered donkey and a colt with her. Untie them and bring them to me. If anyone says anything to you, you are to say, The Master needs them and will send them back directly.' This took place to fulfil the prophecy: Say to the daughter of Zion: Look, your king comes to you; he is humble, he rides on a donkey and on a colt, the foal of a beast of burden. So the disciples went out and did as Jesus had told them. They brought the donkey and the colt, then they laid their cloaks on their backs and he sat on them. Great crowds of people spread their cloaks on the road, while others were cutting branches from the trees and spreading them in his path. The crowds who went in front of him and those who followed were all shouting: 'Hosanna to the Son of David! Blessings on him who comes in the name of the Lord! Hosanna in the highest heavens!' And when he entered Jerusalem, the whole city was in turmoil. 'Who is this?' people asked, and the crowds answered, 'This is the prophet Jesus from Nazareth in Galilee.'

CHRIST THE LORD The Pharisees had put a price on Jesus' head by this time. The natural reaction to that kind of enmity would be for him to shy away from public attention. But Jesus does just the opposite. As the most sacred of Jewish feasts approached (the Passover), over a million Jewish pilgrims would have been swelling the already crowded city of Jerusalem. Jesus chooses just such a moment to draw all eyes to himself. Fulfilling Zechariah's prophecy (entering the Holy City on a colt never before mounted) and with the people imitating past celebrations of mighty Jewish victories (paving the road with palm branches), Jesus Christ becomes a living billboard announcing his claim to be the Messiah, the Anointed One of God come as the prophets had promised to reestablish the Davidic Kingdom. It is worth noting as well that the event was not a spontaneous one; the throngs did not suddenly and without reason feel moved to rally around Jesus and proclaim him their king. Jesus himself organized the demonstration; he is the first one to assert his Lordship.

CHRIST THE TEACHER In ancient times, kings of the Middle East would frequently ride on donkeys, which were (and are) much more impressive and respected animals there than in the West. During times of war, the king would ride on a horse, but not during times of peace. Christ's gesture, then, indicates that he has come to bring peace. His sacrificial death on the cross, just a few days ahead, would reestablish peace between man and God; his Eucharist, instituted during the Last Supper and perpetuated throughout the centuries by the ministry of the Church, would sow that peace in the hearts of men, whence it would overflow into peace among peoples.

The palm branches symbolized military victory and its subsequent order and prosperity. Christ was coming to conquer sin, selfishness, and death – a victory unmatched and unmatchable by any other king.

The people shouted "Hosanna," a cry for deliverance and salvation (literally, it meant "Save now!"). They acclaimed him "Son of David," a title for the Messiah and an allusion to the hopes they put on him, hopes that he would bring back to Israel its ancient glory and fulfill the promises God made in ages past. This signified God's faithfulness to his people.

Palm Sunday, when the Church commemorates this triumphal occasion in its liturgy is a preview of the Kingdom of Christ. If we welcome him each day as he was welcomed then, then his peace, victory, and faithfulness will enter our hearts as gloriously as he entered Jerusalem.

CHRIST THE FRIEND Wherever Jesus goes, he brings his disciples with him. He could easily have gone himself to untie the colt, or even made it miraculously appear at his side, but he didn't. Instead, "he sent two disciples" to do it for him. In Christ, God wants to enter into our lives and involve us in his works of love and salvation. The Incarnation is God's way of relating to us as the human beings we truly are. In the Church, God continues this same tactic, touching us with human hands and calling us to be his hands for others.

Jesus: That day the people of Jerusalem welcomed me into the city, but not all of them welcomed me into their hearts. Even today, many of my followers look like Christians by their outward actions, but they haven't let me become the Lord of their lives. It is not enough to be known as a Catholic; I want to make you into a saint. The gates of the city mean less to me than the gates of your heart. Only you can open those gates, because when I created you I gave you the only key.

CHRIST IN MY LIFE Lord, many times I have proclaimed my faith in you; I do so again right now. You are the fulfillment of all the prophecies, the answer to every heart's quest, and the hope of every searching soul. You are my Lord and my God, my Savior and my closest, most faithful friend. I want to walk with you each day of my life, sharing your triumphs and your sorrows. I believe in you. I want to be faithful to you, as you have been to me...

You came to bring your peace to my soul. You came to bring your victory over sin and hopelessness and selfishness into my heart. I have experienced your peace and your victory, but you know how much I still need your grace. Come and be the Lord of my heart, Jesus; teach me to follow you more closely, to love you more fully...

Only you know how many people still haven't accepted your offer of salvation and friendship. But I know one thing: you have asked for my assistance in helping some to do so. Give me, Lord, the prudence, charity, and fortitude I need to be your faithful messenger. Give my words, deeds, and example the stamp of authentic Christianity: self-forgetting love for my neighbor...

QUESTIONS FOR SMALL GROUP DISCUSSION

1) What struck you most about this passage? What did you notice that you hadn't noticed before?

2) How would this experience have altered (if at all) the Twelve Apostles' understanding of Jesus and of their role as his closest followers?

3) What thoughts and feelings would have been in Christ's heart throughout this dramatic event?

4) If you had to explain to a non-believer what Christ's title of Messiah means, what would you say?

Cf. Catechism of the Catholic Church, 557-560, 569, 570 on the meaning of the Triumphal Entry into Jerusalem and Palm Sunday

64. TOUGH TIMES IN THE TEMPLE (MT 21:12-27)

"Holy Scripture is the table of Christ, from whence we are nourished, from whence we learn what we should love and what we should desire, to whom we should have our eyes raised."

- Blessed Alcuin

Matthew 21:12-27

Jesus then went into the Temple and drove out all those who were selling and buying there; he upset the tables of the money changers and the chairs of those who were selling pigeons. 'According to scripture' he said 'my house will be called a house of prayer; but you are turning it into a robbers' den'. There were also blind and lame people who came to him in the Temple, and he cured them. At the sight of the wonderful things he did and of the children shouting, 'Hosanna to the Son of David' in the Temple, the chief priests and the scribes were indignant. 'Do you hear what they are saying?' they said to him. 'Yes,' Jesus answered 'have you never read this: By the mouths of children, babes in arms, you have made sure of praise?' With that he left them and went out of the city to Bethany where he spent the night.

As he was returning to the city in the early morning, he felt hungry. Seeing a fig tree by the road, he went up to it and found nothing on it but leaves. And he said to it, 'May you never bear fruit again'; and at that instant the fig tree withered. The disciples were amazed when they saw it. 'What happened to the tree' they said 'that it withered there and then?' Jesus answered, 'I tell you solemnly, if you have faith and do not doubt at all, not only will you do what I have done to the fig tree, but even if you say to this mountain, Get up and throw yourself into the sea, it will be done. And if you have faith, everything you ask for in prayer you will receive.'

He had gone into the Temple and was teaching, when the chief priests and the elders of the people came to him and said, 'What authority have you for acting like this? And who gave you this authority?' 'And I' replied Jesus 'will ask you a question, only one; if you tell me the answer to it, I will then tell you my authority for acting like this. John's baptism: where did it come from: heaven or man?' And they argued it out this way among themselves, 'If we say from heaven, he will retort, Then why did you refuse to believe him?; but if we say from man, we have the people to fear, for they all hold that John was a prophet.' So their reply to Jesus was, 'We do not know.' And he retorted, 'Nor will I tell you my authority for acting like this.'

CHRIST THE LORD No place in the world was as holy as the Temple. The one true God of all creation had deigned to take up his abode with the Chosen People of Israel, and Solomon's original Temple had been the place of that abode. At the time of Christ, a new structure had been built on Solomon's site, since the first Temple had been razed in 586 B.C. by the Babylonians, but the Jews and Jesus still regarded it as the spiritual center of the world. Even the Gentiles would come there to worship, though they had to stay in the outermost courtyard. This courtyard is where Jesus finds the businessmen who were selling sacrificial animals to the ceaseless flow of pilgrims. But turning that courtyard into an outdoor mall hampered the Gentiles' worship. How could they pray surrounded by bleating sheep and haggling bankers? This disrespect, condoned by the Temple authorities, degraded the one chance these visitors had to adore the true God.

When Jesus drives out the money changers, therefore, he demonstrates once again the universality of his Lordship. He implicitly declares his superiority over the Temple authorities, and so over the Temple itself, and he also shows his concern for the Gentiles. No wonder the Jewish leaders confront him. They demand to know by what authority he performed so audacious an action. But Jesus knows that their real interest lies in trying to make him look like a fool. If he tells them the truth, they will scoff indignantly, just as the Pharisees have done in the face of all his miracles and declarations. So the Lord makes them a counter-challenge instead, once again trying to jar their consciences. Maybe, just maybe, one or two of them will be shamed by their hypocrisy and open their hearts to the truth.

CHRIST THE TEACHER The lesson of the fig tree seems obscure. At first Jesus' words and actions appear out of synch, but a closer look proves otherwise.

Jesus is hungry and hopes to find some figs, but the apparently healthy tree is barren. Just so, the leaders of the Temple and the Holy City of Jerusalem have all the right appearances, but no matter what Jesus does or says, they lack the most important things: faith, repentance, and obedience. They try to intimidate Jesus by challenging his authority, and then they won't even answer his question, because the truth holds no interest for them. They just care about getting (or keeping) what they want. They scorn the spontaneous, simple faith of the children and the crowds who welcome Jesus as truly sent from God, exposing their tragedy: mere children detect the truth more readily than these great intellectual and religious leaders. Thus, the barren fig tree stands for the Jewish establishment that bears no fruit of faith in Christ's coming. Their love for power, wealth, and honor has crowded out faith and humility.

But what does all that have to do with Christ's lesson about throwing mountains into the sea? When Jesus turns to his apostles, the future pillars of his Church, and praises the power of faith, he is warning them to beware of the Pharisees' fall. Church leaders – and every Christian disciple – will always be tempted to use their privileges for selfish aims, to put money changers in the Temple courts. But if instead they keep their faith robust, never doubting or losing sight of Christ's truth, they will do the truly wonderful things Jesus has called them to do.

CHRIST THE FRIEND In difficult times, God's presence often evades us. But he is there all the same – in fact, he is the one who sends or permits those difficulties. It's his way of driving self-centeredness, arrogance, sensuality, and superficiality out of his disciples' hearts, just as he drives these vendors out of the Temple. Jesus sees the true beauty and purpose of our lives more clearly than we do. We have become used to things – habits of the heart and mind, unhealthy attachments, subtly self-seeking desires and false justifications – that in fact hinder our growth in holiness.

Jesus: Your soul is infinitely more precious to me than the Temple ever was. Your soul is where you dwell, and I am interested in you. I want you to live in intimate friendship with me now, and for all eternity. The sinful world and your own sins have cluttered and defaced your soul. My grace is purifying you, healing you, helping you become the person I created you to be. You can help purify your soul through self-denial and growth in virtue, but even so, sometimes I have to take things into my own hands. Sometimes I have to pull out some deep roots of selfishness with my own strength. At those times, I send you troubles, which, if you let them, do for your soul what a scalpel in the hands of an expert surgeon does for your body. Trust me in times of trouble; turn to me. I love you too much to be satisfied until you are all you were meant to be.

CHRIST IN MY LIFE What attitudes and habits are crowding, clogging, and distracting my heart, keeping me from loving you and my neighbor as I ought? Whatever they are, I don't want them anymore. I want only to seek and to do your will. You are the Lord, the Savior, the One sent to lead me to paradise. Jesus, I beg of you, come into every corner of my soul, not only the outer courtyard, and cleanse it through and through.

Jesus, you always knew what to say and do, and when to say it and do it… You had been to the Temple before without driving out the money changers, but this time you did. You always know! Often I don't know what to say or what to do to bring others closer to you. I need you to guide me. Teach me, Lord. I will just do my best, counting on you to do the rest…

Am I that barren fig tree? Or is my faith so alive and fervent that I am bearing abundant fruit? Help me, Lord, to reject without delay the small doubts that creep into my heart and mind. I want to stay true to you, never sliding down the slippery slope of self-sufficiency that can destroy my faith. United firmly to you, make my faith firm…

QUESTIONS FOR SMALL GROUP DISCUSSION

1. What struck you most about this passage? What did you notice that you hadn't noticed before?

2. What aspects of popular culture most threaten our faith? What can we do to combat them and keep our faith healthy?

3. What are the biggest challenges you face to have a healthy prayer life? What are some tactics for meeting those challenges?

4. What kind of fruit does Jesus want our lives to bear?

Cf. Catechism of the Catholic Church, 2729-2733 on vigilance of the heart; 2742-2745 on persevering in the love of Christ

65. TWO TYPES OF SINNERS (MT 21:28-32)

"I already have a spouse, and I will not offend him by pretending that another might please me. I will give myself only to him who first chose me. So, executioners, what are you waiting for?"

- St Agnes, martyr

Matthew 21:28-32

'What is your opinion? A man had two sons. He went and said to the first, My boy, you go and work in the vineyard today. He answered, I will not go, but afterwards thought better of it and went. The man then went and said the same thing to the second who answered, Certainly, sir, but did not go. Which of the two did the father's will?' 'The first' they said. Jesus said to them, 'I tell you solemnly, tax collectors and prostitutes are making their way into the kingdom of God before you. For John came to you, a pattern of true righteousness, but you did not believe him, and yet the tax collectors and prostitutes did. Even after seeing that, you refused to think better of it and believe in him.'

CHRIST THE LORD Christ beats Israel's best sophists at their own game. This interchange takes place in Jerusalem right after the chief priests and the elders of the people had tried to trap Jesus in his own words by asking him the origin of his authority. Jesus deflects their attack, and turns the tables, so that they end up accusing themselves of infidelity to God.

Jesus Christ is more than a quick-witted debater. He is the Lord, the Word of God; his teaching "comes from above" (John 8:23) and ought to be accepted. The Church has never asked its children to have blind faith, to believe in Christ's words without good reasons, but it has always asked her to have healthy faith, to believe in Christ's words even when reason cannot completely explain them. Can a five-year-old child understand why he must eat beans and rice as well as candy and ice cream? Hardly, but he knows that his mother loves him, so he trusts that her menu will serve him well. Likewise, when we approach the Lord and his Church, we come not as his equals, but as his beloved and loving followers.

Faith means trusting in someone else's authority. The Pharisees trusted only in themselves, so they closed their minds first to John the Baptist's preaching, and then to Christ's. They even closed their minds to the results of this preaching: the conversion of sinners. We can never truly encounter Christ the Lord unless we are open to becoming his subjects.

CHRIST THE TEACHER This parable's lesson supposes that doing God's will is always the best course of action, a premise accepted by all parties in the discussion. Because we live in a secularized society that does not share this premise, it will be useful to take a quick look at it.

Usually, we determine the best course of action by first applying our own personal analysis and standards. Then, if what the Church or our superiors teach happens to be in agreement with our judgment, we accept it. If it doesn't, we tend to question them rather than ourselves. The Christian attitude should be exactly the opposite; it recognizes the weakness and limits of human nature (and therefore of oneself), and seeks to align its judgment with the assurance of God's revelation in Christ. It lets the warm and gentle sunlight of faith brighten the shadows cast by the quivering lamplight of natural reason. The result, as the unparalleled flowering of human thought in the Christian West evidences, is certainty without close-mindedness, understanding without cynicism, and confidence without arrogance.

The actual lesson of the parable follows this premise. If God's will is the best course of action, who is more worthy of praise – those who promise to fulfill it or those who really do fulfill it? Jesus despised hypocrisy more than almost every other sin. He called those who preach the truth but live falsely "white-washed tombs, serpents, brood of vipers, blind guides" (Mt 23). He went so far as to declare that salvation depends precisely on what we do, not merely on what we say or believe: "It is not those who say to me, Lord, Lord, who will enter the kingdom of heaven, but the person who does the will of my Father in heaven" (Matthew 7:21). St James put it quite bluntly, "For just as a body without a spirit is dead, so faith without works is dead" (James 2:26).

Neither son in the parable treated his father with due respect and obedience, just as neither hypocrisy nor greed and lust (the sins associated with tax collectors and prostitutes) please God, but clearly the one who "changed his mind" (with all the humiliation and humility that entailed) and went into the fields cheered his father's heart more than the other. Even if we tend to grumble at God's will when first we discover it, we can make his heart rejoice if we obey.

CHRIST THE FRIEND As followers of Christ, we can easily relish scenes like this for the wrong reasons: we like it when our Leader defeats his opponents. But Jesus cared little for such vain victories; he told this parable hoping to stir the consciences of those who needed to repent. He told this parable because he desperately wanted the chief priests and leaders of the people to "enter the Kingdom of heaven," and so far they were not doing so. Christ always has our ultimate good in mind. He seeks not his own glory and "success," but only the glory of his Father, which shines most brightly in the salvation of souls. Would that we followed more closely in the footsteps of our Friend!

CHRIST IN MY LIFE Have you been trying to tell me something, Lord? Have I been deaf to your message, like the Pharisees, because I am too attached to my own ideas, my own desires? I want to follow you. I want to love you. I want to know you better. Teach me to do your will...

Sometimes I am like the older son, and then there are times when I am like the younger son, but I want to be like you, the perfectly faithful Son. Thank you for always forgiving me and giving me another chance. I know your will for me: my responsibilities, my conscience, my commitments, your commandments, your Church's teaching. To make your Kingdom come, I have only to make your will be done...

You went out of your way to convince the Pharisees and chief priests to follow you. Throughout your whole ministry they resisted, and yet you never stopped reaching out to them through your miracles, your teachings, your discussions, and your parables. Give me that same zeal and charity to bring those around me closer to you. With the love of your heart, inflame my heart...

QUESTIONS FOR SMALL GROUP DISCUSSION

1. What struck you most about this passage? What did you notice that you hadn't noticed before?

2. If a Catholic you know came to you and said, "I am definitely Catholic, but there are some teachings I just don't agree with," how would you respond?

3. In discussions about the faith with non-Catholics and non-believers, how can we be both charitable (sincerely wanting to draw others to Christ) and sincere (defending the truth of the Catholic faith)?

4. How do you think Christ spoke to his Father about the chief priests and leaders of the people when he prayed for them?

Cf. Catechism of the Catholic Church, 2468-2505 on hypocrisy; 35, 153-162 on the relationship between faith and reason

66. A VALUABLE VINEYARD (MT 21:33-46)

"My daughter, all your miseries have been consumed in the flame of My love, like a little twig thrown into a roaring fire."

- Words of Jesus to St Faustina Kowalska

Matthew 21:33-46

'Listen to another parable. There was a man, a landowner, who planted a vineyard; he fenced it round, dug a winepress in it and built a tower; then he leased it to tenants and went abroad. When vintage time drew near he sent his servants to the tenants to collect his produce. But the tenants seized his servants, thrashed one, killed another and stoned a third. Next he sent some more servants, this time a larger number, and they dealt with them in the same way. Finally he sent his son to them. They will respect my son he said. But when the tenants saw the son, they said to each other, This is the heir. Come on, let us kill him and take over his inheritance. So they seized him and threw him out of the vineyard and killed him. Now when the owner of the vineyard comes, what will he do to those tenants?' They answered, 'He will bring those wretches to a wretched end and lease the vineyard to other tenants who will deliver the produce to him when the season arrives'. Jesus said to them, 'Have you never read in the scriptures: It was the stone rejected by the builders that became the keystone. This was the Lord's doing and it is wonderful to see? I tell you, then, that the kingdom of God will be taken from you and given to a people who will produce its fruit.' When they heard his parables, the chief priests and the scribes realised he was speaking about them, but though they would have liked to arrest him they were afraid of the crowds, who looked on him as a prophet.

CHRIST THE LORD In this parable, Christ himself is one of the characters. The servants of the vineyard's owners represent all the prophets and teachers sent by God to the people of Israel before the coming of Christ – from Moses to Micah. They represent the whole history of God's attempt to bring men back into friendship with him through a loving call to repentance. How patient God has been! But even such patience could not transform men's hearts. So God sent his son, Jesus Christ. The parable emphasizes the difference between the servants and the son. If ever Christ's hearers had doubted his claim to be more than just another prophet, more than just another rabbi, more than just another great teacher and philosopher, this parable would surely cure them. Jesus Christ is Lord not just because he is better than any other religious or political leader, but because he is qualitatively different; he is the Son of God.

The Pharisees and chief priests understand the parable. They concede the point; they see and condemn the tenants' diabolical injustice. They also recognize that Jesus is applying the parable to them: he is the Messiah and they have failed to welcome him. But they don't repent. Here St Matthew is preparing us to recognize the true greatness of our Lord. Jesus will continue to explain, argue, exhort, and warn these men who refuse to believe in him. And they will continue to refuse. So then Jesus will put aside words and arguments and miracles. Instead, he will take up his cross. He will make a final assault on their entrenched hearts with the irresistible weapon of total love, total self-giving, total forgiveness. Jesus is the only Lord that conquers by surrender.

CHRIST THE TEACHER In these few sentences, Jesus sums up the history of salvation, past, present, and future. The vineyard is the world, given to men by God for them to "cultivate and care for" (Genesis 2:15). The tenants are the leaders of God's Chosen People. The owner is God himself. The servants and the son are the prophets and Christ himself. Sin is the tenants' "wretchedness," by which they rebel against the owner out of utter selfishness and greed. Could Jesus have given a clearer warning to these men? Could he have given a simpler explanation of his own identity and mission, a more understandable presentation to the Pharisees of the reality and consequences of their desires to kill him?

The parable applies just as easily to every man and woman. We are each given a vineyard: our own life. We are each given all the means necessary (the hedge, the tower, the winepress) to live that life in accordance with God's plan for us. We are each given many, many chances to put our lives right with God, honoring him and loving him by living as he designed us to live. And each of us, in some way, has been introduced to the owner's son, Jesus Christ. It seems from the Gospel texts that few chief priests and elders actually repented and accepted Christ's message. It's easy for us to deplore such hardheartedness, but before doing so, we should see what kind of fruit our own vineyards are producing, and how much our lives are giving glory to God instead of trying to steal glory for ourselves.

CHRIST THE FRIEND The owner of the vineyard would have had every right to punish the tenants after they had done away with the first batch of servants. But he didn't. He sent more, and more, and finally he sent his son. Only when we have made a definitive decision against him and held fast to that decision in the face of abundant gestures of his love will he let us have what we have wrongly chosen. Christ, the true friend, does not condemn those who refuse his friendship; they condemn themselves.

Jesus: I will never give up on you. If only you knew how much I love my Church, and every person in it. If only you knew how patient my Father is, how magnificently and unabashedly he loves each one of his children! Since I will never give up on you, you must never give up on yourself. No matter how many times you offend me, fail, or reject me, I am always ready and willing to renew our friendship. I am always taking the first step, moving you and inspiring you to come back to me.

CHRIST IN MY LIFE I pray for those who are far from you, for those who don't recognize the hardness of their own hearts. Conquer them with your grace. Don't let them perish, but grant them eternal life. All things are possible for you, Lord, so soften their hearts. Reach out to them through me. I too want to give my life for the salvation of others. For the sake of your sorrowful Passion, have mercy on us and on the whole world…

What are you saying to me that I am not hearing? What relationship do I need to reform? What responsibility am I neglecting? What mission am I ignoring? Lord, I know that following you will always require the painful steps of humility. Never let me take any other path. Never let me be separated from you…

Thank you for never giving up on me. Thank you for being so patient with me. Thank you for inspiring good desires in my heart. Lord, teach me to be truly humble, to place all my confidence in you, and to learn the secret of lasting joy. Make me a channel of your peace…

QUESTIONS FOR SMALL GROUP DISCUSSION

1. What struck you most about this passage? What did you notice that you hadn't noticed before?

2. What is our role in taking care of the "vineyard" of the Church? How can we more effectively fulfill it?

3. What are the "fruits" that the owner of the vineyard demanded? What fruits should the life of a Christian bear for the world?

4. What more could Jesus have done to convince the Pharisees to accept him? What more could he have done to convince us to trust him completely?

Cf. Catechism of the Catholic Church, 153-165 on the mystery of how we can believe or reject Christ and salvation; 470-478 on how Christ is both Son of God and a man

THE GOSPEL OF MATTHEW CHAPTER 22

"Alas for the street in which no one walks, in which the voice of man is not heard; it is a lurking place for wild beasts. Alas for the soul in which the Lord does not walk and put to flight by his voice the spiritual beasts of wickedness. Alas for the house in which its master does not dwell. Alas for the land which has no farmer to till it. Alas for the ship which has been abandoned by its steersman: it is tossed about by the winds and waves of the ocean, and perishes. Alas for the soul which does not have its true steersman Christ in it: it lives in the bitter darkness of the sea and is tossed by the waves of passions. It is buffeted by the wicked spirits as by winter tempests, and finally comes to destruction."

- St Macarius

67. A THANKLESS BANQUET (MT 22:1-14)

"Alas for the soul which is without Christ to cultivate it so that it will bring forth the fruits of the Spirit. When it is deserted it becomes full of thorns and thistles…"

- St Macarius

Matthew 22:1-14

Jesus began to speak to them in parables once again, 'The kingdom of heaven may be compared to a king who gave a feast for his son's wedding. He sent his servants to call those who had been invited, but they would not come. Next he sent some more servants. Tell those who have been invited he said that I have my banquet all prepared, my oxen and fattened cattle have been slaughtered, everything is ready. Come to the wedding. But they were not interested: one went off to his farm, another to his business, and the rest seized his servants, maltreated them and killed them. The king was furious. He despatched his troops, destroyed those murderers and burnt their town. Then he said to his servants, The wedding is ready; but as those who were invited proved to be unworthy, go to the crossroads in the town and invite everyone you can find to the wedding. So these servants went out on to the roads and collected together everyone they could find, bad and good alike; and the wedding hall was filled with guests. When the king came in to look at the guests he noticed one man who was not wearing a wedding garment, and said to him, How did you get in here, my friend, without a wedding garment? And the man was silent. Then the king said to the attendants, Bind him hand and foot and throw him out into the dark, where there will be weeping and grinding of teeth. For many are called, but few are chosen.'

CHRIST THE LORD This king's generosity depends not primarily upon what the people deserve, but upon his own abundant goodness. No one had earned an invitation to the feast; it was purely the king's initiative – a beaming example of true nobility and magnanimity.

Christ's is a feast of grace, an overflowing banquet of divine life. No one can deserve that; it springs from his bountiful generosity, from his longing to share the indescribable joy of his own existence. By the mere act of accepting such an invitation we honor and please him, because we allow him to share with us the delight of his feast. The evil of sin, of self-centeredness, stems ultimately from its ingratitude. Those who declined the invitation checked the king's flow of generosity; they forbade it from reaching them. They frustrated the king's munificence, even though it was meant for their own good. So too, our first duty in relation to God consists in humbly accepting his generous gifts, in letting him be for us the kind of King he really is.

Jesus tells this parable in the hearing of those Jewish leaders who had been consistently rejecting his signs and teachings for the last three years. He shows them the ugliness of their ingratitude, hoping it will jar them into a last minute acceptance of Christ as the Messiah. Even if they fail to understand or accept it right away, maybe after the coming crucifixion (which Jesus foresees) they will remember the parable's vivid image of violence being done to the king's servants. Perhaps then they will repent. Christ's generosity is illustrated by the meaning of the parable; it is exemplified by his decision to tell it in the first place.

CHRIST THE TEACHER God invites, but he does not coerce; he will never force us into his friendship, nor into heaven. This parable and the ones he spoke immediately before it address the mysterious topic of human freedom. In light of the parable, we clearly perceive how foolish those men were who preferred their own little businesses to the king's feast. Not only did they end up being destroyed, but they also missed out on the royal celebration. They loved good things so much (their work and their profit) that they tragically declined the much better thing. If they had only been willing to admit their indebtedness to the king, whose rule made the peace and prosperity they were enjoying possible in the first place, they would have easily adjusted their own plans to honor him. In that case, they could have enjoyed both the good things and the better things. In the parable their mistake is clear, but in our own lives we often fall into the same trap: God's plans seem to interrupt our own, and we forget that ours have no meaning except inside of his.

Even one of those who did accept the invitation somehow responded insufficiently.

In ancient times, when a wedding was announced the actual day and hour were not immediately disclosed. Guests were alerted that they would be invited to a wedding, and that they should stay ready. Likewise, Christ's first coming announced the wedding feast of the Kingdom, but we do not know the actual day and hour when we will be summoned to it. By continually living in a vital and personal friendship with Christ we stay ready. In ancient times, the host provided his guests with wedding garments as part of the celebration; the man who is at the banquet without one must have refused the host's gesture of welcome. Likewise, if we neglect our friendship with Christ – if we continue to put our whims and preferences ahead of God's will, believing without putting our faith into action, we may end up excluded from the banquet. The reality of human freedom, the awful possibility that you or I may reject God's gracious invitation, should be always in our minds, motivating us to take care of our own life of grace, and spurring us on to summon others to the feast.

CHRIST THE FRIEND Wedding feasts in first-century Palestine lasted for about seven days. The guests, the families, and sometimes the entire village treated the bride and groom like royalty for the entire length of the feast. It was the epitome of joy, celebration, and total contentment. It is also Jesus' favorite image for heaven – for his Kingdom.

Jesus Christ calls us to authentic joy. He invites us to follow the way of his cross (obedience to his will) only so that we can join him in the Resurrection. The joy he has in store for us far outweighs the sufferings we endure while following him now. He reaches out to us, through the voice of our conscience, through the teachings of the Church, through the inspiration of the Holy Spirit, in order to draw us closer to the feast, closer to the source of gladness, deeper into an intimate friendship with the eternal God himself.

CHRIST IN MY LIFE Do I know anyone who is more dedicated to their work or their hobbies than to seeking life's true meaning in Christ? Are you sending me as a messenger to them, Lord? How can I speak to them of you? Why am I afraid of their rejecting me, more than I am afraid of their rejecting you? Have patience with me, Lord, and make me into the saint you created me to be…

Why don't I look forward to heaven as much as I look forward to my favorite pastimes? You spoke so often of heaven, and you suffered so much to open heaven's gates to those who believe in you – why is it so far from my mind? Stir up the virtue of hope in my heart, Lord. Stir up my gratitude to you. Never let me desire or seek anything in place of you or before you. Be my heart's whole quest…

I never want to be like the ungrateful invitees, preferring my own comfortable routine and little dreams to your great and adventurous plans. Thy will be done, my Lord, thy Kingdom come in my heart…

QUESTIONS FOR SMALL GROUP DISCUSSION

1. What struck you most about this passage? What did you notice that you hadn't noticed before?

2. The banquet of the parable can also be understood as the Celebration of the Eucharist at Sunday Mass. What are some common excuses people give for skipping Mass? What light does the parable shed on those excuses?

3. St Gregory the Great interpreted the two excuses offered by the invitees as being too engrossed in work (going off to the farm) and being too covetous of riches (going off to the business). Which of these attitudes is more prevalent in popular culture today?

4. If you had to describe the Christian idea of heaven to a non-believer, how would you do it?

Cf. Catechism of the Catholic Church, 150-165 on God's invitation and the response of human freedom; 456-460 on what Jesus wants; 543-546 on the nature of the Kingdom

68. FOILED AGAIN (MT 22:15-21)

"Alas for the soul which has not Christ for its Lord dwelling in it, for when it is deserted and filled with the stench of passions it becomes a den of vice."

- St Macarius

Matthew 22:15-21

Then the Pharisees went away to work out between them how to trap him in what he said. And they sent their disciples to him, together with the Herodians, to say, 'Master, we know that you are an honest man and teach the way of God in an honest way, and that you are not afraid of anyone, because a man's rank means nothing to you. Tell us your opinion, then. Is it permissible to pay taxes to Caesar or not?' But Jesus was aware of their malice and replied, 'You hypocrites! Why do you set this trap for me? Let me see the money you pay the tax with.' They handed him a denarius, and he said, 'Whose head is this? Whose name?' 'Caesar's' they replied. He then said to them, 'Very well, give back to Caesar what belongs to Caesar – and to God what belongs to God.' This reply took them by surprise, and they left him alone and went away.

CHRIST THE LORD Jesus is master of every situation. He recognizes hypocrisy and exposes it with the floodlight of truth. He steadfastly faces his enemies courageously, knowing well what they seek – to discredit him in the eyes of the people – but taking their challenge and beating them at their own game. In encounters like this, the Gospel reveals the power of Christ's personality, the immense force of his intelligence, and the piercing lucidity of his wisdom. Such is the Son of God made man, such is this man who has called us by name and invited us to follow him.

Nevertheless, St Matthew continues to highlight Jesus' refusal to humiliate his enemies utterly (which they deserved) or violate their freedom by forcing their allegiance; he keeps on inviting them to believe in him. Bearing with the hypocritical Pharisees yet again, he puts up with their underhanded ruse and gives a response that stirs even their hardened hearts to admiration. His language is no longer soft (he calls them hypocrites), because time is running short, but he still hasn't given up on them. Again we see that the Lord of the universe is truly the Good Shepherd, no matter how stubborn the sheep.

CHRIST THE TEACHER The lesson Jesus taught his enemies twenty centuries ago still abides today: Give to Caesar what belongs to Caesar, and to God what belongs to God. Every Christian holds dual citizenship, each with its own benefits and duties: our birth makes us citizens of an earthly nation; our baptism makes us citizens of a heavenly Kingdom. Christ commands us to live out both with justice and responsibility. The protection and public services rendered us by the political community rightly demand a response of obedience, gratitude, and active collaboration. A Christian should be the most engaged and dependable of citizens – unless of course "Caesar" tries to claim rights that belong only to God.

A less obvious lesson also emerges from this encounter. The opposition against Jesus is increasing. The Pharisees join forces with the Herodians; the former disapproved of paying taxes to Rome and still pursued political independence for Israel, while the latter were loyal to the Empire. That two such disparate parties come together against Jesus shows the magnitude of his threat to the sinful status quo. This pattern of growing opposition is repeated wherever Christian holiness thrives; the lives of the saints and the history of the Church reproduce it again and again, like an ever-expanding crystal. It embodies the last and greatest of the Beatitudes: "Blessed are those who are persecuted for righteousness' sake, for theirs is the Kingdom of Heaven" (Mt 5:10). If Christ was a sign of contradiction in a self-centered world, authentic Christians will be too.

CHRIST THE FRIEND The coin belongs to Caesar, but what exactly belongs to God? Do we owe any taxes to the heavenly IRS? All that we are and all that we possess has come to us from God. Just as the Roman coin bears the image of the Emperor who made it, so the human soul bears the "image and likeness" (Genesis 1:26) of God who calls each of us into existence so as to live in personal communion with him. "Coming from God, going toward God, man lives a fully human life only if he freely lives by his bond with God" (Catechism of the Catholic Church, 44). Freely living by our bond with God means living as he created us to live, and he has shown us how to do that by sending us his Son, the model of every Christian life, the Friend of every human soul. Ignoring God, making our decisions, and living out our relationships as if he were far away and uninterested is a kind of spiritual thievery, like stealing the Emperor's coins. Will we be so ungrateful?

CHRIST IN MY LIFE I am glad to be your follower, Lord. You are the fount of wisdom and life, the source of every good thing. You have called me by name. You hold me in existence. You give me work to do in your Kingdom, the work of love, self-giving, and self-sacrifice. Teach me your wisdom, Lord; teach me your love…

How easily I lose patience! You continue to converse with your enemies, you continue to teach your apostles, you continue to heal the sick and suffering crowds – your heart is an inexhaustible fountain of goodness. Come with your grace to make my heart like that. With the patience of your heart, bear with my stubborn heart, and teach me to love my brothers and sisters as you have loved me…

This world offers me so many opportunities for doing good. Nothing is perfect here, not the Church, not the political community, not my local community, not my family. Why am I so blind to the needs around me? Why is my sphere of interest so reduced? Remind me of my mission in life, Lord. I am not the Savior of the world, but I am your disciple; show me what more I can do to build your Kingdom…

QUESTIONS FOR SMALL GROUP DISCUSSION

1. What struck you most about this passage? What did you notice that you hadn't noticed before?

2. What does it mean to be responsible citizens of our country and of this world? How can we fulfill this duty more completely?

3. What does it mean to be a responsible citizen of heaven? How can we fulfill this duty more completely?

4. How should Christians respond when a society's laws overstep their rightful limits and infringe upon the law of God, trying to claim for the state what rightly belongs to God?

5. If a non-believer asked you what Christians think of politics, how would you answer?

Cf. Catechism of the Catholic Church, 2238-2343 on the Christian vision of our duties to secular society

69. AMAZING TEACHER; AMAZING TRUTH (MT 22:23-33)

"I pray you, noble Jesus, that as you have graciously granted me joyfully to imbibe the words of your knowledge, so you will also of your bounty grant me to come at length to yourself, the found of all wisdom, and to dwell in your presence forever."

- St Bede the Venerable

Matthew 22:23-33

That day some Sadducees – who deny that there is a resurrection – approached him and they put this question to him, 'Master, Moses said that if a man dies child-less, his brother is to marry the widow, his sister-in-law to raise children for his brother. Now we had a case involving seven brothers; the first married and then died without children, leaving his wife to his brother; the same thing happened with the second and third and so on to the seventh, and then last of all the woman herself died. Now at the resurrection to which of those seven will she be wife, since she had been married to them all?' Jesus answered them, 'You are wrong, because you understand neither the scriptures nor the power of God. For at the resurrection men and women do not marry; no, they are like the angels in heaven. And as for the resurrection of the dead, have you never read what God himself said to you: I am the God of Abraham, the God of Isaac and the God of Jacob? God is God, not of the dead, but of the living.' And his teaching made a deep impression on the people who heard it.

CHRIST THE LORD More enemies draw near, and another battle ensues. This time the attackers are representatives of the wealthy political leaders, who had different religious views than the Pharisees, but once again, Jesus prevails. His enemies still refuse to be converted. And the listening crowd is filled with awe.

That same crowd had long submitted to the harsh and demanding rule of the Pharisees and Sadducees. Both groups of leaders were far superior to the vast majority of the working population in knowledge, influence, education, and wealth. And they made their superiority felt. In Christ these searching souls find something entirely different. He neither fears the leaders' power nor bows to their prowess. He confronts them, argues with them, and repeatedly sends them away confounded. And all the while he generously heals and teaches the ordinary people, so despised by the others. Jesus is right down there among them. They sense in Christ something much greater than any earthly leader, and they also perceive him as someone much closer to them, interested in them, and capable of helping them. This is how the Lord behaved; this is how his Church continues to behave; this is how his disciples ought to behave.

CHRIST THE TEACHER Instead of calling the Sadducees "hypocrites," as he did with the Pharisees, Jesus simply tells them, "You are wrong." The Pharisees erred in their willful denial of Christ's claims, a denial that sprang from malice, from envy and jealousy; the Sadducees err merely in ignorance. They truly think this Nazarene rabbi is just a popularizer of mistaken doctrine, and they try to set him straight. So Jesus instructs them.

First, he tells them the reasons for their error: their knowledge of Scripture is incomplete, and their conception of God's power is too limited. These are the same errors behind every heresy and doctrinal deviation in the history of the Church. As soon as someone thinks his own interpretation of God's revelation is superior to the Church's constant and divinely guaranteed teaching, his conception of God shrinks, because he is depending less and less on God's own revelation and more and more on his own puny, human intellect. Division, confusion, and tragedy ensue. Staying in step with the Magisterium is the only sure way to stay in tune with God.

Next, Jesus explains the essence of their error. We can look forward to life after death, but that life will be substantially different from earthly life. In affirming these truths, Jesus confirms the faltering hope of his listeners (except the Sadducees themselves), who have long sensed that the passing joys of this life, so tainted by the world's many sorrows, were only whiffs of the good life to come. Jesus speaks with such cogent logic and irrefutable authority that as the questioners abandon the battlefield, stunned, the onlookers' attention stays fixed on Jesus, filled with wonder and anticipation. Perhaps we too should let the truth of the Resurrection sink a bit deeper into our minds.

CHRIST THE FRIEND Why is Jesus spending his last days in the Temple? Why is he taking so much time to teach, to argue, to heal, to preach, and to be bothered with all the attacks and questions and requests? Because Jesus came for us, not for himself, not for his own comfort, not for any earthly glory – he came to be our salvation, to be a sure light in our persistent darkness. Jesus still does the same thing. His Church is the extension of this same mission. He "never ceases to draw man to himself" (Catechism of the Catholic Church, 27), he is always thinking of each one of us, always reaching out to us, always hearing our pleas and queries, always eager to respond. And the better we get to know him, the more we become like him: full of saving wisdom that can satisfy the thirstiest soul, and full of active love that goes out to deliver the drink.

CHRIST IN MY LIFE I am proud to be your disciple. You are a worthy Lord.

You are the only Lord. You have all the answers. I want to know you better each day, to follow you more closely each day, to love you more passionately and truly every single day. With the knowledge of your heart, make my heart wise...

Am I looking forward to the Resurrection as eagerly as you want me to? To be honest, Lord, I rarely think about it, and yet, it is the cornerstone of our faith. Stir up my hope in you, Lord. Teach me to live in light of the big picture, in light of the whole story, which you went to so much trouble to reveal...

Are you pleased with how I spend my time? Do I keep too much of it to myself? Should I be giving more time to others, to your Church, to you? You tirelessly dedicated your life to fulfilling the Father's will. Your agenda was full, but only with things that helped you accomplish your mission in life. Teach me to do the same; teach me to do your will...

QUESTIONS FOR SMALL GROUP DISCUSSION

1. What struck you most about this passage? What did you notice that you hadn't noticed before?

2. If you had to explain to a non-believer (someone you know) the Christian doctrine of the resurrection of the body, how would you do it? What might some of this person's objections be?

3. How do you think Jesus' apostles (who are keeping a remarkably low profile at this point in St Matthew's Gospel) were feeling after these first couple of days in Jerusalem: the Triumphal Entry, then the series of successful verbal skirmishes, first with the Pharisees, then with the Pharisees' disciples and the Herodians, and now with the Sadducees?

4. Why do you think there won't be any marriage after the final resurrection? What does this tell us about God's purpose for marriage? What implications does this doctrine have for the value of priestly celibacy and consecrated virginity?

Cf. Catechism of the Catholic Church, 988-1013 on the resurrection of the body; 366 on the body and soul at the final resurrection; 2697-2699 on the Church's recommendation for spending time in prayer

70. THE ANSWER (MT 22:34-46)

"If we desire to live in the dwelling-place of his kingdom there is no means of reaching it except by the way of good deeds."

- St Benedict

Matthew 22:34-46

But when the Pharisees heard that he had silenced the Sadducees they got together and, to disconcert him, one of them put a question, 'Master, which is the greatest commandment of the Law?' Jesus said, 'You must love the Lord your God with all your heart, with all your soul, and with all your mind. This is the greatest and the first commandment. The second resembles it: You must love your neighbour as your-self. On these two commandments hang the whole Law, and the Prophets also.' While the Pharisees were gathered round, Jesus put to them this question, 'What is your opinion about the Christ? Whose son is he?' 'David's' they told him. 'Then how is it' he said 'that David, moved by the Spirit, calls him Lord, where he says: The Lord said to my Lord: Sit at my right hand and I will put your enemies under your feet? 'If David can call him Lord, then how can he be his son?' Not one could think of anything to say in reply, and from that day no one dared to ask him any further questions.

CHRIST THE LORD The "law and the prophets" was considered by the Jews to contain the absolutely unique self-revelation of the one, true God to his only Chosen People. In possessing this revelation, Israel excelled over all other na-tions and peoples: the Creator of heaven and earth had entered into a personal covenant with them, promising to bless all nations through them. Therefore, when this Pharisee (who happened to be an expert in "the law and the proph-ets") queries Jesus as to the greatest among the 613 commandments of the law, he is really ferreting out Christ's interpretation of the entire history and reality of the Israelite nation – a daunting task. We can imagine Christ fixing his eyes on those of the questioner, wondering if perchance this question were asked sincerely. Once again, he rises to the occasion, giving us in two sentences the perfect program for our entire life.

After responding, Jesus decides the time has come to end the interminable debate with the Pharisees. Throughout St Matthew's Gospel they have ob-structed, insulted, doubted, confronted, and tried to humiliate and discredit Jesus. As the hour of Christ's passion approaches, he turns the tables. He asks them about the first verse of Psalm 110, a psalm that, as all the rabbis agreed, dealt specifically with the Messiah. Jesus asks them to interpret how David can address the Messiah, who is David's son and by that standard ought to be inferior to David, as his superior, calling him Lord. Some commentators see this challenge as a final discrediting of the Pharisees by Jesus. Up to this time, they have tried to demean him with their supposedly superior knowledge of the Law, but now Jesus denigrates them in the eyes of all the people, inviting the crowds to retract their confidence in these false teachers who are not even able to decipher the meaning of a simple, well-known Scripture passage. Other commentators say Jesus was indicating one final time that their concept of the Messiah was too worldly; it didn't leave room for God's wonderful plan of send-ing the Second Person of the Trinity. In this case too, their small-mindedness destroys their credibility.

In either case, this final exchange marks a turning point: the Lord will no longer tolerate the Pharisees' stubborn resistance; the time has come to put them in their place so as to open the hearts of the people to the Savior's grace.

CHRIST THE TEACHER The novelty of Christ's answer to the Pharisee's query comes not in identifying the greatest commandment, about which the rabbis had already come to a consensus, but in linking it to the second greatest commandment – in binding together in his New Covenant love for God and love for neighbor. They had asked him for one commandment; he gave them two, as if to say that these two are really only one: how can you truly love God with all your heart if you do not also love your neighbor? This is where the Pharisees were always falling short. And, how can you truly love your neighbor if you do not love God with all your heart? This is where many modern humanitarians tend to fall short. What possible reason would there be to love my neighbor, that neighbor who contradicts me and gets on my nerves and treats me badly and uses up my resources, if my neighbor were not loved by God, if my neighbor were not my brother? If God loves him, and I love God… well, as true friends say: any friend of yours is a friend of mine.

CHRIST THE FRIEND The social action of the Church throughout the centuries proves the power of this double dimension of love, lived out first by Christ, and subsequently, through the Holy Spirit, by his followers. The saints have been the ones to found hospitals, orphanages, schools, and countless other works of charity ("charity," by the way, traditionally refers to both these dimensions of Christian love – for God and for neighbor because of God). Their love for God burned so wildly that it spread into love for all of God's children, and whatever they could do for the spiritual and material benefit of those children was never enough. The dignity of every human person, a dignity that demands that they be loved, stems only from the image they bear within of God himself, most worthy of all our love. True love of God yields love for our neighbor; without it, love for our neighbor may temporarily relieve our conscience, but it will never bear lasting fruit. In identifying himself with each of his children, then, Christ has become the truest friend of all.

Jesus: So many people are searching for easy formulas that will simplify their lives. So many people are trying to find a clear answer to the questions that torment their souls. If only they would listen to my words! If only they would trust me and accept my teaching! If only they would try, just a little bit, to make the slightest effort to put it into practice, then my grace would sweep them off their feet and lead them to the meaningful life they long for.

CHRIST IN MY LIFE Lord, is it possible that some of the leaven of the Pharisees has penetrated my life? I know the right answers, and everyone identifies me as a faithful Christian, but are there relationships or habitual ways of thinking in my life that conform more to selfish standards than yours? Show me where my attitudes and actions need to be touched by your grace. Teach me, Lord, to do your will...

Your program of life is so simple. Why is it that I complicate things? How I long for the peace of living in communion with you! Cleanse my heart of every other desire, so that it's only full of love for you and for my neighbor...

Why must I love my neighbor as myself? I so readily make excuses for myself; I always put up with myself – but my neighbor is so hard to tolerate, so full of faults. How do you see that person, Lord? Open my eyes to see as you see. No one is so faulty that you can't make them into a saint...

QUESTIONS FOR SMALL GROUP DISCUSSION

1) What struck you most about this passage? What did you notice that you hadn't noticed before?

2) What are the most common ways we fail to keep each of these two commandments?

3) What aspects of popular culture encourage the following of these two commandments? What aspects discourage it?

4) What has helped you most in your efforts to love your neighbor as yourself?

5) What is the greatest thing you (or anyone) can do for your neighbor?

Cf. Catechism of the Catholic Church, 1822-1826 on the nature of Christian charity; 1878-1889 on the social dimension of human life; 1928-1942 on social justice

THE GOSPEL OF MATTHEW CHAPTER 23

"So long as we continue to behave as sheep, we are victorious. Even if ten thousand wolves surround us, we conquer and are victorious. But the moment we become wolves, we are conquered, for we lose the help of the shepherd. He is the shepherd of sheep, not of wolves. If he leaves you and goes away, it is because you do not allow him to show his power."

- St John Chrysostom

71. LEARNING FROM THE PHARISEES (MT 23:1-12)

"The man who loves God thinks it enough to please him whom he loves, for no greater reward can be sought than that love itself."

- Pope St Leo the Great

Matthew 23:1-12

Then addressing the people and his disciples Jesus said, 'The scribes and the Pharisees occupy the chair of Moses. You must therefore do what they tell you and listen
to what they say; but do not be guided by what they do: since they do not practise
what they preach. They tie up heavy burdens and lay them on men's shoulders, but
will they lift a finger to move them? Not they! Everything they do is done to attract
attention, like wearing broader phylacteries and longer tassels, like wanting to take
the place of honour at banquets and the front seats in the synagogues, being greeted
obsequiously in the market squares and having people call them Rabbi. 'You, however, must not allow yourselves to be called Rabbi, since you have only one master,
and you are all brothers. You must call no one on earth your father, since you have
only one Father, and he is in heaven. Nor must you allow yourselves to be called
teachers, for you have only one Teacher, the Christ. The greatest among you must
be your servant. Anyone who exalts himself will be humbled, and anyone who
humbles himself will exalted.'

CHRIST THE LORD St Matthew has just described the last encounter between
Jesus and the Jewish authorities, the scribes and Pharisees. During the long
series of encounters in which they sought to trick Jesus, humiliate and discredit
him, Jesus patiently but firmly parried their every blow and repeatedly directed
their attention to the saving truth about himself and the frightening truth about
themselves. They continually refused to accept the Lord, until finally Jesus was
forced to silence his enemies by posing them a question in his turn, one that
left them speechless and confused. Now, as they go off to fume and concoct
other plans, he turns to those who had been watching and listening to this
verbal bout. They have long looked up to their religious leaders, but Jesus
now has to definitively repeal those leaders' credentials, so that his followers can be free to embrace his doctrine fully. The Lord's insatiable desire
to *teach them the way of salvation* overflows in a lesson that he longs for us
all to learn, a lesson that the scribes and Pharisees rejected – the lesson of
humility.

The contrast between the picture Jesus paints of the scribes and Pharisees and
his own style of life highlights what kind of a king he really is. These men did
things out of love for themselves in order to elevate themselves and aggrandize
themselves. Their leadership consisted in crushing those beneath them, intimidating them, or devouring them into acknowledging the pharisaical greatness.
Jesus' whole public ministry demonstrates the exact opposite approach. He
sought only to elevate those around him. His teaching and his miracles were

always aimed at the good of those around him. He is the Lord of self-forgetful love, dethroning the idol of self-indulgent hypocrisy.

CHRIST THE TEACHER The Pharisees were the self-proclaimed elite of Palestine; they were the perfect ones who dedicated themselves to the fulfillment of every detail of the Jewish law, while the common people only fulfilled the broad precepts. The Pharisees thought themselves superior and gloried in this; they used it to humiliate others and thus perpetuate their superiority. Theirs was an extreme case of arrogance and hypocrisy, for the more they posed as God's friends, the further they fell from God's true friendship.

How much of the Pharisee is in us? How often do we pose and posture and seek recognition? We who are fallen always seek to climb the ladder of success. We scheme and strive and maneuver our way to praise, attention, recognition, and admiration as eagerly as children battle for candy at a parade. *Oh, that they will think highly of me! Oh, that they will accept me! Oh, that I will meet their expectations! Oh, that I will "succeed"!*

Some seek recognition in their profession, while others seek it in artistic and intellectual achievement. Some seek to be recognized in the public eye; others strive to obtain political power, still others in petty, local vanity. We tend to exalt ourselves in as many eyes as possible, caring a great deal about the opinions of our fellow men, when what Christ longs for is that we seek only to be pleasing in the sight of God: "Set your hearts on his kingdom first, and on his righteousness, and all these other things will be given you as well" (Matthew 6:33). To humble ourselves, to give God his rightful place in our lives, realizing that all the good we have is God's gift – this is the secret to Christian success. After all, what, besides our sin, can we call our own? Do not our successes stem from circumstances, opportunities, and talents that we have received? What we *should* set our hearts on, what Christ wants us to seek, is pleasing God, obeying him, letting him be our Master, our Father, our Friend. If God is pleased with us, what will we care about the opinion of the world?

CHRIST THE FRIEND It must have been difficult for Jesus to speak so harshly about the Pharisees and scribes. He only did so for the sake of the crowds and disciples who had witnessed the ongoing controversy. Jesus had done everything within his power – while still respecting his enemies' freedom – to win over his attackers, to meet them on their own ground, to open their closed minds to his saving truth. Only then does he pronounce judgment on them. Even this harsh task of uprooting the Jewish authorities – a task Jesus had the right and duty to perform, for the sake of those whom the authorities were leading astray – is performed with generosity, in the context of teaching a lesson that will serve the good of all.

Christ taught this lesson many times with words, all the time with his actions, and one time forever with his passion, the ultimate expression of his love: "…he emptied himself, taking the form of a slave, coming in human likeness; and found human in appearance, he humbled himself, becoming obedient to death, even death on a cross" (Philippians 2:7-8).

CHRIST IN MY LIFE Never let me deceive myself, Lord. Help me to see myself as I truly am. I want to follow you, to hear your voice each moment, to see your providential, loving action in every happening and encounter of my life. Teach me to walk by faith, Lord, not by sight…

I can only strive to please you if I know what truly pleases you. And I can only know what pleases you if I study and pray. I need you to keep me humble, Lord. I tend so easily to slip into that self-destructive thirst for recognition and superiority. That tendency goes deep – only your love goes deeper. Purify my heart, Lord. Teach me to think first of others, and then of myself, just as you did. Jesus, I trust in you…

Sometimes I have to point out others' faults. Teach me to do so with true Christian charity. Teach me to separate the sin from the sinner. Teach me to seek the good of my enemies, the return of the lost sheep, just as you always do – just as you did with me. I don't want to judge my brothers; that's your job. I want to speak the truth in love. Mary, Queen of peace, pray for me…

QUESTIONS FOR SMALL GROUP DISCUSSION

1. What struck you most about this passage? What did you notice that you hadn't noticed before?

2. Christ was angry with the Pharisees for more than one reason. What were the reasons? Can he reprimand us for any of the same reasons that he reprimanded them?

3. To what extent does the society around us encourage Christian humility? To what extent does it encourage vanity and arrogance?

4. In what ways is hypocrisy (attending to appearances but not to the heart) most tempting for the Catholics I know? How can we arm ourselves against falling into this deadly sin?

Cf. Catechism of the Catholic Church, 768, 771, 2219, 2540, 2546, 2554, 2559, 2613, 2631, 2753, and 2779 on the importance of humility in the spiritual life

72. THE FOOLISHNESS OF BEING FALSE (MT 23:13-26)

"For surely the confidence of a notorious sinner honors God most of all, for he is so convinced of God's infinite mercy that all his sins seem no more than an atom in its presence."

- St Claude de la Colombière

Matthew 23:13-26

'Alas for you, scribes and Pharisees, you hypocrites! You who shut up the kingdom of heaven in men's faces, neither going in yourselves nor allowing others to go in who want to. 'Alas for you, scribes and Pharisees, you hypocrites! You who travel over sea and land to make a single proselyte, and when you have him you make him twice as fit for hell as you are. 'Alas for you, blind guides! You who say, If a man swears by the Temple, it has no force; but if a man swears by the gold of the Temple, he is bound. Fools and blind! For which is of greater worth, the gold or the Temple that makes the gold sacred? Or else, If a man swears by the altar it has no force; but if a man swears by the offering that is on the altar, he is bound. You blind men! For which is of greater worth, the offering or the altar that makes the offering sacred? Therefore, when a man swears by the altar he is swearing by that and by everything on it. And when a man swears by the Temple he is swearing by that and by the One who dwells in it. And when a man swears by heaven he is swearing by the throne of God and by the One who is seated there. 'Alas for you, scribes and Pharisees, you hypocrites! You who pay your tithe of mint and dill and cummin and have neglected the weightier matters of the Law – justice, mercy, good faith! These you should have practised, without neglecting the others. You blind guides! Straining out gnats and swallowing camels! 'Alas for you, scribes and Pharisees, you hypocrites! You who clean the outside of cup and dish and leave the inside full of extortion and intemperance. Blind Pharisee! Clean the inside of cup and dish first so that the outside may become clean as well.'

CHRIST THE LORD In the rest of Chapter 23, St Matthew records one of the harshest excoriations in all literature. Having defeated the Pharisees in the controversies they initiated and having unsuccessfully tried again and again to open their hearts to his message, Jesus now pronounces the Seven Woes (or curses). In his denunciation of the Pharisees, Jesus shows an aspect of his Lordship that often goes unnoticed: how well he knows his subjects. His examples reveal a heart that has long contemplated the hypocritical practices of these men and sorrowed over them. God's interest in and attention to the details of our lives, both our sufferings and our decisions, is a leitmotif of the whole Bible (e.g., Ps 32:8 - "I will watch over you and be your adviser"). We have become so used to God's care that we gloss right over it most of the time. God is interested in mankind. Each person matters to him. He watches over us like a loving Father, eager for us to choose the good and pained when we choose evil. Christ is the Lord, true, but he is a Lord who knows and loves.

CHRIST THE TEACHER Jesus uses specific, concrete examples of Pharisaic practice – convoluted vows that leave comfortable wiggle room for deception, minute attention to exterior propriety that masks interior barbarity, a self-seeking piety that leads others to reverence them instead of God – to illustrate both the root of the Pharisees' sin (hypocrisy – the epithet "hypocrites" serves as a refrain for the entire discourse) and also the extent to which it has corrupted every aspect of their lives. Much research has elucidated the pharisaical practices Jesus refers to, but the point of his invective lies elsewhere.

This discourse of the Seven Woes is his last speech in the Temple, his last public teaching before his Passion. It parallels his first public teaching, the Sermon on the Mount, which began with the Seven Beatitudes (many commentators separate the last into two parts, counting eight). In both cases, Jesus addresses himself to the crowds and to his disciples. His own life and works have exemplified the beatitudes for them – a code of conduct marked by humility, reverence for God, and service to others. The hypocritical scribes and Pharisees exemplify the opposite code of conduct, condemned in the Seven Woes and characterized by allegiance only to conceit, self-sufficiency, and arrogance under the appearance of righteousness. The Beatitudes show religion and the meaning of life as being matters of the heart; the pharisaic approach disregards the heart and overemphasizes exterior practices, which lose their meaning by being cut off from a coherent interior intention – external perfection has become an idol.

Jesus' examples were apt for the Pharisees, their times, and their way of life, but the principle behind them applies to all times and all ways of life. To reach maturity as a human being takes sincerity and coherence – there is a striving for complete harmony between ideals, desires, words, and actions; the whole person, the inside of the cup as well as the outside, has to be in sync. It is not enough to achieve great things professionally, to win the admiration of peers and the anonymous throngs. It is not enough to fit in with the chic and the elite, to be considered a success. For the human soul to be strong and at peace, exterior achievements must flow out of interior integrity; the ship must be shipshape through and through, not just have a flashy coat of paint. To reach Christian maturity requires going even one step further: bringing one's whole self into sync not just with basic moral truth, but *with the truth of Christ* – so much in sync, in fact, that nothing can turn the soul away from its friendship with the Lord: "Blessed are you when people abuse you and persecute you and speak all kinds of calumny against you falsely on my account. Rejoice and be glad, for your reward will be great in heaven" (Mt 5:11-12). Hypocrisy divides a man on the inside and sparks violence between men on the outside; Christ and his truth bring the monolithic force of unity to both.

CHRIST THE FRIEND The Greek word translated here as "Alas for you!" is often translated as "Woe to you!" The first reflects the Greek better, since it includes the connotation of sorrow. Christ's anger in the face of the Pharisees' stubborn resistance is shot through with sorrow and regret. In listing their modes of hypocrisy, Jesus isn't merely letting off steam – in fact, the leaders of the people had actually left Christ's presence before this discourse began. At this point, the Lord is addressing the crowds and his disciples. St Matthew doesn't show him staring his enemies down and terrorizing them. Rather, we witness the outpouring of Jesus' heart, his burning regret and righteous anger in the face of the absurd and self-destructive behavior of these men whom God had called to be leaders of his people.

Jesus: When people reject me, it pains me more than angers me. I don't want to lose anyone. Every child of my Father was created to be good and to add to the glory of heaven. I am the Good Shepherd who sets out to rescue every soul. I denounced the rulers of the people because I had to pour out my sorrow, because I had to warn the crowds and my disciples from following the same path of destruction, and because I had to try to jar the few remaining Pharisees into repentance. Whatever I say, whatever I do, it's always with the best for others in mind.

CHRIST IN MY LIFE You know me through and through. Enlighten my mind now, so I can see my own hypocrisy. Help me make a list of the ways I put on a show in order to win empty human praise and give myself an excuse to look down on others. Help me to know myself as you know me, to accept myself as you accept me, and to better myself in accordance with your dream for my life. Jesus, I trust in your mercy…

How many people around me are sinking in the quicksand of hypocrisy! Trends, public opinion, peer pressure, social acceptance… All these leeches are draining souls of the true joy and meaning they can have from a simple, honest life of friendship with you. Save them, Lord, as you have saved me! And show me how to reach out to them in your name…

QUESTIONS FOR SMALL GROUP DISCUSSION

1. What struck you most about this passage? What did you notice that you hadn't noticed before?

2. What aspects of popular culture encourage hypocrisy, deception, and insincerity?

3. If Jesus were to give this discourse today, what examples might he use to make the same point?

4. There is a healthy pride and a sinful pride. How would you describe the difference?

5. Is it possible, in your opinion, to pay attention to external appearances without falling into hypocrisy? If so, how? Is it commendable to try? If so, why?

Cf. Catechism of the Catholic Church, 2482-2487 on the nature and evil of lying; 2514-2516 on our innate tendency to sin; 2514-2519 on purification of the heart

73. THE FINAL CURTAIN (MT 23:27-24:2)

"Only one thing is necessary: Jesus Christ. Think unceasingly of him."

- St John Gabriel Perboyre

Matthew 23:27-39

'Alas for you, scribes and Pharisees, you hypocrites! You who build the sepulchres of the prophets and decorate the tombs of holy men, saying, We would never have joined in shedding the blood of the prophets, had we lived in our fathers' day. So! Your own evidence tells against you! You are the sons of those who murdered the prophets! Very well then, finish off the work that your fathers began. 'Serpents, brood of vipers, how can you escape being condemned to hell? This is why, in my turn, I am sending you prophets and wise men and scribes: some you will slaughter and crucify, some you will scourge in your synagogues and hunt from town to town; and so you will draw down on yourselves the blood of every holy man that has been shed on earth, from the blood of Abel the Holy to the blood of Zechariah son of Barachiah whom you murdered between the sanctuary and the altar. I tell you solemnly, all of this will recoil on this generation. 'Jerusalem, Jerusalem, you that kill the prophets and stone those who are sent to you! How often have I longed to gather your children, as a hen gathers her chicks under her wings, and you refused! So be it! Your house will be left to you desolate, for, I promise, you shall not see me any more until you say: Blessings on him who comes in the name of the Lord!'

Jesus left the Temple, and as he was going away his disciples came up to draw his attention to the Temple buildings. He said to them in reply, 'You see all these? I tell you solemnly, not a single stone here will be left on another: everything will be destroyed.'

CHRIST THE LORD This is Jesus' final exit from the Temple; St Matthew never describes him returning. The whole dramatic discourse and departure echoes the discourse and vision of Ezekiel (Ezek 10, 11), in which the inspired prophet condemned Jerusalem's corrupt leaders, and God's glory physically left the Temple to settle on the Mount of Olives. Soon after, the original Temple was destroyed (586 BC).

Jesus knows that the prophetic events of Ezekiel's time are reaching their fulfillment in him. Cain rejected God's call in murdering his brother Abel at the start of salvation history; the leaders of Jerusalem rejected God's call through murdering the prophet Zechariah as that history approached its culmination in Jesus. When the leaders of the people bring this crescendo of rejection to its pinnacle in condemning Christ, the Messiah, God's grace is transferred to a new Chosen People, his Church, in which both Jews and Gentiles will find communion with God, and once again – this time for good – the Temple is destroyed (by the Romans in 70 AD).

Christ is the Lord of history, and so this drama is played out on a grand scale through the centuries, drawing on whole nations and empires as actors and padding the lists of martyrs. But he is also the Lord of each human heart, more precious and lasting longer than any earthly kingdom. Here too the principle stands: only one lord can rule, either Christ or self. Each soul is a temple built for the reigning and life-giving presence of God, but each person must decide to either let that purpose be fulfilled or hijack his soul for the kingdom of self. In the case of Jerusalem, Ezekiel foretold what the outcome would be, but in the case of each soul, no prophecy holds.

CHRIST THE TEACHER Jesus vividly describes the twofold results of hypocrisy. First, the divided, hypocritical soul inexorably moves from unjust attitudes and words to unjust deeds. The logical progression stems from the hypocrites' rebellion against reality. In their hearts they are greedy, self-centered, and arrogant (full of bones and corruption), but on the outside they put up the appearance of being magnanimous, God-fearing, and humble (handsome, freshly painted tombstones[5]). They show off their religious practices to make everyone think they are good; in truth, they are selfish. This rift between reality and appearances becomes their weapon for conquering esteem, influence, and wealth. Therefore, when they run up against someone they cannot conquer, someone

---

[5] *They kept them freshly painted because many tombs were located on the roadside, and if pilgrims coming to the Holy City unwittingly touched an indistinct tomb, they would be made unclean, and therefore unable to participate in Temple worship.*

who exposes the reality behind their appearances, they either have to repent or destroy; they must either resolve the discrepancy between their internal reality and their external appearances, or obliterate whoever is pointing out that discrepancy – they cannot merely tolerate such a profound threat. Thus, when God sends his prophets, some hypocrites may repent, but the others must destroy (i.e., murder) the messenger who is an intolerable sign of contradiction. Just so, small, interior sins tend to snowball into bigger sins, until the soul rebels directly and violently against God himself (Jesus) in a vain attempt to alter reality to fit his own distorted vision of self.

As if that diabolical progression from sin to greater sin weren't tragic enough in itself, Jesus also points out an even more disastrous result of hypocrisy. Not only does it spread corruption throughout the soul, like a cancer, but it closes the soul off from the possibility of receiving God's grace. When someone rebels against reality, he is exalting himself to a divine level. To murder, in fact, is to ape a divine action, since only God is the Lord of life and death. But if self is enthroned where God ought to be, how can that person recognize God's call, action, or invitation? God is forced to withdraw, dismissed by the sinner's own persistent refusal to heed the Spirit's pleas: "Your house will be deserted… You shall not see me anymore… Jesus left the Temple." Hypocrisy gradually destroys the sinner's own soul and the lives of those around him, and even sends God himself packing. It is the devil's work, and we are wise to shun it as the very antithesis of Christianity.

CHRIST THE FRIEND Not all of the Pharisees and scribes rejected Jesus. The Gospels tell of two men, Nicodemus and Joseph of Arimathea, who were secret disciples of the Lord. Surely they weren't alone. The Book of Acts also records the conversion of a large number of Temple officials in the aftermath of Pentecost. It is reasonable to surmise, then, that Jesus' longsuffering efforts to win over his rivals bore more fruit than St Matthew mentions. Perhaps even this last, scathing speech, delivered to the crowds and the disciples after the defeated departure of Jesus' pharisaical interrogators, was heard by more than a few Pharisees. Probably, however, the overwhelming force of Jesus' passion, death, and resurrection – suffered and carried out for the sake of these very sinners who rejected their Lord – put a chink even in these thick walls of hypocrisy, in some cases letting in just enough grace for the Holy Spirit to work.

Jesus never gives up on anyone. You can hear this loving persistence in his heart-felt plea: "How often I longed to gather your children…!" In the end, salvation is lost only by those who give up on him: "… and you refused!"

CHRIST IN MY LIFE You long for me to stay close to you, as a chick stays close to the hen. You long to be my teacher, my Lord, my leader, my shield, my companion, my friend. You know me through and through, and you still want me to stay with you, to listen to you, to follow you. Open my mind to your wisdom, my heart to your presence, and my will to your grace…

Your condemnations are terrifying, Lord. Our decisions and actions matter so much to you and have such lasting repercussions. I do not trust myself, Lord. The Pharisees couldn't even recognize their sin, they were so hardened. Save me from that. Inspire me to repent daily even of my small selfish acts and thoughts, to take wise advantage of the sacrament of Confession, and to do all things out of love…

You cared so deeply about your people! It hurt you so much when they rejected you – and how much you must have rejoiced in those who trusted you and followed you. I am so indifferent. Why don't I care more about bringing others into your friendship? Why do I look on the apostolate as a pastime instead of an urgent mission? It's because I don't love like you. Teach me, Lord, to love as you love…

QUESTIONS FOR SMALL GROUP DISCUSSION

1. What struck you most about this passage? What did you notice that you hadn't noticed before?

2. Why is hypocrisy a particularly dangerous temptation for people in leadership positions, especially positions of religious leadership?

3. Why do you think the apostles started up a conversation about the impressive beauty and grandeur of the Temple right after hearing this devastating speech?

4. Jesus passionately sought to convince people to believe in and follow him. As his disciples, we are called to do the same. How can we do so better?

Cf. Catechism of the Catholic Church, 591, 674, 1859 on hardening of the heart; 2563 and 2710 on the heart as the place of encounter with God; 573, 583-586, 593 on Jesus and the Temple

THE GOSPEL OF MATTHEW CHAPTER 24

"If he had revealed when he was to come again, his coming would have been made pointless and the peoples and ages in which it will take place would no longer yearn for it. He said that he will come again but he did not say exactly when. Hence, all generations and ages line in eager expectation of him. The Lord pointed out the signs of his coming but we have no knowledge of when they will be completed. In many varied ways they have happened and passed away and are still happening. His last

coming is, in fact, like his first. The just and the prophets longed for him, thinking that he was to appear in their day. So, today, each of the faithful wants to receive him in his own lifetime, just because he did not reveal the day of his coming."

- St Ephraem, Commentary on the Diatessaron

74. THE END OF THE OLD (MT 24:3-22)

"Our Lord Jesus Christ will, then, come from heaven. He will come in glory at the end of this world on the last day. Then there will be an end to this world, and this created world will be made new."

- St Cyril of Jerusalem

Matthew 24:3-22

And when he was sitting on the Mount of Olives the disciples came and asked him privately, 'Tell us, when is this going to happen, and what will be the sign of your coming and of the end of the world?' And Jesus answered them, 'Take care that no one deceives you; because many will come using my name and saying, I am the Christ, and they will deceive many. You will hear of wars and rumours of wars; do not be alarmed, for this is something that must happen, but the end will not be yet. For nation will fight against nation, and kingdom against kingdom. There will be famines and earthquakes here and there. All this is only the beginning of the birth-pangs. Then they will hand you over to be tortured and put to death; and you will be hated by all the nations on account of my name. And then many will fall away; men will betray one another and hate one another. Many false prophets will arise; they will deceive many, and with the increase of lawlessness, love in most men will grow cold; but the man who stands firm to the end will be saved. This Good News of the kingdom will be proclaimed to the whole world as a witness to all the nations. And then the end will come. 'So when you see the disastrous abomination, of which the prophet Daniel spoke, set up in the Holy Place (let the reader understand), then those in Judaea must escape to the mountains; if a man is on the housetop, he must not come down to collect his belongings; if a man is in the fields, he must not turn back to fetch his cloak. Alas for those with child, or with babies at the breast, when those days come! Pray that you will not have to escape in winter or on a sabbath. For then there will be great distress such as, until now, since the world began, there never has been, nor ever will be again. And if that time had not been shortened, no one would have survived; but shortened that time shall be, for the sake of those who are chosen.'

CHRIST THE LORD Jesus has exited the Temple in the wake of his final, definitive encounter with the faithless leaders of Jerusalem. He pronounced the Seven Woes and announced that the Old Covenant would soon come to an end – that their "house will be left desolate" and the Temple, symbol and center of that Covenant, would be destroyed. All of this was said in Jesus' last public discourse, which St Matthew presented as a climax of his whole public ministry. Now Jesus and his closest disciples, the apostles, leave Jerusalem and make their way back towards the town of Bethphage, where they frequently stayed. They descend from Temple mount, cross the Kedron Valley, and climb the Mount of Olives. Near the top they rest, and the apostles question Jesus about his predictions about the Temple's destruction.

We can picture our Lord sitting on the hillside, looking back down at Jerusalem, the City of the King, the golden Temple shining in the sunlight. He is surrounded by the men who have stayed faithful to him, the future leaders and pillars of his Church, representing the Jews who did accept their Messiah, as opposed to the leaders of Jerusalem who rejected him. He knows his passion is only a few hours away – the definitive moment when the Old Covenant will pass away and he will establish the new, everlasting Covenant in his blood. He knows what the future holds. The city and the Temple must be destroyed; they were meant to be the capitol of his Kingdom, but they have opted instead for a different type of kingdom (which the Jewish war of rebellion against Roman rule will try to establish by force in 68 AD), and the consequences will be dire. The Roman general and future emperor Titus will overrun Jewish resistance forces and lay a five-month siege to Jerusalem in 70 AD. Over a million Jews will die, just a few thousand will survive, and the Roman legions will crush the city and raze the Temple.

The Kingdom of Heaven will survive and grow, and the nascent Church will spread quickly, bringing Christ's message "to the whole world, as a witness to the nations," but the casualties will be severe. All of this is in the Lord's mind, and he speaks of it to his disciples, explaining the battle plan, as it were, for his conquest of the world by grace.

CHRIST THE TEACHER Chapter 24 of St Matthew's Gospel has produced more controversy than perhaps any other chapter. The language is obscure to non-Jewish ears, because it is taken from the prophetic and apocalyptic literature, which was well developed at the time of Christ but forgotten during the subsequent centuries. What is Jesus saying to his apostles in this mysterious conversation on the slope of Mount Olivet, overlooking the city that had rejected Jesus and was even now preparing to destroy him, unaware that it would seal its own destruction in the process?

Remember that Jesus is speaking to his Twelve Apostles. He is still preparing them for their mission as leaders of his Church, the new People of God. He has already stated that God will visit destruction on the Old Covenant, and in so doing he has implied the arrival of the long hoped for Day of the Lord that Jewish tradition identified with the beginning of the messianic era. The disciples ask him when it will happen, referring to the event as "his coming" and the "end of the world" – in other words, the definitive foundation of Christ's New Covenant Kingdom and the definitive end of the previous era of salvation history that had prepared for it. The Greek word translated as "world" in "end of the world" refers to epoch or age (i.e., the world built around the promises of the Old Covenant as opposed to the world built around their fulfillment in the New Covenant). Jesus' answer to their question occupies the rest of Chapters 24 and 25.

This answer refers primarily and literally to the coming siege and destruction of Jerusalem, since this was the event that would cap off the transition between Covenants. Until then, even Jewish converts to Christianity would still maintain many Old Covenant practices. The initial list of sufferings prophesized in this passage ("They will hand you over to be tortured…") were fulfilled literally in the martyrdoms, infra-Church dissention, and waves of violent persecution – initially from Jewish groups then from the Romans – that the first generation of Christians experienced before 70 AD. (And during that time, they did indeed bring the gospel to the whole known world.) Then Jesus says "the end will come" and the disciples will recognize it because of the "disastrous abomination" set up in the Temple. This refers to the idol that past conquerors had erected there (Daniel 9: 10-11); a similar desecration reappears during the Jewish rebellion, as the zealots turned the Temple into a fortress and then Roman troops crushed it. The second list of sufferings – from which "those in Judea must escape to the mountains" – refers to the siege of Jerusalem, described by other historical sources as unspeakably hideous. His warnings to escape before the siege begins were heeded by the Christians living there at the time, who fled to the city of Pella on the other side of the Jordan River.

The siege and destruction of Jerusalem, however, are in themselves prophetic events. And so, superimposed on Jesus' prophecy about them, we find another prophecy. In the Old Testament, the Temple was understood to serve as a kind of model of the entire cosmos. Thus Jesus' description of its destruction and related events also has a more universal application. Throughout the whole era of the Church, as the gospel keeps spreading, Christians will continue to suffer for their faith. And as the end of history itself draws near, human suffering will intensify during a siege of evil against the whole world, until the old order is destroyed to make room not for a new covenant, but even for a new heaven and a new earth able to contain the mature Kingdom of Christ.

Thus in answering his disciples' question about the destruction of the unfaithful Temple in 70 AD, Jesus also gives them a first lesson about the destruction of the fallen world at the end of time.

CHRIST THE FRIEND The disciples, who still misunderstand the nature of Jesus' Kingdom, are curious about the spectacular events Jesus has predicted. But in responding, Jesus desires to do much more than just satisfy their curiosity. He wants to prepare them. They need to know ahead of time that their mission will involve suffering and sacrifice; they need to know ahead of time that they have been chosen to be harbingers not just of any good news, but of the Good News of the eternal Kingdom – history from then on will divided into two halves, before Christ and after Christ; they also need to know that Jesus knows everything that will come to pass. When they begin their missionary work after Pentecost, they will be able to recall this conversation – in fact, as events unfold they will understand it more and more completely, and it will thereby increase their confidence in Jesus and in their mission. You can picture them later on, reflecting on the martyrdoms, the persecutions, the razing of Jerusalem – when suddenly a light goes on in their mind: "Yes, it's just as Jesus told us that day on the Mount of Olives…"

Perhaps more than anything, in the midst of their trials and tribulations they would recall verse 13: "but the man who stands firm to the end will be saved." How comforting it is to understand that the Lord knew ahead of time how hard following him would be for our fallen human nature, and to hear those words of encouragement! Jesus knows what we need even before we need it, and he never fails to supply it.

CHRIST IN MY LIFE I have such a narrow view of history; it makes me vulnerable to the tempests-in-a-teacup that swirl around me. Jesus, I believe that you are the Lord of history. You are providentially leading all things towards ultimate fulfillment in you, as an author carefully weaves and then ties together all the strands of his story. How much confidence, hope, and assurance this faith should give me! Jesus, I trust in you…

Some people describe Christians as "once saved, always saved." Yet in these words you regret that many of your Chosen People rejected you, and you warn the very leaders of your Church against doing the same: "The man who stands firm to the end will be saved…" Grant me your grace to keep me firm and to always confirm my brothers and sisters. With the fortitude of your heart, Lord Jesus, strengthen my heart…

QUESTIONS FOR GROUP DISCUSSION

1. What struck you most about this passage? What did you notice that you hadn't noticed before?

2. How would you describe what human history looks like from God's perspective? What do you think he is most interested in as he watches over the unfolding of historical events?

3. Knowing the Christ is the Lord history enables the Christian to have a unique perspective on world events. What light does this vision shed on some of the most important recent headlines? In other words, what's the difference between how a well formed Christian and a non-believer understand those headlines?

4. Does the destruction of Jerusalem after the city's leaders reject Jesus teach us anything about politics?

Cf. Catechism of the Catholic Church, 668-677 on Christ's glorious coming again in glory; 756-757 on the Church as the new Temple

75. THE BEGINNING OF THE NEW (MT 24:23-36)

"The Savior will come not to be judged again but to call to judgment those who called him to judgment. He who was silent when he was first judged will indict the malefactors who dared to perpetrate the outrage of the cross, and say, 'These things you did and I was silent.'"

- St Cyril of Jerusalem

Matthew 24:23-36

'If anyone says to you then, Look, here is the Christ or, He is there, do not believe it; for false Christs and false prophets will arise and produce great signs and portents, enough to deceive even the chosen, if that were possible. There; I have forewarned you. If, then, they say to you, Look, he is in the desert, do not go there; Look, he is in some hiding place, do not believe it; because the coming of the Son of Man will be like lightning striking in the east and flashing far into the west. Wherever the corpse is, there will the vultures gather. Immediately after the distress of those days the sun will be darkened, the moon will lose its brightness, the stars will fall from the sky and the powers of heaven will be shaken. And then the sign of the Son of Man will appear in heaven; then too all the peoples of the earth will beat their breasts; and they will see the Son of Man coming on the clouds of heaven with power and great glory. And he will send his angels with a loud trumpet to gather his chosen from the four winds, from one end of heaven to the other. Take the fig tree as a parable: as soon as its twigs grow supple and its leaves come out, you know that summer is near. So with you when you see all these things: know that he is near, at the very gates. I tell you solemnly, before this generation has passed away all these things will have taken place. Heaven and earth will pass away, but my words will never pass away. But as for that day and hour, nobody knows it, neither the angels of heaven, nor the Son, no one but the Father only.'

CHRIST THE LORD Jesus speaks of these future events with utter assurance, as no merely human leader can. He demonstrates that the ebb and flow of history, so elusive and mysterious for even the most brilliant human intellects, is firmly within his grasp. Here, in fact, with the doctrine of God's providence giving history a rational shape, the idea of progress finds its origin. Only in the Christian West does this idea take root and develop. Pre-Christian and non-Christian philosophies and religions tend to view history as a cycle of recurrence, without origin and without purpose. Jesus, the Lord of history, reveals something else entirely. All will be brought to completion; beneath the seemingly chaotic and destructive surface of the human story the irresistible hand of providence is at work, strong with the strength of the Creator, wise with the wisdom of the Word, but secret and subtle with the breath of the Spirit. For the Christian, realism is optimism, because the Lord is in control.

CHRIST THE TEACHER Jesus is still sitting on Mount Olivet with his apostles, gazing thoughtfully down at the chosen city that has rejected him and answering the disciples' question about when the Temple, the symbol and center of the Old Covenant kingdom, will be destroyed and Christ's new Kingdom will be established. As in the first part of this chapter, Jesus is still describing primarily the destruction of Jerusalem and the events surrounding it. That very destruction is understood as Christ's coming – his coming to end the Old Covenant definitively and inaugurate the New. Before it comes to pass, false Messiahs will appear in Palestine (many did between the death of Jesus and the Jewish rebellion against Rome – in fact, their agitation helped spark the rebellion), whether in the likeness of desert ascetics or basement conspirators. Jesus warns his disciples of them beforehand, telling them not to pay attention to them. The Day of the Lord, the consequences of the leaders' rejection of Jesus played out in the Temple's destruction, will happen in a visible, violent way, like lightning: the siege and toppling of Jerusalem by the Roman army.

Then Jesus shifts focus. He looks to what will come about as a result of Jerusalem's downfall, after "the distress of those days." For this, he marshals language that the prophets (and other apocalyptic literature of the time) used to describe the messianic age, the time when the Kingdom of Heaven would be established. The darkening of the sun and moon, the falling of the stars, the coming of the Son of Man on the clouds of heaven – these indicate primarily the alteration of the cosmic order that comes when the age of promises (Old Covenant) gives way to the age of fulfillment (New Covenant). Jesus is speaking of the age of the Church, when his messengers will make Christ's glory known throughout the world, establishing his Kingdom through their witness, their preaching, their miracles, and their martyrdoms – these are the trumpets that will gather believers into the new, sacramental and spiritual People of God, wherever they may be geographically. Jesus applies messianic language to the expansion of his Church, indicating the true nature of that New Covenant community – the fulfillment of God's promises to Israel.

As in the earlier part of this discourse, the literal references to the destruction of the Old Jerusalem and the expansion of the New Jerusalem (the Church) refer simultaneously to the future destruction of the fallen world and the establishment of the new heavens and the new earth at the end of time. Thus, the experience of the first generation of Christians prior to the Temple's destruction – the alternation between growth and difficulties – establishes a pattern that all future generations will continue to experience, both personally (as individuals receive the gospel, repent, and leave behind their old ways of life to experience the glory of the life of grace) and also communally (as the saints continue to spread Christ's message into pagan societies that will have to shed their old ways in order to be conformed to the truths of God's revelation in Christ). And in the end, just as the first generation of Christians witnessed the destruction of Jerusalem, the last generation of Christians will witness the destruction of history as the everlasting Kingdom flowers into eternity.

CHRIST THE FRIEND Throughout this discourse, Jesus has one thing in mind: preparing his disciples to cope with the challenges their mission will bring. In this passage, he illumines the pattern (not the exact dates and times – only the Father knows the day and hour) of social unrest, growth, dissention, and persecution that will mark the apostles' years of ministry as well as the whole history of the Church. He advises them to learn from the signs of coming fruit put forth by the fig tree – thus, when the things he describes come to pass, they will not surprise his disciples, but only confirm their faith in Jesus, who predicted them. His words should have the same effect on us. Birth pangs are necessary for giving birth; struggle and sacrifice are unavoidable if we want to grow in friendship with Christ. The good Doctor of our souls wants us to be ready for the sometimes painful operation of making us into saints.

CHRIST IN MY LIFE Sometimes I am still amazed that you have shared your mission with me. You have called me to follow you and build your Kingdom in my heart and in the world around me. You have entrusted your message to me and sent me as your ambassador. Don't you know how weak I am? Of course you know. Lord, when I am weak, I am strong, because then I stay closer to you…

Nothing matters to you more than your Church. She is your bride and your body. She is the beginning of your everlasting Kingdom. Earthly kingdoms come and go, but your Church remains, and grows, and pours out the fruits of holiness in every age and place. Thank you for bringing me into your Church. Your power and your wisdom shine forth in her. Bless your Church, her leaders, and all her works…

Lord, I am still surprised when troubles come, but I shouldn't be. They are part of your plan. You experienced them. Your saints experienced them. Your Church experiences them. Increase my faith, Lord, and the faith of those who are suffering more than I. Teach me to perceive your action in all things. Jesus, I trust in you…

QUESTIONS FOR SMALL GROUP DISCUSSION

1. What struck you most about this passage? What did you notice that you hadn't noticed before?

2. What tone of voice do you think Jesus used in speaking of these things with his disciples? How do you think his disciples reacted?

3. What types of persecution are faithful Catholics facing today?

4. What can we do now to prepare ourselves to stay faithful to Christ later, when troubles come?

Cf. Catechism of the Catholic Church, 1040 on not knowing the "day nor the hour"; 1023-1029 on heaven; 863-865 on the universal responsibility of Christians to spread Christ's Kingdom

76. GETTING READY (MT 24:37-51)

"He first came in the order of divine providence to teach men by gentle persuasion, but when he comes again they will, whether they wish it or not, be subjected to his kingship."
- St Cyril of Jerusalem

Matthew 24:37-51

'As it was in Noah's day, so will it be when the Son of Man comes. For in those days before the Flood people were eating, drinking, taking wives, taking husbands, right up to the day Noah went into the ark, and they suspected nothing till the Flood came and swept all away. It will be like this when the Son of Man comes. Then of two men in the fields one is taken, one left; of two women at the millstone grinding, one is taken, one left. So stay awake, because you do not know the day when your master is coming. You may be quite sure of this that if the householder had known at what time of the night the burglar would come, he would have stayed awake and would not have allowed anyone to break through the wall of his house. Therefore, you too must stand ready because the Son of Man is coming at an hour you do not expect. What sort of servant, then, is faithful and wise enough for the master to place him over his household to give them their food at the proper time? Happy that servant if his master's arrival finds him at this employment. I tell you solemnly, he will place him over everything he owns. But as for the dishonest servant who says to himself, My master is taking his time, and sets about beating his fellow servants and eating and drinking with drunkards, his master will come on a day he does not expect and at an hour he does not know. The master will cut him off and send him to the same fate as the hypocrites, where there will be weeping and grinding of teeth.'

CHRIST THE LORD The Church presents us with this passage at the start of Advent. During the season of Advent, we gratefully recall Christ's first coming, we renew our faith in his continual coming in the life of the Church, and we stir up our anticipation of his Second Coming at the end of time. In the context St Matthew provides for these words, Jesus is also referring to three comings: the imminent destruction of Jerusalem (and foundation of the Church), the future destruction (and remaking) of the cosmos at the end of history, and the inevitable end of each individual's earthly existence. In few passages does Christ's universal Lordship – past, present, and future – show itself more clearly.

It is worth contemplating this scene: sitting with Jesus and his apostles on the Mount of Olives in the cool of the evening after a busy day in the Temple, eagerly listening, trying to understand, glad to be there with him. See the gleaming marble and domes of the city, recently refurbished by King Herod the Great. See the busy throngs pouring in and out of the city gates and through the city streets, preoccupied with the hundred-and-one cares of daily living while their Creator and Lord looks on from above. See the sun setting behind the guard towers on the far side of the city walls, silhouetting the taller palaces and sending rays of color through the clouds. Hear the voice of Jesus, instructing his followers. Did he speak slowly, or was he full of eagerness and zeal? Did his voice reveal the sadness he felt at the rejection of the city leaders, or the enthusiasm of knowing that the Church for which he was about to give his life would last for centuries, pouring his grace into the hearts of people throughout the globe? See the faces of his twelve closest disciples and friends. Some are rapt with attention; others perhaps are disturbed by his words and look off into the distance. Some are perplexed. All are simply glad to be at their Master's side...

In our own hearts and imagination, and not just in the Advent season, we can join the apostles there to experience the Lord as they did.

CHRIST THE TEACHER Up until this point, Jesus has been answering his disciples' question about when the destruction of the Temple and the establishment of the new Kingdom would take place. Jesus has explained the signs of those events; he has given a sketch of the apostolic age of the Church, which will serve as a pattern for the whole messianic age until the Second Coming. The time has come to draw some conclusions.

The disciples now know that both exciting growth and painful persecution await them. They know that Jerusalem, the center of the Old Covenant, will be destroyed to make way for the New Covenant, and then the world itself will eventually be destroyed to make way for the new heavens and the new earth at the end of the messianic age – though they don't know exactly when all this will happen. This is the lesson of Noah: a prophetic event.

What should they – indeed, what should *we* do with this knowledge? The answer is: Use it to give sharp focus to how we spend whatever amount of time we have left. The bottom line is that our time is limited. This awareness should keep us awake and dedicated to the mission we have received. Jesus considers this lesson to be so important that he dedicates these and three other parables to getting it across; he knew how easily even the most faithful disciple can fall into the trap of thinking that this life is the goal, not merely the path.

CHRIST THE FRIEND Love is never satisfied. Christ's three comings – originally at his incarnation, continually through the Liturgy, and finally and definitively at his second coming – all have the same purpose: to reestablish and deepen our friendship with God. But even these do not satisfy his desire to be with us. He wants to come into our lives every day. He yearns to encounter his bride, to renew his covenant with the Church and with every individual soul as often as possible. In the Eucharist, he found a way to continue coming to us day after day: a new advent, a new Bethlehem, a renewed communion every time the Eucharist is celebrated. At each Mass, every day, he longs to take up fresh lodging in our hearts; his only hope is that there will be some room in the inn.

Jesus: It is hard for you to imagine how glad I am whenever you take time to pray, to sit with me and listen to my words and speak what is in your heart. This is what my first disciples did; this is what all my followers have done, through the centuries. I am the Lord of history, and I am the Lord of your personal history. I will never rule you by force, however. I love you too much for that. So whenever you look to me and listen to me, my heart rejoices, because it means you want to share your life with me, just as I yearn to share mine with you.

CHRIST IN MY LIFE Thank you for coming to be our Savior. Thank you for taking my sins upon yourself, and for enlightening me with these eternal truths. I can count on your word. You will come again to bring history to its conclusion. And you want me to organize my life with the end in mind. So many people search so anxiously for an answer to this question of what the future holds. I already have the answer. Thank you, Lord…

What aspects of my life need to be reformed by this teaching? I want my whole life to be pleasing to you, to glorify you, and to bear fruit for your Kingdom. If I am close to you, I will be able to do so much more to help those around me. Take me on an inventory of my habits, activities, and attitudes and show me what to change… With the Kingdom of your heart, Lord, reign in my heart …

QUESTIONS FOR SMALL GROUP DISCUSSION

1. What struck you most about this passage? What did you notice that you hadn't noticed before?
2. Why does Christ want us to be ready for his coming? Why would it matter to him?
3. Why do you think God hasn't revealed to us the exact time of his Second Coming?
4. Some non-believers criticize Christians for disengaging from this earthly life because they are so worried about eternal life. How would you respond to this criticism? Do these parables encourage us to disengage from earthly life?

Cf. Catechism of the Catholic Church, 673-674, 1040 on the uncertainty of the time of the Lord's coming; 522-526 on the meaning of Advent and Christmas; 1, 27, 45 on communion with God as the meaning of life

THE GOSPEL OF MATTHEW   CHAPTER 25

But let us see what sort of wisdom he then demands. He calls it the wisdom 'of a serpent.' The serpent abandons everything, even if its body has to be cut off, and does not resist much, provided only it can save its head. In the same way, he says, abandon everything except your faith, even if it means giving up your wealth, you body, your life itself. Your faith is your head and your roots. If you preserve that, you will get everything back again with greater glory. Therefore he commanded that a man should be not only simple and honest, not only wise, but he combined the two qualities to form together virtue. A man should have the wisdom of the serpent, so as not to receive mortal wounds. He should have the innocence of a dove, so as not to take vengeance on those who do him injury, nor bear a grudge against those who plot against him. Wisdom is no use by itself unless there is innocence as well."

- St John Chrysostom

77. STAYING READY (MT 25:1-13)

'It is not enough for us, then, to be content with his first coming; we must wait in hope of his second coming."

- St Cyril of Jerusalem

Matthew 25:1-13

'Then the kingdom of heaven will be like this: Ten bridesmaids took their lamps and went to meet the bridegroom. Five of them were foolish and five were sensible: the foolish ones did take their lamps, but they brought no oil, whereas the sensible ones took flasks of oil as well as their lamps. The bridegroom was late, and they all grew drowsy and fell asleep. But at midnight there was a cry, The bridegroom is here! Go out and meet him. At this, all those bridesmaids woke up and trimmed their lamps, and the foolish ones said to the sensible ones, Give us some of your oil: our lamps are going out. But they replied, There may not be enough for us and for you; you had better go to those who sell it and buy some for yourselves. They had gone off to buy it when the bridegroom arrived. Those who were ready went in with him to the wedding hall and the door was closed. The other bridesmaids arrived later. Lord, Lord, they said open the door for us. But he replied, I tell you solemnly, I do not know you. So stay awake, because you do not know either the day or the hour.'

CHRIST THE LORD Jesus and his apostles are still sitting on the slope of Mount Olivet, looking down on Jerusalem as his passion draws near. The Lord has given his ambassadors a briefing on what will happen in the messianic age, which he was even then inaugurating. In Chapter 25, St Matthew shows our Lord stressing the lessons he wants his disciples to glean from their privileged

287

knowledge of what is to come. He has painted the future in broad strokes: persecution, transformation, dissention, and through it all the glorious sign of the Son of Man shining over the redeemed world through the marvelous growth of the Church. His Kingdom will triumph. It may start small, like a mustard seed, but it will grow to immense proportions, until it attracts the very birds of the air – the farthest nations of the earth – to come and dwell in its branches. His assurance is breathtaking. Perhaps he only spoke this discourse to his Twelve because only they knew him well enough to take seriously such colossal claims – that he knows the future, governs it, and sends the leaders of his Church to conquer the entire world for his Kingdom. If Jesus had left any room for doubt about his being the Lord, he removes it here. No mere philosopher, reformer, political revolutionary, or even prophet could speak so definitively; this Lord is worthy of our faith.

Jesus, however, is more than a Lord; he is also a Bridegroom. The image of a wedding banquet, already present in the Old Testament, appears multiple times in his own preaching. Each soul is his bride; the Church is his bride; and the goal of each individual life and of human history is a spousal union, a complete communion of persons, of hearts, between the Lord and his subjects. The parable reminds us of what Jesus thinks about those he came to save and to rule, and it reminds us that he is looking forward to his wedding day. Are we?

CHRIST THE TEACHER The parable of the ten bridesmaids is the first of three St Matthew records in Chapter 25. Each one amplifies the previous discourse, where Jesus explains the coming destruction of the Temple and the events leading up to and surrounding it – a historical reality that, as we have seen, is prophetic: it foreshadows what will happen to the entire cosmos throughout the messianic age before Christ's Second Coming; it also sets the pattern for what will happen in the life of each person as death approaches. These three levels of meaning (the destruction of Jerusalem, the end of history, and individual death) overlap and reinforce one another. Each of the three parables brings special light to bear on one level of meaning, while still being relevant for all levels.

This first parable illustrates most especially the coming destruction of the Temple and the Old Covenant. The Messiah is Israel's bridegroom. The people of Israel are the bridesmaids: as the Chosen People, they were given a special invitation to accompany the nuptial celebration. In the time of Christ and during the first wave of evangelization before 70 AD (the destruction of the Temple), the Bridegroom arrives and, through his passion, death, and resurrection, consummates the promised communion between mankind and God. Many contemporary Jews (like the apostles) recognize Christ's coming, accept him, and enter into the joy of the Kingdom – the wise bridesmaids. Many others, however, reject him (especially the leaders of the Holy City), and they suffer exile after the Romans destroy Jerusalem – the foolish bridesmaids. The wise bridesmaids stand for those who not only believed in God's promises (this faith is symbolized by the lamp), but also strove to live a life of humility and virtue – of godly actions and good works (symbolized by the extra oil). The Pharisees and Sadducees, on the other hand, had faith, but no virtuous acts; their religion was superficial, and so when the Messiah came they were caught unawares and missed him.

Likewise for every believer: faith in Christ must lead to a life increasingly like Christ's. As St James puts it, "Faith, if good deeds do not go with it, is quite dead" (James 2:17). Jesus wants us all to be integral, mature Christians, ready for his coming at any moment. He warns us as clearly as he can not to be foolish, and he gives us the secret to wisdom. The lamp in this sense stands for *a living knowledge of him,* friendship with him, a vital and personal relationship with him, a relationship that has been lived and cultivated throughout our terrestrial pilgrimage (the extra oil refers to the ongoing cultivation of that relationship). Because of this friendship, this life of grace, how would he ever be able to say to us, "I do not know you"? He will not, and we will find ourselves with lighted lamp in the family of God as it celebrates the wedding of the Lamb.

CHRIST THE FRIEND Christ also paints quite a lively picture of heaven in this passage, and in other similar passages. What produces more intense joy than a wedding and its celebration? In human terms, it is hard to come up with something to top it. When we think of heaven, Christ wants us to think in those terms: joy, delight, pleasure, the communion of hearts and minds, a celebration. Even our wildest imaginary exaggerations will fall almost infinitely short of the reality, but that doesn't mean we shouldn't think about it. The great Christian virtue of hope allows us to envision in our mind's eye the total fulfillment of all the deepest yearnings of our heart upon arrival to the Father's house. Keeping heaven in mind and activating our faith in what Christ has revealed about it should motivate us in our battle to be his faithful friends, to build and spread his Kingdom. After all, it was to open heaven's gates – which sin had closed – that Christ became a man, lived, died, and rose again; and so, to let heaven fade out of our thoughts would be a monstrous insult, at the very least.

CHRIST IN MY LIFE Open my mind to know you better, Lord. I want to know your love as it really is. Only your love for me can cast out my fears and fill me with peace, confidence, and lasting joy in the midst of life's troubles. Why can't I see you more clearly? Show me your face, Lord; show me your heart. I want to see you!...

Am I ready, Lord? Am I really living out my faith, or has it grown cold, superficial, or overly intellectual? Does it give light and meaning to everything I do, to every relationship? If you told this parable to your apostles, it's because you knew they needed to hear it. I am sure I need to hear it too. I'm already good at being foolish, Lord, so help me to be wise…

You tell this parable because you love us. You want us to know how to enter into your grace now and for all eternity. Please pour that same love into my heart, so I will be creative and courageous in spreading your good news. Why doesn't my heart burn more ardently to save souls? With the love of your heart, Lord, inflame my heart…

QUESTIONS FOR SMALL GROUP DISCUSSION

1. What struck you most about this passage? What did you notice that you hadn't noticed before?

2. What more can we do to make sure that our lamps and as many other lamps as possible are lit when Christ comes?

3. In relation to the meaning of the parable, how can you explain why the wise bridesmaids don't share their extra oil with the foolish ones?

4. How would you respond to someone who objected that Jesus is being unfair here, because since the bridesmaids didn't know the bridegroom would be so late, why should they be punished for not being prepared?

Cf. Catechism of the Catholic Church, 1026-1027 on heaven; 142-165 on the nature and importance of faith in our relationship with God, 2558 on the importance of a vital and personal relationship with God

78. TALENTS IN TRUST (MT 25:14-30)

"We preach not one coming only of Christ, but a second also, far more glorious than the first. The first revealed the meaning of his patient endurance; the second brings with it the crown of the divine kingdom."

- St Cyril of Jerusalem

Matthew 25:14-30

'It is like a man on his way abroad who summoned his servants and entrusted his property to them. To one he gave five talents, to another two, to a third one; each in proportion to his ability. Then he set out. The man who had received the five talents promptly went and traded with them and made five more. The man who had received two made two more in the same way. But the man who had received one went off and dug a hole in the ground and hid his master's money. Now a long time after, the master of those servants came back and went through his accounts with them. The man who had received the five talents came forward bringing five more. Sir, he said you entrusted me with five talents; here are five more that I have made. His master said to him, Well done, good and faithful servant; you have shown you can be faithful in small things, I will trust you with greater; come and join in your master's happiness. Next the man with the two talents came forward. Sir, he said you entrusted me with two talents; here are two more that I have made. His master said to him, Well done, good and faithful servant; you have shown you can be faithful in small things, I will trust you with greater; come and join in your master's happiness. Last came forward the man who had the one talent. Sir, said he, I had heard you were a hard man, reaping where you have not sown and gathering where you have not scattered; so I was afraid, and I went off and hid your talent in the ground. Here it is; it was yours, you have it back. But his master answered him, You wicked and lazy servant! So you knew that I reap where I have not sown and gather where I have not scattered? Well then, you should have deposited my money with the bankers, and on my return I would have recovered my capital with interest. So now, take the talent from him and give it to the man who has the five talents. For to everyone who has will be given more, and he will have more than enough; but from the man who has not, even what he has will be taken away. As for this good-for-nothing servant, throw him out into the dark, where there will be weeping and grinding of teeth.'

CHRIST THE LORD Christ is the king of the parable, and we are the servants. Do you think of yourself as a servant? God has given each of us a certain number of "talents." (By a fortuitous linguistic quirk, the word that in the original language refers to a large sum of money refers in our language to a much broader category of skills and abilities.) Christ's return in the context of this discourse means three things: when destruction comes upon Jerusalem sometime after Jesus' ascension, when he comes again at the end of history – which could be tomorrow or could be in another thousand years – and when he comes individually to each of us at the end of our lives, another mysterious moment. And so, we have an unknown amount of time in which to invest those talents and to make them increase the wealth of the Kingdom – or not. Our eternal destiny depends directly upon how much our talents have contributed to the growth of the Kingdom. There will be no room for excuses: if we have tried to invest our talents, we will be welcomed into the Kingdom forever: if not, we will be thrown into the darkness.

Perhaps at first glance the most striking aspect of this parable is how definitive it is. Jesus speaks so unambiguously, even graphically, about heaven and hell. Since he is Lord of life, death, and history, nothing about them is hidden from him. Yet, another glance will show something even more striking: he desires all of us to come and be with him in heaven.

CHRIST THE TEACHER Note first of all that our talents are to be invested *on behalf of the king*, since we will have to give them back to the king in the end. They must increase the wealth of Christ's Kingdom. We are called to use our talents to extend and defend the Kingdom of God, to promote true human values (justice, life, beauty, and peace), to spread the good news of salvation in Jesus Christ, to bring as many people as possible into this Kingdom (which here on earth subsists in the Church), to overtake the remaining bastions of sin and greed, and dismantle every work of the devil. To the extent that I use my talents for these purposes, I will achieve the purpose of my life, please the king, and prove myself his worthy subject, one who has responsibly administered the great gifts I have received. And as a result, I will be rewarded accordingly; the reward will be proportionate to my diligence. (Christ was always talking about rewards.)

Note secondly what the Church has always understood by talents: *every gift* we have received from God, starting with the gift of existence, including all the capabilities of our bodies and minds, extending to education, culture, faith, the sacraments, vocation, and every opportunity and resource within our personal sphere of influence – from money to artistic sensibility, from creative genius to physical prowess, from freedom of speech to the elusive entity of time itself. In other words, we have received *everything* from God, and we are free either to take all our gifts and squander them, burying them in the hole of self-indulgence, fear, laziness, and greed (as did the prodigal son, for instance, in addition to the hapless fellow of the current parable), or to give them back to God by putting them to work for his Kingdom. Nothing escapes the eternal reckoning, so everything is a chance to build up or tear down our relationship with God. In this parable, Christ implores us: "Live for the things that last! Strive for true human and Christian values! Don't be afraid to lay everything on the line for me and for the Church! For others, time is *money*; for you, time is *Kingdom*."

CHRIST THE FRIEND How clearly Christ speaks to us in the Gospels! He does not disguise his saving truth in complicated theological costumes; he does not distort it for fear of offending our over-sensitive egocentrism; he does not greedily hoard it. God *wants* to save *us* and teach us the path of a fulfilling life; Christ is the generous agent of that salvation.

The lazy servant of the parable failed precisely because he had a different concept of the master. He feared him like a slave, maybe even resented him (for only giving him one talent and giving more to the other servants). He thought of his lord as a hard taskmaster; the mission with which he was entrusted seemed too demanding, too unreasonable. We can fall into the same deception. We are exceedingly vulnerable to it, because it gives us an easy excuse for wallowing in our laziness and self-pity. Jesus has proved that he is thoroughly trustworthy, but since trusting him means breaking out of our comfort zone, sometimes we prefer to stay suspicious. Few things pain his heart more.

Jesus: I created you to know me and love me, to live in my friendship now and for all eternity. I have limited my omnipotence in giving you this possibility, because friendship requires freedom, and freedom necessitates the possibility that you will reject my friendship. But you have nothing to fear from me, nothing to lose in following me. You gain everything by accepting my invitation. Enjoy the life and talents I have given you, invest them for eternity, and trust that I will never demand from you more than you are capable of giving.

CHRIST IN MY LIFE My life is a mission. You have given me real responsibility; what I do matters, for me and for others. Sometimes this makes me feel pressured – but that's not what you want. You want me to launch out into the deep with utter confidence in you. Enlarge my heart! Increase my faith! You are worthy of all trust, of all love, of any sacrifice. Thank you for giving me a few talents. Help me to put them to work…

How many people squander their lives, Lord! Just as I was doing before you came to my rescue…. You are so patient with me. You give me plenty of time. And all you ask is that I try my best to serve you, please you, and glorify you by fulfilling my potential and helping as many others as I can fulfill theirs. Through me, may your Kingdom come…

QUESTIONS FOR SMALL GROUP DISCUSSION

1. What struck you most about this passage? What did you notice that you hadn't noticed before?

2. How would a non-believer criticize this parable? How would you respond to the criticism?

3. If all Catholics in this country were to put all their talents directly at the service of the Kingdom of God, how would society change? What if 50 percent did? What if 25 percent did?

4. How does the development of our natural talents, like athletic or artistic ability, glorify God?

Cf. Catechism of the Catholic Church, 1020-1022 on death and the particular judgment; 1038-1041 on the Last Judgment; 1023-1037 on heaven, hell, and purgatory

79. CHEAT SHEET (MT 25:31-46)

"I beg you, join with me in love. Run with me in faith. Let us yearn for our heavenly home. Let us sigh for it. Let us realize that we are strangers here below."

- St Augustine

Matthew 25: 31-46

'When the Son of Man comes in his glory, escorted by all the angels, then he will take his seat on his throne of glory. All the nations will be assembled before him and he will separate men one from another as the shepherd separates sheep from goats. He will place the sheep on his right hand and the goats on his left. Then the King will say to those on his right hand, Come, you whom my Father has blessed, take for your heritage the kingdom prepared for you since the foundation of the world. For I was hungry and you gave me food; I was thirsty and you gave me drink; I was a stranger and you made me welcome; naked and you clothed me, sick and you visited me, in prison and you came to see me. Then the virtuous will say to him in reply, Lord, when did we see you hungry and feed you; or thirsty and give you drink? When did we see you a stranger and make you welcome; naked and clothe you; sick or in prison and go to see you? And the King will answer, I tell you solemnly, in so far as you did this to one of the least of these brothers of mine, you did it to me. Next he will say to those on his left hand, Go away from me, with your curse upon you, to the eternal fire prepared for the devil and his angels. For I was hungry and you never gave me food; I was thirsty and you never gave me anything to drink; I was a stranger and you never made me welcome, naked and you never clothed me, sick and in prison and you never visited me. Then it will be their turn to ask, Lord, when did we see you hungry or thirsty, a stranger or naked, sick or in prison, and did not come to your help? Then he will answer, I tell you solemnly, in so far as you neglected to do this to one of the least of these, you neglected to do it to me. And they will go away to eternal punishment, and the virtuous to eternal life.'

CHRIST THE LORD Jesus Christ makes an unambiguous claim to universal authority. All the nations of the world will come before him to be judged; all the angels make up his royal court; he holds in his hands the eternal destiny of every man and woman of all time. This passage leaves no room for us to wonder about who Christ really is: either he is the Lord of life and history as he claims to be, or he is a lunatic, and the testimony of the Church throughout the last twenty centuries (first of all, its mere longevity, but also the contribution of wisdom and holiness it has made to human culture) eliminates the lunatic option. Jesus Christ is the King of kings and the Lord of lords; he alone is the Holy One and the Most High, as we proclaim every Sunday when we sing the

Gloria at Mass. He is worthy of our allegiance.

Yet, once again he shows that his Lordship is not only grand and majestic, but intimate and accessible. He is a King who identifies himself with each one of his subjects. In fact, he is present in every person. His love is so total, so unabashed, so reckless, that it propels his very self into every human heart. In a mysterious way, he dwells in each one of us. The revolution that this Lord proclaims happens every time we act in accordance with this amazing truth.

CHRIST THE TEACHER He is also the most generous of teachers. At the end of life we will all have to take a final exam, the only exam that really matters. Christ is the examiner, and in this passage he gives us ahead of time not only the questions on the exam, but also the answers.

This lesson uncovers the most precious truth of all, the pearl of great price that men and women have searched for since the very beginning: the meaning of life. In the end, all that will matter is what we have done for Christ and our neighbor. We will not be asked how much money we made, how many awards we won, how famous we became, how many discoveries we made, how many achievements we accomplished, how much we enjoyed ourselves, or how many people we had working under us. We will be asked one question: "What did you do for me in your neighbor?" Christ teaches us repeatedly in the Gospels by word and example that the secret to happiness in this life and the life to come is self-giving, self-forgetful love, serving the spiritual and material needs of our brothers and sisters, through Christ, with Christ, and in Christ. Only self-giving – the mark of authentic love – counteracts the epidemic of self-centeredness, self-indulgence, and self-sufficiency that has scourged the human family ever since the fall.

This third parable specifically references the final judgment at the Second Coming, after the destruction of the cosmos and the end of history. The parable of the bridesmaids applied more directly to the destruction of Jerusalem in the apostolic age, and that of the talents focused on the experience of the individual soul at the moment of death. With this parable, Jesus completes his briefing to the apostles about what the future has in store.

CHRIST THE FRIEND Our God does not sit idly by as we struggle through life, waiting to pass judgment on all our failings. True, judgment will come, because God is fair, but Jesus Christ does all he can to prepare each of us ahead of time. In the first place, he came to earth; he became one of us, so that he could teach

295

us using words and actions that we would understand. Secondly, he stays with us "until the end of time" (Matthew 28:20) through the ministry of his Church. The Church makes his teachings ring out in every age and place, constantly reminding us of the gospel's saving truths; through her the Holy Spirit vivifies the sacraments in order to bring each of her children into intimate friendship with God; above all, through her Christ stays literally at our side in the Eucharist, accompanying us patiently and lovingly in every tabernacle throughout the world. In this way, he hopes to make the Last Judgment a joyful reunion of intimate friends, not a surprise encounter between hostile strangers.

CHRIST IN MY LIFE I know you ascended in heaven after your resurrection, Lord. I know that you are there now, interceding for me and guiding your Church through the Holy Spirit. And yet, you tell me that you are still present in my heart, and in the hearts of all my brothers and sisters here on earth. I can never grasp this truth with my own intelligence. Teach me, Lord. May your grace open the eyes of my soul to see you as you really are…

How could you have been clearer? You care about how I treat my neighbor, what I do for those around me. It seems so burdensome to live with my attention focused on others. I have so many needs, desires, and dreams of my own! But what matters most is not what I do, but who I am. Am I someone who loves, who gives, who serves? Self-giving is the one law of heaven. If I can't learn to obey it now, I won't ever want to obey it later…

In the end, you will make all things right. All the injustice and misery of the world will not escape your goodness and your power. I believe that you will come again, to judge, to rule, and to set things right. You wouldn't have promised this if you weren't planning on doing it. Help me to prepare for that day, and to help everyone around me prepare as well…

QUESTIONS FOR SMALL GROUP DISCUSSION

1. What struck you most about this passage? What did you notice that you hadn't noticed before?

2. According to this parable, the standard by which we will all be judged has to do with what each person *failed to do,* with sins of *omission.* How do sins of *commission* (murder, adultery, etc.) fit into this picture?

3. Why is Jesus so interested in how we treat our neighbor?

4. What aspects of popular culture help us live out the ethic Jesus propounds in this parable? What aspects don't?

Cf. Catechism of the Catholic Church, 668-682 on Christ's second coming and the last judgment; 2443-2463 on love for the poor, the traditional "works of mercy" as ways of loving God and neighbor

THE GOSPEL OF MATTHEW CHAPTER 26

'Fix your minds, then, on the passion of our Lord Jesus Christ. Inflamed with love for us, he came down from heaven to redeem us. For our sake he endured every torment of body and soul and shrank from no bodily pain. He himself gave us an example of perfect patience and love. We, then, are to be patient in adversity. Put aside your hatred and animosity. Take pains to refrain from sharp words. If they escape your lips, do not be ashamed to let your lips produce the remedy, since they have caused the wounds. Pardon one another so that later on you will not remember the injury. The recollection of an injury is itself wrong. It adds to our anger, nurtures our sin, and hates what is good. It is a rusty arrow and poison for the soul. It puts all virtue to flight. It is like a worm in the mind: it confuses our speech and tears to shreds our petitions to God. It is foreign to charity: it remains planted in the soul like a nail. It is wickedness that never sleeps, sin that never fails. It is indeed a daily death. Be peace-loving. Peace is a precious treasure to be sought with great zeal. You are well aware that our sins arouse God's anger. You must change your life, therefore, so that God in his mercy will pardon you. What we conceal from men is known to God. Be converted, then, with a sincere heart. Live your life that you may receive the blessing of the Lord. Then the peace of God our Father will be with you always."

- St Francis of Paola

80. THE DIE IS CAST (MT 26:1-5)

"Do not fear anything; I am always with you."

- Words of Jesus to St Faustina Kowalska

Matthew 26:1-5

Jesus had now finished all he wanted to say, and he told his disciples, 'It will be Passover, as you know, in two days' time, and the Son of Man will be handed over to be crucified'. Then the chief priests and the elders of the people assembled in the palace of the high priest, whose name was Caiaphas, and made plans to arrest Jesus by some trick and have him put to death. They said, however, 'It must not be during the festivities; there must be no disturbance among the people.'

CHRIST THE LORD As St Matthew begins his narration of Christ's passion, he reminds us that Jesus knew exactly what was going to happen. His suffering,

297

humiliation, unjust condemnation, death, and resurrection – Jesus knew what lay before him. Even as the leaders of the people gather to figure out how to do away with Jesus once and for all, the Lord is one step ahead of them; already preparing himself and his disciples for the final battle.

His foreknowledge doesn't mean that his enemies were being forced by fate to act as they did; it simply means that God's Providence is able to take mankind's freedom, respect it, and still weave those free actions into a beautiful tapestry of salvation and eternal glory. In entering into history and submitting to the wicked decisions of men, Jesus doesn't relinquish his Lordship. On the contrary, by bringing victory out of such a defeat and then sharing it with the very men who crucified him, he exhibits the full extent of his Lordship.

CHRIST THE TEACHER This is the fourth time St Matthew shows Jesus explaining to his apostles that he is going to taken and crucified. He wants them to be ready. He refuses to lead them on with false promises of easy victory and earthly glory. His way is the way of the cross. If they want to follow him, they must prepare themselves for opposition, struggle, suffering, and rejection. The gate that leads to salvation is narrow; the road to new life passes through Calvary. Jesus insists on this lesson. Over and over again he warns his apostles. And yet, when the shadow of the cross actually makes its appearance, they will all flee and go into hiding.

Jesus' warnings are for us too. The gospel, if we decide to live it to the full, will hurt. An authentic Christian finds happiness in the midst of struggles, not instead of them. Christ wants us to be ready. If we contemplate his passion and see how he loved amid his sufferings, we will be ready. And whatever crosses may come, they won't separate us from meaning and fulfillment, but rather will lift us closer to the goal.

CHRIST THE FRIEND As we begin to contemplate Christ's passion, we should keep firmly in mind that everything Jesus undergoes is suffered *for us*. Our hearts are so wounded that we often resist this truth of our faith. We take refuge behind generalizations: Jesus atoned for the sins of mankind; Jesus saved the human race; Jesus loved the world so much…. These are true, but their truth only matters if it penetrates each individual heart, which needs so much to know that it's loved. The Eucharist, the memorial of his passion, is the simplest and most eloquent reminder of this truth – that God loves me personally, and Christ suffered for me personally (to atone for *my* sins, to teach *me* the evil of sin, to save *me* from hell, to give *me* hope, to show how much he values *me*).

Millions receive the same sacrament when they receive Holy Communion, and yet each one receives the whole Christ, none more or less than any other. God holds nothing back in loving each of us.

CHRIST IN MY LIFE You came precisely to save me. If I had been the only person in the universe, you still would have come to save me. You know how wounded I am by those who have violated my trust. I throw my wounded heart at your feet: heal me with your love. You are faithful, as trustworthy as the mountains are firm. Sacred Heart of Jesus, I trust in you…

I am amazed at how focused you are on your mission. Your life had such unity of purpose. Why I am so distracted and divided and inconstant and frantic? I am a Christian: your follower. I am counting on your grace to put order in my heart, my mind, and my life. That way, your light and strength will better be able to flow through me to those around me…

QUESTIONS FOR SMALL GROUP DISCUSSION

1. What struck you most about this passage? What did you notice that you hadn't noticed before?

2. Why were the leaders of the people so intent on destroying Jesus?

3. Why did Jesus repeat the prophecy about his passion yet again, after he'd already told his disciples about it multiple times?

4. The Christian view of history centers around Christ's passion as the fulfillment of all that had come before and the origin of all that would come after. How does this vision of history differ from that present in popular culture? Where does the latter come from?

Cf. Catechism of the Catholic Church, 456-460 on why Jesus came to earth; 608 on Jesus as the Lamb of God

81. KEEPING FIRST THINGS FIRST (MT 26:6-16)

"And suddenly and insensibly, as though touched by the gentleness of Christ close at hand, you begin to taste how sweet he is and to feel how lovely he is."

- St Aelred

Matthew 26:6-16

Jesus was at Bethany in the house of Simon the leper, when a woman came to him with an alabaster jar of the most expensive ointment, and poured it on his head as he was at table. When they saw this, the disciples were indignant; 'Why this waste?' they said. 'This could have been sold at a high price and the money given to the poor.' Jesus noticed this. 'Why are you upsetting the woman?' he said to them. 'What she has done for me is one of the good works indeed! You have the poor with you always, but you will not always have me. When she poured this ointment on my body, she did it to prepare me for burial. I tell you solemnly, wherever in all the world this Good News is proclaimed, what she has done will be told also, in remembrance of her.' Then one of the Twelve, the man called Judas Iscariot, went to the chief priests and said, 'What are you prepared to give me if I hand him over to you?' They paid him thirty silver pieces, and from that moment he looked for an opportunity to betray him.

CHRIST THE LORD Jesus is worthy of worship. Have other great philosophers and religious leaders encouraged their followers to worship them, to honor them absolutely, as they would honor God? Only megalomaniacs have made such claims. Here Jesus accepts this act of adoration. It reminds us of the Magi's visit, when the kings prostrated themselves and offered the baby Jesus their precious gifts, signifying their humble adoration.

Worship involves acknowledging our debt to God. We have received everything from him: existence, forgiveness, the desire for happiness, and the hope for its fulfillment. He deserves our praise – not only our gratitude, which is linked to the specific gifts we have received from him, but also our *praise*, by which we acknowledge in awe-filled wonder the immense goodness and power of that Someone who loves us. Of the whole visible creation, only we human beings have the prerogative of praising God; we should learn to do it well, offering to him what is most valuable to us - whatever it is that we keep in our alabaster jars.

CHRIST THE TEACHER St Matthew describes the whole group of disciples disdaining this woman's extravagance. We know from St John's Gospel that Judas was the instigator of the complaint. We can infer, therefore, that Judas had quite an influence over the other disciples. He was the educated one, the only Judean among them, the bright and practical one to whom Jesus had entrusted the community funds. We should keep this in mind as we watch the drama of the Passion unfold.

Jesus defends the woman's extravagance – not only the gesture in general, but its extravagance specifically. Is it ever a waste to give our best to Christ? The disciples argue that the perfume could have been sold and the large sum of money given to the poor. Jesus acknowledges the value of giving to the poor, but he puts gifts offered directly to him on an even higher level. The reason we should serve our neighbor is because every person is created in the image of God. Jesus' parable of the Last Judgment, where the king separates the sheep from the goats, shows that reward and punishment for our deeds comes because whatever we do to our neighbor is as it were done to him; God is present in each man, woman, and child. This is the origin of human dignity and the only reason behind every act of justice or charity.

How much more valuable, then, are those acts of worship by which we honor God directly! Therefore, anyone who criticizes gifts given to God – donations made to adorn churches, support priests, build convents, etc. – simply cannot be doing so out of true love for the poor. The poor are to be loved because they are the image of God, as is every human person. And so, how can someone who truly loves the poor for their own sake, for their intrinsic dignity as human beings, criticize others for praising the God who gave them that dignity? Indeed, Judas, the instigator of the criticism, wasn't thinking about the poor. As St John tells us later, he was thinking about lining his own pockets because he was a thief. A sincere follower of Christ will neglect neither his neighbor nor his God.

CHRIST THE FRIEND This woman is expressing her gratitude to Jesus. Most likely, judging from parallel passages in the other Gospels, she is Mary of Bethany, sister to Jesus' friend Lazarus, whom Christ had resurrected from the dead. Her heart is so full of gratitude that she must publicly honor the Lord. And what is Jesus' response? He answers her small grain of thanks with an avalanche of his own gratitude. He promises that he will remember her act through all eternity, and that he will make it resound to the farthest ends of the earth, from generation to generation. How glad he is to receive her thanks! How disproportionate to her gift is response of the Lord who receives it! Jesus has a human heart, but it overflows with the immensity of divine love; the smallest act of trust, of generosity, elicits from this volcano of love a massive eruption of grace. He loves us so much and longs for us to accept his love, so he can love us even more.

Matthew: Of all the experiences I had with my Lord, this is one of those that has stayed with me the most. I can still picture it as if I were there. It was a joyful dinner. We all knew each other so well, the food was delicious, and we were so comfortable there with Jesus and Lazarus' family. We weren't boisterous though. We all knew that something was going to happen in the next few days. I thought Jesus was going to overthrow the corrupt rulers of Jerusalem. Thomas was worried that Jesus was going to be arrested. Jesus too seemed preoccupied, though his eyes radiated even more than usual his unique warmth and enthusiasm. But he was quieter than normal. And it was during a quiet moment that Martha's sister brought in the ointment. And as she anointed the Lord, we all watched in utter silence. You could see that between her and Jesus there was some kind of understanding that even Peter didn't have – not even John had it. How she loved the Lord! He was everything to her. There was a beauty to that encounter…. And then it was shattered. She had just finished anointing him. Everyone was quiet, pensive. The aroma of the perfume was almost intoxicating. Then Judas mumbled his comment. It was like a brick thrown through a glass window. Only Jesus and Mary kept their composure. That was just like him. Nothing could get the better of him; he always knew what he was about.

CHRIST IN MY LIFE I too want to adore you, Lord. Your goodness is without limit. All the beauty of creation is but a dim and distant shadow of the beauty of your heart. All the good gifts you shower me with each day are only faint whiffs of what you wish me to have forever in heaven. You are my Father, my Savior, my Companion, my Healer, my Friend, my All. Blessed be your name throughout the earth…

How hard it is to avoid the snares of money. I kneel before you now, my Lord, and I ask you, truly and humbly: teach me to use all my money and all my material wealth only for your glory. It all belongs to you. Grant me wisdom and detachment to be generous and frugal. I don't want any regrets on judgment day. I care only about loving you and loving my neighbor. Teach me to love as you love…

Judas exposed what was really in his heart by criticizing this woman: selfishness, greed, and guile. Show me, Lord, what is truly in my heart. What do I criticize? Why? With the purity of your heart, make my heart clean…

QUESTIONS FOR SMALL GROUP DISCUSSION

1. What struck you most about this passage? What did you notice that you hadn't noticed before?

2. When critics accuse the Church of squandering money on elaborate buildings, works of art, and ceremonies, how do you respond?

3. How can we make our worship more worthy of the Lord?

4. This woman gave her most valuable possession to Christ. What are some of our most valuable commodities, and how can we offer them to Christ?

Cf. Catechism of the Catholic Church, 2443-2449 on love for the poor; 2084-2097 on worshiping God

82. THE TASTE OF LOVE (MT 26:17-35)

"I am the same under each of the species, but not every soul receives me with the same living faith as you do, my daughter, and therefore I cannot act in their souls as I do in yours."

- Words of Jesus to St Faustina Kowalska

Matthew 26:17-35

Now on the first day of Unleavened Bread the disciples came to Jesus to say, 'Where do you want us to make the preparations for you to eat the passover?' 'Go to so-and-so in the city,' he replied, 'and say to him, The Master says: My time is near. It is at your house that I am keeping Passover with my disciples.' The disciples did what Jesus told them and prepared the Passover. When evening came he was at table with the twelve disciples. And while they were eating he said, 'I tell you solemnly, one of you is about to betray me.' They were greatly distressed and started asking him in turn, 'Not I, Lord, surely?' He answered, 'Someone who has dipped his hand into the dish with me, will betray me. The Son of Man is going to his fate, as the scriptures say he will, but alas for that man by whom the Son of Man is betrayed! Better for that man if he had never been born!' Judas, who was to betray him; asked in his turn, 'Not I, Rabbi, surely?' 'They are your own words,' answered Jesus.

Now as they were eating, Jesus took some bread, and when he had said the blessing he broke it and gave it to the disciples. 'Take it and eat,' he said, 'this is my body.' Then he took a cup, and when he had returned thanks he gave it to them. 'Drink all of you from this,' he said, 'for this is my blood, the blood of the covenant, which is to be poured out for many for the forgiveness of sins. From now on, I tell you, I shall not drink wine until the day I drink the new wine with you in the kingdom of my Father.'

After psalms had been sung they left for the Mount of Olives. Then Jesus said to them, 'You will all lose faith in me this night, for the scripture says: I shall strike the shepherd and the sheep of the flock will be scattered, but after my resurrection I shall go before you to Galilee.' At this, Peter said, 'Though all lose faith in you, I will never lose faith.' Jesus answered him, 'I tell you solemnly, this very night, before the cock crows, you will have disowned me three times.' Peter said to him, 'Even if I have to die with you, I will never disown you.' And all the disciples said the same.

CHRIST THE LORD Jesus alters the ritual of the Passover meal, which had been established by God himself through the ministry of Moses. In doing so, he confirms yet again his claim to be the Messiah (evident as well in his continued use of the Messiah's prophetic title, Son of Man), and by doing so in his own name, he reiterates his claim to be the Son of God. These changes shed light on just what kind of a King he is.

The unleavened bread commemorates the Israelites' rushed departure from Egypt (they were hurrying too much to have time to bake leavened bread), and the cup – the third ceremonial glass of wine, commemorating past blessings – is drunk right after eating the sacrificial lamb and precedes a long prayer of thanksgiving. This bread and wine become Christ's body and blood, which are given up for the forgiveness of sins (just as the blood of animal sacrifices was poured out at the foot of the altar to atone for sins in the Old Covenant). Jesus also cuts the meal short. He declares he will not drink of the fruit of the vine again until he has entered into his Kingdom, even though normally a fourth cup was drunk at the end of the Passover supper, in anticipation of the future fulfillment of all God's Old Testament promises.

Jesus thus turns this religious meal into an unbloody sacrifice that points towards the bloody sacrifice he will soon make on Calvary. In so doing, he accrues to himself the roles of priest (he offers the sacrifice) and victim (his body and blood are offered). And by inviting his Twelve Apostles to participate in the sacrifice and receive its benefits, he shows that his Kingship will be exercised in the total surrender of himself for the good of his subjects. Not only will his sacrifice wipe away their sins, but it will also elevate them to become, through Holy Communion, sharers in his royal and divine nature. For us as well: if we eat his flesh and drink his blood, we will have his everlasting life within us.

Christ is the one Lord of history, and the only Lord in history to share his royal inheritance with all his people.

CHRIST THE TEACHER We are accustomed to this sharing of natures that Jesus enacts through the Eucharist, but its sharp departure from Jewish custom would have astonished the Twelve. The Mosaic and Levitical Law prohibited all Jews from drinking the blood of their sacrifices, or even eating any meat with the blood still in it. In blood, they believed, was life, and all life belonged to God – it's off-limits for men. So when Jesus commands them to take the cup of his blood and drink from it, the concept would have shocked them.

And yet, that Old Testament command had its purpose. Pagan religions had no prohibition against the consumption of blood. Pagans were accustomed to consuming bloody meat and bloody sacrifices. Just as they worshiped idols (creatures that were considered divine), they believed they could enter into communion with the divine through the consumption of those creatures' blood. But the Jews were protected from such practices. They knew they had been created in God's image, and that there was only one God, Creator of all things. And so, when Jesus proclaims a new covenant in his name – something only God could do – and then commands his followers to consume his precious blood in the Eucharist, the apostles would have gotten the message: the divine life of Christ was about to start flowing in their veins; the pagan sham is giving way to the real thing. The first time in their lives that they consumed blood of any kind was when they received their first Holy Communion.

How fitting it was that God had prepared so carefully, through the Mosaic customs, the men who first consumed Christ's body and blood! It teaches us the reverence and gratitude with which we ought to treat this most Blessed Sacrament.

CHRIST THE FRIEND When Jesus and his disciples celebrate this first Eucharist, the New Covenant is established. In the biblical context, a covenant is a family bond, a mutual commitment that links two parties so that they become one thing. Marriage, for example, is a covenant. God's promise to Abraham is a covenant. In establishing a New Covenant, Jesus abrogates the Mosaic Covenant, which was written on stone tablets, and fulfills Jeremiah's prophecy that after Israel's infidelity to the Old Covenant, God would make a new one – deeper, everlasting, and written on his people's hearts (Jer 31:31).

How curious it is that St Matthew locates the establishment of this everlasting covenant right between two predictions of betrayal, Judas' and Peter's. Jesus is willing to commit himself to us, body and soul; he offers us his undying fidelity, even knowing we will betray him. When he predicts the betrayals, we can hear the sadness in his voice; dipping into the same dish was a sign of close friendship, and that is how he describes his betrayer, as someone close to him, someone trusted by him. And yet, he wants his disciples to realize that he knows what will happen, so that later they will reflect on it, seeing that he loves them no matter what, even knowing their weakness. He wants to remove even the last speck of doubt from our hearts: in Christ we have found an undying, untiring love, the firmest of anchors in the stormy sea of life.

CHRIST IN MY LIFE Will I abandon you too, Lord? You know that I already have. So many times I have failed to trust you, I have ignored your voice speaking in the depths of my soul. I am weak, Lord, and I am inconsistent. Be my rock; be my shield! With the fortitude of your heart, strengthen my heart…

Your generosity humbles me, Lord! Do I deserve the great gift you give me in the Eucharist? Do I deserve the forgiveness you offer me, even before I am aware of all my sins? Do I deserve your friendship, which you promise never to take back, even if I betray you? Do I deserve to be permitted just to speak your holy name, the name which says everything? Jesus: God saves. Lord Jesus, have mercy on me...

I cannot receive you in the Sacrament right now, but at least come into my heart... Come to me, my Lord, and make me like you. You give without counting the cost. You love and forgive without ever demanding your rights. I am so slow to give, so reluctant to forgive. But I know that with you I can do all things. Jesus, I trust in you...

QUESTIONS FOR SMALL GROUP DISCUSSION

1. What struck you most about this passage? What did you notice that you hadn't noticed before?

2. Throughout this passage, which is about betrayal and the sufferings and sacrifice of Christ, Jesus makes references to his resurrection. Why? Is there some lesson in that as to how we ought to bear our own crosses?

3. Is there anything in this passage that helps us understand why later on Judas was not able to recover from his betrayal, while Peter was?

4. Why do you think Jesus chose to leave us his body and blood under the appearances of bread and wine?

Cf. Catechism of the Catholic Church, 1362-1372 on the Eucharist as sacrifice; 1322, 1393-1395 and 1074 on Christ's transforming action through the Eucharist

83. THE STRENGTH OF PRAYER (MT 26:36-46)

"The Lord taught us to pray not only in words, but also in actions; he prayed frequently himself and showed us by example what we must do."

- St Cyprian of Carthage

Matthew 26:36-46

Then Jesus came with them to a small estate called Gethsemane; and he said to his disciples, 'Stay here while I go over there to pray.' He took Peter and the two sons of Zebedee with him. And sadness came over him, and great distress. Then he said to them, 'My soul is sorrowful to the point of death. Wait here and keep awake with me.' And going on a little further he fell on his face and prayed. 'My Father,' he said 'if it is possible, let this cup pass me by. Nevertheless, let it be as you, not I, would have it.' He came back to the disciples and found them sleeping, and he said to Peter, 'So you had not the strength to keep awake with me one hour? You should be awake, and praying not to be put to the test. The spirit is willing, but the flesh is weak.' Again, a second time, he went away and prayed: 'My Father,' he said, 'If this cup cannot pass by without my drinking it, your will be done!' And he came back again and found them sleeping, their eyes were so heavy. Leaving them there, he went away again and prayed for the third time, repeating the same words. Then he came back to the disciples and said to them, 'You can sleep on now and take your rest. Now the hour has come when the Son of Man is to be betrayed into the hands of sinners. Get up! Let us go! My betrayer is already close at hand.'

CHRIST THE LORD   For Christians, obedience is a virtue. Jesus is Lord, not president. We don't impeach him or vote him out of office when he does something we don't like. He rules the universe, and we, first of all through baptism and then again every time we pray the Our Father, have freely and consciously submitted our lives to his rule. This means that we obey his commandments, the teachings of the Church, the voice of conscience, and those who exercise legitimate authority in society, community, and family. The universe is not a democracy.

This obedience is demanding. Even though we have freely taken it upon ourselves, it sometimes hurts. Rampant individualism, consumerism, and the spreading of a democratic mindset into every sector of life only aggravate the difficulty. Jesus knows this. To make it easier for us, he paves the way with his own obedience. Though he is Lord, though he is the Son, he learns obedience by what he suffers (Hebrews 5:8).

Obedience means the union of wills – it's another name for love. It's a virtue, because virtues make us fulfill our vocation to reflect God in the world, and God is Three Persons who share the same will and the same desire to save fallen mankind, no matter what the cost. The Lord is not a dictator, but a Son; in him we obey, but like trusting brothers and sisters, not like slaves.

CHRIST THE TEACHER   Of the many lessons Jesus teaches in Gethsemane, St Matthew emphasizes two.

The first is about Christ himself. Jesus was untouched by original sin; no tendencies to selfishness marred his love or his integrity. And yet, even so, he found it humanly difficult to accept his Father's will – so difficult that St Matthew can barely find strong enough words to describe his suffering: sadness, great distress, sorrow to the point of death. His human nature, perfect and unsullied as it was, nevertheless rebelled violently and persistently at what the Father was asking him to do; God's will was utterly repugnant to him on a natural level. What comfort we find in this simple fact! Now we can be absolutely certain that life's ubiquitous obstacles, difficulties, and sufferings fit inside God's Providence. If even Christ, if even Mary had to travel a hard road, we have no reason to think that our hardships will obstruct our spiritual growth. Christ's sufferings set us free from the vain but tempting ideal of a life without pain.

Second, Jesus teaches us the secret to persevering in the path of holiness and happiness. When his vocation weighs him down and his human will resists the demands of his mission, he seeks solace and strength in prayer. Prayer foils the devil. Prayer conquers evil. Prayer frees the soul to achieve the purpose for which it was created. But prayer is demanding too. Jesus himself had to persevere; three times he went off to pray and came back. The disciples didn't persist, and they will soon abandon their Lord. Prayer is necessary, but its fruitfulness depends on an attitude of docility, on watchfulness, on self-mastery – "the spirit is willing, but the flesh is weak." A heart that seeks God in prayer won't get very far unless it decides to heed what it hears from the Lord.

CHRIST THE FRIEND Jesus is in heaven now, but he is still fully man. He didn't leave his human nature behind. And in his mystical body, the Church, he continues to suffer, even humanly, this agony that he suffered in his physical body in Gethsemane. Then his suffering stemmed from the prospect of taking our sins upon himself and all that would entail. Now his suffering consists in the many wounds that the Church receives from without and from within, from persecution as well as from infidelity. In Gethsemane he asked his closest disciples to stay with him, to comfort him in his agony. They didn't. They failed. They let him down. In the whole Gospel, only here does St Matthew depict our Lord asking for the comfort and support of his disciples. If they could do it again, surely they would do whatever it took to keep awake. But they can't; their chance to suffer with their Lord is over.

We, however, can do it again – we can accompany him in the agony he suffers now, by watching and praying with him, especially in the Eucharist. A Holy Hour is another Gethsemane; he needed his friends to comfort him then, and he chooses to still need them now.

Jesus: Will you stay and watch with me? All was dark on this night. My Father withdrew, my followers withdrew, and the ancient Enemy approached. Many people think I don't understand their dark moments (or weeks, or even years). But I do. I came to earth specifically to enter into the darkness of a fallen world. There my light shines brightest. But not this night! This night all was dark for me. The guilt of your sins crushed me. The infidelity of everyone who would abandon me and reject my Father crashed like a wave over my heart and flooded my mind with an agony that pushed me to the edge of despair. All was dark for me. Will you stay and watch with me?

CHRIST IN MY LIFE It is hard for me to believe that you suffered so much. I don't understand it, Lord. And yet the Gospel couldn't be clearer. You took my sins upon you. All of them. You paid the price for them. You let their guilt saturate your soul. So then, also feel my love. I don't want to fall asleep and leave you alone. I want to be with you, to pray and to watch, to cling to your will each moment of my life, no matter what the cost…

Why do I expect an easy life? Why do I hope for heaven on earth? If you and your Mother had to suffer, why do my sufferings still surprise me? Teach me the wisdom of the cross, Lord. Teach me to pray as you prayed: Thy will be done. Make your will my only quest, my only desire, my only hope. Then I will be your true disciple…

QUESTIONS FOR SMALL GROUP DISCUSSION

1. What struck you most about this passage? What did you notice that you hadn't noticed before?

2. Why is it so hard for us to accept life's sufferings and difficulties?

3. Why do you think the apostles didn't make a greater effort to stay awake with Jesus?

4. Jesus asked the Father to change his plans, but when the Father didn't, Jesus accepted it fully. What can this teach us about true Christian prayer?

5. How can we harmonize Jesus promise of an abundant life with his promise that we will have to bear crosses? Is there a contradiction?

Cf. Catechism of the Catholic Church, 411, 475, 532, 539, 612, 615, 908, and 1009 on Christ's obedience; 2607-2615 on Jesus teaching us to pray

84. PROPHECIES AND KISSES (MT 26:47-56)

"Put Christ first, because he put us first, and let nothing deter us from loving him."

- St Cyprian of Carthage

Matthew 26:47-56

He was still speaking when Judas, one of the Twelve, appeared, and with him a large number of men armed with swords and clubs, sent by the chief priests and elders of the people. Now the traitor had arranged a sign with them. 'The one I kiss,' he had said, 'he is the man. Take him in charge.' So he went straight up to Jesus and said, 'Greetings, Rabbi,' and kissed him. Jesus said to him, 'My friend, do what you are here for.' Then they came forward, seized Jesus and took him in charge. At that, one of the followers of Jesus grasped his sword and drew it; he struck out at the high priest's servant, and cut off his ear. Jesus then said, 'Put your sword back, for all who draw the sword will die by the sword. Or do you think that I cannot appeal to my Father who would promptly send more than twelve legions of angels to my defence? But then, how would the scriptures be fulfilled that say this is the way it must be?' It was at this time that Jesus said to the crowds, 'Am I a brigand, that you had to set out to capture me with swords and clubs? I sat teaching in the Temple day after day and you never laid hands on me.' Now all this happened to fulfil the prophecies in scripture. Then all the disciples deserted him and ran away.

CHRIST THE LORD Now and throughout his passion, Jesus is always in control. In this passage, he knew Judas and the mob were on their way to apprehend him, and yet he steps out to meet them. He responds to Judas' deceptive gesture with perfect composure. He reins in the impulsive Peter. He challenges and intimidates the very guards who arrest him, exposing their bosses' evil intent and pricking their consciences. Above all, he purposely allows the events to play themselves out, instead of calling in supernatural reinforcements. His dignity, his sense of mission, and his respect for all men, including his enemies, never abandons him, even in the face of brutal humiliation and hideous suffering.

Perhaps here, more than anywhere else in the Gospel, we see the real face of our Lord. Perhaps in contemplating him here, we will finally learn to follow his example. Then we will be able to stay by his side no matter how hard it gets, instead of deserting him and running away like the apostles. They didn't have the benefit of meditating on the Passion before their own trial came upon them; we do.

CHRIST THE TEACHER St Matthew is writing primarily for a Jewish audience. He was a Jew, and his post-Resurrection apostolic mission was carried out mostly among the Jews in Palestine and Egypt. As a result, throughout his Gospel, he points out the fulfillment of Old Testament prophecy more frequently than the other evangelists. In this passage, he does so twice: Jesus explains his submission to the arrest as a way of allowing the scriptures to be fulfilled, and then St Matthew summarizes the whole scene by saying the same thing.

The wrong lesson to draw from Matthew's observation is that these events were inevitable. The prophesies foretold these events, but they didn't determine them. God knows the future (what we call the future, that is), because he is already there; he exists outside of time. When Jesus submits to what the scriptures foretold, then, far from violating the Pharisees' freedom, he is respecting it; he knew how despicably they would treat him, but he accepts it. They are free to resist God's will and rebel against his plan. God chooses to show his omnipotence not by constricting that freedom, but by turning even those evil deeds into the agents of salvation and redemption. When he allows us to experience evil and suffering in our lives – which he promises to permit; we can count on it – we have a chance to respond as Jesus did, accepting whatever God allows, knowing that if he allows it, it will redound to his glory and to our growth in wisdom and holiness.

CHRIST THE FRIEND Jesus calls Judas his friend at the very moment of the traitorous kiss. He didn't have to – he didn't have to say anything. What is Jesus interested in at that moment? He isn't thinking of himself. He is think-ing of Judas. He is planting a seed. A word of kindness at the hour of betrayal – maybe that small gesture of love will do what three years of companionship, miracles, and conversations failed to do: convince Judas that Jesus truly cared about him. Jesus' love for his disciple is untiring, unassailable. It is constant, life-giving, and unconditional, like the sun: nothing Judas can do will diminish it or increase it; all he can do is bask in its light or flee to the shadows.

Each of us is in some way like Judas. The same lips that have received Christ's body and blood so many times have also pronounced rash judgments, angry insults, deadly gossip, self-serving lies…. Judas betrays Jesus with his mouth; Jesus reaches out to save him with a word of kindness. Christ never retracts his friendship – never. If our words were habitually worthy of such a Friend, we would probably help save many Judases from their demise.

CHRIST IN MY LIFE Whenever I take time to reflect on your passion, Lord, I shake my head in disbelief. In your brief ministry on earth all you did was heal, teach, and give hope. And yet, the very people you came to save take you prisoner, as if you were a criminal. Every generation, every life repeats that same story. How can we be so ungrateful? How can you be so patient? Teach me gratitude, Lord; teach me patience…

Your chosen disciples run away. Judas hands you over to your enemies. The soldiers take you into custody. And never, not even once, does a glimmer of hatred or selfish anger show in your eyes. You are praying for your enemies; you love those who persecute you. I am one of them. Many times, in many ways, I have abandoned you and imprisoned you. Forgive me, Lord; give me a heart like yours…

Mary, your heart was struck by the arrest of your Son, as if he were an outlaw, a thug. I have treated Jesus like that too. I have wounded your heart too. Mary, refuge of sinners, pray for me, pray for all sinners; make our hearts more like Christ's...

QUESTIONS FOR SMALL GROUP DISCUSSION

1. What struck you most about this passage? What did you notice that you hadn't noticed before?

2. At first, Peter showed courage by trying to defend Jesus with the sword. After Jesus reprimanded him, why do you think he lost courage and fled? Why did the other disciples flee?

3. How do you think the guards reacted when Jesus pointed out that they could have arrested him in the Temple, that he wasn't an outlaw hiding in some cave? Why do you think Jesus made a point of saying this?

4. One of Jesus' first apostles betrayed him completely. What does this fact have to teach us about the Church that Christ is establishing?

5. Some people interpret Jesus' saying about living and dying by the sword as a blanket condemnation of war. Do you agree?

Cf. Catechism of the Catholic Church, 2284-2287 on the sin of scandal; 2302-2306 and 1851 on violence and peace; 2307-2317 on war

85. CONDEMNED AND DENIED (MT 26:57-75)

"Lord, lighten the heavy burden of my sins by which I have seriously offended you. Cleanse my mind and my heart. Like a bright lamp, guide me along the right path."

- St John Damascene

Matthew 26:57-75

The men who had arrested Jesus led him off to Caiaphas the high priest, where the scribes and the elders were assembled. Peter followed him at a distance, and when he reached the high priest's palace, he went in and sat down with the attendants to see what the end would be. The chief priests and the whole Sanhedrin were looking for evidence against Jesus, however false, on which they might pass the death-sentence. But they could not find any, though several lying witnesses came forward. Eventually two stepped forward and made a statement, 'This man said, I have power to destroy the Temple of God and in three days build it up.' The high priest then stood up and said to him, 'Have you no answer to that? What is this evidence these men are bringing against you?' But Jesus was silent. And the high priest said to him, 'I put you on oath by the living God to tell us if you are the Christ, the Son of God.' 'The words are your own,' answered Jesus. 'Moreover, I tell you that from this time onward you will see the Son of Man seated at the right hand of the Power and coming on the clouds of heaven.' At this, the high priest tore his clothes and said, 'He has blasphemed. What need of witnesses have we now? There! You have just heard the blasphemy. What is your opinion?' They answered, 'He deserves to die.' Then they spat in his face and hit him with their fists; others said as they struck him, 'Play the prophet, Christ! Who hit you then?'

Meanwhile Peter was sitting outside in the courtyard, and a servant-girl came up to him and said, 'You too were with Jesus the Galilean.' But he denied it in front of them all. 'I do not know what you are talking about,' he said. When he went out to the gateway another servant-girl saw him and said to the people there, 'This man was with Jesus the Nazarene.' And again, with an oath, he denied it, 'I do not know the man.' A little later the bystanders came up and said to Peter, 'You are one of them for sure! Why, your accent gives you away.' Then he started calling down curses on himself and swearing, 'I do not know the man.' At that moment the cock crew, and Peter remembered what Jesus had said, 'Before the cock crows you will have disowned me three times.' And he went outside and wept bitterly.

CHRIST THE LORD Jesus had the power to defend himself both in word and in deed. And yet, he stays silent. He purposely submits to the injustice of this mock trial. The leaders have decided ahead of time what the verdict will be, and they are simply going through the motions of justice in order to find an excuse to declare it.

The Council chamber is lit with smoky lamps. The leaders of Jerusalem gather around the accused. Witnesses and guards stand in the wings. Torches cast flickering shadows on the stone walls and marble floors. All eyes are intent on Jesus, chained, exhausted from his battle in Gethsemane, but standing straight, firm, and docile. He looks into the eyes of his accusers. He knows their hearts. He speaks to those who will listen merely with the power of his glance. The smoke from the torches and lamps makes the air bitter. The council gets impatient.

How many times throughout St Matthew's Gospel does Jesus confound the Pharisees' subtle attempts to trap him by accusations and verbal tricks! But not now. He has already shown them plenty of evidence to prove his claim to be the Messiah, and they have stubbornly refused to see. Now he lets them have their way with him. Only when the high priest puts him under oath – which the high priest had the right to do – does Jesus speak, reaffirming his claims to be the Messiah and the divine Son of God. His opponents understand the claim – but instead of putting their faith in him, they accuse him of blasphemy; they deny the legitimacy of the claim simply because of its inherent scope, not because of any evidence that it is false. They disbelieve because they don't want to believe. And Jesus lets them have their way.

This is always how it is with the Lord. If he can't convince us by his teachings and the many gifts and wonders with which he surrounds us, he resorts to convincing us by his humility. He allows us to reject him, to banish him from our lives, to bind our conscience and lock it up in the dungeon of our soul. But later, when the consequences of our sin topple the flimsy kingdom of self that we have so energetically erected, he will once again catch our eye. And then, because he didn't condemn us at first, because he submitted to our sentence, we will be able to trust him, to go back to him and be saved.

The first law of this Lord's Kingdom is not justice, but mercy, which leads to salvation.

CHRIST THE TEACHER Peter had recovered a little bit from the fright he took in Gethsemane; he followed Jesus to the scene of his trial, while the other disciples kept their distance. During the Last Supper, all of them had vociferously affirmed their willingness to die for Jesus; their courage fled when they saw that Jesus wasn't going to fight. This shows that they still had one lesson to learn from the Master – Peter especially, since he was to be their leader when Christ had finished his earthly mission.

What was the lesson? When it comes to building and defending the Kingdom of Christ, our own strength is simply not enough. Peter loved Jesus. But the mission Jesus had given him was far beyond his natural powers, as considerable as they were. Only at this tragic moment, when fear of the cross unnerves him completely, after he abandons Jesus and then repeatedly denies his allegiance to him – only then is Peter humbled enough to realize his utter need for God's grace.

Peter and his successors will be faithful not because of their great intelligence, vigor, and talent, but because, for the sake of Christ's Kingdom, the Holy Spirit will reinforce their human weakness. Every disciple must learn the same lesson, since every Christian's mission exceeds merely natural capacities: "'Not by might and not by power, but by my spirit,' says the Lord" (Zechariah 4:14).

How did St Matthew find out about Peter's denials? How did any of the evangelists find out? Only through Peter himself – no other witnesses could have testified to that event. We can picture St Peter explaining this scene to the first groups of Christians, shamed by his weakness, but rejoicing in Christ's forgiveness, and vehemently exhorting the disciples to learn this essential lesson from Peter's infidelity instead of from their own.

CHRIST THE FRIEND How many friendships, even family relationships, have crumbled under the weight of resentment! A brother insults his brother; a friend mockingly exposes another friend's secret; siblings contend over an inheritance; and overnight an immense wall springs up to separate two hearts that only yesterday were graciously united. Nothing is more contrary to Christianity.

See the guards mock Jesus. See them spit on his face, brutally strike him, laugh at him, and insult him, over and over again, as only hardened soldiers know how to do. If any other man were in his place, with his power, would he have had the strength to resist fighting back? But Jesus does resist. Resentment, selfish anger, or even the righteous claims of justice have no power to build walls around his heart. It is for those very offenders, so despicable, so merciless, so inhuman, that Jesus will pray: "Father, forgive them…"

CHRIST IN MY LIFE I insist on justice, but you strive after mercy. I demand respect, and you suffer humiliation to show your love. Jesus, the habits of my heart are programmed for self-protection. But I want to be your faithful disciple. It frightens me to see how you were abused, and yet your nobility and your love touch the core of my being. You are the way, the truth, and the life. Teach me to follow you…

When I mock my neighbor, I am joining the ranks of your persecutors. When I joke bitingly about my neighbor – even about public figures whom I've never met – I am joining their ranks. No more, Lord. Open my eyes to see you in my neighbor, and move my heart to love them as you do…

Mary, how can you stand by and watch as they condemn your Son unjustly, beat him, and make fun of him? How can you endure the suffering of the Innocent One whom you love with the purest love? Share with me your faith, your wisdom, and your hope. By your Immaculate Heart, O Mary, purify and sanctify me…

QUESTIONS FOR SMALL GROUP DISCUSSION

1. What struck you most about this passage? What did you notice that you hadn't noticed before?

2. Do you know of any Christians who have suffered injustice for the sake of the Kingdom? How did they persevere, and what were the results of their faithfulness?

3. In what practical ways can we develop our dependence on God's grace and decrease the kind of self-sufficiency that led to Peter's denial?

4. The leaders of the Sanhedrin had no doubt about Christ's claim to be the Messiah and to be divine – that's why they condemned him. Many contemporary critics of Christianity, however, say that Jesus never made such a claim. How would you respond to such a challenge?

Cf. Catechism of the Catholic Church, 2840-2845 on the importance of forgiving our offenders; 1657 and 2227 on the family as a school of forgiveness; 441-445 on the title "Son of God"

THE GOSPEL OF MATTHEW CHAPTER 27

"If a person on board a ship anchored permanently in the ocean sees his native land from a distance, and also notices the intervening water, such an individual has no way of going ashore. The sea prevents this person from coming to the mainland. Christ comes to the rescue and provides a tree by which such a person may traverse the water. This tree is the Cross of Christ. No one can cross the sea of life unless carried by the Cross. Whoever does not depart from Christ's Cross will arrive at the true native land, Heaven."

- St Augustine

86. WHY HOPE RUNS DRY (MT 27:1-10)

"Our pilgrim life here on earth cannot be without temptation, for it is through temptation that we make progress and it is only by being tempted that we come to know ourselves."

- St Augustine

Matthew 27:1-10

When morning came, all the chief priests and the elders of the people met in council to bring about the death of Jesus. They had him bound, and led him away to hand him over to Pilate, the governor. When he found that Jesus had been condemned, Judas his betrayer was filled with remorse and took the thirty silver pieces back to the chief priests and elders. 'I have sinned,' he said. 'I have betrayed innocent blood' 'What is that to us?' they replied. 'That is your concern.' And flinging down the silver pieces in the sanctuary he made off and hanged himself. The chief priests picked up the silver pieces and said, 'It is against the Law to put this into the treasury; it is blood-money.' So they discussed the matter and bought the potter's field with it as a graveyard for foreigners, and this is why the field is called the Field of Blood today. The words of the prophet Jeremiah were then fulfilled: And they took the thirty silver pieces, the sum at which the precious One was priced by children of Israel, and they gave them for the potter's field, just as the Lord directed me.

CHRIST THE LORD Judas goes to the leaders of the Sanhedrin to repent. He returns his traitor's prize and confesses his sin. How do these supposed representatives of the merciful God of Israel react? They brush him off; they couldn't care less. A soul in dire need comes to them seeking redemption, and they give him a cold word of indifference instead.

How different Jesus is! If only Judas had gone to Jesus to ask forgiveness, he would have found new life. Christ is the first to abide by the lesson he taught Peter and the other apostles: that nothing should limit our forgiveness; seventy times seven times we should forgive those who offend us. And Jesus has never ceased living by this standard; he makes it so palpable and so tangible. Is there a limit to how often a sinner can frequent the confessional? And if he is repentant, even in the slightest, will he ever be denied the Lord's forgiveness?

Judas was ashamed to go to Jesus, because his sin had been against Jesus. And yet, only Jesus could give him the fresh start he so desperately needed. How easy it is to please the heart of Christ by letting him forgive our sins, by letting him be Lord and issue his pardon, which he does so gladly every time we kneel before him in confession.

CHRIST THE TEACHER Sin is self-destructive. Rebelling against God and the moral order he has built into the universe is like a rock climber cutting his own belay. It's like putting sand in your gas tank; a car is made to run on gas, and a person is made to run on truth and goodness. Christ's many exhortations to follow the path of humility, faith, and charity aren't meant to be a random list of dos and don'ts that he uses just to keep his subjects under his thumb. He forbids evil deeds because they are evil – they destroy the sinner first of all, and they damage those around him at the same time.

Judas epitomizes the self-destructive nature of sin. Maybe he thought that his betrayal would only hasten the inevitable conflict that had been brewing between Jesus and the Pharisees, or maybe he thought that Jesus would evade capture in the end anyway, as he had always done in the past. Whatever excuses he used to allay his conscience, they collapse in the face of the Sanhedrin's unjust condemnation and brutal treatment of the Lord, and Judas can no longer escape the clamor of his conscience. He tries to undo his deed, but he can't. And so he despairs. All he needed was the Lord's forgiveness, but by then his habits of self-reliance and arrogance have made it impossible for him to accept help from another, and disaster ensues.

Sin has consequences. It mutilates the soul. It incapacitates the heart. Sin is self-destructive, and the case of Judas is its tragic icon.

CHRIST THE FRIEND *Judas: What could I have done? I saw him give himself up. He didn't* *resist at all. And then I saw that trial. It was a travesty of a trial. And they condemned him to death. He didn't deserve death. I had to give back the money. How could I keep it? It was red with his blood. Where could I have gone? My sin was so colossal. It wasn't just the money. My heart, my lips – the lips that had betrayed him with a kiss of greeting – were stained just as red. It was all my fault. I had failed him. How could he love me after that? How could he ever trust me again? I had failed the other disciples. How could I ever face them again? I had failed myself. I couldn't stand myself, and I couldn't escape myself. I had only one option. What else could I have done? I had failed. It was over. There was nowhere else to turn.*

Jesus: Judas, my son. We had spent so much time together, and still you didn't know me! The times we had walked and talked together on the dirty roads, up and down the hills... There was a time when your heart burned to build the Kingdom of generosity, self-sacrifice, forgiveness, and truth. You were too impatient, though. I watched with sadness as your heart contracted. You wanted everything to be perfect right away. You wanted everyone to change right away. You grew restless. You resented my patience. You resented the ignorance of the other apostles, and their difficulty in understanding my teachings. You began to withdraw into your own dreams of grandeur. When you stopped opening your heart to me, I knew that you had started down a dangerous path. But even then I stayed with you. Did I ever reject you? If only you could have trusted me. Judas, my son, I never stopped loving you. I could have given you a fresh start.

CHRIST IN MY LIFE They bind you and take you off to be sentenced to death, and you let them. What are you thinking as they march you to Pilate's court? You are thinking of me, and that thought drives you forward to fulfill your mission. Scripture tells me that you have loved me from all eternity. On that fateful day, then, you never let your gaze fall away from me. Today I want to think of you. To praise your goodness and learn to follow you – what else could my heart desire? ...

Never let me despair of receiving your forgiveness. At times it's hard for me to forgive myself, just as it was for Judas. Help me to see that this comes from my arrogance and my exaggerated sense of self-importance. You, on the other hand, know my weakness and sinfulness through and through, and yet you love me. Jesus, have mercy on me...

Mary, how many people throughout the world are falling into despair! They have no hope; they are imprisoned in the walls erected by their own sin. But Jesus gave his life to save them. Pray for them, Mary, and pray for me, that I will find ways to be Christ for them...

QUESTIONS FOR SMALL GROUP DISCUSSION

1. What struck you most about this passage? What did you notice that you hadn't noticed before?

2. Why is it often so difficult for us to go to confession? What do you think Jesus thinks when we put this off?

3. What can we do to help make it easier for our Catholic community to experience God's forgiveness both inside and outside of the sacrament of reconciliation?

4. Despair, and even discouragement, are linked to the capital sin of pride. Can you explain why?

Cf. Catechism of the Catholic Church, 1450-1460 on the stages of true penitence; 844, 1501, and 2091 on despair, its causes and consequences; 980 and 1468 on reconciling with God

87. LORD OF ALL, CONDEMNED BY ALL (MT 27:11-26)

The Church likewise believes that the key, the center and the purpose of the whole of man's history is to be found in its Lord and Master."

- Second Vatican Council, Lumen gentium, 10

Matthew 27:11-26

Jesus, then, was brought before the governor, and the governor put to him this question, 'Are you the king of the Jews?' Jesus replied, 'It is you who say it'. But when he was accused by the chief priests and the elders he refused to answer at all. Pilate then said to him, 'Do you not hear how many charges they have brought against you?' But to the governor's complete amazement, he offered no reply to any of the charges. At festival time it was the governor's practice to release a prisoner for the people, anyone they chose. Now there was at that time a notorious prisoner whose name was Barabbas. So when the crowd gathered, Pilate said to them, 'Which do you want me to release for you: Barabbas, or Jesus who is called Christ?' For Pilate knew it was out of jealousy that they had handed him over. Now as he was seated in the chair of judgement, his wife sent him a message, 'Have nothing to do with that man; I have been upset all day by a dream I had about him'. The chief priests and the elders, however, had persuaded the crowd to demand the release of Barabbas and the execution of Jesus. So when the governor spoke and asked them, 'Which of the two do you want me to release for you?' they said, 'Barabbas'. 'But in that case,' Pilate said to them 'what am I to do with Jesus who is called Christ?' They all said, 'Let him be crucified!' 'Why?' he asked 'What harm has he done?' But they shouted all the louder, 'Let him be crucified!' Then Pilate saw that he was making no impression, that in fact a riot was imminent. So he took some water, washed his hands in front of the crowd and said, 'I am innocent of this man's blood. It is your concern.' And the people, to a man, shouted back, 'His blood be on us and on our children!' Then he released Barabbas for them. He ordered Jesus to be first scourged and then handed over to be crucified.

CHRIST THE LORD Jesus is the King of the Jews, as Pilate says and Jesus confirms. But he is also King of the Gentiles. He is the Lord of all. How eloquently this universality of Christ's Kingdom is expressed by a mere quirk of history: under Roman rule, the Jews no longer had the authority to administer capital punishment. The Sanhedrin had to bring their victim to Pilate to achieve their purposes, just as Moses had to bring his message to Pharaoh. Salvation comes from the Jews, but it embraces all peoples. Therefore, representatives of both Jews and Gentiles conspire to bring Jesus to his hour.

The city streets through which they marched Jesus on his way to the governor's insula were the same streets that his Jewish brethren had been traversing for ten centuries or more. Yet, the place of his final condemnation was a new fortress, a Roman barracks and palace for the procurator. The Lord's feet trod the dust of Palestine and the marble of Rome. Jewish eyes watch him as he is brought before the Roman authority. Foreign eyes – Italian, African, Asian, Anatolian – scrutinize him from faces of slaves and guards and soldiers. Jesus knows them all. He is Lord of them all. His Kingdom will one day spread and grow in all their lands – and even some of those eyes will be opened with the light of faith before this day is over.

CHRIST THE TEACHER Pilate was astonished at Jesus' silence. The governor knew very well the tricks the Sanhedrin was up to, the injustice of their sentence, the political power play they were engaged in. If Jesus had only spoken a word in his defense, exposed the false, self-contradictory accusations, Pilate would have found an excuse to set him free. But Jesus is silent. He lets his captors do with him as they please. He is the sacrificial lamb being led docilely to the slaughter.

Jesus will never violate our freedom. These Jewish leaders want to reject him and do away with him, and he lets them. Pilate would prefer that Jesus take the responsibility off his shoulders, but Jesus refuses. He nudges Pilate's conscience through his wife's dream, but he won't take the decision out of Pilate's hands. God's plan of salvation includes human freedom. Abuse of that freedom leads to the worst human tragedies, like the deicide we are witnessing now, but God knows that without freedom there can be no love. And since he created us to love, he won't violate that freedom. He is wise and powerful enough to bring victory out of the defeats caused by sin, so he tolerates the abuse of freedom in order to keep open the possibility of love.

He asks us to do the same. His commandment was to love one another as he has loved us. This means refusing to condemn our neighbors in our heart, even when they deserve condemnation. The Christian will never close the door to love, not even in order to save his own honor and good name. In society at large, justice and order must be maintained through punishing crime, but in the heart of Christ's disciples, even criminals can find a welcome. Blessed are we when we are persecuted for the sake of justice and the Kingdom, our Lord said earlier; even more blessed are those who react to persecution as Christ did.

CHRIST THE FRIEND Barabbas is each one of us. We are scoundrels, experts in selfishness, boasting, lust, violence, and greed. We are bandits, taking God's many gifts and ungratefully neglecting and squandering them. We take for granted the most precious realities of life: family, work, nature, health, faith, and the sacraments. We squander our talents, our money, our time, and the love others offer us. We are quick to criticize and judge, to steal others' honor and sully it with our moral and intellectual myopia. What do we, who are so flawed, so weak, so slow to repent, and so reluctant to serve – what do we deserve? Certainly not God's love, certainly not his continued forgiveness, certainly not redemption, hope, peace, and heaven. Strictly speaking, we deserve to be cut off from the Kingdom against which we have so often rebelled – just like the murderous insurgent, Barabbas.

And yet, Jesus overlooks what we deserve. It is the Passover, and the angel of justice passes over the sinner to wreak his just punishments on the Lamb of God instead. Look at the Lord with the eyes of Barabbas. Is there any heart that loves you more than this Sacred Heart? Is there any heart more trustworthy than the heart that died so you might have abundant life?

CHRIST IN MY LIFE Each day you give me so many opportunities to choose love, to choose to act as you would act, to choose to give glory to God and further your Kingdom by denying my selfish tendencies and putting my life and talents at the service of my neighbor. And yet, like Pilate, I squirm out of these opportunities – or like the chief priests, I self-righteously misuse them. No more, Jesus. Thy will be done...

How magnificently you must love me to suffer all this for my sake! It wasn't enough to give me the universe as my sandbox; you give me yourself as well. How can I number the gifts you have lavished upon me? Of all your immense majesty, what moves me most is this gentle and tireless love you show me. Thank you, Lord...

Mary, did it pain you to hear the crowds ratify their leaders' decision? Did it pain you to see your Son, our Savior, at the mercy of a fickle and ambitious politician? Did you wince when they whipped your Son till the blood flowed? Did you weep when his own people rejected him? Mother of sorrows, teach me to love Jesus and to love as Jesus loved…

QUESTIONS FOR SMALL GROUP DISCUSSION

1. What struck you most in this passage? What did you notice that you hadn't noticed before?

2. What do you think hurt Jesus more, the condemnation or the scourging? Why?

3. St Matthew points out that the crowd had been manipulated by the chief priests and the elders. What does this teach us about popular culture?

4. If a non-believer were to ask you why, if God exists, he permits the innocent to suffer, how would you respond?

Cf. Catechism of the Catholic Church, 595-598 on the trial of Jesus; 1730-1748 on human freedom; 571-573 on the suffering of Jesus; 309-314 on Providence and the scandal of evil

88. MOCKING THE KING (MT 27:27-44)

"None must be ashamed of the cross of Christ, by which he redeemed the world. None must fear to suffer for righteousness' sake. None must doubt that God will fulfill his promises. For through toil comes rest; through death comes life."

- Pope St Leo the Great

Matthew 27:27-44

The governor's soldiers took Jesus with them into the Praetorium and collected the whole cohort round him. Then they stripped him and made him wear a scarlet cloak, and having twisted some thorns into a crown they put this on his head and placed a reed in his right hand. To make fun of him they knelt to him saying, 'Hail, king of the Jews!' And they spat on him and took the reed and struck him on the head with it. And when they had finished making fun of him, they took off the cloak and dressed him in his own clothes and led him away to crucify him. On their way out, they came across a man from Cyrene, Simon by name, and enlisted him to carry his cross. When they had reached a place called Golgotha, that is, the place of the skull, they gave him wine to drink mixed with gall, which he tasted but refused to drink. When they had finished crucifying him they shared out his clothing by casting lots, and then sat down and stayed there keeping guard over him. Above his head was placed the charge against him; it read: 'This is Jesus, the King of the Jews.' At the same time two robbers were crucified with him, one on the right and one on the left. The passers-by jeered at him; they shook their heads and said, 'So you would destroy the Temple and rebuild it in three days! Then save yourself! If you are God's son, come down from the cross!' The chief priests with the scribes and elders mocked him in the same way. 'He saved others,' they said; 'he cannot save himself. He is the king of Israel; let him come down from the cross now, and we will believe in him. He puts his trust in God; now let God rescue him if he wants him. For he did say, I am the son of God.' Even the robbers who were crucified with him taunted him in the same way.

CHRIST THE LORD Even in the midst of mockery and scorn, Christ's Lordship is proclaimed. Three times in this brief passage St Matthew shows Jesus being called a King, and twice he is called the Son of God. It is public proclamation, posted high on the cross for all to see. It comes from Jews and Gentiles alike. They pronounced it as a taunt and jeer, but they pronounced it all the same. And lest we miss it, the pronunciation is even emphasized by the soldiers, who crown him, robe him, and put a scepter in his hand. Here we see our King enthroned on the throne of his choice, the cross, and what kind of King he really is becomes clear.

First of all, his Kingdom is in this world, but not of this world. Until the end of time, conflict will continue to rage between the community of fallen, sin-infected men and the community of those who truly love God. Christ's faithful followers can expect to taste this same mockery and violence at the hands of Christ's enemies.

Secondly, this King conquers by the beauty of his virtue, not the splendor of his might. The One who had the power to destroy his enemies lets his enemies destroy him instead. In the process, he exhibits every virtue to the highest degree: patience, mercy, temperance, fortitude, humility, and above all, love. He loves God his Father enough to suffer unspeakable torments out of obedience, finally untying Adam's knot of disobedience; he loves sinners enough to take the consequences of their sins upon his own body and soul, siphoning off their just deserts. Other kings conquer through self-assertion; Christ conquers through self-oblation.

If the King is like that, so too must be the Kingdom, with all its subjects following his lead, up to Calvary and onto the cross.

CHRIST THE TEACHER Unwittingly, the chief priests expose their own tragic blindness. As they deride and scorn their Savior, they voice the very words of Psalm 22, a psalm that prophesied the crucifixion, one that Jesus himself would quote before he died. Verse 8 of Psalm 22 reads: "He trusted himself to the Lord, let the Lord set him free! ..." It's a phrase more than merely reminiscent of what St Matthew puts in the tormenters' mouths as Jesus hangs there: "He has put his trust in God; now let God rescue him if he wants him…"

Among all the fulfilled prophecies that Matthew points out, perhaps this one contains the most poignant lesson. See Jesus hanging on the cross, seemingly abandoned by God, his life an apparent disaster. If he does what his enemies invite him to do – come down from the cross, show some supernatural pizzazz – he would have everyone cowering at his feet. But his Father's will, God's plan, is different. Jesus sticks to that plan. Contrary to all merely human logic, the all-powerful Creator allows his own weak creatures to crucify his Son. And yet, that event – the atoning sacrifice of Christ on the cross, which so blatantly defied human logic – that event becomes the fulcrum and foundation of all of human history. Jesus trusts against all odds, unconditionally and till the end, and his trust is not betrayed.

We who are wounded by our sins and the sins of others put limits on our trust, even our trust in God. So Christ trusts in our place, and in so doing teaches us that we ought to put no limits on our trust in God.

When our self-love cries out against the discomfort of God's will and the pain of the cross, we need to lift our gaze to Christ crucified. He put his trust in God, and God showed himself worthy; if we do the same, he will surely do so again.

CHRIST THE FRIEND St Matthew seems to be particularly shocked by the universality of the scorn Jesus receives. The soldiers, the chief priests, the passersby, and even the other criminals being crucified all join together in jeering at the Lord. Only one person in the passage doesn't: Simon of Cyrene. Of all the participants in this dark drama, Simon was closest to Christ throughout. He helped him carry the cross. And Simon doesn't mock.

Jesus makes himself weak for a reason. He takes on human nature in order to need us. To be human means to be dependent on others. This is how we're made. From the moment of conception to the moment of death, each of us is dependent, directly or indirectly, on a huge number of other people. When Jesus becomes man, he becomes fully man. As he makes his way to Calvary, weakened, exhausted, almost half-dead already after his violent arrest, night imprisonment, trials, and scourging, he in his true humanity needs help to bring his mission to a close. Simon supplies it. Perhaps that's why Simon doesn't mock him. He is close enough to experience Christ's

ence, overflowing not with anger and hatred and desperation, but with ac-
ance and forgiveness and determination. In helping Christ accomplish his
sion, he entered into a relationship, a friendship, with the Lord.

s elevated that same human nature by taking it into heaven on the day of
Ascension; he rules the universe in his glorified humanity. That means he
needs help to fulfill his mission; he is still dependent, like all men. If we
lder our corner of his cross sincerely, even if at times reluctantly, we will
er fall into mocking him, and he will surely give us the incomparable gift of
unique friendship.

RIST IN MY LIFE Nothing men do to you will change your Kingship.
are the King, the Lord of life and history. I believe in you, my Lord, and
nt to follow you, to know you, to defend and extend your Kingdom. I
w that if they persecuted and humiliated and misunderstood you, they
do the same with your followers. I am willing, Lord. Thy Kingdom
e...

have identified yourself with every person. When I insult my neighbor, I
lt you; when I judge and condemn my neighbor, I judge and condemn
; when I merely use and fail to love my neighbor, I am treating you as these
iers did. Instead, Lord, teach me to love all people as you do...

y, Christ's flesh, torn by the scourging, ripped by the crown of thorns,
ced by the nails, was your flesh. He took it from you, as we all take our
h from our mothers. And so you ached with every wound. But you trusted
God, as Jesus did. Teach me to suffer with love, so as to conquer the death of
with eternal life...

ESTIONS FOR SMALL GROUP DISCUSSION

hat struck you most about this passage? What did you notice that you hadn't noticed
fore?

hy do you think Matthew didn't explain the details of how they crucified Jesus?

a non-believer were to ask you to explain to them the phrase from the Our Father, "Thy
ingdom come," how would you do so?

hy do you think Jesus refused to take the wine mixed with gall – a drink meant to lessen
e pain of crucifixion?

Catechism of the Catholic Church, 1-3 and 396-402 on man's call to trust in God; 356-361 on
an solidarity; 386-387 on the reality of sin

89. THE OLD IS GONE (MT 27:45-56)

"By his obedience shown on one tree he retraced the disobedience which had been shown through another."

- St Irena

Matthew 27:45-56

From the sixth hour there was darkness over all the land until the ninth hour. An about the ninth hour, Jesus cried out in a loud voice, 'Eli, Eli, lama sabachthani?' that is, 'My God, my God, why have you deserted me?' When some of those who stood there heard this, they said, 'The man is calling on Elijah,' and one of them quickly ran to get a sponge which he dipped in vinegar and, putting it on a reed, gave it him to drink. 'Wait!' said the rest of them, 'and see if Elijah will come to s him.' But Jesus, again crying out in a loud voice, yielded up his spirit. At that, th veil of the Temple was torn in two from top to bottom; the earth quaked; the roc were split; the tombs opened and the bodies of many holy men rose from the dea and these, after his resurrection, came out of the tombs, entered the Holy City ar appeared to a number of people. Meanwhile the centurion, together with the oth guarding Jesus, had seen the earthquake and all that was taking place, and they were terrified and said, 'In truth this was a son of God.' And many women were there, watching from a distance, the same women who had followed Jesus from Galilee and looked after him. Among them were Mary of Magdala, Mary the mot of James and Joseph, and the mother of Zebedee's sons.

CHRIST THE LORD St Matthew, always attentive to Christ's fulfillment of th Old Testament prophecies, records in detail the signs and portents that surrounded our Lord's death on the cross. The sun is darkened, the earth quake the dead rise from their graves.... This is the same apocalyptic language that the Old Testament used to refer to the coming Day of the Lord, the end of th Old Covenant and the beginning of the Messianic era. Jesus himself used sim lar language just two days before, when he explained to the apostles the day his coming into his Kingdom.

The crucifixion, the one true redeeming sacrifice in which Jesus' obedience reverses Adam's disobedience and his death atones for all sins, is the watershed of human history. It begins the Last Days, the Age of Grace. It repairs th communion between God and man that Adam's sin had ruptured; thus the huge curtain that separated the inner sanctum of the Temple, where the divi presence had dwelt, is torn apart. It brings new life to those who have faith (holy people who came back from the dead), and it even brings faith to those o had never known the one true God of Israel (the terrified centurion and comrades acknowledge the Christ).

thing can obstruct God's loving plan of salvation; fidelity to God's will ays wins the victory, no matter how horrendous the battle gets. The devil's atest triumph becomes, under the sure guidance of Providence, his irrevers- e downfall. Those who moments ago laughed and taunted and mocked now d their knees in awe and worship. Is there any room for doubt left at all? rist Jesus is, indeed, the Lord.

RIST THE TEACHER Sin has its consequences, and even the Son of God, o had never sinned himself, suffered them in his earthly pilgrimage. All ering, all evil, results from sin. Mankind's original condition was free from ering and death, but original sin shattered that state of harmony like a small ble thrown through a large window shatters the entire pane of glass. And en the Lord comes into our life and we accept his friendship, even though grace renews our fallen nature, the effects of sin remain. The happiness ist offers accompanies the sufferings of this life ("blessed are the poor in it, those who mourn, those who are persecuted…"), it doesn't eliminate m. In their midst we can love more intensely, more purely, like the mother watches day and night over her sick child – it isn't comfortable love, but authentic love, and it brings light and joy to her soul.

s, when Jesus cries out from the cross, "My God, why have you forsaken ?" the first line of Psalm 22, he teaches us that pain and sorrow shouldn't ke our faith – they should strengthen it. The rest of Psalm 22, in fact, is mn to God's faithfulness. If the first line, expressing utter sorrow, was on s' lips, we can rest assured that the next line, expressing utter trust, was in heart: "…in you our ancestors put their trust, they trusted and you set them ." God wants us to bring our troubles to him, so he can bring his grace to

RIST THE FRIEND St Matthew mentions here for the first time the group omen who followed Jesus and looked after him during his years of public istry. They stayed with Christ, standing at a little distance, and watched the na of salvation play itself out; they saw the arrival of the Day of the Lord. y had faithfully served Jesus, who had been their Master and Savior, and r love grew the longer they followed and the more they served. They are souls who stayed in the background, content to put their own needs on the burner if they could only stay close to Jesus. They are the hidden saints.

327

The world forgets them and overlooks them. But not Jesus – He is the faithful friend. They stayed with him until the end; they will be the first to see him at the new beginning, after his resurrection.

Longinus, the soldier: Who would have thought that crucifying a poor Jewish rabbi would cha the whole course of my life? Who could have imagined such a thing? Not even storybooks tell such outlandish tales. But that's what happened. I am a soldier, an experienced soldier. I had seen men die. We were not used to judging them by how they died, but by how they lived. Wh changed me that day, though, was how Jesus died. Everyone and everything around him lost balance, and he, hanging on the cross, stayed firm. The people hurled insults and catcalls at – they were trying much too hard to humiliate him, as if they were desperate to make him ha them. But they couldn't. The earth and the sky rumbled and quaked and shook. It was as if t cross, that man on that cross was the one stable point in the universe. I couldn't take my eyes off him. And he looked at me just before he died. His eyes were so piercing that they startled How could a dying man be so alive? He didn't say a word, but I had the sense that he was sa my name, saying it like no one had ever said it before. He befriended me as I executed him. was the beginning of the rest of my life.

CHRIST IN MY LIFE All of this, Lord, for me. If I had been the only sinner the universe, you still would have suffered it all for me. I deserve to be crus and disfigured by the consequences of my sin, but you take it upon yourself instead. You raise yourself on the cross to be an everlasting sign of your unc querable love for me. Let me know your love for me. As I gaze at you on the cross, let me hear you speak my name...

How little I am willing to suffer for you, Lord! The smallest insult, the least ingratitude, the slightest discomfort – and I complain. How I long to live by faith, as all the saints did, and not by mere sight! All creation and history are in the palm of your hand. Open my eyes so I can find you in all the events a circumstances of my life, so that in living them well, I can love you more...

Mary, you would have died in his place. But it was your task to suffer in sile to be the comfort of all silent sufferers throughout the ages. Stay close to me Speak to me of Jesus. I want to know him more clearly, love him more dear and follow him more nearly...

QUESTIONS FOR SMALL GROUP DISCUSSION

1. What struck you most in this passage? What did you notice that you hadn't noticed befo

2. What most impressed the centurion and guards, do you think? In your experience, what most impresses converts to the Church? What makes them decide to convert?

3. In light of Jesus' passion, crucifixion, and death, what new meaning is given to his word:

one wants to be a follower of mine, let him renounce himself and take up his cross and ow me" (Matthew 16:24)?

ere do you think the apostles were at this point? What might they have been thinking d feeling?

techism of the Catholic Church, 599-605 on Christ's redemptive death in God's plan of salvation

LAYING THE KING TO REST (MT 27:57-66)

has ordained that our hearts will nowhere find rest and that we shall find no nance in this world, except in suffering at the foot of the cross of the Lord."

- St John of Avila

Matthew 27:57-66

When it was evening, there came a rich man of Arimathaea, called Joseph, who had himself become a disciple of Jesus. This man went to Pilate and asked for the body of Jesus. Pilate thereupon ordered it to be handed over. So Joseph took the body, wrapped it in a clean shroud and put it in his own new tomb which he had hewn out of the rock. He then rolled a large stone across the entrance of the tomb and went away. Now Mary of Magdala and the other Mary were there, sitting opposite the sepulchre. Next day, that is, when Preparation Day was over, the chief priests and the Pharisees went in a body to Pilate and said to him, 'Your Excellency, we recall that this impostor said, while he was still alive, After three days I shall rise again. Therefore give the order to have the sepulchre kept secure until the third day, for fear his disciples come and steal him away and tell the people, He has risen from the dead. This last piece of fraud would be worse than what went before.' 'You may have your guard,' said Pilate to them. 'Go and make all as secure as you know how.' So they went and made the sepulchre secure, putting seals on the stone and mounting a guard.

RIST THE LORD Joseph of Arimathaea was a Pharisee, a member of the edrin. He was a disciple of Jesus, but secretly, because he had been afraid amaging his standing and reputation. Strangely, after Jesus' apparent ise, while the apostles are hiding lest they too be arrested, Joseph makes a lic display of his faith – at the very moment when such a display could be t dangerous. What had come over him?

essing Christ's passion and crucifixion had lifted Joseph's confidence to a level. Before, he had been convinced by the truth of Jesus' teachings, or power of his miracles, but now he sees things in a new light. The prophecies been fulfilled, the portents have been seen by all, and Jesus' self-offering as the Lamb of God has been accomplished. St Matthew points out that Christ's death took place around the sixth hour, somewhere near three o'clock in the afternoon. At that time, the Temple officials would have been blowing the trumpets to call the faithful to the evening sacrifice, maybe even to the sacrifice of the Passover lamb. Maybe those trumpet calls stirred Joseph's hesitant heart. Maybe at that moment he realized that Jesus had truly brought in a new era. Maybe for him those were the trumpets announcing the coming of his King, his crucified Lord.

In any case, something awoke in Joseph's spirit in the wake of the crucifixion, and he too left his old, tentative, fearful, compromising ways behind and took charge of laying the King to rest. Perhaps if we contemplate a bit more this side of the Son of Man – the crucifixion – we too will hear the trumpets of the new era calling in our hearts and be moved to leave our old ways behind.

CHRIST THE TEACHER The leaders who had engineered Christ's condemnation and execution can't rest once their sin has been accomplished. The next day they go again to Pilate to get permission for further precautions. They mocked this imposter on Thursday and Friday, and yet they still fear him on Saturday.

Sin never leads to peace. Temptation promises fulfillment and satisfaction, but the human heart was made for truth and love, not deception and self-indulgence, and so sin can never win. The liar has to spin more lies to cover the earlier ones; the murderer has to kill again to do away with witnesses; the thief soon finds himself preferring the darkness lest his deeds be spotted in the light… As attractive and compelling as sin often appears, it can no more quench the yearnings of the human spirit than the chief priests' machinations could keep Jesus in his tomb. The best way to avoid being stuck in the tangled and sticky webs that adorn the many rooms of evil is never even to open its front door in the first place.

CHRIST THE FRIEND Often suffering makes us question God's goodness. If he really loves me, why does he permit such horrible things to happen? Maybe he made a mistake, maybe he forgot about me, maybe… No. Jesus makes no mistakes, and he never forgets about us. His mother Mary and the other Mary who had accompanied him throughout his ministry and as he hung on the cross, loved Jesus more than we can know. And yet he made them pass through the harrowing and heart wrenching experience of watching him be humiliated, unjustly condemned, beaten, scourged, and crucified. He made them witness him writhing on the cross, scorned by aristocrats and criminals alike. Imagine

w devastated they must have been. Words fail. St Matthew merely states that
ary Magdalene and the other Mary sat there, speechless, dazed, numbed with
e pain of loss, looking at the sealed tomb.

t only because they had suffered his loss, only because they had experienced
hat it was like to be without him (though in truth he was watching over them
en when they felt alone and abandoned), only because of their sufferings
re they able to experience the joy of the Resurrection, the joy of new life in
rist. Losing him for a time purified their love. The wounds God inflicts are
vays wounds of love, incisions made by the Doctor who heals our sick and
ak souls. With Christ, every Good Friday is permitted to take center stage
y because Easter Sunday is eagerly waiting in the wings.

RIST IN MY LIFE You know I believe in you. You know I am your disciple.
u alone deserve my praise, and you alone can give me the grace I need so
ich. I need your grace to be more courageous, more persevering, more
ative, and more ingenious in my discipleship. Let me hear the call of your
mpets; stir my heart to serve you with greater determination, greater joy, and
ove all, greater fidelity…

w many souls are wasting away in the futile struggle to free themselves from
tangles of sin! Only you can free them. And you have sent me to them as
ir messenger, your ambassador. You will work through me; for this you have
osen me. With the zeal of your heart, inflame my heart…

ry, no love is greater than a mother's love. And no mother has ever loved
h a purer heart than yours. Who can know, then, how much you suffered
en they killed your Son? Blessed are those who mourn, for they shall be
nforted. Comfort sinners, console the afflicted, teach us to find joy amid sor-
vs. Life is too mysterious for us. Walk beside us, take our hands, teach us…

ESTIONS FOR SMALL GROUP DISCUSSION

/hat struck you most in this passage? What did you notice that you hadn't noticed before?

o you think a Christian should fear death?

hat are some practical things we can do to help people overcome their self-perpetuating
abits of sin?

sus was born in a cave that belonged to someone else (the shepherds), and he is buried in
cave that belongs to someone else (Joseph of Arimathaea). What can we learn about him,
nd about following him, from these two facts?

*Catechism of the Catholic Church, 1005-1014 on Christian death; 627-635 on Christ's death and
ent into hell; 614-618 on the significance of Christ's death; 1865-1869 on the proliferation of sin*

THE GOSPEL OF MATTHEW CHAPTER 28

"It is truly meet and right to proclaim with all affection of heart and mind, and with the service of our voice, the invisible God, the Father Almighty, and his only-begotten Son, our Lord Jesus Christ, who paid for us to his eternal Father the debt of Adam, and by his merciful blood cancelled the guilt incurred by original sin. For this is the Paschal solemnity in which that true Lamb is slain, by whose blood the doorposts of the faithful are hallowed. This is the night in which thou didst first cause our forefathers, the children of Israel, when brought out of Egypt, to pass through the Red with dry feet. This, therefore, is the night which purged away the darkness of sinners by the light of the pillar. This is the night which at this time throughout the world restores to grace and unites in sanctity those that believe in Christ, and are separated from the vices of the world and the darkness of sinners. This is the night in which, destroying the bonds of death, Christ rose victorious from the grave. For it would have profited us nothing to have been born, unless redemption had also been bestowed upon

- Easter Exultet, from the Liturgy for the Easter

91. THE NEW HAS COME (MT 28:1-10)

"Eternal life is the perfect fulfillment of desire; inasmuch as each of the blessed will have more than he desired or hoped for."

- St Thomas Aqu

Matthew 28:1-10

After the sabbath, and towards dawn on the first day of the week, Mary of Magd and the other Mary went to visit the sepulchre. And all at once there was a viole earthquake, for the angel of the Lord, descending from heaven, came and rolled away the stone and sat on it. His face was like lightning, his robe white as snow. The guards were so shaken, so frightened of him, that they were like dead men. the angel spoke; and he said to the women, 'There is no need for you to be afraid know you are looking for Jesus, who was crucified. He is not here, for he has ris as he said he would. Come and see the place where he lay, then go quickly and his disciples, He has risen from the dead and now he is going before you to Gal it is there you will see him. Now I have told you.' Filled with awe and great joy women came quickly away from the tomb and ran to tell the disciples. And the coming to meet them, was Jesus. 'Greetings' he said. And the women came up to and, falling down before him, clasped his feet. Then Jesus said to them, 'Do not be afraid; go and tell my brothers that they must leave for Galilee; they will see me th

CHRIST THE LORD Many great historical figures have led exemplary lives, taught wise doctrines, and even died for the truth. But only one has risen again. Among the vast array of humanity's greatest heroes, Christ alone bears the epithet: "He rose again on the third day, in fulfillment of the scriptures." In Christ's resurrection, goodness and power finally unite. In Christ's resurrection, love proves that it is stronger than death. In Christ and in his resurrection, a wildly new hope dawns for all mankind – the hope that if we stay united to him through faith and grace, we will rise with him, rise from the very tombs where we are buried, and live with him forever in the vast and eternal adventure of heaven. No one else offers such a hope, because no one else has risen from the dead to be able to offer it – only the Lord.

The Resurrection delineates an important moment in the history of religions, the moment when reality exceeds the wonders of myth. Without the reality of the Resurrection, the history of the Church is utterly inexplicable. A few weak, noninfluential, unlettered fishermen from Galilee, frightened out of their wits when Jesus was arrested, suddenly become world travelers, phenomenally successful preachers, and valiant martyrs. And the Church they spread continues to grow after they die, holding fast to the exact same doctrine they preached, century after century, in nation after nation. Only the abiding presence of the Lord can explain this, a presence guaranteed by his resurrection from the dead.

CHRIST THE TEACHER St Matthew has carefully traced the actions of these two women who first saw the resurrected Lord. They witnessed the crucifixion at a distance, they accompanied their Lord at his burial, and they stayed with him when everyone else had left the tomb, loving and sorrowing still. And now, as soon as the law allows them to return, they come back. When the angel appears and gives them the good news, they believe it immediately and rush off to fulfill the mission the angel gave them. On their way, Jesus himself comes to meet them, rewarding their fidelity, and above all their faith.

Why didn't Jesus himself appear to them at the tomb? Why did he send an angel if he was just going to give them the same message a little way down the road? Jesus refuses to force his way into our hearts. Only after the women had believed and obeyed did Jesus reveal himself to them in all his glory. It was a lack of trust in God that led to mankind's fall, and it is only by trusting God that fallen man can rise – and so Jesus leaves room for us to trust, and then rewards that trust so that we will trust even more. When the Marys had believed and obeyed, Jesus rewards them. He longs for our friendship, but even so, he refuses to force it.

CHRIST THE FRIEND For the first time in St Matthew's Gospel, Jesus calls his apostles "my brothers." This marks a qualitative leap in their relationship with the Lord. Now that they have partaken of the Eucharist, they have Christ's own life within them; they are the first fruits of the New Covenant.

In Christ, we are no longer merely members of a chosen people, as in the Old Covenant, but we are sons with the Son; we are children of Gods' family; members of the household of God. Christ's restoration of communion between man and God has actually elevated man's dignity. This is why we sing on the Easter Vigil, "O Happy fault [the sin of Adam] that won for us so great a Redeemer!" As St Augustine explained as the mighty Roman Empire was crumbling all around him, God only permits evil because in his wisdom, goodness, and omnipotence, he can bring an even greater good out of it. What a friend we have in Jesus!

CHRIST IN MY LIFE You have been faithful unto death, Lord – death on a cross. And you have risen on the third day, just as you predicted. I believe in you. I put all my hopes in you. I thank you for the gift of faith. I thank you for your saving sacrifice and resurrection. You have promised to prepare a place for me in heaven – my own place in your household. Make me worthy of your promises, Lord…

Many people are slow to believe and obey – slower even than myself. I can help them. If my life is a mirror of your love, if my words are always worthy of you, then through me, as through the angel, you will roll away the stones that block so many hearts from receiving your grace. Here I am, Lord; I come to do your will…

Mary, how blessed was your reunion with Jesus! He is faithful, and he rewarded your fidelity. Mother, pray for me and for all Christians, that our hearts will overflow with the hope, the courage, the assurance that only Christ can give. Cause of our joy, pray for us…

QUESTIONS FOR SMALL GROUP DISCUSSION

1. What struck you most in this passage? What did you notice that you hadn't noticed before?

2. Jesus tells the women, "Do not be afraid." Why?

3. St Matthew makes a point of mentioning that the angel rolled the stone away from the tomb and then sat on it. Do you think there is any significance in that? What might the stone symbolize?

4. Why do so many people refuse to believe in the doctrine of Christ's resurrection? Can you think of any other ways to explain it besides the one mentioned in the commentary?

Cf. Catechism of the Catholic Church, 651-655 on the meaning of saving significance of the Resurrection; 648-650 on the Resurrection as a work of the Holy Trinity

92. GO (MT 28:11-20)

"…God alone satisfies and infinitely surpasses man's desire, which for that reason is never at rest save in God."

- St Thomas Aquinas

Matthew 28:11-20

Now while they [the women to whom Christ had appeared] were on their way, some of the guards went off into the city to tell the chief priests all that had happened. These held a meeting with the elders and, after some discussion, handed a considerable sum of money to the soldiers with these instructions, "This is what you must say, 'His disciples came during the night and stole him away while we were asleep.' And should the governor come to hear of this, we undertake to put things right with him ourselves and to see that you do not get into trouble." So they took the money and carried out their instructions, and to this day that is the story among the Jews.

The eleven disciples went to Galilee, to the mountain to which Jesus had ordered them. When they saw him, they worshiped, but they doubted. Then Jesus approached and said to them, "All power in heaven and on earth has been given to me. Go, therefore, and make disciples of all nations, baptizing them in the name of the Father, and of the Son, and of the Holy Spirit, teaching them to observe all that I have commanded you. And behold, I am with you always, until the end of the age."

CHRIST THE LORD Jesus Christ has received "all power in heaven and on earth." And what does he do with it? He shares it. He delegates his apostles to extend his Kingdom to all nations, promising to be present with them and to act through them. Jesus makes it abundantly clear that he is the Lord, and yet his Lordship differs profoundly from any other: instead of constricting the lives of his subjects through oppression and arrogance, he expands their horizons, giving them a meaning and purpose far beyond anything they could have ever come up with on their own. Through obedience to Christ, these eleven Galileans have become collaborators with the Blessed Trinity, ambassadors of God himself. Such is the generosity of the one who is our Lord.

How ironic it is that the chief priests and Pharisees, so eager for glory and influence, passed up the chance to be given such an exalted role! The irony doesn't escape St Matthew. He tells us exactly what happened. Having closed their

335

eyes to Christ's light over and over again, they ended up blinding themselves completely to the truth. They refuse to accept even the very sign they had twice asked for – the sign of Jonah. How small their self-absorbed world ends up being, just at the moment when the apostles receive their commission to conquer the entire globe for Christ.

CHRIST THE TEACHER The Incarnation was God's saving invasion into this fallen world. The Church is the extension of that invasion throughout all time and space. Christ came to reunite God and men, to lead us back into communion with the ineffable joys of the Trinitarian life.

By putting his power behind the Church's effort of baptizing, teaching, and making disciples, Jesus teaches us the proper scale of values. He could have put his power at the service of urban planning or space exploration or archeology. Such human endeavors are worthwhile, even noble. But Christ is focused on building his Kingdom, which consists of human hearts united to God through friendship with him. And where human hearts are united to God, they will also be united to one another; the inexpressible unity of the three Divine Persons will spread through those hearts and bring unity among men as well.

If building that Kingdom was and is Christ's primary concern, it needs to be ours too. As he had taught earlier, "Seek first the kingdom of God, and all else will be given you besides" (Matthew 6:33). When he puts his power behind the mission of the Church, he is practicing what he preached.

CHRIST THE FRIEND Baptism inaugurates the soul's life of grace, its life of intimate friendship with God. When we are baptized, we inherit individually Christ's promise to be with us "until the end of the age." He is with us through the other sacraments (to which baptism is the door), which strengthen and sustain us throughout our difficult and wonderful earthly pilgrimage. He is with us through his Scriptural Word as well as through the living word of his Church's teaching. And he is with us by being always within us. We have become temples of the Holy Trinity, as St Paul put it; through the blessed waters of baptism, the Triune God has taken up his dwelling in the very core of our being.

Jesus: You never have to be alone. I am the one who knows you better than you know yourself and loves you with an infinite, crucified, unconditional love, and I am your constant companion. None of the restrictions of human friendship (time, space, miscommunication, selfishness, inconstancy, etc.) apply. You are wholly mine, and I am wholly yours. The perfect family of the Trinity has adopted you into our midst; such is the love of your incomparable Friend.

CHRIST IN MY LIFE I believe in your presence and your power, and I want to walk in your light. And yet, I feel as if something is holding me back. Show me what it is. I want to be the saint you made me to be. Only saints do anything for your Kingdom, and only your Kingdom will last. Show me, Lord, the way I need to go. With the knowledge of your heart, make my heart wise…

Building up the Church, expanding your Kingdom, leading others to your friendship… You have given me a share in this mission. Such a wonderful, exhilarating mission! Thank you for calling me to follow you. Teach me to put things in this perspective – little amusements and petty pleasures have their place, but not your place. Lift my gaze up from the mud of the earth. I hope in you, Lord, my Savior and King…

Mary, Jesus left you to nurse the infant Church. Jesus is my brother, so you are my mother too. Such a wise and beautiful mother, sitting at the King's right hand, arrayed in gold. You were firm and faithful to the end, because your love was true and total. Teach me to be like that…

QUESTIONS FOR SMALL GROUP DISCUSSION

1. What struck you most in this passage? What did you notice that you hadn't noticed before?

2. All Christians are living Temples of the Holy Trinity. How should that show itself in our attitudes and actions?

3. How should Christians celebrate their baptism?

4. How might a Christian method for time management differ from a good but strictly secular method?

Cf. Catechism of the Catholic Church, 238-260 on the Trinity; 50-67 on God's plan of loving goodness; 849-856 on the missionary mandate of the Church

THE GOSPEL ACCORDING TO
ST. MARK

THE GOSPEL OF MARK CHAPTER 1

"You are one with Jesus as the members are one with the head, so you must have with him one spirit, one soul, one life, one will, one intention, one heart. It is he himself who is to be spirit, heart, love, life, everything for you. In the life of a Christian all these marvels have their origin in baptism, are increased and strengthened by confirmation and the good use of the other graces in which God makes him share, and are perfected above all by the holy Eucharist."

- St John Eudes

93. PROPHECIES FINALLY FULFILLED (MK 1:1-6)

"We must therefore get to work, and follow the Lord; we must break the chains which impede our following him."

- St Augustine

Mark 1:1-6

The beginning of the Good News about Jesus Christ, the Son of God. It is written in the book of the prophet Isaiah: Look, I am going to send my messenger before you; he will prepare your way. A voice cries in the wilderness: Prepare a way for the Lord, make his paths straight, and so it was that John the Baptist appeared in the wilderness, proclaiming a baptism of repentance for the forgiveness of sins. All Judaea and all the people of Jerusalem made their way to him, and as they were baptised by him in the river Jordan they confessed their sins. John wore a garment of camel-skin, and he lived on locusts and wild honey.

CHRIST THE LORD St Mark gets right to the point. The Old Testament quotation with which he introduces his Gospel would have been familiar to his readers. They would have recognized that it began one of Isaiah's descriptions of the promised Messiah. Thus, Mark makes clear from the very beginning who Jesus Christ is: the long-awaited Savior, the fulfillment of the Father's ancient promise, the one mightier than even the greatest of prophets.

Here is more of Isaiah's prophecy, a prophecy that, as the rest of Mark's Gospel will show, comes true in Jesus Christ: "Here comes with power the Lord God, who rules by his strong arm; Here is his reward with him, his recompense before him. Like a shepherd he feeds his flock; in his arms he gathers the lambs, carrying them in his bosom, and leading the ewes with care" (Isaiah 40:10-11). The awesome power of God flowing through the loving care of a gentle shepherd – this is Christ the Lord.

All the physical characteristics St Mark describes about St John the Baptist echo his message; they also point to the Savior. He is baptizing in the Jordan River, a symbol of universal salvation, both for the Jews and for the Gentiles. The Israelites had miraculously crossed that river in order to enter into the Promised Land; Naaman the Syrian had bathed in the Jordan to induce his miraculous cure from leprosy. St John is wearing clothes reminiscent of those worn by the prophet Elijah, who was expected to reappear at the start of the messianic age. He also ate the only insect permitted by the Jewish law to be used as food – this fidelity to Old Testament regulations gives credibility to his preaching. The Lord is coming, and his precursor is worthy of his role.

CHRIST THE TEACHER John the Baptist is celebrated repeatedly throughout the liturgical year. He especially occupies a central role in the liturgy of Advent, because during Advent the Church does what John taught the Israelites to do: get ready for Christ's coming.

John is described as the one who "prepares a way for the Lord" and "makes his paths straight." His example of humility and poverty (he ate the poorest of food, dressed in the poorest of clothes, and lived in the wilderness) gave weight to his words when he told people to repent of their arrogance and greed. The baptism he administered symbolized the people's desire to turn away from selfishness and be faithful to God's will – a desire he could stir up because he was already living that kind of fidelity.

This same interior conversion is ongoing for all Christians, as we strive to become more like Christ each day. The Church emphasizes this part of Christian spirituality during its two penitential seasons, Advent and Lent. Advent, St John the Baptist's most visible liturgical season, is the beginning of the liturgical year, a time to examine our hearts and to remove from them all selfishness, impatience, and laziness, so that they can become worthy dwelling places – wide, smooth, well kept roads – for the King who is on his way. And not only should we prepare our own hearts, but also, like John, the sincerity of our repentance should embolden us to invite and assist others to make room for Christ in their lives. If John had not announced Christ's coming with his words and example, many of his peers would have been unprepared for God's action in their lives; so too, if we keep Christ's message, the Good News of Christmas and Easter, to ourselves, many of our peers will be deprived of the grace of God, which they need so badly.

CHRIST THE FRIEND As that wise and revered devotion, the Rosary, instructs us, it is not only during Advent that we should turn our hearts and minds in a special way to that first Christmas, when Christ was born in Bethlehem and the New Covenant began. The lessons of Christ's incarnation and birth should always be nourishing our hearts and minds.

That holy night he became one of us; he entered into the sorrows, joys, hopes, and fears of human life. Why? To be able to administer a baptism that would not only symbolize our desire for God's friendship, as John's did, but actually make it happen. He came to reunite us with God and to make it possible for us to experience the intense meaning and joy that God has wanted for us from the beginning, which sin destroyed. He came because he knew we needed a friend who would never fail us, a heart that would always love us, and a strength that would constantly support us. Every Christmas, and every day, he wants to come again, and he hopes that there will be room in our inn.

CHRIST IN MY LIFE You didn't have to come and save me, Lord. I had freely abandoned you, and I deserved to receive what I had chosen. But you didn't give me what I deserved. You love me too much. It's hard for me to fathom that. Help me know your love. There are no strings attached to it; it's pure interest in me. You have to be my light and salvation. Thank you, Lord...

You are always reaching out to me with your wisdom and guidance, but I am not always ready to listen. I get so preoccupied with my own things; I forget that my primary and most important identity is that of being your disciple. Everything else is secondary. Help me clear away the clutter in my mind and heart, so that I am always ready to receive whatever graces you want to send...

Dear Jesus, if I believed more deeply that you are the only Good News that really matters, I would be more eager to share it with those around me who don't know it yet, or haven't yet believed in it. Increase my faith, Jesus; with the zeal of your heart, inflame my heart...

QUESTIONS FOR SMALL GROUP DISCUSSION

1. What struck you most in this passage? What did you notice that you hadn't noticed before?

2. St John the Baptist practiced what he preached; he showed forth Christ's message in word and deed. How can we be better witnesses of Christ to our community?

3. Why do you think God decided to send someone to announce that the Messiah was on his way? Why didn't he just have Jesus announce himself?

4. When you were baptized and confirmed, you received the Holy Spirit. What difference have those sacraments made in your life? How can you take even better advantage of them?

Cf. Catechism of the Catholic Church, 422-424 and 456-460 on the mission of Christ, 426-429 on the centrality of Christ for the life of every Christian; 522-526 on the preparations for the coming of Christ, the roles of John the Baptist and Advent, and the mystery of Christmas

94. WHAT PLEASES GOD (MK 1:7-13)

"Jesus came to John, and received baptism at his hands. Could anything be more wonderful? The boundless river that gladdens the City of God is washed by a few drops of water. The source without limits that engenders life for all mankind and is beyond all understanding is covered by the poor waters of this world."

- St Hippolytus

Mark 1:7-13

In the course of his [St John the Baptist's] preaching he said, 'Someone is following me, someone who is more powerful than I am, and I am not fit to kneel down and undo the strap of his sandals. I have baptised you with water, but he will baptise you with the Holy Spirit.' It was at this time that Jesus came from Nazareth in Galilee and was baptised in the Jordan by John. No sooner had he come up out of the water than he saw the heavens torn apart and the Spirit, like a dove, descending on him. And a voice came from heaven, 'You are my Son, the Beloved; my favour rests on you.' Immediately afterwards the Spirit drove him out into the wilderness and he remained there for forty days, and was tempted by Satan. He was with the wild beasts, and the angels looked after him.

CHRIST THE LORD St John the Baptist was the first prophet to have arisen in Israel for almost three centuries. He was such an impressive figure that the people thought he might be the Messiah. He had so much influence that King Herod eventually had to imprison him in order to avoid a popular revolt against the King's scandalous behavior, which John was denouncing. Even a hundred years after Christ's resurrection this prophet's disciples continued to carry on his mission of preaching repentance and baptizing. Christ himself called John "a prophet and more than a prophet… the greatest among men born of women."

Yet John himself points out that "someone is following me" (i.e., Jesus) who is "more powerful than I." To emphasize his point, he adds that he "is not worthy to kneel down and undo the strap of his sandals." Taking off someone's sandals, in the ancient near east, was a task reserved for slaves. Coming in from a journey, the dust of the roads mixed with manure from the many pack and harness animals caked a traveler's feet (sandals were the preferred footwear, with no socks). It was a slave's job to clean those grimy extremities, for which he would

343

need to remove the sandals. So John the Baptist, the greatest of prophets and the greatest of men, claims to be less than a slave in relation to Christ's greatness. His example should give us plenty of food for thought regarding how we treat the Lord and where we are on the scale of humility.

Maybe John thought that the Messiah would make his appearance with majesty and impressive glory. That's how God had shown himself to his people in the Old Testament. But the actual encounter between the Lord and his herald is gentler, more intimate. Jesus converses with John as an equal, as a friend. Maybe this was the most shocking part of Christ's revelation. The Lord appears, but instead of bowling over sinners with a rumble of divine thunder, he calmly submits to taking his place among sinners, and the Holy Spirit alights just as calmly, just as gently, in the form of a dove.

CHRIST THE TEACHER Jesus already knew that he was the Father's "beloved son" on whom the Father's "favor rests." The voice from heaven that announced this did so for our benefit. There are only a few times in the New Testament when God's voice speaks from heaven, and each time it does, it says the same thing. It reiterates that Jesus is the chosen one, the beloved, and that we are to heed him.

Among the many lessons hidden in those few words is the one that teaches us what pleases God. Up to this point, Jesus had done nothing extraordinary – no miracles, no great speeches, no massive conversions. He had spent thirty years living in a hut in Nazareth, helping his foster-dad in the carpentry shop and doing chores and errands for his mother. And yet, the Father's favor rests on him; the Father is well pleased with him. Why? Because Jesus has been doing what God asked him to do, and he has been doing it with love.

We don't need to try and impress God with our shocking sacrifices and earth-shaking apostolic endeavors. All he desires from us is a heart centered on him, seeking to do his will. If all Christians were to focus on doing God's will for their lives, the whole Church would swiftly move forward in perfect harmony, spreading Christ's Kingdom like a forest fire. God's will – nothing more, nothing less, nothing else. When we make this our motto, just as it was for Christ, we too fulfill our vocation of being "beloved children" of the Father, on whom his "favor rests."

CHRIST THE FRIEND Jesus did not need to be baptized. He had not sinned, and baptism was a sign of repenting from sin. Yet he chose to be baptized anyway. It is the recurring theme of his life. He didn't have to come to earth at all; he didn't have to suffer and die on the Cross. He didn't have to leave us his real presence in the Eucharist, his Holy Spirit, and the Church to be our guide. In fact, he didn't have to create us in the first place. But he chose to do all these things, simply out of love. Everything God does is motivated by love – everything. He even willingly goes into the wilderness to be tempted by the devil for forty days, not because he needed to be purified (he was without sin), but because he wanted to share our lot as wholly as possible. He is the friend without compare, because he is completely unselfish, and therefore totally trustworthy.

CHRIST IN MY LIFE Thank you for reminding me of your greatness, Lord Jesus. You are the Father's only begotten Son. You are the Eternal Word. When I turn my thoughts to you, the light of your wisdom penetrates and nourishes my soul, like sunlight that streams through a window with its shutters opened. Jesus, you are the Lord of life and history; be my Lord and friend as well.

Thank you for not overpowering me. You are meek and humble of heart. You are close to me, guiding me, entering into my daily life so calmly, so unexpectedly. Keep me tuned in to your action in my life, so I can always welcome and obey you, just as John the Baptist did.

If you had refused to come and save me, I would never have discovered the meaning of life. But because of you I know it: I was created to love God and experience his love for me. All I need to do in life is seek and heed your will for me, in big things and little things. Thank you, Lord for coming to enlighten and strengthen me. Thy Kingdom come, thy will be done!

QUESTIONS FOR SMALL GROUP DISCUSSION

1. What struck you most in this passage? What did you notice that you hadn't noticed before?

2. What enabled John to stay focused on his mission in the midst of receiving praise and adulation from the crowds? How can we do the same?

3. In our present circumstances, how can we make our lives more and more pleasing to the Father?

4. Why do you think the Holy Spirit appears in the form of a dove?

Cf. Catechism of the Catholic Church, 535-537 on the meaning of Christ's baptism; 456-460 on why Christ came among us; 430-451 on the names of Jesus and how they incite us to know, love, and imitate him

95. FISHING FOR FISHERMEN (MK 1:14-20)

"Indeed, as all know, for the spread of God's kingdom Jesus Christ used no other weapon than the preaching of the gospel, that is, the living voice of his heralds, who diffused everywhere the celestial doctrine."

- Pope Benedict XV

Mark 1:14-20

After John had been arrested, Jesus went into Galilee. There he proclaimed the Good News from God. 'The time has come,' he said, 'and the kingdom of God is close at hand. Repent, and believe the Good News.' As he was walking along by the Sea of Galilee he saw Simon and his brother Andrew casting a net in the lake – for they were fishermen. And Jesus said to them, 'Follow me and I will make you into fishers of men.' And at once they left their nets and followed him. Going on a little further, he saw James son of Zebedee and his brother John; they too were in their boat, mending their nets. He called them at once and, leaving their father Zebedee in the boat with the men he employed, they went after him.

CHRIST THE LORD Jesus Christ ushers in the third age in the history of humanity. First there was the age of creation, when mankind lived in the fullness of communion with God and the freshness of an absolute beginning. This ended with original sin and the subsequent fall from grace, after which the second age began, the age of the Promise. God promised Adam and Eve that he would send a Savior to free the human family from domination by the devil (cf. Genesis 3:15). In this second age, God gradually prepares the world through the education of his chosen people, Israel, for the arrival of Jesus Christ, whose advent marks the time of fulfillment ("the time has come" – the third age), when God actually enters into time and space in order to rescue it from sin and destruction. The end of this third age will yield the new heavens and the new earth, the definitive and final victory of Christ's eternal Kingdom.

As pressing and absorbing as current affairs may seem to the men and women of every historical epoch, it is the presence and action of Jesus Christ in and through his Church that gives the human story its true meaning and propels its fundamental drama. All things hinge on Jesus Christ, because he alone holds the key to communion with God, and only that can satisfy the human heart.

Evidence of his continuing intervention in history surrounds us. One of the most eloquent signs is the ongoing flow of vocations to the priesthood and consecrated life. Just as Jesus called his apostles to leave everything and follow him two thousand years ago, so he continues to call men and women today.

Each vocation is proof of his Lordship, proof that the King still reigns. Asking the Lord to keep calling, and asking him to give courage and faith to those he calls, should be a part of every Christian's prayer life – nothing bolsters the Kingdom more.

CHRIST THE TEACHER "The Kingdom of God" is one of Christ's most frequently used phrases. He came to establish it, he rules it, and he taught us to pray constantly for its coming ("Thy Kingdom come, Thy will be done…"). In his initial announcement of its arrival, Jesus gives us the first lesson about what it entails.

"The Kingdom of God is close at hand," he proclaims, and then he adds, "repent and believe the Good News." The "Kingdom of God" merely refers to wherever things are done God's way, wherever his will and his heart infuse life into the souls of men and women. To repent means to turn away from doing things our own, selfish way (which is the way we tend to do things ever since Adam and Eve set the unfortunate precedent). To believe in the Good News means to trust that God's way, God's will, is the best choice. If we trust in the love, wisdom, and power of God, we will have the courage to fashion our lives according to his standards (which are made clear and practical in the Church's teachings). If we recognize our own limitations and selfish tendencies, we will have the necessary humility to repent. If we want to enter this Kingdom and share in its unequaled vitality and meaning, we simply need to trust in God more than ourselves – over and over again.

CHRIST THE FRIEND From St John's Gospel we know that Jesus had already met and spent time with the four apostles whom he calls so suddenly in this passage. It's important to keep this in mind: far from unexpectedly demanding an irrational abandonment of family, career, and previous plans, Jesus built up a relationship of mutual knowledge and trust before he invited Peter, Andrew, James, and John to become his full-time disciples.

Likewise, only as we cultivate a true friendship and an intimate and ongoing exchange of hearts with our Lord will we be able to hear and heed his call in our life. This is not a God who demands blind obedience to his awesome power; this is Jesus Christ, true man, who meets us right where we are and walks along the shore of our lives, who wishes to get to know us, to spend time with us, and to call us by our names. This is a Lord and God who wants our friendship, so that he can share his life with us.

CHRIST IN MY LIFE It's so easy to lose sight of you in my life, Lord. You exercise your authority so gently. I know that history hinges on you, and yet, I still let myself get worried and angry and perturbed by minutiae. Jesus, increase my faith, strengthen my hope, and enlighten my mind – make me your convinced and formidable disciple.

I have heard your call in my life, Jesus, more than once. You have looked into my eyes and invited me to follow you more closely, just as you did with the apostles. Thank you for coming into my life. I am sorry for the times I have been unfaithful. Call me again, Lord, today, so that I can show you my love and loyalty by leaving behind everything that's not your will.

You called these apostles because you wanted to give them a mission in life, something so worthwhile that you didn't hesitate to invite them to leave their careers and their families. You have given me a mission too. Thank you, Lord, for giving me direction and meaning. Make me a fisher of men for your Kingdom.

QUESTIONS FOR SMALL GROUP DISCUSSION

1. What struck you most in this passage? What did you notice that you hadn't noticed before?

2. Jesus Christ wants to be the number one influence in our lives. Which aspects of popular culture are in harmony with that influence, and which work against it?

3. How does "repenting and believing in the gospel" translate into the reality of our day-to-day lives?

4. What can we do to help each other cultivate a deeper intimacy with Christ, a more personal and real friendship with him, so that we will always be able to "leave our nets behind" whenever he calls us?

Cf. Catechism of the Catholic Church, 541-546 on the Kingdom of God and its proclamation; 51-67 on the plan of God for human history and the stages of its revelation; 142-165 on our response to God's revelation, to God's call; 914-931 on the nature of special vocations within the Church

96. THE DEVIL CARES (MK 1:21-28)

"Here it is fitting for us to think of that great, true, eternal light… namely Christ our Savior, the Redeemer of the world, who was made man and came to the last extremity of the human condition."

- St Gregory Agrigentinus

Mark 1:21-28

They went as far as Capernaum, and as soon as the sabbath came he went to the synagogue and began to teach. And his teaching made a deep impression on them because, unlike the scribes, he taught them with authority. In their synagogue just then there was a man possessed by an unclean spirit and it shouted, 'What do you want with us, Jesus of Nazareth? Have you come to destroy us? I know who you are: the Holy One of God.' But Jesus said sharply, 'Be quiet! Come out of him!' And the unclean spirit threw the man into convulsions and with a loud cry went out of him. The people were so astonished that they started asking each other what it all meant. 'Here is a teaching that is new' they said 'and with authority behind it: he gives orders even to unclean spirits and they obey him.' And his reputation rapidly spread everywhere, through all the surrounding Galilean countryside.

CHRIST THE LORD Authority: coming from the "author." Those who heard and saw Jesus were impressed most by his authority. The "scribes," the teachers of the Jewish law, prided themselves on a detailed knowledge of the scriptures and on the myriad scriptural commentaries that rabbis and teachers had made through the centuries, but their words lacked the force of Christ's. Jesus Christ in himself is the fulfillment of all previous and partial revelation. He "has seen the Father" (John 6:46) and reveals him.

Whether we realize it or not, in our hearts we yearn for God, and so when we come into contact with someone close to God, our hearts are moved. When the crowds came into contact with Jesus Christ, the Son of God become man, their hearts burst with astonished joy. Jesus is no average teacher, nor even a great human preacher. Jesus Christ is Lord, the "Holy One of God," and when he began his public ministry, the people could tell.

CHRIST THE TEACHER We are only in the first chapter of St Mark's Gospel, and already the devil makes his appearance. One of his minions has taken possession of a child of God and cries out in panic at the Savior's approach.

The story of Christ's life and ministry cannot be told without giving due space to Satan's activity. The Gospel writers carefully distinguish between cases of mere physical ailments and cases of a demonic character (both of which Jesus cures). Jesus frequently refers to the devil in his parables and other teachings, and the devil himself tempts Jesus in the desert and returns again later to engineer Judas' betrayal (cf. John 13:2).

This Gospel motif teaches us an undeniable, if uncomfortable lesson: the devil is real, and he is interested in countering the work of grace. In one sense, accepting this fundamental truth, and keeping it always in the back of our minds, can comfort us tremendously: it helps us make sense of all the unpleasant influences at work in and around us. We are not crazy; we are not failures; we are simply engaged in a spiritual battle. If we believe in Jesus Christ, we must also believe in the devil – doomed as he is, he would love to take as many souls as he can along with him.

CHRIST THE FRIEND Imagine how the man with the unclean spirit would have felt after this incident. He had been tormented by an evil presence perhaps for years. His life was a series of momentary respites from unending and violent demonic attacks. He had no comfort in family, no rest in friendships, no capacity to carry on a normal, peaceful existence. To a great extent he had lost his most precious gift, freedom. His only hope in the face of such a hell on earth was the direct intervention of God – a miracle.

Perhaps while he was listening to Jesus in the synagogue he felt the agitation of the evil spirit. Perhaps he could sense that the demon felt threatened; perhaps he moved closer to the Lord, drawn by a mysterious, subconscious hope. Suddenly the spirit exerts his usual power and takes over the man's body and senses (who can describe the agony of such an experience?) in order to lash out at the Holy One. With a mere word, Jesus silences him and orders him to depart. The man is thrown to the ground in a final burst of evil fury and then, silence. Peace. Dare he believe it? He opens his eyes and knows that he is now himself again, freed at last from the unspeakable torment. His eyes meet Christ's…. What gratitude fills his heart! What love and gladness he finds in the glance of Jesus! Jesus Christ came to bring new life and new hope to every human heart, and he rejoices whenever we let him have his way.

CHRIST IN MY LIFE Lord Jesus, please help me to experience the power of your grace. Let me hear the words that astonished your listeners when you first came to earth; let me witness the divine authority that flowed out of your every decision and deed. Dear Jesus, it's so hard to stay in tune with your truth; please let me see you, hear you, and love you more and more…

Parts of me are still in chains, Lord. I am still possessed by selfishness. Free me, Lord. Free me from this weight of egoism that keeps me from being all that you created me to be! You are the Lord; come rule in my heart, my mind, my words, and my actions. Rule them all today, tomorrow, and forever…

How many souls are enslaved to sin and unknowingly under Satan's evil spell – confused, depressed, headed for destruction! Jesus, you came to save them all. Your Church is your sacrament of salvation. Here I am, Lord – send me as your ambassador. Fill me with love so I might bring your light to those around me who are in need…

QUESTIONS FOR SMALL GROUP DISCUSSION

1. What struck you most in this passage? What did you notice that you hadn't noticed before?

2. In what ways should we see the authority of Jesus acting or present in our lives?

3. Without being morbid or fearful (after all, Christ has conquered evil and Satan), how can a healthy awareness of the reality of the devil help us fulfill our Christian mission in life?

4. Each Sunday we profess to believe in God the "Father" and in Jesus who came to earth "for us men and for our salvation." If this faith in the goodness and love of God were more robust and lively, how would that affect our daily lives?

Cf. Catechism of the Catholic Church, 391-395 on the devil and his works; 547-550 on the "signs of the Kingdom," including the casting out of devils; 581-582 on the authority of Jesus

97. PRAYER AND ACTION (MK 1:29-39)

"If you seek to know where you can stay, stay close to Christ, because he is the way."

- St Thomas Aquinas

Mark 1:29-39

On leaving the synagogue, he went with James and John straight to the house of Simon and Andrew. Now Simon's mother-in-law had gone to bed with fever, and they told him about her straightaway. He went to her, took her by the hand and helped her up. And the fever left her and she began to wait on them. That evening, after sunset, they brought to him all who were sick and those who were possessed by devils. The whole town came crowding round the door, and he cured many who were suffering from diseases of one kind or another; he also cast out many devils, but he would not allow them to speak, because they knew who he was. In the morning, long before dawn, he got up and left the house, and went off to a lonely place and prayed there. Simon and his companions set out in search of him, and when they found him they said, 'Everybody is looking for you.' He answered, 'Let us go elsewhere, to the neighbouring country towns, so that I can preach there too, because that is why I came.' And he went all through Galilee, preaching in their synagogues and casting out devils.

CHRIST THE LORD Christ is a man whose whole attention is focused on others. Simon and his disciples come to him the morning after a day like none they had ever known before. Christ's popularity was at a zenith, after his immensely successful preaching, his casting out a demon in the synagogue, and his evening of miraculous cures and exorcisms. They surely thought that he would claim the Messianic kingship right away and gather an army to cast off the despicable Roman rule, or something to that effect. When they awoke to find him gone, they searched apprehensively for him, lest they miss their chance for glory (the townspeople were already rallying and demanding his presence). But when they find him, alone in prayer on the mountaintop, and they tell him that everyone is looking for him, Christ answers with what was to be the first of many surprises: it is not for personal glory that he has come, but to fulfill a mission received from another, and so he must move on. They are welcome to come with him, but whether they do or not, he will be faithful to his Father's will.

In a world inundated with the ethos of "success" and "achievement," where great souls are withered by the rat race of petty promotions and vaporous rewards, the selfless, transcendent purpose of a man entirely focused on fulfilling someone else's plan (i.e., God's) may perhaps furrow our brow, but doesn't it also stir us to admiration? Such is our Lord, who hopes that our admiration will evolve into heartfelt emulation.

CHRIST THE TEACHER   Jesus Christ was God become man. His human nature was united with the power of his divine person. He was perfect, sinless, without any selfishness, laziness, or pride. His character was flawless, as firm as the mountains and as gentle as a mother's caress. His mind was beyond brilliant, filled with the radiance of divine light and understanding. No emotional scars from a difficult family upbringing (Mary was without sin too, and Joseph was a saint), no personality disorders or imbalanced self-esteem – no lacks, no wounds, no imperfections at all. And yet, over and over again in the Gospels, we see him go off to be alone in prayer: "In the morning long before dawn, he got up and left the house, and went off to a lonely place and prayed there."

Christ was perfect, God from God and light from light, and yet he needed to reserve time just to be alone with his Father; he needed to go off and pray. He even had to get up early to make time for it. Sometimes he had to stay up late in order to make time for it. But he always did it.

If he, who was perfect, needed prayer in order to fulfill his life's mission, what does that imply for us, who are so imperfect, so weak, so vulnerable to every sort of temptation and wounded by every kind of sin? Christ was a man of prayer, and, as he himself put it, "no disciple is greater than his master" (John 15:20).

CHRIST THE FRIEND   It's not only the simple fact of Christ's miracles that demonstrates his personal love, but even the manner in which he performs them. Simon's mother-in-law is sick in bed with a fever. In the ancient world, fevers posed greater threats than they do today. If the fever was the result of an infection (which fevers frequently are), it could indicate an impending death, since there were no antibiotics; this explains the apostles' concern. Jesus could have snapped his fingers and immediately cured her; but instead, he goes over to the bed where she lay, grasps her sweaty, feverish hand in his own firm, gentle grip, relieving her sickness with his touch, and then helps her up. In Jesus Christ, God comes to meet us in the reality of our humanity, bringing the warmth of his divine light into its most ordinary nooks and crannies.

Simon's mother-in-law: When I woke from the fever, I felt… well, how can I describe how I felt? Normally such a long, severe fever wears you out, but when I woke from this one I felt buoyant, glad, strong. I felt a healthy, invigorating warmth flowing through me, banishing the fever's enfeebling heat. And then I realized that this new strength was flowing into me. Only then did I turn and look to see who was holding my hand: Jesus.

Simon had told me about him, but I had never met him before. And yet, his smiling eyes told me he knew me. He didn't have to speak any words. Right away he was my oldest friend as well as my newest friend. It sounds so strange, but it's true. Suddenly, under his gaze, with his hand holding mine, all the different parts of my life fell into place. My heart and mind came into focus as they never had before. I wasn't just cured from the fever; I was somehow new. Without even thinking, I smiled back at him and rose to start preparing some supper for him and his companions. Healthy? Yes, I was healthy again, healthier than I had ever been before.

CHRIST IN MY LIFE Lord, by making me your disciple, you have shared your mission with me. I am your missionary. You want to reach out to others through me; I am part of your mystical body. O Lord, fill me with enthusiasm and zeal for this wonderful and daunting mission of building your Kingdom! It is far beyond my capacities, but that doesn't matter, as long as you lead me.

Prayer is a mystery to me, Jesus. Sometimes I seem to pray well, while other times I'm completely lost. But I know that you have given me the gift of the Holy Spirit, who dwells within me, teaching me and coaching me. Lord Jesus, I believe in you, and I know that without a healthy, growing life of prayer, my soul will wither. Dear Lord, teach me to be docile to the promptings of your Holy Spirit.

You continue to touch me, just as you touched Peter's mother-in-law, whenever I receive you in the Eucharist. Thank you, Lord, for staying so close to me, for bringing your saving grace into my life in such a human way. Teach me this same gentle, caring manner as I reach out to help my neighbors.

QUESTIONS FOR SMALL GROUP DISCUSSION

1. What struck you most in this passage? What did you notice that you hadn't noticed before?

2. Christ lived his entire life under the light of the mission he had received from his Father – that light informed all his decisions and actions. How would our lives be different if we imitated more closely this characteristic of our Lord?

3. What prevents us from feeling a more intense need for a deep prayer life? How can we better follow our Lord's example in this area? How can we encourage each other to do so?

4. Our concern for other people should be as attentive, sincere, and gentle as Christ's. In what areas can we improve the quality of our Christian charity?

Cf. Catechism of the Catholic Church, 2558-2567 on the importance of prayer; 2598-2606 on the prayer of Jesus; 2725-2733 on difficulties in prayer; 456-560 on the mission of Christ; 1145-1155 on the way God enters into contact with us

98. WHAT CHRIST WANTS (MK 1:40-45)

"How merciful the Lord Jesus is towards us, how abundantly kind and good!"

- St Cyprian

Mark 1:40-45

A leper came to him and pleaded on his knees: 'If you want to' he said 'you can cure me.' Feeling sorry for him, Jesus stretched out his hand and touched him. 'Of course I want to!' he said. 'Be cured!' And the leprosy left him at once and he was cured. Jesus immediately sent him away and sternly ordered him, 'Mind you say nothing to anyone, but go and show yourself to the priest, and make the offering for your healing prescribed by Moses as evidence of your recovery.' The man went away, but then started talking about it freely and telling the story everywhere, so that Jesus could no longer go openly into any town, but had to stay outside in places where nobody lived. Even so, people from all around would come to him.

CHRIST THE LORD Leprosy was widespread and incurable at the time of Jesus. Besides being highly contagious, this bacterial skin infection produces paralysis, nauseating deformities such as the wasting away of fingers, facial features, and entire limbs, and a revolting stench (akin to rotting flesh). Ancient societies gathered lepers into "colonies" isolated from other occupied centers. They required anyone suffering from the disease to stay a hundred yards away from noninfected people and carry a bell, which could be rung to avert a close encounter with the healthy.

Lepers thus lived in isolation, filth, and poverty until the disease progressed sufficiently to cause their death. It was (and still is) a powerful analogy for sin, which is a widespread, contagious disease with similar effects on the spiritual plane: it isolates people from one another, causes deformities in character and understanding, and yields a moral stench unbearable to one's own conscience and the consciences of others. It also leads to death – spiritual death – and at the time of Christ, it too was incurable.

When Christ looks upon this leper and cures him with the mere touch of his hand, he manifests not only his astonishing power over the physical cosmos, but also the ultimate reason behind his coming to earth: to return the outcast hearts of mankind to a living communion with God by taking away our sins. Jesus Christ is the saving Lord of lepers and sinners – if only we kneel before him with faith.

CHRIST THE TEACHER What if this leper had been afraid to come to Jesus? What if he had fearfully remained in his isolation, afraid to come out in the open with his sickness, afraid to break with social protocol and kneel at the Master's feet? He would have stayed stuck in his gruesome affliction. The first lesson, then, consists in admitting our need for help, coming to know that we are infected by sin and sinful tendencies, and that we need to be healed of this spiritual disease. Since (with the devil's help) we have become experts in muffling our conscience, however, we can easily convince ourselves that we don't really need God. But if that were the case, why would Christ have come to earth?

This holy leper also teaches us two secrets to effective prayer: confidence and humility. He has no doubt that Christ can cure him: "If you want to, you can cure me." But he also knows that he has no right to demand a cure; he doesn't say, "Cure me!" He says, "If you want to…" (i.e., "you know what will be best for me and for your Kingdom; if curing me will give you glory, please do so, but if not, I will still believe and trust in you.") Confidence and humility un-leash the roaring flood of power and compassion that streams from the heart of God: "Feeling sorry for him…"

If our prayer weaves together a healthy awareness of our need for God's grace and assistance, a real confidence in his power and love, and the elegance of humility, God will be able to do wonders in us as well.

CHRIST THE FRIEND Few phenomena are as disgusting as leprosy in its ad-vanced stages. Thus, when Christ responds to this man's plea by stretching out his hand and actually touching him, he shows a love that's real, that comes to meet us in the absolute depths of our human misery. God wants to be with us, so that he can raise us up to be with him.

When he orders the cured leper to keep the incident under wraps and go present himself to the priests, who performed a special ceremony to verify a cure from leprosy, Christ shows that his love is also sincere. It was concern and compassion for this man's suffering that moved him to perform the miracle, not a thirst for fame and recognition (although these inevitably followed). Christ's love is real, it is sincere – it is the love of a friend we can count on no matter what.

Jesus: Many people are suffering from invisible leprosy, a leprosy of the soul. They consider themselves outcasts, and although on the surface they appear to be just like everyone else, inside they slowly disintegrating, slowly being consumed by regret, guilt, confusion, sorrow. You know how pure my love is, how powerful. You have welcomed it and experienced it, and you have let my grace touch your heart. Tell these others about it. Convince them to let me touch them, to come to me. I long to save them.

CHRIST IN MY LIFE Lord, thank you for coming to save me from my sin. Thank you for creating and redeeming me, for giving me the gift of faith, and for drawing me closer to you every day. All the good that I have received is your gift, Lord. Why do I still fret and fear? Why do I doubt your love? Forgive my fearful heart, my selfish tantrums. With the Kingdom of your heart, reign in my heart...

I am short on both humility and confidence. I believe, but my faith is weak. I know that without you I can do nothing, but I spend most of my time acting like I can do it all on my own. Have mercy on me, Lord. Teach me the great lesson of humility. Grant me the peace of soul that comes from living in the palm of your hand...

I am amazed at the depth and delicacy of your love. Teach me to love as you love. It is beyond my power. Teach me to reach out to my neighbor, to recognize their needs, to care about them. Tear away the blinders of selfishness that hinder me from building your Kingdom. With the love of your heart, inflame my heart!...

QUESTIONS FOR SMALL GROUP DISCUSSION

1. What struck you most in this passage? What did you notice that you hadn't noticed before?

2. What are some of the ways we tend to disguise (especially from ourselves) our need for God?

3. In what ways can we tell if our prayer (both personal and liturgical/communal) is humble and confident? Is it wrong to go to Mass only in order to "get something out of it"?

4. How do you think Christ's apostles would have reacted during and after this encounter?

*. Catechism of the Catholic Church, 547-550 on the meaning of Christ's miracles; 1-3, 26-29 on
d's sheer goodness (unconditional love) as expressed in his plan of salvation

HE GOSPEL OF MARK CHAPTER 2

*ate have I loved you, O Beauty so ancient and so new; late have I loved you! For
*hold you were within me, and I outside; and I sought you outside and in my ugli-
*ss fell upon those lovely things that you have made. You were with me and I was
*t with you. I was kept from you by those things, yet had they not been in you, they
*ould not have been at all. You called and cried to me and broke open my deafness;
*nd you sent forth your beams and shone upon me and chased away my blindness;
*u breathed fragrance upon me, and I drew in my breath and do now pant for you; I
*sted you, and now hunger and thirst for you; you touched me, and I have burned for
ur peace."

- St Augustine

9. GOING THROUGH THE ROOF (MK 2:1-12)

*nd we too can only serve the Lord energetically if our faith thrives and is present in
undance."

- Pope Benedict XVI

Mark 2:1-12

When he returned to Capernaum some time later, word went round that he was
back; and so many people collected that there was no room left, even in front of
the door. He was preaching the word to them when some people came bringing
him a paralytic carried by four men, but as the crowd made it impossible to get
the man to him, they stripped the roof over the place where Jesus was; and when
they had made an opening, they lowered the stretcher on which the paralytic lay.
Seeing their faith, Jesus said to the paralytic, 'My child, your sins are forgiven.' Now
some scribes were sitting there, and they thought to themselves, 'How can this man
talk like that? He is blaspheming. Who can forgive sins but God?' Jesus, inwardly
aware that this was what they were thinking, said to them, 'Why do you have these
thoughts in your hearts? Which of these is easier: to say to the paralytic, Your sins
are forgiven or to say, Get up, pick up your stretcher and walk? But to prove to you
that the Son of Man has authority on earth to forgive sins,' – he said to the paralytic
– 'I order you: get up, pick up your stretcher, and go off home.' And the man got up,
picked up his stretcher at once and walked out in front of everyone, so that they
were all astounded and praised God saying, 'We have never seen anything like this.'

CHRIST THE LORD Many critics of Christianity claim that Christ was just one of those great philosophers or religious teachers like Confucius and Socrates – that he was only raised to divine status by later generations of his followers. This passage is one of the many New Testament scenes that prove such a position untenable.

Christ's divine authority shines through clearly in the Gospels. Jesus does not deny that the authority to forgive sins belongs only to God, since every sin, every evil deed is primarily an offense against God, the source of all goodness and truth, and unjustly uses God's great gift to men, free will, as an instrument of rebellion against the Giver, but he uses a miracle to prove that he possesses that divine authority. He claims to be not only the Messiah sent by God ("the Son of Man" is a Messianic title taken from the Jewish Scriptures), but to possess God's own divinity. He himself forgives the man's sins in his own name. He leaves no room for doubt; he is the Lord of both earth and heaven.

St Mark gives us another detail that illustrates what kind of a Lord he is. Jesus knows exactly what his critics are thinking; he can read their souls. They are offended by him; they are irked, even outraged, at his apparently blasphemous claim to forgive sins. Instead of voicing their objections, however, they grumble in their hearts. But Jesus sees the entire interior drama. What does he do with this privileged knowledge? Does he brandish it to humiliate his unjust critics? No, he much prefers to use it for their good. Knowing how difficult it is for them to accept his claims, and how reluctant they are to engage in honest dialogue with him, he gives them irrefutable evidence to validate those claims. Our Lord wants to rule by love and truth, not by force.

CHRIST THE TEACHER The paralytic emerges from this encounter healed in soul and in body. Why did Christ heal him? Because he "saw their faith." This group of friends believed in Christ's power to heal, to make whole, to right what was wrong. And they showed the sincerity of that faith in their ingenious, determined efforts to meet him. How easy it would have been for them not to take the first step of lugging the paralytic all the way over to the place where Jesus was preaching! How easy it would have been for them to become discouraged when they realized that the crowd was impenetrable! And yet, their faith prevailed; they found a way to bring the paralytic to the Master's feet. In a sense, their faith had already performed the physical miracle; the paralyzed man had made his way closer to Christ than most of the others who were in the crowd. And it was this faith – clearly authentic because it produced action – that opened the suffering man's soul to receive Jesus' gift of peace.

In an age when Christ is only a stone's throw away, right there in the tabernacle of the nearest Catholic chapel; in an age when confession is available upon request down the street at the local parish; in an age when the revealed Word of God and the teachings of the Church can fit into a handheld computer – in such an age we need to relearn this lesson of faith. What we take for granted the presence of the Living God among us – these men struggled and sacrificed and risked their reputations to find. The next time we have difficulty getting out of bed for Mass (or getting someone else out of bed for Mass), we should call to mind the picture of this paralytic, who wanted to get to "Mass" so badly that he had his friends bring his bed along with him.

CHRIST THE FRIEND Does Christ let anyone down in the Gospels? Does anyone who comes to Christ with a sincere, docile, and generous attitude go away disappointed? Not a one. And yet, they had much less to bolster their faith than we have. They had only rumors of miracles; we have the whole New Testament, the Resurrection, and twenty centuries of miracles through the action of the Church and its countless saints.

Jesus Christ wants to unlock for us life's secret treasures, to unleash on earth the abundance of heavenly joy. That's why he came –to give us what we long for, to lead us where we yearn to go. He asks only that we heed his call: "Follow me." He'll take care of everything else.

Jesus: Their faith opened up the flow of my grace into their lives. Their faith gave them an experience of my presence that no one else in that huge crowd had. They believed in me. But before they arrived, they didn't believe so strongly. Their faith increased a little bit when they realized that they couldn't come close to me through the crowd, and then decided not to give up but to search for some other way. And when they couldn't find any other way and kept searching anyhow, their faith grew even more. Then, when they hit upon the idea of climbing up onto the roof with their paralyzed friend, and they made the effort to open up the roof and lower him down in front of me – when that happened, their faith flowered, and they received their reward… Whenever I allow you to face obstacles in life, remember their example. Remember that the more you have to exercise your faith, the more it will grow, and the more my grace will be able to flow.

CHRIST IN MY LIFE I believe in you, Lord, but my faith is so weak! It's like Charlie Brown's Christmas tree: there, but scrawny. Strengthen it, Lord, please. How can I be the saint you want me to be, how can I live the fruitful, meaningful life you created me to live, how can I fulfill the mission – unique and unrepeatable – that you have entrusted to me, unless you increase my faith?

At times I feel as though my soul is paralyzed, like this man's body. I'm unable to do the good that I know I should do and that I long to do. My sinful habits inhibit me. My selfishness, my arrogance, my laziness, and my love for pleasure – I have cultivated these so well that virtue is held in check. Heal me, Jesus, please; reanimate my capacity to love, because that's what you created me for...

So many people around me are even more paralyzed than I am. They need me and my fellow Christians to bring them to you, so they can meet you, and you can pour your grace into their souls. Who do you want me to bring to you? I will do it, Lord, even if I have to strip a hole in the roof – I only ask that you fill my heart with your very own courage and goodness...

QUESTIONS FOR SMALL GROUP DISCUSSION

1. What struck you most in this passage? What did you notice that you hadn't noticed before?

2. Why did the Pharisees not believe in Jesus even after seeing him perform miracles like this one? How can we tell if that pharisaical attitude is present at all in our relationship with Jesus Christ?

3. Why did these men make such an extraordinary effort to come closer to Christ, and why are we so often reluctant to make even a small effort to do so?

4. The men who carried the paralytic to Jesus were instrumental in his cure: Jesus forgave his sins upon seeing "their faith" – plural, not singular. How can we more effectively show that kind of concern for others in the concrete circumstances of our lives?

Cf. Catechism of the Catholic Church, 547-550 on the meaning of Jesus' miracles; 1440-1449 on sin and forgiveness

100. FOLLOW ME – IF YOU DARE (MK 2:13-17)

"Why do you have so low an opinion of yourself, when you are so precious to God? Why do you so dishonor yourself when you are so honored by God?"

- *St Peter Chrysologus*

Mark 2:13-17

He went out again to the shore of the lake; and all the people came to him, and he taught them. As he was walking on he saw Levi the son of Alphaeus, sitting by the customs house, and he said to him, 'Follow me.' And he got up and followed him. When Jesus was at dinner in his house, a number of tax collectors and sinners were also sitting at the table with Jesus and his disciples; for there were many of them among his followers. When the scribes of the Pharisee party saw him eating with sinners and tax collectors, they said to his disciples, 'Why does he eat with tax collectors and sinners?' When Jesus heard this he said to them, 'It is not the healthy who need the doctor, but the sick. I did not come to call the virtuous, but sinners.'

CHRIST THE LORD Tension between Jesus and the Pharisees is quickly becoming a central theme in St Mark's Gospel, as it is in all the Gospels. The Pharisees were the religious leaders of Israel at the time of Christ. They dedicated themselves to a scrupulous following of the letter of the law (both the divine law as handed down in the Scriptures and the merely human traditions derived from them) with the hopes that their ritual perfection would bring God's favor on Israel and liberate it from Roman rule. Many of them were sincerely religious, but their religiosity was so external that it lent itself to hypocrisy, arrogance, and self-centeredness. Nevertheless, they knew the letter of the law and followed it strictly, thus gaining moral and spiritual ascendancy over the rest of the populace.

Jesus is neither afraid of nor intimidated by them. He understands them perfectly, and tirelessly tries to get them to see their own error, so that they will be free to see him as their Savior. They are perhaps the most pitiful sinners of all those Jesus came to save, because they fail to recognize their own sin – a persistent phenomenon in the history of salvation. One of the greatest proofs that Christ is a Lord whose power shows itself in mercy is the tireless patience with which he treats these Pharisees, such stubborn enemies of his reign. It should give comfort to all of us, and serve as an example for those of us who claim to be the Lord's disciples.

CHRIST THE TEACHER Jesus defends his apostles from the insidious criticism of the Pharisees. The Pharisees, St Mark points out, went up to the *apostles* to criticize Jesus; they were trying to damage the Lord's credibility in the eyes of his followers. They felt that if they could undermine the disciples' confidence, they would render their master powerless. But Jesus comes quickly to his own defense, in order to safeguard his disciples' faith. Two lessons can be drawn from the encounter.

First, we need to be on our guard against destructive criticism. The Pharisees have no interest in Christ's disciples; they are interested in getting rid of this new rabbi who poses a threat to their position and reputation. To get what they want, they resort to crafty criticism, subtly sowing doubts. Whenever we find ourselves criticizing other people, we need to be careful that we haven't fallen into the trap of the Pharisees: lowering others in the eyes of our peers so as to elevate our own image. But we also need to be careful to avoid accepting or tolerating destructive criticism from others – too often it stems from impure motives and is tinged with the poison of falsehood, detraction, or exaggeration.

Second, we need to remember that the sure defense in the face of any doubt or difficulty is Christ's word. Whenever confusion about the faith threatens to weaken our conviction, all we need to do is turn our gaze to the teaching of Christ's Church. Jesus continues to guide his followers on the sure path of truth and holiness through the trustworthy doctrine of the Church. Anything that contradicts the Catechism, no matter how attractive or convincing it may appear, can simply be discarded. Jesus protected his first apostles from the fatal errors of the Pharisees; he will do nothing less for us, as long as we turn to him for that protection.

CHRIST THE FRIEND Jesus sits at table with sinners, with people who aren't part of the "in crowd." Dining with someone in ancient Palestine was a symbolic gesture as well as a nutritive one; it signified acceptance and communion among those who partook of the same meal. Jesus wants to come and dine with us, knowing full well our sinful, selfish souls. He wants to be part of our everyday life, despite our imperfections, to accompany us in all our adventures, trials, triumphs, and defeats. The same Jesus who is Lord of the universe eagerly desires to be with those he came to save; in this passage he actually makes a point of it. A divine Savior who saves sinners by intimate friendship – only a God of love could come up with such a combination.

But Jesus refuses to force himself on anyone. He invites Levi (called Matthew in the other Gospels) to follow him, but Levi has to accept the invitation. He has to decide to leave behind his old life and let Jesus into his circle of friends. The future apostle does so – and changes the course of history with his decision. St Mark deftly juxtaposes Levi's generous acceptance with the Pharisees' rejection of Christ. God wants our friendship, and he gives us many chances to accept it, but in the end, he leaves it up to us to take it or leave it. Would that we all followed in Matthew's footsteps, every day of our lives!

CHRIST IN MY LIFE You know my tendency to criticize unnecessarily and unconstructively. I am often like the Pharisees, Lord: cold, judgmental, looking down on my neighbor so as to inflate my self-esteem. I don't know how you put up with me, but you do. You are patient, generous, and loving. I want to follow you more faithfully, Lord. I want you to come and dine with me, and heal me. Forgive me, Jesus, and come stay with me...

You called St Matthew to serve you in a special way, to be a particularly close companion. You have called me to a unique mission in life as well. No one else has the same mission field as I do. And maybe you are asking me to follow you ven more closely... Whatever the case, please let me hear your voice, let it esound in my heart and stir all the generosity I can muster...

Lord Jesus, how your Church needs men and women who will leave all things to follow you, as St Matthew and all the apostles did! Call them, Lord! Call many young people to give their lives for your Kingdom. Call valiant soldiers into your ranks. Let them hear your call loud and clear, and enable them to respond with the same noble courage as St Matthew...

QUESTIONS FOR SMALL GROUP DISCUSSION

1. What struck you most in this passage? What did you notice that you hadn't noticed before?

2. Why do you think Jesus chose to call Levi while he was right in the middle of a workday at his tax collector's office?

3. How can a young man or woman recognize the call of God to a special vocation in the Church?

4. St Matthew's first reaction to his encounter with Christ was to invite his friends to meet the Lord. In the last two weeks, what have we done to invite our friends to meet the Lord? Why haven't we done more? What more can we do?

Cf. Catechism of the Catholic Church, 545, 589, 1439, 1846 on how Jesus reveals the Father's mercy; 1473 on the necessity of works of mercy; 1864 and 2091 on sinners refusing God's mercy

101. FASTING FOR THE BRIDEGROOM (MK 2:18-22)

We should live as temples of God so that men may see that God dwells in us."

- St Cyprian

Mark 2:18-22

One day when John's disciples and the Pharisees were fasting, some people came and said to him, 'Why is it that John's disciples and the disciples of the Pharisees fast, but your disciples do not?' Jesus replied, 'Surely the bridegroom's attendants would never think of fasting while the bridegroom is still with them? As long as they have the bridegroom with them, they could not think of fasting. But the time will come for the bridegroom to be taken away from them, and then, on that day, they will fast. No one sews a piece of unshrunken cloth on an old cloak; if he does, the patch pulls away from it, the new from the old, and the tear gets worse. And nobody puts new wine into old wineskins; if he does, the wine will burst the skins, and the wine is lost and the skins too. No! New wine, fresh skins!'

CHRIST THE LORD Two details of this exchange reiterate the utter unique-ness of Jesus, advancing his continual claim to be much more than just another prophet or rabbi.

363

First, he likens himself to "the bridegroom." The prophets of the Old Testament often referred to the relationship between God and Israel as a spousal one. The Lord was the bridegroom and Israel was the bride – an unfaithful spouse, but one whom God would not repudiate. It was more than mere poetry, since the Covenant between Israel and God was more than a poetic covenant. Thus, when Christ calls himself the bridegroom, he is using an image to make a point certainly, but he is also appropriating for himself a role that had in the past been reserved for God alone.

Second, he presents himself and his doctrine as something entirely new – a new cloth, a new vintage of wine. His coming marks a new age, a quantum leap in relations between God and man. To try and fit him into the categories that preceded him, the ones that had served as spiritual training wheels, can only yield frustration and destruction. Jesus Christ is unique; he alone is the Lord; in him we have all our hearts could ever desire.

CHRIST THE TEACHER Fasting, making sacrifices, or acts of self-denial, are spiritual disciplines that help detach us from our disordered love of God's gifts in order to live more fully in God's presence, in communion with him, the Giver of those gifts. Fasting is one means of spiritual growth, of strengthening our awareness of God and our need for him. Jesus points out that as long as he is with his disciples in the visible, tangible way of his incarnation, they have no need of such practices, because they are already in God's presence – he's right in front of them, right beside them.

The mistake that John's disciples and the Pharisees were making was twofold: they did not accept Jesus as the Savior, and they had grown proud of their strict spiritual disciplines, thinking themselves superior to others because they fasted more. If they only would believe in Jesus, they could rejoice with the other disciples to be in the presence of the God whom they sought so arrogantly through their elaborate rituals of self-denial!

In teaching us the true reason for fasting, Christ once again invites his critics (along with all of us whose faith is weak) to believe in him, to trust in him, and to direct all the efforts of our spiritual lives toward coming closer to him. In Christ, something new has come into the world. The relationship with God and neighbor that he offers us is qualitatively new. He doesn't simply refill the old wineskins; he brings an entirely new wine, a new kind of intimacy with God, a brand New Covenant. Later, St Paul draws the logical conclusion when he claims that in Christ we are entirely new creatures: "And for anyone who is in

Christ, there is a new creation; the old creation has gone, and now the new one is here" (2 Cor 5:17).

CHRIST THE FRIEND Some Christians give the impression that following Christ is a somber affair, or that the Christian life consists above all of dour sacrifices and boring obligations. Joyless, dreary, dull. No wonder their friends want to stay as far away from Christianity as possible!

Although it is true that the cross is never absent from an authentically Christian life, it is equally true that the God who meets us on that cross is the same God who created the heavens and the earth, the oceans and the mountains, laughter, sunlight, friendship, and every earthly delight. When Christ calls himself the bridegroom, he conjures up images of a wedding banquet, which was the most festive of occasions, according to ancient Semitic customs. He does not choose this allusion by mistake. The "narrow gate" and the "hard way" that Jesus traces out for his followers lead to life – a life of abundant joy, peace, and vigor. As St Theresa of Avila put it, a sad saint is a bad saint. If our friendship with Christ does not fill us with contagious enthusiasm, we're probably being a half-hearted friend.

CHRIST THE LORD Thank you for the gift of faith. I am sorry for taking it for granted so often. This world sometimes reminds me of you, but many times it distracts me from you. Keep teaching me, Lord, keep guiding me. I want to be the saint you created me to be. And please grant the gift of faith to those who don't believe in you. Only you can satisfy their longings...

Do I fast enough? Do I exercise enough self-governance and self-discipline to keep my soul in shape, so I can easily detect your presence and respond to your nudging? I am not sure, Lord. You know I want to follow you. Show me the path to take, teach me to be detached from everything except you, so as to love all things in you, and you in all things...

I believe in you, Jesus, but sometimes the crosses you send me stifle the joy I ought to have knowing that you love me and gave yourself for me. Don't let that happen, Lord. Let me always experience your joy in the depths of my heart, so that it will overflow in everything I say and do, attracting everyone I meet to your friendship...

QUESTIONS FOR SMALL GROUP DISCUSSION

1. What struck you most in this passage? What did you notice that you hadn't noticed before?

2. For the Jews of Jesus' time, the "old wineskins" were the Old Testament practices. In our day, what are the "old wineskins" we can be tempted to use to tame Christ's demands on our lives?

3. Jesus said that his followers are like a city on the hill. In what ways should our lives attract those around us to Christ?

4. How can we make sure that the sacrifices we have taken on as a result of our commitment to Christ and his Church (how we spend our time, the activities we avoid, the self-discipline we inculcate) always flow from love for Christ and a desire to imitate and get closer to him, and never degenerate into dry duties performed in order to foster an attitude of self-righteousness?

Cf. Catechism of the Catholic Church, 1691-1709 on a profile of "life in Christ"; 1803-1832 on the virtues that should characterize Christian life

THE GOSPEL OF MARK CHAPTER 3

"This Sacred Council… teaches and declares that Jesus Christ, the eternal Shepherd, established His holy Church, having sent forth the apostles as He Himself had been sent by the Father; and He willed that their successors, namely the bishops, should be shepherds in His Church even to the consummation of the world. And in order that the episcopate itself might be one and undivided, He placed Blessed Peter over the other apostles, and instituted in him a permanent and visible source and foundation of unity of faith and communion."

- The Second Vatican Council, Lumen gentium, 18

102. THE CONDESCENDING CRITICS CLUB (MK 2:23-3:6)

"For the word of God is light to the mind and fire to the will, enabling man to know and to love God."

- St Laurence of Brindisi

Mark 2:23-3:6

One sabbath day he happened to be taking a walk through the cornfields, and his disciples began to pick ears of corn as they went along. And the Pharisees said to him, 'Look, why are they doing something on the sabbath day that is forbidden?' And he replied, 'Did you never read what David did in his time of need when he and his followers were hungry – how he went into the house of God when Abiathar was high priest, and ate the loaves of offering which only the priests are allowed to eat, and how he also gave some to the men with him?' And he said to them, 'The sabbath was made for man, not man for the sabbath; the Son of Man is master even of the Sabbath.'

He went again into a synagogue, and there was a man there who had a withered hand. And they were watching him to see if he would cure him on the sabbath day, hoping for something to use against him. He said to the man with the withered hand, 'Stand up out in the middle!' Then he said to them, 'Is it against the law on the sabbath day to do good, or to do evil; to save life, or to kill?' But they said nothing. Then, grieved to find them so obstinate, he looked angrily round at them, and said to the man, 'Stretch out your hand.' He stretched it out and his hand was better. The Pharisees went out and at once began to plot with the Herodians against him, discussing how to destroy him.

CHRIST THE LORD Jesus was making enemies. The Pharisees were the "separated ones" in ancient Israel, those who knew the Jewish law inside and out and had committed themselves to following not only the broad regulations of the Sacred Scriptures, but also the innumerable demands of the traditional interpretations of those regulations. They had their seats on the Sanhedrin (the ruling body of the Jewish state), and they were determined to rule the common people and instruct them in what they considered to be true piety. If a man wanted to make a name for himself in the Israel of Jesus' day, crossing the Pharisees would be the last thing on his agenda. And yet, Jesus does just that, over and over.

His challenges are both attempts to shake them out of their complacent and illusory self-righteousness, and also opportunities to teach his disciples about true religion. He is fearless in the face of their intimidations and unperturbed by their imposing presence. On top of it all, he backs up every challenge, every lesson with a miraculous sign, speaking but a word to cure horrible afflictions. He shows clearly that he has full authority over human life, and he continually demonstrates that he wields this authority always and everywhere for the good of his brothers and sisters to help their lives flourish.

Christ was making enemies, but only of those who refused to recognize him as the Lord he truly is. That pattern still occurs today, and we would do well to learn how to spot it.

CHRIST THE TEACHER For the Pharisees, the law of the Sabbath had become the touchstone of devotion to God. The original commandment (the third of the Ten Commandments – "Thou shalt keep holy the Lord's Day") reserved one day a week to be devoted exclusively to worship and fellowship. It was meant to remind God's people that they belonged to him, that they received all their blessings from him, and that their relationship with him was the bedrock of their happiness.

367

Through the centuries, the rabbis had vied with one another in coming up with exact and exhaustive definitions of what kind and amount of work were permitted on the Sabbath. They established distances that the people were permitted to travel, weights they were permitted to lift, and medicinal actions they were allowed to perform. For example, they could keep a wound from getting worse, but they were forbidden from making it better until the Sabbath was over. In short, the Sabbath rest was guarded by hundreds of detailed specifications. To the Pharisees, these assured proper devotion; in fact, they had come to inhibit it, becoming an end in themselves.

Jesus tries to teach this to them when he asks, "Is it against the law on the Sabbath day to do good, or to do evil; to save life, or to kill?" They knew the proper answer, but they also knew that giving such an answer would require that they accept Christ's standards and relinquish their exclusive hold on the spiritual care of the nation – their jealously hardened their hearts, and they would not let themselves be taught.

Pharisaical nitpicking can easily creep into the practicing Catholic's self-perception. Saying prayers, attending Mass, going to confession, accepting and practicing the Church's teaching – sometimes the devil will try to turn these necessary and beneficial expressions of our love for God into monuments of self-righteousness. When we perform them in order to be good Catholics instead of in order to encounter and please Jesus Christ, we sometimes end up looking down at others because they are not practicing, or because they pay less attention to certain liturgical details, or because they dress differently. Such criticism is the sign of a hardening heart. True religion is not about following rules just to follow rules; it's about loving God and loving our neighbor. May we never forget this!

CHRIST THE FRIEND Jesus looked at these Pharisees, "grieved to find them so obstinate...." Christ came to give them life, true life, divine life, a life of intimacy and freedom and joy – and they refused the gift. What could cause him greater sorrow? Here is the mysterious tragedy that accompanies the life of our Lord: "He, through whom the world was made, was in the world, and the world treated him as a stranger. He came to what was his own, and they who were his own gave him no welcome" (John 1:10-11).

If the Pharisees would only let him, he would give life to their withered hearts, just as he restored the crippled man's withered hand right before their eyes. But they were afraid. They feared relinquishing control of their lives. They preferred driving alone to giving the steering wheel to a friend who was a much better driver. What fools we can be!

Jesus: So many souls are withered and paralyzed. They are trapped in cages erected by their own sins, or bruised by wounds inflicted through the sins of others. I came to restore them and heal them. I came to restore and heal you. Parts of your soul are still withered. Come to me and hold out your needs just as this man held out his withered hand, and I will meet them.

CHRIST IN MY LIFE Lord Jesus, if you made enemies in your own day, if you were unable to win over everyone even while you walked the earth and performed miracles, why do I get frustrated when my efforts to spread your Kingdom don't always meet with immediate success? Teach me to see all things in the light of faith, so that the peace you promise me at every Mass can really take hold of my heart...

What can I do to soften the hard hearts of those who are afraid to let you into their lives? Teach me, Lord. Give me words of wisdom and comfort; inflame my heart with prudence and charity; hear my prayers for all those who resist your love. Lay siege to their souls and don't let them die without your grace...

The greatest and only law of your Kingdom, Lord, is charity – Christian love. The most common law of this world is conflict and selfish confrontation. I fall into this too. I think I'm right all the time. Probably I'm right less often than I realize. Teach me to concede in all nonessentials, to affirm my neighbors, never to wound your mystical body. Thy Kingdom come...

QUESTIONS FOR SMALL GROUP DISCUSSION

1. What struck you most in this passage? What did you notice that you hadn't noticed before?

2. If the Pharisees were members of the present-day Catholic Church, in what ways would their self-righteousness and hypocrisy probably show themselves?

3. How can we combat the threat of empty ritualism as we practice our faith?

4. How can we help each other to avoid looking at priests, bishops, and maybe even the Pope in order to judge them, the way the Pharisees looked at Christ, and instead really strive to encounter Christ through their God-given ministry?

Cf. Catechism of the Catholic Church, 1859 and 1864 on "hardness of heart"; 574-582 on Jesus, the Pharisees, and the Law

103. PICKING TEAMS (MK 3:7-19)

"We who have set out to follow, admittedly from afar, the footsteps of the holy apostles and the other soldiers of Christ, should not be unwilling to share in their sufferings as well."

- St Anthony Zaccaria

Mark 3:7-19

Jesus withdrew with his disciples to the lakeside, and great crowds from Galilee followed him. From Judaea, Jerusalem, Idumaea, Transjordania and the region of Tyre and Sidon, great numbers who had heard of all he was doing came to him. And he asked his disciples to have a boat ready for him because of the crowd, to keep him from being crushed. For he had cured so many that all who were afflicted in any way were crowding forward to touch him. And the unclean spirits, whenever they saw him, would fall down before him and shout, 'You are the Son of God!' But he warned them strongly not to make him known. He now went up into the hills and summoned those he wanted. So they came to him and he appointed twelve; they were to be his companions and to be sent out to preach, with power to cast out devils. And so he appointed the Twelve: Simon to whom he gave the name Peter, James the son of Zebedee and John the brother of James, to whom he gave the name Boanerges or 'Sons of Thunder'; then Andrew, Philip, Bartholomew, Matthew, Thomas, James the son of Alphaeus, Thaddaeus, Simon the Zealot and Judas Iscariot, the man who was to betray him.

CHRIST THE LORD We may get the impression that Jesus is beginning to enjoy a kind of "rock star" status, with adoring crowds begging him for favors and frenzied fans following him everywhere he goes just to able to touch the wonder-working Rabbi from Nazareth. That kind of a conception might be attractive to nonbelievers, who are always looking for an excuse to avoid a personal encounter with the Lord. But it doesn't fit the facts as St Mark relates them.

If Jesus' appeal were only operating on a natural level, why would the demons make such a fuss? Whenever Christ comes close to someone possessed by a demon, the evil spirit gets nervous and cries out against this man who is clearly much closer to God than your ordinary rabbi. (The title "Son of God" is used in the Old Testament to refer to angels and even righteous men, as well as in some Messianic allusions, so it is ambiguous. That the demons used it doesn't necessarily mean they understood that Christ was the incarnate Second Person of the Holy Trinity; rather, it shows a recognition of God's presence being manifest in a unique way.) If the devil feels threatened by this carpenter from Nazareth, we can be sure there's good reason: the Lord has come to reclaim what Satan's lies had stolen; evil is doomed.

CHRIST THE TEACHER The great lesson of this passage has to do with the nature of the Church. At this point in his narrative, St Mark shows Jesus surrounded, even hounded, by huge crowds of people, both Jews and Gentiles (Tyre, Sidon, Idumea, and Transjordan were all regions with a high percentage of non-Jewish inhabitants). He teaches them; he heals them; they press all around him, yearning for his wisdom and his grace, anxious for salvation. It is an image of the fallen, wounded world in desperate need of God.

After giving us a vivid snapshot of the clamoring crowd of humanity, St Mark relates that Jesus climbs the side of the mountain, where he spends the whole night in prayer (we know this from St Luke's Gospel). Then he appoints his Twelve Apostles. The appointment is presented as a direct response to the overwhelming swarm of people in need. We can't help being impressed by the multitudes swirling around the Lord. The question pops into our minds: How will Jesus reach all these people? He answers it by appointing his Twelve Apostles and laying the foundation of his Church.

Just as the Old Covenant was built on the twelve patriarchs for whom the twelve tribes of Israel were named, so the New Covenant will start with twelve new patriarchs – in a sense the first bishops of the Church. St Mark repeats the number twelve. At first he says that Jesus "appointed twelve"; then he specifies, saying that the Lord "appointed the Twelve." This is more than a mere group of disciples; this is the embryo of a structured, organized, hierarchical community purposely established by Christ. Throughout the rest of the Gospel, we will see the Twelve continuing to exercise their special role, and Peter will further emerge as their leader (every time the New Testament lists the apostles, Peter is named first, though the order of the others changes).

The Church is Christ's idea, and so it's God's idea. Jesus didn't just leave the world a book; he also left the world twelve apostles, with Peter in charge. Following Christ completely, faithfully, eagerly, and honestly entails submitting to the Church that Christ himself established. At times we may grumble against the discomfort it causes, but as St Mark clearly shows, Jesus long ago – even before his passion and resurrection – decided that he would pour out his wisdom and his saving grace on the world through the ministry of those whom he appointed to be his messengers. And if he chose to do it this way, we can be sure he had some very good reasons.

CHRIST THE FRIEND St Mark emphasizes Jesus' personal touch in naming his Twelve Apostles. Jesus "summoned those he wanted." From the immense crowds that were following him Jesus singles out twelve individuals. He gives them a special role, first of all "to be his companions." Mark even repeats the phrase "he appointed twelve"; he wants to make sure his readers get the message: Jesus himself purposely chose these men, whom he would train and equip to be the pillars of his Church. And finally, we read the list of names, with plenty of little details added to show just how personal and intimate his relationship with these chosen apostles really was.

Jesus: This is how I started my Church: personally calling the Twelve. And this is how I continue to build up my Church: by personally calling each of my followers into its ranks, giving each of you a unique role, a personal vocation in my Kingdom. Following me means entering into a personal relationship with me, entering into my family. It is not a generic thing. It is not a cog-in-the-machine thing. I know your name; I call you by your name. In me, the God who created the entire universe asks if he can walk alongside of you as you make your journey through life. What more could your heart desire?

CHRIST IN MY LIFE Thank you for your Church, Lord. Continue to guide your priests and bishops and continue to raise up many holy priests and bishops. Enlighten all of us so that we can see you at work in and through your Church. My life as your disciple has meaning only in the Church, because that is where you have chosen to dwell. Teach me, Lord, to love, esteem, and build up your Church...

You know my name, Lord. You are thinking of me right now. You are watching over me, accompanying me. You never get tired of me. You made me. You love me; you give yourself to me completely in Holy Communion whenever I wish to receive you. O Jesus, purify my heart of all my petty selfishness and paralyzing doubts and fears. I only want to follow you...

The world is full of people who desperately need your truth and your grace. I have been privileged to receive these precious gifts. Sometimes I take them for granted. Forgive me, Lord. You want to give them to others through me. Teach me the way to go, show me what to do. Make my faith grow by giving me the courage to share it...

QUESTIONS FOR SMALL GROUP DISCUSSION

1. What struck you most in this passage? What did you notice that you hadn't noticed before?
2. Why do you think Christ chose to establish one Church instead of administering his salvation in some other way?

3. In this passage Jesus calls his apostles verbally and physically. How does he call those who have vocations these days?

4. Is there anything more we can do to help those around us who are suffering, as Jesus helped the suffering crowds in this passage?

Cf. Catechism of the Catholic Church, 871-887 on the hierarchical structure of the Church; 517, 550, 1673 on the role of exorcisms in Christ's ministry and in the Church's

104. CONQUESTS AND CONFLICTS (MK 3:20-35)

"And the mere mention of the name of Christ instantly chased Satan away, like a sparrow before a hawk."

- St Athanasius

Mark 3:20-35

He went home again, and once more such a crowd collected that they could not even have a meal. When his relatives heard of this, they set out to take charge of him, convinced he was out of his mind. The scribes who had come down from Jerusalem were saying, 'Beelzebul is in him' and, 'It is through the prince of devils that he casts evils out.' So he called them to him and spoke to them in parables, 'How can Satan cast out Satan? If a kingdom is divided against itself, that kingdom cannot last. And if a household is divided against itself, that household can never stand. Now if Satan has rebelled against himself and is divided, he cannot stand either – it is the end of him. But no one can make his way into a strong man's house and burgle his property unless he has tied up the strong man first. Only then can he burgle his house. I tell you solemnly, all men's sins will be forgiven, and all their blasphemies; but let anyone blaspheme against the Holy Spirit and he will never have forgiveness: he is guilty of an eternal sin.' This was because they were saying, 'An unclean spirit is in him.' His mother and brothers now arrived and, standing outside, sent in a message asking for him. A crowd was sitting round him at the time the message was passed to him, 'Your mother and brothers and sisters are outside asking for you.' He replied, 'Who are my mother and my brothers?' And looking round at those sitting in a circle about him, he said, 'Here are my mother and my brothers. Anyone who does the will of God, that person is my brother and sister and mother.'

CHRIST THE LORD Ever since the fall of Adam and Eve, Satan had been the "ruler of this world" (John 12:31). The law of sin, injustice, and selfishness had governed human affairs, even though the presence and promise of God kept love alive. With the arrival of Christ, we are faced with someone who repeatedly outmatches Satan: he casts out demons effortlessly, repairs physical evil (leprosy, paralysis, and even death) with a mere word or touch, and, above all, he forgives sin, freeing souls from the most dire of Satan's entrapments. Christ performed these deeds in the open air, for all to see.

The "scribes who had come down from Jerusalem," representatives of the Sanhedrin (Israel's governing body) sent to ascertain the legitimacy of this Galilean preacher's dubious (in their minds) doctrine, had to offer some kind of explanation for these phenomena. They could not, however, explain Jesus' special powers as coming from God, since that would require them to accept his teaching as well. But his teaching contradicted much of their own, and so to accept it would be to relinquish their status and influence. So they attributed his works to a pact made with the devil.

Jesus calmly but clearly points out the absurdity of their claim: obviously, his consistent reversal of the devil's conquests shows that he is not only at odds with the ancient enemy, but also more powerful than him. After witnessing the words and actions of the Lord, the only way to deny that "the ruler of this world [Satan] has been condemned" (John 16:11) is to deliberately blind one-self to the facts – a good strategy, if you prefer the illusory advantages you get from relishing the devil's false promises.

CHRIST THE TEACHER Many commentators struggle to explain Jesus' seem-ingly heartless treatment of his mother and his relatives (the term used for "brothers and sisters" often refers back to a Semitic term indicating "relative" in general). Perhaps after his rather caustic reply to the news that they were asking for him, he took his leave from the crowd and went to spend time with them; perhaps he waited until finishing his discourse and then went to be with them; perhaps he simply denied himself the natural pleasure of spending time with his family in order to dedicate himself more completely to his mission. In any case, the evangelist (the writer of the Gospel) is much less interested in giving an explanation for how he treated his relations than in highlighting the lesson Christ gives in this tense moment: the secret to intimacy with God.

What human relationship is more intimate, more familiar, more solid than the relationship between a child and his mother, or that between brothers and sis-ters? These relationships never end, and they lead to an incomparable mutual knowledge. Jesus tells us how our relationship with him, with God, can reach equal depths: "Whoever does the will of God is my brother, and sister, and mother." Seeking, embracing, and fulfilling God's will in our lives leads us into intimate knowledge and familiar intercourse with God – something he yearns for. Do you wish to know God, to be close to him? God's will is the foolproof formula for supernatural success.

CHRIST THE FRIEND Jesus was a man for others. Such a crowd gathered around Jesus and his disciples that they had no time even to eat. Nothing mattered more to Jesus than feeding the souls of his neighbor with the nourishment of his love and his truth, so much so that he neglected to feed himself. This self-sacrificing attitude permeated every moment of his earthly existence, culminating in the complete oblation of his life on the cross at Calvary. "This is the greatest love a man can show, that he should lay down his life for his friends" (John 15:13). By that standard, Jesus shows himself the friend of us all.

CHRIST IN MY LIFE It's hard for me to understand why you yearn for my friendship, why you want me to be as close as your brother and sister and mother. But you do. I want that too, Lord. Only you can fill my heart and my mind with the fullness of life that I long for so achingly. And I know that the way to intimacy with you is to fulfill your will each moment, out of love. Teach me to do your will...

You were so busy – not for your sake, but for the sake of those around you. I want to love like that. I want to be worthy to bear the name of Christian. Jesus, teach my heart to love as you love. Open my eyes to see my neighbors as you see them, and make serving others the default setting of my will. With the zeal of your heart, set my heart on fire...

Mary, you fulfilled your mission in life because you accepted God's plan and fulfilled his will. It wasn't easy for you. A sword pierced your heart; you had to suffer. But you loved your Son, and you trusted him. Teach me to love and trust him. Teach me true humility; teach me to care only about fulfilling the mission he has given me: loving God with all my heart and my neighbor as myself...

QUESTIONS FOR SMALL GROUP DISCUSSION

1. What struck you most in this passage? What did you notice that you hadn't noticed before?

2. What other "success formulas" are we tempted to follow, instead of the one Christ gives us: "doing the will of God"?

3. How would Jesus' self-sacrificing attitude manifest itself if he were in our place?

4. Why do you think the Pharisees were so resistant to faith in Christ? Have they fallen into the "eternal sin" that Jesus refers to?

Cf. Catechism of the Catholic Church, 391-395 and 407-409 on the power of Satan; 142-149 on the role of obedience to God's will in Christian life

THE GOSPEL OF MARK CHAPTER 4

"The waves are many and the surging sea dangerous. But we are not afraid we may be drowned. For we are standing on the rock. Let the sea rage as it will, it cannot split the rock asunder. Though the waves tower on high, they cannot overwhelm the boat of Jesus. What, pray, are we afraid of? Death? 'For me life is Christ, and death gain.' But tell me, is it exile? 'The earth is the Lord's, and all it contains.' Is it the loss of property? 'We brought nothing into the world. It is certain we can take nothing out of it.' The terrors of the world I despise, its treasures I deem laughable. I am not afraid of poverty, I do not long for wealth. I do not dread death, I do not pray to live, except to help you advance in virtue."

- St John Chrysostom

105. HIGH HOPES FOR A HARVEST (MK 4:1-20)

"The soul's entire holiness and perfection lies in love for Jesus Christ, our God, our highest good, our Redeemer."

- St Alphonsus Liguori

Mark 4:1-20

Again he began to teach by the lakeside, but such a huge crowd gathered round him that he got into a boat on the lake and sat there. The people were all along the shore, at the water's edge. He taught them many things in parables, and in the course of his teaching he said to them, 'Listen!, Imagine a sower going out to sow. Now it happened that, as he sowed, some of the seed fell on the edge of the path, and the birds came and ate it up. Some seed fell on rocky ground where it found little soil and sprang up straightaway, because there was no depth of earth; and when the sun came up it was scorched and, not having any roots, it withered away. Some seed fell into thorns, and the thorns grew up and choked it, and it produced no crop. And some seeds fell into rich soil and, growing tall and strong, produced crop; and yielded thirty, sixty, even a hundredfold.' And he said, 'Listen, anyone who has ears to hear!'

When he was alone, the Twelve, together with the others who formed his company, asked what the parables meant. He told them, 'The secret of the kingdom of God is given to you, but to those who are outside everything comes in parables, so that they may see and see again, but not perceive; may hear and hear again, but not understand; otherwise they might be converted and be forgiven'. He said to them, 'Do you not understand this parable? Then how will you understand any of the parables? What the sower is sowing is the word. Those on the edge of the path where the word is sown are people who have no sooner heard it than Satan comes and carries away the word that was sown in them. Similarly, those who receive the seed on patches of rock are people who, when first they hear the word, welcome it at once with joy. But they have no root in them, they do not last; should some trial come, or some persecution on account of the word, they fall away at once. Then there are others who receive the seed in thorns. These have heard the word, but the worries of this world, the lure of riches and all the other passions come in to choke the word, and so it produces nothing. And there are those who have received the seed in rich soil: they hear the word and accept it and yield a harvest, thirty and sixty and a hundredfold.'

CHRIST THE LORD In this parable Jesus outlines his view of politics, so to speak. It's very simple. He promises that everyone who accepts his rule will yield an abundant harvest in life. We know from other New Testament passages that the harvest consists of the fruits of the Spirit: love, joy, peace, patience, kindness, goodness, gentleness, faithfulness, and self-control (Galatians 5:22). In other words, by following Christ we become the kind of persons we yearn to be, both now and in eternity, and we are able to help others do the same.

But accepting Christ's rule involves refusing to vote for other candidates. The parable identifies three types of alternative candidates. The first is superficial- ity – the seed that falls on the path; this candidate promises to just go with the flow, like a lemming. The second is laziness – the seed that falls on the shallow soil; this candidate makes comfort, pleasure, and acceptance the highest priori- ties. The third is self-centeredness – the seed that falls among the thorns; this candidate is obsessed with personal plans, goals, and achievements… in short, a personal agenda (kingdom) so consuming that Christ's Kingdom loses all attraction.

Jesus is fair. He doesn't trick us into accepting his rule under false pretenses. Ultimately, a kingdom can only have one King. He wants to be our King because he wants our lives to bear abundant fruit, but he won't use violence to conquer our hearts – he prefers to wield only goodness, love, and truth to win that battle.

CHRIST THE TEACHER Jesus begins to use parables, as the Old Testament prophets did, because he wants to overcome his opponents' hard-hearted- ness. The Pharisees and their followers are so fixed in their wrong ideas about the Kingdom of God that they refuse to accept Jesus' straightforward teaching, since it contradicts their errors. So Jesus changes his tactics. He tells them the truth about his Kingdom using small stories and vignettes. His listeners, he hopes, will therefore be able to understand the message of each parable and accept it before they realize that it entails changing their own ideas – thus making the necessary change more palatable. We can draw at least two lessons from this approach.

First, we need to be careful about our fixed ideas. On the surface, the Pharisees looked like exemplary Jews. They did all the right things, wore all the right clothes, said all the right words, and yet their minds and hearts were actually far from God. Sometimes our tendencies to self-satisfaction can lead us to a similar place. We think we know it all. We think we have it all figured out. Of course everyone else is wrong; anyone who disagrees with me is a poor ignoramus…. That Jesus had to resort to parables reminds us that we need to make a point of staying humble, of staying open to what Christ and his Church still have to show us. God always knows more than we know, and he always has more to teach us.

Second, we need to be ingenious in our efforts to bring others to Christ. Jesus didn't give up on those people who refused to heed him. He looked for new ways to reach out to them. In the end, he would even forego arguments altogether and show his love for them by dying on the cross. By using parables to convince his listeners to accept his Kingdom, Jesus exemplifies the patient and determined apostle. All Christians worthy of the name will never rest until they have tried every means possible to bring everyone around them at least one step closer to Christ.

CHRIST THE FRIEND One of the biggest threats to our friendship with Christ is superficiality.

In a media centered culture, our minds easily become like the parable's hardened dirt path on the side of the field. A constant, unrelenting, numbing flow of information and images travels through our minds. Like an endless column of marching soldiers, this flow pounds the fertile soil of our soul, making it harder and harder for us to reflect deeply on our life experiences, to mull over the gifts and challenges that life brings us, or to cultivate a rich interior life. Our minds lose their receptivity to truth and beauty, and the good thoughts, the graces, the inspirations God sends us fall onto this hardened surface, unable to penetrate it, drowned out by the continual din of news, gossip, scores, fashions, products, parties, and the thousand other meaningless items and vain desires that mysteriously appear on our mental agenda as a result of all this media bombardment.

How happy the devil is wh en we join the ranks of educated drones for whom every headline is equally important! How tragic for us when we lose the youthful, human capacity to reflect deeply, to dream joyfully, and to hear the words of life and wisdom that our loving Friend never tires of whispering in our heart!

CHRIST IN MY LIFE I feel as if you spoke this parable just for me. You know my heart so well. It's full of so many obstacles: hardened soil, rocky soil, thorn-choked soil… But part of me is also eager to welcome you, Lord. The very core of my heart is all yours. You have taken up your residence there. Keep expanding your rule, plowing away all the other obstacles. Thy Kingdom come…

Every day you sow new seeds of holiness in my life – or at least you want to. How can I keep the soil of my heart receptive? You have to do it, Lord. I too easily am mesmerized by the seductions of this world. But you can keep watering and digging and fertilizing my heart with your Holy Spirit. Teach me to hear your voice amid the noise of my daily life…

So many men and women through the centuries have welcomed your word into their lives. Use me to sow that same word in everyone around me, through my prayer, my example, my actions, and my conversation. Raise up a new generation of saints, Lord! Come and save your people…

QUESTIONS FOR SMALL GROUP DISCUSSION

1. What struck you most in this passage? What did you notice that you hadn't noticed before?

2. Which of the three obstacles is most prevalent in our society?

3. Why do you think God doesn't force everyone to believe in him?

4. What are some telltale signs of each of the bad types of soil? In other words, how can someone tell which soil predominates in one's own life?

Cf. Catechism of the Catholic Church, 142-175 on the nature and necessity of man's response of faith to God's revelation; 29 on reasons for atheism; 51-67 on God's gradual self-revelation.

106. GIVING MORE AND GETTING MORE (MK 4:21-34)

"… Love him and let your whole aim and intention be directed to pleasing him always. Have no fear, for even if all the saints and every creature abandon you, he will always be ready to help you in your needs."

- St Cajetan

Mark 4:21-34

He also said to them, 'Would you bring in a lamp to put it under a tub or under the bed? Surely you will put it on the lamp-stand? For there is nothing hidden but it must be disclosed, nothing kept secret except to be brought to light. If anyone has ears to hear, let him listen to this.' He also said to them, 'Take notice of what you are hearing. The amount you measure out is the amount you will be given – and more besides; for the man who has will be given more; from the man who has not, even what he has will be taken away.' He also said, 'This is what the kingdom of God is like. A man throws seed on the land. Night and day, while he sleeps, when he is awake, the seed is sprouting and growing; how, he does not know. Of its own accord the land produces first the shoot, then the ear, then the full grain in the ear. And when the crop is ready, he loses no time: he starts to reap because the harvest has come.' He also said, 'What can we say the kingdom of God is like? What parable can we find for it? It is like a mustard seed which at the time of its sowing in the soil is the smallest of all the seeds on earth; yet once it is sown it grows into the biggest shrub of them all and puts out big branches so that the birds of the air can shelter in its shade.' Using many parables like these, he spoke the word to them, so far as they were capable of understanding it. He would not speak to them except in parables, but he explained everything to his disciples when they were alone.

CHRIST THE LORD Christ's favorite topic, it could be argued, was "the Kingdom of God." His first public sermon began with "The Kingdom of God is at hand," and from then on he kept talking about it. If there is a Kingdom, there must also be a King, and if there is a King, there must be subjects. Such is the image that Jesus chose to describe the community of his disciples, the Church. We would do well to ask ourselves if we share that vision of the Church. When we pray, "Thy Kingdom come," is what we mean in tune with what Christ means? God's Kingdom is the realm where hearts obey him; the kingdom of this world is the realm where hearts serve themselves; if we want to conquer the latter and spread the former, we need only hearken to the King, so that we can carry out his commands.

Obeying someone else, though, is almost always a challenge. Jesus knows this. And so he motivates his listeners to trust in him. He promises that if we are generous with him (the amount we measure out), he will be generous with us. Then he assures us that even if we trust him just a little bit, if we exercise our faith in him even a small amount, it will give his grace enough room to make those virtues grow, "for the man who has will be given more."

Being generous with this Lord yields very different results than any other brand of generosity. The more we seek and fulfill his will in our lives – following the voice of our conscience, the teachings of the Church, and the example of Christ and his saints – the more abundant and fruitful will our experience of life become. And that makes perfect sense, considering that God was the one who invented human life in the first place.

CHRIST THE TEACHER The growing parables reveal three essential characteristics about living in communion with Christ. First, the life of our relationship with him comes not from ourselves, but from God. The power of growth in the "seeds" does not come from the farmer; it comes from the Creator. Likewise, if God were not constantly breathing his grace into our lives, no matter how hard we might try, we would never be able to grow in intimacy with him – just as the farmer could never make a rock grow into an ear of corn. Our life of union with God depends primarily on God; we cannot achieve Christian success based solely on our own efforts – but the good news is that we don't have to, since God is always at work, even while we're asleep.

Second, growth in holiness (life in communion with God) is a gradual process. Unlike Hollywood heroes, who become world champions in the course of a two-hour movie, Christians develop their incomparable wisdom, joy, and virtue through a patient and consistent effort to cooperate with God for the long haul. This is why discouragement is such an effective assassin of saints – if our prayer life doesn't produce spiritual fireworks right away, if our bad habits don't go away with a snap of our fingers, if we don't understand all of Catholic doctrine after a weekend seminar, we tend to slack off in our efforts. That is the effect of a culture built on the shaky foundations of immediate gratification. We need to learn that when it comes to our friendship with God, the full-grown, healthy plant that will attract and nourish those around us is the fruit of constant, patient effort and an unshakable confidence in God – which is exactly what the devil wants to undermine.

Third, spiritual growth takes time. Imagine a farmer or gardener standing out in the field and yelling down at some recently planted seeds: "Grow faster, you fools! Faster!!" It's an absurd picture, but a common one: every time we get frustrated at our slow progress, we're futilely screaming at the seeds to speed up their growth.

CHRIST THE FRIEND Christ continues to "explain everything in private" to his disciples. In the intimate privacy of prayer, he shines the light of Christian truth on the particular circumstances of our lives. Most especially, he stays present, addressing us intimately and personally in the Gospels and in the Eucharist. There we can always find exactly what our souls need. No matter how often we turn to him, we can always have access to his advice, his comfort and his guidance. Christianity is the most person-to-person of religions; it is God addressing each one of us personally through his Son, which is why the Church tirelessly encourages all of her children to make personal prayer an essential ingredient in their lives. Without spending time alone with God, we rob him of the chance to "explain everything in private" that he is constantly looking forward to

CHRIST IN MY LIFE Teach me to pray, Lord. I want to learn to recognize your voice speaking in my heart and mind. I want to live in your presence so that you can make my life into what you created it to be, so that my life can be a bright lamp shining in a dark world…

How I need patience, Lord! You are patient, humble, wise. Stay close to me. Hold me back. Let me know when I'm being ridiculous. You know that I want my life to bear fruit for your Kingdom, and I want to taste the fruit of your Kingdom in my own soul. So teach me, Lord; in your kindness, show me how to cultivate the grace you have planted in my soul…

I want to spend my days sowing the seeds of your Kingdom everywhere I go. I believe in you, and I believe that only you can satisfy the human heart. The happiness we all seek can only be found in friendship with you. Fill me with that happiness, Lord, so much that it overflows into the lives of those around me. Jesus, meek and humble of heart, make my heart more like yours…

QUESTIONS FOR SMALL GROUP DISCUSSION

1. What struck you most in this passage? What did you notice that you hadn't noticed before?

2. In what areas of our Christian life do we especially need to apply the lessons of patience and confidence in God so eloquently taught by these parables?

3. Jesus' contemporaries were familiar with farming, so they could grasp his agricultural parables. If he were teaching in your community, what other daily life reality might he have chosen to illustrate these points?

4. How does the parable of the mustard seed apply to the history of the Church?

Cf. Catechism of the Catholic Church, 2558-2565 on prayer in the Christian life; 541-542, 546 on the nature of the Kingdom of God

107. THE SWEETNESS OF A STORM (MK 4:35-41)

"Rejoice that you have escaped the manifold perils and shipwrecks of this storm-tossed world."

- St Bruno

Mark 4:35-41

With the coming of evening that same day, he said to them, 'Let us cross over to the other side'. And leaving the crowd behind they took him, just as he was, in the boat; and there were other boats with him. Then it began to blow a gale and the waves were breaking into the boat so that it was almost swamped. But he was in the stern, his head on the cushion, asleep. They woke him and said to him, 'Master, do you not care? We are going down!' And he woke up and rebuked the wind and said to the sea, 'Quiet now! Be calm!' And the wind dropped, and all was calm again. Then he said to them, 'Why are you so frightened? How is it that you have no faith?' They were filled with awe and said to one another, 'Who can this be? Even the wind and the sea obey him.'

CHRIST THE LORD To grasp the awesome power Christ displays in this scene, we need to activate our imagination. Few situations leave men so helpless as storms at sea. The Lake of Galilee, where the disciples were sailing in this case, is still known for the violence of its squalls, which arise and subside rapidly and unpredictably due to its peculiar geographical situation. In the midst of these gales, the forces of nature unleash their full, terrifying force, and human fragility is nakedly exposed.

St Mark makes it quite clear that the disciples feared for their lives, so we can safely infer that this storm was no minor agitation. That a mere word from the Lord reins in nature's primeval brawn shocks the helpless fishermen even more than the stormy lake had frightened them just moments before. They had seen his miracles, they had heard his wisdom, they had witnessed his power over the human heart, but to see the most unruly powers that flow through the bowels of the universe submit like a well-trained golden retriever – this was a Lordship they had not yet even conceived of; this is Christ our Lord.

CHRIST THE TEACHER "Why are you so frightened? How is it that you have no faith?" What is the lesson here? Was it unreasonable for the disciples to be afraid? Was it cowardly for them to wake up their leader when it seemed like they were going to perish? It wasn't unreasonable, nor was it cowardly, but it showed a lack of faith. They did not trust in him completely. They still thought it would be possible to sink, even though Christ himself was in their boat; they still thought that something (in this case, the forces of nature) was more powerful than the love of God.

We still doubt too: when we hesitate to follow a particular Church teaching; when we hesitate to obey the voice of conscience or look for expert advice to clarify a foggy moral issue; when we delay going to confession; when we make excuses to avoid the duties of our state in life or the commitments of our Christian discipleship; when we let frustration and anxiety carry us away in the face of difficulties… In these ways and in many others, we show that we don't know Christ as well as we should, that we don't trust him as we ought to.

Each Sunday we profess our belief in the Creed, which begins: "We believe in one God, the Father all-powerful…" If we truly believe that God is our Father (that we are his beloved children), and that he is all-powerful, why would we ever give in to fear? Why would we ever doubt that following his will, as difficult as it may sometimes be, is the surest path to happiness and fulfillment? If we truly believed that, no storm would shake our confidence. Unfortunately, we, like the apostles, often become anxious, nervous, doubtful, and even just plain scared. And sometimes, unlike the apostles, this fear and doubt lead us to abandon ship, to put our trust in someone else (usually ourselves). The lesson Christ teaches here, both with his words and with his actions, is simple: when he is with us, we are safe.

CHRIST THE FRIEND *James: He was in our boat. He was with us when we encountered a storm. He came to our rescue when we had nowhere else to turn… How often I remembered this experience in the years that followed. It always spoke to me so powerfully – and it always made such an impression on people who were hearing about the Lord for the first time! It was an image for me of the life of every Christian. Christ is always with each one of us, and he has the power to protect us from every evil, to bring us safely through the most trying of times. Although sometimes he seems to be asleep in our boat while our lives are swirling in a hurricane of struggles and confusion, he is truly there. And when we go to him, when we put our faith in him, he will always come through for us – always. His only hope is that we too will come through for him, that we will not abandon him (the way I did a little while later in the Garden of Gethsemane) when he asks us to stay by his side.*

CHRIST IN MY LIFE Your power and majesty come across so vividly in the Gospels, Lord. Why don't I think more often about your greatness? You are the Creator and Lord of the entire universe; you gave the proton its weight and the electron its charge; you inspire every artist and strengthen every saint. Blest be your name throughout the earth! Thank you for calling me to follow you…

Even the wind and sea obey you, Lord. How foolish I am to resist you! I want to want what you want, because you want it, in the way you want it, for however long you want it. With the will of your heart, govern my heart…

You are in my boat; you are in my heart. As I stumble through life, trying to live out my responsibilities as you would have me, trying to discover your will in every storm, you are with me. I believe it, Lord, but help my weak faith! I won't say "Don't you care?" because I know you do care. But I will say: Convince my heart that you care, so I can be free to love as you love…

QUESTIONS FOR SMALL GROUP DISCUSSION

1. What struck you most in this passage? What did you notice that I hadn't noticed before?

2. How should we express our reverence for Christ, who is Lord of life and history?

3. Does popular culture encourage us to trust in Christ? If not, who or what does it encourage us to trust?

4. Why do you think Christ didn't just keep this storm from coming up in the first place? Why does he allow storms in the life of the Church? In our individual lives?

Cf. Catechism of the Catholic Church, 547-550 on the meaning of Jesus' miracles, 302-314 on the workings of divine Providence; 397, 222-227 on the importance of trusting in God

THE GOSPEL OF MARK CHAPTER 5

"Christ is with me, whom shall I fear? Though waves rise up against me, the seas, the wrath of rulers: these things are no more to me than a cobweb… For I always say, 'Lord, thy will be done'; not what such a person, and such, wishes, but whatever you wish. This is my fortress, this is my immovable rock; this is my firm staff. If God wishes this to be, let it be. If he wishes me to be here, I give thanks to him. I give thanks wherever his will is I should be."

- St John Chrysostom

108. RESTORED AND REWARDED (MK 5:1-20)

"Jesus Christ will give me my liberty, and in him I shall rise again as a free man."

- St Ignatius of Antioch

Mark 5:1-20

They reached the country of the Gerasenes on the other side of the lake, and no sooner had he left the boat than a man with an unclean spirit came out from the tombs towards him. The man lived in the tombs and no one could secure him any more, even with a chain; because he had often been secured with fetters and chains but had snapped the chains and broken the fetters, and no one had the strength to control him. All night and all day, among the tombs and in the mountains, he would howl and gash himself with stones. Catching sight of Jesus from a distance, he ran up and fell at his feet and shouted at the top of his voice, 'What do you want with me, Jesus, son of the Most High God? Swear by God you will not torture me!' – For Jesus had been saying to him, 'Come out of the man, unclean spirit.' 'What is your name?' Jesus asked. 'My name is legion,' he answered 'for there are many of us.' And he begged him earnestly not to send them out of the district.

Now there was there on the mountainside a great herd of pigs feeding, and the unclean spirits begged him, 'Send us to the pigs, let us go into them'. So he gave them leave. With that, the unclean spirits came out and went into the pigs, and the herd of about two thousand pigs charged down the cliff into the lake, and there they were drowned.

The swineherds ran off and told their story in the town and in the country round about; and the people came to see what had really happened. They came to Jesus and saw the demoniac sitting there, clothed and in his full senses – the very man who had had the legion in him before – and they were afraid. And those who had witnessed it reported what had happened to the demoniac and what had become of the pigs. Then they began to implore Jesus to leave the neighbourhood. As he was getting into the boat, the man who had been possessed begged to be allowed to stay with him. Jesus would not let him but said to him, 'Go home to your people and tell them all that the Lord in his mercy has done for you'. So the man went off and proceeded to spread throughout the Decapolis all that Jesus had done for him. And everyone was amazed.

CHRIST THE LORD Jesus and his disciples have made their way into a zone of Palestine occupied largely by non-Jews (the Jews never kept pigs, since the Mosaic law had declared them unclean). Outside the borders of Jewish civiliza-tion, the devil seems to have more influence than he does among God's Chosen People. At least, this is how St Mark depicts it. He emphasizes the violence, danger, and uncontrollable strength of the demon-possessed Gentile. Like the pagan religions, which worshipped many so-called gods who were actually no more than demons, this man is under the destructive influence of a whole slew of evil spirits. But in the presence of Christ, they cower, they grovel, and they reluctantly obey.

If anything could be more frightening than the life-threatening storm the Apostles have just traveled through, it would be this bloody and berserk victim of Satan's diabolical hatred. According to St Mark's timeline, the boat must have arrived at the shore, in the neighborhood of the tombs, around dusk, just as it was getting dark – only adding to the eeriness of the encounter. But just as Jesus showed himself Master of the wind and sea, he also commands and controls the powers of spiritual darkness; they only have as much rein as the Lord permits. Once again the demons recognize that Christ is especially privileged with God's presence (though it seems from their appeal to "the name of God" that they don't recognize him as the Incarnate Word), and once again the Lord sends them packing. If God is for us, who can stand against us?

CHRIST THE TEACHER This dramatic encounter discloses an impediment to growth of Christ's Kingdom in our lives, as well as a non-impediment to that growth.

The impediment is an inordinate attachment to the goods of the earth. The townspeople, in spite of the liberation of their brother from his horrendous captivity, ask Jesus to leave. It seems that they were more awed by the loss of the herd of pigs than impressed by the salvation of a soul. Instead of inviting Jesus to stay and teach them, heal their sick, and drive away evil, they keep the Lord at arm's length. They recognize immediately that if he comes into their lives, their whole scale of values will be turned upside down. So to avoid incurring more economic and material losses, as well as lifestyle changes, they turn away from the spiritual things that Jesus represents. Their love for the status quo blinded them to the light of grace. How easy it is for us to foolishly clutch the Creator's many gifts (which will pass away), but turn away from the Creator himself (who lives forever)!

The non-impediment is the devil. The devil loses all his power in the presence of Christ. If we stay united to Christ through all the normal means the Church offers us – a healthy prayer life, frequent Holy Communion and confession, obedience to God's will, a robust effort to grow in all the Christian virtues – he is kept at bay. This is why sanctity is possible. The saints demonstrate Christ's definitive victory over the devil in the here-and-now of life on earth. In any walk of life, in any vocation, *if we stay as close to Christ as we can,* nothing can hinder our rapid advance on the infinitely rewarding road to holiness.

CHRIST THE FRIEND The man who had been possessed begged Jesus to let him come along with the other disciples. But Jesus had another mission in mind for him. And the man accepts it. He doesn't insist on his own plans or his own will; instead, he trusts Jesus. Whatever Jesus wants will be best. No whining, no resistance, no reluctance: this new and faithful disciple overcomes his disappointment through trust in his Lord and takes up with gusto the task Christ gives him. And he is rewarded with fantastic results. All throughout the region, people hear the Good News of Christ, believe it, and are amazed – the hope and light Christ has given him grows exponentially, rejuvenating countless other lives.

We can imagine the demoniac's satisfaction as through his witness more and more people are infected with joyous reverence for Jesus. More than once he must have thanked Christ in his heart for giving him that mission instead of letting him come along in the boat with the other disciples. It proves yet again that Jesus is concerned first and foremost about what's best for each one of us. Whatever task or mission he assigns us will not only advance his Kingdom in the world, but – and this is most important from his perspective – it will rapidly advance his Kingdom in our own hearts. Among all possible friends, only Jesus is infinitely wise, perfectly powerful, and unfailingly faithful.

CHRIST IN MY LIFE You know my fears, Lord; you know them even better than I do. I lay them at your feet. You are my refuge, my fortress, my rock. Stay close to me, so that in your name and with your strength I can overcome my fears. Never let them keep me from living the life you created me to live, from fulfilling the mission you have called me to fulfill. With you, I can do all things…

At times the mission you have given me weighs me down. But even that is your gift; it's a share in your grace-giving cross. You have never let me down, Lord. You can't let me down. You are all-wise, all-loving, all-knowing, and all-powerful. Whatever you ask of me is the best thing I can do. I want to follow you eagerly and faithfully. Teach me, Lord, to do your will…

My God, you conquer evil and make all that is good grow. You are the giver of all good gifts. Free me and all my brothers and sisters from our doubts. Help us see through the deceptions of the devil. Give me a love for my neighbor so strong that I am willing to give my life for their salvation…

QUESTIONS FOR SMALL GROUP DISCUSSION

1. What struck you most in this passage? What did you notice that you hadn't noticed before?

2. Was it inconsiderate of Jesus to allow the demons to destroy the herd of pigs? What did he teach in allowing that to happen?

3. What do we learn about the devil's agenda from this passage? What does the devil want?

4. Why do you think Jesus so meekly granted the townspeople's request that he depart from them? What relevance does this fact have for our own efforts at evangelization?

Cf. The Catechism of the Catholic Church, 2850-2854 on deliverance from the devil; 407 and 409 on our struggle against the powers of evil

109. FEAR OR FAITH? (MK 5:21-43)

When the woman suffering from a flow of blood believed and touched the hem of the Lord's clothing, her flow of blood dried up. In the same way, every soul wounded by sin and punished by a flood of evil thoughts will be saved it if draws near to the Lord in faith."

- St Ammon

Mark 5:21-43

When Jesus had crossed again in the boat to the other side, a large crowd gathered round him and he stayed by the lakeside. Then one of the synagogue officials came up, Jairus by name, and seeing him, fell at his feet and pleaded with him earnestly, saying, 'My little daughter is desperately sick. Do come and lay your hands on her to make her better and save her life.' Jesus went with him and a large crowd followed him; they were pressing all round him.

Now there was a woman who had suffered from a haemorrhage for twelve years; after long and painful treatment under various doctors, she spent all she had without being any the better for it, in fact, she was getting worse. She had heard about Jesus, and she came up behind him through the crowd and touched his cloak. 'If I can touch even his clothes,' she had told herself 'I shall be well again.' And the source of the bleeding dried up instantly, and she felt in herself that she was cured of her complaint. Immediately aware that power had gone out from him, Jesus turned round in the crowd and said, 'Who touched my clothes?' His disciples said to him, 'You see how the crowd is pressing round you and yet you say, Who touched me?' But he continued to look all round to see who had done it. Then the woman came forward, frightened and trembling because she knew what had happened to her, and she fell at his feet and told him the whole truth. 'My daughter,' he said 'your faith has restored you to health; go in peace and be free from your complaint.'

While he was still speaking some people arrived from the house of the synagogue official to say, 'Your daughter is dead: why put the Master to any further trouble?' But Jesus had overheard this remark of theirs and he said to the official, 'Do not be afraid; only have faith'. And he allowed no one to go with him except Peter and James and John the brother of James. So they came to the official's house and Jesus noticed all the commotion, with people weeping and wailing unrestrainedly. He went in and said to them, 'Why all this commotion and crying? The child is not dead, but asleep.' But they laughed at him. So he turned them all out and, taking with him the child's father and mother and his own companions, he went into the

389

place where the child lay. And taking the child by the hand he said to her, 'Talitha, kum!' which means, 'Little girl, I tell you to get up'. The little girl got up at once and began to walk about, for she was twelve years old. At this they were overcome with astonishment, and he ordered them strictly not to let anyone know about it, and told them to give her something to eat.

CHRIST THE LORD Few passages show so clearly the character of Jesus' Lordship. Jesus is powerful and wise with God's own power and wisdom, and yet he puts himself completely at the service of others. He calls on his followers to put their faith in him not for his own self-aggrandizement or self-satisfaction, but for the sake of their salvation – in order to put them in a right relationship with God, so that they can experience fullness and meaning in life. Thus he heals the woman with a hemorrhage; he raises Jairus' daughter from the dead; he never once denies a request made of him with a sincere and humble faith. He is a Lord at the service of his subjects, just as we who are his followers must lead others into the Kingdom not by coercing them, but by serving them. Christian leaders are servant-leaders, mere stewards in God's houseful of invited guests.

He is also a Lord who knows his subjects. He knows what we need, what we do, what we hope for… When the woman touched his cloak, he knew it. Amid the large, jostling crowd, he felt the touch of faith, the touch of someone who was in need. And when he reassures her, he calls her "my daughter" – was ever a Lord so close to his people?

CHRIST THE TEACHER "Do not be afraid; only have faith." If we really learned this one lesson, it would revolutionize our lives. Do not be afraid of what other people will think of you: follow the way of Christ. Do not be afraid of failure: following God's will is the only path to everlasting success. Do not be afraid of changing your personal plans in order to follow God more closely: his plans are even better. Fear, confusion, lack of trust in Christ – these are the kinds of things that tie our souls into knots, causing untold needless suffering and keeping us from experiencing the life-giving power of God's grace.

It was faith that brought Jairus to his knees in front of Christ – and that faith raised his daughter back to life. It was faith that propelled the woman to touch Jesus' cloak, even though doing so was a risk (by the Mosaic Law, her hemorrhage made her ritually unclean, so touching Christ would him make unclean as well), and it was faith that cured her and gave her peace, after a dozen years of uncertainty and fear. Faith, trust in God no matter what, in spite of appearances (Jairus's daughter, by all accounts, was already gone), in spite of the limited vision of our natural reason (the doctors had concluded that this woman's sickness was incurable): this kind of childlike trust is what Christ longs for from us; it alone frees him to unfurl the power of his love in our lives.

CHRIST THE FRIEND The woman with the hemorrhage knew that if she could only touch Jesus' cloak she would be healed. She had the same amount of faith before she touched the cloak as afterwards. So why didn't God cure her without her having to touch him? And why did Jesus go all the way to Jairus's house and take the little girl by the hand in order to bring her back to life? Why not just do it from a distance? It is because God wants to be close to us; he wants to live in friendship with us. And since we are human beings, that closeness, that friendship requires not only spiritual contact, but physical contact as well.

This is the core of the Church's sacramental vision of faith: God doesn't have to operate through material elements like water, oil, bread, and wine, but he chooses to do so, because it better fits our spiritual/material human nature. The sacraments, the church buildings, the vestments, the liturgy, the blessings, the art, the music… These are all places where we encounter God, instruments through which he enters into the very flesh and blood of our daily lives – just as Jesus entered into the very flesh and blood of the Virgin's womb. Our God doesn't keep his distance; he walks by our side.

CHRIST IN MY LIFE I know people whose souls are sick and dying because they need you in their lives. Like Jairus, right now I ask you to come and heal them. I know you love them even more than I do, even more than they love themselves. You seek the salvation of all people. Please open their hearts to your grace, and make me a bold and gentle ambassador to them of your truth and love…

Thank you for the gift of your Church and all the spiritual riches therein. You are always thinking of me, and always coming into my life in one way or another. Open my eyes to see more clearly your presence and action in my life, and increase my faith, so that the power of your grace will touch me where I need it most…

This woman had been suffering for twelve years. You permitted that suffering. Lord, your timing and your providence are beyond my comprehension. I believe that you govern every life and happening of all times. Increase my faith, Lord, so that I can see things as you do, and always rejoice in whatever trial you may send my way…

QUESTIONS FOR SMALL GROUP DISCUSSION

1. What struck you most in this passage? What did you notice that you hadn't noticed before?

2. What opportunities do our current circumstances provide us to exercise true Christian leadership?

3. In what practical ways can we increase our love for and participation in the Church, God's chosen sign and instrument of salvation?

4. Jairus' daughter was twelve years old, and the woman had been sick for twelve years. Do you think there is some significance to this coincidence?

Cf. Catechism of the Catholic Church, 1145-1162 on the sacraments as a fitting way for God to interact with the human family; 198-227 on why we should have unlimited faith in God

THE GOSPEL OF MARK CHAPTER 6

"My Savior, illumine the darkness of my heart, and grant me grace rather to die than to offend your Divine Majesty any more. Guard, O Lord, my affections and my senses, that they may not stray, nor lead me away from the light of your face, the satisfaction of every afflicted heart. I ask you, Lord, to receive all my self-will that by the infection of sin is unable to distinguish good from evil. Receive, O Lord, all my thoughts, words, and deeds, interior and exterior, that I lay at the feet of your Divine Majesty. Although I am utterly unworthy, I beseech you to accept all my being."

- St Angele Merici

110. FAMILY TROUBLES (MK 6:1-6)

"Christ humbled himself; the Christian has his example to imitate."

- St Augustine

Mark 6:1-6

Going from that district, he went to his home town and his disciples accompanied him. With the coming of the sabbath he began teaching in the synagogue and most of them were astonished when they heard him. They said, 'Where did the man get all this? What is this wisdom that has been granted him, and these miracles that are worked through him? This is the carpenter, surely, the son of Mary, the brother of James and Joset and Jude and Simon? His sisters, too, are they not here with us?' And they would not accept him. And Jesus said to them, 'A prophet is only despised in his own country, among his own relations and in his own house'; and he could work no miracle there, though he cured a few sick people by laying his hands on them. He was amazed at their lack of faith. He made a tour around the villages, teaching.

CHRIST THE LORD Jesus Christ forces himself on no one. In him, God purposely limits his omnipotence in order to respect human freedom. He gives countless signs and indications that he is to be trusted, that he is who he says he is, but he refuses to give any evidence that will eliminate the need for trust and faith. He invites; he does not compel. He is a Lord who wages his wars by appealing to the heart, by showing love, and by speaking the truth, but if we refuse his advances, he will leave us free to go our own way. He wants followers who are friends, not slaves – a kingdom of freedom, not bondage.

If we as Christians truly respect and follow our Lord, we will exercise our discipleship in the same way. Instead of browbeating and cajoling others to follow Christ and accept his doctrine (and criticizing, condemning, and disdaining them when they refuse our advances), we will appeal to them on a deeper level, finding creative ways to show them how much Christ loves them and how satisfying and fulfilling it is to follow him, both now and forever. In this regard, the most eloquent and effective testimony is our own example of Christian love. The more we love others as Christ has loved us – serving ingeniously and without looking for recompense, being equally kind with everyone no matter how costly it is to our natural feelings, forgiving quickly and without conditions, always speaking positively and never gossiping, detracting, or destructively criticizing – the more his grace flourishes in our souls. Then virtue takes root and grows. Then we begin to experience in our own lives the happiness, peace, and "joie de vivre" Christ wants for us. That, in turn, attracts others to the Lord. We must invite those around us to follow Jesus more closely, but our words will be hollow if our lives are devoid of grace.

CHRIST THE TEACHER Jesus' hardest mission field was his own backyard. His own family and neighbors, the people who knew him best on a strictly human level, rejected him. (By the way, the "brothers and sisters" mentioned by the evangelist here and elsewhere were not blood siblings – that would contradict the dogma of Mary's perpetual virginity. They were cousins. This is more explicitly shown in parallel passages where the same people are described as children of a different Mary. See, for instance, Matthew 27:56.)

If Jesus himself had such difficulty in bringing his nearest and dearest into the Kingdom, we should not be discouraged if we experience similar resistance from our closest relatives and friends. Many saints have had to endure opposition from mother and father, brother and sister in order to be faithful to God's call in their lives; sometimes honoring our father and mother means opting to please God even if it displeases them. And even if our hearts suffer when others refuse to follow Christ, we should never give in to frustration or despair – even Jesus himself didn't convert everyone he tried to.

CHRIST THE FRIEND Jesus was "amazed at their lack of faith," which made it almost impossible for him to perform any miracles. Sometimes we think that miracles, blessings, and spiritual consolations ought to be given to us to inspire us to believe – to take away the risk factor that comes with following Jesus. The opposite is the case. Christ appeals to us on a personal level, as a friend: inviting us to come and follow him, to get involved in his life and to let him get involved in ours. Then, once we have taken a step of faith, a step of trust, he will reward us with signs that confirm our faith and blessings that boost our trust. To demand assurances from God before following God is to treat Christianity like a business, not a friendship – like a contract, not a covenant.

CHRIST IN MY LIFE You have given me so much, Lord, and I can't help wondering if because of your closeness and generosity I have let my faith wane. Maybe I am like your hometown companions: so familiar with you that I forget what a grace and gift your friendship really is. Never let me fall into routine, Lord, never let me be separated from you. Jesus, I trust in you; increase my faith…

How can I trust you more? What are you asking of me that I am not giving you? What worry do you want me to surrender? What fear do you want to uproot from my heart? Lord Jesus, guide me and teach me, so I can grow closer to you. With the knowledge of your heart, Lord, make my heart wise…

Your love is like a rushing fountain that nothing can stop. Maybe some people will refuse to come and take a drink, or will set up dams so the water doesn't reach them, but your love keeps on flowing. I believe in the power of your love. Teach me, Lord, to welcome your love more and more into my life, and to love more and more as you love…

QUESTIONS FOR SMALL GROUP DISCUSSION

1. What struck you most in this passage? What did you notice that you hadn't noticed before?

2. Why did the inhabitants of Nazareth find it so difficult to believe in Jesus? Do "Catholics in general" tend to exhibit any similar attitudes?

3. Do you know of any cases where faithful followers of Christ have run into opposition from friends or family members?

4. Have you ever thought deeply about why you believe in Jesus and in the Catholic faith and why so many other people don't? How should concern for those who don't believe show itself in the life of a believing, practicing Catholic?

Cf. Catechism of the Catholic Church, 142-175 on the nature and role of faith; 2214-2233 (especially 2232-2233) on duties of family life and duties to God

111. A MISSION FROM GOD (MK 6:7-13)

"Bury yourselves therefore in the heart of Jesus crucified, desiring nothing else but to lead all men to follow his will in all things."

- St Paul of the Cross

Mark 6:7-13

Then he summoned the Twelve and began to send them out in pairs giving them authority over the unclean spirits. And he instructed them to take nothing for the journey except a staff – no bread, no haversack, no coppers for their purses. They were to wear sandals but, he added, 'Do not take a spare tunic.' And he said to them, 'If you enter a house anywhere, stay there until you leave the district. And if any place does not welcome you and people refuse to listen to you, as you walk away shake off the dust from under your feet as a sign to them.' So they set off to preach repentance; and they cast out many devils, and anointed many sick people with oil and cured them.

CHRIST THE LORD Jesus is not a megalomaniac. He delegates his authority; he is a team player. He is the head and foundation of his Kingdom, but he gives his followers real responsibility in spreading and defending that Kingdom. This first missionary trip of the Twelve Apostles shows that Christ is already preparing them to be his messengers, to teach and administer his healing power (grace) in his name. In recent centuries, many critics of the Catholic Church have accused it of imposing a visible, hierarchical structure on the body of Christ's followers that Christ himself never intended. Nothing could be further from the truth. It is the purely spiritual and intangible conceptions of the Church that have no basis in Scripture or history. Jesus Christ is God, but he is also fully human, and his Kingdom, his Church, evidences that in its human structure, informed, empowered, and guided by the Holy Spirit. A faithful follower of Jesus Christ has no choice but to be a faithful child of the Church.

Christ launches this structured hierarchy in order to extend his own mission of preaching, instructing, and healing, not in order to dominate others in a political sense. St Mark makes a point of highlighting how the apostles anointed the sick, and they were healed. This is the origin of the sacrament of anointing, a vivid and eloquent example of the type of power wielded by this Lord – a power of building up, not tearing down.

CHRIST THE TEACHER Every Christian shares in Christ's mission. When we were baptized, we became members of his body, that same body that reaches out to men and women in every age in order to lead them to God. Every Christian shares in this apostolate. Every Christian is sent out to bear witness to Christ, to bring his wisdom and his healing touch to those who are in need, spiritually and physically. Under the supervision of the bishops (the successors to these first Twelve Apostles), we are all called to spread the Kingdom, to be agents of evangelization. Therefore, the missionary instructions that Christ gives to his first followers apply, in analogous ways, to all his followers, us included.

These instructions can be summed up in two words: trust and perseverance. Besides the clothes on their backs, the apostles are only instructed to bring a walking stick and their sandals. Every need they have along the way will be met, but it will be met by God's providence, not by their own self-sufficiency. They are to trust in God to sustain their efforts. The walking stick and the sandals symbolize a determination to continue moving forward, to persevere in their efforts to fulfill God's will. They must not give up. Even when they face opposition, persecution, and a cold welcome (which they will – Christ leaves no room for doubt about that), they are not to be deterred; they are to persevere. Trust and perseverance – these are two qualities of the Christian missionary (and we are all Christian missionaries, in one way or another) whose relevance will never run out.

CHRIST THE FRIEND Sometimes we might consider the obligation of spreading and defending the faith a burden, an unpleasant duty that interferes with our plans and encroaches on our comfort zone. In reality, it is just the opposite. Because Christ has put his Kingdom under our care, our lives matter. No other endeavor has, by its very nature, eternal consequences, so nothing else we can do matters as much as building the Kingdom. And when we are engaged in something that matters, our lives take on meaning – real, existential weight. And, ultimately, we all yearn for that – for meaning, for a life that really matters, one that has a real impact.

If Jesus had selfishly reserved all Kingdom affairs to himself, we would have to occupy ourselves with nothing but trivialities like business, politics, and entertainment; because he has generously put the Kingdom into our hands, these trivialities take on eternal dimensions. Because we are gifted with being men and women of the Kingdom, our actions and decisions reverberate beyond the boundaries of time and space – either for good or for ill.

John: I was just a teenager when he sent me out on my first mission. I was a fisherman from a family of fishermen, and he put the message and power of salvation into my hands and asked me to go out and deliver it in his name. No one else had ever trusted me so much. No one else had ever thought so much of me. Who would have guessed that God would be so generous with me, to make me his ambassador, to put his saving gospel into my care so I could hand it on to my brothers and sisters. That day I became not only a follower of the Lord, but his coworker. It was the dawn of a new era in my life.

CHRIST IN MY LIFE Thank you for the gift of your Church, Lord. It is your chosen way of being present and continuing your mission in all times and places. I believe that you work through your Church. I believe that you love her and that you gave yourself up for her. Teach me to see the Church as you do, with love, with faith, and with affection. Never let me grow bitter because of the sins of her children…

Are you pleased with how I am living out the missionary aspect of my vocation? Am I attentive enough to the opportunities you give me to bring your truth and grace to others? I am quick to make excuses. Give me courage, Lord. Increase your love in my heart, so that I will truly love my neighbors, seeking creative ways to give them what they need most: You….

Lord Jesus, never let me relegate our friendship to an isolated corner of my life. You are interested in everything that happens in my life, and you can give all my activities, decisions, and relationships eternal value, if only I trust you enough to discard the false scale of values that society is always promoting. Thy will be done, Lord; Thy Kingdom come…

QUESTIONS FOR SMALL GROUP DISCUSSION

1. What struck you most in this passage? What did you notice that you hadn't noticed before?

2. What can we do to deepen our identification with the mission of the Church, to share more in its sufferings and triumphs?

3. In what ways is it especially hard to "persevere and trust" in carrying out our missionary activity? Why doesn't Christ make it easier for us?

4. What might Christ think of our present efforts to carry on the Church's missionary activity?

Cf. Catechism of the Catholic Church, 551-553 on the conferral of the Kingdom to his apostles; 1267-1270 on the baptismal commitment to spread and defend the Kingdom; 874-896 on the hierarchical structure of the Church

112. HEROD'S HEDGING HEART (MK 6:14-29)

"But to such men the endurance of temporal torments for the truth was easy and desirable: they knew they would be rewarded with everlasting joys."

- St Bede the Venerable

Mark 6:14-29

Meanwhile King Herod had heard about him, since by now his name was well-known. Some were saying, 'John the Baptist has risen from the dead, and that is why miraculous powers are at work in him.' Others said, 'He is Elijah'; others again, 'He is a prophet, like the prophets we used to have.' But when Herod heard this he said, 'It is John whose head I cut off; he has risen from the dead.'

Now it was this same Herod who had sent to have John arrested, and had him chained up in prison because of Herodias, his brother Philip's wife whom he had married. For John had told Herod, 'It is against the law for you to have your brother's wife.' As for Herodias, she was furious with him and wanted to kill him; but she was not able to, because Herod was afraid of John, knowing him to be a good and holy man, and gave him his protection. When he had heard him speak he was greatly perplexed, and yet he liked to listen to him. An opportunity came on Herod's birthday when he gave a banquet for the nobles of his court, for his army officers and for the leading figures in Galilee. When the daughter of this same Herodias came in and danced, she delighted Herod and his guests; so the king said to the girl, 'Ask me anything you like and I will give it you.' And he swore her an oath, 'I will give you anything you ask, even half my kingdom.' She went out and said to her mother, 'What shall I ask for?' She replied, 'The head of John the Baptist' The girl hurried straight back to the king and made her request, 'I want you to give me John the Baptist's head, here and now, on a dish.' The king was deeply distressed but, thinking of the oaths he had sworn and of his guests, he was reluctant to break his word to her. So the king at once sent one of the bodyguards with orders to bring John's head. The man went off and beheaded him in prison; then he brought the head on a dish and gave it to the girl, and the girl gave it to her mother. When John's disciples heard about this, they came and took his body and laid it in a tomb.

CHRIST THE LORD How different King Herod is compared to Christ the Lord! Herod uses his power and influence to indulge his own desires for pleasure and to advance his own prestige. First he used his position to induce Herodias to abandon her lawful husband (Herod's brother Philip), while his own lawful wife fled to avoid the disgrace of a divorce. Then he used his power to forcibly silence the one man courageous enough to call him to order, John the Baptist. Next he uses his wealth to throw a party that will impress his peers and flaunts his royalty by making a rash oath to Salome after her dance. Finally, he wields the sword of justice falsely in order to curry favor with his courtiers and protect his supposed honor. In Herod's life, everything is about *him* and *his worldly desires*, while in Christ's case, the exact opposite is true. He puts his wisdom at the service of the ignorant, his divine power at the service of the destitute, and his saving grace at the service of all sinners.

This exceeds a mere divergence in leadership styles. The juxtaposition holds a mirror up to each one of us: who do we resemble more, the self-centered and self-indulgent King Herod who puts all his natural and supernatural talents to work inflating his egoism, or the magnificently selfless Lord Jesus who lives exclusively for the sake of bringing true happiness to others? If we call ourselves followers of the Lord, we should do our utmost to bring our lives in line with our epithet.

CHRIST THE TEACHER St John the Baptist's example of integrity and courage teaches us the pattern of Christian living. His fidelity to the prophetic mission he had received from God led him to unjust condemnation and a violent death. This foreshadowed Christ's own suffering, and sets the standard for New Covenant discipleship. In the Old Covenant, it was most often infidelity that led to punishment; in the New Covenant faithfulness yields confrontation. Every single one of the thousands of saints that the Church has given to the world suffered for their faith in Christ. A Christian cannot follow Christ without taking up a share of Christ's cross. The happiness and fulfillment Christ promises rise from the fertile soil of suffering. In a fallen world that exists to be a battlefield between the forces of self-giving and self-indulgence, those who love like Christ will certainly be attacked and wounded – but if they stay faithful, their wounds will be transformed into miracles for the Kingdom.

The contrast between Herod and John only drives this lesson home. John is willing to sacrifice everything for the truth, to be true to his mission and to God's will. He is a model of integrity. Herod is willing to sacrifice the truth – willing to sacrifice justice – to his vanity. He is so concerned about what his peers think of him, so concerned about his reputation, that he commits the heinous crime of executing an innocent, righteous man. Every day, multiple times, we too have to choose between vanity and integrity. We need to decide beforehand that we will be faithful, so as not to be swept away by fear when the moment of truth arrives.

CHRIST THE FRIEND Here again Herod provides a counter-example for what friendship with Christ is really like. What kind of a friend was Herod? He betrayed his brother, he betrayed his wife, and his birthday guests only mattered to him because of what they would think and say about him – and for this reason he won't renege his offer in front of them. Herod is incapable of authentic friendship because he is completely wrapped up in himself.

Jesus is just the opposite. He cares about others only because... well, because he cares about others. He wants to give his grace and wisdom to them. He is entirely unconcerned about what they can give him, because as God he already has all things. He alone, unlike any other man who ever lived, is completely free to love with absolute selflessness, because he alone knows himself as perfectly loved by the Father. The more we let this pure, crystalline, invigorating love that Christ has for each one of us penetrate our souls (which is no easy thing, given our habitual suspicions regarding anyone who vies for our friendship), the freer we in turn will be to love like that, to be that kind of friend to others. And being loved unconditionally and loving unconditionally is the only God-given formula for lasting happiness.

CHRIST IN MY LIFE I want to put the gifts I have received from you at the service of your Kingdom. But I need you to show me how! Teach me to do your will, Lord. Help me to discover your will in the depths of my heart, in my conscience, in the teachings of the Church, and in the circumstances and events of daily life. May your will be my only quest...

The cross still scares me. I know it shouldn't... I think it's only scary when I look at it from a distance; whenever I actually pick it up and do your will, even if it hurts, my heart is always happier and better for it. I trust in you, Lord. So teach me to recognize you in my crosses, so that I will be able to embrace them as you embraced yours, and keep building up your Kingdom...

Love is a mystery to me. I know you are love. Your very life is love. You created me out of love, you hold me in existence because you love me, you redeemed me because of love. Teach me to love. I need to know that you love me, and I need to learn to love as you love. Be my refuge and my shield, Lord; arm my heart with the weapons of your heart...

QUESTIONS FOR SMALL GROUP DISCUSSION

1. What struck you most in this passage? What did you notice that you hadn't noticed before?

2. If St John the Baptist were a member of our society today, which aspects of popular culture might he criticize, and which ones might he praise?

3. Have you ever experienced persecution because of your faith in Christ? Have you known someone who has?

4. Why do we tend to fear being criticized or ostracized because of our faith? What can we do to strengthen ourselves against future persecutions?

Cf. Catechism of the Catholic Church, 1816 on persecution from professing the faith; 2473 on the significance of martyrdom; 1716-1717 on the characteristics of a faithful Christian

113. HUNGRY HEARTS (MK 6:30-44)

"For we do not receive this food as ordinary bread and as ordinary drink; but just as Jesus Christ our Savior became flesh through the word of God, and assumed flesh and blood for our salvation, so too we are taught that the food over which the prayer of thanksgiving, the word received from Christ, has been said, the food which nourishes our flesh and blood by assimilation, is the flesh and blood of this Jesus who became flesh."

- St Justin Martyr

Mark 6:30-44

The apostles rejoined Jesus and told him all they had done and taught. Then he said to them, 'You must come away to some lonely place all by yourselves and rest for a while'; for there were so many coming and going that the apostles had no time even to eat. So they went off in a boat to a lonely place where they could be by themselves. But people saw them going, and many could guess where; and from every town they all hurried to the place on foot and reached it before them. So as he stepped ashore he saw a large crowd; and he took pity on them because they were like sheep without a shepherd, and he set himself to teach them at some length.

By now it was getting very late, and his disciples came up to him and said, 'This is a lonely place and it is getting very late, So send them away, and they can go to the farms and villages round about, to buy themselves something to eat'. He replied, 'Give them something to eat yourselves.' They answered, 'Are we to go and spend two hundred denarii on bread for them to eat?' 'How many loaves have you?' he asked. 'Go and see.' And when they had found out they said, 'Five, and two fish.' Then he ordered them to get all the people together in groups on the green grass, and they sat down on the ground in squares of hundreds and fifties. Then he took the five loaves and the two fish, raised his eyes to heaven and said the blessing; then he broke the loaves and handed them to his disciples to distribute among the people. He also shared out the two fish among them all. They all ate as much as they wanted. They collected twelve basketfuls of scraps of bread and pieces of fish. Those who had eaten the loaves numbered five thousand men.

CHRIST THE LORD Every kingdom resembles its king; Jesus is a King who gives himself entirely for the welfare of his people; therefore his Kingdom overflows with justice, peace, and matchless prosperity – both materially and spiritually. First we see Christ himself working so hard to teach and heal the crowds that he doesn't even have enough time to eat. Then the Twelve return from their first mission, brimming with excitement – but Jesus sees that they are exhausted and need a rest, so he invites them to go on a little getaway. When the crowds refuse to be put off, his heart is moved yet again, and he can't help himself from taking care of them. Such is our Lord. He lived for us; he died for us; he intercedes for us – he is for us, even to the point of becoming our food in the Eucharist, the sacrament foreshadowed by the miraculous multiplication of the loaves. What better response can there be to this love, to this example, than to imitate it? And what else would our Lord expect from the citizens of his Kingdom?

It is not always easy to be followers of such a Lord. He often demands more from us than we think we can give. In this case, he demands that the apostles surrender to him all their food, which isn't much, and then distribute it to the crowds. They must have felt like fools as they started the distribution – so little food for so many people! The Lord, however, can see the big picture. To be his follower means to trust that his vision is better.

CHRIST THE TEACHER Jesus' apostles had completed their first successful missionary endeavor. After being with him for a long time, under his tutelage and guidance, they had been sent out to be his ambassadors, to announce his message and testify to its truth. Now they returned to report their progress. We know from the other evangelists that this moment of reunion is full of rejoicing and energy – they had experienced the power of God working through them, moving people's hearts through their words and deeds. And how does Christ respond? He takes them aside to rest, to be with him again in the quiet intimacy of their small community.

The lesson is clear, but so hard to put into practice: active apostles, Christians who are energetically engaged in evangelizing the world around them, need to complement their activity with contemplation, with time spent in personal dialogue with the Lord. Without prayer and study and time alone with God, our well will soon run dry – we will have nothing substantial to offer others. But without action, without giving freely to others what we have freely received from God, our spiritual waters will become stagnant, lifeless – like a lake with no outlet. Contemplation and action, prayer and work – such was Christ's way, and such should be every Christian's way.

CHRIST THE FRIEND "His heart was moved…" Jesus has a human heart; he took one on purpose – so that he could be close to us. He truly cares for us; he feels our needs and our struggles even more deeply than we feel them ourselves. And he continually reaches out to be our light and our strength. When we accept these offerings of his love, he is pleased, truly gratified; and when we reject them, he is hurt, truly stung by our ingratitude.

This is the lesson of the Sacred Heart of Jesus, which has, through the centuries, confided its sorrows to certain chosen souls, like St Gertrude and St Margaret Mary Alacoque.[1] When we are dealing with Jesus Christ we are not dealing with an idea, a concept, or a philosophical "unmoved mover," as Aristotle described God. In Christ, God has become a man, someone just like us; in heaven, this very moment, he exists as a man, body and soul, and he is "preparing a place" for us (John 14:2). Through the Holy Spirit and the Church, he extends his friendship to us, trying to draw us more fully into the indescribable joys of his own divine life, so that someday, when the time is right, we may enjoy the place he is preparing for us. Every human person seeks to live in communion with God; only those who find Christ get to live out that communion in the form of a real, human friendship.

The greatest summary and manifestation of God's desire to be close to us, to share our every breath, is the sacrament of the Eucharist. The miraculous multiplication of the loaves and fishes in this passage prefigures the Eucharist, the sacrament in which Jesus miraculously transforms blood and wine into his body and blood, and gives himself to each of his followers in Holy Communion. The reason why Jesus multiplied the loaves is the same reason why he gives us the Eucharist: his heart goes out to us; he wants to give us true life. In each Holy Communion Jesus comes to renew his commitment to be our Shepherd, our own personal trainer for the soul. What more could he have done for us?

CHRIST IN MY LIFE You are always thinking of others' needs – mine included. My heart tends to center on my own needs. But I know you can continue to change me. Keep teaching me, Lord. Keep making my heart more like yours: meek, humble, generous, and willing to give my life for the sake of your Kingdom…

---

[1] *For basic information on these saints, and on other saints, an excellent place to start is the following web site: http://www.catholic-forum.com/SAINTS/indexsnt.htm*

Thank you for the gift of the Eucharist. Thank you for wanting to stay on earth for twenty centuries, so that you could come into my heart in Holy Communion. I cannot receive you now in the sacrament, but somewhere you are right now offering yourself again through your priests. Come spiritually into my heart and fill me to overflowing with your grace...

Who around me is like a sheep without a shepherd? Who is hungry and thirsty for meaning, truth, and love? You know, Lord. Show me. I want to tell them about you; I want to lead them to you. Guide my words and my example and draw others to your side through me...

QUESTIONS FOR SMALL GROUP DISCUSSION

1. What struck you most in this passage? What did you notice that you hadn't noticed before?

2. How can we know if we have the proper balance between prayer and activity in our life?

3. How would you explain the Eucharist to a non-believing friend who asked you what it was?

4. The heart of a Christian should imitate the heart of Christ. If Christ were living among us today, who would he identify as the "sheep without a shepherd" and how would he reach out to them?

5. How can we insure that our relationship with Christ stays fresh and personal, so that it doesn't fall into a dry and heartless routine?

Cf. Catechism of the Catholic Church, 422-429 on the love of God made flesh in Christ; 456-460 on the motivations behind Christ's own mission; 2558-2567 on prayer and our personal relationship with God in Christ

114. CHRIST AMID TROUBLES (MK 6:45-56)

"A man can bear all things provided he possesses Christ Jesus dwelling within him as his friend and affectionate guide."

- St Theresa of Avila

Mark 6:45-56

Directly after this he made his disciples get into the boat and go on ahead to Bethsaida, while he himself sent the crowd away. After saying good-bye to them he went off into the hills to pray. When evening came, the boat was far out on the lake, and he was alone on the land. He could see they were worn out with rowing, for the wind was against them; and about the fourth watch of the night he came towards them, walking on the lake. He was going to pass them by, but when they saw him walking on the lake they thought it was a ghost and cried out; for they had all seen him and were terrified. But he at once spoke to them, and said, 'Courage! It is I! Do not be afraid.' Then he got into the boat with them, and the wind dropped.

They were utterly and completely dumbfounded, because they had not seen what the miracle of the loaves meant; their minds were closed. Having made the crossing, they came to land at Gennesaret and tied up. No sooner had they stepped out of the boat than people recognised him, and started hurrying all through the countryside and brought the sick on stretchers to wherever they heard he was. And wherever he went, to village, or town, or farm, they laid down the sick in the open spaces, begging him to let them touch even the fringe of his cloak. And all those who touched him were cured.

CHRIST THE LORD To get the full impact of this encounter, you have to picture it. The apostles are struggling against a strong headwind. The boat is tossing and turning, and they are all getting frustrated and tired. The wind simply won't let them make any progress. All night long – from evening through the fourth night watch, which took place between 3:00 to 6:00 a.m. – they struggle to no avail. Then in the first, dim light of morning, or perhaps in the light of a bright moon, someone in the boat suddenly cries out. He points towards a mysterious, humanlike figure passing by. A little ways off, the figure walks along *on top of* the waves and the sea. Everyone looks. An eerie silence falls over each member of the crew in turn for a split second, until each sees the frightening phenomenon – then, like dominos, one after another they pipe up with exclamations of panic. They are being pursued by a ghost; this difficult journey has just become horrific, and everyone in that boat is wondering if they will ever see land again.

In the midst of such dire situations, the full impact of Christ's Lordship can be felt. He calls out to them. Now their fear turns to confused awe – Jesus is the one walking on the water. He comes towards them. They are wide-eyed with wonder. He reaches the boat and steps lightly onto the deck, rebuking them for their lack of faith, and the wind dies down. A few hours ago he had miraculously multiplied the loaves and fishes, even as the apostles were distributing them. Now he walks on the water and calms the squall, with equal ease. Who is this man whom they have come to love and follow? Little by little it's beginning to dawn on them: Jesus is the Lord.

We only need to remember that he lived through these events, performed these actions, and had the Holy Spirit inspire the Gospel writers to record them *for us*. He wants our allegiance, our faith, and our trust. He doesn't want to be a generic Lord; he wants to be *our* Lord.

CHRIST THE TEACHER One of Jesus' favorite ways to show himself in our lives is through storms. In this case, he purposely waits – or so St Mark makes it seem, by pointing out that Jesus finished praying in the evening, but didn't come out to the boat until the very early morning – while the apostles struggle all night long. Then he actually terrifies them with his water-walking appearance; St Mark uses that very word: "They were terrified." Only then, when they are exhausted with struggling against the adverse conditions and stupefied with paranormal fright – only then does he make himself known. He tells them to have courage and fear not, because he is with them.

When we are out of our range – when we find ourselves in situations that, humanly speaking, are beyond our capacity to control – then we are especially open to seeing the truth of Christ. In fact, only in those moments can we actually exercise the great virtues of hope, courage, and perseverance – because in those moments the challenges require an effortful, virtuous response. On the other hand, while we are cozy and smug inside the confines of our well-constructed comfort zone, we have less reason to exercise our hope and our faith – and if we don't exercise them, they won't grow. Every fear and crisis that brings us to our knees is a precious gift from God, because it sobers up the false intoxication of self-sufficiency, one of the greatest and subtlest obstacles to spiritual growth.

CHRIST THE FRIEND After the big miracle of feeding five thousand people with a few loaves and fishes, Jesus dismisses the crowds and sends his apostles ahead of him in the boat, while he goes up onto the mountainside to pray. Let's go with him.

The sun is going down. Jesus has spent the day working and teaching, and now he climbs the hill to his appointment with the Father. Maybe he prays standing. Maybe he sits on a rock and watches the sun set and the moon rise over the lake below as he converses in prayer. He is true God, but he is also true man. He has to spend time alone with his Father, reflecting on how things are going, unburdening his heart, asking for grace and light for himself and those entrusted to him. His heart yearns to be with the Father, and at the same time he recommits himself to his mission, determined to do the Father's will till the very end.

And among those for whom he prays are you and me. We are on his mind. He worries over us. He intercedes for us. He knows exactly what we need, and he hopes that each of us will respond generously when he nudges our consciences – but all the same, it's up to us. It's possible that we will refuse to accept the gift of grace he has come to earth to give us. Maybe his heart aches at the thought. No matter – he renews his love for the Father and for each of the souls under his care as the Good Shepherd. He draws his prayer to a close and begins heading back down the mountainside. He is more determined than ever to do his part. So he comes to the rescue of his apostles, and then puts himself once again at the service of the crowds. He even heals whoever just touches a tassel on his cloak – if they just reach out to him, he heals them… Indeed, he is determined to do as much as he possibly can – to do his part to the max. Are we determined to do ours?

CHRIST IN MY LIFE Jesus, help me to recognize you in the storm, in the midst of my fears and confusion. I know you never abandon me. You walk by my side, knowing all my troubles, just as you did with your apostles. Increase my faith, Lord! I don't want to walk through life alone! I want to be your companion, to discover the adventure hidden in your will…

You are so gentle – working silently in your sacraments, quietly through the ministry of your Church, and softly through the beauties of nature and culture. You are so gentle, Lord, that sometimes I forget about your greatness and your majesty. You are the Lord of life and history, the Creator of all things. May your named be blessed throughout the earth!…

You came to earth for me. You suffered on the cross for me. You gave me the gifts of faith, of prayer, of the Church, of the Eucharist, of the Gospels. You have done your part in my life and you continue to do it every day. Thank you, Lord. Thank you! And I promise: now I will do my part, if only you give me your hand and guide me…

QUESTIONS FOR SMALL GROUP DISCUSSION

1. What struck you most in this passage? What did you notice that you hadn't noticed before?

2. Jesus walks on the water right after multiplying the loaves. Do you think there is any connection between the two miracles? One has to do with bread, the other with Christ's body…

3. St Mark tells us that the apostles still didn't really understand Jesus, or the meaning behind his miracles. Why do you think it was taking them so long? Why does it take us so long to learn to trust in Christ?

4. The crowds brought their sick to Jesus so he could heal them. How can we do the same?

Cf. Catechism of the Catholic Church, 2742-2745 on the need for perseverance in prayer; 2735-2741 on filial trust in prayer

THE GOSPEL OF MARK CHAPTER 7

115. HARD-HEARTED HYPOCRISY (MK 7:1-23)

"Be courageous; be not puffed up by prosperity nor cast down by adversity. Keep humble in this life so that God may exalt you in the next."

- St Stephen of Hungary

Mark 7:1-23

The Pharisees and some of the scribes who had come from Jerusalem gathered round him, and they noticed that some of his disciples were eating with unclean hands, that is, without washing them. For the Pharisees, and the Jews in general, follow the tradition of the elders and never eat without washing their arms as far as the elbow; and on returning from the market place they never eat without first sprinkling themselves. There are also many other observances which have been handed down to them concerning the washing of cups and pots and bronze dishes. So these Pharisees and scribes asked him, 'Why do your disciples not respect the tradition of the elders but eat their food with unclean hands?' He answered, 'It was of you hypocrites that Isaiah so rightly prophesied in this passage of scripture: This people honours me only with lip-service, while their hearts are far from me. The worship they offer me is worthless, the doctrines they teach are only human regulations. You put aside the commandment of God to cling to human traditions.'

And he said to them, 'How ingeniously you get round the commandment of God in order to preserve your own tradition! For Moses said: Do your duty to your father and your mother, and, Anyone who curses father or mother must be put to death. But you say, If a man says to his father or mother: Anything I have that I might have used to help you is Corban (that is, dedicated to God), then he is forbidden from that moment to do anything for his father or mother. In this way you make God's word null and void for the sake of your tradition which you have handed down. And you do many other things like this.'

He called the people to him again and said, 'Listen to me, all of you, and understand. Nothing that goes into a man from outside can make him unclean; it is the things that come out of a man that make him unclean. If anyone has ears to hear, let him listen to this.' When he had gone back into the house, away from the crowd, his disciples questioned him about the parable. He said to them, 'Do you not understand either? Can you not see that whatever goes into a man from outside cannot make him unclean, because it does not go into his heart but through his stomach and passes out into the sewer?' (Thus he pronounced all foods clean.) And he went on, 'It is what comes out of a man that makes him unclean. For it is from within, from men's hearts, that evil intentions emerge: fornication, theft, murder, adultery, avarice, malice, deceit, indecency, envy, slander, pride, folly. All these evil things come from within and make a man unclean.'

CHRIST THE LORD Once again Jesus opposes the Pharisees, correcting their distorted doctrine privately and publicly. His confidence in confronting men who had the power to condemn him to death reveals the seriousness of his claims. The people of Israel could not follow both Jesus and the Pharisees; it became clearer by the day that Christ was demanding an undivided allegiance. His teachings were not optional addenda; he called for a total commitment. Such was Jesus then, and so he is now: the Lord, not the Consultant.

CHRIST THE TEACHER God wants our hearts. It is quite possible to appear perfectly Christian on the outside – going to Mass, avoiding drunkenness and obviously lewd behavior, saying prayers – while giving in to evil thoughts and entertaining selfish desires over and over again on the inside. That kind of divided life cannot endure for long. Where our hearts are, there our treasure is, as our Lord says elsewhere in the Gospels (cf. Matthew 6:21). We can never be satisfied with merely exterior piety, and we can never consider ourselves superior to others just because our sins are less visible. The heart that loves is never satisfied with how much it can do for its beloved; if we find ourselves smug in our life of faith, like the Pharisees, chances are we're running low on love.

CHRIST THE FRIEND Sometimes we forget how frequently and explicitly Jesus spoke of evil and sin. He was (and is) full of mercy, but that's because we need his mercy. A good friend tells us when we're in the wrong; only wolves in sheep's clothing console the sinner in his sin. Because Christ is so demanding with us, because he tells us directly how much we need to change our lives, we can trust that he has our best welfare in mind. He wants to be with us in heaven, so he sternly warns us against everything that could lure us in the opposite direction.

Most of all, however, he wants us to avoid the double life that the Pharisees are living. They are full of selfishness on the inside, even while they appear to be model Jews on the outside. In this passage, Jesus exhorts the Pharisees, showing that he understands perfectly their shrewd tactics for maintaining appearances while simultaneously indulging their inordinate desires – pretending to commit their property to the Temple, for instance, so that while they maintain use of it they still have a good excuse for not letting others benefit from it at their inconvenience. He also exhorts the people under the Pharisee's leadership. This shows that the temptation to hypocrisy is universal, and dangerous. Mere appearances fail to reach into the soul. True religion has exterior manifestations, certainly, but it flows from the heart, the place where we decide for or against our conscience, for or against God's will. Our friendship with Christ, and the purpose, strength, and vigor that flows out of that friendship, depends on our inner allegiance to him; looking like goody-two-shoes on the outside can never substitute for that. Jesus doesn't care what we look like to others; he cares about who we really are.

CHRIST IN MY LIFE Do I pay too much attention to appearances, Lord? I want others to see you in me, and so I want my outward behavior and appearance to reflect the joy, the purpose, and the goodness you've put in my heart. Please keep me from falling into vanity – from caring more about what others think than what you think. Take care of my heart, Lord; teach me to love as you love…

How you despised hypocrisy! But Lord, I fall into it every day! I say I am your follower, and yet look at some of the things I say! The criticisms, the double entendres, the tacit condoning of degrading comments…. In so many ways, Lord, I am still so far from the integrity you want for me. Change me, Jesus; teach me to do your will…

I wonder why many of the people around me are so unhappy. Is it because they are seeking fulfillment in mere appearances, in social acceptance, in having the right reputation and possessions? You have taught me the futility of that lifestyle. Give me the courage, wisdom, and love to pass the lesson on…

QUESTIONS FOR SMALL GROUP DISCUSSION

1. What struck you most in this passage? What did you notice that you hadn't noticed before?

2. In what ways can we as Catholics fall into the error the Pharisees fell into, the tendency toward a predominantly external piety? What can we do to make sure we avoid this type of behavior?

3. Read the second-to-last sentence again. In what ways does popular culture encourage or discourage this type of behavior?

4. Christ would not have instituted the sacrament of confession if no one needed it. How can we take better advantage of this sacrament and help others to do so as well?

Cf. Catechism of the Catholic Church, 2514-2533 on the importance of and way to purity of heart; 2534-2557 on the sin of interior covetousness; 1846-1876 on the definition and different kinds of sins

116. VICTORY TO THE UNDERDOG (MK 7:24-30)

"Rejoice then, my dear brethren for your blessed lot and for God's abundant gift of grace to you."

- St Bruno

Mark 7:24-30

He left that place and set out for the territory of Tyre. There he went into a house and did not want anyone to know he was there, but he could not pass unrecognised. A woman whose little daughter had an unclean spirit heard about him straightaway and came and fell at his feet. Now the woman was a pagan, by birth a Syrophoenician, and she begged him to cast the devil out of her daughter. And he said to her, 'The children should be fed first, because it is not fair to take the children's food and throw it to the house-dogs.' But she spoke up: 'Ah yes, sir,' she replied, 'but the house-dogs under the table can eat the children's scraps.' And he said to her, 'For saying this, you may go home happy: the devil has gone out of your daughter.' So she went off to her home and found the child lying on the bed and the devil gone.

CHRIST THE LORD The territory of Tyre was outside of ancient Palestine, just northwest of Galilee. It was a pagan area where few Jews lived. Most commentators surmise that Jesus was heading in this direction in order to spend some more time alone with his apostles, to put the finishing touches on their formation before heading back down to Jerusalem to suffer his passion. But his reputation had preceded him even there, and a bold Gentile woman comes to plead with him on behalf of her possessed daughter. Two characteristics of the Lord shine out in this encounter, one having to do with his heart, and the other a lesson for our hearts.

First, his love has no boundaries. We can hardly imagine how rigidly the Jews stayed clear of the Gentiles. Being ruled by the Romans, they couldn't completely avoid contact with non-Jews, but they had procured a whole series of legal exemptions: they could collect their own annual temple tax from Jews throughout the Empire, they could refuse to work on the Sabbath, they were dispensed from obligatory military service, etc. Additionally, they made a point of following their many dietary laws, as well as the regulations limiting their contact with Gentiles, upon pain of defilement. This atmosphere of segregation between Gentile and Jew (thus the comparison between the "dogs" and the "children") was intensified anytime the Gentile happened to be a woman. So the mere fact of Jesus engaging in a conversation with this suppliant (he didn't have to say anything to her at all) shows that the boundaries set up by men have no place in the heart of the Lord.

Jesus transferred this universality to his Church. No other institution is and has been so inclusive. Just take a look at the roster of her saints. Sainthood is the highest honor the Church can bestow on any of her members. Among the thousands of saints, you'll find every walk of life represented – both genders, every race, every culture, every age, every continent.... Like the papal Masses at World Youth Day, or the synod of bishops which meets every few years in Rome, the Kingdom of Christ is universal – it's truly Catholic. If that's the way our King is, and that's the way his Kingdom is, shouldn't that be the way each Christian is?

CHRIST THE TEACHER Second, this encounter teaches us a precious truth about how to stay close to Christ. The benefits of his rule can be enjoyed only by the humble. The humble recognize both their littleness and God's greatness. They understand that they are wholly dependent upon God for everything, but they also understand that God is generous, good, and all-powerful, so their dependence is secure. Jesus grants this woman's request after she admits these two truths. She takes no offense at being relegated to a lower social level than the Jews; in fact, she accepts it readily. But she also acknowledges Christ's capability to perform a miracle; she has no doubt at all that he can do it, if he only says the word.

Humility unleashes God's power in our lives. It is the opposite of that diabolical pride that refuses to acknowledge either one's own limitations or God's greatness. Pride and God's grace simply can't go together, just as night and day can't. But humility draws in God's grace like a vacuum. "Blessed are the poor in spirit, for theirs is the Kingdom of Heaven" (Mt 5:7).

CHRIST THE FRIEND Jesus' exchange with this woman is a real conversation. She expresses to Jesus all the sorrow and desire of her heart, begging him to help her daughter. Jesus hears her, and gives a response that is neither a denial nor an acceptance. He seems to be fishing for something, trying perhaps to induce her to a deeper act of faith or humility. So he gives her a reason why he should deny her request: he is the Messiah of the Jews, and the mission to the Gentiles has yet to begin. Her response in turn reveals her heart. She accepts what could have been taken as an insult without the slightest umbrage, and she even turns it to her advantage. She knows that she has no claim on Christ's generosity; she has no right to demand that he perform the miracle. But at the same time, in his manner and his conversation she senses the throbbing good-ness of his heart, and she appeals directly to that. Her intuition was right on target, and Jesus is unable to hold back the torrent of his love.

Jesus wants to converse with us, in all honesty and without any pretenses. He wants to meet us on our own turf. He came to save us, not from being human, but from being self-centered. Our relationship with Christ, then, should have all the sincerity, reality, spontaneity, and charm of a real friendship, blended easily with the reverence and gratitude we owe to our Creator and Redeemer. It is a real friendship, and Jesus longs for us to treat him as a real friend.

Jesus: I didn't come to earth for me – I came for you. I came to convince you that I want to be close to you, to walk with you. I am with you now; I am always at your side, in your heart. You don't need to impress me to earn my love. You already have it – all of it. Come to me. Unburden yourself to me. Trust me. I came for you.

CHRIST IN MY LIFE   Teach me to pray, Lord. My faith is so weak. It is so hard for me to find you, to hear you, to open my heart to you. I am so easily dis-tracted. Doubts and fears make a constant ruckus in my soul. I want to be like this Syro-Phoneician woman; she knew her own unworthiness and helpless-ness, and she recognized your omnipotence and goodness…

Nothing matters more than staying close to you. Without you, nothing I do will last; with you, everything I do has eternal significance. But I still depend too much on my own puny talents to fulfill my life's mission. My heart is not humble, Lord. This is why I get so perturbed, so distracted. Blessed humility! Jesus, meek and humble of heart, make my heart more like yours…

You are always open and sensitive to the needs of those around you – no matter their looks, likes, or social class. Teach me to be like that. I want to be your representative for everyone around me. I want to spread your goodness, your encouragement, and your grace. Make me a channel of your peace, Lord…

QUESTIONS FOR SMALL GROUP DISCUSSION

1. What struck you most in this passage? What did you notice that you hadn't noticed before?

2. How do you think this woman reacted when she came home and found her daughter well?

3. To what extent and in what ways is humility valued and encouraged by popular culture? To what extent and in what ways is it denigrated?

4. What are some ways in which humility should express itself in our daily lives?

Cf. Catechism of the Catholic Church, 2546, 2559, 2631, and 2713 on humility in prayer; 1784 1866, 2094, 2317, 2514 2540, and 2728 on pride, battling pride, and the consequences of pride

117. THE TOUCH OF THE LORD (MK 7:31-37)

"Oh, I praise that mercy of yours which is beyond praising and I adore in thanksgiving your most loving kindness from the depths of my nothingness."

- St Gertrude

Mark 7:31-37

Returning from the district of Tyre, he went by way of Sidon towards the Sea of Galilee, right through the Decapolis region. And they brought him a deaf man who had an impediment in his speech; and they asked him to lay his hand on him. He took him aside in private, away from the crowd, put his fingers into the man's ears and touched his tongue with spittle. Then looking up to heaven he sighed; and he said to him, 'Ephphatha,' that is, 'Be opened.' And his ears were opened, and the ligament of his tongue was loosened and he spoke clearly. And Jesus ordered them to tell no one about it, but the more he insisted, the more widely they published it. Their admiration was unbounded. 'He has done all things well,' they said. 'He makes the deaf hear and the dumb speak.'

CHRIST THE LORD Even though Jesus knew that reports of miracles and prodigious events would lead people to think of him merely as a wonder-worker and consider his Kingdom to be merely another earthly reign, he couldn't resist the pleas of those who were suffering. He wanted more time to explain his vision, to convince people that the Kingdom of God went far beyond politics and economics, touching people's hearts and bringing them back into communion with God. Thus he tried to get them to refrain from broadcasting his miracles, but to no avail. The more the crowds heard about his wondrous deeds, the less it seems they understood them. The miracles were meant to be signs, confirmations of the truth of his teachings, and invitations to trust and obey him. Unfortunately, although many people were willing to be cured by him, few were willing to suffer with him – that became clear at the time of his passion.

And yet, to be a citizen of his Kingdom means both enjoying his benefits and living under his rule – i.e., bringing thoughts, words, and actions into line with his standard and example. We really can't have the latter without the former. Unfortunately, we often try to do just that: when the Lord gives, we rejoice; when the Lord asks us to give, we balk – much to his chagrin, and even more, to our loss.

CHRIST THE TEACHER We should never despair of the power of God. No soul is too hardened to be penetrated by Christ's love and forgiveness; the greatest sinners often make the greatest saints. Though someone appears deaf to the Word of Life and unable to respond to the invitations of the Holy Spirit, our confidence must never be shaken, for Jesus "makes the deaf hear and the dumb speak."

This applies even to the lives of believers. Often we seem to be stuck in our spiritual lives, unable to advance, incapable of overcoming certain defects or sinful habits. Sometimes this discourages us, and we slack off in our efforts to practice self-discipline and to live a vibrant life of prayer. That's when the devil can make a bold move on us, luring us into a relationship or an activity that actually obstructs the flow of God's grace in our lives. Precisely then, when we seem to have reached a spiritual plateau, we need to let Christ take us "away from the crowd" (perhaps on a retreat) to renew our interior hearing. His power is never lacking, but our faith oftentimes is.

CHRIST THE FRIEND Did Jesus need to go through that whole ritual of touching this poor man's ears and tongue and speaking the word of command? Certainly not. More than once Jesus performed miracles without any tangible contact with the beneficiary. What comes across in this encounter is God's humility. Christ deigns to bring the healing power of God into this man's life through symbolic gestures and visible signs. He continues using this tactic through the ministry of his Church: the sacraments (as well as many of the Church's other ministries) are tangible connections between concrete individuals and divine grace. God made us to exist in the unity of body and soul, and he comes to save us in a way appropriate to that nature. We should be grateful for his patience and condescension, and we should be careful to imitate it as we try to bring Christ to those around us.

CHRIST IN MY LIFE I want to follow you through thick and thin, Lord. You are faithful, and you govern my life and the entire world with perfect wisdom. Open my eyes, enlighten my mind, so that I will discover your presence and your will in each moment, in every circumstance. You never cease to draw me to yourself; never let me stop seeking your face…

Sometimes the obstacles to making your Kingdom grow seem insurmountable, but in truth they never are. You made the deaf hear and the mute speak, Lord! You can give me all the grace I need to overcome every sinful habit and fulfill my mission in life. Make me a channel of your peace, Lord…

Thank you for the sacraments, and thank you for the beauties of nature and culture. You show your patience and gentleness by speaking to me through these things, in ways that I can understand. Help me to take advantage of every moment in order to know and serve you better. In all my relationships, Lord, especially the ones most difficult for me, grant me the grace to be like you: patient, humble, and generous...

QUESTIONS FOR SMALL GROUP DISCUSSION

1. What struck you most in this passage? What did you notice that you hadn't noticed before?

2. In what areas of our lives do we sometimes prefer to be "deaf and mute" in our relationship with God? What clues can we find in this passage about how we can overcome that?

3. How can we increase our understanding of and appreciation for the Church's rich liturgical and sacramental heritage?

4. The crowds said of Jesus, "He has done all things well." Why don't today's crowds say that about Catholics? What can we do to improve the Church's witness in our own community?

Cf. Catechism of the Catholic Church, 1084, 1145-1155 on the strategy behind the sacraments and signs and symbols in the Church's life; 1803, 1833, 2733 on the need for fortitude and constancy in the spiritual life; 547-550 on the true meaning of Christ's miracles

THE GOSPEL OF MARK CHAPTER 8

"So I set about finding a way to gain the strength that was necessary for enjoying you. And I could not find it until I embraced the mediator between God and man, the man Christ Jesus, who is over all things, God blessed forever, who was calling unto me and saying: I am the way, the truth, and the life; and how brought into union with our nature that food which I lacked the strength to take: for the Word was made flesh that your wisdom, by which you created all things, might give suck to our souls' infancy."

- St Augustine

118. FOOD FOR THE JOURNEY (MK 8:1-10)

"We ask that this bread be given to us each day. We are in Christ and we receive his Eucharist daily as the food of salvation..."

- St Cyprian

Mark 8:1-10

And now once again a great crowd had gathered, and they had nothing to eat. So he called his disciples to him and said to them, 'I feel sorry for all these people; they have been with me for three days now and have nothing to eat. If I send them off home hungry they will collapse on the way; some have come a great distance.' His disciples replied, 'Where could anyone get bread to feed these people in a deserted place like this?' He asked them, 'How many loaves have you?' 'Seven,' they said. Then he instructed the crowd to sit down on the ground, and he took the seven loaves, and after giving thanks he broke them and handed them to his disciples to distribute; and they distributed them among the crowd. They had a few small fish as well, and over these he said a blessing and ordered them to be distributed also. They ate as much as they wanted, and they collected seven basketfuls of the scraps left over. Now there had been about four thousand people. He sent them away and immediately, getting into the boat with his disciples, went to the region of Dalmanutha.

CHRIST THE LORD Jesus detects the people's needs before anyone makes a request of him. How he pays attention to us! He is constantly taking the first step, making the first move, coming to our aid, providing for our needs. He truly is the Good Shepherd. Human history is crammed with kings and prime ministers who sought and used power for their own advancement. Jesus establishes and rules his Kingdom only for our sake, so that we will have the light and the strength necessary to complete our life's journey and make our way back home to the Father's house. Everything in the Church exists for the sake of the faithful, to bring us closer to Christ. His Kingdom is, far beyond our full comprehension, *our* Kingdom.

But to be citizens of this Kingdom requires taking on the characteristics of the king. If he anticipated our needs, we should anticipate our neighbor's. If he took the initiative to come and teach us the truth and invite us to follow him, we should do the same with others. When we pray, "Thy Kingdom come," we should back up our words with our lives.

CHRIST THE TEACHER What we give to Jesus is wildly disproportionate to what he will do with whatever we decide to give him. What matters to him is the generosity and faith with which we treat him – the results of our discipleship are in proportion to that, not to our natural, human calculations or abilities. The apostles had seven measly little loaves of bread and a couple of fish. They themselves were just as hungry as the crowds all around them, and yet Jesus asks them to give their food to four thousand people. Their first thought must have been, "Then what are *we* going to eat?" Their second thought: "Yeah, right – it would take another miracle to feed this many people with this meager fare."

They must have been reluctant to give up their bread and anxious about what the crowds would do if their hopes were raised and then dashed. Even after recalling the last miraculous multiplication, they would still waver a bit now – Jesus rarely performed his miracles to meet everyday needs. But the Lord is the one asking, so they pile up their little store of food in front of Jesus. He blesses it and gives thanks to the Father, and then the distribution begins. Christ gives the food to the disciples from the baskets, and they in turn take it to the small groups of people scattered across the countryside. And each time that they return to Christ, expecting to find nothing, he pulls out more. The results, once again, boggle the mind. Every one of those four thousand people went away with a full stomach, and the apostles themselves had ten times as much left over for themselves as what they had started with!

How absurd it is to deny Jesus when he asks something of us! Whatever it may be – money, time, moral obedience, or even one's entire life – if we put it into his hands, it will flourish and blossom and be transformed into marvels far beyond our wildest imagination, guaranteed.

CHRIST THE FRIEND Jesus made the crowds sit down, and then he blessed and broke the bread, but he didn't distribute it himself. Instead, he gave his disciples that task; he worked through them. He always wants to include us in his work. He knows us well, because he created us, and he knows that we need a task in life, a worthwhile task, a mission – we were created to make a difference in the world, and our hearts yearn to do so. What greater mission could there be than Christ's own mission, saving souls and readying them for heaven? Of all the wonderful things we can and should do in this world, no task is more worthwhile than feeding hungry souls with the saving truth and grace of Jesus Christ. We are his hands and feet in this world, just as his disciples were his hands and feet on that miraculous day of the feeding of the four thousand. What we do makes not just a difference, but an eternal difference, if only we follow our Friend's generous lead.

CHRIST IN MY LIFE Lord, I want to follow you more closely. I want to be as generous and as tireless in doing good as you are. You have seen my hunger and exhaustion, and you have come to my aid, giving me the gift of faith, the sacraments, and a sense of purpose. Thank you, Lord. Never abandon me, always accompany me, always look after me. And through me, feed everyone who hungers for you…

Thank you for including me in your mission. You know how inept I am at this. If you leave it all up to me, I'll ruin it in one way or another. Protect me from all varieties of selfishness: envy, lust, greed, arrogance, rejoicing in others' failures, and useless criticism. Teach me to be so busy feeding your beloved souls that I taste the true joy of self-forgetful love…

What are you asking me to put into your hands? Whatever it may be, Lord, here it is; I give it you, just as the apostles gave their loaves of bread. Bless it, Lord; take it. Whatever you do with it will be better than the best I can do. Take my whole life into your hands. Give me a generous heart, like yours – you gave me the universe, so I give it back to you, along with myself…

QUESTIONS FOR SMALL GROUP DISCUSSION

1. What struck you most in this passage? What did you notice that you hadn't noticed before?

2. Some commentators say that this miraculous multiplication of the loaves is actually the same one that St Mark described back in Chapter 6. What textual evidence can you find against such a view?

3. This miracle obviously prefigures the Eucharist. How does Christ's phrase, "If I send them off home hungry they will collapse on the way" apply to Holy Communion in the life of the Church?

4. Jesus gave thanks before he distributed the bread. What is the meaning of our own grace before and after meals? How can we live that small act of faith with more gusto?

Cf. Catechism of the Catholic Church, 1324-1327 on the Eucharist as the source and summit of ecclesial life; 1384-1390 on Holy Communion; 1391-1401 on the fruits of Holy Communion

119. SEEING THE SIGNS (MK 8:11-26)

Therefore stay close to Christ if you want to be secure. You will not be able to stray from the way since he is the way."

- *St Thomas Aquinas*

Mark 8:11-26

The Pharisees came up and started a discussion with him; they demanded of him a sign from heaven, to test him. And with a sigh that came straight from the heart he said, 'Why does this generation demand a sign? I tell you solemnly, no sign shall be given to this generation.' And leaving them again and re-embarking he went away to the opposite shore. The disciples had forgotten to take any food and they had only one loaf with them in the boat. Then he gave them this warning, 'Keep your eyes open; be on your guard against the yeast of the Pharisees and the yeast of Herod.' And they said to one another, 'It is because we have no bread.' And Jesus knew it, and he said to them, 'Why are you talking about having no bread? Do you not yet understand? Have you no perception? Are your minds closed? Have you eyes that do not see, ears that do not hear? Or do you not remember? When I broke the five loaves among the five thousand, how many baskets full of scraps did you collect?' They answered, 'Twelve.' And when I broke the seven loaves for the four thousand, how many baskets full of scraps did you collect?' And they answered, 'Seven.' Then he said to them, 'Are you still without perception?' They came to Bethsaida, and some people brought to him a blind man whom they begged him to touch. He took the blind man by the hand and led him outside the village. Then putting spittle on his eyes and laying his hands on him, he asked, 'Can you see anything?' The man, who was beginning to see, replied, 'I can see people; they look like trees to me, but they are walking about.' Then he laid his hands on the man's eyes again and he saw clearly; he was cured, and he could see everything plainly and distinctly. And Jesus sent him home, saying, 'Do not even go into the village.'

CHRIST THE LORD Jesus responds to the Pharisees with "a sigh that came straight from the heart." It pains him that they refuse to believe. They have recognized his Messianic claims and even his claims to be divine, and they have consciously decided to reject them. If they were open to hearing God's call through Christ, they would have been more than satisfied with the signs he had already performed – his miracles, healings, and exorcisms. Their demand for yet another sign – something fancy, something just for them, unconnected with healing or helping others, just something to show off his power – exposes their ill will. They are trying to discredit him in the eyes of his followers. His refusal to give them the type of sign they want, something so dramatic that will obviate the need for faith and trust, affords them another chance to criticize him. The whole exchange wrings Jesus' heart. He only longs to do good, and these men oppose him in every way.

Why did the Pharisees refuse to believe? Among the many tragic reasons, one is certainly their reluctance to change. They like the way things are. They find themselves in a good situation as respected and influential leaders. This newcomer threatens to disrupt their routine, their pleasures, their status, and their plans. In recognizing this threat, they are right on target. Christ is indeed a revolutionary. To welcome his Kingdom means changing one's life radically, inside and out. But the change will always be for the better, even if it does mean detaching oneself from old ways. Jesus is loving and wise and trustworthy, but he is still the Lord; following him means leaving our idols behind.

CHRIST THE TEACHER Jesus gives his apostles two important lessons in this passage, one directly and one indirectly.

First, he tells them outright to avoid the leaven of the Pharisees and of Herod.

He uses the term leaven as a metaphor. Just as a little bit of leaven affects a whole loaf, so the hypocritical arrogance and rationalistic doubt of the Pharisees, as well as the self-indulgent sensuality of Herod, spread like a contagion throughout the people under their influence. Both lifestyles inhibit the growth of the Kingdom, and Jesus is clearly mulling over this opposition as they make their way across the lake. By warning his disciples, he shows them that they too are vulnerable. And if they were, so are we. We need to be aware of the subtle, self-centered, and sophisticated critics who try to turn us away from the simple truths of our faith and our vocation. We need to be on our guard against the pleasure and comfort-seeking mentality that scoffs at the demands of authentic discipleship. We too are vulnerable.

The miracle of restoring the blind man's sight is another lesson, though an indirect one. Jesus could have cured him right away, but instead the cure takes place in stages. Just so, the teaching of Jesus (symbolized by the spittle which came from his mouth) transforms our lives gradually. His grace comes to us through the sacraments (symbolized by the mud mixed with his spittle – the physical materiality of the sacrament enlivened by the formal words spoken in Christ's name) and heals us of ignorance, frustration, and weakness – all things the blind man would have been experiencing due to his handicap. But the healing takes place little by little. The apostles too are taking a long time to recognize fully who Jesus is – they still don't trust him as they ought to, as is evidenced by their misinterpretation of Jesus' comment about the leaven.

This is the spiritual life, the life of every Christian: first Jesus leads us out of the village (the sinful patterns of fallen human society), then he touches our hearts, and then he begins to instruct and guide and strengthen us, until, bit by bit, we become once again what he created us to be: saints. It takes time, and that means it also takes patience and perseverance.

CHRIST THE FRIEND Here for the second time we see Jesus taking an afflicted man outside of the city in order to heal him. He wants to be alone with him, to leave behind the distractions and the bustle of ordinary life. This is still his methodology today. When we go with Jesus away from the noise and the crowds – in the silence of our own personal prayer time, in the recollection and peace of a weekend retreat, in the quiet of an evening of reflection – he can work in our souls. We need to give him our attention in order to see what he wants to show us, to hear what he has to say to us. That's how friendship works. Friends spend time together, and that's where the friendship grows.

One of the devil's favorite tactics is to keep us so busy – and not necessarily with bad things – that we leave our Friend in the lurch; the tempter knows that if he can do that, his seeds of doubt, criticism, self-pity, self-righteousness, and second-guesses will find a much warmer reception.

CHRIST IN MY LIFE This blind man didn't come to you all by himself, Lord. His friends and acquaintances brought him. Surely in my life someone is blind and yearning for the light of your liberating doctrine and grace. Who? Who do you want me to bring to you? Give me wisdom, Lord, and courage, and above all, love: help me to love all my neighbors just as you do, just as you love me..

I don't want to skimp on the time I spend with you. I am surrounded by influences that dim my vision of faith. I need the constant renewal of grace that comes from you alone. Why don't I prize my prayer time more highly? Why am I reluctant to go on retreats and renewals? Lord, you know why: the battle still rages in my soul – I am still not purely and completely yours…

I never want to cause you the pain that these Pharisees caused you. Never let me become so stuck in my own ideas, so in love with my own comfort and prestige that I resist your grace. You keep asking things of me and challenging me in new ways only because you love me. Thy will be done, Lord, not mine…

QUESTIONS FOR SMALL GROUP DISCUSSION

1. What struck you most in this passage? What did you notice that you hadn't noticed before?

2. Why do you think it takes us so long to understand God's action in our lives and learn to trust him?

3. God knew that this man was blind, but Jesus only healed him because his friends had brought him to be healed. What does this teach us about how God wants to work in the world?

4. How would you explain to a non-believing friend Jesus' refusal to give the Pharisees the sign they requested?

Cf. Catechism of the Catholic Church, 547-550 on the role of miracles as signs of the Kingdom; 57 576 on the opposition of certain Pharisees towards Jesus

120. GOD'S WAY (MK 8:27-38)

"Devotedly obey our mother, the Roman Church, and revere the Supreme Pontiff as your spiritual father."

- St Lou

Mark 8:27-35

Jesus and his disciples left for the villages round Caesarea Philippi. On the way he put this question to his disciples, 'Who do people say I am?' And they told him. 'John the Baptist,' they said 'others Elijah; others again, one of the prophets.' 'But you,' he asked 'who do you say I am?' Peter spoke up and said to him, 'You are the Christ.' And he gave them strict orders not to tell anyone about him. And he began to teach them that the Son of Man was destined to suffer grievously, to be rejected by the elders and the chief priests and the scribes, and to be put to death, and after three days to rise again; and he said all this quite openly. Then, taking him aside, Peter started to remonstrate with him. But, turning and seeing his disciples, he rebuked Peter and said to him, 'Get behind me, Satan! Because the way you think is not God's way but man's.' He called the people and his disciples to him and said, 'If anyone wants to be a follower of mine, let him renounce himself and take up his cross and follow me. For anyone who wants to save his life will lose it; but anyone who loses his life for my sake, and for the sake of the gospel, will save it. What gain, then, is it for a man to win the whole world and ruin his life? And indeed what can a man offer in exchange for his life? For if anyone in this adulterous and sinful generation is ashamed of me and of my words, the Son of Man will also be ashamed of him when he comes in the glory of his Father with the holy angels.'

CHRIST THE LORD   Jesus is the Lord. Yet many people do not consider him to be so. The question Christ asks Peter is one that he also asks us repeatedly throughout our earthly pilgrimage: "Who do people say that I am? … Who do you say that I am?" It is not enough, from Christ's perspective, for his Lordship to be something abstract or distant. Sometimes earthly rulers are satisfied with a superficial allegiance – as long as they get our vote, they won't bother themselves with coming into our personal space. Christ's Kingdom doesn't work that way. To be a Christian by name only – a nominal or cultural Catholic, as it is sometimes called – does not suffice. It is not enough to know what other people say about Jesus; we each need to encounter and respond to him personally. Only then, when in our hearts we have accepted Jesus as the Messiah, the savior, the one anointed by God to come and establish the everlasting Kingdom only then will we be ready to hear him explain to our hearts the mysteries of his loving plan of redemption.

When he does, we will find the strength to rejoice in our belonging to him instead of being ashamed and uncertain. Like the martyrs of every age, we will boldly bear witness to the Lord in word, deed, and example, and he will joyfully welcome us home when his glory is revealed.

CHRIST THE TEACHER "The way you think is not God's way but man's." In other words, God's ways differ from our ways, but we need to learn to follow him and not ourselves. Christ teaches this lesson in the context of his own passion and death, which he has just predicted to his band of followers. When Peter tries to convince Christ to have the path of the Kingdom bypass the cross and its terrible sufferings, he is sharply and publicly rebuked. And then Christ affirms, explicitly and uncompromisingly, that he and all his followers must "bear the cross," must experience suffering in this life. He goes so far as to say that those who refuse to accept the sacrifices and sufferings that God sends or allows will "lose their lives."

The joy of following Christ necessarily involves the pain of self-denial and self-sacrifice. It is not easy to be faithful to one's conscience, to the teachings of the Church, to the Ten Commandments, and to the will of God; it involves self-mastery and, sometimes, humiliation and persecution. "No disciple is greater than his master," as Christ says later on (John 13:16); if he had to suffer in order to open the gates to heaven, we will have to suffer as we follow him in. Perhaps no other gospel lesson is more difficult to learn, or more important.

CHRIST THE FRIEND Jesus never sugarcoats his call to discipleship; to be his faithful friend involves sharing in his cross, no way around it. But crosses, when borne together with Christ, always lead to the Resurrection. If we follow him on the path of self-denial, *losing* our self-centered lives (our instinctual tendencies to self-indulgence) in order to be faithful to him and his Kingdom, we will *find* true life, life in communion with God.

Some people reject God because he hasn't eliminated human suffering (though the same critics rarely consider how much suffering God does indeed prevent – suffering we don't know about it, because it never happens). But if God through the Incarnation, Passion, death, Resurrection and Ascension of Jesus Christ, has chosen to give meaning to suffering instead of doing away with it, do we really have a right to complain? So much human suffering springs from our own, free (and selfish) choices. To eliminate it, God would have to eliminate our freedom. But if we were not free to reject him, we would not be free to accept him, and he values our friendship too much to turn us into mere subservient pets.

CHRIST IN MY LIFE Lord, I want you to be everything for me, absolutely everything. I want to love you as I ought to love you. You are my Creator, my

Redeemer, my confidant, my guide, my brother, my King, my friend. All the good things in my life are your gifts. But you are greater than all your gifts. You are the Christ, the Savior, the way – my way…

I am beginning to understand with my mind the reason you send us crosses: we need to exercise our faith and trust so that those virtues will grow, and crosses are opportunities to exercise them. But even so, the cross still hurts. Teach me to love the crosses in my life as a way of uniting myself more to you and filling my soul with your wisdom…

You never let me bear my crosses alone. You are always alongside me, carrying the cross with me. Teach me to help my neighbors bear their burdens. You told us that there is more joy in giving than receiving. Teach me to be a giver, a self-forgetter, an authentic lover – a true Christian…

QUESTIONS FOR SMALL GROUP DISCUSSION

1. What struck you most in this passage? What did you notice that you hadn't noticed before?

2. Why does Christ first ask the apostles what other people are saying about him? Why not ask them first what they are thinking about him?

3. Why does Christ require his disciples to "take up their cross and follow" him? In other words, why can we only follow Christ by taking up our cross?

4. How can we strengthen our faith so that we can discover Christ even in the midst of suffering and help others to do so as well?

Cf. Catechism of the Catholic Church, 440 on the link between the messianic kingship and suffering; 595-618 on the meaning of Christ's sacrificial death on the cross; 768, 943, 1427-1439 on the need for self-denial in Christian living

THE GOSPEL OF MARK CHAPTER 9

"Therefore if you want to begin to receive this divine light, pray. If you have begun to make progress, pray. And if you have reached the summit of perfection, and want to be super-illuminated so as to remain in that state, pray. If you want faith, pray. If you want hope, pray. If you want charity, pray. If you want poverty, pray. If you want obedience, pray. If you want chastity, pray. If you want humility, pray. If you want meekness, pray. If you want fortitude, pray. If you want any virtue, pray. And pray in this fashion: always reading the Book of Life, that is, the life of the God-man, Jesus Christ, whose life consisted of poverty, pain, contempt, and true obedience."

- St Angela of Foligno

121. LISTENING UP (MK 9:1-13)

"Realize that in this life we are travelers on a journey: our true home is in heaven."

- St Cajetan

Mark 9:1-13

And he said to them, 'I tell you solemnly, there are some standing here who will not taste death before they see the kingdom of God come with power.' Six days later, Jesus took with him Peter and James and John and led them up a high mountain where they could be alone by themselves. There in their presence he was transfigured: his clothes became dazzlingly white, whiter than any earthly bleacher could make them. Elijah appeared to them with Moses; and they were talking with Jesus. Then Peter spoke to Jesus: 'Rabbi,' he said, 'it is wonderful for us to be here; so let us make three tents, one for you, one for Moses and one for Elijah.' He did not know what to say; they were so frightened. And a cloud came, covering them in shadow; and there came a voice from the cloud, 'This is my Son, the Beloved. Listen to him.' Then suddenly, when they looked round, they saw no one with them any more but only Jesus. As they came down from the mountain he warned them to tell no one what they had seen, until after the Son of Man had risen from the dead. They observed the warning faithfully, though among themselves they discussed what 'rising from the dead' could mean. And they put this question to him, 'Why do the scribes say that Elijah has to come first?' 'True,' he said, 'Elijah is to come first and to see that everything is as it should be; yet how is it that the scriptures say about the Son of Man that he is to suffer grievously and be treated with contempt? However, I tell you that Elijah has come and they have treated him as they pleased, just as the scriptures say about him.'

CHRIST THE LORD We glimpse through the eyes of Christ's three closest disciples the true glory of this humble carpenter from the small town of Nazareth. The transfiguration of Christ on Mt Tabor unveils for a shining moment Christ's divinity, so subtly disguised during the rest of his earthly days. In Jesus Christ, heaven and earth meet; time and eternity mingle. St Mark points out that the brilliance of Christ's countenance, and even of his clothes, surpassed the brightest imaginable experience of earthly light. He conversed with God's closest Old Testament collaborators, Moses and Elijah, whose law and prophecies had prefigured him. The entire scene culminates in the descent of a cloud (the Holy Spirit) and the voice of God the Father... Jesus Christ is more than just another rabbi; in him we behold the "fullness of grace and truth," the "glory of the father," and the face of everlasting love (cf. John 1, 3:16). And yet, at the same time, he is just plain Jesus, the rabbi from Galilee. Christ indeed is a Lord unlike any other, full of divine power but gentle as the humblest friend, as the Sacrament of the Eucharist so eloquently bears witness.

CHRIST THE TEACHER When God the Father speaks from heaven, we ought to listen. No doubt he chooses his words carefully: "This is my beloved Son. Listen to him." Throughout all of history, mankind has sought answers to the pressing questions that simmer deep within the human heart: Why are we here? How can we find the happiness we long for so desperately? Why is there suffering and evil? What is the ultimate meaning of existence? Often, as attested by the great literature of human history, man has addressed these questions directly to God, and God has responded. But his response is a surprising one: his answer is a living person, not a formulaic philosophy – the person of his beloved Son," Jesus Christ. Through Christ's life, teachings, death, and resurrection, God has answered all our questions more thoroughly than we could ever have imagined. Christ himself is the answer. As Pope John Paul II put it in his first encyclical letter, "The Redeemer of man, Jesus Christ, is the center of the universe and of history" (*Redemptor hominis,* 1).

By enjoining the three apostles to "listen to him," the Father seems to imply that even though Christ is his beloved Son, not everyone will easily accept him. We hear a kind of plea in that command, a plea that should give us pause. Christ is the answer, but is he my answer? Do I listen to him? Do I follow him? He is the center of the universe, but is he the center of my life? The Father wants him to be – that's why he sent him in the first place – but he leaves us free to make the choice.

The apostles' question to Jesus about Elijah exemplifies our tendency to misinterpret God's action in our lives. They are finally convinced that Jesus is the Messiah, after years of following him, listening to him, seeing his miracles, and now witnessing the Transfiguration. But a question lingers in their minds. The ancient prophecies said that Elijah would return to announce the Messiah's arrival. So, if Jesus is the Messiah, where is Elijah? Jesus reaffirms the prophecy (we know from other Gospel passages that St John the Baptist, who had come in the spirit of Elijah, fulfilled that prophecy), but then he turns his companions' minds once again to his coming passion. He asks them a rhetorical question, as if to say, "True, the prophecy about Elijah was not so easy to understand, but if you didn't grasp the meaning of that one, how will you grasp the meaning of my coming passion, which is also prophesied in the Old Testament?" Jesus tells them repeatedly about his coming passion and resurrection, but they are unable to understand; they simply don't listen – the idea of suffering turns them off. How like us they are!

CHRIST THE FRIEND At times, God grants us exceptional clarity, joy, and satisfaction along our path of Christian discipleship. He does so because he knows that we need foretastes of the happiness he has in store for us if we are to endure the crosses that mark our way. But sometimes, like spoiled children, we hold on to those good feelings as if they were God himself. We echo Peter's petition: "Lord, it is good for us to be here! Let's just put up some tents and never leave!" But earth is not heaven, and God loves us too much to let us settle for anything less than the fullness of his friendship. And so, he leads us down from our high mountains and walks with us to Calvary, where he teaches us to love him and not just his gifts, to give of ourselves, and to store up our treasure in heaven.

CHRIST IN MY LIFE Why do I take you for granted? You are too patient with me. Maybe I need a dramatic, Transfiguration-type experience to wake me up. I believe in you, Lord. I believe that you are the Eternal King, the Lord, the Son of God, the Second Person of the Holy Trinity. And I believe that you – the same Lord, God and Savior – are really and truly present in the Eucharist…

I want to keep listening to you, Lord…. Please speak to my heart. Help me to know what you would have me say and do in each moment, in each relationship of my life. Make me like you, so that the right thing, the true thing, the fruitful thing is my natural preference in every situation. Thy will be done, Lord, in every corner of my life…

You promise crosses, but you also promise resurrection. Get me ready for my crosses, because I want to experience the new life you won for me through your Resurrection. Teach me to die to everything that is selfish and petty, so that your grace and your life can flow through me and spread your Kingdom among everyone around me…

QUESTIONS FOR SMALL GROUP DISCUSSION

1. What struck you most in this passage? What did you notice that you hadn't noticed before?

2. What are some of your most powerful mountaintop experiences (the times you have experienced God's presence and love in a dramatic way)? How can you make sure that their influence continues to encourage you and doesn't just disappear?

3. What can we do concretely to improve our "listening to Christ" this week?

4. How can we know if we have truly accepted the necessity of sharing in Christ's cross (difficulties, persecution, suffering) in order to share in his Resurrection?

Cf. Catechism of the Catholic Church, 444,459 554-556 on the meaning of the Transfiguration

122. BELIEF AMIDST UNBELIEF (MK 9:14-29)

"Jesus flooded the darkness of my soul with torrents of light… Love filled my heart, I forgot myself, and henceforth I was happy."

- St Thérèse of Lisieux

Mark 9:14-29

When they rejoined the disciples they saw a large crowd round them and some scribes arguing with them. The moment they saw him the whole crowd were struck with amazement and ran to greet him. 'What are you arguing about with them?' he asked. A man answered him from the crowd, 'Master, I have brought my son to you; there is a spirit of dumbness in him, and when it takes hold of him it throws him to the ground, and he foams at the mouth and grinds his teeth and goes rigid. And I asked your disciples to cast it out and they were unable to.' 'You faithless generation,' he said to them in reply. 'How much longer must I be with you? How much longer must I put up with you? Bring him to me.' They brought the boy to him, and as soon as the spirit saw Jesus it threw the boy into convulsions, and he fell to the ground and lay writhing there, foaming at the mouth. Jesus asked the father, 'How long has this been happening to him?' 'From childhood,' he replied 'and it has often thrown him into the fire and into the water, in order to destroy him. But if you can do anything, have pity on us and help us.' 'If you can?' retorted Jesus. 'Everything is possible for anyone who has faith.' Immediately the father of the boy cried out, 'I do have faith. Help the little faith I have!' And when Jesus saw how many people were pressing round him, he rebuked the unclean spirit. 'Deaf and dumb spirit,' he said 'I command you: come out of him and never enter him again.' Then throwing the boy into violent convulsions it came out shouting, and the boy lay there so like a corpse that most of them said, 'He is dead.' But Jesus took him by the hand and helped him up, and he was able to stand. When he had gone indoors his disciples asked him privately, 'Why were we unable to cast it out?' 'This is the kind,' he answered, 'that can only be driven out by prayer.'

CHRIST THE LORD Christ's Kingdom offers health and wholeness, freedom from the oppression of evil – as he shows by acceding to this man's request. The devil's kingdom offers false pleasures that lead to destruction – even violent destruction, as this demon had tried to do multiple times with its victim. Clearly, everyone should prefer Christ's rule. But – just as clearly – many people reject Christ. Why? Jesus gives citizenship in his Kingdom on one uncomfortable condition: faith. In order to bring his grace to bear on our lives, we have to *trust in him* – we have to let him. That means obeying his will, whether it shows itself in our conscience, in Church teaching, or in the Ten Commandments.

That's where the spiritual battle really takes place. We find ourselves in situations like this man with the possessed son: we do have faith, but we need Jesus to help the little faith we have. And he will, if we – again like this man – come to him with our needs and problems and hopes and helplessness. Jesus instructs us all when he looks at this suppliant and tells him, "Everything is possible for anyone who has faith." How it pains Jesus when we don't trust him! The only complaint he makes in the entire Gospel is when he rues our lack of faith. But if we stay close to him and exercise the little faith we have, the Lord will find ways to make it grow, because he wants us to experience the blessedness of his Kingdom.

CHRIST THE TEACHER As Christ's followers advance along the path of discipleship, they constantly face new kinds of temptations. By this time, the apostles had all been out on missionary trips, where they cured the sick and cast out demons in the name of Jesus. Then, while Jesus is up on the mountain with his chosen companions, a man with a possessed son comes to the rest of the disciples, asking them to cast out the demon. (Demon possession often manifests itself in part with signs of clinically recognizable illnesses – in this case, epilepsy. Obviously, if a demon wants to make his victim suffer, he has to do so within the confines of human nature, so the disorders it engineers will resemble natural disorders. In any case, the Gospels constantly and precisely distinguish cases of illness from cases of demon-possession, making it clear that possession is not the same thing as mental illness.) We can imagine the apostles' response to the request. Sure, they say, no problem. And they prepare to send the devil packing…. But it doesn't work. The young man remains there, writhing. The demon doesn't depart. The apostles try again, and fail again. A crowd begins to gather…

Later, after Jesus has saved the young man, the apostles ask why they couldn't expel the demon. Jesus explains that prayer was necessary. In other words, the apostles had let their earlier successes go their heads. They had fallen into the trap of thinking they could achieve results for Christ using their own natural abilities. They needed a humiliation to remind them that the disciple does all things in Christ's name, not in his own name. When we start depending solely on ourselves, we are sure to stop bearing fruit, because, as the Lord said during the Last Supper, "Cut off from me you can do nothing" (Jn 15:5).

CHRIST THE FRIEND Picture Jesus bending over the young man after casting out the demon. The violent convulsions and other-worldly shrieks that accompanied the exorcism threw the crowd into shock. The sudden silence and the victim's deathly stillness make the crowd hold their breath. Jesus steps over to him, bends down, and takes him by the hand. He looks into his eyes, smiles, and invites him to try to stand up. Leaning on the Lord, the young man, freed from the torment he had been undergoing since he was a boy, stands up, weak but radiant. His father, overjoyed beyond expression, rushes over and embraces him.

The boy's father: They had told me that Jesus was divine, but when he cured my son what struck me most was how human he was. I believe he is the divine Messiah, and yet he was so approachable. He poured out his salvation in ways that everyone could understand, in ways we could touch and experience. I know now that he came to elevate us to the life of grace, by which we become sons of God too. That day, though, he just wanted to restore my son's human integrity. He wants to do that with everyone. He wants to teach us to live a healthy, full life here on earth – though never exempt from crosses. He wants to be our Friend forever: not just in heaven, but starting right now.

CHRIST IN MY LIFE Lord, why is it so hard for me to trust you? Why is my faith so small? I believe in you, Lord. I trust in you. You are the Lord of life and history; you are truly present in the Sacrament of the Eucharist. I do have faith, Jesus, but to live the life of fulfillment and fruitfulness that you created me to live, I need you to increase my faith…

Keep me humble, Jesus. Grant success to the work of my hands, for the glory of your name and the good of your Kingdom, but please keep me humble. Without you I can do nothing. Never let me be separated from you. Let all my failures and frustrations throw me to my knees in prayer, and let all my successes and joys do the same…

You never stop thinking of me. You are always coming close to me, drawing me closer to you. You have done so much for me. Give me a heart like yours, generous like yours. Teach me to love my neighbor as you have loved me, show me how to bring them the health and hope you won for them through your Incarnation, Passion, Resurrection, and Ascension…

QUESTIONS FOR SMALL GROUP DISCUSSION

1. What struck you most in this passage? What did you notice that you hadn't noticed before?

2. How would you define or describe Christian faith to a non-believer who asked you about it?

3. If someone came up to you, knowing you were a Christian, and told you that they want to believe but simply can't, how would you respond?

4. Cut off from Jesus we can't do anything. What kinds of activities cut us off from Jesus? What types of events dampen our faith? What keeps us united to him?

Cf. Catechism of the Catholic Church, 153-165 on the characteristics of faith; 517, 550, 1237, 1506 and 1673 on casting out demons

123. LEADERS LIKE CHRIST (MK 9:30-37)

"I desire to love you, O my God, with a love that is patient, with a love that abandons itself wholly to you, with a love that acts, and most important of all, with a love that perseveres."

- St Theresa Margaret of the Sacred Heart

Mark 9:30-37

After leaving that place they made their way through Galilee; and he did not want anyone to know, because he was instructing his disciples; he was telling them, 'The Son of Man will be delivered into the hands of men; they will put him to death; and three days after he has been put to death he will rise again.' But they did not understand what he said and were afraid to ask him. They came to Capernaum, and when he was in the house he asked them, 'What were you arguing about on the road?' They said nothing because they had been arguing which of them was the greatest. So he sat down, called the Twelve to him and said, 'If anyone wants to be first, he must make himself last of all and servant of all.' He then took a little child, set him in front of them, put his arms round him, and said to them, 'Anyone who welcomes one of these little children in my name, welcomes me; and anyone who welcomes me welcomes not me but the one who sent me.'

CHRIST THE LORD The lesson Jesus has been teaching by his example since the very start of the Incarnation he now teaches with words. The Christian leader leads in the same way that Christ did – by serving, by taking care of those who are weak and helpless, those who are in need, like little children. Greatness in Christ's Kingdom is equated with humility, an attitude that puts the good of others ahead of one's own preferences. By defining Christian greatness in this way, the innate human desire to excel and achieve is not stifled, but channeled. He doesn't tell his apostles, "You shouldn't strive to be great, to achieve great things," but he does point out where true, lasting, fulfilling greatness lies – in loving one's neighbor as Christ has loved them. Jesus is the Servant-Lord; his greatest disciples follow in those demanding footsteps.

That children were so comfortable around Jesus shows yet another aspect of his personality. Jesus too had been a child, and he never forgot or disdained the sensitivity and enthusiasm that characterize children. He never stifled their innate zest for life. The Lord always knew how to meet everyone exactly where they were, inviting them to take a step closer to his Kingdom.

CHRIST THE TEACHER Jesus is once again trying to explain to his disciples the true nature of his Kingdom. They are still hoping for Jesus to take Israel's throne as David did in the old days, and bring political freedom and economic prosperity back to the Jewish people, who were suffering under oppressive Roman occupation. And they imagined that they would be right there with him, his closest companions and most trusted advisors (they were arguing about exactly that – which of them would be prime minister, which would be defense minister, etc…).

But Christ knows that his Kingdom is not like all the other kingdoms of the world; it is the reign of God's will in the hearts of his followers, which involves self-denial and the cross (a topic that continues to puzzle the apostles); it is a spiritual kingdom that will act like a leaven within the earthly kingdom, bringing souls back into communion with the God who loves them and setting them on the road to heaven, the Resurrection, and eternal life. They just don't understand it. Even now, after twenty centuries of demonstrable proof, many times we still don't get it either; many times we want to experience the pure joys of heaven while we're still on earth, and we resent it when God keeps insisting on the cross. Isn't the Father wise? Shouldn't we trust him? Jesus did, and Good Friday paved the way to Easter Sunday.

CHRIST THE FRIEND Children are basically energetic balls of needs. They can't survive on their own; they need someone to take care of them, to watch over them, to teach them – all the time. By setting a child in the midst of his disciples and telling them that when they accept a child they are welcoming him, Christ is explaining that the Christian heart reaches out to others who are in need. It strives not primarily for its own advancement, but looks for ways to meet the needs of others, be they physical or spiritual. Just as Christ saw us wallowing in the confusion and helplessness of sin, and came to save us, so Christians are called to reach out to the needs of those around them.

Jesus: It is easy to serve others when they can offer something in return. But that's not my way. After all, what could a fallen humanity offer to an infinitely perfect God? I came to rescue you who were more helpless in the spiritual realm than even a child is in the physical realm. I want all my followers to do likewise, whether by giving the unpopular colleague a sample of Christian hospitality, or by making the saving truths of Christ palatable to peers who prefer the taste of immorality and false doctrines, or in whatever way my Holy Spirit inspires you. When you welcome those in need, you welcome me.

CHRIST IN MY LIFE I don't know why humility is so hard for me, Lord. It seems that the dominant décor of my heart is a self-portrait. Why don't you change me? Lord Jesus, I know you are changing me. But you want me to exercise my love and my virtue by making what little effort I can. Okay, help me to do it: help me to put others before myself. Jesus, I trust in you...

You insist so much on the cross. The world I live in hates the cross. I have to admit, Lord; the world rubs off on me. Reach into my mind and my heart and teach me the mysterious wisdom of the cross. In self-forgetful love lies the fullness of life and meaning. I believe it, Lord Jesus, because you teach it. Increase my faith…

You were always thinking about those around you. Teach me to do the same. You promise to give me the satisfaction I can never find in a frenzied search for ultimate self-indulgence if I follow your example of self-forgetful love. Thank you, Jesus, for guiding and strengthening me. Never take your eyes off of me; show me the way to go…

QUESTIONS FOR SMALL GROUP DISCUSSION

1. What struck you most in this passage? What did you notice that you hadn't noticed before?

2. Every Christian is called to lead by serving others. What are some of the prime opportunities available to us now for exercising Christian leadership?

3. We have heard the lesson of the cross many times. Why is it still so difficult for us to accept suffering and adversity when God permits us to face them?

4. Why is it so much easier to serve those whom we like, or find pleasant, or who can return our favors than those who, like children, have nothing with which to repay us?

Cf. Catechism of the Catholic Church, 536, 541, 555, 565 on Jesus as servant; 1822-1829 on the law and virtue of charity

124. SIN MATTERS (MK 9:38-50)

"There is a crown for those who in times of persecution fight the good fight; there is a crown too for those who in times of peace keep true to their conscience."

- St Cyprian

Mark 9:38-50

John said to him, 'Master, we saw a man who is not one of us casting out devils in your name; and because he was not one of us we tried to stop him.' But Jesus said, 'You must not stop him: no one who works a miracle in my name is likely to speak evil of me. Anyone who is not against us is for us. If anyone gives you a cup of water to drink just because you belong to Christ, then I tell you solemnly, he will most certainly not lose his reward. But anyone who is an obstacle to bring down one of these little ones who have faith, would be better thrown into the sea with a great millstone round his neck. And if your hand should cause you to sin, cut it off; it is better for you to enter into life crippled, than to have two hands and go to hell, into the fire that cannot be put out. And if your foot should cause you to sin, cut it off; it is better for you to enter into life lame, than to have two feet and be thrown into hell. And if your eye should cause you to sin, tear it out; it is better for you to enter into the kingdom of God with one eye, than to have two eyes and be thrown into hell where their worm does not die nor their fire go out. For everyone will be salted with fire. Salt is a good thing, but if salt has become insipid, how can you season it again? Have salt in yourselves and be at peace with one another.'

CHRIST THE LORD Jesus is generous. The slightest (or mightiest) good deed done for him or for his Kingdom will not go unrewarded. Our King lavishes his blessings on everyone who lets him. We, as his followers, ought to do the same. Unfortunately, many times we, like the apostle John in this passage, are less generous than our Lord, and concern ourselves with hoarding the grace of God, refusing to give freely what we have freely received (cf. Matthew 10:8), or pettily envying the good that others are doing as if it somehow detracted from the good we are doing. But it is not for us to limit the range of divine benevolence; it is for us to extend it.

With some great leaders it is not necessary to take sides, you can just admire from a distance, but Christ leaves no room for neutrality: "Anyone who is not against us is for us." Sooner or later, everyone must take sides with Christ or against him; since he alone is the everlasting Lord, no other option remains. The choice must be made. Everything else in life comes and goes, but the gaze of Christ is steady: beckoning, inviting, challenging, and hoping that we will give in to the reign of his Divine Heart.

CHRIST THE TEACHER St Mark spared no words. Here, as in many other passages, he sprays his readers with monumental lessons one right after the other, like machine-gun fire. First he specifies the grave responsibility of those who lead others astray by their teaching or bad example – he clearly recognizes that it will occur; otherwise he wouldn't have been so vehement in his warning. Second, he vividly describes sin as what it really is: an invitation to hell. (Gehenna was the public incinerator on the outskirts of Jerusalem, a valley that had been used for human sacrifice during royal apostasies in Old Testament times. Since then it was considered good only for worthless and rotten refuse, which smoldered stubbornly and refused to be completely burnt up – a striking image for the state of eternal separation of a soul from God, and the unending spiritual frustration such a separation entails.)

435

The point about sacrificing one's eye or hand if they cause you to sin in order to avoid sin would have been perfectly understood by his hearers. Eyes and hands don't cause sin; sin is a decision of the heart to prefer one's own will against God's will. It always indicates that we are attached to some good and valued thing (after all, these members of our body are most precious to us) so much that we prefer it to something much better – friendship and communion with God. Thus, at times a certain relationship provides us with comfort or pleasure, even though it leads us to violate God's commandments. Or perhaps we treasure our reputation or popularity so much that we compromise our Christian values in order to protect it. To give up such obstacles to our friendship with Christ hurts – as if we were cutting off our hand or gouging out our eye. But our Lord teaches us that pain is nothing compared with the sorrow of cutting ourselves off forever from God's love.

CHRIST THE FRIEND Real friends tell each other the truth – even when it hurts. Here Christ shows that he is a real friend, making it perfectly clear even for the most obtuse of his listeners that sin is real, hell is real, and unchecked sin leads to hell. These are harsh sounding words for us gentle moderns. And yet, sometimes, modern gentility is a mask for selfish fear: we are afraid to tell our friends the truth about Christ because they might reject us. Christ faced the same fear (Do you think everyone who heard him welcomed his teachings? Certainly not those who crucified him), but he overcame it with the strength of his love. He knows that we need to know the whole story; the truth will set us free – if we let it. He's hoping that we will.

CHRIST IN MY LIFE We are so used to sin, Lord. It swirls all around us and constantly lulls us into a dangerous mediocrity. You hated sin – you still hate sin, because you know what it does to our souls and to your heart. Teach me to call sin by its true name, first and foremost in my own life. Teach me to hate it out of love for you and your Kingdom. Never let me fear seeking your forgiveness…

You often talked to your followers about rewards. It is no sin to look forward to heaven. You are leading me there. All of earth's joys are whiffs of heaven. Dear Jesus, I believe that you died on the cross just so we could look forward to eternal life with you in heaven. Thank you for the invitation. I accept: Thy will be done…

I am foolish to be reluctant to bear witness to you with my words and actions. What greater thing could I do for my neighbor than shine a little bit of your light around them, seasoning their life with the salt of your love? I am still attached to others' opinions of me. Purify my heart, Lord. Give me courage, humility, and zeal. With the love of your heart, inflame my heart…

QUESTIONS FOR SMALL GROUP DISCUSSION

1. What struck you most in this passage? What did you notice that you hadn't noticed before?

2. In what ways can we fall into the same petty envy that St John exhibits in this passage? In what ways can we guard against that?

3. Why does popular culture tend to laugh at the concept of "sin," as if it were a childish, anti-quated idea? How would you explain the idea of sin to a non-believing friend who told you they didn't believe in it?

4. What tone of voice do you think Christ used when he uttered his warnings about sin and hell? What expression do you think his face had? Why?

Cf. Catechism of the Catholic Church, 1849-1864 on the definition, kinds, and gravity of sin; 1033-1037 on hell; 2284-2287 on "scandal" or causing others to fall into sin

THE GOSPEL OF MARK CHAPTER 10

"When a farmer sets out to till the ground he has to take proper tools and clothing for work in the fields: so when Christ, the heavenly king and the true husbandman, came to humanity laid waste by sin, he clothed himself in a body and carried the cross as his implement and cultivated the deserted soul. He pulled up the thorns and thistles of evil spirits and tore up the weeds of sin. With fire he burnt up all the harvest of its sins. When thus he had tilled the ground of the soul with the wooden plow of his cross, he planted in it a lovely garden of the Spirit; a garden which brings forth for God as its master the sweetest and most delightful fruits of every sort."

- St Macarius

125. MARRIED LOVE: MEANT TO LAST (MK 10:1-16)

"Indeed the garden of the Lord contains not only the roses of martyrdom but also the lilies of virginity, the ivy of marriage, and the violets of widowhood. So no one, my dear brethren, need despair of his vocation. Christ suffered for all."

- St Augustine

Mark 10:1-16

Leaving there, he came to the district of Judaea and the far side of the Jordan. And again crowds gathered round him, and again he taught them, as his custom was. Some Pharisees approached him and asked, 'Is it against the law for a man to divorce his wife?' They were testing him. He answered them, 'What did Moses command you?' 'Moses allowed us,' they said, 'to draw up a writ of dismissal and so to divorce.' Then Jesus said to them, 'It was because you were so unteachable that he wrote this commandment for you. But from the beginning of creation God made them male and female. This is why a man must leave father and mother, and the two become one body. They are no longer two, therefore, but one body. So then, what God has united, man must not divide.' Back in the house the disciples questioned him again about this, and he said to them, 'The man who divorces his wife and marries another is guilty of adultery against her. And if a woman divorces her husband and marries another she is guilty of adultery too.' People were bringing little children to him, for him to touch them. The disciples turned them away, but when Jesus saw this he was indignant and said to them, 'Let the little children come to me; do not stop them; for it is to such as these that the kingdom of God belongs. I tell you solemnly, anyone who does not welcome the kingdom of God like a little child will never enter it.' Then he put his arms round them, laid his hands on them and gave them his blessing.

CHRIST THE LORD Jesus is the perfect King. He is absolutely superlative in nobility, wisdom, and authority, as he evidences here by once again interpreting and fixing up the law of Moses – thus showing himself superior to the greatest prophet of all Jewish history. At the same time, though, he is supremely available to all his subjects: the high-class intellectuals (the Pharisees) approach him freely and he converses with them easily, but the young mothers and children swarm around him with equal familiarity, and he is likewise at ease with them (so much so that he has to rebuke his disciples for thinking that he wouldn't want to be bothered with such trivialities). No fairy tale prince or poet's adventurer can match the greatness of our Lord. And if he has exemplified such dignity and goodness, surely he will teach his ambassadors (us) to do the same, if we make the effort to learn.

CHRIST THE TEACHER At the time of Christ, the Jewish world had all but destroyed the institution of marriage. Convenient interpretations of the Mosaic precept that a man could divorce his wife if he found an "indecency" in her that had destabilized marriage – to the point where many women simply avoided marriage (women had a much harder time divorcing their husbands than men did their wives). A man could put away his wife if she cooked a tasteless meal, if she raised her voice, if he met someone whom he found more attractive…. Some voices could be heard objecting to such heinous practices, which were ultimately based on the view that a wife was closer to a piece of property than a person. So the Pharisees posed this question to Christ hoping to embroil him in the irresolvable controversy, thereby discrediting him. Once again, Jesus meets his challengers head-on, and teaches them (and us) an invaluable lesson in the process.

First, he puts the Mosaic law of divorce in its proper perspective. Many scholars agree that Moses had defined the parameters for divorce in order to protect the institution of marriage from total degeneration. In other words, his people were already debasing the marriage bond in myriad ways, and his decree was the first step to regulating and recovering the primeval dignity of marriage – it was limiting abuses by setting parameters, not by giving in to the desire for fluidity. Second, Jesus – who has come to reestablish the communion between man and God that original sin had wrecked – reaffirms and reestablishes God's original design for marriage: a permanent and exclusive union of a man and woman who share equally in the dignity of being created in God's image. Jesus' vision of human love and the beauty of the family had not been blurred by the prevailing clouds of selfishness, lust, and sexism. In his Kingdom, he will settle for nothing less than the pristine brilliance of selfless love, and to enable his subjects to live out such a high calling, he even elevated the natural institution of marriage to the supernatural level of a sacrament. With the help of his grace, his followers can brave every storm and gradually grow into the fullness of spousal love.

CHRIST THE FRIEND Children naturally trust. It is hard for them to be suspicious, even though they are often shy. For this reason they are very vulnerable; many people are not worthy of trust and will abuse the trusting soul. Jesus Christ longs to find this childlike trust in our hearts. If we put ourselves entirely into his care, he will be free to teach and guide and coach us in the art of living. When we are suspicious of him, demand proofs, and doubt his wisdom and love, we limit the range of his action – he has to spend time convincing us of his goodness before we are willing to follow his lead unhesitatingly.

Picture our Lord with these babies (at the time, it was customary for Jewish women to have their babies blessed by a respected rabbi on their first birthday) and their brothers and sisters; if they were so eager to be close to him, it tells us a lot about his personality. Dour and serious types rarely attract children - kids much prefer grown-ups that have a twinkle in their eye and a quick and generous smile. If we approach Jesus with childlike trust, maybe we will more easily perceive this part of his character and catch a bit more of his joy.

CHRIST THE LORD Marriage is sacred to you, Lord. You know we can't live it as you designed it unless we have your help. Jesus, be the strength of all married couples. Fill my heart with your grace and burn away the dross of self-centeredness and woundedness that cripples my capacity for spousal love. With you, Lord, all things are possible…

You have earned my trust. All I have to do is look around at the beauties of this awe-inspiring world, and glance at the purest expression of your trustworthiness there in the crucifix. I trust you, Lord, and I trust in your Church, the Bark of Peter, guaranteed to come safely to shore. Blessed be your name throughout the earth…

I want to know you better; I want to admire your incomparable nobility and inexhaustible generosity. I want to gaze at the wisdom and love of your heart. Let me see your face, Jesus. Let me see you – let the light of your face shine on me, so I can be more like you…

QUESTIONS FOR SMALL GROUP DISCUSSION

1. What struck you most in this passage? What did you notice that you hadn't noticed before?

2. What is the Church's teaching on divorce and remarriage? Why is it so difficult to accept for so many people? What should faithful Catholics do if they have doubts or problems with this teaching in theory and in their daily lives?

3. What are some common obstacles to our trusting fully (like a child) in Jesus Christ and his Church? How can we overcome them?

4. How do you think the Pharisees reacted to Jesus' answer? Why?

Cf. Catechism of the Catholic Church, 1601-1620 on marriage in God's plan; 142-165 on the nature and importance of trust and faith in man's relation to God

126. MONEY, MONEY, MONEY (MK 10:17-31)

"If you wish to talk to Christ and to accept all the truth of his testimony, you must on the one hand 'love the world' – for God 'so loved the world that he gave his only Son' (Jn 3:16) – and at the same time you must acquire interior detachment with regard to all this rich and fascinating reality that makes up 'the world.'"

- Pope John Paul II

Mark 10:17-31

He was setting out on a journey when a man ran up, knelt before him and put this question to him, 'Good master, what must I do to inherit eternal life?' Jesus said to him, 'Why do you call me good? No one is good but God alone. You know the commandments: You must not kill; You must not commit adultery; You must not steal; You must not bring false witness; You must not defraud; Honour your father and mother.' And he said to him, 'Master, I have kept all these from my earliest days.' Jesus looked steadily at him and loved him, and he said, 'There is one thing you lack. Go and sell everything you own and give the money to the poor, and you will have treasure in heaven; then come, follow me.' But his face fell at these words and he went away sad, for he was a man of great wealth.

Jesus looked round and said to his disciples, 'How hard it is for those who have riches to enter the kingdom of God!' The disciples were astounded by these words, but Jesus insisted, 'My children,' he said to them, 'how hard it is to enter the kingdom of God! It is easier for a camel to pass through the eye of a needle than for a rich man to enter the kingdom of God.' They were more astonished than ever. 'In that case,' they said to one another, 'who can be saved?' Jesus gazed at them. 'For men,' he said, 'it is impossible, but not for God: because everything is possible for God.' Peter took this up. 'What about us?' he asked him. 'We have left everything and followed you.' Jesus said, 'I tell you solemnly, there is no one who has left house, brothers, sisters, father, children or land for my sake and for the sake of the gospel who will not be repaid a hundred times over, houses, brothers, sisters, mothers, children and land – not without persecutions – now in this present time and, in the world to come, eternal life. Many who are first will be last, and the last first.'

CHRIST THE LORD The rich aristocrat came to Christ and threw himself at his feet. It doesn't surprise us; it didn't surprise anyone at the time. The truly surprising thing is that everyone didn't throw themselves at his feet. Though he tempers this man's enthusiasm, which may be based too much on mere emotion (as ours so often is), Jesus answers his question – he knows what this man needs in order to achieve the fullness of life for which he thirsts, and he tells him. Christ is the Lord; he has the answers we seek. Going to him and his delegates in the Church is the right thing to do when we need direction and light for our lives, but unlike the man in this encounter, we also need to be ready to accept whatever Christ tells us. After all, he is the Lord.

This man had felt God calling him to experience the "eternal life" of a deeper, definitive divine intimacy. He went to Christ to find out how to follow that call. Christ makes it very simple: give your wealth to the poor and become my disciple. The man balks, and, sadly, rejects the invitation. He had built his happiness around his wealth; it had become his idol, his lord, the god without whom he could not live. Jesus recognized that and opened to the door to freedom, but the rich young man preferred his comfortable chains; he could not let go of his gold in order to grasp the hand of his Lord.

CHRIST THE TEACHER This tragic occasion, which no doubt pained Christ deeply, offers Jesus a chance to put forth his teaching on material goods and the virtue of Christian poverty.

Jewish teaching at the time considered material prosperity a sign of God's favor, which is why the disciples were "more astonished than ever" when Jesus said that it would be hard for the rich to live in communion with God. Thus Jesus needed to use a vivid, unforgettable image to drive his point home: a camel will have a better chance to get through the eye of a needle than a rich person will have of getting into Christ's Kingdom. (Some scholars contend that this "eye of the needle" referred not to the sewing instrument, but to a narrow gate in Jerusalem's city walls, which only skinny camels carrying no baggage could squeeze through. Either way, the message is the same.) The Lord is merely explaining what just happened in his conversation with this rich man (a young man, in fact, as we learn from the accounts in the other Gospels).

Material wealth is not evil in itself – God made the universe and filled it with good things for our use and enjoyment. But because of our fallen nature we tend to attach ourselves too closely to things, to link our hopes too tightly to them. Wealth can easily give us the illusion of being self-sufficient, of being totally in control of our happiness and our destiny. The truth always remains, however, that we are dependent on God for everything; we are fragile, unable to achieve total, lasting fulfillment by ourselves. It is easier to keep that in mind when it is hard to make ends meet.

Out of this hard truth rises the Christian virtue of poverty. It doesn't necessarily imply choosing to live in misery. Rather, it involves the conscious decision to live with dignity, but responsibly and frugally. Material wealth needs to be put to work for the extension of Christ's Kingdom, while at the same time hedging the natural tendency to excess and self-indulgence with habits of self-discipline and voluntary sacrifices in order to avoid becoming money's slave. The heart that is detached from things is freer to love others. It may attract the sneers of worldly peers, but it attracts the smile of God, and in any case, it's worth being looked down upon now if it means enjoying God's approval for all eternity.

CHRIST THE FRIEND St Mark points out that Jesus looked at this young man and "loved him" and then invited him to give up what he held most dear. Christ knows, as he explains to Peter, that he himself is a reward far greater than anything this world has to offer. Thus, when he shows a special love for certain souls, he often asks them to forsake the passing goods of the world and consecrate themselves totally to him, the eternal good. That invitation, as Mark makes so clear, is a result of his *love*. He doesn't call people to serve him more closely in order to punish them – his heart is not cruel. Unfortunately, however, it is not just the rich young man in this passage who turns away from Christ's love: many of us have riches of our own (plans, pleasures, hopes, relationships, etc.) that hold us back from answering a special call to follow the Lord more closely. He wants a closer friendship, and we foolishly hang back.

CHRIST IN MY LIFE I too thirst for the eternal life that every human heart desires. I too come to you, again, right now, and I throw myself at your feet. What more can I do, Lord, to live more fully the life you created me to live? What more can I do to love you as you ought to be loved? Teach me, Lord, in your goodness, to do your will with all my heart, soul, mind, and strength…

It is hard to keep money matters in perspective. Wealth makes so many promises. But only you are faithful. You are perfect wisdom and perfect goodness, and you would never deceive me. I accept your warning, Lord: love of money can block the action of your grace. Have mercy on me and everyone tempted by this distraction from you. Jesus, I trust in you…

Are you calling me to leave something behind and follow you more closely? Are you gazing at me with love and inviting me to a new level of discipleship? Help me to hear your voice; help me to be generous; let me see the love in your gaze. And please do the same for all the young men and women whom you are calling to consecrate their lives to your service…

QUESTIONS FOR SMALL GROUP DISCUSSION

1. What struck you most in this passage? What did you notice that you hadn't noticed before?

2. What can we do to make sure that we never follow in the terrible footsteps of this rich young man?

3. How does Christ's view of material wealth differ from the view held and put forth by popular culture? (Try to think of concrete examples.)

4. What can we do to help those people Christ is calling to complete consecration respond generously to his love?

Cf. Catechism of the Catholic Church, 2052-2055 on the place of the commandments in pursuing eternal life; 2401-2449 on the Christian view of material goods

127. THE HARD ROAD TO JERUSALEM (MK 10:32-45)

"Poverty is true riches. So precious is poverty that God's only-begotten Son came on earth in search of it. In heaven he had superabundance of all goods. Nothing was lacking there but poverty."

- St Anthony of Padua

Mark 10:32-45

They were on the road, going up to Jerusalem; Jesus was walking on ahead of them; they were in a daze, and those who followed were apprehensive. Once more taking the Twelve aside he began to tell them what was going to happen to him: 'Now we are going up to Jerusalem, and the Son of Man is about to be handed over to the chief priests and the scribes. They will condemn him to death and will hand him over to the pagans, who will mock him and spit at him and scourge him and put him to death; and after three days he will rise again.'

James and John, the sons of Zebedee, approached him. 'Master,' they said to him 'we want you to do us a favour.' He said to them, 'What is it you want me to do for you?' They said to him, 'Allow us to sit one at your right hand and the other at your left in your glory.' 'You do not know what you are asking,' Jesus said to them. 'Can you drink the cup that I must drink, or be baptised with the baptism with which I must be baptised?' They replied, 'We can.' Jesus said to them, 'The cup that I must drink you shall drink, and with the baptism with which I must be baptised you shall be baptised, but as for seats at my right hand or my left, these are not mine to grant; they belong to those to whom they have been allotted.'

When the other ten heard this they began to feel indignant with James and John, so Jesus called them to him and said to them, 'You know that among the pagans their so-called rulers lord it over them, and their great men make their authority felt. This is not to happen among you. No; anyone who wants to become great among you must be your servant, and anyone who wants to be first among you must be slave to all. For the Son of Man himself did not come to be served but to serve, and to give his life as a ransom for many.'

CHRIST THE LORD Few times does Jesus so clearly contrast the world's standard with his own standard. He is the Lord, the Eternal King of Kings, and yet he puts all his power, all his wisdom, all his energy, and all his talents at the service of those he rules. He seeks nothing for himself. Most men and women of this world do just the opposite. They put all their gifts at the service of themselves, often to the point of treating those around them unjustly. Thinking that we deserve comfort and honor, we demand it whenever we can – from the waiter at the restaurant, to the telephone operator, to our siblings, to those who work under our supervision. "My will be done!" is the world's motto; "Thy will be done!" is Christ's. Jesus the Lord serves others; he gives his life for their sakes (especially on the cross and in the Eucharist), and he calls us to do the same.

This ethos is most eloquently displayed in Christ's repeated prediction of his Passion. In this passage, he goes into more detail about his coming fate. In fact, he gives a play-by-play account of what will happen to him – the unjust condemnation, the physical torture, the mockery…. He knows what awaits him in Jerusalem. And yet, he freely marches towards that ignominious encounter, almost with an eager determination. This shows that everything he will suffer will be suffered willingly, not for any benefit to him, but for you and me and for all our brothers and sisters in the human race – past, present, and future. Jesus lived and died *for their sake*. He had no personal items on his agenda; he came to serve and to give his life for others. That's the law that ruled this King's conquest, and the same law ought to rule the lives of all his followers.

CHRIST THE TEACHER Notwithstanding their selfish ambition, James and John truly want to be as close to Christ as possible. They trusted him enough to approach him with their petition. Jesus recognizes this, and he tells them a precious secret: to be close to him requires suffering with him. Jesus' "cup" and "baptism" refer to the self-offering he makes in order to reestablish friendship between mankind and God, a self-offering which culminates in his passion and death, which he has just predicted to his apostles for the third time. To be near to him, to enter into an intimate union of hearts with him, requires joining him on the cross. To embrace Christ is to embrace the cross, to retrace in the circumstances of our own lives the steps he took on the way to Calvary. As he put it in another passage, "For whoever wishes to save his life will lose it, but whoever loses his life for my sake will find it" (Mt 16:25). He saved the world through his obedience to the Father's will, which caused him untold suffering before he won his Kingdom. If we would be his disciples, we can expect much of the same – both the painful suffering (which even non-Christians can't avoid in this life), and also the victory.

CHRIST THE FRIEND Sometimes we think that the apostles were born saints. Passages like this one disprove such an idea. First, James and John expose their selfish thirst for glory (though it is certainly mixed with a sincere desire to be as close to the Lord as possible). Then the others show their envy and jealousy by becoming indignant when they hear about it. This kind of interpersonal friction and conflict, as petty as it may seem, was present among the first group of disciples, just as it is among today's disciples, and will be among tomorrow's. And Jesus lives right in the middle of it. How odd of God to lower himself so far that he mediates such trivial squabbles! And yet, that is the lesson of the Incarnation: Jesus wants to live in friendship with us, even if it means putting up with (and helping us overcome) our childish shenanigans. Nothing we can do will alter the love and devotion of this unique Friend.

CHRIST IN MY LIFE My heart is still divided, Lord. I know and I believe that a meaningful, happy life entails self-giving, even to the point of self-sacrifice, but in my daily actions I still fall into self-centeredness. I take offense so easily; I am so preoccupied with how I feel and what I want… Teach me, Lord, to follow in your footsteps, to drink your cup…

If you send me suffering, if you permit troubles in my life, it's only because you know that they can bring me closer to you. They chisel away at my pride, my arrogance, my self-satisfied vanity – at everything that keeps me from hearing your voice and seeing your face clearly. Send me all the crosses you can, Lord, but only if you promise to help me bear them…

Teach me to walk with you, Lord. I am surrounded by a world that doesn't believe, by a culture that seeks happiness in sin. Keep me on your path, and make me your good ambassador to others who are searching…

QUESTIONS FOR SMALL GROUP DISCUSSION

1. What struck you most in this passage? What did you notice that you hadn't noticed before?

2. In our present circumstances, how can we exercise true Christian greatness by serving one another? In other words, what form should Christian leadership/service take in our stage of life?

3. Where can we find the courage to accept Christ's "cup" and "baptism" of self-sacrifice in order to come closer and closer to him? Also, what form does this self-sacrifice usually take in our current life situation?

4. If Christ can put up with our pettiness and selfishness, why do we have such a difficult time putting up with the faults of others?

Cf. Catechism of the Catholic Church, 599-618 on the meaning and nature of Christ's suffering; 440 & 786 on leading by service

128. BLIND EYES, SEEING HEART (MK 10:46-52)

"All my hope is naught save in your great mercy."

- St Augustine

Mark 10:46-52

They reached Jericho; and as he left Jericho with his disciples and a large crowd, Bartimaeus (that is, the son of Timaeus), a blind beggar, was sitting at the side of the road. When he heard that it was Jesus of Nazareth, he began to shout and to say, 'Son of David, Jesus, have pity on me'. And many of them scolded him and told him to keep quiet, but he only shouted all the louder, 'Son of David, have pity on me.' Jesus stopped and said, 'Call him here.' So they called the blind man. 'Courage,' they said, 'get up; he is calling you.' So throwing off his cloak, he jumped up and went to Jesus. Then Jesus spoke, 'What do you want me to do for you?' 'Rabbuni,' the blind man said to him, 'Master, let me see again.' Jesus said to him, 'Go; your faith has saved you.' And immediately his sight returned and he followed him along the road.

CHRIST THE LORD Jesus is the "Son of David." Under King David's rule, the Twelve Tribes of Israel were politically, socially, and religiously united, took full possession of the Promised Land (definitively ousting rival peoples), and became an international political and economic powerhouse. Under King Solomon (David's son and successor), Israel expanded its borders, its wealth, and its influence even more. When Solomon died, internal strife divided the Kingdom. Ten tribes split off from the tribes of Judah and Benjamin, which had their capital in Jerusalem, and formed the Northern Kingdom. Subsequently, through the prophets, God promised to send a Messiah (someone anointed to rule God's people, as Kind David had been) to reunite the Twelve Tribes and reestablish the Davidic Kingdom in even greater glory than before. Bartimaeus recognized that Jesus was this Messiah, and so he addresses him loudly as "Son of David." And Jesus responds with a miracle, as if to confirm the blind man's intuition.

Christ is truly the Promised One; through him God's covenant with Abraham – to bless all peoples through Abraham's descendents – is fulfilled. He is God's appointed King, indeed, the King of kings, who has enlightened the world with his teaching and example, and whom we all ought to follow as eagerly as the blind beggar who was healed. Jesus is the King who will come again in glory, and his Kingdom, unlike all other kingdoms, will have no end. May our hearts also cry out to him, gladly and confidently, "Son of David, Jesus, have pity on me."

CHRIST THE TEACHER Christ teaches two obvious lessons through this incident. First, he shows us that persistent prayer will find its reward. Bartimaeus knew that the heart of Christ was open to all and full of compassion. He knew that his prayer would be heard, if only he persisted in offering it - and he was right.

Behind this persistence is the second lesson, the lesson of faith. We can only know Christ truly by faith. Bartimaeus knew the heart of Christ so well because he believed in him. He knew him better than those who could see him by the natural light of day, because he saw him by the supernatural light of faith. When we trust in God, we detect his presence, power, and love; when we trust in ourselves, he often seems far away. Without the light of faith, we are blind to the brilliance of God's grace; with faith – which often requires us to go against the pressure of the crowds – our eyes are opened.

Bartimaeus himself teaches us yet a third lesson. The Gospel points out that when Jesus called him, he threw aside his cloak, jumped up, and went to his Lord. The cloak was the most versatile item of Palestinian clothing at the time. It was protection against the rapid and frequent temperature changes, insulation against the harsh Judean winds, and at night it doubled as a blanket. The Fathers of the Church have seen in it a symbol of self-sufficiency, of those things in our lives that we depend on – things that can hold us back when we hear God calling. By leaving it behind, Bartimaeus teaches us that our only sufficiency should be Jesus Christ.

CHRIST THE FRIEND Christ's question to the blind man seems out of place. "What do you want me to do for you?" he queries. What else? Cure him of his blindness, of course! And yet, he lets Bartimaeus ask. He respects the man's freedom and evokes an explicit act of faith. Bartimaeus must have been breathless with excitement and exertion. He must have been disoriented even more than usual after being led about quickly by the disciples who brought him to Jesus. He couldn't see the warmth and gentleness and sincerity of Christ's eyes, so the Lord chose to communicate those things with his voice. The question he asked and the way he asked it stripped away all nervousness, fear, and hesitation. Somehow, Bartimaeus knew immediately that Jesus cared, that Jesus wanted to listen, to help. The brief exchange draws these two hearts together: the beggar is freed from any possible inhibitions and given a chance to bare his deepest longings to the Lord. And the Lord welcomes them, takes them into his own soul, and grants them. It is a prototype of all prayer, which God wants to be eminently personal and sincere. He is our God, and yet he wants to be our ally, our friend, and our confidant. Will we let him?

CHRIST IN MY LIFE Thank you for making me a citizen of your Kingdom. I know and I believe that your Kingdom will never end. You are the Lord of all people and all time. Your Kingdom is growing, little by little, through your Church. Make it grow more, Lord. Make it grow in my heart; make it grow in the hearts of those around me; make me an instrument of its growth…

You have given me the precious gift of faith, Lord. Please grant me as well the gift to persevere until death in this faith. How mysterious it is, that some people believe in you and others refuse to believe! How can I help others believe? Have mercy on us all, Lord; we are small and weak and weighed down with selfishness. Jesus, I trust in you…

Teach me to pray, Lord. I want to stay close to you. Only you have the words of everlasting life. Only you have the wisdom and love that can fill my aching heart. Only you can teach me to be all that you created me to be. Master, let me see again, let all of us see you! You are calling me to come to you, every day, in prayer. Teach me, Lord, to do your will…

QUESTIONS FOR SMALL GROUP DISCUSSION

1. What struck you most in the passage? What did you notice that you hadn't noticed before?

2. Why did the disciples around Jesus try to silence Bartimaeus? Why did Bartimaeus resist them?

3. Why did Jesus have his disciples bring the beggar to him, instead of going over to where he was sitting by the roadside?

4. What are some common "cloaks" that can hold us back from answering the Lord's summons?

Cf. Catechism of the Catholic Church, 153-165 on the importance and characteristics of faith; 27-30 on our need for God; 2558-2567 on prayer as an intimate exchange of hearts

THE GOSPEL OF MARK CHAPTER 11

Man is created to praise, reverence, and serve God our Lord, and by this means to save his soul. All other things on the face of the earth are created for man to help him fulfill the end for which he is created. From this it follows that man is to use these things to the extent that they will help him to attain his end. Likewise, he must rid himself of them in so far as they prevent him from attaining it. Therefore we must make ourselves indifferent to all created things, in so far as it is left to the choice of our free will and is not forbidden. Acting accordingly, for our part, we should not prefer health to sickness, riches to poverty, honor to dishonor, a long life to a short one. And so in all things we should desire and choose only those things that will best help us attain the end for which we are created."

- St Ignatius of Loyola

129. THE PRINCE OF PEACE ATTACKS (MK 11:1-11)

Do you want to speak the praise of God? Be yourselves what you speak. If you live good lives, you are his praise."

- St Augustine

Mark 11:1-10

When they were approaching Jerusalem, in sight of Bethphage and Bethany, close by the Mount of Olives, he sent two of his disciples and said to them, 'Go off to the village facing you, and as soon as you enter it you will find a tethered colt that no one has yet ridden. Untie it and bring it here. If anyone says to you, What are you doing? say, The Master needs it and will send it back here directly.' They went off and found a colt tethered near a door in the open street. As they untied it, some men standing there said, 'What are you doing, untying that colt?' They gave the answer Jesus had told them, and the men let them go. Then they took the colt to Jesus and threw their cloaks on its back, and he sat on it. Many people spread their cloaks on the road, others greenery which they had cut in the fields. And those who went in front and those who followed were all shouting, 'Hosanna! Blessings on him who comes in the name of the Lord! Blessings on the coming kingdom of our father David! Hosanna in the highest heavens!' He entered Jerusalem and went into the Temple. He looked all round him, but as it was now late, he went out to Bethany with the Twelve.

CHRIST THE LORD Many times the Old Testament prophets complemented their prophetic words with prophetic action. Jeremiah walked the streets of Jerusalem with a yoke around his neck in order to illustrate the coming conquest of Judah; Hosea married an unfaithful wife in order to represent the kind of spouse Israel had been to the Lord. On the Sunday before his passion, Jesus follows suit: instead of merely saying, "I am the Messiah you have been waiting for" (which he did in his conversation with the Samaritan woman, for instance), he performs a dramatic gesture that makes the claim for him.

Zechariah had prophesied (Zech 9:9) that the conquering Messiah would come to save Jerusalem riding on a donkey colt. (The donkey was a noble animal in first century Palestine, not merely a servile beast of burden, as we tend to conceive of it.) The greenery and cloaks strewn along his path were reminiscent of the welcome given hundreds of years before to the military kings Jehu and Simon Maccabaeus. The shouts that rang out alluded to the Messianic promises of the Old Testament: "Hosanna," meaning "Save now!" was a cry for the king's help and protection (cf. 2 Samuel 14:4); "him who comes" was a title for the Messiah, just as the "coming kingdom of our father David" was a name for the Messianic kingdom. Every detail of the scene announces that Jesus Christ is the Messiah, the Savior whom long ago God had promised to send his chosen people. If the miracles had not convinced them, if Christ's words had not convinced them, now at least they should have understood that Jesus is God's anointed, the Lord.

CHRIST THE TEACHER Many of Jesus' contemporaries expected the Messiah to be a military conqueror who would liberate Israel from Roman occupation. But Jesus purposely does not come riding on a horse, the mount preferred by kings who rode to war; he comes on a donkey, the traditional mount for kings who come in peace.

The Kingdom of Christ, as the angels had pointed out on Christmas, was one of "peace on earth to men who are God's friends." God sent the Savior to heal the wounds in men's hearts, to repair the injustice that sin had done to mankind's relationship with God. His Kingdom is in hearts, not in swords. He conquers heart by heart, starting with our own. He had explained this many times to his disciples and even to the Pharisees: "Upon being asked by the Pharisees, when the kingdom of God was to come, he answered, The Kingdom of God comes unwatched by men's eyes; there will be no saying, See it is here, or See, it is there; the Kingdom of God is here, within you" (Luke 17:20-21). Christ conquers evil, sin, and selfishness by patience, truth, and sacrificial love – as he would show even more dramatically through the ordeal of Calvary. His Kingdom is "not of this world," which is a lesson that we, like the cheering crowds of Palm Sunday, can too easily forget.

CHRIST THE FRIEND Two details of this passage reiterate the strategy of the Incarnation, God's desire to encounter us in the reality of our humanity.

First, he sends two of his disciples to get the colt. He could have supernaturally inspired the owner of the colt to bring it to him, or he could have had an angel lead the colt to him: instead, he involves his disciples. God does not save us from the outside; he enters into our lives and renews them from within, engaging us in the very work of spreading his heavenly Kingdom on earth.

Second, St Mark points out that this event took place near Bethphage, Bethany, and the Mount of Olives – real geographical locations referred to in other historical documents and, in the case of the Mount of Olives, open to visitors even today. Our God is not somewhere "out there," looking down upon us from some lofty mythological perch. In Christ, God himself enters into our lives, our histories, and our relationships, and he unfolds his loving plans in words and actions that we can perceive with our senses. It is his chosen pedagogical method, perfectly adapted to human nature, a method that continues today through the ministry of his Church: a fully human institution, endowed with divine prerogatives through the power of the Holy Spirit – a historical extension, as it were, of Christ's own incarnation.

CHRIST IN MY LIFE These people were so eager to welcome you, so glad to put their hope in you. And I? Each time I go to Mass, you come once again to your people, to me, as Savior and King. My heart and my mind can be so dulled to it all. I fall into routine, or I blame the priest for being "boring"... Lord, you, your very self, my King and Creator and Redeemer, come to me in the Eucharist. Blessed be your name...

Come again into my heart, Lord. Rule my life from within. Guide me. You are Wisdom itself and Goodness. You know me through and through. You know my desires and my needs. Purify me, put order in my heart, my affections, my hopes. With the love of your heart, purify me Lord...

Do I take advantage of the many ways you wish to fill me with grace through your Church? Do I know the Church, its teachings, its history...? Somewhat. But I tend to take it for granted. Open my eyes to the beauties of your Church; move me to seek you in all the places you wish to be found – the sacraments, the teaching, the saints, the buildings...

QUESTIONS FOR SMALL GROUP DISCUSSION

1. What struck you most in this passage? What did you notice that you hadn't noticed before?

2. What do you think was in Christ's heart and mind during this procession – knowing, as he did, that soon some of these same people would soon clamor for his crucifixion?

3. In what ways are we vulnerable to the temptation of expecting "heaven on earth" as strive to follow Christ?

4. If you had to explain the meaning of Palm Sunday to a non-believing friend who asked you about it, how would you do so?

Cf. Catechism of the Catholic Church, 557-560, 569, 570 on the meaning of Palm Sunday

130. OF FIGS AND FORGIVENESS (MK 11:12-26)

"Nothing is colder than a Christian who does not care for the salvation of others."
- St John Chrysostom

Mark 11:12-25

Next day as they were leaving Bethany, he felt hungry. Seeing a fig tree in leaf some distance away, he went to see if he could find any fruit on it, but when he came up to it he found nothing but leaves; for it was not the season for figs. And he addressed the fig tree. 'May no one ever eat fruit from you again,' he said. And his disciples heard him say this. So they reached Jerusalem and he went into the Temple and began driving out those who were selling and buying there; he upset the tables of the money changers and the chairs of those who were selling pigeons. Nor would he allow anyone to carry anything through the Temple. And he taught them and said, 'Does not scripture say: My house will be called a house of prayer for all the peoples? But you have turned it into a robbers' den.' This came to the ears of the chief priests and the scribes, and they tried to find some way of doing away with him; they were afraid of him because the people were carried away by his teaching. And when evening came he went out of the city. Next morning, as they passed by, they saw the fig tree withered to the roots. Peter remembered. 'Look, Rabbi,' he said to Jesus, 'the fig tree you cursed has withered away.' Jesus answered, 'Have faith in God. I tell you solemnly, if anyone says to this mountain, Get up and throw yourself into the sea, with no hesitation in his heart but believing that what he says will happen, it will be done for him. I tell you therefore: everything you ask and pray for, believe that you have it already, and it will be yours. And when you stand in prayer, forgive whatever you have against anybody, so that your Father in heaven may forgive your failings too.'

CHRIST THE LORD The withering fig tree is another action-parable. In the Old Testament, Israel was compared to a fig tree. The tree, then, stands for the people of the Old Covenant. Jesus' physical hunger images his burning desire for the Chosen People to accept their Messiah by showing forth fruits of repentance, faith, and the good works that faith produces. But as we near the end of Jesus' earthly journey, he knows that the leaders of the people are poised to reject him instead. And the result will be the destruction of the Old Covenant and the establishment of a New Covenant with a New People of God, the Church. This destruction was palpably manifested by the Roman army's conquest and razing of Jerusalem in 70 AD, which the withering fig tree foreshadows.

This striking miracle, therefore, illustrates two remarkable truths about the Lord. First, Jesus knew that he would be rejected by the majority of those he came to save, at least at first. And yet, knowing how they were going to treat him, he still went through with his mission. He loved them more than his own life. Second, Jesus had the power to destroy his enemies instead of letting them have their way with him (if his mere word dried up this tree, surely he could defend himself against the puny power of the Temple guards, if he wanted to), but he decided to submit to their decision anyway. He shows his power now (with the fig tree), as a reminder on the eve of his passion, so as to give his disciples food for thought later. They will reflect on why he didn't use that same power to defend himself, and maybe then they will learn that hard lesson about forgiveness, and come to appreciate even more the goodness and wisdom of their Lord.

CHRIST THE TEACHER The vehemence and effectiveness with which Jesus cleanses the outer Temple area, destroying the business stands that changed pilgrims' money and sold animals for pilgrims' sacrifices, echoes the demonstration of power that withered the fig tree. But it also teaches us what Jesus dislikes most: hypocrisy.

The Temple was meant to be a house of prayer – indeed, this outer courtyard was meant to be a place where Gentiles could come to the one true Temple and pray (thus his quotation of the prophetic text, "a house of prayer for all the peoples"). But the Temple officials had turned it into a mall, and a dishonest mall at that. This is double-faced. It is an external, visible manifestation of the internal, invisible incoherence of the Jewish leaders. They too, like the Temple, were meant to be especially devoted to God and his people, and on the outside they looked the part. But their reaction to Jesus and his teaching, which we will see again throughout the rest of this chapter, shows that their real interest is neither in God nor in the truth. Rather, they care only about maintaining their position of power and influence and about keeping intact their reputations for holiness and intelligence.

Hypocrisy is easier to fall into than we may think. We all are naturally concerned about appearances. We fear others' disdain – maybe not everyone's, but there are some people whose praise and approval it appears we can barely live without. This can lead us to give lip service to what's most important – fidelity to Christ and his friendship, efforts to build up his Kingdom in ourselves and in those around us – while in our behavior we scramble, like the scribes and chief priests, to hang onto our overly prized reputation. We rush through our personal prayer commitments, but we take plenty of time conversing with our boss at work or the popular neighbor down the road, and we easily laugh at their crude jokes and join in a bit of gossip. We throw on whatever clothes are nearby to go to Mass, but we check ourselves in the mirror five or six times before that important meeting at work or lunch at the club, and we tuck our crucifix under our collar too, just in case. Jesus warns against playing that dangerous game; it's much better simply to be who we claim to be.

CHRIST THE FRIEND Peter and the other apostles are awestruck by how fast the fig tree withered. Jesus takes advantage of their shock by issuing a plea for them to put their faith in him. He instructs them about the power of faith-filled prayer: it can obtain anything at all from God's omnipotence. Jesus wants us to trust fully in him, so that he can unleash his power in us. Can you hear his eagerness to work wonders in our lives, his plaintive encouragement to believe in him without reserve? He wants us to approach him with all our needs, hopes, and dreams, which he longs to fulfill.

But there is one condition. In order for our faith in God to be authentic, we have to forgive anyone who has offended us. Failing to forgive is tantamount to putting ourselves in God's place, on the throne of judgment that only he can occupy. And doing that is a flat contradiction of trust in him; if we trusted in him, we would leave judgment up to him and obey his command to forgive. Jesus yearns for us to tap into the unimaginable power of authentic faith-filled prayer that all the saints have discovered, but in order to do so we have to release our self-righteous anger and resentment. To enjoy Christ's friendship fully, we have to be willing to befriend everyone else whom Jesus loves.

CHRIST IN MY LIFE My heart is your Temple, Lord. You want to find sincerity, fidelity, fortitude, patience, humility, and all the other virtues within me. But I think there are still some money changers in there. I am still full of selfishness - uncontrolled desires and unsurrendered fears. Come into my heart and purify me with your passion. Destroy whatever is obstructing your grace in my life…

Whom do I need to forgive, Lord? Never let the bitter poison of self-righteous resentment infect my heart. You have forgiven me – so many times! – for rebelling against you, my Creator and Redeemer. Teach me to forgive those who are unjust or ungrateful towards me. Soften all hearts darkened by hate. Where there is injury, Lord, teach me to sow pardon…

I ask you once again: teach me to pray! Teach me to discover your presence and your will in all the circumstances and events of every day. You never cease drawing me to yourself, sending me gifts and messages of your love, lessons of your wisdom. Open my eyes, Lord! Teach me to pray, to confide in you, to trust in you and throw all my cares upon you…

QUESTIONS FOR SMALL GROUP DISCUSSION

1. What struck you most in this passage? What did you notice that you hadn't noticed before?
2. Considering that the cursing of the fig tree was an action-parable, do you think it was unfair to curse it, since it wasn't the season for figs?
3. What more do you think Jesus could have done to make the scribes and chief priests believe in him? Why did they refuse to believe?
4. How can we help people who refuse to believe receive the gift of faith?

Cf. Catechism of the Catholic Church, 2840 and 2845 on forgiving others so we can be forgiven; 1657 and 2227 on the family as a school for learning forgiveness; 576, 583-586, 593, and 1197 on Christ and the Temple; 2609-2610 on praying with boldness and filial trust

THE GOSPEL OF MARK CHAPTER 12

"Be sure to be warmly affable toward everyone. Speak to and answer everyone with very great gentleness and deference. Keep in mind the way the Lord spoke and replied to others even when he was most harshly treated. Never comment on the faults or the behavior of your neighbors. When others speak of them, put a good interpretation on their actions. If you cannot, say nothing at all. In short, decide never to speak of the failings of others nor to reprimand them no matter how serious they seem to you. When you see someone fall into some fault, call to mind the gospel saying, 'You can see the splinter in your brother's eye, but you cannot see the beam in your own' (Mt 7:3)."

- St John Baptist de la Salle

131. FREE FALL (MK 11:27-12:12)

"His love is grace and faithfulness, mercy and truth! By setting us free from the darkness of sin and death, he has become the firm and unshakeable foundation of the hope of every human being."

- Pope John Paul II

Mark 11:27-12:12

They came to Jerusalem again, and as Jesus was walking in the Temple, the chief priests and the scribes and the elders came to him, and they said to him, 'What authority have you for acting like this? Or who gave you authority to do these things?' Jesus said to them, 'I will ask you a question, only one; answer me and I will tell you my authority for acting like this. John's baptism: did it come from heaven, or from man? Answer me that.' And they argued it out this way among themselves: 'If we say from heaven, he will say, Then why did you refuse to believe him? But dare we say from man?' – they had the people to fear, for everyone held that John was a real prophet. So their reply to Jesus was, 'We do not know.' And Jesus said to them, 'Nor will I tell you my authority for acting like this.'

He went on to speak to them in parables, 'A man planted a vineyard; he fenced it round, dug out a trough for the winepress and built a tower; then he leased it to tenants and went abroad. When the time came, he sent a servant to the tenants to collect from them his share of the produce from the vineyard. But they seized the man, thrashed him and sent him away empty-handed. Next he sent another servant to them; him they beat about the head and treated shamefully. And he sent another and him they killed; then a number of others, and they thrashed some and killed the rest. He had still someone left: his beloved son. He sent him to them last of all. They will respect my son he said. But those tenants said to each other, 'This is the heir. Come on, let us kill him, and the inheritance will be ours.' So they seized him and killed him and threw him out of the vineyard. Now what will the owner of the vineyard do? He will come and make an end of the tenants and give the vineyard to others. Have you not read this text of scripture: It was the stone rejected by the builders that became the keystone. This was the Lord's doing and it is wonderful to see? And they would have liked to arrest him, because they realised that the parable was aimed at them, but they were afraid of the crowds. So they left him alone and went away.

CHRIST THE LORD Few passages in the Gospel show Christ's nobility better than this one. On the one hand, he handles this hypocritical attack, obviously meant to discredit him in the eyes of his followers, with superb composure and astonishing brilliance, but on the other hand, he does so with the gentle delicacy of a surgeon: he avoids compromising the truth, he sidesteps damaging his adversaries' pride, and at the same time he generously gives them a chance to change their rebellious ways and accept him without losing face.

The trap the Jewish leaders laid was subtle. They knew Jesus respected the Jewish authorities and institutions. They also knew that he had banished the money changers from the Temple without prior authorization from the chief priests who had jurisdiction over the Temple area. So they simply ask him by what authority he did this, trying to make him look like a childish, temperamental rabble-rouser. But Jesus turns the tables. He presents them with a dilemma. By whose authority did John the Baptist baptize? He hadn't received his authority from the chief priests either, and yet his work had caused a true spiritual revival in Israel, so it must have been from God. But if so, then what he said about Jesus (that he was the Messiah) was also from God.

You can see Jesus' eager gaze directed at these men as they ponder how they should respond. St Mark tells us what they were thinking – and they got it right. They recognized the subtle lesson Jesus wanted to teach them: he really is the Messiah; it's not too late to accept him. In fact, it was the perfect chance for them to do so, using the occasion as an opportunity to admit that they had never thought about it that way before, thus saving face in the eyes of the crowd. And yet, they still refuse.

Jesus did everything he could to bring his enemies into the fold of truth and light. Only when they stubbornly refused his rule, over and over again, did he honor their wishes and exclude them from his Kingdom. What a noble, generous Lord we have in Jesus! May all his followers prove to be worthy of such a Lord.

CHRIST THE TEACHER As we begin the final showdown between the Jewish leaders (a conglomeration of scribes, Sadducees, Herodians, chief priests, elders, and Pharisees), we touch upon the second greatest mystery of the universe: human freedom. (The first greatest mystery is the Trinity – how one God is three Persons.)

The leaders of the people want to do away with Jesus, because they fear losing the personal advantages they have in the status quo. But here on the threshold of his passion and death, Jesus pours out a flood of teaching that shows fully the mistake they are making. Could the parable in this passage, for instance, be any clearer? The leaders understand exactly what he is saying to them: Jesus is the Son of God, the final and overwhelming gesture of love sent by the Father to win them over to the truth, and though they maybe have lived unfaithful lives up to now, they still have time to reform. And yet, in spite of the blinding clarity of the teaching, in spite of the three years' worth of miracles and exorcisms, in spite of the overwhelming support of the common people, and in spite of Jesus' own riveting personality and undeniable holiness, these men still "would have liked to arrest him," and in their cowardice they simply "left him alone and went away."

How can this be? How can the human soul, created by God to find its fulfillment in God, reject the very God it can't help desiring? Jesus doesn't give us a full answer, probably because only God himself can penetrate this mystery completely. His many confrontations with his enemies make it clear that these men freely chose not to believe in Jesus, because they wanted to cling to their own ideas and way of life, which Jesus' doctrine denounced. But why and how they were able to resist the advances of his love and grace remains a question mark. We who have received the gift of faith can only pray for the hard-hearted, begging the Lord to save them – and us – from a dire fate.

CHRIST THE FRIEND Although this parable applies primarily to the Jewish leaders who through the centuries rejected God's prophets and finally did away with the Messiah, secondarily it applies to the life of every Christian, and every person. The Catechism teaches us that "at every time and in every place God draws close to man" (cf. Catechism of the Catholic Church, 1). He is always reaching out to each one of us. He sends us his messengers in many ways – through the teaching of the Church, the examples of the saints, and the beauties of nature. He offers his grace over and over again, sometimes through simple conversations and invitations and nudges of conscience, other times through suffering and tragedy and interior restlessness. Over and over again Jesus reaches out with his offer of friendship, a friendship that can fill our hearts like no other, a friendship that will only grow brighter, deeper, and more joyful the closer we come to eternity. But, just like in the parable, he will never force us to accept that offer.

In justice we owe him everything, as the tenants owed absolutely everything to the owner of the vineyard. Nevertheless, he demurs from demanding that justice – at least not until he has asked for friendship, over and over and over again.

Jesus: Think back on all the times I have come to you, all the times I have asked you to follow me, to give me something, to show me your love. I am always thinking of you, but you are not always thinking of me. When I send you a message, when I try to get your attention, so often you turn the other way and focus your attention on other things. Am I not the one who loves you? Am I not the one who knows you through and through? Why do you ignore me? Who else can give you what I long to give you?

CHRIST IN MY LIFE I am amazed at you, Lord. Your wisdom, your love, your vigor, your passion, your self-mastery… You are everything I want to be. Fill me with your grace and teach me to follow in your footsteps. May my heart seek instructions only from your Holy Spirit, so that I too can make the Father's glory shine through my words, actions, and example…

I tremble when I think of the power you have placed in my hands by making me free. And yet, I thank you for the gift of freedom! It is my ticket to love, and I want to love you and all those whom you love, giving myself for them, never thinking of my preferences or needs, pouring out this life you have given me in your honor, just as you poured yours out for my salvation…

Many times I have rebelled against your action in my life. Many times I have tried to claim the vineyard for myself. How foolish, how futile! Lord, all I am and all I have come from you. You love me more than I love myself. Forgive my ingratitude. I offer you the fruits of my life, paltry as they are. Take them, Lord, as an offering of justice and of love…

QUESTIONS FOR SMALL GROUP DISCUSSION

1. What struck you most in this passage? What did you notice that you hadn't noticed before?

2. Why didn't Jesus force his enemies to accept the truth of his claims? What lessons can his example teach us for our own efforts at evangelization?

3. What can we do to grow in Christian wisdom and prudence?

4. What are some signs we can look for in our own lives that will tip us off to encroaching hypocrisy and help us get back on track?

Cf. Catechism of the Catholic Church, 1731-1738 on freedom and responsibility; 1742, 1993, 2008 on how God's grace doesn't eliminate human freedom; 587-591 on the refusal of Jerusalem's leaders to accept Jesus

132. KEEPING FIRST THINGS FIRST, AND LAST THINGS TOO (MK 12:13-27)

"The man who is united interiorly to the Son of the living God also bears Christ's image in his outward behavior."

- St Paul of the Cross

Mark 12:13-27

Next they sent to him some Pharisees and some Herodians to catch him out in what he said. These came and said to him, 'Master, we know you are an honest man, that you are not afraid of anyone, because a man's rank means nothing to you, and that you teach the way of God in all honesty. Is it permissible to pay taxes to Caesar or not? Should we pay, yes or no?' Seeing through their hypocrisy he said to them, 'Why do you set this trap for me? Hand me a denarius and let me see it.' They handed him one and he said, 'Whose head is this? Whose name?' 'Caesar's' they told him. Jesus said to them, 'Give back to Caesar what belongs to Caesar – and to God what belongs to God.' This reply took them completely by surprise. Then some Sadducees – who deny that there is a resurrection – came to him and they put this question to him, 'Master, we have it from Moses in writing, if a man's brother dies leaving a wife but no child, the man must marry the widow to raise up children for his brother. Now there were seven brothers. The first married a wife and then died leaving no children. The second married the widow, and he too died leaving no children; with the third it was the same, and none of the seven left any children. Last of all the woman herself died. Now at the resurrection, when they rise again, whose wife will she be, since she had been married to all seven?' Jesus said to them, 'Is not the reason why you go wrong, that you understand neither the scriptures nor the power of God? For when they rise from the dead, men and women do not marry; no, they are like the angels in heaven. Now about the dead rising again, have you never read in the Book of Moses, in the passage about the Bush, how God spoke to him and said: I am the God of Abraham, the God of Isaac and the God of Jacob? He is God, not of the dead, but of the living. You are very much mistaken.'

CHRIST THE LORD Jesus' patience is remarkable. His enemies have been provoking him and trying to trip him up since the very beginning of his public ministry. Here in the Temple as his passion approaches, they increase their efforts, and Jesus continues to meet them on their own ground, bearing with their false flattery and subtle traps alike. He understands their questions, their motives, and their process of argumentation. He enters into it, putting the truth in terms that they would understand clearly. He corrects them without condemning them – repeatedly.

Judging from the quickness and intelligence of his replies, it is clear that, if he had wanted to, he could have publicly humiliated them. Another man with equal superiority and less love would have done so. But Jesus isn't interested in elevating himself by criticizing and disgracing others. He yearns for them to accept the truth. So he argues with them, responds to them, and patiently abides their malice and obstinacy. Only when they have definitively closed themselves off will he denounce them – and even then, the denouncement will be couched in such a way that it is presented as a warning to the crowds instead of a face-to-face denunciation – he will turn to the multitude and exhort them to steer clear of hypocrisy, lest their hearts too shut out the light.

The Lord seeks to conquer, but he conquers only to save.

CHRIST THE TEACHER Two lessons emerge from this exchange. The first has to do with how Christ's everlasting Kingdom, present here in embryonic form through the Church, is related to the passing human kingdoms where Christians live their daily lives. In dodging the Pharisees' subtle attack (they wanted him to denounce Caesar so they could report him to the Roman authorities as a dangerous revolutionary), Jesus indicates that his followers are to be responsible citizens of this world, while at the same time giving priority to their relationship with God. The coin bore Caesar's image, but the human soul bears God's image. The latter duty, therefore, will take precedence in case of irreconcilable conflicts. This lesson was lived out magnificently in the first three centuries of the Church's existence, as generation after generation of Christians – who were model citizens in every way – refused to give divine honor to the Roman emperor, even in the face of death. As Christians, our first allegiance must always be to Christ and his Church; for us, Sunday, not Saturday night, is the high point of the week.

The second lesson has to do with heaven. We will have our bodies in heaven, but they will be different. At the final judgment, we will all receive our bodies back; we will not be angels (who are pure spirit by nature) for all eternity. Nevertheless, Jesus goes on to teach us that God's power will somehow transform those resurrected bodies. Life in heaven will not be the same as life on earth; we will be in direct communion with God, like the angels. We will be fully human, with body and soul (and so at our entrance into the Kingdom at the end of time, Jesus will welcome us both body and soul), but our humanity will have been swept up into a much grander and more magnificent adventure than we could ever have imagined. Jesus talked a lot about heaven. It may do us good to give it a bit more thought and to ask the Holy Spirit to give us some insights.

CHRIST THE FRIEND Jesus points out that the Lord "is God, not of the dead, but of the living." Mull that over. God gave us life, and he wants us to live life to the full. Later in the New Testament, Jesus even sums up his whole mission by saying, "I have come so that they may have life, and have it to the full" (John 10:10). When Jesus looks at us and thinks of us (which he never stops doing), that's what he sees: the fullness of life that each of us long for. All that he has done and continues to do has this same aim – our fulfillment. In growing into human and spiritual maturity and experiencing the meaning, joy, and wisdom such maturity entails, we give him glory, just as the mature fig tree gives God glory by bearing luscious, tasty figs. He is the God of life, the God who wants us to live life to the hilt. If only we would follow his will more closely!

CHRIST IN MY LIFE You patiently endure your enemies' attacks, just as you patiently endure my superficiality, infidelities, and persistent selfishness. How I long to have a heart like yours! Teach me to care more about your Kingdom than my comfort, and teach me to think as much about others' needs and desires as I do about my own…

What will heaven be like, Lord? Are the earthly joys you give me any indication? I know that the law of heaven is love. So there I will be free to love to the full, as you created me to. Everyone will be fully loving. Love yields joy, fruitfulness…

I think about you thinking about me. Knowing that you see me only through the eyes of love makes me smile. It gives me such pleasure, Lord, to know that you are always thinking of me. Whatever you permit in my life, whatever you ask of me, it always has one purpose: to fulfill your dream for me, making my life overflow with your goodness. Thank you, Lord, for thinking of me and for coming to give me the fullness of life…

QUESTIONS FOR SMALL GROUP DISCUSSION

1. What struck you most in this passage? What did you notice that you hadn't noticed before?

2. What relevance does the doctrine of the Resurrection have for your daily life?

3. Some people maintain that Christianity's exclusion of marriage from heaven demeans marriage even here on earth. How would you respond to such an argument?

4. How would you explain the Christian idea of heaven to a non-believing friend who asked you about it?

Cf. Catechism of the Catholic Church, 1042-1050 on heaven; 326, 1024-1026, 2794-2795, 2802 on the significance of heaven; 1601-1620 on marriage in God's plan

133. LIFESTYLE BY CHRIST (MK 12:28-37)

"For our sakes he suffered all the agonies of body and mind, and did not shrink from any torment. He gave us a perfect example of patience and love."

- St Francis of Paola

Mark 12:28-37

One of the scribes who had listened to them debating and had observed how well Jesus had answered them, now came up and put a question to him, 'Which is the first of all the commandments?' Jesus replied, 'This is the first: Listen, Israel, the Lord our God is the one Lord, and you must love the Lord your God with all your heart, with all your soul, with all your mind and with all your strength. The second is this: You must love your neighbour as yourself. There is no commandment greater than these.' The scribe said to him, 'Well spoken, Master; what you have said is true: that he is one and there is no other. To love him with all your heart, with all your understanding and strength, and to love your neighbour as yourself, this is far more important than any holocaust or sacrifice.' Jesus, seeing how wisely he had spoken, said, 'You are not far from the kingdom of God.' And after that no one dared to question him any more.

Later, while teaching in the Temple, Jesus said, 'How can the scribes maintain that the Christ is the son of David? David himself, moved by the Holy Spirit, said: The Lord said to my Lord: Sit at my right hand and I will put your enemies under your feet. David himself calls him Lord, in what way then can he be his son?' And the great majority of the people heard this with delight.

CHRIST THE LORD This is the last in a series of questions that the "experts" in

Jerusalem posed in order to discredit Jesus. Their efforts failed. In the end, "no one dared to question him anymore."

Sometimes we become so familiar with the figure of Christ as he appears in the Gospels that we forget the surpassing dignity and authority of his personality. If we were to meet him on the street, we would immediately sense something about him that set him completely apart. If we were to engage in a conversation with him in an airport waiting area or at a bus station, we would be impressed and attracted by the magnetism and quiet strength of his character. We should try to picture the marvelous figure of the Lord as he vanquishes Israel's most intelligent and powerful leaders in this battle of wits. These elite intellectuals and trendsetters intimidated the average citizen into obsequious obedience and cowering respect, but they met their match in the Lord.

CHRIST THE TEACHER Jesus' first lesson in this passage came in linking forever the commandment to love God with the commandment to love one's neighbor as oneself. If all we did in our spiritual lives were to strive to our utmost to fulfill these commandments, we would very soon be saints.

In Jesus' time, this answer was most likely surprising because it put love for neighbor on par with love for God. No one had ever done that before; everyone simply agreed that loving God came first. In our day, perhaps the more surprising aspect is the priority Jesus gives to loving God. The postmodern world has, in many ways, given up on the idea of God. The sheer quantity of religions and denominations and their inability to agree on doctrines has created a cynical indifference to God. What the seculars do agree about, however, is the importance of loving one's neighbor. Tolerance, diversity, random acts of kindness: these are things we can sink our teeth into, so they say. And yet, is it really possible to make the sustained effort necessary for a truly Christian love of neighbor without staying connected to the reason why our neighbor ought to be loved? If I don't love the God in whose image my neighbor is created, how long and how deeply can I really love my neighbor?

After exhorting his listeners to love, Jesus right away backs up his words with a deed. He has silenced his detractors, having answered all the questions they put to him; now he asks a question of his own. If they had been sincere in their questioning, by his answers they would have already recognized in him the Messiah, but instead they only seethed with resentment. So Jesus gives them yet another chance. He quotes a passage from the Psalms that implies that the Messiah will not only be a descendent of King David, but will also be somehow superior to the great king. He is turning their minds to the Old Testament scriptures in order to open their minds to his New Testament claims. It was a generous move, one they didn't deserve, giving them one last chance to think things through. He really did practice what he preached: he loved his neighbors, even his enemies, until the end, when he tried to win over their hearts with the warmth of the truth.

CHRIST THE FRIEND By the response of this questioner, we can tell that he was not a hypocrite, like Jesus' other interrogators. Perhaps he had his suspicions about this rabbi from Galilee who was making such a stir in Jerusalem, and so he came to find out for himself if Jesus was just another flash-in-the-pan demagogue or the real thing. So he poses a question that makes the perfect litmus test: which is the greatest commandment? The commandments that governed Israel's relationship with God were many. The Jewish leaders at the time of Christ were in an ongoing discussion about the relative importance of them. The most influential rabbinic schools agreed that "You shall love the Lord your God with all your heart, soul, mind, and strength" was indeed the greatest of all commandments. If Jesus had stated something else, this scribe would have known that he could not be trusted.

But, much to the inquirer's delight, Jesus gives him the right answer – expressing it forcibly. And the scribe acknowledges Christ's wisdom and acumen, reiterating the answer in his own words (the hypocritical Pharisees would never have done something like that). And because of this sincerity and sound conviction, Christ approves of the scribe and encourages him to continue serving God as he has been doing. We can almost hear the surprised pleasure in Christ's voice, finally having found a leader in Israel who cares more for what is true than for power and prestige. We can also imagine the surprised satisfaction of the scribe at receiving such a glowing commendation from Jesus. What started as a cold, suspicious encounter became the planting of the seed of friendship.

When we come to the Lord with a sincere, open heart, we will always find a welcome – after all, that's why he came, to give seeking hearts an everlasting home.

CHRIST IN MY LIFE I am sure you have much more you want to teach me, more you want me to do. But I can't help wondering: am I really listening to you? Or am I kind of like the Pharisees, who had plenty of contact with you but were so absorbed by their own plans, hopes, and ideas that their minds were closed to what you had to say? O Jesus, open my eyes; let me hear you and follow you…

You make things so simple, Lord. All I have to do is love God with all my strength, and love my neighbor as myself. How I long to want only that in life! That is what you created me for. You are infinitely loveable, the source of all good things. And my neighbor – all my neighbors, without exception, are created by you and loved by you. O Jesus, make my heart overflow with love…

Teach me to pray, Lord. I know I have asked you this before, but I ask again: really teach me to pray, please. I long for your wisdom to shed its light in my mind. I long for your love to inflame my heart. I long for your strength to steel my weak will…. You have called me to be your apostle – now please, make me what you want me to be…

QUESTIONS FOR SMALL GROUP DISCUSSION

1. What struck you most in this passage? What did you notice that you hadn't noticed before?

2. These two commandments are meant to be the basic program for every Christian's life. What would you say makes up the basic program for life as expressed in popular culture?

3. What can we do to make our love for God grow – to make it the occupation of "all our heart, mind, soul, and strength"?

4. How can we "love our neighbors as ourselves" more effectively? How can we avoid being so wrapped up in our own plans and problems that everyone else fades into the background?

Cf. Catechism of the Catholic Church, 1822-1829, 2086, 2093-2094 on the love of God; 1878 on the love of neighbor; 2096-2097 on worship and adoration; and 2031 on the union of love of God and neighbor in the Eucharist

134. A MIGHTY HEART (MK 12:38-44)

"… You have been created for the glory of God and for you own eternal salvation; this is your end, this is the object of your soul and the treasure of your heart."

- St Robert Bellarmine

Mark 12:38-44

In his teaching he said, 'Beware of the scribes who like to walk about in long robes, to be greeted obsequiously in the market squares, to take the front seats in the synagogues and the places of honour at banquets; these are the men who swallow the property of widows, while making a show of lengthy prayers. The more severe will be the sentence they receive.' He sat down opposite the treasury and watched the people putting money into the treasury, and many of the rich put in a great deal. A poor widow came and put in two small coins, the equivalent of a penny. Then he called his disciples and said to them, 'I tell you solemnly, this poor widow has put more in than all who have contributed to the treasury; for they have all put in money they had over, but she from the little she had has put in everything she possessed, all she had to live on.'

CHRIST THE LORD The scribes were the experts in interpreting the Law of Moses (the Pharisees were the experts in upholding it), and the Law of Moses was the heart of Jewish culture; it separated the Jews from all other peoples. Therefore, the people of Israel respected and reverenced the scribes. But Jesus was unhappy with them. Their natural intellectual gifts (the Law and its voluminous commentaries were no Dr Seuss picture book!) and elevated social function had gone to their heads. Instead of exercising their leadership as a service to the nation and to their neighbors, they were flaunting it to stoke their vanity, increase their comfort, and enhance their reputation. No figure earned Christ's disdain more than the proud, self-seeking religious leader, because no other figure so disfigures people's idea of God, and a disfigured idea of God will alienate people from him (as the devil knew even way back in the Garden of Eden). Christ's entire life, and especially his death, was the proclamation of a different type of religion, and a different style of leadership: a religion of intimacy with God, and a leadership of sincere, sacrificial service.

The scribes felt they were being generous with God by giving him their money, their knowledge, and their talents – all those things they had received from him in the first place. What God truly wants is something different. We can only give the Lord one thing that he really needs and desires: our love. Out of love, we can trust him, like the poor widow; we can seek to know him and make him known. This is the gift most worthy of the Lord.

CHRIST THE TEACHER The lesson is plain – no parable here: "Beware of the scribes." We have seen why the scribes are in trouble (because of their selfish, abusive religious leadership), but why should we beware of them? Jesus knows that his disciples will become religious leaders. Every Christian by virtue of their baptism is called to be a leader of souls, an evangelizer, a prophet of the gospel to the world in word and in deed. Therefore, we will be exposed to the same temptation to which the scribes succumbed: self-righteousness. How easy it is to consider oneself superior to others for all the wrong reasons! Because we are faithful to the true teaching of the Church; because we follow liturgical norms with perfection; because we don't wear risqué clothes; because we don't engage in this or that type of behavior; because we say our prayers and go to

Mass… if God has kept us so close to him in these ways, can we congratulate ourselves? Rather, we ought to thank him, and all the more energetically reach out to those around us who need God's grace and are far from it. "Beware of the scribes," because it is so very easy to become self-indulgently religious, and that's the first step to idolatry. May God preserve us from becoming scribes like them.

CHRIST THE FRIEND Some supposed friends are dazzled by appearances. For them, being in the right social circles matters more than deep bonds of trust and love. Christ is not among them. He is not impressed by the flashy shows of the rich almsgivers; he looks to the heart. He looks to our hearts – he wants to find openness there, confidence in God, generosity in following and serving him. The poor widow gave all she had to the Lord, and it was pleasing to him; the popular, wealthy folks made huge donations – that didn't even make them feel the pinch – in order to pump up their egos. This saddened the Lord. He wants our hearts and our hopes, because he wants to fill them with the meaning and love that only he can give. He wants the gift of our friendship, so that he can give his in return.

The poor widow: Whenever I had any coins left over after buying my daily bread, I always put them in the box at the Temple. What did I want with extra coins? The Lord was my shepherd, and he never took his eye off me. Once when I was a young wife I thought to myself that it might be nice to have a lot of extra money and beautiful clothes and a palace to live in. But then I thought, well, I can't take any of that with me. And besides, doesn't the whole world belong to me? Am I not one of God's chosen people? He is enough for me. He always was.

CHRIST IN MY LIFE Do the people in my life see your goodness reflected in how I treat them? The scribes and Pharisees thought they were glorifying you, but in fact they were displeasing you and driving other people away from you. How could they have been so blind! Lord, I don't want to be blind. Please keep me humble; please keep me true…

Success in your eyes is so different than success in the world's eyes. Both ideas of success blend together in my own mind. Make yours win out, Lord, so that I always can love as you love. You are faithful and wise. Never let me fall into the hypocrisy of caring more about my status in others' eyes than about your status in their hearts…

Thank you for giving me faith and the precious gift of your friendship. This is my treasure. I know you will never take it away. You who placed the stars in the sky and carved out the ocean depths are at my beck and call. Whenever I call your name, you listen to me. What more can I desire, Lord? Thank you. I trust in you. Thy will be done…

QUESTIONS FOR SMALL GROUP DISCUSSION

1. What struck you most in this passage? What did you notice that you hadn't noticed before?

2. In what ways do we tend to fall into the self-righteousness Christ warns us about?

3. Christ praised the widow for holding nothing back from God. In today's society, what types of things do we tend to hold back most? Why is it so difficult for us to tithe as the Church recommends?

4. Why does Jesus care more about the heart than about appearances?

Cf. Catechism of the Catholic Church, 571-591 on Jesus' relationship with the Jewish leaders; 2558-2565 on prayer as a personal encounter between God and the soul

THE GOSPEL OF MARK CHAPTER 13

"Would that mortal men might know how wonderful is divine grace, how beautiful, how precious; what riches are hidden therein, what treasures, what joys, what delights. If they but knew, surely they would direct their energy with all care and diligence to procuring sufferings and afflictions for themselves. Instead of good fortune all men everywhere would seek out troubles, illnesses and suffering that they might obtain the inestimable treasure of grace. This is the final profit to be gained from patient endurance. No one would complain about the cross or about hardships coming seemingly by chance upon him, if he realized in what balance they are weighted before being distributed to men."

- St Rose of Lima

135. BATTLE READY (MK 13:1-13)

"If God sends you tribulation, you ought to endure it, giving thanks, realizing that it is for your good, and that, perhaps, you have deserved it."

- St Louis

Mark 13:1-13

As he was leaving the Temple one of his disciples said to him, 'Look at the size of those stones, Master! Look at the size of those buildings!' And Jesus said to him, 'You see these great buildings? Not a single stone will be left on another: everything will be destroyed.' And while he was sitting facing the Temple, on the Mount of Olives, Peter, James, John and Andrew questioned him privately, 'Tell us, when is this going to happen, and what sign will there be that all this is about to be fulfilled?'

Then Jesus began to tell them, 'Take care that no one deceives you. Many will come using my name and saying, I am he, and they will deceive many. When you hear of wars and rumours of wars, do not be alarmed, this is something that must happen, but the end will not be yet. For nation will fight against nation, and kingdom against kingdom. There will be earthquakes here and there; there will be famines. This is the beginning of the birthpangs. Be on your guard: they will hand you over to sanhedrins; you will be beaten in synagogues; and you will stand before governors and kings for my sake, to bear witness before them, since the Good News must first be proclaimed to all the nations. And when they lead you away to hand you over, do not worry beforehand about what to say; no, say whatever is given to you when the time comes, because it is not you who will be speaking: it will be the Holy Spirit. Brother will betray brother to death, and the father his child; children will rise against their parents and have them put to death. You will be hated by all men on account of my name; but the man who stands firm to the end will be saved.'

CHRIST THE LORD Jesus describes the events that will take place before the fall of Jerusalem (70 AD) – wars, famines, false Messianic movements, and natural disasters. And then he says something curious: "Do not be alarmed; this is something that must happen…" He calls these horrible sufferings the beginning of the birth pangs. In a post-original sin world, new life can't emerge without birth pangs. Just so, the fullness of Christ's Kingdom can't emerge from history without these tragedies.

Somehow, Christ's lordship over history includes these types of events. They are needed in order to shake people lose from their petty desires of merely earthly happiness. This was the desire that had led to original sin – Adam and Eve tried to achieve total fulfillment by their own unaided efforts – and this is the desire that must be uprooted in order to make way for Christ's New Creation. Experiencing the passing nature of earthly realities does the uprooting. Jesus is at work in the midst of the horrors of human history, turning the bitter fruits of original sin into medicine for eternal life.

The apostles were mesmerized by the beauty of the Temple, just as we so easily become too attached to our earthly pleasures and achievements, but all such things are destined to pass away. Jesus is teaching us to set our sights on something higher, something that will last forever. That way, we won't be alarmed by this world's tragedies, and we will be able to "stand firm to the end" and be saved. We'll be able to enter fully into the Kingdom of the Lord who is greater than history, because he rules history.

CHRIST THE TEACHER Imagine the apostles' reaction to Christ's predictions of their suffering. He tells them they will be arrested and turned in to the authorities; they will be publicly beaten; they will be put on trial in front of the world's most powerful leaders; they will experience betrayal at the hands of loved ones; they will be universally hated because they are Christ's followers… Not exactly the rosiest of job descriptions. All those things came to pass in the lives of the apostles, who brought Christ's teachings and grace to the ends of the known world at the time, but suffered torments and martyrdoms because of it. And the same warnings apply to all Christians.

Christ's lesson on the eve of his passion is precisely this: his followers will be asked to bear their crosses in union with the Crucified One. The fallen world violently rejected Christ, and until the final regeneration at the end of time, the same world will continually do violence to Christ's followers and his Church. Tradition calls the members of Christ's family who are still battling here on earth the Church Militant. It can be no other way; the criteria of selfishness will only give way to the criteria of Christ gradually, kicking and screaming, like a spoiled child who wants his own way. We are a fighting Church (whose greatest weapon of offense and defense is Christian charity); we should expect opposition. Jesus wants us to be ready: "Be on your guard," he tells us. How much peace of mind we would have in the midst of life's difficulties if we really took his admonishment to heart!

CHRIST THE FRIEND Amidst these dire predictions, we hear a word of comfort and strength. Jesus tells us, "Do not worry beforehand about what to say" when we are brought into tight spots because of our faith. We are his followers, his ambassadors. If our fidelity to him leads us into difficulties, will he abandon us? *Could* he abandon us? Certainly not. This has been the experience of the Church's thousands of martyrs through the centuries. In the face of cruelty, torture, injustice, intimidation, and death, their faith filled them with a courage and an eloquence that repeatedly turned their apparent defeats into occasions of winning more converts to Christ. The hotter the crucible and the tighter the spot, the brighter they shone and the firmer their faith became.

Wherever our journey of faith leads us, however the enemies of the Kingdom may assail us, the Holy Spirit will always be with us. Jesus is the most faithful of friends. We have absolutely nothing to fear if we stay close to him. "The Lord is my shepherd… Though I pass through a gloomy valley, I fear no harm; beside me your rod and your staff are there, to hearten me" (Psalm 23). How he yearns to be everything for us, so that our lives can be all that he created them to be!

471

CHRIST IN MY LIFE You have the whole world in your firm, wise, and loving grasp. Nothing happens without your permission. You are working everything out for the best. How hard it is for me to believe this sometimes! Speak these words to my heart, just as you spoke to your apostles: "Be on your guard… Do not be alarmed… Do not worry…" Jesus, I trust in you…

You have walked the way of the cross before me, because you want to be my strength as I follow after you. Somehow, this is part of the story. You send me crosses so I can exercise my love. You teach me that love is the currency of your Kingdom, the secret to meaning and fruitfulness, the key to lasting joy. May I give my life to you through whatever martyrdom you call me to…

You are my good shepherd. How could I ever lack anything? I am such a jittery sheep, Lord. Stay close to me. In your goodness, in your wisdom, guide me and never let me stray from your side. You will lead my soul to grassy meadows and clear, refreshing streams. You are faithful, you are true, and I put my hope in you…

QUESTIONS FOR SMALL GROUP DISCUSSION

1. What struck you most in this passage? What did you notice that you hadn't noticed before?

2. What has your experience of suffering for Christ been like? What has the experience of others you know or have heard of suffering for Christ been like?

3. Why do you think Jesus didn't reveal to his Church the exact date of his second coming and the end of history?

4. In what ways does popular culture encourage us to have Christ's visions of the good things of this world? In what ways does it discourage that view?

Cf. Catechism of the Catholic Church, 1130 on sacraments and Christ's second coming; 1179-1186 on the new Temple (where the Church's liturgy is celebrated); 2816-2812 on the nature of Christ's Kingdom

136. HISTORY UNVEILED (MK 13:14-27)

"The final age of the world has already come upon us. The renovation of the world has already been irrevocably decreed and in this age is already anticipated in some real way."
- Second Vatican Council, Lumen Gentium, 48

Mark 13:14-27

'When you see the disastrous abomination set up where it ought not to be (let the reader understand), then those in Judaea must escape to the mountains; if a man is on the housetop, he must not come down to go into the house to collect any of his belongings; if a man is in the fields, he must not turn back to fetch his cloak.

Alas for those with child, or with babies at the breast, when those days come! Pray that this may not be in winter. For in those days there will be such distress as, until now, has not been equalled since the beginning when God created the world, nor ever will be again. And if the Lord had not shortened that time, no one would have survived; but he did shorten the time, for the sake of the elect whom he chose. And if anyone says to you then, Look, here is the Christ or, Look, he is there, do not believe it; for false Christs and false prophets will arise and produce signs and portents to deceive the elect, if that were possible. You therefore must be on your guard. I have forewarned you of everything. But in those days, after that time of distress, the sun will be darkened, the moon will lose its brightness, the stars will come falling from heaven and the powers in the heavens will be shaken. And then they will see the Son of Man coming in the clouds with great power and glory; then too he will send the angels to gather his chosen from the four winds, from the ends of the world to the ends of heaven.'

CHRIST THE LORD This discourse takes place as St Mark's Gospel is reaching its climax, when Jesus and his apostles are relaxing on the Mount of Olives overlooking Jerusalem after a busy day teaching and contending with the rabbis in the Temple. Jesus knows that the culmination of his earthly mission is drawing near (echoed in the liturgy by the approaching end of another liturgical year – the passage is read in the Church at the end of Ordinary Time), and he takes advantage of a comment by his disciples about the glory of the Jewish temple to point out to them the passing nature of all worldly glories.

We can picture the Lord explaining these coming events, almost seeing them unfold in his mind's eye, as the disciples stare at him, hardly daring to believe what he is saying, wondering exactly what he means. He speaks of these future events with a sureness and clarity that we have come to expect, but which must have been alarming – if not frightening – for his disciples. If we read these words as if we were hearing them for the first time, we can better understand the sense of urgency that the first Christians had about spreading the gospel. The Lord is speaking about the end as if it's right around the corner, which it is – if not the end of history, at least the end of each of our lives – and he wants his followers to live with that in mind. This is no casual observation; our Lord tells us, "I have forewarned you of everything…" As his faithful followers we know all we need to know about the future – more than enough to keep us focused, balanced, and purposeful in the present.

CHRIST THE TEACHER In this conversation with his apostles Jesus is speaking primarily and literally of the coming destruction of Jerusalem, which occurred before the passing of the disciples' generation in 70 AD. He warns them that the days when the Roman army lays siege to Jerusalem will be full of horrific suffering. It came to pass just as he said. More than a million Jews died in that final rebellion and siege, and only about 30,000 survived, according to the contemporary historian Josephus. But Jesus affirms that the Lord will be in control even of that tragedy – he will "shorten the time" for the inscrutable purposes of his wisdom.

But Jesus goes on to describe "those days" using another kind of language. He speaks of the sun being darkened, the moon going out, stars falling and heaven shaken, the Son of Man coming on clouds, angels gathering the chosen from the ends of the earth… This is the language used by the prophets (and other spiritual writers of the time) to refer to the end of the Old Covenant and the establishment of the promised Messianic Kingdom. In the first part of the discourse Jesus was preparing his disciples for the destruction of Jerusalem and the Temple, and now he is explaining what that coming destruction means. It will be the visible sign that the New Covenant has fulfilled and supplanted the Old Covenant. The apostles, on whom Jesus builds his Church, his New Covenant community, are to be messengers of the end-times, because the New Covenant issues in the last period of human history, which will draw to its close when Jesus comes again to administer the final judgment, banish evil forever, and recreate the heavens and the earth.

In this context, all of Jesus' predictions of disasters and wars and suffering apply directly to the coming destruction of Jerusalem, as the visible inauguration of the end-times, the age of the Church. But they also apply as a kind of pattern for what will continue to happen throughout the age of the Church until the culmination of history. Thus, the lesson he wants the apostles to learn – that they should live with the clear awareness that this life is a time for mission, not for idleness or indulgence – applies equally to all Christians throughout history. They did not know the exact "day or hour" that Jerusalem would be destroyed, but they knew that before it happened the Church would spread throughout the world, winning converts from the four corners of the globe, and they knew they would suffer in myriad ways. Just so, we do not know the exact day or hour that our lives will end, nor do we know when Jesus will wrap up human history as a whole, but do we know that in the meantime the Kingdom will continue to grow and suffer growing pains, in us and throughout the world. Jesus wants us to live with this in mind.

CHRIST THE FRIEND Some critics claim that passages like this were later additions to the Gospels, since they depict Christ as harsh and demanding, not gentle and forgiving. But if Christ knew that he would be coming again "to judge the living and the dead," it would have been cruel *not* to tell us about it. Because he wants to be able to reward us at the end of our earthly pilgrimage, he constantly reminds us to keep first things first while we are still on our way. Sometimes true friends need to be demanding – and Christ is nothing if not a true friend.

His coming in this life already gives us a foretaste of what it will be like at the end. Every time he leads us further along the path of discipleship, it entails some kind of destruction, some kind of loss. A habit of sin, a sinful tendency, an inordinate attachment – to follow Christ more closely, to know and love him better, requires become a new creation, over and over again, and that means leaving the old behind, letting it be destroyed by the flow of God's renewing grace.

CHRIST IN MY LIFE I am envious of the apostles, Lord. They had you at their side; they could hear your voice and see your face as you taught them. I want to know you better. I know you are always speaking to my heart and guiding me, but I am so hard of hearing! Lord Jesus, teach me to do your will, teach me to follow your path, teach me to hear your voice always and everywhere…

This world is so beautiful and full of so many good things. Thank you for this life, this earth, and the many blessings you never fail to shower upon me. And yet, you are leading me to something much more beautiful. Why do I think of it so rarely? You are looking forward to welcoming me into your heavenly Kingdom. Thy Kingdom come…

I believe in you. I believe that you are the Lord of life and history, that you are the way, the truth, and the life. I believe that you will come again to judge the living and the dead. I believe that you love me and have revealed the path of salvation to me through the Church. I believe in you, Lord; now help me to put my faith into action…

QUESTIONS FOR SMALL GROUP DISCUSSION

1. What struck you most in this passage? What did you notice that you hadn't noticed before?

2. Following Christ's own indications, the Church teaches that "before Christ's second coming the Church must pass through a final trial that will shake the faith of many believers." (Catechism of the Catholic Church, 675) How can we prepare ourselves for this, in case it happens in our lifetime?

3. How should the doctrine that Christ will come again and history will end affect our daily lives?

4. If we knew that the end of the world (or the end of our world – death) would come tomorrow, how would that change the way we live today?

Cf. Catechism of the Catholic Church, 668-682 on Christ's second coming; the order of events preceding it; and the last judgment

137. STAYING READY (MK 13:28-37)

"Not all of us are called to undergo martyrdom, but we are all called to a life of Christian virtue. Now virtue demands courage… It demands from us daily, assiduous, unremitting effort to our very last breath, and so it can be called a slow and continuous martyrdom."

- *Pope Pius XII*

Mark 13:28-37

'Take the fig tree as a parable: as soon as its twigs grow supple and its leaves come out, you know that summer is near. So with you when you see these things happening: know that he is near, at the very gates. I tell you solemnly, before this generation has passed away all these things will have taken place. Heaven and earth will pass away, but my words will not pass away. 'But as for that day or hour, nobody knows it, neither the angels of heaven, nor the Son; no one but the Father. Be on your guard, stay awake, because you never know when the time will come. It is like a man travelling abroad: he has gone from home, and left his servants in charge, each with his own task; and he has told the doorkeeper to stay awake. So stay awake, because you do not know when the master of the house is coming, evening, midnight, cockcrow, dawn; if he comes unexpectedly, he must not find you asleep. And what I say to you I say to all: Stay awake!'

CHRIST THE LORD Christ is the "master of the house," but ever since he ascended into heaven (forty days after his resurrection), he has ruled through his "servants." The Church is Christ's household, and all its members (i.e., us) are his servants. This passage (read in the Church on this first Sunday of Advent, the beginning of the new liturgical year) reminds us that this present arrangement will not last forever, and when the Lord returns he will hope to find each of us working hard at whatever chores we have been assigned.

People often accuse Christianity of self-contradiction: it claims that the Savior has already come into the world, and yet the world (and even some Christians) is still full of suffering, evil, and sin. What kind of a Savior would leave the world no better than he found it? Yet, Christ has consciously chosen to insert the "age of the Church" between his first and second coming. In this age, every human person is given the opportunity to please God and merit a heavenly reward by following Christ. As vehemently asserted in this passage, Christ the Lord longs for us to use this opportunity well, and we have no one to blame but ourselves if we don't.

CHRIST THE TEACHER Christ keeps things simple – the better for us to understand them. In these few lines, he provides a snapshot of what it means to be a Christian. To follow Christ is to honor him by serving and obeying the Church (the "house"). Each of us is a member of this household, and our membership constitutes the most important aspect of our lives on earth. If we live accordingly, we will be ready to welcome him when he comes again. If we neglect to "watch," however, and let other concerns take precedence over our relationship with God in the Church, we may be unpleasantly surprised by the eventual outcome. So simple – and yet, at times so difficult!

Exactly when these events will occur is shrouded in mystery; no one but the Father knows. We can only recognize the signs that they are on the way in general, broad strokes (thus the fig tree analogy). What Jesus wants to make sure his apostles understand is that his second coming *will* occur, and he wants them to be ready for it at all times: "Be watchful! Be alert! You do not know when the time will come." We do not know, because we do not need to know. God has seen fit to assure us that history has a purpose, that it will come to an end, and that we should always keep this eventuality in mind. Through the ages, many Christians have become obsessed with the details of how and when this will occur, often neglecting the whole point of this datum of revelation. It suffices for us to know that we are part of a story that has meaning and that it will come to a definitive end, such that the sun and moon and stars will be darkened – the whole order of creation will be transformed. At that time, we will receive just recompense for how we carried out our role in the story. It's that simple, and it's that momentous.

CHRIST THE FRIEND Christ is our Judge, but he is also our Savior. "Heaven and earth will pass away, but my words will not pass away." If we build our lives on the rock of Christ and his teaching, we will outlive "heaven and earth." Jesus doesn't speak about these events in order to scare us, but in order to motivate us. It is so easy to fall into a purely natural outlook on life, getting so wrapped up in our daily to-do lists that we forget the big picture. When we do that, we push our relationship with Christ further and further into the background. For example, our prayer life is the first thing to go out the window when a time crunch occurs. However, Jesus knows that nothing could be worse for our happiness, now and forever. Therefore, he reminds us to keep the end in sight, so that we can keep everything else in proper perspective.

CHRIST IN MY LIFE Why do I get so distracted with so many things and forget how simple life is from your perspective? All you ask of us is to do your will each moment. And most of the time your will is so clear! The normal duties and relationships and responsibilities, the basic virtue of Christian charity… Just as you and Mary lived in Nazareth. So why do I get distracted? You are in charge Lord, not I…

You are perfect wisdom and perfect goodness. You hold all of history in your hands. Remind me, Lord, that I am a traveler. Remind me, every day, that this is not my final resting place. I don't want to do in eighty years what I could have done in only twenty. Help me to fulfill the mission you have given me: to make your goodness and wisdom known to as many people as possible through my words, actions, and lifestyle…

What would I do without you, Lord? Never let me be separated from you. Only you have the words of eternal life, only you have suffered and died to win forgiveness for my sins, and only you have risen from the dead to open the gates of heaven to those who believe in you. Increase my faith, Lord, and make me a channel of your grace…

QUESTIONS FOR SMALL GROUP DISCUSSION

1. What struck you most in this passage? What did you notice that you hadn't noticed before?

2. How should we carry out Christ's vehement command to "Watch!" in the present circumstances of our lives?

3. As Christians, our self-images should be dominated by knowing that Christ died for us out of love, and that we have a mission in life as his followers. How should this manifest itself in our daily lives? What self-images does popular culture propagate?

4. How might Christ's apostles have reacted to these words of Christ, spoken towards the end of his earthly ministry?

Cf. Catechism of the Catholic Church, 668-682 on Christ's second coming; 1021-1022 and 1038-1041 on the particular and final judgment

THE GOSPEL OF MARK CHAPTER 14

'He was led as a sheep to the slaughter, but he was not a sheep; he was as a lamb without a voice, but he was not a lamb. The figure has passed away, the reality has come: it is God who has come in place of the lamb, man in place of the sheep, and in the man is Christ, who contains all things. So the immolation of the sheep, and the solemn rite of the Pasch, and the letter of the law have come to accomplishment in Christ Jesus. Everything in the old law, and more particularly everything in the new, was directed towards him. For the law has become the Word and the old new (each coming from Sion and Jerusalem); the commandment has become grace, and the type reality, the lamb has become the Son, the Sheep a man, and the man has become God."

- St Melito of Sardis

138. LOVED AND BETRAYED (MK 14:1-11)

"By his words and actions Christ has showed himself to be true God and Lord of the universe..."

- St Anastasius of Antioch

Mark 14:1-11

It was two days before the Passover and the feast of Unleavened Bread, and the chief priests and the scribes were looking for a way to arrest Jesus by some trick and have him put to death. For they said, 'It must not be during the festivities, or there will be a disturbance among the people.' Jesus was at Bethany in the house of Simon the leper; he was at dinner when a woman came in with an alabaster jar of very costly ointment, pure nard. She broke the jar and poured the ointment on his head. Some who were there said to one another indignantly, 'Why this waste of ointment? Ointment like this could have been sold for over three hundred denarii and the money given to the poor'; and they were angry with her. But Jesus said, 'Leave her alone. Why are you upsetting her? What she has done for me is one of the good works. You have the poor with you always, and you can be kind to them whenever you wish, but you will not always have me. She has done what was in her power to do: she has anointed my body beforehand for its burial. I tell you solemnly, wherever throughout all the world the Good News is proclaimed, what she has done will be told also, in remembrance of her.' Judas Iscariot, one of the Twelve, approached the chief priests with an offer to hand Jesus over to them. They were delighted to hear it, and promised to give him money; and he looked for a way of betraying him when the opportunity should occur.

CHRIST THE LORD Jesus is about to offer up the only true atonement for sin that mankind has ever offered to God: his self-sacrifice on the cross at Calvary. Sacrifice, the giving up of something to acknowledge one's dependence on and gratitude to God, has always been essential to religion, no matter the particular creed. It was also essential to the Old Covenant. But even those Old Covenant sacrifices, and even more so the pagan sacrifices of every epoch, failed to make a just offering to God. God deserves what fallen man was unable to give him: total allegiance, unbridled and loving obedience free from even the slightest contamination of sin or selfishness. The lamb, the meekest and most docile of animals, symbolized this totality of love and obedience that Jesus embodied throughout his life and especially during his passion. A spotless lamb was sacrificed in the Passover celebration. As St Mark points out, in that pivotal year of redemption, precisely as this Passover celebration got underway, God's own Lamb, Jesus, was to fulfill the prophetic meaning of the ancient Passover. He was giving his life in atonement for mankind's sins, offering a worthy sacrifice and thereby freeing those who believe in him from slavery to selfishness and the devil.

In spite of the ancient prophecies, and in spite of Jesus' own predictions and warnings, few recognized this singular event as it was happening. But even so, Jerusalem and the whole area around the city were teeming with festive, enthusiastic pilgrims; upwards of three million people filled the city for the Passover celebration and the following seven-day Feast of Unleavened Bread. (This is why the chief priests and scribes were trying to apprehend Jesus by some trick – they wanted to grab him before the crowds could do anything to protect him.) This situation is the background for Jesus' passion: a city overflowing with worshippers of the one true God, recalling God's past saving action and looking forward to the promised salvation of the future. The ignorance, blindness, and opposition of men, as real as they are, can never obstruct the plans of our all-powerful Lord who rules every heart and "makes all things work together for the good of those who love him" (Romans 8:28).

CHRIST THE TEACHER It was customary in Palestine to welcome guests by anointing them with a drop or two of perfume when they entered your house or when they reclined at table (meals then were taken reclining on couches; you leaned on your left elbow and took your food with your right hand). This woman takes the custom to an extreme by anointing Jesus with an entire flask of expensive perfume (at the time, nard-based ointment was manufactured only in India). We can imagine the depth of understanding between them. Jesus knows her heart, and she knows that he knows, and with utter simplicity and confidence she expresses what is in her heart and what she can no longer contain. He looks into her eyes as she approaches him, and smiles. She adores him, thanks him, and praises him through the sincerity and simplicity with which she performs this gesture of welcome and appreciation. This rich exchange of hearts is inaccessible to the others. The disciples, blind to the real meaning of what is happening, are scandalized by the opulence of the gesture. When Jesus praises it, he teaches them, and us, the characteristics of true love.

The woman's gesture was *generous*, and true love is generous. Love flows like a waterfall, like a rushing fountain; it doesn't measure itself out in a miserly way with an eyedropper. The woman's gesture was *costly*, and true love is costly. Since love by definition is self-giving, when one loves one necessarily feels a certain loss, a certain self-sacrifice. The loss yields a profound joy, because the beloved benefits (and because we are created to love), but it remains a kind of loss nonetheless. Christ himself asserted this paradox: "… Anyone who loses his life for my sake, and for the sake of the gospel, will save it" (Mk 8:35). The woman's gesture was *beautiful*, and true love is the most beautiful reality of all. St Mark tells us that Jesus called her homage "one of the good works." Greek has two words for "good," *agathos* and *kalos*. *Agathos* connotes strict moral goodness, while *kalos* connotes moral goodness with a winsome, elegant, charming twist. St Mark uses *kalos* in transcribing Jesus' compliment. True love goes beyond the cold exactitude of dry duty; true love gives with a smile, a flourish, and a delicacy that not only meets the beloved's needs but meets them in a lovely, pleasing way.[2]

Jesus will perfectly exhibit these characteristics of love in his passion. He generously pours out all his blood, not just a symbolic drop; he suffers betrayal, rejection, humiliation, injustice, physical torment, and mockery – a costly gesture indeed; he goes to the cross forgiving his enemies all the while, showing such an attractive nobility and humility that he even wins over the battle-hardened Roman guards. Jesus comes to this woman's defense because he always defends true love, because his love is always true.

CHRIST THE FRIEND Commentators have speculated extensively about Judas' motives. What moved him to betray his Messiah and friend? St John points out greed as a primary factor; others surmise it was jealousy; still others say that Judas merely wanted to give Jesus an opportunity to show his stuff and throw down his enemies. St Mark ventures no explanation, but simply records the fact.

---

[2] *See* **William Barclay's** Daily Study Bible: The Gospel of Mark

Whatever specific reason Judas may have had, one thing is certain: he was dissatisfied with the Kingdom Jesus was offering; he wanted Jesus to be different than he was. Judas had his own idea of what a Savior should be like. He had become Christ's follower harboring that idea. When he gradually discovered that Jesus had a different idea, instead of adjusting his own and trusting in Christ, he made an idol of his own idea and crushed Christ. Here is the essence of every sin and the opposite of authentic friendship: independence and a stubborn attachment to doing things our way or no way, as if we were God. Jesus offers us his friendship, but it is friendship with God. Accepting it means letting God be God. Judas refused. Whenever we sin, in big things or small, we echo the ancient, hellish, and foolish rebel's cry: "I will not serve!" (Jeremiah 2:20).

CHRIST IN MY LIFE You alone give hope to the human soul. You have given me hope. Your sacrifice on Calvary and in every Mass links my heart to your divine heart. How much you must love me! How can you love me enough to willingly offer yourself as the lamb to be slaughtered in reparation and atonement for my sins? Touch my heart, Lord, and help me glimpse the light of your love…

How valiantly you defended this woman who loved you so deeply! Teach me to love truly. My love is weak, inconstant, partial. But your Holy Spirit is at work in my soul. I know that in you I can love as you love, and I know that loving as you love is the secret to the fulfillment and fruitfulness I long for. With the love of your heart, Lord, inflame my heart…

How many times have I betrayed you? How many times have I rebelled against your will? How foolish I am to prefer my petty, narrow, self-centered ideas to the pure, eternal wisdom of your will. Your will is full of your wisdom, as the ocean is full of water. Make your will my heart's only quest, my mind's one delight! My heart is restless until it rests in you…

QUESTIONS FOR SMALL GROUP DISCUSSION

1. What struck you most in this passage? What did you notice that you hadn't noticed before?
2. How does the concept of love promoted by popular culture compare to Christ's conception of love?
3. What are some ways in which society commonly tempts us to betray Jesus?
4. Can you think of any reasons why perfume is such an eloquent symbol of love?

Cf. Catechism of the Catholic Church, 599-605 on Christ's redemptive death in God's plan of salvation; 606-611 on Jesus as the sacrificial Lamb

139. SHADOWS FALL (MK 14:12-25)

"I have found the paradox that if I love until it hurts, then there is no hurt, but only more love."

- Blessed Mother Theresa of Calcutta

Mark 14:12-25

On the first day of Unleavened Bread, when the Passover lamb was sacrificed, his disciples said to him, 'Where do you want us to go and make the preparations for you to eat the passover?' So he sent two of his disciples, saying to them, 'Go into the city and you will meet a man carrying a pitcher of water. Follow him, and say to the owner of the house which he enters, The Master says: Where is my dining room in which I can eat the passover with my disciples? He will show you a large upper room furnished with couches, all prepared. Make the preparations for us there,' The disciples set out and went to the city and found everything as he had told them, and prepared the Passover. When evening came he arrived with the Twelve. And while they were at table eating, Jesus said, 'I tell you solemnly, one of you is about to betray me, one of you eating with me.' They were distressed and asked him, one after another, 'Not I, surely?' He said to them, 'It is one of the Twelve, one who is dipping into the same dish with me. Yes, the Son of Man is going to his fate, as the scriptures say he will, but alas for that man by whom the Son of Man is betrayed! Better for that man if he had never been born!' And as they were eating he took some bread, and when he had said the blessing he broke it and gave it to them. 'Take it,' he said 'this is my body.' Then he took a cup, and when he had returned thanks he gave it to them, and all drank from it, and he said to them, 'This is my blood, the blood of the covenant, which is to be poured out for many. I tell you solemnly, I shall not drink any more wine until the day I drink the new wine in the kingdom of God.'

CHRIST THE LORD The Jewish feast of the Passover commemorated and renewed the foundational experience of God's Chosen People: the liberation from slavery in Egypt. The first Passover occurred in the aftermath of Pharaoh's repeated refusals to let the Israelites free to worship the one, true God. Nine horrible and miraculous plagues wouldn't budge the stubborn Egyptian leader, so finally God sent his angel of death to slay every Egyptian firstborn male. On that very night, every Israelite family was told to sacrifice a spotless lamb, mark the doorjambs of their dwellings with its blood, and feast upon it. The blood of the lamb signaled the presence of God's favor, and so the angel of death knew to "pass over" those families in the course of its mission.

When Moses had successfully led his people out of Egypt, God gave the Israelites

483

detailed instructions for the annual commemoration of this event. Such a commemoration, the Passover Seder (or "supper," still celebrated by Jews) was the occasion for Christ's institution of the sacrament of the Eucharist. St Mark records the words of Jesus by which he reveals that he is the true Passover lamb. Just as the Israelites in Egypt were saved from slavery by the lamb's sacrifice, so all men and women would be saved from sin by the sacrifice of Christ on Calvary, by the breaking of his body and the pouring out of his blood out of love for us. And just as the Israelites were to partake of the feast of the lamb, so all of Christ's followers are called to feast on his living body and blood through the Eucharist in order to share intimately in his divine life. The Eucharist manifests Christ's Lordship over life and history – it extends his once-for-all sacrifice through all time and space – and shows what kind of Lord he is: one who gives his life for those entrusted to his care, even for his betrayer. It is, truly, the bread that frees us from death. Do we treat it that way?

CHRIST THE TEACHER   St Mark spends as much time describing the odd events that immediately led up to the Last Supper as he does describing the institution of the Eucharist itself. What does the man carrying the water jar have to do with Christ's saving sacrifice? Some scholars surmise that Jesus kept the location of the Last Supper secret in order to insure that his enemies wouldn't be able to apprehend him there. If he had said openly where they would be gathered, Judas would have been able to tip off the Jewish leaders. Other scholars point out that carrying water was a woman's task in ancient Palestine, so finding a man carrying water subtly indicates the new order of things that Christ is about to establish.

Whatever scholars may say, however, one thing is clear: Jesus knew exactly how this last evening with his apostles was going to pan out. His instructions about finding the place for their celebration show that the occurrences of that evening were not left up to chance. Every word, every action was part of a drama being directed by God, most especially the highlight – the institution of the Eucharist. This was no ordinary supper, no traditional celebration: the images and shadows of the Old Covenant would give way this night to the fullness of the New Covenant. The Eucharist, the sacramental foreshadowing and prolongation of Calvary, is no abstract symbol; it is the ultimate reality towards which all other symbols converge.

CHRIST THE FRIEND   Christ gave his disciples bread, which had become his own body. Then he gave them wine, which had become his blood. He did this for their sake, and for the sake of all who would be saved from the slavery to sin. What greater gift could he have given them, and through them, to us? Christ continues to take, bless, break, and give the bread and wine that are his body and blood – he does it through his priests of his Church, because he wants to stay with us and be our life. And this gift has no strings attached. Jesus gives it even though we are undeserving; like Judas, we have betrayed our Lord countless times. Every time we ignore or discard the voice of conscience, every time we pick and choose among the Church's teachings, every time we judge our neighbor and fail to love others as Christ as loved us, we echo Judas' betrayal. Christ's love doesn't depend on our being worthy; Christ's love depends only on his burning desire to give us the fullness of life. What a relief to have such a friend, one who cares only about giving, and one who can give such an incomparable gift!

CHRIST IN MY LIFE Thank you for the Eucharist, your quiet, dependable presence in every Tabernacle. What more could I desire, having you so close to me, waiting for me, adoring the Father in every moment on my behalf? And thank you for the great gift of Holy Communion, in which you come into my very being to be my nourishment and joy. Teach me to receive these gifts worthily…

You, Lord, are all-knowing and all-powerful. All the events of my life, whether big or small, are equally under you loving, wise care. Please open my eyes so that I can see you in all things, love you in all things, and thank you and serve you as I ought to. Save me from the meaningless routine of a superficial, frenetic, giddy life. Teach me to live as you created me to live…

How my soul needs your pure love! You alone can love perfectly. When you look at me you want only one thing: that I become what you created me to be. Your smile has no hidden agendas. You are love! You love me! How strange, how hard for me to accept this truth, to bring it from my head to my heart! Pound my heart with your love, my Lord, until it fills me to overflowing…

QUESTIONS FOR SMALL GROUP DISCUSSION

1. What struck you most in this passage? What did you notice that you hadn't noticed before?

2. Why would Christ have chosen to leave us his body and blood under the appearances of bread and wine, instead of some other way?

3. If Christ himself, his entire being and life, is truly present in the Eucharist and reserved in

the tabernacles of all our Catholic Churches, why do so few people spend significant time with him there?

4. When we have an important meeting or event to attend (an interview, a ball, a wedding, etc.), we usually take plenty of time to prepare ourselves. Why do we generally take so little time to prepare ourselves to encounter the King of kings in Mass and Communion?

Cf. Catechism of the Catholic Church, 1322-1340 and 1406-1419 on the Eucharist; 1391-1401 on Holy Communion; 1345-1390 on the Mass

140. A GARDEN AT NIGHT (MK 14:26-42)

"Now I am beginning to be a disciple. Come fire and cross and grapplings with wild beasts, cuttings and manglings, wrenching of bones, hacking of limbs, crushing of my whole body, come cruel tortures of the devil to assail me. Only may I attain to Jesus Christ."

- St Ignatius of Antioch, martyr

Mark 14:26-42

After psalms had been sung they left for the Mount of Olives. And Jesus said to them, 'You will all lose faith, for the scripture says: I shall strike the shepherd and the sheep will be scattered, however after my resurrection I shall go before you to Galilee'. Peter said, 'Even if all lose faith, I will not.' And Jesus said to him, 'I tell you solemnly, this day, this very night, before the cock crows twice, you will have disowned me three times.' But he repeated still more earnestly, 'If I have to die with you, I will never disown you.' And they all said the same.

They came to a small estate called Gethsemane, and Jesus said to his disciples, 'Stay here while I pray.' Then he took Peter and James and John with him. And a sudden fear came over him, and great distress. And he said to them, 'My soul is sorrowful to the point of death. Wait here, and keep awake.' And going on a little further he threw himself on the ground and prayed that, if it were possible, this hour might pass him by. 'Abba (Father)!' he said 'Everything is possible for you. Take this cup away from me. But let it be as you, not I, would have it.' He came back and found them sleeping, and he said to Peter, 'Simon, are you asleep? Had you not the strength to keep awake one hour? You should be awake, and praying not to be put to the test. The spirit is willing, but the flesh is weak.' Again he went away and prayed, saying the same words. And once more he came back and found them sleeping, their eyes were so heavy; and they could find no answer for him. He came back a third time and said to them, 'You can sleep on now and take your rest. It is all over. The hour has come. Now the Son of Man is to be betrayed into the hands of sinners. Get up! Let us go! My betrayer is close at hand already.'

CHRIST THE LORD As his hour draws near, Jesus warns his disciples that they will be thrown into confusion by his apparent defeat, quoting an Old Testament prophecy (Zechariah 13:7-9). But Peter refuses to believe either the prophecy or Jesus' interpretation of it. He has thrown in his lot completely with the Lord, and he is passionately determined to hold true to his pledge. Jesus sees the depths of Peter's soul, however, and knows that Peter is still depending too much on his own strength and on a false idea of the Kingdom. Even after the Lord reiterates and specifies his prediction of the Apostles' flight and denial, they still protest. Jesus is sure of his mission and determined to carry it out, but the disciples, like Peter, are still thinking of the Kingdom in merely worldly terms. Jesus makes these predictions and calls to mind the scriptures so that later, when the disciples are reflecting back on this conversation, they will realize that Jesus went into his Passion with full awareness and consent.

They will realize then that although he knew they were going to abandon him in his hour of need, he wasn't going to hold it against them – he even looks forward to seeing them again after his resurrection. Somehow, they will later see, their abandonment too was part of the plan. To establish his Lordship in their hearts once and for all, he had to strip them of every last scrap of self-sufficiency that still contaminated those hearts. His Kingdom is not of this earth, and so his apostles and all his followers need to learn that to be a citizen of this Kingdom takes more than simply natural affection, determination, and talent. It has to be based on the unshakable conviction of Christ's love, which frees the soul to trust in God and fulfill God's will, in spite of earthly fears and repugnance. The Christian has to trust Christ even more than he trusts himself; the apostles' coming failure will purify them of their last vestiges of pride and prepare them to spend the rest of their lives following the Lord's way of humility, obedience, and self-sacrifice. May the Holy Spirit teach us the same lesson without having to send us through the same trial!

CHRIST THE TEACHER Jesus went off to pray in order to align his tormented will with the Father's will. He didn't pretend that what God was asking him was easy – it wasn't. But he wants to be faithful. Just wishing for fidelity, however, is not enough; fidelity has to be won by persistent prayer. St Mark tells us that Jesus went off to pray, came back to his disciples, and then went off to pray again. He did that three times. Three times in the course of an hour or more, Jesus literally threw himself on the ground in order to wrest grace from the Father to bolster his flagging human nature.

The lesson couldn't be clearer: fidelity to our mission in life takes perseverance in prayer. Jesus suffered unspeakable fear, distress, and sorrow as the guilt of all human sin slowly seeped into his soul and the shadow of the cross darkened his mind. He experienced this Gethsemane for us: to atone for our sins, but also to blaze a trail that we could follow through our own Gethsemanes. We each have them. Christ's passion, death, and resurrection – the Paschal Mystery – is the pattern of each Christian life. If we are to abide in God's will and accomplish our mission in life, we too must develop sincerity and persistence in our life of prayer. Everyone's Gethsemane is tailor-made, but the secret to endurance is always the same: persevering in prayer. The spirit is willing, but the flesh – our fallen human nature with its tendencies to comfort and self-centeredness – is weak; it needs the constant nourishment and strengthening that comes from contact with God.

CHRIST THE FRIEND How did St Mark and the other evangelists find out about Christ's Gethsemane experience? The other nine apostles were farther off, and these three were sleeping, so who saw our Lord in his agony? Jesus himself probably told his disciples about it later, after the Resurrection. Imagine that conversation... Jesus asks them if they remember the fateful night and how tired they were. He anxiously hoped for the moral support of their friendship, but they couldn't stop dozing off. And so he was alone, and the burden of humanity's sin was laid upon his soul, and the prospect of humiliation, torment, and death was presented to him in all its utter horror, such that his will was assailed and he had to battle with all the strength of his spirit to accept the Father's will.

Jesus bares his heart to us in this passage. He wants his disciples – us included – to know beyond any possible doubt that his love is faithful. He wants us to know that he understands what it means to suffer, that he took on and experienced every kind of suffering we could ever encounter. He wants us to believe in the possibility of love, of faithfulness, no matter how impossible it may seem. Christ's strength, which encountered and endured the worst of sufferings, can be our strength, and the strength of those around us, if only we stick by his side as faithful friends. Hail Gethsemane, the Christian's greatest hope!

CHRIST IN MY LIFE It's hard for me to picture this, Lord. It's hard for me to imagine you suffering. You are the Lord! And yet, there it is – you were sorrowful to the point of death. What does that mean? Sorrowful to the point of death... I have sorrows too, Lord. Teach me about yours, so that I can bear mine with your love. Teach me to comfort you in yours, so I find your comfort in mine...

My Gethsemane is so dull, Lord. It's the daily routine. It's the unpleasant colleague. It's the nagging money problem…. Do these count? Do you care about these struggles? Of course you do. These too are chances for me to exercise love, the love of fidelity and perseverance in my life's mission, and the love that consists in trusting you. Teach me to do your will…

You are God, and yet you experienced the same confusion and oppression and anxiety that plague me. You did it for me. You shared my lot. Thank you, Lord. Teach me to be that generous with those around me. Teach me to be with them as you are with me: patient, self-forgetful, self-sacrificing, dependable, forgiving. Make my heart more and more like yours…

QUESTIONS FOR SMALL GROUP DISCUSSION

1. What struck you most in this passage? What did you notice that you hadn't noticed before?

2. Jesus went to prayer in his toughest moments. Where does popular culture encourage us to go in our toughest moments? Where should we go?

3. The disciples – especially Peter – were completely convinced that they would stay faithful to Christ no matter what. What do you think went wrong? Why didn't they stay awake and pray?

4. St Mark said Jesus used the same words each of the three times he went off to pray. Why do you think Jesus did that? Is there a lesson in that for us?

Cf. Catechism of the Catholic Church, 2779-2785 on addressing God as "Father"; 598 on who was responsible for Christ's Passion; 609 and 612 on the agony in Gethsemane; 2697-2699 on the life of prayer

141. GRACE UNDER FIRE (MK 14:43-52)

"Christ is the way: Christ is the door. By Christ we mount, by Christ we are borne… A man should look at Christ hanging on the cross, should look with faith, hope, love, wonder, joy appreciation, praise and jubilation."

- St Bonaventure

Mark 14:43-52

Even while he was still speaking, Judas, one of the Twelve, came up with a number of men armed with swords and clubs, sent by the chief priests and the scribes and the elders. Now the traitor had arranged a signal with them. 'The one I kiss,' he had said, 'he is the man. Take him in charge, and see he is well guarded when you lead him away.' So when the traitor came, he went straight up to Jesus and said, 'Rabbi!' and kissed him. The others seized him and took him in charge. Then one of the bystanders drew his sword and struck out at the high priest's servant, and cut off his ear. Then Jesus spoke. 'Am I a brigand,' he said, 'that you had to set out to capture me with swords and clubs? I was among you teaching in the Temple day after day and you never laid hands on me. But this is to fulfil the scriptures.' And they all deserted him and ran away. A young man who followed him had nothing on but a linen cloth. They caught hold of him, but he left the cloth in their hands and ran away naked.

CHRIST THE LORD The agony in Gethsemane reveals the human side of our Lord as no other Gospel passage does. We see him sorrowful, terrified, anxious – in a crisis more severe than we can ever imagine. And yet, after those horrific hours of prayerful struggle, Jesus emerges strengthened, noble, and serene. In the moment of his arrest, and throughout the tragedy that is soon to unfold, Jesus stays one hundred percent on task. His captors and tormentors, so eager and almost desperate to humiliate and do away with him, have no power over his mind or his heart. Even while surrendering his body into the hands of sinners, Jesus remains the Lord: he instructs his captors and foes even at the moment of his capture.

Grace under fire is a mark of Christ's Lordship, because he truly is always in control, in spite of tempest of evil and sin that swirls around him. It's also a mark of every authentic Christian, because they don't have to depend solely on their own wits and strength to fulfill their mission; the Lord himself is at work within them.

CHRIST THE TEACHER English only has one word for kiss, but Greek has two. The normal kiss of greeting is *philein*, and St Mark uses this word when quoting Judas instructing the soldiers. The other word, *kataphilein*, implies a more meaningful, respectful kiss, the kind of greeting given not out of strict formality, but between intimates.[3] St Mark uses this word to refer to the actual kiss with which Judas betrays Jesus. Judas was on intimate terms with Jesus; he was "one of the Twelve," as St Mark repeatedly and poignantly reports. Otherwise, he could not have betrayed the Lord. Only those close to us, those to whom we are linked by the bond of trust and love, can betray us. This kiss hurt the heart of Christ more deeply than all the other torments he was to endure. A prophecy in the Book of Psalms anticipated this heartrending blow: "Were it an enemy who insulted me, that I could bear; if an opponent pitted himself against me, I could turn away from him. But you, a person of my own rank, a comrade and dear friend, to whom I was bound by intimate friendship in the house of God!" (Psalm 55:12-14)

---

[3] *Cf. William Barclay,* The Daily Study Bible: The Gospel of Mark

It is always this way. Those who are closest to us wound us most. Those whom Christ has graced with a special intimacy, a special mission, a special vocation, can give him either great joy or great sorrow. We should never belittle our sins. In the realm of love and intimacy, where Christ has held nothing back, our indifference, ingratitude, and betrayals, so mundane from the world's perspective, echo Judas' kiss. This was the risk Jesus took by becoming man: If he is able to love and be loved in his human nature, he is also able to suffer the surpassing pangs of unrequited love. The kiss in the Garden throws into high relief both the heights of evil man can attain and the exquisite goodness of God's incarnate love. Each of us needs to bewail the one and bask in the other.

CHRIST THE FRIEND St Mark adds a curious detail lacking in all the other Gospel accounts of this scene: the young man in his nightgown who was almost apprehended with Jesus and had to flee naked. Most biblical scholars surmise that this young man was the John Mark mentioned in the Book of Acts (Acts 12:12), son of the Mary whose house seems to have been the center of the first Jerusalem Christian community – the same house, most likely, where the Last Supper had taken place. (This would be the same Mark who authored the Gospel.) Maybe he trailed the Master and his band from the Last Supper room and hid in the shadows to watch Jesus. Maybe he was the one who witnessed Jesus' prayer in Gethsemane. Whatever the details, the fact remains there, recorded in the Gospel and given to us to ponder.

Spiritual writers rarely comment on it, but it bears eloquent witness to one of Christ's most endearing characteristics, his universal openness. Do the Gospels ever tell us of a case when Jesus refused to make himself available to people who wanted to speak with him or spend time with him? On the contrary, Jesus is so available that often he doesn't even have time to eat, and even when he tries to resist people's entreaties (as when he wanted to take his disciples away to a quiet place for a while, or when the Canaanite woman asked him to exorcise her daughter), his heart simply can't remain unmoved. This young man (probably in his early teens) wanted to spend the Passover night close to his favorite rabbi, and Jesus lets him. On this most significant night in all human history, the King of the universe deigns to let this pesky whippersnapper tag along. The boy's nascent love for Christ wanted to see everything; the same love, matured in the Holy Spirit, would move him to write the second Gospel. Wherever there is love, wherever there is a smidgeon of sincerity in one's desire to see Jesus, the Lord simply can't say no. This was Jesus on the first Holy Thursday, and this is still Jesus in every Tabernacle throughout the world: eager to make himself available to everyone that longs for his friendship.

CHRIST IN MY LIFE You are fearless and gentle as the minions of evil close in on you like a pack of wolves. Why am I so fearful and temperamental? Are you not my Lord? Do you not dwell in my heart? Jesus, I don't understand myself. I know that you understand me, though, and that you want to guide me and coach me. Teach me to do your will, Lord, to be more like you…

I picture Judas betraying you with a kiss… How many of your chosen souls, the men and women you have called to special intimacy, have done the same! But how can I judge them? Have you not given me a vocation of my own, a mission of my own, a call of my own? And have I been faithful? Jesus, never let me betray you again, never let me pain your heart…

Thank you for always being available. I never have to be alone. How much suffering and how many sins spring from loneliness! Jesus, you are the faithful friend, but so many people still haven't found you. Don't you want them to? Teach me to teach them about you! I do nothing more for my neighbor than help them see that you love them and seek their friendship...

QUESTIONS FOR SMALL GROUP DISCUSSION

1. What struck you most in this passage? What did you notice that you hadn't noticed before?

2. Why do you think Jesus admonished his captors about their dastardly method of apprehending him in the dead of night when he had been teaching in public places all week long?

3. If a non-believing friend asked you, "Why didn't Jesus defend himself?" how would you answer?

4. Do you think Judas' betrayal sheds any light on the Church's discipline that anyone who finds himself in mortal sin, or that anyone who doesn't fully share the Catholic faith should not receive Holy Communion?

Cf. Catechism of the Catholic Church, 2142-2155 on betraying the Lord's name; 1786-1789 on the proper role of conscience in our choices

142. THE COURAGE OF LOVE (MK 14:53-65)

"He came therefore of his own set purpose to his passion, rejoicing in his noble deed, smiling at the crown, cheered by the salvation of mankind; not ashamed of the cross for it was to save the world."

- St Cyril of Jerusalem

Mark 14:53-65

They led Jesus off to the high priest; and all the chief priests and the elders and the scribes assembled there. Peter had followed him at a distance, right into the high priest's palace, and was sitting with the attendants warming himself at the fire. The chief priests and the whole Sanhedrin were looking for evidence against Jesus on which they might pass the death-sentence. But they could not find any. Several, indeed, brought false evidence against him, but their evidence was conflicting. Some stood up and submitted this false evidence against him, 'We heard him say, I am going to destroy this Temple made by human hands, and in three days build another, not made by human hands.' But even on this point their evidence was conflicting. The high priest then stood up before the whole assembly and put this question to Jesus, 'Have you no answer to that? What is this evidence these men are bringing against you?' But he was silent and made no answer at all. The high priest put a second question to him, 'Are you the Christ,' he said 'the Son of the Blessed One?' 'I am,' said Jesus, 'and you will see the Son of Man seated at the right hand of the Power and coming with the clouds of heaven.' The high priest tore his robes, 'What need of witnesses have we now?' he said. 'You heard the blasphemy. What is your finding?' And they all gave their verdict: he deserved to die. Some of them started spitting at him and, blindfolding him, began hitting him with their fists and shouting, 'Play the prophet!' And the attendants rained blows on him.

CHRIST THE LORD St Mark, with his typical clarity, removes any doubt about who Jesus is. The Lord held himself in silence as the illegally convened court (the Sanhedrin was forbidden to meet at night; it was forbidden to meet anywhere besides its proper room in the Temple precincts) threw itself into a frenzy trying to incriminate him. Finally, the high priest, speaking on the authority of his legitimate office, demands a proclamation from the accused: Do you really claim to be not only the promised Messiah, but also the Son of God, someone who has a special identification with the Most High Lord of Israel? Jesus looks directly at him and says yes. To make it even clearer, he quotes the Messianic prophesies in reference to himself, as if in explanation of his claim. If the Sanhedrin had understood the scriptures, they would have realized that the Messiah, in God's plan of salvation, had to have a unique relationship to the divine nature.

In response to such a clear answer, the Sanhedrin had only one choice: accept his claims or condemn him for blasphemy. It is curious to note that among all the evidence brought against Jesus, the court members didn't call any of the many witnesses who could have proven his Messianic identity: the lepers he

493

healed, the blind and deaf he restored, the dead he raised to life, the crippled he made whole... how willingly blind the Sanhedrin was! (How willingly blind all of us can be!) They at least recognized that Jesus wasn't just claiming, as Socrates had done, for example, to be a good teacher, a wise philosopher, a social reformer... Those more modern accusations are false too. Jesus is either what he claims to be, the Lord of all, or he is a deluded lunatic – and lunatics don't found churches that continually influence and shape civilization – transforming saints for more than two thousand years.

CHRIST THE TEACHER Jesus did not pick this fight, but now that it has begun, he courageously and nobly defends the truth in spite of the consequences it may have for his own well-being. It must be the same for every Christian. Jesus sent his disciples to carry his message to the ends of the world, to all peoples. He also promised that those who faithfully carry out this mission will run into trouble. His own life sets the pattern for the life of every Christian – humble, hidden work at Nazareth; bold, fruitful teaching and healing; conflict, suffering, and death at the hands of those who refuse to heed God's call; and, finally, glorious resurrection. We are to follow in his footsteps. And that includes speaking the truth in moments when the forces of falsehood and evil surround us and bait us and humiliate and torment us. Jesus is the Messiah, the one Savior of mankind, the Lord of life and history; to know, love, and follow him is to find the everlasting life so ardently sought by every human soul. We don't pick fights, but when our faith spurs opposition we, like our Lord, courageously and nobly bear him witness, no matter what the cost.

CHRIST THE FRIEND Some of the guards, bystanders, or members of the Sanhedrin, St Mark informs us, started spitting at Jesus. Then some blindfolded him and beat him, mocking him all the while. What started off as a game became a sadistic rout, as "the attendants rained blows on him."

Picture these petty men spitting at Jesus. How does Jesus respond? With his mouth he says nothing. Is he saying anything in his heart? "Forgive them, Father, they don't know what they are doing." Picture them blindfolding him, toying with him, battering him, mocking him, and laughing cruelly at him. How does he respond? "Forgive them, Father... You know that I love them." He is deeply saddened, not for himself, but for them. They are in darkness. Ignorance, malice, selfishness – evil has blinded them. Jesus harbors no resentment, no desire for vengeance, no anger – only forgiveness. Only an eagerness to sacrifice all his dignity, all his blood to the last drop, so as to make amends for these sins, so as to open the gates of heaven to these very thugs who are railing against him.

We are those tyrants. Every idle word, every mocking look, every evil thought, every illicit pleasure, every outburst of anger, every festering notion of resentment, jealousy, and envy – they are all present in these wicked blows that mar the Holy Face of Christ. And Jesus looks at each of us, with no self-pity, with no accusation: "Forgive them, Father... You know that I love them." Has the world ever known such a friend?

CHRIST IN MY LIFE I believe in you, Lord. I stand in place of all those men and women throughout the world who don't believe in you and who reject your love, and I say for them, in their stead: I believe in you, Jesus; I thank you and I love you. You are the Son of the living God, the Messiah, the Savior of all people. Have mercy on us. Your Kingdom come, your will be done...

You know how weak and fearful I can be. I am downright feeble when it comes to bearing witness to you in certain circumstances. But I know that when I am weak, I am strong, because your strength has more room to shine whenever I lean less on my own resources and more on your grace. With the courage of your heart, Lord, sustain my vocation...

I am unworthy of your friendship. For that very reason, I thank you even more for it. You know the depths of evil that my heart can reach, and still you want to love me and accompany me and guide me and lead me to your side in heaven. I claim your friendship, Lord! May it be my only treasure, and may I always show my gratitude by loving others as you have loved me...

QUESTIONS FOR SMALL GROUP DISCUSSION

1. What struck you most in this passage? What did you notice that you hadn't noticed before?

2. Why do you think Jesus didn't defend himself more amply during this trial?

3. How can we know when to defend truth and justice and when to submit to injustice, as Christ does here?

4. Why do you think the chief priests and other members of the Sanhedrin didn't wait until daylight so as to hold a legitimate, legal trial?

Cf. Catechism of the Catholic Church, 595-598 on the trial of Jesus; 2284-2301 on respecting human dignity; 1929-1933 on charity and respect for the human person

143. THE FORCE OF FORGIVENESS (MK 14:66-72)

"In this way, in Christ and through Christ, God also becomes especially visible in his mercy."

- Pope John Paul II, Dives in Misericordia, 2

Mark 14:66-72

While Peter was down below in the courtyard, one of the high priest's servant-girls came up. She saw Peter warming himself there, stared at him and said, 'You too were with Jesus, the man from Nazareth.' But he denied it. 'I do not know, I do not understand, what you are talking about,' he said. And he went out into the fore-court. The servant-girl saw him and again started telling the bystanders, 'This fellow is one of them.' But again he denied it. A little later the bystanders themselves said to Peter, 'You are one of them for sure! Why, you are a Galilean.' But he started calling down curses on himself and swearing, 'I do not know the man you speak of.' At that moment the cock crew for the second time, and Peter recalled how Jesus had said to him, 'Before the cock crows twice, you will have disowned me three times.' And he burst into tears.

CHRIST THE LORD In the world, rulers and kings make much of sheer power. Without power, without force, a worldly kingdom cannot endure. Christ's king-dom is wildly different. Sheer power has no place in it, and yet it has outlasted (and will continue to outlast) even the most glorious earthly empires. What holds this remarkable Kingdom together? What is its secret source of strength? The Lord's mercy – mercy is the unbreakable binding force of the Kingdom of Christ.

Peter was Christ's most loyal follower. Jesus had been grooming him for the top leadership position in his Church. Peter had even shown courage where the other disciples had balked: he drew his sword in the Garden of Gethsemane, as if he would be able to take on single-handedly the whole cohort sent to appre-hend Jesus; then he actually followed the Lord into the high priest's courtyard, where the very servant whose ear he had wounded was probably residing; finally, when someone recognized him, instead of hightailing it out of that nest of enemies, he stuck around, just to be as faithful to Jesus as circumstances would allow. But his natural reserves of courage ran out. The terror of that most infamous and most glorious night in human history weighed upon him, and as the little crowd began to harangue him, he denied his association with Jesus, three hideous times.

But then the cockcrow – either the bugle call known by that name, or the second crow of the rooster, both of which marked the start of fourth watch of the night – reminded him that Jesus had known all along how weak Peter was and had loved him and stayed faithful even so. That's when Peter's life changed. He relinquished his earthly hopes and self-reliance, and he embraced Christ's everlasting hopes and supernatural grace. It was the Lord's mercy that fit the rock foundation of his Church firmly into place, and it is his mercy that keeps it there.

CHRIST THE TEACHER Jesus is never surprised by our sins. He is not afraid of sin. He knows we are weak. He accepts that as an unavoidable fact. He is willing to work with it, to work in spite of it, and to work through it, thus transforming us at a deeper level than we could ever suspect. He did so with Peter, and he does so with all his saints. So why are we surprised at our weakness? Why do we fall into discouragement and depression at our inability to overcome our faults more quickly? Why are we not satisfied with God's omnipotence and with the pace of growth and transformation that he chooses to take?

Jesus needs all his followers to learn humility. Without humility, without a serene and mature acceptance of our utter dependence on God, we can make no progress at all in the spiritual realm. If God allows us to fall, if he allows us to face our weakness, again and again, it's because that rich soil of humility needs constantly to be turned over, plowed under, and fertilized. If the tears we shed at our falls keep us from getting back up again and surging onward, they don't come from the Lord.

CHRIST THE FRIEND Every Christian is called to be another Christ. This is Jesus' strategy for redeeming the world; he makes himself present in every family, community, intimate circle of friends, business, country, and courtroom through his ambassadors – through Christians. We make him visible by the lives we live. Christ's love made itself known most surely in his mercy, in his forgiveness. As his messengers and representatives, then, forgiveness and mercy have to be our bottom line. If we don't forgive, we can't love as Christ loves. But we can't move ourselves to forgive only by our natural powers – we need to contemplate Jesus' example and let his grace reach into the darkest corners of our souls where we harbor resentment and anger. Those are the weak and self-centered sentiments; the noble and strong works of Christian soldiers are works of mercy. Christ showed proved the mettle of his friendship by his unconditional forgiveness of our every sin; we will prove ours by forgiving our neighbor from our hearts.

Jesus: Peter could never have preached the Kingdom if he had never experienced my forgiveness. He would have become like the Pharisees – proud of his talents and privileges, but cold and hard in his condemnation of those blessed with fewer natural gifts. For a long time I had prepared him for this moment. It was his great test – not the test of whether or not he would deny, but the test of whether or not he would be humble enough to accept my forgiveness and let himself start over, leaning more completely on my grace. I want you to accept my forgiveness too.

CHRIST IN MY LIFE Peter was so sure of himself, and yet the mission you gave him was beyond his natural capacities, as great as they were. At times I am too sure of myself. In spite of my insecurities and complexes, I still think I'm always right, and I still want everyone to do things my way. Teach me to mourn for my sins and sinfulness, to find all my joy in your most precious will…

How different my life would be if I were to accept my weakness as a fact of life! How much peace would invade my soul! How much freer I would be to make better use of the graces you send me to strengthen me in my journey towards holiness! I am just a little speck in this immense universe, Lord, and I only matter because you love me – teach me to live from your love…

Countless hearts are closed and hardened in resentment, hate, and envy. Are there any corners of my heart infected with these diabolical diseases? Dear Lord, cleanse my heart; fill me with a burning desire to love you. Make me a channel of your peace; where there is hatred, let me sow your love, and where there is injury, your pardon…

QUESTIONS FOR SMALL GROUP DISCUSSION

1. What struck you most in this passage? What did you notice that you hadn't noticed before?

2. The early Christians could only have learned of this happening through Peter's own telling of the story. Why do you think he told it? How do you think he told it, and how often? How do you think he felt when he told it?

3. Jesus warned Peter about what was going to happen. Why do you think Peter didn't keep his guard up better?

4. Compare and contrast Judas' and Peter's betrayal. What did they have in common and what didn't they have in common? Why do you think Peter was able to recover and Judas wasn't?

Cf. Catechism of the Catholic Church, 1425-1429 on our need for ongoing conversion; 1430-1433 on interior penance; 2838-2845 on God's forgiveness and our forgiveness

THE GOSPEL OF MARK CHAPTER 15

"The liberation of the children of Israel, and the journey by which they were led to the

homeland they had long ago been promised, correspond to the mystery of our redemption, through which we make our way to the brightness of our heavenly home, with the grace of Christ as our light and our guide. The light of grace is symbolized by the pillar of cloud and fire which throughout their journey protected them from the darkness of the night, and led them along their secret path to their home in the promised land."

- St Bede the Venerable

144. AN ELOQUENT SILENCE (MK 15:1-20)

'Let us then not be ashamed of the cross of our Savior, but rather glory in it… For it was not a mere man who died for us, but the Son of God, God made man."

- St Cyril of Jerusalem

Mark 15:1-20

First thing in the morning, the chief priests together with the elders and scribes, in short the whole Sanhedrin, had their plan ready. They had Jesus bound and took him away and handed him over to Pilate. Pilate questioned him, 'Are you the king of the Jews?' 'It is you who say it,' he answered. And the chief priests brought many accusations against him. Pilate questioned him again, 'Have you no reply at all? See how many accusations they are bringing against you!' But, to Pilate's amazement, Jesus made no further reply. At festival time Pilate used to release a prisoner for them, anyone they asked for. Now a man called Barabbas was then in prison with the rioters who had committed murder during the uprising. When the crowd went up and began to ask Pilate the customary favour, Pilate answered them, 'Do you want me to release for you the king of the Jews?' For he realised it was out of jealousy that the chief priests had handed Jesus over. The chief priests, however, had incited the crowd to demand that he should release Barabbas for them instead. Then Pilate spoke again. 'But in that case,' he said to them, 'what am I to do with the man you call king of the Jews?' They shouted back, 'Crucify him!' 'Why?' Pilate asked them. 'What harm has he done?' But they shouted all the louder, 'Crucify him!' So Pilate, anxious to placate the crowd, released Barabbas for them and, having ordered Jesus to be scourged, handed him over to be crucified.

The soldiers led him away to the inner part of the palace, that is, the Praetorium, and called the whole cohort together. They dressed him up in purple, twisted some thorns into a crown and put it on him. And they began saluting him, 'Hail, king of the Jews!' They struck his head with a reed and spat on him; and they went down on their knees to do him homage. And when they had finished making fun of him, they took off the purple and dressed him in his own clothes. They led him out to crucify him.

CHRIST THE LORD Why do so many people refuse to accept Christ's rule in their lives? In Christ's Kingdom, only Christ can be king. In Christ's Kingdom, everything depends on him, and our lives take on meaning only insofar as we are collaborating with him, under his orders, in the fulfillment of his will. His is the Kingdom of salvation, but he is the Savior, not us. Our own achievements avail us nothing apart from him. And that is hard for the arrogant to accept.

The streak of diabolical pride that we all inherited with original sin prefers to build up one's own kingdom, by one's own efforts, on one's own terms. This was the attraction of Barabbas. He was no petty, groveling thief. He was a violent criminal, most likely a member of the band of Sicarii, known for the concealed daggers they carried around with them. This was one of numerous insurrectionist groups that wanted to throw off the Roman yoke once and for all, using lawlessness, intimidation, and violence. In other words, they used their own strength, willpower, and wits exclusively, regardless of God's plan or will. We too always have a tendency to want to do things our own way. We may even say we want to build up Christ's Kingdom, but if we are not willing to obey God's law and Christ's Vicar, we can be sure we are falling into this blinding and destructive error of personal judgment.

When we choose Christ and his Lordship, we choose to humble ourselves and obey. Self-reliance may appear more glorious and worthy, but self-forgetfulness is true greatness. In the end, that is the only path to authentic, lasting fulfillment. Jesus himself stressed it: "Anyone who exalts himself up will be humbled, and anyone who humbles himself will be exalted" (Matthew 23:12).

CHRIST THE TEACHER Two parties are responsible, immediately and historically, for Christ's condemnation (although theologically and more profoundly, every sinner is responsible): the Jewish leaders and Pilate. They each make the wrong decision. They each exemplify two selfish tendencies that often lead us as well to make wrong decisions.

Pilate is anxious and frustrated because Jesus remains silent. The one answer Jesus gives ("It is you who say it") throws the responsibility back onto Pilate – as if Jesus is saying, "You know in your heart that my Kingdom is no threat to you or Caesar; it is a Kingdom of the heart. So you decide what to do." Pilate recognizes that justice would dictate setting Jesus free, because he has done nothing against the Roman laws. But he knows that if he doesn't accommodate the Jewish leaders and the crowd, he risks causing a public outcry. That could wind him up in trouble with his superiors and endanger whatever hopes he had for professional advancement. He is ambitious. He cares first about his career; only secondly is he concerned with the reason his career exists in the first place: the promotion of justice and the common good. How frequently ambition rides roughshod over truth and justice, to the tragic detriment of the common good! Even otherwise faithful Christians often compromise their consciences in order to pursue a Machiavellian course of justifying good ends by accepting – actively or passively – evil means.

St Mark tells us explicitly that the Jewish leaders were acting out of jealousy. They had achieved their position of influence through long and exhausting effort, and they weren't about to let this upstart rabbi from Nazareth turn their comfortable order of things topsy-turvy. They held the allegiance and admiration of the common people, they held the purse strings of the Temple, and they maintained a certain hold on the Roman authorities. If this Jesus was given free rein, they might lose all that. And so they violate their own laws of justice and then strong-arm Pilate into doing away with him. How destructive a force jealousy can be! We are so attached to our superior position, to the praise we receive, that we lower ourselves to calumny, insults, manipulations, and even violence in order to stay on top. And when we find ourselves on the bottom, the other side of the jealousy coin, envy, leads us to pursue the same despicable tactics to climb a little bit higher.

Ambition, jealousy, envy – the devil made use of these passions to consummate his destruction of the Savior two thousand years ago, and they are still some of his favorite weapons today.

CHRIST THE FRIEND St Mark relates only briefly the sufferings of Christ between the moment of condemnation and the picking up of his cross, but we should pause a little and consider them more thoroughly. They, as with all his sufferings, reveal the heart of our most faithful friend.

Pilate had Jesus scourged, and then he followed the Roman ritual of sentencing someone to crucifixion, which meant that Jesus was put into the hands of the guards for a brief period while the cross was readied. This is when the soldiers put on their little play, their game of mock worship. In the scourging and the mockery, Jesus enters more deeply into the two most common arenas of human suffering. He wants to experience everything we experience, even more intensely, so that we never have to suffer alone.

The scourging was the high point of physical suffering. The evangelists refrain from describing it in detail – they didn't need to; it was such a common public punishment in ancient times that all their readers would have seen more than one scourging with their own eyes. The leather whip that was used to tear into the victim's bare back was tipped with pieces of sharp bone or rough metal, so that it literally shredded the flesh. It is recorded that men had eyes torn out during a scourging. Others were scourged to death, and it drove some men completely insane. Jesus is no stranger to physical suffering, that constant and debilitating companion of human life. He wanted to assure us that he suffers with us, and that our physical suffering is never in vain if we unite it to his. In his acceptance of physical torture he exercised the sacrificial, loving obedience that undid Adam's disobedience and redeemed mankind from sin. Through prayer and the Eucharist, our acceptance of physical suffering can repair the sins of disobedience and self-indulgence that still abound and can apply Christ's grace to our own needy souls and those we pray for.

The soldiers' mockery involved physical suffering too, but it added a new element. They laughed at Jesus. They made fun of him. They cut him with sarcasm and disdain. They ridiculed him, scorned him, and humiliated him. Have you ever been laughed at? Have you ever been made fun of? Have you ever been spat at? Many times ridicule is even more painful than a physical blow; many times we would prefer the worst physical torments to vicious taunts from those we love. Jesus chose to suffer both. Never, not even in our loneliest, saddest moments, do we have to suffer alone. Jesus has trod this path too ahead of us, because he wants his friendship to be total. We can always find comfort and meaning no matter how anguished and hopeless life appears, because Christ has descended as far as we can go, letting the light of his love shine even there. There too the Savior reigns.

CHRIST IN MY LIFE I am glad to claim you as my King. I know that in obeying you I reach the fullness of life that you created me to enjoy. It is no shame to obey the Lord of life and history, whose wisdom is deeper than the ocean and whose goodness is broader than the sky. You are my Creator, my Redeemer, my Teacher. Thy Kingdom come, Lord, in my heart and through my heart...

I tremble when I consider the easy sin of Pilate and the Jewish leaders. I could so easily go down that path – and in fact, many times I have. How vain are my petty ambitions and jealousies and search for praise from fickle men! And yet, my heart goes there sometimes. Purify me, Lord; teach me to make your will and your Kingdom my only quest, my one desire...

Teach me to suffer with faith. You have given meaning to suffering – you alone have done that. No philosopher, no religious leader, no scientist has ever cracked the mystery of suffering, but you have embraced it and transformed it into the path of salvation. Open my eyes, Lord, so I will learn to unite my sufferings to yours, and to lighten those of my neighbor…

QUESTIONS FOR SMALL GROUP DISCUSSION

1. What struck you most in this passage? What did you notice that you hadn't noticed before?

2. There is an old phrase that Catholics have long used to describe how we should react to sufferings that come our way: "Offer it up." In the context of Christ's passion, what does this really mean, and how does one do it?

3. In your own sufferings, how have you found comfort? Have you ever had the experience of giving comfort to others who suffer? Why do you think the Church numbers "comfort the sorrowing" among her privileged works of mercy?

4. What do you think pained Christ more: the jealousy of the Jewish leaders, the ambition of Pilate, or the cruelty of the soldiers? Which of those three sins do you think is most common today?

Cf. Catechism of the Catholic Church, 571-573 on the meaning of Jesus' suffering; 309, 385, and 395 on the mystery of evil; 1851 on violence and the many forms of sin manifested in the Passion

145. THE LORD ENTHRONED (MK 15:21-39)

"But the glory of the cross led those who were blind through ignorance into light, loosed all who were held fast by sin, and ransomed the whole world of mankind."

- St Cyril of Jerusalem

Mark 15:21-39

They enlisted a passer-by, Simon of Cyrene, father of Alexander and Rufus, who was coming in from the country, to carry his cross. They brought Jesus to the place called Golgotha, which means the place of the skull. They offered him wine mixed with myrrh, but he refused it. Then they crucified him, and shared out his clothing, casting lots to decide what each should get. It was the third hour when they crucified him. The inscription giving the charge against him read: 'The King of the Jews.' And they crucified two robbers with him, one on his right and one on his left.

The passers-by jeered at him; they shook their heads and said, 'Aha! So you would destroy the Temple and rebuild it in three days! Then save yourself: come down from the cross!' The chief priests and the scribes mocked him among themselves in the same way. 'He saved others,' they said 'he cannot save himself. Let the Christ, the king of Israel, come down from the cross now, for us to see it and believe.' Even those who were crucified with him taunted him. When the sixth hour came there was darkness over the whole land until the ninth hour. And at the ninth hour Jesus cried out in a loud voice, 'Eloi, Eloi, lama sabachthani?' which means, 'My God, my God, why have you deserted me?' When some of those who stood by heard this, they said, 'Listen, he is calling on Elijah.' Someone ran and soaked a sponge in vinegar and, putting it on a reed, gave it him to drink saying; 'Wait and see if Elijah will come to take him down.' But Jesus gave a loud cry and breathed his last. And the veil of the Temple was torn in two from top to bottom. The centurion, who was standing in front of him, had seen how he had died, and he said, 'In truth this man was a son of God.'

CHRIST THE LORD Jesus has just proclaimed his Lordship to the leaders of Jerusalem at the trial in the chief priest's palace. He has just been crowned King (albeit the crown was of thorns) within the city walls. But now he is led outside the city. There he is enthroned on the cross; there they post the announcement: The King of the Jews.

Even in these tragic hours when Jesus is rejected by those he came to save, when sin and evil are given free rein, even then God's Providence is at work laying the foundation for the eternal, universal Kingdom. Jesus is King and Messiah both of the Jews and of the Gentiles. He is King of all people, all times, all places. All things were made through him, and though sin tried to wrench his kingdom from his grasp, all things remain firmly under his sway. Thus, crowned inside Jerusalem, because he is King of the Jews, and enthroned outside the city walls, because he is King of the Gentiles, in the moment of conquest, when his obedience unto death dissolves Adam's disobedience unto death, God reveals the mystery hidden since the dawn of history: that all things are to be united in Christ, the Lord. The centurion, the Roman officer, is the first human being in the entire Gospel of Mark to affirm faith in Christ as the Son of God – "In truth this man was a son of God" – the New Covenant has been inaugurated.

CHRIST THE TEACHER Christ's every word and deed is instructive; he lived them all for our sake, and each one is steeped in his eternal wisdom. And yet, this saving eloquence takes on an even greater intensity during the Passion. This is the pivotal moment of all human history. In Adam's sin, mankind fell; in Israel, God prepared mankind's recovery; in Christ's loving obedience, we were redeemed; in the Church, that redemption is brought to the remotest corners of the world. This is the summary of human history. And at this point, at Golgotha, when the wrong is righted and saving grace is merited, every detail is a torrent of instruction:

- *They had a passerby help Jesus carry his cross.* Jesus makes himself weak so that we can have a share in the glorious work of saving souls and building up his eternal Kingdom.

• *They offered him myrrh as a painkiller.* Jesus refused. He doesn't want any person who suffers physical pain to feel that he isn't with them even in the worst moments.

• *They divided up his clothes.* Jesus is completely detached from every worldly desire. How much time and money we spend on clothes, on appearances! Jesus puts them in their proper place.

• *They crucified two robbers next to him.* To the last, Jesus takes his place among sinners, his beloved sinners, whom he came to save.

• *The passersby jeered at him, and the leaders of the people continued to mock him.* Nothing, not even the most constant and resilient antagonism, can deter him from fulfilling the Father's will.

• *Darkness covered the land.* Christ is the Lord of all creation, the light of every life, and when we reject him, our souls descend into the cold shadows of self-absorption; we are lost to the darkness.

• *Jesus cries out to his Father, expressing the agony of his heart.* In quoting the first line of Psalm 22, Jesus invokes the entire Psalm, a song of near despair that transforms into steadfast hope. What a lesson of prayer is here! Christ found his deepest motivations and convictions expressed in God's Word, transformed into prayer. How God longs for us to be honest in our prayers! Why do we pose and posture with God, when he already knows what's in our hearts?

• *The famous veil of the Temple, the symbolic wall of separation that sin erected between the human family and God, is torn completely in two.* Jesus had finally done what no one since Adam could have done: lived a sinless life, reestablishing communion between man and God and giving the lost and wounded human race a new and substantial hope.

• *The centurion, gazing on the dying Christ, receives the gift of faith.* Do we want to bring others to friendship in Christ? Arguments will avail little; we must bring them to Christ himself in the Eucharist, in the Gospel, in our own witness of self-forgetful love, and Jesus will do the rest.

And there is more, much more. How glad our Lord is when we take a few minutes to consider his love, painted into every scene of the Gospels, and most especially the scene at Calvary! How much good it does to our own soul! Like Mary, we have only to "treasure all these things and ponder them" in our hearts (Luke 2:19), and we too will discover the surpassing love of God in which "all the jewels of wisdom and knowledge are hidden" (Colossians 2:3).

CHRIST THE FRIEND Jesus' gauntlet of suffering continues as he takes up his cross, climbs the hill of Golgotha, and is crucified. Again, he takes upon himself more genres of pain so as to be able to accompany all sufferers throughout history, no matter the manner or intensity of their sorrow. Jesus' hands and feet are nailed through with metal spikes. The spikes in his hands, low down on the palms or in the wrists, pierce the nerve bundle that gives the fingers all their sensitivity. And each time he takes a breath, he pushes his whole body up to fill his lungs with air, forcing those raw, exposed nerves to grate against the spikes. But now, hanging on the cross, barely recognizable and barely alive, yet another type of suffering is added to the excruciating physical pain and crescendo of mockery and taunts: the feeling of utter helplessness. Now he is pinned to the cross. Now he can only watch and wait; he can do nothing for himself or for those around him. He must simply endure to the end.

Often this is the most trying of all suffering, because it shackles love. Love always wants to do something, to reach out, to give. But often the other heart – the beloved's – is closed, and so love is left helpless. Or the situation is so completely out of our hands that, like Christ, all we can do is watch, wait, pray, and suffer. How well Jesus knows this brand of pain too! When he visited Nazareth, he couldn't perform miracles because his fellow townspeople had no faith. He experienced it as he wrestled for the souls of the Pharisees and Saducees. The wound of rejected love was still fresh where Judas had kissed him. How much that loving heart must have agonized over such tragic resistance! And here on the cross that agony is made visible. His hands and feet are immobilized, his mouth is parched – he hangs there, dying, utterly helpless.

He wanted to experience this; he wanted to prove that his friendship is so complete that he accompanies us even in our deepest frustration. Truly we have no friend like this friend, if only we would open our eyes to see. Let us be still awhile, and gaze up at love incarnate, nailed to a cross for love of you and me.

CHRIST IN MY LIFE I believe in you, Lord. Truly, you are the Son of God, the Savior of the world, the Redeemer of the whole human family, and the one who rescued me from my sins. Your love was constant. Your faithfulness never wavered. Sin and evil unleashed their worst assault and still you loved, forgave, and endured. Jesus, my Lord! Teach me to love as you love, teach me to do your will…

You have made the cross the central sign of the Church. We have crosses everywhere. You want us to think about the cross. You want us to bless ourselves with the sign of the cross. You want us to learn the wisdom of the cross, the science of the cross. Lord, unveil for me the mystery of the cross. How I long to know you better, to love you more, to follow you…

Once again you assure me that I never have to be alone. No matter what, no matter how dark the valley I'm traveling through, you are there beside me. Thank you, Lord. But what about the people who don't know you or don't trust you? Don't let them languish in their loneliness. Make me a channel of your peace, an ambassador of your friendship…

QUESTIONS FOR SMALL GROUP DISCUSSION

1. What struck you most in this passage? What did you notice that you hadn't noticed before?

2. Of the many lessons Christ teaches on Calvary, which one has meant the most to you so far in your Christian journey?

3. If a non-believing friend were to ask you, "Why did Jesus die on the cross? Why didn't he come down from the cross, as they asked him to do?" how would you respond?

4. What should we be thinking about when we make the sign of the cross?

Cf. Catechism of the Catholic Church, 606-618 Christ's offering for the liberation from mankind's sins; 1113-1116 on Christ's saving presence in the sacraments; 555, 1816, and 2015 on the cross as the way to follow Christ and the way to holiness

146. DYING FOR LOVE (MK 15:40-47)

"We are celebrating the feast of the cross, whereby darkness was dispelled and the light restored."

- St Andrew of Crete

Mark 15:40-47

There were some women watching from a distance. Among them were Mary of Magdala, Mary who was the mother of James the younger and Joset, and Salome. These used to follow him and look after him when he was in Galilee. And there were many other women there who had come up to Jerusalem with him. It was now evening, and since it was Preparation Day (that is, the vigil of the sabbath), there came Joseph of Arimathaea, a prominent member of the Council, who himself lived in the hope of seeing the kingdom of God, and he boldly went to Pilate and asked for the body of Jesus. Pilate, astonished that he should have died so soon, summoned the centurion and enquired if he was already dead. Having been assured of this by the centurion, he granted the corpse to Joseph who bought a shroud, took Jesus down from the cross, wrapped him in the shroud and laid him in a tomb which had been hewn out of the rock. He then rolled a stone against the entrance to the tomb. Mary of Magdala and Mary the mother of Joset were watching and took note of where he was laid.

CHRIST THE LORD Jesus died. And so he was able to enter the realm of the dead. The souls of those faithful men and women who had trusted in God and in God's promise during the centuries before the Incarnation were not yet in heaven. They had died in friendship with God, but the gates of heaven were still closed, because no one had yet atoned for the sin of mankind that had closed them in the first place. Now Jesus comes and achieves the atonement. And the first thing he does is to go and announce the good news to the souls who were awaiting their redemption. Now the King has rescued his faithful subjects: Abraham, Moses, David, and his foster father Joseph. Now the mystery of God's saving love is revealed to them in the piercing, loving gaze of their Savior. Now they can experience what they longed for with vibrant faith and faithful hope, the full presence of God as they await the resurrection of their bodies and the final judgment. What a joyous meeting it must have been! Each of his faithful followers hears him say, "Well done, good and faithful servant, now enter into the joy of your Lord." And how Jesus' own heart must have overflowed to say it! How he had looked forward to the moment when he would give them their crowning gift!

Christ reigns supreme over all his creatures, living and dead, faithful and unfaithful. He truly is the Lord. He is looking forward to welcoming each of us as well when our pilgrimage ends.

CHRIST THE TEACHER Christ's self-sacrifice on the cross reveals that God's love for weak and selfish sinners has absolutely no limit. Imagine if Jesus had conceded to the taunts of the Temple officials, who promised to believe in him if he would just come down from the cross. Such a move would have shown power, but not love. Love is self-giving for the good of the beloved. If Jesus had been willing to suffer in order to atone for our sins, but not to suffer completely, unto death, then he would have left room for doubt: Maybe God loves me a lot, but not so much as to forgive *this* sin, not so much as to forgive me *yet again*… Jesus left no room for doubt. His love has no limits, no conditions, no ifs or buts, only ands: He loved us so much that he become one of us, *and* he lived among us, *and* he worked and suffered the grind of ordinary life, *and* he taught and healed and revealed God's heart, *and* he founded the Church to extend his presence and grace throughout all time, *and* he let himself be betrayed, humiliated, unjustly condemned, made fun of, *and* he subjected himself to excruciating physical torments, *and* he hung helpless on the cross in our place, and he took upon himself our sins, *and* he, the Creator and Lord of life, died, *and* he loves us to the end.

This incomparable display of love achieves more than any display of power ever could. It penetrates walled up hearts and opens them to receive God's grace, hope, and rejuvenation. First the centurion – a battle-hardened veteran who had seen many men die, but none die as Jesus did – receives the gift of faith, and now Joseph of Arimathaea, a wishy-washy would-be disciple of Christ and member of the very Sanhedrin that condemned Jesus, is finally emboldened to declare his allegiance to the Lord. Joseph was most likely present at Jesus' trial, and he may have been the source of the Gospels' accounts of it, but there he feared to speak up even though he had seen Jesus' power and wisdom and felt attracted to the Lord. Only now, after the crucifixion, after seeing the extent of Christ's love, the extreme, inexhaustible flow of his mercy, only now does Joseph find enough courage to become a full-fledged follower of Christ.

For Christ, the greatest power is the power of God's love; for Christians, it ought to be just the same.

CHRIST THE FRIEND Every person can count on two things in life: suffering and death. Everything else is up for grabs, but these are unavoidable. Jesus knows this, and he also knows that these are the very things we most fear. And so he strides right into them, taking upon himself their full brunt. He already knows that he is always with us, that he understands us completely, that his compassion towards each of us is more perfect than anyone can imagine, but he also knows that we don't know this. He has to show it to us, because he yearns for us to trust him. Ever since original sin, we have had a tough time trusting God; we have been suspicious and fearful. Jesus takes advantage of his Incarnation to wipe away every last vestige of mistrust. He freely and lovingly shares in every brand of human suffering, and even in that great, looming mystery of death.

Mary: We buried him then. My heart sorrowed for him. How could I not? I sorrowed for those who had rejected him. I sorrowed because I had not been able to die instead of him. I sorrowed for the high price he had to pay to win us his grace…. And yet, somehow I felt a certain comfort, a certain peace. I knew that he had won and his victory would soon appear. And I also knew that now, everyone would be able to discover, beyond a shadow of a doubt, that even the greatest mystery of human life, suffering and death, has meaning. He had given it meaning by loving through the worst of it. Yes, even death, that most bitter fruit of the human family's rebellion against God, has been redeemed. With Jesus as our companion in life, there is simply nothing left to fear.

CHRIST IN MY LIFE I believe in what you teach us about purgatory, Lord. You will provide for your friends who die without having purified all their selfishness. You will not exclude them from heaven, but you will purify them yourself, so that they can join the eternal banquet of charity. Don't let me neglect them in my prayers; they too are my brothers and sisters, because you died for them as well…

What do I see when I look up at your cross? How can I look upon you and remain unmoved? I am so used to the crucifix, Lord. But have I learned what you want to teach me there? Open my eyes to your love. Your love is the balm that will heal all the ugly wounds that still fester in my soul. Your love will release my capacity to live as you created me to live. With the love of your heart, Lord, inflame my heart…

I must not be afraid of death. I must remember that death will come for me, and for all those I love. I must get ready for death. That sounds so strange! The world around me flees death as the greatest evil, but you embraced it willingly and lovingly. Fill me with your courage, your humility, your wisdom. Thy will be done, Lord…

QUESTIONS FOR SMALL GROUP DISCUSSION

1. What struck you most in this passage? What did you notice that you hadn't noticed before?

2. Some critics claim that Jesus never really died, and so his resurrection was only a pseudo-resurrection. How would you answer that objection? Is there anything in this passage that disproves such a theory?

3. Why do you think the women St Mark mentions stayed to watch the whole crucifixion, but the apostles weren't there? Is there a lesson in that for us?

4. Some people claim that thinking about death is morbid. As a Christian, do you agree? Why or why not?

Cf. Catechism of the Catholic Church, 1005-1014 on the meaning of Christian death; 1030-1032 on the final purification (purgatory); 632-635 on Christ's descent into the place of the dead

THE GOSPEL OF MARK CHAPTER 16

The only-begotten Son of the Eternal Father, who came on earth to bring salvation and the light of divine wisdom to men, conferred a great and wonderful blessing on the world when, about to ascend again into heaven, he commanded the Apostles to go and teach all nations, and left the Church which He had founded to be the common and supreme teacher of the peoples. For men whom the truth had set free were to be preserved by the truth; nor would the fruits of heavenly doctrines by which salvation comes to men have long remained had not the Lord Christ appointed an unfailing teaching authority to train the minds to faith. And the Church built upon the promises of its own divine Author, whose charity it imitated, so faithfully followed out his commands that its constant aim and chief wish was this: to teach religion and contend forever against errors."

- Pope Leo XIII, Aeterni patris, 1

147. IRREVERSIBLE VICTORY (MK 16:1-8)

"...the path of each single Christian, like that of the Church as a whole, leads to new life, to eternal life, through the imitation of Christ and the experience of his cross."

- Pope Benedict XVI

Mark 16:1-8

When the sabbath was over, Mary of Magdala, Mary the mother of James, and Salome, bought spices with which to go and anoint him. And very early in the morning on the first day of the week they went to the tomb, just as the sun was rising. They had been saying to one another, 'Who will roll away the stone for us from the entrance to the tomb?' But when they looked they could see that the stone – which was very big – had already been rolled back. On entering the tomb they saw a young man in a white robe seated on the right-hand side, and they were struck with amazement. But he said to them, 'There is no need for alarm. You are looking for Jesus of Nazareth, who was crucified: he has risen, he is not here. See, here is the place where they laid him. But you must go and tell his disciples and Peter, He is going before you to Galilee; it is there you will see him, just as he told you.' And the women came out and ran away from the tomb because they were frightened out of their wits; and they said nothing to a soul, for they were afraid.

CHRIST THE LORD Jesus, the crucified one, has now been raised from the dead. He is risen. Utter defeat has been transformed into irreversible victory. Evil had its way with God's anointed, and God's anointed came out victorious. The resurrection of Christ is the incontrovertible affirmation of everything he

511

taught and lived: his obedience to God's will in the face of humiliation and injustice; his insistence on the law of mercy and forgiveness, patience, and compassion; and his repeated claims to have authority to wipe away sin and to reestablish communion between God and man. If he had not been raised, his Lordship would have been debunked, which is why those who wish to invalidate his Lordship over their lives start by raising doubts about the reality of the Resurrection. But in the face of twenty centuries filled with a steady stream of saints, an unchecked growth of the Catholic Church, and an unquenchable Christian vitality, is it more reasonable to disbelieve the resurrection of Christ, or believe it? Jesus truly is the Lord, and the Resurrection is the guarantee that his followers do not follow in vain.

CHRIST THE TEACHER On the evening of Good Friday, apparent failure loomed large. Not only was the Lord dead and buried, but the apostles were holed up in a locked room, fearing for their lives. Where were all the miracles now? What did the Master's words mean now? Had God not abandoned their cause, exposed it for a naïve dream?

The Christian life is series of variations on the theme of the Holy Triduum (Holy Thursday through Easter Sunday). We follow Christ; he leads us to the hill of Calvary, where suffering and confusion darkens our hearts; through that very darkness we come into a deeper, more vital relationship with the God who is faithful, who conquers every evil, who cannot be deterred from pouring out his love and his life for our salvation.

The life of every Christian follows the pattern of the life of Christ: Good Friday – Easter Sunday; Good Friday – Easter Sunday; Good Friday – Easter Sunday. When we expect one without the other, it means we have not learned the fundamental lesson of the gospel; when we accept and adapt to that rhythm of life, we finally begin to speed along the road to wisdom, holiness, and lasting happiness.

CHRIST THE FRIEND The women who came to finish anointing Christ's body came out of sheer love. He had become everything for them. We know from other Gospel passages that he had saved them from horrible sins and great suffering, and they had come to know him as their hope and their sustenance. Now they sought him – even in his death – because they loved him, and their love could not stop seeking him.

Jesus: I rewarded their love. The huge boulder that sealed my tomb symbolizes sin, the efficient

cause of my crucifixion and the primary obstacle separating the human heart from my friend-
ship, which every heart desires so anxiously. When these women pursued me out of love, I myself
had the boulder removed; whenever you search for me out of love, or even out of a sincere desire
to love, I remove the obstacles that inhibit you from entering into intimate communion with me.
All I need is for you to truly to want to love; I will do all the rest. The message of my resurrection
is that love is stronger than death. If you love me, I will conquer your sin; if you seek me, you
will find me; if you come to me, as I am already drawing your hearts towards me, I will come to
you and share my joy with you.

CHRIST IN MY LIFE Sometimes little doubts creep into my mind, Lord. The logic of this world seems so convincing at times. But you have conquered this world; your wisdom rules it and will bring it to an end. You made me for something greater, greater even than the many beautiful pleasures of earthly life. Teach me to enjoy this life but to store up my treasures in heaven…

Clear my mind of all the false promises consumerism makes, all those illusions of pure happiness on earth that clog my faith. You have revealed the rhythm of life. Help me to find your presence and your will in all my Good Fridays and in all my Easter Sundays. May I desire Mt Calvary as much as Mt Tabor. Make me a true Christian. Teach me to perceive, embrace, and accomplish your will…

I want to love you as you ought to be loved. I want to love you so much that your angels roll away the stones that block out your light from thousands of hearts. Make me a channel of your peace. Where there is hatred, let me bring love, and where there is darkness, pour out your light through me…

QUESTIONS FOR SMALL GROUP DISCUSSION

1. What struck you most in this passage? What did you notice that you hadn't noticed before?

2. What kind of impact do you think the reality of Christ's resurrection should have on our daily lives?

3. What would popular culture say about the law of "Good Friday – Easter Sunday"? If you had assimilated that law more completely, in what way would your life change?

4. The authenticity of our love for Christ can be measured by how earnestly and actively we seek to know him and imitate him. How can we seek him better?

Cf. Catechism of the Catholic Church, 638-655 on the meaning of Christ's Resurrection; 599-618 on the meaning of Christ's death

148. SENT TO CONQUER (MK 16:9-20)

"... That missionary responsibility must once again become strong within us: if our faith makes us glad, let us feel bound to speak of it to others. The extent to which people will be able to accept it will then be in God's hands."

- *Pope Benedict XVI*

Mark 16:9-20

Having risen in the morning on the first day of the week, he appeared first to Mary of Magdala from whom he had cast out seven devils. She then went to those who had been his companions, and who were mourning and in tears, and told them. But they did not believe her when they heard her say that he was alive and that she had seen him. After this, he showed himself under another form to two of them as they were on their way into the country. These went back and told the others, who did not believe them either. Lastly, he showed himself to the Eleven themselves while they were at table. He reproached them for their incredulity and obstinacy, because they had refused to believe those who had seen him after he had risen. And he said to them, 'Go out to the whole world; proclaim the Good News to all creation. He who believes and is baptised will be saved; he who does not believe will be condemned. These are the signs that will be associated with believers: in my name they will cast out devils; they will have the gift of tongues; they will pick up snakes in their hands, and be unharmed should they drink deadly poison; they will lay their hands on the sick, who will recover.' And so the Lord Jesus, after he had spoken to them, was taken up into heaven: there at the right hand of God he took his place, while they, going out, preached everywhere, the Lord working with them and confirming the word by the signs that accompanied it.

CHRIST THE LORD With the Resurrection, Christ completed his mission on earth. All that remains is for him to enter into the eternal Tabernacle of heaven, clearing the final stretch of the path he wants us to follow. On the cross, Jesus made himself into mankind's definitive offering to God, the sacrifice that reconciles our rebellious human family with God, our creator and the source of our true meaning. By ascending bodily into heaven, Christ shows that this offering – himself – is truly acceptable to God. No longer do we need to question whether or not God is pleased with us, whether or not he has forgiven us, whether or not we can live in the communion with him that our hearts long for. If we remain in Christ (through baptism and an active life of prayer, virtue, and sacramental grace) we can be certain that our lives are already linked to heaven. As St Paul put it, "our citizenship is in heaven" (Philippians 3:20). Jesus Christ, victim of our sin, has now taken his place "at the right hand of God," which simply means that he has received all power and authority over heaven and earth. If we are faithful followers of such a Lord, we will soon take our own places at his side.

CHRIST THE TEACHER Christ came to conquer. Before he ascends into heaven, Jesus commissions his Apostles (the "Eleven" now, instead of the "Twelve,") to proclaim the gospel (meaning literally, the "good news") to the entire world. He promises that whoever believes their proclamation and is baptized will be saved. He assures them that "signs" will accompany their work, to indicate to the world that God is with them.

In these few lines, St Mark summarizes the whole history the Church. Jesus Christ is the Commander-in-Chief of an army of faithful followers on earth. His apostles are his generals (among whom Peter is the Chief of Staff), carrying out his orders to defend and extend the Kingdom of God's truth and grace to every corner of the earth. Since Christ himself commissions his generals, we can be assured that he will work through them; in fact, for the soul who really wants to discover the newness of life in Christ, the only sure way to do so is by believing in the apostolic preaching and receiving the sacraments through the apostolic succession. The Church, which the Holy Spirit guides through the apostles and their successors, the bishops, is the visible presence of Christ in time and space: as he ascends into the heavenly realm, the apostles in turn bring him (through their mission of preaching and baptizing, and the guaranteed authority and sacramental system that fulfilling such a mission presupposes) into the hearts of men on earth. As baptized Catholics ourselves, we ought not only to give due thanks to God for having reached out to our own souls through the ministry of the Church, but also eagerly fulfill our duty to take an active part in the Church's perennial mission.

CHRIST THE FRIEND Jesus knows that at times it will be hard for us to carry out this mission – just as it was hard for the apostles to believe in the Resurrection. So he promises to accompany our faith with signs that will "confirm" the gospel that we hear and pass on. These signs have never been lacking in the Church at large, and even in our own lives. Every age has boasted of its saints, those men and women who have generously heeded God's call and filled the world with miracles both visible and invisible. The Church itself has steadily increased in extension, in vitality, and in beauty, and it is still the world's most vibrant spiritual and moral force.

In our own lives too, we have experienced the presence of God in countless ways, not the least of which is the consistent and dependable sacred signs of the sacraments. So many quiet, refreshing moments in front of the Tabernacle, so much strength and consolation from Holy Communion, such deep and liberating peace after every confession… Our own experience of the Risen Lord, the Friend who never fails us, should move us to bring others closer to him, just as the apostles were moved.

Christ has been a faithful friend who fulfills his promise; the "signs" have not waned. But have we really learned to read them?

CHRIST IN MY LIFE I believe that you are enthroned and reigning even now in heaven. From there, you are working tirelessly to extend your Kingdom on earth. You are present in your Church, in every Christian, drawing each person closer to you in every moment. Your love continues to flow out upon this fallen world. You are with us; you are with me. You will never abandon me. I believe in you, Lord…

I believe in your Church, Lord. I want to stay close to you and be faithful to you, I want to do things your way, not my way, and thus I cling to your Church. You have given me a role in the Church's mission. What a mysterious yet marvelous reality. I have my own mission within the Church's mission, and only I can fulfill it. Thank you for giving it to me. Help me to accomplish it with love…

I know you fill our lives with signs of your love and power and forgiveness. You have given me so many signs in my life! How you must love me! Why do you care so much about me? O Lord, make my entire life a sign of your goodness and truth. Teach me to do your will, always with docility…

QUESTIONS FOR SMALL GROUP DISCUSSION

1. What struck you most in this passage? What did you notice that you hadn't noticed before?

2. How much should the thought of Christ's victorious presence in heaven encourage our fidelity to him here on earth?

3. Why do you think Christ chose to administer salvation through a Church made of normal (and therefore imperfect) human beings?

4. What can we do in order to become more aware of and more positively influenced by the many signs that God uses to confirm us in the faith?

Cf. Catechism of the Catholic Church, 659-667 on the meaning of our Lord's Ascension; 748-750 and 758-769 on the Church's origin, foundation, and mission, 802-810 on Christ's presence in the Church

THE GOSPEL ACCORDING TO
ST. LUKE

THE GOSPEL OF LUKE CHAPTER 1

"The Son of God himself,
who is before all ages,
the invisible, the incomprehensible, the bodiless,
the beginning from the beginning,
the light from the light,
source of life and immortality,
image of the archetype,
immoveable seal,
unchangeable image,
the Father's definition and Word,
he it is who came to his own image and took to himself
flesh for the sake of our flesh."

- St Gregory Nazienzen, Oration

149. DOING OUR PART (LK 1:1-4)

"The only-begotten Son of God, wishing to enable us to share in his divinity, assumed our nature, so that by becoming man he might make men gods."

- St Thomas Aquina

Luke 1:1-4

Seeing that many others have undertaken to draw up accounts of the events that have taken place among us, exactly as these were handed down to us by those who from the outset were eyewitnesses and ministers of the word, I in my turn, after carefully going over the whole story from the beginning, have decided to write an ordered account for you, Theophilus, so that your Excellency may learn how well founded the teaching is that you have received.

CHRIST THE LORD St Luke is the only non-Jewish author to write part of the New Testament (he wrote both the Gospel of Luke and the Acts of the Apostles). He was a doctor, a scholar (as is evident in his elegant writing style), and an artist who converted to Christianity during the first wave of evangelization after Jesus' ascension. He accompanied St Paul on his journeys and during his imprisonment, and he had the chance to meet all the major figures of the early Church. He addresses this manuscript to a high-ranking Roman official (the title "your Excellency" was reserved for such well-positioned men), who may have been financing its publication.

This background information itself speaks volumes about Jesus. He never left Palestine, he died on a cross as a criminal, and only a handful of simple fisherman continued to preach his message after he left this earth. In spite of such star-crossed beginnings, in a matter of just a few years the gospel of Jesus Christ had spread like a storm throughout the Roman Empire. It penetrated the social strata of rich and poor alike, the educated and the ignorant, shedding its saving light into human hearts of every kind.

History can boast of no similar case, unless we count the many instances of saints who brought the gospel to pagan lands. They too started infinitesimally small and soon imbued entire societies and whole cultures with Christ's truth and grace. No greater proof of Christ's universal, saving Lordship can be found than that history of his Church.

CHRIST THE TEACHER Sometimes we mistakenly think that the Bible came right from Christ's lips. Christ established his Church, the living community of his followers gathered around and "built upon the foundation of the apostles and prophets" (Ephesians 2:20). He commissioned that Church to hand on (the same term that gives the etymological root for "tradition") his message. The Bible followed, as disciples like St Luke realized a need to record the events and teachings of Christ's life and the early Church for the sake of having common reference points to guide the Church's growth. The Bible truly is the Word of God, a uniquely inspired compendium of God's own self-revelation, but it doesn't exist in a vacuum. It is a sacred text whose full meaning only shines through when read and interpreted in the context of the living Church, which preserves the tradition from which the Bible itself sprang.

That's why the term "biblical Christian" is a misnomer – the Bible is not enough to make a mature Christian. And that's why all Christians need to stay tuned to what the Church is saying; we all need to feed our souls on God's Word as served up by the Church.

CHRIST THE FRIEND St Luke is about to begin telling the most important, wonderful story in all human history. He obviously feels a need to do so, to write it out in a way that others can understand it and reflect on it. Just so, each Christian should sense a need to hand on the story of Christ.

Did Luke know that the Holy Spirit was inspiring him to write one of the infallible books of the New Testament? Probably not. He just knew that he had to do this, and he had to do it as well as he could – asking all the eyewitnesses, putting things together clearly and truly, doing his homework. He rolled up his sleeves and got to work, and that's what God used in order to achieve his plan for Luke's life, and to reach out through him to millions of thirsty, searching souls.

The Christian life is always like that. The partnership between each Christian and the Holy Spirit is a collaboration between true friends. Jesus doesn't do everything himself, leaving us with some symbolic but useless gesture, like a dad who lets his son follow behind him with a plastic lawnmower. Instead, Jesus has given us the mysterious gift of freedom, and when we join his team, he wants us to put all our creativity, talents, and love into action on his behalf. If we do, the results will far outstrip our natural capacities, but our natural capacities will still be the basis of those results. It's like the bread used at Mass. It's small, flimsy, plain, and weak, but without our giving it to God, Christ's Eucharistic presence would never come to pass.

CHRIST IN MY LIFE Your Church is so human, Lord. Its history can only be explained by your gentle, sure hand guiding and protecting it in every era. Thank you for the Church. Thank you for this Gospel. Thank you for making sure that I would have a chance to hear the Good News of your salvation. Thank you for the gift of faith. Jesus, never let me be separated from you.

So many voices clamor for my attention. Jesus, teach me to tune in to your voice. Show me how to listen to the teachings of the Church, to the advice of the saints. My life is so short! I have so little time! Help me to keep first things first. Teach me to do your will, Lord.

Sometimes it's hard for me to believe that you have made your Kingdom depend in some small way on my efforts. But it's true. You have called me, and you lead and inspire me, as you did with St Luke, to make my own unique contribution. Make me docile to heed your guidance; strengthen my spirit to persevere in doing your will; inflame my heart with true Christian zeal.

QUESTIONS FOR SMALL GROUP DISCUSSION

1. What struck you most in this passage? What did you notice that you hadn't noticed before?

2. What do you think might have been the most exciting thing about living in the first Christian communities?

3. Some critics deride the Church because of its many cases of corruption throughout history. How would you respond to someone who made such an argument to you?

4. In general, how can you tell if an inspiration or an idea really comes from God?

Cf. The Catechism of the Catholic Church, 4-10 on the nature of handing on the faith; 36-43 on knowing God through the Church and speaking of God within the limits of human language; 106-07 on the inspiration and truth of Sacred Scripture

150. THE TIME HAS FINALLY COME (LK 1:5-25)

When I read the Gospel and find there testimonies from the Law and from the Prophets, I see only Christ."

- St Jerome

Luke 1:5-25

In the days of King Herod of Judaea there lived a priest called Zechariah who belonged to the Abijah section of the priesthood, and he had a wife, Elizabeth by name, who was a descendant of Aaron. Both were worthy in the sight of God, and scrupulously observed all the commandments and observances of the Lord. But they were childless: Elizabeth was barren and they were both getting on in years. Now it was the turn of Zechariah's section to serve, and he was exercising his priestly office before God when it fell to him by lot, as the ritual custom was, to enter the Lord's sanctuary and burn incense there. And at the hour of incense the whole congregation was outside, praying. Then there appeared to him the angel of the Lord, standing on the right of the altar of incense. The sight disturbed Zechariah and he was overcome with fear. But the angel said to him, 'Zechariah, do not be afraid, your prayer has been heard. Your wife Elizabeth is to bear you a son and you must name him John. He will be your joy and delight and many will rejoice at his birth, for he will be great in the sight of the Lord; he must drink no wine, no strong drink. Even from his mother's womb he will be filled with the Holy Spirit, and he will bring back many of the sons of Israel to the Lord their God. With the spirit and power of Elijah, he will go before him to turn the hearts of fathers towards their children and the disobedient back to the wisdom that the virtuous have, preparing for the Lord a people fit for him.'

Zechariah said to the angel, 'How can I be sure of this? I am an old man and my wife is getting on in years.' The angel replied, 'I am Gabriel who stand in God's presence, and I have been sent to speak to you and bring you this good news. Listen! Since you have not believed my words, which will come true at their appointed time, you will be silenced and have no power of speech until this has happened.' Meanwhile the people were waiting for Zechariah and were surprised that he stayed in the sanctuary so long. When he came out he could not speak to them, and they realised that he had received a vision in the sanctuary. But he could only make signs to them, and remained dumb. When his time of service came to an end he returned home. Some time later his wife Elizabeth conceived, and for five months she kept to herself. 'The Lord has done this for me,' she said, 'now that it has pleased him to take away the humiliation I suffered among men.'

CHRIST THE LORD The entire history of the Old Covenant made sense only because it converged on the promised Messiah. John the Baptist, the child promised to Zechariah, is to be the Messiah's first herald, and Israel's last and greatest prophet, the final link in the Old Covenant's chain. So it is highly appropriate that when the moment comes for the Messiah to be announced, the first movement of the Messianic age takes place inside the priests' court of the Temple (where only priests could go), in accordance with the daily rhythm of prayer and sacrifice that the Old Testament had prescribed. The liturgy of the Old Covenant centered on thanking God for his past blessings and imploring him for future blessings, especially the greatest blessing of all, the arrival of the promised Messiah. St Luke begins his Gospel by plugging the story of Jesus into the very heart of the story of Israel, showing the continuity of God's action throughout the history of salvation.

But St Luke also provides another context for the beginning of the Messianic era. He provides specific references to rulers and places in the pagan world (in this passage: Herod, the King of Judaea), references that historians have cross-checked and corroborated with nonbiblical sources. In Jesus, then, the age of preparation comes to its conclusion, and the hope offered to Israel is also held out to all nations. Just as Jesus, the Savior and Redeemer, comes to dwell in and among the Jews living in Palestine, so he comes to dwell in and among the Romans, who ruled Palestine and most of the civilized world at the time.

St Luke is already cluing us in to a key characteristic of the Lord's leadership style: it has a personal, incarnational touch, but a universal extension.

CHRIST THE TEACHER Why did Zechariah hear God's voice *inside* the Temple *during* the liturgical ceremony? Why didn't God send him the message in the quiet of his garden at home, while he was meditating in comfort and contemplating the beauty of nature? Why didn't God send the angel while Zechariah was pouring over the Scriptures early in the morning, in his study, by the light of a lantern? God can speak to our hearts at any time and in any place, but he has established some normal channels, and we would be wise to attend to them: they are the various seasons and celebrations of the liturgy.

Ancient Israel had them, and it had a clergy to go along with them. All of that Old Covenant liturgical establishment was a precursor for the Church's liturgy. Just as God prepared the way for Christ through setting aside a Chosen People – an entire nation that served and followed him as a community – so Christ himself established a New Chosen People: the believing community of his Church.

Often, perhaps, we would prefer something more individualistic, something more comfortable and amenable to our personal tastes, but God is a family (the Trinity), and his salvation is administered and experienced through the family of the Church. If we are serious about seeking and fulfilling God's plan for our lives, and coming to full maturity as Christ's followers, then participating deeply in the life of the Church – above all the liturgical life of the Church: the sacraments, the seasons, the Mass – will be among our top priorities. And if it is, we will surely hear God's voice guiding and strengthening us, just as Zechariah did.

CHRIST THE FRIEND Elizabeth and Zechariah were both pure Jews and faithful to God. In fact, St Luke makes a point of saying they were exemplary in every way. And yet, God had sent them a weighty cross, one that also brought with it a social stigma in ancient Israel: they were childless. This was their great burden. Jews of the time considered it a curse to be without children. How often they must have begged God to give them the blessing of a child! How often they must have shed secret tears at the disdain of their neighbors! How it must have wrung Elizabeth's heart at times to see her neighbor's children! They must have wondered why God didn't answer their prayer. But God had heard their prayer – this is the first thing the angel Gabriel says to Zechariah, that his prayer has been heard. And God's plan was unfolding. Elizabeth's long barrenness and miraculous pregnancy were part of God's plan, just as the couple's suffering had been.

The example of God's dramatic action in their lives should fill us with comfort and confidence even in the midst of our own struggles. Any burden that God permits or sends us is part of his wise, providential plan for our good and the good of his Kingdom. He doesn't ask us to ignore our sufferings, but to bear them with trust and faith, bringing our needs and concerns to him in prayer, confident that his love knows how to work everything out in the end.

CHRIST IN MY LIFE You are the center and goal of all human history, Lord. You are enthroned even now in heaven, ruling over all creation. You are guiding all hearts and nations towards the definitive culmination of the human story. I believe in you, Lord. I believe that history has meaning, and that you forget no one. Help me to be your instrument of grace in my part of the story...

I wish I could hear your voice more clearly. But you are always speaking to my heart, drawing me closer to you, guiding me. I know this. Maybe I look too eagerly for special signs, like the one you gave to Zechariah – but even that didn't convince him. Lord, I want to believe with a fresh, simple, robust faith. Lord Jesus, increase my faith and open my heart to hear your voice...

I beg you, Lord, once and for all, please teach me to recognize your hand in the sufferings and hardships that come my way. You are all-powerful and all-good, all-knowing and all-loving. Nothing is outside of your purview. I trust in you, Lord. Increase my trust. And teach me to bolster my neighbors' trust and help them journey towards you...

QUESTIONS FOR SMALL GROUP DISCUSSION

1. What struck you most in this passage? What did you notice that you hadn't noticed before?

2. Why do you think Zechariah doubted Gabriel's message, even after seeing the glorious signs of the angel's presence?

3. Two daily liturgical sacrifices were offered in the Temple, one in the morning and one in the evening. Do you think it's significant that God chose to announce John the Baptist's arrival during the evening sacrifice instead of during the one in the morning?

4. Why do you think Gabriel made Zechariah mute as a result of his doubt? Does the "punishment fit the crime," so to speak?

Cf. Catechism of the Catholic Church, 1066-1075 on the nature, role, and importance of the Church's liturgy; 269, 304, and 450 on Christ as the Lord of history; 388 and 1040 on grasping the ultimate meaning of history

151. THE GREATEST YES (LK 1:26-38)

"Therefore, though it is God who takes the initiative of coming to dwell in the midst of men, and he is always the main architect of this plan, it is also true that he does not will to carry it out without our active cooperation."

- Pope Benedict XVI

Luke 1:26-38

In the sixth month the angel Gabriel was sent by God to a town in Galilee called Nazareth, to a virgin betrothed to a man named Joseph, of the House of David; and the virgin's name was Mary. He went in and said to her, 'Rejoice, so highly favoured! The Lord is with you.' She was deeply disturbed by these words and asked herself what this greeting could mean, but the angel said to her, 'Mary, do not be afraid; you have won God's favour. Listen! You are to conceive and bear a son, and you must name him Jesus. He will be great and will be called Son of the Most High. The Lord God will give him the throne of his ancestor David; he will rule over the House of Jacob for ever and his reign will have no end.' Mary said to the angel, 'But how can this come about, since I am a virgin?' 'The Holy Spirit will come upon you,' the angel answered, 'and the power of the Most High will cover you with its shadow.

And so the child will be holy and will be called Son of God. Know this too: your kinswoman Elizabeth has, in her old age, herself conceived a son, and she whom people called barren is now in her sixth month, for nothing is impossible to God.' 'I am the handmaid of the Lord,' said Mary; 'let what you have said be done to me.' And the angel left her.

CHRIST THE LORD Of whom can it be said, "His reign will have no end"? Only of Jesus Christ, the Son of God and the son of David (from whose descendents the promised Messiah was to be born), and the only man ever born of a virgin. Gabriel's brief announcement to Mary foretells the advent of someone absolutely unique: the Davidic king who will rule over all the nations, the one who would save mankind from their sins ("Jesus" means "God saves"), and the one who would fulfill all the Old Testament prophecies about the reunification of Israel and Judah (the "House of Jacob"). The entire Gospel is packed into this Annunciation of the Archangel Gabriel to Mary.

It is a Gospel that at times is hard to believe. Sometimes it seems almost too good to be true – too simple, too easy. On the other hand, when the sufferings and tragedies of life and the tumultuous twists and turns of human history oppress us, it seems more like a fairy tale, a pipe dream. For Mary too the announcement was almost overwhelming. But her faith and purity sensitized her to God's truth. She accepted the angel's message and all its implications for her own life – a radical, unforeseen change in her plans. She was able to do so because she had long ago assimilated a doctrine we too often ignore, one that Gabriel reminded her of: "Nothing is impossible for God."

CHRIST THE TEACHER Christmas, the part of Christ's life this Gospel passage is connected to, presents us with the mystery of God who became man, but it also includes the mystery of man cooperating in the saving action of God. God sends his messenger to Mary in order to invite her to become the mother of the Savior. She accepted the invitation, and history has never been the same. But it would have been possible for her to reject it. Like the parable Christ tells of the many townspeople who decline the king's invitation to attend his son's wedding feast, Mary could have considered God's intervention just a disruption of her plans, an inconvenience. But she did not.

When God asked her to take on a role in his plan of salvation, she said yes: "I am the handmaid of the Lord, let what you have said be done to me." Her question to the archangel, "But how can this come about, since I am a virgin?" was different than the similar sounding question Zechariah had posed: "How can I be sure of this? I am an old man and my wife is getting on in years." Zechariah was asking for proof that God could do what he promised; Mary was merely asking what God wanted her to do – she had promised her virginity to God, and she wanted to know if God was asking her something else. She didn't doubt God's wisdom or power; she just wanted more instructions. This is why the angel's response to her was generous, while his response to Zechariah was harsh. Zechariah answered God's call by saying, "Prove it to me"; Mary answered saying, "Show me the way to go."

We can learn no greater lesson than how to say yes to God. Mary's "yes" reversed Eve's "no," and paved the way for Christ's undoing of Adam's fall. Likewise, when God disrupts our lives – through the voice of conscience, the normal responsibilities and demands of our state in life, or the indications of Church teaching – our "yes" can echo Mary's and make more room for Christ in this fallen world. But our "no" – or even our "maybe" – can just as easily shut him out.

CHRIST THE FRIEND Many friends exchange gifts, but only Christ has given us his own mother, to be our solace and our refuge as we strive to follow in his footsteps.

As he was dying on the cross, Jesus entrusted his mother to the care of his "beloved disciple," and he entrusted the disciple to her care: "When Jesus saw his mother and the disciple there whom he loved, he said to his mother, 'Woman, behold, your son.' Then he said to the disciple, 'Behold, your mother.' And from that hour the disciple took her into his home" (John 19:26-27).

From its earliest days, the Church has interpreted this passage in a deeply spiritual way: since Jesus has desired to have us as his brothers and sisters, he has also desired to share with us his mother, to give us a mother in the order of grace. Through the ages, Christians in all walks of life have been inspired by Mary's example, comforted by her spiritual solicitude, and aided by her heavenly intercession. Wherever one finds true devotion to Mary (which consists primarily in the imitation of her "yes" to God, not just in pious expressions and pretty pictures), one finds as well a passionate love for Jesus Christ, the Savior. She accompanied him on every step of his earthly sojourn, and she accompanies his little brothers and sisters (that's us) with equal love and concern.

CHRIST IN MY LIFE Thank you for making me a Christian. You are the one Savior, the promised Messiah, and your Kingdom will have no end. You have called me into your Kingdom. What more could I ask for? You have given me your friendship. Lord, teach me to live closer to you, to have the same scale of values that you have, and to see all things with your eyes.

Mary, you were just a girl when God came and invited you to be the mother of the Savior. Even then you knew that God's will was the highest and wisest calling. You didn't fear missing out on all that the world had to offer, because you only wanted to stay close to the world's Creator. Teach me to trust and love Christ, and teach me to give him to others, as you gave him to us.

How strange, Lord, that you made the history of salvation depend not only on your own actions, but also on the free cooperation of your creatures! You waited for Mary to say yes before coming to be our Savior. You wait for each of us to say yes before coming to save us. I renew my "yes" right now. Teach me to help others say yes too; only what I do for your Kingdom will last forever.

QUESTIONS FOR SMALL GROUP DISCUSSION

1. What struck you most in this passage? What did you notice that you hadn't noticed before?

2. What can we do to renew our appreciation of the wonderful miracle of Christmas, which we so often take for granted?

3. How can we benefit more from Mary's motherly interest in our Christian discipleship?

4. Christ asked something difficult from Mary. Do you think she ever regretted her answer? Do you know anyone else who has said yes to something difficult that God asked of them?

Cf. Catechism of the Catholic Church, 484-507 on the privileges and role of Mary in Christ's Kingdom; 456-478 on the mission and uniqueness of Jesus Christ, Son of God and man

152. MARY'S SONG (LK 1:39-56)

"The Holy Spirit heated, inflamed and melted Mary with love, as fire does iron, so that the flame of the Spirit was seen and nothing was felt but the fire of the love of God."
- St Ildefonsus of Toledo

Luke 1:39-56

Mary set out at that time and went as quickly as she could to a town in the hill country of Judah. She went into Zechariah's house and greeted Elizabeth. Now as soon as Elizabeth heard Mary's greeting, the child leapt in her womb and Elizabeth was filled with the Holy Spirit. She gave a loud cry and said, 'Of all women you are the most blessed, and blessed is the fruit of your womb. Why should I be honoured with a visit from the mother of my Lord? For the moment your greeting reached my ears, the child in my womb leapt for joy. Yes, blessed is she who believed that the promise made her by the Lord would be fulfilled.' And Mary said: 'My soul proclaims the greatness of the Lord, and my spirit exults in God my saviour; because he has looked upon his lowly handmaid. Yes, from this day forward all generations will call me blessed, for the Almighty has done great things for me. Holy is his name, and his mercy reaches from age to age for those who fear him. He has shown the power of his arm, he has routed the proud of heart. He has pulled down princes from their thrones and exalted the lowly. The hungry he has filled with good things, the rich sent empty away. He has come to the help of Israel his servant, mindful of his mercy – according to the promise he made to our ancestors – of his mercy to Abraham and to his descendants for ever.' Mary stayed with Elizabeth about three months and then went back home.

CHRIST THE LORD Elizabeth knows what's going on. After years of infertility, God has seen fit to make her the mother of John the Baptist, the Messiah's herald, whom she is still carrying in her womb. In response to such a privilege she has drawn closer to God, filled as she is with humble gratitude and a new appreciation of his mercy and generosity. Therefore, God begins to fill her with the Holy Spirit, who in turn keeps drawing her deeper into the mysterious and wonderful events taking place through and around her. This intimate union with God enables her to perceive God's presence in Christ, even though he is only an embryo in Mary's womb. And she calls him "my Lord."

Before he ever worked any wonders, before he mesmerized the crowds with his preaching, before he rose from the dead, indeed, from all eternity, Jesus is "the Lord."

CHRIST THE TEACHER It's impossible to tell the story of Christmas without including Mary. As Christ's first and most faithful disciple, the first one to welcome him into the world, she shows all of us how to live every Advent and Christmas season – indeed, every season of our Christian life – with faith. Through her example, Christ teaches us how to respond to God's action in and around us: by believing in him and by trusting that whatever he may be asking of us is the best available option.

Who are we to argue with God, to disobey him? Will he deceive us? Will he lead us astray? Mary, partially enlightened by her heartfelt knowledge of God's plan as revealed in the Old Testament scriptures, could not see clearly how God's plans would work themselves out in the end. Even so, humbly and trustingly she put her faith in them, and for that wise faith she was "blessed among women," as Elizabeth exclaimed. The Lord is constantly hoping that we will put our trust in him in the same way, so that he can shower his blessings upon us as well.

What was Mary's secret? Why was she able to believe so firmly and to fulfill her vocation so magnificently? Why did she succeed where Eve had failed? She reveals her secret in this hymn of praise that bursts from her heart as soon as she greets Elizabeth.

During the whole journey from Nazareth to the hill country outside Jerusalem where Elizabeth and Zechariah lived, she had been joyfully contemplating all that God had done in her life and in the whole history of salvation. When she meets Elizabeth and realizes that God has revealed his plans to her as well, she feels free to give full expression to her thoughts and sentiments. She sings the Magnificat, a prayer that still echoes throughout the world every day through the liturgy of the Church. In its simple words, imbued with the prayers of the Old Testament, we glimpse Mary's vision of reality, in which God rules all things with perfect power and with a wisdom that confounds the vain ambition of men. Humility, a serene recognition of our utter dependence on God, unleashes the power of divine grace in the world. Those who depend on themselves – the rich, the self-satisfied, the proud, the powerful – thwart God's action in and through them. This is Mary's secret – and it is a secret no longer. She teaches it to all who are willing to learn.

CHRIST THE FRIEND God is already caring for us long before we realize it. He has had a plan in mind for us, a particular vocation, a unique role in his Kingdom, from before we were born, before we were ever conceived. In discovering and living out that plan we find our true and lasting joy. Why else is John the Baptist able to "leap for joy" while he is still in his mother's womb? Only because God had made him the herald, the precursor, the one who would announce the imminent manifestation of the Messiah – this was his God-given mission in life, his vocation. Before he is aware of it, he is already fulfilling it.

Likewise, before we hear God's call in our life, he is already preparing us to follow it – and hoping that when the call comes we will respond generously, so that he can make our hearts leap continually with joy until he welcomes us into his heavenly Kingdom.

CHRIST IN MY LIFE Lord, are you still at work in the world the way you were back when these wonderful happenings were unfolding? I know you are. I know that every time Mass is celebrated, it's a new Annunciation, a new Bethlehem, a new Calvary. I know that you never cease drawing us to yourself. Open my eyes, increase my faith! I want to see you at work in all things...

Humility is a mystery to me, Lord. How humble Mary must have been! Unspoiled, uncontaminated by original sin and the slew of selfish tendencies it sets loose in our souls! Mary, my Mother, teach me your secret. Teach me to be truly humble, truly great in God's eyes, so that my life will bear fruit for Christ's Kingdom...

Lord, I know that you really do have something in mind for me. You created me to know you and love you as only I can. My concept of my vocation may not be in perfect sync with yours. But even so, I want to follow you. I want to discover and fulfill your will for me. I want to perceive it and understand it more deeply every day, so that I can embrace it more fully each moment...

QUESTIONS FOR SMALL GROUP DISCUSSION

1. What struck you most in this passage? What did you notice that you hadn't noticed before?

2. How can we be more sensitive, like Elizabeth, to the action of God in our lives? How can we cultivate the beautiful virtue of gratitude?

3. What more can we do to discover our true vocation? How can we follow it more energetically?

4. What aspects of popular culture encourage us to think of life in terms of our God-given mission, as God thinks of us? What aspects discourage that?

Cf. Catechism of the Catholic Church, 484-507 on the privileges and role of Mary in Christ's Kingdom; 456-478 on the mission and uniqueness of Jesus Christ, Son of God and man

153. THE FRUITS OF OBEDIENCE (LK 1:57-80)

"After the fullness of time had come, there came too the fullness of the Godhead."

- St Bernard of Clairvaux

Luke 1:57-66

Meanwhile the time came for Elizabeth to have her child, and she gave birth to a son; and when her neighbours and relations heard that the Lord had shown her so great a kindness, they shared her joy. Now on the eighth day they came to circumcise the child; they were going to call him Zechariah after his father, but his mother spoke up. 'No,' she said 'he is to be called John.' They said to her, 'But no one in your family has that name,' and made signs to his father to find out what he wanted him called. The father asked for a writing-tablet and wrote, 'His name is John.' And they were all astonished. At that instant his power of speech returned and he spoke and praised God. All their neighbours were filled with awe and the whole affair was talked about throughout the hill country of Judaea. All those who heard of it treasured it in their hearts. 'What will this child turn out to be?' they wondered. And indeed the hand of the Lord was with him.

His father Zechariah was filled with the Holy Spirit and spoke this prophecy: 'Blessed be the Lord, the God of Israel for he has visited his people, he has come to their rescue and he has raised up for us a power for salvation in the House of his servant David, even as he proclaimed, by the mouth of his holy prophets from ancient times, that he would save us from our enemies and from the hands of all who hate us. Thus he shows mercy to our ancestors, thus he remembers his holy covenant, the oath he swore to our father Abraham that he would grant us, free from fear, to be delivered from the hands of our enemies, to serve him in holiness and virtue in his presence, all our days. And you, little child, you shall be called Prophet of the Most High, for you will go before the Lord to prepare the way for him. To give his people knowledge of salvation through the forgiveness of their sins; this by the tender mercy of our God who from on high will bring the rising Sun to visit us, to give light to those who live in darkness and the shadow of death, and to guide our feet into the way of peace.' Meanwhile the child grew up and his spirit matured. And he lived out in the wilderness until the day he appeared openly to Israel.

CHRIST THE LORD Christ the Lord fulfills both God's promises and the human heart's deepest longings.

The beginning of Zechariah's prophecy links his son's mission of announcing the Messiah's arrival with the whole history of Israel. Ever since our first parents fell from grace, God had been preparing the world for a Savior. The events, personalities, and prophesies of the Old Covenant were orchestrated with Christ in mind; they always pointed towards the Redeemer and Savior. Zechariah recognizes this. After his nine months of muteness, during which he had plenty of time to reflect, pray, and listen to God's words (instead of drowning them out with his own idle chatter), he mulled over the marvelous history of Israel, and God was able to give him a clear vision of what the Messianic age consisted in: the fulfillment of God's many faceted, ancient, and constantly renewed promise of salvation.

The second half of his prophecy takes a different angle on things. It looks into the longings of the human spirit that had been alienated from God and exiled from its true homeland because of sin. The human soul yearns for forgiveness – we long to know that we are loved unconditionally, generously, no matter what. The human mind longs for light – we hunger to know the truth of things, the reason we exist, where we are going, the meaning of life, and the path to fulfillment. And all of us pine above all for peace – the peace that is so much more than a mere absence of war, the peace that is fullness, prosperity, goodness, social harmony, creative expansiveness, and cultural flourishing.

God's Savior comes to bring all of these mighty gifts. He comes, as John the Baptist will announce, to inaugurate a New Creation, a New Covenant that will end in an everlastingly fruitful life.

CHRIST THE TEACHER Elizabeth and Zechariah are put to the test when the time comes to name their child. It was customary to give firstborn boys names that would link them to their families, their fathers, and their fathers' fathers. But this elderly couple chooses a name foreign to their family. They do so because that's what God asked them to do through the angel's message. Fidelity to God's will in this case means causing a stir. It means bucking social convention. It means risking the gossipmongers' epithets. But they do the right thing – and as a result, Zechariah miraculously recovers his speech, and the whole region is thrown into awestruck admiration of God. Elizabeth's and Zechariah's fidelity to God's will in spite of social pressure plants the seeds that John the Baptist will later harvest when he begins his mission of preaching and baptizing.

Whenever God makes his will known to us, through the voice of conscience, Church teaching, or even strong interior motions of the Holy Spirit, he does so for a reason. Our obedience will draw us closer to God personally, but it will also cause a domino effect of grace and blessing to those around us. Trusting obedience to God and his Church is always the best policy.

CHRIST THE FRIEND We take for granted John the Baptist's role in the story of Christ – we are so used to it. But isn't there something strange about it? Was it absolutely necessary to send a herald ahead of the Messiah? Couldn't the Messiah handle the job himself? Probably he could have, but his choice to send a forerunner reveals something essential about his personality.

Jesus never forces his way into our lives. He is too polite, too respectful. He refuses to conquer hearts by compulsion. He acts gently, gradually. He prepares us for the special graces he has in store for us. Since he is always thinking of us, he guides us little by little. The more generously we respond to the many messengers and signs he sends ahead of him, the more he will pick up the pace of his action in our lives. But even then, his grace warms our soul like sunlight: silently, gently, but surely. Such is our Lord, who longs to be our closest friend.

CHRIST IN MY LIFE I believe in you, Lord Jesus. I believe that you are the only Son of the Father, the Savior of all people, the way, the truth, and the life. I believe that you were born of the Virgin Mary, that you came to earth for our salvation, that only in your name can we find salvation. And I believe that you will come again to judge all of us and that your Kingdom will have no end...

I often feel pressure to conform to social patterns instead of being faithful to my call to holiness. How can I love you wholly and still be prudent? Lord, it's so hard to keep the balance. I want to fulfill the life-mission you have given me, but at times I just don't see things clearly. But I trust in you, Lord. You will guide me, in spite of my clumsiness and egoism. You are faithful...

Sometimes I wish you would be less polite with me – force your way into my heart, Lord! I want to love you more and to love others as you love me, but my selfishness clings to my soul and weighs me down. Purify me, Lord. Strip away every stain of egoism and self-absorption so that I can be truly free to live as you created me to live, to fulfill the mission you have given me in life...

QUESTIONS FOR SMALL GROUP DISCUSSION

1. What struck you most in this passage? What did you notice that you hadn't noticed before?

2. What are the most dependable ways to identify God's will in our lives?

3. Zechariah's song rejoices in the salvation God sends through the Messiah. How should this healthy desire for salvation manifest itself in a Christian's life in our day and age?

4. According to this passage, the Messiah will bring satisfaction to all the longings of the human heart. Where does popular culture claim such satisfaction can be found?

Cf. Catechism of the Catholic Church, 1-3 on God's long-term plan of salvation; 27-30 on the human heart's natural desire for God; 51-53 on God's loving plan of salvation; 54-64 on all the stages of revelation leading up to Christ

THE GOSPEL OF LUKE CHAPTER 2

"For this cause he came down upon earth, that by pursuing death he might kill the rebel that slew men. For one underwent the judgment, and myriads were set free. One was buried, and myriads rose again. He is the mediator between God and man. He is the resurrection and salvation of all. He is the guide of the erring, the shepherd of men who have been set free, the life of the dead, the charioteer of the cherubim, and the king of kings, to whom be the glory for ever and ever. Amen."

- St Alexander of Alexandria

154. THE PROMISE OF PEACE (LK 2:1-14)

"He does not want to overwhelm us with his strength. He takes away our fear of his greatness. He asks for our love: so he makes himself a child."

- Pope Benedict XVI

Luke 2:1-14

Now at this time Caesar Augustus issued a decree for a census of the whole world to be taken. This census – the first – took place while Quirinius was governor of Syria, and everyone went to his own town to be registered. So Joseph set out from the town of Nazareth in Galilee and travelled up to Judaea, to the town of David called Bethlehem, since he was of David's House and line, in order to be registered together with Mary, his betrothed, who was with child. While they were there the time came for her to have her child, and she gave birth to a son, her first born. She wrapped him in swaddling clothes, and laid him in a manger because there was no room for them at the inn. In the countryside close by there were shepherds who lived in the fields and took it in turns to watch their flocks during the night. The angel of the Lord appeared to them and the glory of the Lord shone round them. They were terrified, but the angel said, 'Do not be afraid. Listen, I bring you news of great joy, a joy to be shared by the whole people. Today in the town of David a sav-iour has been born to you; he is Christ the Lord. And here is a sign for you: you will find a baby wrapped in swaddling clothes and lying in a manger.' And suddenly with the angel there was a great throng of the heavenly host, praising God and sing-ing: 'Glory to God in the highest heaven, and peace to men who enjoy his favour.'

CHRIST THE LORD The universe is not a democracy. Rather, it is ruled directly by God, who is a King, and his Kingdom is one of peace – the interior peace that comes from a clean conscience and the knowledge that our heavenly Father loves us, and the exterior peace that comes from communities built on humility, generosity, charity, and solidarity. Just as David (who was also one "anointed" by God) brought peace to ancient Israel, so his descendent, Jesus Christ, born in David's city, will bring universal peace to all mankind. Those who submit to his rule will begin to experience that peace even now, while his Kingdom is still incomplete. Those who rebel against his rule, ignoring or disdaining his wisdom and authority, will never experience the peace they long for – neither in this world, nor in the world to come. Jesus is the Prince of Peace, but the peace he came to give can only be had if we obey him as our wise and loving Lord.

As his followers, we often wonder how we can more effectively communicate this message of peace. Through the mystery of his birth, Jesus teaches us that eloquence in announcing the message comes from obedience in doing God's will. Jesus obeys the divine decision to become a human being, to be born as an infant, unable to utter a word. Yet, at that very moment of his seeming weakness, the angels come and announce the message with a superhuman power and beauty. The Lord is the one who builds his Kingdom; our task is simply to carry out whatever orders he gives us.

CHRIST THE TEACHER We tend to search for elaborate methods to get into contact with God. We often expect to find God in extraordinary circumstances. But we're usually wrong. The shepherds were responsibly fulfilling their normal, unglamorous duties when the angels appeared to them. Joseph and Mary welcomed the Son of God in a poor stable-cave while they were waiting to register for the census. The great lesson of the Incarnation is precisely that God wants to meet us – and befriend us – right where we are. With Christ, the everyday circumstances of the human condition become occasions of divine revelation and grace-filled salvation. St Theresa of Avila used to say that she found the Lord among the pots and pans; with a simple, childlike faith, we can do the same.

The shepherds were shivering in the cold, watching over their tranquil flocks, gazing at the stars, mulling over their worries. They had no reason to expect that anything special would happen that night. But God finds a way to break through the routine.

Joseph was concerned for his wife, who had to give birth in a grotto used to shelter livestock. How he would have longed to give Jesus a worthier welcome! Yet he had to do the best he could under the circumstances, and God took his best and turned it into the most eloquent story in human history. God throws off his glory and power and wraps himself in humility and poverty, because he wants to walk with his people and lead them home to heaven.

Mary, whose heart had been beating in sync with Christ's Sacred Heart for nine months now – nurturing in her womb the sacred humanity of our Savior and nurturing in her mind the unfathomable love of God – was most likely not distracted at all by the circumstances. Her gaze was fixed entirely on Jesus. Every detail of the night was emblazoned on her memory, and each one spoke to her of God. The hay, the manger, the cave, the cold, the swaddling clothes, the animals, the darkness… Jesus had chosen to be born in their midst, and that was enough of an explanation for one who believed.

CHRIST THE FRIEND God is all-powerful. He is all knowing. He could have come to us in any way at all, but he chose to do so quietly. He chose to give us a "sign" by becoming an "infant wrapped in swaddling clothes and laid in a manger."

Small, weak, and helpless – that's how our Lord comes to us, because he wants us to welcome him, to let him into our lives. Would we feel drawn to him if he had come in the form of a powerful giant? Probably not. But who can resist the charm of a helpless baby? By making himself weak, in need of constant care and attention, he draws us into a relationship with him, a relationship that God has longed to restore ever since it was shattered in the Garden of Eden. Each Christmas, and each day, when the Bethlehem event is renewed on the altar during Mass, God reissues his gentle invitation. Will we accept? Will we let Christ come into our lives anew, or will we keep him at a distance, afraid to risk our self-sufficiency and comfort for the sake of a helpless, needy child? It's cold in that Bethlehem cave, and he's hoping to be warmed by our embrace.

CHRIST IN MY LIFE I believe in you, and I want to follow you. I don't want to rule you or rule the universe, or even rule my own life and the lives of those around me. I am your ambassador, your servant, your messenger, your soldier. Do with me as you will, Lord. I ask only that you bring your peace to my heart each day, and make me an instrument to bring that same peace to those around me...

Sometimes it's easy for me to find you among the pots and pans, but other times I feel quite alone. How can I see your hand at work in the normal events of my daily life? I want to find you there, to embrace you there, to converse with you there, to obey you and follow you there. Lord, I believe, but help my unbelief...

You are so gentle, so respectful. You never force your way into my heart. Teach me to be like you, Lord: full of strength, but a strength that acts with respect, gentleness, and humility. Teach me to love my neighbors, to treat them with the same sincere and attentive kindness with which you have always treated me. And teach me to love all my neighbors, not just the ones who are easy to love...

QUESTIONS FOR SMALL GROUP DISCUSSION

1. What struck you most in this passage? What did you notice that you hadn't noticed before?
2. How can we live our normal responsibilities with greater fidelity, so that we will be more attuned to God's presence and action in and through them?
3. What evidence should there be in the daily life of Christians that Christ is really the Lord of their life?
4. What can we do to live the liturgical seasons (like Christmas) in a way more pleasing to God, more in accord with the reason for which they exist?

Cf. Catechism of the Catholic Church, 2544-2547 on poverty of heart (which the shepherds had); 525-526 on the Christmas Mystery; 456-463 on why Jesus came to earth in the Incarnation

155. PRAISING AND PONDERING (LK 2:15-21)

"God made himself small so that we could understand him, welcome him, and love him."

- Pope Benedict XVI

Luke 2:15-21

Now when the angels had gone from them into heaven, the shepherds said to one another, 'Let us go to Bethlehem and see this thing that has happened which the Lord has made known to us.' So they hurried away and found Mary and Joseph, and the baby lying in the manger. When they saw the child they repeated what they had been told about him, and everyone who heard it was astonished at what the shepherds had to say. As for Mary, she treasured all these things and pondered them in her heart. And the shepherds went back glorifying and praising God for all they had heard and seen; it was exactly as they had been told. When the eighth day came and the child was to be circumcised, they gave him the name Jesus, the name the angel had given him before his conception.

CHRIST THE LORD When Jesus was born, the angels of heaven could not restrain their joy, so they appeared to some humble shepherds and gave them a Christmas concert they would never forget. The birth of Christ shows that its consequences are unlimited by time and space, and the same goes for his Lordship. This child, this infant, holds the universe in his hands – which is why we sometimes see the infant Jesus depicted as a king, holding a sphere in his left hand (symbolizing the world) and a scepter in his right hand (symbolizing power and authority). Christ is Lord because he is God's Anointed, even when lying in a lowly little manger.

Perhaps the most beautiful thing about this absolute, universal Lordship is that it exists entirely for our sake. St Luke makes a point of telling us about Christ's circumcision day, the day when he shed his first drop of blood, taking his place among sinners so that he could redeem them. It was traditional to give a boy his name on the same day he was circumcised. And so Mary and Joseph give him the name that God had assigned him through Gabriel's message: Jesus, which means "God saves." Luke reminds us that this name was given to him even before he was conceived in Mary's womb. The Word of God created us because he knew we would like it, and now he comes to redeem us because he knows we need it. Christ's whole life, his whole mission, is for our good, for our salvation.

Jesus' us-centered orientation wasn't an afterthought; we are the reason Jesus came to earth, lived, taught, healed, suffered, died, and rose again. Perhaps this is why saints throughout the ages have found in the simple name of "Jesus" one of their favorite and most fruitful prayers. Merely invoking our Lord, repeating his name over and over again, gives rest to our souls, because that's exactly what he came to do.

CHRIST THE TEACHER How are we to respond to the wonders God has done and is doing in the world and in our own lives? We can respond by following the shepherds' example. First, we should "hurry away" to find Christ, go in haste to seek him out in the midst of his family, the Church, here represented by Mary and Joseph. Second, as the shepherds "repeated what they had been told" about Christ, we should make known the message we have received. Third, we should "glorify and praise" the God who comes to save. We must allow the wonder of God's love to burst into our lives, as the shepherds did. We too must let God's marvelous works amaze us, never falling into a blasé attitude, a routine, been-there-done-that Christian mediocrity. Children get excited every Christmas, so why shouldn't we – who know so much more about the real meaning of the story – let it fill us with spiritual enthusiasm every single day?

We should also respond as Mary did: "Mary treasured all these things, and pondered them in her heart." God did not tell Mary his entire plan. We know much more than she did about how everything was going to work out. She had to walk in the dim light of faith, one step at a time, trusting in God, witnessing his action, and seconding it whenever she could. But she paid attention. She knew that the life and mission of Christ eclipsed in importance any other concern or event that might surface. She pondered in her heart all of God's gifts to her, all of his words, all of his actions and plans… She was truly a woman of the Kingdom. We need to learn this lesson as well, to be men and women who "seek first the Kingdom," and let everything else fall comfortably (and properly) into second place (cf. Matthew 6:33).

CHRIST THE FRIEND God wants to give us the fullness of life. And he can give it to us – as a matter of fact, he is the only one who can give it to us. The problem is that we tend not to pay attention to him. His love, however, is determined. So he came up with a radical solution: he became a little baby, a helpless infant. Everyone pays attention to babies. So now we will look at him, even if only to see how cute he is. That's a start. Let's not belittle this reality! Coming to the baby Jesus and letting ourselves be charmed by his simplicity and innocence should be a frequent practice of our spiritual life – not something reserved exclusively to the Christmas season. We should, like the shepherds, gather around the manger with Mary and Joseph, and bask in the warm light of God's love radiating out from the infant Lord.

CHRIST IN MY LIFE You have revealed your name to me, because you want to stay close to me. Whenever I speak your name from my heart, you turn your attention to me. When I call you, you always come to me. You want to be available, to be close, to stay near. Why don't I call you more often? Why do I let the hustle and bustle of life drown you out? Jesus, please walk with me...

More than half the people in this world still don't know you or believe in you. I am one of the privileged minority who has received the Good News. Teach me, Lord, to be full of joy and generosity, like the shepherds, full of wonder and contemplation, like Mary, and full of the eager desire to spread the word...

How odd this Christmas story really is! The Creator and Sustainer of the universe becoming a little infant! No other religion has such a strange event. Dear Jesus, let me hold you in my arms. You are so small, so helpless. Let me take care of you. I adore you, Lord. I will never leave you; I will never abandon you. You are my life and my joy. You are safe with me, and you know that I love you. You can trust me, my Child; I love you, and I will watch over you...

QUESTIONS FOR SMALL GROUP DISCUSSION

1. What struck you in this passage? What did you notice that you hadn't noticed before?

2. Why aren't we as eager as the shepherds to share with others our knowledge and experience of Christ?

3. How can we encourage each other to better imitate the Blessed Virgin in her prayerful spirit, "pondering all these things" in our hearts?

4. What do you think St Joseph's reaction to these events was?

Cf. Catechism of the Catholic Church, 2673-2679 on praying the way Mary prayed; 2544-2547 on poverty of heart (which the shepherds had); 525-526 on the Christmas Mystery

156. THE FIRST CHRISTIAN HOMILY (LK 2:22-40)

"The patriarchs and prophets longed and prayed and yearned with all their hearts for this time. That just man Simeon at long last saw this time and his joy was boundless."

- St Charles Borromeo

Luke 2: 22-40

And when the day came for them to be purified as laid down by the Law of Moses, they took him up to Jerusalem to present him to the Lord – observing what stands written in the Law of the Lord: Every first-born male must be consecrated to the Lord – and also to offer in sacrifice, in accordance with what is said in the Law of the Lord, a pair of turtledoves or two young pigeons.

Now in Jerusalem there was a man named Simeon. He was an upright and devout man; he looked forward to Israel's comforting and the Holy Spirit rested on him. It had been revealed to him by the Holy Spirit that he would not see death until he had set eyes on the Christ of the Lord. Prompted by the Spirit he came to the Temple and when the parents brought in the child Jesus to do for him what the Law required, he took him into his arms and blessed God; and he said: 'Now, Master, you can let your servant go in peace, just as you promised; because my eyes have seen the salvation which you have prepared for all the nations to see, a light to enlighten the pagans and the glory of your people Israel.' As the child's father and mother stood there wondering at the things that were being said about him, Simeon blessed them and said to Mary his mother, 'You see this child: he is destined for the fall and for the rising of many in Israel, destined to be a sign that is rejected – and a sword will pierce your own soul too – so that the secret thoughts of many may be laid bare.'

There was a prophetess also, Anna the daughter of Phanuel, of the tribe of Asher. She was well on in years. Her days of girlhood over, she had been married for seven years before becoming a widow. She was now eighty-four years old and never left the Temple, serving God night and day with fasting and prayer. She came by just at that moment and began to praise God; and she spoke of the child to all who looked forward to the deliverance of Jerusalem. When they had done everything the Law of the Lord required, they went back to Galilee, to their own town of Nazareth. Meanwhile the child grew to maturity, and he was filled with wisdom; and God's favour was with him.

CHRIST THE LORD Under the influence of the Holy Spirit, Simeon joyfully explains who this newborn child really is. Christ is "God's salvation": God had long ago promised to save fallen mankind (thus he is a "light for revelation to the Gentiles"; i.e., the non-Jews), and he had promised to save a remnant from unfaithful Israel (thus he is "glory for your people Israel").

But Christ is also a sign of contradiction. God will not save us against our will. Many respond to Christ with humility and gladness, pushing aside their selfishness to follow him. Yet others respond with suspicion and disdain; they prefer to clutch their own little kingdoms instead of submitting to the true King. Throughout the Gospels, we see both reactions, and in the world today we also see them. Even in our own hearts we often vacillate between rising up to follow the Lord and falling away from his friendship. The only constant in this equation is Christ himself, the everlasting Lord; we can always count on him.

CHRIST THE TEACHER Mary and Joseph are obliged to follow the dictates of Jewish law in regards to their firstborn son. Because children are a gift from God, ultimately they belong to God. The Jewish law prescribed a ritual by which the parents could acknowledge this truth: they would offer God a gift in symbolic exchange for their child. This is what St Luke refers to when he writes that Mary and Joseph "consecrated" Jesus to God. (This ritual is also related to the Passover, when God slew the firstborn sons of Egypt, but spared those of Israel.)

After giving birth, women were required by Jewish law to wait for a specified amount of time before they could appear in the Temple or participate in any religious ritual. Once the time had elapsed, they rejoined community worship by offering two sacrifices (this is what the "pair of turtledoves" was for). This requirement reflects the religious value that God's people have always put upon human life, a way of acknowledging the sacredness of life. When a woman gave birth, she was participating intimately in a mystery that touched God directly, since he was the creator and sustainer of all life (most especially human life, since the Jews believed that all men and women were created "in the image of God"). So it was appropriate that she remain segregated from normal activities immediately afterwards.

Christ's submission to these religious laws shows that he verifies the reverential view of human life that they reflect. Every child, every human life, is a gift from God, a participation in the mystery of God's infinite power and unwearied love. We cannot own, nor govern the life of an individual person, even those of our own children. Jesus is pro-life, because he is the author and protector of life – of each of our lives.

CHRIST THE FRIEND Mary offers two pigeons instead of the normal combination of a lamb and a pigeon. A stipulation of the Jewish law allowed this for those families too poor to afford a lamb (pigeons cost much less than lambs).

Jesus Christ, King of the universe, not only became man, but he became a member of a normal, humble, working-class family. Mary, Queen of heaven and earth, lived her incomparably holy life as a wife and mother in a poor family. Joseph, patron of the universal Church and greatest of all Patriarchs, worked hard just to keep enough bread on the table. Such a normal family, such an ordinary life… God wants us to know that his Kingdom is within us; we can find him in the midst of our normal occupations, where he wants to be with us as our friend. Though we may be ordinary people, by letting Christ into our lives we can end up doing extraordinary things.

Jesus: You don't need as much as you think you need to be happy. True happiness comes from a kind of wealth that no one sees, the wealth of a heart set on knowing and loving me. If I had come among you as a worldly prince, surrounded by luxury and comfort, I would have given you reason to believe that such things bring meaning and happiness. But I didn't. Have you thought deeply about my poverty? Do material things have too tight a hold on your heart? Look at me, look at my example. Come and live with me in Nazareth, and I will show you the path to lasting happiness.

CHRIST IN MY LIFE It's a good thing you are patient with me, Lord; I am so inconsistent. Every day is a little war between my selfishness and my faith. You know that I wish the war were over, but I know that it's part of your plan. Somehow, my efforts to follow you in spite of my selfish tendencies give you glory, extend your Kingdom, and make my soul grow and mature. And you never leave me to fight alone…

You despise no human life, because you see every person as they truly are: unique reflections of infinite beauty. You died for every person. Your love has no exceptions. Am I following your example? Is my heart open to all people? You know I have a tendency to play favorites, but I want to love as you love, because that's what you made me for. Teach me to love, Lord…

Wealth, pleasure, and luxury items are always attracting me, and yet you chose to live in poverty and simplicity. You could have chosen any lifestyle, yet you and your family lived simply, detached from the beautiful things of this world. Teach me to follow in your footsteps. Have mercy on the countless people who idolize money. Make me a good steward of your gifts…

QUESTIONS FOR SMALL GROUP DISCUSSION

1. What struck you most in this passage? What did you notice that you hadn't noticed before?

2. What can we do to live more fully the Church's uniquely fruitful and beautiful teaching on family life?

3. How can we increase our sincere reverence for God's gift of life to us and to those around us, instead of taking it so much for granted?

4. How have you let Christ enter more into the nitty-gritty of your most mundane struggles and joys, instead of reserving him just for the times when you go to Church or when you're really in trouble?

Cf. Catechism of the Catholic Church, 2201-2206 on the Family in God's Plan; 527-530 on the meaning of Christ's infancy

157. THE SECRETS OF NAZARETH (LK 2:41-52)

By giving us his Son whom, in order to spare us he did not spare, he gave us everything: graced, love, heaven; for all these indeed are less than his Son."

- St Alphonsus Liguori

Luke 2:41-52

Every year his parents used to go to Jerusalem for the feast of the Passover. When he was twelve years old, they went up for the feast as usual. When they were on their way home after the feast, the boy Jesus stayed behind in Jerusalem without his parents knowing it. They assumed he was with the caravan, and it was only after a day's journey that they went to look for him among their relations and acquaintances. When they failed to find him they went back to Jerusalem looking for him everywhere. Three days later, they found him in the Temple, sitting among the doctors, listening to them, and asking them questions; and all those who heard him were astounded at his intelligence and his replies. They were overcome when they saw him, and his mother said to him, 'My child, why have, you done this to us? See how worried your father and I have been, looking for you.' 'Why were you looking for me?' he replied 'Did you not know that I must be busy with my Father's affairs?' But they did not understand what he meant. He then went down with them and came to Nazareth and lived under their authority. His mother stored up all these things in her heart. And Jesus increased in wisdom, in stature, and in favour with God and men.

CHRIST THE LORD At the age of twelve Jewish boys took their place in their community as young men. Up till then, they were not strictly under the law, but upon coming of age, they were expected to carry their own weight religiously and begin to do so socially and economically. Thus this trip to Jerusalem for the Passover was probably Jesus' first; previously he would have stayed at home with the other young children. Certainly the throngs of pilgrims, the glory of the big city, and the pageantry of the religious ritual fascinated him (especially because of his unique mission and identity), inducing him to stay behind when the caravan from Nazareth headed home – the women traveling ahead of the men, which is why Joseph probably thought Jesus was with Mary, and vice versa.

During the Passover festival, the Jewish leaders (members of the Sanhedrin) gave open lectures and led public discussions in the Temple precincts. Jesus participated in these, his unusual interest and uncanny intuition making a dramatic impression upon the other youngsters as well as the rabbis.

What was on Jesus' mind as he spent these three days alone in the City of David? St Luke gives us a clue. When Joseph and Mary finally catch up to him, Mary says, "Your father and I have been looking for you..." and Jesus answers, "I must be in my Father's house." At some point in his young life, Jesus the human boy, the son of Joseph the carpenter, must have begun to understand who he was as Jesus the Son of God. And even if he had known it long before, now that he had officially come of age, it was high time that he begin to act in accordance with it.

Once again, we see that Christ's Lordship is not an exterior tag, a romantic title tacked on to a great philosopher by sycophant disciples. He is Lord of men because he is God become man, come to live with us and establish his eternal Kingdom.

CHRIST THE TEACHER For thirty of his thirty-three years of earthly life, Jesus "was obedient to" his parents in Nazareth. In other words, he lived the most normal, unglamorous life that can be imagined: he worked in a carpenter's shop in a small town on the edge of the Roman Empire. He did chores, he studied his lessons, he went to the Synagogue on Saturdays, he played with his cousins, he helped his mother fetch the water... for thirty years. He did nothing miraculous or spectacular... for thirty years. Is he trying to teach us something? Isn't he showing us that to be a Christian, to be a saint, begins with the faithful fulfillment of the normal responsibilities of life? God created us to be human, and he expects us to reach our potential by living fully human lives. A Christian should be a model son, daughter, father, mother, student, carpenter, athlete, bricklayer, statesman, marketing director – whatever our situation in life, we should live it deeply, conscious that by taking upon himself our human nature, Christ sanctified the human condition. He made the ordinary activities and duties of life into channels of divine grace.

CHRIST THE FRIEND Often we are afraid to be honest in our prayer. We feel that our everyday struggles, needs, questions, and frustrations are too petty for God. But Christ proves that attitude wrong. He grew up in a family – a poor family, in fact – and he did not magically protect them from all the mundane concerns that buffet the daily struggle of such families. Mary and Joseph didn't understand what he was saying; they were worried sick when they couldn't find him – they reacted the way any healthy parents would react to a crisis situation. It is precisely in the midst of these seemingly petty experiences that God can work in our souls, on one condition: that we, like Mary, "store up all these things" and ponder them in our hearts. God is always drawing close to us, drawing us closer to himself – we need only make an effort to detect his action, and his action will be able to take its effect.

Joseph: I really never knew what was going to happen next. Most days followed the same pattern of work and rest. Mary made our home the brightest and neatest in the town, and Jesus was the most energetic, healthiest, and most helpful boy you could imagine. Our little place was always buzzing with activity. Everyone who needed help or comfort came by, knowing that Mary would find a solution – and that kept me busy too. They were both docile, always finding ways to make me happy. Yet, this normal, strenuous, beautiful life was lit up every once in a while by flashes of the extraordinary, like when we lost Jesus in the Temple. I knew I was part of a bigger story, and God kept reminding me of it. I always felt that it was something far beyond what I could understand. I listened to the Lord; I did every task as best I could, and I simply had to trust that he would work everything out in the end.

CHRIST IN MY LIFE Thank you for coming to be my Savior, Lord. Thank you for becoming Mary's child, so that I could become a child of God. When I take time to think of all that you have done and all that you are doing, my worries and concerns shrink down to their proper size. You are busy about your Father's work – teach me to be busy doing your will in my life…

I think I have lost some of my ability to enjoy the simple pleasures and challenges of life. I think I have fallen into the trap of consumerism – always needing new toys to feel stimulated and happy. Purify me, Lord. You were happy amid the work and suffering of Nazareth. Blessed be Nazareth, blessed by your holy name…

Mary, how were you able to keep believing the words of the angel when for thirty years you saw no advances of your son to claim his Kingship…. Teach me to live with faith. I always want so badly to understand everything. Did you want that too? You bore Wisdom himself in your womb, and you raised him and taught him and loved him. He clung to you and depended on you. Mary, teach me to live with Jesus, to learn from him…

QUESTIONS FOR SMALL GROUP DISCUSSION

1. What struck you most in this passage? What did you notice that you hadn't noticed before?

2. Jesus was eager to hear the rabbis' teaching and learn all that the experts in the Law had to say. How should a similar eagerness manifest itself in the life of today's Christian?

3. How should we be living out the Fourth Commandment ("Honor your father and mother") in the particular circumstances of our lives?

4. How can we make our prayer life more sincere?

Cf. Catechism of the Catholic Church, 564 on life in the Holy Family; 1655 on the Holy Family as a prototype of the Church; 531-534 on the mysteries of Jesus' hidden life in Nazareth

THE GOSPEL OF LUKE CHAPTER 3

"How privileged is water in the sight of God and of his Christ, that it should so bring out the meaning of Baptism! Christ made use of it constantly. He himself was baptized in the Jordan, and when invited to a wedding, it was by means of water that he inaugurated his miracles. Does he preach the word? He calls upon those who are thirsty to drink of his eternal water. Does he speak of charity? He recognizes as a work of love the cup of water given to a neighbor. Near a well, he rested. He walked on the water. He washed the feet of his Apostles with water. This witness in favor of Baptism is found even in his Passion; at his condemnation, Pilate washed his hands in water. When his side was pierced with a lance, water flowed from his side with blood."

- Tertullian, On Baptism

158. PREPARING THE WAY (LK 3:1-6)

"For Jesus Christ reigns over the minds of individuals by his teachings, in their hearts by his love, in each one's life by the living according to his law and the imitating of his example."

- Pope Pius XI

Luke 3:1-6

In the fifteenth year of Tiberius Caesar's reign, when Pontius Pilate was governor of Judaea, Herod tetrarch of Galilee, his brother Philip tetrarch of the lands of Ituraea and Trachonitis, Lysanias tetrarch of Abilene, during the pontificate of Annas and Caiaphas the word of God came to John son of Zechariah, in the wilderness. He went through the whole Jordan district proclaiming a baptism of repentance for the forgiveness of sins, as it is written in the book of the sayings of the prophet Isaiah: A voice cries in the wilderness: Prepare a way for the Lord, make his paths straight. Every valley will be filled in, every mountain and hill be laid low, winding ways will be straightened and rough roads made smooth. And all mankind shall see the salvation of God.

CHRIST THE LORD Great personages announce their official visits ahead of time. This provides people with an opportunity to prepare for the visit, so as to be able to take be ready for it. John the Baptist is Christ's precursor, the one sent to announce his coming and get people ready to welcome him. He plays a central role in the liturgy of Advent, the season during which the Church recalls Christ's first coming, readies itself to welcome him at his new, spiritual coming each Christmas, and looks forward to his definitive, second coming at the end of history ("Advent" derives from the Latin for "coming towards"). Luke emphasizes the incomparable importance of Christ's coming by pointing out how Isaiah had prophesied not only the arrival of Jesus but even the appearance of the precursor, John. God had long been preparing this pivotal moment in the world's history, and wanted to do everything possible to alert his people of its imminence.

Although Christ has come to the earth, and although he has come to dwell in many human hearts and societies, many more have still not heard of him or welcomed him. The Lord has his eye on those and is planning advents for each one of them. With each person, he continues to use this same methodology: he sends his heralds ahead of him. We are those heralds. Every Christian is another John the Baptist, boldly drawing others' attention to the truth and grace of Christ with his words, deeds and example. Among the many responsibilities each of us has, none is greater or more rewarding than teaming up with the Holy Spirit to prepare hearts for the Lord.

CHRIST THE TEACHER Isaiah's prophecy, which summarizes John's message, offers us two lessons. First it tells us *what* to do in order to get ready for Christ's comings in our lives and those around us. We are to "prepare the way," filling in valleys, leveling hills, straightening crooked roads, and smoothing out rough paths. The imagery comes from a typical scene in the ancient world (before concrete and asphalt highways). Roads were notoriously unreliable in Isaiah's time, long before the establishment and spread of the Roman Empire. When a king or emperor made the rounds of his territories, his officials would travel ahead of him, making sure that the roads were safe and in good condition so that he wouldn't be delayed and would be less vulnerable to enemy ambushes. Likewise, we are called to examine our own souls on a regular basis, especially in the penitential seasons of Advent and Lent, to see where selfishness has encroached upon our relationships with God and with other people, and where laziness and self-indulgence have worn away our self-discipline. We may need to fill in some spiritual potholes or clear away some unwelcome debris, so that the graces God has in store for us during each season of our lives will be able to stream unhindered into our hearts.

Second, Isaiah tells us *why* we should prepare our hearts for Christ's comings: "All flesh shall see the salvation of God." He reminds us that we (the entire human family, as well as each of us individually) need God's grace. The peace, meaning, and joy that we thirst for above all else is out of our sinful reach; we need someone to bring it us, to search us out in this desert of our earthly exile and give us the waters of eternal life. Christ is the one to do this. He always wants to bring us closer to God, closer to the fullness of life that we long for. But he won't force his way in; we need to ready ourselves to welcome him.

CHRIST THE FRIEND St Luke begins this chapter of his Gospel curiously: with a list of names and places that seem irrelevant at first glance. Twenty centuries after the fact, we are interested in Jesus, not in tetrarchs and obsolete geography. But these details reveal something crucial about Jesus: he is not an abstract God. He weaves his action and presence into the fabric of our day-to-day lives; he takes up his stance on the crossroads of everyone's personal history and addresses us there. And he does it because he wants to. Jesus Christ is a God who is our friend, not a faceless, aloof divine architect.

Jesus: I know where you were born and when. I remember every moment of your childhood, every one of your experiences growing up. I have been with you through it all. I will continue to be with you. Nothing about you is indifferent to me; all the circumstances of your life matter, and I am using them all to draw you closer to me, to show you your mission and guide you to its fulfillment. If you look for me, you will always find me, right there beside you.

CHRIST IN MY LIFE Am I a good messenger, Lord? Do my words stir up noble sentiments? Do my actions clear the way for your grace? Does my manner point people to the goodness of Christ? Do I even try to help bring others a step closer to you? Life is so busy, Lord. Can I be your ambassador in the midst of my busy-ness? Of course I can, if you will show me the way…

I know that my fears and self-centered habits obstruct your action in my life. I want to be free of them. Thank you for always being ready to forgive me and supply me with your grace. I want to take advantage of your generosity, to make use of confession and all the other ways you give me to grow, little by little but surely and constantly, into the saint you created me to be…

You teach me so clearly that the drama of salvation history is played out in the mundane reality of my life and the lives of those around me. Tune me in to this drama. Open my eyes. I want to see you in every event and every person. I want to detect and seize every opportunity to love you and make you known. You are my hope, my light, my Lord…

QUESTIONS FOR SMALL GROUP DISCUSSION

1. What struck you most in this passage? What did you notice that you hadn't noticed before?

2. Who were the "John the Baptists" in your own story of becoming a disciple of Christ, and how did they do their job of bringing Jesus into your life?

3. How can we take more seriously the Church's continual call to prepare ourselves for Christ's coming?

4. What can we do to foster the kind of intimate, personal relationship with Christ that God wants us to have (and avoid a distant, abstract, impersonal religiosity)?

Cf. Catechism of the Catholic Church, 717-720 on the role of John the Baptist in the mystery of salvation; 1430-1433 on interior penance; 2566-2567 on the mysterious mutual desire of man for God and God for man

159. BASIC TRAINING (LK 3:10-20)

… So far as I am concerned, to die in Jesus Christ is better than to be monarch of earth's widest bounds. He who died for us is all that I seek; he who rose again for us is my whole desire."

- St Ignatius of Antioch, martyr

Luke 3:10-18

He said, therefore, to the crowds who came to be baptised by him, 'Brood of vipers, who warned you to fly from the retribution that is coming? But if you are repentant, produce the appropriate fruits, and do not think of telling yourselves, We have Abraham for our father because, I tell you, God can raise children for Abraham from these stones. Yes, even now the axe is laid to the roots of the trees, so that any tree which fails to produce good fruit will be cut down and thrown on the fire.' When all the people asked him, 'What must we do, then?' he answered, 'If anyone has two tunics he must share with the man who has none, and the one with something to eat must do the same'. There were tax collectors too who came for baptism, and these said to him, 'Master, what must we do?' He said to them, 'Exact no more than your rate'. Some soldiers asked him in their turn, 'What about us? What must we do?' He said to them, 'No intimidation! No extortion! Be content with your pay!' A feeling of expectancy had grown among the people, who were beginning to think that John might be the Christ, so John declared before them all, 'I baptise you with water, but someone is coming, someone who is more powerful than I am, and I am not fit to undo the strap of his sandals; he will baptise you with the Holy Spirit and fire. His winnowing-fan is in his hand to clear his threshing-floor and to gather the wheat into his barn; but the chaff he will burn in a fire that will never go out.' As well as this, there were many other things he said to exhort the people and to announce the Good News to them. But Herod the tetrarch, whom he criticised for his relations with his brother's wife Herodias and for all the other crimes Herod had committed, added a further crime to all the rest by shutting John up in prison.

CHRIST THE LORD Many great teachers and leaders have come and gone throughout human history, but there is only one Jesus Christ. Even John the Baptist, whom Jesus later called "more than a prophet… the greatest of those born of women," can only "baptize with water." In other words, he can only work with souls on a natural level, strengthening them in virtue and helping them understand the requirements of a good life, but that pales in comparison with what Christ does. Jesus "baptizes with the Holy Spirit and fire." In him, we come into contact with God himself, and we are completely transformed (as the saints testify), just as fire completely transforms whatever it burns. This is why he is the Messiah, the "anointed one" sent to fill the breach that sin opened between God and man. No one else can be the Messiah, because no one else can bridge that infinite gap. His coming into our midst is an utterly unique event. St Luke wants to make that clear – over and over again – so that we stop taking it for granted.

CHRIST THE TEACHER Often John the Baptist is depicted as an ill-tempered, fire-and-brimstone preacher who scared the people into repentance. First of all, such a conception fails to explain how he was able to attract such huge crowds and win over so many hearts. And secondly, it neglects the main point of his message: that salvation is at hand. Salvation, friendship with God, the fullness and security of living in communion with our Creator and Redeemer, of being "gathered into the barns" of his eternal and sublime Kingdom… this is John the Baptist's true message.

John teaches his listeners how to please Christ, how to live in communion with the God who wants to save us. His lesson is nothing new (though his personal integrity gives it new weight); he merely applies the Ten Commandments to the particular situations of his hearers. He appeals to the demands of justice and the demands of humility – we are not to take undue advantage of anyone, and we are to help those in need. How different the world would be if everyone followed these simple directives! And how open our souls would be to God's grace if we would combat our selfishness in these apparently trivial ways! Often people reject Christianity not because its theology is too difficult to comprehend, but because its moral demands are too basic. Isn't it much more romantic and titillating to perform esoteric rituals and commune with invisible forces through crystals and spells than to be honest and hardworking? And yet, the glitz of pseudo-religion can't nourish the soul. The real path that leads to life is steep and narrow, as Christ himself would put it later, but why would we want to take any other?

CHRIST THE FRIEND The human heart longs for a purpose and a joy that no earthly experience can supply; John brings the Good News that Christ is on his way, and that he can provide our hearts with everything they yearn for if we will accept his offer of friendship. Indeed, it is in our ongoing, growing, changing, maturing, personal, relationship with Jesus that our yearning souls will find what they seek. The Christian life is a journey with Christ. The Christian answer to the human heart's search for happiness isn't a drug or a pill you take once in order to enter into an altered state of bliss. The human heart is made for greater things, and the adventure of friendship with Christ will gradually show us what they are.

The heart of this adventure consists in following Christ's example of self-giving, of emptying ourselves, of putting ourselves at the service of Christ and our neighbors. When it becomes our way of life, this Christian charity, this giving away our tunics and sharing our food, leads us to discover the meaning and joy that Christ came to give, which only experience can describe.

CHRIST IN MY LIFE Why is my life not as fruitful as the lives of the saints? I know you have called me to real holiness, and I believe that the fulfillment I long for will only be found there. But something is still holding me back. I want to see your glory, Lord. I want to experience your love and your greatness so thoroughly that my whole life is polarized around your Kingdom, and all my pettiness and selfishness falls away…

Okay, Lord, I believe in you – you know I do. And so I believe the lesson of this Gospel, that I can fulfill your dream for my life simply by living out my normal activities with responsibility, generosity, and faith. Help me to take my sights off some abstract, pie-in-the-sky holiness. I want to love you in the here and now of my life. I know I am not worthy even to untie your sandal strap, but you have given me a chance to serve you by doing all things as you would have me…

If I found myself completely alone, I wouldn't quit, because I would still have you. If I found myself kidnapped and thrown into prison, I wouldn't panic, because you would still be with me. If I found myself drowning in failure and rejection or submerged in endless pain, I wouldn't despair, because even there your friendship would be my meaning and salvation…

QUESTIONS FOR SMALL GROUP DISCUSSION

1. What struck you most in this passage? What did you notice that you hadn't noticed before?

2. How does the daily life of someone who really believes in the uniqueness of Christ differ from that of someone who doesn't?

3. John the Baptist knew about the gospel, and he made sure that everyone around him found about it as well. We know about the gospel, but are we being as effective as John in making sure others know about it? If not, why not?

4. How can we keep our hearts filled with fresh joy and the hope of the "good news" of Jesus Christ? In other words, how can we keep ourselves from falling into routine, from becoming "used to" the saving message of Christ?

Cf. Catechism of the Catholic Church, 410, 436-445, 453, 547 on the meaning of Christ as the "Messiah"; 524 on John the Baptist as a model for Advent living; 1803-1845 on the virtues

160. SON OF GOD, SON OF MAN (LK 3:21-38)

"The promise of a Redeemer brightens the first page of the history of mankind, and the confident hope aroused by this promise softened the keen regret for a paradise which had been lost."

- Pope Pius XI

Luke 3:21-38

Now when all the people had been baptised and while Jesus after his own baptism was at prayer, heaven opened and the Holy Spirit descended on him in bodily shape, like a dove. And a voice came from heaven, 'You are my Son, the Beloved; my favour rests on you.'

When he started to teach, Jesus was about thirty years old, being the son, as it was thought, of Joseph son of Heli, son of Matthat, son of Levi, son of Melchi, son of Jannai, son of Joseph, son of Mattathias, son of Amos, son of Nahum, son of Esli, son of Naggai, son of Maath, son of Mattathias, son of Semein, son of Josech, son of Joda, son of Joanan, son of Rhesa, son of Zerubbabel, son of Shealtiel, son of Neri, son of Melchi, son of Addi, son of Cosam, son of Elmadam, son of Er, son of Joshua, son of Joshua, son of Eliezer, son of Jorim, son of Matthat, son of Levi son of Syme-on, son of Judah, son of Joseph, son of Jonam, son of Eliakim, son of Melea, son of Menna, son of Mattatha, son of Nathan, son of David, son of Jesse, son of Obed, son of Boaz, son of Sala, son of Nahshon, son of Amminadab, son of Admin, son of

Arni, son of Hezron, son of Perez, son of Judah, son of Jacob, son of Isaac, son of Abraham, son of Terah, son of Nahor, son of Serug, son of Reu, son of Peleg, son of Eber, son of Shelah, son of Cainan, son of Arphaxad, son of Shem, son of Noah, son of Lamech, son of Methuselah, son of Enoch, son of Jared, son of Mahalaleel, son of Cainan, son of Enos, son of Seth, son of Adam, son of God.

CHRIST THE LORD At the time of Jesus' baptism, which marked the beginning of his public ministry, the people were filled with expectation (cf. Luke 3:15) for two reasons. First, rumor had it that according to the prophecies of Daniel, the first century AD (although they didn't call it that at the time) was to witness the arrival of the promised Messiah, the King anointed by God to restore the Davidic kingdom. The identifying marks of that Messiah were much disputed among scholars of the time, but a sense that the time had come was widespread. Second, no true prophet had arisen in Israel in over two centuries. Therefore, when John the Baptist came onto the scene, they knew something big was afoot; many hoped that he himself was the Messiah.

God certainly supplied plenty of signs to indicate the coming of Jesus. Even so, Christ found a welcome in only a few hearts; the others gave him up to be crucified. We need to ask ourselves why, lest we make the same mistake. Could it be that the people of Israel were expecting one kind of Lord, and God wanted to give them another? We often fall into the same trap; we know clearly the things we want, but God sends us something else, and we resent it. If Christ is truly the Lord, however, and the greatest prophet of all time was not even worthy to "loosen the thongs of his sandals" (Luke 3:16 – this was a slave's job, because ancient roads were nothing but dirt, mud, and animal manure, and the condition of one's sandals often proved it), why do we expect him to do things our way? And why do we expect them to fit our schedule? Isn't it possible that he knows better?

CHRIST THE TEACHER What God the Father tells Jesus is what he wants to say to each one of us: "You are my son, today I have fathered you." Jesus came to earth in order to call forth God's pleasure on sinful mankind, to lift us back into membership in God's family. Adam is described here as the "Son of God" yet our rebellion against God in the Garden of Eden made it impossible for us to continue to be members of his family. Jesus, through his loving obedience to the Father's will, even to the point of accepting death on a cross, reversed that rebellion. Now, by uniting ourselves to Christ, we can become God's beloved children and live in communion with him.

How do we unite ourselves to Christ? By taking three steps: knowing him, loving him, and imitating him. (The prerequisite, of course, is baptism, which unites us to God as branches are united to the vine, making our friendship with Christ possible.) The more fully we come to know Christ, especially through prayerful reading of the Gospels and time spent with him in the Eucharist, the more we will come to love him. And the more we love him, the more we will want to follow him and imitate him, especially in his perfect fulfillment of the Father's will and his tireless love for all people. If we let these three motifs set the rhythm for our daily living, we too can please the heart of God and be filled with his life-giving love.

CHRIST THE FRIEND John was baptizing "all the people" as a way to help them prepare their hearts to welcome Christ. Their hearts needed preparing, because they were full of selfishness, doubt, arrogance, greed, etc. Christ's heart, however, was pure; he did not need to be baptized. And yet, he got in line with the rest of the sinners and submitted to the ritual.

Jesus: I came to earth to be Emmanuel, God with you. I eagerly desired to reunite you with the Father, and so I became your brother – just as human as anyone else, whether Jew or Gentile, as the list of my ancestors shows. Do you see how deeply I long for your friendship? I knew how hard it was for you to accept my offer and give me your friendship. So I decided to come and walk beside you along the rough and dangerous paths of life, to be your strength in times of struggle, to meet your glance, and assure you that I will never forsake you. I took your place in the waters of baptism, and I took your place on the wood of the cross. What more could I have done to gain your trust?

CHRIST IN MY LIFE I want to do things your way, but it seems so hard! Lord, why does my nature rebel against your will? Have mercy on me, Lord. Your faithfulness is as firm as the mountains. Send your wisdom and your grace into my soul to help me follow you as both you and I want. Come to my aid, Lord. I can do nothing without you...

The world doesn't understand you. I want to understand you, to seek you, to know you, to love you. I believe that you are the Creator and the Savior of the world, and that all the urgent and absorbing cares that tend to overwhelm me are only secondary. You are primary; your Kingdom is what matters most. Make me a true Christian, a true ambassador of that Kingdom...

Thank you for coming to take my part and be my companion. I want to walk with you, to follow you, to learn from you. But Jesus, I know many people who are trying to journey through life alone, on their own strength. Don't you want to walk with them too? Please come to them, as you came to me. Make me your messenger, your instrument…

QUESTIONS FOR SMALL GROUP DISCUSSION

1. What struck you most in this passage? What did you notice that you hadn't noticed before?

2. How can we make a constant effort to know Christ better every day? Why should we?

3. How can we help one another to know, love, and imitate Christ better?

4. Each of us should evaluate frequently the status of our friendship with Christ - what kind of a friend we are being towards Jesus. The following question may help: If the friend I love most treated me the way I treat Christ, would I be pleased or saddened?

Cf. Catechism of the Catholic Church, 535-537 on the meaning of Christ's baptism; 456-460 on why Christ came among us; 430-451 on the names of Jesus and how they incite us to know, love, and imitate him

THE GOSPEL OF LUKE CHAPTER 4

"Come, Holy Spirit. May the union of the Father and the will of the Son come to us. You, Spirit of truth, are the reward of the saints, the refreshment of souls, light in darkness, the riches of the poor, the treasury of lovers, the satisfaction of the hungry, the consolation of the pilgrim Church; you are he in whom all treasures are contained. Come, you who, descending into Mary, caused the Word to take flesh: effect in us by grace what you accomplished in her by grace and nature. Come, you who are the nourishment of all chaste thoughts, the fountain of all clemency, the summit of all purity. Come, and take away from us all that hinders us from being absorbed in you."

- St Mary Magdalene of Pazzi

161. FIRST VICTORY (LK 4:1-13)

"When temptation comes, turn straight to God, and he will help you."

- St Leonard of Port Maurice

Luke 4:1-13

Filled with the Holy Spirit, Jesus left the Jordan and was led by the Spirit through the wilderness, being tempted there by the devil for forty days. During that time he ate nothing and at the end he was hungry. Then the devil said to him, 'If you are the Son of God, tell this stone to turn into a loaf'. But Jesus replied, 'Scripture says: Man does not live on bread alone'. Then leading him to a height, the devil showed him in a moment of time all the kingdoms of the world and said to him, 'I will give you all this power and the glory of these kingdoms, for it has been committed to

me and I give it to anyone I choose. Worship me, then, and it shall all be yours.'
But Jesus answered him, 'Scripture says: You must worship the Lord your God, and
serve him alone.' Then he led him to Jerusalem and made him stand on the parapet
of the Temple. 'If you are the Son of God,' he said to him, 'throw yourself down
from here, for scripture says: He will put his angels in charge of you to guard you,
and again: They will hold you up on their hands in case you hurt your foot against
a stone.' But Jesus answered him, 'It has been said: You must not put the Lord your
God to the test.' Having exhausted all these ways of tempting him, the devil left
him, to return at the appointed time.

CHRIST THE LORD Jesus' temptation in the desert, which the liturgy locates
in the first Sunday of Lent, vividly reminds us that Christ came "to destroy
the works of the devil" (1 John 3:8). Since the dawn of time, the devil had
mastered the human heart, leading every man and woman more or less into
the tangle of selfishness and sin, encouraging them to use power to procure
pleasure, to compromise principles for the sake of popularity, and to disobey
the voice of conscience in favor of convenience. But Christ was too much for
him. In this first combat, the devil tried "every way of putting him to the test,"
but they glanced off Jesus like so many plastic darts. The almost irresistible
lure of temptation that causes such anguish and struggle in us has no power
over our Lord. Staying close to him, therefore, leaning on him and filled with
his grace, we can experience the victory over sin. In him we can attain freedom
from slavery to our own evil tendencies. Christ indeed is the Lord, and he has
come to conquer. If we follow him, we will share the spoils.

CHRIST THE TEACHER By letting himself be tempted, Jesus teaches us how
the devil works, and how to overcome him. The devil appeals to our selfish
tendencies in order to draw us away from God. We all desire physical pleasure
and comfort ("Tell this stone to turn in to a loaf"), but sometimes we need to
subordinate that desire to a higher ideal ("Man lives not on bread alone"). We
all desire to be self-sufficient, to have power to do whatever we want whenever
we want, free from natural limitations ("I shall give you all this power"), but
only God is self-sufficient. Our existence depends on him – we need him to
sustain and guide us ("God alone you must serve"). We all desire recognition,
popularity, and praise (a swan dive from the Temple parapet would have won
Jesus instant fame), but these are no substitute for the true meaning and happiness given by humble friendship with God; it's not worth risking the latter to
gain the former ("You must not put the Lord your God to the test"). The devil
wants us to keep "self" in the center of our lives, so that we feed our egoism

and eventually become a moral black hole. But as long as we keep God at the center, "seeking first the Kingdom," we will be safe from his wiles.

The devil doesn't change his agenda of temptations as the years go by, because he knows that human nature stays the same. For the same reason, the three great Christian virtues of poverty, obedience, and chastity (lived most fully by those called to the religious or consecrated life) are always in season as antidotes to the tempter's poison.

CHRIST THE FRIEND Jesus Christ was tempted, and so he redeemed temptation. What a relief! Now we know that our own temptations can give glory to God. We know that feeling the attraction of evil and the tug of selfishness is no cause for despair; rather it provides an opportunity to exercise our love. Every time we resist a temptation, we extend the Kingdom of God, winning back territory from the devil. Christ didn't come to exempt us from spiritual combat, but to give us strength to fight valiantly for his cause. He is the great champion, and he invites us to battle at his side, sharing in his sufferings and his triumphs. He has become one of us, so as to make us just like him.

CHRIST IN MY LIFE You conquered sin and evil. You want to extend your conquest into every human heart. I intercede for all those hearts that resist you. Lord, convince them of your goodness! Make them trust in you! Wash them in your mercy, and make my life a billboard for the power of your love…

What interests you most is what happens in my heart. The world and other people see only appearances; I can fool them. You see the decisions that determine my character and the direction of my moral journey. You are interested in that, because you want me to choose to spend eternity in your palace in heaven, with Mary and all the saints, on the everlasting adventure…

Mary, you know that sometimes I get tired of the battle and simply want to rest. I know you humbled yourself every day, conquering sin with the grace you had received and living solely for Christ in spite of discomfort, obstacles, and opposition. You are the school of every virtue. Teach me to persevere in my mission, as you did, until the very end…. And doing so you showed me that life on earth is not mean to be a cakewalk, but a mission. Thy will be done, Lord; you can count on me…

QUESTIONS FOR SMALL GROUP DISCUSSION

1. What struck you most in this passage? What did you notice that you hadn't noticed before?

2. The season of Lent lasts for forty days, just as long as Christ's temptation in the desert, the rains that led to Noah's flood, and the years Israel spent wandering in the desert… How would you explain the relationship between these events?

3. The devil quoted the Bible in order to tempt Jesus. Is there a lesson in that for us?

4. How can we get and keep our conscience "in shape," able to recognize easily the difference between an innocent desire, a temptation, and a sin?

Cf. Catechism of the Catholic Church, 391-395 on Satan and the other fallen angels; 538-542 on Jesus' temptations and his first sermon; 1427-1433 on Jesus' call to repentance and on our need for constant conversion

162. MORE THAN A HUMAN MISSION (LK 4:14-21)

"As there are many kinds of persecution, so there are many forms of martyrdom. You are a witness to Christ every day."

- St Ambrose

Luke 4:14-21

Jesus, with the power of the Spirit in him, returned to Galilee; and his reputation spread throughout the countryside. He taught in their synagogues and everyone praised him. He came to Nazara, where he had been brought up, and went into the synagogue on the sabbath day as he usually did. He stood up to read and they handed him the scroll of the prophet Isaiah. Unrolling the scroll he found the place where it is written: 'The spirit of the Lord has been given to me, for he has anointed me. He has sent me to bring the good news to the poor, to proclaim liberty to captives and to the blind new sight, to set the downtrodden free, to proclaim the Lord's year of favour.' He then rolled up the scroll, gave it back to the assistant and sat down. And all eyes in the synagogue were fixed on him. Then he began to speak to them, 'This text is being fulfilled today even as you listen.'

CHRIST THE LORD Here we have Jesus' first sermon. He reads a passage from the Old Testament that refers to the Messiah, to the descendent of David whom God promised to raise up to establish a Kingdom of justice and peace that would never end. When he finishes reading it, he sits down (the recognized posture for official teaching in Jewish culture at the time) and pauses, meeting the expectant gazes of everyone gathered in the synagogue. Probably he had read the scripture passage with a force of expression that they had never heard before, and so their attention was riveted on what he was going to say. He looks at them, and speaks: "This passage is fulfilled today, right now: I am that Messiah, that promised Savior, that King whose Kingdom will never end." If they had difficulty believing it (and they did), and if others throughout the centuries would have the same difficulty (and they would), at least Jesus made clear what exactly it was he wanted them to believe – that he is the Lord.

It is a worthy spiritual exercise every once in a while to examine our faith in Jesus as Lord. Often we get so caught up in our efforts to follow him, to fulfill our responsibilities, to imitate his virtues, and to spread the faith that we forget about the majesty and nobility of our God. Jesus is King of the universe. He is the promised Messiah God had promised to send since the beginning of salvation history. He will come again to judge all people, living and dead, and bring this fallen world to an end, resolving once and for all the struggle between good and evil. Reflecting on this bigger picture can do wonders for putting our little pictures in proper perspective – the Lord's perspective.

CHRIST THE TEACHER Here St Luke begins his description of Jesus' public ministry. Jesus will spend the coming two or three years traveling throughout Palestine, teaching, healing, and gathering his Twelve Apostles, whom he will put in charge of the Church after his passion, resurrection, and ascension. His itinerant career is a pattern for every Christian life, in a sense, and for the Church as a whole. He is the light of the world, and through his disciples – through their words, actions, and example – he brings that light to shine in all the sin-darkened corners of the globe. He wants to bring his truth (what he taught) and his grace (that which heals both body and soul) to every human heart, of every epoch and to every nation. This is his mission; this is our mission.

But notice how Jesus set up this pattern of Church life. St Luke points out that Jesus entered Galilee "with the power of the Spirit in him, and the first line of the prophecy he quotes is "the Spirit of the Lord is upon me," Jesus' mission was more than a merely human mission, and so is ours. We received that very same Spirit in baptism, and we received a further outpouring of the Spirit in confirmation. Our mission in life, in the Church, and in the world is one that we must carry out depending on God's supernatural grace and following his supernatural lead. Much of the frustrations, conflicts, and discouragements that Christians experience come from forgetting this fact. We are instruments, foot soldiers, and ambassadors, but the Holy Spirit is coordinating all of our efforts. If each of us is docile to him, when the last battle comes to its close, we will be amazed at the hidden progress that blossoms forth in the definitive establishment of Christ's Kingdom. The most fundamental lesson the active Christian needs to learn is to see all things with eyes enlightened by the Spirit.

CHRIST THE FRIEND Jesus came to bring "good news" to those who suffer, to free captives, and to cure the blind – he came because we needed him to come. We suffer the moral agony of incurable selfishness; we are shackled by our strong tendencies to sin; we are blinded by the sparkling allure of temptation. He came to be our Savior. And when we truly contemplate him, he attracts us with a force that leaves all other material realities far behind. If we want to experience life as God means it to be lived, all we need to do is call upon the name of Jesus and follow where he leads; he is all for us, the perfect friend, the one we can trust without limits.

CHRIST IN MY LIFE Many people consider you to be just one more great philosopher. I know better, Lord. You have given me the gift of faith. I know that you are God made man, the source of all existence, and you come to dwell among your creatures. You stay with us in the Tabernacle; you feed us in Holy Communion. You are all-powerful and all-loving. Never let me be separated from you...

Teach me to lean on you, to listen for your instructions, to pay attention to the teachings and directives of the pope, to live, as you lived, "by the power of the Spirit." Why do I fear failure when I know you can bring glory out of grime? Why do I fear loneliness when I know you have made me a Temple of the Holy Spirit? Reign fully in me, Lord, for the glory of your name...

I need your grace. What can I do on my own? You know what happens when I try to follow you and build your Kingdom and be faithful to your teaching depending on my own strength alone. I don't even want to think about it. I am glad to admit that I need you. Without you, I wouldn't even exist. I would simply disappear, be obliterated. Be my light and my refuge, Lord...

QUESTIONS FOR SMALL GROUP DISCUSSION

1. What struck you most in this passage? What did you notice that you hadn't noticed before?

2. What evidence should there be in our daily living that we believe Christ's Kingdom "will have no end"?

3. How can we foster a more responsible and reverential love for Scripture and for the Church?

4. How can we develop the confidence in God that we need in order to be sincere with him in prayer, instead of vainly putting on a show?

Cf. Catechism of the Catholic Church, 430-440 on who Christ is; 456-460 on why Christ came; 74-95 on the transmission of divine revelation

163. TROUBLES AT HOME (LK 4:22-30)

If you search for the reason why a man loves God, you will find no other reason at all, save that God first loved him.

-St Augustine

Luke 4:22-30

And he won the approval of all, and they were astonished by the gracious words that came from his lips. They said, 'This is Joseph's son, surely?' But he replied, 'No doubt you will quote me the saying, "Physician, heal yourself" and tell me, "We have heard all that happened in Capernaum, do the same here in your own countryside."' And he went on, 'I tell you solemnly, no prophet is ever accepted in his own country. There were many widows in Israel, I can assure you, in Elijah's day, when heaven remained shut for three years and six months and a great famine raged throughout the land, but Elijah was not sent to any one of these: he was sent to a widow at Zarephath, a Sidonian town. And in the prophet Elisha's time there were many lepers in Israel, but none of these was cured, except the Syrian, Naaman.' When they heard this everyone in the synagogue was enraged. They sprang to their feet and hustled him out of the town; and they took him up to the brow of the hill their town was built on, intending to throw him down the cliff, but he slipped through the crowd and walked away.

CHRIST THE LORD In the sermon Jesus has just finished giving to the hometown synagogue-crowd he explained that he was the Messiah. He identifies himself with the Savior that the prophets foretold would come to restore Israel's greatness and fulfill God's promise of an everlasting Kingdom under the rule of David's son. Unfortunately, the people of Nazareth were expecting something a bit more dramatic from the Messiah. They were hoping for military might and political glory, not wisdom from the lips of a carpenter's son. And so they reject his claim. It is a pattern that history will repeat countless times. Few people question Jesus' *claim* to be the Lord, but many reject him because they find his Lordship uncomfortable. They don't want him to be *their* Lord.

We need to ask ourselves continually: am I satisfied with Jesus' style of leadership? Am I willing to accept his way of saving humanity and making me a saint – the way of patience, mercy, self-giving, and suffering? Unless we consciously keep the Lord's criteria in mind, especially through prayer and study, we may easily fall prey to devilish whispers that encourage us to branch out on our own instead of banking on the one Lord of life and history, who loved us and gave himself for our happiness, both here on earth and forever in heaven.

CHRIST THE TEACHER To receive God's grace we need to be open to it. One of the great obstacles to that openness is routine and familiarity. The people of Israel became so accustomed to the remarkable favors that God showered upon them (like parting the Red Sea and feeding them with manna in the desert), that they began to take him for granted. Foreigners (like Naaman the Syrian and the widow of Zarephath), however, were not used to experiencing God's miracles, and did not take the supernatural for granted. Consequently, they were open to the action of God; their humility and faith allowed his grace to work.

The citizens of Jesus' hometown made the same mistake Israel had made. They refused to believe that God could work among them through one of their own; they had become so used to Christ that they became incapable of putting supernatural faith in him, even when he showed by his words and miracles that he was worthy of such faith.

We can also make this mistake. We can take God's truly marvelous actions for granted, closing ourselves off from the grace they afford. It takes effort on our part not to fall into routine and boredom at Mass – the most remarkable event that takes place in the world today. It takes faith and humility to appreciate the gift of the Church and its Magisterium, a sure guide through the oppressive moral fog of our times. It takes childlike trust to find God supernaturally at work in the simple symbols of the sacraments and in the people his providence has put alongside us – a spouse, a spiritual director, a boss…. The more we fall into a merely superficial, going-through-the-motions type of faith, without concentrating and putting our whole mind and strength into it, the more exposed we are to the danger of falling into routine. Only heartfelt prayer and humility will enable us – like Mary – to give Christ a fresh welcome into the hometown of our hearts every day.

CHRIST THE FRIEND *John: I often wondered why Jesus didn't claim his rights. He could have – there were many times when I wanted him to. If he had stayed more aloof in public, perhaps more people would have believed in him – people are funny that way. If he had insulated himself behind hundreds of servants and deputies and courtiers, letting himself be seen and heard only on the rarest of occasions and performing an impressive miracle every once in a while, he would have appealed more readily to the human appetite for sensationalism. But he didn't do it that way. He wanted to walk among his people, to touch and heal their diseases, to hear their stories and speak to them of his Kingdom, to be with them. How he loved to be among people! That was always his desire. He always risked being rejected as ordinary in order to be accepted as a friend. When my turn came to go out and spread the good news, I thought to myself: If that's the way our Lord did it, then that's the way his followers should do it as well.*

CHRIST IN MY LIFE To be completely honest, Lord, I have to admit that I am often weighed down by problems – problems in the world, problems in my own life, problems in my family. I know that you have chosen to save us by meeting us in the midst of our problems, but I also know that not all suffering is necessary, healthy, or desired by you. Help me to see the difference, so I can live in your peace…

I never want to fall into an empty routine. I never want my faith to dim or my love to grow cold. Only you can keep my commitment fresh, Lord. And any of your followers who are just going through the motions, or who are giving into selfishness – I pray for them now. Especially your priests and consecrated souls. Keep their love fresh; stir their hearts with your wisdom and zeal…

You have given me such a treasure in my Catholic faith. Show me how to share it. Often I don't know when to speak and when to stay silent. I don't know what others are thinking or suffering. But you do. You know exactly what everyone needs. Guide me; give me courage and simplicity. Make me a channel of your peace…

QUESTIONS FOR SMALL GROUP DISCUSSION

1. What struck you most in this passage? What did you notice that you hadn't noticed before?

2. How do you think Christ felt at this reaction of his friends and extended family, a reaction so vehement that he had to exercise his messianic powers in order to escape execution?

3. Which of God's gifts do we tend to take most for granted? How can we break out of the routine?

4. How do you think his disciples reacted to this incident?

Cf. Catechism of the Catholic Church, 543-546 on the proclamation of the Kingdom of God; 587-591 on Israel's rejection of Jesus; 150-165 on the nature and necessity of faith

164. AUTHORITY AND POWER (LK 4:31-44)

"If you seek to know where you are going, stay close to Christ, because he is the truth that we long to reach."

- St Thomas Aquinas

Luke 4:31-44

He went down to Capernaum, a town in Galilee, and taught them on the sabbath. And his teaching made a deep impression on them because he spoke with authority. In the synagogue there was a man who was possessed by the spirit of an unclean devil, and it shouted at the top of its voice, 'Ha! What do you want with us, Jesus of Nazareth? Have you come to destroy us? I know who you are: the Holy One of God.' But Jesus said sharply, 'Be quiet! Come out of him!' And the devil, throwing the man down in front of everyone, went out of him without hurting him at all. Astonishment seized them and they were all saying to one another, 'What teaching! He gives orders to unclean spirits with authority and power and they come out.' And reports of him went all through the surrounding countryside. Leaving the synagogue he went to Simon's house. Now Simon's mother-in-law was suffering from a high fever and they asked him to do something for her. Leaning over her he rebuked the fever and it left her. And she immediately got up and began to wait on them. At sunset all those who had friends suffering from diseases of one kind or another brought them to him, and laying his hands on each he cured them. Devils too came out of many people, howling, 'You are the Son of God.' But he rebuked them and would not allow them to speak because they knew that he was the Christ. When daylight came he left the house and made his way to a lonely place. The crowds went to look for him, and when they had caught up with him they wanted to prevent him leaving them, but he answered, 'I must proclaim the Good News of the kingdom of God to the other towns too, because that is what I was sent to do.' And he continued his preaching in the synagogues of Judaea.

CHRIST THE LORD In this brief passage, St Luke describes a flurry of activity that sets the tone for the rest of Jesus' public ministry. He also profiles Christ's qualifications as Redeemer, as the second Adam who came to restore and renew the fallen world. Adam's sin had caused the human family to fall under the influence of ignorance, sickness and death, and the devil. Jesus proves his Lordship by overcoming all three of those curses. His teaching makes a deep impression on normal people who are usually full of doubts, questions, and conflicting opinions, because his grasp of the truth is firm and complete. He cures the sick and diseased with a simple word or gesture. The demons flee his very presence, recognizing in him a unique closeness to God and an unassailable spiritual strength (theologians differ on whether the devil knew that Jesus was the incarnate Second Person of the Holy Trinity – the titles "Holy One of God" and "Son of God" could refer, in the Semitic mindset, to a merely human Messiah).

What comes across in these encounters is Christ's authority. Where even strong and intelligent men have to guess and labor, Jesus simply acts. The same fearlessness and effectiveness are exhibited throughout the centuries in the lives of the Church's many saints. He is truly a King, and his Kingdom is already well advanced.

CHRIST THE TEACHER Jesus has had great success in his first appearances at Capernaum. Yet he decides to move on. Purely human logic fails to explain such a move, but Jesus leaves behind the adoring crowds and takes his disciples to the next town, because "That is what I was sent to do."

Every Christian shares in Christ's mission. We have all received a commission, something to do in this world to advance Christ's Kingdom. As we make our way through life trying to accomplish it, sometimes we are unsure what the next step should be. Should I move on, or should I stay here? Human logic can shed a bit of light on those decisions, but ultimately, since God is the commander-in-chief who alone has a view of the entire spiritual war, I can only make those decisions wisely if my prayer life is in good shape (and if I make humble use of the advice God sends through his representatives). This is how Jesus discerned when it was time to leave Capernaum: "When daylight came he left the house and made his way to a lonely place." He went off to pray. In the quiet of prayer, he was able to detect his Father's will.

And it wasn't easy to find the time to pray. He had to get up early enough to avoid the crowds, even after what was surely a busy and tiring schedule the day before. He had to find a "lonely place" where he could recollect his spirit and converse peacefully with the Father.

It is possible to picture a faithful Christian who never travels the globe or converts thousands or builds cathedrals – indeed, plenty of saints have lived outwardly normal and unspectacular lives. But it is not possible to picture a faithful Christian who doesn't give God the time he deserves every day in prayer. If Christ needed it, we all need it.

CHRIST THE FRIEND Simon Peter's mother-in-law knew what it meant to be Christ's friend. As soon as he healed her, she "immediately got up and began to wait on them." She learned from Jesus, who came to serve. When we experience his saving power in our lives, the most natural way to respond is to stand up and join his team, loving and serving others as Jesus has loved and served us.

Friendship is, among other things, a kind of partnership. Jesus has a mission to win over hearts for his Kingdom, to bring lost and frustrated souls back into communion with God. When he offers us his friendship, he also offers us a share in his work. He wants us to experience the joy of loving as he loves, because that's what he created us to do. Simon Peter's mother-in-law got the picture; Jesus hopes that we get it too.

CHRIST IN MY LIFE Sometimes I think that if I could just see you and hear your voice, my life would take on an entirely different sheen. But that's not true. It's not lack of knowledge that hinders my discipleship – in fact, you are always speaking to me – it's my persistent selfish tendencies. They weaken my confidence in you and make me deaf to your words. Give me the strength to rein in my self-centeredness, so you can work more freely in and through my life…

Thank you for the gift of prayer. It's something I take for granted. At any time, at any place, I can turn to you and know for certain that you hear me and pay attention to me. No busy numbers, no voicemails, no crammed inboxes – you are always attentive and eager to hear and answer me. I have a direct line. Teach me to pray, Lord. Teach me to live always in the light of your truth and love…

I can't imagine what life would be like without your friendship. What hope would I have? Where would I go to repent of my sins, to get the light and strength I need for my life's mission, to restore my soul? And what would I look forward to after death? But many, many people haven't accepted your offer of friendship. Make me an instrument of your grace…

QUESTIONS FOR SMALL GROUP DISCUSSION

1. What struck you most in this passage? What did you notice that you hadn't noticed before?
2. How do you think the disciples might have reacted when Jesus said it was time to move on to another town?
3. Why do you think Jesus ordered the demons to stay quiet about his identity as Messiah?
4. Many people don't believe in the devil, but the Gospels clearly show the reality of demonic action and presence in the world. How would you explain the devil's existence to a skeptical, agnostic friend?

Cf. Catechism of the Catholic Church, 397, 413, 1707, 2583, 2851 on the devil as the origin of evil; 394-395, 398, 2851-2852 on the works of the devil; 547-550 on the signs of the Kingdom of God

THE GOSPEL OF LUKE CHAPTER 5

"Jesus Christ, our God and our Redeemer, is rich in the fullest and perfect possession of all things: we, on the other hand, are so poor and needy that we have nothing of our own to offer him as a gift. But yet, in his infinite goodness and love, he in no way objects to our giving and consecrating to him what is already his, as if it were really our own; nay, far from refusing such an offering, he positively desires it and asks for it: 'My son, give me your heart' (Proverbs 23:26). We are, therefore, able to be pleasing to him by the good will and the affection of our soul. For by consecrating ourselves

to him we not only declare our open and free acknowledgment and acceptance of his authority over us, but we also testify that if what we offer as a gift were really our own, we would still offer it with our whole heart."

- Pope Leo XIII, Annum Sacrum, 149

165. CATCHING FISH AND LEAVING BOATS (LK 5:1-11)

'Christ is the light and the lamp stand is Peter."

- St Ephraem

Luke 5:1-11

Now he was standing one day by the Lake of Gennesaret, with the crowd pressing round him listening to the word of God, when he caught sight of two boats close to the bank. The fishermen had gone out of them and were washing their nets. He got into one of the boats – it was Simon's – and asked him to put out a little from the shore. Then he sat down and taught the crowds from the boat. When he had finished speaking he said to Simon, 'Put out into deep water and pay out your nets for a catch'. 'Master,' Simon replied 'we worked hard all night long and caught nothing, but if you say so, I will pay out the nets.' And when they had done this they netted such a huge number of fish that their nets began to tear, so they signalled to their companions in the other boat to come and help them; when these came, they filled the two boats to sinking point. When Simon Peter saw this he fell at the knees of Jesus saying, 'Leave me, Lord; I am a sinful man.' For he and all his companions were completely overcome by the catch they had made; so also were James and John, sons of Zebedee, who were Simon's partners. But Jesus said to Simon, 'Do not be afraid; from now on it is men you will catch.' Then, bringing their boats back to land, they left everything and followed him.

CHRIST THE LORD Jesus shows his mastery over the hearts of men (the crowd was "pressing round" him to hear him speak) and over the forces of nature (they caught a "huge number of fish"). Yet when he asks Peter to "put out into deep water and pay out your nets for a catch," the future Apostle complains before he obeys. However many times God shows himself worthy of our trust (creation, the Incarnation, the Passion, the Resurrection, the sacraments – what more could he have done to win us over?), we still hesitate to do things his way. We need to acknowledge him as Lord not only with our lips, but with our hearts as well, and with our decisions. Like Peter, we need to apply all our natural effort (they had been fishing all night), but then take the extra step of faith: "Master… if you say so, I will…"

567

This applies to our apostolic endeavors, but it also applies to our moral lives. Many times the Church's teaching on controversial moral issues (for example, artificial and assisted reproduction, contraception, divorce and remarriage) is hard to understand on a merely natural level, especially when the prevailing culture bombards us with contrary views. In those moments especially, we need to realize that the life we are called to live surpasses our natural capacities. Jesus could never have proved to Peter beforehand that he would take in a miraculous catch in the middle of broad daylight, but that's what the Lord had in store for his disciple. To experience the wonderful action of God's grace in our lives, we have to bolster our natural understanding with supernatural faith (we need both faith and reason – either one without the other is not Christianity), and then we, like Peter, will draw in a wondrous catch.

CHRIST THE TEACHER Whenever we trust Jesus sufficiently to admit the limits of our merely human judgment, God rewards us in multiple ways. He gives us a greater experience of his goodness (the enormous catch of fish); he gives us a deeper knowledge of ourselves (in the wake of the miracle Peter sees clearly, maybe for the first time in his life, how arrogant and headstrong he really is: "I am a sinful man…"); he brings us closer to him, giving us a more intimate knowledge of him and the mission he has entrusted to us ("from now on you will be catching men… they left everything and followed him…").

Whenever God asks anything of us, it is always for our good and for the good of his Kingdom. This is the experience of all the saints – as soon as they launch themselves into the enterprises of God, life takes on an entirely new and indescribable dimension. On the other hand, when we hesitate, or demand proofs, or measure God by the undersized standards of human reason, we inhibit him from showing forth his goodness and love. But when we make an act of trust in God, obeying his will even when our human nature resists, God rewards us beyond our wildest imaginations.

CHRIST THE FRIEND God doesn't want to do everything by himself; he wants us to help him. He wants it so much that he makes himself weak in order to actually need our help. In this passage, he asks Peter to take him out from the shore so he can more effectively address the crowds – God enlists the help of a fisherman to make his voice heard! Since that moment, the advance of Christ's cause has been linked to an unbroken chain of men and women generous enough to lend their boats to the Lord, just as Peter did – or even to dock their boats, to "leave everything, and follow" him. He doesn't want to impose his

Kingdom from above; he wants us to enter freely into it, and help others to do the same, walking right beside him.

Andrew: It was mid-morning, my least favorite time of day. We were fixing our nets on the shore – my least favorite task. Everyone was tired and surly. As Jesus came by with the crowds I didn't even look up, I was in such a rotten humor. But he came over to us. I could tell Simon didn't want to oblige the Master, but sometimes it was simply impossible to say no to Jesus. We rowed out a little way. You should have seen the faces of the people as they listened to Jesus. They didn't miss a syllable. You could see their souls in their eyes, begging him for solace. I was barely listening to him. I couldn't look away from the crowd. Some of their faces were full of joy and enthusiasm. Others were yearning for something. Others were trying to hide, but unable to pull themselves away. When Jesus asked us to put out for a catch, I was still thinking about all those people. And then, when we drew in the overflowing nets, and when he told Simon that he would make us into fishers of men, it all came together. The fish were like the crowd of people; the boat was like his Kingdom. From then on I wanted only one thing: to go wherever Jesus went.

CHRIST IN MY LIFE I believe in you, Lord, and I believe in your Church. You continue to teach and guide the human family in every era and in every place through the living Magisterium of your Church. I want to follow you, and I want to experience the life you created me to live, and so I commit myself once again to be a faithful child of the Church, your chosen sacrament of salvation…

I am impressed by Peter's faith. He resisted at first, but when he saw the light in your eyes, he did what you asked him. And he did it only because it was you who were asking. I want to be like that. I want to see the light in your eyes and obey your every command, your every indication. You are the Lord; you are my Savior; Thy will be done…

Take my boat, Lord; enter into my life and use it to preach your saving message. I will go wherever you ask me. I will do whatever you require of me. Give me the strength to persevere in your will, no matter how dull or how painful it may become. You alone have the words of eternal life; turn my life into an amplifier that will make them resound to the ends of the earth…

QUESTIONS FOR SMALL GROUP DISCUSSION

1. What struck you most in this passage? What did you notice that you hadn't noticed before?

2. Why do you think Christ told Peter, "Do not be afraid"?

3. Why do you think Christ decided to give the men a miraculous catch of fish?

4. Is Christ asking us (or me personally) to "put out in the deep" in any way? If so, is he pleased with our (my) response?

Cf. Catechism of the Catholic Church, 547-550 on the signs of the Kingdom; 551-553 on the primacy of Peter (from whose boat Jesus taught) among the Apostles

166. HINTS OF A STORM (LK 5:12-26)

"There are many who study humanity and the natural world; few who study the Son of God."

- Pope Leo XIII

Luke 5:12-16

Now Jesus was in one of the towns when a man appeared, covered with leprosy. Seeing Jesus he fell on his face and implored him. 'Sir,' he said 'if you want to, you can cure me.' Jesus stretched out his hand, touched him and said, 'Of course I want to! Be cured!' And the leprosy left him at once. He ordered him to tell no one, 'But go and show yourself to the priest and make the offering for your healing as Moses prescribed it, as evidence for them.' His reputation continued to grow, and large crowds would gather to hear him and to have their sickness cured, but he would always go off to some place where he could be alone and pray.

Now he was teaching one day, and among the audience there were Pharisees and doctors of the Law who had come from every village in Galilee, from Judaea and from Jerusalem. And the Power of the Lord was behind his works of healing. Then some men appeared, carrying on a bed a paralysed man whom they were trying to bring in and lay down in front of him. But as the crowd made it impossible to find a way of getting him in, they went up on to the flat roof and lowered him and his stretcher down through the tiles into the middle of the gathering, in front of Jesus. Seeing their faith he said, 'My friend, your sins are forgiven you.' The scribes and the Pharisees began to think this over. 'Who is this man talking blasphemy? Who can forgive sins but God alone?' But Jesus, aware of their thoughts, made them this reply, 'What are these thoughts you have in your hearts? Which of these is easier: to say, "Your sins are forgiven you" or to say, "Get up and walk?" But to prove to you that the Son of Man has authority on earth to forgive sins,' – he said to the paralysed man – 'I order you: get up, and pick up your stretcher and go home.' And immediately before their very eyes he got up, picked up what he had been lying on and went home praising God. They were all astounded and praised God, and were filled with awe, saying, 'We have seen strange things today.'

CHRIST THE LORD This passage marks a turning point in the Gospel. Luke explains that Jesus' teaching and miracles were drawing huge crowds, and his reputation was spreading like wildfire. But even so, Jesus himself continues to carefully circumscribe his work. He heals the leper, a social and religious outcast, but he orders him to keep the miracle quiet and respectfully follow all the normal Jewish rules surrounding cures from leprosy. And although massive throngs gather around him, he still makes a point of going off to be alone to pray when he is finished teaching them and healing the sick. In other words, Jesus is not stirring up some kind of political revolution. He is not trying to gather an army to execute a coup d'état against the Pharisees, the Scribes, the Sadducees, and the Elders who made up Israel's ruling body, the Sanhedrin. Jesus is not instigating conflict.

Immediately after making this clear, however, St Luke points out that while Jesus is teaching one day, representatives of those ruling parties were in the crowd, listening to him and judging him. His work had sparked their interest, because they saw in him a rival for the people's allegiance. Then, in the course of his teaching, Jesus makes claims to forgive the paralytic's sins – something that, in the Old Covenant, could only be done through the proper Temple sacrifices carried out by the Levitical priests. Immediately these rulers of the status quo grumble in opposition. A conflict begins to brew. But Jesus recognizes their disquiet, and so right away he sets out to allay their suspicions. For the Jews, physical suffering was a result of sin. So Jesus knows that if he demonstrates enough power to cure this man's paralysis, it will be a clear indication that he also had the authority to forgive sins. And that's precisely what he does. This clear and obvious sign, however, won't be sufficient for many Pharisees and other Jewish leaders. Unfortunately, they are more interested in maintaining their influence than discovering the truth of Christ's identity.

This first inkling of the coming storm illustrates a pattern that the whole history of the Church will follow. Christ's faithful disciples will not seek out conflict with worldly rulers, but their fidelity to Christ's teaching and mission will inevitably challenge the powers that be, since those powers all too often seek self-aggrandizement in the place of truth and justice, and from that tacit challenge conflict will ensue. In the end, there can be only one Lord, and anyone unwilling to accept his rule will perish in their vain, but violent, attempts to crush it. A mature Christian is never surprised at opposition.

CHRIST THE TEACHER Christ was both active and contemplative. He spent his days teaching, preaching, and healing, but he spent his nights and mornings in prayer.

Every Christian is called to be another Christ. And so every Christian must also be active *and* contemplative. We find it hard to keep the balance. Everybody has a natural affinity for one or the other, which creates a tendency to over-emphasize the one we naturally like. A central component, therefore, of every Christian's cross is keeping the balance between prayer and action. Without filling our souls with God's grace and light in prayer, we have nothing worth-while to offer our neighbors. But without bringing Christ to our neighbors, our own spiritual lives stultify, like noxious swamps that have no outlet. The Master prayed and the Master worked, and where the Master is, there too his disciples will be found.

CHRIST THE FRIEND Lepers were unfortunate victims of a virus that gradu-ally and inexorably rotted the diseased person's flesh. Leprosy was highly contagious, so lepers were not permitted to come even within a hundred yards of uninfected people. Besides the sickness itself, then, lepers suffered the agony of social ostracism and isolation. When this leper comes up to Jesus to beg for a miracle, he breaks all the rules, so desperate is he for a cure. And Jesus not only saves him from the disease, but he reaches out and touches him, ending his exile from human companionship. Jesus knew that the man was suffering in his body, but also in his soul, and he is interested in both.

The same thing happens with the paralyzed man. According to the understand-ing of the times, this man would have considered his illness to be punishment for some sin. When his friends bring him to Jesus for healing, Jesus sees right away that the man's deepest suffering comes from the consciousness of this sin. The Lord sees his repentance and rewards the faith of the whole group of friends by offering God's forgiveness. Only then does he heal the man's body.

Jesus always knows what we need. The more we get to know him, the more his saving grace will heal us where we truly need to be healed, a place we may not even know about ourselves. Over and over again the Gospels show Jesus performing his miracles as ways of displaying God's goodness to suffering individuals. He is no showman out for applause; he is a loving shepherd tending his needy sheep.

CHRIST IN MY LIFE Why can't building your Kingdom in this world be a peaceful affair? Why must there always be opposition, conflict, and misun-derstanding? Your patience astounds me, Lord. You put up with all our petty squabbles and wasteful, self-righteous arguments. Teach me to leave them all behind and be just like you, forging ahead and spreading your truth and love…

I want to do something for your Kingdom, but I also simply want to know you better. I want to learn to contemplate your greatness and majesty in the midst of life's hustle and bustle, and I want to learn to conquer dying hearts with your grace. I want to follow in your footsteps, Lord. Teach me to pray, and teach me to build your Kingdom…

You told us to learn from you, because you are meek and humble of heart. Can I love those around me as you love me? You banished the leper's loneliness and set the paralytic's conscience at ease. Give my heart the wisdom and gentleness of your heart, so I can detect and help meet the real, interior needs of my neighbors and not just live on the surface…

QUESTIONS FOR SMALL GROUP DISCUSSION

1. What struck you most in this passage? What did you notice that you hadn't noticed before?

2. Surely Jesus was praying at all times, but St Luke explicitly and repeatedly mentions that he also went off to places where he could be alone to pray. What are some of the common obstacles to a healthy prayer life, and how can we overcome them?

3. St Luke tells us that Jesus forgave the paralytic when he saw "their" faith, the faith of the whole group of friends. What lesson can we learn from this detail?

4. The four men who brought in the paralytic had to go to quite a bit of trouble to do so. What are some common excuses we make in order to avoid going out of our way to bring others closer to Christ? How do they hold up in light of this Gospel passage?

Cf. Catechism of the Catholic Church, 514-521 on Christ's whole life as mystery; 574-576 on Jesus and Israel; 1440-1449 on how God forgives sin in the New Covenant

167. MAKING ALL THINGS NEW (LK 5:27-39)

"As the tree is known by its fruits, so they who claim to belong to Christ are known by their actions; for this work of ours does not consist in just making professions, but in a faith that is both practical and lasting."

- St Ignatius of Antioch

Luke 5:27-39

When he went out after this, he noticed a tax collector, Levi by name, sitting by the customs house, and said to him, 'Follow me.' And leaving everything he got up and followed him. In his honour Levi held a great reception in his house, and with them at table was a large gathering of tax collectors and others. The Pharisees and their scribes complained to his disciples and said, 'Why do you eat and drink with tax collectors and sinners?' Jesus said to them in reply, 'It is not those who are well who need the doctor, but the sick. I have not come to call the virtuous, but sinners to repentance.' They then said to him, 'John's disciples are always fasting and saying prayers, and the disciples of the Pharisees too, but yours go on eating and drinking.'

Jesus replied, 'Surely you cannot make the bridegroom's attendants fast while the bridegroom is still with them? But the time will come, the time for the bridegroom to be taken away from them; that will be the time when they will fast.' He also told them this parable, 'No one tears a piece from a new cloak to put it on an old cloak; if he does, not only will he have torn the new one, but the piece taken from the new will not match the old. And nobody puts new wine into old skins; if he does, the new wine will burst the skins and then run out, and the skins will be lost. No; new wine must be put into fresh skins. And nobody who has been drinking old wine wants new. The old is good, he says.'

CHRIST THE LORD Christ's invitation to Levi (aka Matthew) is odd. In fact, the word "invitation" doesn't describe it very well. It's more like a command. Jesus doesn't say, "Levi, would you like to join my band of disciples?" or "Levi, how would you feel about taking some time off work to come and learn how to save your soul?" Instead, he simply looks at Levi and orders him, with no explanation, to follow him: "Follow me."

Jesus is either a megalomaniac or the Lord. Who else would issue such a definitive, personal command? This is no cajoling philosopher; this is a King exercising his rights over his beloved subjects. And Levi makes the right response: when your King sends for you, you come. He is our King too, and he is daily sending for us – how he hopes that we will have the same courage and love that Levi had, so he can make us too into the saints he created each one of us to be.

CHRIST THE TEACHER Following Jesus involves change. Levi the tax collector makes himself into a living parable of this fundamental Christian truth – Jesus called him, and Levi responded the way everyone must respond if they want to enter Christ's Kingdom. First, St Luke tells us that Levi's response required "leaving everything." Jesus is not a TV show that you can turn on and off when you feel like it, or a website you can visit at your leisure and forget about the rest of the time. Jesus is God. To make room in one's life for his voice, his action, means taking a huge risk. We have to be willing to give up whatever Jesus demands that we give up. Second, St Luke mentions that Levi "got up" and followed the Lord. He had to step out of his comfort zone. Christ teaches us that life on earth is a mission, not a vacation – a journey, not a destination. Jesus is constantly demanding more from his followers, constantly upsetting their plans and their ease, because love does that: it settles only for the very best, which means inciting continual growth in virtue and wisdom (along with the required growing pains).

Levi's response is a living parable about what the Christian life involves, but to make sure the lesson sticks, Jesus complements Levi's example with some normal parables. Old clothes are comfortable; old, familiar wine is pleasant. When Christ comes into our lives, he brings new clothes and new wine, and responding generously to his call means making an uncomfortable and at first unpleasant adjustment. And as our friendship with Christ grows, he continues to surprise us with another set of new clothes, with another new batch of wine. Earth is not heaven, so while we are on earth making our way to heaven, we can never rest on our laurels. The authentic Christian never conforms to what he has already accomplished, because Christ always has more for us to learn, to do, and to become.

CHRIST THE FRIEND St Luke paints a vivid picture of the encounter between Jesus and Levi. Jesus is walking downtown, probably with his disciples, and sees Levi there at his office. Luke says that Jesus "noticed a tax collector, Levi by name." Isn't it just like Jesus to *notice* someone – what a torrent of instruction rushes out of that one little verb! It means that the Lord is always on the look-out. It means that Jesus is thinking not of himself, but of us and of our needs. It means that Jesus recognizes the needs and desires and yearnings of our hearts. Jesus notices this unhappy tax collector, a social pariah, and calls him, renews his life, and gives him a mission and a meaning.

That's what Jesus does. He is the doctor of every soul; he detects our every need and hope, and he prescribes the perfect medicine. He is the bridegroom of every heart; he gazes on us with personal, determined love and leads us into the everlasting adventure of indescribable intimacy and communion with God. Jesus is a friend, true – but what a friend he is, and what great friends he teaches us to be!

CHRIST IN MY LIFE You deserve my whole allegiance and my unconditional obedience. You created me. You placed me on this wonderful, mysterious earth. You gave me faith and showed me the purpose of my life: to know you and love you, and to help build up your Kingdom. I don't need to know anything else, Lord. Your word is enough for me. Thy will be done in every corner of my life…

Lord, sometimes I wonder why you keep asking me for more, why you keep sending me more crosses, more missions. Why can't we relax and take it easy? I know the answer: because you love me too much, and you love every person too much – you suffered and died to win us grace, and you want that grace to fill us and lead us to true meaning and lasting happiness. Lord Jesus, I trust in you…

I remember the first time I heard your voice in my heart. I was like Levi, living an average life, wanting more but not knowing where to find it. And you noticed me. You notice me every day, every moment. Give me a heart like yours, one that responds like Levi to your every wish, and in turn reaches out to others as you have reached out to me. Teach me, Lord…

QUESTIONS FOR SMALL GROUP DISCUSSION

1. What struck you most in this passage? What did you notice that you hadn't noticed before?

2. What have been some of the more difficult changes Christ has asked of you in your life?

3. Levi followed Jesus generously and enthusiastically. What can inhibit us from doing the same?

4. How can we reach out to sinners who need Christ without falling into their sins?

Cf. Catechism of the Catholic Church, 1500-1513 on Christ the physician; 545 and 588 on the universality of Christ's mercy; 796 on Christ as the bridegroom of the Church

THE GOSPEL OF LUKE CHAPTER 6

"My friends, in the heart of every man there is the desire for a house. Even more so in the young person's heart there is a great longing for a proper house, a stable house, one to which he cannot only return with joy, but where every guest who arrives can be joyfully welcomed. There is a yearning for a house where the daily bread is love, pardon and understanding. It is a place where the truth is the source out of which flows peace of heart. There is a longing for a house you can be proud of, where you need not be ashamed and where you never fear its loss. These longings are simply the desire for a full, happy and successful life. Do not be afraid of this desire! Do not run away from this desire! Do not be discouraged at the sight of crumbling houses, frustrated desires and faded longings. God the Creator, who inspires in young hearts an immense yearning for happiness, will not abandon you in the difficult construction of the house called life.

"My friends, this brings about a question: 'How do we build this house?' Jesus… encourages us to build on the rock… Building on rock means first of all to build on Christ and with Christ… In short, building on Christ means basing all your desires, aspirations, dreams, ambitions and plans on his will. It means saying to yourself, to your family, to your friends, to the whole world and, above all to Christ: "Lord, in life I wish to do nothing against you, because you know what is best for me. Only you have the words of eternal life" (cf. John 6:68). My friends, do not be afraid to lean on Christ! Long for Christ, as the foundation of your life! Enkindle within you the desire to build your life on him and for him! Because no one who depends on the crucified love of the Incarnate Word can ever lose."

- Pope Benedict XVI

168. THE CHANGING OF THE GUARD (LK 6:1-16)

For we can have no life apart from Jesus Christ; and as he represents the mind of the Father, so our bishops, even those who are stationed in the remotest parts of the world, represent the mind of Jesus Christ."

- St Ignatius of Antioch

Luke 6:1-16

Now one sabbath he happened to be taking a walk through the cornfields, and his disciples were picking ears of corn, rubbing them in their hands and eating them. Some of the Pharisees said, 'Why are you doing something that is forbidden on the sabbath day?' Jesus answered them, 'So you have not read what David did when he and his followers were hungry – how he went into the house of God, took the loaves of offering and ate them and gave them to his followers, loaves which only the priests are allowed to eat?' And he said to them, 'The Son of Man is master of the sabbath'. Now on another sabbath he went into the synagogue and began to teach, and a man was there whose right hand was withered. The scribes and the Pharisees were watching him to see if he would cure a man on the sabbath, hoping to find something to use against him. But he knew their thoughts; and he said to the man with the withered hand, 'Stand up! Come out into the middle.' And he came out and stood there. Then Jesus said to them, 'I put it to you: is it against the law on the sabbath to do good, or to do evil; to save life, or to destroy it?' Then he looked round at them all and said to the man, 'Stretch out your hand'. He did so, and his hand was better. But they were furious, and began to discuss the best way of dealing with Jesus. Now it was about this time that he went out into the hills to pray; and he spent the whole night in prayer to God. When day came he summoned his disciples and picked out twelve of them; he called them 'apostles': Simon whom he called Peter, and his brother Andrew; James, John, Philip, Bartholomew, Matthew, Thomas, James son of Alphaeus, Simon called the Zealot, Judas son of James, and Judas Iscariot who became a traitor.

CHRIST THE LORD Jesus is Lord, but he exercises his Lordship through normal human channels. For the duration of the Old Covenant, he governed his Chosen People through prophets, judges, and kings – through flesh and blood human beings. He established his Covenant with Israel through Abraham; he sent them the Law through Moses; he led them into the Promised Land through Joshua; he made them into a Kingdom through Samuel, Saul, and David. God most often sends his grace into human lives through human instruments.

At this point in his ministry, however, Jesus is seeing that the current religious leaders of Israel, who were supposed to be acting as those instruments for that generation, were closing themselves off to his teaching. He answers their objection to the disciples' picking and eating corn on the Sabbath; he explains why their conception of Sabbath regulations is wrong (they have forgotten the reason behind it) and proves the validity of his explanation and his claim to be Lord of the Sabbath by a dramatic miracle. But in spite of these and other proofs and arguments, the Pharisees and Scribes become outraged and harden their minds and hearts even more to the Messiah.

So Jesus goes off to pray. And in his prayer he sees that the time has come to prepare a new generation of leaders who will be his instruments of grace for the New Covenant. The leaders of the Old Covenant have relinquished their roles by rejecting Jesus, who will now name a new generation of shepherds. When his night vigil comes to a close, he chooses twelve of his disciples to be his special envoys, and the Apostolic College, the first bishops of the Church, is established. The Lord changes the Covenant, but he doesn't change his methodology: in the New People of God, just as in the Old People of God, he will administer his grace and his salvation through human instruments. He likes to treat us like the people we are.

CHRIST THE TEACHER The Pharisees had become obsessed with their appearance of holiness. They were convinced that external formalities sufficed; if they followed all the rules, that was all that mattered. But in truth they were missing the very point of the rules. The Law of the Old Covenant was a gift of God to his Chosen People. It was aimed at helping them learn to love God and their neighbors better. At the time of Christ, the Pharisees, the experts in interpreting this Law and in carrying it out to the minutest external detail, had forgotten this essential purpose. And so, when Jesus performs a work of mercy (a miraculous work that could only have been performed with God's direct intervention) that contradicts the Sabbath rules (you could heal mortal wounds on the Sabbath, but not illnesses or wounds that weren't putting one's life in immediate danger), the Pharisees become violently indignant, "furious" St Luke tells us. Their self-righteousness had blinded them completely to God's action, God's presence, and the real needs of their neighbors.

It is easy to point fingers at these Pharisees. It is easy to see how foolish and hard-hearted they were. But the Gospels don't remind us of them just so we can shake our heads in disdain. We too can fall into the exact same trap. How many divisions in the Church happen because we are so attached to appearances (to our appearance) that we neglect the substance! How many times arguments drive divisions deeper just because we are concerned about keeping up vain appearances!

The human heart easily gets too attached to its own practices and preferences, so that other practices and preferences are looked upon not simply as different, but as inferior. Does it please Christ when we break into cliques and quarreling camps? Didn't he give us the papacy to guarantee unity by identifying and protecting what must be maintained and held by all his followers and to determine where variety is allowed? The ancient Pharisees destroyed Christ; modern Pharisees continue, tragically, to wound his Body.

CHRIST THE FRIEND Jesus spends the whole night in prayer. It's clear that he is praying about his next day's choice of the Twelve Apostles. He chooses carefully, purposely – not randomly. He chooses each one by name.

Christianity is the most personal of religions. True, Christians become members of Christ's Body, of the family of the Church, but their individuality is not destroyed – it is liberated. Jesus knows each of his followers by name. That list of names that St Luke records assures us that in God's eyes none of us is a mere statistic. None of us is overlooked or chosen by mistake. God is the God of the entire universe, but he knows each of us through and through, and he calls each one of us to follow him individually. We are not generic soldiers in a zombie army. Christ's followers are, first and foremost, his personal friends.

CHRIST IN MY LIFE Sometimes I think that it would be more convenient if I could follow you without the Church, in a purely one-on-one religion. I wouldn't have to bother with other people, many who rub me the wrong way. But you want to send your grace through human instruments. Teach me why, Lord, so that I can love as you love…

The law of your Kingdom is self-giving, not self-assertion. The Pharisees didn't understand that. Lord, I am afraid of becoming like those Pharisees. I see that I too have a tendency toward self-righteousness, a tendency to think I am always right, a tendency to get stuck in my opinions. Keep me humble, Lord. Teach me to love my neighbor as you have loved me. Never let me be separated from you…

You know my name, and you have told me yours. How much peace this should give me! You call me by name! You have gone to heaven to prepare a place there just for me, with my name on it. No one else can love you or know you in quite the same way as I can. Thank you, Lord. Teach me to live in the peace of your love and leave behind the pressure of merely keeping up appearances…

QUESTIONS FOR SMALL GROUP DISCUSSION

1. What struck you most in this passage? What did you notice that you hadn't noticed before?

2. In all the lists of Apostles that appear in the New Testament, Peter is always put first and Judas last. Do you think that arrangement is significant?

3. Once again we see Jesus going off to pray, all by himself. What is the biggest obstacle in your prayer life? What has been the biggest help?

4. If a non-Catholic Christian friend asked you why you don't just "go right to God" instead of "going through a priest or the pope," how would you respond?

Cf. Catechism of the Catholic Church, 857-865 on the Apostolicity of the Church; 758-769 on the Church's origin and mission; 587-591 on the conflict between Jesus and the Pharisees

169. THE WAY TO GO (LK 6:17-26)

"The more one contemplates him with sincere and unprejudiced mind, the clearer does it become that there can be nothing more salutary than his law, more divine than his teaching."

- Pope Leo XIII

Luke 6:17-26

He then came down with them and stopped at a piece of level ground where there was a large gathering of his disciples with a great crowd of people from all parts of Judaea and from Jerusalem and from the coastal region of Tyre and Sidon who had come to hear him and to be cured of their diseases. People tormented by unclean spirits were also cured, and everyone in the crowd was trying to touch him because power came out of him that cured them all. Then fixing his eyes on his disciples he said: 'How happy are you who are poor: yours is the kingdom of God. Happy you who are hungry now: you shall be satisfied. Happy you who weep now: you shall laugh. Happy are you when people hate you, drive you out, abuse you, denounce your name as criminal, on account of the Son of Man. Rejoice when that day comes and dance for joy, for then your reward will be great in heaven. This was the way their ancestors treated the prophets. 'But alas for you who are rich: you are having your consolation now. Alas for you who have your fill now: you shall go hungry. Alas for you who laugh now: you shall mourn and weep. Alas for you when the world speaks well of you! This was the way their ancestors treated the false prophets.'

CHRIST THE LORD We have reached a turning point in the Lord's career. He has just been up on the mountaintop, where he spent the whole night in prayer.

When morning dawned, he gathered his disciples and chose twelve of them to be his intimate coworkers, his apostles. Now, with them, he descends to the crowds below and takes his place on a wide plain, where St Luke locates his first open air sermon, a summary of his new and spiritually revolutionary doctrine.

The picture Luke paints reminds us of Moses, who went up to the top of Mt Sinai to be with God and to receive the divine law, which he then taught to the people of Israel in the plain below; it is a picture of God-given authority, of someone who teaches with power. Luke also gives inklings of the universality, the definitiveness of Christ's authority: the crowds hail not only from Judea and Jerusalem (the territory of the Jews), but also from Tyre and Sidon (pagan lands and Gentile territories). Christ's law, unlike Moses' law, will extend God's covenant to all people. Finally, Luke provides a detail that turns these "statements" of Jesus into challenges, into commands: "And raising his eyes toward his disciples…." Christ presents his doctrine while looking us right in the eye - this is no mere professor, no theoretician; this is One who comes to conquer, this is the Lord. When we read these familiar words with that in mind, it makes all the difference.

CHRIST THE TEACHER In this context "blessed" means truly happy, filled with lasting joy. In a shocking reversal of ordinary standards, Jesus links true happiness with struggle and hardship, suffering and opposition. Those who set their sights merely on what this world has to offer and pursue it with all their heart, soul, mind, and strength will attain it, but that is all they will attain - and it won't be enough to satisfy them. Those who are full now will be hungry later; those who make merry now will be sad later; those who are popular now will experience rejection later. In other words, the human spirit was made to find its fulfillment by living in communion with God, and that can only happen if we use created realities in order to bring us closer to God. If, on the other hand, we set our hearts on the gifts of God in and of themselves (all the pleasures of the created world), we will certainly find enjoyment in them, but we will miss the point; our reservoir of happiness will eventually run dry, because we will have cut ourselves off from their source.

This lesson has to be relearned continually. Because of our fallen nature, we always tend to think we can find heaven on earth by putting together just the right combination of possessions, esteem, and power. But since we can't, as our Lord makes perfectly clear, the mature Christian will always need to avoid the

581

temptation to put his faith and his virtue on cruise control. There is no such amenity in the spiritual life. We are members of the Church militant for as long as we journey here on earth, and that means we need to keep our armor on and our supply lines protected, lest we fall into the enemy's traps.

CHRIST THE FRIEND In Christ's coming down from the mountain, looking his disciples in the eye, and telling them the secret to a meaningful and fulfilling life, we are presented with the entire pattern of salvation history in miniature. In becoming man, God descended from heaven to enter into the realities of our daily life. He did this in order to bring the light and grace of heaven into the darkness of a fallen earth. Why did he do it? Only out of love. He longs to look into our eyes, to catch our attention, and to convince us to join him in the adventure of eternal life. Is it not possible that when Jesus "lifted his eyes to his disciples" there was more than fire burning in them, more than determination and authority? Is it not possible that his power and certainty were softened with a rush of tenderness, with the hint of a knowing smile? If so, it was the smile of one who would be our friend – if we'll accept him.

CHRIST IN MY LIFE I believe in you, Lord, and I believe in all that you teach through your Scriptures and your Church. I have to admit that sometimes your teaching makes me uncomfortable, but because I know that your wisdom is always one and the same as your love, I gladly welcome it. I want to follow your path, and I want to help everyone I can to follow it too. Jesus, I trust in you...

Teach me to put all of the good things of this world in their proper place. Teach me to avoid making any created thing – money, pleasure, praise, success, influence, feelings – into an idol. You alone are the Lord, and you created this world to teach me about you and to give me an arena to exercise love. Thank you, Lord! Blessed be your name throughout the world...

Come again down into my life. Come again into my heart with your grace and into my mind with your truth. Never fail to come to me, never abandon me, Lord; never leave me to walk alone. I have put all my trust in you. I need you to teach me how to love, how to endure, how to understand. Thank you for coming to save me and befriend me; make my heart like yours...

QUESTIONS FOR SMALL GROUP DISCUSSION

1. What struck you most in this passage? What did you notice that you hadn't noticed before?

2. How could we translate these lessons of Christ (the Beatitudes) into language that would apply

to our specific situation? In other words, if he were to explain the Beatitudes to us right here and now, applying their principles to our lives, what would he say?

3. Where does popular culture encourage us to look for happiness? How does that compare with where Christ tells us to look for it?

4. If someone in your life-situation were 100 percent committed to Christ's plan of life, how would their weekly schedule differ from the average, non-believer's weekly schedule in the same life-situation?

Cf. Catechism of the Catholic Church, 1716-1729 on the Beatitudes and the secret to Christian happiness

170. LOVE, GIVE, AND LIVE (LK 6:27-38)

The measure of love is to love without measure."

- St Augustine

Luke 6:27-38

'But I say this to you who are listening: Love your enemies, do good to those who hate you, bless those who curse you, pray for those who treat you badly. To the man who slaps you on one cheek, present the other cheek too; to the man who takes your cloak from you, do not refuse your tunic. Give to everyone who asks you, and do not ask for your property back from the man who robs you. Treat others as you would like them to treat you. If you love those who love you, what thanks can you expect? Even sinners love those who love them. And if you do good to those who do good to you, what thanks can you expect? For even sinners do that much. And if you lend to those from whom you hope to receive, what thanks can you expect? Even sinners lend to sinners to get back the same amount. Instead, love your enemies and do good, and lend without any hope of return. You will have a great reward, and you will be sons of the Most High, for he himself is kind to the ungrateful and the wicked. Be compassionate as your Father is compassionate. Do not judge, and you will not be judged yourselves; do not condemn, and you will not be condemned yourselves; grant pardon, and you will be pardoned. Give, and there will be gifts for you: a full measure, pressed down, shaken together, and running over, will be poured into your lap; because the amount you measure out is the amount you will be given back.'

CHRIST THE LORD In this portrait of a true Christian, Jesus indirectly gives us a portrait of himself. He shows us what kind of Lord he really is: a lavish one. Nothing limits his generosity – not ingratitude, not opposition, not concern for himself – nothing. Only because he is unlimited in his generosity can he demand that his followers follow suit. If we truly know him, we will delight in serving such a Lord, and we will go out of our way to be worthy of him.

In the midst of this portrait, Jesus also teaches us one of the most basic laws of his Kingdom: the amount we measure out is the amount we will be given back. The more generous we are to others, the better we learn the art of self-giving, of self-forgetful love, the more intensely we will experience the fulfilled and fulfilling life we long for. The reason for this is simple. We are created in God's image and God is love; his very divine nature is all about self-giving. So the more we develop our capacity for love – authentic, self-forgetful love – the more we mature into what God created us to be. And just as a mature, healthy apple tree bears abundant fruit, so a mature, healthy human soul overflows with the spiritual fruits of profound joy, peace, and enthusiasm. This is the number one reason heaven will not be boring (contrary to what the devil does his best to make us think) – there's just too much overflowing life and love to leave even a tiny nook or cranny for boredom to creep in!

CHRIST THE TEACHER Through baptism, Christians become members of the body of Christ, brothers of the Lord, and children of God. In our journey through life we either stay faithful to that vocation or abandon it (and sometimes we go back and forth). In this passage, Christ gives us the touchstone of our fidelity, the sign by which we can know that we are living up to our vocation. It isn't vast theological knowledge, nor is it personal charm or professional success. Neither is it having ecstasies in prayer or taking on extreme penances. Rather, the identifying mark of a Christian is treating others – all others – the way God does, the way God treats us. God is kind and merciful "even to the ungrateful and the wicked." If we are his children, his followers, we will be kind and merciful too. We will be quick to forgive, quick to make excuses for others, quick to avoid judging and condemning them. We will think well of others, speak well of them, and treat them like the children of God (and thus our brothers and sisters) that they truly are.

God never holds back his love, and neither should we. God is like the sun, tirelessly emanating the goodness of love as the sun radiates light and heat. When we were baptized, he came to dwell within us, so that he could emanate his goodness to the world through us. Unfortunately, our pettiness, selfishness, and partiality often obscure his light instead of transmitting it. Learning to let his love and light shine more and more, in every moment and in every relationship, is the only task that really matters – the only lesson that Christ is hoping we will learn (with plenty of his help) perfectly.

CHRIST THE FRIEND Jesus presents us with a new way of living so that our reward will be great" and "there will be gifts" for us. Sometimes we mistakenly think that a Christian ought somehow to be indifferent to the human desire for happiness, as if wanting to be happy were some kind of sin. The truth is much more realistic: the desire for happiness is a gift from God, a homing device that impels us towards God, the only source of true and lasting happiness. If Christ demands sacrifice and generosity, if his way of life seems hard, if the cross is painful, it's only a temporary pain, like that of someone recovering from reconstructive surgery: the doctor demands a long and arduous rehabilitation program so that the patient can once again enjoy a healthy, active, and happy life. Christ is the doctor of our fallen, selfish souls, and he eagerly looks forward to the day when we will join him on the tennis courts in heaven.

CHRIST IN MY LIFE You want me to be truly happy. You will never be satisfied with the counterfeit happiness this world offers, the kind I sometimes would prefer. You love me too much. I believe in you, Lord, but it's hard to follow your path. I need your grace. You know I do. You will never hoard your help. Thank you, Lord. Teach me to do your will...

Your standard of love is much too high for me. So if you want me to live that way, you are going to have to come and be my light and my strength. Send your Holy Spirit into my soul and into the souls of all the members of your Church. Grant us a renewal of authentic Christian charity. You are all-powerful, Lord – you can do it! Come Holy Spirit, enkindle in me the fire of your love...

Dear Lord, a strange opinion about life is circulating out there. People seem to think it is dishonorable to follow you in order to be happy. But that's not what you teach. You came precisely because you wanted to show us – and open up for us – the path to true human fulfillment, both here on earth and forever in eternity. I trust you, Lord; teach me to spread your truth...

QUESTIONS FOR SMALL GROUP DISCUSSION

1. What struck you most in this passage? What did you notice that you hadn't noticed before?

2. What one thing has most hindered you from living Christian charity (treating others "as I would have them treat me," as God would have you treat them)? What one thing has most helped?

3. In what ways can we better imbue our community with the ethic of Christian charity?

4. Clearly, the world would be a better place if everything followed Christ's commandment to "Do unto others as you would have them do unto you." So why doesn't everyone follow it?

Cf. Catechism of the Catholic Church, 1-3, 26-29 on God's sheer goodness (unconditional love) as expressed in his plan of salvation; 1822-1829, 1844 on the primacy and nature of Christian charity

171. SURVIVING LIFE'S STORM (LK 6:39-49)

"To build on the rock means to build on Christ and with Christ, who is the rock."

- Pope Benedict XVI

Luke 6:39-49

He also told a parable to them, 'Can one blind man guide another? Surely both will fall into a pit? The disciple is not superior to his teacher; the fully trained disciple will always be like his teacher. Why do you observe the splinter in your brother's eye and never notice the plank in your own? How can you say to your brother, Brother, let me take out the splinter that is in your eye, when you cannot see the plank in your own? Hypocrite! Take the plank out of your own eye first, and then you will see clearly enough to take out the splinter that is in your brother's eye. There is no sound tree that produces rotten fruit, nor again a rotten tree that produces sound fruit. For every tree can be told by its own fruit: people do not pick figs from thorns, nor gather grapes from brambles. A good man draws what is good from the store of goodness in his heart; a bad man draws what is bad from the store of badness. For a man's words flow out of what fills his heart. Why do you call me, Lord, Lord and not do what I say? Everyone who comes to me and listens to my words and acts on them – I will show you what he is like. He is like the man who when he built his house dug, and dug deep, and laid the foundations on rock; when the river was in flood it bore down on that house but could not shake it, it was so well built. But the one who listens and does nothing is like the man who built his house on soil, with no foundations: as soon as the river bore down on it, it collapsed; and what a ruin that house became!'

CHRIST THE LORD By applying Jesus' parable to himself, we can better understand the nature of his Kingdom. What kind of fruit has his tree produced? Saints. Those who have followed Christ and his teaching are the saints, the men and women who have given a moral compass to the world, who have filled the world with hope, light, and enthusiasm. And the culture that was nourished on the love and sacrifice of the saints has given the world much of what it treasures most: hospitals (even the initial idea of hospitals), public education, equal rights, freedom from slavery, universities, technological progress.... These and many other institutions and values have flourished only in the wake of the gospel. To judge our Lord by his fruits, we would have to conclude that his Lordship is incomparable. And if we come to that conclusion, we will want to do all we can to live under his Lordship ourselves and extend it to as many others as possible.

Some critics often point to the sins of Christians as a way to discredit Christianity. Some Christians have sinned and caused as much destruction in the world as some non-Christians, they claim, which shows that Christianity is a pleasant but unsubstantial myth, like every other religion. This argument is shockingly illogical (revealing that those who purport it are being irrational – some other motive really lies behind their vehement opposition to God). Jesus warned his followers that if they heard his teaching and didn't put it into practice, their lives would collapse like a house built on sand collapses in a flood, damaging itself and ruining everyone in it. On the other hand, those disciples who hear *and heed* his teaching will stand solidly when the storm comes, providing shelter and stability. Discarding his doctrine because some hypocritical disciples proved that sand-grounded houses will indeed collapse in a flood is simply foolish and nonsensical. In the same way, accepting his doctrine because of the fruitfulness and happiness exemplified in the lives of thousands of saints is wise and commonsensical.

CHRIST THE TEACHER St Luke links four different lessons together in this brief speech. First, Jesus points out that disciples become like their teachers. Consequently, we need to choose our teachers well. (Of course, the obvious conclusion is to become a disciple of Christ – the greatest teacher of all). Second, he warns us about the inanity of useless criticism. We are all flawed and ignorant, so we have no prerogative to go around passing judgment on others for their flaws and ignorance. When we do, we make ourselves out to be fools. (Picture in your mind how foolish a man with a plank in his eye would look trying to remove a speck from his friend's eye – that's what we are like when we take on a "holier-than-thou" type of attitude, which we so easily tend to do.)

Third, we must be careful to be Christians who not only talk the talk, but also walk the walk. The world has plenty of preachers, but precious few saints. If we really want to bring others into the Kingdom, to lead others to Christ, words will not be enough; our lives have to bear the irresistible fruit of real virtue. Finally, Jesus points out that we give ourselves away by what we say. If we really want to know the state of our souls, all we have to do is pay attention to the words that come out of our mouths – especially when we are speaking spontaneously; what we say reveals what we care about. If we really want to improve the state of our souls, we should start by practicing self-control in our speech. In fact, merely starting to pay attention to the loose comments that stream out of our mouths will mark a big step in the right direction.

Any one of these lessons is enough to build a life around; unfortunately, few of us really bear down and study any of them well. We hear them, approve of them, and complain when the people around us don't follow them, but is our effort to learn and implement them as concerted as our effort to learn the ins and outs of our favorite hobby? It's so easy to look at other people and conclude that they are shamefully building on sand. But judging by these standards, wouldn't they be tempted to say the same thing about us?

CHRIST THE FRIEND Try to imagine the tone of Christ's voice as he spoke to the gathering on the plain. Was it like a professor expostulating in a classroom, enamored of his own voice? Was it brittle and fierce, like a harsh taskmaster? Or was it perhaps warm, eager, and exuberant? Most likely the latter – Jesus did not come to earth to flatter himself or to flex his divine muscles; he came to win our hearts back to God, and that's still the one item on his to-do list.

Jesus: You need a solid foundation, a firm anchor, a dependable, unchanging reference point. You need a rock on which to build your life. I have given you your life, along with the desires for meaning, fruitfulness, and adventure that go with it. And I have come to be your rock. The world is full of shifting sands. Opinions change, friends are unfaithful, circumstances take you where you would never have chosen to go – but through it all, I never leave you. My words, my example, my presence, my Church…. You can count on them all. Listen to me, walk with me, confide in me, and follow me. How could I ever lead you astray, when I gave my life for you?

CHRIST IN MY LIFE The fruits you are looking for in my life are the fruits of virtue. It is the heart that interests you most: what I desire in my heart and what I seek with my actions based on those desires. You know that in the very core of my being I want your friendship to be my highest priority. I want to reflect your goodness, your saving goodness, in everything I think, say, and do…

I think it's odd that you didn't teach us about political and economic systems. That's all we think about these days. But you brought us salvation and the secret to happiness, and you never talked about either one of them. Instead, you talked about how to love God and neighbor. That's the rock-solid foundation of a meaningful life, and of any political or economic system. I believe in you, Jesus, and I trust in you…

Jesus, I need you so much. When I am honest with myself, I see that in my heart and in my words I am still very far from following your teaching. I criticize, I judge, I look down on others, I am closed to their points of view. You know this. You can change me. You already have. Stay with me, Jesus. Keep teaching me to do your will…

QUESTIONS FOR SMALL GROUP DISCUSSION

1. What struck you most in this passage? What did you notice that you hadn't noticed before?

2. In what ways do Christ's four lessons in this passage apply to us? Which lesson is particularly applicable to you?

3. When Jesus first began to preach in public, he drew huge crowds. Do his words still attract? Why or why not?

4. Everyone chooses to follow someone, some teacher, in life. Who are some of the most revered "teachers" according to popular culture? How can a person know if he has really chosen Christ to be his teacher?

Cf. Catechism of the Catholic Church, 1691-1698 on Life in Christ; 1701-1724 on human nature and our vocation to happiness; 2464-2503 on the proper use of words and communication

THE GOSPEL OF LUKE CHAPTER 7

'Come here, then, my soul, and tell me – in God's name, I ask you – what hinders you from following wholly after God with all your strength? What do you love if not God, your spouse? Why don't you have great love for him who has so greatly loved you? Had he nothing else to do on earth except to give himself up for you? And seek your benefit even to his own hurt? What is there for you to do on earth except to love the King of heaven? Don't you see that all these things must come to an end? What do you see? What do you hear? What do you touch? Taste? Handle? Don't you see that all these things are but a spider's web that can never clothe you or keep you from the cold? Where are you when you are not in Jesus Christ? What do you think about? What do you value? What do you seek beyond the one perfect good? Let us rise, my soul, and put an end to this evil dream. Let us awaken, for it is day, and Jesus Christ, who is the light, has come."

- St John of Avila

172. TRUSTING THE LORD (LK 7:1-10)

"Hold fast to the rudder of faith, that you may not be shaken by the heavy storms of this world."

- St Ambrose

Luke 7:1-10

When he had come to the end of all he wanted the people to hear, he went into Capernaum. A centurion there had a servant, a favourite of his, who was sick and near death. Having heard about Jesus he sent some Jewish elders to him to ask him to come and heal his servant. When they came to Jesus they pleaded earnestly with him. 'He deserves this of you,' they said, 'because he is friendly towards our people; in fact, he is the one who built the synagogue.' So Jesus went with them, and was not very far from the house when the centurion sent word to him by some friends: 'Sir,' he said 'do not put yourself to trouble; because I am not worthy to have you under my roof; and for this same reason I did not presume to come to you myself; but give the word and let my servant be cured. For I am under authority myself, and have soldiers under me; and I say to one man: Go, and he goes; to another: Come here, and he comes; to my servant: Do this, and he does it.' When Jesus heard these words he was astonished at him and, turning round, said to the crowd following him, 'I tell you, not even in Israel have I found faith like this.' And when the messengers got back to the house they found the servant in perfect health.

CHRIST THE LORD Implicit in the title "lord" is superiority. Lords deserve to be obeyed. In human society, this obedience is based on a person's position, not on his intrinsic worth. With Christ it is different. He deserves to be obeyed because he is the Lord; he actually possesses within his very nature as God the authority that commands all things: "God said, 'Let there be light,' and there was light" (Genesis 1:3). And yet, Jesus refuses to force people to obey him; his power is wedded to love, and his love seeks a heartfelt, joyful obedience, not one that's compelled or robotic. The centurion recognizes both of these characteristics. Because he has come to believe in Christ's true Lordship, he knows that all forces in the universe will obey him, and because he has perceived Christ's love, he knows that Jesus will gladly use his power to cure this slave who was so valuable to him. Christ is a Lord both incomparably powerful and inestimably loving, and when we approach him with this in mind, he will work wonders for us.

Whenever we are given authority over others, we should keep Christ's example as our standard. Christ always uses his power for serving others; his followers should do the same.

CHRIST THE TEACHER It is possible to amaze Jesus. The centurion did it by having more faith in him than those who should have had the most faith of all. This brief incident instructs us about one of life's greatest mysteries: human freedom. Certainly God knows all things, but not because he directly determines them. He knows what we will do tomorrow only because for him there is no tomorrow; every "tomorrow" is present to him. We have difficulty understanding this, just as a blind man has difficulty understanding color, but our difficulty doesn't alter the fact: God's omnipotence and omniscience *respect our freedom*. In the core of our being we remain free to accept or reject God's action in our lives – and to accept or reject it more or less intensely. God wants us to accept him with all our "heart, soul, mind, and strength" – in other words, as intensely as possible. But he also knows that we are burdened with selfishness and beset by the devil, so it will take a great effort on our part to correspond to his grace. When the centurion, who had no prior contact with Jesus and no tangible reasons to put his faith in him, shows that he has made that effort, Jesus is amazed – and, most likely, immensely gratified. If we can learn from the centurion, we too can amaze and please our Lord.

Sometimes we put too much distance between faith and daily life. The centurion was facing the kind of crisis that happens only once in awhile, but we can imitate his faith even in normal situations. Every time our conscience nudges us to refrain from sharing or tolerating that little bit of gossip, every time we feel a tug in our hearts to say a prayer or give a little more effort, every time we detect an opportunity to do a hidden act of kindness to someone in need, we are faced with an opportunity to please the Lord by putting our faith in his will.

CHRIST THE FRIEND The words of the centurion have echoed down through the centuries as few others – "Lord, I am not worthy to receive you, but only say the word and I shall be healed" has been repeated in every Mass on every continent for almost 2000 years. In putting them on our lips before we receive Holy Communion, the Church helps us to come to Christ with both reverence and confidence: reverence, because he is God and we have rebelled against God, and confidence, because instead of punishing our rebellion, he wants to come and win back our friendship.

We should be grateful for Christ's willingness to come into our lives, as the centurion was surely grateful for all Jesus had done for him. But having received Christ, having become his brothers and sisters, his ambassadors, we should also imitate his example. The people around us who don't know Jesus should find in us an advertisement for following him. The centurion sensed Christ's divinity and his goodness without ever having met him personally – he knew Jesus only from hearing about others' experience of him and seeing the lives that Jesus had changed. Would that we were such effective messengers to the centurions all around us! Our friend deserves that we at least give it our best shot – he'll take it from there.

CHRIST IN MY LIFE When I take time to reflect on the beauties of the world around me, I can't help but marvel at your power and your wisdom. All of this came forth from your heart and your hands. You are the Creator and Sustainer of all things, and yet you deign to dwell with us in the humble silence of the Eucharist. Come and reside in my heart, come to rule me gently...

I do believe in you, Lord. I have put my trust in you. You know I have. But my faith is scrawny. I know you have wonderful things you want to do in my life and through my life. You have called me to be a saint, an oasis of virtue and fruitfulness in this fallen world. You just need me to trust you more. Increase my faith, Lord; teach me to follow you and do your will...

How many needy hearts are yearning for your light, your grace, and your forgiveness! You long to hear everyone express a firm and simple faith like the centurion's. When I repeat his words before receiving Holy Communion, let me speak them with a vibrant faith. And make me an instrument through which you can stir up faith in hardened hearts...

QUESTIONS FOR SMALL GROUP DISCUSSION

1. What struck you most in this passage? What did you notice that you hadn't noticed before?

2. Did Christ grant the centurion's miracle for the same reasons the Jewish leaders used to persuade him to do so? If not, why did he grant it?

3. What practical things can we do to increase our faith?

4. How can we approach Holy Communion with more reverence and confidence? How can we help others do so as well?

Cf. Catechism of the Catholic Church, 142-165 on the nature and necessity of faith; 547-550 on the meaning of Christ's miracles

173. LOVE CONQUERS DEATH (LK 7:11-17)

"He was indeed the true God and hence brought it about that the blind saw, the lame walked, the deaf heard, he cleansed those afflicted with leprosy, and by a simple command called the dead back to life."

- St Gregory Agrigentinus

Luke 7:11-17

Now soon afterwards he went to a town called Nain, accompanied by his disciples and a great number of people. When he was near the gate of the town it happened that a dead man was being carried out for burial, the only son of his mother, and she was a widow. And a considerable number of the townspeople were with her. When the Lord saw her he felt sorry for her. 'Do not cry,' he said. Then he went up and put his hand on the bier and the bearers stood still, and he said, 'Young man, I tell you to get up.' And the dead man sat up and began to talk, and Jesus gave him to his mother. Everyone was filled with awe and praised God saying, 'A great prophet has appeared among us; God has visited his people.' And this opinion of him spread throughout Judaea and all over the countryside.

CHRIST THE LORD Jesus commands a dead man to rise, and he is obeyed. He shows that he is the Lord of life. And yet, when he commands us, "Do unto others as you would have them do unto you," or "Do not worry about tomorrow," or "Follow me," we resist. Does his Lordship work only on the dead? Hardly. Rather, he refuses to force his way into our hearts; he is Lord, but he is also Love. He makes his Lordship known, and then he invites us to fight under his banner – but there are no mercenaries in his army, only friends who serve the Lord of Love out of love for the Lord.

When he asks us something difficult, we should remember this passage. The same power which raised this dead man to life is at work in his commands to us. In baptism, this power floods our soul with grace through the words of the priest and the sign of water. In confession, this same power cleanses and renews our souls. Every word that Jesus speaks to us has the power to raise us up, to lift us into the kind of life we long to live.

CHRIST THE TEACHER The lesson is so simple that we may miss it: God cares. "Do not cry," he tells the woman, as if to say, "I can't bear to see you suffer. Let me help." No one asked him to perform this miracle – not even his disciples, who should have. The same motive behind his journey from heaven to earth through the Incarnation moves him to comfort this lonely widow. And the same motive is behind everything else he did before that moment and everything he accomplished since then: he cares. Such a simple lesson – but one that's so easy to forget!

Another more subtle lesson is hidden in this passage as well. The woman was a widow, like Jesus' own mother, Mary. (Joseph had died, tradition tells us, before Jesus set out on his public ministry.) The woman had only one son, again like Mary. Mary too will watch her only son die and be buried. Jesus' reaching out to this suffering woman reveals one of the most attractive characteristics of his Sacred Heart: his truly filial love for his Mother. How could Mary not have an entirely unique place in the perfect heart of the Redeemer? The Church's ancient practice of invoking Mary's intercession is, in this sense, an act of reverence made to Christ's Incarnation: only because he shares completely our humanity does he have a mother in the first place, and because faithful sons honor and respect their mothers – all the more so when the son is a perfect King and the mother a wise and selfless Queen – Jesus gives Mary a throne at his side. And just as he couldn't resist the heart's desire of this weeping widow of Nain, how can he resist Mary's heartfelt intercession on our behalf?

CHRIST THE FRIEND We never have to suffer alone. Some time before, the widow had lost her husband, and now she loses her only son; she certainly must have felt as alone as a person can feel, inconsolable in her grief even while surrounded by the crowd. Who can fathom the depths of a mother's love? And yet, she found someone who shared her pain – Jesus. Not only did he perceive her moral agony, her utter loneliness, but he had compassion on her; he suffered *with* her (which is what the word compassion means). Because of this, he knew how to relieve her suffering; when he came over to her and placed her resurrected son's hand in hers, she was no longer alone.

Sometimes we do feel like we are suffering alone – Christ seems far away; at least he doesn't intervene so dramatically as he did in Nain. But indulging such feelings shows a lack of faith. This poor widow did not know about Calvary; she had never seen a crucifix. The only way Christ had to show her his compassion was to restore her son to life. But we have seen Calvary. We know to what depths God's compassion has gone. And we can always go to the Tabernacle, where we find the Eucharist, the living memorial of Calvary – the revelation of God's unfathomable compassion, his "suffering with" each and every one of us. Truly, we never have to suffer alone. And so, when we choose to do so anyway, we not only increase our own pain, but we double Christ's as well, by turning a blind eye to his cross.

CHRIST IN MY LIFE Lord, I know I have to obey someone in life: either myself, with all my ignorance and limitations, or some other teacher or guru, or the shallow advice of popular culture (which only cares about turning me into a good consumer) – or you. I want to obey you. I choose once again to follow you. Lord Jesus, I believe that you are the way, the truth, and the life…

I know that you are with me in every moment of my life, the good moments and the bad ones. You suffer with me, because you know that having to suffer alone would double my pain. Why do I insist on walking alone? Why do I insist on resisting your compassion and comfort and the soothing balm of your Church's doctrine? Jesus, teach me to bear my cross with you…

Mary, you are my mother as well as Christ's, because my baptism made me a child of God. Teach me to be like Jesus. Teach me to trust in him, to know his goodness and his power so deeply that I never doubt him – so that I never fall back into self-absorption and angry frustration. Teach me to be bold and faithful ambassador of his Kingdom. Queen of peace, pray for me…

QUESTIONS FOR SMALL GROUP DISCUSSION

1. What struck you most in this passage? What did you notice that you hadn't noticed before?

2. What evidence should there be in a Christian's day-to-day life that says to other people around him: "God really does care"?

3. What can we do now to learn how to suffer as a Christian, uniting our sufferings to Christ's on the cross, so as to be ready for bigger crosses that will come later?

4. Every committed Christian makes a definitive option to fight under Christ's banner no matter how difficult the battle may get. What aspects of popular culture make it hard to stay true to that decision?

Cf. Catechism of the Catholic Church, 1-3, 27-30, 50-67 on how much God cares; 901, 1508, 556 on the role of trials and tribulations in the Christian life

174. IT'S UP TO YOU (LK 7:18-35)

"For this reason the Word of God became man and the Son of God became the son of man, in order that man, being mingled with the Word of God and being granted adoption, should become the son of God."

- St Irenaeus

Luke 7:18-35

The disciples of John gave him all this news, and John, summoning two of his disciples, sent them to the Lord to ask, 'Are you the one who is to come, or must we wait for someone else?' When the men reached Jesus they said, 'John the Baptist has sent us to you, to ask, Are you the one who is to come or have we to wait for someone else?' It was just then that he cured many people of diseases and afflictions and of evil spirits, and gave the gift of sight to many who were blind. Then he gave the messengers their answer, 'Go back and tell John what you have seen and heard: the blind see again, the lame walk, lepers are cleansed, and the deaf hear, the dead are raised to life, the Good News is proclaimed to the poor and happy is the man who does not lose faith in me.'

When John's messengers had gone he began to talk to the people about John, 'What did you go out into the wilderness to see? A reed swaying in the breeze? No? Then what did you go out to see? A man dressed in fine clothes? Oh no, those who go in for fine clothes and live luxuriously are to be found at court! Then what did you go out to see? A prophet? Yes, I tell you, and much more than a prophet: he is the one of whom scripture says: See, I am going to send my messenger before you; he will prepare the way before you. 'I tell you, of all the children born of women, there is no one greater than John; yet the least in the kingdom of God is greater than he is.' All the people who heard him, and the tax collectors too, acknowledged God's plan by accepting baptism from John; but by refusing baptism from him the Pharisees and the lawyers had thwarted what God had in mind for them. 'What description, then, can I find for the men of this generation? What are they like? They are like children shouting to one another while they sit in the market place: We played the pipes for you, and you wouldn't dance; we sang dirges, and you wouldn't cry. 'For John the Baptist comes, not eating bread, not drinking wine, and you say, He is possessed. The Son of Man comes, eating and drinking, and you say, Look, a glutton and a drunkard, a friend of tax collectors and sinners. Yet Wisdom has been proved right by all her children.'

CHRIST THE LORD John the Baptist has already recognized and acknowledged Jesus as the promised Messiah. But some of his disciples are still not convinced. Nothing John tells them can shake their doubt, so he sends them to ask Jesus directly, point blank, whether he is the Messiah. Jesus' answer seems evasive; he doesn't simply say, "Yes, I am." In fact, however, the answer is much more convincing than such a direct statement would be.

St Luke has just described all the remarkable healings and exorcisms that Jesus was performing at this time. So Jesus invites John's disciples to simply look around them and see the evidence: the prophets all announced that the Messianic era would be marked by giving the blind their sight, the deaf their hearing, the lame their health, the imprisoned freedom, and the dead new life (e.g., Isaiah 35:4-6, 61:1). These are the exact signs that Jesus is performing. Jesus lets his actions speak for themselves, and leaves it up to his questioners to accept or reject his claim. And he does the same thing today.

CHRIST THE TEACHER This passage teaches a harrowing lesson. St Luke points out that the sinners who believed in John the Baptist's preaching have also come to believe in Christ; they have "acknowledged God's plan" for salvation and for their own lives. As a result, God's plan is unfolding itself for them. But the apparently pious and religious people, the Pharisees and scribes, "thwarted what God had in mind for them," and so found themselves excluded from the Kingdom. Jesus himself gives a portrait of those resistant souls. They are like immature children who care only about satisfying their whims, regardless of how much God tries to accommodate them.

The lesson is clear, but so frightening that we can easily miss it: it is possible for a human person – for me – to thwart God's purpose for my life. We can, by abusing our freedom through self-indulgence and arrogance, shut out God's grace from our lives. When we live focused on our feelings, our petty desires, and our whims, we blind ourselves to God's will (which always demands self-mastery and self-sacrifice), and we frustrate his glorious plan and beautiful hopes for us. The scariest part of this lesson, however, isn't merely the fact of this possibility; it's the fact that the Pharisees, who had fallen into just such a state, truly thought they were doing the right thing by rejecting John and Jesus. They were so full of self-importance that they were literally blinded to the truth. May God save us from such a tragedy!

CHRIST THE FRIEND Jesus explains that, although John was the greatest of prophets, "the least in the Kingdom of God is greater than he is."

Jesus: This shows how much I want to give you. I not only want you to become citizens of my everlasting Kingdom, but I want to be your brother. I want you to dwell with me forever – not just as guests, but as members of my family; I came to make that possible. If you truly understand this generosity, this desire of my heart, you will begin to grasp how much I really love you. And knowing that will set you free from your fears and from your self-imposed (and unnecessary) pressure to try and earn my love. It also equips you to love others on a whole new level, since you are able to give them something that has everlasting value – you are able to help them come into the Kingdom.

CHRIST IN MY LIFE All of history was leading up to your appearance, Lord, and now all of history points to your final victory. I believe in you, Lord; I believe you are the Messiah sent by God to atone for our sins and to teach us the way to go. I believe that you govern all things with your providential wisdom and love. I believe that you will come again. Thy Kingdom come, thy will be done…

It scares me to think that I could become so self-absorbed as to be completely deaf to your voice. Never let me be separated from you, Lord. Many times your teaching and your will go against my whims and personal preferences, but these are just opportunities to show you that I love you and trust you. Hold me close to your side, Lord; keep me on the path of life…

Grant me, Lord, a clearer vision of your dream for my life. Sometimes I just don't know what to do with all the yearnings that I find in my heart. But you put them all there. They have their true object in you and your Kingdom. Help me to live entirely for my true vocation, and help me help those I love find theirs…

QUESTIONS FOR SMALL GROUP DISCUSSION

1. What struck you most in this passage? What did you notice that you hadn't noticed before?

2. In what ways does popular culture encourage us to give first priority to our passing whims and fancies, like the immature children Jesus uses in his parable?

3. If you had to explain "the Kingdom of God" to a non-believing friend, how would you do it?

4. Jesus performed many signs that indicated he was the Messiah. Why do you think it was so hard for the John's disciples to accept him?

Cf. Catechism of the Catholic Church, 456-460 on why the Word became flesh, 436-440 on Jesus as the "Christ" or "Messiah"; 547-550, 560, 670, 1505 on the signs of the Kingdom of God

175. HUMBLE PIE (LK 7:36-50)

"There will be no defense left to you on the day of judgement, when you will be judged according to the sentence you passed on others and you will be dealt with as you have dealt with others."

- St Cyprian

Luke 7:36-50

One of the Pharisees invited him to a meal. When he arrived at the Pharisee's house and took his place at table, a woman came in, who had a bad name in the town. She had heard he was dining with the Pharisee and had brought with her an alabaster jar of ointment. She waited behind him at his feet, weeping, and her tears fell on his feet, and she wiped them away with her hair; then she covered his feet with kisses and anointed them with the ointment. When the Pharisee who had invited him saw this, he said to himself, 'If this man were a prophet, he would know who this woman is that is touching him and what a bad name she has.' Then Jesus took him up and said, 'Simon, I have something to say to you.' 'Speak, Master' was the reply. 'There was once a creditor who had two men in his debt; one owed him five hundred denarii, the other fifty. They were unable to pay, so he pardoned them both. Which of them will love him more?' 'The one who was pardoned more, I suppose,' answered Simon. Jesus said, 'You are right'. Then he turned to the woman. 'Simon,' he said 'you see this woman? I came into your house, and you poured no water over my feet, but she has poured out her tears over my feet and wiped them away with her hair. You gave me no kiss, but she has been covering my feet with kisses ever since I came in. You did not anoint my head with oil, but she has anointed my feet with ointment. For this reason I tell you that her sins, her many sins, must have been forgiven her, or she would not have shown such great love. It is the man who is forgiven little who shows little love.' Then he said to her, 'Your sins are forgiven'. Those who were with him at table began to say to themselves, 'Who is this man, that he even forgives sins?' But he said to the woman, 'Your faith has saved you; go in peace.'

CHRIST THE LORD How did this woman enter the dining room? Sheepishly? If she were self-conscious, she wouldn't have come at all. She must have swept into the room, searching the faces with an alarming intensity, until she saw Jesus. Then her eyes lit up, her frown relaxed into a smile, and she rushed to his feet. He had given her something she had long been searching for. We don't know how she had met him. Maybe she had only seen him from a distance and listened to his teaching. However it happened, the power of his grace had reached through the layers of self-protection that she had erected around her heart and touched her soul. She had finally found someone who truly knew her, who truly valued her the way she had yearned to be valued, and who wanted nothing from her except trust and friendship. She had been searching for her self – her true self, her true worth – all these years, in all the wrong places. Now Jesus had shown her the way.

Jesus also reveals himself in this encounter. He shows his full identity in response to this woman's humble love and faith. No longer could people simply call him a great teacher, or a mighty prophet, or a wonderworker. No, he had publicly forgiven this woman's sins, something that God alone can do. Now the die was definitively tossed: either Jesus was the divine Messiah, or he was a lunatic pretending to be God. There is no evidence at all for lunacy, so we must conclude that he is, indeed, the Lord.

How much confidence and peace this conviction would give to our souls if we would simply let it sink in! Jesus is the Lord. He is Lord of history, of life, of good, of circumstances, hopes, and obstacles. And he is my Lord. His Lordship is exercised on my behalf, for the sake of my salvation, to free me from my sins and set me on the path of true love and joy – a path so fulfilling that this fashionable and pleasure-loving woman wept for happiness when she found herself upon it.

CHRIST THE TEACHER Jesus teaches us how he wants to forgive our sins: through real words spoken with a real, audible voice: "Your sins are forgiven." Just as this incomprehensibly mundane and human way of administering divine forgiveness shocked and scandalized Simon and his fellow Pharisees, so it continues to shock people today. If God has chosen to send his forgiveness through the tangible ministry of the sacrament of confession, he must have his reasons (and you can probably think of plenty). Of course, that doesn't make it any easier to go to confession. The sinful woman was doubly shamed, having to lay bare her guilt and repentance not only to her Lord (whom she trusted), but to everyone there at the table with him. We can feel the same shame and humiliation when we have to honestly tell our sins to the priest in the confessional. But Jesus wants to give us that chance. He wants to make it possible for us to confess our sins and our repentance in a physical, tangible way – that's why he became man in the first place. And he also wants us to be able to receive his forgiveness in a physical, tangible way. Christ's final words, "Your sins are forgiven… Your faith has saved you, go in peace" are quoted almost verbatim in the sacrament of confession. And just as we can imagine how deeply pleased he was at this encounter, so is his heart filled with joy whenever we give him a chance to shower us with his love in the confessional.

One thing that often keeps us away from this precious sacrament is the same thing that kept Simon from understanding why Jesus let this woman bathe his feet: we think we don't need God's forgiveness. We belittle our sin and selfish tendencies; we trust in our own strength to keep us on track; we readily admit others' weaknesses, but purposely ignore our own. Regular and frequent confession is one the surest signs of spiritual growth – skipping it is usually an equally trustworthy sign of spiritual stagnation.

CHRIST THE FRIEND How gently Jesus rebukes and teaches Simon the Pharisee! He doesn't yell or humiliate him; instead, he simply asks a couple of questions that quietly light up his conscience. And it had its effect. Many spiritual writers identify this Simon with the Simon who later threw a banquet for Jesus in Bethany just before his passion (it was common for the wealthy to have more than one house in Palestine). We know that by the time of the second banquet this Simon believed in Jesus and honored him. But even if the two Simons are different, the example of Christ's eagerness to win souls over to his Kingdom and the sweet meekness of his manner remains. St Frances de Sales used to say that one drop of honey will attract more flies than a whole barrel of vinegar. Jesus is dripping honey all over the place in the Gospels – which shows that he is more concerned about our good than his own vanity (patience, gentleness, and mercy aren't typical ways to assert one's self-esteem).

This is how Jesus dealt with Simon, and this is how he deals with us. Just recall how he has acted in your life up to now – steadily, surely, but very gently and respectfully. And if he does so with us, showing himself to be a true friend, shouldn't we do the same with the Simons we run across?

CHRIST IN MY LIFE You know I believe in you, but you also know how shaky my faith can be. Jesus, convince me of your wisdom, your nearness, your greatness. Help me to see your hand at work in all things. Pour your Holy Spirit upon me again, with his gifts of understanding and knowledge. My mind is so caked with the mud of this fallen world! Lord Jesus, be my light…

I don't know why it's still hard for me to go to confession. Shouldn't I be used to it by now? I'm glad I'm not. I'm glad I feel humiliated at confessing my petty selfishness and tantrums of self-indulgence – I should feel humiliated by such things. And what better way to become humble than to exercise humility? Thank you, Lord for your wise and mysterious mercy…

Jesus, you told me to learn from you because you are meek and humble of heart. I want to be a faithful ambassador of your Kingdom. And that means reaching out to those around me with the same gentleness and humility that you always showed. But I need your grace to control my temper, my tendency to arrogance, and my impatience. Lord Jesus, help me…

QUESTIONS FOR SMALL GROUP DISCUSSION

1. What struck you most in this passage? What did you notice that you hadn't noticed before?

2. How do you think Christ feels when we make a good confession? How do you think he feels when we systematically avoid or put off confession?

3. What aspects of popular culture encourage us to be like the sinful woman (recognizing our sins and our need for God), and which aspects encourage us to be like Simon the Pharisee (oblivious of our sins and full of self-righteousness and arrogance)?

4. When Christ comes to us in Holy Communion, how can we better welcome him with the love and attention of the sinful woman instead of the cold aloofness of Simon the Pharisee?

Cf. Catechism of the Catholic Church, 1420-1484 on the sacrament of confession; 3, 863-865 on the need God has of our collaboration to extend his Kingdom

THE GOSPEL OF LUKE CHAPTER 8

"We live in an age of inventions. We need no longer climb laboriously up flights of stairs. And I was determined to find an elevator to carry me to Jesus, for I was too small to climb the steep stairs of perfection. So I sought in Holy Scripture some idea of what this lift I wanted would be, and I read, 'Whoever is a little one, let him come to me' (Lk 8:16). I also wanted to know how God would deal with a "little one," so I searched and found: 'You shall be carried in her arms and fondled in her lap; as a mother comforts her son…' (Is 66:12-13) It is your arms, Jesus, which are the

elevator to carry me to heaven. So there is no need for me to grow up. In fact: just the opposite. I must become less and less."

- St Thérèse of Lisieux

176. IN PARTNERSHIP WITH GRACE (LK 8:1-15)

"Obedience is the backbone of faith."

- St Francis of Paola

Luke 8:1-15

Now after this he made his way through towns and villages preaching, and proclaiming the Good News of the kingdom of God. With him went the Twelve, as well as certain women who had been cured of evil spirits and ailments: Mary surnamed the Magdalene, from whom seven demons had gone out, Joanna the wife of Herod's steward Chuza, Susanna, and several others who provided for them out of their own resources.

With a large crowd gathering and people from every town finding their way to him, he used this parable: 'A sower went out to sow his seed. As he sowed, some fell on the edge of the path and was trampled on; and the birds of the air ate it up. Some seed fell on rock, and when it came up it withered away, having no moisture. Some seed fell amongst thorns and the thorns grew with it and choked it. And some seed fell into rich soil and grew and produced its crop a hundredfold.' Saying this he cried, 'Listen, anyone who has ears to hear!' His disciples asked him what this parable might mean, and he said, The mysteries of the kingdom of God are revealed to you; for the rest there are only parables, so that they may see but not perceive, listen but not understand 'This, then, is what the parable means: the seed is the word of God. Those on the edge of the path are people who have heard it, and then the devil comes and carries away the word from their hearts in case they should believe and be saved. Those on the rock are people who, when they first hear it, welcome the word with joy. But these have no root; they believe for a while, and in time of trial they give up. As for the part that fell into thorns, this is people who have heard, but as they go on their way they are choked by the worries and riches and pleasures of life and do not reach maturity. As for the part in the rich soil, this is people with a noble and generous heart who have heard the word and take it to themselves and yield a harvest through their perseverance.

CHRIST THE LORD Jesus is humble. He has all knowledge and all power, and he wants to give us a share for our happiness and salvation, but he constantly shows an attentive respect for our freedom. The passage illustrates this characteristic respect in two ways.

First, St Luke has Jesus start using parables. A parable presents a truth in brilliant clarity, but leaves it up to the listener to apply that truth to his own life. Jesus wants us to do this, saying, "Listen, anyone who has ears to hear!" At the same time, he knows that many who hear him are so attached to their own ideas and way of living that they are not really looking for wisdom, and so they will not search the parable for how it applies to their lives – "They may see but not perceive, listen but not understand…" If Jesus had taught more directly, those who were eager to learn would have assimilated it less completely – because when we have to make an effort to understand, we learn more deeply – and those who were just hanging around to see the show would have been immediately turned off, losing even the small chance they had of getting hit by a stray spark of grace.

Second, the parable itself reveals God's astonishing methodology of salvation. His grace is the seed, and our souls are the soil. Without the soil, the seed is completely useless. But without the seed, the soil is utterly barren. Each is made for each other. God's grace cannot work in our lives unless we receive it with a "noble and generous heart," unless we recognize our need for God, even if only in a vague and partial way, and seek his guidance. But no matter how intensely we may be seeking answers and wisdom and meaning, unless God intervenes with his grace, we will remain completely in the dark, like the barren blackness of a lifeless field.

How humble the Lord is to enter into an equal partnership with the very sinners who banished his grace from their souls!

CHRIST THE TEACHER God always supplies his grace. He always does his part in our spiritual lives. We can count on it. But we don't always do our part. Our attitude towards God's will determines the fate of his grace. If we are "noble and generous," his grace will have plenty of room to fill our lives with the fruits of holiness and happiness. If we give up when God's will requires us to persevere through tough times, his grace will wither. If we try to two-time God and the world, as if the cares and pleasures of life on earth were on an equal footing with our friendship with Christ, his grace will be sterile. Unless we make God's will – especially as discerned in our conscience and through Church teaching – our highest priority, we aren't really letting God be God, and so he can't make our life what he created it to be.

But the parable has yet another lesson. The first obstacle to God's grace appears to be the devil – represented by the birds that pick the seed up off the path.

Actually, however, the occasion that gives the devil a chance to get in there is, once again, due to the quality of the soil, the attitudes of our soul. The soil on the path is hardened. The seed can't sink in. This is the superficial soul, the person who never takes time to reflect, to pray, to think deeply, the person who lets himself be "distracted from distractions by distractions," as T. S. Eliot put it. In a culture more and more dominated by information and mass media, this is perhaps the greatest danger of all. The constant flow of images, ideas, opinions, advertisements, chats, noise, music, entertainment, news, and everything else can, if we let it, create such a quantity of traffic in our minds that we become unable to savor truth, even on the off chance that we recognize it amidst the din. The same mind we use all day long, the one we fill with idle chatter and sensationalized news and everything else – that's the same mind we bring to prayer. Unless we put a fence around what we attend to in our minds, unless we practice self-mastery and discipline in our thoughts, the graces God constantly sends us will bounce onto the top of the beaten track and sit there, easy pickings for the devil.

CHRIST THE FRIEND *Susanna: Many things were different about Jesus. His words, his miracles, his presence…. But from the very first time I met him, what struck me most was how he treated women. He had no fear of us, and he put on no airs of superiority or false dignity. He treated us as equals. He knew us. He respected us. He let us help him and take care of him. With Jesus we were colleagues; we shared in his projects, in his work. And we were also friends, because we shared his needs. He depended on us. He chose to need us. In him, I learned that real friendship with God is possible. All distances collapsed. Much later, after he had risen from the dead and gone back to his Father, some of the disciples were frightened and, well, confused and hesitant. Mary told us then that we should be afraid of nothing; he left us with a mission, because he wanted to continue in our friendship. He left his Kingdom in our hands because he wanted to continue needing us. He gave us the most precious gift he could think of: he entrusted to us the task of leading others into eternal life. For Jesus, everyone mattered; everyone was worthy.*

CHRIST IN MY LIFE I want to kneel down and thank you for being so patient with me. You want to save me, but not at the cost of obliterating my humanity. How wise you are, Lord! But how slow and distracted I am in response to your wisdom! Teach me, Jesus; I want to learn the secrets of your Kingdom. I have ears, and I want to hear you, but I need you to take me by the hand, every day…

Once and for all, Lord, I want to take control of how I use the mass media. My spiritual progress depends on it. Help me, guide me, teach me, somehow show me the way to make good use of these wonderful inventions, which you surely want to be put at the service of our good, but which are so easy to abuse. Give me the strength of will and mind to guard the soil of my heart…

Thank you for coming into my life. Lord, I think of the thousands, maybe millions, of people who don't know you, who don't know that they can be friends with God and sharers in your incomparable mission. Send messengers to bring them your truth and grace! Send me! I want to want what you want, to do what you want, to want what you do…

QUESTIONS FOR SMALL GROUP DISCUSSION

1. What struck you most in this passage? What did you notice that you hadn't noticed before?

2. We all have all three of the bad types of soil in our souls, but one of them predominates. How can we discover which one?

3. What tactics can we come up with to make good use of mass media in our lives, so we can make sure that the media culture doesn't devour us?

4. Is there anything we can do for the people who really seem to have no interest at all in discovering transcendent meaning in life?

Cf. Catechism of the Catholic Church, 683-686 on God's action in our souls; 164 on temptations and difficulties on the path of faith; 412, 679, 1861 on the refusal and privation of grace; 2729-2733 on humble vigilance of heart

177. FEARLESS FAITH (LK 8:16-25)

"Christ has dominion over all creatures, a dominion not seized by violence nor usurped, but his by essence and by nature."

- St Cyril of Alexandria

Luke 8:16-25

'No one lights a lamp to cover it with a bowl or to put it under a bed. No, he puts it on a lamp-stand so that people may see the light when they come in. For nothing is hidden but it will be made clear, nothing secret but it will be known and brought to light. So take care how you hear; for anyone who has will be given more; from anyone who has not, even what he thinks he has will be taken away.'

His mother and his brothers came looking for him, but they could not get to him because of the crowd. He was told, 'Your mother and brothers are standing outside and want to see you.' But he said in answer, 'My mother and my brothers are those who hear the word of God and put it into practice'. One day, he got into a boat with his disciples and said to them, 'Let us cross over to the other side of the lake.' So they put to sea, and as they sailed he fell asleep. When a squall came down on the lake the boat started taking in water and they found themselves in danger. So they went to rouse him saying, 'Master! Master! We are going down!' Then he woke up and rebuked the wind and the rough water; and they subsided and it was calm again. He said to them, 'Where is your faith?' They were awestruck and astonished and said to one another, 'Who can this be, that gives orders even to winds and waves and they obey him?'

CHRIST THE LORD Imagine how the disciples would have remembered this event. It must have left a particularly deep impression on them. So many of them were fishermen, experts in working a boat and navigating rough waters. And yet in the face of this squall, they panic. It must have been a terrible storm. It must have been humbling for them to admit that their experience and skill failed them, but fail they did.

We are all fragile and small, no matter how much success we may have experienced in life. Sooner or later we have to face this truth, and when we do, we should follow the example of the apostles. They did the right thing when their resources ran out – they went to the Master. He is always near, even if he seems asleep. And no storm is too great for his calming touch. In fact, the most elemental and uncontrollable powers of nature, in the face of which even modern technology has to bow its proud head, meekly obey the word of the Lord.

Some spiritual writers see in this passage a prequel to the Resurrection. Jesus asleep in the boat anticipates his sleep of death in the tomb. The storm corresponds to the fears and doubts that beset the scattered disciples after the tragedy of the cross. Jesus waking up and calming the wind and water is his resurrection on the third day, which renews the apostles' confidence. In the face of our own storms, we should make a point of keeping the Lord's resurrection in mind – it's our lifetime warranty and everlasting guarantee.

CHRIST THE TEACHER The light of Christ's doctrine, which is only penetrating the apostles' hearts bit by bit as they have a chance to question him in private about his parables and teachings, will one day shine out for the whole world to see, through the work of the Church. And throughout the epoch of the Church, Christ's disciples are called to boldly spread that light. He has given it to us for our own good, but also so that we in turn will light up the whole household of mankind.

Jesus related this parable of the lamp because he knew we would be tempted to keep what we have received to ourselves. We hide things under bowls and under beds when we are afraid that other people will see them. When it comes to our Christian beliefs, fear of mockery, disdain, and rejection often make us hesitate when we should speak forth. The possibility of persecution throws us into a panic, just as the storm on the lake threw the apostles into a panic. The solution for our cowardice is the same as the solution Christ gave the apostles – faith: "Where is your faith?" God has given us more than enough reasons to believe in him and trust in him – now we just have to exercise the little faith we already have, and it will soon grow into a robust, joyful, and fruitful virtue: "Anyone who has will be given more." Otherwise, hiding the lamp under a bowl may protect the lamp, but it will snuff out the flame; our timorous efforts to avoid ridicule and persecution will have deprived even our own lives of Christ's saving light: "From anyone who has not, even what he thinks he has will be taken away."

CHRIST THE FRIEND In this passage, Jesus reiterates his Kingdom's fundamental law of generosity, the only law that makes sense in a Kingdom where all the King's subjects are also his friends, brothers, and sisters. He states this law in a slightly different way than he has before by saying, "Anyone who has will be given more" – a little trust and obedience can quickly grow into an abundant harvest of all the virtues. Then he points to a living illustration: Mary, his mother. She and some of his relatives have come looking for him, and Jesus makes the most of the opportunity to remind his listeners of what he really wants for them. He came to earth to atone for our sins and win us a place inside God's family. If only we trust him enough to fulfil God's will, to live as Jesus teaches we should live, "hearing the word of God and putting it into practice," then we will become his very brothers and sisters and mothers.

This is exactly what had happened with Mary. She trusted in God; she lived with the consciousness of being "the handmaid of the Lord" (Luke 1:38). And because of her faith, God was able to give her much more; he made her into the mother of the Lord. From handmaid to mother, from village girl to Queen of the Universe – this is the "anyone who has will be given more" rule at its best, and Jesus wants us to give him a chance to apply it in our lives as well.

CHRIST IN MY LIFE I wonder why I don't think about your Resurrection more often. Why doesn't that victory make a bigger difference in my attitudes and reactions? You rose from the dead. You showed your power over the wind and the sea, and over death itself. You are the same Lord who comes to me in Holy Communion, who waits for me patiently in the Tabernacle. Lord, increase my faith…

I know I am supposed to trust you in the midst of the storms, but Lord, it's not easy. The storms come and I often cave in. Where is my faith in those moments? You asked your apostles that question, but I ask you: why don't I

607

believe more firmly? Why don't I trust more easily? Why, Lord, do I advance so slowly? Have mercy on me, Lord. Teach me. I trust in you, I really do…

Mary, you learned perfectly the most important lesson – the path to true happiness: to hear God's word and put it into practice. Teach me what you learned. That's all I want to do. In my work, to work as he would have me; in my family, to be patient and selfless as he would have me; in my prayer, to be humble; in my relationships, helpful, kind, and forgiving. Mary, Seat of Wisdom, make me wise…

QUESTIONS FOR SMALL GROUP DISCUSSION

1. What struck you most in this passage? What did you notice that you hadn't noticed before?
2. Have you ever been "awestruck and astonished" at something God did in your life or the life of someone you know?
3. What are some common fears we have to overcome in order to share our faith? What has helped you most to overcome them in particular situations?
4. In one sense, following Christ is so simple: "Hear the word of God and put it into practice." Why do think so many people refuse to do so?

Cf. Catechism of the Catholic Church, 148, 490, 494 on Mary's assent; 2030 on Mary as the exemplar of holiness; 257, 1077 and 2009 on our filial adoption in Christ

178. COLD RECEPTION (LK 8:26-39)

"We proclaim the Crucified, and the devils quake. So don't be ashamed of the cross of Christ."

- St Cyril of Jerusalem

Luke 8:26-39

They came to land in the country of the Gerasenes which is opposite Galilee. He was stepping ashore when a man from the town who was possessed by devils came towards him; for a long time the man had worn no clothes, nor did he live in a house, but in the tombs. Catching sight of Jesus he gave a shout, fell at his feet and cried out at the top of his voice, 'What do you want with me, Jesus, son of the Most High God? I implore you, do not torture me.' For Jesus had been telling the unclean spirit to come out of the man. It was a devil that had seized on him a great many times, and then they used to secure him with chains and fetters to restrain him, but he would always break the fastenings, and the devil would drive him out into the wilds. 'What is your name?' Jesus asked. 'Legion,' he said – because many devils had gone into him. And these pleaded with him not to order them to depart into the Abyss. Now there was a large herd of pigs feeding there on the mountain, and the devils pleaded with him to let them go into these. So he gave them leave. The devils came out of the man and went into the pigs, and the herd charged down the cliff into the lake and were drowned. When the swineherds saw what had happened they ran off and told their story in the town and in the country round about; and the people went out to see what had happened. When they came to Jesus they found the man from whom the devils had gone out sitting at the feet of Jesus, clothed and in his full senses; and they were afraid. Those who had witnessed it told them how the man who had been possessed came to be healed. The entire population of the Gerasene territory was in a state of panic and asked Jesus to leave them. So he got into the boat and went back. The man from whom the devils had gone out asked to be allowed to stay with him, but he sent him away. 'Go back home,' he said, 'and report all that God has done for you.' So the man went off and spread throughout the town all that Jesus had done for him.

CHRIST THE LORD The people's response to Christ's action is odd. He performs a miracle of staggering proportions, restoring one of their townspeople to full health and ridding the region of a violent and dangerous demonic presence. You would think the townspeople would honor him and ask him to become their king, or at least bring him the rest of their sick and demon-possessed confreres. But instead, "they were afraid… in a state of panic, and they asked Jesus to leave…"

These people were Gentiles. They didn't have the privilege of knowing the one true God, the Creator and Redeemer. Their idea of divine power was the pagan idea, in which the gods have no genuine concern for mankind at all. When they do interact with puny humans, it's only to their own advantage. Jesus' demonstration of power makes them realize, rightly, that one of these unpredictable (to their minds) divinities is at work in him – only a divine power could have cast the demon out of the raving man and into the tranquil herd of pigs, which in turn began raving to the point of self-destruction. Word of the supernatural deed spreads. The people gather around Jesus and the restored man. Knowing (so they think) that the gods have nothing good in store for men, they are scared out of their wits. They don't know what to expect from this man-god who is so powerful that he can cast out mighty demons with only a word. As he shows no sign of aggression, some of the more bold townspeople hesitantly, tremulously ask him to spare their town from divine destruction, to simply pass them by. Jesus obliges them, and gets back into the boat with his apostles.

How it must have pained Christ's heart when they asked him to go away! But at the same time, how it must have inflamed him with renewed zeal to accomplish his mission! This is what fallen humanity had come to – they lived in a state of helpless terror in their relationship with God, instead of in one of loving intimacy. Satan's reign and the widespread contagion of sin had so distorted men's understanding of God that they actually feared their Father and Creator, like an orphaned child that has been so abused that he shrinks even from the loving touch of a genuine benefactress.

Jesus came precisely to rectify the fallen human family's mistaken notion of God, to reestablish communion between God and man. He can't wait to get started, so he sends the man he saved to spread the word among those pagans who aren't quite ready for the Good News from his own lips. The restored man goes off on the first missionary trip to Gentile territory, enthusiastically announcing: "God loves us and wants to fill us with abundant life; I know it for a fact, because he saved me from the tortures of a thousand devils – we need not fear any longer!"

CHRIST THE TEACHER Many times we experience a similar rejection in our apostolic endeavors. We think we are bringing something great to a community or an institution. We start out enthusiastically and see a flurry of progress. And then, all of a sudden, someone balks, and our work is cut short. Just so, the people of this region had seen with their own eyes Christ's transforming power, and then they asked him to leave. At such times we have to trust in God. He has his plan, and human freedom is part of it. Ours is simply to obey God's call in our lives as best we can, stay humble, and never tire of finding new ways to express our love for Jesus Christ.

CHRIST THE FRIEND Jesus tells the man he cured to "report all that God has done for you." He tells us the same thing. And so, unless we have experienced deeply the love God has for us, we will have little to say. Our effectiveness as disciples, as Christ's ambassadors in the world around us and to whomever Providence puts in our path, depends entirely on our personal experience of Christ. Our friendship with him, our relationship with him has to be far and away the most important priority of our lives. Our hearts were made for him, so we will only find meaning and fulfilment in knowing and loving him. Our life-mission is to spread his Kingdom, which means "reporting all God has done" for us, but unless we let him transform our lives, we'll simply have nothing to report, and our mission will never be accomplished.

The healed demoniac: I spent the rest of my life telling people about Jesus. Some people laughed at me. Others shook their heads in disbelief. But many wanted to hear more. At first I was sur-

prised – the more I spoke about him, the more I seemed to know of him. Only much later did I come to know that he was truly divine, and then I understood that he was accompanying me and speaking through me, and that's why people listened. When I told them about him, many of them opened their hearts. I discovered that many, many people – many more than I ever would have imagined – had their own demons that they were battling with. They had been wounded and maltreated and oppressed in ways that only they knew. The more I learned, the more my heart went out to them. I saw these wounds heal in his name. He had freed me from my imprisonment, and then he sent me to free others. He had given me a fresh start, and he showed me the way to make the most of it.

CHRIST IN MY LIFE The world is in dire need of your truth and your grace. I know this, and you know it. Lord, don't abandon us to our ignorance and egoism. Send your light among us, raise up apostles and missionaries who will boldly report all that you have done and wish to do in people's lives. Cast out our fears, cast out our sins, cast out the devil who never tires of tempting us…

Nothing matters but your will, Lord. I can't control other people's hearts. Even you were rejected by many of the people you came to save, many of the people who heard you speak and saw your miracles. Can I expect anything less? Many friends, relatives, and other Christians don't understand my relationship to you or why I follow you. Jesus, help me to seek first your Kingdom…

What was it like to walk with you along the roads of Galilee and Judea, to hear your voice and see the look in your eyes? I want to know you more intimately, Lord. What do you think about all the time? What do you think about world events? What do you want for me? What do you want from me? Teach me, Lord, to know you and to follow you…

QUESTIONS FOR SMALL GROUP DISCUSSION

1. What struck you most in this passage? What did you notice that you hadn't noticed before?
2. How do you think the disciples might have reacted to the cold welcome the people gave to Jesus?
3. If a non-believing friend of yours came up to you and said that the devil doesn't exist, how would you respond?
4. What does popular culture say about the existence and cause of evil? How does that compare with the Christian view?

Cf. Catechism of the Catholic Church, 2850-2854 on deliverance from the devil; 2110-2117 on idolatry and recourse to demons; 407-409 on man's struggle against the power of evil; 397, 413, 1707, 2583, and 2851 on the origin of evil

179. DETERMINED FAITH (LK 8:40-56)

"Christ gives us help and strength, never deserts and is true and sincere in his friendship."

- St Theresa of Avila

Luke 8:40-56

On his return Jesus was welcomed by the crowd, for they were all there waiting for him. And now there came a man named Jairus, who was an official of the synagogue. He fell at Jesus' feet and pleaded with him to come to his house, because he had an only daughter about twelve years old, who was dying. And the crowds were almost stifling Jesus as he went. Now there was a woman suffering from a hemorrhage for twelve years, whom no one had been able to cure. She came up behind him and touched the fringe of his cloak; and the hemorrhage stopped at that instant. Jesus said, 'Who touched me?' When they all denied that they had, Peter and his companions said, 'Master, it is the crowds round you, pushing.' But Jesus said, 'Somebody touched me. I felt that power had gone out from me.' Seeing herself discovered, the woman came forward trembling, and falling at his feet explained in front of all the people why she had touched him and how she had been cured at that very moment. 'My daughter,' he said 'your faith has restored you to health; go in peace.' While he was still speaking, someone arrived from the house of the synagogue official to say, 'Your daughter has died. Do not trouble the Master any further.' But Jesus had heard this, and he spoke to the man, 'Do not be afraid, only have faith and she will be safe.' When he came to the house he allowed no one to go in with him except Peter and John and James, and the child's father and mother. They were all weeping and mourning for her, but Jesus said, 'Stop crying; she is not dead, but asleep'. But they laughed at him, knowing she was dead. But taking her by the hand he called to her, 'Child, get up.' And her spirit returned and she got up at once. Then he told them to give her something to eat. Her parents were astonished, but he ordered them not to tell anyone what had happened.

CHRIST THE LORD St Luke presents us with the finale in a series of miracles. Earlier in the chapter, Jesus had calmed a storm at sea. Then he exorcised an army of demons from a possessed man. Now he cures a hopeless illness and, finally, brings a dead child back to life. Jesus' résumé is complete: he is Lord of the physical universe, of the powers of evil, of sickness, and even of death. This is Christ. This is the Savior-King who claimed us as his own when we were baptized, who gave us a position in his court when we were confirmed, who dwells in our hearts at all times, who feeds us with his own divine life whenever we receive Holy Communion, and who is always ready to receive us when we call at the Tabernacle.

The Gospel portrait of Christ brings out his majesty and his greatness – we are not surprised to see that he was "welcomed by the crowd" who had been await-ing his return, and that the "crowds were almost stifling Jesus as he went." But it should surprise us that we, having him so close to us and having his teaching so available, sometimes relegate him to a small corner of our day. Why aren't we yet the saints God wants us to be? Because we haven't let the Lord come and rule over every aspect of our lives; we circumscribe his action because, like stubborn adolescents, we still want to do everything our own way. It is time to let the Lord be the Lord.

CHRIST THE TEACHER In these encounters Jesus teaches us how to release his power in our lives. He has the power to heal our wounds, as he did with the woman suffering from the hemorrhage, and he has the power to reach out to those we love through our intercession, as he did with Jairus and his daugh-ter. What permits his saving grace to flow into and through our lives is faith: "Your faith has restored you…. Do not be afraid, only have faith…."

Faith is a mysterious virtue. It is a living thing, hard to pin down and compre-hend. The examples in this passage show us two characteristics of faith. First, authentic faith moves us to action. Believing in Christ and his capacity and willingness to intervene in our lives always implies some kind of action. As St James puts it, "Faith without works is dead" (James 2:17). Merely wish-ing isn't really faith, because it takes no risk. Faith always involves trust, and trust always involves stepping out. So we see the woman with a hemorrhage determined to touch Jesus. She has to fight through the huge crowd that is almost stifling the Lord; she has to get down on her knees maybe, getting shoved and kneed and stepped on and pushed aside – but she does it. She touches his cloak, and she is healed. If our faith in Christ isn't driving us to take concrete steps in the direction we need to go, it's not authentic Christian faith.

Second, faith perseveres when confronted with obstacles. When Jairus' servants come to tell him that his daughter is already dead, his hope vanishes. What can be done? Jesus tells him to believe. At that point, the only reason to believe is Jesus' own command. Rationally speaking, the story is over. But Jairus, seeing the look in Christ's eyes when the Lord tells him, "Do not fear…" decides to bank on Jesus. Imagine the long walk back to his house, walking side by side with Jesus. What was he thinking? How he must have had to battle a rush of doubts and sadness, putting his trust in the word and presence of Christ alone. And his faith in the Lord, in the end, is rewarded.

True believers in Jesus, those who want his power and grace to transform their lives and the lives of those around them, put their faith into action and never give up. These are the people who see God work wonders. A flaccid or pie-in-the-sky piety never actually touches Jesus, so it can never see the beauty of holiness or really plug into his love.

CHRIST THE FRIEND Why did Jesus insist on finding the woman who had touched him? He didn't want to take her to task, although she was afraid he did. According to Jewish law, her hemorrhage made her unclean, so consequently those she touched were also made ritually unclean – and so when Jesus demands to see her, she's thinks she's in trouble. And it seems like he didn't want to set her up as an example for everyone else, since he doesn't say anything to that effect. Jesus just wanted to see her and to speak to her. He wanted to assure her of his personal love for her. He doesn't want her to think he is just some kind of magician. Trembling, she falls at his feet. Jesus looks at her and calls her "My daughter…" Then he assures her that she truly is healed because she has believed in him, and he sends her home, saying, "Go in peace." How Jesus' eyes must have shined with tenderness and gladness! So many of his followers and opponents had little or no faith in him, but this woman trusted him completely. And the glance of love and tenderness he gave her must have been indelibly fixed in that woman's memory: "He called me his daughter! He knows me, and he cares for me. He sent me away in peace, healed. How good he is! How glad I am that I made the effort to touch his cloak!"

Jesus continues to act in the same way today. It is not enough for him to do things generically. He himself gives us Holy Communion, one-on-one, through the hands of his chosen priests. He wants to speak the words of absolution out loud to us, so that we leave the confessional assured and relieved, as this woman left the scene of the miracle. In countless ways, God makes that extra effort to personalize our experience of him. He longs to see us, to look us in the eye and speak with us. He is our Creator, who created us to be his everlasting friends.

CHRIST IN MY LIFE You truly are the Lord of life and history. All good things come from you. You showed your lordship in the Gospels, you continue to show in the Church, and you have shown it countless times in my own life. Jesus, I beg you, please teach me to put everything else in my life in second place, so that I can truly be your disciple, your ambassador, and your companion…

You performed these miracles for my benefit. You were thinking of me when you healed. You are trying to convince me to trust in you more. How can I trust in you when I don't know what to do? So many problems swirl around me, and I am so helpless, so ignorant! But you know everything. You know how much I need you. I do believe; I do trust in you, Lord. Teach me what to say; show me what to do…

I live in a noisy world, Lord. I have to shove my way through crowds and chaos to touch you. I need you to clear the crowd away so I can see you look at me and hear you speak to me. Lord, my heart is longing for your grace, for your love. Please, Lord, let me touch you, let me find you in all things, in all people, in every moment…

QUESTIONS FOR SMALL GROUP DISCUSSION

1. What struck you most in this passage? What did you notice that you hadn't noticed before?

2. Why do you think Jesus only took his three closest disciples with him into Jarius' house?

3. Does popular culture help or hinder the development of authentic Christian faith? What can we do to grow in this key virtue?

4. If a non-believing friend came up to you and said, "I want to believe in Christ, but I simply can't," what would you say to them?

Cf. Catechism of the Catholic Church, 26,144-149 on the nature of faith; 153-165 on the characteristics of faith; 65-67 on Christ as the fullness of God's revelation

THE GOSPEL OF LUKE CHAPTER 9

"All who in the whole world bear the name of Christian and truly understand the Christian faith know and believe that Saint Peter, the prince of the apostles, is the father of all Christians and their first shepherd after Christ, and that the holy Roman Church is the mother and mistress of all the Churches."

- Pope St Gregory VII

180. A TEST OF FAITH (LK 9:1-17)

"Christ sent out the apostles as the ministers of his divine will. They were to proclaim

that spiritual gospel which runs above natural law and written codes, and to call men to himself."

- St Procopius of Gaza

Luke 9:1-17

He called the Twelve together and gave them power and authority over all devils and to cure diseases, and he sent them out to proclaim the kingdom of God and to heal. He said to them, 'Take nothing for the journey: neither staff, nor haversack, nor bread, nor money; and let none of you take a spare tunic. Whatever house you enter, stay there; and when you leave, let it be from there. As for those who do not welcome you, when you leave their town shake the dust from your feet as a sign to them.' So they set out and went from village to village proclaiming the Good News and healing everywhere. Meanwhile Herod the tetrarch had heard about all that was going on; and he was puzzled, because some people were saying that John had risen from the dead, others that Elijah had reappeared, still others that one of the ancient prophets had come back to life. But Herod said, 'John? I beheaded him. So who is this I hear such reports about?' And he was anxious to see him.

On their return the apostles gave him an account of all they had done. Then he took them with him and withdrew to a town called Bethsaida where they could be by themselves. But the crowds got to know and they went after him. He made them welcome and talked to them about the kingdom of God; and he cured those who were in need of healing. It was late afternoon when the Twelve came to him and said, 'Send the people away, and they can go to the villages and farms round about to find lodging and food; for we are in a lonely place here.' He replied, 'Give them something to eat yourselves.' But they said, 'We have no more than five loaves and two fish, unless we are to go ourselves and buy food for all these people.' For there were about five thousand men. But he said to his disciples, 'Get them to sit down in parties of about fifty.' They did so and made them all sit down. Then he took the five loaves and the two fish, raised his eyes to heaven, and said the blessing over them; then he broke them and handed them to his disciples to distribute among the crowd. They all ate as much as they wanted, and when the scraps remaining were collected they filled twelve baskets.

CHRIST THE LORD Imagine the apostles' impression as Jesus sent them out on their first missionary journey. He hands them over a share of his own divine power, instructing them to cast out demons, perform miracles, and preach to the crowds. Which of the Twelve was naturally qualified for that kind of an assignment? And just to make sure they don't get cocky, Jesus tells them to travel without supplies – they are to depend entirely on God's providence. You can picture them furrowing their brows in consternation as they set out, eager but nervous. Even bold Peter must have been shaking a little bit the first time he took on a demon all by himself. But the apostles obey and trust, and the results are substantial – even King Herod hears about their goings on.

Then, imagine the apostles' reaction when Jesus commanded them to feed dinner to those thousands of people. They utter a whimpering protest, pointing out that they don't have nearly enough food for that many people. But when Jesus tells them to have the crowds sit down in groups, they do it. What must have been going through their minds? Jesus just keeps stretching their faith. And then he takes their loaves and fish and miraculously multiplies them.

More than our brilliant minds, rich personalities, and fabulous organizational skills, God needs us to give him our trust and our faith. With those, he can expand our small efforts and ideas into miraculous proportions, extending his Kingdom to thousands of souls – many more than we could have reached by trusting merely in our paltry human qualities. He is the Lord; we are only his ambassadors.

CHRIST THE TEACHER Sometimes we are afraid of giving ourselves completely to God because we think we won't have anything left for ourselves. When he asks us to give up the things that we think make us the happiest, we hesitate. Jesus knows that we struggle with this. In the multiplication of the loaves, he teaches us a lesson to allay those fears.

The apostles were no doubt hungry after a long day of ministry. They had little enough food for themselves (five large loaves and two fish would hardly satisfy a dozen brawny men). Jesus asks them to give it all away. They probably handed them over reluctantly, mouths watering. But Jesus took the food, blessed it, broke it, and gave it back to the disciples to distribute to the crowds (the same four verbs used in the consecration of the bread during the Mass). And at the end, each disciple had an entire basket full of food for his own little feast.

Christ will never, never be outdone in generosity. The more we give to him, the more we will receive. As St Luke put it in another passage of his Gospel, Jesus said: "Give, and there will be gifts for you: a full measure, pressed down, shaken together, and running over, will be poured into your lap; because the amount you measure out is the amount you will be given back" (Luke 6:38). When God asks us to empty ourselves, it's only so he can have room to fill us up with something better.

CHRIST THE FRIEND When Jesus walked the dusty trails of Palestine, he did so for the sake of the people who lived there. He "talked to them about the kingdom," he "healed those who needed to be cured," and he fed them when they were hungry. His whole life was for others. The mere fact that he came to earth at all tells us that much. The fact that he has remained with us not only in the Holy Scriptures, not only in the living Church, not only in the examples of the saints, but even under the humble and silent appearances of bread and wine in the Eucharist, only makes it that much clearer. Christ came for us! He lived for us, died for us, and rose for us, and he is still here with us, for our sakes. He has not changed since the day he multiplied the loaves for the hungry crowds. He has not all of a sudden become selfish, harsh, and unforgiving. And yet, we often act as if he had. We keep ourselves at a distance; we let doubts and hesitations mar our friendship with him; we leave him alone in the Tabernacle, not even dropping by to say hello. What more could he have done for us to declare his love?

CHRIST IN MY LIFE I wonder how many times my small-mindedness has inhibited your action in and through my life. I get tangled up in complicated considerations and excuses that simply don't take into account the primacy of your grace. Lift me out of the swamp of foolish self-sufficiency! You are the general; I am just a soldier on the battlefield. Teach me to trust, obey, and give my all…

I want to be generous with you, Lord. Most of the time, when I'm honest with myself, I know what you are asking of me. But many times I am simply afraid to make the sacrifice. I keep thinking that the result will be boring, unpleasant, or uncomfortable. But would you ever ask of me something that wasn't best for me? Jesus, I trust in you…

You are always thinking of me. Teach me to think of you more often. Teach me to live life deeply and wisely, in constant contact with you, talking things over with you, keeping close to you. Lord Jesus, be my refuge and my strength…

QUESTIONS FOR SMALL GROUP DISCUSSION

1. What struck you most in this passage? What did you notice that you hadn't noticed before?

2. What are the "five loaves and two fish" that Christ is asking us to give him?

3. If Christ himself, his entire being and life, is truly present in the Eucharist and reserved in the tabernacles of all our Catholic Churches, why do so few people spend significant time with him there?

4. When we have an important meeting or event to attend, we usually take plenty of time to

prepare ourselves. Why do we generally not take time to prepare ourselves for Mass and Communion? How can we prepare ourselves better?

Cf. Catechism of the Catholic Church, 1322-1340 and 1406-1419 on the Eucharist; 1391-1401 on Holy Communion; 1345-1390 on the Mass

181. CROSSES WITH CHRIST (LK 9:18-27)

The only petition I would have you put forward on my behalf is that I may be given sufficient inward and outward strength to be as resolute in will as in words, and a Christian in reality instead of only in repute."

- St Ignatius of Antioch, martyr

Luke 9:18-27

Now one day when he was praying alone in the presence of his disciples he put this question to them, 'Who do the crowds say I am?' And they answered, 'John the Baptist; others Elijah; and others say one of the ancient prophets come back to life.' 'But you,' he said, 'who do you say I am?' It was Peter who spoke up. 'The Christ of God,' he said. But he gave them strict orders not to tell anyone anything about this. 'The Son of Man,' he said 'is destined to suffer grievously, to be rejected by the elders and chief priests and scribes and to be put to death, and to be raised up on the third day.' Then to all he said, 'If anyone wants to be a follower of mine, let him renounce himself and take up his cross every day and follow me. For anyone who wants to save his life will lose it; but anyone who loses his life for my sake, that man will save it. What gain, then, is it for a man to have won the whole world and to have lost or ruined his very self? For if anyone is ashamed of me and of my words, of him the Son of Man will be ashamed when he comes in his own glory and in the glory of the Father and the holy angels. 'I tell you truly, there are some standing here who will not taste death before they see the kingdom of God.'

CHRIST THE LORD "Christ" means "anointed" (and in Hebrew, "Messiah"). The term is used in reference to King David, who was anointed by the prophet Samuel to show that he had been chosen and sent by God to lead his people to peace and prosperity. (Olive oil comes from olives, and the healthy olive tree was always a symbol of peace and prosperity.) The same term is used in reference to God's promise to reestablish the Kingdom of David forever under one of his descendents (the Davidic Kingdom fell after the reign of Solomon, David's son). Jesus is that descendent. He is the one God has chosen and sent to lead all mankind to the spiritual peace and prosperity of life in communion with God, which had been symbolized by the material peace and prosperity of the Davidic Kingdom. Peter and the other disciples recognized this, and when they asserted it, Jesus did not contradict them. Critics still say that Christ was merely "a prophet" or a "great religious teacher," but Jesus himself made it clear that he claimed to be nothing less than the Lord.

CHRIST THE TEACHER Jesus knew that the general public still associated the title "Christ" with an image of political and military victory. After all, David's kingdom was political, and he had established it through force of arms. But Christ's Kingdom was of a different stamp. It was built around the cross, around suffering, sacrifice, and self-denial. True, he was the Messiah, God's anointed, and his Kingdom would stand forever, but he would establish it through obedience to the Father's will, even unto death by crucifixion. And everyone who wished to enter that Kingdom would have to follow the same path: obedience to God's will, no matter how difficult it might be: "If anyone wants to be a follower of mine, let him renounce himself and take up his cross every day and follow me."

So Jesus told his disciples not to use the term Christ for the time being, allowing him a chance to instruct the crowds, to elevate their hopes and adjust their expectations, to explain how it was that an apparently weak, submissive, suffering Jesus could be the Lord of life and history. We also need time to learn this lesson. We need time spent in prayer, contemplating Christ's teachings and example in the Gospel. We need time spent in study, looking into the history of the Church and the lives of the saints. We need to desire Mt Calvary as much as Mt Tabor. Only then will this hardest of all lessons – that earth isn't heaven and never will be, that the path to abundant meaning and happiness passes through a daily cross, that unless we are willing to sacrifice our personal preferences and worldly desires we will never reach the goal for which we were created – only then will this lesson be able to seep down into our hearts and spread into every corner of our minds.

CHRIST THE FRIEND True friends tell friends the hard truth; flatterers don't. In this intimate exchange with his chosen disciples, Jesus looks them in the eye and tells them a very hard truth – that their lives will only take on real meaning if they are willing to sacrifice whatever is necessary (dreams, hopes, comfort, plans) in order to follow him. If we don't take the time to learn this lesson, we run the risk of discarding our friendship with Christ when it starts to cost us. Jesus warns us that if we are ashamed of him and our identification with him, if we prefer acceptance by the world and worldly success to being a faithful

Christian, then we may, tragically, end up with what we have preferred. In the end, Christ's Kingdom will come in all its glory (now in the Church it is still in embryonic form), and our allegiance to him in spite of suffering and rejection will prove to have been, as he promises us, the wiser course.

If Christ had not traveled that path ahead of us, climbing the hill of Calvary and dying on a cross, it would be hard to believe him. But he has, and so it shouldn't be that hard after all.

CHRIST IN MY LIFE And if you were to ask me this question, "Who do you say I am?" how would I answer? I would say the right words: you are the Messiah, the Son of God, the Lord of life and history. But I think you would keep looking at me, because you see beyond words into my heart. And in my heart, Lord, I have still not surrendered completely to your love. Lord Jesus, help me…

You know I am afraid of the cross. I know that I don't have to be. So why don't you take this fear away? I have a crucifix. I see it all the time. Open my eyes, Lord, so that I not only see the cross, but also the crucifix. May I understand with all my being the immensity of your love that the crucifix communicates. If I truly believe in your love for me, no cross will make me hesitate…

What are you asking of me, Lord? Okay, I give it to you. I will follow where you lead. If you went to Calvary for me, I will go there for you. Help me to see everything with faith. If I know it's your will, I can embrace it, but my faith is sometimes so weak that I forget to look for your hand in the circumstances and responsibilities of my life. Lord, increase my faith…

QUESTIONS FOR SMALL GROUP DISCUSSION

1. What struck you most in this passage? What did you notice that you hadn't noticed before?

2. What does this dialogue reveal to us about the heart of Jesus?

3. How would the agents of popular culture answer the question Jesus puts to his disciples? How would popular culture react to Jesus' doctrine of the cross?

4. What are the most common "crosses" that we need to "take up daily" in our present life-situations?

Cf. Catechism of the Catholic Church, 436-440 on the meaning of the term "Messiah"; 409 & 2015 on the necessity of the cross in the life of every Christian

182. GLIMPSES OF GLORY (LK 9:28-36)

"No music soothes the ear, no words so sweet to hear, no memories half so dear, as Jesus, Son of God."

- St Bernard of Clairvaux

Luke 9:28-36

Now about eight days after this had been said, he took with him Peter and John and James and went up the mountain to pray. As he prayed, the aspect of his face was changed and his clothing became brilliant as lightning. Suddenly there were two men there talking to him; they were Moses and Elijah appearing in glory, and they were speaking of his passing which he was to accomplish in Jerusalem. Peter and his companions were heavy with sleep, but they kept awake and saw his glory and the two men standing with him. As these were leaving him, Peter said to Jesus, 'Master, it is wonderful for us to be here; so let us make three tents, one for you, one for Moses and one for Elijah.' He did not know what he was saying. As he spoke, a cloud came and covered them with shadow; and when they went into the cloud the disciples were afraid. And a voice came from the cloud saying, 'This is my Son, the Chosen One. Listen to him.' And after the voice had spoken, Jesus was found alone. The disciples kept silence and, at that time, told no one what they had seen.

CHRIST THE LORD For a brief moment, Christ reveals a smidgeon of his true glory. Gathered on the mountaintop with his closest apostles and with the greatest prophets from the Old Testament, speaking with them about the most important event in history (his coming passion and death), he lifts the veil cloaking his divinity, and his disciples become "awake" and "afraid." If a passing glimpse of Jesus' splendor fills them with amazement, just imagine how easy it would have been for him to win all of Palestine to his cause if he had fully unveiled his divinity. And yet, he doesn't. He refuses to overpower us into obedience, preferring to win us over with his love and goodness. Christ indeed is the Lord; he is all-powerful, the Father's "Chosen Son," but he wields his power gently, like a shepherd, so that we won't be scared away.

CHRIST THE TEACHER When these three disciples went off to be alone with Jesus and pray, they saw his glory and came to know him better. Here Jesus teaches us how to come closer to him, how to hear the voice of the Father and encounter the glory of God: by taking time to go off and be alone with him in prayer. In such moments of intimacy with God we will find the light and strength we need to convert the world instead of being converted by it. God has something to say to us; he wants us to discover him and his plan for our lives. But if we refuse to go "up the mountain to pray," we won't be able to hear him.

In the liturgy, the Church presents us with this challenge at the beginning of Lent, reminding us that the best way to prepare for Holy Week and the Solemnity of Solemnities (Easter), the commemoration of the most important event in the history of the human race, is by dedicating ourselves more than usual to prayer, to heartfelt conversation with Christ. But the lesson applies equally for our daily preparation for whatever adventures he sends our way as well as our regular preparation for our own participation in his sacrifice during Mass. Christ has so much he wants to tell us – at all times and in so many ways – that all we need to do is "listen to him," which is impossible unless we set aside time to pray.

CHRIST THE FRIEND As always, in this scene Christ shows how personal his love is. Jesus knew what was going to happen on top of the mountain. And he brought three of his apostles with him to witness it – only three. He knew that in the future they would need to draw on this experience to bolster their faith. Of course, they didn't really understand; they just followed along, dozed off in their prayer, made a senseless remark, and then kept quiet about the whole thing. But Jesus is preparing them for the mission they will have to carry out later. His love for each of us is just as personal and just as wise. He knows what we need when we need it. He gives us moments of consolation in prayer to propel us through dark periods of dryness. All he asks is that we follow along, trusting him, even when we don't understand or when we feel clumsy and ig- norant. Peter, James, and John didn't become saints overnight, and neither will we. But if we stay close to the Lord, we will eventually – he will make sure of it.

CHRIST IN MY LIFE You are the Good Shepherd. You know exactly what I need. I remember the times I thought things were going badly, but later I realized that your wisdom had been guiding them all along. Your rule is gentle but sure. Teach me to be docile, to trust in you. I know what you want of me: fidelity to my life's mission, my responsibilities, and my conscience. You will take care of the rest…

I want to pray better. It can't be that hard, because prayer is a gift you give to everyone, young and old, smart and not-so-smart, holy and sinful. So teach me to pray, Lord. Teach me to tune in to your voice. Not only during specific prayer commitments, but all throughout the day. Are you not always with me, a faithful friend at my side? Well then, let's talk…

Even now you are preparing me for future tasks. I want to live each current moment to the full, pouring my love into your will, dedicating myself to whatever you ask of me with all my heart, soul, mind, and strength. If I do, I know you will take my efforts and make them fruitful, both for me and for the Church. I may see the results only later – that's okay. All for your glory…

QUESTIONS FOR SMALL GROUP DISCUSSION

1. What struck you most in this passage? What did you notice that you hadn't noticed before?

2. What can we do to live more intensely and fruitfully during the liturgical seasons in general and the particular season we are in right now?

3. Why do you think mountaintops are consistently referred to as preferred places of prayer in the Bible? What can we learn for our own lives from that?

4. Why do you think Christ talked with Elijah and Moses about his "passing"?

Cf. Catechism of the Catholic Church, 444,459 554-556 on the meaning of the Transfiguration

183. BACK TO THE ROUTINE (LK 9:37-50)

"I resolved always to prefer labors to comforts, contempt to honors. And, in particular, if on one side a kingdom were offered and on the other the washing of dishes, I would refuse the kingdom and accept the dishwashing so as to be truly like Christ, who humbled himself."

- St John Berchmans

Luke 9:37-50

Now on the following day when they were coming down from the mountain a large crowd came to meet him. Suddenly a man in the crowd cried out. 'Master,' he said 'I implore you to look at my son: he is my only child. All at once a spirit will take hold of him, and give a sudden cry and throw the boy into convulsions with foaming at the mouth; it is slow to leave him, but when it does it leaves the boy worn out. I begged your disciples to cast it out, and they could not.' 'Faithless and perverse generation!' Jesus said in reply 'How much longer must I be among you and put up with you? Bring your son here.' The boy was still moving towards Jesus when the devil threw him to the ground in convulsions. But Jesus rebuked the unclean spirit and cured the boy and gave him back to his father, and everyone was awestruck by the greatness of God.

At a time when everyone was full of admiration for all he did, he said to his disciples, 'For your part, you must have these words constantly in your mind: The Son of Man is going to be handed over into the power of men.' But they did not understand him when he said this; it was hidden from them so that they should not see the meaning of it, and they were afraid to ask him about what he had just said. An argument started between them about which of them was the greatest. Jesus knew what thoughts were going through their minds, and he took a little child and set him by his side and then said to them, 'Anyone who welcomes this little child in my name welcomes me; and anyone who welcomes me welcomes the one who sent me. For the least among you all, that is the one who is great.' John spoke up. 'Master,' he said, 'we saw a man casting out devils in your so name, and because he is not with us we tried to stop him.' But Jesus said to him, 'You must not stop him: anyone who is not against you is for you.'

CHRIST THE LORD Jesus has work to do. He is a King at war, conquering lost and rebellious hearts by renewing them with his love. The era of the Church, before Christ's second coming, is the era of work and conquest. So his apostles are necessarily called to keep moving, building, and spreading the Kingdom. We all need our mountaintop moments, as Jesus gave to Peter, James, and John at his Transfiguration. These come in many forms – insights and consolations that arrive uninvited at the oddest times, retreats and sabbaticals and vacations that revitalize our minds and hearts with fresh experiences of God's love and goodness, even particular liturgies or moments of prayer when God makes his presence felt in especially intense ways.

God sends these experiences to us because we need them, but they are not the goal, at least not as long as we are members of the Church Militant here on earth. There is always "the following day when they were coming down the mountain," when the demands of our daily life and mission clamor once again for attention. When the moments of bliss give way to moments of battle, we can take comfort that for Christ too the mission was demanding, and even at times exasperating: "How much longer must I be among you and put up with you?" The Lord worked and sweated and suffered, and his earthly joys were only vista points on an uphill journey. His ambassadors (that's us!) are on the same track.

CHRIST THE TEACHER As the time of Jesus' ministry in the district of Galilee is drawing to its conclusion, St Luke explains that Christ's popularity reaches an all-time high: "Everyone was full of admiration for all he did." Precisely at that moment Jesus pulls his disciples aside and reminds them of his coming passion and death. The apostles still fail to understand what he means; they feel the surge of his popularity and are already looking forward to his victory – in fact, they are arguing who will get which positions of honor once the Lord takes his rightful throne. But Jesus insists: it's not about self-aggrandizement, it's about self-giving. He tells them that they must keep the Passion, the ultimate model of self-giving, "constantly in your mind."

Jesus says the same thing to us. We are continually beset by the temptation that led Adam and Eve to their demise, the one at the root of every sin: trying to make earth into heaven, trying to find satisfaction in life apart from God and his commands. Suffering, opposition, toil, hardship – these are the bread and

625

butter of human life in a fallen world, and we will never avoid them completely. Jesus doesn't save us *from* them; he saves us *through* them. He takes the wafers of bread that are made from the grinding and pounding and baking of the wheat, and he turns them into his Body. We are the grains of wheat, and the sufferings of life are the sickle, the millstone, and the oven that make us into hosts with the Host. They turn our lives into other Christs by giving us a chance to rehabilitate our trust in God and develop all the Christian virtues that such trust entails, that make us into fruitful and fulfilling channels of his wisdom and power. Only self-sacrificial, self-forgetful love can give his grace room to work, and that kind of love always involves the cross.

Christians in the Middle Ages had a beautiful phrase that we should all make our own: *per crucem ad lucem* – "through the cross to the light." Deciphering the mystery of human life means keeping those words "constantly in mind."

CHRIST THE FRIEND True friendship can't be earned, it simply happens. Two people discover in each other a soul mate, and that's that. That's what we're like for Jesus. He doesn't choose us because we have certain talents, or because we're popular, useful, or beautiful. He chooses us simply because we are who we are and we delight him. He tries to convince us of this over and over again.

In this passage, while his apostles are arguing about who deserves more recognition and prestige, Jesus puts a little child beside him – in the place of honor. It's as if he is saying, "Look, I didn't choose you because of what you deserve. You are like this little child, who by yourself can do nothing to build my Kingdom except delight the King. I chose you because I delight in you, because I love you. I want you with me. That's the kind of love I have for you, and that's the kind of love that will be the sole law of my Kingdom. If you want to be great in my Kingdom, accept my love and love others like that. Think not of yourself, but think of others – delight in them, and serve them."

CHRIST IN MY LIFE You are all I need, Lord. I only need to know that you are near me and that I'm on the path you want me to be on. With that I am satisfied. At least, I want to live like that. I don't want my joy to depend on external circumstances. I want to experience truly Christian joy, rooted in your unchanging love for me. Teach me to find you in the moments of calm and in the heat of the battle…

I am struck by how often you warned your apostles about the coming drama of the cross, and how little they understood. But then I have to ask myself, have

I understood? I react so violently when my will or my plans or my hopes are contradicted. In your cross is my salvation and that of the whole world. Teach me the wisdom of your cross, Lord…

I know that you love me without any strings attached. Even so, at times I'm afraid. I have been wounded so often. I recoil from such love. Don't let me, Lord. Come after me. Convince me, Lord, that you love me just because I exist. Convince me, Lord, that nothing I can do will every increase or decrease the love you have for me right now. Reign in my heart with your peace…

QUESTIONS FOR SMALL GROUP DISCUSSION

1. What struck you most in this passage? What did you notice that you hadn't noticed before?

2. How can we keep our hopes up in the middle of life's trials and tribulations and daily grind?

3. Why do you think it took the apostles so long to learn the lesson of the cross? How have we learned this lesson in our own lives?

4. What opportunities to exhibit Christian greatness are provided by our daily life-situation?

Cf. Catechism of the Catholic Church, 853, 863 on how to spread Christ's Kingdom; 699, 1244, and 1261 on Jesus and the little children; 607 and 713 on the meaning and necessity of Christ's Passion

184. BAD EXCUSES (LK 9:51-62)

"You who have been present at this bloody tragedy, learn that all torments seem as nothing to one who has an everlasting crown before his eyes. Your gods are not gods; renounce their worship. He alone for whom I suffer and die is the true God. To die for Him is to live."

- Last words of St Arcadius, fourth-century martyr

Luke 9:51-62

Now as the time drew near for him to be taken up to heaven, he resolutely took the road for Jerusalem and sent messengers ahead of him. These set out, and they went into a Samaritan village to make preparations for him, but the people would not receive him because he was making for Jerusalem. Seeing this, the disciples James and John said, 'Lord, do you want us to call down fire from heaven to burn them up?' But he turned and rebuked them, and they went off to another village. As they travelled along they met a man on the road who said to him, 'I will follow you wherever you go.' Jesus answered, 'Foxes have holes and the birds of the air have nests, but the Son of Man has nowhere to lay his head.' Another to whom he said, 'Follow me', replied, 'Let me go and bury my father first.' But he answered, 'Leave the dead to bury their dead; your duty is to go and spread the news of the kingdom of God.' Another said, 'I will follow you, sir, but first let me go and say good-bye to

627

my people at home.' Jesus said to him, 'Once the hand is laid on the plough, no one who looks back is fit for the kingdom of God.'

CHRIST THE LORD   Two of Jesus' closest disciples (James and John) still hadn't understood their leader. Even as Jesus "resolutely took" the road to Jerusalem, where he would allow himself to be rejected, humiliated, tortured, and executed, they were eager to defend his Lordship by violence and force. On the one hand, they were right: Jesus was the Lord, and he deserved to be welcomed and treated with the highest respect. Therefore, in rejecting him, the Samaritan village deserved censure. But on the other hand, Christ had repeatedly explained that he was on his way to Jerusalem precisely to accept the people's rejection. Christ reveals God's mercy precisely by not giving his enemies what they deserve, but by patiently bearing with them. Christ's Lordship is real, but it differs from what we tend to expect: for Christ, and thus for the Christian, success means fulfilling God's will, even if that requires suffering, humiliation, rejection, and total failure in the eyes of the world.

CHRIST THE TEACHER   These three encounters with these would-be disciples teach us three tough lessons about what it means to follow Christ.

First, we have to give up our security. Christ is trustworthy, but when we follow him, we have to do so one step and one day at a time – he refuses to give us a full outline in advance. Even foxes and birds have the security of their instincts and natural habitats, but Christians are on an unpredictable adventure.

Second, we have to take risks. The words of the Lord to this young man seem harsh, but in the idiom of the time, they probably weren't. The man's father was probably not dead at all. Rather, the young man simply said that he wanted to follow the Lord, to leave behind the spiritually dead environment he lived in, but he would do so once his father had grown old and died. He felt the tug of Christ calling him, but he also felt the pull of his comfortable life, of the relationships, hopes, and projects that he had long been attached to. Christ warns him that he needs to heed God's voice without delay – as risky as it may be.

Finally, we can expect difficulties. Plowing fields by hand was no easy task, and to do it well, to plow a straight and deep furrow, required dedication, perseverance, and just plain hard work. Following Christ is no different. Once we get into it, we discover how demanding it really is, and we are tempted to look back at the ease and comfort of a self-centered life (conveniently forgetting, of course, about the hardships that go along with that too). But if we go back, we lose. Only Christ's Kingdom lasts forever, only God can fill the deepest longings of our hearts – the hard work that fidelity to God's will requires pays for itself with eternal returns.

CHRIST THE FRIEND Christ invites these potential disciples to follow him, just as he invites us to follow him. This is no insignificant detail. If he invites us, it is because he wants us to be with him; he is interested in us, in bringing us into his Kingdom. What we do, whether we follow him or not, matters to him. God really cares about each one of us. As the Catechism (#30) puts it, "[God] never ceases to call every man to seek him, so as to find life and happiness." If we understood how much we matter to him, it would solve an awful lot of our problems.

Jesus: Would you approve of a doctor who ignored his patient's illness? Would you hire a coach who never pushed his players to excel? Then why do you resist when I ask you to leave things behind in order to follow me? Unless you make room in your heart for my grace by emptying it of selfishness, how can you be my follower? Remember, whenever I ask something of you, I am the doctor of your soul, the coach of your pursuit of happiness and holiness.

CHRIST IN MY LIFE Why am I so afraid of failure and rejection? You chose exactly those realities as your path of glory. You only cared about fulfilling the Father's will, so why do I care so much about what others think of me, about performing better than my neighbor? Lord, free my heart from vanity and arrogance and insecurity. Free me to love and give myself as totally and gladly as you did…

I really do want to be your disciple. You know my limits and my circumstances, and you know my possibilities – much better than I do. So teach me to trust in you and your will more than in my own judgment. Teach me to find the balance between sensibility (I know you don't want me to abandon common sense, since you invented it) and courage…

Since you are God, you think unceasingly of those you love. And since you love me, you must think of me unceasingly. Lord, help me to believe that! Help me to live knowing that you are always surrounding me with your wise, merciful, and loving providence. Inspire me with your love, so I will be generous and courageous in spreading the treasures of your truth and grace…

QUESTIONS FOR SMALL GROUP DISCUSSION

1. What struck you most in this passage? What did you notice that you hadn't noticed before?

2. In what circumstances are we tempted to react to others' rejection of Christ (or of Church

teaching) as James and John did? How can we learn to be more Christlike in those situations?

3. How does popular culture encourage us to react to the demands and difficulties involved in following Christ? How does Christ want us to react?

4. How can we deepen our appreciation and awareness of God's personal interest in each of us? How can we transmit it to those who have no awareness of it all?

Cf. Catechism of the Catholic Church, 2340, 1734, 2015 on the need for effort in following Christ; 1846-1848 and 218-221 on God's mercy and love

THE GOSPEL OF ST LUKE CHAPTER 10

"Adapt yourself with gracious and charitable compliance to all your neighbor's weaknesses. In particular, make a rule to hide your feelings in many inconsequential matters. Give up all bitterness toward your neighbor, no matter what. And be convinced that your neighbor is in everything better than you. This will not be difficult if you keep even a little aware of yourself. It will give you the ability to overcome your feelings of resentment. Each day look for every possible opportunity to do a kindness for those you do not like. After examining yourselves on this matter every morning, decide what you are going to do, and do it faithfully with kindness and humility."

- St John Baptist de la Salle

185. WORKING FOR THE LORD (LK 10:1-12)

"I am convinced that there is a great need for the whole Church to rediscover the joy of evangelization, to become a community inspired with missionary zeal to make Jesus better known and loved."

- Pope Benedict XVI

Luke 10:1- 20

After this the Lord appointed seventy-two others and sent them out ahead of him, in pairs, to all the towns and places he himself was to visit. He said to them, 'The harvest is rich but the labourers are few, so ask the Lord of the harvest to send labourers to his harvest. Start off now, but remember, I am sending you out like lambs among wolves. Carry no purse, no haversack, no sandals. Salute no one on the road. Whatever house you go into, let your first words be, Peace to this house! And if a man of peace lives there, your peace will go and rest on him; if not, it will come back to you. Stay in the same house, taking what food and drink they have to offer, for the labourer deserves his wages; do not move from house to house. Whenever you go into a town where they make you welcome, eat what is set before you. Cure those in it who are sick, and say, The kingdom of God is very near to you.

But whenever you enter a town and they do not make you welcome, go out into its streets and say, "We wipe off the very dust of your town that clings to our feet, and leave it with you. Yet be sure of this: the kingdom of God is very near." I tell you, on that day it will not go as hard with Sodom as with that town.'

CHRIST THE LORD Appointing seventy-two disciples to be collaborators in his mission is an action with deep biblical significance. When Moses was leading the people of Israel into the Promised Land, God had him bring seventy elders to the door of the Tabernacle (the tent where the Ark of the Covenant was kept, and where Moses used to meet with God), so that they could receive the spirit of Moses and become his assistants. Later the Sanhedrin, the ruling body of post-exilic Israel, was made up of seventy-one elders. By following this pattern, Christ once again shows that he is bringing the Old Covenant to its fulfillment. The number seventy-two may even have yet another level of meaning. The Book of Genesis described the division of the non-Jewish world into seventy nations. So Jesus' choice of seventy-two disciples includes those seventy Gentile nations, the nation of Israel, and, perhaps, his Church, the new People of God. In any case, the allusion is clear. Christ is the new Moses; he is bringing a New Covenant and extending it to a new Israel, the Church.

We also see in this passage Jesus' insistence on his methodology of mediation. He had chosen his twelve closest companions, the apostles, the forerunners of the bishops. He had already sent them out on their first missionary journey. Now that their training has advanced, he gathers another group of assistants and sends them out on a similar mission. The structure of the New People of God is already taking shape, and it is even now hierarchical. Jesus is at the top of the pyramid, his Twelve Apostles come next, and beneath them there is another rung of ministers. Each of these in turn would reach out to others and engage them in building the Kingdom. The Lord came not only to announce the Good News, but to set up the ecclesial structure that would insure its ongoing announcement to the ends of the earth until the end of time, setting a pattern for apostleship that brings the principles of effectiveness and multiplication onto center stage.

CHRIST THE TEACHER Among the many lessons Jesus teaches in this lecture on how to be a Christian apostle, the last one is too often overlooked. He tells his disciples how to react when they are rejected, when their efforts appear to bear no fruit, when they run into opposition, and when they seem to fail in their attempts to win people over to Christ. When that happens, they are simply to shake the dust from their feet and move on.

Everyone remains free to accept or reject God's grace. If Christ himself suffered seeming failures in the apostolate (the Pharisees weren't exactly pushovers), should we expect anything more? The greatest danger for an apostle is discouragement. But discouragement comes from unfulfilled expectations. To avoid discouragement, therefore, Jesus points out what our expectations need to be. If we seek only to please the Lord, the Lord will indeed be pleased, even if no one else is.

CHRIST THE FRIEND "The harvest is abundant, but the laborers are few." Imagine the emotion behind those words. They express a sense of urgency, a burning desire to reach out to all the men and women who so desperately need direction, meaning, and true love in their lives, and to lead them into the Kingdom. So many needs, so many souls ripe for the Good News! And yet, so few of Christ's followers are willing to go out and gather them in. The true friends of Christ, the ones he can really count on, will let his yearning love echo in their hearts, and reverberate in their actions.

Priests share this mission in a special way, and Christ therefore allows them to share his yearning love more closely. They are the extension in time and space of Christ himself, who in his wisdom has chosen to work through them to infuse sacramental grace into the Church. Friendship with Christ, then, includes a supernatural appreciation for his priests, an attitude of respect and cooperation, and an eagerness to help those whom Christ is calling hear and heed him.

CHRIST IN MY LIFE You want your saving message to reach every human heart and society. But you also desire to spread that message through the words and actions of your disciples. I am a bit puzzled by your confidence in us, but even so, Lord, I renew my willingness to go wherever you want me to go and do whatever you want me to do to build your Kingdom. Teach me to do your will…

I tend to measure my Christian life in non-Christian terms, as if I could earn more of your love by showing more results in my efforts to build your Kingdom. I know you want the contrary: you want me to work for your Kingdom out of love for you, not in order to earn your love. But my heart is infected with the upside-down insecurity of this fallen world. Heal me with your love…

Your heart is burning with love. Why else would you have left heaven in order to come and suffer and die on earth? You eagerly desire the friendship of people just like me. Jesus, I can do nothing greater for my neighbors – the ones

I know well and the ones I barely know at all – than to bring them deeper into your friendship. With the zeal of your heart, inflame my heart…

QUESTIONS FOR SMALL GROUP DISCUSSION

1. What struck you most in this passage? What did you notice that you hadn't noticed before?

2. How do the guidelines that Christ gave the seventy-two apply to us today?

3. What are the biggest obstacles we face in trying to spread Christ's Kingdom and what would Christ say about them?

4. If Christ asked me to give my life completely to "gathering the harvest," would I be willing to? If not, why not?

Cf. Catechism of the Catholic Church, 857-865 on the apostolic nature of the Church; 3 and 1267-1270 on the responsibility of each Christian to spread the Kingdom

186. JOY AND HOPE (LK 10:13-24)

'What more do we want than to have at our side a friend so loyal that he will never desert us when we are in trouble or in difficulties, as worldly friends do?'

- St Theresa of Avila

Luke 10:13-24

'Alas for you, Chorazin! Alas for you, Bethsaida! For if the miracles done in you had been done in Tyre and Sidon, they would have repented long ago, sitting in sackcloth and ashes. And still, it will not go as hard with Tyre and Sidon at the Judgement as with you. And as for you, Capernaum, did you want to be exalted high as heaven? You shall be thrown down to hell. Anyone who listens to you listens to me; anyone who rejects you rejects me, and those who reject me reject the one who sent me.'

The seventy-two came back rejoicing. 'Lord,' they said, 'even the devils submit to us when we use your name.' He said to them, 'I watched Satan fall like lightning from heaven. Yes, I have given you power to tread underfoot serpents and scorpions and the whole strength of the enemy; nothing shall ever hurt you. Yet do not rejoice that the spirits submit to you; rejoice rather that your names are written in heaven.' It was then that, filled with joy by the Holy Spirit, he said, 'I bless you, Father, Lord of heaven and of earth, for hiding these things from the learned and the clever and revealing them to mere children. Yes, Father, for that is what it pleased you to do. Everything has been entrusted to me by my Father; and no one knows who the Son is except the Father, and who the Father is except the Son and those to whom the Son chooses to reveal him.' Then turning to his disciples he spoke to them in private, 'Happy the eyes that see what you see, for I tell you that many prophets

633

and kings wanted to see what you see, and never saw it; to hear what you hear, and never heard it.'

CHRIST THE LORD Jesus identifies himself with his chosen missionaries. To demonstrate what a high privilege that is, St Luke records some of the boldest claims that Jesus ever made.

First, we hear him reprimand the towns that refused to accept his teaching and apply it to their lives. His reaction to their rejection is passionate and dramatic; he prophesies that their cold reception will lead to their demise on the Day of Judgment. The implication is clear: Jesus is the One sent by the Father, and the way we treat Jesus is the way we treat God, for good or for ill.

Second, he exults in the faith-filled welcome the seventy-two gave to his grace, which enabled them to push back Satan's conquests and advance Christ's eternal Kingdom. In the course of that exultation he actually identifies himself with the Father; he explains that although they are two separate persons, they are completely united in the knowledge and love they share – knowledge and love being the two characteristics that bring persons into communion with each other. Here we have a protolesson on the Blessed Trinity.

Third, after celebrating the return of the seventy-two, Jesus speaks alone with his apostles. We can picture his eyes shining with an eager light, his gladness at the seventy-two's faith still overflowing in his countenance. And then it overflows again in his words as he explains that his mission, his presence in Israel, and the establishment of his Church are what all human history and all salvation history had been looking forward to. He is the "center of the universe and of history."[1]

CHRIST THE TEACHER Commentators vary on their interpretation of the striking phrase, "I watched Satan fall like lightning from heaven." Some read it as if Jesus were smiling and affirming the reports from the seventy-two disciples that the devils submitted to them. It would be like Jesus saying, "Yes, while you were preaching and healing, I was here and I saw Satan's rule rolling back wherever you spread the Good News." Others read the saying as a preface to the rest of his mini-discourse, as a warning against unhealthy pride, which was the cause of Satan's original fall from grace. In this case, the phrase would mean, "Well, it's good that you have experienced the power of my salvation, but be careful. If you forget that this power comes not from yourselves but from on high, you may fall into

---

[1] *Pope John Paul II*, Redemptor Hominis, *1*

the tragic trap that the devil fell into, thinking that you are on par with God."

In either case, the lesson of his conversation with the returning disciples remains the same. Those who trust in God and obey his call in their lives, as did the seventy-two, will experience God's power acting in and through their lives, and that is exactly what Christ is hoping for. And as long as they remember that their fruitfulness and effectiveness is based on God's initiative and grace working in them, thus staying humble and trusting like "mere children," all will be well. But if they begin to think too highly of themselves, as if their own greatness were yielding these remarkable results, thus considering themselves "the learned and the clever," they will self-destruct.

How easy it is, even for those who have spent long years working faithfully in the Lord's vineyard, to become dangerously proud and self-satisfied! The secret to perseverance in friendship with Christ is to draw our satisfaction not primarily from what we do, but from what God has done for us, and that requires the daily mental discipline of directing our thoughts again and again to God's goodness, cultivating an attitude of gratitude. After all, what can give us greater happiness than knowing that our "names are written in heaven," just as the names of citizens in the Greek cities at the time of Christ were carefully kept on regularly updated lists?

CHRIST THE FRIEND The disciples come back "rejoicing." Jesus catches their spirit, and his acclamation of praise to the Father is given while he is "filled with joy by the Holy Spirit." The Lord rejoices in our joys, just as much as he sorrows in our sorrows. We have a hard time understanding how deeply interested he is in our lives, but the fact remains, as this passage makes clear – he is deeply interested. This is one of Christianity's great differences. The God of the Bible cares passionately about every single human soul. Was Jesus' reaction to Bethsaida and Capernaum's failure to repent one of indifference? Hardly – it was as full of pathos as his reaction to the successful mission of the seventy-two was full of joy. Christ's heart beats with our hearts, because it is one with ours, because it came to earth and started beating in the first place in order to save our hearts from loneliness, frustration, and despair. He is the Friend beyond all imagining.

Philip: I will never forget that day when everyone came back from the second mission trip. We were all exhausted but overflowing with enthusiasm. Everyone wanted to tell Jesus about all the wonderful things that had happened. Everyone had some remarkable stories. As we came together, I was thinking to myself that Jesus wouldn't be as eager to hear our stories as we were to tell them. After all, his own miracles were far beyond the scope of anything we were doing. But I was wrong. As we approached him he came out towards us. It was as if he had been waiting for us. His eyes were full of welcome – and questions. He wanted to know everything. No detail was too slight for him. It made a lasting impression on me. I remembered it frequently in later years, when we had all gone out to spread the Church. When I prayed, I would remember how eagerly he had listened to the seventy-two, and I would tell him everything, absolutely everything that was going on. He would always answer me, somehow. That's the way I stayed close to him.

CHRIST IN MY LIFE   You have given me the universe. All that I see around me, Lord, is mine, because it is yours. You have given me your very self, and you continue to give me yourself every time I receive Holy Communion. You hold me in the palm of your hand. You, the all-powerful, all-knowing God, shower me with gifts. Thank you, Lord. Blessed be your name through all the earth…

I bear your name, and you have anointed my forehead with the sign of the cross. You have given me a mission in life, just as you gave one to the seventy-two. I am to bring the sweet aroma of your truth and love into the world where I live and work. Make me your faithful disciple, Lord, so that I can experience the joy of your victory, and so bring joy to your heart…

Why do I insist on walking alone through life? You are always thinking of me, like a lover in the full, fresh bloom of love. You are interested in me, wanting to teach and guide me in all my responsibilities, activities, and relationships. You are on the edge of your seat, waiting to see how I will respond to all the blessings and opportunities for growth that you send me. Thank you, Lord…

QUESTIONS FOR SMALL GROUP DISCUSSION

1. What struck you most in this passage? What did you notice that you hadn't noticed before?

2. How does Christ expect us to build his Kingdom in our current life-situation? What can help us do it more effectively?

3. Christ promises to protect those who trust him and strive to do his work. Have you ever felt that protection? Do the examples of the martyrs contradict Jesus' promise that "nothing shall every hurt you"?

4. What does popular culture encourage us to "rejoice" in? What would Christ say about that?

Cf. Catechism of the Catholic Church, 27, 30, 384, 1028, 1035, 1723 on how God gives happiness; 774-776 on the Church as the sacrament of salvation; 1554-1571 on the three degrees of holy orders

187. THE GOOD LIFE (LK 10:25-37)

"Remember that the Christian life is one of action, not of speech and daydreams. Let there be few words and many deeds and let them be done well."

- St Vincent Palliotti

Luke 10:25-37

There was a lawyer who, to disconcert him, stood up and said to him, 'Master, what must I do to inherit eternal life?' He said to him, 'What is written in the Law? What do you read there?' He replied, 'You must love the Lord your God with all your heart, with all your soul, with all your strength, and with all your mind, and your neighbour as yourself.' 'You have answered right,' said Jesus, 'do this and life is yours.' But the man was anxious to justify himself and said to Jesus, 'And who is my neighbour?' Jesus replied, 'A man was once on his way down from Jerusalem to Jericho and fell into the hands of brigands; they took all he had, beat him and then made off, leaving him half dead. Now a priest happened to be travelling down the same road, but when he saw the man, he passed by on the other side. In the same way a Levite who came to the place saw him, and passed by on the other side. But a Samaritan traveller who came upon him was moved with compassion when he saw him. He went up and bandaged his wounds, pouring oil and wine on them. He then lifted him on to his own mount, carried him to the inn and looked after him. Next day, he took out two denarii and handed them to the innkeeper. "Look after him, he said, and on my way back I will make good any extra expense you have." Which of these three, do you think, proved himself a neighbour to the man who fell into the brigands' hands?' 'The one who took pity on him,' he replied. Jesus said to him, 'Go, and do the same yourself.'

CHRIST THE LORD This parable is so familiar to us that we often see only one of its dimensions. Certainly it presents a model for us to follow – "Go and do the same yourself" – but it also presents us with a self-portrait of Christ; it reveals what kind of a Lord he is. Each of us has been robbed of our original holiness by original sin. Our own selfishness and sins (and the sins of others) have deeply wounded our souls. We lay on the side of life's path in need of a Savior. We have been bruised and broken and wounded; the Lord kneels down and lifts us up with his healing touch. Christ is the Good Samaritan, the merciful Lord who heals and restores us with the balm of his sacraments, who pays for our salvation with the boundless riches of his grace, poured out generously on Calvary's cross and entrusted to the innkeeper of the Church, who watches over our convalescence until he comes again. He is the Lord, yes, but the truly noble Lord, who cares enough to come meet us in our need and carry us safely to his Father's inn.

CHRIST THE TEACHER   Christ's lesson is so simple! "Love God with all your heart and love your neighbor as yourself, and you will live." It is within everyone's reach to live out this simple lesson, even within the reach of a Samaritan, who according to local customs of the time was not supposed to have anything to do with Jews. It summarizes the entire Gospel, the entire meaning of life. But we are not satisfied with simplicity. We pester him for clarifications, "Yes, but who actually is my neighbor? ..." And he obliges us with further explanations, with the explanation given by the words and examples of thousands of saints, by the teaching of the Church in every age, by the nudges of our own conscience.... And still we find it hard to learn the lesson. One would venture to think that perhaps we don't really want to learn it. What holds us back from deciding once and for all to make Christ's standard our own? The complicated shadows of self-absorption have become too comfortable; the simple, bright light of Christ's truth hurts our eyes. But in our hearts we know what we should do. The time has come to pack up our books and leave the classroom behind; the lesson of how to live only makes sense when we let it change the course of our life.

CHRIST THE FRIEND   The Good Samaritan put himself out to save the half-dead traveler. First of all, it was risky: playing dead was a popular ploy of Palestine's experienced brigands. Second, it was costly: he had to expend his own oil and wine, and he had to leave money with the innkeeper. Third, it was inconvenient: certainly the Samaritan was on the road for business, maybe very important business, and stopping at the scene of the accident and then taking the fellow to a place of safety would delay his trip. The whole thing was really a bad investment, practically speaking. But friends do that; they put themselves out for their friends, they take risks for them and make sacrifices for them. That's what Christ did for us (just look at a crucifix), to prove what kind of friend he is. And if we value his friendship, and want to be his friend, we will "go and do the same."

Jesus: Life is so short. It is so easy to forget that. It is so easy for you to get caught up in the stream of activities that seem so urgent but in fact are secondary. Your primary task, the mission I have given you, is to follow in my footsteps. Open your eyes and your heart to the people around you. See their needs and reach out to them as I have seen yours and reached out to you. If this is hard for you, if the stream of urgencies keeps sweeping you away, don't worry. Keep contemplating my example, keep thinking of the love I have for you and all that I have done and still do for you. Little by little the weight of my love will give you stability, strength, and peace. My wisdom will be the balm that heals your anxiety.

CHRIST IN MY LIFE Jesus, thank you for coming to earth, paying the price of my sins, and inviting me to your heavenly banquet. I don't thank you enough for all you have done for me. You didn't pass me by when you saw me in need. You never do. You are always with me, no matter how hard life may get. Keep me faithful to you, Lord, just as you are always faithful to me…

How I yearn for clarity of mind! Life seems so complicated sometimes, Lord. I know it's because I'm too self-absorbed. Help me, teach me, send me the wisdom of your Spirit, clean out the junk drawer of my soul. I want to be completely free to live life as you created me to live it. I love you, Lord; teach me to do your will…

Being a Good Samaritan at times seems too hard, too demanding. But I know, even from my own experience, that it's really not so hard at all – once I decide to do it. Help me to be courageous in those critical moments of decision. If I can resist the temptation to self-centeredness right when a chance to love presents itself, the rest will be smooth sailing…

QUESTIONS FOR SMALL GROUP DISCUSSION

1. What struck you most in this passage? What did you notice that you hadn't noticed before?

2. What can we do to increase our reverence for and appreciation of Christ?

3. When we have moral or religious questions, as did this scholar, where should we go with them?

4. What would the "Good Samaritan" be doing if he were in our place today?

Cf. Catechism of the Catholic Church, 1822-1829 on charity; 1846-1848 on mercy; 1939-1942 on human solidarity

188. CHOOSING THE BETTER PART (LK 10:38-42)

"From the top of a hill the rain flows down to the valley. Just as more water collects at the bottom of the hill, so Mary, sitting in a low place at the feet of Jesus, listening to His words, receives more than Martha, standing and serving the temporal needs of her Master. Mary, loving Jesus, the one thing needed, is in port. Martha, occupying herself about many things, is still at sea."

- St Augustine

Luke 10:38-42

In the course of their journey he came to a village, and a woman named Martha welcomed him into her house. She had a sister called Mary, who sat down at the Lord's feet and listened to him speaking. Now Martha who was distracted with all the serving said, 'Lord, do you not care that my sister is leaving me to do the serving all by myself? Please tell her to help me.' But the Lord answered: 'Martha, Martha,' he said, 'you worry and fret about so many things, and yet few are needed, indeed only one. It is Mary who has chosen the better part; it is not to be taken from her.'

CHRIST THE LORD If Christ truly is the one Lord of life and history, the one Savior, the one Way, Truth, and Life (and he is), then it is certain that "only one" thing is needed for a fulfilling, meaningful, and fruitful life: to stay as close to him as possible at all times. When we address Christ from our hearts as Lord, we acknowledge our conviction that he truly is our one thing necessary, and he will be as pleased with us for doing so as he was with Mary.

The Lord already is the one thing needed. Our task is to choose to shape our lives accordingly. Jesus doesn't congratulate Mary because she won the spiritual lottery or had received a particularly beautiful soul from God. He praises her because she has "chosen the better part." She chooses it. She chooses to submit to the Lord, to let him be for her what he in truth is for everyone – that one needed thing.

Once again, we are confronted with this amazing truth about Christ's Kingship: he offers the benefits of his rule to all people, but he leaves each person supremely free to accept or reject them. And the offer is not a one-time affair. Martha had chosen to busy herself with her own plans on this occasion, but you can bet she adjusted her behavior the next time the Lord came around. Mary had chosen to adore the Lord this time, but she would still be free to make the same or a different choice the next time. Each and every time we choose to give Christ and his will priority in our lives, we are pleasing him and extending the borders of his Kingdom in our lives. And every time we bring his message to others, we give them a chance to do the same.

CHRIST THE TEACHER We shouldn't berate Martha too much – she also is a saint, and she was also much loved by the Lord. But she needed to learn a lesson. She needed to learn that what we do for Christ has to flow out of what we are for him – his true and devoted friends. It is easy to overload our agenda with so many activities and commitments – good and beneficial as they may be – that we lose sight of our goal: to know, love, and imitate Christ more each day.

Only that will give meaning to our lives; only that will equip us to help others find meaning; only that will fill us with the joy we long for. If we are separated from the vine, we cannot bear fruit (cf. John 15:5), but if we seek first the Kingdom, everything else will fall into place (cf. Matthew 6:33).

The crucial sign that we may be following Martha's footsteps a little too closely is a waning life of prayer. When we skimp on our prayer life, on that precious time that we spend, as Mary did, "at the Lord's feet listening to him speaking," we need to stop and check our spiritual vital signs. Maybe we have allowed ourselves to become so "distracted with all the serving" that we have forgotten why we should be serving in the first place.

CHRIST THE FRIEND Christ was glad to be served, but he was even gladder to be loved. He yearns for our love. When we come before him at the final judgment, he will be less interested in our résumé of achievements than in the love with which we achieved them. He was happy that Mary wanted to listen to him, wanted to sit beside him and spend time with him. That is why he became man in the first place – to make himself available, to offer his friendship. This desire was so strong that he invented a way to extend his real presence to all times and places through the sacrament of the Eucharist. In every tabernacle throughout the world he is available 24/7, just for us, just because he loves us.

CHRIST IN MY LIFE I want to choose the better part every day – every moment of every day. I believe in you completely; I want to live wholly for you. Whose kingdom could I possibly prefer? My own? Save me from that! Someone else's? But who is as wise as you, who is as powerful as you? Who is as loving as you? Thy Kingdom come, Lord, thy will be done…

I want to build your Kingdom, fulfill my apostolate, and win souls over to your friendship. I want to do so much for you! But I know that my heart is not yet completely pure. The infection of egoism is still there, albeit on the wane because of your grace. So keep me humble, Lord. Keep me focused on you and your Kingdom – not on myself and my achievements…

Thank you for staying with me in the Eucharist. Now I always have a chance to sit at your feet and listen to your words and your heartbeats. I need that. I need a real place, a real presence. Thank you, Lord. Never let me take this great gift for granted. With the love of your heart, inflame my heart…

QUESTIONS FOR SMALL GROUP DISCUSSION

1. What struck you most in this passage? What did you notice that you hadn't noticed before?

2. Why do you think Martha had enough confidence to issue such a mundane complaint to Jesus about her sister? What does this tell us about her relationship with Jesus?

3. What substitutes do people come up with for the "one thing needed" when they don't have Christ?

4. What are some tactics that have helped you regularly make time in your busy schedule to sit at the Lord's feet and listen to him? What keeps us from being more like Mary?

Cf. Catechism of the Catholic Church, 2558-2567 on the importance and nature of prayer; 2709-2719 on contemplative prayer; 1373-1381 on Christ's prayer in the Eucharist

THE GOSPEL OF ST LUKE CHAPTER 11

"The man who prays looks above to the goods of heaven whereon he meditates and which he desires; his whole being is plunged in the contemplation of the marvelous order established by God, which knows not the frenzy of earthly successes nor the futile competitions of ever increasing speed; and thus automatically, as it were, will be reestablished that equilibrium between work and rest, whose entire absence from society today is responsible for grave dangers to life physical, economic and moral."

- Pope Pius XI

189. PRAYER SCHOOL (LK 11:1-13)

"One can always enter into inner prayer, independently of the conditions of health, work, or emotional state. The heart is the place of this conquest and encounter, in poverty and in faith."

- Catechism of the Catholic Church, 2710

Luke 11:1-13

Now once he was in a certain place praying, and when he had finished one of his disciples said, 'Lord, teach us to pray, just as John taught his disciples.' He said to them, 'Say this when you pray: Father, may your name be held holy, your kingdom come; give us each day our daily bread, and forgive us our sins, for we ourselves forgive each one who is in debt to us. And do not put us to the test.' He also said to them, 'Suppose one of you has a friend and goes to him in the middle of the night to say, My friend, lend me three loaves, because a friend of mine on his travels has just arrived at my house and I have nothing to offer him; and the man answers from inside the house, Do not bother me. The door is bolted now, and my children and I are in bed; I cannot get up to give it you. I tell you, if the man does not get up and give it him for friendship's sake, persistence will be enough to make him get up and give his friend all he wants. So I say to you: Ask, and it will be given to you; search, and you will find; knock, and the door will be opened to you. For the one who asks always receives; the one who searches always finds; the one who knocks will always have the door opened to him. What father among you would hand his son a stone when he asked for bread? Or hand him a snake instead of a fish? Or hand him a scorpion if he asked for an egg? If you then, who are evil, know how to give your children what is good, how much more will the heavenly Father give the Holy Spirit to those who ask him!'

CHRIST THE LORD We, though we tend to be selfish, are still eager to give good things to those we love. God, who is unhampered by even the slightest smidgeon of selfishness, is certainly more eager than we can imagine to give good things to us, whom he loves tirelessly and without measure. Just as Christ answered his disciples' request to teach them how to pray, so he will hear every request we ask of him and answer it even more generously than we could have hoped for. He is a lavish Lord, abounding in every good thing – most especially in forgiveness and faithfulness, the two deepest needs of the human heart – and ready to pour them out upon us, if only we really want him to.

In a sense, the history of salvation is a history of God answering the prayers of his people. The Old Testament is a litany of answered prayers: Moses repeatedly intercedes for the Israelites, and God delivers; the Lord answers their pleas for deliverance by sending them judges and prophets and finally a king; Hannah is granted a son; Judith and Esther are granted victory in the face of overpowering enemies through their heartfelt prayers, and the list goes on. Certainly, God is the initiator of salvation. He created us and guides us through the labyrinth of life, but he guides us in accordance with our nature, and that means respecting our freedom and listening to our entreaties. He is not a Dictator, but an all-powerful Father.

CHRIST THE TEACHER The words of the Our Father, abridged here in St Luke's version, are God's own instructions on prayer. Each phrase is a gushing stream of grace and wisdom; if we spend our lives tuning our hearts to their inexhaustible meaning (and not just mindlessly rattling them off), we will discover every secret of peace and happiness. They show us how God wants us to approach him and be with him.

In addition to fostering the attitudes and desires woven into the Our Father, however, Jesus teaches us two other qualities of Christian prayer: persistence and confidence. In the Garden of Eden, Adam and Eve failed the Lord by letting the devil trick them out of these two attitudes. Instead of having confidence in God's command not to eat the forbidden fruit, they let their trust in the creator die in their hearts; and instead of turning to God in their moment of trial and hardship, they depended solely on their own wits. Though baptism has overcome in our souls the alienation from God inherited from original sin, the weakness, the tendency to distrust God and give up on him, remains. God allows it to remain because he wants to give us a share in the all-important work of building up his Kingdom, which is an interior kingdom of the heart. Our prayer life is a privileged place to accomplish that work. By exercising these attitudes in our prayer, we have a chance to rehabilitate our persistent confidence in the Lord, so that we can return to intimacy with him.

CHRIST THE FRIEND "Search and you will find; ask, and it will be given to you." The funny thing about friendship is that it can't be forced. As much as God wants to regain our friendship and deepen it day after day, he can only do so if we share (at least a little bit) that same desire, if we yearn for his friendship as he yearns for ours. He does everything he can to stir it up within us (even descending from heaven to become man and live among us), but ultimately, because he will settle for nothing less than true friendship, he willingly limits his own freedom in order to respect ours.

Jesus: Prayer is much simpler than you think. I am always with you, always at your side and in your heart. I am always paying attention to you, thinking of you. I am always interested in what you are going through and what is on your mind and heart. Remember this, believe it, and prayer will become as natural as breathing. You never have to be alone. I am the one who knows you wholly and loves you no matter what. Live in the awareness of my presence; let me be your life's companion.

CHRIST IN MY LIFE I trust in you, Lord. Send me the gifts of your Holy Spirit. Fill my soul with your light and your peace; wipe away all the stains of selfishness. I want to live each new day with the freshness of your everlasting love. I want to live with the joy of the simple child and the wisdom of old age. I want my life to be a window, clear and spotless, that faces the vista of your Sacred Heart…

Teach me to pray, Lord. I believe in the necessity and importance of prayer. I thank you for the gift of prayer. I want to learn to search for you in prayer, so that I can find you. I want to learn to pray at all times, so that I can always know what's best to do, what's the most effective way to build your Kingdom in my life and my neighbors' lives…

Lord, I still want to follow you. I want you to be Lord of my life, just as you are Lord of history. Thank you for offering me your friendship. But what about all those other people who haven't accepted the offer? Have mercy on them, as you had mercy on me, and move their hearts to trust in you. And teach me what to say and do to bring them closer to your Kingdom…

QUESTIONS FOR SMALL GROUP DISCUSSION

1. What struck you most in this passage? What did you notice that you hadn't noticed before?

2. St Luke tells us, "Jesus was praying in a certain place." Many times throughout his Gospel he shows Jesus at prayer. If Christ was God, why did he need to pray? What does this teach us about our own need for personal prayer?

3. What are the most common difficulties facing Christians today who want to have a healthy prayer life? How can Christ's lessons in this passage help us overcome them?

4. How do you think the disciples reacted when Jesus said to them, "If you then, who are evil, know how to give your children what is good…"? Those same words are meant for each of us; how do you react to them? How do you think Christ wants you to react to them?

Cf. Catechism of the Catholic Church, 2759-2865 on the deep meaning of the Our Father; 2734-2745 on trust and persistence in prayer

190. A CLOSER LOOK AT THE DEVIL (LK 11:14-26)

To choose rightly it is necessary to concentrate on the end for which I am created, that is, for the praise of God and for the salvation of my soul."

- St Ignatius Loyola, *Spiritual Exercises, 169*

Luke 11:14-26

He was casting out a devil and it was dumb; but when the devil had gone out the dumb man spoke, and the people were amazed. But some of them said, 'It is through Beelzebul, the prince of devils, that he casts out devils.' Others asked him, as a test, for a sign from heaven; but, knowing what they were thinking, he said to them, 'Every kingdom divided against itself is heading for ruin, and a household divided against itself collapses. So too with Satan: if he is divided against himself, how can his kingdom stand? – Since you assert that it is through Beelzebul that I cast out devils. Now if it is through Beelzebul that I cast out devils, through whom do your own experts cast them out? Let them be your judges then. But if it is through the finger of God that I cast out devils, then know that the kingdom of God has overtaken you. So long as a strong man fully armed guards his own palace, his goods are undisturbed; but when someone stronger than he is attacks and defeats him, the stronger man takes away all the weapons he relied on and shares out his spoil. He who is not with me is against me; and he who does not gather with me scatters. When an unclean spirit goes out of a man it wanders through waterless

645

country looking for a place to rest, and not finding one it says, I will go back to the home I came from. But on arrival, finding it swept and tidied, it then goes off and brings seven other spirits more wicked than itself, and they go in and set up house there, so that the man ends up by being worse than he was before.'

CHRIST THE LORD The crowds around Jesus ask him to show them an additional sign to disprove the critics who say he is in league with the devil. Jesus shows how superficial that question is. The devil's goal is to enslave men and make them suffer, to keep them from believing in, trusting, and obeying God. Demonic possession is one way of working towards this goal. What could the devil possibly gain from pretending to be his own enemy? Jesus sends the devils out of possessed people as a way of reducing their suffering and restoring their freedom. Doing so inspires people to believe his teaching, which is all about trusting and obeying God. Therefore, no sincere observer could mistake his actions as a deceitful plot of the devil. Those who accuse him of being on the devil's side are obviously not sincere observers, and those who are asking for more signs do so vainly; if they can't rightly interpret the signs Jesus has already given, they won't be able to interpret any sign.

Anyone who looks honestly at the figure of Christ in the Gospels and in the lives of those saints throughout history who have faithfully followed his teachings and example is forced to admit that in him the Kingdom of righteousness (the "stronger man") has overcome the kingdom of evil (the "strong man"). But not everyone takes that honest look. It is the Christian's job to give wavering believers and non-believers countless chances to do so. The Lord will take care of the rest.

CHRIST THE TEACHER Jesus is involved in a spiritual battle. The devil and his minions play an important part in the history of salvation and in the Gospels, as uncomfortable as that may make us feel. In fact, "This was the purpose of the appearing of the Son of God, to undo the work of the devil" (1 Jn 3:8). In our struggles to grow in Christian virtue and build up Christ's Kingdom, we have to always keep this in mind. We are not fighting only against natural obstacles. We are not working in a vacuum. "For it is not against human enemies that we have to struggle, but against the principalities and the ruling forces who are masters of the darkness in this world, the spirits of evil in the heavens" (Eph 6:12).

The most important theater of this war, as Jesus makes clear in his parable, is the human heart, the place where we make decisions. Each day we make thousands of decisions. Every decision is based on a criterion, a goal. If the criteria and goals are in harmony with the true goal of human existence and with Christ's Kingdom, those decisions will be good and thus will contribute to individual and social well-being. The devil wants to stir up selfish motives and self-centered attitudes, so that our decisions will be made as if we were God and everything depended only on ourselves. Christ, through his teaching and his grace, through our conscience and the inspirations of the Holy Spirit, wants to stir up noble and true motives. But neither the devil nor Christ will make our decisions for us. We can make the most of Christ's grace (especially through prayer and the sacraments) to obtain forgiveness and be strengthened in virtue, but as long as we remain on this earth, we will still have to make our own decisions, and we will still be influenced by temptation as well as grace. Life on earth is a mission and an adventure, but it's also an ongoing battle.

CHRIST THE FRIEND Jesus is willing to discuss things with his enemies and with those who doubt, just as the Church is always ready to explain her teachings and listen to the problems and complaints of her children and inquirers. Jesus has been facing opposition since the beginning of his life, but he never loses patience, just as the Church is always willing to receive repentant sinners, no matter how many times they need to repent. Jesus teaches, forgives, invites, and sometimes warns, but he never closes the door to salvation. His love won't let him. Even on the cross itself, as his enemies taunt and deride him, he still showers them with his patient and forgiving love: "Father, forgive them, they do not know what they are doing" (Luke 23:34). His whole life is one huge billboard: "You can trust in me no matter what."

We need to relearn this lesson every day. And we need to do all we can so that our lives continue that same advertising campaign – the salvation of souls depends on it.

CHRIST IN MY LIFE Sometimes I hem and haw about what you are asking me. I ask for signs because I don't want to accept what I know your will is. I don't know how you put up with me, Lord. Teach me humility and docility. Teach me the strength and courage to follow you through thick and thin, trusting all the way…

I know that life is a battle between good and evil, but in the rush of everyday life I forget about it. I don't want to live life on the surface! Save me from skimming along on fashionable and passing preoccupations. I want to go deeper. I want to discover and spread your wisdom, your goodness, and your love…

Patience is so hard for me. But you are perfect in your patience, remaining in the Tabernacle day after day. And you nourish me with your own life, feeding my soul with your virtues in Holy Communion. Activate in my heart the strength of your virtue, so that all I do and say will draw others closer to you instead of pushing them away…

QUESTIONS FOR SMALL GROUP DISCUSSION

1. What struck you most in this passage? What did you notice that you hadn't noticed before?

2. Why do people continue to resist Christ's teaching so vehemently?

3. What's the difference between temptation and sin?

4. What does popular culture say about spiritual warfare? How does that fit into Christ's teaching?

Cf. Catechism of the Catholic Church, 2087-2094 on faith, hope, and love and the sins against them; 2115-2117 on divination and magic

191. THE MOST PRECIOUS SECRET (LK 11:27-36)

"Man has a noble task: that of prayer and love. To pray and to love, that is the happiness of man on earth."

- St John Vianney

Luke 11:27-36

Now as he was speaking, a woman in the crowd raised her voice and said, 'Happy the womb that bore you and the breasts you sucked!' But he replied, 'Still happier those who hear the word of God and keep it!' The crowds got even bigger and he addressed them, 'This is a wicked generation; it is asking for a sign. The only sign it will be given is the sign of Jonah. For just as Jonah became a sign to the Ninevites, so will the Son of Man be to this generation. On Judgement Day the Queen of the South will rise up with the men of this generation and condemn them, because she came from the ends of the earth to hear the wisdom of Solomon; and there is something greater than Solomon here. On Judgement Day the men of Nineveh will stand up with this generation and condemn it, because when Jonah preached they repented; and there is something greater than Jonah here. No one lights a lamp and puts it in some hidden place or under a tub, but on the lamp-stand so that people may see the light when they come in. The lamp of your body is your eye. When your eye is sound, your whole body too is filled with light; but when it is diseased your body too will be all darkness. See to it then that the light inside you is not darkness. If, therefore, your whole body is filled with light, and no trace of darkness, it will be light entirely, as when the lamp shines on you with its rays.'

CHRIST THE LORD Jonah's preaching to the Gentile Ninevites led to their repentance and salvation. Solomon's wisdom attracted the Gentile Queen of Sheba and made her into a believer in the one true God. Jesus' preaching and wisdom is far superior to either of theirs, and yet many (and many of the most influential) of his contemporary Jews simply refused to accept him.

The particular greatness of these two Old Testament prophets was that they both brought God's salvation even to non-Jews. In declaring his superiority to both of them, Jesus makes it clear that in him the Messianic era has come; in him the Kingdom of God will be established in such a way so as to fulfill the promise to Abraham that *all peoples* would be blessed through his descendents. It is possible to become so used to Jesus Christ, that we forget the utter extravagance of his claim. He is the King of all times and places. If we let that truth sink in a bit more thoroughly every day, our lives as his followers and friends will take on a whole new perspective.

CHRIST THE TEACHER Jesus uses an image he has already used – that of the lamp. But he expands on its meaning. Lamps are not meant to be hidden away; they ought to spread light. Just so, each person's life should be full of goodness and generosity, shining with the light of virtue. This is what we were created for – to be full of light ourselves and spread that light around us. But our lives, unlike physical lamps, can fail to achieve their purpose. Instead of being full to overflowing with selfless virtue, we can become full to overflowing with selfish vice. How? What makes the difference?

Jesus makes the answer clear. It depends on our eye. The eye is the organ by which we see. As such, it is a metaphor for our desires, for what we seek – we can only desire what we see. If we desire to love God and love our neighbors, then our eye is bright; if we desire or seek our own self-indulgence and exaltation, then our eye is dark. Our hearts, the seat of our desires and decisions, determine the state of our souls and the fruitfulness of our lives on earth. Jesus is trying to convince us to desire to give, to be like the sun, instead of desiring only to receive, which makes us like a black hole.

CHRIST THE FRIEND It must have warmed Christ's heart to hear the cheer this woman let loose in the middle of his homily. She had detected his goodness and his beauty and couldn't hold back her praise. What a contrast with the many self-righteous intellectuals who sneered at the humble rabbi from Nazareth! But Jesus doesn't luxuriate in the compliment. He seizes the opportunity to reveal the secret that mankind had been seeking since before history began: what makes for a happy life.

The human heart was made to find its true, lasting satisfaction only by living in communion with God, by knowing God and loving God – hearing and heeding God's word. The blessedness that comes from that outstrips even the most profound and worthy natural delights, like that of being parent to a great and wise rabbi. Jesus came to once again make that kind of happiness possible. Whoever trusts in him, follows his teachings, and stays close to him will experience it, just as the example of his closest friend of all time – his mother Mary, whose moral and spiritual beauty he subtly complements in his response to the cheer – eloquently attests to.

CHRIST IN MY LIFE When I take time to think about who you really are, Creator and Redeemer of all things, the infinite One, the all-powerful and all-loving and all-knowing God, I am filled with wonder. And to think that you want to walk with me, to guide my life. You suffered every kind of sorrow and humiliation in order to be able to prepare me a place in your Kingdom. Blessed be your name…

The pace of life often carries me away, and I forget to keep you in my sights. I have to admit, the seductions of pleasure, wealth, popularity, power – they still attract me. Part of me still reaches out to those things. But my eye, the eye of my soul, recognizes that only you and your will can give lasting meaning and fruitfulness. I want you, Lord. Teach me to do your will…

Mary, you treasured in your heart every word of God that came into your life. You sought only to discern and fulfill his will. You are the Queen of all saints and the Seat of Wisdom. Pray for me, and pray for all those people who have been entrusted to my care, in however small a way. Thank you for being our mother and nursing us into the image of Christ. Queen of peace, pray for us…

QUESTIONS FOR SMALL GROUP DISCUSSION

1. What struck you most in this passage? What did you notice that you hadn't noticed before?
2. Where does popular culture indicate happiness can be found? How does that square with what Christ says?
3. If a non-believing but sincerely open friend asked you how he could discover what God was saying to him, how would you respond?
4. Where can we hear God's word, and how can we prepare ourselves better to heed it once we do hear it?

Cf. Catechism of the Catholic Church, 1697, 1718, 2546 on the path to happiness; on the human desire for happiness; 27, 30, 384, 1028, 1035, 1723 on happiness coming from God

192. THE PHARISEES' FAILURE (LK 11:37-54)

"And even if I would not confess to you, what could be hidden in me, O Lord, from you to whose eyes the deepest depth of man's conscience lies bare? I should only be hiding you from myself, not myself from you."

- St Augustine

Luke 11:37-54

He had just finished speaking when a Pharisee invited him to dine at his house. He went in and sat down at the table. The Pharisee saw this and was surprised that he had not first washed before the meal. But the Lord said to him, 'Oh, you Pharisees! You clean the outside of cup and plate, while inside yourselves you are filled with extortion and wickedness. Fools! Did not he who made the outside make the inside too? Instead, give alms from what you have and then indeed everything will be clean for you. But alas for you Pharisees! You who pay your tithe of mint and rue and all sorts of garden herbs and overlook justice and the love of God! These you should have practiced, without leaving the others undone. Alas for you Pharisees who like taking the seats of honor in the synagogues and being greeted obsequiously in the market squares! Alas for you, because you are like the unmarked tombs that men walk on without knowing it!'

A lawyer then spoke up. 'Master,' he said, 'when you speak like this you insult us too.' 'Alas for you lawyers also,' he replied, 'because you load on men burdens that are unendurable, burdens that you yourselves do not move a finger to lift. Alas for you who build the tombs of the prophets, the men your ancestors killed! In this way you both witness what your ancestors did and approve it; they did the killing, you do the building. And that is why the Wisdom of God said, I will send them prophets and apostles; some they will slaughter and persecute, so that this generation will have to answer for every prophet's blood that has been shed since the foundation of the world, from the blood of Abel to the blood of Zechariah, who was murdered between the altar and the sanctuary. Yes, I tell you, this generation will have to answer for it all. Alas for you lawyers who have taken away the key of knowledge! You have not gone in yourselves, and have prevented others going in who wanted to.' When he left the house, the scribes and the Pharisees began a furious attack on him and tried to force answers from him on innumerable questions, setting traps to catch him out in something he might say.

CHRIST THE LORD Jesus seems to treat his host and the other guests harshly. Their furious reaction seems perfectly reasonable. Was our Lord disrespectful and out of place in this diatribe? Not at all.

In the first place, Jesus is now reaching the end of his public ministry, and still the Pharisees, scribes, and other leading Jews of the time, in spite of being perfectly aware of Jesus' impeccable selflessness, his incomparable wisdom and knowledge of the scriptures, and his truly divine power (he has healed every kind of disease, raised people from the dead, commanded the forces of nature, and sent scores of demons scuttling back to hell) – in spite of being witnesses of all this, many of the Jewish leaders still refuse to believe in him. Time is running short. Jesus knows that to win over any of them who aren't yet believers, he must change tactics. No longer the patient argument and indirect evidence, the time has come to rattle their self-confidence. He will shake them up and make them face their own consciences. His harsh critique flows from his determined love, not from a self-indulgent loss of composure.

In the second place, St Luke informs us that the conversation took place in a Pharisee's private residence. Jesus levels his criticisms to his opponents' faces. He confronts them head-on, not by launching attacks through third parties or public declarations. To the end, Christ tempers his Lordship with the tact and respect shown only by the most faithful of friends, even to those (including us) who resist his rule and who don't really deserve his friendship.

CHRIST THE TEACHER The Pharisees and the scribes (called "lawyers" here) were the religious leaders of ancient Palestine. The scribes dedicated themselves to studying the scriptures (the law of Moses and the prophets). They knew them backwards and forwards, and through the centuries they had derived an elaborate code of conduct that applied those scriptures to every possible permutation of daily living. For instance, it was forbidden to lift and carry items on the Sabbath. But what if you were to lift just a feather, or lift some food to your mouth? Or what if you were to carry something on the back of your hand instead of in your hand? The scribes' expertise could cover every scenario. And the Pharisees carried out what the scribes taught. The immense code of religious rituals that had accumulated through the ages was too demanding for most normal people to fulfill, but the Pharisees (their name means "the separated ones") were zealously dedicated to being exemplary in every detail.

Together, then, the Pharisees and scribes were supposed to inspire and guide the Jews in Palestine, bringing them closer to God and maintaining religious fervor among the people. But, as is clear from Jesus' description, they had utterly failed to do so. The scribes had turned their intellectual expertise inside out by weaving loopholes into every corner of the law, loopholes that only they could understand and take advantage of. The Pharisees had become so obsessed by their minute attention to externals that they had emptied their religion of its essence: "to act justly, to love tenderly and to walk humbly with your God" (Micah 6:8). They condemned the great bulk of the population that tried to love God and neighbor but couldn't keep up with the morass of external regulations. Thus these leaders were like "unmarked tombs" – by law touching such a tomb, even if you didn't know it, would make you ritually unclean. (Tombs were usually next to major roads, so it was easy to come into contact with old, overgrown ones.) Just so, the majority of Jews at the time who came into contact with the Pharisees and scribes thought they were learning from them the principles of true religion, but in fact they were being poisoned with false ideas about God. An important lesson for us is to learn to live more out of love than by the law, looking seriously into our own lives before condemning the Pharisees and scribes, lest we unknowingly condemn ourselves with them.

CHRIST THE FRIEND   *A Pharisee: When I first heard this young rabbi excoriate us, I was deeply offended. But something about his words and manner struck me. He was gaining nothing for himself by laying bare our hypocrisy. The light that flashed from his eyes as he spoke was the light of righteousness, but not self-righteousness. Although his lesson was bitter, it was true. Throughout our history, many of Israel's mainstream leaders rejected, disobeyed, and even murdered the prophets God sent to guide them. There was no denying this. We had tried to make up for it by honoring those previously rejected prophets. We even decorated their tombs, just as he said. Yet, John the Baptist spoke and lived as a prophet, and we turned up our noses at him. Jesus himself, as ordinary and unschooled as he seemed to be, performed works that only someone with God's favor could perform, but we never tired of looking for ways to discredit him. It occurred to me then that maybe he was right – maybe we were following the example of the wrong ancestors in rejecting him. Subsequent events proved that this was indeed the case. Our rejection was even graver than the previous ones, since Jesus was the Lord himself and not merely the Lord's ambassador. It also had a greater repercussion: the end of the Old Covenant, the destruction of the Temple, and the scattering of the Jews in a new Diaspora. Repeatedly he tried to show us, but our arrogance blinded us. He offered us a friendship that would last forever, but we preferred the passing glory of popularity and earthly power.*

CHRIST IN MY LIFE   I don't think I am like the Pharisees. But maybe I am. I am quick to judge people who have a different idea of what it means to follow you. I am quick to pay attention to other people's faults so that my own good points stand out. And that's not what you want from me. With the love of your heart, Lord, inflame my heart…

Sometimes I don't know whether to speak out or keep quiet. Sometimes I can't tell whether my anger is righteous or disordered. I need your guidance, Lord! I want to be courageous, but prudent. I want to be sincere, but respectful. I want to be coherent, but kind. This is what you were like, and I just want to follow in your footsteps. Teach me to do your will…

I am afraid that I am not hearing your voice, Lord, just as the Pharisees didn't hear it. Is my arrogance making me deaf? Are you correcting and guiding me through the words of my spiritual guide, my spouse, my boss, my teachers? You are all-powerful, Lord. You can break through my barriers. Teach me to be docile, to hear your word, no matter how much it hurts…

QUESTIONS FOR SMALL GROUP DISCUSSION

1. What struck you most in this passage? What did you notice that you hadn't noticed before?

2. Jesus' critique shows that he understood these men inside and out. Why do we tend to judge others without first striving to know them as best as we can?

3. Everything Jesus said about the Pharisees and scribes was true. Why do you think they reacted by attacking him instead of by repenting?

4. In what situations are we most frequently tempted to react to Christ as the Pharisees did?

Cf. Catechism of the Catholic Church, 1581-1589 on a portrait of Church ministers; 2546 on humility of heart

THE GOSPEL OF ST LUKE CHAPTER 12

"… I went across the garden one afternoon and stopped on the shore of the lake; I stood there for a long time, contemplating my surroundings. Suddenly, I saw the Lord Jesus near me, and he graciously said to me, 'All this I created for you, my spouse; and know that all this beauty is nothing compared to what I have prepared for you in eternity.' My soul was inundated with such consolation that I stayed there until evening, and it seemed to me like a brief moment."

- St Faustina Kowalska

193. COURAGE AND CONFIDENCE (LK 12:1-12)

"God does not expect us to be successful but to be faithful."

- Blessed Mother Teresa of Calcutta

Luke 12:1-12

Meanwhile the people had gathered in their thousands so that they were treading on one another. And he began to speak, first of all to his disciples. 'Be on your guard against the yeast of the Pharisees – that is, their hypocrisy. Everything that is now covered will be uncovered, and everything now hidden will be made clear. For this reason, whatever you have said in the dark will be heard in the daylight, and what you have whispered in hidden places will be proclaimed on the housetops.

'To you my friends I say: Do not be afraid of those who kill the body and after that can do no more. I will tell you whom to fear: fear him who, after he has killed, has the power to cast into hell. Yes, I tell you, fear him. Can you not buy five sparrows for two pennies? And yet not one is forgotten in God's sight. Why, every hair on your head has been counted. There is no need to be afraid: you are worth more than hundreds of sparrows. I tell you, if anyone openly declares himself for me in the presence of men, the Son of Man will declare himself for him in the presence of God's angels. But the man who disowns me in the presence of men will be disowned in the presence of God's angels. Everyone who says a word against the Son of Man will be forgiven, but he who blasphemes against the Holy Spirit will not be forgiven. When they take you before synagogues and magistrates and authorities, do not worry about how to defend yourselves or what to say, because when the time comes, the Holy Spirit will teach you what you must say.'

CHRIST THE LORD As Jesus makes his way to Jerusalem for his final showdown and the consummation of his mission, St Luke takes pains to show us the gradual but substantial increase in the number of people following him. In the previous chapter, St Luke wrote, "The crowds got even bigger…" (11:29) – implying that the already huge gathering was still growing. Now the massive audience is stadium-sized or bigger (the Greek term translated here as "thousands" literally means "tens of thousands"), so much so that "they were treading on one another."

With such a following, Jesus could have easily organized a revolt and usurped power from the corrupt Sanhedrin and maybe even from the Roman procurator (no more than two legions of soldiers, 12,000 men, were stationed throughout the entire province of Palestine). But his Kingdom is not of this world, and so he wields his Lordship in a different way. He continues to instruct his apostles privately, still training them for their future mission as leaders of the Church. And he continues teaching the crowds publicly, making sure that they learn how to set their sights on eternal life. This Lord's weapons are truth and love, not bullets, bombs, and bludgeons. We who are his ambassadors should take careful note.

CHRIST THE TEACHER The lesson Jesus gives his apostles at the beginning of this passage should instill a healthy fear in every Christian heart. He tells them to beware of the leaven of the Pharisees (with whom he has just had another verbal tussle) – i.e., their hypocrisy. The Pharisees were posers. They cared

655

only about the external appearance of religion and what people thought and said about them, not about the state of their souls, the virtue in their hearts, or the truth in their minds. That much is clear, but why warn the apostles about it– why warn those who believe in him? Because the apostles too were called by God to be leaders, to be the little bit of leaven that affects the whole loaf for good or ill. And the great temptation of anyone in a position of leadership, however small the position may be, is hypocrisy.

The power and esteem that goes with leadership can be intoxicating. It can lead to a reversal of values: instead of using one's influence strictly for the good of others, you begin to care more about simply staying in power. Then the truth – and the true good – inevitably takes a backseat to expediency. And the worst aspect of all is that it's almost irreversible. The Pharisees had completely lost touch with what was right, because they were completely fixated on what was useful to themselves. Every leader, including the leaders of Christ's Church, must be on their guard "against the leaven of the Pharisees," because in the end, the truth will come out.

CHRIST THE FRIEND Jesus' message to the vast crowd is different. He exhorts them to confidence and courage. Our confidence in the face of life's trials should be unlimited, because God cares more about us than we can possibly imagine, numbering even the hairs on our heads. If he keeps an eye even on the fifth sparrow that's thrown into the bag without charge when a person pays enough for four – a sparrow worth absolutely nothing – how could he not keep his watchful, loving eye on each one of us, for whom he went to such trouble in order to save? And our courage should be unflinching. If we are in friendship with God, and if we boldly bear witness to that friendship in word and deed, then what could we possibly have to fear? Will God's loyalty be outmatched by man's hostility? Even if at times it seems so, in the end God's fidelity will shine forth like the sun.

"Do not be afraid… There is no need to fear… Do not worry…" If anyone else were to repeat this comforting injunction so insistently, we would do well to be skeptical. But when the Lord is the one making the point, we don't have to hesitate at all. He is in charge of our lives. However much responsibility or influence we wield, we will always be at peace and never go astray if we always keep that simple fact in mind. Humble courage and unshakable confidence are par for the course when we're at the side of this Friend.

CHRIST IN MY LIFE You are so familiar to me. I go to Mass with humdrum regularity; I receive Holy Communion so mechanically; I open the Bible so casually. Remind me, Lord, of your majesty, your greatness, and your infinite attraction. I need to be reminded, not because I want to live my life based on fickle feelings, but because I am weak and self-absorbed and forget. Lord, increase my faith…

I could become a hypocrite, a Pharisee. It's true. How can I be on my guard? I never want to become so attached to my personal preferences that I completely drown out your voice. And yet, you warn me that I can. Lord, let's make a deal right now: I will always say yes to whatever you ask of me, and you promise never to abandon me…

There's something that seems too good to be true about the sparrows and the numbering of each hair on my head. And yet I know that the truth is even more magnificent, more marvelous! Your love is beyond my wildest imagining, and it's personal. You know my name, you think of me unceasingly, and you guide me untiringly. I believe in you, Lord; I love you…

QUESTIONS FOR SMALL GROUP DISCUSSION

1. What struck you most in this passage? What did you notice that you hadn't noticed before?

2. In what situations is it particularly hard to bear witness to Christ? How can we do better in those situations?

3. Why is it so hard to accept that Christ's love for each of us is total and unconditional? And if we accept it, why do we not always obey his will manifested through the Church and through our conscience?

4. If an agnostic friend of yours came up to you and asked how he could know that God loves him, how would you respond?

Cf. Catechism of the Catholic Church, 1805, 1808 on fortitude as a cardinal virtue; 712, 1303, 1831, 2846 on fortitude and courage as gifts of the Holy Spirit; 1864 on blasphemy against the Holy Spirit

194. NOT OF THIS WORLD (LK 12:13-21)

"All Christians, rich or poor, must keep their eye fixed on heaven, remembering that 'we have not here a lasting city, but we seek one that is to come' (Heb 13:14)."

- *Pope Pius XI*

Luke 12:13-21

A man in the crowd said to him, 'Master, tell my brother to give me a share of our inheritance.' 'My friend,' he replied – 'who appointed me your judge, or the arbitrator of your claims?' Then he said to them, 'Watch, and be on your guard against avarice of any kind, for a man's life is not made secure by what he owns, even when he has more than he needs.' Then he told them a parable: 'There was once a rich man who, having had a good harvest from his land, thought to himself, What am I to do? I have not enough room to store my crops. Then he said, This is what I will do: I will pull down my barns and build bigger ones, and store all my grain and my goods in them, and I will say to my soul: My soul, you have plenty of good things laid by for many years to come; take things easy, eat, drink, have a good time. But God said to him, Fool! This very night the demand will be made for your soul; and this hoard of yours, whose will it be then? So it is when a man stores up treasure for himself in place of making himself rich in the sight of God.'

CHRIST THE LORD At the end of his earthly life, Jesus will point out to Pontius Pilate, "My Kingdom is not of this world." He gives the same answer to this man's request for probate justice – he refuses to usurp the normal functions of earthly, human justice. Christ came not to take over the world, but to imbue it with a new spirit, to redeem it from within through grace. Jesus came to establish a Kingdom – a heavenly Kingdom, a Kingdom unlike any other kingdom of this world. This was his mission, and through the Church, it remains his mission.

By refusing to arbitrate this man's legal complaint, Jesus exemplifies the kind of mission-centered mindset that all of his disciples should share. Jesus refuses to be sidetracked. He knows exactly what his task in life is, and he dedicates himself to it with unwavering love and total focus. He directs all his words and actions to laying the foundations of his eternal Kingdom. The more closely we follow Christ and imitate his example, the more focused our own lives will be. We too are called to make the eternal Kingdom our first priority (cf. Matthew 6:33). If we do, the rest of our lives will fall into place; we will be able to navigate more surely through shoals and straits of our earthly pilgrimage. If we know clearly where we are headed (our heavenly destination), we will be better equipped to make decisions at every juncture along the way. Either we follow the Lord, or we wander aimlessly through an empty life.

CHRIST THE TEACHER Perhaps this inquirer was sincerely interested in justice, and his brother was being unfair, or perhaps he was just being greedy. In either case, Jesus makes the most of this encounter to teach one of the most basic (though not the most popular) Christian lessons: "Man's life is not made secure by what he owns" – our lives do not consist in having possessions.

Earlier in the Gospel, Jesus had put this lesson into action in order to resist the devil's temptation, when he averred, "Man does not live on bread alone" (Luke 4:4). We can almost hear a pleading tone in Christ's response to this man: "Watch, and be on your guard against avarice of all kind…" He knows how easily we tend to equate happiness with things and security with wealth. But he also knows, better than anyone, how wrong we are when we do. We are pilgrims on this earth, travelers. This life is a preparation for heaven, an opportunity to discover the beauty of God and opt for it. But our hearts will be ever restless here on earth until they rest completely in him (cf. St Augustine's *Confessions,* 1:1), which will never happen if we keep them too firmly attached to other things.

We need possessions and material things of all kinds in order to live, and it is certainly no sin to enjoy them, but if we strive after them to the exclusion or neglect of our relationship with God, the Church, and our neighbors, we will come to a tragic end, just like the rich man in the parable. The way to true fulfillment and stability is to make oneself "rich in the sight of God."

CHRIST THE FRIEND Jesus calls his interlocutor "My friend," and then proceeds to refuse his request. Was he just being polite by saying "friend"? Maybe. But maybe he was saying exactly what he meant: "I have come to be the true Friend and Savior of your soul, which doesn't always include managing your bank account for you. You can count on me to give you light, guidance, and strength, and to walk with you along life's path, but you still must walk."

Sometimes we doubt God's love because he doesn't remove all the obstacles along our way, but does a truly loving father take the easy way out and spoil his children? God seeks the true good of his children, and that often differs from what appears to us to be our immediate good. Jesus saw that this man was too attached to material things, and his refusal to resolve the difficulty helps spur the man to reorder his priorities. Christ is our Friend precisely because he never loses sight of our real goal, communion with God starting now and finishing in heaven, and because he never tires of leading us closer to it.

CHRIST IN MY LIFE I get sidetracked too easily. Sometimes I feel like the salvation of the whole world, the resolution of every conflict, the righting of every wrong is up to me. But it's not – it's up to you. And you give me a share of your work. Help me to be as serenely and energetically focused on my mission as you were on yours. Teach me to do your will…

What should I think about money, Lord? In this world, I can't do much without it. But whether I have it or not, it's constantly trying to take hold of me. Teach me to be responsible and smart. Save me from slavery to wealth and the things it can buy. I became your soldier on the day of my confirmation. Help me to persevere every day in fighting for the Kingdom that does not end...

How many times I have been like this man, who wanted you to resolve all his difficulties! But you will never do that. My difficulties are opportunities to get to know myself, to exercise virtue, and to grow in my discipleship. Others' difficulties are my opportunities to show them your goodness and build your Kingdom. Instead of getting discouraged in the face of difficulties, help me to turn to you who will always be there to show me the path and the way to follow it...

QUESTIONS FOR SMALL GROUP DISCUSSION

1. What struck you most in this passage? What did you notice that you hadn't noticed before?

2. What can we do to become more aware of our mission in life, and how can we stick to it with the same focus and dedication that Christ had?

3. What is popular culture's view of material wealth? (Try to think of some examples.) What would Christ say about it?

4. What are the most common difficulties we face in living out our faith? To what extent do they stem from objective hardship and to what extent do they stem from immature expectations?

Cf. Catechism of the Catholic Church, 2401-2418 on a Christian view of material possessions; 1854-1869 on the gravity and proliferation of sin

195. SETTING OUR HEARTS STRAIGHT (LK 12:22-31)

"Through love for man he created all these things, so that all those creatures should serve man, and that man in gratitude for so many gifts should return love for love to his Creator."

- St Alphonsus Liguori

Luke 12:22-31

Then he said to his disciples, 'That is why I am telling you not to worry about your life and what you are to eat, nor about your body and how you are to clothe it. For life means more than food, and the body more than clothing. Think of the ravens. They do not sow or reap; they have no storehouses and no barns; yet God feeds them. And how much more are you worth than the birds! Can any of you, for all his worrying, add a single cubit to his span of life? If the smallest things, therefore, are outside your control, why worry about the rest? Think of the flowers; they never have to spin or weave; yet, I assure you, not even Solomon in all his regalia was robed like one of these. Now if that is how God clothes the grass in the field which is there today and thrown into the furnace tomorrow, how much more will he look after you, you men of little faith! But you, you must not set your hearts on things to eat and things to drink; nor must you worry. It is the pagans of this world who set their hearts on all these things. Your Father well knows you need them. No; set your hearts on his kingdom, and these other things will be given you as well.'

CHRIST THE LORD Jesus is still speaking to the enormous crowds that have gathered around him as he makes his way to Jerusalem. In this part of his discourse, he wants to tell them about God. The people listening to him already believed in God, and they were even familiar with God's self-revelation in the Old Testament, but judging from Christ's words here, they had yet to grasp God's most important quality.

Our idea of God affects how we relate to God. That idea has been played upon by myriad influences, many of them bad. Unless we constantly purify and rectify our idea of God, we will simply never flourish the way he wants us to, because our relationship with him will never be able to mature. At this point in the Gospel, Jesus has proven his privileged relationship with the Father. And by his own actions and manner, he has made God's goodness visible, tangible to everyone who has seen him. But still the idea of a distant, harsh taskmaster lingers. So now Jesus complements his actions with these words. We have heard them many times, but we can never get enough of them. To follow the Lord as he wants to be followed, we have constantly to renew our vision of his utter goodness.

CHRIST THE TEACHER Jesus understands the Father as sheer, ever-present goodness. Christ himself, by the way he treated others and the way he carried out his mission, imaged the sheer part of that goodness – totally unconditional, a pure outpouring of generosity, that's what God is. But creation, often called "the first book of revelation" by the Church Fathers, illustrates the ever-present part. Jesus turns his listeners' gazes to the simple realities of nature – flowers, birds, growth – and unveils their real meaning: God is the one who upholds every atom of it. He does so effortlessly, wisely, generously, not looking for anything in return. The beauty and fruitfulness of nature – which are completely outside our control – flow directly from the power and love of God. If the Father is so attentive to the rest of creation, which will all pass away, how much more attentive will he be to his own children, who will live forever – us!

Having made the concept clear – God's goodness is sheer, endless, attentive, all-powerful, ever-present – Jesus then goes on to apply this point of doctrine to our lives. If God is upholding and guarding and guiding us in each moment, then why do we give in to worries and anxieties? Every worry, every anxiety about the material things of life – health, sickness, money, food, success, reputation – stems from a lack of trust in God. These things are all passing, and if we are faithful to our normal responsibilities, God will provide whatever we need for our life's mission. Instead of living as if the meaning of life were to be found in such things, Jesus invites us – in fact, he commands us – to live with our hearts "set on his Kingdom." Our first and sole concern in life, according to Christ, should be to know and follow him better, to discover, embrace, and fulfill his will. And if he commands this of us, then it must be possible. In this lies the entire spiritual life: training ourselves under the guidance and grace of the Holy Spirit to pay more and more attention to loving God and our neighbors and focusing less and less attention on our natural tantrums of self-absorption.

CHRIST THE FRIEND Jesus simplifies everything with this discourse. He brings the whole complicated, intimidating, impenetrable mystery of the human predicament into perfect focus. All we need to do on our journey through life is let God be God and follow where he leads. But Jesus is never satisfied with mere book lessons. His incarnation, the example he gives by his life, ministry, death, and resurrection, reveals what "setting your hearts on the Kingdom" looks like in practice. And just in case that wasn't enough, he decided to establish his Church so that his teaching could be kept intact even as historical and cultural conditions changed through time. But even that left him unsatisfied, so he stayed with us in the Tabernacle. With just a little bit of faith, then, we can make good use of all these gifts in order to delight our Savior and become what he has always hoped we would be.

CHRIST IN MY LIFE At times the beauty of your creation overwhelms me. It shows your majesty and your delicacy – mountains and mockingbirds. And you who made and uphold that immense menagerie, you care about me too. In fact, because your love is divine, you care about me as if I were the only one here. Help this truth sink in, Lord, so that I can live freely and love as you love…

What worries me most often and most intensely? And what do you think about that? It should be enough that I do what I can do and leave the rest to you. Aren't my worries, sometimes at least, a subtle type of self-indulgence? Jesus, I don't understand myself. I put myself at your service. Lord Jesus, I believe that you are the Lord of life and history – and of my life and history…

How can I love you more than simply trusting in you at all times? Is that not the best expression of my love for you? Why do I still seek to love you by my achievements when I can't even add an inch to my height or a minute to my life? I want to love you, and I want to trust you. Your love and goodness have no end. Jesus, I trust in you…

QUESTIONS FOR SMALL GROUP DISCUSSION

1. What struck you most in this passage? What did you notice that you hadn't noticed before?

2. Why do we tend to worry about things we have no control over?

3. How can we learn to benefit more from "the first book of God's revelation," his creation?

4. If God is our Father who takes care of all our needs, why are there so many natural disasters and privations in the world (starvation, war, drought…)? How could he possibly be loving us even in and through these?

Cf. Catechism of the Catholic Church, #s 313-314 and 322 on God's providence, 396-401 on the role of trust in original sin, 222-231 on the implications of having "faith in one God," 2544-2550 on the secret to happiness.

196. TRUE TREASURE (LK 12:32-48)

"To become what the martyrs, the apostles, what even Christ himself was, means im-mense labor – but what a reward!"

- St Jerome

Luke 12:32-48

'There is no need to be afraid, little flock, for it has pleased your Father to give you the kingdom. Sell your possessions and give alms. Get yourselves purses that do not wear out, treasure that will not fail you, in heaven where no thief can reach it and no moth destroy it. For where your treasure is, there will your heart be also. See that you are dressed for action and have your lamps lit. Be like men waiting for their master to return from the wedding feast, ready to open the door as soon as he comes and knocks. Happy those servants whom the master finds awake when he comes. I tell you solemnly, he will put on an apron, sit them down at table and wait on them. It may be in the second watch he comes, or in the third, but happy those servants if he finds them ready. You may be quite sure of this, that if the household-er had known at what hour the burglar would come, he would not have let anyone break through the wall of his house. You too must stand ready, because the Son of Man is coming at an hour you do not expect.'

Peter said, 'Lord, do you mean this parable for us, or for everyone?' The Lord replied, 'What sort of steward, then, is faithful and wise enough for the master to place him over his household to give them their allowance of food at the proper time? Happy that servant if his master's arrival finds him at this employment. I tell you truly, he will place him over everything he owns. But as for the servant who says to himself, My master is taking his time coming, and sets about beating the menservants and the maids, and eating and drinking and getting drunk, his master will come on a day he does not expect and at an hour he does not know. The master will cut him off and send him to the same fate as the unfaithful. The servant who knows what his master wants, but has not even started to carry out those wishes, will receive very many strokes of the lash. The one who did not know, but deserves to be beaten for what he has done, will receive fewer strokes. When a man has had a great deal given him, a great deal will be demanded of him; when a man has had a great deal given him on trust, even more will be expected of him.'

CHRIST THE LORD In these parables, Christ portrays himself as the master of the house, his apostles as the stewards (the head servants), and his other disciples as the servants. Even when the master is absent (as during the age of the Church, when Christ delegates his authority to the successors of his apostles), he is still in charge, and he expects his servants to be faithful. He wants to return to his estate and see them working hard, full of joy and enthusiasm as they strive not only to keep the estate going, but to make it thrive. He didn't have to go away. He could have stayed and taken care of things himself, but he wanted to share his responsibility with us. He wants us to be his responsible followers, freely and energetically putting our talents at the service of something that will last forever.

Although he gives us real responsibility as his coworkers, he still remains the Lord. Christ's Kingdom is truly a Kingdom, with an authoritative King – not an elected president. His Church is the seed of this Kingdom in history, and so it too is hierarchical, with real authority. When we call ourselves Christians, we acknowledge ourselves as followers of Christ, trusting that he knows how and where to lead.

We can easily forget that being entrusted with work in Christ's Kingdom is a blessing and a grace. As in the case of the first Apostles, the mission of building up the Church gives our ordinary, earthly lives an extraordinary, heavenly dimension. Being a servant in the Kingdom of Christ is such a precious gift that the Queen of Heaven herself glories in being called "the handmaid of the Lord" (Luke 1:38).

CHRIST THE TEACHER This part of Jesus' discourse balances out what he said a few verses earlier about not worrying. He instructed his listeners not to fret about worldly concerns, but lest they take that as an excuse for irresponsible and hedonistic living, he now shows the other side of the coin.

"You too must stand ready," is the first lesson of this passage. You can't cram for life's final exam. If we want to live in communion with God forever, we need to start cultivating that friendship now, making it our first priority. After all, what could be more important than our friendship with God? The good things of this earthly life, its pleasures, challenges, and occupations, will come to an end. To live as if they won't, therefore, is foolish. Christ wants to make sure we don't act like fools.

"When a man has had a great deal given him, a great deal will be demanded of him; when a man has had a great deal given him on trust, even more will be expected of him." Each human life has a task, a mission to know, love, and serve God in a particular way. Our lives will take on their true meaning to the extent that we carry out that task and fulfill that mission – to the extent that our "treasure" (what we value and desire) consists of that task and mission. We are responsible for making good use of the gifts we have received from God (our lives, our talents, our education) in order to accomplish our mission. Christ's view of the universe doesn't include reincarnation – a concept which takes away all personal responsibility, since everyone is just recycled over and over again until they have no choice but to hit on the right combination of circumstances and decisions. The Christian view involves responsibility, and this enables us to love, because love means freely choosing to put oneself and one's talents at the service of another's good. That's what God created us for, and that's how we image God. If, on the other hand, we squander our time, talents, and gifts in self-indulgence and egoism, we will miss out on what Christ wants to give us.

CHRIST THE FRIEND "There is no need to be afraid, little flock…." Jesus came to bring us back into communion with God, to plug us in to heaven, so that even now we can begin to taste the joy and peace that will never end. But he doesn't force us to receive this gift of the Kingdom that it has pleased the Father to give us. We need to let go of the false idols that can't give us the happiness we seek ("sell your possessions and give alms") and realign our hearts so that they lean more consistently towards God. If we store up our hopes (our "treasure") in the heart of Christ, we will certainly not be disappointed; if we store them up anywhere else, we certainly will.

Jesus: In my eyes, the Church is still a little flock, my little flock. Though it includes millions of members throughout the world, and millions more if you include past and future centuries, my heart is big enough to love each one of you personally, intimately. You are my little flock. You have nothing to fear. I am your shepherd, and I am leading you to the grassy pastures and cool, refreshing streams around my Father's house.

CHRIST IN MY LIFE Bless the Pope, Lord, and all the bishops and priests. Calm the winds of infidelity and disobedience and pour out the Spirit of wisdom and piety on your Church. I want to be faithful to you and to the friendship you offer me, and I know that means being faithful to your Church. Make me a builder of your Kingdom, Lord, not a nitpicker and complainer…

You have given me a mission in life, and you have given me the freedom to put all my talents and gifts at the service of fulfilling that mission. I am not a squirrel, which isn't free to abandon its little mission. You have given me your greatest gift, the capacity to love. Lord Jesus, with the love of your heart, inflame my heart…

What is holding me back from being all that you created me to be? Is it an unrestrained selfish desire, maybe one I don't even recognize? Is it a self-indulgent relationship? Is it a continuous refusal to give you something you are asking me? Shed light into my heart and conscience, Lord, so that I don't deceive myself and squander this wonderful life you have given me…

QUESTIONS FOR SMALL GROUP DISCUSSION

1. What struck me most in this passage? What did I notice that I hadn't noticed before?

2. Where does popular culture advise us to "store up our treasure"?

3. Why do you think the "master of the house" goes away for a while, leaving his household in charge of the stewards and servants?

4. What is the "great deal" that we have been given, and how can we insure that it yields what the Giver is expecting?

Cf. Catechism of the Catholic Church, 1038-1050 on the Last Judgment and the New Heaven and the New Earth; 1020-1022 on death and the particular judgment; 1023-1037 on heaven, hell, and purgatory

197. READING THE SIGNS (LK 12:49-59)

"Very many out there fail to become Christians simply because there is nobody available to make them Christian."

- St Francis Xavier

Luke 12:49-59

'I have come to bring fire to the earth, and how I wish it were blazing already! There is a baptism I must still receive, and how great is my distress till it is over! Do you suppose that I am here to bring peace on earth? No, I tell you, but rather division. For from now on a household of five will be divided: three against two and two against three; the father divided against the son, son against father, mother against daughter, daughter against mother, mother-in-law against daughter-in-law, daughter-in-law against mother-in-law.' He said again to the crowds, 'When you see a cloud looming up in the west you say at once that rain is coming, and so it does. And when the wind is from the south you say it will be hot, and it is. Hypocrites! You know how to interpret the face of the earth and the sky. How is it you do not know how to interpret these times? Why not judge for yourselves what is right? For example: when you go to court with your opponent, try to settle with him on the way, or he may drag you before the judge and the judge hand you over to the bailiff and the bailiff have you thrown into prison. I tell you, you will not get out till you have paid the very last penny.'

CHRIST THE LORD From the vantage point of twenty centuries of the Church's growth, it is easy for us to understand what Christ meant when he said he came "to set the earth on fire." He was speaking of the fire of Christian charity that will bring souls back into communion with God and gradually build up the civilization of justice and love. But imagine the reaction of the apostles and the other disciples – they must have been perplexed, perhaps frightened, maybe energized by such a claim. Though the fire has spread since it first appeared, the whole earth has certainly not yet been set ablaze. So the same zeal to extend his Kingdom that animated him then still animates him now, and if we truly love our Lord, it will burn in our hearts too.

We find it easy to criticize the people of Christ's day for not recognizing more readily the signs of God's action – John the Baptist's preaching, Christ's own ministry. Yet the same Christ is unceasingly at work in our little worlds each day, and we still continue to put off those decisions that will give his grace free rein in our lives. We truly are like that man walking to court with his opponent, because we are journeying through the world to heaven, where we will discover, to our dismay, all the opportunities for doing good that we casually passed by, overly preoccupied as we were with the sports page, the latest fashion trends, the stock index, and any number of other worthy but secondary realities. If we think it's easy to spot the blindness of Christ's contemporaries, just imagine what the saints in heaven think of us as we amble through life satisfied with spiritual mediocrity.

CHRIST THE TEACHER Nothing is more important than our friendship with Christ. When he calls us, when he makes his will known, not even the closest natural ties (like those we have with our mother and father) are worthy constrainers. The peace that comes with following Christ is the peace of a heart in communion with God and of a conscience cleansed of all self-deprecation. If we expect some other, exterior peace – a smooth ride through life, for instance – we are in for a shock. The demands of Christ are so absolute that they will necessarily bring us into conflict with the demands of the fallen world, of other people, and even of our own sin-struck nature. This conflict of interests is built into the heart of Christianity; it appears on the cross itself, which is an intersection of the vertical and the horizontal, the heavenly and the earthly, God's will and my will. Of course, if we are faithful to him, he will be faithful to us, and what we thought we had lost for his sake we will receive back a hundredfold.

CHRIST THE FRIEND The word "baptize" comes from the Greek word for dip or submerge (it also has other uses, such as to wash), and it was often used to refer to a tribulation or a trial through which one had to pass. Christ's choice of the term shows us what he felt about his journey to Calvary and the cross – it was not going to be easy. The thought of it was always with him: "… how great is my distress till it is over…" Although we will never be able fully to understand the depth of suffering that our Lord has endured for our sake, we can acknowledge the fact that he has endured it, and welcome the love this fact implies.

Yet, his self-sacrifice on our behalf is more than a sign of his love, and more than an example to follow. In a mysterious way, his fidelity actually becomes our fidelity. Because he has been our faithful Friend, we can be his faithful friend. The grace we receive through the sacraments nourishes our souls with Christ's very life. He is faithful, and in him we can be faithful too.

CHRIST IN MY LIFE Why is it so hard for me to read the "signs of the times" in my own life? I know they are there, and I know you are always wanting to guide me and teach me and show me the way to go. I believe that. So why don't I see them more clearly? Maybe I'm looking for the wrong kind of signs. Teach me, Lord, to be simple, like a child, satisfied with knowing your will for me each moment…

It's hard for me to disregard what others think and say of me. I still hope for the kind of peace that I mistakenly think will satisfy me – relief from all opposition, discomfort, and suffering. Fill my heart so full of love for you, Lord, that I jump at every chance to show that love, thinking less and less of my comfort zone, and more and more of your Kingdom…

You came to earth for me. You left heaven behind and worked and toiled and sweat for thirty years, just so you could be close to me. And then, to make sure I would never doubt your unconditional love for me, you freely accepted the indescribable suffering of Good Friday. Thank you, Lord. I believe in you. Jesus, I trust in you…

QUESTIONS FOR SMALL GROUP DISCUSSION

1. What struck you most in this passage? What did you notice that you hadn't noticed before?

2. What can we do to more deeply share Christ's zeal for the salvation of souls and the extension of his Kingdom?

3. What "divisions" have you experienced as a result of following Christ? What would be the hardest thing for you to give up in order to remain faithful to him?

4. Why do you think Christ spoke so openly about his "wish" and his "distress"? Why did St Luke consider it important enough to include in his Gospel?

Cf. Catechism of the Catholic Church, 456-460 on the mission of Jesus; 606-618 on the "baptism" of Jesus

THE GOSPEL OF LUKE CHAPTER 13

"Wake up, O man – it was for you that God was made man! Awake, O sleeper, and arise from the dead, and Christ shall give you light. For you, I say, was God made man. Eternal death would have awaited you had he not been born in time. Never would you be freed from you sinful flesh, had he not taken to himself the likeness of sinful flesh. Everlasting would be your misery, had he not performed this act of mercy. You would not have come to life again, had he not come to die your death. You would have broken down, had he not come to help you. You would have perished, had he not come. Let us joyfully celebrate the coming of our salvation and redemption."

- St Augustine

198. THE MEANING OF DISASTER (LK 13:1-9)

"What dignity, what security to leave this life with joy, triumphant over trials and tortures, one moment to close those eyes with which we used to gaze on men and one the world, the next to open them to see God and Christ!"

- St Cyprian

Luke 13:1-9

It was just about this time that some people arrived and told him about the Galileans whose blood Pilate had mingled with that of their sacrifices. At this he said to them, 'Do you suppose these Galileans who suffered like that were greater sinners than any other Galileans? They were not, I tell you. No; but unless you repent you will all perish as they did. Or those eighteen on whom the tower at Siloam fell and killed them? Do you suppose that they were more guilty than all the other people living in Jerusalem? They were not, I tell you. No; but unless you repent you will all perish as they did.' He told this parable: 'A man had a fig tree planted in his vineyard, and he came looking for fruit on it but found none. He said to the man who looked after the vineyard, Look here, for three years now I have been coming to look for fruit on this fig tree and finding none. Cut it down: why should it be taking up the ground? Sir, the man replied leave it one more year and give me time to dig round it and manure it: it may bear fruit next year; if not, then you can cut it down.'

CHRIST THE LORD Christ spoke with authority not only about heavenly things, but also about the true meaning of earthly events. His Lordship, after all, is universal. Thus he gives the definitive interpretation of these two tragic events, and he points out the real meaning behind them. When Christ decided to exercise his Lordship through the ministry of his Church, he delegated the authority to continue announcing the meaning behind earthly events. No voice in the world speaks so frequently and directly about the critical issues of every age as the Magisterium of the Catholic Church. Just as Jesus himself was "the light of the world" when he walked the dusty roads of Palestine, so through his Church he remains a beacon of truth shining brightly amid the dark fog of the world's confusion.

Unfortunately, however, not everyone heeded his voice back then, and not everyone heeds his voice today. The world is always seeking the fruits of justice, peace, and prosperity. Individuals are always seeking happiness. Without digging into human hearts and fertilizing them with the truth about who we are and what we were created for, however, society will be barren of these most valuable fruits. Imagine how different the world community would be if everyone simply followed the Ten Commandments. The global culture would flourish in every way. Our Lord knows the way to fulfillment and fruitfulness. As his disciples, we know it too, and we should strive to make it known.

CHRIST THE TEACHER An influential school of Jewish thought at the time of Christ drew a direct line of causality from people's sufferings back to their personal sins. The more someone sinned, supposedly, the more they suffered. By this logic, the Galileans who were killed by Pilate's soldiers must have deserved it because of their sins. (Scholars are not in agreement about the incident being referred to. Many think, however, that it was Pilate's violent suppression of a demonstration in Jerusalem. Demonstrators had gathered in the Temple area to protest Pilate's use of Temple money to construct new aqueducts. Pilate then sent armed soldiers among them in disguise. At a signal, the soldiers dispersed the mob with clubs, killing many more than Pilate had anticipated.) Likewise, those who were killed in the construction accident in Siloam (some scholars think the tower being constructed was a part of those same aqueducts), so it was thought, were paying the penalty for their sins.

The Church has often pointed out, however, that personal suffering is not necessarily a result of personal sin (if it were, how could we explain Christ's Passion and death?), and that suffering is often a sign of God's blessing ("Those whom I love, I reprove and chastise" – Revelation 3:19). But Christ's lesson in the passage stands: everyone who refuses to repent (the barren fig tree symbolizes someone who lacks the fruits of repentance) will stay separated from God, and if they die in such a state of alienation (and death can come at any time), they will continue in it for all eternity. Even if the consequences of our actions do not always make themselves completely felt in this life, they will do so eventually – both for good and for ill; earthly tragedies should remind us of the passing nature and relative meaning of earthly life. It is a hard truth, but one that the Church wants us to consider deeply, especially during the penitential season of Lent, when this passage is read in the Sunday liturgy.

CHRIST THE FRIEND God is not indifferent to our lives. He wants them to bear fruit; he wants us to live fully. As our Creator, he has a right to expect us to live as he intended us to, just as the owner of the orchard has a right to expect his fig tree to grow figs. And yet, he doesn't demand his rights. Rather, he sends his Son to "cultivate the ground" of our hearts, to fertilize it with his love, his doctrine, and his sacraments. He does everything he possibly can to convince us to live in friendship with God, a friendship that will yield the lasting fruits of meaning and happiness. In the end, however, he leaves the decision up to us. After all, a forced friendship is no friendship at all.

CHRIST IN MY LIFE Thank you for making your voice resound even into my lifetime through the teachings of your Church. You are present in your ministers, your liturgy, and your Word. You want to point out to me what things mean. You want me to adjust my choices and priorities to the true scale of values. Thank you for thinking of me and staying with me…

No one likes to talk about Judgment Day. But you spoke often about it, and you inspired the Gospel writers to record what you said. I love this world, with all its wonder and beauty, but it is passing away. The struggles and sufferings that you permit should remind me of that. Help me to think as you think and see all things as you see them…

Thank you for your patience. You never give up on me; you keep working with me so I will bear the fruit you created me to bear. Teach me to do the same with those around me. They too are called to bear eternal fruit. How can I fertilize and trim and tend them, how can I help them discover and follow your will for their lives? Teach me to do your will…

QUESTIONS FOR SMALL GROUP DISCUSSION

1. What struck you most in this passage? What did you notice that you hadn't noticed before?

2. God instituted the sacrament of confession because he knew that we would need to repent again and again. How can we better take advantage of this sacrament?

3. How can we pay more attention to the Church's voice in national and world affairs?

4. What do you think Christ would say if someone were to ask him about today's world crises? What do you say when you are asked about them?

Cf. Catechism of the Catholic Church, 214, 218-221 on God's mercy; 888-892 on the teaching office of the Church (the Magisterium); 1033-1037 on the consequences of not repenting from sin

199. THE LORD'S DAY, THE LORD'S WAY (LK 13:10-21)

"This divine heart is an ocean full of all good things wherein poor souls can cast all their needs; it is an ocean full of joy to drown all our sadness, an ocean of humility to overwhelm our folly, an ocean of mercy for those in distress, an ocean of love in which to submerge our poverty."

- St Margaret Mary Alocoque

Luke 13:10-21

One sabbath day he was teaching in one of the synagogues, and a woman was there who for eighteen years had been possessed by a spirit that left her enfeebled; she was bent double and quite unable to stand upright. When Jesus saw her he called her over and said, 'Woman, you are rid of your infirmity,' and he laid his hands on her. And at once she straightened up, and she glorified God. But the synagogue official was indignant because Jesus had healed on the sabbath, and he addressed the people present. 'There are six days' he said 'when work is to be done. Come and be healed on one of those days and not on the sabbath.' But the Lord answered him. 'Hypocrites!' he said 'Is there one of you who does not untie his ox or his donkey from the manger on the sabbath and take it out for watering? And this woman, a daughter of Abraham whom Satan has held bound these eighteen years – was it not right to untie her bonds on the sabbath day?' When he said this, all his adversaries were covered with confusion, and all the people were overjoyed at all the wonders he worked. He went on to say, 'What is the kingdom of God like? What shall I compare it with? It is like a mustard seed which a man took and threw into his garden: it grew and became a tree, and the birds of the air sheltered in its branches.' Another thing he said, 'What shall I compare the kingdom of God with? It is like the yeast a woman took and mixed in with three measures of flour till it was leavened all through.'

CHRIST THE LORD The Sabbath is the Lord's Day. In the Old Covenant, it echoed the seventh day of Creation, the day when God's work was finished. As such, it also pointed towards the fulfillment of God's promise to lead Israel into a future age of prosperity, freeing them from toil and suffering. In Jesus that promise is fulfilled. He is the Lord; wherever he is, the Lord's Day is too. His healing of this crippled woman exemplifies this. On the Sabbath, he takes away her burden and restores her to communion with God. The opposition this miracle stirs up shows once again that Jesus' adversaries have lost their perspective. To them, the Sabbath was an end in itself, and so the complicated rules about what work could be performed on the Sabbath were followed rigidly. They had forgotten the purpose of the Lord's Day: to renew Israel's faith and trust in God, and to refresh their hope in the deliverance he promised them.

When we find ourselves spouting criticism and self-righteous complaints, like the synagogue official, it may be that we too have lost our perspective. In Christ's Kingdom, the only rule that matters is the rule of love, the rule of self-giving. Everything else exists for the sake of enabling us to love God and our neighbor better and better, and thus following more closely the Lord.

CHRIST THE TEACHER Besides reminding the crowd and the leaders about the true meaning of the Old Covenant's Sabbath (and therefore, by association, of the whole body of Old Covenant law), Jesus also teaches them about the New Covenant. He likens it to a mustard seed and a bit of yeast. The comparisons emphasize the contrast between small beginnings and big results. It aptly follows up his lesson about the Sabbath.

The code of conduct that through the centuries Israel had extrapolated from the

Law of Moses was big, complex, and highly visible – and the Sabbath regulations formed an important part of it. Those who followed it most closely, the Pharisees, were almost entirely focused on its flamboyant visibility. They made sure that all their religious practices were seen and appreciated. Jesus advocates a different type of religiosity. He focuses on the interior attitude of self-forgetful love for God and neighbor. The Christian way is the way of the heart. But who can see the heart? No one – only oneself and God. This law of love and self-giving, therefore, is like the mustard seed and the leaven: barely perceptible to anyone at the beginning, but magnificent when it matures.

The parables remind us of another image Jesus used when talking about the law of his Kingdom: "Unless a wheat grain falls on the ground and dies, it remains only a single grain; but if it dies, it yields a rich harvest" (John 12:24). The Pharisees cared about their appearances, and their lives were barren. Christians should care about the heart, even if it means self-mastery and abnegation. If they do, their lives will flourish.

CHRIST THE FRIEND Friends go beyond the narrow call of duty; they take the initiative to help and please their friends. Jesus did this with the crippled woman. St Luke makes no mention of anyone asking Jesus for a cure. Jesus simply sees the woman, knows how long she has suffered, and can't hold himself back from showing her the power and the love of God. He reaches out to her as soon as he becomes aware of her need. After eighteen years of walking bowed, looking only at the ground, she can now look once again to the heavens.

He did the same thing with us. When Adam and Eve sinned, they didn't go looking for God so they could set things straight; it was God who came looking for them, to save them. Ever since, it has been God who constantly invites and guides us. Every good thing is a gift from him, a message written by his love. If he had limited himself to his strict duty, we would never have been created in the first place – he had no need or obligation to make the universe – and we would certainly never have been given the hope of redemption (we were the ones who rebelled, not him). When Christ becomes man, our centuries of crippled, earthly existence are over, and we can rise once again to our heavenly vocation.

We can evaluate the status of our friendship with Christ by this standard. The closer we are to him, the more we will treat others the way he has treated us – taking the initiative to come to their aid.

CHRIST IN MY LIFE I am glad I exist. I am glad you created me and invited me to become a citizen of your Kingdom. Thank you, Lord. You have already taken away so many of my burdens – the guilt of my sins, the weight of ignorance and anxiety, the insecurity of wondering what life is all about. I believe in you, Lord, and I am looking forward to the day when I will see you face to face…

Sometimes I get too caught up in the nonessentials – sometimes they look flashier than the essentials. But I want to stay focused, Lord. I want to love as you love, and to build your Kingdom in my heart and in those around me. To love you, to love my neighbor, to love by forgetting myself – this is the mustard seed; plant it firmly in my heart…

It is hard for me to step out of my comfort zone for the sake of my neighbor, even in little things. I want to please you; feed the good desires in my heart. I need you to strengthen me, to push me, to fire my heart with your love. With the zeal of your heart, set my heart on fire…

QUESTIONS FOR SMALL GROUP DISCUSSION

1. What struck you most in this passage? What did you notice that you hadn't noticed before?

2. Why do you think the reaction of the people to this miracle was so different than the reaction of Jesus' adversaries? After all, everybody saw the same thing….

3. What can we do to celebrate the Lord's Day better, more the way Jesus wants us to?

4. What are some commonly overlooked opportunities to live out the law of Christian charity in our life-situations?

Cf. Catechism of the Catholic Church, 577-582 on Jesus and the Law; 2816-2821 on the coming of the Kingdom; 1694 and 2013 on the call to charity; 1844 and 1973 on charity as the perfection of Christian life

200. HEAVENLY FEAST OR HELLISH ISOLATION (LK 13:22-35)

"No misfortune should distract us from this happiness and deep joy; for if anyone is anxious to reach a destination, the roughness of the road will not make him change his mind."

- Pope St Gregory the Great

Luke 13:22-35

Through towns and villages he went teaching, making his way to Jerusalem. Someone said to him, 'Sir, will there be only a few saved?' He said to them, 'Try your best to enter by the narrow door, because, I tell you, many will try to enter and will not succeed. Once the master of the house has got up and locked the door, you may find yourself knocking on the door, saying, Lord, open to us, but he will answer, I do not know where you come from. Then you will find yourself saying, We once ate and drank in your company; you taught in our streets, but he will reply, I do not know where you come from. Away from me, all you wicked men! Then there will be weeping and grinding of teeth, when you see Abraham and Isaac and Jacob and all the prophets in the kingdom of God, and yourselves turned outside. And men from east and west, from north and south, will come to take their places at the feast in the kingdom of God. Yes, there are those now last who will be first, and those now first who will be last.'

Just at this time some Pharisees came up. 'Go away,' they said. 'Leave this place, because Herod means to kill you.' He replied, 'You may go and give that fox this message: Learn that today and tomorrow I cast out devils and on the third day attain my end. But for today and tomorrow and the next day I must go on, since it would not be right for a prophet to die outside Jerusalem. Jerusalem, Jerusalem, you that kill the prophets and stone those who are sent to you! How often have I longed to gather your children, as a hen gathers her brood under her wings, and you refused! So be it! Your house will be left to you. Yes, I promise you, you shall not see me till the time comes when you say: Blessings on him who comes in the name of the Lord!'

CHRIST THE LORD   Christ alone is the Lord of life and history. There is only one eternal banquet, only one eternal Kingdom, and it is his. He came to earth in order to tell us about it, and to blaze a trail that would lead us to it. And he doesn't want to leave anyone out of it – which is why he speaks so vehemently about its importance in passages like this – but neither will he force us into it. He is the Lord, and he invites us to follow him, but he will respect our response to his invitation. This is why we should respond with great care.

Christ himself is the way to salvation and fulfillment. Salvation comes from actually following him, from striving to know him better and from obeying his teaching. This is the narrow door, because he is demanding. It is possible to be labeled a Christian on the outside without really making an effort to follow the Christian way in our hearts, or to go to Church and be seen frequently at the parish without ever really entering into a committed, life-changing, personal relationship with Christ. It may be comfortable for awhile, but in the end only those who have followed the Lord will be welcomed to the banquet.

CHRIST THE TEACHER   This innocent question, "Will only a few people be saved?" afforded Christ the perfect opportunity to tell everyone, "Relax – all you have to do is be a good guy, more or less, and you'll get to heaven." But he didn't. He told us to "try your best" to enter into his Kingdom, because many will try to enter and will not succeed." Certainly, the Church teaches that without the help of divine grace no one can live in eternal friendship with God, but Jesus is emphasizing here that we each must do our part as well. If we settle for a comfortable, self-satisfying Christianity, we may be deceiving ourselves – instead of building up God's Kingdom, we may in fact be erecting an idolatrous house of cards. The spiritual life is a battle, as the Church never tires of telling us, and we are not to take victory for granted. The entrance door is "narrow," and the Lord will refuse entry altogether to "wicked men" – even those who thought they were good. Bottom line: Salvation matters, and it's not just a consolation prize.

CHRIST THE FRIEND Because Christ is a true friend, he sees the heart. Many times those who seem great or holy by the world's standards are filled with selfishness and arrogance, while those whom the world despises are filled with humility and wisdom. But Jesus will correct this injustice: "There are those now last who will be first, and those now first who will be last." Christ sees each of us as we truly are, and warns us not to trust in appearances – neither our own appearance of righteousness, nor others' appearance of dishonor. If we trust only in Christ, in his goodness and love, we will learn to see as he sees, and when judgment day comes, we won't have to worry about any surprises.

But Jesus knows that many will indeed reject him, including the leaders of Jerusalem who fear losing their privilege and power. His expression of how much their rejection pains him shows his yearning for our friendship. We can picture him looking towards Jerusalem, the earthly center of God's saving action for so many centuries, soon to become the stage of the Atonement itself (Christ's passion and resurrection). Then a sigh of yearning escapes him, "Jerusalem, Jerusalem… How often I have longed…!" When we look at our own lives and our often tepid or even rebellious responses to God's invitations, we can see him sighing in the same way over us. Just as a hen cannot help gathering her brood – it's built into the very fiber of her being – so God cannot help desiring our companionship. But if we refuse it, we too will be left on our own, and just as the unwelcoming earthly Jerusalem will soon be completely destroyed, so those without God will lose even the little happiness they think they have – not because God shut the door, but because they chose not to go through it when they could.

CHRIST IN MY LIFE I want to be with you for your eternal banquet, and I know you want me to be there too. You want everyone to be there! What more can I do to bring others into your friendship? What can I do to deepen my friendship with you? Teach me to try my best to enter the narrow door. In the end, nothing else matters…

Why do people think and talk so little about what is sure to happen to us all, death and judgment? Why do people think it's a sign of weakness to look forward to heaven and to live on earth in such as way as to prepare for heaven? I know that earth is not heaven, and I know I need you to lead me to the fulfillment I long for. Never let me be separated from you, Lord…

It should bother me more that so many people reject you. Lord, my heart is still contracted and selfish. Pour your Spirit into my soul and fill me with your love. Real love, deep love, self-forgetting love – that's what you lived, that's what you taught, that's what I was made for. With the love of your heart, inflame my heart…

QUESTIONS FOR SMALL GROUP DISCUSSION

1. What struck you most in this passage? What did you notice that you hadn't noticed before?

2. The tone of this discourse seems to be "negative." How do you think it sounded when Christ himself was giving it?

3. Why do you suppose Christ spoke so "threateningly" about salvation, when God is supposed to be "merciful"?

4. What can we do to make sure everyone around us gets to heaven? What will we have to sacrifice in order to do that?

Cf. Catechism of the Catholic Church, 668-679 on the end of history and Christ's final judgment; 1023-1037 on heaven, hell, and purgatory; 1021-22 and 1038-41 on the particular and universal judgment

THE GOSPEL OF LUKE CHAPTER 14

"Lord, who can grasp all the wealth of just one of your words? What we understand is much less than what we leave behind, like thirsty people who drink from a fountain. For your word, Lord, has many shades of meaning just as those who study it have many different points of view. The Lord has colored his words with many hues so that each person who studies it can see in it what he loves. He has hidden many treasures in his word so that each of us is enriched as we meditate on it. The word of God is a tree of life that from all its parts offers you fruits that are blessed. It is like that rock opened in the desert that from all its parts gave forth a spiritual drink… The thirsty man rejoices when he drinks and he is not downcast because he cannot empty the fountain. Rather let the fountain quench your thirst than have your thirst quench the fountain. Because if your thirst is quenched and the fountain is not exhausted you car

drink from it again whenever you are thirsty."

- St Ephraem

201. AIMING REALLY HIGH (LK 14:1-14)

Only when we meet the living God in Christ do we know what life is. We are not some casual and meaningless product of evolution. Each of us is the result of a thought of God. Each of us is willed, each of us is loved, each of us is necessary."

- Pope Benedict XVI

Luke 14:1-14

Now on a sabbath day he had gone for a meal to the house of one of the leading Pharisees; and they watched him closely. There in front of him was a man with dropsy, and Jesus addressed the lawyers and Pharisees. 'Is it against the law,' he asked, 'to cure a man on the sabbath, or not?' But they remained silent, so he took the man and cured him and sent him away. Then he said to them, 'Which of you here, if his son falls into a well, or his ox, will not pull him out on a sabbath day without hesitation?' And to this they could find no answer.

He then told the guests a parable, because he had noticed how they picked the places of honour. He said this, 'When someone invites you to a wedding feast, do not take your seat in the place of honour. A more distinguished person than you may have been invited, and the person who invited you both may come and say, Give up your place to this man. And then, to your embarrassment, you would have to go and take the lowest place. No; when you are a guest, make your way to the lowest place and sit there, so that, when your host comes, he may say, My friend, move up higher. In that way, everyone with you at the table will see you honoured. For everyone who exalts himself will be humbled, and the man who humbles himself will be exalted.' Then he said to his host, 'When you give a lunch or a dinner, do not ask your friends, brothers, relations or rich neighbours, for fear they repay your courtesy by inviting you in return. No; when you have a party, invite the poor, the crippled, the lame, the blind; that they cannot pay you back means that you are fortunate, because repayment will be made to you when the virtuous rise again.'

CHRIST THE LORD Jesus addresses himself to the leading Pharisees (Israel's religious and intellectual elite) and other high-class personnel as their superior. No earthly power can intimidate him; nothing can deter him from announcing the truths of the Kingdom. That he was even invited in the first place shows that he was as comfortable interacting with Palestine's leaders as he was tending to their poor and lame. That he seized the opportunity of the invitation to sow the seeds of the gospel shows that the glitz of power, wealth, and fame held no sway over his heart. Such is our Lord; so he would have his followers be.

Viewed in light of Christ's passion, the advice he gives these Pharisees takes on a deeper meaning. He followed this advice – radically. He took the lowest place here on earth, that of a criminal. He took on the most humiliating form of death, that of crucifixion. He was stripped of every honor, even the honor of his reputation, which was defamed and dragged through the mire by his enemies' lies and corruption. And yet, because he humbled himself, the Lord was glorified – this is the law of his Kingdom.

CHRIST THE TEACHER At first glance, the lessons of this passage seem simple and straightforward; at second glance, they are shocking. On the surface, they advocate humility and generosity: don't assume your importance by sitting in the seat of honor on your own initiative; don't give your hospitality just to people who can pay you back. Certainly Jesus intends to teach these lessons, and certainly the pompous and vain, hoity-toity Pharisees needed to learn them. But isn't it curious that Jesus doesn't say, "You should not want to be honored at all," and "You should seek no reward for your good deeds"? That is what the modern secular humanist would tell us: true charity means absolute selflessness – they would fault us even for doing right, if it makes us happy. But Christ doesn't condemn the natural desire for honor and reward; he elevates it. We should seek our reward in heaven – the reward of lasting happiness that comes from living in friendship with God. And we should put ourselves in "the lowest place" now, serving others while we can, so that we can be lifted higher later. Christ is the ultimate realist; he knows the human heart (after all, he made it), and he doesn't want to stifle it – he wants to set it free.

CHRIST THE FRIEND Christ's method of teaching reveals how sincerely he cares for us. By telling the parable to the dinner party, he exposes everyone's vanity without embarrassing anyone. He teaches and corrects us not to humiliate us, but to gently lead us towards the freedom of truth. When he instructs the host on how to win eternal favors, he doesn't condemn him for doing something bad (inviting one's friends to a banquet is hardly an evil deed), but he invites him to do something even better. Every word of Christ, every gesture and deed, has our good as its aim. He is the ever-faithful friend.

Perhaps it was this unblemished goodness of God that the Pharisees most needed to perceive. Their objections to Christ's Sabbath miracles reflect a very different idea of God. The Sabbath was the Lord's Day, and honoring the Lord, from their perspective, meant a strict, harsh, cold obedience to the letter of the law – as if God were a stern judge who was just waiting to pounce on anyone who stepped out of place. For Jesus, on the other hand, honoring the Lord on the Lord's Day meant relieving people of their sufferings and sorrows, giving them a glimpse and a taste of the Father's omnipotent love, emphasizing that the highest place of honor in every heart should belong to the Giver of all good gifts. Two different ideas of God produced two different ways of relating to God. We should make sure our idea is as close to Christ's as possible, so we can live as he wants us to live.

CHRIST IN MY LIFE I know you planted the desire for happiness in my heart for a reason. I know you want my happiness. Untangle all the complicated ideas linked to the meaning of life that bombard me from here and there. You are my Lord. Your gospel is my plan of action. Help me to know you better each day, so I can follow you more closely and love you more deeply…

Sometimes I still doubt your care and concern for me. Not in my mind, but in my heart. Part of me still recoils at your tenderness. Heal my wounded heart, Lord. Let me love you more by trusting you completely. Let me glorify you by confiding in you wholly…

I am your ambassador – you made it so on the day of my confirmation. I should have the same purposeful but humble confidence in all my encounters as you did. Why don't I? Why do I get nervous, hesitant, uncertain? I still have a divided heart. Make your will into my only desire, and teach me to walk in your ways…

QUESTIONS FOR SMALL GROUP DISCUSSION

1. What struck you most in this passage? What did you notice that you hadn't noticed before?

2. In what ways can we fall into seeking "the places of honor" in opposition to the humility of heart that the gospel calls for?

3. Why do you think Christ accepts an invitation to a dinner party given by one of the leading Pharisees, when they had already openly declared their opposition to him?

4. Christ is at home with the rich and the poor, with the leaders of society and the large crowds of ordinary citizens. How was he able to be so universal? How can we follow in his footsteps?

Cf. Catechism of the Catholic Church, 22 and 1718-1719 on the natural human desire for happiness; 2544-2547 on humility

202. RSVP (LK 14:15-24)

"If we let Christ into our lives, we lose nothing, nothing, absolutely nothing of what

makes life free, beautiful and great… Only in this friendship are the doors of life
opened wide. Only in this friendship is the great potential of human existence truly
revealed. Only in this friendship do we experience beauty and liberation."

- Pope Benedict XVI

Luke 14:15-24

On hearing this, one of those gathered round the table said to him, 'Happy the man who will be at the feast in the kingdom of God!' But he said to him, 'There was a man who gave a great banquet, and he invited a large number of people. When the time for the banquet came, he sent his servant to say to those who had been invited, Come along: everything is ready now. But all alike started to make excuses. The first said, I have bought a piece of land and must go and see it. Please accept my apologies. Another said, I have bought five yoke of oxen and am on my way to try them out. Please accept my apologies. Yet another said, I have just got married and so am unable to come. The servant returned and reported this to his master. Then the householder, in a rage, said to his servant, Go out quickly into the streets and alleys of the town and bring in here the poor, the crippled, the blind and the lame. Sir, said the servant, your orders have been carried out and there is still room. Then the master said to his servant, Go to the open roads and the hedgerows and force people to come in to make sure my house is full; because, I tell you, not one of those who were invited shall have a taste of my banquet.'

CHRIST THE LORD One of the guests at the dinner responds to Jesus' previous comment about giving feasts and inviting the poor, and about taking the last seat when you're invited to a feast, by calling to mind the great Jewish idea of the Messianic Feast. The Jews believed that when the Messiah finally came, he would organize a huge feast for all of the faithful Jews. Jesus' response must have been sobering. He acknowledges the man's comment and explains that those who were originally invited to the Messianic feast were already in the process of declining to come – the very Pharisees and other exteriorly righteous Jews were the ones who rejected Jesus. And so Jesus invites the poor and indigent of the town – the tax collectors, the ignorant, and the public sinners of Palestine who welcomed Christ's message. But there is still room for more, so Jesus sends messengers outside of the town, into the highways and byways, and the Gentiles too are brought into the banquet. In short, those who were supposed to be the guests of honor ended up missing the event entirely, while those who didn't even know about the feast were the ones who enjoyed it.

Jesus tells this parable to the Pharisees hoping it will wake them up to Christ's truth. But it tells us a lot about the Lord as well. It tells us that he considers himself incomplete unless his subjects come and celebrate with him. He is the antithesis of a lone ranger. (Here is the root of the Church's admonition that all her children faithfully attend Sunday Mass.) It tells us that he respects our freedom – the line about forcing people to come in alludes to the compulsion of love, not to injustice. It tells us that he desires to bring as many people as possible into his Kingdom. This is our Lord, and as his ambassadors, we should be the same.

CHRIST THE TEACHER The Pharisees' rejection of Jesus is mysterious. Why were they so blind? Why did they persist in their blindness? Maybe many more than we realize eventually become believers and followers of Christ, but many of them held out against him to the bitter end. How could that be? The three refusals in the parable explain.

One man was occupied with his business deals – he's the man of *power*. Another was excited about his new purchase – he's the man of *possessions*. And a third was engrossed in the raptures of a newlywed – he's the man of *pleasure*. To understand their situations completely, it's important to realize how these ancient banquets worked. When a banquet was to be held, two invitations went out. The first merely announced the host's intention of throwing the party; it didn't give the details of date and time. When those were arranged, servants would be sent out to announce the actual hour of the banquet, and those who had accepted the first invitation would now come and enjoy the feast. To say yes to the first invitation and then decline the second was considered a grave insult. All three of these men had accepted the original invitation. They valued the host enough to commit to coming to his banquet. But then the weeks went by, and they became absorbed in their own affairs. By the time the second invitation arrives, their own preoccupations – whether power, possessions, or pleasure – have crowded out their allegiance to the host.

From this perspective, the Pharisees' failure to welcome Jesus makes sense. It was God who had chosen the Chosen People; his call and covenant came out of his initiative. Therefore, following through on it necessarily involves putting God's plans ahead of one's personal plans. And who of us hasn't experienced the difficulty in that? Put in those terms, the parable applies to all of us. The first invitation is our baptism, by which we are put on the roster of God's family. But later in life, the Lord comes and asks each one of us to follow through, and unless we have kept in touch with God, with his wisdom and goodness, we too can easily ignore his voice in favor of self-absorption. The tragedy is double: we not only miss out on the feast, but if we simply trusted in God, we could have both the feast and our personal interests – the businessman didn't have to lose his land in order to come to the feast, he only had to delay his appointment, and likewise with the others. So the Pharisees' rejection of Christ is not so mysterious after all – it was just like ours.

CHRIST THE FRIEND   Jesus' favorite image for his Kingdom is the banquet, the feast. Not just a little dinner party, but a huge festival, worthy of the kind of King he is. Banquets are full of enjoyment, communion, conversation, and delight; they are icons of fulfillment. This is what Jesus has in store for his friends. We would do well to contemplate this image so that it sinks deeply into our hearts and minds, especially because we know that his banquet lasts forever, whereas our little earthly plans and pleasures are quickly coming to an end. Contemplating this image will help us begin to value our friendship with Christ the way it deserves to be valued – and cherish and nourish it as we ought.

Jesus: The banquet I am preparing for you is beyond what you can imagine. Remember all of the most beautiful sunsets, landscapes, and night skies that you have enjoyed – they are a dim, colorless shadow compared to heaven. Remember the most satisfying discoveries you have made through your books, travels, hobbies, and education – they are just a title page compared to all that you still have to discover. Remember your greatest and purest pleasures: the summer sun warming your shoulders, a glass of cool lemonade after a long afternoon's work, the hard-fought victory won by a dramatic comeback, the embrace of a loved one after a long time apart – these are just whiffs of the pleasures to come. Remember the more substantial joys of friendship, of forgiveness, of loving and being loved in return, of knowing and being known by the one you love – all these are my gifts to you here on earth, and they are but a prelude to their fulfillment in heaven. I promised to go and prepare a place for you in my Father's house. It is almost ready. I am looking forward to showing it to you. I hope you are looking forward to coming.

CHRIST IN MY LIFE   You invite me to your banquet every day: the Eucharist. What more could I desire than to enter into such intimate communion with you? You are all I need. The troubles and sufferings of life can't take you away from me; you are faithful. Teach me to live as you lived, to love as you love, and to think as you think. Make me a channel of your peace…

I shake my head at those three men in the parable who foolishly miss their chance to come to the banquet. But you know that I too decline your invitations many, many times. You are always inviting me to follow you more closely, to be more like you. Yet I decline. I am so slow to reach out to those who rub me the wrong way, so reluctant to forgive, so quick to criticize, so swift to pass judgment. Forgive me, Lord. Never let me be separated from you…

I am that servant you sent out to gather people for your banquet. Teach me what to say. Teach me how to bring others closer to you. Show me how to use my talents and opportunities to give you glory and to benefit my neighbor as much as possible. Make me more aware of the mission you have given me, so I can throw myself into it with all the love of my heart…

QUESTIONS FOR SMALL GROUP DISCUSSION

1. What struck you most in this passage? What did you notice that you hadn't noticed before?

2. Which of the three excuses is commonly heard today?

3. What are some of the most common excuses people make for not going to Mass, the banquet of the Eucharist? How do they hold up in light of this parable?

4. Why do you think it's so easy for us to discard God's invitations?

Cf. Catechism of the Catholic Church, 1023-1029 on what heaven will be like; 2794-2796 on the significance of heaven; 1720-1724 on Christian beatitude

203. CHRISTIAN CONDITIONS (LK 14:25-35)

"But above all things maintain peace of heart which surpasses every treasure. For maintaining this peace nothing is more effective than to renounce one's own will and to set in its place the will of the Sacred Heart…"

- St Margaret Mary Alacoque

Luke 14:25-35

Great crowds accompanied him on his way and he turned and spoke to them. 'If any man comes to me without hating his father, mother, wife, children, brothers, sisters, yes and his own life too, he cannot be my disciple. Anyone who does not carry his cross and come after me cannot be my disciple. And indeed, which of you here, intending to build a tower, would not first sit down and work out the cost to see if he had enough to complete it? Otherwise, if he laid the foundation and then found himself unable to finish the work, the onlookers would all start making fun of him and saying, Here is a man who started to build and was unable to finish. Or again, what king marching to war against another king would not first sit down and consider whether with ten thousand men he could stand up to the other who advanced against him with twenty thousand? If not, then while the other king was still a long way off, he would send envoys to sue for peace. So in the same way, none of you can be my disciple unless he gives up all his possessions. Salt is a useful thing. But if the salt itself loses its taste, how can it be seasoned again? It is good for neither soil nor manure heap. People throw it out. Listen, anyone who has ears to hear!'

CHRIST THE LORD We easily become familiar with Christ; we lose our sense of wonder and amazement of him. But the people of his time knew that it was no ordinary man who walked among them – rather, they knew that he was an ordinary man who at the same time was extraordinary. Thus we run into brief phrases like "great crowds accompanied him on his way" strewn throughout the Gospels. Try to picture that. A rabbi walking the dusty streets of Palestine, drawing thousands of people in his wake…. Even if later some of the people in these crowds were also in the crowd that convinced Pilate to crucify him on Good Friday, we should credit them with recognizing that Christ was more than a name in one of Western culture's great books – indeed, he was and is the Lord.

CHRIST THE TEACHER At this point in Luke's Gospel, Jesus is steadfastly making his way to Jerusalem, where he knows that he can expect nothing but betrayal, condemnation, humiliation, torture, and death, but he knows that on the third day he will rise again. He also knows that everyone who wants to be his follower, everyone who has tasted the incomparable meaning and deep joy of his Kingdom and wants its fullness, will have to follow the same path – every Christian has to die with Christ in order to rise with him. (cf. Romans 6:8) Death in this sense will not necessarily take the form of physical crucifixion, although for many of his closest followers (the martyrs) it did. But whatever form the cross takes in a particular Christian's life, it will require a painful renunciation of things dear to us. Like a good surgeon, Christ has to cut away whatever holds us back from him, and that can hurt. The Church has always understood that Christ's exhortation to hate father and mother and brothers and sisters simply points out that a true Christian can prefer nothing to Christ.

Jesus also teaches us that following him involves more than feelings and inspirations. We are meant to use our minds. The builder and the warring king had to channel their enthusiasm through the cool filter of reason. Christians must do the same. The emotional excitement that comes from a retreat or a pilgrimage or a special grace-filled encounter with the Lord is like the blossoms on a cherry tree. They bloom quickly and fill our souls with a sweet aroma, but then the long summer comes, and we have to persevere patiently, following an intelligent plan of spiritual and apostolic work, before the fruit matures. Love is often born amidst intense emotions, but it matures through suffering and sweat, and these are only endured through the aid of reason and conviction. Following Christ is more than following a whim; it is a long-term project that engages the whole person.

CHRIST THE FRIEND Jesus didn't want his followers to be under any illusions. Perhaps some people in that crowd were hoping for a sweeping political victory to overthrow the hated Roman yoke as soon as they would arrive in Jerusalem. Perhaps some were entertaining fanciful illusions about effortless prosperity – after all, hadn't Jesus multiplied five loaves so as to feed more than five thousand people? Jesus knew that his Kingdom was of a different stripe. He knew that it was much greater, much better than anything they could imagine, but he also knew that attaining it would be more demanding than they thought. If they would be his friends, then, he would tell them right from the outset what such a friendship would entail. "None of you can be my disciple unless he gives up all his possessions…" Jesus isn't advocating delay or hesitation in following him, but he is advocating firm resolution. Salt that loses its flavor is good for nothing, just so a disciple who loses his fervor when fidelity to Christ gets tough. Jesus is no fair-weather friend, and he's looking for more than fair-weather followers.

St Luke doesn't tell us what tone of voice our Lord used when speaking these words, nor does he say how the crowds reacted, but we don't really need him to. As always, Jesus was inviting these people to trust in him, and in his eyes was the fire of love and the warm hope of a heart that longs to give.

CHRIST IN MY LIFE Open my eyes, Lord. I want to know you better. I fall into routine so easily. Grant me the grace to perceive your majesty, your goodness, and your wisdom. If you don't let me see your beauty, I will be turned aside by the passing fancies of this world. Open my eyes, Lord; increase my faith…

I want to be your follower, cross and all. But it's hard for me to recognize my crosses. The contradictions and struggles of every day seem so petty – where is the redemption in them, Lord? I know it's there somewhere, but where? Teach me to see my crosses, so that I can bear them, united to yours, with faith, hope, and love…

I know that following you will be costly. It's much easier to go with what's popular, easy, and pleasurable. But as long as you walk beside me, I would never desire another path. What would life be like without you? A tumbleweed, a passing cloud, a firecracker. You plug my life into eternity, and I know in my heart that's where I belong…

QUESTIONS FOR SMALL GROUP DISCUSSION

1. What struck you most in this passage? What did you notice that you hadn't noticed before?

2. What are the hardest sacrifices we face in following Christ on a day-to-day basis? Why are they hard?

3. If God really wants us to follow Christ, why doesn't he make it easier?

4. In the Gospel of Matthew, Jesus says, "My yoke is easy and my burden is light." (Matthew 11:30) How can we reconcile that statement with, "Whoever does not carry his own cross and come after me cannot be my disciple"? After all, crosses are not exactly easy and light.

Cf. Catechism of the Catholic Church, 409 and 2015 on the difficulties of Christian discipleship

THE GOSPEL OF LUKE CHAPTER 15

"What greater proof could he have given of his mercy than by taking upon himself that which needed mercy? Where is there such fullness of loving-kindness as in the fact that the Word of God became perishable like the grass for our sakes?… Let man infer from this how much God cares for him. Let him know from this what God thinks of him, what he feels about him. Man, do not ask about your own sufferings, but about what he suffered. Learn from what he was made for you, how much he makes of you, so that his kindness may show itself to you from his humanity. The lesser he has made himself in his humanity, the greater has he shown himself in kindness. The more he humbles himself on my account, the more powerfully he engages my love."

- St Bernard of Clairvaux

204. WHAT GOD THINKS OF SINNERS (LK 15:1-10)

"The Word spoke, and by these words he turned man away from disobedience, not enslaving him by force or necessity, but inviting him to choose freedom of his own accord."

- St Hippolytus

Luke 15:1-10

The tax collectors and the sinners, meanwhile, were all seeking his company to hear what he had to say, and the Pharisees and the scribes complained. 'This man' they said 'welcomes sinners and eats with them.' So he spoke this parable to them: 'What man among you with a hundred sheep, losing one, would not leave the ninety-nine in the wilderness and go after the missing one till he found it? And when he found it, would he not joyfully take it on his shoulders and then, when he got home, call together his friends and neighbours? Rejoice with me, he would say I have found my sheep that was lost. In the same way, I tell you, there will be more rejoicing in heaven over one repentant sinner than over ninety-nine virtuous men who have no need of repentance. Or again, what woman with ten drachmas would not, if she lost one, light a lamp and sweep out the house and search thoroughly till she found it? And then, when she had found it, call together her friends and neighbours? Rejoice with me, she would say I have found the drachma I lost. In the same way, I tell you, there is rejoicing among the angels of God over one repentant sinner.'

CHRIST THE LORD If one of the self-righteous Pharisees had possessed the power and authority of Christ, he would have destroyed all the "sinners." But Christ deploys all his power and authority to bring them back into communion with God. Once again we see that the Pharisees' idea of God is off base. They see God as harsh and judgmental, when the truth is that God is a dedicated shepherd. The return of a sinner actually makes God rejoice – as the shepherd rejoices upon retrieving his sheep, and as the woman rejoices upon recovering her coin. The parables show us that God feels anxiousness in regards to sinners, not anger; he wants them back, he doesn't want to condemn them. The Pharisees can't understand this, because they have painted their image of God in their own likeness. They enjoy condemning others for being less perfect than themselves, because it feeds their vanity, making them feel superior. But the Lord has no vanity, only love. If we are to be his followers, we need to see him as he really is and work to become more like him.

The Pharisees were impossible to please. They found fault with everything Jesus did. But he never gave up trying to win them over. Here, when they complain about his rubbing shoulders with tax collectors and sinners, he responds by telling them some of the most beautiful stories in all of Scripture – pleading with them to soften their hearts and accept God's mercy. The Lord rules, but he rules wisely and mercifully, and his patience never wears thin, no matter how sorely we try it.

CHRIST THE TEACHER The parables always teach us about ourselves. The lost sheep is helpless and vulnerable; it needs the flock and the shepherd to protect and guide it. Just so, every person is created to find meaning and fulfillment in communion with God and others – thus the two great commandments of loving God and loving neighbor. The lost coin is completely without value unless it is possessed by its owner. Even if it had been a gold piece worth 1000 drachmas, it would be completely worthless buried in the dust under the sofa

– of absolutely no use to anyone. Likewise, each of us has a mission in life, a purpose and a task, but its proper place is within Christ's Kingdom. Outside of the Kingdom we can do wonderful things and have exciting adventures, but everything we do is utterly unsubstantial, like a puff of smoke, unless it's plugged into eternity through God's saving grace. Our lives only have real meaning through Christ, with Christ, and in Christ – otherwise they're just tasteless wafers of unleavened bread.

These parables also show the truth about the sacrament of confession. Far from a drudgery or manipulative coercion, this sacrament is God's way of making it as simple and direct as possible for us to come back into the fold and set the bells of his heart ringing.

CHRIST THE FRIEND These two parables teach us more about the heart of God than a whole library full of theological treatises. God cares about each one of us (he will not rest if only one sheep is missing, or one coin is lost). He cares deeply enough to go out of his way to save us when we are lost (it was certainly an inconvenience to go bushwhacking after the foolish stray sheep, and to light the lamp and sweep the dirt-floored house trying to find the lost coin). He rejoices when we return to him – he actually rejoices. Every sinner who returns to God causes joyful celebration in the halls of heaven and in the heart of the Father.

A shepherd counts his sheep after a long day of grazing, as the sun goes down. One is missing. He counts again. Yes, one sheep has wandered away from the flock. High on the mountainside pasture, the air is already getting cold as daylight fades. The flock huddles together. The shepherd leads them into a natural hollow under an overhanging cliff. He turns around and retraces his steps; he sets out to find the lost sheep. He stumbles over sharp rocks in the lengthening shadows. He has to climb off the path, pushing through brambles and thorns. He pulls his cloak tighter around him to keep out the chill. It starts to drizzle. Will the wolves come out in the rain? There is no moon tonight, and the clouds block out the stars. Maybe he should turn back while he can still find his way. He will come and search for the lost sheep in the morning. A wolf howls. The morning may be too late. He trudges on. The mud is slippery. The wind picks up. Water drips down the back of his neck. Soon he is soaked to the skin. The night crawls on. He will find his sheep. That's what matters. He is a good shepherd.

CHRIST IN MY LIFE Unless you make my heart more like yours, I will continue judging my neighbor just like the Pharisees. Unless you give me a deeper experience of your goodness, I will keep slipping into the wrong idea about you. I see the Pharisee in myself, Lord, and I don't want him to win out. I want to be your ambassador, not your adversary...

I was that lost coin, and you found me. I have been the lost sheep many times, and you have always come after me. Thank you, Lord. I don't thank you as often as I should. I am glad you haven't given up on me. Now, please teach me to be like you, to seek and find lost coins and lost sheep, so I can repay your love to me by bringing joy to your heart...

How patient you were with the stubborn, self-righteous Pharisees! Pour some of that patience into my heart, Lord. I have too short a fuse. I know I'm acting like a fool when I harp on others and become exasperated with them – as if I were perfect. Help me to think more about the good of my neighbor than the satisfaction of my own desires. Teach me to love as you love...

QUESTIONS FOR SMALL GROUP DISCUSSION

1. What struck you most in this passage? What did you notice that you hadn't noticed before?

2. In what areas of my life do I tend to try God's patience?

3. As faithful followers of Christ, we should do our best to go after the lost sheep and look for the lost coins on his behalf. In what ways can we improve our imitation of Christ the Good Shepherd?

4. What does popular culture tell us to base our self-esteem on? How does that compare with Christ's message in these parables?

Cf. Catechism of the Catholic Church, 1468-1470 on the effects of sacramental confession; 210-227 on God's mercy and other qualities

205. COMING HOME (LK 15:11-32)

"On the basis of this way of manifesting the presence of God who is Father, love and mercy, Jesus makes mercy one of the principal themes of his preaching."

- Pope John Paul II

Luke 15:11-32

He also said, 'A man had two sons. The younger said to his father, Father, let me have the share of the estate that would come to me. So the father divided the property between them. A few days later, the younger son got together everything he had and left for a distant country where he squandered his money on a life of debauchery. When he had spent it all, that country experienced a severe famine, and now he began to feel the pinch, so he hired himself out to one of the local inhabitants who put him on his farm to feed the pigs. And he would willingly have filled his belly with the husks the pigs were eating but no one offered him anything. Then he came to his senses and said, How many of my father's paid servants have more food than they want, and here am I dying of hunger! I will leave this place and go to my father and say: Father, I have sinned against heaven and against you; I no longer deserve to be called your son; treat me as one of your paid servants. So he left the place and went back to his father. While he was still a long way off, his father saw him and was moved with pity. He ran to the boy, clasped him in his arms and kissed him tenderly. Then his son said, Father, I have sinned against heaven and against you. I no longer deserve to be called your son. But the father said to his servants, Quick! Bring out the best robe and put it on him; put a ring on his finger and sandals on his feet. Bring the calf we have been fattening, and kill it; we are going to have a feast, a celebration, because this son of mine was dead and has come back to life; he was lost and is found. And they began to celebrate.

'Now the elder son was out in the fields, and on his way back, as he drew near the house, he could hear music and dancing. Calling one of the servants he asked what it was all about. Your brother has come replied the servant and your father has killed the calf we had fattened because he has got him back safe and sound. He was angry then and refused to go in, and his father came out to plead with him; but he answered his father, Look, all these years I have slaved for you and never once disobeyed your orders, yet you never offered me so much as a kid for me to celebrate with my friends. But, for this son of yours, when he comes back after swallowing up your property – he and his women – you kill the calf we had been fattening. The father said, My son, you are with me always and all I have is yours. But it was only right we should celebrate and rejoice, because your brother here was dead and has come to life; he was lost and is found.'

CHRIST THE LORD Many leaders in the world are "in it for themselves." Christ isn't. His greatest glory is winning people's hearts for God, which also happens to be the best thing for them. When the Pharisees complained about his generosity to sinners, he made the most of their attention to try and teach them a lesson. He didn't have to – they certainly didn't deserve his mercy, but he chose to. Then, within the parable itself, Christ profiles his own heart – the heart of God – in the behavior of the father, who lived only for his sons' well-being. "All I have is yours" is no empty rhetoric: in Christ, in the Church, in the Eucharist, God has held absolutely nothing back from us. Jesus is Lord, but he is the Lord of love, longing for hearts that will submit to his gentle and life-giving reign.

CHRIST THE TEACHER This parable teaches us that it is possible to live "in the father's house" without really getting to know the Father. If the younger son had truly known how much his father loved him, how generous his father was, how eagerly he wanted to bequeath to him prosperity and joy, he would never have paid him the insult of asking for his share of the inheritance while his father was still alive. That was equivalent to saying that his father would be of more use to him if he were dead. And if the older son (the dutiful one who seemed to do everything just right) had known how much his father cared for him, he would not have resented the celebration at this brother's return. So although they had lived their entire lives under the same roof, they had not opened their hearts to their father; instead they had closed themselves into the little world of their egoism.

We can easily do the same – spend our whole lives as "practicing" Catholics, going through all the right motions and looking great on the outside, but not opening our hearts to the grace and love of God, not getting to know him on a personal, intimate level. If we operate this way, we run the risk of some day abandoning the Father, convinced that he is treating us unjustly, when the truth is that he is giving us everything he owns.

CHRIST THE FRIEND "While he was still a long way off, his father caught sight of him…" God never stops hoping that we will come to him. He has his eyes on us all the time – not to pounce on us when we mess up, but to run to us, embrace us, kiss us, and clothe us with the robe of his grace and the sandals of divine sonship (servants went barefoot in ancient households, but family members wore sandals). The devil likes to make us forget about this – especially when we most need to remember it; let's not give him that pleasure.

We can also please the father by going in search of our prodigal brothers and sisters. The rebellious son abandons his father, and his father respects that – he won't go out and try to force his son to come back home. But if the older brother had really cared for both his father and his younger sibling, he could have made a trek or two in search of the unfortunate youth. We can imagine the conversation they would have had at the pig farm. The older brother, "We miss you and we would love for you to come back." The younger brother, "But how can I, what I did was so horrible?" "Don't worry, just come back – trust me, we'll work it out. You don't have to stay here eating corn husks…"

How many lost and sorrowful younger brothers are all around us, if only we would open the eyes of our hearts to see them! And how easy it would be to invite them back to the father's house, if only we could see beyond our self-centered preoccupations!

CHRIST IN MY LIFE While the Pharisees needed to understand your goodness and mercy, I think that at times I need to be more aware of the evil of sin. I have been infected by the prevailing mentality that forgets about personal responsibility, and about the wounds selfishness causes to others. Lord, why do I act as if self-centeredness were okay? Free me, Lord, to love…

Something made that younger son come back to his senses. You are working in mysterious, hidden ways in every heart. I have placed my hope in you, because I believe that you are the way, the truth, and the life. But sometimes I have less confidence in your ability to help others, who seem so far from the truth, to come to their senses. Increase my hope, Lord…

I don't have to go far to find people who are in trouble, who are sad, who need to come back to you and don't know the way. Open my heart so I can reach out to them. Will you not use my slightest effort, even if it's clumsy, as a channel of grace? I don't want to hoard the treasure you have given me – knowing your love. The more I give away, the more you will give to me…

QUESTIONS FOR SMALL GROUP DISCUSSION

1. What struck you most in this passage? What did you notice that you hadn't noticed before?

2. Which son do you think caused the father more sorrow? Which son do you tend to resemble more?

3. In what ways does our society encourage us to fall into a merely exterior, routine living out of our faith, instead of a heartfelt, loving relationship with God?

4. What do you think made the younger son "come to his senses"? Does that apply to us in any way?

Cf. Catechism of the Catholic Church, 1461-1470 on God's forgiveness in the sacrament of confession; 2084-2100 on what it means to love God

THE GOSPEL OF LUKE CHAPTER 16

"Despite all the mysteries and wonders which have been discovered by holy doctors and understood by holy souls in this state of life, there still remains more for them to say and to understand. There are depths to be fathomed in Christ. He is like a rich mine with many recesses containing treasures, and no matter how men try to fathom them the end is never reached. Rather, in each recess, men keep on finding here and there new veins of new riches."

- St John of the Cross

206. SERVING ONE MASTER (LK 16:1-13)

"Christian charity ought not to be content with not hating our enemies and loving them as brothers; it also demands that we treat them with kindness."

- Pope Benedict XV

Luke 16:1-13

He also said to his disciples, 'There was a rich man and he had a steward denounced to him for being wasteful with his property. He called for the man and said, What is this I hear about you? Draw me up an account of your stewardship because you are not to be my steward any longer. Then the steward said to himself, Now that my master is taking the stewardship from me, what am I to do? Dig? I am not strong enough. Go begging? I should be too ashamed. Ah, I know what I will do to make sure that when I am dismissed from office there will be some to welcome me into their homes. Then he called his master's debtors one by one. To the first he said, How much do you owe my master? One hundred measures of oil was the reply. The steward said, Here, take your bond; sit down straight away and write fifty. To another he said, And you, sir, how much do you owe? One hundred measures of wheat was the reply. The steward said, Here, take your bond and write eighty. The master praised the dishonest steward for his astuteness. For the children of this world are more astute in dealing with their own kind than are the children of light.

'And so I tell you this: use money, tainted as it is, to win you friends, and thus make sure that when it fails you, they will welcome you into the tents of eternity. The man who can be trusted in little things can be trusted in great; the man who is dishonest in little things will be dishonest in great. If then you cannot be trusted with money, that tainted thing, who will trust you with genuine riches? And if you cannot be trusted with what is not yours, who will give you what is your very own? No servant can be the slave of two masters: he will either hate the first and love the second, or treat the first with respect and the second with scorn. You cannot be the slave both of God and of money.'

CHRIST THE LORD "No servant can be the slave of two masters." Jesus doesn't give a third alternative; we have to serve someone. In another place he puts it like this: "He who does not gather with me scatters" (Luke 11:23). We cannot be morally neutral in life. If we live selfishly, we contribute to the culture of selfishness; we extend the kingdom of money and follow the lord of selfishness, Satan. If we live for Christ, on the other hand, we extend the Kingdom of justice and love, the eternal Kingdom. He doesn't give us any alternative: either we follow a lord, or we follow the Lord.

At the same time, Jesus reminds us that our lives are extended through time; the Christian life consists in an ongoing series of decisions in which we reinforce or undermine our basic choice to follow Christ. How we use money (since it represents power – the ability to do and acquire things) can serve as a trustworthy thermometer of our commitment to Christ. If his Kingdom is our true priority, our checking account will show it, because we will put that power (money) at the service of the Kingdom as much as we can.

CHRIST THE TEACHER "For the children of this world are more astute in dealing with their own kind than are the children of light." We see that every day. The great men and women of the world, the CEOs, the athletes, the movie stars, the political leaders – many of them are exemplary in their tenacity, their determination, and their astuteness. They set a goal and let nothing stop them from achieving it. They turn everything into an opportunity to advance their cause. No sacrifice is too great. Imagine how different the Church (and the world) would be if every Catholic pursued holiness as energetically as most people pursue pleasure, honor, and wealth. Jesus is not rebuking us for striving after excellence in worldly pursuits, but he is rebuking us for not dedicating ourselves with equal conviction to advancing his Kingdom. After all, the former will pass away, but the latter will endure forever – so which is the better investment?

Jesus uses a curious image to instruct us about how to use money. First he says that money is "tainted" – but he doesn't condemn it outright. It's tainted because it is so easily abused by fallen human nature. Then he tells us to use it to win friends, so that when money fails (the moment of death) those friends will welcome us into heaven. In other words, we should marshal our wealth to serve others, not to indulge ourselves. Certainly he doesn't mean that a Christian should abstain from all the world's pleasures and entertainments, but those should be kept under control. The end goal of life is to reach heaven, not to fabricate it here on earth. Using money wisely means investing in the former, not the latter.

CHRIST THE FRIEND Jesus gives this advice so that his disciples might be welcomed into "tents of eternity." The advice may be hard to follow, but the results are worth it.

Nothing Christ demands of us is gratuitous. God doesn't make up rules just for fun. Every word of the Lord is spoken for our benefit, to guide us along the path of eternal life. Every teaching that the Church puts forward is meant to be a beacon of light in a dark and confused world. Unfortunately, we often ignore them as if they were arbitrary no-parking signs. Whenever Christ or the Church seems too demanding, all we need to do is look at a crucifix.

Christ gave everything for our sake, absolutely everything. We are his one love. He became a servant, a criminal, a victim, just for us. That means we can trust him without hesitation, even when he is demanding. He is the friend who will never fail.

CHRIST IN MY LIFE I am glad to be a citizen of your Kingdom, and to have received from you the call to help spread that Kingdom. I can't imagine any other occupation in life that would be more worthwhile. Thank you, Lord. So please help me see all that I do – my normal responsibilities, my apostolic initiatives, my relationships – from this perspective: Thy Kingdom come, thy will be done…

Money is a tough topic, Lord. Everywhere I turn, I am being invited to spend it – and even to spend more than I have. I am part of this culture, Lord, this consumerist culture in which the highest priority is a robust economy. Teach me self-discipline and generosity, so I never fall prey to idols…

Once again you remind me of heaven, of the "tents of eternity." You were always talking about that. O Lord, give me a foretaste of heaven, give me the wisdom that sees this earthly life from the proper perspective. Stir up in my heart a desire for that definitive encounter with you that will take place when my terrestrial pilgrimage reaches its fulfillment. Hallowed be thy name…

QUESTIONS FOR SMALL GROUP DISCUSSION

1. What struck you most in this passage? What did you notice that you hadn't noticed before?

2. Why do we tend to be more ingenious and proactive when it comes to worldly pursuits than when it comes to spiritual things?

3. What has helped you most in keeping your financial life as Christian as possible? What has hindered you? How can we know where to draw the line between responsibility and generosity?

4. We call ourselves Christians, followers of Christ. If someone were to follow us around for a day, what evidence would there be that this is truly the case? What evidence might they find that could the opposite – that we serve some other lord?

Cf. Catechism of the Catholic Church, 50-67 and 2822-2827 on what God wants; 2850-2854 on the Prince of this World; 2401-2418 on a Christian's proper relationship to "mammon"

207. GOD SEES THE HEART (LK 16:14-18)

"It is for love of him that I do not spare myself in preaching him."

- Pope St Gregory the Great

Luke 16:14-18

The Pharisees, who loved money, heard all this and laughed at him. He said to them, 'You are the very ones who pass yourselves off as virtuous in people's sight, but God knows your hearts. For what is thought highly of by men is loathsome in the sight of God. Up to the time of John it was the Law and the Prophets; since then, the kingdom of God has been preached, and by violence everyone is getting in. It is easier for heaven and earth to disappear than for one little stroke to drop out of the Law. Everyone who divorces his wife and marries another is guilty of adultery, and the man who marries a woman divorced by her husband commits adultery.'

CHRIST THE LORD Imagine Jesus being laughed at. Imagine God being laughed at – the Creator of the oceans, the earth, the solar system, the sculptor of mountains, volcanoes, and daffodils, the fashioner of the Pharisees themselves. And why did the Pharisees laugh at him? Because they loved money, St Luke tells us, and Jesus had just put money in its place, which was not a very high one.

How does Jesus respond to this scorn? He takes no offense; rather he warns his interlocutors that they are dangerously wrong. They have one set of priorities: reputation, influence, wealth; but these coveted goods are "loathsome" in the sight of God. The literal translation of the Greek at that point is "stinks in God's face." It's as if Jesus were saying that they may laugh at God's standards, but in so doing they separate themselves from the God they claim to serve. God has a different set of priorities: moral integrity (thus his comment about the endurance of the law), fidelity (thus his reminder about the evil of divorce), and self-forgetfulness (thus the reference to getting into the Kingdom of God by violence – by the self-mastery and renunciation exemplified by John the Baptist, not the self-indulgent prosperity exemplified by the money-loving Pharisees).

Few passages make so clear the clash between the values promoted by a worldly society and those promoted by the Lord. Since we live both in the world and in Christ, we have to make a point of setting our sights on God so that this world's standards won't blind us to the truth, as they did with the Pharisees.

CHRIST THE TEACHER The Pharisees would have held the Old Covenant view that economic prosperity was necessarily a sign of God's favor and poverty a sign of his disfavor. They drew this conclusion from the many promises in the Old Testament where God encourages Israel to look forward to fruitful vines and bountiful harvests. But the Pharisees' interpretation of this imagery went off track. They used it as an excuse to justify hoarding, indulgence, and even injustice – the more wealth they could accumulate, the more they would appear blessed by God. Thus they used the Law and the Prophets (the Old Testament) to legitimate their self-aggrandizement.

Jesus corrects their misinterpretation. Now that the Kingdom of God is being preached, the Old Testament can be understood in its fullness (thus the extension of Moses' limits on divorce to a complete exclusion of divorce, for example). Just as John the Baptist, who was a bridge between the Old and New Covenants, lived a life of austerity and self-mastery, so the true prosperity that indicates God's favor is that of virtue. The virtuous, those who do what is right and true even when it is costly to their worldly tendencies, those whose *hearts* are pleasing to God, experience interior peace and vigor; they enter God's Kingdom (a Kingdom of the heart) by doing violence to their selfish tendencies, not by indulging them.

The world today is still obsessed with appearances. Today's Pharisees still laugh at Jesus and call his followers weaklings. Yet God still looks to the heart, hoping to find good soil where he can raise a bumper crop of authentic joy, peace, and spiritual prosperity. At times it is painful to live in the world without giving in to the world's standards, but in the end it is well worth it. There is nothing in this world that can satisfy us as much as the love of Christ.

CHRIST THE FRIEND It was impossible for the Pharisees who rejected Jesus to be true friends to anyone, because they were self-centered. Jesus, on the other hand, was completely self-forgetful. What interested him was the mission he had received from his Father to lay the foundation of his Kingdom, which would bring light into darkened souls until the end of time. He preaches about selflessness, and he exemplifies it in every detail of his life. He continues to exemplify it in the Church, in his saints, and especially in the Eucharist. He patiently waits in every Tabernacle across the globe, glad to be able to adore the Father in our name, and willing to put up with hours and hours of loneliness in order to still be there when one of his followers needs to talk.

Surely it is more beautiful and fulfilling to be a true friend than to be a Pharisee. If we let Christ be the friend he wants to be, maybe we will learn to be that kind of friend for others.

CHRIST IN MY LIFE When I look into my soul, I find a clash. I do love you and want to follow you, but I also love my comfort and the praise of my peers. It's so hard to strike the right balance between giving the good things of this world their due, and keeping on the high road to holiness. Thank you for walking this path at my side. I know you will guide me; you have guided me so faithfully already...

Help me to want what you want, Lord. Help me to do what you want. Help me to want what you do. I don't want to deceive myself the way the Pharisees did. I want to hear your word and obey it. I don't care what other people say about me – only you have the words of eternal life. You are the Lord, my Savior and Guide. Thy will be done...

You are more interested in how I treat my colleague down the hall than in the biggest headlines of the biggest newspaper in the world. You are more interested in my heart than in wars and disasters. Everything here is passing away, but every human soul will live forever, either in light or darkness. Lord, make me a lantern and a flame to spread your light...

QUESTIONS FOR SMALL GROUP DISCUSSION

1. What struck you most in this passage? What did you notice that you hadn't noticed before?
2. Which aspects of our popular culture reflect Christ's scale of values? Which reflect the Pharisees' scale of values?
3. In what way is it easiest for us to fall into hypocrisy, to look virtuous on the outside but actually be selfish on the inside at the same time?
4. Why do you think God doesn't always reward holiness with earthly prosperity?

Cf. Catechism of the Catholic Church, 1750-1761 on the morality of human acts; 1804-1811 on the moral virtues

208. MONEY AND FIRE (LK 16:19-31)

"Girding our loins then with faith and the observance of good deeds let us so follow his paths under the guidance of the gospel that we may be worthy to see him who has called us into his kingdom."

- St Benedict

Luke 16:19-31

'There was a rich man who used to dress in purple and fine linen and feast magnificently every day. And at his gate there lay a poor man called Lazarus, covered with sores, who longed to fill himself with the scraps that fell from the rich man's table. Dogs even came and licked his sores. Now the poor man died and was carried away by the angels to the bosom of Abraham. The rich man also died and was buried. In his torment in Hades he looked up and saw Abraham a long way off with Lazarus in his bosom. So he cried out, Father Abraham, pity me and send Lazarus to dip the tip of his finger in water and cool my tongue, for I am in agony in these flames. My son, Abraham replied, remember that during your life good things came your way, just as bad things came the way of Lazarus. Now he is being comforted here while you are in agony. But that is not all: between us and you a great gulf has been fixed, to stop anyone, if he wanted to, crossing from our side to yours, and to stop any crossing from your side to ours. The rich man replied, Father, I beg you then to send Lazarus to my father's house, since I have five brothers, to give them warning so that they do not come to this place of torment too. They have Moses and the prophets, said Abraham, let them listen to them. Ah no, father Abraham, said the rich man, but if someone comes to them from the dead, they will repent. Then Abraham said to him, If they will not listen either to Moses or to the prophets, they will not be convinced even if someone should rise from the dead.'

CHRIST THE LORD Jesus knew what was going to happen to him. He knew that he would suffer, die, and "rise from the dead." And he knew that even then many would not believe in him. He is like a King who is determined to free a captive people from slavery, knowing that once he does, many of them will go off and enslave themselves again. So why go to all the trouble? For the few who will not leave him. Even if one person – you – could be reunited to God through his passion, death, and resurrection, it would be worth it. The value of one soul is a concept that eludes the modern mind, affected so profoundly by polls and percentages, but it is at the center of God's heart. Because his love is not limited by time and space, he is able to love each person with a personal, intimate, determined attention.

This simultaneous universality and individuality of God's love is mirrored in the two great vocations of the Church: marriage and celibacy. Marriage establishes the deep and almost unbreakable bond of family love, highly personal and intimate. Celibacy shows forth the universal extension of God's love, which plays no favorites and excludes no one.

"Yes, God loved the world so much that he gave his only Son, so that everyone who believes in him may not be lost but may have eternal life" (John 3:16). Love moves our Lord, and love never gives up. If we are faithful followers, we should faithfully follow in his steps of self-forgetful love.

CHRIST THE TEACHER Jesus told this parable to the Pharisees. A few verses earlier, St Luke points out that they "loved money, heard all this, and laughed at him." They were the religious and intellectual elite of Palestine. Everyone respected them; everyone revered them. They were sought after as teachers and leaders of synagogues – they were the ones who had all the right degrees, had gone to all the right schools, got all the top jobs…. They had it made. And Christ reminds them of a lesson that the successful of this world too easily forget: this world is not all there is. In fact, it is bound to disappear, giving way to either eternal reward or regret. The purpose of this world is to prepare us for heaven, but if we get attached to it, we may never make it to heaven.

And that would be the real tragedy, because heaven is where the soul lives in perfect communion with God – which is what the soul was created for. Outside of heaven, there is only the frustration of unfulfilled longings – more painful than even the most parched physical thirst. Christ could not have been clearer about this, and yet so many still refuse to listen.

CHRIST THE FRIEND Perhaps Christ's greatest act of charity was his patient effort to win over the hearts of the self-satisfied Pharisees. Many of them showed no sign of respect or even mild interest in the truth of his claims, and yet he kept buffeting them with parables and miracles, desperately hoping that they would let in the light of his grace. Christ commanded his disciples to love their enemies, to forgive those who persecuted them, and he shows them how – by being a true friend to his most vicious antagonists.

He continues this conquest of love. Yesterday, today, and tomorrow, Jesus continues to go after every single soul. He wants to hold each one close to his heart, just as Lazarus was held close in Abraham's bosom. It is God's will that none be lost. His mission is to draw all men to himself. This is the desire in the heart of our Friend, and if we are to be faithful, it should become our desire too, for he has given us a share in this same mission of gathering souls to the bosom of the Father.

CHRIST IN MY LIFE Because you love me, you created me. Because you love me, you gave me the gift of faith. Because you love me, you surround me with innumerable gifts of love, you involve me in your own mission of building up the eternal Kingdom, and you never tire of guiding me to a more fruitful, virtuous life. Open my eyes, Lord, so that I can see the beauty of your love…

So many people live as if this life were all there is. Why? Why don't we believe in heaven and hell? I admit, it's possible to get obsessed with the afterlife, but it would be a foolish traveler who kept moving ahead every day without ever thinking about his destination. Keep me in tune with the truth, Lord, and teach me to bear witness with courage and love…

Who are my enemies, my antagonists? Do I love them as you loved yours? The Pharisees didn't give you warm, fuzzy feelings, but you loved them all the same. You went out of your way to give them what they most needed – a vision of your love and truth. Teach me to love as you love and to give as you give…

QUESTIONS FOR REFLECTION

1. What struck you most in this passage? What did you notice that you hadn't noticed before?

2. How do you think Jesus hoping the Pharisees would react to this parable? How is he hoping we will react to it?

3. Why do you think inordinate love for money make it so hard for the Pharisees to receive Christ's message?

4. How should the reality of heaven, hell, and purgatory (all revealed doctrines of the Church) impact our day-to-day lives?

Cf. Catechism of the Catholic Church, 2443-2449 on love for the poor; 2405-2418 on a Christian's use of material goods; 2534-2550 on love for money; 1020-1050 on death, judgment, hell, purgatory, and heaven

THE GOSPEL OF LUKE CHAPTER 17

"Our king, though he is most high, came for our sake in great humility, but he could not come empty-handed. He brought with him, as it were, a great bonus for his soldiers, which not only made them abundantly rich, but also gave them strength to fight and conquer. The gift he brought was love, and which brings men into fellowship with the Godhead…. Love, therefore, is the origin and source of all good things; it is a most excellent defense, the road that leads to heaven. Whoever walks in love can neither stray nor be afraid. Love guides, love protects, love leads to the end. Christ our Lord, brethren, set up for us this ladder of love, and by it every Christian can climb to heaven. You must, therefore, keep a firm hold on love, you must show it to one another, and by progress in it climb up to heaven."

- St Fulgentius of Ruspe

209. REAL HUMILITY (LK 17:1-10)

"Wherever we find ourselves we not only may, but should, seek perfection."

- St Francis de Sales

Luke 17:1-10

He said to his disciples, 'Obstacles are sure to come, but alas for the one who provides them! It would be better for him to be thrown into the Sea with a millstone put round his neck than that he should lead astray a single one of these little ones. Watch yourselves! And if he wrongs you seven times a day and seven times comes back to you and says, I am sorry, you must forgive him.' The apostles said to the Lord, 'Increase our faith.' The Lord replied, 'Were your faith the size of a mustard seed you could say to this mulberry tree, Be uprooted and planted in the sea, and it would obey you. Which of you, with a servant ploughing or minding sheep, would say to him when he returned from the fields, Come and have your meal immediately? Would he not be more likely to say, Get my supper laid; make yourself tidy and wait on me while I eat and drink. You can eat and drink yourself afterwards? Must he be grateful to the servant for doing what he was told? So with you: when you have done all you have been told to do, say, We are merely servants: we have done no more than our duty.'

CHRIST THE LORD The easiest thing for us to do is forget that we are not God. When we achieve something great, when we receive applause, we let it go to our heads. One of the very first prayers we all learn is: "Glory be to the Father, and to the Son, and to the Holy Spirit, as it was in the beginning, is now, and ever shall be, world without end. Amen." All good things come from God, so ultimately all praise should go to him as well. Even our talents and our opportunities are gifts of God, so if we bear fruit because of them very little of the credit should go to us. When we start to take more credit than is our due, we are forgetting who really is Lord. That was Satan's mistake; let's not repeat it.

This kind of humility can sound harsh to us. Isn't Jesus being a bit hard on that servant of the parable? The servant works hard, obeys, submits, and Jesus says he should look for no recompense; he's just doing his duty. It seems rather cold. But in fact, it's just the opposite. Imagine how unstable our lives would be if the intensity of God's love for us depended on the efficiency of our service in his Kingdom. If we could increase or decrease God's love for us just by our performance rating, what would be the difference between God's Kingdom and this world? We would be just as anxious, ambitious, and self-centered working for Christ as we tend to be working for money and promotions.

In the Lord's Kingdom, the opposite is true. God's love for each of us is already so total, so personal, so unconditional, and so untiring that nothing we do can increase or decrease it. And so the servant in God's Kingdom does his work energetically, joyfully, and peacefully as a response to that gratuitous love of God. God's love doesn't depend on our achievements; our achievements flow from knowing how much God loves us and from wanting to thank him. This is true humility; this is what the Lord wants us to learn.

CHRIST THE TEACHER The two lessons of the passage are unrelated, except that St Luke reports them together in a section of his Gospel where he summarizes several of Jesus' lessons. The first lesson stresses the power and importance of faith. Faith unleashes God's power in our lives. When we let ourselves be won over by God, he can do wonders with us; when we doubt him, trusting ourselves and our ideas more than his infinite wisdom and love (e.g., filtering out Church teaching that we find uncomfortable), we cut ourselves off from his grace. He won't force his way in; he respects us too much for that. But if we invite him in, and give him full control over our lives, amazing things begin to happen.

The second lesson is the hardest one to learn: the lesson of humility. Simply put, all we have comes from God; it is all a gift. So strictly speaking, we deserve nothing (except recompense for our sins). And yet we think we deserve everything. Even our basic human rights stem from our existence, which is a gift of God and not a personal achievement. Our duty is not to rule the universe, but to serve God, to get to know him, and discover his plan for us. If we do that, we will experience the peace and meaning we long for – just as flowers achieve their beauty only when they grow as God designed them to.

CHRIST THE FRIEND The apostles did the right thing. When they detected a flaw in their spiritual life (a lack of faith), they humbly approached the Lord and asked him to take care of it. They trusted him. They knew that he was sincerely interested in making them men of his Kingdom, so they did not hesitate to come to him with their needs. The answer he gives is indirect, and somewhat unsatisfying, which probably means that they weren't ready for the full answer yet, but we can be sure that it only drew them closer to him. Whenever we come to Christ in sincerity and humility, he draws us closer to him – which is why we should come to him more often.

The warning against scandal – putting obstacles in the way of others' faith and trust in God – couldn't be more frightening. This too shows how intensely Jesus is interested in each one of us. In the first place, he gives us a chance to help build his Kingdom, to bring others to Christ. In the second place, he vehemently warns us against abusing that privilege. This shows that our friendship is real – Jesus takes a risk with us. All real friendship involves risk, the risk of having one's trust betrayed. And it also gives us a glimpse of heaven, where our friendship with Christ will have automatically made us into friends with everyone else he has befriended.

CHRIST IN MY LIFE The default position of my self-conception is still me-centered, Lord. I don't like considering myself a mere servant. But it's true. You didn't have to create me, you didn't have to redeem me, you didn't have to give me the talents and gifts you gave me – in short, everything I am and everything I have depends on you. Jesus, teach me the joy and freedom of humility…

Increase my faith, Lord. I want to do great things for your Kingdom. You have put in my heart a burning desire to make a difference in the world, to bring others into your friendship. But I am so clumsy, so blind. Increase my faith, Lord. Teach me to do your will…

Because you have made me a free person, I am equally capable of both good and evil. I know that my impatience and self-centeredness offends you and pushes others away from you. But I also know that the power of your grace is infinite. You are working in my soul, recreating me in your own image. Make me more attentive to your words, Lord…

QUESTIONS FOR SMALL GROUP DISCUSSION

1. What struck you most in this passage? What did you notice that you hadn't noticed before?

2. How should a Christian react to praise? How can we learn to do that?

3. What hinders us from having a stronger faith?

4. How would our lives be different if we really, truly believed that we were just "mere servants," that God doesn't really need us in the way we need him, but that he passionately desires us to come into his Kingdom?

Cf. Catechism of the Catholic Church, 142-184 on faith; 2083-2141 on the proper relationship between God and the human person

210. A RARE FLOWER (LK 17:11-19)

"Compelled by his great love, or rather, as the apostle says, by the excess of his love for us, he sent his beloved Son that he might make satisfaction for us, and recall us to the life which sin had taken away."

- St Alphonsus Liguori

Luke 17:11-19

Now on the way to Jerusalem he travelled along the border between Samaria and Galilee. As he entered one of the villages, ten lepers came to meet him. They stood some way off and called to him, 'Jesus! Master! Take pity on us.' When he saw them he said, 'Go and show yourselves to the priests.' Now as they were going away they were cleansed. Finding himself cured, one of them turned back praising God at the top of his voice and threw himself at the feet of Jesus and thanked him. The man was a Samaritan. This made Jesus say, 'Were not all ten made clean? The other nine, where are they? It seems that no one has come back to give praise to God, except this foreigner.' And he said to the man, 'Stand up and go on your way. Your faith has saved you.'

CHRIST THE LORD To this day, leprosy is an incurable disease. It can be controlled preventively, through proper hygiene, but it can't be cured. (Leprosy is a bacterial infection that causes loss of sensation and eventual paralysis, along with the grotesque disintegration of a person's extremities – fingers, facial features, etc.) Yet Christ cures these ten lepers with a mere command. Showing oneself to the priest was a requirement of Old Testament law for anyone who claimed to have been cured from leprosy. This law had been instituted in order to insure a full cure. They took this precaution because leprosy was thought to be highly contagious, and a miscalculation in an individual case could cause a severe outbreak among a whole village or city. Christ's Lordship rarely appears so clearly and nobly as when he commands the powers of nature for the benefit (never for the harm) of the people he came to save – Jews and foreigners alike.

This encounter stands in sharp contrast, however, to the ongoing verbal fencing between Jesus and the stubborn Pharisees. They refused to call Jesus "Master"; they refused to accept his grace – simply put, they refused him. Why? Because the Pharisees were successful, strong, healthy, and talented, so it was easy for them to consider themselves self-sufficient. The lepers, on the other hand, had no alternative but to acknowledge their utter helplessness. Those who think they can make something truly worthy of their lives depending only on their own resources shut out the authentically transforming grace of God. What's more, the Pharisees didn't even see their error; they thought they were in communion with God. That kind of tragic self-deception should make each one us take a closer look at our own relationship with the Lord.

CHRIST THE TEACHER At the end of his Gospel, St John tells us that if everything Christ did during his brief earthly life were written down, the entire world would not contain the books. We can infer, therefore, that many of Christ's miracles were not recorded in the New Testament. Why did St Luke include this one? Clearly because of the lesson that Christ teaches us by it: the ugliness of ingratitude and the beauty of gratitude.

The ten lepers had no hope but Christ. Even their closest relatives dared not come near them. They were required to live in isolated colonies, and if they had to travel, the law obliged them to ring a bell wherever they went, shouting out, "Unclean! Unclean!" to warn people of their approach (which is why they addressed Christ from a distance). On top of that, they had to live with the repulsion of their own decaying bodies – the pain and the stench of leprosy are almost unbearable. Leprosy was a long, humiliating, and dismal agony, the most horrible of ancient diseases. Jesus frees these ten lepers entirely from their hopelessness and dread, and only one comes back to thank him for it – and that one happens to be a Samaritan (the Samaritans were archenemies of the Jews, racially and religiously).

We are all moral lepers. The human race was infected with mortal selfishness by original sin. Christ saved us, not with a mere command, but by his Incarnation, life, suffering, and painful death on a cross. How many of us render him sincere, heartfelt thanks for all he has done for us? Not to live with an attitude of gratitude towards God is more than being impolite – ingratitude is ugly because it's positively unjust. Gratitude, on the other hand, is one of the most beautiful flowers in the whole garden of virtue. It directly contradicts self-centeredness, self-indulgence, and self-absorption. It builds bridges, unites communities, and softens hearts. It encourages and inspires. It cuts through discouragement and counteracts depression. It opens the soul to the truth and releases anxiety. It brings smiles and gladness wherever it blooms. What a pity that it is as rare as it is lovely!

CHRIST THE FRIEND Jesus cannot resist a cry for pity. For him, a soul in need is an obligation to help. He needed no convincing, no cajolery – these lepers cried out to him from the depths of their hearts and automatically his heart was moved. We see it over and over again in the Gospels – his heart being moved to miraculous action by the needs of those around him. Of course, that same sensitivity was the motive for his coming to earth in the first place – love simply can't hold back when it sees others in need. This truth about Jesus can be the source of our confidence in him, but it should also be the source of our own activity in the world. We who feast on Christ's very own body and blood in the Eucharist need to share also the beatings of his heart, his desire to do as much good as possible; otherwise, our hearts will beat in vain.

CHRIST IN MY LIFE It's easy for me to forget about my sins, my sinfulness, and my need for you. The slightest success puts me into a preening mode.

Lord, never let me forget that all that I have and all that I am is a gift of your goodness. Teach me to live with the attitude of humble wonder and gratitude that you praised in the Samaritan. For all those people who never thank you, I thank you now…

It is a mystery to me that I am still nervous about exposing my "leprosy" to you in the sacrament of confession – you wouldn't have instituted the sacrament if we didn't need it. I can't help feeling ashamed at my egoism, but I ask you to always use that shame to drive me closer to you, my hope and my salvation…

It doesn't take much to detect the moral leprosy affecting our world; it only exacerbates the poverty and sickness that afflict so many people. It moves your heart so much – why does it move mine so little? What more would you have me do, Lord, to relieve my neighbors' suffering? Jesus, meek and humble of heart, make my heart more like yours…

QUESTIONS FOR SMALL GROUP DISCUSSION

. What struck you most in this passage? What did you notice that you hadn't noticed before?

. Gratitude has been called "the rarest flower in the garden of the virtues." Why do you think that is? What can we do to increase this beautiful virtue in our lives?

. Why do you think the other nine lepers didn't come back to thank Jesus?

. People who have grown up Catholic often take the beauty and greatness of the Church for granted, or don't even recognize it, whereas converts to the Church are some of its most avid fans. Why is this? Is there any relationship between this phenomenon and the fact that the one leper who thanked Jesus was not a Jew?

Cf. Catechism of the Catholic Church, 1359-1361 the Eucharist and gratitude; 2097, 2099, 2637-2638 on gratitude owed to God; 396-412 on original sin and God's response to it

211. THY KINGDOM COME! (LK 17:20-37)

He is the man of sorrows and of hope. It is he who will come and who one day will be our judge and – we hope – the everlasting fullness of our existence, our happiness."

- *Pope Paul VI*

Luke 17:20-37

Asked by the Pharisees when the kingdom of God was to come, he gave them this answer, 'The coming of the kingdom of God does not admit of observation and there will be no one to say, Look here! Look there! For, you must know, the kingdom of God is among you.' He said to the disciples, 'A time will come when you will long to see one of the days of the Son of Man and will not see it. They will say to you, Look there! or, Look here! Make no move; do not set off in pursuit; for as the lightning flashing from one part of heaven lights up the other, so will be the Son of Man when his day comes. But first he must suffer grievously and be rejected by this generation.

As it was in Noah's day, so will it also be in the days of the Son of Man. People were eating and drinking, marrying wives and husbands, right up to the day Noah went into the ark, and the flood came and destroyed them all. It will be the same as it was in Lot's day: people were eating and drinking, buying and selling, planting and building, but the day Lot left Sodom, God rained fire and brimstone from heaven and it destroyed them all. It will be the same when the day comes for the Son of Man to be revealed. When that day comes, anyone on the housetop, with his possessions in the house, must not come down to collect them, nor must anyone in the fields turn back either. Remember Lot's wife. Anyone who tries to preserve his life will lose it; and anyone who loses it will keep it safe. I tell you, on that night two will be in one bed: one will be taken, the other left; two women will be grinding corn together: one will be taken, the other left.' The disciples interrupted. 'Where, Lord?' they asked. He said, 'Where the body is, there too will the vultures gather.'

CHRIST THE LORD "The Kingdom of God is among you," Jesus tells the inquiring Pharisees. Obviously, he didn't mean that they had already entered the Kingdom, because they hadn't believed in him or accepted his rule. So what does Jesus mean? He means that in the epoch of the Son of Man – the New Covenant – God's grace is at work in the midst of our everyday life. Just as through the Incarnation, Jesus – the King – came to dwell among the people of Palestine, among the Pharisees, so throughout the whole of the Church's era, God will be inviting and inspiring and knocking on the doors of people's hearts from within. This is the Lord's methodology throughout his Palestinian ministry, and through the Church, it will continue to be his methodology. When will the Kingdom come? Whenever we care to listen. Praying for the coming of the Kingdom, then, means praying for hearts to be docile to the Lord.

CHRIST THE TEACHER The Pharisees ask a question we all long to ask: when will the Kingdom come? And Jesus answers: it already has come. Where Jesus is accepted, believed in, and obeyed, there he reigns; there the Kingdom can be found. But then he goes on to explain to his disciples that although it is primarily a Kingdom of the heart, it will have a visible manifestation as well.

Many Jews at the time of Jesus were expecting a Messiah to come and restore a highly visible Kingdom, a political and social arrangement in which the Jews would once again have independence and international influence, as they did in the time of David. From their perspective, these were key ingredients for the beginning of the Messianic era, what Jesus calls the "days of the Son of man." But Jesus corrects their mistaken conception. He describes in this passage the symbolic end the Old Covenant, the fall of Jerusalem, which took place in 70 AD after a horrific siege of the city left more than a million Jews dead. Jesus warns his disciples to leave the city as soon as the enemy appears to avoid suffering in this siege. And that's exactly what the Christian community in Jerusalem did when the Roman legions appeared on the horizon; they fled to a town across the Jordan, and they survived. The Roman legions were the vultures bent on tearing apart the city of Jerusalem, which by its official rejection of Jesus had become a spiritual corpse. The Church then took up the baton, and continued to embody and spread Christ's reign.

But this discourse has a lesson for us as well. The end of the Old Covenant and the destruction of Jerusalem foreshadowed the end of history, just as the end of Sodom and Noah's flood foreshadowed the end of Jerusalem. Then, all of creation will "wear out like a garment" (Heb 1:11). It will be destroyed just as Jerusalem was, and in its place Jesus will establish the new heaven and the new earth, in which the interior Kingdom of his reign will be perfectly manifested on the outside as well. That ending will come as swiftly and surprisingly and definitively as the ending of the Old Covenant, so we too should be ready, and we should let nothing distract us from following the Lord in the meantime.

CHRIST THE FRIEND Jesus knows what we need to know, and he knows what we don't need to know. He answers these thorny questions, therefore, without giving all the details. Dates and times won't help the disciples to be more faithful, so he doesn't reveal them.

Jesus: Sometimes you wonder why I don't show you my master plan for your life. I do have one. I have a dream for you. I know what will satisfy you and how you can achieve it. If it would help to tell you everything at once, do you think I would hesitate for the slightest instant to do so? You need to live out my plan for your life one day and one decision at a time. In my wisdom and love, I can tell you that what matters most is that you learn to trust me more and more. Your acts of trust, your obedience to my will, your docility – that is your contribution in making my plan a reality. I know that sometimes you feel frustrated because you can't figure out what I am up to. That's when you need to remember that good friends know how to administer the right medicine one dose at a time, and I am the very best of friends.

CHRIST IN MY LIFE How many times I pray this prayer, "Thy Kingdom Come!" O Lord, I want to pray it from my heart. I want everyone, starting with me, to be docile to your will, to respond generously and trustingly to the nudges and invitations you constantly give. Teach me to make this the real motto of my life: Thy Kingdom come, thy will be done...

So often I want to be able to put everything into a nice little package, to be able to understand everything and live placidly with all the answers. You don't want that. You want me to exercise virtue, trust, and faith. Somehow, you prefer to work that way. Life is an adventure, a journey. Keep me on the right path, going at the right pace...

I trust in you, Lord. When a cathedral is being built, it looks like a mess, but a master plan is guiding that mess and turning it into something beautiful, something magnificent. I know you are the master architect of my life and my efforts to build your Kingdom. Teach me to trust in you at all times and never doubt your wisdom...

QUESTIONS FOR SMALL GROUP DISCUSSION

1. What struck you most in this passage? What did you notice that you hadn't noticed before?

2. If a non-believing friend were to ask you the same question the Pharisees asked Jesus, "When will the Kingdom come?" – how would you answer them?

3. Why do you think Jesus described all these horrible things that would happen at the fall of Jerusalem? When these events actually occurred and some of the Pharisees who had heard Jesus' explanation saw them, what might they have thought?

4. What has been hard for you to trust Jesus about? What has helped you most to trust in difficult moments?

Cf. Catechism of the Catholic Church, 667-677 on Christ already reigning in the Church; 2816-2821 on what the petition "Thy Kingdom come!" really means

THE GOSPEL OF LUKE CHAPTER 18

"For he who will reward us on judgment day for our works and alms will even in this life listen mercifully to those who come to him in prayer combined with good works."
-St Cyprian of Carthage

212. NEVER LOSING HEART (LK 18:1-8)

Luke 18:1-8

Then he told them a parable about the need to pray continually and never lose heart. 'There was a judge in a certain town' he said 'who had neither fear of God nor respect for man. In the same town there was a widow who kept on coming to him and saying, I want justice from you against my enemy! For a long time he refused, but at last he said to himself, Maybe I have neither fear of God nor respect for man, but since she keeps pestering me I must give this widow her just rights, or she will persist in coming and worry me to death.' And the Lord said 'You notice what the unjust judge has to say? Now will not God see justice done to his chosen who cry to him day and night even when he delays to help them? I promise you, he will see justice done to them, and done speedily. But when the Son of Man comes, will he find any faith on earth?'

CHRIST THE LORD The judge in the parable, although an unworthy fellow, has real authority. He can issue a decision that will have actual repercussions both for the widow and for her adversary. Christ also has real authority – "all authority in heaven and earth," as a matter of fact (Matthew 28:18). He is able to influence our lives and history, and he has chosen to put this influence at our disposal. Just as the judge would not have given the widow a fair decision if she had not pleaded with him to do so, God also has decided to make his graces depend (at least in part) upon our initiative. "Ask, and it will be given to you," our Lord pointed out earlier (Luke 11:9); "Search and you will find…" It seems that Christ refuses to be a dictator, but delights in being a generous and responsive King.

CHRIST THE TEACHER Jesus is politely telling us that we are weak petition-ers. He probably detected impatience behind the Pharisees' question about when the kingdom would come, an impatience we too are familiar with. We give up too easily; we approach God with less confidence than this determined widow had in approaching a crooked judge. We doubt God. We think that just because he doesn't answer us in the way we expect him to, he isn't answering us at all. That shows a lack of faith, a truncated vision of God. No prayer that we utter goes unheard. God is never out of his office; he's never on vacation. He is longing for us to bombard him with our prayers. He is eagerly searching for hearts that trust him enough to ask him unceasingly for everything they need. He always answers our prayers, even when the answer is "no."

On judgment day, one of our greatest regrets will be how little we prayed – prayer costs us nothing and can be done anywhere and any time; it's an invest-ment that simply can't go wrong, and yet we relegate it to a few minutes here and there. It's like refusing to turn on the lights because we're afraid they might not work, or because we have become oddly attached to the dark.

CHRIST THE FRIEND In Jesus' last sentence, we detect a tinge of sadness. It is a rhetorical question: when he comes again, will he find any faith? Will he find anyone who recognizes him and is glad to welcome him? He certainly hopes so. He wants to be able to grant us the intense joy of eternal life, but he knows that not everyone will accept the gift, and it pains him.

Jesus: Love is always a risk. I risked it when I came to find you and invite you to follow me in my Kingdom. I knew that in order to offer myself in friendship, I had to become vulnerable; it had to be possible for you to reject me. Look at me hanging from the cross. Look at my side, pierced to my heart with the soldier's lance. This is what love risks; this is love's vulnerability. I am willing to take the risk, because I long for your friendship; I long for you to follow me, day after day. If you accept my invitation, you will have nothing to fear. When it comes to friendship with me, the vulnerability only goes in one direction: you may hurt me by preferring your own will and being unfaithful to me, but I will never be unfaithful to you.

CHRIST IN MY LIFE Thank you for the gift of prayer, Lord. Thank you for giving me a share in your work, for not doing it all yourself. Now my life can have eternal repercussions as you want it to. Dear Lord, teach me to use my freedom well. I don't want to live at the mercy of passing fancies or stock market fluctuations. I want to live grounded in you, grounded in your love and truth…

Teach me to pray, Lord. My faith is so weak. Teach me to pray at all times, to never tire of conversing with you about everything. Help me to develop the habit of lifting my heart and mind to you in the midst of a meeting, a traffic jam, or a chore. Help me to confide in you with all my heart, as you want me to, so that you can work through me to bring many souls into your Kingdom…

I believe in you, Lord. I have put my hopes in you. I love you, though my love is weak and scrawny. If thousands ignore you, I at least want to stay close to you. Guide me, lead me along the path of your wisdom and your peace, and make me a channel of your grace…

QUESTIONS FOR SMALL GROUP DISCUSSION

1. What struck you most in this passage? What did you notice that you hadn't noticed before?

2. What experience or conversation might have prompted Jesus to tell this parable?

3. Why are we less persistent in our prayers than the widow was with her case?

4. What things tend to hold us back from being perfectly docile to God's will? Jesus lived his whole life for us, for the Kingdom. How can we better follow his example?

Cf. Catechism of the Catholic Church, 2742-2745 on the need for perseverance in prayer; 2725-2737 on difficulties in prayer and the "battle" of prayer

213. THE ABCS OF SUCCESS (LK 18:9-17)

Confession heals, confession justifies, confession grants pardon of sin. All hope consists in confession."

- *St Isidore of Seville*

Luke 18:9-17

He spoke the following parable to some people who prided themselves on being virtuous and despised everyone else, 'Two men went up to the Temple to pray, one a Pharisee, the other a tax collector. The Pharisee stood there and said this prayer to himself, I thank you, God, that I am not grasping, unjust, adulterous like the rest of mankind, and particularly that I am not like this tax collector here. I fast twice a week; I pay tithes on all I get. The tax collector stood some distance away, not daring even to raise his eyes to heaven; but he beat his breast and said, God, be merciful to me, a sinner. This man, I tell you, went home again at rights with God; the other did not. For everyone who exalts himself will be humbled, but the man who humbles himself will be exalted.' People even brought little children to him, for him to touch them; but when the disciples saw this they turned them away. But Jesus called the children to him and said, 'Let the little children come to me, and do not stop them; for it is to such as these that the kingdom of God belongs. I tell you solemnly, anyone who does not welcome the kingdom of God like a little child will never enter it.'

CHRIST THE LORD God has the right to be Lord. He is eternal, all-power-ful, all-knowing, all-good, and all-loving. He created all things, and he keeps all things in existence. Everything (and everyone) else owes everything to him. Without God, we would not even be able to sin – because to sin, first of all we have to exist, and second of all, we have to possess free will. Without God, who supplies both of these requisites, we are nothing. When we address Christ as "Lord," we acknowledge this utter dependence on him, and we express our trust that he will continue showering his blessings upon us – not because we deserve them, but because who he is: abounding in generosity and loving-kindness.

When we address Christ as "Lord," we also acknowledge that he deserves our complete fidelity and obedience. And since we are not completely obedient to God (even the just man falls "seven times" a day, cf. Proverbs 24:16), address-ing him as Lord needs to include a confident plea for his mercy. This is the bedrock of all true prayer, because it is the bedrock of the truth about us and about God. In this light, the Pharisee's sin was much greater than "greed, dis-honesty, or adultery"; it was the sin of thinking he didn't need God, that he was independent of the Lord.

By this standard, the Pharisee was not going to make it into the Kingdom of God, because that requires being like children – serenely aware of our dependence. Children aren't angels, but they certainly are dependent on their parents, and they know it. This is basic humility, and without it we can never live in communion with the Lord.

CHRIST THE TEACHER Through the centuries, the prayer of the publican (i.e., tax collector: a Jew who collaborated with the occupying Roman forces by collecting taxes from fellow Jews, often looked upon as the epitome of infidelity to God and a betrayer of the Covenant) has been described as a complete summary of Christian spirituality. There are even cases of monks who made this prayer the only words that they spoke, and who reached the heights of sanctity by means of it.

First of all, it recognizes God's greatest quality – in relation to fallen mankind, that is – his mercy. Mercy is the form love takes in the face of suffering. The word "mercy" comes from the Latin misericors: *miser* (wretched, miserable) plus *cor* (heart) – to take someone else's wretchedness into one's heart. Because of original sin, and because of our personal sins, we are miserable creatures, and when we bring our misery to God, he takes it up into his heart. Second, the publican's prayer recognizes his own need: he accuses himself for being a sinner, someone who has abused the gifts of God, someone who has given into selfishness.

The Pharisee's prayer shows no knowledge either of God's mercy or of his own need for God. In truth, it is no prayer at all – there is no connection between God and the one who is praying: it is just an exercise in narcissism, in self-admiration. God wants to connect with us, but he can only do so if we let him.

CHRIST THE FRIEND Jesus went after the big sinners – you don't get much bigger than "people who prided themselves on being virtuous and despised everyone else." He didn't just preach to the choir (which, in fact, is why his enemies had to have him killed; his influence was simply becoming too widespread). This shows how much he cared about others, and how little he worried about himself. If he had been after comfortable self-satisfaction, he would never have gone after big sinners. This is confirmed by our own experience: when we don't go after those who need Christ most, isn't it because we care more about our own comfortable self-satisfaction than about expanding Christ's Kingdom?

His concern for big sinners also gives us another reason to trust him without limits. No sinner is too big for Christ's mercy. His mercy is infinite, like an ocean; even the greatest sins are finite, like a thimble. How foolish we would be to think our thimble was too deep for his ocean!

CHRIST IN MY LIFE You are my Lord. I understand what that means – I owe everything to you. You hold my entire existence in the palm of your hand. You never cease thinking of me and drawing me closer to you. You are my Lord, but you are also my Father, my Brother, and my Friend. Jesus, I trust in you…

I ask you to have mercy on me, for all the selfishness I know about, and for all the selfishness I'm unaware of. And I ask you to have mercy on all sinners. It is your mercy that makes your glory shine! Teach me to confide in your mercy no matter what, and to be merciful, forgiving, gentle, and meek – especially with those who don't deserve it…

Pour your courage into my heart, Lord. I am hampered in my apostolate and my testimony because I still care too much about what other people will think. I'm glad you didn't give in to those temptations. Teach me to be adventurous in building your Kingdom and spreading it, even to the "big sinners" who seem so hopeless…

QUESTIONS FOR REFLECTION

1. What struck you most in this passage? What did you notice that you hadn't noticed before?

2. How would you describe the proper basic attitude that should be used when we approach God in prayer? What does this parable teach us about God's attitude towards us when we pray?

3. How can we become less like the Pharisee and more like the publican in our prayer? Why should we want to?

4. If an open-minded non-believing friend asked you how to pray, what would say?

Cf. Catechism of the Catholic Church, 2558-256 on the prerequisites for prayer; 2568-2589 on models of prayer from the Old Testament; 2779-2785 on how we should approach God in prayer; 1846-1851 on mercy and sin

214. RIGHT QUESTION – TOUGH ANSWER (LK 18:18-30)

"It is not those who commit the least faults who are most holy, but those who have the greatest courage, the greatest generosity, the greatest love, who make the boldest efforts to overcome themselves, and are not immoderately apprehensive of tripping."

- St Francis de Sales

Luke 18:18-30

A member of one of the leading families put this question to him, 'Good Master, what have I to do to inherit eternal life?' Jesus said to him, 'Why do you call me good? No one is good but God alone. You know the commandments: You must not commit adultery; You must not kill; You must not steal; You must not bring false witness; Honour your father and mother.' He replied, 'I have kept all these from my earliest days till now.' And when Jesus heard this he said, 'There is still one thing you lack. Sell all that you own and distribute the money to the poor, and you will have treasure in heaven; then come, follow me.' But when he heard this he was filled with sadness, for he was very rich. Jesus looked at him and said, 'How hard it is for those who have riches to make their way into the kingdom of God! Yes, it is easier for a camel to pass through the eye of a needle than for a rich man to enter the kingdom of God.' 'In that case,' said the listeners, 'who can be saved?' 'Things that are impossible for men,' he replied, 'are possible for God.' Then Peter said, 'What about us? We left all we had to follow you.' He said to them, 'I tell you solemnly, there is no one who has left house, wife, brothers, parents or children for the sake of the kingdom of God who will not be given repayment many times over in this present time and, in the world to come, eternal life.'

CHRIST THE LORD Throughout the Gospels Jesus repeats the phrase, "I tell you solemnly" (often translated as "Amen, amen, I say to you"). It is another sign of Christ's incomparable stature. Others could use the phrase for rhetorical emphasis, but Christ can speak it with utter exactitude. He is the very Word of God made man – the idea God has of himself, so vibrant and unique that it shares the divine nature and is eternally begotten as the Son. Christ can make solemn declarations, indubitable statements about things inscrutable to even the most illustrious, but still only human, intellects.

When Jesus prefaces statements with this phrase, he is preparing his listeners for a flash of divine revelation. In this case, he makes the unambiguous claim that a life devoted entirely to him is both more fruitful and more fulfilling than a life devoted to anything else, no matter how good and noble it may be. He doesn't disdain prosperity ("house") and family, but he puts them in their proper context. They are gifts from God meant to provide us with arenas for choices where we can exercise virtue and learn to live in communion with God. But too often they become rivals for our hearts, and we become so attached to them that they usurp the place God ought to have – as was the case for this rich young man. Those who trust God, obeying and following him even under the shadow of the cross and self-sacrifice, will find that all the yearnings of the human heart will be abundantly fulfilled, starting in this life and overflowing in the next. It has to be that way, because that's the way of our Lord.

CHRIST THE TEACHER Jesus recognizes the man's sincerity and openheartedness, and he immediately teaches him a preliminary lesson: the question of life's meaning, of eternal life, what every heart knowingly or unknowingly longs for, can only be resolved by God: "Only God is good." Who has not asked this question in their heart? Who has not gazed on a moonrise or a sunset and felt that plaintive ache in their soul, that yearning to reach out and touch the source of all that beauty? This is the burden Jesus' interlocutor lays at the Lord's feet.

How wise he was to lay it there! How foolish so many others have been through the ages (and how foolish many still are today), seeking the answer to this question anywhere else but in the Word of God! But even though this rich young man asked the right question of the right Master, he ended up making the same mistake as those who ask it of the wrong masters. This young man thought he could achieve meaning and fulfillment by some formula, by some action of his own, by his own natural powers. He had faithfully obeyed the commandments Jesus lists, all having to do with how he treated his neighbor, but it seems he was still depending on his own resources. He had neglected the very first commandment, to love God with all his heart, soul, and mind. He was still in the driver's seat of his life. And when Jesus asks him to give us his false sense of security and self-sufficiency – symbolized by his money – he simply can't do it. He won't let God drive.

Jesus draws out the lesson after this saddening refusal: those who are rich in this world's goods easily fall into the deception that they can achieve life's meaning on their own, without God's help. But when they buy into this deception, they sabotage their chance at fulfillment, because "man is made to live in communion with God, in whom he finds happiness" (Catechism of the Catholic Church, 45). Only God satisfies.

CHRIST THE FRIEND *Jesus: My child, if only you knew how much I want to give you. I created the whole universe just to show you a little bit of what I want you to have. I am glad you are here with me now, taking time to consider what I came to earth in order to teach you. But do you really believe it with all your heart? The more you follow me and trust me, the more space you give me to lavish my gifts upon you. How it pains me when people prefer passing wealth to the everlasting wealth I created them to enjoy! You trust in me, I know. Never let the desire for the good things of this world sway you from the path of my will. I will always let you know which way to turn on your journey through life, and if you trust me, you will always recognize* *my voice, because you will know I am always at your side. You belong to my Kingdom, and I am your Shepherd; stay close to me.*

CHRIST IN MY LIFE Lord, thank you for giving me the Gospels. I am so thirsty to know the truth. I have asked this question about life's meaning so many times. And now I know that I am on the right path, because it is your path. O Lord, grant me the gift of wisdom, so that I can always taste the sweetness of your truth and prefer it to every false deception of this fallen world...

I know that money tempts me, and you know it too. You know that I love the good things of this world, all the pleasures and comforts that money can buy. Sometimes I think it would be easier to just live with absolutely nothing, but I know that you want me to live the virtue of detachment while still using these good things. Help me, Lord, to do your will...

I love the phrase you say to St Peter, "Things that are impossible for men are possible for God." O Jesus, burn that into my mind and my heart! Never let me forget it! I am so easily daunted and discouraged, but how can I be when I know that you are my Lord, my champion? I want to give my whole heart to you through doing your will today. Be my strength, Lord Jesus...

QUESTIONS FOR SMALL GROUP DISCUSSION

1. What struck you most in this passage? What did you notice that you hadn't noticed before?

2. What has helped you most as you strive to live the spirit of Christian poverty and detachment in the midst of a consumer-crazed world?

3. What light does this passage shed on the first beatitude, "How happy are the poor in spirit; theirs is the Kingdom of Heaven"?

4. Besides wealth, what are some of the other most common obstacles to following God's will in our lives?

Cf. Catechism of the Catholic Church, 2112-2114, 2172, 2424, 2536 on idolatry and the divinizing of what is not God; 2402-2406 on the universal destination of all earthly goods; 2426-2436 on economic activity and social justice

215. THINGS ARE NOT AS THEY SEEM (LK 18:31-43)

"Everyone – whether kings, nobles, tradesmen or peasants – must do all things for the glory of God and under the inspiration of Christ's example."

- St Francis Borgia

Luke 18:31-43

Then taking the Twelve aside he said to them, 'Now we are going up to Jerusalem, and everything that is written by the prophets about the Son of Man is to come true. For he will be handed over to the pagans and will be mocked, maltreated and spat on, and when they have scourged him they will put him to death; and on the third day he will rise again.' But they could make nothing of this; what he said was quite obscure to them, they had no idea what it meant. Now as he drew near to Jericho there was a blind man sitting at the side of the road begging. When he heard the crowd going past he asked what it was all about, and they told him that Jesus the Nazarene was passing by. So he called out, 'Jesus, Son of David, have pity on me'. The people in front scolded him and told him to keep quiet, but he shouted all the louder, 'Son of David, have pity on me.' Jesus stopped and ordered them to bring the man to him, and when he came up, asked him, 'What do you want me to do for you?' 'Sir,' he replied 'let me see again.' Jesus said to him, 'Receive your sight. Your faith has saved you.' And instantly his sight returned and he followed him praising God, and all the people who saw it gave praise to God for what had happened.

CHRIST THE LORD Jesus predicts his passion yet again, instructing his apostles in even more detail than before, mentioning the Roman ("pagan") involvement this time. St Luke makes it painfully clear, however, that the apostles still understood absolutely nothing of this. Why does Jesus keep repeating it when it's clear they simply can't grasp what he's telling them?

He was arming them for the crisis they would face in the aftermath of the event. At that moment (which is just around the corner), in the midst of their fear and confusion, they would remember that Jesus went to Jerusalem with full knowledge of what was going to befall him. Reflecting on Jesus' prior knowledge and his willingness to suffer will prepare them to accept the Resurrection and to understand the sacrificial meaning of his death. It will also help them appreciate more fully the great truth that will make such an impact on St Paul – that Jesus took the punishment for our sins upon himself *while we were still sinners*, before we had asked for forgiveness or repented. This is the mightiest proof that the Lord's love and saving mercy are entirely dependable and always accessible, because they are entirely independent of our worthiness. The Lord loves us madly simply because we are.

CHRIST THE TEACHER This last miracle before his passion is particularly eloquent. St Luke has just emphatically explained that Jesus' predictions were "quite obscure" to the apostles – they couldn't see what he meant; they were blind to the coming storm. And upon Christ's entry into Jerusalem, St Luke will go on to describe a series of encounters with the leaders of the city in which they continually refuse to see the glaring credentials of the Messiah – they too are blind, unable to recognize Jesus for who he is. And in the middle of all this spiritual darkness, we find a man who is physically blind but spiritually brilliant. He believes in Jesus whom he has never seen. He has never seen any of his miracles and has probably never heard him preach before – if he had, he would have asked for his cure then.

How is it that the blind man of Jericho can see so clearly? What illuminates for him the priceless lamp of faith? He alone recognizes his need for Christ's grace. The leaders of Jerusalem don't recognize their need for anything – the status quo is profitable and under their complete control. Even the apostles don't recognize their real need for Christ's grace, because they don't yet recognize the true, supernatural essence of their mission. They will soon profess their undying loyalty, basing it on their natural strength, only to fall away and abandon him when things get uncomfortable. The Gospels never tire of telling us that humility alone frees God to do miracles in our lives. And maybe that's because God knows we are ceaselessly tempted to think we know better than him.

CHRIST THE FRIEND *Jesus: My child, the hour of my passion is drawing near. I am eager for it to come. Too many hearts will never trust me unless I show them that nothing they can do can diminish even a nanometer of my love for them. But we will talk more of that later.*

Look at this blind man who moved my heart. He had once been able to see, but now all was dark to him. He is like the whole human race, which had seen my goodness and wisdom in all its beauty at the dawn of creation but had fallen into darkness at the rebellion of original sin. Every heart still harbors a memory of that intimacy we enjoyed before the Fall, because I made every heart for that intimacy. Why do so many hearts seek the light they long for in the shadows? Why don't they come to me, who came to bring it to them? I will open their eyes, as I opened this man's eyes. Ask me to give you back more and more of that original light. I will fulfill your deepest desires, because you believe in me.

CHRIST IN MY LIFE I am sometimes afraid that I am just like the apostles, Lord. You told them the same thing over and over again – about your passion and resurrection – and they were still shocked when it happened. You keep telling me the same things over and over again too, and I think I am just as slow a learner. But you didn't give up on them, and I know you will never give up on me…

Why is humility so hard, Lord? I want to depend on you, to be like a little child in his mother's arms. I know that your grace can give me that trust, confidence, and littleness. How full of peace and joy is the humble heart! That's what you want for me. Jesus, meek and humble of heart, make my heart more like yours…

Send me to bring your torch into the darkness, Lord. I don't have to be the light; I just have to carry it. You are the light. I want to spread your light to the farthest corners of the world – geographically and spiritually. Fill me with your light, and then send me to those of your children who are in darkness. Make me generous and docile, and I will go wherever you want me to go…

QUESTIONS FOR SMALL GROUP DISCUSSION

1. What struck you most in this passage? What did you notice that you hadn't noticed before?

2. What does popular culture think about the virtue of humility, and how does it compare to Christ's view? How can we make sure to keep Christ's vision fresh in our minds?

3. Do you think Christ's foreknowledge of his passion diminished or increased his suffering when it actually began? Why and in what way?

4. Why do you think the crowd tried to keep the blind man away from Jesus? Is there a lesson here for us?

Cf. Catechism of the Catholic Church, 27-30 on man's desire for God; 153-165 on the nature of faith

THE GOSPEL OF LUKE CHAPTER 19

"Why, dearest daughter, do you waste time in sadness when time is so precious for the salvation of poor sinners? Get rid of your melancholy immediately. Don't think any more about yourself. Do not indulge in so many useless and dangerous reflections. Look ahead always without ever looking back. Keep your gaze fixed on the summit of perfection where Christ awaits you. He wants you despoiled of all things, intent only on procuring his greater glory during this brief time of your existence. For the short time that remains, is it worthwhile to lose yourself in melancholy like those who think only of themselves, as if all were to end with this life? Ah no. We must not even desire that our pilgrimage on this earth be a short one because we do not yet know the infinite value of every minute employed for the glory of God. Carry your cross then but carry it joyfully, my daughter. Think that Jesus loves you very much. And in return for such love, don't lose yourself in so many desires, but accept daily with serenity whatever comes your way. May the heart of Jesus bless you and make you holy not as you want but as he desires."

- St Frances Xavier Cabrini

216. SEEK AND YOU WILL FIND (LK 19:1-10)

"Help me, O Lord, that my eyes may be merciful, so that I may never suspect or judge from appearances, but look for what is beautiful in my neighbors' souls and come to their rescue."

- St Faustina Kowalska

Luke 19:1-10

He entered Jericho and was going through the town when a man whose name was Zacchaeus made his appearance; he was one of the senior tax collectors and a wealthy man. He was anxious to see what kind of man Jesus was, but he was too short and could not see him for the crowd; so he ran ahead and climbed a sycamore tree to catch a glimpse of Jesus who was to pass that way. When Jesus reached the spot he looked up and spoke to him: 'Zacchaeus, come down. Hurry, because I must stay at your house today.' And he hurried down and welcomed him joyfully. They all complained when they saw what was happening. 'He has gone to stay at a sinner's house' they said. But Zacchaeus stood his ground and said to the Lord, 'Look, sir, I am going to give half my property to the poor, and if I have cheated anybody I will pay him back four times the amount.' And Jesus said to him, 'Today salvation has come to this house, because this man too is a son of Abraham; for the Son of Man has come to seek out and save what was lost.'

CHRIST THE LORD Leaders, to be effective, need to base their leadership on something deeper than opinion polls and popularity ratings. Jesus had attracted a crowd as he made his way to Jerusalem (previous passages call it a "great crowd"). Perhaps it was a member of this crowd who pointed Zacchaeus out to Jesus and mentioned what an evil man he was. (Tax collectors made their handsome livings by requiring the people to pay more taxes than Rome demanded and then skimming off the excess for themselves – that's how the Roman authorities kept the tax collectors in tow.) In any case, when Jesus decided to go over to Zacchaeus' house, the crowd was appalled. They all "began to grumble, saying, 'He has gone to stay at a sinner's house.'" If Jesus had cared more for what people said about him than for what God was asking of him, Zacchaeus would have continued in his sin, and the countryside would have continued to suffer from his injustice. But Jesus knew his mission, and he didn't let vain gossip and opposition deter him from it. He is the Lord, and he will rule his Kingdom according to his own standards, whether or not everyone else is comfortable with it. True Christians will do likewise.

But truly effective leadership, from Christ's perspective, also requires truly caring for others, a trait Jesus exemplifies here yet again. Zacchaeus didn't know that he was in dire need of a spiritual renewal (or perhaps he did know, deep down), but Christ recognized it immediately. And even though he had intended to pass through the town, Christ changes his plans and invites himself over for dinner at the unpopular tax collector's house. "...Come down. Hurry..." he told Zacchaeus, expressing his eager desire to bring "salvation" to this man's house.

And Zacchaeus "hurried down and welcomed him joyfully." Jesus continues to do the same thing with us, going out of his way to bring us the light and strength we need to live in accordance with God's hopes for us – and if we, like Zacchaeus, come quickly and receive God's advances with joy, salvation will come to our house too.

CHRIST THE TEACHER In this passage Jesus teaches us about himself. He provides a living parable that illustrates the entire meaning of the Incarnation, and then, just in case we didn't get the message, he summarizes it for us: "The Son of Man has come to seek out and save what was lost."

Christ's whole life while he was on earth was dedicated to bringing people back into friendship with God, and to establishing his Church to continue that mission throughout history. If that is the mission of Christ, and if that is the mission of the Church, than it ought also to be the mission of every Christian, of every member of the Church. And when we make it the mission of our lives, we, like Christ, will become messengers of deep and lasting peace, both for the hearts of troubled souls and for the hearts of troubled societies. Zacchaeus's conversion affected not only himself, but also the entire region – all the poor and all those who "grumbled" when Jesus went to stay at his house. The path to social justice follows the path of one-on-one reconciliation with God.

CHRIST THE FRIEND *Zacchaeus: I wanted to see this man that everyone was talking about. At first, it felt like normal curiosity. But then, when I went out into the streets and saw the crowds, when I felt the intensity of emotion and expectation, it became more than curiosity. Something inside of me pushed me, drove me, propelled me to find a way to see this rabbi from Nazareth. One of the soldiers helped me climb up into the crook of that tree – and it was just in time, too. As soon as Jesus came into sight, I couldn't take my eyes off him. It was as if the rest of the world receded and only he existed. I watched him make his way slowly through the throngs. He was coming closer. I could feel my heart beating. Suddenly a voice seemed to tell me to get down from the tree, to hide before he saw me. I don't know why I didn't do that. I only know that something even deeper in my heart kept me riveted to him. Then he stopped, right beside the tree. He looked up. Even before he said my name, I could sense his goodness rising up to me. I know it sounds strange.... It was – the whole encounter was strange. But it was real; it was true. I spent the day with him. He brought my soul back to life. He freed my heart from chains that I didn't even know were there. That's how he was.*

Jesus: My child, do you see what happens whenever you make even a little effort to find me, to see me more clearly, like Zacchaeus? He was joyful because salvation came to his heart, but I think I was even more joyful, because the shepherd loves the sheep more than the sheep can ever love the shepherd. You bring joy to my heart whenever you welcome me into your home, your soul, and your mind. When you receive me in Holy Communion, I bring all my grace to strengthen your soul for doing good and living in the light, just as when Zacchaeus took me into his household. How I long for more souls who would receive me in Holy Communion! So many don't even know I'm there, and many who do know don't take full advantage of this gift. I am glad that you do. Now, speak to me of your plans, your hopes, and your struggles.

CHRIST IN MY LIFE I am vulnerable to other people's opinions – a bit too vulnerable. If I loved you more and if my faith were stronger, I would care less about what they think and more about what you think. That's what I want, Lord. Increase my faith! Increase my love! Make me passionate about the mission you have given me, as you were passionate about the mission the Father gave you…

You know I want to bring many souls into your friendship; I want to go out and find the Zacchaeuses, the ones everyone else has given up on. I want to speak to them about your goodness and your love, your forgiveness, and the meaning you give to life. But I am clumsy and inconsistent – you knew that when you made me your disciple. You can be my strength, Lord…

What did you create me for? You made me to live in communion with you. You want me to get to know you, more and more, for all eternity, as best friends keep getting to know each other better – and the more they do, the more enjoyable the friendship becomes. I want that too. I want to share in your work. Whatever you want me to do, I want to do, because I want to follow you…

QUESTIONS FOR SMALL GROUP DISCUSSION

1. What struck you most in this passage? What did you notice that you hadn't noticed before?
2. Why do you think Christ was able to resist popular trends and "peer pressure"? Why do we often find it difficult to do so?
3. If Christ were with us now, how would he be fulfilling his mission to "seek and save what was lost"? In other words, how does that essential mission translate into the "here and now" for us? Who are the Zacchaeuses in our lives?
4. Christ went out of his way – changed his plans even – to take advantage of an opportunity to bring Zacchaeus back to God. How can we become more sensitive to such opportunities and take better advantage of them?

Cf. Catechism of the Catholic Church, 456-460 on Christ's mission; 976-983 on Christ and the forgiveness of sins; 1886-1889 on conversion and society

217. LORD OF HISTORY, LORD OF HEARTS (LK 19:11-27)

"That man is your best servant who is not so much concerned to hear from you what he wills as to will what he hears from you."

- St Augustine

Luke 19:11-27

While the people were listening to this he went on to tell a parable, because he was near Jerusalem and they imagined that the kingdom of God was going to show itself then and there. Accordingly he said, 'A man of noble birth went to a distant country to be appointed king and afterwards return. He summoned ten of his servants and gave them ten pounds. Do business with these he told them until I get back. But his compatriots detested him and sent a delegation to follow him with this message, We do not want this man to be our king. Now on his return, having received his appointment as king, he sent for those servants to whom he had given the money, to find out what profit each had made. The first came in and said, Sir, your one pound has brought in ten. Well done, my good servant! he replied Since you have proved yourself faithful in a very small thing, you shall have the government of ten cities. Then came the second and said, Sir, your one pound has made five. To this one also he said, And you shall be in charge of five cities. Next came the other and said, Sir, here is your pound. I put it away safely in a piece of linen because I was afraid of you; for you are an exacting man: you pick up what you have not put down and reap what you have not sown. You wicked servant! he said Out of your own mouth I condemn you. So you knew I was an exacting man, picking up what I have not put down and reaping what I have not sown? Then why did you not put my money in the bank? On my return I could have drawn it out with interest. And he said to those standing by, Take the pound from him and give it to the man who has ten pounds. And they said to him, But, sir, he has ten pounds . . . I tell you, to everyone who has will be given more; but from the man who has not, even what he has will be taken away. But as for my enemies who did not want me for their king, bring them here and execute them in my presence.'

CHRIST THE LORD Up to the very end, St Luke tells us, Jesus' followers still mistakenly thought that Jesus was going to take possession of Israel like the return of an Old Testament political leader. You can't blame them. Even though Jesus had been predicting his fate – betrayal, passion, and death in Jerusalem – for a while now, the immense crowds, the festive atmosphere (it is estimated that several million pilgrims were in and around Jerusalem for the Passover festival), and the crescendo of miracles and verbal defeats of the Pharisees all seemed to indicate an impending, dramatic, glorious emergence of Jesus as the new David. But Christ has his sights set on something even greater.

His Kingdom, of which David's was but a shadowy forerunner, will include all people, and it will last forever. It won't be a Kingdom of military might and political prudence, but one of deep, definitive renewal of the human spirit by plugging it back into communion with God. It is the Kingdom of grace, the New Covenant community, the Church, which will spread through every land for all of history until Jesus comes again to inaugurate its fullness. Its foundation, therefore, must go deeper than merely political maneuverings. Jesus is going up to Jerusalem to lay that foundation by performing his own redemptive sacrifice on Calvary. By suffering, dying, and rising from the dead in perfect love and obedience to the Father, Jesus – the second Adam – will conquer not merely political enemies, but the archenemy of the human race, Satan himself, who instituted the reign of death by instigating the first Adam to mistrust and disobey the Father.

Christ is Lord of life and history because he makes himself Lord of human hearts, which, by their choices, lead lives and history either to their fulfilment or to their frustration. As we walk with Jesus from Jericho to Jerusalem, up the dusty roads of Judea, we should thank him for setting his sights so high, renew our allegiance to his Kingdom, and ask for the grace to have the same priorities in our lives that he had in his.

CHRIST THE TEACHER Jesus, always patient and understanding, explains to his misconstruing followers yet again the Kingdom that they continue to confuse. Since it is a Kingdom of hearts, they themselves will be primary players in it. Jesus will give them the three tools they will need to perform their role in the Kingdom.

First, Jesus will give them the grace of redemption, an interior renewal of their souls, a fresh start in their relationship with God and their fellow men – this is the sanctifying grace that comes to us from his passion, death, and resurrection through the sacraments of his Church. The "pound" that the king in the parable gives his servants represents this grace, the same gift received by all. Second, Jesus gives them an unspecified period of time in which to make this grace grow by living out his teachings and his commandments – most especially the commandments of love and evangelization. This corresponds to the time in the parable during which the new king is traveling to be invested with his kingship, the period after Christ's ascension. Third, Jesus gives his disciples the knowledge that he will come again at the end of history in order to reward his faithful followers, but those who have been selfish and wicked, sticking to their old way of life in spite of the gift of grace, will have forfeited their membership in his Kingdom.

This parable should be one of the most highly prized treasures of every Christian. It brings all of the human condition into sharp, refreshing, unmistakable focus. We are here to receive God's gifts and make them bear fruit for his Kingdom, to invest our lives in giving witness to Christ in our thoughts, words, deeds, and manner. This life is brief and only has meaning in relation to the life to come. How clear our Lord makes it for us! How eager he is for us to use our freedom wisely, so that he can reward us richly when the time comes!

CHRIST THE FRIEND *Jesus: My child, many people, like the third servant in the parable, think I am angry, irrational, unpredictable, selfish, and irascible. But what evidence have I given for such a characterization? Is my creation not a beautiful abode? Do I not maintain the laws of physics and chemistry and biology, so that humanity can continue to live without descending into chaos? And when my children rebelled against me and lost the harmony I had given them at first, did I not continue to care for them and then come and teach them with my gospel the meaning of life, suffering, and death? Am I not willing to forgive them at any moment, no matter how horrendous their offenses? Did I myself, all-powerful and all-knowing, not suffer humiliation, rejection, betrayal, scourging, beating, and crucifixion just to prove to them that I am not an evil, selfish King, but their brother as well as their Lord?*

When they accuse me of being harsh and unyielding, they accuse themselves; they continue living in the self-destruction of self-centeredness and self-indulgence. I will wait as long as possible for them to become disenchanted with that life and turn again to the light. I will send my messengers to them over and over, in myriad ways. But I will not force them to trust me. No, I gave them freedom, the capacity to love, and I will never take it away.

CHRIST IN MY LIFE Lord Jesus, I have placed all my hopes in you. I have confessed my faith in you and I have committed myself to doing your will and living as you would have me live. And I am glad I have! You are a generous Lord – you are generosity itself! Whatever you ask of me, I will give you, because all I have, you have given to me…

I have precious few things, but they are all I need. I have the grace you have given me, my faith, my friendship with you, the pearl of great price. I have my life, however long or short it may be – only you know, Lord. And I have the knowledge that you have given me a mission to accomplish. I need nothing more, except the strength to say each day, "Thy will be done…"

I will go to those who are hiding their pound because they are lazy and self-absorbed. I will be your goodness to them. I will be your voice to them. Teach me what to say, what to do, what to write, how to act – so that your Kingdom will triumph in the hardest of hearts…

QUESTIONS FOR SMALL GROUP DISCUSSION

1. What struck you most in this passage? What did you notice that you hadn't noticed before?

2. Why do you think his followers still misunderstood the nature of his Kingdom? Do you think we are really as free from this error as we think we are?

3. Jesus is basically instructing his followers to live diligently and responsibly in this earthly life, but to focus on the life that is to come. Why do you think so many contemporaries make fun of this view of reality? How can we respond to their objections?

4. If an agnostic friend came up to you and asked how to get to heaven, what would you tell them?

Cf. Catechism of the Catholic Church, 678-679 on Jesus' judgment at the end of history; 668-677 on Christ's second coming in glory

218. PALMS AND STONES (LK 19:28-40)

"Sing with your voices, sing with your hearts, sing with your lips, sing with your lives."

- St Augustine

Luke 19:28-40

When he had said this he went on ahead, going up to Jerusalem. Now when he was near Bethphage and Bethany, close by the Mount of Olives as it is called, he sent two of the disciples, telling them, 'Go off to the village opposite, and as you enter it you will find a tethered colt that no one has yet ridden. Untie it and bring it here. If anyone asks you, Why are you untying it? you are to say this, The Master needs it.' The messengers went off and found everything just as he had told them. As they were untying the colt, its owner said, 'Why are you untying that colt?' and they answered, 'The Master needs it.' So they took the colt to Jesus, and throwing their garments over its back they helped Jesus on to it. As he moved off, people spread their cloaks in the road, and now, as he was approaching the downward slope of the Mount of Olives, the whole group of disciples joyfully began to praise God at the top of their voices for all the miracles they had seen. They cried out: 'Blessings on the King who comes, in the name of the Lord! Peace in heaven and glory in the highest heavens!' Some Pharisees in the crowd said to him, 'Master, check your disciples,' but he answered, 'I tell you, if these keep silence the stones will cry out.'

CHRIST THE LORD The King is coming to take possession of his Kingdom. The King happens to be God's only Son, the Anointed One, the Messiah, and the Kingdom happens to be the eternal Kingdom of God himself. It is the first act of the sacred drama of Christ's greatest work: his passion, death, and resurrection. That drama is the crux of all history: everything that came before was leading up to it, preparing for it; everything that has come since has flowed from it. If Christ had not obeyed the Father by loving his disciples "to the end" (John 13:1), mankind would still be alienated from God. The salvation of the universe was at stake, and though the King's throne would be a cross and his crown would be of thorns, even so, that throne and that crown would outlast every other earthly king's and be glorified even into eternity. Indeed, as much as the Pharisees were disturbed by talk of kings and heavenly glory, if they had been silent, the stones would surely have had to cry out.

Yet, were the crowds shouting and singing in recognition of this eternal Kingdom, the Kingdom of grace, redemption, and spiritual renewal? They were hoping for a different kind of prosperity, unfortunately, as would become evident when they all abandoned Jesus in fear and confusion later in the week. They looked at Christ and knew that he was their King, their Deliverer, but they looked at him through the filter of their own narrow, mundane expectations. Jesus had something much greater that he wanted to give them. As he scanned their ecstatic faces, did his own expression betray a hint of sadness? The Lord was being misunderstood by the people he came to save. Is he perhaps still being misunderstood by us?

CHRIST THE TEACHER When we were baptized, we became sharers in Christ's Kingship; we became "coheirs" with Christ the King, as St Paul would put it (Romans 8:17). In his royal entry into Jerusalem, Jesus gives us a model for the kind of kings we are to be. First, we are to be faithful to God's will. It was Zechariah who prophesied in God's name that the Messiah would enter Jerusalem riding on a colt, so Christ made sure to do so. Second, we are to be bearers of peace. When kings in the ancient near East rode on donkeys (which were considered much nobler animals there than they were in the West), it was a sign that they traveled in times of peace and came in peace; when they rode on horses, they rode to war. Third, we are to pay attention to the little things. Perhaps Christ had previously arranged a "password" with the owners of the colt; perhaps he simply knew that they would understand when his disciples said "The Master has need of it." In any case, he had planned ahead; he had done his homework. We should strive to be worthy of such a Master, showing our Christian love in the little things, where love matters most.

CHRIST THE FRIEND *Jesus: My child, notice how I had it recorded exactly where this* *great event occurred: "near Bethphage and Bethany, close by the Mount of Olives." I am not the abstract deity that so many make me out to be. I am not just a divine architect who holds creation at arm's length. I am present in the real, day-to-day flow of your life. That's where I want to bring my victory. What good would it do if I were to stay far away from you? How would I be able to convince you of my love, of the offer of my friendship? I want to walk with you through life. I want to share your joys and sorrows and have you share mine. You can find me always at your side – this is the whole reason behind my Incarnation. I am with you, loving you, guiding you, teaching you – even when you forget about me, I never forget about you: in the library, on the racquetball courts, in the nursery, at the office. I told you my name because I already knew yours, even before you were born. Thank you for letting me walk with you. Let me accompany you in your daily life.*

CHRIST IN MY LIFE I believe in you, Lord. I believe that you are the Savior sent by the Father to lead us home to heaven. You know that this is not the most popular belief these days. But I don't care about what's popular; I care about what's true. I believe in you, and I want to follow you. Thank you for the gift of faith, Lord. Teach me to live it radically, totally, like the saints…

You knew your mission so thoroughly. Is it possible for me to know mine as thoroughly? Sometimes it seems so vague to me. Maybe it will always have that layer of mystery, but I know that it can't be too mystical, because then I wouldn't be able to carry it out. Help me to understand my mission better, Lord, so that I can fulfill it more energetically and completely…

I know you walk with me every step of my life. What would I without you? But what about all my neighbors, and what about the thousands of others who don't even know your name? They need your presence and your strength and wisdom just as much as I do. Reach out to them, Lord. Make me your messenger. I give you my feet to follow your path…

QUESTIONS FOR SMALL GROUP DISCUSSION

1. What struck you most in this passage? What did you notice that you hadn't noticed before?

2. The "Holy, holy, holy…" that we pray every Mass is taken from this Gospel event. Considering its original context, why do you think the Church inserted it into the Mass in the place we find it today? What should the attitude of our hearts be when we pray it?

3. What could have been in Christ's heart and mind during this procession – knowing, as he did, that soon some of these same people would clamor for his crucifixion?

4. How can we avoid treating Jesus as an abstract deity? In other words, how can we learn to find him near the "Bethphage and Bethany" of our everyday lives?

Cf. Catechism of the Catholic Church, 557-560, 569, 570 on the meaning of Palm Sunday

219. THE SACRED HEART UNFURLED (LK 19:41-48)

"Do not be afraid of Christ! He takes nothing away, and he gives you everything. When we give ourselves to him, we receive a hundredfold in return. Yes, open, open wide the doors to Christ – and you will find true life."

- Pope Benedict XVI

Luke 19:41-48

As he drew near and came in sight of the city he shed tears over it and said, 'If you in your turn had only understood on this day the message of peace! But, alas, it is hidden from your eyes! Yes, a time is coming when your enemies will raise fortifications all round you, when they will encircle you and hem you in on every side; they will dash you and the children inside your walls to the ground; they will leave not one stone standing on another within you – and all because you did not recognise your opportunity when God offered it!' Then he went into the Temple and began driving out those who were selling. 'According to scripture,' he said, 'my house will be a house of prayer. But you have turned it into a robbers' den.' He taught in the Temple every day. The chief priests and the scribes, with the support of the leading citizens, tried to do away with him, but they did not see how they could carry this out because the people as a whole hung on his words.

CHRIST THE LORD Some kings wish destruction on their enemies; the Lord desires his enemies' salvation. Few passages of the Gospels reveal so emphatically the love Christ bore the people he came to save: "As he drew near… he shed tears…" Amidst the jubilation of the crowds, Jesus weeps. He looks down upon this city, chosen by God to be a lantern for the world, whose vocation is to be frustrated by the stubborn refusal of its leaders to admit God's sovereignty. Jesus weeps not because his pride is wounded, but because he knows that those who reject God's rule and the peace it brings simultaneously submit themselves to Satan's (we only have two options), and that means destruction. The devastation he describes here will eventually take place just as he predicted it, in 70 AD under the merciless siege engines of the Roman army.

The all-powerful King weeps over his rebellious subjects because he is unwilling to force them into subjection and freely accepts their rejection of him, drinking it to the bitterest dregs, just to show forth the extent of his love. If we truly contemplated this portrait of our Lord, it would change our hearts forever.

As his followers, our hearts too should resonate with the needs of the world. If Jesus wept over ancient Jerusalem, how would he react upon coming to modern New York, or Paris, or Tokyo? We should know, because our hearts are one with his, and the concerns and desires of our Lord should be reflected in those who love him.

CHRIST THE TEACHER Shrewd businessmen bent the rules of Temple purity during Passover time, and the Temple officials let them. To take advantage of the huge amount of pilgrims coming from all over the Mediterranean world, all of who had to change money so they could buy sacrificial animals for the worship ceremonies, they set up commerce booths inside the outermost courtyard of the sacred precincts – the only place where Gentile pilgrims were allowed to pray. Jesus scatters them. His action prefigures the approaching scattering of the Temple itself that will happen at the end of the siege of Jerusalem – that too will be the result of the leaders of Jerusalem preferring worldly desires to God's plans.

But the action has a deeper lesson as well. Every Christian soul is a temple of the Holy Spirit (1 Cor 6:19). We too can defile ourselves by letting habits of self-indulgence and self-centeredness disrupt the communion with God we are called to enjoy. We can even transform our religious actions into subtle tactics for self-aggrandizement, seeking profit in the eyes of others instead of the eyes of God. When our friendship with Christ becomes one more item on our to-do list instead of the motivation behind all we do, it's a sign that we have set up money changer booths in our hearts. When we ignore the voice of our conscience, treat the apostolate as a favor we do for Jesus, and start blaming the faults of others for our own shortcomings, we can be sure that the temple of our soul is being defiled.

Few times in the Gospels does Jesus act so forcefully and angrily as in this scene. We should take the lesson to heart now and do regular spring-cleaning willingly, lest we suffer worse consequences unwillingly later on.

CHRIST THE FRIEND *Jesus: When I saw the city of Jerusalem, gleaming in the sunlight as I descended Mount Olivet, I saw all its history and all its future. How could I not weep? Certainly it pained my heart to be rejected by so many of my Chosen People, but many of them also recognized their Messiah and welcomed me – Mary did, and Peter, James, the other apostles, Nicodemus, and many others. But this city meant so much more. It was the symbol of my Father's fidelity and love for all mankind, the symbol of his untiring effort to lead the stray sheep back home to the sheepfold, of his eternal plan of salvation. And just as so many in Jerusalem turned a deaf or fearful ear to my words that week, spurning my Father's generosity, just so many others would do the same all along the centuries in many other cities throughout the world.*

That is why you should never doubt my commitment to you, my joy at your "Yes" to my invita-

tions. If I wept so openly at others' rejections, do you not think I rejoice even more at your trust-ing acceptance? Follow me, and I will show you the way to the life you long to live.

CHRIST IN MY LIFE Lord Jesus, why do I not weep for those souls who reject you? Why do I not burn with a desire to bring them closer to you? You know why. My heart is still stained and tainted with too much selfishness. But you knew that when you called me to follow you. You can work with that. You are all powerful. I put my heart in your hands. Teach me to love as you love…

It is hard to keep first things first in this world, Lord. I think a few money changers have sneaked their way into the Temple of my heart. But you know that I want to follow you. You know I want to be the saint you created me to be. So let's get to work, Lord. Show me what has to change, and give me the strength to change it…

Thank you, Lord, for your persistent love. Thank you, Father, for sending your Son to walk with me. Look me in the eye and teach me about your greatness and your mercy. Thank you for giving me the Church through which I can still see Christ's eyes and hear his voice. How you must love me to give me so much! Blessed be your name forever…

QUESTIONS FOR SMALL GROUP DISCUSSION

1. What struck you most in this passage? What did you notice that you hadn't noticed before?

2. How do you think the apostles reacted when Jesus was cleansing the Temple?

3. What are some of the common "money changers" that we let set up shop in our hearts these days?

4. Jesus' cleansing of the Temple is an image of what happens in the individual soul during confession. Does it help explain in any way why going to confession is always difficult? How can we make the most of this sacrament?

Cf. Catechism of the Catholic Church, 583-586 on Jesus and the Temple; 2083-2094 on keeping the First Commandment in the Era of the Church; 1763-1770 on passions (like anger and sadness) and the moral life; 2302 on the sin of anger

THE GOSPEL OF LUKE CHAPTER 20

"Prayer, then, and penance are the two potent inspirations sent to us at this time by God, that we may lead back to him mankind that has gone astray and wanders about without a guide: they are the inspirations that will dispel and remedy the first and prin-cipal cause of every form of disturbance and rebellion, the revolt of man against God."

- Pope Pius XI

220. FRUITFUL VINES AND SHRIVELED HEARTS (LK 20:1-19)

"The Lord said to me, 'I want to give myself to souls and to fill them with my love, but few there are who want to accept all the graces my love has intended for them.'"

- St Faustina Kowalska

Luke 20:1-19

Now one day while he was teaching the people in the Temple and proclaiming the Good News, the chief priests and the scribes came up, together with the elders, and spoke to him. 'Tell us' they said 'what authority have you for acting like this? Or who is it that gave you this authority?' 'And I,' replied Jesus, 'will ask you a question. Tell me: John's baptism: did it come from heaven, or from man?' And they argued it out this way among themselves, 'If we say from heaven, he will say, Why did you refuse to believe him?; and if we say from man, the people will all stone us, for they are convinced that John was a prophet.' So their reply was that they did not know where it came from. And Jesus said to then, 'Nor will I tell you my authority for acting like this.'

And he went on to tell the people this parable: 'A man planted a vineyard and leased it to tenants, and went abroad for a long while. When the time came, he sent a servant to the tenants to get his share of the produce of the vineyard from them. But the tenants thrashed him, and sent him away empty-handed. But he persevered and sent a second servant; they thrashed him too and treated him shamefully and sent him away empty-handed. He still persevered and sent a third; they wounded this one also, and threw him out. Then the owner of the vineyard said, What am I to do? I will send them my dear son. Perhaps they will respect him. But when the tenants saw him they put their heads together. This is the heir, they said let us kill him so that the inheritance will be ours. So they threw him out of the vineyard and killed him. Now what will the owner of the vineyard do to them? He will come and make an end of these tenants and give the vineyard to others.' Hearing this they said, 'God forbid!' But he looked hard at them and said, 'Then what does this text in the scriptures mean: It was the stone rejected by the builders that became the keystone? Anyone who falls on that stone will be dashed to pieces; anyone it falls on will be crushed.' But for their fear of the people, the scribes and the chief priests would have liked to lay hands on him that very moment, because they realised that this parable was aimed at them.

CHRIST THE LORD Picture Jesus at the end of telling this parable, when, as St Luke writes, "… he looked hard at them…" What does that mean? What did that look contain? The full fire of Christ's burning love! He has put up with his opponents since the very start of his ministry. Now that his time is running out, he is becoming more and more explicit in exposing the true, and truly heinous, state of their souls. Just when they try to discredit him in the eyes of the crowd with their shrewd question about authority, Jesus tells this parable to that same crowd, while his adversaries sit listening in. The parable unmistakably identifies Jesus as the Son of God in a unique sense (this is the very claim that his enemies had latched onto as grounds for blasphemy) and also paints a sad picture of the history of Israel. Generation after generation of Israelite leaders (the tenants in the parable) have refused to respond to God's goodness with gratitude and fidelity, or even with basic justice. Now, when God (the vineyard owner in the parable) sends his own Son, the current generation of leaders goes even one step further, murdering him in hopes of being able to usurp complete power over the nation.

That hard look of Jesus was meant to shake up those closed-hearted listeners into not only understanding the parable – it was impossible to avoid that – but also into letting it sink in. The warm-up was over, and the final clash was about to begin. Even at such a moment – especially at such a moment – Jesus makes yet another effort to win his enemies over to the truth.

CHRIST THE TEACHER This parable teaches us valuable lessons about God and about man. God goes beyond the demands of justice in order to give all people the chance of salvation. The owner of the vineyard had every right to get rid of the greedy and rebellious tenants after their first refusal to pay what they owned their master. But the owner waits patiently and then sends another messenger, and then finally a third. At that point, who would have blamed him for throwing the tenants out, or even for putting them in prison? But he waits yet another amount of time, and then he sends his very own son to plead with them, hoping beyond all hope that they will come to their senses, realize that the master is generous and longsuffering, not harsh and intransigent, and put things to rights. This is how God was with Israel, how he has been with all mankind, and how he never ceases to be with each soul. Whoever ends up spending eternity without Christ as his friend will have only himself to blame – that much we know for sure.

Regarding the human person, this parable illustrates (but fails to explain fully) the great mystery of freedom. Why did the tenants consistently and deliberately refuse to do the right, fair, and just plain sensible thing? Why did the Pharisees refuse to welcome Jesus? Why do so many Christians refuse to follow Christ's teachings? How can anyone who has received life, and all the good things that go with it as a pure gift from on high, turn their back on God as if he didn't even exist? Jesus offers no explicit answer, but the bottom line remains clear: the end of the story, for each person, isn't determined by fate, destiny, or some incontrovertible, meta-historical force; the end of our story is up to each one of us.

CHRIST THE FRIEND *Jesus: My child, I only want one thing. I only want you to flourish, to become the saint I created you to be. Your life is like the vineyard, and the fruit I ask from you is the fruit of the Spirit: love, joy, peace, patience, kindness, goodness, faithfulness, gentleness, and self-control. The more you seek and follow my will for you, the more abundant your harvest will be, and the more fulfilled and fulfilling your life will become. The leaders of Jerusalem who resisted my grace were afraid of losing the passing things of this world that they had spent so much time and energy acquiring: wealth, position, reputation, power. But those fruits are bitter unless they are seasoned with the fruits of the spirit.*

I set up my vineyard in your heart when you were baptized. I have tended it faithfully through the rest of the sacraments and through the teaching of my Gospels. Often I have come and requested a harvest by asking you to act in accordance with my will. Many times you have treated me just as the tenants in the parable treated the owner of the vineyard. You have squandered my grace. But I haven't given up on you. Many other times you welcome my inspirations and commands, and you have experienced the joy of doing so. You always know what I am asking of you – my will is no great enigma. Be courageous, be generous, continue trusting me, one step at a time, and we will enjoy your eternal harvest together.

CHRIST IN MY LIFE Lord, I don't understand how so many people reject you. I don't understand why I sometimes refuse to follow your will, disobey my conscience, skirt along the edges of Church teaching. I don't so much ask you to help me understand it; I ask you to help me overcome it. Let me know you so clearly that I can't help loving you with all my heart, mind, and strength…

Thank you for your patience and mercy. You never give up on me – you never have, and you never will. You have adopted me into your own family. Now you are my brother, my friend, my companion! Thank you, Lord. Now teach me to be generous and strong and merciful, just like you…

When I see how little you are loved, and when I see how they treat your representatives and how they lead your faithful astray, my heart sinks. Then it burns with desire to react. I want to do something! I love you, and I want to show you my love. I want to do your will, Lord. I can only do a little bit, here and now, today, of what you ask of me, but I want to put in all the love I can…

QUESTIONS FOR SMALL GROUP DISCUSSION

1. What struck you most in this passage? What did you notice that you hadn't noticed before?

2. In your experience, what is the real reason behind the disbelief of those people who refuse to accept Christ?

3. Why would Jesus answer these leaders' question about his authority with another question, instead of giving them the real answer?

4. What has been the one thing that has helped your friendship with Christ most in the last six months?

Cf. Catechism of the Catholic Church, 1846-1848 on mercy and sin; 1854-1864 on the different kinds of sins (especially the sin against the Holy Spirit, 1864)

221. CUNNING DOVES (LK 20:20-26)

"Each of you will stand in the presence of God, before countless hosts of angels. The Holy Spirit will set a seal upon your souls, and you will be enlisted into the service of the great King."

- St Cyril of Jerusalem

Luke 20:20-26

So they waited their opportunity and sent agents to pose as men devoted to the Law, and to fasten on something he might say and so enable them to hand him over to the jurisdiction and authority of the governor. They put to him this question, 'Master, we know that you say and teach what is right; you favor no one, but teach the way of God in all honesty. Is it permissible for us to pay taxes to Caesar or not?' But he was aware of their cunning and said, 'Show me a denarius. Whose head and name are on it?' 'Caesar's' they said. 'Well then,' he said to them, 'give back to Caesar what belongs to Caesar – and to God what belongs to God.' As a result, they were unable to find fault with anything he had to say in public; his answer took them by surprise and they were silenced.

CHRIST THE LORD Jesus' enemies try to trap Jesus with an astute ploy. About twenty years prior to this conversation, a dispute about whether or not the Jews should pay taxes to Rome erupted in a rebellion, ending with the crucifixion of 2000 Jews. Some Jews thought such taxes impeded efforts to achieve Israel's independence. Others thought that evading these taxes would bring down an even harsher Roman rule. By presenting the question to Jesus, therefore, they scribes were showing their acumen.

Jesus' answer, in addition to confounding his enemies, reveals a central characteristic of his Kingdom: it is not of this world. Christianity consists in renewing the human heart through Christ's grace. This is the work of the Church. In turn, this interior renewal gradually overflows into a hidden renewal of every arena of human endeavor, as leaven gradually works its way into the whole loaf as its being kneaded. (The energetic kneading of human culture is performed by the seemingly inscrutable flow of history, guided by Providence.)

Christians sometimes fail to make this distinction, and they can fall into committing injustices in the name of Christ when they do, but the distinction is there, in Christ's teaching and that of the Church. The Lord cannot be pigeon-holed into a single political party or agenda; instead, he sends his disciples to rectify and edify them all.

CHRIST THE TEACHER Jesus provides both a negative and a positive lesson about how to deal with hypocrites. First, we are to avoid being naïve. The Christian life and mission is not a walk in the park. The devil cares infinitely more about what the Christian is doing to spread the faith than about whatever else he's doing, and he continually throws up opposition. The experience of two millennia leaves no room for doubt: if you would like to start a tennis club, you will find no out of the ordinary obstacles popping up every step of the way; if, however, you try to start a Catholic kids club, or an apostolate dedicated to retrieving fallen-away Catholic businessmen, watch out.

The dynamics of human history, on the small scale and the large scale, really are what Hollywood tells us they are: the forces of good (Christ, his angels, his followers) pitted against the forces of evil (the devil, his angels, fallen human nature and the culture it produces). Christians who take their mission seriously automatically become threats to men and women who have set their hearts on manipulating their sphere of influence towards their own self-aggrandizement – just as Christ posed a threat to the leaders of Jerusalem.

So we should expect attacks from duplicitous people – we should not be naïve – but how should we respond to them? Shrewdly. Jesus used his wits. He never lowered himself to the lying and deceptive tactics of his enemies, but he crossed verbal swords with them, outdoing them in their own canniness. He doesn't answer their question directly, because he sees that they don't care about the truth anyway. He answers it in a way that will make them think and maybe open their minds and hearts to his message. Jesus is following his own advice to "be cunning as snakes" with hypocrites, but "innocent as doves" by not adopting their sinful ways (Mathew 10:16). He is neither intimidated nor distracted by obstacles and opposition; he forges ahead, continuing to do good, to find creative ways to communicate his message. As his disciples, we should do the same.

CHRIST THE FRIEND God created us in his own image. He created us to be able to live in friendship with him, to know truth, goodness, and beauty, and to be able create our own expressions of them. Unfortunately, we often see the sinful side of human nature so clearly that we forget how noble the human soul really is. We need the reminder that Christ gives us in this conversation with the Pharisees; we need to make an effort to call to mind repeatedly that every man, woman, and child is created in God's image, noble beyond description and destined for eternal life. The most beautiful and magnificent parts of creation will all pass away, but the human person will live forever. Each one will be resurrected, either to eternal life or eternal death.

Jesus: When I look at you, I see the true you – I can see how you will be when I have purified you from all your selfishness and you have let my grace renew each corner of your soul. Little babies have no idea how wonderful it will be when they grow up and come into full possession of all their faculties, but their mothers do, and they delight in the thought of it and care for their children with that in mind. Your soul is like that little child, and I am as attentive and delighted in you as the most tender of mothers.

CHRIST IN MY LIFE I am a citizen of two kingdoms, Lord – this world and your everlasting reign. You want me here, like leaven, influencing my circle of activity with your grace. I am your ambassador. Lord Jesus, make me a good one. I want to bring you to many hearts. I want to be a light to those around me. May your light shine through me…

Sometimes the challenges of being faithful to your will and to your mission intimidate me. Sometimes they tire me out. Sometimes they rile me up. Lord, whatever my reaction, you know that the only way I can persevere is if you fill me with your wisdom and strength in each challenge. I don't care how I feel; I care only about being faithful to what you are asking of me…

Why do I so easily forget the bigger picture? Lord Jesus, I get so discouraged, so distracted. Be patient with me, Lord, and teach me to be patient with those around me. You have designed things to take time, and your design is wise. Teach me to be docile, to do your will…

QUESTIONS FOR SMALL GROUP DISCUSSION

1. What struck you most in this passage? What did you notice that you hadn't noticed before?

2. What difference should there be between a Christian and a non-Christian when it comes to political opinions and activity? Why?

3. What has helped you in the past to be shrewd with hypocrites while at the same time extending Christian charity and justice?

4. If a non-believing acquaintance were to come up to you with the following question, how would you respond: "Why should I follow Christ? He's supposed to be all about a nice afterlife, but he hasn't even been able to fix this earthly life."

Cf. Catechism of the Catholic Church, 1897-1904 on legitimate political authority; 1905-1912 on the common good; 356-361 on man being created in the image of God

222. SAVING THE SADDUCEES (LK 20:27-47)

"Living faith working through love – this is what leads mean to put aside the goods of the present in the hope of those of the future, and to look to the future rather than to the present."

- Pope Benedict XIV

Luke 20:27-47

Some Sadducees – those who say that there is no resurrection – approached him and they put this question to him, 'Master, we have it from Moses in writing, that if a man's married brother dies childless, the man must marry the widow to raise up children for his brother. Well then, there were seven brothers. The first, having married a wife, died childless. The second and then the third married the widow. And the same with all seven, they died leaving no children. Finally the woman herself died Now, at the resurrection, to which of them will she be wife since she had been married to all seven?' Jesus replied, 'The children of this world take wives and husbands, but those who are judged worthy of a place in the other world and of the resurrection from the dead do not marry because they can no longer die, for they are the same as the angels, and being children of the resurrection they are sons of God. And Moses himself implies that the dead rise again, in the passage about the bush where he calls the Lord the God of Abraham, the God of Isaac and the God of Jacob. Now he is God, not of the dead, but of the living; for to him all men are in fact alive.' Some scribes then spoke up. 'Well put, Master,' they said because they would not dare to ask him any more questions.

He then said to them, 'How can people maintain that the Christ is son of David? Why, David himself says in the Book of Psalms: The Lord said to my Lord: Sit at my right hand and I will make your enemies a footstool for you. David here calls him Lord; how then can he be his son?' While all the people were listening he said to the disciples, 'Beware of the scribes who like to walk about in long robes and love to be greeted obsequiously in the market squares, to take the front seats in the synagogues and the places of honour at banquets, who swallow the property of widows, while making a show of lengthy prayers. The more severe will be the sentence they receive.

CHRIST THE LORD Imagine the scene. We are in the Temple courtyards, where rabbis continuously discuss, instruct, and debate with peers and public alike. Jesus has been spending the last few days there, teaching the people and gallantly repelling crafty attacks from envious Pharisees, the religious leaders of contemporary Jewry. Worn out and exasperated, the Pharisees bring in reinforcements, the Sadducees, to continue trying to discredit this incorrigible young Galilean rabbi. (Usually the Sadducees and Pharisees were rivals, but the common threat posed by Christ's new teaching brings them together.) The Sadducees slip into the circle of disciples gathered around Jesus. They are Israel's political leaders, eager collaborators with their Roman overlords; they are in love with the pleasures of this present world and disdain many of the common Jewish beliefs and practices, like the resurrection of the dead. At just the right moment, one of them steps forward to issue the challenge, posing a previously unanswerable theological conundrum. With a rhetorical flourish he finishes stating his case, certain that everyone there now clearly perceives how ridiculous the resurrection doctrine really is. A hush ensues as the crowd now turns to Jesus. Will he be able to respond? He is gazing steadily at the self-satisfied Sadducee, but he offers no reprimand, as he did to the Pharisees. Rather, he takes up the challenge directly and points out their mistake.

St Luke's concise description of this dramatic encounter brings to light the weight of Christ's authority, the incomparable power of Christ's presence and words, which in this case silences Israel's most accomplished sophists. Why else would St Luke include a discussion about Jewish doctrinal nitpickings when his primary readership was non-Jewish? Once again, the Gospel gives us a glimpse of the magnificent but munificent Lordship of Christ.

CHRIST THE TEACHER The lesson Jesus teaches his attackers strikes home as much for us as for them. They were conceiving of heaven in earthly terms and applying human restrictions to God. The doctrine of eternal life and the resurrection of the dead threatened the worldly lifestyle of the Sadducees; if there really is life after death, then they would have to adjust their pattern of life on earth to be ready for it – something they were reluctant to do. Christ's answer points out both their theological and their moral blunders.

God has revealed himself as the living God, powerful enough to give eternal life and raise us from the dead, just as Christ's own Resurrection would prove definitively. Furthermore, the pleasures and obligations of this life will be transformed in the life to come. Even marriage, one of the most sacred of human institutions, will fall away in the newness of heaven, where the love we practiced on earth will be caught up into a higher love, bringing our longing for union with God and one another to its utter fulfillment.

Christianity is not a mass of restrictions and rules, but the true path to peace, joy, life, and fulfillment. If only we had more strength to trust in the God who shaped the mountains and carved out the seas instead of trying all the time to avoid his wise law, we would find the peace we long for but vainly search for everywhere else.

CHRIST THE FRIEND *Jesus: My child, if I didn't love you with all the strength of my heart, I wouldn't challenge you. I wouldn't push you to grow, expand your views, and go beyond your limited understanding and assumptions. Some think of me as a weakling, a starry-eyed dreamer - I know. It is because my mercy is boundless, and they mistake mercy for weakness. But my mercy is the elemental building block of the universe. Look into my eyes. You will see my love – I will show it to you. And you will see that it is burning and determined. Listen to my voice. Is it wavering and noncommittal and superficial? It is compassionate, but my compassion grips your heart and demands that you change. You know this, because you have had the courage to listen. You know that when you follow my footsteps, you feel hope and joy, but the kind that flourishes in the shadow of the cross. I am the Lamb of God, but I am also the Lion of Judah. And the only reason you should let me into your life more deeply each day is because I love you even more than you love yourself.*

CHRIST IN MY LIFE I am bewildered and frustrated by the resistance the leaders of Jerusalem showed you, Lord, but even more than that, I am mesmerized by your wisdom and your majesty. Lord, teach me to be wise. Attract me to your heart. I want my words to reflect your goodness. I know I will not be able to open every heart to your gospel, because even you didn't open every heart, but I want to give you my mouth to speak your words…

I know you want me to be faithful to my daily responsibilities. You are not some strange guru with weird, otherworldly practices – you are Jesus of Nazareth, and you know what it means to work and sweat. But you also want me to think of the Resurrection. This life has a purpose. I believe it, Lord. Increase my faith…

Challenge me, Lord. Lead me forward. Why do I want to stay comfortable when there is so much for me to do for you, so many ways for me to give myself to you by giving myself to those around me? Challenge me, Lord, and never let me forget that you are with me, that you are the very strength you demand of me…

QUESTIONS FOR SMALL GROUP REFLECTION

1. What struck you most in this passage? What did you notice that you hadn't noticed before?

2. What factors in popular culture tend to reduce Jesus Christ to an abstract concept or historical artifact instead of a living person? How can we minimize their influence in our lives?

3. How should our reverence for Christ's authority as exercised through the Church's teaching manifest itself? What are some telltale signs that we might be falling into subjectivism, preferring our own version of the gospel (maybe one that fits well with our personal likes and dislikes, our personal "comfort zones")?

4. How should the doctrine of the resurrection from the dead, which we profess to believe every Sunday when we recite the Creed at Mass, impact our lives, our decisions, and our perception of what is important?

Cf. Catechism of the Catholic Church, 638-658 on Christ's Resurrection; on 988-1004 Christians' resurrection; 577-582 on Jesus and the Law

THE GOSPEL OF LUKE CHAPTER 21

223. A WIDOW'S MIGHT (LK 21:1-7)

"We cannot all do great things, but we can do small things with great love."

- *Blessed Mother Theresa of Calcutta*

Luke 21:1-7

As he looked up he saw rich people putting their offerings into the treasury; then he happened to notice a poverty-stricken widow putting in two small coins, and he said, 'I tell you truly, this poor widow has put in more than any of them; for these have all contributed money they had over, but she from the little she had has put in all she had to live on.' When some were talking about the Temple, remarking how it was adorned with fine stonework and votive offerings, he said, 'All these things you are staring at now – the time will come when not a single stone will be left on another: everything will be destroyed'. And they put to him this question: 'Master,' they said 'when will this happen, then, and what sign will there be that this is about to take place?'

CHRIST THE LORD The widow who depends entirely on God throws into sharp relief the lesson Jesus has just been teaching – that his Kingdom transcends this world, and only those who recognize their need for God will enter into it. Jesus' prediction of the destruction of the Temple, the symbol of the earthly Kingdom of Israel, which Jesus' enemies mistakenly thought would last forever, calls to mind this contrast between Christ's Kingdom and all earthly kingdoms. The things of the earth will pass away, but the things of God will remain.

This is why Jesus can say that the widow put more into the treasury than the rich people, even though her gift was only a small sum of money. Jesus saw into her heart. She was a widow, alone in the world, having lost the husband she had loved and cherished. She was poverty-stricken, with nothing to attract the attention of a possible future husband. She had experienced the loss of what was most precious to her as well as the fragility of her own existence, and this had led her to abandon herself completely to God. As she dropped her last two pennies into the treasury box, Jesus saw both the tears of sorrow and helplessness in her eyes, and also the trust and gratitude in her heart. Her monetary gift was the embodiment of her gift of self. It expresses the wisdom her suffering had taught her, the wisdom God wants all of us to acquire through our own suffering: only the Lord's love endures, so only his Kingdom is worth living for.

CHRIST THE TEACHER Jesus wants to make sure we are never deceived by the appearances of this world. Certainly it is filled with good and beautiful things, and human culture adorns it even more magnificently. The Temple of Jerusalem was known throughout the ancient world as a towering artistic achievement, even this reconstructed Temple. However, the rightful pleasure taken in good worldly achievements can lead us astray, because it can make us start looking for heaven on earth. But heaven is heaven, and earth is earth, and the glories of the former will not last, "not a single stone will be left on another; everything will be destroyed." This prediction applies both to the Temple at Jerusalem and to the earth itself and all the achievements of human hands. What will last forever, on the other hand, is what we do for God and what we do for our neighbor – these are the two coins the widow puts into the treasury.

In contrast to the well-educated, well-respected, well-to-do people who ostentatiously pour into the coffers objectively large amounts of money that are subjectively worthless to them, she puts in an objectively minuscule amount (two "lepta" coins, the lowest value coin in circulation at the time), in which consists, subjectively, her whole entire livelihood. In other words, she gives her whole self to God. Jesus says this is the worthy and lasting gift. To give ourselves to God by seeking and fulfilling his will (summed up by the commandment to love) is the only investment we can make that will bring in everlasting dividends.

CHRIST THE FRIEND *Jesus: Do you see this widow? She is alone in the world, and she is poor, and yet she has more wisdom and strength than the rich, the powerful, and the popular. She gives all she has to me in humble gratitude, knowing that since she has received everything from me, I will take care of her. The only worries in her heart are worries about others' needs. I want you to learn from her. I want you to trust me as she trusted me. She is the model of all my saints, who have realized that the good things of this world pass quickly. They all know that what pleases my heart and enriches the treasury of my Kingdom are the two seemingly tiny little coins: love for God and love for neighbor. These coins are looked down upon by the powerful of this world, those who think they can bring heaven to earth with their great projects and programs. But without self-forgetful love, what good is any organization or any political platform? I want you to look at this widow, look into her heart. Learn to see the world and the people in the world as I do, and you will discover the wisdom I want to give you.*

CHRIST IN MY LIFE Thank you for giving me enough of your eternal wisdom, Lord, to know that nothing beautiful on this earth will last forever. All the toys and trinkets and achievements are like flowers; they bloom and wither. But your grace bears fruit that never dies. Thank you for the gift of life and faith, and thank you for giving me a mission in life that really matters, the mission of love…

I love the scene of this destitute widow dropping everything she has into the treasury. She doesn't care about the greedy chief priests who will probably steal from the collection – she cares only about you. She wants to give everything she has to you. What a noble soul! Teach me to give you everything I have by throwing myself into your will for me here and now…

I feel in my heart the desire to make a difference in the world. Where did that desire come from if it didn't come from you? You put it there, Lord, and then you taught me how to fulfill it: Love God and love my neighbor. Yes, Lord, this is what I want. Show me the way to go; I will follow you, and you will make my life bear fruit…

QUESTIONS FOR SMALL GROUP DISCUSSION

1. What struck you most in this passage? What did you notice that you hadn't noticed before?

2. What helps you to keep in mind the passing nature of the things of this world?

3. In what ways do we tend to follow in the footsteps of the rich people Jesus observes in this passage – appearing to give a lot to God, but really holding back the only thing he wants us to give?

4. If everything in the world is going to pass away, why does the Church still encourage us to be fully engaged in society and culture?

Cf. Catechism of the Catholic Church, 1913-1917 on responsibility and participation in society; 2095-2103 on giving worship to God; 1052-1074 on a summary of the two great commandments

224. STAYING FAITHFUL IN THE FRAY (LK 21: 8-24)

"The charms of prosperity must not lead us astray; for only a foolish traveler, when he sees pleasant fields on his way, forgets to go on towards his destination."

- Pope St Gregory the Great

Luke 21:8-24

'Take care not to be deceived,' he said, 'because many will come using my name and saying, I am he and, The time is near at hand. Refuse to join them. And when you hear of wars and revolutions, do not be frightened, for this is something that must happen but the end is not so soon.' Then he said to them, 'Nation will fight against nation, and kingdom against kingdom. There will be great earthquakes and plagues and famines here and there; there will be fearful sights and great signs from heaven. But before all this happens, men will seize you and persecute you; they will hand you over to the synagogues and to imprisonment, and bring you before kings and governors because of my name and that will be your opportunity to bear witness. Keep this carefully in mind: you are not to prepare your defence, because I myself shall give you an eloquence and a wisdom that none of your opponents will be able to resist or contradict. You will be betrayed even by parents and brothers, relations and friends; and some of you will be put to death. You will be hated by all men on account of my name, but not a hair of your head will be lost. Your endurance will win you your lives.

'When you see Jerusalem surrounded by armies, you must realise that she will soon be laid desolate. Then those in Judaea must escape to the mountains, those inside the city must leave it, and those in country districts must not take refuge in it. For this is the time of vengeance when all that scripture says must be fulfilled. Alas for those with child, or with babies at the breast, when those days come! They will fall by the edge of the sword and be led captive to every pagan country; and Jerusalem will be trampled down by the pagans until the age of the pagans is completely over.'

CHRIST THE LORD Imagine the tone of this conversation. One of the bystanders makes an offhand comment, a little bit of small talk about the beauty of the Temple. Christ takes up the theme as a chance to voice what has been on his heart. He describes the coming destruction of the Temple by the Roman army (this was to occur in 70 AD), which will mark the definitive end of the former age, the Old Covenant epoch. And then, in response to that description, one of the disciples asks him when this will occur. That question is what immediately precedes this speech of the Lord. He tells them that other claimants to his Messianic title will appear – and they did appear. He tells them that wars and natural disasters will occur – and they did occur between the years of his death and the destruction of Jerusalem, all over the Mediterranean basin (e.g., the Parthians moved against the eastern border of the Roman Empire; Laodicaea was devastated by an earthquake in 60 AD; a famine ravaged Rome during the reign of Claudius, etc.). He tells them that foreign armies will surround Jerusalem and lay a horrible siege to it, and he tells them that they should get out before the siege begins. And then he tells them that before Jerusalem is destroyed, they themselves will suffer fierce persecution from all sides, but that very persecution will afford them an opportunity to spread the Good News.

Maybe his listeners didn't grasp the whole meaning of his prediction until the events began to play themselves out, but as Jesus spoke they would have had no doubt that Christ was declaring himself to be the lynchpin of time and eternity. With the completion of his earthly mission, human history takes its final turn; the Old Covenant is being brought to its definitive end ("Jerusalem will be trampled down by the pagans until the age of the pagans is completely over"), and the New, Everlasting Covenant is about to be inaugurated by the Lord.

CHRIST THE TEACHER Although this speech was the response to a question about when the Temple would be destroyed, Jesus doesn't really give a specific date and time. He is more interested in explaining the pattern of events so that his disciples will have reference points as they experience life in the era of the Church. He's interested in pointing out the three most critical facts about the future: 1) He is going back to the Father's house, but he will return to bring to fruition the eternal Kingdom that he founded through the Church (thus the reference to the "age of the pagans" being "completely over"); 2) In the meantime, he is sending his disciples to announce that Kingdom to all peoples; and 3) Although this mission will bring with it a crescendo of suffering and humiliation and opposition of all kinds, he will be with his Church always, working in and through his followers by the power of the Holy Spirit.

CHRIST THE FRIEND Christ's mission is much greater than many people think. It isn't only to make life on earth a bit easier; it is cosmic and eternal. His bottom line is not measured in dollars and cents, but in salvation itself

– in everlasting life for real people like our neighbors, our family members, and us. He calls all his followers to share in this mission, to make it their priority, and to persevere in it by leaning on him and not on themselves as they weather storms of pain and violent rejection. They may even suffer rejection at the hands of their closest relatives, but he assures them that if he permits that to happen, it's only because it will redound in the end for a greater good. Consciously, actively sharing in Christ's mission grows our friendship with him, because it leads us to continue seeking his will and trusting in him. And when all the battles are over, the victory will come. He is looking forward to sharing that victory with us. After all, that's why he came.

CHRIST IN MY LIFE   I am struck by how vivid these future events were to you, long before they occurred. All knowledge of the universe is yours by divine right. And yet, the teaching you left us was so simple, understandable, and straightforward – above all, your commandment of love. I want to know your teaching better, Lord. I want to follow it. You are the Lord of history; be also the Lord of my life...

What do the petty concerns of my typical day matter in light of the great events of history? Sometimes I let myself listen to the seductive gospel of the news programs, and I think that my petty concerns don't matter at all. But I know better. What matters to you is that I choose in each moment of the day to love you by doing your will. If I do, I will be a true revolutionary...

Persecution isn't my favorite thing, Lord, but you promised it would come. Sometimes I think it would be easier if it came in the form of a sword or a gun – being talked about behind my back, laughed at, and criticized wounds my vanity and self-love so deeply. Teach me to overcome evil by doing good, and to love even my enemies as you have loved me...

QUESTIONS FOR SMALL GROUP DISCUSSION

1. What struck you most in this passage? What did you notice that you hadn't noticed before?

2. "He will come again in glory to judge the living and the dead, and his Kingdom will have no end." What impact do you think this doctrine should have on our daily lives?

3. Knowing that fidelity to Christ and his Church will bring with it persecution, misunderstanding, and opposition, how should we prepare ourselves for these eventualities? What form will they take in our current life situation?

4. How can we avoid falling into the frustrating trap of trying to tackle the difficulties and challenges of life all by ourselves, forgetting that Christ is always with us, working in our hearts and in others through us?

Cf. Catechism of the Catholic Church, 780 on the Church as the sign and instrument of salvation; 668-682 on the Second Coming and the Day of Judgment

225. ENDGAME (LK 21:25-38)

"He hid the time from us so that we would be on the watch and so that each of us might think that the coming will happen in his own lifetime."

- St Ephraem

Luke 21:25-38

'There will be signs in the sun and moon and stars; on earth nations in agony, bewildered by the clamour of the ocean and its waves; men dying of fear as they await what menaces the world, for the powers of heaven will be shaken. And then they will see the Son of Man coming in a cloud with power and great glory. When these things begin to take place, stand erect, hold your heads high, because your liberation is near at hand.' And he told them a parable, 'Think of the fig tree and indeed every tree. As soon as you see them bud, you know that summer is now near. So with you when you see these things happening: know that the kingdom of God is near. I tell you solemnly, before this generation has passed away all will have taken place. Heaven and earth will pass away, but my words will never pass away. Watch yourselves, or your hearts will be coarsened with debauchery and drunkenness and the cares of life, and that day will be sprung on you suddenly, like a trap. For it will come down on every living man on the face of the earth. Stay awake, praying at all times for the strength to survive all that is going to happen, and to stand with confidence before the Son of Man.'

In the daytime he would be in the Temple teaching, but would spend the night on the hill called the Mount of Olives. And from early morning the people would gather round him in the Temple to listen to him.

CHRIST THE LORD In this second half of Jesus' speech answering the question about when the destruction of the Temple would occur Jesus changes his imagery. He employs phrases and allusions that all of his Jewish listeners would have recognized as referring to the Day of the Lord that the Old Testament prophets had predicted. The Day of the Lord referred to the coming of the Messiah and the inauguration of the new Messianic Kingdom, which also included the end of the Old Covenant. From the Jewish perspective, this would be the line of demarcation for all human history. By making these allusions, therefore, Jesus associates the events that will occur in the first Christian generation ("Before this generation has passed away all will have taken place") and conclude with the destruction of Jerusalem as that fateful Day of the Lord. But the Day

751

of the Lord doesn't end with the fall of the Temple; it is extended throughout the rest of human history. During that time, the experience of the first generations of Christians – persecution, growth, conversions of whole cities and cultures, wars and disasters – will be repeated by successive generations until Jesus comes again. So Jesus' comments about those days apply to every age of the Church, and the destruction of Jerusalem and the Temple at the end of Old Covenant history is a foreshadowing of the destruction of heaven and earth at the end of New Covenant history.

Jesus Christ is the Lord of history. When we read the history books and watch the daily news it may not seem so, but in reality he is. At some point in the future, the story that mankind has been putting together since the dawn of time will come to an end; the way things are will be radically changed. Thus the imagery Jesus provides of "signs" in the sun, the moon, and the waves of the sea indicate that the stable order of the universe in which we make history will be uprooted and history will end. When that happens, Christ's Lordship will be fully manifest to everyone (he will come again in "a cloud with power and great glory") and will bring to fruition his eternal reign. All human history is moving towards that final, climactic moment. Everyone's personal contribution to the human story will be made known to all at the end, when the Lord renews heaven and earth and takes his place on the everlasting throne.

CHRIST THE TEACHER Jesus doesn't tell us the exact day and hour of his second coming. He prefers for us to stay ready for it at every moment; this is the lesson of the fig tree. If we keep our hearts awake, resisting the sweet lullaby of earthly pleasures and concerns, we will recognize the signs of his approach and be prepared to greet him when he comes. He also warns us that we will have to face tribulations before we are able to stand before him in glory; it will not be easy to stay faithful to God throughout the trials of life. (Otherwise, why would he tell us to pray for "strength to survive all that is going to happen"?)

Though millennia have already passed without his appearance, his warnings are as urgent as ever. For even if another millennium or two unfold before history as a whole concludes, our personal histories have a much more predictable endpoint. As individuals, we could find ourselves standing before him any day. It is up to each one of us to heed his warnings now, before "that day is sprung on [us] suddenly, like a trap." Every year the Church reminds us of this as the Solemnity of Christ the King concludes the liturgical year. We will have no one to blame but ourselves if we don't take the reminders to heart – and that doesn't mean shivering with fright and terror, but simply staying faithful to God's will for our lives, the true source of joy and meaning both in time and in eternity.

CHRIST THE FRIEND *Jesus: Do you think I had fire and brimstone in my eyes when I spoke these warnings? Do you think I spoke them quietly, in intimate conversation with my disciples? You know that I never take pleasure in the destruction of sinners. I only seek their salvation, as I have sought yours. I wanted you to know what the human heart has always wondered about – the end of history will come, and I will make a new creation, and the justice that was not given during the course of your earthly life will be given, and my mercy will shine out in all of its infinite glory. I want you to know that, so that you are able to stand up to the trials that following me always brings with it. I know you trust me, but now you have one more reason to do so. You don't have to fear the future; you already know what it holds. You can be ready, and be at peace, and you can dedicate yourself to loving me and loving those I give you to love. And even though I am with you all the time now, you can already start looking forward to that day when we will be together without the veil of faith.*

CHRIST IN MY LIFE I have to thank you again for the gift of these Gospels. Here you speak to me directly – you who created me and love me more than I love myself. And you nourish my soul with the truth of your words and examples. Lord, I want to become an expert in the Gospels – not an academic expert, but a loving expert in knowing and following you, my Lord and my God…

It isn't easy to stay ready, Lord. Why do you delay your coming? You don't need to tell me – I already know. In your love and your wisdom you are waiting until the right moment. I want to live faithfully while my life lasts. I want to experience your love and your joy, and I want to spread it to those around me. Fill my heart with your grace and my mind with your truth…

I know that being faithful to you, to what is true and right and good, will bring trouble upon me, just as it brought trouble upon you. But you will never let me be tempted beyond my power to endure, and you will always give me whatever strength I need. I am not afraid, Lord. I keep seeing you on the cross, gazing down at me, telling me not to fear, telling me just to be faithful, courageous…

QUESTIONS FOR SMALL GROUP DISCUSSION

1. What struck you most in this passage? What did you notice that you hadn't noticed before?

2. What influences around us tend to "make our hearts coarsened"? In other words, how do Christ's examples of "debauchery, drunkenness, and the cares of life" apply to us?

3. How can we better follow Christ's advice about "staying awake, praying at all times"?

4. At the risk of scaring us off, Christ has told us about the seriousness of our life decisions in

light of his second coming. We should be equally charitable in telling those around us about these fundamental truths. What are some good ways and appropriate times to do so?

Cf. Catechism of the Catholic Church, 673-674, 1040 on the uncertainty of the time of the Lord's coming; 522-526 on the meaning of Advent and Christmas

THE GOSPEL OF LUKE CHAPTER 22

"Thus the passion of the Saviour is salvation for mankind. This was why he willed to die for us, that we should believe in him, and live forever. He willed to become for a time what we are, so that we should receive the promise of his eternity and live with him forever. This is the feast of the year for which we long, the beginnings of life-giving realities. Here is given us the grace of the heavenly mysteries, the gift of the Pasch."

- Homily of an ancient author

226. THE PASSION BEGINS (LK 22:1-13)

"Let us fix our thoughts on the blood of Christ; and reflect how precious that blood is in God's eyes, inasmuch as its outpouring for our salvation has opened the grace of repentance to all mankind."

- Pope St Clement I

Luke 22:1-13

The feast of Unleavened Bread, called the Passover, was now drawing near, and the chief priests and the scribes were looking for some way of doing away with him, because they mistrusted the people. Then Satan entered into Judas, surnamed Iscariot, who was numbered among the Twelve. He went to the chief priests and the officers of the guard to discuss a scheme for handing Jesus over to them. They were delighted and agreed to give him money. He accepted, and looked for an opportunity to betray him to them without the people knowing. The day of Unleavened Bread came round, the day on which the passover had to be sacrificed, and he sent Peter and John, saying, 'Go and make the preparations for us to eat the Passover.' 'Where do you want us to prepare it?' they asked. 'Listen,' he said 'as you go into the city you will meet a man carrying a pitcher of water. Follow him into the house he enters and tell the owner of the house, The Master has this to say to you: Where is the dining room in which I can eat the passover with my disciples? The man will show you a large upper room furnished with couches. Make the preparations there.' They set off and found everything as he had told them, and prepared the Passover.

CHRIST THE LORD St Luke points out that Satan "entered into Judas" and crowned Judas' decision to betray Jesus. All that follows, therefore, will be orchestrated by the evil one. As such, it will reveal to us what Satan desires – destruction, suffering, dissention, dishonesty, selfishness. He stirs up all that is evil in the human heart in order to bring sorrow and pain. At the same time, however, St Luke describes Jesus' minute knowledge of everything that is going to take place. Isn't this a contradiction? If Jesus is in control of each detail, if God is really guiding the events of history and especially these events of history's fulcrum moment, why does Satan have free rein? Only because God's omnipotence embraces even the freedom of his creatures; so powerful and wise is our Lord, that while Satan freely enters Judas and Judas freely decides to betray his Master and Peter and John freely decide to obey him, all four of them equally "prepared the Passover" in accordance with God's will.

The kingdom of evil is not on par with the Kingdom of Christ. The forces are not even; the battle does not hang in the balance. Christ is Lord, and those who follow him triumph.

CHRIST THE TEACHER Peter and John provide a beautiful example of Christian obedience, thrown into special relief by Judas' disobedience immediately preceding it. Jesus gives them a simple task, and they ask for some specific clarifications – "Where do you want us to prepare the meal?" Jesus answers them with a cryptic prediction of an encounter with an unnamed man. Did it strike them as odd that Jesus wouldn't simply tell them where the house was? Maybe he wanted to keep it secret from Judas so as to insure a peaceful Last Supper, but he doesn't give any such explanation. He simply expects his two closest disciples to trust him and carry out the task. They have no idea that this is going to be the famous Last Supper, during which they will be ordained priests and the Old Covenant will give way to the New Covenant with its new, redemptive sacrifice. No, they don't know any of the details or the greater meaning. Yet, it is enough for them to know that this is what the Master wants them to do. And so they go off, trusting simply in their Lord like children, waiting for what he said to come to pass. And it does – they "found everything as he had told them."

Sometimes it is vain and selfish to ask for complete explanations of why God wants us to do things his way or the Church's way. Sometimes we just need to trust in him, and in his chosen instruments (his bishops and priests, the spiritual directors his providence provides for us…) so he can be free to make salvation history.

CHRIST THE FRIEND *Jesus: I knew what was going on in Judas' heart... how he had lost*

755

faith in me and was using his intelligence to arrange a profitable way to manipulate events in accordance with what he thought were his own plans. But what he didn't know was that as soon as he started to live a double life – appearing to be a faithful disciple on the outside, but really scheming deceptively on the inside – he opened his soul to the influence of the evil one. If only he had come to me with his frustrations, anger, and disappointment! The others had come at different times. They had opened their hearts to me, admitting their weakness and accepting my grace. But he wanted to work everything out himself, and he wanted solutions right away.

Many others through the years have done the same. Even many of my priests and religious have run into difficulties and tried to resolve them all by themselves, keeping up false appearances on the outside and nurturing rebellion in their hearts. Why didn't they come to me and open their hearts? I know how weak the human heart can be. You will never give up on me, I hope. You know I will never give up on you. Keep your heart crystal clear. Never live a double life. Come to me in confession, in prayer. Stay close to me, as I am always close to you.

CHRIST IN MY LIFE When I try to understand the mystery of evil, Lord, it is so hard to fathom. But I know that it's more important to relish your goodness, spreading it and making it known. How can I ever understand everything that you understand? It is enough for me to follow you each day, to let you teach me at the pace you want me to go. Make me a channel of your peace…

You know, Lord, that obedience is not considered a virtue by anyone in the world today. And yet, you achieved our salvation by obeying your Father's will, and Mary won her crown through her faith-filled obedience. I want to obey you because I know that you are trustworthy. Align my will with yours…

Jesus, never let me fall into the hypocrisy that Judas fell into. Never let me be one thing on the outside and another thing on the inside. I want to be wholly yours, consistent, a Christian with integrity. I don't have to tell everyone about all my interior struggles and temptations, but yes, I do have to live in complete sincerity with you and with myself. Teach me to follow your path…

QUESTIONS FOR SMALL GROUP DISCUSSION

1. What struck you most in this passage? What did you notice that you hadn't noticed before?

2. If Jesus knew what Judas was up to, why didn't he pull him aside and confront him about it? Is there a lesson in this for us?

3. In what areas of life does popular culture make it hard to be authentic, to be sincere?

4. What do you think the apostles (besides Judas) were thinking as this Passover drew near?

Cf. Catechism of the Catholic Church, 144-149 on the obedience of faith; 2465-2470 on living in the truth; 1790-1794 on erroneous conscience

227. GIVEN FOR YOU (LK 22:14-27)

"In the Eucharist we receive something that we cannot do, but instead enter something greater that becomes our own, precisely when we give ourselves to this thing that is greater, truly seeking to celebrate the Liturgy as the Church's Liturgy."

- Pope Benedict XVI

Luke 22:14-27

When the hour came he took his place at table, and the apostles with him. And he said to them, 'I have longed to eat this passover with you before I suffer; because, I tell you, I shall not eat it again until it is fulfilled in the kingdom of God'. Then, taking a cup, he gave thanks and said, 'Take this and share it among you, because from now on, I tell you, I shall not drink wine until the kingdom of God comes.' Then he took some bread, and when he had given thanks, broke it and gave it to them, saying, 'This is my body which will be given for you; do this as a memorial of me.' He did the same with the cup after supper, and said, 'This cup is the new covenant in my blood which will be poured out for you. And yet, here with me on the table is the hand of the man who betrays me. The Son of Man does indeed go to his fate even as it has been decreed, but alas for that man by whom he is betrayed!' And they began to ask one another which of them it could be who was to do this thing. A dispute arose also between them about which should be reckoned the greatest, but he said to them, 'Among pagans it is the kings who lord it over them, and those who have authority over them are given the title Benefactor. This must not happen with you. No; the greatest among you must behave as if he were the youngest, the leader as if he were the one who serves. For who is the greater: the one at table or the one who serves? The one at table, surely? Yet here am I among you as one who serves!'

CHRIST THE LORD The Passover meal was a ritual commemorating God's liberation of his people from Egyptian slavery through the ministry of Moses. God had initiated and accomplished the liberation, and he had established the way of celebrating it, so that the Israelites would never forget all that God had done for them. The blood of the lamb sacrificed at Passover was the mark by which God's favor was shown to Israel and by which the Old Covenant would come to be established. Now, during the Last Supper, Jesus reshapes the ritual, reveals the true meaning behind the old symbols (he is the Lamb; he is the Savior), and establishes a new ceremony that will commemorate his own immolation on Calvary until the end of time. If this were the only passage of the Gospels that history had preserved, it would be enough to corroborate Jesus' claim to be divine – only God had the authority to alter the most sacred Passover ritual that God himself had established.

It is the culminating moment of history. Now communion between God and man – the only source of authentic human happiness – is to be reestablished, because from now on men will be able to partake of the body and blood of God. Whenever we approach the Lord in this sacrament, he wants to deepen this communion, drawing us closer to his heart, uniting us more firmly with the rest of the Church, and activating our own vocation to become bridges between him and those who still don't know him. He is uniting the scattered and divided human family in himself through the breaking of his body and the pouring out of his blood. When we receive and adore him with this in mind, we help his Kingdom come.

CHRIST THE TEACHER St Luke mentions that Jesus "gave thanks" before he consecrated the bread. From this Greek term we derive the name Eucharist. On the eve of Christ's passing over to death he leaves us the gift of the Eucharist, a gift that will enable him to enter into intimate communion with each one of his followers throughout human history, to be their strength, their comfort, and their joy. This is why he says, "I have longed to eat this Passover with you before I suffer." He has longed to leave us the sacrament of his love, the guarantee of his presence and forgiveness and fidelity. What more could he have given us?

And yet, even in that solemn moment, the Apostles are still bickering about their privileges. We should be glad they did, because it gave Jesus a chance to explain once again the fundamental law of his Kingdom, a law embodied perfectly in the Eucharist, the law of self-giving. Greatness for the Christian means giving oneself for the good of the other, just as Christ has given himself, literally and heroically, in the sacrament of the Eucharist. It is a lesson we should never tire of hearing, because it is a lesson we should never stop striving to learn.

CHRIST THE FRIEND *Peter: How could we have been so oblivious? We all felt that it was a special night, but none of us guessed what was really at stake. Jesus seemed pensive, but he was still our familiar leader, our teacher and friend. I was just glad to be sitting beside him. It never occurred to me that this would be our last dinner together. He knew, and that's why he said what he said and did what he did. How could I have been so slow to recognize the importance of what was going on? It was always like that. I was always so preoccupied with my own things that I missed the Lord's hints. And he was so gentle, so patient.*

Jesus: How eagerly I had been looking forward to that supper! When we had the sacrificial lamb on our plates, I thought of my own imminent sacrifice, my own suffering that would remove once and for all any shadow of doubt about my love. How my heart overflowed when I was finally able to give to my first priests and followers the Sacrament of intimate communion – all of the sufferings that had already happened and all that were still to come were worth suffering a thousand times more so that I could leave for you this New Testament, this New Covenant, this bridge between time and eternity.

Do you know that I still look forward just as eagerly to each sacramental celebration of that Supper, to each Holy Communion? I long to give myself to you in this Sacrament. I am wholly present in it, and I bring all my grace and all my wisdom and all my love when you receive me. You can't see all of this, because your faith is still small, still growing. But as you come to know me better, I will show you more and more, and you will see how every Tabernacle in the world shines more brightly than the sun, spreading goodness and hope and redemption all around it.

CHRIST IN MY LIFE Sometimes I think you should have given me a more dramatic way to commemorate your suffering and redemption, Lord. But then I remember that you don't want to impress me; you want to walk with me. You want to be my strength and life. You want to be my daily bread, my daily companion. There, in the midst of the normal daily dramas, you teach and guide me…

I want to be able to give myself to others as completely and generously as you give yourself to me. But I am so hampered by all my selfish tendencies, my oversensitivity, and my complexes and fears! You are my only hope, Lord. Only you can renew my heart and give me whatever it is I need in order to become your true, faithful, persevering disciple…

I want to appreciate your gift of the Eucharist more, Lord. Draw me to your Tabernacles and altars. Increase my faith! You come in such simplicity, such silence, such gentleness! Like the sunshine and the drizzling rain, you come into my heart, and I barely know you're there. Open my eyes of faith, so that I can see more clearly your goodness and love and power and proclaim it more wisely and boldly…

QUESTIONS FOR SMALL GROUP DISCUSSION

1. What struck you most in this passage? What did you notice that you hadn't noticed before?

2. The Church teaches that Jesus is truly present in the Sacrament of the Eucharist, not just symbolically present. How would you explain that difference to a child preparing for First Communion?

3. If a stranger were to gauge your Eucharistic life during a typical week (your visits to the Lord in the Eucharist, your Communions – their frequency and their fervor – and your spiritual communions…), what kind of a conclusion would they make about the importance of the Eucharist in your life?

4. What more can we do to promote Eucharistic life among our peers?

Cf. *Catechism of the Catholic Church*, 1333-1344 on the Eucharist in the economy of the salvation; 1345-1355 on the Mass as the celebration of the Eucharist

228. THE BESTOWAL OF THRONES (LK 22:28-38)

"As for me, my spirit is now all humble devotion to the cross: the cross which so greatly offends the unbelievers, but is salvation and eternal life to us."

- St Ignatius of Antioch

Luke 22:28-38

'You are the men who have stood by me faithfully in my trials; and now I confer a kingdom on you, just as my Father conferred one on me: you will eat and drink at my table in my kingdom, and you will sit on thrones to judge the twelve tribes of Israel. Simon, Simon! Satan, you must know, has got his wish to sift you all like wheat; but I have prayed for you, Simon, that your faith may not fail, and once you have recovered, you in your turn must strengthen your brothers.' 'Lord,' he answered, 'I would be ready to go to prison with you, and to death.' Jesus replied, 'I tell you, Peter, by the time the cock crows today you will have denied three times that you know me.' He said to them, 'When I sent you out without purse or haversack or sandals, were you short of anything?' 'No,' they said. He said to them, 'But now if you have a purse, take it; if you have a haversack, do the same; if you have no sword, sell your cloak and buy one, because I tell you these words of scripture have to be fulfilled in me: He let himself be taken for a criminal. Yes, what scripture says about me is even now reaching its fulfilment.' 'Lord,' they said 'there are two swords here now.' He said to them, 'That is enough!'

CHRIST THE LORD Jesus is troubled by Judas' betrayal, but he is also encouraged by the others' fidelity and loyalty, in spite of their clumsiness and slowness to understand. In his gratitude, he reminds his apostles that he has promised them a Kingdom, and he assures them that he is conferring it on them even now. And his promise is literally fulfilled in the establishment of the Church, which can only take place at the conclusion of the atoning sacrifice of Calvary. When the spear is thrust through his heart as he hangs dead on the cross, the blood and water that flow out are the blood and water of the Church's birth. The Church is the start of Christ's Kingdom, and he bestows it upon his Apostles by making them its first leaders, the overseers and rulers of this new people of God – and once again in his discourse, at this solemn moment, he gives special attention to Peter, entrusting him with the role of confirming the others. Just as Kind David had thrones in his palace for the ministers who assisted him in ruling his Kingdom, so Jesus will rule through the ministry of his bishops. Just as the Davidic Kingdom had a prime minister who bore the keys in the king's absence, so also would the Church.

Thus, the apostles truly do become the judges (an Old Testament term used for rulers in general, not only court justices as we understand them today) of all the tribes of the new Israel, the Church. And they eat and drink at the Lord's Table there, in that Kingdom, by celebrating the sacrament of the Eucharist.

Once again, Jesus reminds us that every step of his passion is meaningful – is part of the Father's plan to redeem fallen humanity through his everlasting Church. We are the heirs of this immensely beautiful, richly mysterious plan, and as heirs, it is up to us to carry forward and carry high its banner.

CHRIST THE TEACHER With this final discourse before his suffering begins, he is once again providing his apostles with what they will need to brave the coming storm – advice about how to understand what will come to pass in the next few hours. When he sent them on mission trips without supplies, he gave them instructions to depend on the goodwill of the people to whom he was sending them. But tonight is different. Tonight they will not be able to depend on the goodwill of anyone, because their Master will be taken away as a criminal. In telling them this, he did not mean for them to gather swords, he simply meant for them to understand that he knew beforehand what was going to happen. When they reflected back on it as the crisis was unfolding, his foreknowledge and willing acceptance would provide enough assurance to give them at least a glimmer of hope during the dark three days to come.

Just so, the memory of Jesus' passion should give us the amount of strength we need to persevere in fidelity and in doing what's right even in the face of trials, persecution, and suffering. All that Jesus did, he did for our sake to encourage us to stay the course. It remains up to us to take advantage of our inheritance and make it bear fruit by keeping it always in mind along the twists and turns of our own journey through life.

CHRIST THE FRIEND *James: We still didn't understand what was going to happen, even though he had told us so many times. We didn't want to believe him, and so we simply failed to understand. At least, that's how it was with me. I still had my hopes on an easy victory and a taste of worldly glory. I still thought we would be able to fulfill our mission as his disciples with our own natural strengths and talents. I thought I could stay faithful to him by depending on my-self. We were all like that – so attached to our own ideas that we weren't listening to him. That's when we were most vulnerable. That's always when his followers are most vulnerable, when they lean on their own strength and forget that without him we can do nothing.*

Jesus: I created you to need me, so that you would feel drawn to the eternal life that I can give you. I want you to enjoy my friendship for all eternity, and that's something you can't achieve with your own talents. (I know, I gave those to you too.) Sometimes I have to remind you that you need me, as I had to remind Peter. You never need to be ashamed of your weakness; it's no surprise to me. I am always ready to come to your aid. It's never too late to call my name – but it's even better if you just let me keep walking by your side all the time.

CHRIST IN MY LIFE Thank you for the gift of the Church. Maybe because I'm inside it that I sometimes forget how remarkable and how wonderful it really is. Thank you for all your sacraments. Thank you for the pure, crystalline teaching where I can always relieve my thirst for truth. Are you happy with how I treat the Church? Bless your Church, Lord, and make us all her faithful children...

In the same breath, Lord, you promised to give your apostles the Kingdom, and then you told them they would be shaken and scattered like wheat by the onslaught of evil. You rejoice to give me good gifts, in spite of my faults and sins and failings! Your love doesn't depend on my perfection – how many times must you remind me! My happiness depends solely on your love...

I know that without you I can do nothing. But I also know that you have given me a role in your mission of salvation. You don't want me to just sit back and enjoy the ride. Thank you for this gift. I am glad to have something to do, some way I can grow in my love and serve my neighbor. Keep me faithful, Lord...

QUESTIONS FOR SMALL GROUP DISCUSSION

1. What struck you most in this passage? What did you notice that you hadn't noticed before?

2. How can we foster, in ourselves and in those around us, a more vibrant and supernatural love and respect for the Pope and our bishops?

3. What should be the immediate reaction of Christians when they fall or fail, as Peter is about to do?

4. Why do you think Jesus doesn't protect us from every fall and failure?

Cf. Catechism of the Catholic Church, 551-553 on Jesus' establishment of the Church hierarchy; 874-896 on the hierarchical structure of the Church; 1430-1433 on interior penance

229. A DARK GARDEN (LK 22:39-54)

"I've had these temptations for forty-one years now – do you think I'm going to give up after all this time? Absolutely not. I'll never stop hoping in God, though he kill me, though he grind me in the dust of eternity."

- St Jane de Chantal

Luke 22:39-54

He then left to make his way as usual to the Mount of Olives, with the disciples following. When they reached the place he said to them, 'Pray not to be put to the test.' Then he withdrew from them, about a stone's throw away, and knelt down and prayed. 'Father,' he said 'if you are willing, take this cup away from me. Nevertheless, let your will be done, not mine.' Then an angel appeared to him, coming from heaven to give him strength. In his anguish he prayed even more earnestly, and his sweat fell to the ground like great drops of blood. When he rose from prayer he went to the disciples and found them sleeping for sheer grief. 'Why are you asleep?' he said to them. 'Get up and pray not to be put to the test.' He was still speaking when a number of men appeared, and at the head of them the man called Judas, one of the Twelve, who went up to Jesus to kiss him. Jesus said, 'Judas, are you betraying the son of Man with a kiss?' His followers, seeing what was happening, said, 'Lord, shall we use our swords?' And one of them struck out at the high priest's servant, and cut off his right ear. But at this Jesus spoke. 'Leave off!' he said 'That will do!' And touching the man's ear he healed him. Then Jesus spoke to the chief priests and captains of the Temple guard and elders who had come for him. 'Am I a brigand,' he said, 'that you had to set out with swords and clubs? When I was among you in the Temple day after day you never moved to lay hands on me. But this is your hour; this is the reign of darkness.' They seized him then and led him away, and they took him to the high priest's house.

CHRIST THE LORD One of the most remarkable things about the Passion narratives is how Jesus remains composed and in control the whole time. As the petty wrath and duplicity of his enemies break against him, his fidelity and assurance, his love and self-mastery are completely undiminished, while their hatred surges and splatters and gathers for more and more useless assaults. His betrayer acts so nonchalant and unassuming, but the words of the Master lay bare his heart – "Is it with a kiss you betray me, Judas?" His disciples lash out with their swords, stirred to a worldly fury, but Jesus calms them with a word and restores order, healing his maimed and panicking enemy with a miracle. Faced with the gang of hirelings sent to arrest him, he reminds them that he has not been hiding in caves like an outlaw and thus exposes what they had not wanted to face up to – that something dishonorable and even despicable hovers all around this late-night, secret arrest. Even when he prays in the Garden, while every fiber of his human nature is pulling him away from the Father's will, even then the earnestness and force of his will presides, bringing every emotion and fear and doubt under the sweet yoke of loving obedience.

Jesus lived his passion this way because he lived it with love and purpose, as he lived every moment of his earthly life. We have received the same love and purpose through his grace, and as a result, as the countless martyrs have shown, we can find the same strength and nobility in the midst of our own passions simply by exercising our faith in him.

CHRIST THE TEACHER Our Lord's sweat pouring out in great drops of blood is more than St Luke waxing poetic. In extreme states of anxiety, clinical studies have shown that the capillaries near the surface of the skin will burst, and blood will mingle with the perspiration exuded by the sweat glands. What is Jesus teaching us by suffering this kind of anxiety? One simple lesson: fulfilling God's will in a fallen world will require self-sacrifice. It did for him, it did for his mother the Blessed Virgin Mary, and it did for every one of his followers who has been courageous enough to persevere in seeking and carrying out God's will. If it isn't demanding, it isn't the gospel.

Jesus wants us to know that, but he also wants us to know how to endure the suffering: by prayer. This is what he does, and this is what he tells his disciples to do, "Get up and pray not to be put to the test." If we pray, we will receive whatever grace we need to continue along the right path – just as Jesus here in Gethsemane received comfort from the angel.

Suffering and prayer – these are two of the three weapons available to us for spreading Christ's Kingdom. The third is a Christlike love for our neighbor.

CHRIST THE FRIEND *Jesus: I was thinking of you when I prayed in the Garden. I was thinking of what would happen to you if I were to reject the Father's will. You would have never discovered my love for you. You would have been stuck in those sins, hopelessly, for the rest of your life. You would have suffered interior remorse with no hope of forgiveness. You would have had to harden your heart so much just in order to survive that you would have lost the ability to love and let yourself be loved. None of your wounds that I have started to heal would have ever healed. None of the hopes that shine so brightly in your heart would be shining at all. I was glad to say yes to my Father so that you wouldn't have to suffer the darkness of everlasting regret and despair.*

I was also thinking of all the times you would to say yes to me. That was how the angel comforted me. He showed me the times you would confess your sins and accept my forgiveness. He showed me the times you would trust me enough to follow the voice of your conscience, even when the easier, more popular thing was to ignore it. He showed me all your prayers, your Holy Communions, your deeds of selflessness, fidelity, and generosity. He showed me your room in my Father's house, still waiting there for you. How much it thrilled me to see those things! I was glad to go to the cross for you. I would do it again a thousand times.

CHRIST IN MY LIFE If you are for me, Lord, who can be against me? Jesus, give me your courage and your wisdom. This world I live in is in such need of your grace, and by myself I am such a weak grace-dispenser. But you have called me into your Kingdom. And you can work through me. With the zeal of your heart, inflame my heart, and with the fortitude of your heart, make my heart strong…

You suffered and you prayed. Teach me to suffer and to pray. I am afraid of suffering; I run from it. You didn't. You ran towards it. How can I understand these mysteries without the light of your Holy Spirit? How can I learn to pray as I ought without your help? Jesus, I trust in you; let your will be done, not mine…

I can't help thinking about all the people who have to suffer without the comfort of your friendship. Jesus, come to their aid. Some suffer physically, others only in the secret of their souls. Send your messengers to them. Send me to them. Who can I bring your friendship to today, Lord? Show me how to be a better instrument of your grace today…

QUESTIONS FOR SMALL GROUP DISCUSSION

1. What struck you most in this passage? What did you notice that you hadn't noticed before?

2. What tone of voice do you think Jesus used to address Judas? What did he mean by his question?

3. The Church teaches that Jesus suffered, died, and rose *for us*. What different ways can you think of for interpreting what "for us" really means?

4. If an agnostic acquaintance asked you why Jesus, if he was really God, had so much trouble accepting the Father's will in the Garden of Gethsemane, what would you say?

Cf. Catechism of the Catholic Church, 609-61 on Jesus' self-offering at the Last Supper and in Gethsemane; 2824-2827 on the meaning of Jesus' prayer in Gethsemane

230. MYRIAD SINS, MULTIFACETED LOVE (LK 22:55-71)

"Therefore let no one presume on his own powers when he speaks; let no one trust in his own strength when he undergoes temptation, since in order to speak well and prudently, we must have wisdom from the Lord; and in order to bear misfortune bravely, we must receive the gift of endurance from him."

- St Augustine

Luke 22:55-71

Peter followed at a distance. They had lit a fire in the middle of the courtyard and Peter sat down among them, and as he was sitting there by the blaze a servant-girl saw him, peered at him, and said, 'This person was with him too.' But he denied it. 'Woman,' he said, 'I do not know him.' Shortly afterwards someone else saw him and said, 'You are another of them. But Peter replied, 'I am not, my friend.' About an hour later another man insisted, saying, 'This fellow was certainly with him. Why, he is a Galilean.' 'My friend,' said Peter, 'I do not know what you are talking about.' At that instant, while he was still speaking, the cock crew, and the Lord turned and looked straight at Peter, and Peter remembered what the Lord had said to him, 'Before the cock crows today, you will have disowned me three times.' And he went outside and wept bitterly. Meanwhile the men who guarded Jesus were mocking and beating him. They blindfolded him and questioned him. 'Play the prophet,' they said. 'Who hit you then?' And they continued heaping insults on him. When day broke there was a meeting of the elders of the people, attended by the chief priests and scribes. He was brought before their council, and they said to him, 'If you are the Christ, tell us.' 'If I tell you,' he replied 'you will not believe me, and if I question you, you will not answer. But from now on, the Son of Man will be seated at the right hand of the Power of God.' Then they all said, 'So you are the Son of God then?' He answered, 'It is you who say I am.' 'What need of witnesses have we now?' they said. 'We have heard it for ourselves from his own lips.'

CHRIST THE LORD During his passion, Jesus seems to make a point of suffering in every way possible, just so we will never have to suffer alone, no matter what brand of hardship life throws at us. By letting evil have free rein with him, and by persevering in love through it all, he shows his Lordship over the kingdom of darkness. And even in this final battle of his earthly life, he has us in mind, so that the revelation of his love exposes the face of sin as well. Every type of suffering that Jesus undergoes is caused by its own type of sin. As we contemplate his sorrows, then, he purifies our multifaceted selfishness, so that we who get a chance to share his sorrows here in this fallen world can also share his victories.

In this passage Peter causes Christ the immense sorrow of being abandoned by his closest friend. Peter, Jesus' privileged disciple, disowns his Master. Why did Peter do it? Unlike Judas, Peter didn't premeditate his betrayal. He hadn't fondled and coddled and nourished his feelings of self-righteousness and self-pity to the point where he thought turning Christ in was a justifiable and even, perhaps, virtuous act. No, Peter's sin was simple weakness. Disoriented by the arrest in the Garden, intimidated by the Sanhedrin's show of force, and surprised by the aggressive accusations made at him around the fire, he unthinkingly falls back into a self-centered self-defense mode. His true self was still caked with egoism, in spite of his acclamations to the contrary just hours before and his authentic desire to be faithful to Christ. We all share this weakness, and when we lean on our own strength as if we didn't, our inevitable falls grieve the heart of the Lord.

CHRIST THE TEACHER The guards were "mocking and beating him." We should not overlook the raw physical suffering this treatment caused our Lord. Just because the suffering of his heart was deeper and more painful, that doesn't mean that the suffering of the body ought to be minimized. Jesus had come to save these very men who are beating him; he came to pay the price for their sins and give them the light and grace that would renew their spirits and lead them to the happiness they yearn for. But they treat him cruelly. Theirs is the sin against charity, against the love we ought to have for our neighbors. Perhaps they had no way to recognize Christ as Lord, but they still had before them a fellow man, and yet they treated him like an animal, sporting with him. How often we do the same to our fellow men! Our careless words and pointed criticisms, our unforgiving judgments and arrogant gossip – these are cruel blows leveled against Christ himself, because "I tell you solemnly, in so far as you did this to one of the least of these brothers of mine, you did it to me" (Matthew 25:40).

The leaders of the Sanhedrin, the Jewish governing body in Palestine at the time, simply refuse to listen to him. "If I tell you, you will not believe me, and if I question you, you will not answer." By far, this causes Jesus the greatest suffering, that of unrequited love. Jesus is the pure love of the Father who has come to dwell among us. He is the Father's final and definitive declaration of love, and yet "his own people did not accept him" (John 1:11). Whenever we sin, in little things or big, we echo the Sanhedrin's proud refusal to accept their Savior. Whenever we say no to the voice of conscience, whenever we set ourselves up as judges of the Church's teaching, we join the ranks of "his own people, who did not accept him."

CHRIST THE FRIEND *Jesus: Many people think I must have been angry as my enemies destroyed me piece by piece. But how could I be angry? I was sad. I knew each one of my persecutors; I had created them, I was holding them in existence even as they rejected me. I knew that in destroying me, they were working their own destruction. Have you ever watched a loved one work his own destruction? Then you can feel a tinge of the sadness that drowned my heart during my Passion. But even as they crushed me, body and soul, underneath the sadness I was still able to rejoice because I knew that the supreme witness of my love on the cross would break open some of those tightly closed hearts, and at the very culmination of their colossal crimes, they would feel remorse and turn to me in repentance, and all would be well.*

You were with me then too. Your sins were raining down upon me, but your repentance gave me joy. It was all worth it, because my sacrifice would convince you of my love, and it would bring you onto my team and into my heart. Stay close to me, and offer your sufferings for the conversion of the many hearts that remained closed, and let us rejoice together in the victory of love.

CHRIST IN MY LIFE I don't want to forget about my sins, Lord, because your love shines brightest in your mercy. I believe in your mercy, and I am sorry for my sins. But if your mercy has overcome my sins, and if the sun of your mercy still shines even after my many attempts to blot it out with my sins, then what could ever steal my peace of soul? In your love I find all that my heart desires…

Why is it so hard for me to control my words, Lord? I am like those brutal soldiers, completely oblivious to the effect my criticisms and jibes have on those around me. What would we talk about all the time if we didn't criticize people? I want to know, Lord; I want to discover how to spread peace and light with the precious gift of speech, not bitterness and darkness…

Mary, you know I believe in Jesus. I have put my hopes in him. I don't want to cause him any suffering. Teach me to please him with my faith, my hope, and my efforts to build his Kingdom. Mother of mercy, pray for the many people who still refuse to believe in him. Help me to make his goodness visible to them, as you made it visible by standing by him at Calvary, so that his grace will win over their hearts…

QUESTIONS FOR SMALL GROUP DISCUSSION

1. What struck you most in this passage? What did you notice that you hadn't noticed before?

2. Why is speaking badly of others such an easy sin to fall into, and why is speaking well of others such a hard habit to form? How can we help each other to make the switch?

3. Why do you think Jesus purposely turned to look at Peter right after his third denial and the crowing of the rooster?

4. If you had to explain the evil of sin to an agnostic acquaintance who asked you about it, what would you tell them?

Cf. Catechism of the Catholic Church, 1846-1848 on mercy and sin; 1849-1853 on sin; 1865-1869 on the proliferation of sin; 2839-2841 on asking God's forgiveness

THE GOSPEL OF LUKE CHAPTER 23

"How precious is the gift of the cross! See, how beautiful it is to behold! It shows no sign of evil mixed with good, like the tree of old in Eden; it is all beautiful and comely to see and to taste. For it is a tree which brings forth life, not death. It is the source

of light, not darkness. It offers you a home in Eden; it does not cast you out. It is the tree which Christ mounted as a king his chariot, and so destroyed the devil, the lord of death, and rescued the human race from slavery to the tyrant. It is the tree on which the Lord, like a great warrior with his hands and feet and his divine side pierced in battle, healed the wounds of our sins, healed our nature that had been wounded by the evil serpent."

- St Theodore the Studite

231. UNRULY RULERS (LK 23:1-12)

"O man, rouse yourself! Learn to know the dignity of your nature. Remember that image of God in which you were created, which, though defaced in Adam, is now restored in Christ."

- Pope St Leo the Great

Luke 23:1-12

The whole assembly then rose, and they brought him before Pilate. They began their accusation by saying, 'We found this man inciting our people to revolt, opposing payment of the tribute to Caesar, and claiming to be Christ, a king.' Pilate put to him this question, 'Are you the king of the Jews?' 'It is you who say it,' he replied. Pilate then said to the chief priests and the crowd, 'I find no case against this man.' But they persisted, 'He is inflaming the people with his teaching all over Judaea; it has come all the way from Galilee, where he started, down to here.' When Pilate heard this, he asked if the man were a Galilean; and finding that he came under Herod's jurisdiction he passed him over to Herod who was also in Jerusalem at that time. Herod was delighted to see Jesus; he had heard about him and had been wanting for a long time to set eyes on him; moreover, he was hoping to see some miracle worked by him. So he questioned him at some length; but without getting any reply. Meanwhile the chief priests and the scribes were there, violently pressing their accusations. Then Herod, together with his guards, treated him with contempt and made fun of him; he put a rich cloak on him and sent him back to Pilate. And though Herod and Pilate had been enemies before, they were reconciled that same day.

CHRIST THE LORD We too often doubt God's powerful action in the course of human events simply because it is hidden. This passage gives us one of the great examples of the omnipotence of Providence. Pilate and Herod were rivals. Galilee and Judea were under different Roman jurisdictions – Judea was part of a procuratorship directly under Roman rule, while several of the neighboring areas, including Galilee, were under the rule of Herod, an semi-independent king allied with Rome. Because of the proximity of these territories and the constant flow of commerce and culture between them, the people often took advantage of Herod's policies to wheedle out of complying with Pilate's, and vice versa. You can imagine how doubly glad Pilate must have been to be able to slough off this tough case onto Herod's shoulders, taking advantage of a jurisdictional detail.

On the great day of Christ's passion, however, this rivalry ends. St Luke doesn't explain the reason behind Pilate and Herod's reconciliation; he just says it happened as a result of their both being involved with Christ in his passion. Already, even before the consummation of his sacrifice, the leaven of redemption is bringing together the peoples (Pilate was Roman; Herod was part Jew and part Samaritan) and the hearts that original sin had antagonized. How great should the confidence of the Christian be in the face of the greatness of the power of Christ! No challenge is too great for him; only his followers can imbue the frustrated world with the real, fruitful hope of lasting progress.

CHRIST THE TEACHER Jesus is faced with false charges. He is given two opportunities to defend himself, and he doesn't use them to his advantage. He humbly accepts the injustice (from Pilate) and the mockery (from Herod). Reflect a moment on the strength of soul that this requires. Think about how hard it is for us to enact this virtue in much smaller things. How quickly we justify ourselves in the eyes of others! How deftly we shift the responsibility for failures onto other shoulders! We take such delicate care of what other people think of us, and here our Lord, for the good of the Kingdom, lets his enemies annihilate his reputation in a dozen different ways and says nary a word in his own defense.

Often our determined demands for justice or recognition are really desperate attempts to save face. We would have more peace in our hearts, and we would be freer to do more for the Kingdom, if we cared less about the opinions of others and about getting the credit for doing good. What should matter to the Christian is God's opinion.

CHRIST THE FRIEND When Jesus spoke with Pilate, he saw a man whose soul had been starved by his ambition. Pilate was no longer able to defend truth and justice, because he had sold his heart to the idol of success. So many Pilates still walk the halls of government today. Christ longs for his faithful disciples to take the truth and light of virtue into the midst of the world's rulers! With his grace in their hearts and his teachings giving light to their minds, they will be able to do so much good for the human family. But many of them lack courage.

God has doled out to plenty of his children the talents for government, but too many of them have preferred a comfortable life.

He has given talents to each one of us. We know what some of them are; others are still waiting to be discovered. They are meant to be put at the service of the Kingdom. Christ's true friends know they are never alone, and so they never lack the courage to rejoice in the talents he has given to others and to use generously those they have received. The time is short. There is no time to be afraid. We should tirelessly forge ahead with whatever he inspires us to do for the good of the Church and of our neighbor. He is close beside us, guiding our every step.

CHRIST IN MY LIFE I believe in your Providence, Lord. I believe that you are guiding all things to their glorious conclusion in your Kingdom. Sometimes I am discouraged by the lack of visible progress, but I know that's only a temptation. Help me to do my part. Help me to give my best in everything I do, and to do only what I know you want me to do. Jesus, I trust in you…

This world is an expert at enticing me, Lord. How attractive it makes everything look! The pull of ambition, pleasure, popularity – it's constant, it's strong, it's seductive. I guess I still need a lot of help to keep things in proper perspective. Increase my virtue, Lord, so that I can do the right thing better, faster, more often, and with greater satisfaction…

I believe that you care about the course this world is taking. Raise up more leaders after your own heart, Lord. Remember how much you suffered for us, how much you love us, and don't abandon us to the whims of selfish and dishonest rulers. Thy Kingdom come…

QUESTIONS FOR SMALL GROUP DISCUSSION

1. What struck you most in this passage? What did you notice that you hadn't noticed before?

2. Why do you think we don't find more virtuous Catholics in leadership positions throughout the world?

3. Herod was interested in a good show and Pilate wanted to climb the ladder of success, while Christ was focused on the mission he had received from the Father. Which of the three approaches to life do you think resonates most with popular culture? Why?

4. What are some of the most common ways we can fall into the sin of wasting time? How can we help ourselves make better use of this precious commodity?

Cf. Catechism of the Catholic Church, 302-314 on God's providence and how it works; 898-900 and 2442 on Catholics' intervention in political life; 2520 on purity of intention

232. CARRYING THE CROSS (LK 23:13-32)

"Throughout history the most wonderful events have been only the symbols and fore-shadowings of this cross."

- St Theodore the Studite

Luke 23:13-32

Pilate then summoned the chief priests and the leading men and the people. 'You brought this man before me,' he said, 'as a political agitator. Now I have gone into the matter myself in your presence and found no case against the man in respect of all the charges you bring against him. Nor has Herod either, since he has sent him back to us. As you can see, the man has done nothing that deserves death, So I shall have him flogged and then let him go.' But as one man they howled, 'Away with him! Give us Barabbas!' (This man had been thrown into prison for causing a riot in the city and for murder.) Pilate was anxious to set Jesus free and addressed them again, but they shouted back, 'Crucify him! Crucify him!' And for the third time he spoke to them, 'Why? What harm has this man done? I have found no case against him that deserves death, so I shall have him punished and then let him go' But they kept on shouting at the top of their voices, demanding that he should be crucified. And their shouts were growing louder. Pilate then gave his verdict: their demand was to be granted. He released the man they asked for, who had been imprisoned for rioting and murder, and handed Jesus over to them to deal with as they pleased. As they were leading him away they seized on a man, Simon from Cyrene, who was coming in from the country, and made him shoulder the cross and carry it behind Jesus. Large numbers of people followed him, and of women too, who mourned and lamented for him. But Jesus turned to them and said, 'Daughters of Jerusalem, do not weep for me; weep rather for yourselves and for your children. For the days will surely come when people will say, Happy are those who are barren, the wombs that have never borne, the breasts that have never suckled! Then they will begin to say to the mountains, Fall on us! to the hills, Cover us. For if men use the green wood like this, what will happen when it is dry?' Now with him they were also leading out two other criminals to be executed.

CHRIST THE LORD Jesus is the Word of God made flesh. As the Word of God, he is the creator of all that exists, including the moral order of human nature. That very moral order is what makes Pilate hesitate to condemn Jesus to death, because it is wrong to punish the innocent and even worse to kill the innocent. Pilate holds out against the crowd for a little while, but in the end he gives in. He violates his conscience, and in so doing condemns Christ to be crucified.

This is a snapshot of the whole moral life. Our conscience, formed and informed by Church teaching and the just laws and traditions of human society, indicates the right thing to do. It is one of God's great gifts, an internal chip that tells us his will and how we can live our lives in communion with him. When we disobey it, we are doing exactly what Pilate did – crucifying Christ, executing God, and banishing him in order to eliminate the discomfort his presence can cause. The same factors that influenced Pilate's decision influence ours: he was afraid to lose his position, his reputation, his livelihood, his hopes for promotion, and his cushy retirement. The shouts of the crowds – like the shouts of our passions and emotions – inflated the value of his temporal welfare, so much so that he was willing to sacrifice his own moral integrity to protect it.

Where was Christ in the midst of the battle? Why didn't he rescue Pilate? Jesus was right there. Pilate was looking at him the whole time. He knew exactly what he was doing. Just so, Jesus is with us every time we are faced with a moral decision, big or small. And when we are honest with ourselves, we know very well that we are fully responsible for each one of those decisions. This is why it is so important to reflect and pray about why we should stay faithful to God's will, to what is right, *before* the moments of conflict. Only then will we be able to resist the violent pressure of our emotions and fears in order to stay faithful to the Lord.

CHRIST THE TEACHER What is going on in Jesus' mind as he shoulders the cross and begins the long, excruciating, humiliating march to Calvary? Thanks to his encounter with the compassionate women who were walking beside him, we know the answer. He was thinking of us, of his beloved brothers and sisters for whom he was offering his life as an atoning sacrifice. Amazingly, even in a furious hurricane of personal suffering, his mind is not on himself, but on those whom he loves. He tells these women not to weep for him. He tells them to think of those who are rejecting him, and what will happen as a result of their rejection. Once again he uses language reminiscent of the Old Testament prophets, language used by those prophets to predict the fall of Jerusalem to the Babylon armies in 586 BC and the fall of the Northern Kingdom of Israel to the Assyrian armies in 733 BC. Those who refuse God's grace are cutting themselves off from the source of existence itself, and only one result can ensue.

This conversation teaches us how to carry our crosses – and Jesus promised that his followers will have crosses to carry, every day. We are to remember that our acceptance of God's will when it's costly is the only way to exercise the virtues of faith, hope, and love that will restore our souls to health and holiness.

We are to remember that when God sends us crosses, they too can be redemptive—just as Christ won grace by carrying and dying on his cross. We can win graces for the lives of those around us, the lives of those who need them most, through carrying and dying on our crosses with Christ, uniting our imperfect fidelity and trust to his perfect surrender. Jesus wanted to teach us that salvation comes not in spite of or instead of suffering, but through suffering. And he wanted to give us a chance not only to be saved ourselves, but to become agents of salvation for others, to become other Christs.

CHRIST THE FRIEND *Jesus: Do you realize what Barabbas was in prison for? He had rebelled against the Roman authority. Do you remember what crime my enemies accused me of in front of Pilate? Of raising up anti-Roman rebellions. Barabbas had committed the crime that I was accused of but had not committed, and he went free while I suffered his just punishment. Now do you see how my justice and mercy go together? I take upon myself the just punishments that others deserve, so that I can forgive their sins and give them a fresh start. I did the same with your sins—every one of them. The disorder they caused had to be set right – I did that during my passion, and I do it at every Mass. I am the Lamb of God who takes away the sins of the world.*

Would you be willing to do the same? Are you willing to suffer what others deserve to suffer, so that they can go free and have a fresh start? I know that you love me and want to show me your love. I also know that the more you show me your love, the happier you will be. Here is a vast arena where you can love. Every time I permit a small suffering to come your way, if you accept it the way I accepted mine, you can offer it to the Father in reparation for the sin of someone who is still imprisoned in sin, and if you do this in my name, you will help set that person free. I have put the power of my Kingship in your hands.

CHRIST IN MY LIFE If I don't follow your will, Lord, who else's can I follow? There's mine, but I know how ignorant and selfish I am. There are other people's, but who is a wiser guide than you? There's the trend of popular culture, or any of the sub-cultures, but who's behind those trends if not some other self-proclaimed guru, or maybe even the devil? I want to follow your will, Lord; show me the way…

I see you carrying your cross, thinking about the mission the Father has entrusted to you. You are engrossed in the needs of others. You are glad to sacrifice yourself for me. O Jesus, give me a heart like that! Make me love as you love! I tend to turn in on myself when the going gets rough. Help me, Lord. Teach me to embrace my crosses as you embraced yours…

Mary, your love and fidelity helped Jesus redeem the world. Jesus wanted you to help. I know he wants me to help too. I know that my own prayer and fidelity can really help undo the evil of sin – mine as well as others'. I am not only an adopted child of God, but a real child of God. His life, nurtured in your womb, is my life. You are my mother too. Teach me to understand the dignity of being a Christian, and teach me to live in accordance with that dignity…

QUESTIONS FOR SMALL GROUP DISCUSSION

1. What struck you most in this passage? What did you notice that you hadn't noticed before?

2. How can we better help each other carry our crosses?

3. Why do you think we resist suffering even though we know that it's an essential ingredient of human life?

4. How can we strengthen our consciences so that we make fewer and fewer sinful choices and more and more virtuous choices?

Cf. Catechism of the Catholic Church, 1750-1756 on the morality of our actions; 1776-1789 on the conscience; 602-605 on Christ's atoning sacrifice; 901-903 and 2099-2100 on offering sacrifices to God in union with Christ

233. THE KING'S PARDON (LK 23:33-43)

'O wonderful cross, upon whose branches hung the treasure and redemption of captive men, through you the world is redeemed by the blood of the Lord."

- Liturgy of the Hours

Lk 23:33-43

When they reached the place called The Skull, they crucified him there and the two criminals also, one on the right, the other on the left. Jesus said, 'Father, forgive them; they do not know what they are doing.' Then they cast lots to share out his clothing. The people stayed there watching him. As for the leaders, they jeered at him. 'He saved others,' they said 'let him save himself if he is the Christ of God, the Chosen One.' The soldiers mocked him too, and when they approached to offer vinegar they said, 'If you are the king of the Jews, save yourself.' Above him there was an inscription: 'This is the King of the Jews.' One of the criminals hanging there abused him. 'Are you not the Christ?' he said. 'Save yourself and us as well.' But the other spoke up and rebuked him. 'Have you no fear of God at all?' he said. 'You got the same sentence as he did, but in our case we deserved it: we are paying for what we did. But this man has done nothing wrong. Jesus,' he said, 'remember me when you come into your kingdom.' 'Indeed, I promise you,' he replied 'today you will be with me in paradise.'

CHRIST THE LORD We are gazing at the pivotal moment of human history: Jesus Christ being crucified on the hill of Calvary. In the Church's liturgy, this passage is read on the Solemnity of Christ the King at the end of liturgical year C. It's as if the Church directs our gaze to this pitiful man, wounded, dying, and rejected, and says to us: "Behold your King." A King enthroned upon a cross? Yes. Christ reigns from the cross. What is a King but the one responsible for bringing peace and prosperity, justice and order to a people? On the cross, Christ does just that for us. The human family had fallen from grace when our first parents gave in to temptation and rebelled against God. Thereafter the proliferation of sin demolished the order, the peace, and the joy of God's original design for creation. Jesus Christ came to earth to put things right, to "undo the work of the Devil" (1 John 3:8). His obedience "unto death, and death on a cross" (Philippians 2:8) reversed the disobedience of Adam and Eve and closed the breach opened by man's rebellion against God, making possible once again intimate friendship between them, the friendship which alone can produce true peace and order in the heart of men and human societies.

One of the thieves detected this somehow. He watched as Christ carried his cross to Calvary. He saw the Lord nailed to the wood and lifted up from the earth. And through it all, he saw how differently Jesus suffered. There was pain and humiliation, but no fear, no panic, no hatred. The Lord bore it all with purpose, determination, and serenity; he bore it like the King he truly is. And the good thief recognized this. Hope kindled in his heart, even at that darkest hour. He looked into Christ's eyes and made an act of faith, a promise of loyalty, and he did not go unrewarded.

Indeed, Christ the King does reign from the cross, the perfect expression of his unconditional yes to the Father, the yes that conquered sin, death, and the devil, the yes of unconditional forgiveness that opened for us the gates of Heaven: "Father, forgive them… Today you will be with me in Paradise."

CHRIST THE TEACHER At Calvary, Christ teaches us what he meant when he proclaimed "Mine is not a Kingdom of this world" (John 18:36) and "If anyone wants to be a follower of mine, let him renounce himself and take up his cross every day and follow me" (Luke 9:23). Jesus faithfully obeyed the Father's will. In this fallen world, such obedience led him to experience physical torture, abandonment by his friends, mockery and misunderstanding from his peers, humiliation, sorrow, and death.

When we decide to follow Christ, we can expect much of the same. Only through death to ourselves, to our selfishness and vanity, can the new life of Christ take root in us: "If then we have died with Christ, we believe we will also live with him" (Romans 6:8). Each time we see a crucifix, not only do we see our King enthroned, but we see the path we must follow to enter his Kingdom.

CHRIST THE FRIEND *Jesus: The people watched and stared at me hanging and dying on the Cross; do you see them? I saw them so clearly. The rulers sneered at me; the soldiers mocked me; one of the thieves abused me… You were there too, along with all of those who have called themselves Christians. Every time my followers fail to come to their neighbor's aid, they join Calvary's passive spectators; when they disdain the teachings of the Church, they join the sneering rulers and mocking soldiers; when they give up their faith or let it smolder because they prefer the passing kingdoms of this world, they join the abusive thief.*

I saw your face looking up at me as I hung upon the cross. At first you laughed and mocked; you were distracted and careless, just like the others. Then you saw that I was looking at you, waiting for you, hoping in you, and your expression changed. A flash of recognition flitted across your eyes. I knew that you had glimpsed my love and that you were sorry. And even then, in my agony, I smiled. As soon as you repent, as soon as you come to me in your need and ask me to be your King, I take you by the hand and rejoice in leading you to Paradise.

CHRIST IN MY LIFE If you reign from a cross, why do I still look for earthly glory and pleasure? Am I not your follower? I only have a short time to work for you here on earth, Lord. Help me to spend it well. Help me to love and rejoice in you and to help as many others as possible to do the same. With the Kingdom of your heart, reign in my heart…

Please purify my heart, Lord. I still desire fruitfulness and fulfillment without self-mastery and self-sacrifice. How many times I make the sign of the cross! And yet I still run from so many of the crosses that you send me. Teach me to embrace my cross. Teach me to trust in your truth, to do what is right, to put you first, my neighbor second, and myself third…

My sins crucified you, Lord. When I sin, I banish you from my world, just as the Pharisees tried to banish you from theirs. I hate sin, Lord. Even as I say it, I know that I will be tempted, but you know that my heart is yours. I am still full of selfishness, which holds me back from loving you, but I trust in you. You can renew me…

QUESTIONS FOR SMALL GROUP DISCUSSION

1. What struck you most in this passage? What did you noticed that you hadn't noticed before?

2. What can we do to avoid getting so used to seeing the crucifix that we become oblivious to the inexhaustible lessons Christ has to teach us from the cross?

3. What has helped you the most in your efforts to imitate Christ by accepting and responding

ingeniously to difficulties, persecution, ridicule, or resistance, without getting frustrated or discouraged? What tends to encourage you to adopt the mentality of those who will serve Christ only if he comes down from the cross and does things "my way"?

4. What most inhibits us from trusting Christ enough to regularly bring our sins and sinfulness to him in the sacrament of reconciliation, instead of making him wait for us while we continue rejecting his grace?

Cf. Catechism of the Catholic Church, 606-618, 550, 853, 440 on the meaning of Christ' sacrifice at Calvary; 1430-1433 on the importance of repentance; 2015, 1816, 2427 on the role of sacrifice and self-denial in the Christian walk

234. THE PERFECT DEATH (LK 23:44-56)

"We are celebrating the feast of the cross, and with the crucified one we are raised up, leaving behind us the earth and sins so that we may possess what is above."

- St Andrew of Crete

Luke 23:44-56

It was now about the sixth hour and, with the sun eclipsed, a darkness came over the whole land until the ninth hour. The veil of the Temple was torn right down the middle; and when Jesus had cried out in a loud voice, he said, 'Father, into your hands I commit my spirit.' With these words he breathed his last. When the centurion saw what had taken place, he gave praise to God and said, 'This was a great and good man.' And when all the people who had gathered for the spectacle saw what had happened, they went home beating their breasts. All his friends stood at a distance; so also did the women who had accompanied him from Galilee, and they saw all this happen. Then a member of the council arrived, an upright and virtuous man named Joseph. He had not consented to what the others had planned and carried out. He came from Arimathaea, a Jewish town, and he lived in the hope of seeing the kingdom of God. This man went to Pilate and asked for the body of Jesus. He then took it down, wrapped it in a shroud and put him in a tomb which was hewn in stone in which no one had yet been laid. It was Preparation Day and the sabbath was imminent. Meanwhile the women who had come from Galilee with Jesus were following behind. They took note of the tomb and of the position of the body. Then they returned and prepared spices and ointments. And on the sabbath day they rested, as the Law required.

CHRIST THE LORD At the very moment of his apparent defeat, our King begins to enjoy the abundant spoils of his eternal victory – the allegiance of loving hearts. The centurion, who had overseen Christ's whole condemnation, torture, mockery, and expiration, opens his heart with an act of faith; he becomes a soldier of Christ. The bystanders, who minutes before had been laughing and berating, repent as they stumble home. His friends and followers stand gazing at their Lord, unable to turn away from this horrendous scene, which has become beautiful to them and has changed their hearts forever. Joseph of Arimathaea, a member of the Sanhedrin, risks his own reputation as he publicly defies the enemies of Christ and pays homage to his crucified Lord. The women of Galilee show their fierce and constant fidelity, obeying the Law while they also obey the law of love by preparing spices to anoint their beloved Jesus. As much as the powers of darkness tried to shatter once and for all the Kingdom of Christ, his followers continue to serve him, like iron filings that just keep converging on a magnet.

Love – Christ's love – is stronger than death.

CHRIST THE TEACHER Jesus taught us how to live, seeking and fulfilling God's will in all things, loving God and loving our neighbor. Now he teaches us how to die. He dies so well that in the very moment of death he wins a convert: "When the centurion saw what had taken place, he gave praise to God…."

Death will come for each of us. It is one of the few things the future holds that we can be absolutely sure of. And yet we spend precious little time considering it and preparing for it. Christians are not meant to be obsessed with death, but neither should they join the swelling ranks of those who frantically distract themselves from this simple truth.

Jesus dies well because he dies in perfect communion with the Father. At the end of his earthly mission, as he feels his life slipping away from him, he is able to pray, "Father, into your hands I commit my spirit." It is a phrase from the Psalms (Psalm 31:5). It shows us the two qualities of a good death. First, Jesus was close to the Father. In the moment of final crisis, God is not a stranger to him. God is not someone Jesus has been trying to deceive, avoid, or play games with. God is his Father. Second, it shows Jesus' total trust in God's goodness. Few realities instill fear like death, when our very lives, our very selves seem to be drifting outside our grasp. Panic and despair often take over, but not for Jesus. Quietly, confidently, surely, he commits his soul and all that will come after into the Father's hands.

Staying close to God through daily prayer and frequent sacramental life, especially frequent confession, is the best preparation we can make for this all-important event. And spending at least as much time filling our minds with thoughts of God's goodness (drawn from reflection, readings, and conversations) as we do filling it with the flotsam and jetsam of news and useless chatter will help store up inner peace and strength for our final battle. But if death comes and finds us unprepared, we need not fear. If we say with Jesus his own last prayer, how could the Father not honor it?

CHRIST THE FRIEND *Mary: It is over. He has done it. He has revealed everything. The world now knows that God is not a tyrant, not a cold architect, not a fickle force. Now they know that he is a Lover. Lovers give their lives for the ones they love. He has given his life. He has given it in such a way that anyone who sees him will be attracted by his meekness and mercy, just as you have been. His mercy is more powerful than all the greatness of this passing world. Now you know that you can trust him. He seeks nothing for himself – do you see him on the cross? He cares nothing for himself; all his teaching and all his will is for your good, for your happiness. Now you don't have to be suspicious. Trust him. Tell others that they can trust him. And you will see that this cross, erected to deal out death, has become the new and everlasting Tree of Life.*

CHRIST IN MY LIFE I am one of your followers, Lord, and I want to follow you to the end. Who else is there to follow? Who else has done so much for me? Thank you for being completely faithful. How I have longed for someone who will be faithful! Teach me to be faithful – faithful to my family and friends, faithful to my conscience, faithful to my mission in life, just like you…

When will my death come, Lord? What will it be like? You know. I don't need to know. I only need to know that it will come. Of course I am afraid of it a little bit. But you have gone before me, and you have shown me how to go there. Help me to remember that this life is only a journey. Jesus, I hope in you…

Love is more than feelings – it is self-giving, it is the cross. I want to learn to love the way you created me to love, and I want to experience the immense joy and meaning that come from a life given to loving. I can't receive you in Communion right now, but come at least spiritually into my heart as I unite myself to your sacrifice of love. Teach me to love…

QUESTIONS FOR SMALL GROUP DISCUSSION

1. What struck you most in this passage? What did you notice that you hadn't noticed before?

2. What is the significance of the sky going dark during the last hours of Christ's agony? Of the Temple veil being torn in two at the moment of his death?

3. Why do you think St Luke makes a point of twice mentioning the women from Galilee in this passage?

4. What is your favorite artistic depiction of the crucifixion and why?

Cf. Catechism of the Catholic Church, 440, 550, 617, 813, 1505, 1741, 1992, and 2305 on the effects of the sacrifice of the cross; 1323, 1364-66, and 1382 on the Eucharist as the ever present sacrifice of the cross; 1005-1014 on the Christian vision of death; 1684-1690 on the celebration of funerals

THE GOSPEL OF LUKE CHAPTER 24

"Though Lord, he became man; he suffered for those who were suffering, he was bound
for the captive, judged for the condemned, buried for the one who was buried; he rose
from the dead and cried out: 'Who shall contend with me? Let him stand up to face
me. I have freed the condemned, brought the dead to life, raised up the buried. Who
will speak against me?' 'I am the Christ,' he says, 'It is I who destroyed death, who
triumphed over the enemy, who trampled Hades underfoot, who bound the strong one
and snatched man away to the heights of heaven; I am the Christ."

- St Melito of Sardis

235. LOVE AND LIFE (LK 24:1-12)

"You are alive! Your murderers handled your life like farmers: they sowed it like grain
deep in the earth, for it to spring up and raise with itself a multitude of men."

- St Ephraem

Luke 24:1-12

On the first day of the week, at the first sign of dawn, they went to the tomb with
the spices they had prepared. They found that the stone had been rolled away
from the tomb, but on entering discovered that the body of the Lord Jesus was not
there. As they stood there not knowing what to think, two men in brilliant clothes
suddenly appeared at their side. Terrified, the women lowered their eyes. But the
two men said to them, 'Why look among the dead for someone who is alive? He
is not here; he has risen. Remember what he told you when he was still in Galilee:
that the Son of Man had to be handed over into the power of sinful men and be
crucified, and rise again on the third day?' And they remembered his words. When
the women returned from the tomb they told all this to the Eleven and to all the
others. The women were Mary of Magdala, Joanna, and Mary the mother of James.
The other women with them also told the apostles, but this story of theirs seemed
pure nonsense, and they did not believe them. Peter, however, went running to the
tomb. He bent down and saw the binding cloths but nothing else; he then went
back home, amazed at what had happened.

CHRIST THE LORD No one escapes death. Emperors die, geniuses die, business tycoons die – death is the great equalizer, the great reminder that we are
not gods. But Christ rose from the dead; he conquered the grave. He died, yet
he is still alive. He lives and reigns now, in this very moment. He is as alive as
anyone walking the earth today, even though he truly died. No other historical
figure has even made such a claim, let alone given proof, century after century

(through the otherwise inexplicable vitality of the Church), to substantiate the claim. The Resurrection is Christ's trump card, Christian life's unshakable foundation. This is our Lord, the definitive conqueror of sin and death. We, like Peter, should be "amazed." If we are not, we don't really know our Lord.

CHRIST THE TEACHER The Resurrection validates all of Christ's other lessons. Without it, they would be nice pieces of advice, beautiful ones even, but ultimately impractical. If his doctrine doesn't lead to true life, why make the sacrifices necessary to follow it? By rising from the dead, he confirms that his doctrine does lead to life. The Resurrection is his "most marvelous work," as St Augustine put it. The odd thing is that he entrusts the announcement of this all-important message to his weak and fragile followers. Unless we spread the news, it won't get spread at all.

The news of this most marvelous work doesn't come from his own lips. He entrusts the message first to the angels, then to the women who came to his tomb. Only after the women hear the news from the angels does he appear to them (cf. St Matthew's version); and only after the women have announced the news to the Apostles does he appear to them. This is the pattern of evangelization in all times and places: a personal, life-changing encounter with the living Lord is always mediated by Christian witness. We who have met the risen Jesus through the gift of faith have to announce the good news to those who have not. As St Paul put it: "But how can they call on him in whom they have not believed? And how can they believe in him of whom they have not heard? And how can they hear without someone to preach?" (Romans 10:14)

CHRIST THE FRIEND *Joanna: When the angels spoke to us, they called Jesus "someone who is alive." The words struck me, though I only had time to reflect on them later. At the time, we were so exhausted by our sadness and shocked by the bright angels and the open tomb that we couldn't think at all. I am sure we were quite incoherent when we went to tell the apostles. How beautiful are the angel's words! Jesus truly is the one most alive, because he is the one who loves the most. The cross was the testament to his immense love; the Resurrection is the testament to his overflowing life. God is love, and God is also the source of all life. True life and true love are inextricably intertwined. When Jesus offered me his friendship, he was inviting me to share in his life. That meant experiencing his love so that I could learn to love as he does, which is the path to the indescribable life he wishes to give us.*

Jesus: I want my life to be your life. Imagine an iron rod being thrust into a blazing fire. Just as the cold, hard rod becomes red-hot and supple, taking on the characteristics of the fire, so your life, united in friendship to mine, will take on the intensity of my life. I came for this, that you might have life and have it in all its abundance.

CHRIST IN MY LIFE How little I think about your Resurrection, Lord! And yet, you really did rise from the dead. Only you have done it. I believe in your goodness, and I believe in your power. And so I will continue to seek your will for my life, because your will is both your goodness and your power custom-fitted to the needs and yearnings of my soul. Teach me to do your will…

Sometimes I am intimidated by the commission you have given me to spread your Kingdom. But you don't ask me to convert the world, you just ask me to bear witness right here and right now, with my life, and when necessary with words, to all that you have done for me. All I need to do is make myself available, and you will take care of the rest. Jesus, I trust in you…

Mary, your heart still beats with Christ's. I want to burn with the love that consumes your heart. I want to live the life of overflowing abundance, unlimited surrender, and uncontainable joy that Jesus gave to you and gives to all his saints, to everyone who trusts in him unconditionally. Let it be done to me according to his word…

QUESTIONS FOR SMALL GROUP DISCUSSION

1. What struck you most in this passage? What did you notice that you hadn't noticed before?

2. Why do you think the reality of the Resurrection doesn't have a bigger impact on our lives? Why don't we think it about it more often?

3. How concerned should we be about spreading the good news of Christ's Resurrection (and all that it implies)? How should we show that concern?

4. How can we deepen our friendship with Christ this week – allowing him to be more alive in our daily lives?

Cf. Catechism of the Catholic Church, 638-655 on the meaning of Christ's Resurrection; 599-618 on the meaning of Christ's death

236. THE LORD DRAWS NEAR (LK 24:13-35)

"This glorious son of the carpenter, who set up his cross above the all-consuming world of the dead, led the human race into the abode of life."

- St Ephraem

Luke 24:13-35

That very same day, two of them were on their way to a village called Emmaus, seven miles from Jerusalem, and they were talking together about all that had happened. Now as they talked this over, Jesus himself came up and walked by their side; but something prevented them from recognising him. He said to them, 'What matters are you discussing as you walk along?' They stopped short, their faces downcast. Then one of them, called Cleopas, answered him, 'You must be the only person staying in Jerusalem who does not know the things that have been happening there these last few days.' 'What things?' he asked. 'All about Jesus of Nazareth,' they answered, 'who proved he was a great prophet by the things he said and did in the sight of God and of the whole people; and how our chief priests and our leaders handed him over to be sentenced to death, and had him crucified. Our own hope had been that he would be the one to set Israel free. And this is not all: two whole days have gone by since it all happened; and some women from our group have astounded us: they went to the tomb in the early morning, and when they did not find the body, they came back to tell us they had seen a vision of angels who declared he was alive. Some of our friends went to the tomb and found everything exactly as the women had reported, but of him they saw nothing.'

Then he said to them, 'You foolish men! So slow to believe the full message of the prophets! Was it not ordained that the Christ should suffer and so enter into his glory?' Then, starting with Moses and going through all the prophets, he explained to them the passages throughout the scriptures that were about himself. When they drew near to the village to which they were going, he made as if to go on; but they pressed him to stay with them. 'It is nearly evening' they said 'and the day is almost over.' So he went in to stay with them. Now while he was with them at table, he took the bread and said the blessing; then he broke it and handed it to them. And their eyes were opened and they recognised him; but he had vanished from their sight. Then they said to each other, 'Did not our hearts burn within us as he talked to us on the road and explained the scriptures to us?' They set out that instant and returned to Jerusalem. There they found the Eleven assembled together with their companions, who said to them, 'Yes, it is true. The Lord has risen and has appeared to Simon.' Then they told their story of what had happened on the road and how they had recognised him at the breaking of bread.

CHRIST THE LORD Leaders know how to motivate, how to inspire. The greater their leadership capacity, the deeper the motivations they stir up. A great teacher not only knows the subject well, but also spreads a passion for it among the students. A great statesman buoys up the hopes of citizens in times of trouble and inspires them to self-sacrifice for the common good. How much more in the case of Christ the Lord! These downcast disciples had given up. They had left everything to follow Jesus, but the events of Good Friday had dashed their hopes, and they were walking sadly back to their old lives. A few words from their Leader, however, an opening of their eyes to share his vision, and suddenly their heavy hearts were "burning" again, so much so that they retraced their seven-mile trek in the dark without complaint.

If we truly wish to follow Christ, he will lead us as no one ever could; if we attentively listen to him, he will stir up our hearts with a wisdom this world can never give.

CHRIST THE TEACHER The Risen One was recognized "at the breaking of the bread." That was one of the names the early Church used to refer to the celebration of the Eucharist. The gestures of Christ at supper with these two disciples mirror those of the Last Supper and have been perpetuated in those of the Mass: "He took the bread and said the blessing; then he broke it and handed it to them. And their eyes were opened and they recognized him." Do you want to find the Lord? Do you want to know him? Do you want to discover the inexhaustible riches of life in communion with him? He teaches us how: come to him in the Eucharist.

Our primary encounter with Christ in the Eucharist takes place through the sacrifice of the Mass, which makes Christ's unique sacrifice offered on the cross at Calvary present for us in the here-and-now of our lives. Notice how closely the structure of the Mass follows the structure of this encounter between Christ and the disciples on the road to Emmaus: Christ comes to meet them on the road; through the priest, Christ comes to meet us right where we are. In the midst of our sorrows and joys he is present, veiled behind the personality of the priest, but really there through the sacrament of Holy Orders. Christ then explains the scriptures to them, showing how they point to him, and relating them to the disciples' present needs; and what is the first part of Mass (the readings and the homily) if not a reenactment of this walk to Emmaus? Finally, Christ joins them for the evening meal and breaks bread with them; here is the second part of Mass, the Eucharistic prayers, the consecration of the bread and wine into Christ's body and blood, and the reception of Holy Communion. To have the privilege of participating in the celebration of the Eucharist is to encounter the Crucified and Risen One, and to let him set our hearts on fire.

CHRIST THE FRIEND "Jesus himself came up and walked by their side." Christ continues to do this every day in the Blessed Sacrament. In every Mass, in every Tabernacle, he draws near to us and walks by our side. In Holy Communion, he continues to share his life with us. He is truly present, reaching out to us, speaking to our hearts, behind the thin veil of faith. If only we, like these two disciples, are honest and courageous enough to open our hearts to him and invite him into the secret places of our souls, we will see him anew, and his love will burn within us.

Jesus: I know when you are downcast and sad. I know when the shadow of the cross and Good Friday make you turn away from Jerusalem and head back to your old ways. I know, and I care, more than you can imagine. I am always drawing near to you. I speak in the quiet voice of your conscience, where only you can hear me. Sometimes I speak to you through the words of a friend or a verse from the Bible. Whenever you hear my voice, and you know when you do, you have only to welcome it, to make your prayer the same as these two disciples who pressed me to stay with them. Will I ever deny such a request, I who came all the way down from heaven just because I couldn't stand being far away from you? This is why I came; this is why I died; this is why I rose again – to stay with you.

CHRIST IN MY LIFE I have chosen to follow you, Lord, and no one else. I know it's only because you called me, but I have made the choice. You didn't force me. And I want to be true to that choice. You are the Lord. You are the fount of wisdom, forgiveness, love, and life that fills the world with whatever goodness it has. Make me a channel of your grace, a riverbed for your flowing fountain…

The struggles of my life seem so irrelevant sometimes when I go to Mass. But how could they be? Do you not care about them? Dear Lord, it's a mystery to me, this passing life, so busy but so out of focus. Help me to know in each moment what I should do and how I should be. I have only this life to live, and I want to live it well…

Stay with me, Lord. How I need a friend who knows me through and through and doesn't judge me! How I need a coach who knows my strengths and weaknesses and who knows how to profit from the former and shore up the latter! I feel such a burning desire to do something worthwhile, to do more – you put that desire in my heart. Now show me what to do with it…

QUESTIONS FOR SMALL GROUP DISCUSSION

1. What struck you most in this passage? What did you notice that you hadn't noticed before?

2. Why do you think Christ appeared to these two disciples but didn't reveal his identity until the end of the encounter? Why did he disappear at that point?

3. What was the real reason that these two disciples were "downcast"?

4. Why did Christ give the impression that he was going on further ("He made as if to go on…")? What lesson is there in that for us?

Cf. Catechism of the Catholic Church, 1322-1405 on the meaning of the Eucharist

237. AMAZING PEACE (LK 24:36-48)

"He submitted to death and endured it of his own free will, in order to destroy death against death's will."

- St Ephraem

Luke 24:36-48

They were still talking about all this when he himself stood among them and said to them, 'Peace be with you!' In a state of alarm and fright, they thought they were seeing a ghost. But he said, 'Why are you so agitated, and why are these doubts rising in your hearts? Look at my hands and feet; yes, it is I indeed. Touch me and see for yourselves; a ghost has no flesh and bones as you can see I have.' And as he said this he showed them his hands and feet. Their joy was so great that they still could not believe it, and they stood there dumbfounded; so he said to them, 'Have you anything here to eat?' And they offered him a piece of grilled fish, which he took and ate before their eyes. Then he told them, 'This is what I meant when I said, while I was still with you, that everything written about me in the Law of Moses, in the Prophets and in the Psalms has to be fulfilled.' He then opened their minds to understand the scriptures, and he said to them, 'So you see how it is written that the Christ would suffer and on the third day rise from the dead, and that, in his name, repentance for the forgiveness of sins would be preached to all the nations, beginning from Jerusalem. You are witnesses to this.'

CHRIST THE LORD In describing this appearance to his disciples, St Luke emphasizes the reality of Christ's resurrected body. They were not seeing a ghost; it was not a mass hallucination; it was far too shocking to be wishful thinking – Jesus makes all of this abundantly clear by his gestures and actions. As the reality of his complete, physical, personal presence sinks in, the disciples are overcome with joy and amazement. Their Lord had turned the worst of defeats into a definitive victory; he had conquered injustice, violence, hatred, rejection, and death itself by taking them all upon himself and then dissolving them in the Resurrection. If such an unparalleled event had failed to elicit joy and amazement on behalf of those who love him and put his trust in him, something would have been very wrong.

The level of our spiritual joy and amazement when we contemplate these same realities can in turn give us an inkling of the level of our love and trust. We cheer with gusto when our favorite team wins the championship; how enthusiastically do our hearts cheer at the Resurrection of our Lord, the pledge of our own resurrection?

CHRIST THE TEACHER Christ's glorified body suffers none of the limitations of our natural body, but it still bears the marks of his sacrifice on the cross. He shows his wounds to the disciples to prove to them that it really is he. To this day, as he reigns in heaven, he still bears those wounds; he will bear them throughout all eternity. They are God's remarkable answer to the perennial question of human suffering: he doesn't explain the mystery with a syllogism or a philosophical discourse; he explains it by taking it upon himself and bathing it in everlasting glory. If we unite our sufferings to those of Christ, if we attach our crosses to his, then all of our wounds will be found in his, and they all will share in his eternal splendor. The hardship of following Christ – the cross – is only half the story; the joy and glory of following Christ – the Resurrection – is the other half. If we accept the one, it's only because we believe firmly in the other.

CHRIST THE FRIEND *Jesus: Do you remember what I said most often after my resurrection? "Peace be with you." Peace. Peace is my antidote to modern man's most endemic diseases: stress, depression, and anxiety – and I know you have been affected by those diseases. If you trust in me, I will give you all the peace you need: peace for your mind, because when you look at my wounds that are now sharing my everlasting life, you can know for certain that my unbounded forgiveness lasts forever; peace for your heart, because when you see those nail marks and my pierced side, you know for certain that I love you with an undying, unconditional, personal, determined love – and that too will never change; peace for your soul, because I who am your King reign now and always, and I have given you a task worthy of the restlessness that stirs your will. You are to be my witness, both among those close at hand in your own Jerusalem, and to all peoples everywhere through your surrender to my will, your prayers, your example, and your apostolic activity. I want to give you my peace. Trust me, and you will be able to accept it.*

CHRIST IN MY LIFE I am like your disciples, Lord: reluctant to believe. I see the bad side, the hard side, the problems. These come easily to mind. But at times it seems almost impossible for me to smile, to laugh, to rejoice in the victory that I know you have shared with me. Teach me, Lord. Train me. Open my eyes. Fill me with your light. With the joy of your heart, expand my heart…

You are in heaven right now, body and soul. And you are preparing a place for me there. You want me to come and spend eternity in the adventure of your friendship. You will resurrect my body too and will give me a share in your glory. Help me to taste the joy and amazement that your goodness and power should stir up in my mind. Blessed be your name in all the earth…

Not only do I want to experience your peace, the peace that goes deeper than emotions and passing moods, but I want to be a channel of your peace. Fill me with your abundant fullness of life, Lord; fill me so much that I overflow with it, spreading it to everyone I meet, work, and live with. With the Kingdom of your heart, reign in my heart…

QUESTIONS FOR SMALL GROUP DISCUSSION

1. What struck you most in this passage? What did you notice that you hadn't noticed before?

2. If an non-believing acquaintance were to challenge you by claiming that Christ's resurrection was just a hoax, how would you respond?

3. What can we do to live more fully the steady, deep, consistent peace that comes from a solid and vibrant friendship with Jesus Christ?

4. Spiritual writers often tell us to unite our sufferings to Christ's. What has helped you to do that? What difference does this make in your life?

Cf. Catechism of the Catholic Church, 631-658 on the nature and meaning of the Resurrection; 1047, 1468, 1784, and 2302 on peace of heart and the Christian life; 609, 440, 601, 1505 and 1521 on the meaning of suffering

238. ANCHORED IN HEAVEN (LK 24:49-53)

"Let us keep ever before our eyes this great thought – everything in this world comes to an end, whether it be prosperity or adversity. Eternity alone never ends."

- St Alfonsus Ligouri

Luke 24:49-53

'And now I am sending down to you what the Father has promised. Stay in the city then, until you are clothed with the power from on high.' Then he took them out as far as the outskirts of Bethany, and lifting up his hands he blessed them. Now as he blessed them, he withdrew from them and was carried up to heaven. They worshipped him and then went back to Jerusalem full of joy; and they were continually in the Temple praising God.

CHRIST THE LORD In Luke's Gospel, this scene takes place immediately after Jesus appeared to his apostles, showed them his wounds, and ate with them in order to assure them that he was no mere ghost. Thus, his ascension into heaven shares in the earthy reality of the rest of his Resurrection appearances. It is not an ethereal dissipation into some shadowy realm of vague symbols; it is the establishment of his Kingship on unshakable ground. Earthly kings and emperors always remain vulnerable; if their enemies don't usurp them, death surely will. But Christ's reign will never come to an end. Because he has ascended into heaven, his Kingdom is firm; his Church will never be destroyed. If we stay faithful to this King, our victory over sin, evil, and injustice (and the happiness that such a victory implies) is assured. Christ's ascension should fill us with joy, as it did his disciples, because now we know for certain that the Christian cause is unassailable and that Christ's Lordship is imperturbable.

CHRIST THE TEACHER Christ's entire life – his words and works, and above all his suffering, death, and resurrection – is a lesson. It teaches us the way to repentance for the forgiveness of sins. Nothing is more important, since sin separates us from God, the only source of lasting happiness. This lesson must be preached in his name to all nations, as Christ instructed his apostles before this parting scene. For that reason, the apostles were called upon to be witness of these things. Of course, they would not be able to carry out their witness all by themselves; they would need the Holy Spirit. They would need to be "clothed with power from on high," which happened at Pentecost. Thus, in the ascension of our Lord, we come face-to-face with the core of the entire Gospel: Christ's saving message being transmitted to all people through the ministry of the Church.

Sometimes we become so involved in related but secondary issues (theological squabbles, new projects and ministries…) that we forget about this core. We shouldn't need to wait for the annual liturgical Solemnity of the Ascension to return to it – to focus once again on the essentials and cut away any superfluities that might have been accumulating in the décor of our Christian life.

CHRIST THE FRIEND *Jesus: Before I left them, I blessed them. Do you realize that the same blessing continues to radiate throughout the world today? What is my Church, if not the extension of my blessing, my life-giving love and grace, into every time and place, to all the nations? Isn't that how you discovered my love for you, through my Church? How I long to bless you even more! How I long to draw you closer and closer to my heart. My fullness of life is no good to me alone. I want to share it with you, to fill you to overflowing with my abundant, fruitful life. I have no hidden agendas, no second, selfish intentions. What more could I desire than what I already have, unless it is your heart, the full flourishing of your soul? I want to bless you, and I want the blessing of your friendship…*

CHRIST IN MY LIFE Who else can say, "My Kingdom will last forever"? No one. Absolutely no one else can say that. Only you. And you are mine, and I am yours. Dear Lord, thank you for giving me the gift of faith. Never let me take it for granted. Never let me be discouraged by the trials of life. You are reigning right now from a throne that will never pass away…

I am your messenger, Lord. Your triumph over sin and evil is my message. But so often, I really have no idea how to get the message across. I want to spread your Kingdom; I want to bear witness boldly, with words of truth and deeds of love. Be my strength, Lord, be my help; be my hands and feet and mouth. I give myself wholly to you – do with me as you please...

You know that I want to follow you. You know that the burdens and troubles of my life sometimes make me forget about that. Aren't you here in the midst of them? I know you are, but I need help to find you. You have given me so much, but I need even more, Lord. I need you to open my eyes so I can discover and embrace your will and love in every moment of every day...

QUESTIONS FOR SMALL GROUP DISCUSSION

1. What struck you most in this passage? What did you notice that you hadn't noticed before?

2. What impact should this great mystery of the Ascension have on our lives?

3. How can we help each other stay focused on the important things in life – most especially defending and spreading Christ's Kingdom in our own hearts and in the hearts of those around us – and not be distracted by lesser concerns?

4. Why do you think Christ took his apostles out of Jerusalem before blessing them and ascending into heaven?

Cf. Catechism of the Catholic Church, 659-667 on the meaning of our Lord's Ascension; 748-750 and 758-769 on the Church's origin, foundation, and mission; 802-810 on Christ's presence in the Church

THE GOSPEL ACCORDING TO
ST. JOHN

THE GOSPEL OF JOHN CHAPTER 1

"Moreover, you belong to God's Son: you should, therefore, be in him what members of a body are to the head. All that is in you must be grafted on to him, so that from him you may draw life and by him be ruled. True life is nowhere to be found by you except in him, who is the only source of life. Apart from him you will find naught save death and destruction. Let him be the only principle of all your actions, emotions, powers. You must live by him and for him…"

- St John Eudes

239. AN UNWELCOME SUNRISE (JN 1:1-18)

"Though he was rich, yet for our sake he became poor, so that by his poverty we might become rich."

- St Augustine

John 1:1-18

In the beginning was the Word: and the Word was with God and the Word was God. He was with God in the beginning. Through him all things came to be, not one thing had its being but through him. All that came to be had life in him and that life was the light of men, a light that shines in the dark, a light that darkness could not overpower.

A man came, sent by God. His name was John. He came as a witness, as a witness to speak for the light, so that everyone might believe through him. He was not the light, only a witness to speak for the light. The Word was the true light that enlightens all men; and he was coming into the world. He was in the world that had its being through him, and the world did not know him. He came to his own domain and his own people did not accept him. But to all who did accept him he gave power to become children of God, to all who believe in the name of him who was born not out of human stock or urge of the flesh or will of man but of God himself.

The Word was made flesh, he lived among us, and we saw his glory, the glory that is his as the only Son of the Father, full of grace and truth. John appears as his witness. He proclaims: 'This is the one of whom I said: He who comes after me ranks before me because he existed before me.' Indeed, from his fullness we have, all of us, received – yes, grace in return for grace, since, though the Law was given through Moses, grace and truth have come through Jesus Christ. No one has ever seen God; it is the only Son, who is nearest to the Father's heart, who has made him known.

CHRIST THE LORD St John wrote his Gospel towards the end of his long life. He addressed it primarily to those coming from a Hellenistic (pagan Greek) background, and only secondarily to his fellow Jews. But by calling Jesus the "Word of God made flesh," John wields a term shocking to both categories of readers.

For the Hellenistic Greeks, "Logos," here translated as "Word," referred to the one unifying principle that linked together and put order in the entire cosmos. At the time when St John was writing, Greek philosophers had developed elaborate behavioral codes that they hoped could put them in touch with this unifying force. Similarly, for the Hebrew mentality, the "Word of God" connoted God's wisdom, often personified in the Old Testament, which informs and directs all his works, including the creation and sustenance of the universe.

St John includes both these dimensions in using the term to refer to Christ, but he corrects and elevates them by adding two additional dimensions. In showing that through the Word "all things were made," he reveals that the Hellenistic concept of Logos had missed the mark: the unity of the cosmos, its order and beauty and glory, is not drawn from some force within itself, but from a transcendent, personal, creating God. Then, in asserting that "the Word became flesh," he challenges his Jewish brethren to broaden their conception of the Messiah from a mere human king to God himself taking on human nature.

In the liturgical year, the Church offers us this tightly packed biography of our Savior on Christmas day, so that we can be justly amazed at beholding all of God's infinite power and majesty wrapped in a few strips of swaddling cloth, sleeping helplessly in his mother's arms: Jesus Christ, truly God and truly man, come gently to walk with us. Here indeed is a noble Lord, worthy of our heart-felt praise and silent adoration.

CHRIST THE TEACHER The little cave at Bethlehem, where the Incarnation of God's Word first became visible, is a torrential fountain of Christ's doctrine. Today, however, St John draws our attention to a less romantic, more uncomfortable lesson that we often ignore. Jesus Christ came to those who had been created in his image, and they "did not know him." He came to those who had received centuries of preparation through the Old Covenant, and they "did not accept him."

Human history is a dramatic struggle of man's attempts to discover meaning in life. It narrates the mostly unsuccessful but always passionate search for order, prosperity, and lasting happiness. You would think that when God himself decided to dwell among us to give us the answer and show us the way, we would welcome him eagerly and gladly. Such was not the case. The answer didn't fit our categories, and the way led out of our comfort zone, and therefore many turned their backs on the Savior. We are all tempted to cling to the darkness and flee the light, and St John teaches us that overcoming this temptation can be harder than we think, though it's well worth the effort.

God will not force salvation upon us. Christ did not come to bring heaven to earth, but to lead those who would accept him from earth to heaven. Of all the world's religions, Christianity is the most respectful of human freedom – which makes perfect sense, considering that the law of Christ's Kingdom is authentic love, the perfect fulfillment of that particularly human characteristic.

CHRIST THE FRIEND *Jesus: Many people complain that I haven't made myself clear enough, that I haven't done enough to convince everyone to believe in and follow me. But they don't understand the gentle force of love that binds my Kingdom together. Have you ever turned on bright lights after being in a dark room for a long time? You know how it hurts your eyes. If I had come exactly as I am, I would have blinded you. You would have submitted, but out of fear and pain. I didn't create you for that. I created you to live in my friendship. Everything I do is to win back that friendship, which sin destroyed. So I came to meet you right where you are, right in the middle of your normal life. I came to live among you. And through my Church and my missionaries, I do the same thing in every generation all throughout the earth. My presence is bright but soft, like Christmas lights, because I know that your soul is wounded and sensitive. Trust me. Follow me. Let me guide you. I am here for that.*

CHRIST IN MY LIFE All that exists has come from you. Help me grasp this truth, Lord. You, who call me by my name, who have gone to heaven to prepare a place for me, who suffered on the cross to redeem me from sin, who come to me humbly and quietly in the Eucharist – you are the very same One who created and sustains every molecule, every sub-atomic particle, every galaxy, every activity of this vast, beautiful, incomprehensible universe…

It is a terrible thought: you came to give us the fullness of life that every heart longs for, but not every heart is willing to accept it. Lord Jesus, I too resist the inklings of your grace too often. Help me to be strong in doing what is right and resisting temptation. Help me to follow you, to be your messenger to everyone in my life…

You are so gentle with me, Lord. You always forgive; you always nudge; you always wait with infinite patience. Thank you. Make me more like you. I want to be your light and your goodness to everyone around me. I want to attract them to you, however far away they may be, as the star of Bethlehem attracted the wise men. Jesus, meek and humble of heart, make my heart more like yours…

QUESTIONS FOR SMALL GROUP DISCUSSION

1. What struck you most in this passage? What did you notice that you hadn't noticed before?

2. The fact of the Incarnation radically altered the course of history. What facts have most radically altered the course of your personal history? What should be influencing most your personal history right now?

3. Why do you think so many people refuse to welcome Christ into their lives, even when they hear about his love and know others who have welcomed him?

4. Christ has come to meet us in very human ways, through family, friends, priests, and other members of the Church. How can we be better channels for bringing him to others?

Cf. Catechism of the Catholic Church, 525-534 on the Christmas mystery; the mysteries of Jesus' infancy and the mysteries of his hidden life; 456-463 on why Jesus came to earth in the Incarnation; 897-913 on the mission of lay people in the Church

240. A GENEROUS KING (JN 1:19-28)

"God's providence of mercy, having determined to save in the last days the world which was perishing, foreordained the salvation of all nations in Christ."

- Pope St Leo the Great

John 1:19-28

This is how John appeared as a witness. When the Jews sent priests and Levites from Jerusalem to ask him, 'Who are you?' he not only declared, but he declared quite openly, 'I am not the Christ.' 'Well then,' they asked 'are you Elijah?' 'I am not,' he said. 'Are you the Prophet?' He answered, 'No.' So they said to him, 'Who are you? We must take back an answer to those who sent us. What have you to say about yourself?' So John said, 'I am, as Isaiah prophesied: a voice that cries in the wilderness: Make a straight way for the Lord.' Now these men had been sent by the Pharisees, and they put this further question to him, 'Why are you baptising if you are not the Christ, and not Elijah, and not the prophet?' John replied, 'I baptise with water; but there stands among you – unknown to you – the one who is coming after me; and I am not fit to undo his sandal-strap.' This happened at Bethany, on the far side of the Jordan, where John was baptising.

CHRIST THE LORD John the Evangelist (the writer of this Gospel) had to counteract a misconception that lingered for a long time among the early Christian communities. For more than a hundred years after Christ's resurrection, pockets of John the Baptist's disciples continued to claim and preach that the Baptist himself was the true Messiah. Correcting this mistake is one of the minor motifs of John's Gospel. In this first chapter, the Gospel writer makes abundantly clear that John is not the Messiah. The inquirers query him point blank. They ask him if he is the Messiah, and he says no; they ask him if he is the Prophet promised long ago by Moses (and often identified with the promised Messiah), and he says no; they ask him if he is Elijah (who was supposed to come again to announce the Messiah's arrival, but whom some thought would be the Messiah), and again John denies it, lest they misunderstand. Jesus Christ is the Messiah, the Prophet greater than any prophet, the One who came to set all things right – he alone, and no one else. John had clear and distinct ideas about Jesus. Do we?

The bickering about John the Baptist's identity may seem like an anachronistic squabble, but if it were, the Holy Spirit would not have included it in the Gospels. In fact, Christ's disciples fall into the same kind of bickering all the time. We are always taking sides and arguing among ourselves about which preacher or bishop or religious order or pious group is better than another. How happy this makes the devil! The mature Christian knows that there is one Lord whom we all are meant to serve, and if we hang our hat on anything else, it's due to our own pride, vanity, or narrow-mindedness.

CHRIST THE TEACHER The "priests and Levites" had charge of Jerusalem's Temple worship. John came from a family of priests, so it was only natural for them to come and find out why he – one of their own coterie – was acting so abnormally and making such a stir among the people. The Pharisees were members of the ruling body of Israel, the Sanhedrin. The Sanhedrin took charge of reining in false prophets, so they sent a delegation to investigate this new rabble-rouser. Both groups who questioned John listened to his message only through the filter of their personal agendas, and both groups missed the point. Their own preconceived notions impeded their acceptance of God's word spoken through John.

How often we fall into the same trap! We take refuge in our own exaggerated sense of self-sufficiency and sit in judgment over the Church's teaching. In many ways, we are trained to do this. Humility, simplicity, faith – these essential Christian virtues are in scant supply at most institutes of higher learning; we prefer to make truth conform to our own wishes rather than adjust our lives to the demands of truth. God "never ceases to draw man to himself," as the Catechism says (#27), but man (and that includes all of us) tends to resist the tug. From now on, let's not.

CHRIST THE FRIEND Generous kings hoard neither their wealth nor their privileges; they multiply and distribute their royal abundance, extending their friendship to all who will welcome it. Christ is a generous King, offering every man and woman his friendship and renewing the offer each day. He sent John the Baptist to announce his arrival, generously giving him a role in building up the Kingdom. In the same way, he has entrusted the defense and expansion of his Kingdom to the Church and therefore to each of us as members of the Church. Just as he gave John the honor and responsibility to announce his coming, so he gives us the chance to spread his reign. Ever since our baptism we have been members of his royal court, and from the moment of our confirmation, we accepted our appointment as ambassadors of the Eternal King. We have nothing to fear, because our natural powers did not earn this honor (it was a gift of grace), and our natural powers alone will not win success (Christ's grace is at work in and through us). He has involved us so intimately in his plan (in fact, we are his plan) because he wants our friendship, and friends share their most important occupations. His consists in rescuing his lost sheep.

CHRIST IN MY LIFE I want to be a true Christian, Lord. I want to follow you. Anyone who is trying to follow you and spread your Kingdom is my ally, not my adversary – even if they use methods I may not prefer or emphasize different aspects of your message than I do. I want to be an agent of unity and charity in your family of believers. Teach me to curb my tongue, and to open my heart as wide as you have opened yours…

How can I take away my filter of subjective prejudices and half-baked ideas in order to hear your voice loud and clear? How can I wipe away the film of preconceived opinions that are clouding my mental vision without my realizing it? I can't. I need your grace to come and cleanse my heart and my mind. You can do it, Lord. You can cut through the grime. Give me a new heart and a new mind, full of your light and your love…

St John the Baptist, pray for me. I too have been given a role in Christ's Kingdom, just as you were. I am glad to have something to do that can please him and deepen our friendship. With your prayers, protect and guide me as I strive to fulfill my life's mission. With your example, help me to see God's providential hand in all the events and people that swirl around me, so that I may always be faithful to whatever he asks of me…

QUESTIONS FOR SMALL GROUP DISCUSSION

1. What struck you most in this passage? What did you notice that you hadn't noticed before?

2. Christ's persona and mission are inexhaustible sources of study and meditation. What should we be doing to understand him more deeply each day?

3. What are some influences around us that encourage intellectual pride – that tendency to require everyone, even the Church, to measure up to one's personal standards, trusting more in one's own understanding than in the revealed truth of Jesus Christ – and how can we counteract them?

4. What are some of the factors that keep Christians from engaging fully in their mission to spread the Kingdom of Christ, and what can we do this week to help overcome them?

Cf. Catechism of the Catholic Church, 523 on the role of John the Baptist; 554-555 for Jesus' own revelation of his glory; 1267-1270 on our responsibility to participate in the mission of the Church due to our baptism

241. THE FIRST STEP (JN 1:29-34)

"Today the Holy Spirit floats over the waters in the form of a dove, so that by this sign it might be known that the world's universal shipwreck has ceased, as the dove had announced to Noah that the world's flood had subsided."

- St Peter Chrysologus

John 1:29-34

The next day, seeing Jesus coming towards him, John said, 'Look, there is the lamb of God that takes away the sin of the world. This is the one I spoke of when I said: A man is coming after me who ranks before me because he existed before me. I did not know him myself, and yet it was to reveal him to Israel that I came baptising with water.' John also declared, 'I saw the Spirit coming down on him from heaven like a dove and resting on him. I did not know him myself, but he who sent me to baptise with water had said to me, The man on whom you see the Spirit come down and rest is the one who is going to baptise with the Holy Spirit. Yes, I have seen and I am the witness that he is the Chosen One of God.'

CHRIST THE LORD John the Baptist's favorite title for Jesus is "the Lamb of God." Clearly it also became one of John the Evangelist's favorite titles, since he used it twenty-nine times in the Book of Revelation. It brings together three images that would have been familiar to the Jews of that time, and by being ap-plied to Christ, it indicates that in him those images find their full meaning.

God required the Jews to sacrifice a lamb twice a day to expiate the sins of the people (cf. Exodus 29:39). Thus the lamb symbolized the price to be paid for sin. The primary holy day of the Jews was (and remains) the Passover. In the Passover ceremony, each family sacrifices and eats a lamb to recall their libera-tion from Egypt in the days of Moses. On that night, God killed all the firstborn children and animals of the Egyptians, but spared those of the Hebrews. In order to indicate which households the angel of death was to skip over, God commanded the Hebrews to kill a lamb and mark their doorposts with its blood. Thus the Passover lamb signified God's merciful and saving love. Finally, the Messiah announced by the prophets was described as a lamb who went silently to the slaughter, to take the sins of his people upon himself and wipe them away.

John proclaims: "Behold the Lamb of God," and we turn our eyes to Christ, the real lamb of God, the Incarnation of God's desire and power to free us from the slavery of selfishness, vanity, lust, and greed, and to lead us to the promised land of joyful friendship with him. So apt is this title that the Church repeats it every time Mass is celebrated: "Lamb of God, you take away the sins of the world, have mercy on us."

CHRIST THE TEACHER John tells his disciples about Jesus. Some of the future Apostles had originally been John's disciples. They were there with him on the banks of the Jordan, helping him baptize, when he first pointed out who the Master was. They heard his testimony about Jesus, and it sparked their interest, and so they went to meet the Lord for themselves.

Jesus chooses to use the testimony of those who believe in him to draw others into his friendship. If John had kept quiet about what God had shown him, his disciples might never have found the Lord. Likewise, Christ is counting on us to introduce him to others.

This takes humility. John was not looking for his own glory, but for God's. His own popularity and success didn't go to his head. His mission mattered more. In our efforts to build Christ's Kingdom, we can hardly choose a better model than John, who teaches us never to work merely for our own satisfaction or for the esteem of our peers. Our goal is Christ and our path is his will – and in the end, nothing else matters.

CHRIST THE FRIEND John saw "Jesus coming towards him."

Jesus: How much I love to do this. I never force my way into anyone's life, but I come towards everyone. I want to attract their attention because I want their friendship and happiness. I am always taking the first step. Isn't that what happened with you and me? Don't you remember? I caught your attention. Even before that, I had been coming towards you in many ways. It's like when you are in love, and you go out of your way to run into the person you love, just to get a glimpse of them, just hoping that they will stop and talk to you. I love you like that. I even come right up to your heart and knock, hoping you will let me in. I always have more to give you, more to teach you, more for us to do. My love never runs out of words, attention, encouragement, projects – my love never runs out, period. Keep welcoming me; keep looking out for me. I am still coming towards you, and I will never stop coming towards you.

CHRIST IN MY LIFE   You are the Savior of all people. You are the light of the world. You are the Lamb of God. I don't want these words to become meaningless phrases in my heart. Keep my faith fresh, Lord. Just because I sometimes get tired or fall into routine, that doesn't mean that you have changed. You are still God, still the Lord, still the Teacher. Open my eyes to see all the wonders of your love...

I think of all the people in my life: family, friends, colleagues, acquaintances.... You have a mission for each one of them. You are calling each one of them to be saints. And I can either help them discover and fulfill that mission or hinder them. I want to help them. I want to encourage them in whatever way I can to hear and heed your call in their life. With the zeal of your heart, set my heart on fire...

Thank you for coming into my life, Lord. Before you came I was like an unlit candle. Jesus, never let me be separated from you. O Lord, what would I do without my faith in you? How vulnerable I would be to the lies and destructive seductions all around me! Keep me faithful to your will, Lord, and make me an instrument of your peace...

QUESTIONS FOR SMALL GROUP DISCUSSION

1. What struck you most in this passage? What did you notice that you hadn't noticed before?

2. At Mass, when we pray "Lamb of God, you take away the sins of the world, have mercy on us," what should be on our hearts and minds? Why do you think the Church puts the title "Lamb of God" on our lips right before we receive Holy Communion?

3. What most often inhibits our taking advantage of opportunities to speak about Christ and the Church to others who need God? What can we do to overcome this?

4. How can we pay closer attention to God, so as not to miss the times when he "comes towards us"?

Cf. Catechism of the Catholic Church, 608 on "The Lamb of God"; 863-865 and 897-913 on the role of the laity in the mission of the Church; 27 and 30 on God taking the initiative in our friendship with him.

242. WANTING THE RIGHT THING (JN 1:35-42)

"If, then, you seek to know what path to follow, take Christ because he is the way."

- St Thomas Aquinas

John 1:35-42

On the following day as John stood there again with two of his disciples, Jesus passed, and John stared hard at him and said, 'Look, there is the lamb of God.' Hearing this, the two disciples followed Jesus. Jesus turned round, saw them following and said, 'What do you want?' They answered, 'Rabbi,' – which means Teacher – 'where do you live?' 'Come and see' he replied; so they went and saw where he lived, and stayed with him the rest of that day. It was about the tenth hour. One of these two who became followers of Jesus after hearing what John had said was Andrew, the brother of Simon Peter. Early next morning, Andrew met his brother and said to him, 'We have found the Messiah' – which means the Christ – and he took Simon to Jesus. Jesus looked hard at him and said, 'You are Simon son of John; you are to be called Cephas' – meaning Rock.

CHRIST THE LORD In these few verses St John gives us three key titles of Christ, each of which should stir our hearts to gratitude, praise, and adoration.

First, John reemphasizes that Jesus is the "Lamb of God," a title worth reflecting on again and again. The lamb appeared over and over in the Jewish scriptures and in their traditions. The central allusion, however, was to the Passover, when the Israelites sprinkled the blood of the Passover lamb on the lintels of their doors (cf. Exodus 12). The lamb had been sacrificed in order to save the Israelites, so that Moses would be able to lead them out of slavery. Christ was to be slain as well – on the cross of Calvary – and his blood was to be sprinkled on the lips of his faithful when they receive Holy Communion. In this way, Christians would be saved from the slavery of sin and led into the freedom of eternal life, the unquenchable abundance of heaven, by Jesus Christ, the Lamb of God. Christ is not only Lord; he is also Savior.

Second, Jesus is called "the Messiah," or "the Anointed One" (the Greek word for this gives us the title "Christ"). This title referred to the promised successor to the throne of David, whom God had anointed king of his Chosen People. Under David's kingship Israel had become a world power, reaching its peak of greatness and influence. God had promised that the line of David would never entirely fail, and he promised that a son of David would ascend to the throne to reinstate a new and even greater golden age for Israel. This Messiah (kings were "anointed" as a sign of their being chosen and strengthened by God for their divine mission on his behalf) would save Israel from all her sufferings and oppression, from all the misery that her sin had heaped upon her.

It is to save us, to rescue us from our own ignorance, weakness, and confusion that Jesus came. In relation to mankind, God's glory consists in the human race reaching its full potential, in all people discovering the joy of a life lived in communion with God. Christ is the bearer of this glory, the King who comes to establish the sovereignty of God – with the peace and the fullness it entails – in every human heart.

CHRIST THE TEACHER Third, St John points out that the two disciples called Jesus "Rabbi," which means "teacher" or "master." Rabbis were popular Jewish leaders, not by position or birth, but by their knowledge of the things of God and their ability to teach and pass on that knowledge. In Matthew 19 and John 13, Christ makes an explicit and exclusive claim to this title, affirming that he is the definitive teacher of the things of God and demanding the absolute allegiance of his followers.

Even in this passage, we detect the unprecedented authority Jesus claims when he renames Simon. In the Jewish scriptural tradition, only God gave new names to people, and he only did so when he gave them a prominent role in his plan of salvation and connected them in a special way to his covenantal promise. Christ's exercise of such authority during his first meeting with Simon certainly would have given these disciples a hint that this Galilean was no average rabbi. (It also is one of the many indications in the gospels that the preeminent role of Peter, and thus of the Papacy, was instituted and intended by Christ himself, and not merely an invention of the early Church.) Christ is Lord and Savior, but he is also the Master, a Teacher unlike any other. To follow him and learn from him should be our greatest joy.

Although Christ's titles bespeak his greatness, his behavior in this first encounter with John and Andrew shows his simplicity and humility. He walks by the place where they and John the Baptist are baptizing. He simply walks by. He makes no grand entrance, employs no intimidating tactics. When John and Andrew finally decide to go after him, he turns around to welcome them. He makes no demands, gives no orders, and passes no judgment. Rather, he engages them in a conversation and issues an invitation to come and spend time with him. This is how Jesus works. This is how he calls us, gently, unexpectedly, personally. The era of flashing fire on the mountaintop is over; the era of good-hearted friendship and intimate companionship with the eternal God has begun.

CHRIST THE FRIEND This is Jesus' first encounter with his first disciples. It is the beginning of the second half of human history – an important occasion.

Surely the evangelist is describing every detail with care, most especially the very first words that Jesus speaks in this Gospel. He asks his future Apostles a simple question: "What do you want?" (What do you seek? What are you hoping for?) It is still one of Christ's favorite questions. Jesus already knows the deepest desires of every heart, but many people never take the time to reflect on their own deepest desires. Jesus poses the question in order to spur that kind of reflection. Unless we take time to examine ourselves and our lives, we can easily end up looking for meaning and happiness in the wrong places, mindlessly latching onto every passing fancy and popular guru, bouncing from fashion to fad, never drinking of the living water that only he can give.

Jesus: My first two disciples gave the right answer to this question. They asked where I was staying. What did they want? They only wanted to come and stay with me. That is how you answered the question too. How it pleases me to find humble, thirsting hearts – what a feast I have in store for them! What do you want? What are you seeking? If you want the right thing, everything else will fall into place. If you don't, nothing you do will give rest to your soul.

CHRIST IN MY LIFE Where do you live, Lord? I want to find you and stay with you. You are the creator of the mountains, the ocean, the clouds, and the stars. You are the wisdom that gives order to the universe. You are the spark of light that gives man a knowing mind and a loving heart. You are the source and goal of all things. And you have come to live in my heart. You are mine, and I am yours. Let me stay with you…

I need a Teacher, Lord, and I choose to sit at your feet and listen to you. Sometimes I find myself yearning so much to understand things – to have true wisdom – that I am almost in pain. You made me with a need for truth. You are the Truth. Speak to my heart, Lord. Send your Spirit to teach and guide me. Never take your eyes off of me…

What do I want? I want so many things! I want happiness, Lord. I want happiness for myself and for those around me. Fulfillment, meaning, satisfaction. I want my life to bear the fruit you created it to bear. I want to look into your eyes and see you smile on the day you call me home to eternity, and I want to hear you say, "Well done, good and faithful servant…"

QUESTIONS FOR SMALL GROUP DISCUSSION

1. What struck you most in this passage? What did you notice that you hadn't noticed before?

2. Jesus' first words in the Gospel of John are: "What do you want?" What would the voice of popular culture say in response to that question?

3. Why did Jesus wait until the two disciples came after him? Why didn't he go after them first?

4. Every one of the disciples who comes to Jesus in this first chapter of John's Gospel does so at the invitation of an intermediary. When was the last time you invited someone to come and meet Jesus? What happened? Why don't we invite people more often?

Cf. Catechism of the Catholic Church, 602, 613, 1137 on the meaning of the title "Lamb of God"; 436-440 on the meaning of the title "Messiah"; 512-521 on the life of Christ as a definitive "teaching" of the things of God

243. YOU WILL SEE GREAT THINGS (JN 1:43-51)

"We have been granted by the good Lord the privilege of sharing in that greatest, most divine, chief of all names, so that, honored with the name of Christ, we are called Christians."

- St Gregory of Nyssa

John 1:43-51

The next day, after Jesus had decided to leave for Galilee, he met Philip and said, 'Follow me.' Philip came from the same town, Bethsaida, as Andrew and Peter. Philip found Nathanael and said to him, 'We have found the one Moses wrote about in the Law, the one about whom the prophets wrote: he is Jesus son of Joseph, from Nazareth.' 'From Nazareth?' said Nathanael, 'Can anything good come from that place?' 'Come and see,' replied Philip. When Jesus saw Nathanael coming he said of him, 'There is an Israelite who deserves the name, incapable of deceit.' 'How do you know me?' said Nathanael 'Before Philip came to call you,' said Jesus 'I saw you under the fig tree.' Nathanael answered, 'Rabbi, you are the Son of God, you are the King of Israel.' Jesus replied, 'You believe that just because I said: I saw you under the fig tree. You will see greater things than that.' And then he added 'I tell you most solemnly, you will see heaven laid open and, above the Son of Man, the angels of God ascending and descending.'

CHRIST THE LORD Jesus issues bold commands. He says to Philip, "Follow me." Imagine the look in his eyes as he gazed at Philip and said those words. Imagine how much force and love and vibrant life must have been in that look. It was no generic, philosophical observation. It was a penetrating, life-changing encounter.

This is the heart and soul of Christianity. Not its creed, not its ceremonies, not even the Bible, but the person of Christ the Lord, looking into the eyes of every man and woman, and inviting them to follow him. If he is the Lord, then he is to be followed; he is to be obeyed. Not because after much study and reflection we have concluded that he is worthy of our standards, but because he is the Lord. Our hearts were made to know, love, and follow him, which is why his call stirred Philip so radically, and which is why we always know when he's asking something of us. His call to our hearts often takes place in the most unglamorous ways, because he's not trying to impress us (he's from Nazareth, after all – the boondocks of Palestine); he simply wants to lead us; he wants to befriend us.

CHRIST THE TEACHER Jesus' first actions in his ministry consist in gathering around himself a group of followers – not dramatic speeches, or dozens of miracles, or clashes with his enemies. No, first he wants to shape the nucleus of his Church. Right from the beginning, this is his priority. These men will become his Apostles. For the next three years, he will spend the vast majority of his time – almost all his time, in fact – with them. He will teach them with his words and example. He will let them get to know him, reveal his thoughts and desires to them, train them for their mission in his Kingdom, and gradually reveal to them what that mission is.

Christ's Kingdom is the rule of his love and wisdom in the hearts of his followers. It is the family of those who believe in him; it is the Church, militant, suffering, and triumphant. And just as the foundation of the Church occurred through his one-on-one attention to and formation of his Apostles, who would go and do the same in other places, multiplying themselves in others just as Christ had multiplied himself in them, so the growth of the Church throughout the centuries has taken place in the same way. And if we want to help the Church grow in our day, we will follow the same methodology. We will gather around the successors to the Apostles, the Pope and the bishops, by studying and obeying the teachings of the Church, in order to come to know Christ and to love him. We will spend time with him in prayer and the sacraments. And then we, like other Christs, like new apostles, will invite those around us to come and follow the Lord.

CHRIST THE FRIEND *Jesus: When I told Nathaniel that I had seen him under the fig tree, I was referring to a moment of spiritual crisis and enlightenment that he had had a few months earlier. It was something that occurred as he was meditating and reflecting in the shadow of a fig tree. Only he and God knew about it. It was a moment of preparation that I sent him, readying him for this encounter with me. When I mentioned it, he knew immediately that he was to come and be my follower.*

You have had many moments like his under the fig tree: those times, brief or long, of intimate spiritual sensitivity, of spiritual struggle, of interior growth and discovery. I have been with you for each of them. They are my action in your soul. I am always thinking of you and working in your heart – I can't help it, because my love draws me to you every moment of the day and night. I want you to have the confidence in me that Nathaniel had. I want you to follow me more closely, because it pains me more than I can describe to see you looking for satisfaction in places where you can never find it – comfort and pleasure, your own achievements and success, outdoing others. Come and follow me more closely, and you will see heaven laid open, and even greater things…

CHRIST IN MY LIFE I have heard you say to me what you said to Philip, "Follow me." I have heard it so many times! Never let me stop being amazed that you, the creator of all things, came into my life, looked me in the eye, smiled, and invited me to be your royal companion, your collaborator, and your ambassador. I want to be generous with you, Lord; I want to be your worthy disciple…

How I love your Church! Bless the Pope, Lord, and bless all your bishops and priests. Keep your Church united around you. Calm the erosive winds of infidelity and disobedience. And give me, I beg you, the courage, confidence, and humility to take up my mission within the Church and carry it out. Blessed be your name throughout the earth…

Thank you for stirring my heart so many times. I don't want to live on the surface of life, giggling and bantering and chatting and skipping along aimlessly. I don't want to throw myself into the latest distractions laid out on the smorgasbord of popular culture, without a thought for the purpose for which you created me. I want to enjoy the good things of this world profoundly, as you created me to. Grant me wisdom, Lord…

QUESTIONS FOR SMALL GROUP DISCUSSION

1. What struck you most in this passage? What did you notice that you hadn't noticed before?

2. Why do you think Jesus didn't give Philip any reasons to follow him – why did he just say, "Follow me"? Why didn't Philip argue in response to Nathaniel's objection to following Christ – why did he simply say, "Come and see"?

3. Why do you think Jesus chose to reach out to the world through his Church? Why not just go directly to each soul without any intermediaries?

4. Who did in your life what Philip did in Nathaniel's life, inviting you to "come and see" the Lord?

Cf. Catechism of the Catholic Church, 874-896 on the hierarchical structure of the Church; 1533 and 1962 on holiness and the Gospel as the vocation of all the disciples of Christ; 897-913 on the laity's mission in the Church and the world; 914-933 on the different manifestations of the mission of consecrated persons in the Church and the world

THE GOSPEL OF JOHN CHAPTER 2

'At rest on the heights of virtue, rich beyond measure with divine gifts, she who surpassed all others in grace lavishly pours out streams of graces on thirsty souls. She bestows healing for bodies and souls, powerful to save men from both spiritual and corporal death. What man ever went away from her sick or sad or without heavenly light to guide him? Who has not returned home glad and rejoicing having obtained what he prayed for from Mary, the Mother of our Lord?'

- St Amedeus of Lausanne

244. GLORY DAWNS (JN 2:1-12)

"By her maternal charity, Mary cares for the brethren of her Son who still wander through this world in the midst of dangers and difficulties until they are led to the happiness of their heavenly home."

- Second Vatican Council, Lumen gentium 61

John 2:1-12

Three days later there was a wedding at Cana in Galilee. The mother of Jesus was there, and Jesus and his disciples had also been invited. When they ran out of wine, since the wine provided for the wedding was all finished, the mother of Jesus said to him, 'They have no wine.' Jesus said 'Woman, why turn to me? My hour has not come yet.' His mother said to the servants, 'Do whatever he tells you.' There were six stone water jars standing there, meant for the ablutions that are customary among the Jews: each could hold twenty or thirty gallons. Jesus said to the servants, 'Fill the jars with water,' and they filled them to the brim. 'Draw some out now' he told them 'and take it to the steward.' They did this; the steward tasted the water, and it had turned into wine. Having no idea where it came from – only the servants who had drawn the water knew – the steward called the bridegroom and said, 'People generally serve the best wine first, and keep the cheaper sort till the guests have had plenty to drink; but you have kept the best wine till now.' This was the first of the signs given by Jesus: it was given at Cana in Galilee. He let his glory be seen, and his disciples believed in him. After this he went down to Capernaum with his mother and the brothers, but they stayed there only a few days.

CHRIST THE LORD Mary knew how to treat the Lord: there was a crisis, and she went to him for a solution. The vast majority of Jews living in Palestine were poor. Wedding feasts and religious festivals were their sole respite from a life of hard labor and simple survival. In fact, wedding feasts often lasted for days at a time (they took the place of our honeymoons, which didn't exist in first-century Israel), and the entire town participated. To run out of wine in the middle of it would not only deflate the festive atmosphere, but it would also deeply shame the newlyweds and their families, turning what should be the most joyous days of their lives into an embarrassment. Attentive to the needs of those around her, Mary saw the crisis coming, and she knew just what to do. Even when the words of Jesus' answer seemed like a rebuff, she knew that he would come through. Jesus will never reject the humble appeal of faith – he is a Lord who "came not be served but to serve" (Matthew 20:28), and he's hoping that we will have as much confidence in him as his mother did.

We shouldn't overlook the power Jesus shows in this miracle. It was the "first of his signs," and by it he "let his glory be seen," to the benefit of his disciples, whose faith it deepened. Picture what happened. Pretend you are one of the servants. You fill up six huge stone kegs with water (no easy task when you have to go back and forth to the well). Then this young rabbi from the neighboring town tells you to draw some out (some of the water, remember – you know it's water, because you put it in there yourself) and bring it to the steward in charge of testing the wine before serving it. Imagine how dumbfounded you would be by such an order. But you do it. And you're carrying the water over to the steward, glancing nervously back over your shoulder at Mary and Jesus, who motion for you to keep going. You hand the gourd to the boss, looking down, maybe even closing your eyes in anticipation of his wrathful rebuke. And then, all of a sudden, he smacks his lips and hums with pleasure.... Jesus turned a hundred gallons of water into excellent wine, effortlessly. This is our Lord.

CHRIST THE TEACHER Jesus treated his mother with love and respect. He sees her not only as God's chosen instrument, but also as the woman who brought him into the world, took care of him when he was a helpless infant, and taught him to speak, to pray, to work, and to live. Both Jesus and Mary were free from sin, but that made them more human, not less. And so the natural, incomparable bond that forms between a mother and her son was deeper, purer, and more binding in their case than in any other case in human history. Since baptism has brought us into Christ's family, our love and respect for Mary should echo Christ's.

On the other hand, no one knows Jesus better than his mother. She bore him in her womb, nursed him at her breast, and raised him from childhood to manhood. Thirty of his thirty-three years on earth were spent in almost constant contact with her. When he begins his public ministry, she fades into the background but remains faithful: when he was in agony on the cross, she was there beside him. When she says something about him, therefore, we should take it to heart (just as he took to heart her hint that he should do something about the wine crisis), and in this passage she gives us an unambiguous lesson about how to relate to Jesus.

The Bible is inspired, so it is no coincidence that Mary's last biblical words say everything that needs to be said: "Do whatever he tells you." If we followed that one piece of advice, heeding Christ's every order and suggestion (those in the Scriptures, those of his Church, and those in our conscience), the water of our normal, everyday activities would quickly be turned into the wine of supernatural joy and fruitfulness. We would no longer be mere men and women; we would be saints.

CHRIST THE FRIEND *Jesus: I brought my disciples to a wedding feast. Think about that for a moment. Do you think it is something that happened by chance? Not at all. Too often people think of me as a stern taskmaster, distant and removed from the healthy joys and activities of the human experience. But I was the one who invented those joys and activities!*

I came to earth not just to teach you theology and not to douse your zest for life, but to bring everything about life back to its fullness, back to its complete and rightly ordered fruition. I know much better than anyone else that it is part of human nature to celebrate, to enjoy the good things of creation, like marriage and wine. But only I can teach you how to do so in a balanced, healthy way, in a way that will deepen your joy and not cheapen it. Stay close to me, seek to know me better, and I will show you how to experience more fully the life I have given you.

CHRIST IN MY LIFE Lord, I am so used to this miracle – too used to it. I have heard about it so many times. But when I stop to really reflect on what you did, I am amazed. Why do I live on the mundane surface of things so much? Why can't I keep in mind the wonders of your love, the gift of your presence, the assurance of your wisdom? You are all mine, Lord, and I am all yours. Keep me closer to your heart…

If I don't seek out and fulfill your will, whose will is left? Mine is ignorant and narrow-minded. No one else has your wisdom, love and fidelity. I want to know your will, your teaching, and your criteria. I want to learn to hear your voice. I want to live out all the normal responsibilities of my life as you would have me live them out, because I know that if I do, you will make my life bear abundant fruit…

I don't want to be one of those sad, cold, self-righteously pious, proper people. I want to be a saint, the saint you created me to be. The true saints, the ones your Church encourages me to look at, are so full of life that wherever they go they cause a revolution. Fill me with life, Lord, with your life, with true life. Make my words and my glance glow with the warmth of your love. Teach me to do your will…

QUESTIONS FOR SMALL GROUP DISCUSSION

1. What struck you most in this passage? What did you notice that you hadn't noticed before?

2. What characterized the relationship between Jesus and Mary? How would you venture to describe it?

3. If "Do whatever he tells you" is the motto of Christian culture, what would you define as the motto of popular culture?

4. What has helped you carry on your social life with the joy, spontaneity, and self-dominion that a Christian ought to have, without falling into excesses or superficiality?

Cf. Catechism of the Catholic Church, 487-507 on Mary's role in the Kingdom; 2288-2291 on respect for health and temperance

245. SPRING CLEANING (JN 2:13-25)

"He is the center of history and of the world; he is the one who knows us and who loves us; he is the companion and friend of our life."

- Pope Paul VI

John 2:13-25

Just before the Jewish Passover Jesus went up to Jerusalem, and in the Temple he found people selling cattle and sheep and pigeons, and the money changers sitting at their counters there. Making a whip out of some cord, he drove them all out of the Temple, cattle and sheep as well, scattered the money changers' coins, knocked their tables over and said to the pigeon-sellers, 'Take all this out of here and stop turning my Father's house into a market.' Then his disciples remembered the words of scripture: Zeal for your house will devour me.

The Jews intervened and said, 'What sign can you show us to justify what you have done?' Jesus answered, 'Destroy this sanctuary, and in three days I will raise it up.' The Jews replied, 'It has taken forty-six years to build this sanctuary: are you going to raise it up in three days?' But he was speaking of the sanctuary that was his body, and when Jesus rose from the dead, his disciples remembered that he had said this, and they believed the scripture and the words he had said. During his stay in Jerusalem for the Passover many believed in his name when they saw the signs that he gave, but Jesus knew them all and did not trust himself to them; he never needed evidence about any man; he could tell what a man had in him.

CHRIST THE LORD In the chronology of John's Gospel, this event takes place at the beginning of Jesus' public ministry. John's point of view, however, rightly interprets it in light of Christ's entire life. Here Jesus is already speaking of his resurrection. Thus we see how clearly Jesus understood his mission from the very start.

Christ is the ultimate defender of mankind's authentic relationship with God, and therefore he cleanses the Temple (an architectural symbol of that relationship) of everything that detracts from true faith and heartfelt worship. The officials in charge of the Temple take umbrage at this flouting of their authority, and Christ responds by explaining, albeit indirectly, his own identity and his reason for coming to earth. He calls himself the Temple (the word Jesus used, "sanctuary," was the inner part of the Temple, the most important part), because as true God and true man, he is the paradigmatic meeting place of the divine and the human. This meeting place, this communion between God and man, will be rejected at first (at the crucifixion), but he will assure us that in the end it will take root and endure (from the Resurrection into the age of the Church).

God had revealed himself directly to only one ancient nation, the nation of Israel. He had instructed them to build a Temple, a place of worship and communion between the one true God and his Chosen People. Solomon's Temple had housed the altars of sacrifice as well as the Ark of the Covenant itself, the box containing the tablets of the Ten Commandments. No holier place existed on earth – until the coming of Christ. Now, in the aftermath of Christ's coming, the presence of God has spread throughout the globe; every Christian heart is a sanctuary of the Holy Spirit, and every Catholic Tabernacle contains the living presence of the very author of the new and everlasting Covenant. Christ would later say that he was "greater than Solomon," for as magnificent as Solomon's Temple was (it was considered one of the wonders of the ancient world), it only foreshadowed the true Temple, the one that human hands could never destroy.

CHRIST THE TEACHER Few times in the Gospels do we see Christ act or speak out in anger, and when he does, it is always to condemn hypocrisy. By all appearances, the Temple officials were directing their fellow Jews in proper rituals of worship. In actual fact, however, they were adulterating that worship.

God had given his people the Temple to be a house of prayer and worship. The buying, selling, and money changing that went on in the Temple area had long been happening there. When pilgrims came to worship, they had to offer victims to the priests, who would sacrifice them to the Lord on their behalf. Strict

813

rules governed the qualifications of the victims – not just any animal would do. Therefore, businesses cropped up that specialized in making the right beasts easily available. Likewise, pilgrims came from all over the civilized world and brought money of various mintages. These had to be weighed, valued, and exchanged in order to be used for purchasing the sacrificial victims. Gradually, greed had infiltrated even these sacred services – the money changers demanded exorbitant fees and the vendors overcharged.

In this way, what was meant to be heartfelt service to God became a path to worldly success. The Temple officials were by all appearances exemplarily religious, but actually they were greedy merchants. This contradiction between appearances and reality is hypocrisy. The frightening thing is how easily we fall into it; we are experts at finding ways to project ourselves as exemplary Catholics, while on the inside we still seek the kingdom of "me" rather than the Kingdom of Christ.

CHRIST THE FRIEND St John tells us that the Lord knew human nature well; he "could tell what a man had in him."

Jesus: This should comfort you: I know the contradictions that disturb your mind and heart, the temptations that beset you, the streak of falls and failures that mark your path of discipleship. None of that surprises me. In fact, I came because of them. If you hadn't needed someone to save you, to redeem you, to renew your weary and dying soul, why would I have had to come? You don't need to make yourself perfect before you can have confidence in me. Your trust can be vast, joy-filled, and unrestrained right now, if only you will be honest and open. I came because I want your friendship – but I want your friendship, the one that comes from your heart, not from your masks. Approach me in prayer – just as you are!

CHRIST IN MY LIFE Lord, only through my friendship with you can I live in communion with God. You are the one Mediator, Lord – the one true Temple. I believe in you, and I have put all my hopes in you. I want to know, love, and follow you more each day, because in you I will become what I long to be: rich in virtue and wisdom, free from selfishness and sin, strong in love and purified from greed, lust, envy, and arrogance…

I wish you would come and cleanse the money-grubbing, pleasure-grabbing tendencies out of my heart once and for all. You know that I want to be patient, generous, and wise. So why am I so often impatient, selfish, and foolish? My only comfort is that you know me through and through, and even so, you chose me. No task is too great for you, not even bringing light and order to my dark and disordered soul…

I want my life to be fully at the service of what is good, true, and right – of your Kingdom. I want to give myself to you. I believe in you, Lord. All the energy and vitality you have given me, I put back in your hands. The tasks you have given me to do, I do for love of you. I am a Temple dedicated entirely to your glory and your goodness, because all I have I have received from you…

QUESTIONS FOR SMALL GROUP DISCUSSION

1. What struck you most in this passage? What did you notice that you hadn't noticed before?

2. What are some of the hypocrisies that easily creep into our lives as Catholics today?

3. What has helped you most in making your friendship with Christ more heartfelt and personal, and less superficial and mechanical?

4. As Christians, we consider our bodies to be Temples of the Holy Spirit. How should that affect the way we treat our bodies? What does popular culture think of the human body, and how does that affect how popular culture encourages us to treat our bodies?

Cf. Catechism of the Catholic Church, 583-586 on Jesus and the Temple; 2468 and 2505 on hypocrisy; 2559-2564 on praying from the heart

THE GOSPEL OF JOHN CHAPTER 3

"Sin which destroyed the divine life within us demands a satisfaction, an expiation without which it would be impossible for divine life to be restored to us. Being a mere creature, man cannot give this satisfaction for an offense of infinite malice, and, on the other hand, divinity can neither suffer nor expiate. How is this problem to be solved? The Incarnation gives us the answer. Consider the babe of Bethlehem. He is the Word-made-Flesh. The Word asks of us a human nature to find in it wherewith to suffer, to expiate, to merit, to heap graces upon us. It is through the flesh that man turns away from God; it is in becoming flesh that God delivers man. The flesh that the Word of God takes upon himself, is to become the instrument of salvation for all men."

- *Blessed Columba Marmion*

246. NIGHT LINES (JN 3:1-15)

"Eternal Trinity, you are like a deep sea, in which the more I seek, the more I find; and the more I find, the more I seek you."

- *St Catherine of Siena*

John 3:1-15

There was one of the Pharisees called Nicodemus, a leading Jew, who came to Jesus by night and said, 'Rabbi, we know that you are a teacher who comes from God;

for no one could perform the signs that you do unless God were with him.' Jesus answered: 'I tell you most solemnly, unless a man is born from above, he cannot see the kingdom of God.' Nicodemus said, 'How can a grown man be born? Can he go back into his mother's womb and be born again?' Jesus replied: 'I tell you most solemnly, unless a man is born through water and the Spirit, he cannot enter the kingdom of God: what is born of the flesh is flesh; what is born of the Spirit is spirit. Do not be surprised when I say: You must be born from above. The wind blows wherever it pleases; you hear its sound, but you cannot tell where it comes from or where it is going. That is how it is with all who are born of the Spirit.' 'How can that be possible?' asked Nicodemus. 'You, a teacher in Israel, and you do not know these things!' replied Jesus. 'I tell you most solemnly, we speak only about what we know and witness only to what we have seen and yet you people reject our evidence. If you do not believe me when I speak about things in this world, how are you going to believe me when I speak to you about heavenly things? No one has gone up to heaven except the one who came down from heaven, the Son of Man who is in heaven; and the Son of Man must be lifted up as Moses lifted up the serpent in the desert, so that everyone who believes may have eternal life in him.'

CHRIST THE LORD Christ's mission is universal. He was sent so that everyone who believes in him may receive eternal life. Nicodemus was a leader of the Jewish nation. He would have known the Old Testament prophecies about the promised Messiah not only restoring the Kingdom of Israel, but also being a "light for the nations." God had entrusted Israel with a universal mission to be the firstborn son of all the nations, a priestly people that would channel God's blessings to all the other peoples of the world. Therefore, when Christ spoke of himself as the one sent to save the world, Nicodemus would have recognized the Messianic claim. All that remained was for him to accept it. We know from later passages that eventually he did accept it and became a secret disciple.

Nicodemus needed a large dose of faith to believe and live in accord with Christ's claim. After all, at the time Jesus appeared to be nothing more than a rough-and-ready rabbi from Galilee. For us, it should be much easier. Christ's prediction that he would be raised up like Moses' bronze serpent has come true. (When the Israelites were wandering in the desert, they were plagued by an infestation of poisonous serpents. To cure them, God had Moses make a bronze image of a serpent on a stick and hold it up; everyone who looked upon the image was saved.) In every corner of the globe, the crucifix looks down upon mankind, and the entire world looks up at it. These looks of love fill thousands of churches, chapels, and classrooms, millions of living rooms and bedrooms. Christians are fingering their crucifix necklaces on subways and airplanes, in hospitals and army camps. Other fingers are touching it on innumerable rosaries, stirring lips and hearts to constant prayer. Truly, the universality of Christ's claim has been verified by the unconquerable universality of his Church.

CHRIST THE TEACHER Nicodemus was a member of Israel's ruling body, the Sanhedrin. He had come to speak with Jesus in secret, to find out the truth about this controversial rabbi from Galilee. In their conversation, Jesus wins over his heart, so much so that, as we know from other passages, Nicodemus became an undercover disciple.

The Lord knew how to speak to the poor. He knew how to clothe the mysteries of God in language accessible to the humblest of workers, but he also knew how to reach out to those who were educated, sophisticated, and in charge. The gospel breaks through all boundaries of race, class, and rank. Christ's wisdom is universal, just as his Church is Catholic (catholic means "universal"). No other message or body of doctrine is more worth studying through and through than the science of Christ. It is the fullness of truth, because Christ himself is Truth. It never stops satisfying every kind of thirst the soul can have, like a fountain that everyone in the city can go back to again and again and always be refreshed.

That the Church's saints, religious, bishops, cardinals, and popes have come and still come from every race, class, and rank continuously shows that it is carrying Christ's unflagging, universal torch, a torch that every Christian should also carry.

CHRIST THE FRIEND Nicodemus was like so many of us. He was only able to take small, hesitant steps towards the Lord. Why? He hadn't understood the depths of God's love. He thought the Messiah was only coming to put the finishing touches on what had already been done throughout salvation history, when Christ's true mission was the complete renewal of the human spirit.

This is still his mission; this is still his dream for every human heart.

His Spirit comes not only to heal our wounds but to give us an entirely new birth, an entirely new life – not just once, but continually, until we are ready for heaven. It takes faith and trust to accept Christ's agenda. At times, like Nicodemus we are tempted to stop at whatever point we have already reached, clinging to the well-known comfort of our well-known world. But Jesus has more to give us, more to show us, more for us to do. He has more life for us to grow into. He has spoken to us of earthly things, and maybe we have learned his lessons well; now he wishes to speak to us of heavenly things.

CHRIST IN MY LIFE Thank you for the gift of faith, Lord. You are the Savior of the world. You created this world, and when our sin cut it off from your friendship, you came down to live among us so you could win that friendship back. Make me like that. Make me generous. Make me eager to do good for my neighbor, to spread the soothing balm of goodness and understanding in this world that is so full of bitterness…

Your words are nourishment for my soul and for every soul. The world is full of so many words, Lord. We are drowning in them. Yet that doesn't take away the value of your wisdom. Today, your Church still speaks in your name to the rich and poor, the educated and uneducated, the young and old. Give me a share of your wisdom too, so that I can plant seeds of faith with the words that come from my mouth…

I have known you for a long time, Lord, and you have given me so much. Yet, I feel as if I still need much more. How can it be that as I grow older, I feel a heightened need for your enlightenment and guidance? I want to be born yet again, to experience the freedom of mature virtue, the fruitfulness of flourishing love. With the knowledge of your heart, Lord, make my heart wise…

QUESTIONS FOR SMALL GROUP DISCUSSION

1. What struck you most in this passage? What did you notice that you hadn't noticed before?

2. How should our being born again from above through baptism affect our daily living?

3. In the context of our lives, what would constitute a generous response to God's generous offer of salvation in his only Son? In other words, for us right now, what does "believing in Jesus" really entail?

4. When popular culture mentions God, what characteristics does it usually highlight?

Cf. Catechism of the Catholic Church, 599-618 on the meaning of Christ's death on the cross; 2567, 30, 142, and 1-3 on God's unceasing invitation of love to all mankind

247. GOD'S GAME PLAN (JN 3:16-21)

"How precious must man be in the eyes of the Creator, if he gained so great a Redeemer, and if God 'gave his only Son' in order that man 'should not perish but have eternal life.'"

- *Pope John Paul II*

John 3:16-21

'Yes, God loved the world so much that he gave his only Son, so that everyone who believes in him may not be lost but may have eternal life. For God sent his Son into the world not to condemn the world, but so that through him the world might be saved. No one who believes in him will be condemned; but whoever refuses to believe is condemned already, because he has refused to believe in the name of God's only Son. On these grounds is sentence pronounced: that though the light has come into the world men have shown they prefer darkness to the light because their deeds were evil. And indeed, everybody who does wrong hates the light and avoids it, for fear his actions should be exposed; but the man who lives by the truth comes out into the light, so that it may be plainly seen that what he does is done in God.'

CHRIST THE LORD   You never really know someone until you know what's in their heart – what motivates them, what they're looking for, why they do what they do. In this conversation with Nicodemus, Jesus lays bare the heart of God.

The history of salvation, from the fall of Adam and Eve until the final judgment, revolves around the coming of Jesus Christ, the Savior, the Son of God. Why did he come? Because the Father sent him. Why did the Father send him? Because he "loved the world so much." He simply couldn't bear to see us perish in our sins; he longed to share with us his everlasting life. God cares. And Jesus Christ is the definitive proof that he cares. He cares so much that he is willing to sacrifice his only Son to atone for the sins that have separated man from God, the source of all good things. We need look no further to find the very core of the gospel: "God loved the world so much that he gave his only Son, so that everyone who believes in him may not be lost but may have eternal life." No hidden agenda, no selfish undertones – pure generosity. This is the heart of God, of the Lord who longs for our friendship.

Only when a Christian internalizes this fundamental and overarching motive of God does Christian discipleship really begin to mature. This is Christ's revolution. That disinterested, self-forgetful love has the power to overcome all evil and renew every human heart and the human race as a whole. The rules and rituals of Christianity are not its core, but its leaves. Joy, the kind of joy that none of life's contrarieties can diminish, as the lives of countless saints from every walk of life so powerfully attest to, is its flower. But its root is God's love, and its fruit is God's love lived out in the humdrum routine of daily life by the followers of Christ.

CHRIST THE TEACHER   With these few sentences, Jesus lifts the veil of heaven and gives us a brief glimpse into the life of God himself.

The conversation between Father, Son, and Holy Spirit that led to the Incarnation and the salvation of sinful mankind was one of love. Love spoke to Love, and

Love answered, and Love himself came to earth to teach us love. God is a relationship of eternal love between the Three Divine Persons.

Theologians reflecting on the Trinity see its image in the human family. The love of husband and wife in an embrace of complete and mutual self-giving yield a child. It is love that brings them together and love that brings new life. Similarly, but in an even more marvelous way, the Father and the Son look upon each other with such love that the love itself is another Person, another source of love, the Holy Spirit.

CHRIST THE FRIEND Jesus has proven his love by coming to earth "for our sake and for our salvation." He invites us to believe, so that we might not perish but have eternal life. He did not come for his own sake, but for ours. This is the epitome of friendship. "No one has greater love than this, to lay down one's life for one's friends" (John 15:13). But in his conversation with Nicodemus, Jesus once again points out that we remain free to accept or reject his offer of friendship, his offer of salvation. He makes it starkly clear: "Whoever does not believe in him has already been condemned." Salvation depends on God and on us; God has done his part, now we must do ours.

Nicodemus: I remember the tone of the Lord's voice that night. We were talking quietly, almost alone. Only one of his young disciples was there with us. We were sitting outside near a fire on a hillside under the stars. How could I forget this, my first conversation with the Master? His voice resonated with the very love of which he spoke. His eyes glimmered in the firelight with eager enthusiasm. I knew even then that it was the enthusiasm that had been at the origin of his mission to earth. As he spoke of those who believed in him, he grew joyful and glad. Then his words trembled with sadness and disappointment when he spoke of those who did not believe. How could I not be convinced by his wisdom, brighter and hotter than the fire between us? It was a risk for me to come to him that night, but I am ever grateful that I took it.

CHRIST IN MY LIFE I am so glad to be loved, Lord, and yet I am so slow to love. My heart is so inconstant. If I like someone, I treat them the way you would have me treat them, but if they rub me the wrong way, I bristle and gripe. Teach me to be a mature Christian. Teach me to love in word and deed, in thought and action. Teach me to love everyone the way you love…

I praise you, Father all-powerful, Christ, Lord and Savior, Holy Spirit of love. You have revealed yourself to me, and you have drawn me to share in your life and your love. Stay near to me, God. You have created me in your image and you have given life to this world because of your love. In your goodness make me an instrument of your mercy…

Lead me, Lord, to the pinnacle of love. I don't ask to be taken to new places or given new tasks. I ask you to unveil your beauty here where I live and work, where you have placed me. I ask you to infuse me with your love in the tasks you have already given me to do. I believe in you, Lord. Thy will be done...

QUESTIONS FOR SMALL GROUP DISCUSSION

1. What struck you most in this passage? What did you notice that you hadn't noticed before?

2. As Christians, how can we cultivate our relationship with a God who is a Trinity, not just with a generic God? How does our Trinitarian God differ from the gods of other religions?

3. When life and faith present us with difficult questions, where does popular culture encourage us to look for answers? How can we be more like Nicodemus in those moments, bringing our problems to Christ, and how can we encourage those around us to be more like Nicodemus?

4. If a non-believing friend of yours asked you, "If God is so loving, why does he let bad things happen to good people?" how would you respond?

Cf. Catechism of the Catholic Church, 238-260 on the Trinity; 50-67 on God's plan of "loving goodness"; 144-152 on what it means to "believe"

248. GREAT AND LITTLE (JN 3:22-36)

"He was to be manifested visibly, so that the world would see him and be saved."

- St Hippolytus

Jn 3:22-36

After this, Jesus went with his disciples into the Judaean countryside and stayed with them there and baptised. At the same time John was baptising at Aenon near Salim, where there was plenty of water, and people were going there to be baptised. This was before John had been put in prison. Now some of John's disciples had opened a discussion with a Jew about purification, so they went to John and said, 'Rabbi, the man who was with you on the far side of the Jordan, the man to whom you bore witness, is baptising now; and everyone is going to him.' John replied: 'A man can lay claim only to what is given him from heaven. You yourselves can bear me out: I said: I myself am not the Christ; I am the one who has been sent in front of him. The bride is only for the bridegroom; and yet the bridegroom's friend, who stands there and listens, is glad when he hears the bridegroom's voice. This same joy I feel, and now it is complete. He must grow greater, I must grow smaller. He who comes from above is above all others; he who is born of the earth is earthly himself and speaks in an earthly way. He who comes from heaven bears witness to the things he has seen and heard, even if his testimony is not accepted; though all who do accept his testimony are attesting the truthfulness of God, since he whom

God has sent speaks God's own words: God gives him the Spirit without reserve. The Father loves the Son and has entrusted everything to him. Anyone who believes in the Son has eternal life, but anyone who refuses to believe in the Son will never see life: the anger of God stays on him.'

CHRIST THE LORD Jesus is everything. First, John tells us, he is the bridegroom. This is an image taken from the Old Testament, which often referred to Israel as God's chosen bride. Imagine God calling himself a bridegroom. How passionately he must love each human soul, the whole human family! This is not the language of a cold architect or a distant watchmaker.

Second, he is the one who "comes from above… who comes from heaven… he… speaks God's own words." Only Jesus can speak definitively about the things of God. The fullness of God's own self-revelation is found in him. In this especially, Christianity differs from the rest of the world's religions: Christ is God himself come to reveal to man – in language man can understand – the truths that are beyond his natural knowledge. Therein lies the unique authority of the Catholic Church, the preserver and loudspeaker of God's self-revelation.

Third, he has "the Spirit without reserve." Those who consider Jesus to be just another guru among many, and who measure his teachings against the reams of merely human wisdom that history has churned out through the centuries are making a terrible mistake.

Finally, "The Father loves the Son and has entrusted everything to him." Jesus and God the Father are a perfect unity.

Could John have been any clearer in bearing witness to the full divine identity of Jesus Christ, the rabbi from Nazareth? Even those of us who already believe in him should never tire of savoring the fullness of his glory, letting it nourish our minds and hearts. The better we know the Lord, the fuller our lives will be.

CHRIST THE TEACHER In John the Baptist, Jesus gives us an icon of humility.

Every Christian has the same mission, basically, as John the Baptist. We are called to bear witness to Christ, to help people understand who he really is, and to bring them into the circle of his disciples. Essential to this mission is the virtue of humility, summed up perfectly by John in his greatest phrase: "He must grow greater, I must grow smaller." Our mission in life is to know, love, and follow Christ ourselves and to make him known, loved, and followed by as many others as possible. In this we will find our fulfillment, because we were made to love, and love is self-giving – giving of ourselves for the good of the beloved – not self-aggrandizing. In this we will also find our joy, as John the Baptist did: "This same joy I feel, and now it is complete" (Jn 3:29).

Jesus is the center of the universe. He is the focal point of history. We are simply his friends, his ambassadors, and his assistants. He loves us as passionately as a bridegroom loves his bride, but we cannot experience that love unless we first truly realize that we are not at the center of things, that we don't strictly deserve his love – rather it is freely given to us. Just as Mary became the Mother of God because she saw herself as "the handmaid of the Lord" (Luke 1:38), and just as John the Baptist could experience the joy of Christ only because he freely ceded his own glory to Christ, just so, life for us will only click into place when we learn to look beyond the mirror.

CHRIST THE FRIEND *Jesus: How faithful a friend and messenger John the Baptist was for me! Look at him now, as his disciples come back, rankled from conversations in which they were complaining about John's diminishing and my rising popularity. But John was not fazed by their comments. He sought nothing for himself. He, the greatest of all prophets, had more to be proud of than any of his disciples, and yet he graciously accepts a lower status. If only all my followers would learn from him! The body of my Church is always being lacerated by divisions, rivalries, envy, and even intrigue. This above all is what keeps many more of my beloved souls from believing in me. They look at those who claim to believe already, see them posturing and backbiting just like everyone else, and turn away.*

Am I not enough for your soul? Is my friendship not enough to give you joy as it gave joy to John? Why do you seek approval from others when I have already given you my whole heart? Stay a while with me. Let me in, so I can conquer your heart.

CHRIST IN MY LIFE Lord, all throughout these first chapters of John's Gospel, the constantly recurring theme is that many refuse to believe in you. Today is no different. Those whom you came to save refuse to believe in you. Move their hearts, Lord! Why did you give me the gift of faith and not them? I understand very little of these mysteries. Teach me, Lord, to do your will and build your Kingdom…

You are meek and humble of heart. John was meek, gladly fading into the background once his part had been played. And I? I am full of a burning desire for recognition, praise, and influence. Purify my heart, Lord. How can I conquer souls for your Kingdom by using the enemies' weapons? Jesus, meek and humble of heart, make my heart more like yours…

I want to love you, and I want to show you my love in every detail of this day. I want to give myself to the mission you have entrusted to me. I am limited – I

823

have limited time and resources, but your love is unlimited. Pour your love into my heart so that it can overflow in how I do my work today, all for the glory of your name and the triumph of your Kingdom…

QUESTIONS FOR SMALL GROUP DISCUSSION

1. What struck you most in this passage? What did you notice that you hadn't noticed before?

2. Why do you think it is so easy even for Christians to divide up into factions? What can we do to avoid this kind of thing?

3. If an agnostic friend came up to you and asked how you would define humility and why it was important, what would you tell them?

4. What are some ways in which we can exercise and grow in the virtue of humility?

Cf. Catechism of the Catholic Church, 456-460 on why the Son of God became man; 461-463 on the meaning of Christ's Incarnation; 464-469 on how it is possible for Jesus to be both human and divine at the same time

THE GOSPEL OF JOHN CHAPTER 4

"In your spiritual ascent and your search for a closer union with God, you must allow yourself no rest, no slipping back. You must go forward till you have obtained the object of your desires. Follow the example of mountain climbers. If your desires turn aside after objects that pass below, you will lose yourself in byways and your mind will be drawn in all directions. Your progress will be uncertain. You will not reach your goal. And you will not find rest after your labors. But if your heart and mind, led by love and desire, withdraw from the distractions of the world, you will grow strong. Your recollection will deepen the higher you rise on the wings of knowledge and desire. Little by little as you abandon baser things to rest in the one true and unchangeable Good, you will dwell there, held fast by the bonds of love."

- St Albert the Great

249. QUENCHING CHRIST'S THIRST (JN 4:1-30)

"To show that he was not different from us, he undertook hard work, he went hungry and thirsty, he took rest and sleep, he did not shirk suffering, he revealed the Resurrection."

- St Hippolytus

John 4:1-30

When Jesus heard that the Pharisees had found out that he was making and baptising more disciples than John – though in fact it was his disciples who baptised, not Jesus himself – he left Judaea and went back to Galilee. This meant that he had to cross Samaria. On the way he came to the Samaritan town called Sychar, near the land that Jacob gave to his son Joseph. Jacob's well is there and Jesus, tired by the journey, sat straight down by the well. It was about the sixth hour. When a Samaritan woman came to draw water, Jesus said to her, 'Give me a drink.' His disciples had gone into the town to buy food. The Samaritan woman said to him, 'What? You are a Jew and you ask me, a Samaritan, for a drink?' – Jews, in fact, do not associate with Samaritans. Jesus replied: 'If you only knew what God is offering and who it is that is saying to you: Give me a drink, you would have been the one to ask, and he would have given you living water.' 'You have no bucket, sir,' she answered, 'and the well is deep: how could you get this living water? Are you a greater man than our father Jacob who gave us this well and drank from it himself with his sons and his cattle?' Jesus replied: 'Whoever drinks this water will get thirsty again; but anyone who drinks the water that I shall give will never be thirsty again: the water that I shall give will turn into a spring inside him, welling up to eternal life.'

'Sir,' said the woman 'give me some of that water, so that I may never get thirsty and never have to come here again to draw water.' 'Go and call your husband,' said Jesus to her, 'and come back here.' The woman answered, 'I have no husband.' He said to her, 'You are right to say, I have no husband; for although you have had five, the one you have now is not your husband. You spoke the truth there.' 'I see you are a prophet, sir,' said the woman. 'Our fathers worshipped on this mountain, while you say that Jerusalem is the place where one ought to worship.' Jesus said: 'Believe me, woman, the hour is coming when you will worship the Father neither on this mountain nor in Jerusalem. You worship what you do not know; we worship what we do know: for salvation comes from the Jews. But the hour will come – in fact it is here already – when true worshippers will worship the Father in spirit and truth: that is the kind of worshipper the Father wants. God is spirit, and those who worship must worship in spirit and truth.' The woman said to him, 'I know that Messiah – that is, Christ – is coming; and when he comes he will tell us everything.' 'I who am speaking to you,' said Jesus, 'I am he.' At this point his disciples returned, and were surprised to find him speaking to a woman, though none of them asked, 'What do you want from her?' or, 'Why are you talking to her?' The woman put down her water jar and hurried back to the town to tell the people. 'Come and see a man who has told me everything I ever did; I wonder if he is the Christ?' This brought people out of the town and they started walking towards him.

CHRIST THE LORD Passing through Samaria was not the only route from Judea to Galilee, but Jesus chose that route. He knew the bigger picture. He is always attentive to our needs, just as he was attentive to the needs of this woman and her countrymen. He never uses his knowledge and power to oppress and abuse, but only to amplify his love.

Christ is the Savior of the World, the Messiah, the long-awaited King greater even than Jacob, inheritor of the Promise and father of the Twelve Tribes of Israel, so he tells this divorcee. He graces the Samaritan woman with one of the richest descriptions of himself and his work that appear in all the Scriptures. Why? Why tell so much to someone so insignificant? Because to him, she wasn't insignificant at all. He wanted to be known by her, to give her hope, to save her. Ours is a Lord who wishes to shower us with his love, to fill us with the "living waters" of "the Spirit and truth," and to "tell us everything." This is the God in whom we believe; this is the Lord we serve.

CHRIST THE TEACHER Jesus was tired after his journey. He sat down by the well, thirsty, hungry, worn out. He was so thirsty that he skirted all social protocol and asked a Samaritan woman to give him a drink. But his tiredness doesn't hold back his love. He had come to rescue the lost sheep – this was his mission. The Samaritan woman came to the well at noon, the hottest hour of the day. The other women of the village would have come in the cooler hours of early morning and evening. This one was obviously avoiding contact with her peers. Jesus certainly notices this, seeing in her eyes the anxiety that comes from an unstable life, but he also sees a spark of sincerity – her rocky path through life had worn down any façade of self-righteousness or self-delusion. She was a woman in search of answers and direction, though she had perhaps given up on finding them. Jesus sees all this in her eyes, and he can't contain the love that overflows in his heart. He sees a soul in need, and he can't help reaching out. This is why he came.

Jesus became one of us on purpose with a mission in mind. Because of our sin, we could no longer raise ourselves up to friendship with God; so God comes down to meet us. In the Incarnation of Christ and the Church (which is the extension of that Incarnation throughout history) God continues to come down to meet us. He addresses us, he walks with us, he humbles himself so much that he even needs us to give him a drink: "Whatever you did for one of the least brothers of mine you did for me" (Matthew 25:40). When the Samaritan woman encountered this God who was man, she was so transported with joy and so eager to spread the news that she forgot to bring back her water jar, the very reason she came to the well in the first place. Christ is the kind of friend who can make a real difference in our lives, one who can put things in perspective – if we let him.

CHRIST THE FRIEND *The Samaritan woman: I knew something was different about that man as soon as I came up to the well. He looked at me in a way that* *men didn't usually look at me. I met his eyes for just a second, and then I looked away. But I wanted to look again. I had seen in his glance something that I had only dreamed about before: he knew me completely – he knew exactly what kind of person I was. Yet it didn't bother him; in fact, it was as if he was glad to see me – not because he wanted anything from me, but because he seemed to want something for me, as if he were pure kindness. So when I looked away, because that was the proper thing to do, I was just dying to look at him again, to see that kindness in his eyes, to drink it in.*

But then I thought, no, it's only my imagination. And then he spoke to me. He asked me for a drink. And that was the beginning of a conversation that changed my life. I didn't understand everything he told me, but I understood that he knew me – he knew me through and through and he still cared about me, he was interested in me. For him, I was important, not just because I could give him something, but just… well, just because. In his eyes, I mattered. Even then I knew that what he said about being the Messiah was true. How else could I explain the change that was already happening in my heart? It was as if a door had opened in my life where before there had only been a thick, dark, high wall protecting my broken heart. He freed me. I had to tell the others in the town. I knew he was the Savior, and I just had to tell everyone. I knew that as soon as they met him they too would realize it. And they did! Before that day I was just surviving; after that encounter with his words, his glance, his presence – from then on I began to live.

CHRIST IN MY LIFE Jesus, tell me everything. Tell me about myself and the meaning of my life; tell me about your love and your wisdom and your plan for my life. Lord, give me your living water – how thirsty I am! I have tasted your gifts; I know at least a little bit about what you are offering. I want to know more. I want to live closer to you. I want to lead others to your heart, just as you led me…

I believe in you, Lord, and in your eagerness to save souls who are stuck in sin and darkness. And I believe that you can save them, just as you turned this woman's life around – just as you have turned my life around. Thank you for guiding me. Thank you for not giving up on me. Thank you for giving me a mission in life…

What does it mean, Lord, to worship in "Spirit and truth"? You want it; you came to make it possible. To worship is to acknowledge your greatness, majesty, and goodness. You want me to do so not only in external ceremonies but in my heart, in my attitudes, in my choices. You want me to live as you would have me live, Lord, trusting in you, seeking your will always. Teach me to do so, because this is what you desire…

QUESTIONS FOR SMALL GROUP DISCUSSION

1. What struck you most in this passage? What did you notice that you hadn't noticed before?

2. Would you say that your community of believers has come to believe in Christ with as much conviction as the Samaritan woman, who told the whole town about Christ? If not, what is holding you back?

3. In your Christian journey so far, what moment or experience has been most similar to the experience of this Samaritan woman?

4. The Samaritan woman was looking forward to the coming of the Messiah to get answers to life's questions. Where does popular culture encourage us to seek those answers?

Cf. Catechism of the Catholic Church, 2560-2562, 2652 on the encounter at Jacob's well as an image of prayer; 436-440 on the meaning of the title "Messiah"

250. FOOD FOR LIFE (JN 4:31-42)

"The best way to become a saint is to plunge ourselves in the will of God, as a stone is immersed in the water. We must allow ourselves to be tossed like a ball here and there according to his good pleasure."

- St Clement Hofbauer

John 4:31-42

Meanwhile, the disciples were urging him, 'Rabbi, do have something to eat; but he said, 'I have food to eat that you do not know about.' So the disciples asked one another, 'Has someone been bringing him food?' But Jesus said: 'My food is to do the will of the one who sent me, and to complete his work. Have you not got a saying: Four months and then the harvest? Well, I tell you: Look around you, look at the fields; already they are white, ready for harvest! Already the reaper is being paid his wages, already he is bringing in the grain for eternal life, and thus sower and reaper rejoice together. For here the proverb holds good: one sows, another reaps; I sent you to reap a harvest you had not worked for. Others worked for it; and you have come into the rewards of their trouble.' Many Samaritans of that town had believed in him on the strength of the woman's testimony when she said, 'He told me all I have ever done,' so, when the Samaritans came up to him, they begged him to stay with them. He stayed for two days, and when he spoke to them many more came to believe; and they said to the woman, 'Now we no longer believe because of what you told us; we have heard him ourselves and we know that he really is the savior of the world.'

CHRIST THE LORD The Samaritans recognized Jesus as the "Savior of the world." The Samaritans were descended from Jews who had intermarried with non-Jews and abandoned the Jewish faith when the Kingdom of Israel was splitting up. They didn't get along well with the Jews. Jesus' stop here in Samaria, their generous response, and the phrase "Savior of the world," therefore, all come together to point to the universality of Jesus' mission. He has come to reestablish communion between God and all mankind. He has come to plug all lost hearts back into the source of true happiness: the love, truth, and mercy of God.

Jesus is consumed with longing to fulfill this mission. His hunger, which St John just mentioned a few verses ago, has vanished, because he has been doing what he is passionate about: saving souls. And he wants his disciples to share the joy by dedicating themselves to the same mission. He paints a picture of it for them, likening the spiritual harvest of bringing sinful and estranged people back into communion with God to the physical harvest of wheat. When a crop is ready for harvest, the farmers work eagerly and enthusiastically to gather it in; when a crop fails and the harvest is meager, the farmers are grieved – they wish they had more work. Jesus shows his disciples that the world is full of men and women like these Samaritans who are searching for the truth, whom God has prepared to hear the message of truth. The leaders of Jerusalem were indignant at Christ's claims to be the Messiah, but the outcast Samaritans drink it all in. Seeing such a huge harvest ready to be gathered in should fill Christ's disciples with a keen desire to roll up their sleeves and get to work. The Lord came to conquer hearts – the hearts of all men.

CHRIST THE TEACHER Whenever we encounter great individuals, we want to know what makes them tick. We want to discover the source of their greatness, so we can tap into it. St John knows what makes Jesus tick. John is "the beloved disciple," who reclined next to Jesus during the Last Supper, leaning against him and listening to the beatings of his heart. As he finishes narrating this fascinating scene of Jesus' encounter with the Samaritan woman, he makes clear what Jesus is all about, what is in his heart. In so doing, he teaches us the key to being Christ's disciples: "My food is to do the will of the one who sent me, and to complete his work." Christ is a man consumed by his mission. Only that mission matters. To fulfill the Father's will, to complete the mission (the "work") – this is Christ's passionate desire. It pushes him on; it fills him with purpose and energy…. It is his food.

When we were baptized, we also were anointed in the name and the Spirit of Christ. When we were confirmed, we were anointed again and sent out as ambassadors of Christ and of his Church to gather in the abundant harvest of souls like the Samaritan woman, who are looking for Jesus and just need someone to point him out. As Christians, we are other Christs, continuing his saving mission in the world, and our food too should be none other than God's will.

CHRIST THE FRIEND Jesus explains that sometimes those who plant and those who harvest celebrate together. Other times, however, those who plant may never see the harvest, and those who gather may not have labored in the planting. In this way, he gives courage and comfort to those who have decided to accept his offer of friendship and work with him to build the Kingdom; he prepares them for two possible scenarios as they try to gather the harvest.

Jesus: At times you will see success and results right away; your efforts to build my Kingdom will yield abundant fruit quickly and easily. In those times, you must not give in to the temptation that will surely come, that of thinking that your talents and efforts alone have brought in the crop. I was the one who prepared those people to find me and hear my call through your voice. Rejoice then, but remember that the soil had been fertilized, tilled, and planted by other hands, and that I was the one who made the seeds grow. Other times I will ask you to do the fertilizing, tilling, and planting, and you may never see the results. Are you ready for that? I ask that of you because I know you love me, and I want to purify your love. If you persevere even when you don't see results, you will have to exercise that love, and you will no longer be working for the praise and recognition of others, but solely for me and my Kingdom. Then, as your love grows, you will begin to experience true joy and true freedom. I will be able to fill your soul with my wisdom and love, because it will have been emptied a little bit more of the vanity and pride that clogs the flow of my grace.

CHRIST IN MY LIFE I believe that you are the Savior of the world, Lord. And I believe that the world needs a Savior. We are all thirsty for the living water of your Spirit. I am thirsty, Lord. Increase my faith. Deepen my conviction. What does it really mean for me to say that I believe you are the Savior of the world? It made a difference in the lives of these Samaritans. Help it make a bigger difference in my life, Lord…

You lived wholly for the mission your Father had given you. I too have a mission. You have given me life and faith and relationships and responsibilities. You have made me a member of your Church, the extension of your Incarnation. How I long for my life to be focused and ordered, as yours was! Teach me to make your will the compass of my life, the quest of my heart, my anchor and my guiding star…

I want to build your Kingdom. I want to put my talents at the service of the men and women you love so much, the ones you came to save. But you know that my motives are not pure. So much selfishness is still mixed in. Purify me, Lord. Remind me that you are the Lord of the harvest and I am only one worker among many. Help me to find all my satisfaction in loving you by doing your will…

QUESTIONS FOR SMALL GROUP DISCUSSION

1. What struck you most in this passage? What did you notice that you hadn't noticed before?

2. All Christians are called to have one constant and burning desire in life – one "food" – to discover and fulfill the mission God has in mind for them. What other desires tend to seep into our lives and drain us of its force?

3. What more can we do to gather in the harvest that God has prepared around us?

4. What things tend to make us hesitant to bring others closer to Christ and how can we overcome them?

Cf. Catechism of the Catholic Church, 606-618 on the centrality of obedience to the Father's will in Christ's life and mission; 904-913 on the mission of the laity to exercise Christ's priestly and kingly offices in the world

251. A JOURNEY IN FAITH (JN 4:43-54)

"What is it that made the holy apostles and martyrs undergo fierce struggles and terrible agonies, if not faith, and above all faith in the Resurrection?"

- Pope Benedict XIV

John 4:43-54

When the two days were over Jesus left for Galilee. He himself had declared that there is no respect for a prophet in his own country, but on his arrival the Galileans received him well, having seen all that he had done at Jerusalem during the festival which they too had attended. He went again to Cana in Galilee, where he had changed the water into wine. Now there was a court official there whose son was ill at Capernaum and, hearing that Jesus had arrived in Galilee from Judaea, he went and asked him to come and cure his son as he was at the point of death. Jesus said, 'So you will not believe unless you see signs and portents!' 'Sir,' answered the official 'come down before my child dies.' 'Go home,' said Jesus, 'your son will live.' The man believed what Jesus had said and started on his way; and while he was still on the journey back his servants met him with the news that his boy was alive. He asked them when the boy had begun to recover. 'The fever left him yesterday,' they said, 'at the seventh hour.' The father realised that this was exactly the time when Jesus had said, 'Your son will live'; and he and all his household believed. This was the second sign given by Jesus, on his return from Judaea to Galilee.

CHRIST THE LORD Few passages show the sheer power of Jesus as eloquently as this miracle. In response to the courtier's request, Jesus simply tells him to go home, his son will live. And it happens exactly as Christ said it would. He spoke just one word, sickness and death fled, and life was restored. The effortlessness of the miracle is reminiscent of the Creation narrative in Genesis, where God simply says the word, "Let there be," and the infinite variety of existing things come into being out of nothing. This divine power continues to work in the Church today. When an ordained priest pronounces, in the person of Christ, the words of consecration, "This is my body... this is the cup of my blood," the bread is immediately transformed into Christ's body and the wine into his blood – just as easily and gently as Christ's word restored health to the courtier's son. When the priest pronounces the words of absolution in the confessional, "I absolve you from your sins in the name of the Father..." a moral healing, as real and as miraculous as the healing of the courtier's son, really takes place.

We easily take Christ's Lordship for granted. He is so gentle and patient with us that we can lose the sense of wonder that should accompany our journey of faith. Is it so small a thing to create a daffodil out of nothing, to bring solar systems and galaxies into existence where a moment before there was only nothingness, not even empty space? Is it so small a thing to transform bread and wine into Christ, the Son of God made man, and to do so in such a way that Christ himself becomes the nourishment of Christians? To recover and to nurture a healthy sense of wonder at who the Lord is and all that he does is pleasing to God and good for the soul. Children are full of wonder, and our Lord promised that unless we become like children, we will not enter into his Kingdom (Mark 10:15).

CHRIST THE TEACHER The court official is a paradigm of how difficult it can be to follow Christ, and how rewarding it is to persevere in the midst of such difficulties.

He is a high-ranking courtier in the royal palace of King Herod. And yet, with all his influence and wealth, he is helpless in the face of his son's illness. As he looks at his son, feverish and wasting away, he acutely feels this helplessness. He feels for the first time how trifling the honors and powers of high society really are – they can do nothing to help him in the things that really matter. He hears that Jesus, the wonder-working rabbi from Nazareth, is back in Capernaum. The thought occurs: maybe he should go and ask Jesus to heal his son.

But it would mean humbling himself in front of a simple carpenter. It would mean ridicule and talking behind his back from his colleagues at court, who mock the simple faith of the common people. It would mean admitting that this working-class, uneducated rabbi is God's chosen one when all the sophisticated Jewish leaders were calling him an imposter and a rabble-rouser. To go to Jesus would mean losing his carefully cultivated reputation, and maybe even compromise his chances at promotion. It is a high price to pay, he thinks. But then he looks at his son, and his father's heart yearns and cries out. No, he thinks again, it is a small price to pay for the life of my son.

And so the fashionable courtier makes the twenty-mile trip from Capernaum to Cana, humbles himself, and begs Jesus to come and heal his child. Jesus looks at him and seems to decline the request. He seems to reproach the courtier, and those around him, for needing to see signs and miracles in order to believe in him. Something in Jesus' voice and look invites the courtier to insist, however, and he does. This insistence shows that he already believes, that he has already relocated his trust. No longer does he rely on his own strength and position; now he has put all his confidence, all his hope, in Jesus. And Jesus answers his prayer. Then, without seeing the result, but taking Jesus at his word, the court official "believed what Jesus had said and started on his way."

CHRIST THE FRIEND The tragedy of his son's illness detached the courtier's heart from the vain promises of the world and impelled him to seek out Christ. As a result, he and all his family were brought into the saving realm of grace. Such is the unchanging pattern of growth in Christ. Whenever we admit the limits of our own resources and turn to Jesus for help, we give God's grace room to work.

Jesus: I performed this miracle for the courtier and his family, but I also did it for you. The miracle showed them how much I cared about them. Once they realized that, their lives blossomed. I care for you as much as I cared for them. I know you as fully as I knew them. I want you to believe in me, and I want you to believe that whatever I ask of you, I ask because I love you. If you believe in me more each day, your life will blossom more each day. I have so much I want to show you and teach you. Follow me; listen to me. I know you are still sick with selfish tendencies. Do you believe I can heal you? Ask me. Trust me. Let me walk with you.

CHRIST IN MY LIFE Lord, I praise you for your glory. All the wonders of this world, from the smallest buttercup to the farthest star, sing of your goodness. I am surrounded by gifts of your love. Why don't I think of this more often, Lord? Guide my thoughts to you. Help me to see your love at work in all things. Thank you for coming to earth to show us your face. Hallowed be thy name…

I am so often torn between following your path of trust and humility and gliding along the wide road of doing what everybody else is doing. Why do I care so much about what others think and say? Why is it so hard for me to do what I know you are asking and inviting me to do? You know, Lord; you know how weak I am. But what does my weakness matter when I have you all to myself to be my strength…

I know you and I believe in you. But what about all the courtiers in the world today who don't know you? Their lives are full of suffering, and they don't know where to go to find relief, meaning, and strength. Draw them to yourself, as you drew this court official. Move their hearts, and make me your ambassador. I will tell them of you…

QUESTIONS FOR SMALL GROUP DISCUSSION

1. What struck you most in this passage? What did you notice that you hadn't noticed before?

2. Which personal occurrences have taught you the most about or given you the most intense experience of God's goodness?

3. Why do you think Jesus didn't offer to go to the courtier's home to cure his son, as he did other times in the Gospels?

4. How do you think life in the court official's family might have changed after this encounter with Christ?

Cf. Catechism of the Catholic Church, 150-152 on what it means to believe in Christ; 153-165 on the characteristics of faith; 547-550 on the signs of the Kingdom of God

THE GOSPEL OF JOHN CHAPTER 5

"Suppose you want to fill some sort of bag, and you know the bulk of what you will be given, you stretch the bag or the sack or the skin or whatever it is. You know how big the object that you want to put in and you see that the bag is narrow so you increase its capacity by stretching it. In the same way by delaying the fulfillment of desire God stretches it, by making us desire he expands the soul, and by this expansion he increases its capacity."

- St Augustine

252. STIRRING THINGS UP (JN 5:1-18)

"Whether I receive good or ill, I return thanks equally to God, who taught me always to trust him unreservedly."

- St Patrick

John 5:1-18

Some time after this there was a Jewish festival, and Jesus went up to Jerusalem. Now at the Sheep Pool in Jerusalem there is a building, called Bethzatha in Hebrew, consisting of five porticos; and under these were crowds of sick people – blind, lame, paralysed – waiting for the water to move; for at intervals the angel of the Lord came down into the pool, and the water was disturbed, and the first person to enter the water after this disturbance was cured of any ailment he suffered from. One man there had an illness which had lasted thirty-eight years, and when Jesus saw him lying there and knew he had been in this condition for a long time, he said, 'Do you want to be well again?' 'Sir,' replied the sick man, 'I have no one to put me into the pool when the water is disturbed; and while I am still on the way, someone else gets there before me.' Jesus said, 'Get up, pick up your sleeping-mat and walk.' The man was cured at once, and he picked up his mat and walked away.

Now that day happened to be the sabbath, so the Jews said to the man who had been cured, 'It is the sabbath; you are not allowed to carry your sleeping-mat.' He replied, 'But the man who cured me told me, Pick up your mat and walk.' They asked, 'Who is the man who said to you, Pick up your mat and walk?' The man had no idea who it was, since Jesus had disappeared into the crowd that filled the place. After a while Jesus met him in the Temple and said, 'Now you are well again, be sure not to sin any more, or something worse may happen to you.' The man went back and told the Jews that it was Jesus who had cured him. It was because he did things like this on the sabbath that the Jews began to persecute Jesus. His answer to them was, 'My Father goes on working, and so do I.' But that only made the Jews even more intent on killing him, because, not content with breaking the sabbath, he spoke of God as his own Father, and so made himself God's equal.

CHRIST THE LORD   Jesus is back in Jerusalem, where the Jewish leaders continue to resist his teaching and ignore his signs. St John gives no explanation for why these leaders refused to believe in Jesus, but he explains clearly what they refused to believe: "It was because he did things like this on the Sabbath that the Jews began to persecute Jesus…. He [Jesus] spoke of God as his own Father, and so made himself God's equal."

The complicated tangle of laws restricting the kind of work that could be done on the Sabbath was the Jewish leaders' pride and joy. It had become so complex and convoluted over the years that normal people had no hope of complying in every detail. Only the Pharisees, an important faction in the Sanhedrin, Israel's ruling body, kept faithful to all the restrictions, and this gave them moral and spiritual ascendancy over the populous. When Jesus returns to the pristine spirit of the Sabbath law, performing deeds that reveal God's goodness and give reason to praise him (that was the primary purpose for keeping the Sabbath holy, so that it would be a day dedicated to thanking and praising God), he threatens the Pharisees' ascendancy. Jesus, then, became an enemy to the status quo and to the leaders who had the power and influence therein. When the leaders challenge him, he uses the opportunity to reveal his identity as the Son of God. His comment about the Father who goes on working during the Sabbath refers to God's omnipotence that sustains the universe at all times – the rivers continue to flow, the sun continues to shine, and the crops continue to grow whether or not it's the Sabbath. God's love has no time limits, and Jesus' every word and action is a revelation and manifestation of God's love, so he too continues to work, Sabbath or no.

Jesus' Sabbath miracles manifest and validate his claim to be the divine Messiah. The Pharisees and other Jewish leaders recognized the claim but rejected its validity. They preferred being petty princes in their own little kingdoms to becoming disciples of the true King whose rule brings everlasting life. Today many people still reject Christ's claim. We who have chosen – by the light of his grace – to become his disciples should constantly renew our commitment. It's always possible to start clinging to the status quo so tightly that we end up missing the miracles he wants to send us.

CHRIST THE TEACHER Jesus asks this lame man a strange question, "Do you want to be well again?" How could the man not want to be well again? After thirty-eight years, his hope may have shriveled. Jesus stirs it up. Christ will never act in our lives unless we hope. Hope is the virtue of desiring the right things, confident in God's willingness and ability to give them. Hope can be cultivated. We have a responsibility to consciously steer our desires for happiness and fulfillment towards Christ and God's will. Do we want to leave behind our selfishness and learn to love? Do we really want to? Jesus has to ask this question first, because he will never force his way into our lives. We must want to be his followers, because all his followers are his friends, and friendship can't be forced.

Then he tells the man to get up. For almost forty years, the man had been unable to get up. He was lame. But Jesus asks him to get up all the same. When he makes the effort, simply because Jesus told him to, the miracle kicks into action. It is true that in the spiritual life we are helpless. Without God's grace we will never be made whole, never be forgiven, never achieve the spiritual maturity we were made for and that we long for. And yet, God's grace always requires our cooperation. We must obey, we must follow, we must trust – sometimes beyond the high-visibility range of our reason. We must respond to God's invitation in whatever little ways he may ask us in order for him to do wonderful, amazing things in and through us.

CHRIST THE FRIEND This man had been ill for thirty-eight years. It seems from Jesus' later comment when they meet in the Temple that his own sins had been the cause of his illness. It was an illness that made him an invalid, helpless and incapable of contributing to the society around him. And to top it all off, he was a lonely man. He didn't have any friend or family member who could help him down to the pool after the stirring of the waters. And then one day a young rabbi comes up to him. He squats down beside him, looks into his eyes, and asks him if he wants to be cured. Jesus is always taking the initiative in our lives. He knows what we need more than we do. He knows how much we have suffered and how our sins have damaged our souls. He comes to heal and renew us.

The sick man: Of course I wanted to be cured. That's why I was still waiting at the pool. It seemed an odd question to me. So I looked up at this man. I looked into his eyes as I told him that I wasn't fast enough to make it to the healing waters. What I said didn't seem to matter. He looked at me intently, but gently. I don't know how else to describe it. And then he seemed to smile, and there was a fire in his eyes. And he told me to get up, pick up my sleeping mat, and walk. I thought to myself, "Doesn't he see that I can't get up, that I can't carry anything, let alone my sleeping mat? I can't even walk! Doesn't he see me?" For thirty-eight years I had been lame, unable to do any of those things, and this man was telling me to stand up. It was a crazy thing to say. But his eyes weren't crazy. He just kept looking at me intently. I was going to tell him what a crazy idea it was, but his eyes wouldn't let me. Somehow, the fire in his eyes kindled one in my own, and all of a sudden I knew that I just had to do what he was telling me. But how could I? I had to try. Even as part of me objected – it was such an absurd thing that he was saying – I couldn't help but start to hope. And he kept looking at me and, well, I don't know how it happened, but I just started to get up, and all of a sudden I could. And then I picked up my mat. And I started walking. After thirty-eight years! I turned to thank him – but he was gone.

CHRIST IN MY LIFE Why didn't the leaders of Jerusalem believe in you? They saw your miracles, but even that couldn't pry their hearts away from their own self-centeredness. It seems so unreasonable. And yet, can I say that my faith is robust and confident? Am I not like those leaders, unable to free myself from my own self-centeredness, in spite of all you have done for me? Teach me, Lord, to do your will. Increase my faith…

Many times, the little things you ask me to do seem impossible. How can I be patient and kind to people who irritate me, who are ungrateful? How can I overcome the repugnance I feel sometimes in the face of my responsibilities? How can I simply trust you when so many things go wrong and nothing seems to work? Lord, I believe in you. If you tell me to get up and walk, I will. Thy will be done…

I want to be as generous as you are, Lord. You saw this man, knew his suffering and came to his rescue. You have made me your ambassador; you want me to do the same for everyone around me. You want me to keep my eyes open for opportunities to serve, help, and do good. You want me to make that my obsession, as it was yours. Give me your grace, Lord, so that I too can "go on working"…

QUESTIONS FOR SMALL GROUP DISCUSSION

1. What struck you most in this passage? What did you notice that you hadn't noticed before?
2. Why do you think so many of the leaders of Jerusalem refused to believe in Jesus, even in the face of miracles?
3. What would you say is the most common reason that people today, in your community, refuse to believe in Jesus?
4. What are some things we can do to stir up and keep healthy the right desires in our hearts?

Cf. Catechism of the Catholic Church, 27-30 on the natural human desire for God; 65-67 on Christ as the definitive revelation of God; 172-175 on the oneness of our faith in Christ

253. AIMING AT GOD'S WILL (JN 5:19-30)

"There is one most priceless pearl: the knowledge of the Savior, the mystery of his Passion, the secret of his Resurrection."

- St Jerome

John 5:19-30

To this accusation Jesus replied: 'I tell you most solemnly, the Son can do nothing by himself; he can do only what he sees the Father doing: and whatever the Father does the Son does too. For the Father loves the Son and shows him everything he does himself, and he will show him even greater things than these, works that will astonish you. Thus, as the Father raises the dead and gives them life, so the Son gives life to anyone he chooses; for the Father judges no one; he has entrusted all judgement to the Son, so that all may honour the Son as they honour the Father. Whoever refuses honour to the Son refuses honour to the Father who sent him. I tell you most solemnly, whoever listens to my words, and believes in the one who sent me, has eternal life; without being brought to judgement he has passed from death to life. I tell you most solemnly, the hour will come – in fact it is here already – when the dead will hear the voice of the Son of God, and all who hear it will live. For the Father, who is the source of life, has made the Son the source of life; and, because he is the Son of Man, has appointed him supreme judge. Do not be surprised at this, for the hour is coming when the dead will leave their graves at the sound of his voice: those who did good will rise again to life; and those who did evil, to condemnation. I can do nothing by myself; I can only judge as I am told to judge, and my judging is just, because my aim is to do not my own will, but the will of him who sent me.'

CHRIST THE LORD Prior to this discourse, the Jewish leaders Jesus is speaking with had recognized Jesus' claim to be one with God the Father. That made them mad, and it confirmed their determination to do away with Jesus. This was the perfect opportunity, then, for Christ to clarify himself. Now was the time to explain that he wasn't saying he was one with God, but that he was just closer to God than other people, and so he had some special insights into the meaning of life. That would have put him on the same level as other rabbis and relieved the tension.

But Jesus doesn't do that. In fact, he amplifies and reiterates his claim to be one with the Father. Jesus is God made man. He is the one true God come to dwell among his people to save and instruct them, to give them life. Jesus is God, and he will exercise the divine prerogative of judging men and awarding eternal life or condemning to eternal death. This is his mission. The Word of God became incarnate in order to redeem sinners and bring them eternal life. And since there is only one God, anyone who believes in the true God will also believe in Jesus, because he and the Father are one.

The Lord is so much more than a great philosopher, a mighty king, or a flashy leader. Jesus, the same Jesus who comes to us each day in Holy Communion, who forgives our sins through the priest in the confessional, and who waits patiently for us in the Tabernacle – this same Jesus is God, creator of all things, redeemer of all people, omniscient, omnipotent, all-loving, all-good. It is too much for us to understand. He knows that. And so he gives us once again the clue to living in accordance with these overwhelming truths. "My aim is to do not my own will, but the will of him who sent me," he explains. If the Father's will was the Lord's rule of life, the same should be true of his faithful subjects.

CHRIST THE TEACHER The eternal life that Jesus came to win for us doesn't begin in heaven; it begins on earth. Life in Christ is life in communion with

God, and life in communion with God is what we were made for. It's where our happiness and fulfillment lie. It begins in this life and continues for all eternity, as we profess every Sunday: "We look for the resurrection of the dead and the life of the world to come."

Through the centuries, Christians have clashed over how this life is to be obtained. Some have claimed that faith alone brings the soul into friendship with Christ; others have claimed that good deeds will do it. But the Church's teaching has always been clear: friendship with Christ and the eternal life that comes with it requires both faith and good works. In fact, although we can distinguish conceptually these two sides of the Christian life, in the reality of daily living there simply is no separation between them. This is because the human person is a unity of spirit and matter. Consequently, whatever one truly believes and commits to (in one's mind and will) necessarily manifests in actions. What we care about automatically affects the choices we make and the actions we perform. This is why Jesus can say in the same discourse, "Whoever listens to my words, and believes in the one who sent me, has eternal life," and then a few lines later, "Those who did good will rise again to life; and those who did evil, to condemnation."

Only by God's grace can we receive eternal life. But God's grace comes only to those who believe in Jesus. And to believe in Jesus is to live as Jesus would have us live. The life he gives us renews the whole person – mind, heart, and behavior. This fundamental truth explains why so many people who would like to believe in Christ can't seem to make the act of faith. They know instinctively that to say to Christ, "I believe in you" means saying at the same time, "I will follow you." But if they follow Christ, they have to leave their selfish ways behind. Here is the core of the spiritual battle. Only when a person comes to see that friendship with Christ offers more fulfillment than an atomized, self-centered existence will they be able to believe and follow the Lord.

CHRIST THE FRIEND Jesus only wants one thing – for us to have life. Death was the consequence of original sin and continues to be the consequence of all sins. Spiritual death ensues from sin, because sin is rebellion against God, a willful separation of oneself from communion, from friendship with God. But since God alone is the source of all life, separation from him means separation from life, from the fullness of that meaningful and fruitful life that he created us to experience. And if friendship with God is not reestablished while one's earthly, biological life lasts, the separation from God will endure in an eternal "condemnation." But those who believe and trust in Jesus regain communion and friendship with God, and so they can be reborn to a meaningful and fruitful life here on earth. And if they stay faithful to their friendship with God until the end of their earthly sojourn, they will "rise again to life" at the end of history, and they will enjoy that friendship for all eternity.

Jesus: When I look at you and think of you, which I am always doing, I picture you living the life I created you to live. I know that now you still struggle and suffer, but this is only a passing stage. You are still recovering from sin. You are still in rehabilitation, and that always hurts. Keep going. Keep seeking my will. Keep getting up every time you fall. I am right at your side. I am leading you to a life that will fill you with more joy and wisdom and love than you can possibly imagine. I am the life, and I want you to spend forever with me.

CHRIST IN MY LIFE When I try to understand you, Lord, I am blinded by the immensity of your mystery. And yet I know that you came to earth and walked among men and that you continue to stay with me now in your Church and through your sacraments, precisely because you didn't want to keep your distance. You want me to know you. Little by little, Lord, reveal yourself to me. Open my eyes; I want to see your glory…

I know that you want to give me eternal life. You want to give me what I yearn for, passionately, in the very core of my being. You created me for that. But you can only give it to me if I am willing to follow you, if I am willing to seek and fulfill your will, no matter what. I want to, Lord. I want to spend my days doing good for those around me, just as you did, helping others to find life in you, now and for all eternity…

Thank you for becoming my Savior. Thank you for renewing my life. Sometimes I forget that I need you. But right now, I know that without your grace my life would have no meaning, like a lamp that's unplugged. Jesus, fill me with your life and make me a channel through which your life can flow into others and renew them too. Nothing matters more. Come, Lord Jesus, be my Savior…

QUESTIONS FOR SMALL GROUP DISCUSSION

1. What struck you most in this passage? What did you notice that you hadn't noticed before?

2. Why do you think Jesus so emphasizes his union with the Father in this discourse?

3. How would you explain to an inquiring, non-believing acquaintance the relationship between faith and good deeds in the pursuit of salvation? How would you explain the Christian idea of "eternal life"?

4. Some people criticize Christians for being too focused on the afterlife. How would you respond to such a criticism?

Cf. Catechism of the Catholic Church, 1811 on how to persevere in friendship with Christ; 1739-1742 on the relationship between grace and freedom; 1021-1022 on judgment and reward according to faith and works; 1038-1041 on the last judgment; 2006-2011 on the relationship between salvation, merit, and good deeds

254. EASY TO PLEASE (JN 5:31-47)

"… This love for Christ must ever be the chiefest and most agreeable result of a knowledge of Holy Scripture."

- Pope Benedict XV

John 5:31-47

'Were I to testify on my own behalf, my testimony would not be valid; but there is another witness who can speak on my behalf, and I know that his testimony is valid. You sent messengers to John, and he gave his testimony to the truth: not that I depend on human testimony; no, it is for your salvation that I speak of this. John was a lamp alight and shining and for a time you were content to enjoy the light that he gave. But my testimony is greater than John's: the works my Father has given me to carry out, these same works of mine testify that the Father has sent me. Besides, the Father who sent me bears witness to me himself. You have never heard his voice, you have never seen his shape, and his word finds no home in you because you do not believe in the one he has sent. You study the scriptures, believing that in them you have eternal life; now these same scriptures testify to me, and yet you refuse to come to me for life! As for human approval, this means nothing to me. Besides, I know you too well: you have no love of God in you. I have come in the name of my Father and you refuse to accept me; if someone else comes in his own name you will accept him. How can you believe, since you look to one another for approval and are not concerned with the approval that comes from the one God? Do not imagine that I am going to accuse you before the Father: you place your hopes on Moses, and Moses will be your accuser. If you really believed him you would believe me too, since it was I that he was writing about; but if you refuse to believe what he wrote, how can you believe what I say?'

CHRIST THE LORD Jesus makes no effort to overpower his antagonists. He reaches out to them using their own language, their own form of argumentation. The Jewish scribes and Pharisees and other leaders in Jerusalem at that time were scholars. They dedicated themselves to study and memorize the scriptures and the many commentaries and interpretations of them that had accumulated through the centuries. This was an important work for these leaders, because the scriptures were the record of the special revelation that God had given to them and to no other nation. It was a rigorous work, too – copies of the text had to be handwritten; no printing press was around to help supply everyone with personal libraries.

Part of this rabbinic intellectual culture included a legal system in which at least two witnesses were required to affect a verdict, and the accused person was not permitted to witness in his own defense. Jesus graciously admits and accepts these criteria as he defends his own claims to be the divine Messiah. He points to three witnesses that all of his interlocutors should recognize: John the Baptist, whom everyone agreed was a prophet, and who had explicitly declared Christ to be the Messiah; the Father, whose divine power is evident in Christ's miracles; and the Scriptures themselves, which record the revelation that was directed in its every detail towards the coming of Jesus Christ.

Jesus seeks to conquer hearts and minds – to rescue them from the darkness of self-absorption and lead them into the light of truth – but he does so by coming into our lives and speaking our language, reaching out to us in ways we will understand. This has always been, still is, and ever will be the way of the Lord.

CHRIST THE TEACHER Jesus' case is already complete and incontrovertible because of his three witnesses, but he goes even one step further, hoping to win over these reluctant rabbis. He tells them exactly why they find it difficult to accept his message: "…You have no love of God in you… you look to one another for approval and are not concerned with the approval that comes from the one God." The Pharisees and scribes who rejected Jesus did so because they had let themselves be carried away by their own successes. In their zeal for perfection, they had begun to pay too much attention to being more respected and popular than the other guy. This kind of religiosity was attractive to them because it provided a standard of success that was within their own, natural reach: if they only have to be better than their neighbor, they have no need of God's assistance in order to be successful. If they had been seeking the kind of success God wanted, however, they would have had to admit their sins and failings and come to depend on God's help. But depending on God was an uncomfortable thing, because it meant that God would get the glory; it was much more satisfying, in the short term, to achieve success by their own efforts and claim all the glory for themselves.

The Gospel writers spent so much time describing Jesus' clashes with these self-righteous and self-seeking antagonists because the Holy Spirit knows that we are just like them. Why are we not yet the saints that God wants us to be? Why has God's grace not yet yielded the over-abundant harvest of spiritual fruit that he promises us? Because the love of God in our hearts is still not pure, we still seek our satisfaction too much in being thought well of by our neighbors, in beating our competitors, and in achieving great things by our own power. Even in the apostolate, our self-giving and love for the Church is often tainted with a vain thirst for success and a jealous desire to appear more pious than others. Inasmuch as we still seek glory for ourselves, we handcuff the transforming power of God in our lives.

CHRIST THE FRIEND Jesus is a faithful friend. Once again he publicly praises John the Baptist, who had dedicated his life to serving Christ and bearing him witness. Jesus never forgets deeds done to please him and build up his King-dom. He is interested in everything we do, because he loves us more than the most loving parent, more than the most faithful spouse. He appreciates every effort we make in his name, for his sake. How much confidence this should give us! Even if no one ever knows or sees our sacrifices, our small acts of self-denial and self-giving, Jesus is gathering them up like beautiful flowers and enjoying each one of them. Each one weaves the patchwork of our life. How much freedom this truth can give to our souls! We no longer have to scratch and fight our way to the honors platform in order to win prizes that perish and recognition that withers. In Christ, we can flourish without fear.

Christ: My love is enough for you. Live in the light of my love. Live for loving me. Seek my ap-proval in all you do; I am so easy to please, and no whims or selfishness or bad moods cloud my appreciation. I lived and died and rose for you. I want to give you the kind of peace and joy that doesn't wear away. All you need is my love.

CHRIST IN MY LIFE I believe in you, Lord, but I know so many people who don't believe in you. They are still looking for meaning in awards and money and reputation. They are stuck on that thankless merry-go-round. Thank you for taking me off that and putting me on the path of life. Forgive me for my ingratitude, for the times I resent your demands. Make me your disciple, your spokesperson, to bring many others to your friendship…

I know that you are always speaking to me, arranging all the events and en-counters of my day in order to draw me closer to you. You love me that much. I know it, Lord, and yet I am still a bad listener. Teach me to find you, to see you, to hear your voice in all the happenings of my busy life. Teach me to detect your will and do it, gladly, eagerly, simply because I love you…

Sometimes I am afraid that I am not doing enough for you, Lord. But that's because I keep thinking that I need to earn your love the way I have had to earn the love of others. But you are not like that. You already love me, and nothing I do can increase or decrease that love. Cast out my fears and fill me with the courage and energy that comes from knowing I am loved unconditionally and infinitely by you…

QUESTIONS FOR SMALL GROUP DISCUSSION

1. What struck you most in this passage? What did you notice that you hadn't noticed before?

2. The people Jesus was addressing knew the scriptures backwards and forwards, and yet they couldn't recognize that Jesus was the fulfillment of all the prophecies they knew so well. How can we avoid falling into this kind of subjective understanding of God's revelation?

3. Which elements of popular culture encourage us to seek the approval of other people instead of God's approval? How can we avoid this?

4. In what ways have you discovered God coming and speaking to your heart in a language you understand particularly well, just as he came and spoke to the Jewish leaders using arguments that they were experts in?

Cf. Catechism of the Catholic Church, 80-83 on sacred scripture; 84-95 on the proper way to interpret sacred scripture; 101-104 on Christ as the center of sacred scripture; 109-119 on the levels of meaning in sacred scripture and criteria for interpreting it; 2123-2128 on reasons behind disbelief; 1459 on the consequences of sin for our spiritual lives

THE GOSPEL OF JOHN CHAPTER 6

"It was his will that his gifts should remain among us; it was his will that the souls which he had redeemed by his precious blood should continue to be sanctified by sharing the pattern of his own passion. For this reason he appointed his faithful disciples the first priests of his Church and enjoined them never to cease to perform the mysteries of eternal life. These mysteries must be celebrated by every priest in every church in the world until Christ comes again from heaven, so that we priests, together with the congregation of the faithful, may have the example of Christ's passion daily before our eyes, hold it in our hands, and even receive it in our mouths and in our hearts and so keep undimmed the memory of our redemption."

- St Gaudentius of Brescia

255. FEEDING THE HUNGRY (JN 6:1-15)

"This is the food which sustains and nourishes us on our journey through life, until we depart from this world and are united with Christ."

- St Gaudentius of Brescia

John 6:1-15

Some time after this, Jesus went off to the other side of the Sea of Galilee – or of Tiberias – and a large crowd followed him, impressed by the signs he gave by curing the sick. Jesus climbed the hillside, and sat down there with his disciples. It was shortly before the Jewish feast of Passover. Looking up, Jesus saw the crowds approaching and said to Philip, 'Where can we buy some bread for these people to eat?' He only said this to test Philip; he himself knew exactly what he was going to do. Philip answered, 'Two hundred denarii would only buy enough to give them a small piece each'. One of his disciples, Andrew, Simon Peter's brother, said, 'There is a small boy here with five barley loaves and two fish; but what is that between so many?' Jesus said to them, 'Make the people sit down.' There was plenty of grass there, and as many as five thousand men sat down. Then Jesus took the loaves, gave thanks, and gave them out to all who were sitting ready; he then did the same with the fish, giving out as much as was wanted. When they had eaten enough he said to the disciples, 'Pick up the pieces left over, so that nothing gets wasted.' So they picked them up, and filled twelve hampers with scraps left over from the meal of five barley loaves. The people, seeing this sign that he had given, said, 'This really is the prophet who is to come into the world.' Jesus, who could see they were about to come and take him by force and make him king, escaped back to the hills by himself.

CHRIST THE LORD Before dying, Moses promised that some day God would send another leader to the people of Israel, someone as great as himself, who had been the greatest and humblest of God's servants. This figure was referred to as "the prophet": "I will raise up a prophet like yourself for them from their own brothers; I will put my words into his mouth and he shall tell them all I command him. The man who does not listen to my words that he speaks in my name, shall be held answerable to me for it" (Deuteronomy 18:18-19). Through the centuries, the Jewish people had come to identify this figure with the promised Messiah, the one who would liberate their nation from oppression and usher in a new golden age, similar to the one they had enjoyed under King David.

The magnitude of the miracle Jesus performs by multiplying the loaves and fishes, added to the many other miracles that he had already done, convinces the crowds that he is indeed the promised Savior, the one whom God had sent into the world to finish the job of salvation that had begun with Moses and the Exodus. They recognized him, but they did not listen to him. He showed by his miracles that he was God's chosen one, but with his words he spoke of a new kind of Kingdom, an everlasting Kingdom that was within men's hearts, not in political platforms. The crowds refused to understand this, and so Christ refused to let them make him their King.

CHRIST THE TEACHER Five loaves and two fish cannot feed a crowd of five thousand men (plus at least as many women and children). It is impossible. Not even a year's salary (the equivalent of two hundred denarii) could buy enough for such a feast, as Philip nervously points out. And yet, when the Apostles hand over their paltry resources to the Lord, they become more than enough to do the job.

The same goes for every Christian apostle. Whose natural talents and wisdom are sufficient to defeat the forces of evil that hold the world in tow? Whose innate strength is sufficient to put an end to the selfishness, lust, and greed that rage within the human heart? How can the meager resources of a single parish or diocese suffice to do battle with media moguls, corrupt politicians, international banking cartels, and other agents of the culture of death? We only have five loaves and two fish; by ourselves we can do nothing. Only if we put all we have into Christ's hands, trusting in him and not ourselves, can we hope to make a real difference for the good of the Kingdom – in our hearts and in society at large. Every small act of charity adds to the Church's much-needed reservoir of grace and strength. What we could never achieve on our own, we can immeasurably surpass with God. As Jesus himself put it, "For God everything is possible" (Mt 19:26).

CHRIST THE FRIEND Friends look out for each other. "Looking up," Jesus saw that the crowd following him didn't have any food; that he remedied the situation demonstrates his desire for our friendship. He wants to be our partner in life, our companion; our confidant. He is looking out for us, always keeping his eyes open for an opportunity to feed our hungry hearts with his beauty and truth. He wants to supply for our needs; it is his greatest joy. As he puts it later in this same Gospel, "I have come so that they may have life, and have it to the full." Those are the words of a friend we can count on.

Philip: How could I ever forget that day? None of us wanted to bother with the needs of that huge crowd of people. We were exhausted and just wanted to get away and relax. I was especially exhausted. Maybe that's why he teased me a bit and tested me with the question about where we could buy some bread for that huge mass of hungry people; he knew I would be exasperated. But our tiredness didn't impede us from learning the lesson he wanted to teach. In fact, it helped. He wanted us to learn what love is. He looked out at those people, who had sacrificed their own comfort in order to come and be with him, and he saw how hungry they were. He couldn't hold back his yearning to feed them. He was always like that. He was always looking for ways to fill our starving minds and hearts with his abundant truth and wisdom. He was totally for us. Actually, most of the time I felt as if he was totally for me. He knew me so well; he always knew exactly what I needed, and he always took the first step to give it to me.

CHRIST IN MY LIFE I know that you are most interested in what happens inside me, in my heart and in my mind. You care about what I think about, pay attention to, and decide to do. You want to be King of my heart, because you know exactly what my heart needs in order to experience the satisfaction and meaning that it longs for. Lord Jesus, Savior of all people, make your Kingdom come in my mind and heart...

So often I let myself be carried away by nervousness, stress, worry, and fear. How I need you to increase my faith, Lord! You are God; you are omnipotent! All I need to do each day is put my five loaves and two fish into your wise and powerful hands, and you will make my life a fountain of light and hope and goodness. Teach me to trust in you, to rejoice in you, to fear only whatever could separate me from you...

Your heart never tires of giving. You are a furnace of love that never grows cold. When you look at me, you think only of all that you want to do for me. Why am I not more like you, Lord? What is keeping me from loving others with that kind of energy, constancy, and creativity? I give you my meager five loaves and two fish. Lord Jesus, show me how to follow you more closely, teach me to love as you love, giving myself to others as you give yourself to me...

QUESTIONS FOR SMALL GROUP DISCUSSION

1. What struck you most in this passage? What did you notice that you hadn't noticed before?
2. What are the differences between the benefits that we could expect from a prosperous worldly kingdom and the benefits we should hope for from God's Kingdom?
3. In what ways are we often tempted to hoard our few loaves, instead of giving them to Christ so he can multiply them?
4. How can we tell if we are really counting on Christ to give our lives meaning – as he wants us to – instead of depending on our own efforts?

Cf. Catechism of the Catholic Church, 27-30 on God as the only source of true happiness; 430-440 on Christ as the fulfillment of God's plan of salvation, begun in the Old Testament; 2816-2821 on the meaning of the "Kingdom"

256. WORKING FOR BREAD THAT LASTS (JN 6:16-35)

"... In the same way we call Christ our bread, because he is the food of those who are members of his body."

- St Cyprian

John 6:16-35

That evening the disciples went down to the shore of the lake and got into a boat to make for Capernaum on the other side of the lake. It was getting dark by now and Jesus had still not rejoined them. The wind was strong, and the sea was getting rough. They had rowed three or four miles when they saw Jesus walking on the lake and coming towards the boat. This frightened them, but he said, 'It is I. Do not be afraid.' They were for taking him into the boat, but in no time it reached the shore at the place they were making for.

Next day, the crowd that had stayed on the other side saw that only one boat had been there, and that Jesus had not got into the boat with his disciples, but that the disciples had set off by themselves. Other boats, however, had put in from Tiberias, near the place where the bread had been eaten. When the people saw that neither Jesus nor his disciples were there, they got into those boats and crossed to Capernaum to look for Jesus. When they found him on the other side, they said to him, 'Rabbi, when did you come here?' Jesus answered: 'I tell you most solemnly, you are not looking for me because you have seen the signs but because you had all the bread you wanted to eat. Do not work for food that cannot last, but work for food that endures to eternal life, the kind of food the Son of Man is offering you, for on him the Father, God himself, has set his seal.' Then they said to him, 'What must we do if we are to do the works that God wants?' Jesus gave them this answer, 'This is working for God: you must believe in the one he has sent.' So they said, 'What sign will you give to show us that we should believe in you? What work will you do? Our fathers had manna to eat in the desert; as scripture says: He gave them bread from heaven to eat.' Jesus answered: 'I tell you most solemnly, it was not Moses who gave you bread from heaven, it is my Father who gives you the bread from heaven, the true bread; for the bread of God is that which comes down from heaven and gives life to the world'. 'Sir,' they said 'give us that bread always.' Jesus answered: 'I am the bread of life. He who comes to me will never be hungry; he who believes in me will never thirst.'

CHRIST THE LORD Jesus is not flattered by the adulation of the crowds. He is acutely aware that his mission is not to bring people a paradise on earth (which is what they want – "You are… looking for me… because you had all the bread you wanted to eat"), but to bring them "bread from heaven," the truth and freedom of living in communion with God. He will not accept their allegiance unless they accept his message; he will not compromise his undertaking to enjoy an ego trip. Christ is a Leader entirely focused on his mission, not on himself. If we are to be faithful to him, we need to follow in those footsteps.

CHRIST THE TEACHER The Jewish rabbis had long predicted that the Prophet who would come to carry on Moses' work of salvation would prove himself through a miracle similar to that of the manna, the bread which God miraculously sent his people each morning during their forty years of wandering through the desert – bread "from heaven" as they called it, meaning from the sky. Such a sign is what the people are asking for here. Christ responds by explaining that the miraculous bread they are talking about – the promised Messianic sign – is much more than an abundance of bread that will feed the body; it is bread that actually comes from heaven (not just from the sky) and imbues the world with divine life. The people's eager response, "Give us that bread always," shows that they have understood the elevated nature of this new manna, and they desire it.

Through that conversation, and through the miracle of the multiplication of loaves that took place the previous day, Jesus has prepared them for this crucial moment, the first announcement of the Sacrament of the Eucharist, the living sacrifice of and communion with Christ's own body and blood which will inundate the world with his very life. He had been looking forward to telling them. Now the time had come. We can imagine the moment in which he speaks the next phrase, how he paused to search their faces, looking into their eyes, hoping that they would respond with faith and trust, but knowing that many of them would not. Finally, as they gaze on him with keen anticipation, he speaks: "I am the bread of life. He who comes to me will never be hungry; he who believes in me will never thirst." He spoke those tremendous, mysterious words and then stood looking intently into their faces, eagerly hoping for a trusting response of childlike faith. What went through their minds? What goes through our minds?

CHRIST THE FRIEND Jesus knows the deepest yearnings of our hearts; he knows what we hunger for, what we thirst for: happiness, meaning, and fulfillment. He knows it, because he made us to desire lasting joy and satisfaction. When we achieve that, we are achieving the purpose for which he created us. But he also knows that we cannot do it alone. Ever since original sin separated us from friendship with God, our most fundamental desire has been frustrated. That's why he came to earth; that's why he established his Church; that's why he constantly embraces us through the sacraments, especially the Eucharist. In Christ, the human heart feasts on the abundance of life for which it was made; without Christ, it slowly starves.

Jesus: Your heart is restless, I know. That's good. You want more out of your life; I do too. I am what you're looking for. Know me better; listen to me; trust me more. Why do you keep trying to be a saint on your own? Your efforts can do nothing alone. I am not asking you to go off and become perfect and then come back to me so I can let you into my Kingdom. My Kingdom is not something you get into by submitting a résumé, as if you were applying for a job. My Kingdom is my family. You don't have to earn my love; I love you already. You only have to trust me, lean on me, and follow me. Why else would I give my own life to be your food? Be at peace. I am with you.

CHRIST IN MY LIFE Thank you for caring more about my salvation than your reputation, Lord. Thank you for staying faithful to your mission. Thank you for refusing to flatter the crowds and insisting on teaching the truth. O Lord, you have made me your ambassador, so give me that same burning desire to build your Kingdom. Cleanse my desires, purify my heart, and teach me to seek your will above all things...

I believe that you are truly present in the Eucharist. I believe that you want to give me your own life, to enable me to share in your divine nature, to bring me into your family. I want to eat this bread, Lord. I want to eat it worthily, to receive you with faith, hope, and love, not just out of routine, not just because everyone else does it. O Lord, stir up in my mind a deep awareness of your gift in the Eucharist...

Okay, Lord, I admit it once again: I cannot follow you by relying only on my own strength. I need your grace. You want it that way. You created me to need you, so that I would be drawn by my own inner yearnings to live in a communion of knowledge and love with you. Be my strength, Lord; be my light, my food, my joy, my all...

QUESTIONS FOR SMALL GROUP DISCUSSION

1. What struck you most in this passage? What did you notice that you hadn't noticed before?

2. Where do you think Christ gets the strength to stay "on task" (i.e., doing his Father's will) even when it means giving up his popularity among the crowds?

3. How can we appreciate more Christ's great gift of the Eucharist, both individually and as a community?

4. If Jesus Christ really is the bread of life, we who know this should be eager to take advantage of every opportunity to bring others closer to him. In what ways should this eagerness manifest itself? What opportunities do we tend to squander?

Cf. Catechism of the Catholic Church, 1382-1405 on the benefits of devotion to the Eucharist; 1333-1338 on the meaning of "bread" in the Eucharist, and the Catholic interpretation of John 6

257. BELIEVING OR COMPLAINING (JN 6:36-51)

"He gave himself to be our food; unhappy is the one who is unaware of so great a gift."

- St Cajetan

John 6:36-51

'But, as I have told you, you can see me and still you do not believe. All that the Father gives me will come to me, and whoever comes to me I shall not turn him away; because I have come from heaven, not to do my own will, but to do the will of the one who sent me. Now the will of him who sent me is that I should lose nothing of all that he has given to me, and that I should raise it up on the last day. Yes, it is my Father's will that whoever sees the Son and believes in him shall have eternal life, and that I shall raise him up on the last day.' Meanwhile the Jews were complaining to each other about him, because he had said, 'I am the bread that came down from heaven'. 'Surely this is Jesus son of Joseph' they said. 'We know his father and mother. How can he now say, I have come down from heaven?' Jesus said in reply, 'Stop complaining to each other. No one can come to me unless he is drawn by the Father who sent me, and I will raise him up at the last day. It is written in the prophets: They will all be taught by God, and to hear the teaching of the Father, and learn from it, is to come to me. Not that anybody has seen the Father, except the one who comes from God: he has seen the Father. I tell you most solemnly, everybody who believes has eternal life. I am the bread of life. Your fathers ate the manna in the desert and they are dead; but this is the bread that comes down from heaven, so that a man may eat it and not die. I am the living bread which has come down from heaven. Anyone who eats this bread will live for ever; and the bread that I shall give is my flesh, for the life of the world.'

CHRIST THE LORD   Jesus is no ordinary leader. He is not even the greatest king among all kings. He is absolutely unique. When he speaks of God, he speaks of "my Father," whom he alone has "seen," who sent him, whose will Jesus fulfills perfectly. To hear Christ, to know him, and to follow him means to hear, know, and follow God himself. That is why "whoever believes" in him "has eternal life." To believe in Christ is to give one's life to him, to entrust oneself to his care – and when we do that, he faithfully leads us to his Father's house.

Through the centuries, many have continued to "complain" about Jesus, contending that he is only a man, only a great teacher, or only a great religious leader: "We know his father and mother...." Only when we allow ourselves to be drawn by the love of God, when we give in to God as he tugs at our hearts ("No one can come to me unless he is drawn by the Father"), only then can we see beyond the confines of our limited understanding; only then does Jesus of Nazareth become for us Jesus the Christ, Christ the Lord.

CHRIST THE TEACHER Christ packs three momentous lessons into this discourse. First, he points out the mystery of faith, that no one can believe in him "unless he is drawn by the Father." Faith in Jesus Christ supplies us with life's only dependable fuel, and yet, faith in Christ is God's gift. For this reason, we need to pray ceaselessly for an increase of faith, both for ourselves and for those who have yet to believe.

Second, faith in Christ leads to "eternal life." Later in the Gospel, Jesus tells us that eternal life consists in knowing "you, the only true God, and Jesus Christ whom you have sent" (John 17:3). In Biblical language, "knowing" implies deep interpersonal intimacy, the kind of relationship that we all yearn for. That we can have this with God himself, who is more lovable, more beautiful than any other person is or ever could be, is the Good News of Jesus Christ.

Third, Jesus himself is the "bread" of this eternal life, its source and sustenance. Without bread, without food, physical life perishes; without Jesus, without his "flesh for the life of the world" in the Eucharist, our life of intimate communion with God will perish. It's that simple – and it's that crucial. Eleven times in this discourse Jesus speaks of himself as the bread of life; you'd think we would get the message. But if someone were to measure our real devotion to the Eucharist – our active and prayerful involvement in Mass, our recollection in receiving Communion, the frequency and sincerity of our visits to the Tabernacle – would they conclude that this Sacrament is, in actual fact, our bread of life?

CHRIST THE FRIEND Those who believe in Jesus will have "eternal life"; they will "not die" but "will live forever"; those who come to him will be "raised on the last day." How odd for Jesus to be thinking of that even before he himself has been raised! And yet, it is why he came; it is the goal of all his sufferings and efforts. He wants to bring each of us into the everlasting Kingdom of light and joy, and he never lets that goal drift into the background. Friendship with Christ is not a temporary fix, a psychological gimmick to make our little trip through life a bit livelier. When Jesus Christ extends his hand in friendship (which he never stops doing), he means to walk with us in time and in eternity – if we're willing.

Jesus: So many people still think of me as a harsh taskmaster. They think of Christianity as a list of dos and don'ts (mostly don'ts). But my desire, the Father's desire, is to give everyone the fullness of life that they yearn for. Everything I taught and did, everything my Church teaches and does, is directed to that goal. You know this. You believe it. Let my love seep more and more into your heart; let the hope I bring overflow in the enthusiasm of your glance and the simple joy of your smile. You know the truth about what is in store for those who believe in me. Always remember it and think about it. When sadness or discouragement creeps up on you, turn back to me and my promises, and I will renew your peace, your joy, your confidence, and your enthusiasm.

CHRIST IN MY LIFE I don't want to complain anymore, Lord. I want to listen to you, to believe in you, to let myself be drawn to you. O Lord, I feel so contradictory! My selfishness, my resistance to believing without understanding completely, my tendency to make everything and everyone bow down to my own standards and ideas – all of this holds me back. Free me from myself, Lord; teach me to do your will...

I don't know how I'm supposed to remember all that you have taught me, Lord. The supply of your wisdom is too deep and too rich for me to keep it all in my mind. And yet, I want to live wholly engaged by your gospel, wholly enthralled by your message. Take my life in your hands, Lord. Guide my thoughts, desires, and decisions, so that I live entirely docile to your inspirations and your will...

You keep talking about raising up on the last day those who believe in you. It was on your mind. Why is it not more on my mind? Increase my faith, Lord. Teach me to see the world as you see it, to want the true and lasting good of my neighbor (and my family, and my colleagues) as much as you do. With the burning love of your heart, inflame my heart...

QUESTIONS FOR SMALL GROUP DISCUSSION

1. What struck you most in this passage? What did you notice that you hadn't noticed before?

2. Why do you think so many people consider Jesus Christ to be just one more great (or not so great) historical personage, when the Gospels make it so clear that he claimed to be the one and only Son of God and Messiah?

3. What evidence is there in our daily lives that we conceive of the Eucharist as necessary food for our spiritual life, as Christ conceives of it? What evidence should there be?

4. How would you describe your relationship with Christ? Is it more like an antidote to personal problems, or is it an adventure of friendship, one of mutual self-revelation and discovery?

Cf. Catechism of the Catholic Church, 55, 161-165 on faith and eternal life; 166-175 on the nature of faith; 1337-1344 on the institution of the Eucharist

258. EATING RIGHT (JN 6:52-59)

"This sacrament is operative to produce both love and union with Christ. The greatest showing of love is to give oneself as food."

- St Albert the Great

John 6:52-59

Then the Jews started arguing with one another: 'How can this man give us his flesh to eat?' they said. Jesus replied: 'I tell you most solemnly, if you do not eat the flesh of the Son of Man and drink his blood, you will not have life in you. Anyone who does eat my flesh and drink my blood has eternal life, and I shall raise him up on the last day. For my flesh is real food and my blood is real drink. He who eats my flesh and drinks my blood lives in me and I live in him. As I, who am sent by the living Father, myself draw life from the Father, so whoever eats me will draw life from me. This is the bread come down from heaven; not like the bread our ancestors ate: they are dead, but anyone who eats this bread will live for ever.' He taught this doctrine at Capernaum, in the synagogue.

CHRIST THE LORD History is replete with kings and emperors who put up with no opposition. If the subjects of Ivan the Terrible had ever been caught "arguing with one another" about the veracity or wisdom of one of his declarations, they would have met with a quick and speedy death. But Jesus leaves each one free to accept or reject him, to trust him or abandon him. Our Lord is all-powerful, but he refuses to abuse his power; he called the Jews to believe in him and follow him – just as he calls each one of us – but he never forces us. His is a Kingdom of justice, but also one of love.

Jesus describes himself as being sent from the Father, as sharing the very life of Father. Christ is a man, and he is God. These are remarkable claims. But they don't stop there. He claims that he will give his own flesh as our food, so that we might enter into that divine life as well. We will remain men and women, but we will have the life of God within us. Jesus claims a Lordship unlike any ever claimed before or since. He is Master both of earth and of heaven; he is the Lord of both human and divine life. No wonder his claims caused his listeners to argue amongst themselves; it is no ordinary thing to believe in such a Lord.

CHRIST THE TEACHER Great teachers know that "repetition is the mother of learning," as the old saying goes. If they deem a certain lesson more important than others, they will repeat it over and over again, in different ways perhaps, until the students pick it up. In this discourse, responding to his audience's understandable difficulty in grasping how it will be possible for all of them to "eat his flesh," Jesus clarifies what he means.

This was the perfect opportunity for Christ to say, "Wait a minute, what I really meant was that my body and blood will just be symbolized by bread and wine. Of course I didn't mean that bread and wine really would become my body and blood. Don't be foolish!" The strange thing is he doesn't say that. He does not water down his claim, as if eating his flesh were just a metaphor for believing in his doctrine; on the contrary, he reiterates the importance of really eating his flesh and drinking his blood. Seven times throughout his speech he repeats that his flesh is to be eaten and his blood to be drunk by those who wish to have eternal life. *Seven times.* None of his listeners concluded that he was speaking with poetic imagery; they all understood him to mean what he said. Many of them did not accept it, and they abandoned him. Those who stayed were rewarded much later, when at the Last Supper Jesus showed how this strange saying was to play out: through the Sacrament of the Eucharist – his flesh made into our food, his blood made into our drink, so as to flood this dying world with the eternal life of God.

CHRIST THE FRIEND Love gives itself; it shares itself completely. Christ loves to the extreme: he gives us his own life. He shares with us his own divine existence – "Whoever eats me will draw life from me." This is the meaning of the Eucharist, which the Church calls the "source and summit" of Christian life. It is the sacrament of love par excellence, because there Love makes himself available 24/7. We will never be able to comprehend exactly how it happens, but we know that it does happen, and we know why: so that we will "live forever." In the face of such love, the only appropriate response is to humbly accept this precious gift, relish it, and give our own love in return.

Jesus: When your friends go away, you often give them a gift or a keepsake to remember you by; when I returned to heaven, I left you my very self to remember me by. When you are separated from friends for extended periods, you occasionally make yourself present to them through letters and calls and e-mails; while I am reigning in heaven, I stay with you all the time in the Tabernacle. You may think that my love is kind of generic, because the Eucharist is so simple and ordinary, and because everyone gets the same kind of host. But that's not how it is at all. I am fully present in every host. And each one of you receives me personally from the hands of the priest – one-on-one. And don't forget that I am God, so nothing limits my love – not time, not space, not tiredness, not bad moods, nothing: I love you as if you alone were loveable. When I come to you in Holy Communion, and when I wait for you in the Tabernacle, all my thought and all my desire is focused on you. I know it's hard for you to understand this, but it's true. Think about me waiting for you there in the Tabernacle, interceding for you, offering myself for you at every moment... for you. You never have to doubt my love again.

CHRIST IN MY LIFE Thank you for creating me free and respecting my freedom. Because you made me free, I can love, and in loving, I come to resemble you and enter into your friendship. O Lord, purify my heart. Help me to choose more often, more definitively, and more passionately to give myself to those you have put under my care. I want to love with all the force of my freedom, just as you do...

Bread is such a simple food, Lord. It's so normal, so basic. And that's how you come to me. O Lord, open my eyes so that I will see you as you truly are in this mysterious sacrament. And open my eyes so that I will see you as you truly are, present and active in the normal, basic activities and events of my life. You came to walk with me and accompany me through life. I don't want to walk alone anymore...

I want to be like the Eucharist. I want my life to nourish the hearts and souls of those around me. I want to pour out all my energy, all my talent, and all my love for the sake of your Kingdom, bringing others closer to you and closer to the happiness you created them to enjoy. How can I give myself more? How can I be more like you? Teach me to do your will, Lord, and to seek first your Kingdom...

QUESTIONS FOR SMALL GROUP DISCUSSION

1. What struck you most in this passage? What did you notice that you hadn't noticed before?

2. Why do you think so many of his listeners don't accept Christ at his word? How do you think Christ reacts when we take time to visit him in the Eucharist, to go there and thank him – to pour out our troubles to him and ask for his help?

3. If Christ himself, his entire being and life, is truly present in the Eucharist and reserved in the Tabernacles of all our Catholic Churches, why do you think so few people spend significant time with him there?

4. If an unbelieving but inquiring acquaintance asked you about the difference between receiving communion in the Catholic Church and receiving it in other Christian churches, what would you tell them?

Cf. Catechism of the Catholic Church, 1324-1327 on the Eucharist as the source and summit of ecclesial life; 1373-1381 on the real presence of Christ in the Eucharist; 1382-1401 on the nature and benefits of Holy Communion; 1345-1390 on the Mass

259. FREE TO STAY OR GO (JN 6:60-71)

"Do not, my child, approach Jesus Christ with the hope of bending his will to yours: what I desire is that you yield yourself to him and that he receive you, so that he, your Savior, may do with you and in you whatever he pleases."

- St Cajetan

John 6:60-71

After hearing it, many of his followers said, 'This is intolerable language. How could anyone accept it?' Jesus was aware that his followers were complaining about it and said, 'Does this upset you? What if you should see the Son of Man ascend to where he was before? It is the spirit that gives life, the flesh has nothing to offer. The words I have spoken to you are spirit and they are life. But there are some of you who do not believe.' For Jesus knew from the outset those who did not believe, and who it was that would betray him. He went on, 'This is why I told you that no one could come to me unless the Father allows him.' After this, many of his disciples left him and stopped going with him. Then Jesus said to the Twelve, 'What about you, do you want to go away too?' Simon Peter answered, 'Lord, who shall we go to? You have the message of eternal life, and we believe; we know that you are the Holy One of God.' Jesus replied, 'Have I not chosen you, you Twelve? Yet one of you is a devil.' He meant Judas son of Simon Iscariot, since this was the man, one of the Twelve, who was going to betray him.

CHRIST THE LORD Why do many disciples leave Christ, while the Twelve stay with him? The question touches one of the great mysteries of our faith: human freedom. Somehow, in the depths of the human heart, God leaves us free to accept or reject the gift of faith. It always begins with God ("no one could come to me unless the Father allows him"), but the choice to stay or "leave" remains with each individual: "Do you want to go away too?" Jesus Christ is the Lord of life and history, but he refuses to impose his rule on hearts that want to "stop going with him" and return to their former way of life. God has given us the gift of life, but he leaves us free to administer it as we wish. In the Kingdom of Christ, there are no misanthropes.

CHRIST THE TEACHER For the Christian, difficulties are opportunities. In the face of this "intolerable language," Christ turns to his closest followers and invites them to make an explicit act of faith, to believe in him not because it makes perfect sense to do so, but simply because of who he is. He elicits their trust by assuring them that his words are "spirit and life," but not by removing all obstacles from their understanding. (By saying, "It is the spirit which gives life, not the flesh," he is not reneging on his assertion that his flesh is real food, just explaining how it can be living food.) For those who reassert their faith in him, trusting in him more than in their own understanding, this crisis becomes a milestone. Likewise, when we face moments of crisis, when the demands of faith outstrip the powers of understanding, we can either lean on ourselves and fall, or lean harder than ever on Christ and rise to the heights of love.

CHRIST THE FRIEND Try to imagine how Jesus spoke the words, "Do you want to go away too?" Try to picture his expression as he looked into the faces of his chosen Twelve. He cared deeply about them; he had handpicked them to be his closest companions. He had given them his heart, and now, as other followers gave up on him, he looked to them with a tinge of sadness, perhaps even with apprehension. Would they too abandon him? How near God draws to us in Jesus Christ! He humbles himself – he makes himself weak, almost powerless, in the face of our freedom. He doesn't want mindless robots or heartless slaves; he wants friends, forever.

CHRIST IN MY LIFE You know that I don't understand everything you ask of me – I don't understand the half of it, I am afraid. But you also know that I trust in you. You have the words of eternal life, and no one else does. I know I don't. I am counting on you, Lord, on your example and your teaching. I want to be like you and follow you in all of my relationships and responsibilities. Never let me be separated from you...

Many people react to your Church's teaching just the way these listeners did that day in Capernaum – since it makes them uncomfortable and it doesn't fit into their expectations, they reject it. I am tempted to do the same thing sometimes; the vocation you have given me isn't easy or smooth; I often get flustered. But I know that you love me, and I never want to go back to living with you just on the sidelines...

You can count on me, Lord. I don't promise that I will never fall or fail, because I know that I am weak and full of selfishness. But I promise that I will always turn to you for help, take your hand, and get up again. It's so simple, really. Only you have the words of eternal life. So what else is there for me to do except listen to you, follow you, and do whatever you ask of me? Teach me to do your will...

QUESTIONS FOR SMALL GROUP DISCUSSION

1. What struck you most in this passage? What did you notice that you hadn't noticed before?

2. How can we become more aware of our gift of freedom and use it more responsibly?

859

3. Why do you think Jesus chose to leave us his body and blood under the form of bread and wine?

4. It wounds Christ's heart when people reject him. By exercising our faith, especially in a solid and deep Eucharistic devotion, we can, in a sense, make up for those rejections. In what specific ways can we thus console the heart of Christ in our present circumstances?

Cf. Catechism of the Catholic Church, 396, 1738-1742 on the reality and mystery of human freedom; 153-165 on the importance and nature of faith

THE GOSPEL OF JOHN CHAPTER 7

"Happy the soul to whom it is given to attain this life with Christ, to cleave with all one's heart to him whose beauty all the heavenly hosts behold forever; whose love inflames our love; whose contemplation is our refreshment; whose graciousness is our delight; whose gentleness fills us to overflowing; whose remembrance gives sweet light; whose fragrance revives the dead; whose glorious vision will be the happiness of all the citizens of that heavenly Jerusalem. For he is the brightness of the eternal glory, the splendor of eternal light, the mirror without spot."

- St Clare of Assisi

260. FOCUSING ON THE MISSION (JN 7:1-19)

"What food, what honey could be sweeter than to learn of God's providence, to enter into his shrine and look into the mind of the creator, to listen to the Lord's words at which the wise of this world laugh, but which really are full of spiritual teaching?"

- St Jerome

John 7:1-19

After this Jesus stayed in Galilee; he could not stay in Judaea, because the Jews were out to kill him. As the Jewish feast of Tabernacles drew near, his brothers said to him, 'Why not leave this place and go to Judaea, and let your disciples see the works you are doing; if a man wants to be known he does not do things in secret; since you are doing all this, you should let the whole world see.' Not even his brothers, in fact, had faith in him. Jesus answered, 'The right time for me has not come yet, but any time is the right time for you. The world cannot hate you, but it does hate me, because I give evidence that its ways are evil. Go up to the festival yourselves: I am not going to this festival, because for me the time is not ripe yet.' Having said that, he stayed behind in Galilee. However, after his brothers had left for the festival, he went up as well, but quite privately, without drawing attention to himself. At the festival the Jews were on the look-out for him: 'Where is he?' they said. People stood in groups whispering about him. Some said, 'He is a good man'; others, 'No, he is leading the people astray'. Yet no one spoke about him openly, for fear of the Jews. When the festival was half over, Jesus went to the Temple and began to teach. The Jews were astonished and said, 'How did he learn to read? He has not been taught.' Jesus answered them: 'My teaching is not from myself: it comes from the one who sent me; and if anyone is prepared to do his will, he will know whether my teaching is from God or whether my doctrine is my own. When a man's doctrine is his own he is hoping to get honor for himself; but when he is working for the honor of one who sent him, then he is sincere and by no means an impostor. Did not Moses give you the Law? And yet not one of you keeps the Law!'

CHRIST THE LORD Jesus is a man with a mission. In this passage, he shows this focus on the mission in two ways. First, he explains to his relatives who were going to Jerusalem for the annual, weeklong celebration commemorating Israel's entrance into the Promised Land why he won't be going with them. (This was the Feast of Tabernacles, which coincided with the autumn harvest. It was called the Feast of Tabernacles because the residents and pilgrims who participated in it would erect huts or tents [the word tabernacle means, literally, tent] to live in during the festival as a way of recalling the years during which the Israelites wandered in the desert after being liberated from Egypt and before entering the Promised Land.) At this point in his ministry, Jesus has already traveled throughout Galilee, curing the sick, casting out demons, performing miracles, and preaching to huge crowds of Jewish and Gentile followers. His relatives think that it's time for him to make the same kind of showing in Jerusalem – if he really wants to become famous, he will have to make a name for himself with the educated and sophisticated leaders of the big city. But Jesus doesn't travel with the family caravan. Instead, he waits until the midpoint of the eight-day festival, when the huge crowds of pilgrims are already gathered, when the festival is well underway, when the preparations, the small talk, and the mutual catching up of friends and relatives is over, and everyone's attention is focused on the activities in the Temple. Jesus chose carefully the "right time" to go up to the festival. He took his mission seriously, and he marshaled all his intelligence, prudence, and strategic judgment in order to bring it to completion.

Second, he explains once again that he is not seeking honor and recognition for himself but is carrying out the will of the Father who sent him. This explains why he doesn't raise an army and stage a violent takeover of the city – which he easily could have done, judging by the crowds' reaction to his preaching. This also explains why he continues to teach and argue and explain instead of just forcing his will on the antagonistic Jewish leaders. His mission at this point is merely to deliver a message – the Father's message.

Jesus is a man with a mission, and when we were baptized and confirmed, we became his accomplices in fulfilling that mission. We should be as focused and determined and energetic in carrying it out as he was.

CHRIST THE TEACHER Two key lessons come out in this speech. First, Jesus explains to his relatives that since his job is to expose the self-seeking ways of the world and invite men to repent, he will constantly experience opposition and resistance. People don't like to be told that they are selfish, and they will often show their animosity to that message by persecuting the messenger. This was true for Jesus, and it is true for his followers. If we are faithfully bearing witness to Christ and his message, we too will incur resentment and opposition. All Christians who are true to their vocation to be other Christs can say with Jesus that the world "does hate me, because I give evidence that its ways are evil." Opposition is part of the Christian's daily bread.

Second, Jesus reveals the prerequisite for understanding his doctrine: "… If anyone is prepared to do his [the Father's] will, he will know whether my teaching is from God or whether my doctrine is my own…" The disposition of our will determines our capacity to recognize the truth. A heart free from inordinate attachments to selfish desires will be docile to God's action and inspirations. That docility will give the Holy Spirit room to work, enlightening and strengthening the soul. A heart that has idolized something, however, whether it be money, pleasure, position, power, popularity, or success of any kind – or even just comfort and ease – that heart is not free to respond to God's action; it is chained to its idol. The wind of the Holy Spirit blows, but the idolatrous soul is tied to the shore and makes no progress towards the light. Often God has to send a storm to break the moorings and detach that soul from its idol. Only then can grace begin to work.

CHRIST THE FRIEND Jesus was willing to risk his own life in order to accomplish his mission, to save us and give us hope. That is love. That is friendship. St John reminds us at the beginning of this chapter that Jesus had been forced to restrict his ministry to Galilee because the authorities in Judea had put a price on his head. But Jesus knows that he has to preach in the Temple if he is going to fulfill the Father's will. The Temple and the earthly Jerusalem were the privileged places of God's revelation and Covenant; the Messiah had to go and insistently proclaim his message there. He had to walk into the lion's den in order to save the lost sheep.

Jesus: I come to you in Holy Communion because I want to give you my own courage. I feed you with my own fortitude. I nourish you with my love. If only you knew how it saddens me when my disciples are afraid to take up their mission, to launch out to where I have sent them! And if only you knew how I rejoice – and all heaven with me – whenever one of my disciples is willing to brook opposition and rejection in order to be faithful to the truth, in order to advance the Kingdom! My Church is adorned with countless martyrs and virgins and confessors and saints who broke free from the shackles of worldly fear because they discovered my love and took the risk of letting it flood their lives. Do you think that perhaps some of them regret it? I want you to follow in their path. Trust me, be courageous, and fill each moment of your day with faith and love. I guarantee you won't regret it.

CHRIST IN MY LIFE You were entirely dedicated to your mission – the mission the Father had given you. Remind me, Lord: what is my mission? I am your disciple, your ambassador to the people around me, your messenger, just as you were the Father's messenger to Israel. O Lord, I believe that the happiness I long for can only come from living in synch with the purpose for which you created me, from fulfilling my mission in life…

I can't help wondering, Lord. Is part of me still not well disposed to your will? Do I have some secret idols stashed away in the closet of my soul? I believe in you, Lord, and I want to be wholly yours. All my hopes are in you and in your goodness. Who else can teach me and guide me to the life I long to live? Come and show me what I need to change; come and break any chains that hold me back from loving you…

Thank you for not thinking of your own personal preferences and comfort. Thank you for giving yourself entirely to fulfill the mission you had received from the Father. Teach me to do the same. Give me courage, Lord, the courage to live out all my relationships and responsibilities just as you would have me, the courage to be passionately faithful to the vocation you have given me, no matter what the cost…

QUESTIONS FOR SMALL GROUP DISCUSSION

1. What struck you most in this passage? What did you notice that you hadn't noticed before?

2. What were the different ways that people reacted to Christ's teachings? Which of those reactions do we still run across today?

3. Why are we so afraid of stirring up opposition or disdain by giving witness to Christ?

4. The people who heard Jesus teach were amazed at his eloquence and wisdom, especially since they knew he had not studied in any of the rabbinic schools that churned out scholars and preachers. Do you think there is a lesson in this for all of us?

Cf. Catechism of the Catholic Church, 1816 on the necessity of every Christian bearing witness to

Christ; 769 on the necessity of suffering persecution; 675-677 on the final persecution the Church will experience; 1817-1821 on hoping in God alone; 2112-2114, 1723, 2289, and 2424 on the different types of idolatry

261. CONFLICT AND CONTRADICTION (JN 7:20-36)

"When we consider that Christ is the true light far removed from all falsehood, we realize that our lives too should be lit by the rays of the sun of justice, which shine for our enlightenment. These rays are the virtues…"

- St Gregory of Nyssa

John 7:20-36

'Why do you want to kill me?' The crowd replied, 'You are mad! Who wants to kill you?' Jesus answered, 'One work I did, and you are all surprised by it. Moses ordered you to practise circumcision – not that it began with him, it goes back to the patriarchs – and you circumcise on the sabbath. Now if a man can be circumcised on the sabbath so that the Law of Moses is not broken, why are you angry with me for making a man whole and complete on a sabbath? Do not keep judging according to appearances; let your judgement be according to what is right.' Meanwhile some of the people of Jerusalem were saying, 'Isn't this the man they want to kill? And here he is, speaking freely, and they have nothing to say to him! Can it be true the authorities have made up their minds that he is the Christ? Yet we all know where he comes from, but when the Christ appears no one will know where he comes from.' Then, as Jesus taught in the Temple, he cried out: 'Yes, you know me and you know where I came from. Yet I have not come of myself: no, there is one who sent me and I really come from him, and you do not know him, but I know him because I have come from him and it was he who sent me.'

They would have arrested him then, but because his time had not yet come no one laid a hand on him. There were many people in the crowds, however, who believed in him; they were saying, 'When the Christ comes, will he give more signs than this man?' Hearing that rumours like this about him were spreading among the people, the Pharisees sent the Temple police to arrest him. Then Jesus said: 'I shall remain with you for only a short time now; then I shall go back to the one who sent me. You will look for me and will not find me: where I am you cannot come.' The Jews then said to one another, 'Where is he going that we shan't be able to find him? Is he going abroad to the people who are dispersed among the Greeks and will he teach the Greeks? What does he mean when he says: You will look for me and will not find me: where I am, you cannot come?'

CHRIST THE LORD Jesus is teaching in the Temple precincts, where long colonnades and porticos provided outdoor, spontaneous classrooms that were especially busy during the great festivals. A crowd of pilgrims surrounds him, including some of the Pharisees and Scribes and other leaders who are seeking his demise. He knows very well that ever since his earlier trip to Jerusalem and the miraculous cure of the lame man on the Sabbath, many of these leaders were contriving his death. Some pilgrims in the crowd who resided in other cities were unaware of the vehement malevolence with which the leaders viewed Jesus. But Jesus doesn't direct his remarks to them; instead, he addresses his enemies.

Once again we see Jesus practicing what he preaches. He instructed his followers to love their enemies and do good to those who hate them, and Jesus does exactly that in this and the many other conversations he has with the very men who want to do away with him. He spares no pains to open their minds to the truth. In this case, he points out the superficiality of their objection to his supposed Sabbath-breaking cure. Although the Law of Moses, which they esteemed so highly, demanded that no work be done on the Sabbath (not even medical work unless death was imminent), the Pharisees and chief priests themselves allowed for circumcision to be performed on that day, because newborn male babies were circumcised on the eighth day after their birth, which often fell on the Sabbath. If this sign of their Covenant with God was permitted to trump the Sabbath restrictions, why were they so indignant at Jesus for restoring a crippled man's health and faith – thus exercising that same Covenant – on the Sabbath? His critics were so obsessed with external piety that they had lost sight of its real meaning; they were "judging according to appearances" instead of "according to what is right."

Jesus doesn't condemn those who condemn him; he instructs them. Jesus is the King who reaches out to those who reject him, meeting them on their own terms in hopes that a little bit of his light will shine through a chink in their self-righteous armor. If our Lord acts like that, we should do the same.

CHRIST THE TEACHER Jesus' teaching impresses the crowds, as does his courage – because they know that the authorities are out to get him, and yet he stands up in public and continues to preach. Reflecting on what they have seen and heard, some members of the crowd believe in him. Others raise an interesting objection, which affords Jesus an opportunity to explain once again his divine origin and mission. The objectors refer to a popular Jewish belief that the Messiah will emerge on the scene publicly, suddenly, mysteriously, and dramatically. By this standard, Jesus doesn't fit. They knew where he came from. They knew his relatives and his background. Jesus admits that, but he goes on to say that his true origin is not known to them. He has been sent by God to do God's work. He claims once again a unique knowledge of and relationship with the Father, whom they do not really know at all. If they did, they would recognize Jesus as Messiah.

Often we fall into this same mistake. We think that God's action in our lives has to be dramatic and mysterious, when most often it reaches us through the ordinary experiences of life. Jesus is both Son of God and Son of Mary; Word of God and Nazarene carpenter. God is not a tyrant, eager to show off his power and cow us into obedience. That conception was in the back of the minds of these objectors, and sometimes it lingers in the back of our minds as well. But Jesus is proof that the truth is quite different. God came into the world in the quiet of Bethlehem. He redeemed the world in the workshop at Nazareth and by suffering and dying – experiences common to all of us. He spreads his grace through normal, everyday water, oil, bread, and wine, using words and gestures that are simple and easy to understand. If we are looking for God in the extraordinary things, we may completely miss his constant love that flows continually through the ordinary things.

CHRIST THE FRIEND A touch of sadness seems to color Jesus' words when the guards show up to arrest him. The time for his Passion has not yet arrived, however, and so they do not arrest him. But their arrival makes Jesus think ahead to what he knows will happen in just a few months. He is painfully aware that his time is limited. We can hear the longing in his voice as he alludes to his Ascension – he wants people to believe in him before their hearts become so hardened that they will no longer even be able to believe. Jesus still longs for us to believe in him, to trust him, to accept him. Life is so short; time is so limited. God showers every soul with his graces and invitations, but still many souls refuse to believe.

Christ: You are a comfort to me. You have listened to my voice in your conscience and you have followed me. You have trusted me. You have let me heal you and guide you with my grace. I am preparing a place for you in my Father's house. But I wish I could describe to you how it pains my heart to see so many souls turn their backs on me. What more could I have done for them? Each one of them is looking for me, but they keep looking in the wrong places. And the farther they distance themselves from me, the less distinct my voice becomes. Go to them and tell them that I am what they are looking for. I will be with you.

CHRIST IN MY LIFE Keep my heart open to you, Lord. It's so easy to go to the right or the left, to fall into legalism or laxity, like the Pharisees and the Sadducees, those leaders of Jerusalem who tried to destroy you. Keep me on the right path, Lord. Teach me to do your will. Teach me to keep striving to love you with all my heart and my neighbor as myself. Push me, Lord; draw me closer to you…

I praise you for your gentle love. You come to me in the simple things of life. It delights you to show your love and your majesty in the quiet beauty of a sunset, the simple joy of a child's smile, the embrace of a loved one, the refreshing caress of a cool breeze. Teach me the wisdom I need to live in constant contact with you, so I can be a channel of your grace…

I know I only have a little time left on this earth. I want to do so much. But my job is not to save the world – that's your job, Lord. All I have to do is fulfill your will with trust and love. I ask only that you make your will clear to me each day, and then give me the strength to carry it out with love. When my last day comes, I want to be able to say: I love you Lord, and that's why I always sought to do your will…

QUESTIONS FOR SMALL GROUP DISCUSSION

1. What struck you most in this passage? What did you notice that you hadn't noticed before?

2. What has most helped your faith to grow over the years, and what has hindered it?

3. What can we do to help each other become more sensitive to God's action in the normal occurrences of everyday life?

4. If an agnostic acquaintance came up to you and asked how it is possible for Christ to be both true man and true God, how would you explain it to them?

Cf. Catechism of the Catholic Church, 464-469 on Jesus as true God and true man; 470-478 on how Jesus' divine and human faculties and knowledge coexisted; 1114-1116 on Christ at work in the sacraments

262. WATER FROM THE ROCK (JN 7:37-8:1)

"Jesus Christ is the beginning and the end, the Alpha and the Omega; he is the king of the new world; he is the secret of history; he is the key to our destiny."

- Pope Paul VI

John 7:37-8:1

On the last day and greatest day of the festival, Jesus stood there and cried out: 'If any man is thirsty, let him come to me! Let the man come and drink who believes in me!' As scripture says: From his breast shall flow fountains of living water. He was speaking of the Spirit which those who believed in him were to receive; for there was no Spirit as yet because Jesus had not yet been glorified. Several people who had been listening said, 'Surely he must be the prophet', and some said, 'He is the Christ', but others said, 'Would the Christ be from Galilee? Does not scripture say that the Christ must be descended from David and come from the town of Bethlehem?' So the people could not agree about him. Some would have liked to arrest him, but no one actually laid hands on him. The police went back to the chief priests and Pharisees who said to them, 'Why haven't you brought him?' The police replied, 'There has never been anybody who has spoken like him'. 'So,' the Pharisees answered, 'you have been led astray as well? Have any of the authorities believed in him? Any of the Pharisees? This rabble knows nothing about the Law – they are damned.' One of them, Nicodemus – the same man who had come to Jesus earlier – said to them, 'But surely the Law does not allow us to pass judgement on a man without giving him a hearing and discovering what he is about?' To this they answered, 'Are you a Galilean too? Go into the matter, and see for yourself: prophets do not come out of Galilee.' They all went home, and Jesus went to the Mount of Olives.

CHRIST THE LORD The Feast of Shelters was one of the most important feasts in the Jewish year. The words Christ speaks in this passage were spoken to the thousands of pilgrims who gathered in Jerusalem to celebrate that feast. On each day of the feast (and with greater drama on the last day, the day referred to in this passage), the people held a procession during which they marched around the altar of the Temple and sang hymns while the priest drew water from an ancient pool (the pool of Siloam) and poured it over the altar as an offering and a prayer to God, thanking him for the harvests that had recently been taken in and asking him to bless them with sufficient rain for the coming months. The ritual also called to mind the miracle in the desert when God had Moses draw water from a rock for his people as they made their way to the Promised Land. This ceremony provided the backdrop for Jesus' exclamation: "If any man is thirsty, let him come to me!" He will provide them with rivers of living water flowing within their thirsty hearts.

In Christ, all the events of the Old Testament find their true meaning, for they had only been shadows of future events, as St Paul calls them. All of God's self-revelation to mankind is summed up in Jesus Christ; he is the only rock on which it is safe to build a life, the only water that will quench the universal thirst for meaning and lasting happiness, and the new Moses who has come to turn our sin-hardened hearts into flowing fountains of life-giving love – he is the Lord.

CHRIST THE TEACHER St John points out that the "fountains of living water" flowing within the hearts of those who come to Christ refer to the Holy Spirit, who was to make his appearance only after Jesus had ascended to the Father. The Feast of Pentecost, the tenth day after the Ascension, witnessed the descent of the Holy Spirit on the apostles, who had been gathered in expectant prayer with Mary throughout those ten days. The feast of Pentecost, in addition to being relived each year in the liturgical calendar, is also made present at the celebration of the sacrament of confirmation. When we are confirmed, we receive a renewed outpouring of the Holy Spirit, strengthening us for our life mission of giving public testimony to Christ.

By likening the Holy Spirit's presence and action to "fountains of living water," Jesus uses imagery that would have evoked a powerful reaction from his listeners. Jewish traditions involved elaborate ceremonial cleansings, many of which occurred on a daily basis, and the Jewish scriptures are replete with references to flowing water as a sign of God's fidelity, of life and fecundity, of happiness and promise. If the Holy Spirit is likened to water that flows within our hearts, it means that he is the source of intimate, spiritual purification, health, life, and zest. If he is "living" water, he is a constantly self-renewing source of those gifts – inexhaustible. If he is "fountains" of living water, he is a dynamic, energetic, powerful source of interior renewal, not passively pious and timidly hesitant. This is the Spirit that we who are members of Christ through baptism and soldiers of Christ through confirmation have received. We have a spring of pure and abundant spiritual invigoration flowing freely within us. As St Paul puts it: "Didn't you realize that you were God's temple and that the Spirit of God was living among you?" (1 Corinthians 3:16)

CHRIST THE FRIEND St John was present when Christ announced the coming of the Spirit. He mentions that on the last and greatest day of the feast, Jesus "stood there and cried out: 'If any man is thirsty, let him come to me!'" Every detail expresses the intensity of Christ's desire to give away the precious gift of meaning and fulfillment that he alone can give. He waited until the climax of the eight-day celebration. He stood up, which means that he took a very visible posture, where the immense crowds couldn't help but see him. And then he "exclaimed," as if to say he shouted, he cried out, he did everything he could to make himself heard. And what did he say? "Come to me if you are thirsty, and I will give you a drink like one you have never had before!" Clearly, he meant more than physical thirst; he was addressing himself to the thirst of the human soul, the thirst for meaning and true happiness that drives every decision and action of every man and woman of every time and place. The deepest longing of the human heart – that is what Christ came to fulfill, and how he craves to fulfill it!

Nicodemus: The Sanhedrin was shocked beyond description when the guards returned empty-handed. They couldn't understand how Jesus was able to move the hearts of everyone who listened to him. They simply refused to confront the truth – they shut it out. I tried to make them see, but they turned on me with such violence that I was disoriented. Wherever Jesus went, people either loved him or hated him. But he always loved. He even loved those who despised him. I warned him and encouraged him to go away, but he was determined to show how much he loved them. When people asked me about him afterwards, that's what I always said, that he only wanted to convince everyone that they were loved.

CHRIST IN MY LIFE I am thirsty Lord. I have already tasted the living water that you offer. Your Holy Spirit, your wisdom, your truth, and your love alone satisfy the yearnings of my heart. I was made for you – I was made to know you, to feel your love, and to love you in return. But the more I taste the living water of your grace, the more I want to drink. Send your Spirit, Lord, to be my constant companion, my light, and my refreshment…

If your Spirit is flowing within me, refreshing me with grace at every moment, why do I get tired? Why, Lord, do I keep falling into discouragement and frustration? O Jesus, I know that you have the answers, but sometimes I wish I had them too. Instruct me, Lord; teach me and guide me. Show me the way to go; purify me of everything that blocks the flow of grace in me and through me…

Why do you care so much about me? Why does it matter to you whether I come and drink from the springs of your grace? You hold the whole universe in your hand, and I am just a little speck in the midst of it. And yet, you have made this invitation resound through twenty centuries until it has reached my ears: "Come to me!" You know my name. You want me beside you. I look at you and I know that I am loved…

QUESTIONS FOR SMALL GROUP DISCUSSION

1. What struck you most in this passage? What did you notice that you hadn't noticed before?

2. Do I eagerly strive to understand God's revelation, making an effort to know and grasp the Old Testament in the light of the New Testament, or am I a passive Catholic, taking only what comes to me and making little personal effort to delve into the riches of my faith?

3. The Holy Spirit is the third person of the Blessed Trinity, the one responsible for our growth in intimacy with God, the one who has made his dwelling in our hearts and remains there as our guest. How can we cultivate our relationship with him, learning to recognize his voice and follow his inspirations?

4. If Christ can truly quench the thirst of the human heart, why don't more people come to him? If I believe he can, why don't I bring more people to him?

Cf. Catechism of the Catholic Church, 731-741 on the meaning of Pentecost and the Holy Spirit's role in the Church; 694-701 on the Holy Spirit's individual action in each soul

THE GOSPEL OF JOHN CHAPTER 8

For this cause he came down upon earth, that by pursuing death he might kill the rebel that slew men. For one underwent the judgment, and myriads were set free. One was buried, and myriads rose again. He is the mediator between God and man. He is the resurrection and salvation of all. He is the guide of the erring, the shepherd of men who have been set free, the life of the dead, the charioteer of the cherubim, and the king of kings, to whom be the glory for ever and ever. Amen."

- St Alexander of Alexandria

263. GETTING WHAT WE DON'T DESERVE (JN 8:2-11)

"His attitude towards sinners was full of kindness and loving friendship."

- St John Bosco

John 8:2-11

At daybreak he appeared in the Temple again; and as all the people came to him, he sat down and began to teach them. The scribes and Pharisees brought a woman along who had been caught committing adultery; and making her stand there in full view of everybody, they said to Jesus, 'Master, this woman was caught in the very act of committing adultery, and Moses has ordered us in the Law to condemn women like this to death by stoning. What have you to say?' They asked him this as a test, looking for something to use against him. But Jesus bent down and started writing on the ground with his finger. As they persisted with their question, he looked up and said, 'If there is one of you who has not sinned, let him be the first to throw a stone at her.' Then he bent down and wrote on the ground again. When they heard this they went away one by one, beginning with the eldest, until Jesus was left alone with the woman, who remained standing there. He looked up and said, 'Woman, where are they? Has no one condemned you?' 'No one, sir,' she replied. 'Neither do I condemn you,' said Jesus, 'go away, and don't sin any more.'

CHRIST THE LORD The scribes and the Pharisees – the religious leaders of Israel at the time – were constantly trying to discredit Jesus. This trap was particularly shrewd. If he forgave the woman, they could accuse him of contradicting Moses (who had taught that all women caught in adultery should be

871

stoned to death), which was tantamount to blasphemy. If he condemned her, he would lose his popular support. Christ escapes, however, by turning the tables, showing the hypocrisy of their supposed zeal for righteousness. Christ's uncanny ability to beat these cunning adversaries at their own game is a subtle indication of his extraordinary personality. It doesn't directly prove his divinity, but it certainly shows him to be a Lord among men. The more we let ourselves be filled with his Spirit, the more we will share his deftness in building the Kingdom and defending the truth.

The scene must have been alarming. Picture the small crowd of pilgrims gathered around Jesus in the Temple courtyard, while the Lord speaks to them from a seat under the colonnade. The morning sunlight makes the marble sparkle and gives the atmosphere a clear, golden tint. The people are intent on Jesus; he is intent on them. Those sitting farther inside the courtyard, away from Jesus, hear a commotion outside the gate. They turn to see a large group of Pharisees and scribes dressed in their tassels and robes, with some Temple guards roughly escorting a frightened and disheveled woman. The crowd clears a path for the newcomers. They station themselves in front of the Master, who takes in the whole situation with his penetrating gaze. He sees the woman's scared, ashamed expression; he sees the leaders of the Pharisees with their stern look of defiance; he sees the younger ones smiling with satisfaction: finally, they have Jesus in a bind. But the Lord sees beneath their facial expressions into their hearts. His wisdom and his mercy reach out to them all, defusing their self-righteousness and pardoning their guilt with merely a word. The Lord comes to save, not to destroy.

CHRIST THE TEACHER Biblical scholars have long wondered what Christ was writing on the ground as he bent down during this encounter. Some say it was the sins of all the accusers. Others say that he was merely giving them a chance to reconsider their position so that he wouldn't have to embarrass them. In any case, the fundamental lesson is clear: we are all in need of God's mercy; we have all "sinned and forfeited God's glory" (Romans 3:23), and Christ knows it.

Significantly, the oldest accusers were the first to walk away; the younger ones were more reluctant to admit their need for God. Old and young alike, however, admitted it eventually. And so the adulteress was free to go. This brings out the corollary to the lesson that everyone is in need of God's mercy: realizing that we need God's mercy enables us to forgive others and treat them with the charity that Christ requires. The more profoundly we have experienced God's forgiveness and the free gift of his mercy, which we don't deserve, the more readily we will communicate it to others by releasing resentment and letting grudges go – not because their sins don't matter, but because God came to save sinners.

Living on the level of God's mercy not only fills our souls with peace and supernatural strength, it also gives lost, lonely, angry, and closed hearts a whiff of God's love – and that's the only thing that can save them. If we throw stones by condemning and criticizing and judging, we drive others and ourselves away from Christ; if we give others a fresh start, whether they deserve it or not, we become the peacemakers that Jesus declared blessed: "for they will be called the sons of God" (Mt 5:9).

CHRIST THE FRIEND *Jesus: I came not to condemn the world, but to save the world. If I just wanted to condemn you, I would have had no reason to come. I know your sins and your weakness, and still I called you and continue to call you. Think for a moment about the one reason behind my incarnation, life, passion, death, resurrection, and ascension. Why would I follow such an itinerary? It was only because I want your friendship. Every page and word of the Gospels, every faithful action and teaching of my Church has one, single purpose: to convince you that I want to walk with you now and spend eternity showing you the splendors of my Kingdom. I am all for you, and I ask in return only one thing, the same thing I asked of this adulterous woman: trust me, accept my love, and turn away from your sin.*

CHRIST IN MY LIFE Make me a channel of your mercy, Lord. Your mercy means that even when I offend you, you keep on loving me and wanting what's best for me. I want to be like that. I want to be like gravity: continually pulling no matter what; I want to keep on showing people your goodness and wisdom. I want to keep on leading them to you, to keep on loving even those I find hard to love…

Forgive me, Lord, for judging my neighbor. How foolish it is for me to pass judgment and criticize and pigeonhole! Can I see their hearts? The Pharisees are quick to condemn, because it makes them feel important and superior. But I am even quicker to make excuses for myself and my failings. Teach me to see others as you see them and to speak about them as I would want them to speak about me…

I want to be able to defend your truth and the teachings of your Church, but so often I am at a loss for words. In the midst of conversations and encounters, I get flustered. Afterwards, I think up great responses. You always had the right response. You always knew what to say. Fill me with your grace and your wisdom, Lord, so that I can be your faithful friend and true ambassador…

QUESTIONS FOR SMALL GROUP DISCUSSION

1. What struck you most in this passage? What did you notice that you hadn't noticed before?

2. Why do we sometimes find it hard to forgive others? What can we do to develop the capacity to forgive more fully and more freely, as Christ forgives us?

3. In what ways do our present circumstances encourage us to fall into pharisaical (hypocritical) self-righteousness?

4. How do you think the disciples reacted to this encounter?

Cf. Catechism of the Catholic Church, 456-460 on why Jesus came to earth; 1846-1851 on God's mercy and the need to admit our sinfulness

264. LIGHT FROM LIGHT (JN 8:12-20)

"That is to say, if a man follows Christ in all things, he will cross over in Christ's steps to the very throne of eternal light."

- Homily of an ancient author

John 8:12-20

When Jesus spoke to the people again, he said: 'I am the light of the world; anyone who follows me will not be walking in the dark; he will have the light of life.' At this the Pharisees said to him, 'You are testifying on your own behalf; your testimony is not valid.' Jesus replied: 'It is true that I am testifying on my own behalf, but my testimony is still valid, because I know where I came from and where I am going; but you do not know where I come from or where I am going. You judge by human standards; I judge no one, but if I judge, my judgement will be sound, because I am not alone: the one who sent me is with me; and in your Law it is written that the testimony of two witnesses is valid. I may be testifying on my own behalf, but the Father who sent me is my witness too.' They asked him, 'Where is your Father?' Jesus answered: 'You do not know me, nor do you know my Father; if you did know me, you would know my Father as well.' He spoke these words in the Treasury, while teaching in the Temple. No one arrested him, because his time had not yet come.

CHRIST THE LORD One of the most exciting rituals associated with this festival took place at night in the second court of the Temple where the Treasury was. This courtyard was surrounded by porticoes that housed thirteen large alms-boxes, where pilgrims and worshippers could make the various offerings that Temple worship required. During the festival, a kind of grandstand was erected all around the porticoes, which could hold huge numbers of spectators. In the center of the courtyard, four gigantic candelabras were erected. When the full darkness of night had descended and the galleries were full, the candelabras were lit, creating a blaze so bright that, ancient sources record, the light spread to all the streets and courtyards throughout the city. (The Temple was located on a higher level than the rest of the city, so light there would be visible from afar.) This firelight commemorated the pillar of fire that God used to guide Israel through the desert every night during their forty-year sojourn from Egypt into the Promised Land. Throughout the night, Israel's holiest and wisest teachers would perform ceremonies of worship that included singing of psalms and dancing in praise and thanksgiving to God, whom the Scriptures repeatedly referred to as the light of his Chosen People. The faithful pilgrims would join in the celebration and enjoy the dramatic ceremony until the sun came up.

This setting gives Christ's words, "I am the light of the world," spectacular eloquence. With this experience fresh in the minds of his rapt listeners, speaking in the very courtyard where the ceremony of light had taken place, Jesus proclaims that he is the light of the world. Just as the pillar of fire had led the people of Israel into the Promised Land, and just as the great candelabras illuminated the holy city of Jerusalem, Jesus himself, his person and his teachings, is the pillar of saving fire that shines throughout the entire world, leading whoever believes in him to the fullness of life itself. That is what Jesus says about himself. Is it what we think about him?

CHRIST THE TEACHER Jesus claims to be the saving light of the world, and then he says that anyone who follows him will have the light of life. In that one phrase, he teaches us both what he came to give us, and how we can go about getting it.

He came to give us the light of life. Our lives are a journey through this wonderful but confusing and treacherous world. We live each day in search of happiness and fulfillment, but the vast majority of roads and paths and side streets lead only to frustration, futile toil, and dead ends. How true it is, as Thoreau put it, that most men lead lives of quiet desperation, knowing that there is more to life, but unable to find it. We walk in darkness, groping tentatively and anxiously – unless we have Jesus. His example, his teaching, and his presence are a "lamp to our feet and a light to our path" (Ps 119:105). With Jesus, we know where we are going and how to get there. Who are the people in history who have lived the most fulfilling, fulfilled, and fruitful lives if not the saints, who abandoned the comfort of darkness in order to launch out on the path of Christ's light? Only the saints learn the secret of rejoicing in the midst of suffering; only they conquer the conundrum of how to be happy in a fallen world.

In Jesus, with him and through him, our lives grow, flourish, and blossom, like wildflowers in the sunlight of spring. Without him our potential never matures, like a seed planted in cold soil and starved of light by shadows.

CHRIST THE FRIEND How do we go about getting that light of life? By following him. The Greek word translated as "follow" has a rich deposit of overlapping meanings. It is used to describe soldiers following their commanders into battle; it is used to portray slaves who stay always at their master's side, ready to do whatever task he sets them; it is used to describe heeding the advice or verdict pronounced by a wise counselor; it is used to describe obedience to the laws of a city or a state; and it is used to indicate someone who makes the effort to understand a teacher's line of argument.

Jesus wants to be everything for us. He wants to be our leader and teacher, our counselor and coach, our doctor and brother and friend. Most of all, he wants to walk by our side, guiding each of us along this adventure of life. He knows every road and every path, and he knows where we should go and what we should avoid. He knows where we will flourish, where we will discover our mission, and what steps we must take to fulfill it. We have to learn to listen only to his voice, which we have already learned to discern in our hearts and conscience. He has so much in store for us, so much to show us and teach us, so much for us to do. We just have to follow him, to keep following him, to trust him and not look back. He is the light of the world, the only light that will never go out.

CHRIST IN MY LIFE You are the light of the world, Lord. I believe it, and I am amazed at how easily I take you for granted. Why do the passing fancies of the world grab my attention so easily and distract me from your Kingdom and your will? You are the light that never goes out, and you have given yourself to me. Thank you, Lord. Teach me to follow you more closely. Teach me to love you and cherish your light…

The Pharisees and scribes didn't believe in you, because they didn't want to. Why did you give me the desire to believe in you? How is it that you have given me the gift of faith, but so many others still don't believe? Lord Jesus, I believe in you, and I want to follow you and you alone. Only you have the light of life, and that is what I yearn for. Lead me, Lord, one step at a time; you are the light that will never fail…

You have kindled a fire in my heart, Lord. I want to spread it to other hearts. I know you want to enlighten them as well. Teach me to keep the flame of faith burning brightly. Teach me to be your witness and your herald. Make me a torch, a lamp, a star that will guide others into your embrace. How else can I show you my love, Lord, but by loving those whom you love?...

QUESTIONS FOR SMALL GROUP DISCUSSION

1. What struck you most in this passage? What did you notice that you hadn't noticed before?

2. Jesus makes it quite clear that the power exhibited by his words and deeds demonstrated that the Father was at work in and through him, and yet his enemies still refused to believe. Why?

3. Christians are those who follow Christ. What does the phrase "following Christ" mean to you? If you had to explain it to a non-believing acquaintance, how would you do so?

4. Which aspects of popular culture tend to obscure the light of Christ from our lives, and which aspects tend to magnify it?

Cf. Catechism of the Catholic Church, 2465-2470 on living in the truth of Christ's light; 781-786 on the Church's mission to continue being the light of the world; 2104-2109 on the duty of all Christians to be the light of the world

265. CHRIST'S PROGRAM OF LIFE (JN 8:21-30)

"For God, as I have said, does not work in those who refuse to place all their trust and expectation in him alone."

- *St Jerome Emilian*

John 8:21-30

Again he said to them: 'I am going away; you will look for me and you will die in your sin. Where I am going, you cannot come.' The Jews said to one another, 'Will he kill himself? Is that what he means by saying, Where I am going, you cannot come?' Jesus went on: 'You are from below; I am from above. You are of this world; I am not of this world. I have told you already: You will die in your sins. Yes, if you do not believe that I am He, you will die in your sins.' So they said to him, 'Who are you?' Jesus answered: 'What I have told you from the outset. About you I have much to say and much to condemn; but the one who sent me is truthful, and what I have learnt from him I declare to the world.' They failed to understand that he was talking to them about the Father. So Jesus said: 'When you have lifted up the Son of Man, then you will know that I am He and that I do nothing of myself: what the Father has taught me is what I preach; he who sent me is with me, and has not left me to myself, for I always do what pleases him'. As he was saying this, many came to believe in him.

CHRIST THE LORD Jesus keeps telling his critics (and the crowds) that he is the Messiah. He keeps telling them that he is one with the Father, that he is

877

the one the Father has sent, and that he is not just another rabbi. "I am from above… I am not of this world…" The force of his words must have been immense. In spite of the difficult concepts, "many came to believe in him." But some still resisted. They were so caught up in their own ideas and expectations, so centered on themselves, that this wave of heavenly light and wisdom crashed against their closed minds and hearts as uselessly as the surf crashes against cliffs on the seashore. But Jesus had a plan to penetrate even those hardened hearts: "When you have lifted up the Son of man, then you will know that I am He…" He is referring to his crucifixion, which is still six months down the road. He knows that only limitless love can win over proud, arrogant, and self-centered hearts, and by going to the cross he will show that his love has absolutely no limits. The Lord came to conquer rebellious minds and hearts and lead them into his Kingdom of light, and he is willing to go to the extreme of self-sacrifice to bring about his victory.

CHRIST THE TEACHER In this passage, Jesus reveals his program of life: "I always do what pleases him [the Father]." Sometimes we resist the virtue of obedience because we are afraid that always doing God's will is somehow going to stifle our creativity or our true self. Just the opposite is the case.

Jesus repeatedly explains that he is not doing his own thing, but what the Father has given him to do. He teaches not his own wisdom, but what he has learned from the Father, seeking only to please the one who sent him. And this is what makes his life the most fruitful and beautiful life that has ever been. Following his example has made the lives of countless saints, men and women, rich and poor, religious and laity, resound with meaning and wisdom and the kind of joy that no amount of self-seeking and self-centeredness can ever produce. The reason is simple: we were created to love and be loved, to live in relation with God and others. That ongoing relationship of love implies turning our attention away from getting things *for* ourselves, instead focusing on giving *of* ourselves for the good of the beloved. This is what it means to "always do what pleases" God. God loves us, and his love is made concrete in his will – he communicates his love by guiding us to the fulfillment we seek; we accept his love and love him in return by obeying and by following his guidance.

Far from stifling our true selves, loving God – always doing what is pleasing to him – frees us to be much more than we ever dreamed we could be, and it liberates us to be all that God has always dreamt for us to be.

CHRIST THE FRIEND *Christ: I and my Father are one. When I called you to be my disciple, I called you to live in communion with me just as I do with my Father. And just as my Father "is with me, and has not left me to myself," I am always with you, and I will never abandon you. In your heart you know this, but even so, you often let yourself be carried away by worries and fears. When I let a cloud block out the sun, does the sun disappear? The sun is always there, and just so I am always watching over you. Every worry and fear that comes across the sky of your soul is a chance for you to exercise your faith and trust in me. That is what pleases me, and that is what sets my grace free to transform you and strengthen you and release your full potential for living as you ought to live. Seek always to do what pleases me, as I always sought to do what was pleasing to my Father, and you will discover anew my presence and grace, over and over again.*

CHRIST IN MY LIFE I too am sometimes hardhearted, like the Pharisees and scribes, who loved their own plans so much that they couldn't even see your plan. Cure me, Lord. Purify my heart. Show me my prejudices and selfish tendencies. Shine the light of your love into all the shadows of my soul. I want to be completely yours. I want to become your faithful disciple, a soldier you can count on...

How simple your program of life is! You seek always and everywhere to do what is pleasing to the Father. Teach me to live like that. Free me from my obsession with pleasing myself. You didn't design me to find fulfillment by navel-gazing – you created me to flourish by self-forgetting love. With the love of your heart, Lord, inflame my heart...

Are you really always with me? Why do you let me feel alone? Why do you let so many clouds block out the sun? You want me to grow up, to mature. You want me to love you for you and not for the light and gifts that you give to me. You want me to exercise the precious virtues of faith, hope, and love, which have to be based on trust. Teach me to leave behind my cold calculations and abandon myself to your goodness...

QUESTIONS FOR SMALL GROUP DISCUSSION

1. What struck you most in this passage? What did you notice that you hadn't noticed before?

2. Why is Jesus so patient and persistent with these people who resist his teachings so systematically? Why is it so hard for us to patient and persistent with people who resist faith in Christ?

3. In general, how can we follow Christ's example to do always what is pleasing to the Father? How can we discern what is pleasing to God in the different situations of life?

4. What has most helped you to remember that Christ never leaves you alone, that he is always with you and always in control? How can we develop this awareness?

Cf. Catechism of the Catholic Church, 2822-2827 and 2196 on what is pleasing to God; 1813 and 1817-1821 on the virtue of hope; 2656-2658 on increasing the theological virtues through prayer and the liturgy; 2779-2785 on having confidence in God the Father

266. HOME FREE (JN 8:31-41)

"This Lord of ours is the one from whom and through whom all good things come to us."

- St Theresa of Avila

John 8:31-41

To the Jews who believed in him Jesus said: 'If you make my word your home you will indeed be my disciples, you will learn the truth and the truth will make you free'. They answered, 'We are descended from Abraham and we have never been the slaves of anyone; what do you mean, You will be made free?' Jesus replied: 'I tell you most solemnly, everyone who commits sin is a slave. Now the slave's place in the house is not assured, but the son's place is assured. So if the Son makes you free, you will be free indeed. I know that you are descended from Abraham; but in spite of that you want to kill me because nothing I say has penetrated into you. What I, for my part, speak of is what I have seen with my Father; but you, you put into action the lessons learnt from your father.' They repeated, 'Our father is Abraham.' Jesus said to them: 'If you were Abraham's children, you would do as Abraham did. As it is, you want to kill me when I tell you the truth as I have learnt it from God; that is not what Abraham did. What you are doing is what your father does.'

CHRIST THE LORD Some of the Jewish faithful listening to Jesus had the wrong idea of what it meant to live in communion with God. They thought it was sufficient to be descended from Abraham – a purely exterior condition. But Jesus demands more than biological descent; he demands spiritual descent. Abraham's greatness lay in his docility to God's will. He left his homeland and family en route to an unknown destination simply because God asked him to. He was even willing to sacrifice his own son, Isaac, when God commanded it. This faith, this docile trust in God that had enabled Abraham to recognize God's action in his life, is what made him great. The true children of Abraham and inheritors of his promise, therefore, are those who imitate his trust and docility: "If you were children of Abraham, you would do what Abraham did." But Jesus' interlocutors, by their failure to recognize Jesus as sent from God and by their desire to do away with him, exposed their self-seeking (unlike Abraham's God-seeking) hearts.

Jesus was the Word of God made flesh, a much greater revelation than Abraham had ever received, and yet these Pharisees and Scribes stubbornly rejected him. They had put their trust in themselves and were seeking their own glory. Thus they were no children of Abraham and no disciples of the Lord. In Christ's Kingdom there can be only one King, and if we want to enjoy the prosperity of that Kingdom, we have to relinquish our self-made scepters and trust that King.

CHRIST THE TEACHER Every human heart yearns for freedom – the freedom to live as we suspect we ought to live, the freedom to be masters of our instincts and passions instead of their slaves, the freedom to be all that we were created to be. At the same time, every human heart feels shackled by something. Something holds us back from reaching our potential. We know we can do more, we know we can be better, and yet we find ourselves stuck in spiritual mediocrity. In this passage, Jesus reveals both the nature of our restraints, and the path to the freedom we desire.

The truth sets us free. Freedom is more than the indifferent capacity to choose between various options. Freedom is the possibility we have to achieve excellence through making choices in accordance with truth. Animals and plants and rocks don't have this possibility; only rational creatures (humans and angels) can contribute consciously and meritoriously to their own flourishing and fulfillment. But we can only do so if we direct our conscious actions in harmony with the way things are, with the way God created them to be – in other words, with the truth. This is less complicated than it seems. Think of the converse case. When does human freedom completely collapse? In the instance of insanity. When a person is no longer able to perceive reality, when they are out of touch with the way things are, they can longer grow at all, let alone flourish.

Our inborn capacity to recognize truth – reality, the way things are, the way God designed them to be – gives us the possibility to direct our lives towards the fulfillment we long for. But that possibility is constantly being threatened and hindered by our tendency (inherited through original sin and exacerbated by personal sin – ours and others') to indulge our self-seeking appetites at the expense of what's truly fulfilling. This is sin. It is a rebellion against the way God created us to be. It is preferring our own disordered, shortsighted, and irrational preferences to God's perfectly wise and loving will. This tendency is always at work in us, and whenever we give into it, it tightens its grip, making it harder for us both to perceive our true good and also to pursue it. Thus, "everyone who commits a sin is a slave." The way to overcome our tendency to selfish implosion is to "make Christ's word our home."

CHRIST THE FRIEND Christ's word is the expression of his love. He is God, and God is love, and all his actions and words are the revelation of that love. To make his word our home, then, means to dwell in God's love for us – to relish it, to accept it, to drink it in. It involves hearing and heeding his call in our life. This call takes many forms: the nudge of conscience in little and big dilemmas; the deep, insistent, resounding invitation to a particular vocation; the normal responsibilities of life; the commandments of the Bible and the Church... When Jesus tells us to make his word our home, he is inviting us to dwell in his will and find our comfort, our solace, our rest, and our renewal in it. Jesus comes to rescue us from our vain attempts to concoct some magic formula for self-fulfillment all by ourselves. His will is his word, and his word is the expression of his love, so to dwell in his word is to be in a constant communion with the one who loves us – to live in friendship with Christ. He is the truth, and he will set us free.

CHRIST IN MY LIFE I believe in you, Lord. You are the one, true God. Only you are the Savior. I pray for those who don't believe in you. Show yourself to them. Win over their hearts. Free them from sin. And what about those around me who don't believe in you? Send me to them, Lord. I want to build and spread your Kingdom, but I need your grace to tell me what to say, what to do, and how to love them as you have loved me...

I so easily forget that I am a fallen person in a fallen world. You have redeemed me, but you didn't take away the effects of sin. You want me to exercise my faith and love by resisting my tendencies to self-seeking and by obeying the call of your truth. This is virtue, Lord. Virtue is freedom from the merciless and destructive slavery of self-centeredness. Teach me virtue; show me the way to go...

What is your will for me, Lord? Remind me. Life is so busy. Life is so unpredictable. Events and problems and activities swirl around me, and emotions and desires and temptations churn inside me. Make your word alive for me – I hear and read it so often, in Mass, in spiritual reading, and in my prayer, but I want to listen better. I don't want to dwell in my paltry self, and I don't want to dwell in the passing fads of this fallen world. I want to dwell in you, in your word, and in your will. Teach me to do your will...

QUESTIONS FOR GROUP DISCUSSION

1. What struck you most in this passage? What did you notice that you hadn't noticed before?

2. It seems that many Jews wrongly thought they were in a right relationship with God just

because of their racial identity as Abraham's descendents. In what ways can today's Catholics fall into a similar mistake?

3. Where does popular culture encourage us to "make our home"? In other words, where does it encourage us to seek the meaning, fulfillment, and happiness that we long for? How does that compare with Christ's exhortation?

4. How would you explain the right and wrong views of freedom to a non-believer who claimed that freedom just means doing whatever you feel like?

Cf. Catechism of the Catholic Church, 396-406 on freedom and original sin; 407-409 on the hard battle that ensued after original sin; 144-147 on Abraham as a model of faith

267. LIES AND DEATH, TRUTH AND LIFE (JN 8:42-59)

"You who have now put on Christ and follow our guidance are like little fish on the hook: you are being pulled up out of the deep waters of this world by the word of God."

- St Jerome

John 8:42-59

'We were not born of prostitution,' they went on 'we have one father: God.' Jesus answered: 'If God were your father, you would love me, since I have come here from God; yes, I have come from him; not that I came because I chose, no, I was sent, and by him. Do you know why you cannot take in what I say? It is because you are unable to understand my language. The devil is your father, and you prefer to do what your father wants. He was a murderer from the start; he was never grounded in the truth; there is no truth in him at all: when he lies he is drawing on his own store, because he is a liar, and the father of lies. But as for me, I speak the truth and for that very reason, you do not believe me. Can one of you convict me of sin? If I speak the truth, why do you not believe me? A child of God listens to the words of God; if you refuse to listen, it is because you are not God's children.'

The Jews replied, 'Are we not right in saying that you are a Samaritan and possessed by a devil?' Jesus answered: 'I am not possessed; no, I honour my Father, but you want to dishonour me. Not that I care for my own glory, there is someone who takes care of that and is the judge of it. I tell you most solemnly, whoever keeps my word will never see death.' The Jews said, 'Now we know for certain that you are possessed. Abraham is dead, and the prophets are dead, and yet you say, Whoever keeps my word will never know the taste of death. Are you greater than our father Abraham, who is dead? The prophets are dead too. Who are you claiming to be?' Jesus answered: 'If I were to seek my own glory that would be no glory at all; my glory is conferred by the Father, by the one of whom you say, He is our God although you do not know him. But I know him, and if I were to say: I do not know him, I should be a liar, as you are liars yourselves. But I do know him, and I faithfully keep his word. Your father Abraham rejoiced to think that he would see my Day; he saw it and was glad.' The Jews then said, 'You are not fifty yet, and you have seen Abraham!' Jesus replied: 'I tell you most solemnly, before Abraham ever was, I Am.' At this they picked up stones to throw at him; but Jesus hid himself and left the Temple.

CHRIST THE LORD Jesus continues to intensify his claim to be God made man and thus the unique and everlasting Lord of life and history. In this passage, three statements would have made this claim unmistakably clear to his listeners. That some understood the claim but refused to accept it is made evident by their furious attempt to stone Jesus to death for blasphemy right there in the Temple precincts.

Besides reiterating that he is the one whom God sent (this is the role of the Messiah, the one who will fulfill God's promise to Abraham to bless all nations through his descendents, a promise Abraham rejoiced to contemplate), Jesus attests to a unique knowledge of God and a unique obedience to God's will: "I do know him, and I faithfully keep his word." Knowing and willing are the two capacities that separate spiritual beings from merely physical ones; they differentiate persons from things. By choosing to describe his union with the Father through these two activities, Jesus gives us a glimpse (and that's all we can take) of the inner life of the Blessed Trinity, in which the three divine Persons are perfectly united in knowing and willing the eternal Truth and Goodness of the divine Nature.

But lest this revelation be lost on his listeners, Jesus goes on to make yet another, unambiguous proclamation of his divine sonship: "Before Abraham ever was, I Am." To speak about the historical past in the present tense is something only God can do, because only God exists, unchanging, outside of time. To use the simple, open-ended phrase "I Am" in reference to oneself would have been to the Jewish mind a declaration of godhood; it was the same title God himself used in answering Moses' query about God's name during the encounter at the burning bush. This same Jesus, as much a human person as you and I, as close to us as it is possible to be through his self-giving in Holy Communion, is also at the same time the eternal Son and Word of God, the Second Person of the Blessed Trinity.

CHRIST THE TEACHER Jesus speaks the truth, and "whoever keeps [his] word will never know the taste of death." But the devil "is a liar, and the father of lies" and "was a murderer from the beginning." Truth and life come with

Christ; lies and death come with the devil. Those who seek and heed the truth will live as they are meant to live, while those who falsify their conscience in order to satisfy their thirst for selfish glory will only experience frustration, anxiety, and spiritual infertility. This was the exact progression of original sin: Adam and Eve, tempted by the devil, chose the desire "to be like gods" – a thirst for vain glory – and ended up estranged from their Creator, from each other, and from the world around them. Jesus, on the other hand, doesn't seek his own glory; in fact, he willingly accepts the humiliation of the cross, and as a result, he rises to the fullness of eternal life. These are the two options – truth and life or lies, betrayal of conscience, and death; there is no other.

This is the dramatic structure of the human condition. Philosophers, manu-facturers, entertainers, and politicians can come up with as many worldviews and programs and systems and promises as they like, but ultimately, every human heart is a battleground between two loves: love of self, which seems to promise immediate gratification but requires rebellion against or abandonment of God; and love of God, which requires self-forgetfulness and sacrifice in order to "listen to the words of God" by following Christ but leads to ever-increasing fulfillment in this life and eternal adventure in the life to come. The devil and his angels encourage the false love of self-seeking, and the Spirit of God en-courages the true love of self-giving. Every choice we make, big or little, every day, strengthens one of those loves and weakens the other. One of the greatest Christian privileges consists in being privy to this knowledge of the structure that underlies the whole story of humanity and the story of every man.

CHRIST THE FRIEND *Christ: Whoever keeps my word will never know the taste of death. Do you know what the taste of death is? It is interior darkness and the absence of hope. It is de-pression that gets heavier and heavier until it spawns despair. It is the sense of defeat and mean-inglessness that seeps into every corner of the soul like a cold, dense fog that gets thicker and thicker and thicker. It is discovering that you are alone, that no one truly knows you, and so no one can truly love you. It is seeing the seething ugliness of sin putrefying in one's heart and being unable to do anything to wipe it away. It is watching your dreams slowly wither away, unfulfilled, or seeing them come true only to turn into nightmares as soon you reach out to grasp them.*

No one can live at peace with themselves unless they are willing to follow me. There is no other way. Death is existence without my friendship. It is what I came to destroy. You who have em-braced life, you are my prize and my delight, because you let my victory in.

Keep my word, follow me and I will give you life.

CHRIST IN MY LIFE I have to admit, Lord, that I understand very little when it comes to the mystery of your Incarnation. I know you are true God, and I know you are true man, but how you fit those two things together boggles my mind. But I am content to know that you who created and redeemed me continue to love and accompany me. To have God as my intimate friend is more than I could ever desire…

When I think about how much my daily decisions and actions matter in your eyes, it fills me with enthusiasm. I can build your Kingdom! I know that you care most about what happens in my heart. Many people build impressive worldly empires around shriveled hearts, and when their empires wane, their lives do too. But I want to live from your love, seeking your will, giving you glory…

What would I do without your friendship, Lord? Who would I hope in? Who would I complain to? Who would I learn from? Thank you for coming into my life. Never let me be separated from you. And fill me with your own desire: to save many souls from death, from the hollow existence of life without your friendship. Make me your apostle, your disciple, your ambassador; make me a fisher of men…

QUESTIONS FOR SMALL GROUP DISCUSSION

1. What struck you most in this passage? What did you notice that you hadn't noticed before?

2. What does popular culture say about the devil and how does that compare with what Jesus says about the devil?

3. Why are lying and self-indulgence so tempting to us? What can we do to arm ourselves in advance against these temptations?

4. The Christian view of life sees the dramatic struggle between Christ-centeredness and self-centeredness that is always happening in each human heart as the fundamental structure of the human condition. Which aspects of popular culture mesh with that view, and which ones contradict it?

Cf. Catechism of the Catholic Church: 1861 on eternal death in hell; 1033-1037 on hell as eternal separation from God; 407-409 on the spiritual battle of life; 441-445 on Jesus as the only Son of God

THE GOSPEL OF JOHN CHAPTER 9

"If the new man, made in the likeness of sinful flesh, had not taken our old nature; if he, one in substance with the Father, had not accepted to be one in substance with the mother; if he who was alone free from sin had not united our nature to himself – then

men would still have been held captive under the power of the devil. We would have been incapable of profiting by the victor's triumph if the battle had been fought outside our nature."

- Pope St Leo the Great

268. A BLIND MAN SEES (JN 9:1-17)

"Let us carry bravely the shield of faith, so that with its protection we may be able to parry whatever the enemy hurls at us."

- St Cyprian

John 9:1-17

As he went along, he saw a man who had been blind from birth. His disciples asked him, 'Rabbi, who sinned, this man or his parents, for him to have been born blind?' 'Neither he nor his parents sinned,' Jesus answered 'he was born blind so that the works of God might be displayed in him. As long as the day lasts I must carry out the work of the one who sent me; the night will soon be here when no one can work. As long as I am in the world I am the light of the world.' Having said this, he spat on the ground, made a paste with the spittle, put this over the eyes of the blind man, and said to him, 'Go and wash in the Pool of Siloam (a name that means 'sent'). So the blind man went off and washed himself, and came away with his sight restored.

His neighbours and people who earlier had seen him begging said, 'Isn't this the man who used to sit and beg?' Some said, 'Yes, it is the same one.' Others said, 'No, he only looks like him.' The man himself said, 'I am the man.' So they said to him, 'Then how do your eyes come to be open?' 'The man called Jesus' he answered 'made a paste, daubed my eyes with it and said to me, Go and wash at Siloam; so I went, and when I washed I could see.' They asked, 'Where is he?' 'I don't know' he answered. They brought the man who had been blind to the Pharisees. It had been a sabbath day when Jesus made the paste and opened the man's eyes, so when the Pharisees asked him how he had come to see, he said, 'He put a paste on my eyes, and I washed, and I can see.' Then some of the Pharisees said, 'This man cannot be from God: he does not keep the sabbath.' Others said, 'How could a sinner produce signs like this?' And there was disagreement among them. So they spoke to the blind man again, 'What have you to say about him yourself, now that he has opened your eyes?' 'He is a prophet,' replied the man.

CHRIST THE LORD As Jesus approaches his passion (and as the Church, which reads this passage towards the end of Lent, approaches it liturgically), he shows forth his power more brilliantly, definitively claiming in word and in deed that he is "the Son of Man" (one of the Old Testament titles for the promised Messiah).

In deed, Christ does two things. First, he defies the sacred laws of the Sabbath. No work – or healing, except in case of death – was allowed on the Sabbath, according to reigning Jewish law; making clay was considered work, and anointing eyes with spittle was considered healing. This defiance shows that his authority is higher than that of the Pharisees and scribes who delineated those laws and is even equal to God's authority, since God himself had commanded the Sabbath rest in the first place. Second, he cures a man born blind. As the blind man himself says, no one had ever heard of such a thing; it was a miracle that clearly exhibited divine action. In word, Jesus attributes to himself the Messianic title, calling himself again the "light of the world," and labeling his miracle a revelation of God's glory.

That Jesus had the man wash in the pool of Siloam adds yet another dimension to the revelation of his divine nature and mission. The eight-day Feast of Tabernacles, which was just coming to an end, included a grand ceremony recalling the water that Moses made flow out of a rock during Israel's journey through the desert. During that ceremony, huge amounts of water were poured over the stone altar in the Temple's inner courtyard (the court of priests), so that they flowed through the whole Temple. This water was taken from the pool of Siloam, an artificially constructed basin fed by the only spring that supplied water to the city, a spring located outside the city walls. (The water in the pool had been "sent" from the well through a long tunnel painstakingly excavated through solid rock.) The Feast of Tabernacles also included a spectacular ceremony of light, recalling the Pillar of Fire that had guided the Israelites during the nights of their forty-year trek to the Promised Land.

Jesus' miracle reveals that the power at work in him is the same power that had formed and liberated Israel in the days of Moses: with water from the rock, he brings new light into this man's darkness. The Gospels remind us again and again that Jesus is the fullness of God's revelation, bringing light and life to this world.

CHRIST THE TEACHER Among the many lessons hidden in this passage, one deserves special mention. How odd that Jesus used spittle and mud to make clay, put the clay on the man's eyelids, and told him to go to the pool of Siloam to wash! Did he *have* to perform the miracle like that? Certainly not: he could have merely snapped his fingers (he was God, after all). Yet, it was *appropriate* to do so. Besides the obvious reason that in ancient times saliva was often used in medical procedures, through this method of curing, the blind man felt Christ touching him, heard his voice, and actively participated in the saving deed of God. In this way, Christ shows how he communicates God's grace to us in ways appropriate to our human nature – which includes both body and spirit. Jesus wants to reach into our lives, to lower himself to our level, to touch us, even physically. Christ's touch gave the blind man hope and confidence, making the miracle into a personal encounter, not a magic trick.

The Catholic Church, under the constant guidance of the Holy Spirit, has preserved this method of administering God's grace through the sacraments. The priest's words of absolution at the end of confession provide the consolation we need to bring the reality of God's forgiveness home to our hearts. The water of baptism, the bread and wine of the Eucharist, the chrism… all the material elements of the sacraments extend throughout time the reality of God's eager desire to reach out and touch us. We are not purely spiritual beings; it suits us to encounter God through the mediation of physical realities. God became man not to despoil our humanity, but to bring it to its fullness.

CHRIST THE FRIEND Everything Jesus said and did in his brief life on earth was for us. He was a constant, overflowing gift of truth and grace: "Indeed, from his fullness we have, all of us, received – yes, grace in return for grace…" (John 1:16). We should relish his words, his atoning sacrifice to free us from our sins, the Church that he established as his mediator through time and space, and the example he gives us of how to lead a meaningful, fulfilling, and fruitful life. In this passage, he exemplifies an especially important characteristic of that kind of life: "As long as the day lasts I must carry out the work of the one who sent me; the night will soon be here when no one can work."

Jesus lived a busy life, but his busyness was the fruit of love. The blind man had suffered so long with both the physical inconveniences of blindness and the emotional and spiritual pain of wondering why God had sent him this handicap. When Jesus saw him, he recognized all of this. His heart overflowed with love, and his love drove him to heal the man, on the inside as well as on the outside. Jesus didn't waste time, because love wouldn't let him.

Christ: If only you could understand how brief this earthly life is! Time is so short. Eternity is always at your side. Everything that happens to you now, every opportunity I send you, every invitation I give you, is a chance for you to expand the capacity of your soul for love by exercising self-forgetfulness and self-giving. And the more you expand that capacity, the more I will be able to fill you with the light of my glory when you come home to my Father's house. Think more about this. Work for my Kingdom as if you had little time left to do so, because the truth is that you do have little time left, so little time!

CHRIST IN MY LIFE Never let me forget your majesty and glory. This world seems to delight in watering down your magnificence. But I believe in your greatness and your goodness. I want to live in the reality of your presence, like the saints. I want to learn to hear your voice calling out to me in all things, as I know you are doing, because you have promised that your love for me is constant, personal, and determined...

Too frequently, I take your sacraments for granted. You are so humble and gentle; you want to pour the balm of your grace into my life through signs that I can recognize and understand. I want to be grateful and attentive to your gifts. I want to appreciate them as I should and teach others to do the same. Open my eyes, Lord...

You know that I tend to be lazy, Lord. I gravitate toward idleness and self-indulgence. Please take this tendency away so I can be more energetic and constant in doing good and fulfilling your will. O Lord, please pour your Spirit into my heart, purge my soul from the self-seeking habits that hold me back. Make me an apostle, a soldier, a worker – teach me to live with the fervor of someone whose love never grows cold...

QUESTIONS FOR SMALL GROUP REFLECTION

1. What struck you most in this passage? What did you notice that you didn't notice before?

2. Sometimes we tend to resist Christ's Lordship, like the Pharisees. What causes such resistance, and what can we do to diminish it?

3. What can we do to live the different sacraments better, to make them the kind of personal encounter with Christ that God wants them to be?

4. Think of the liturgical gestures that the congregation performs during Mass (kneeling, standing, making the sign of the cross in different ways at different times...). How would you explain their meaning to a non-Catholic?

Cf. Catechism of the Catholic Church: 2466 on Jesus as the light of the world; 547-550 on the meaning of Christ's miracles; 1076 on the nature of the sacramental economy; 1084-1090 on Christ's continue work through the sacramental economy

269. THE SEEING GO BLIND (JN 9:18-41)

"God is watching us as we battle and fight in the combat of the faith. His angels are watching us, and so is Christ."

- St Cyprian

John 9:18-41

However, the Jews would not believe that the man had been blind and had gained his sight, without first sending for his parents and asking them, 'Is this man really your son who you say was born blind? If so, how is it that he is now able to see?' His parents answered, 'We know he is our son and we know he was born blind, but we don't know how it is that he can see now, or who opened his eyes. He is old enough: let him speak for himself.' His parents spoke like this out of fear of the Jews, who had already agreed to expel from the synagogue anyone who should acknowledge Jesus as the Christ. This was why his parents said, 'He is old enough; ask him'. So the Jews again sent for the man and said to him, 'Give glory to God! For our part, we know that this man is a sinner.' The man answered, 'I don't know if he is a sinner; I only know that I was blind and now I can see.' They said to him, 'What did he do to you? How did he open your eyes?' He replied, 'I have told you once and you wouldn't listen. Why do you want to hear it all again? Do you want to become his disciples too?' At this they hurled abuse at him: 'You can be his disciple,' they said 'we are disciples of Moses: we know that God spoke to Moses, but as for this man, we don't know where he comes from.'

The man replied, 'Now here is an astonishing thing! He has opened my eyes, and you don't know where he comes from! We know that God doesn't listen to sinners, but God does listen to men who are devout and do his will. Ever since the world began it is unheard of for anyone to open the eyes of a man who was born blind; if this man were not from God, he couldn't do a thing.' 'Are you trying to teach us,' they replied 'and you a sinner through and through, since you were born!' And they drove him away. Jesus heard they had driven him away, and when he found him he said to him, 'Do you believe in the Son of Man?' 'Sir,' the man replied, 'tell me who he is so that I may believe in him.' Jesus said, 'You are looking at him; he is speaking to you.' The man said, 'Lord, I believe', and worshipped him. Jesus said: 'It is for judgement that I have come into this world, so that those without sight may see and those with sight turn blind.' Hearing this, some Pharisees who were present said to him, 'We are not blind, surely?' Jesus replied: 'Blind? If you were, you would not be guilty, but since you say, We see, your guilt remains.'

CHRIST THE LORD Jesus continues insisting on his identity as the Son of God and the Messiah. He claims for himself the title of "Son of Man," commonly held to refer to the Messiah and used that way by the prophets. Then he accepts the blind man's calling him "Lord" (the title used by Jews to address God in prayer) and worshipping him – in Israel worship was reserved for God alone. Then Jesus declares that he came for judgment, to set free those who accept his Lordship and to condemn those who refuse to admit their need for him. These unheard of claims stir up the entire city of Jerusalem, throwing its leaders into a frenzy of agitation and its people into a state of excitement.

Jesus Christ came to earth to establish an eternal Kingdom, nothing less; when he comes into our lives, we can also expect him to shake things up – one way or another. That's the way the Lord works.

CHRIST THE TEACHER What did Jesus teach the blind man? He opened the eyes of his soul as well as the eyes of his body. He gave him the joy of physical sight. For the first time in his life, he could see. All of the things that he had known just by words and sound and touch suddenly came alive to him. Color entered his mind like a flood and filled him with wonder. The visual symphony of the sky and the landscape, the subtle beauty of expressions on people's faces emphasizing the meanings of their words, the look of love and tenderness from his mother, which he had never seen – Jesus opened up to this man a new, glorious, awe-inspiring world of human experience. Joy, amazement, and gratitude filled the man's mind and heart so that he experienced an intensity of life that he had never even dreamed of.

But Jesus also gave him spiritual sight - the gift of faith. He enabled the blind man to see God through himself. He enabled him to encounter his Creator knowingly, face to face. And the man worshipped as he had never worshipped before, pouring out all the love and faith he could muster at the feet of Christ, fulfilling the first and greatest commandment more passionately than we can imagine. This too must have overwhelmed him with ineffable spiritual delight.

Which gift did the man value more? Perhaps at first he valued his physical sight, but by the end of the day he was willing to stand up to the powerful Pharisees in order to defend the Lordship of Jesus Christ, knowing that such resistance could incur severe punishment. He did not let the gifts of God blind him to the goodness of God. In this, there is a lesson for us all: God, Jesus Christ, deserves our loyalty, friendship, and worship; if we ever find ourselves forgetting this by following him only for what he can do for us (cure us, give us gifts, work miracles), we will have become spiritually blind.

CHRIST THE FRIEND The blind man was interrogated twice, maligned, and insulted by the Pharisees for his allegiance to Jesus Christ. As soon as Christ found out, he went looking for him, and rewarded him with the gift of a deeper, more complete faith. Jesus must have been pleased and consoled by the man's courage, just as he is pleased and consoled whenever any of his followers stay faithful to him in the face of difficulties or persecution. In hard times, friends show what they're really made of.

Christ: I am always the Good Shepherd, always seeking out and protecting my sheep and leading them to rich pastures and flowing streams. I never abandon you – I never have and I never will. I will never leave you alone. How could I? I died in order to give you life. You can always count on me to feel your needs deeply and hear your prayers, even before you feel them or voice them. Only those, like the Pharisees, who refuse to put aside their illusory, but comfortable, self-suffi-ciency and accept me as their Lord and companion, need ever fear being separated from me.

CHRIST IN MY LIFE I know you love me, Lord. And I know you are always on the lookout to teach me, guide me, protect me, and heal me. Your goodness is a broad as the sky and as deep as the ocean. Your faithfulness is as steadfast as the snow-capped mountains. I beg you, Lord, to increase my faith. Let these truths that I know in my mind seep into the depths of my heart. I want to experience your joy…

I fear spiritual blindness. The Pharisees were the most learned of men, and yet they didn't recognize you. They were experts, consultants, and guides, yet they themselves fell into the dark pit of arrogance. If they fell so low, how can I pretend to be immune from the temptations to self-sufficiency, pride, vanity? Keep me humble, Lord; how much I need your constant help…

You will has never let me down. Make me a faithful friend, a trustworthy worker, loving and dependable in all my relationships, especially in the most ordinary and day-to-day ones. If you were faithful, it was in order to give me an example, a clue to true happiness. With your grace, I can be faithful too. I want to be faithful to you, to the Church, to those around me – faithful unto death…

QUESTIONS FOR SMALL GROUP DISCUSSION

1. What struck you most in this passage? What did you notice that you hadn't noticed before?

2. Christ's miraculous intervention in the blind man's life changed his heart and his behavior as well as his eyesight. Christ still intervenes in our lives. How does he do so, and how should we react?

3. The blind man was willing to defend Jesus even in the face of persecution, knowing that Christ was not going to let him down. What opportunities do our life situations give us to defend Jesus and bear witness to him?

4. What are some circumstances or occurrences that could start moving us in the direction of pharisaical spiritual blindness, and how can we guard against that?

Cf. Catechism of the Catholic Church: 2088-2089 and 2091 on sins against faith and hope; 1420-

1421 on the Christ's continued work of healing through his sacraments of penance and anointing; 1866, 2094, 2733, and 2755 on sloth and not taking advantage of the opportunities God presents during this life

THE GOSPEL OF JOHN CHAPTER 10

"So the sheep find the Lord's pastures; for anyone who follows him with an undivided heart is nourished in a pasture which is forever green. What are the pastures of these sheep if they are not the deepest joys of the everlasting fresh pastures of paradise? For the pasture of the saints is to see God face to face; when the vision of God never fails, the soul receives its fill of the food of life forever. And so, dear brethren, let us seek these pastures and there join in the joy and the celebrations of so many citizens of heaven. Let their happiness and rejoicing be an invitation to us. Let our hearts grow warm, brethren, let our faith be rekindled, let our desires for heavenly things grow warm; for to love like this is to be on the way."

- Pope St Gregory the Great

270. LIFE TO THE FULL (JN 10:1-10)

"Christ my God, you humbled yourself in order to lift me, a straying sheep, on to your shoulders."

- St John Damascene

John 10:1-10

'I tell you most solemnly, anyone who does not enter the sheepfold through the gate, but gets in some other way is a thief and a brigand. The one who enters through the gate is the shepherd of the flock; the gatekeeper lets him in, the sheep hear his voice, one by one he calls his own sheep and leads them out. When he has brought out his flock, he goes ahead of them, and the sheep follow because they know his voice. They never follow a stranger but run away from him: they do not recognise the voice of strangers.' Jesus told them this parable but they failed to understand what he meant by telling it to them. So Jesus spoke to them again: 'I tell you most solemnly, I am the gate of the sheepfold. All others who have come are thieves and brigands; but the sheep took no notice of them. I am the gate. Anyone who enters through me will be safe: he will go freely in and out and be sure of finding pasture. The thief comes only to steal and kill and destroy. I have come so that they may have life and have it to the full.'

CHRIST THE LORD Israel had long been a shepherding people, and none of these details would have been lost on Jesus' listeners. Israel's greatest king was a shepherd (David), and it is one of the favorite images of God in the psalms and the prophets: "The Lord is my shepherd, I lack nothing…" (Psalm 23). By assuming this identity, Christ asserts both our need for his guidance and care and his great willingness to provide it.

When a lamb is particularly rambunctious or adventurous, repeatedly putting itself in danger, a shepherd will sometimes purposely break one of its legs. He then puts the lamb around his neck until its leg is healed. By that time, the little lamb has become attached to the shepherd, and it never again strays far from its master's protection and guidance.

Jesus wants us to know who he is: the Good Shepherd who protects and cares for the people of God just as a shepherd does his sheep. He does not claim to be one among many, but the only one: "All others who have come are thieves and brigands." Some religious leaders and philosophers throughout history have claimed to be saviors, claimed to have all the answers, but they were really consumed by pride, greed, or lust. Others sincerely sought to better this world, but simply did not have enough wisdom or power to provide the human family with the kind of hope we long for and need. Jesus Christ, on the other hand, not only wants to give us abundant life, but he can. Omniscient, omnipotent, and eternal, he combines utter goodness with unlimited wisdom and power. With his flock, the problem is not the shepherd's powerlessness or ignorance, but the sheep's lack of docility: we stray from the flock and trap ourselves in thistles and swamps. As Christians, we don't only have a *good* Shepherd, but the *perfect* Shepherd; now all we need is to be sensible sheep and listen to the voice of the One we know.

CHRIST THE TEACHER A flock of sheep needs both protection and nourishment. The corral (sheepfold) provides the protection, and the fields provide the food and water. Without the corral, they are vulnerable to attack (sheep are notoriously bad at self-defense), and without the pasture, they starve. When Christ calls himself the "gate" for the sheep, he is claiming to provide us with everything we need, both the sheepfold and the pasture.

In Palestine, shepherds often sleep in the opening of the sheepfold, which is made out of a large circle of thick, high shrubbery. In this way, the shepherds both scare away the wolves and keep the sheep together: wolves smell their presence and are afraid to make midnight raids, while the sheep have no desire to walk over the shepherd to escape through the opening, since they recognize him as a sign of security. When day finally dawns, the shepherd will rise and lead his sheep out to pasture. Thus the gate, the door to the sheep pen, symbolizes the complete attention and care given by a good shepherd. Christ chooses this image to teach us what he wants to be for each of us: everything.

CHRIST THE FRIEND Sheep grow accustomed to their shepherd, and vice versa. When a shepherd leads his sheep out to graze, he walks in front of them, speaking or singing to them. They recognize his voice and follow along. Very different is the cattle driver, who pushes the herd from behind by force. A shepherd knows which sheep tend to wander off from the flock, which tend to lead others astray, and which he can count on to stay close beside him – he knows each by name.

Sheep are also infamously dependent. They are defenseless against their carnivorous predators. They will gnaw a little patch of grass down to dirt and then starve instead of looking over the next hill for fresh pasture. They will follow one another to their deaths over the edge of a cliff before breaking ranks. If any animal needs husbanding, it's the sheep; sheep depend on their shepherd. And shepherds always want their sheep to be healthy and happy. They want them to have the best grass, fresh water, and safety, so that they can grow and multiply as much as possible. A sheep has no greater friend than a good shepherd, and we have no greater friend than Christ. He invented life, he gave us life, and he came so that, in him, we might learn to live it "to the full."

CHRIST IN MY LIFE If I believed in you the way I really ought to, I would pray more, study the Scriptures more, and make a more concerted effort to discover and embrace your will in the daily hustle and bustle of life. I'm not a very good sheep, Lord. I get distracted by the seductions of other shepherds – the ones who are thieves and robbers. Forgive me, Lord. Teach me to do your will…

So many people are wandering through life like lost sheep, Lord. They are looking for good pastures, for guidance. They are fearful of wolves, and they don't know how to distinguish friends from enemies or wise counselors from charlatans. Call out to them. They need you. Teach me to be a loudspeaker for your voice, so those around me can find you and come into the fold where they belong…

It is hard for me to admit that I need you as much as I do. Why is that, Lord? Why do I think I can be so self-sufficient, when in fact I know very well that I am constantly stumbling along and messing things up? You are a God who comes to watch over me and guide me. My greatest glory, Lord, is to be loved by you. Free me to trust wholly in your goodness and obey fully your will…

QUESTIONS FOR SMALL GROUP DISCUSSION

1. What struck you most in this passage? What did you notice that you hadn't noticed before?

2. This speech takes place right after Jesus cured the man born blind, when the man defends Jesus as the Messiah in front of the threatening Pharisees. What special relevance does that context give to this speech?

3. In this passage, Christ gives a summary of his life's mission: "I have come so that they may have life and have it to the full." What do you think he means by "life" and "to the full"?

4. Who embodies the role of the good shepherd in our world today? Who do people look to for guidance and protection when they don't look to Christ?

Cf. Catechism of the Catholic Church: 754, 874 on the flock of sheep as an image for the Church; 896 on the image of the Good Shepherd as a model for the ministry of priests and bishops

271. ONE FLOCK, ONE SHEPHERD (JN 10:11-18)

"Death is certain, and life is short and vanishes like smoke. Therefore you must fix your minds on the Passion of our Lord Jesus Christ who so burned with love for us that he came down from heaven to redeem us."

- St Francis of Paola

John 10:11-18

'I am the good shepherd: the good shepherd is one who lays down his life for his sheep. The hired man, since he is not the shepherd and the sheep do not belong to him, abandons the sheep and runs away as soon as he sees a wolf coming, and then the wolf attacks and scatters the sheep; this is because he is only a hired man and has no concern for the sheep. I am the good shepherd; I know my own and my own know me, just as the Father knows me and I know the Father; and I lay down my life for my sheep. And there are other sheep I have that are not of this fold, and these I have to lead as well. They too will listen to my voice, and there will be only one flock, and one shepherd. The Father loves me, because I lay down my life in order to take it up again. No one takes it from me; I lay it down of my own free will, and as it is in my power to lay it down, so it is in my power to take it up again; and this is the command I have been given by my Father.'

CHRIST THE LORD Jesus Christ was sent to the Jews to be their Messiah in accordance with God's ancient promises to his Chosen People. Yet God was not satisfied to save only one group of people – he wants his blessing to reach all nations, every corner of the earth. Christ the Savior, then, receives Lordship not only over the little flock of Israel and Judah but over all the flocks of the earth. In him, we all come under one Lordship, that of the Good Shepherd, who is the one pastor of the one flock. The effect of the wolf (the devil) is to catch and scatter the sheep; Christ frees and unites us. And even if the wolf attacks the shepherd himself, as he will during Christ's Passion, the shepherd has the power both to lay down and raise up his life, so the one flock will never perish, never be scattered, never be captured. Because Christ the Good Shepherd is our Lord, the Church (the one flock) will never fail. Our membership in this flock is perhaps the greatest gift we have received from the Lord after the gift of life itself. Unfortunately, we often take them both for granted.

This is one of the most compelling reasons behind the Church's missionary mandate. We are all called to spread the Good News of Christ, to "make disciples of all nations," bringing everyone into this one flock. Only the Catholic Church has the divine guarantee that it will never fail (never be scattered by wolves). Other churches and other religions may have sincere believers and parts of the truth, but only Christ's one flock gathered around his vicar's staff is guaranteed never to fail. Building the Kingdom of the Lord, then, means building up his Church.

CHRIST THE TEACHER The fall of Adam and Eve came about as a result of their lack of trust in God. Jesus Christ came to win back that trust. By giving up his own life to atone for our sins, he showed that the Father is worthy of our trust, that he will forgive us, protect us, and lead us to rich pastures. God will never abandon us in our need – never. The Passion, death and Resurrection of Jesus Christ are his proof. Though the wolf (the devil) attacked and scattered Christ's disciples on that first Good Friday, Christ did not flee; he gave up his own life, freely suffering what in truth we, because of our sins, deserved to suffer and freely obeying with the total obedience that Adam and Eve had lacked. Because of his docility in embracing the Father's will, the Father rewarded him by raising him from the dead. Christ was faithful to his mission, even knowing what it was going to cost him. That mission consists in saving us from sin and estrangement from God. He is the Good Shepherd, the one we can trust, the one who cares more about our lives than we do ourselves, the Lord who came not to be served, but to serve, and to give his life as a ransom for ours.

Note how this mission of carrying out the Father's plan, of obeying the Father's will, consumes Jesus and constitutes in his mind the entire meaning of his life: "The Father loves me, because I lay down my life in order to take it up again... and this is the command I have been given by my Father." This is how Christ, the perfect man, lived out his human existence, focusing wholly on the Father's will, being passionately faithful to his sonship. To discover and fulfill our own identity as children of God, and thus experience life as he created us to live it¬ – both now and in eternity – Jesus invites us to do the same: "The sheep follow, because they know his voice" (John 10:4).

CHRIST THE FRIEND *Jesus: I know my own and my own know me. When I created you, I built two needs into your soul: the need to love and the need to be loved. If you don't learn to love, you will never flourish, and if you don't discover that you are loved, you will never learn to love. Love is always a two-way street – an exchange, an embrace. It's much harder for you to let yourself be loved than it is to love, because to be loved, you have to let yourself be known. You cannot be loved fully by someone who doesn't know you fully. This is why every earthly love is precarious; you never know if the person who loves you will continue to do so when they know you better.*

I know you through and through, completely, even better than you know yourself. I know all the things you keep hidden from others, all the things about you that you barely understand yourself. I know you so thoroughly because I gave you life, I brought you into existence, and I have been holding you and sustaining you every instant of your life. I know you uniquely and totally, so I can love you as no one else can. You never have to worry about my love waning, because I have already shown you, while you were still a sinner, still a rebel, that my love endures to the end, even to death on a cross. You have nothing left to fear. Nothing is hidden from me, and yet I still love you without an ounce of ambiguity or reluctance. I know you, and now you know me. I love you, so come now and love me...

CHRIST IN MY LIFE How can I thank you for bringing me into your flock and saving me from so many dangers? You have called out to me, and you have given me ears to hear your voice. Never let me be separated from you, Lord. Only you love me enough to lay down your life for my sake. Teach me to be worthy of your love. Teach me to be docile, to stay at your side no matter what...

I am so used to thinking about your sacrificial love. I look at crucifixes all the time. But I know that I haven't plumbed the depths of this lesson. You gave your life because you loved me. How can I discover the full import of that truth? I think it's only by following in your footsteps. Only by giving my own life for your Kingdom, by sacrificing myself for the good of my neighbor and those around me...

How can I love you, Lord? Love wants to give, but what can I give you that you don't already have? I know the answer, Lord. I can love you by loving those you put into my life. Every one of them. You love them, and so you are within them, and when I love them, I am loving you. May our wills become one...

QUESTIONS FOR SMALL GROUP DISCUSSION

1. What struck you most in this passage? What did you notice that you hadn't noticed before?

2. If we were more aware of our need for God, which Christ likens to the sheep's need for the shepherd, how would that affect our everyday attitudes and choices?

3. What can we do to foster a healthier awareness of our membership in the universal Church, by which we should rejoice with our fellow Christians when they rejoice, and mourn with them when they mourn?

4. What more can we do to help those in our community draw closer to the Good Shepherd – or enter into the flock?

Cf. Catechism of the Catholic Church: 754, 874, and 2686 on the flock of sheep as an image for the Church; 830-856 on the universality of the Catholic Church; 396, 397, and 227 on the role of trusting God in the life of a Christian; 846-856 on the Church's missionary responsibility and salvation

272. A SHEPHERD'S LAMENT (JN 10:19-42)

"Let us have recourse to that fatherly love revealed to us by Christ in his messianic mission, a love which reached its culmination in his cross, in his death and resurrection."

- Pope John Paul II

John 10:19-42

These words caused disagreement among the Jews. Many said, 'He is possessed, he is raving; why bother to listen to him?' Others said, 'These are not the words of a man possessed by a devil: could a devil open the eyes of the blind?' It was the time when the feast of Dedication was being celebrated in Jerusalem. It was winter, and Jesus was in the Temple walking up and down in the Portico of Solomon. The Jews gathered round him and said, 'How much longer are you going to keep us in suspense? If you are the Christ, tell us plainly.' Jesus replied: 'I have told you, but you do not believe. The works I do in my Father's name are my witness; but you do not believe, because you are no sheep of mine. The sheep that belong to me listen to my voice; I know them and they follow me. I give them eternal life; they will never be lost and no one will ever steal them from me. The Father who gave them to me is greater than anyone, and no one can steal from the Father. The Father and I are one.'

The Jews fetched stones to stone him, so Jesus said to them, 'I have done many good works for you to see, works from my Father; for which of these are you stoning me?' The Jews answered him, 'We are not stoning you for doing a good work but for blasphemy: you are only a man and you claim to be God.' Jesus answered: 'Is it not written in your Law: I said, you are gods? So the Law uses the word gods of those to whom the word of God was addressed, and scripture cannot be rejected. Yet you say to someone the Father has consecrated and sent into the world, You are blaspheming, because he says, I am the son of God. If I am not doing my Father's work, there is no need to believe me; but if I am doing it, then even if you refuse to believe in me, at least believe in the work I do; then you will know for sure that the Father is in me and I am in the Father.' They wanted to arrest him then, but he eluded them. He went back again to the far side of the Jordan to stay in the district where John had once been baptising. Many people who came to him there said, 'John gave no signs, but all he said about this man was true'; and many of them believed in him.

CHRIST THE LORD "I and the Father are one." When the Jewish leaders heard him say that, they picked up rocks in order to stone him to death – for a man to claim equality with God was, for them, the purest blasphemy, the grossest idolatry. Indeed, what other man in history has claimed to be God – not just "a" god or a "manifestation" of a higher power, but *the* God? It is an outrageous claim, and it makes it impossible to write Jesus off as merely a great teacher, philosopher, or religious leader. Even believing Christians, however, can fall into those errors, at least in practical terms – treating their Christianity like a cold body of doctrine or a mere personal opinion. Therefore, although Christ has made this claim frequently throughout the Gospels, we should never tire of considering it, of letting it sink deeper and deeper into our understanding of the Lord we follow.

Someone who makes such a claim can only be one of two things: a lunatic or exactly what he says he is. The Gospels give no evidence for lunacy in Christ; in fact, his teaching and his behavior are more lucid and brilliant than anyone else's, and his miracles (the "works" he constantly refers to) are incontrovertible. And in the centuries after his Ascension, his followers and doctrine have not waned – as would a lunatic's – but have only grown, contributing immeasurable good to a human race beset with evil. Therefore, we have to conclude that Christ wasn't a lunatic. Only one option remains. But if he is indeed who he says he is, then we must follow him. That takes humility; it takes listening to him and trusting him, as sheep do with their shepherd. Indeed, he is the Lord – that is clear; what's problematic is our reluctance to surrender our personal kingdoms into his hands.

Another level of meaning can be ascribed to this phrase. On the one hand, as the Jews understood it, Jesus was claiming equality with God. On the other hand, Jesus alludes to the Old Testament texts that refer to judges who have been set aside to do God's work as "gods" – i.e., men set aside to represent God to other men through the administration of justice (e.g., Psalm 82:6 and

901

Exodus 21:6). In this sense, then, Jesus' phrase "I and the Father are one" emphasizes the interpersonal union between the Son and the Father, a union of love that Jesus manifests more perfectly than anyone else who has ever been sent by God through his flawless and loving obedience. From this perspective, the Lord's claim to be one with the Father is actually an invitation for his listeners to enter into the same union; if they "listen to [his] voice and follow [him]," they will enter into the "eternal life" that he shares with his Father.

CHRIST THE TEACHER The scene St John describes is picturesque. It is winter, cool and blustery, during the celebration of Hanukah, a commemoration of the cleansing and rededication of the Temple in 164 BC after its three years of being polluted by pagan squatters (this had occurred with the successful completion of the Maccabees' wars against the Greek Hellenistic ruler of Palestine, Antiochus Epiphanes). Jesus is spending his days in the outer courtyard of the Temple precincts. This courtyard was flanked by two huge covered colonnades that were over forty feet high. He and his apostles and other residents and pilgrims are walking up and down the colonnades discussing the meaning of the Scriptures, the nature of the Messiah, and the way of salvation. Jesus is strolling along the porticoes arguing and explaining and teaching and exhorting. It is no dry, difficult to comprehend, boring philosophical lecture, but a passionate, enthusiastic, fiery exchange in which the eager words of Jesus stir his listeners' to question him and themselves. Their comments, questions, and reactions pour out, not waiting for the others to finish, talking over each other, full of intent enthusiasm. God is walking among men, speaking their language, engaging with them on their own turf, joyfully pleading with them to open their minds and hearts to his revelation.

This is still his methodology. Jesus is still walking among men through his ordained ministers and his missionaries, through his catechists and his disciples in every walk of life. He dwells and speaks and accompanies all men through those who by his grace have become his ambassadors. And he still backs up his words with incontrovertible deeds, with signs that prove his credibility and dependability – the greatest of which is the continued existence and expansion of his Church. In spite of twenty centuries of nonstop crises and attacks, the Church marches on, giving light to the world and reminding men and women of all times and places they are loved by a merciful God who invites them to join him in the everlasting adventure of eternal life.

CHRIST THE FRIEND "I give them eternal life." Shepherds want their sheep to thrive. They want their sheep to stay safe, to eat well, to be healthy and happy – the shepherds' livelihood depends on it. Christ is our shepherd.

Christ: All I want is for you to flourish, to experience the fullness and wonder of life as I designed it to be. Every invitation I make, every indication I give through my words, my example, the commandments, the teachings of my Church, the nudges in your conscience, all has but one purpose: to lead you into the incomparably rich pastures of a life in communion with me, a communion that can begin here on earth but will only reach its fulfillment when you come home to heaven. I want to be your Good Shepherd, and my greatest joy is when you decide to be my good sheep.

CHRIST IN MY LIFE You and the Father are one, and you invite me to be one with you. I can't get over how strange it is that you, Creator of all things, deign to come into my life and address me, guide me, and patiently invite me to follow you and assume responsibility in your Kingdom. You and I both know that I don't deserve this kind of attention. It flows from your abundant goodness, which will never run dry…

Only you know how hot the desire for meaning and fruitfulness burns in my heart. How strange this life is! It is so full of joys and sorrows and yet so incomplete. You are the bread of life. Keep guiding me, Lord; keep leading me. You know what I need and hope for – you are my hope. Never let me slow down or be satisfied when you still have more in store for me…

You were eager to dwell among men because you had something to give them – your love, your wisdom, your grace. And now you have made me your messenger. Am I as eager as you were to engage my neighbors, to bring them your light? I am reluctant sometimes. I don't love enough. But you know that I want to love more. And that's all you need – you will work wonders through those who trust in you…

QUESTIONS FOR SMALL GROUP DISCUSSION

1. What struck you most in this passage? What did you notice that you hadn't noticed before?

2. How can we increase our confidence in Christ's unique Lordship enough so that we are able to defend and explain it calmly and charitably (inoffensively) in conversations with those who don't believe it?

3. In what ways can we be true to our need for God throughout the day? In other words, in what situations do we tend to forget about God or act like we don't really need him?

4. When God asks something difficult of us, why is it often so hard to react with faith and trust, obeying promptly and joyfully?

Cf. Catechism of the Catholic Church: 754, 874, and 2686 on the flock of sheep as an image for the Church; 830-856 on the universality of the Catholic Church; 396, 397, and 227 on the role of trusting in God in the life of a Christian

THE GOSPEL OF JOHN CHAPTER 11

"The Lord, our Savior, raised his voice and spoke with incomparable majesty. 'Let all know,' he said, 'that after sorrow grace follows; let them understand that without the burden of affliction one cannot arrive at the height of glory; that the measure of heavenly gifts is increased in proportion to the labors undertaken. Let them be on their guard against error or deception; this is the only ladder by which paradise is reached; without the cross there is no road to heaven.'"

- St Rose of Lima

273. GOD'S TIMING (JN 11:1-16)

"Rather, my dear brothers, let us be ready for all that God's will may bring, with an undivided heart, firm faith, and rugged strength."

- St Cyprian

John 11:1-16

There was a man named Lazarus who lived in the village of Bethany with the two sisters, Mary and Martha, and he was ill. It was the same Mary, the sister of the sick man Lazarus, who anointed the Lord with ointment and wiped his feet with her hair. The sisters sent this message to Jesus, 'Lord, the man you love is ill.' On receiving the message, Jesus said, 'This sickness will end not in death but in God's glory, and through it the Son of God will be glorified.' Jesus loved Martha and her sister and Lazarus, yet when he heard that Lazarus was ill he stayed where he was for two more days before saying to the disciples, 'Let us go to Judaea.' The disciples said, 'Rabbi, it is not long since the Jews wanted to stone you; are you going back again?' Jesus replied: 'Are there not twelve hours in the day? A man can walk in the daytime without stumbling because he has the light of this world to see by; but if he walks at night he stumbles, because there is no light to guide him.' He said that and then added, 'Our friend Lazarus is resting, I am going to wake him.' The disciples said to him, 'Lord, if he is able to rest he is sure to get better'. The phrase Jesus used referred to the death of Lazarus, but they thought that by 'rest' he meant 'sleep,' so Jesus put it plainly, 'Lazarus is dead; and for your sake I am glad I was not there because now you will believe. But let us go to him.' Then Thomas – known as the Twin – said to the other disciples, 'Let us go too, and die with him.'

CHRIST THE LORD Jesus is drawing close to the end of his earthly mission. His disciples have been accompanying him, learning from him, and witnessing his miracles for almost three years. Here once again St John shows that Jesus had knowledge that was not merely human – he knew how Lazarus's sickness would end, and he knew, without any need for a messenger, when Lazarus had died.

And yet, even at this late point in his ministry, even when Jesus shows his divine knowledge, we see that his disciples still don't understand him. They still misconstrue his words and even doubt his good sense and power. Any lesser Lord would have long ago given up on his slow and artless followers, but not Jesus. He is a Lord who serves his subjects, teaching them and guiding them to the fullness of life. The needier they are, the more he condescends to stay with them, put up with them, and give them whatever they need in order to make them believe in, trust, and follow him. And besides all this, he entrusted his greatest gift to their care – his Church. The Lord rules, but he rules with love.

CHRIST THE TEACHER St John points out that "Jesus loved Martha and her sister and Lazarus." And yet he let Lazarus die. He told the messengers, "This sickness will end not in death but in God's glory, and through it the Son of God will be glorified." Jesus loves them, and yet he lets them suffer. He lets them experience their helplessness, their weakness, the separation of death, and the loss of a loved one. Did he do it to punish them? Did he do it because he had no power to remedy the evil? No, he let them suffer precisely because he loved them. He wanted to give them the great gift of knowing him more deeply and more intimately, and he wanted them to experience his power and his love more profoundly. The suffering afforded him an opportunity to act in their lives in a new way, revealing himself to them more completely. This is God's glory – that we know him and love him and experience his love more completely.

We urgently need to contemplate this moment in our Lord's life. Suffering, death, pain, and sorrow touch us all. If we exercise our faith in Christ's wisdom as shown in his relationship with this family from Bethany, we will be more ready to find and embrace him when suffering strikes closer to home.

CHRIST THE FRIEND The messengers arrive tired and breathless; they have traveled in haste. The circle of apostles opens up so they can come close to the Master and deliver their message. Their faces are anxious, fearful, but with a glint of hope that Jesus will come to save the dying Lazarus. And they deliver their message, the simplest and subtlest of messages, composed by Mary and

Martha, close friends of Jesus (and probably relatives on Jesus' mother's side according to the scholars): "Lord, the man you love is ill." The messengers look earnestly and eagerly at Christ's face, and the apostles alternate their gazes between Jesus and the messengers. Silence. Then Jesus, looking warmly at the messengers, smiles and answers: "This sickness will not end in death…"

Christ: Look into my heart at the moment when I heard that message, "The man you love is ill." How it filled my soul with joy! It was the perfect prayer. Martha and Mary knew me so well. They knew that I loved, and they knew that I can't hold back from acting on my love. They could have said, "Lord, the one who loves you is ill," as though because Lazarus loved me, he deserved to be healed. But who loved more, Lazarus or I? I loved him infinitely more than he could ever love me! They could have said, "Lord, come and heal Lazarus, who is ill." But they knew that my love would do much more than they could ever think of. This was the perfect prayer. It throws all their needs and hopes and sorrows into the bottomless ocean of my love. You too can pray this prayer. Do you have a need, a worry, a sin that has to be forgiven? Say to me, "Lord, the one you love is ill," and how will I be able to hold myself back from coming to your aid? Do you have someone else who is in need? Tell me "Lord, the one you love is ill." Can my heart resist that prayer? Is it possible? It may seem that I delay my response, but trust me. My love only seeks fullness of life for you and greater glory for my Father.

CHRIST IN MY LIFE I am slow and artless, clumsy and inelegant by nature, Lord. You have to teach me the same lesson a hundred times before I start getting the gist of it. But you are willing to do that. I think that one of the best ways I can praise you is simply by rejoicing in your love, your patience, and your goodness. You are all-powerful, all-loving, and all-good – you are all mine, so I can always rejoice…

You have something for me to do in your Kingdom, just as you had something for each of your apostles. You have given me a mission in life, and because I am united to you through grace, that mission will resound through all eternity. Without you, what worthwhile thing would I have to do? What could I do that would last? You have given me what I yearn for most: meaning, purpose, a mission…

Lord, I am here, the one you love, and I am ill. I am sick with the infection of selfishness, vanity, arrogance, and self-indulgence. I am weighed down by troubles and worries. Lord, the one you love is ill. I trust in you. You are mercy. You are love…

QUESTIONS FOR SMALL GROUP REFLECTION

1. What struck you most in this passage? What did you notice that you hadn't noticed before?

2. Why is it often so hard to trust in Christ during times of crisis and suffering?

3. How does our popular culture's view of suffering and sickness compare with the Christian view?

4. St John tells us that Jesus said to his apostles, "For your sake I am glad I was not there because now you will believe." That implies that they still did not believe. What did you think they didn't believe, and why didn't they? Does this detail have some kind of a lesson for us?

Cf. Catechism of the Catholic Church: 547-550 on the meaning of Christ's miracles; 551-553 on the special role of the Twelve Apostles in the Kingdom of Christ; 478 on the heart of Christ; 1500-1513 on the place of sickness in the lives of Christians

274. THE FORCE OF FAITH – THE POWER OF LOVE (JN 11: 17-44)

"Since Christ is our peace, we shall be living up to the name of Christian if we let Christ be seen in our lives by letting peace reign in our hearts."

- St Gregory of Nyssa

John 11:17-44

On arriving, Jesus found that Lazarus had been in the tomb for four days already. Bethany is only about two miles from Jerusalem, and many Jews had come to Martha and Mary to sympathise with them over their brother. When Martha heard that Jesus had come she went to meet him. Mary remained sitting in the house. Martha said to Jesus, 'If you had been here, my brother would not have died, but I know that, even now, whatever you ask of God, he will grant you'. 'Your brother' said Jesus to her 'will rise again.' Martha said, 'I know he will rise again at the resurrection on the last day'. Jesus said: 'I am the resurrection. If anyone believes in me, even though he dies he will live, and whoever lives and believes in me will never die. Do you believe this?' 'Yes, Lord,' she said 'I believe that you are the Christ, the Son of God, the one who was to come into this world.' When she had said this, she went and called her sister Mary, saying in a low voice, 'The Master is here and wants to see you'. Hearing this, Mary got up quickly and went to him. Jesus had not yet come into the village; he was still at the place where Martha had met him. When the Jews who were in the house sympathising with Mary saw her get up so quickly and go out, they followed her, thinking that she was going to the tomb to weep there.

Mary went to Jesus, and as soon as she saw him she threw herself at his feet, saying, 'Lord, if you had been here, my brother would not have died.' At the sight of her tears, and those of the Jews who followed her, Jesus said in great distress, with a sigh that came straight from the heart, 'Where have you put him?' They said, 'Lord, come and see.' Jesus wept; and the Jews said, 'See how much he loved him!' But there were some who remarked, 'He opened the eyes of the blind man, could he not have prevented this man's death?' Still sighing, Jesus reached the tomb: it was a cave with a stone to close the opening. Jesus said, 'Take the stone away.' Martha said to him, 'Lord, by now he will smell; this is the fourth day'. Jesus replied, 'Have I not told you that if you believe you will see the glory of God?' So they took away the stone. Then Jesus lifted up his eyes and said: 'Father, I thank you for hearing my prayer. I knew indeed that you always hear me, but I speak for the sake of all these who stand round me, so that they may believe it was you who sent me.' When he had said this, he cried in a loud voice, 'Lazarus, here! Come out!' The dead man came out, his feet and hands bound with bands of stuff and a cloth round his face. Jesus said to them, 'Unbind him, let him go free.'

CHRIST THE LORD Jesus raises Lazarus from the dead. He had been in the tomb for four days, and Jesus Christ calls his name, orders him to come out, and he does. Death itself submits to Christ the Lord. The crowd must have been stupefied, wide-eyed with disbelief, awe, and wonder that gathered in deadly silence as Lazarus stepped out from the tomb and then burst forth in a storm of joy and celebration. Martha and Mary were so full of natural jubilation and supernatural elation that they wouldn't have known who to embrace first, their brother or their Lord. Lazarus, as soon as the cloths were removed, surely gazed into his Lord's shining eyes with the deepest love and most determined, courageous loyalty that he had ever experienced. The whole scene was a prelude to heaven and the final resurrection.

The Church presents this reading to us towards the end of the Lenten liturgical crescendo: Christ told the woman at the well that he was the Messiah; he cured the man born blind, something never done before; and now he tops everything by raising Lazarus from the dead, once again "for God's glory; through it the Son of God will be glorified." Jesus knows that in order to fulfill the Father's plan, he will soon suffer humiliation, torture, and death. As that moment draws near, he performs miracle after miracle to bolster his disciples' faith, so that the coming events of his Passion will not snuff out their hope in him.

How many great figures throughout history have made (and continue to make) wild claims and fabulous promises! And yet none have made such a claim as Christ: "I am the resurrection…" Unlike so many others, however, Jesus Christ backs up his claims with incontrovertible deeds. He is a Leader we can count on – forever.

CHRIST THE TEACHER Martha and Mary had different personalities. Martha was the organizer, the practical one, the quick-thinking one, attentive to details. She doesn't interrupt Mary's prayer when she gets word that Jesus has arrived – she quietly tiptoes away. She comes to Jesus and discusses the situation with him, eliciting explanations and words and instruction from the Master. She is the one who arranges that her sister too can come to be with the Lord. She whispers to Jesus that if they take away the stone the stench of the tomb will be terrific. Mary, on the other hand, was the contemplative one, the intense and more emotional one, the natural, effortless leader. Everyone followed her out of the house when she rushed to see Jesus. She throws herself at his feet when she sees him. She moves his heart and elicits his tears.

Did either one love Jesus more? Did Jesus love either one more? Not at all. The lesson St John teaches us by presenting these distinct portraits is that each one of us has a unique relationship with Christ. Mary and Martha shared a friend in Jesus, but each one's friendship was personal, intimate, and customized. Learning this lesson is essential to achieving peace of heart and maturity in our spiritual lives. What would have happened if Mary had wanted to relate to Jesus the way Martha did? She would have been frustrated and anxious and off balance. And what if Martha wanted to relate to Jesus the way Mary did? She too would have been dissatisfied and experienced insincerity and incompleteness in her relationship with Christ. Too often we fall into that trap, trying to gear our friendship with Christ in accordance with someone else's standard or style. We envy what others have instead of being true to what God has given us.

CHRIST THE FRIEND This passage contains the shortest verse in the New Testament: "Jesus wept." Jesus Christ is not a distant God. Look how intimately and familiarly Martha and Mary treat him! He never relinquishes his Lordship, and they never forget that he is the Lord. But he is unlike any other Lord; he not only gives us protection, security, life, and peace, he gives us his very heart. The heart of Christ yearns for us to give him as much love and confidence as Mary and Martha; he yearns to be let into the presence of our hearts so as to share our sorrows and troubles. "Jesus wept." No other god ever shared our tears; only Christ is Emmanuel, "God with us."

Lazarus: How differently I lived from that day on! It was like a fog had lifted and I could see everything clearly. I wasn't anxious for praise and acceptance and recognition anymore, because I finally realized how fleeting such things were. I thought less about myself and my problems, because I knew so clearly that God was holding me in the palm of his hand. I was so free! I was free to bring joy and comfort to those around me, to be a delight for my sisters and our friends. I was free from the fears that made me hesitate to speak to everyone about Jesus. When he called my name and drew me out of the tomb, it really was a brand new start, a brand new life. And he's willing to do the same for everyone, if only they will trust in him and take the first step towards the opening of the tomb.

CHRIST IN MY LIFE Death is the great equalizer. It comes for everyone, and it brings an end to all illusions. And yet you are Lord over death. You have conquered death. With you, death is just a door to an even truer life. Death – so many fear it; so many avoid thinking about it. With you at my side, Lord, I have nothing to fear, nothing to avoid thinking about. Death is my sister; she will lead me deeper into your presence...

Teach me to be as close to you as Mary and Martha were. Teach me to speak to you right from my heart, to share all my thoughts with you. Teach me to be sincere and spontaneous, yet still full of reverence and respect. I too believe in you, I know you are the Resurrection; you are the life. Teach me to trust in you and do your will...

Do you still weep with me, Lord? Do you still feel the losses I feel, the struggles that weigh me down? Can you understand them? Can you come and rescue me from my sorrow as you did with Mary and Martha? I know you do and I know you can. O Lord, increase my faith! Increase my faith! Increase my faith! You don't want me to suffer alone. Let me know your presence, Lord...

QUESTIONS FOR SMALL GROUP DISCUSSION

1. What struck you most in this passage? What did you notice that you hadn't noticed before?

2. Why do you think Jesus spends so much time questioning Martha?

3. If Jesus already knew that Lazarus was dead even before he reached Bethany, why do you think he suddenly started weeping and sighing once he saw the sorrow of all the mourners?

4. Why do you think Jesus had some of the bystanders remove the stone from the entrance to the tomb and then take off Lazarus's burial cloths? If he had the power to raise the dead man to life, he certainly had to have the power to take care of those details as well, didn't he? Do you think these details harbor any lessons for us and for the Church?

Cf. Catechism of the Catholic Church: 992-1004 on the meaning of the resurrection for Christ and for us; 456-460 on why Jesus became man in the first place; 547-550 on Jesus' miracles as signs of the Kingdom

275. PAR FOR THE CHRISTIAN COURSE (JN 11:45-57)

"He was crucified on behalf of us all and for the sake of us all, so that, when one had died instead of all, we all might live in him."

- St Cyril of Alexandria

John 11:45-57

Many of the Jews who had come to visit Mary and had seen what he did believed in him, but some of them went to tell the Pharisees what Jesus had done. Then the chief priests and Pharisees called a meeting. 'Here is this man working all these signs' they said 'and what action are we taking? If we let him go on in this way everybody will believe in him, and the Romans will come and destroy the Holy Place and our nation.' One of them, Caiaphas, the high priest that year, said, 'You don't seem to have grasped the situation at all; you fail to see that it is better for one man to die for the people, than for the whole nation to be destroyed.' He did not speak in his own person, it was as high priest that he made this prophecy that Jesus was to die for the nation – and not for the nation only, but to gather together in unity the scattered children of God. From that day they were determined to kill him. So Jesus no longer went about openly among the Jews, but left the district for a town called Ephraim, in the country bordering on the desert, and stayed there with his disciples. The Jewish Passover drew near, and many of the country people who had gone up to Jerusalem to purify themselves looked out for Jesus, saying to one another as they stood about in the Temple, 'What do you think? Will he come to the festival or not?' The chief priests and Pharisees had by now given their orders: anyone who knew where he was must inform them so that they could arrest him.

CHRIST THE LORD Caiaphas rightly declared that Christ was to die for the sake of the whole nation, but he declared it without fully understanding what he was saying. In his own mind, he meant the preservation of the status quo in Palestine, the continued occupation by the people of Israel of the Promised Land, even though they were under Roman rule. By doing away with Jesus, he thought he would save that relative stability; by letting Jesus continue his ministry, he feared its annihilation by the Romans. In the mind of God, however, the death of Jesus, by giving him a chance to exhibit utter fidelity and perfect, loving obedience, was the antidote to the death of the human race that had occurred because of Adam's infidelity and disobedience. The salvation that God was working out through the actions of Caiaphas was far beyond Caiaphas's wildest imaginings. Instead of maintaining a precarious, merely political status quo, God was laying the foundation for a new and everlasting covenant between God and man.

This incident is a striking example of the great mystery of Providence. God is able to guide the history of the world and of each person's life towards his own wise and glorious ends without violating the freedom of his spiritual creatures. He is a Lord both just and merciful, all-powerful but all-loving. Though we cannot completely understand how this happens, the coming Passion, death, and Resurrection of Jesus is the most astonishing and incontrovertible evidence that it does indeed happen. Nothing on earth walks aimlessly; all things are working together for the good of those whom God loves.

CHRIST THE TEACHER Think for a minute about the recent sequence of events. Jesus shows up in Bethany to visit some of his closest friends, only to find them and their acquaintances mourning Lazarus's death. He is moved with compassion and asks to be taken to the grave. In the midst of the general gloom and sadness, he performs one of the most dramatic miracles of his whole ministry – one of the most dramatic miracles of all human history. He brings Lazarus back from the dead with a mere word of command. Joy, gratitude, celebration, and amazement abound. The news spreads, people come to see for themselves, and the undeniable evidence leads them to believe in Jesus' claims to be the Messiah. They are filled with hope, joy, and humble faith. But not all are rejoicing. For some of the Jewish leaders, the miracle is the straw that breaks the camel's back. They decide finally and definitively to apprehend and destroy the miracle worker.

Is this a logical reaction? Shouldn't even his enemies realize by this point that Jesus was from God? They should have, but they don't. And they flex their political and social muscles so threateningly that Jesus is forced to go into hiding as he waits for the Passover. Anyone who associates with him or even fails to tell the police where he's hiding is menaced with punishment. All because Jesus raised Lazarus from the dead!

The stark contrast between the pure goodness of Christ and the violent opposition his goodness stirs up is a composite of the history of the Church and of every Christian. Where Jesus Christ is truly being preached and taught, where he is changing lives and raising dead souls to hope and enthusiasm, the forces of evil will not tarry in throwing up clouds of adversity. If this happened to Jesus himself, whose goodness and trustworthiness were incontrovertibly confirmed by his extraordinary miracles, only the most foolish or naïve Christian will ever be surprised, scandalized, or discouraged by the opposition that necessarily shows up wherever serious Kingdom-building operations are under way.

CHRIST THE FRIEND The Pharisees appear monstrous to us. Yet we can be just like them. When we are stuck in our sins or wallowing in self-centeredness, the good deeds of others agitate us; they prick our conscience. We try to stamp them out. We try to minimize them. Instead of rejoicing in goodness wherever we find it, we resent it, and we rejoice instead in our neighbor's fall, since it brings them down to our level. Christ is never like that with us. The more we experience his unquenchable generosity towards us, the more it will purify our stinginess and free us to love our neighbors as he does.

Jesus: Do you think I despised these corrupt men who countenanced my death and scattered my sheep? How could I? They were as much my sheep as the others. They were more lost than the others, and I longed for their hearts to turn around and come to me. It was for them that I went to the cross. They needed to see the extent of my love for them; they needed to see that nothing they could do to me was able to stop me from loving them. Rest in my heart for a moment now, and see how I love those who hate and persecute me. Since you know that I am always with you, always loving and guiding and protecting you, you have the strength to do the same.

CHRIST IN MY LIFE Thinking about your Providence fills my soul with peace. I know that you are always watching over me and guiding me and those around me. In some hidden way, the many Good Fridays of human history, and of my story, will all erupt into Easter Sundays. You are my Father, and in addition to loving me intensely and tenderly, you hold the reins of the universe and put everything at the service of that love…

How do I react to difficulties and opposition in life? How did you react? You accepted them, and you continued steadfastly on the path of the Father's will. Why do they upset me so much? Jesus, increase my faith! Convince me that you can handle these injustices and persecutions and this endless gauntlet of obstacles. Lord Jesus, I believe that you are the Lord of life and history, and I trust in you…

Lord Jesus, I can barely keep myself from lashing out at colleagues who show up late… how can I learn to love actual enemies, people who willfully destroy reputations and good works? And how can I refrain from criticizing those who exert their energy and influence in resisting your action and your Spirit? Teach me the science of the cross, Lord, and teach me the lesson of Christ-like love…

QUESTIONS FOR SMALL GROUP DISCUSSION

1. What struck you most in this passage? What did you notice that you hadn't noticed before?

2. What do you think was really at the root of Caiaphas's and the other leaders' resistance to Christ?

3. In what ways do faithful Christians find themselves opposed and persecuted today?

4. Many people believed in Jesus after this miracle, but many still didn't believe in him. What should that teach us about our own evangelizing efforts?

Cf. Catechism of the Catholic Church: 302-314 on the mystery of God's providence and how it combines with the realities of evil and human freedom; 305, 322, 2215, 2547, and 2830 on childlike abandonment to the providence of God; 2608 and 1825, 2443 and 2844 on loving the poor and one's enemies as Christ did; 595-598 on the leaders of Jerusalem and Jesus' death

THE GOSPEL OF JOHN CHAPTER 12

"When we submit ourselves entirely to Christ Jesus, when we abandon ourselves to him, when our soul only responds, like his own, with a perpetual amen to all that he asks of us in the name of his Father; when, after his example, we abide in this attitude of adoration before all the manifestations of the divine will, in face of the least permissions of his providence, then Christ Jesus establishes his peace in us: his peace, not that which the world promises, but that true peace which can only come from himself. Indeed, such adoration produces in us the unity of all desires. The soul has but one thing in view: the establishing in her of Christ's Kingdom. Christ Jesus, in return, satisfies this desire with magnificent plenitude."

- Blessed Columba Marmion

276. THE SWEET SCENT OF LOVE (JN 12:1-11)

"An egg given during life for love of God is more profitable for eternity than a cathedral full of gold given after death."

- St Albert the Great

John 12:1-11

Six days before the Passover, Jesus went to Bethany, where Lazarus was, whom he had raised from the dead. They gave a dinner for him there; Martha waited on them and Lazarus was among those at table. Mary brought in a pound of very costly ointment, pure nard, and with it anointed the feet of Jesus, wiping them with her hair; the house was full of the scent of the ointment. Then Judas Iscariot – one of his disciples, the man who was to betray him – said, 'Why wasn't this ointment sold for three hundred denarii, and the money given to the poor?' He said this, not because he cared about the poor, but because he was a thief; he was in charge of the common fund and used to help himself to the contributions. So Jesus said, 'Leave her alone; she had to keep this scent for the day of my burial. You have the poor with you always, you will not always have me.' Meanwhile a large number of Jews heard that he was there and came not only on account of Jesus but also to see Lazarus whom he had raised from the dead. Then the chief priests decided to kill Lazarus as well, since it was on his account that many of the Jews were leaving them and believing in Jesus.

CHRIST THE LORD Mary's exquisite gesture of love illustrates in three ways the utter uniqueness of Christ and the corresponding uniqueness of our friendship with him.

First, she gives Jesus her best. The ointment was rare, expensive, and precious. Jesus deserves our complete loyalty, not our leftovers. We have received everything from him; we will live forever in his company because of his mercy and love. The only appropriate response to God's generosity is complete abandonment to his goodness and unflinching obedience to his will. Mary shows that she understands this by pouring out upon him her "very costly ointment."

Second, she anoints his feet. The common way to show honor to a guest was through anointing his head. But Mary understood that she could confer no honor upon Christ; he was the Lord, he already possessed infinite dignity. Instead of bestowing honor from a position of superiority, as hosts could normally presume to do for guests who entered their own homes, she humbles herself. In an absolute sense, we cannot do favors for Christ – what does he lack that we can supply? But we can give thanks to him for the favor he has given to us – his coming among us and taking up residence in the needs of our neighbors provides us an opportunity to return love for love. Serving the Lord requires humility of heart.

Third, she wipes his feet with her hair. In Palestine at the time, women covered their hair in public. Mary defies this protocol. Her love for the Master frees her from the shackles of convention and the fears of ridicule. Christian faith is creative. The Lord always has more to give, so when we follow him sincerely, he shatters our human limitations and leads us to new horizons of generosity, new levels of fruitfulness, and new experiences of his goodness.

CHRIST THE TEACHER Jesus defends Mary's gesture on the grounds that the time for such deeds is short. This applies to every human life. Opportunities for love – for the creative, beautiful, saving deeds of self-forgetful generosity – present themselves each day. But if they are not seized, they disappear. How many times have we regretted not issuing a word of encouragement when the idea occurred to us? How many spouses, children, and friends have gazed sadly on the corpse of a loved one, desperately yearning to turn back the clock, to have just five more minutes to express the love that they had failed to show? How many chances to brighten up our neighbor's day or give glory to God in a detail of fidelity or with a brief prayer hover around us as we rush through life thinking only about ourselves? The time to love, the time to give, the time to be the noble child of God that in our hearts we know we are called to be – that time is now.

CHRIST THE FRIEND "Martha waited on them…"

Martha: How can I describe to you that scene? Something new was in the Lord's eyes in those last days before his Passion. It was a new intensity, a new determination. Maybe "new" isn't the right word – it was just more of what had always been there, more intensity, more determination, more attention, more love. And it spread to everyone around him. I will never forget watching him at dinner, surrounded by his apostles, with Mary, so content, sitting at his feet and the other guests unable to look away from him. He was like a glowing hearth that drew in and warmed everyone around him. His presence filled everyone with light and vigor and a freshness of life. What the aroma of Mary's perfume was for our senses, Jesus had already been for our minds and hearts. Whenever I smelled perfume after that day, it reminded me of the gentle power of his presence, which since then has never left me. And I knew that just as the perfume filled the house with its sweet and delicious scent, just so the Lord's life-giving presence was going to spread and fill every corner of history and the world.

CHRIST IN MY LIFE Teach me to love you as I should, Lord. Turn me around – I don't want to keep gazing in the mirror and worrying about what others think of me and how I can achieve more than them. I want to gaze at you, at your truth, at the beauty of your Kingdom. I want to care only about pouring out my life in your service, like Mary's perfume, so that I can spread the fullness of life to those around me…

I wonder if I have it too easy, Lord. Maybe if my life were a bit less comfortable and pleasant I would more easily remember that I am here to fulfill a mission, not just to have a good time. You lived your life so intensely, focusing on your Father's will and the mission he had given you. And that intensity, that focus, was the source of your joy and fruitfulness. Help me, Lord, to follow your example…

Lord Jesus, you have already given me so much, but I want to ask you to come anew into my life, to make me experience again the sweet aroma of your presence. I forget so easily, Lord. The troubles of life dull my faith and hope. I need you to come and dine with me, to let me sit at your feet and drink in your wisdom. I want to keep fighting for your Kingdom. Lord Jesus, give me strength…

QUESTIONS FOR SMALL GROUP DISCUSSION

1. What struck you most in this passage? What did you notice that you hadn't noticed before?

2. Judas' criticism sounded good on the outside, but in reality it stemmed from his selfishness. Can you think of any criticisms currently being launched against the Church that might fall in the same category?

3. If St John knew that Judas was pilfering from the community bank account, surely Jesus knew as well. Why do you think he hadn't taken that responsibility away from Judas? Do you think there is a lesson in this for us?

4. Some people claim that the Church should sell its works of art and give the money to the poor. Do you think that's a good idea? Why or why not?

Cf. Catechism of the Catholic Church: 2096-2097 and 2626-2628 on adoration of God; 2559-2565 on authentic prayer; 2639-2643 on the prayer of praise

277. THE CONQUEROR COMES (JN 12:12-19)

"Just as what brings heat make things expand, so it is the gift of love to stretch hearts wide open; it is a warm and glowing virtue… For there is nothing which so draws a man to return love, as when he understands that he who loves him is urgently longing for his affection."

- St John Chrysostom

John 12:12-19

The next day the crowds who had come up for the festival heard that Jesus was on his way to Jerusalem. They took branches of palm and went out to meet him, shouting, 'Hosanna! Blessings on the King of Israel, who comes in the name of the Lord.' Jesus found a young donkey and mounted it – as scripture says: Do not be afraid, daughter of Zion; see, your king is coming, mounted on the colt of a donkey. At the time his disciples did not understand this, but later, after Jesus had been glorified, they remembered that this had been written about him and that this was in fact how they had received him. All who had been with him when he called Lazarus out of the tomb and raised him from the dead were telling how they had witnessed it; it was because of this, too, that the crowd came out to meet him: they had heard that he had given this sign. Then the Pharisees said to one another, 'You see, there is nothing you can do; look, the whole world is running after him!'

CHRIST THE LORD Two crowds converged on the Lord as he joined the hundreds of thousands of pilgrims who flooded Jerusalem for the celebration of Passover. With him was the crowd that accompanied him from Bethany. Many of the pilgrims stayed in Bethany during the Passover; Jerusalem was too small to hold the masses of people who came for the festival, and Bethany was designated by law as one of the overflow cities. But another, even larger crowd surged out of the city gates as Jesus approached, riding down the small mountain situated to the east of the ancient city. Word had spread that the wonder-working rabbi from Nazareth, whom the authorities had condemned and put a bounty on, was arriving in full daylight. The common people were stirred by curiosity, but also by an intuitive sense of significance. How could it be that this man, whom the rich and powerful were hunting like an outlaw, was brash enough to make such a public appearance? It was a deliberate challenge, as if Jesus was looking the authorities in the eye and daring them to just try and stop him. Such was the viewpoint of the crowds. A man who could show such courage might indeed be the one who would set Israel free from Roman domination, clear out the corrupt collaborationists who ran the Temple and the Sanhedrin, and reestablish the greatness of the Chosen People. If Jesus could raise the dead to life, maybe he was the new conqueror and deliverer.

Jesus accepted their homage, though it was only partially correct. He was the new conqueror, but he came to conquer evil and sin so as to free men's minds and hearts, not to build a political empire. He was the new deliverer, but he came to deliver God's truth, grace, and love through his self-sacrifice on the cross, not to impose the rule of sword and spear. The shouting and frenzy of the crowd precluded him from speaking, but he told them this all the same: he didn't enter on a mighty horse, as kings who were going to war; he came on a meek donkey colt, as kings who come in times of peace.

To this day the world and even many of his believing disciples continue to mistake the nature of Christ's Kingdom. We keep hoping he will bring us heaven on earth, instead of accepting his message of how to live this passing, earthly life in a way that will prepare us for heaven.

CHRIST THE TEACHER St John, who saw this dramatic event with his own eyes – in fact, he was probably walking right beside the Master the whole time, basking in the Lord's glory – makes a point of telling us that "At the time the disciples did not understand this, but later, after Jesus had been glorified, they remembered…"

This is often the case in our journey of faith. God is always at work in our lives, but we don't always recognize or understand his action until later. Like parents who have to teach children to do certain things even before the children can fully understand the reasons behind them, God is constantly preparing us for the future, filling our spiritual supply depots. The example of the disciples who didn't understand the meaning of what Jesus was doing while he was doing it should encourage us. The important thing is simply to stay with Christ, to continue to live in his presence and fulfill the commitments of our friendship with him. If we do, little by little the Holy Spirit will coach us until we reach the fullness of holiness and happiness that he has in store for us. Jesus can see the whole picture even when we can't, so we should continue following his lead with enthusiasm and trust, no matter where it takes us.

CHRIST THE FRIEND "The whole world is running after him!"

A Pharisee: That was the day I started to believe in Jesus. Up until then I was convinced that he deserved to be silenced. But I was standing on the city walls when he came to Jerusalem, and

I watched the crowds behind and before him surge together like two great tides colliding. As he approached, I could see his face. The look he gave them wasn't the look of a power-hungry and self-absorbed demagogue. It was calm, glad, and, well, it sounds rather anticlimactic, but I think the best word to describe it is - good. His countenance irradiated goodness. The irrepressible ebullience of that immense mass of humanity would have made any normal man drunk with their adoration. But not Jesus. And for some reason, I recognized immediately why he was riding on the donkey. I had just been meditating on the prophesy of Zechariah that described how the Messiah would enter into his reign just this way. I had a kind of intuitive flash as I watched him make his way slowly and gently through the forest of palm branches and the din of cheers. I seemed to see that this was the first swell of something entirely new, of a Kingdom that would surpass all of our small and antiquated expectations. And then – you may not believe me, but I promise you, it's true – then, just before he passed through the gate, he looked up, and his eyes met mine. His gaze gripped me and shone right through me as sunlight shines through glass; I couldn't resist it, but I didn't want to. It was just for a split second. And with that look he said to me, "Yes, it is so" – just as if he had known everything I had been thinking while I watched his triumphal entry! And he had known it. He knew it all, because in his mercy and love he had been inspiring those thoughts. From that day forward, I believed.

CHRIST IN MY LIFE I want your Kingdom to come, Lord. I want your wisdom to drench my mind and your love to infuse my heart. I want to be a riverbed through which your saving grace can flood the world around me. I am not looking for comfort and bliss and ease, but for ways of spreading the good news of your salvation. Teach me to be your faithful disciple, right here where I live. I want to live as you would have me live…

I think I am too intent on understanding everything. I get frustrated if I can't figure everything out. But how could I ever comprehend the immensity of your glory and knowledge? Why am I so greedy as to demand an explanation for everything? Lord Jesus, teach me the sweet wisdom of humility and keep me faithful. Show me the way to go and never let me stray from your path…

I believe in you, Lord. I believe that you are the One the Father sent, that you are the Savior of all people, that you are the way, the truth, and the life. Do you know, Lord, how many people don't believe in you? Give them the gift of faith. Increase my faith, so that I can go and tell them the truth. Every soul is searching for you, Lord. Let them find you. Let them discover your love…

QUESTIONS FOR SMALL GROUP DISCUSSION

1. What struck you most in this passage? What did you notice that you hadn't noticed before?
2. The Church puts this prayer – "Hosanna in the highest, blessed is he who comes…" – on our lips during Mass, right before the prayer of consecration. Why do you think this is so?

3. Why do you think Jesus chose to make his final entry into Jerusalem so dramatic? Why didn't he come quietly, as he had in the past?

4. Do you think Jesus was pleased or displeased by the crowd's welcome? Why?

Cf. Catechism of the Catholic Church: 559-560 on the meaning of Jesus' Messianic entry into Jerusalem; 2302-2317 on the Christian understanding of peace and war; 736, 1424, 1468, and 1832 on peace as the fruit of the Spirit and a gift from God

278. THE HOUR HAS COME (JN 12:20-33)

"In Christ and through Christ God has revealed himself fully to mankind and has definitively drawn close to it…"

- Pope John Paul II

John 12:20-33

Among those who went up to worship at the festival were some Greeks. These approached Philip, who came from Bethsaida in Galilee, and put this request to him, 'Sir, we should like to see Jesus'. Philip went to tell Andrew, and Andrew and Philip together went to tell Jesus. Jesus replied to them: 'Now the hour has come for the Son of Man to be glorified. I tell you, most solemnly, unless a wheat grain falls on the ground and dies, it remains only a single grain; but if it dies, it yields a rich harvest. Anyone who loves his life loses it; anyone who hates his life in this world will keep it for the eternal life. If a man serves me, he must follow me, wherever I am, my servant will be there too. If anyone serves me, my Father will honour him. Now my soul is troubled. What shall I say: Father, save me from this hour? But it was for this very reason that I have come to this hour. Father, glorify your name!' A voice came from heaven, 'I have glorified it, and I will glorify it again.' People standing by, who heard this, said it was a clap of thunder; others said, 'It was an angel speaking to him'. Jesus answered, 'It was not for my sake that this voice came, but for yours. Now sentence is being passed on this world; now the prince of this world is to be overthrown. And when I am lifted up from the earth, I shall draw all men to myself.' By these words he indicated the kind of death he would die.

CHRIST THE LORD We are on the verge of Christ's passion. Jesus knows exactly what is going to happen to him. "His hour" has arrived. He will suffer ignominy, public humiliation, abandonment by his closest companions, betrayal at the hand of an intimate friend, rejection by the very people he came to save, supreme and drawn-out physical torture, even a kind of separation from his Father – and then he will die. By announcing this to his disciples beforehand, he demonstrates to them that he suffers it willingly for the sake of the Father's glory and the eternal Kingdom. Thus, Christ's passion signifies the unbreakable strength of his divine love, the ultimate freedom shown forth by obeying God's will under the most trying circumstances. It is the reversal of Adam's tragic weakness that led him to give in to temptation and disobey God's wise commands. Now the "passing sentence on this world," now, through the unshakable love and trust that he will demonstrate by his obedience unto death on a cross, "the prince of this world [the devil] is to be overthrown." We are on the verge of the climax of human history.

So that the crowds will grasp meaning of this pivotal moment in human history, the Father himself audibly affirms what the Son is going to do. Jesus was speaking to the people, but he must have looked up as he addressed his Father. His listeners had been focused on Jesus throughout his impassioned speech, and suddenly, as he lifts his gaze and utters his prayer to the Father, they hear a voice from heaven respond! It must have been a shock – exhilarating to those who had already come to believe in Jesus and disconcerting to those who doubted him. Jesus Christ is the champion of the human race, the savior of mankind, the everlasting Lord; he knows it; the Father knows it; how deeply do we know it?

CHRIST THE TEACHER During his public ministry, Jesus laid down the condition for being his disciple: "If anyone wants to be a follower of mine, let him renounce himself and take up his cross every day and follow me" (Lk 9:23). Now, as his Passion draws near, he forcibly reiterates this same condition: "Unless a wheat grain falls on the ground and dies, it remains only a single grain; but if it dies, it yields a rich harvest."

To be a Christian is to be where Christ is ("If a man serves me, he must follow me, wherever I am, my servant will be there too"), and Christ is always pouring out his life for others on the cross, giving himself for the good of others through self-forgetful love. St Paul learned this lesson well: "…the only knowledge I claimed to have was about Jesus, and only about him as the crucified Christ" (1 Corinthians 2:2). Love is self-giving: "A man can have no greater love than to lay down his life for his friends" (John 15:13). And Jesus calls us to love: "This is my commandment: love one another as I have loved you" (John 15:12). Therefore, our lives must bear the sign of the cross – of self-giving, of self-sacrifice. When we decide to follow Christ, we should expect crosses, we should expect difficulties, and we should expect persecution: "If they persecuted me, they will persecute you too" (John 15:20). Christ's is the "narrow gate and the hard road" that leads to life (Matthew 7:14), and Christian joy is deep and strong because it sinks its roots into the rich soil of sacrifice, suffering, and sorrow. There is no greater lesson than that of Christ's cross, and there is no better time to learn it than now.

CHRIST THE FRIEND The Greek visitors (non-Jews who were sympathizers with Judaism) wanted to see Jesus. When Jesus hears this, he responds with a long explanation of "his hour." It seems that he denies their request. But his last statement shows that he will grant it: "And when I am lifted up from the earth, I will draw everyone to myself."

By his crucifixion, he reveals himself to everyone (the Greek visitors included). Christ wants everyone to find him, to see him, to learn to know and love him; and so he allows himself to be crucified, he exposes his heart for all to see – a heart blazing with so much love that it is willing to die for our sake, to suffer unspeakable pain in order to reopen for us the gates of heaven. The crucifix is the great revelation of the heart of God; if we want to "see Christ," to see and know God, we have only to raise our eyes to behold him dying on the cross in order to give us true life. There Christ is most attractive to us – and we should always remember that we are no less attractive to him when we bend under the weight of our own cross and weakness.

CHRIST IN MY LIFE Christianity seems so strange, Lord. You saved us from sin by taking sin upon yourself. You conquered evil by absorbing in yourself all the venom that evil could spit out. You ended the tragic meaninglessness of human suffering not by eliminating it, but by turning it into a way to exercise the virtues that reunite our souls to God, faith, hope, and love. Help me to understand this mystery, Lord...

All your saints loved and embraced their crosses. Why do I still resist mine? What is it that makes me carry my crosses reluctantly and halfheartedly? I know that if you gave me a choice, I would probably choose a path without crosses. But you who did have a choice chose the way of the cross. Lord Jesus, purge my heart of the selfishness that clings so desperately to me. I want to live; I want to love as you love...

I take my crucifix in my hands again, Lord, right now. There you are. Agonizing. Your life slowly, excruciatingly ebbing away – only because you love me. You have told your saints, and your Church teaches, that if I had been the only sinner in the universe, you would have suffered all of that just for me, just so I wouldn't have to suffer it, just so I could hope with assurance to enjoy the Father's embrace...

QUESTIONS FOR SMALL GROUP DISCUSSION

1. What struck you most in this passage? What did you notice that you hadn't noticed before?

2. What can we do to participate more fruitfully in the liturgical celebration of Christ's passion, death, and resurrection that happens at every Mass?

3. What has helped you most to bear your crosses as Christ bore his?

4. What should we think when we gaze on a crucifix or make the sign of the cross?

Cf. Catechism of the Catholic Church: 595-623 on the meaning of Christ's Passion and death; 2015, 407-409, and 2725 on the role of the cross and self-denial in the life of Christians

279. BELIEF AND UNBELIEF (JN 12:34-50)

"When I begin to pray I do not see Jesus with my eyes, but I know he is there before me, and my soul finds rest in his presence."

- St Gemma Galgani

John 12:34-50

The crowd answered, 'The Law has taught us that the Christ will remain for ever. How can you say, The Son of Man must be lifted up? Who is this Son of Man?' Jesus then said: 'The light will be with you only a little longer now. Walk while you have the light, or the dark will overtake you; he who walks in the dark does not know where he is going. While you still have the light, believe in the light and you will become sons of light.' Having said this, Jesus left them and kept himself hidden. Though they had been present when he gave so many signs, they did not believe in him; this was to fulfil the words of the prophet Isaiah: Lord, who could believe what we have heard said, and to whom has the power of the Lord been revealed? Indeed, they were unable to believe because, as Isaiah says again: He has blinded their eyes, he has hardened their heart, for fear they should see with their eyes and understand with their heart, and turn to me for healing. Isaiah said this when he saw his glory, and his words referred to Jesus. And yet there were many who did believe in him, even among the leading men, but they did not admit it, through fear of the Pharisees and fear of being expelled from the synagogue: they put honor from men before the honor that comes from God.

Jesus declared publicly: 'Whoever believes in me believes not in me but in the one who sent me, and whoever sees me, sees the one who sent me. I, the light, have come into the world, so that whoever believes in me need not stay in the dark any more. If anyone hears my words and does not keep them faithfully, it is not I who shall condemn him, since I have come not to condemn the world, but to save the world: he who rejects me and refuses my words has his judge already: the word itself that I have spoken will be his judge on the last day. For what I have spoken does not come from myself; no, what I was to say, what I had to speak, was commanded by the Father who sent me, and I know that his commands mean eternal life. And therefore what the Father has told me is what I speak.'

CHRIST THE LORD We who believe in the Lord continue to battle the shadows. Doubts assail us, fears constrain us, and hesitancy and infidelity are always knocking at the door of our hearts. Why? Why has Christ still not conquered our hearts completely?

It is because we are too much like those many Pharisees who believed in Jesus, but who "put honor from men before the honor that comes from God." The human heart has an imperishable need to be accepted, to be loved, and to be valued. We want to be part of the popular crowd, the inner circle, the winning team. In a fallen world, this fundamental need for solidarity, as all of our fundamental needs and desires, has gone awry. It tends to override other values that matter more: truth, justice, and fidelity, to name a few. We want to follow Christ, because his call resonates in the depths of our hearts, but we don't want to risk following him to the cross, because a little voice in the back of our minds still thinks that happiness and meaning can be had by our own efforts, by arranging our lives according to our own natural preferences. It's the old temptation behind every temptation: eat the forbidden fruit and you can be like gods – completely fulfilled – without having to submit to God.

It didn't work for Adam and Eve, and it doesn't work for us. Disobeying the voice of conscience in order to win praise from the voices of peers hardens the heart. Gossiping or welcoming gossip to get into someone's good graces nullifies the grace of God. If we really believe that the Lord is Lord, we will lay aside once and for all anything and everything that interferes with our faithful following of his will.

CHRIST THE TEACHER The unbelief of so many who experienced Jesus face-to-face is one of the most vexing mysteries of the Gospel. Still today, unbelief in the face of twenty centuries of saints and miracles and the ineffable wonder of the Catholic Church's unceasing expansion and fruitfulness boggles the mind. And yet, at first glance, St John's explanation of this phenomenon is entirely unsatisfying. He quotes the prophet Isaiah, who seems to attribute this unbelief to God's own action, as if God had forced these people to reject his Son. Certainly that cannot be the case, since some did believe. God cannot contradict himself, sending Jesus to save his people while at the same time inspiring those people to turn away from Jesus. We can only understand St John's explanation if we understand the context in which Isaiah uttered those words. They came after his own mission of preaching had failed. He was sent to the northern tribes of Israel to convince them to repent from their idolatry, but they refused to repent. And afterwards he writes those words, "He [God] has blinded their eyes…" His prophecy is a bewildered complaint. He can't explain why they won't believe God's message, so he throws up an impassioned complaint, "It's as if God himself didn't even want them to believe!"

Jesus' contemporaries were free to accept or reject Jesus' message, just as every man and woman continues to be. Ultimately, St John is saying, only God knows why and how so many human hearts that were created to live in communion with God freely turn aside from that communion. Only God knows why, and God can still take those refusals and somehow weave them into his plan of salvation. We cannot expect to understand and control all things; it is enough for us to know that God does.

CHRIST THE FRIEND *Jesus: I have not come to condemn the world, but to save the world. My child, have you understood this? So many of my followers have not. They condemn and judge and criticize. I know that most of the time they mean well; they truly think they know what's best. But condemning each other does no good. It hardens hearts. Did I condemn my enemies? Did I condemn sinners? Did I condemn you? I forgave, I taught, I exhorted, I encouraged, I insisted, I invited, I invited again, and that's what I still do. Those who condemn forget that they too ought to be condemned. Those who criticize forget that they too deserve to be criticized. I long for disciples who leave all that behind. I long for followers who bring my light into darkened hearts. I am the light. Let me shine through you. That will scatter the shadows. Leave aside all rancor and useless criticism and condemnation. Build up, plant, work. Say little, do much. You have only a short while – spend it loving, not berating, and teach others to do the same.*

CHRIST IN MY LIFE Father, how can I root out these fears and vain ambitions that infest my heart? You want me to follow in the footsteps of your Son. Pour your Spirit into my mind and my soul, cleanse every vestige of self-seeking, and infuse me with courage and purity of heart and poverty of spirit. Hallowed be thy name…

Jesus, if you don't teach me how to use my words to build up my brothers and sisters, how can I do it? You have never condemned me, although I have so often deserved it. Your patience and your goodness are inexhaustible. You hang from the cross and forgive me, and still I dare to pass judgment on my neighbor. Have mercy on me, Lord, and teach me to love as you love…

Mary, how hard it must have been for you to see so many of your brothers and sisters refuse to believe in Jesus! You were there in Jerusalem during these last days. Did you encourage him? Did he encourage you? You continued to believe and trust. I am your child too; Jesus is my brother. I try to build his Kingdom, but I run into so many dead ends, just like Jesus. Stay by my side, as you stayed by his …

QUESTIONS FOR SMALL GROUP DISCUSSION

1. What struck you most in this passage? What did you notice that you hadn't noticed before?

2. Why do you think Jesus continues to insist so much on his identity with the Father and on his unique link to the Father?

3. According to St John, this was Jesus' last public preaching. Considering that, how does it change your interpretation of his speech?

4. How can we apply Jesus' example of dealing with people who reject his message to our own efforts to spread the gospel?

Cf. Catechism of the Catholic Church: 1084-1090 on the centrality of Christ in the Liturgy; 2598-2616 on the centrality of Christ in prayer; 587-591 on Jesus and Israel's faith; 238-248 on the relationship between the Father, the Son, and the Spirit

THE GOSPEL OF JOHN CHAPTER 13

"Man cannot live without love. He remains a being that is incomprehensible for himself, his life is senseless, if love is not revealed to him, if he does not encounter love, if he does not experience it and make it his own, if he does not participate intimately in it."

- Pope John Paul II, Redemptor hominis, 10

280. THE FINAL LESSON (JN 13:1-20)

"'Consider well,' he says to us, 'that in loving I was first. You had not yet come forth into the light, not even the world itself had come into existence, when already I was loving you. Throughout my eternal existence I have loved you.'"

- St Alphonsus Liguori

John 13:1-20

It was before the festival of the Passover, and Jesus knew that the hour had come for him to pass from this world to the Father. He had always loved those who were his in the world, but now he showed how perfect his love was. They were at supper, and the devil had already put it into the mind of Judas Iscariot son of Simon, to betray him. Jesus knew that the Father had put everything into his hands, and that he had come from God and was returning to God, and he got up from table, removed his outer garment and, taking a towel, wrapped it round his waist; he then poured water into a basin and began to wash the disciples' feet and to wipe them with the towel he was wearing. He came to Simon Peter, who said to him, 'Lord, are you going to wash my feet?' Jesus answered, 'At the moment you do not know what I am doing, but later you will understand'. 'Never!' said Peter 'You shall never wash my feet.' Jesus replied, 'If I do not wash you, you can have nothing in common with me'. 'Then, Lord,' said Simon Peter 'not only my feet, but my hands and my head as well!' Jesus said, 'No one who has taken a bath needs washing, he is clean all over. You too are clean, though not all of you are.' He knew who was going to betray him, that was why he said, 'though not all of you are.'

When he had washed their feet and put on his clothes again he went back to the table. 'Do you understand' he said 'what I have done to you? You call me Master and Lord, and rightly; so I am. If I, then, the Lord and Master, have washed your feet, you should wash each other's feet. I have given you an example so that you may copy what I have done to you. I tell you most solemnly, no servant is greater than his master, no messenger is greater than the man who sent him. Now that you know this, happiness will be yours if you behave accordingly. I am not speaking about all of you: I know the ones I have chosen; but what scripture says must be fulfilled: Someone who shares my table rebels against me. I tell you this now, before it happens, so that when it does happen you may believe that I am He. I tell you most solemnly, whoever welcomes the one I send welcomes me, and whoever welcomes me welcomes the one who sent me.'

CHRIST THE LORD Most of the world's great teachers and philosophers shy away from adulation. They draw people's attention to their doctrine while they themselves shun the spotlight. Jesus Christ, whose doctrine is more complete, powerful, and veracious than anyone's, breaks this mold. He constantly invites people to hear and heed his doctrine, but at the same time, and even more vehemently, he draws his listeners and disciples to himself; he wants them to cling with all their hearts and minds to him. Nowhere is this personal, heart-to-heart appeal of Christ more clearly expressed than in this passage. But to appreciate it properly, we have to put ourselves into the scene.

The Twelve are gathered with their Master for the most sacred meal of the year. The stone walls of the upper room are lit with the warm light of flickering torches and lamps. The apostles and Jesus are reclining at the low table, glad to be together once again, eager to share the lamb, the bread, the wine, and the bitter herbs. They know each other so well by now. They can feel something different in the atmosphere tonight. Something has changed in the Lord's attitude. It has some new sense of urgency. He is looking at them with even greater emotion than usual.

St John's introduction to the Last Supper recreates the atmosphere of solemnity that surrounded that climactic meal. He reminds us that Jesus' mission was coming to its dramatic conclusion, that Jesus knew it, and that he was consciously intensifying the revelation of his love because of it, "... now he showed how perfect his love was." The words of Jesus on this occasion ring with an even greater intimacy, majesty, and solemnity than we have heard throughout this Gospel. The apostles sense the added intensity, and their own expectations rise to a higher pitch then ever before. When Jesus interrupts the Passover ritual by standing up, all their eyes are fixed on him. Conversation ceases. Eating stops. Jesus walks over to the large water jug (water was habitually kept nearby for the many ritual washings), and the silence deepens. They watch Jesus as he puts on the garment used by slaves and, slowly, deliberately, but still without a word, begins washing their feet. Only Peter breaks the silence, but he quickly quiets down. It takes a good amount of time to make the circle of his Twelve Apostles. Then Jesus gets up, replaces his normal outer garment and once again takes his place among them. The apostles are turned to him, their looks are begging for an explanation. They are humbled, all their attention is on the Lord. He doesn't speak right away, but looks at each of them. Then he finally breaks the long silence, which makes his quiet but momentous words reverberate all the more: "... You call me Master and Lord, and rightly; so I am."

CHRIST THE TEACHER In ancient Palestine, washing feet was a job reserved for slaves. It was one of the most unpleasant and humiliating tasks. People wore sandals or went barefoot, and the roads and paths that they walked were the same ones used by herdsmen to drive their animals to market, as well as travelers and traders who moved their goods by ox and camel. The dirt of these unpaved byways, therefore, was blended with dung. Even a short jaunt would cake one's sandal-exposed feet with the pungent mix. This earthy combination of elements, this unattractive mire was what Jesus washed from the feet of his disciples. Jesus, God made man, the King of kings and Lord of the universe, lowered himself to the status of a slave and freely, willingly, and gladly "showed how perfect his love was" by this utterly self-forgetful act of service. He didn't have to do it. He certainly felt no natural pleasure in doing it. But still he did it, at the most solemn moment of his ministry, when common sense would dictate that he be more focused on his coming passion. Why? "... You should wash each other's feet. I have given you an example so that you may copy what I have done to you."

The mark of the Christian is self-forgetful love. Sin divided once and still divides the human family. Christ, the conqueror of sin, reunites all people. He does this through his love, which reaches out to all the ends of the earth through his disciples. And love is not feelings; it is not noble desires; love is self-giving. Love is costly. In Jesus, God came down from heaven to dwell among men, to serve the needs of men, the very men who had rebelled against him and usurped the world he had entrusted to them. In so doing, they ruined themselves. God wanted to save them, even though they deserved to die. So he takes the first step; he reaches out to them by serving them. The washing of his disciples' feet was an icon of Jesus' entire mission and a revelation, a miniature portrait of the heart of God. And so he tells us that if we wish to regain our place in the family of God, we are to enter into the same dimension of self-forgetful love. There is no other way: "You should wash each other's feet…"

For our fallen nature, this is a hard lesson. For that very reason, Jesus taught it so insistently and so graphically. The cross of self-sacrifice repels us, so Jesus climbed onto it before us to make sure that we make no mistake about what he means. But although the lesson is hard, it is not sad. It is the truth that will set us free, and Jesus finishes with a glow in his eyes and a smile on his lips: "Now that you know this, happiness will be yours if you behave accordingly."

CHRIST THE FRIEND Judas was still at the Last Supper at this point. He had already decided to follow through with his plan of betrayal, but he had not yet left to set it in motion. What was in Jesus' mind when he came to Judas, poured water over his feet, and began to wash them? As Jesus finished drying Judas' feet with the towel, and as he laced up the sandals again, he looked into Judas's face and caught his eye. Jesus hadn't given up on him. Jesus never gives up on us; he is the ever-faithful friend. The tragedy is that we are the ones who sometimes give up on him.

Judas: I was more disgusted than ever at this repellent display of weakness. It confirmed yet again all my suspicions: this man had not come to restore Israel to its glory, but to enervate it and despoil it. I wanted nothing to do with such an imposter, such a weak dreamer. I have to admit, though, that when he looked up at me – well, it made me think of the first time we had met, when I heard him speaking in the Temple and my heart surged with hope. He had looked at me then too, and I seemed to see in his eyes all the strength and wisdom and life that I knew existed somewhere but hadn't been able to find. He invited me to come with him then, and I couldn't resist. I had never been moved like that before. And then there were the miracles, and the huge crowds, and his mastery over the Pharisees. It was all so promising, and I could even taste victory just around the corner. But he never took the final step. And then he started talking about the cross. The others ignored it, but I knew he was serious. And how could a crucified rabbi be the Messiah? How could weakness reclaim our glory? That last night, for a split second after he replaced my sandals, it occurred to me that maybe there was more to it than I understood. But then I looked at him again, wrapped in that towel like a slave, washing my feet. It was repugnant. Peter was right – who would ever let a real Messiah sink so low as to wash our feet? But Peter was weak too; he caved in. I could never serve a Lord like that.

CHRIST IN MY LIFE I glory in being able to call you Lord. I know that there is order in the universe. I know that my life has purpose. I know that the world is safe in your hands and history is marching forward according to a law of hidden progress, surely guided by your invincible Providence. Jesus, my Lord, my Master! Here is my life. I put it at your feet and at your service. I offer myself to you...

So many items are on my to-do list. I have so many plans and hopes. I want to do so much for you, Lord. But in the midst of my programs and activities, I too often forget about the only law of your Kingdom: I am to wash my neighbors' feet. Only there will I ever find the happiness you intend for me. I must learn self-forgetful love. And each day you provide so many chances for me to give myself in this way! Give me courage...

You have washed my feet so often, Lord. Every time I go to confession, you humble yourself and wash my feet. Thank you for washing Judas's feet. I am like Judas. Have I not betrayed you at times? You knew I would; you knew my heart as you washed my feet. A Judas is within me; don't let me forget. As soon as I forget it, I will follow his example. Make me faithful, Lord; never let me be separated from you, never...

QUESTIONS FOR SMALL GROUP DISCUSSION

1. What struck you most in this passage? What did you notice that you hadn't noticed before?

2. In our current life situations, what are some ways that we can follow Christ's example of service on a daily basis?

3. Why is it often so hard for us to serve those around us? In your experience, what circumstances have made self-forgetful service easier, and what can we learn from that?

4. If an agnostic acquaintance asked you why you think Christianity is so unique, what would you say?

Cf. Catechism of the Catholic Church: 459, 852, 1022, 1823-1825, 1844, 1337, 2055, 2104, 2196, 2443, and 2822 on the commandment to love one's neighbor as Christ as loved us; 221 on God's nature as an exchange of love

281. THE NEW COMMANDMENT (JN 13:21-38)

"But he was not satisfied with giving us all these beautiful things. He went to such lengths to win our love that he gave himself wholly to us. The Eternal Father gave us even his only Son."

- St Alphonsus Liguori

John 13:21-38

Having said this, Jesus was troubled in spirit and declared, 'I tell you most solemnly, one of you will betray me'. The disciples looked at one another, wondering which he meant. The disciple Jesus loved was reclining next to Jesus; Simon Peter signed to him and said, 'Ask who it is he means', so leaning back on Jesus' breast he said, 'Who is it, Lord?' 'It is the one' replied Jesus 'to whom I give the piece of bread that I shall dip in the dish.' He dipped the piece of bread and gave it to Judas son of Simon Iscariot. At that instant, after Judas had taken the bread, Satan entered him. Jesus then said, 'What you are going to do, do quickly'. None of the others at table understood the reason he said this. Since Judas had charge of the common fund, some of them thought Jesus was telling him, 'Buy what we need for the festival', or telling him to give something to the poor. As soon as Judas had taken the piece of bread he went out. Night had fallen.

When he had gone Jesus said: 'Now has the Son of Man been glorified, and in him God has been glorified. If God has been glorified in him, God will in turn glorify him in himself, and will glorify him very soon. My little children, I shall not be with you much longer. You will look for me, and, as I told the Jews, where I am going, you cannot come. I give you a new commandment: love one another; just as I have loved you, you also must love one another. By this love you have for one another, everyone will know that you are my disciples.' Simon Peter said, 'Lord, where are you going?' Jesus replied, 'Where I am going you cannot follow me now; you will follow me later'. Peter said to him, 'Why can't I follow you now? I will lay down my life for you.' 'Lay down your life for me?' answered Jesus. 'I tell you most solemnly, before the cock crows you will have disowned me three times.

CHRIST THE LORD By issuing a new commandment, Christ manifests unambiguously his unique claim to be sent by God and to be God's own Son. In the Old Testament, only God issued commandments; no one else had the authority to make precepts binding on the whole nation. Repeatedly, the texts in the Pentateuch point out that Moses delivered to Israel the commandments he had received from God. Here, however, Christ says, "I give you a new commandment," not "Here is a commandment that I pass on to you from God." He speaks calmly and confidently with the authority of God himself. Notice that

Christ says he is giving them a "new" commandment. That means that the old commandments were somehow insufficient. (In truth they were a preparation for the new covenant, a first stage towards definitive communion with God in Christ.) If the old ones, however, came from God, only God could enhance them. Thus, in that one sentence, Christ makes clear yet again that he is no mere philosopher or above-average rabbi – he is the Messiah, the Son of God, the only Savior: the Lord. These details would not have been lost on the Twelve Apostles. We should make sure it is never lost on us – Christ is close; he is our intimate friend, but he is also God, all-powerful, all-knowing, and all-loving. He is worthy of our praise and adoration, worthy to be our Lord.

And what is the defining characteristic of Christ's Lordship? Wherein lies his glory? As he has repeated again and again throughout this whole Gospel, it is in his perfect, loving obedience to the Father's will. It is the Father's will that Jesus suffer and die, and Judas is the instrument through which that will be accomplished. Jesus knows this, but his "soul is troubled" at the thought of it. Deeply troubled – anguished, as we see later in the Garden of Gethsemane. And yet, in spite of the repugnance and resistance of his human nature, he accepts his mission. He expresses this acceptance by telling Judas, "What you are going to do, do quickly." And this is what glorifies God. The glory of God and the glory of the human person converge, as the Lord displays, in our loving obedience to God's will, no matter the cost.

CHRIST THE TEACHER This glory of God is, as the catechism tells us, the entire reason behind the existence of all things: "The world was created for the glory of God." It is an inexhaustible concept, but that doesn't mean we shouldn't reflect on it a bit more.

God's glory is different than we might think. We tend to think of it in Hollywood terms – bursts of brilliant light, thunder claps, swirling vortexes of power and color and smoke… Such extraordinary phenomena may be used now and again to call attention to the extraordinariness of God, but his glory is something deeper. When Judas begins to carry out his betrayal, Christ says, "Now the Son of Man is glorified, and God is glorified in him." What's the connection? Love. Love means self-giving; by accepting the suffering and death that Judas's betrayal brings on, Jesus is revealing, making visible, God's immeasurable love for each one of us. He loves us so much that he is willing to suffer in our place, even while we were still sinners (as St Paul later points out). It's like sitting in the electric chair in place of the man who murdered your children so that he doesn't have to suffer and die – crazy love, incalculable love, unfathomable love. And that is God's glory: making known God's love, the love that gives existence to the universe, the love that calls us into being and reaches out to bring us into the eternal Kingdom.

CHRIST THE FRIEND If we value our friendship with Christ, we will try to please him, make him happy, and stay close to him. And he (unlike many human friends) is able to tell us exactly how to do that. If we love him, we will keep his command, and his command is for us to love one another, to put our lives at the service of those around us, just as he did for us. It is the touchstone of the Christian: "By this… everyone will know that you are my disciples…." Without it, no matter how much theology we may know, no matter how good we may be at winning arguments, no matter how many awards we may win – without learning to love as Christ has loved, we simply cannot consider ourselves his friends.

When Judas left Christ to betray him, St John tells us that "night had fallen." It is the counterpoint to Christ's insistent self-appellation throughout the Gospel that he is the light of the world and that whoever heeds his word will not walk in darkness. Only friendship with Christ illuminates the meaning of the human condition and the path to human happiness. To reject this friendship is to willingly plunge into the darkness.

Jesus: I was looking ahead to my sufferings. They loomed over me. Yet I wanted them, because I wanted to glorify the Father; I wanted to show forth his goodness. I wanted them too because of you. They would rebuild the bridge between God and man, a bridge that you could then walk across into my Kingdom. If only you knew how ardent my love for you is! That is what I wanted to show you. Let me show you. Open your mind to see the intensity of my love reflected in the intensity of my suffering.

CHRIST IN MY LIFE Teach me to do your will, Lord. What more could I desire than for your goodness to shine through my life? Your will is love and wisdom. Your will is my salvation, fulfillment, and happiness. I have only to follow your example, the teachings of your Church, and your voice in my conscience. Make your will the whole quest of my heart…

Mary, you knew all the apostles, including Judas. Why was Satan able to enter into him? I want to know. I don't trust myself. I don't want to betray Christ. Maybe I should ask instead why the others, who also abandoned him, were able to come back to him. They fell because of weakness, but Judas initiated his own rebellion. Mother, save me both from weakness and from pride…

Father, you sent us your Son so that we would not have to stumble in the darkness anymore. Yet so many people continue to reject him, and so many others have never known him. Move their hearts, Lord. Send out messengers – convinced, courageous, determined messengers. Send me. Reach into the hearts of those around me through my words, actions, and prayers…

QUESTIONS FOR SMALL GROUP REFLECTION

1. What struck you most in this passage? What did you notice that you hadn't noticed before?

2. How can we live out Christ's new commandment more fully in our present circumstances?

3. In our relationship with Christ, how should we manifest the reverence and respect that we ought to have for the Son of God?

4. How does Christ's commandment to love and serve everyone (not just those people we naturally get along with) compare with the behavior patterns encouraged by popular culture?

Cf. Catechism of the Catholic Church: 2093-2094 on love towards God; 2084-2109 on reverencing God; 2196 on the importance of love for one another; 1822-1829 on the "new commandment"

THE GOSPEL OF JOHN CHAPTER 14

"It is surely unnecessary to prove, what experience constantly shows and what each individual feels in himself, even in the very midst of all temporal prosperity – that in God alone can the human will find absolute and perfect peace. God is the only end of man. All our life on earth is the truthful and exact image of a pilgrimage. Now Christ is the 'Way,' for we can never reach God, the supreme and ultimate good, by this toilsome and doubtful road of mortal life, except with Christ as our leader and guide."

- Pope Leo XIII

282. UNTROUBLED HEARTS (JN 14:1-12)

"Contradictions, sickness, scruples, spiritual aridity, and all the inner and outward torments are the chisel with which God carves his statues for paradise."

- St Alphonsus Ligouri

John 14:1-12

'Do not let your hearts be troubled. Trust in God still, and trust in me. There are many rooms in my Father's house; if there were not, I should have told you. I am going now to prepare a place for you, and after I have gone and prepared you a place, I shall return to take you with me; so that where I am you may be too. You know the way to the place where I am going.' Thomas said, 'Lord, we do not know where you are going, so how can we know the way?' Jesus said: 'I am the Way, the Truth and the Life. No one can come to the Father except through me. If you know me, you know my Father too. From this moment you know him and have seen him.' Philip said, 'Lord, let us see the Father and then we shall be satisfied'. 'Have I been with you all this time, Philip,' said Jesus to him 'and you still do not know me? 'To have seen me is to have seen the Father, so how can you say, Let us see the Father? Do you not believe that I am in the Father and the Father is in me? The words I say to you I do not speak as from myself: it is the Father, living in me, who is doing this work. You must believe me when I say that I am in the Father and the Father is in me; believe it on the evidence of this work, if for no other reason. I tell you most solemnly, whoever believes in me will perform the same works as I do myself, he will perform even greater works, because I am going to the Father.'

CHRIST THE LORD Christ is not Lord just because he is more intelligent than anyone else, or more charismatic, or more ruthless, or filled with magic powers. Christ is Lord because he is God become man. To see him is to see God; he is in the Father and the Father is in him. But seeing him requires more than bodily eyes; it requires faith. Philip had followed Christ for almost three years, and he still did not recognize him. How many Catholics have been going to Mass for years but still do not know the Lord? If we look at Christ and find it hard to see the Father, it is our eyes – our lives – that need adjusting, not him.

If we do adjust them, trusting more in Jesus and less in our own limited understanding and talent, our lives will gradually take on proportions far beyond what we can imagine: "Whoever believes in me will perform the same works as I do myself, he will perform even greater works." To live in a communion of friendship and obedience with Christ is to live united to God himself, the Creator and Sustainer of the universe, the Lord of life and history. His knowledge and power and love become ours; we become sharers in the divine nature (2 Pet 1:4). The lives of the saints, past and present, continue to cry out their confirmation of this promise. They are our brothers and sisters who, under the impulse of God's grace, have relinquished their vain attempts at controlling their destiny and the world and truly believed in Christ, trusting that he, the only Lord, knows better and that his plans, his will, are better than theirs.

Too often we relegate our relationship with the Lord to one section of our agenda. Christ's presence and will should be much, much more for us. He should be everything. As Christians, our life is a mission. We are called to be other Christs in the world – in the specific circumstances, relationships, and possibilities of our own personal worlds. If our first concern is truly to live as

Christ would live in our place, we will release the full power of grace in our lives, and we will become saints. If following the Lord is just one action item among many, grace will have no room to work.

CHRIST THE TEACHER From ancient times philosophers have summed up the human condition as a quest to answer three fundamental queries: What should I do? What can I know? What can I hope for? Jesus Christ answers them all, not merely with doctrine, but with his very person. "I am the way" can translate into: What should you do? Follow me! Do what I have done. "I am the truth" means: What can you know? You can know everything, if only you know me. Knowing me, you know the truth; you know the secret behind the workings of the whole universe and the yearnings of the human heart. "I am the life" means: What can you hope for? In me, through me, you can hope for and expect the fullness of life that you long for, even though you may not be able to put that longing into words. Christ is truly the living water that quenches every thirst. He is truly the light that scatters every kind of darkness. The quest of every man and woman to satisfy the heart's deepest needs is the quest to seek his face, and it leads either to Christ and the place he has prepared for us in heaven or to a dead end.

CHRIST THE FRIEND The atmosphere of the Last Supper was tense. The apostles knew that something was up, and they were afraid, or at least disquieted. Jesus reassures them by inviting them to believe in him, to trust in him. He goes to prepare a place for us in the Father's house, in heaven. And he promises to come back for us, so that he can take us where we will always be with him. Christianity is about entering into the family of God, becoming a member of that family. Jesus wants to dwell with us; he wants to dwell in us, and he longs to share his eternal and ever-new joy with us. This is why he came. He is the friend who "gave his life up for his friends." With a friend like that, how could our hearts be troubled?

Mary: My child, Jesus tells you: "Do not let your hearts be troubled… Trust in me…" If he tells you that, it means that it is possible for you to live in his peace. He does not say that troubling things won't happen – they will. But in him, if you exercise your trust in him, you can keep your heart in peace, like a little child in its mother's arms. He always holds you in his sure embrace. When troubles come, bring your heart back to the sure knowledge of his love and his wise providence. It is a mark of all true followers of Christ that they have learned to be steady in the storm; they have learned to rejoice in the depths of their souls even in the midst of tears. He is worthy of your trust.

CHRIST IN MY LIFE Lord, you wanted to be known, and so you came to reveal yourself to us. I already know you; you have given me the gift of faith. I want to be for you what you were for the Father. When people see me, especially those closest to me, I want them to see you. Make me like you, Lord…

I believe in you, Lord, and I am so grateful to you. What thousands of people for thousands of years have been searching for, you have given me. You have given me the pearl of great price, the hidden treasure. I know the answers to the deepest questions, because I know you. You are not just the endpoint of my search; you are the beginning of my adventure, my way, my truth, my life…

Mary, my mother, how can I trust in Jesus when everything is collapsing around me? How can I be at peace when my mind and heart are in turmoil? You can teach me. On this night of the Last Supper, you were close by. You knew that Jesus' hour had come. Your mother's heart quaked and shook and wept, and yet you never ceased trusting, accepting, or offering. Teach me to not be afraid…

QUESTIONS FOR SMALL GROUP DISCUSSION

1. What struck you most in this passage? What did you notice that you hadn't noticed before?

2. What do you think was most on Jesus' mind and heart during this intense emotional moment of the Last Supper?

3. Why would the Church give us this Gospel passage to read during the liturgical season of Easter?

4. Why do you think Christ invites us to trust in him when our hearts are troubled, instead of just making sure that our hearts never get troubled in the first place?

Cf. Catechism of the Catholic Church, 464-478 on Jesus Christ as true God and true man; 459, 1698, 2037, 2614 on Jesus Christ as "the way, the truth, and the life"

283. THE SUPREME GIFT (JN 14:13-21)

"The spiritual building-up of the body of Christ is brought about by love…"

- St Fulgentius of Ruspe

John 14:13-21

'Whatever you ask for in my name I will do, so that the Father may be glorified in the Son. If you ask for anything in my name, I will do it. If you love me you will keep my commandments. I shall ask the Father, and he will give you another Advocate to be with you for ever, that Spirit of truth whom the world can never receive since it neither sees nor knows him; but you know him, because he is with you, he is in you. I will not leave you orphans; I will come back to you. In a short time the world will no longer see me; but you will see me, because I live and you will live. On that day you will understand that I am in my Father and you in me and I in you. Anybody who receives my commandments and keeps them will be one who loves me; and anybody who loves me will be loved by my Father, and I shall love him and show myself to him.'

CHRIST THE LORD Jesus is gathered with his disciples on the evening before his Passion. The intense intimacy of the moment is marked by his apostles' rapt attention. He begins to speak to them of what is about to happen. He knows that he is going to suffer, die, rise, and ascend into heaven. His earthly mission is coming to a close, and he is preparing them for the next stage, the epoch of the Church, which he will guide through the work of the Holy Spirit, the "Advocate."

To us, this is normal. We know the full story, so we know what Christ is referring to. But put yourself in the position of the apostles. How odd it must have been for them to hear these words – even mystifying! Jesus is predicting the future with an uncanny specificity and confidence. His mastery over other men, over nature, over sickness and demons, all this was familiar to the Twelve. But mastery over future events? Seemingly contradictory references to being unseen and then seen again? Allusions to the Father sending an "Advocate" to be with them always? Surely they must have sounded almost like the words of a madman… or of the Son of God. If with our imagination we try to enter into this scene, placing ourselves at the apostles' side and listening to these words as if for the first time, perhaps we will hear once again the untamed grandeur, tender love, and mysterious truth that radiated from Christ the Lord on the first Holy Thursday.

CHRIST THE TEACHER During the Last Supper discourse, Christ's constant refrain is: if you love me, you will keep my commandment. That commandment is to "love one another as I have loved you" (John 13:34), the commandment of charity. In a sense, the Last Supper is Jesus' last earthly encounter with his beloved companions (the later Resurrection appearances already have an otherworldly feel). These are his parting words, then, the last flow of love from his Sacred Heart before it is broken and pierced. They are special words. We need to hear them; we need to let them sink in.

He knows that these twelve men, so normal and yet so privileged, love him. He earnestly desires to teach them how to live out that love. It is not in pretty words, it is not merely in rituals and prayers, it is not in lengthy theological treatises – it is in obedience to the wishes of his heart; it is in imitating his love for them. Love made into action, into serving our brothers and sisters, giving our lives for them – just like Christ's love from Calvary's cross – is the only mark of a follower of Christ. Jesus never tires of repeating this. He wants to convince us that everything else is in a distant second place. If, having discovered his love for us, we courageously and trustingly leave behind our self-absorption and launch out on the enlivening and everlasting adventure of loving in the same way, we will finally discover and experience what we were created for and what we long for. In the end, we will be judged on our love – our love for God lived out in love for our neighbor.

CHRIST THE FRIEND "I will not leave you orphans." How painful for the Twelve to hear their Lord, their Leader, speaking about his imminent departure! They had left all to follow him, and he was going to leave them. But not really... He would send them the "Advocate to be with them always" - the "Paraclete," the Holy Spirit. In the Holy Spirit, Jesus knows that he will be present to his disciples in a more intimate way than ever before. The Holy Spirit, the third person of the Blessed Trinity, is the love between the Father and Son lived so intensely that it is a person itself. When we are baptized, that same Spirit takes up residence within our souls, and his field of action is increased when we are confirmed. This gift surpasses all other gifts. In the Holy Spirit the prophecy of "Emmanuel" (God-with-us) takes on unimaginable proportions: not merely God among us, as in the Incarnation, but God *within* us, a guest in our souls, a guide for our life's journey, a personal trainer for our spiritual fitness. What greater gift could Christ have left us? What other friend could match such a gift?

Jesus: I was longing to complete my mission go back to the Father, because I was longing to come and live in your heart forever, in an intimacy that only the Spirit can give. And I was longing to go and sit at the Father's right hand so that I could be there interceding for you all the time, so that you could finally ask the Father for all that you need and desire in my name. Now that I have repaired the breach through my sacrifice on the cross, the floodgates of grace are open, and all that I have and all that the Father has is all yours.

CHRIST IN MY LIFE You speak with such assurance, Lord. You are Master of all time and space. You are Master of my life. What confidence this should give me! Increase my faith, Lord. Give me the faith and trust of a child who is incapable of doubting, of being anxious, of wondering what will become of him. You love me more than any human mother or father ever could. And you are all-powerful. Jesus, I trust in you...

Mary, the Church calls you the Mother of Fairest Love. But you didn't do big and impressive things. You did all things with the purest and most humble self-forgetfulness and dedication to God the world had ever seen. You had two mottos: "Let it be done to me..." and "My soul magnifies the Lord." Why do I keep seeking satisfaction in other mottos? Mother, pray for me, teach me to love...

Holy Spirit, pour out your gifts into my soul. My mind is weak and benighted; renew and restore its vigor and clarity. My will is shrunken and misdirected; breathe into it your force and goodness. My heart – I don't even want to talk about it. You know that way down at its very core is a tiny spark of love. Blow on it, feed it, build it into a blazing fire of zeal for God's glory and the salvation of souls...

QUESTIONS FOR SMALL GROUP DISCUSSION

1. What struck you most in this passage? What did you notice that you hadn't noticed before?

2. Why do you think Christ insists so vehemently on loving him through obeying his command? Does that mean that prayer and the sacraments don't really matter? How pleased do you think he is with how his disciples (throughout the ages) have responded to this insistence?

3. Why do you think Christ says that he will reveal himself to those who love him? Why wouldn't he reveal himself so that we would love him?

4. How can we take better advantage of the priceless gift of the Holy Spirit?

Cf. Catechism of the Catholic Church, 539, 1850, 1991, 2087 on the relationship between love and obedience; 683-747 on the nature and role of the Holy Spirit; 232-248 on the nature of the Holy Trinity: "Father, Son, and Holy Spirit"

284. THE GIFT OF PEACE (JN 14:22-31)

"In all this he offered his own self, so that when you suffered you would not lose heart, but rather would recognize that you are a man, and would yourself expect to receive what he received from God."

- St Hippolytus

John 14:22-31

Judas – this was not Judas Iscariot – said to him, 'Lord, what is all this about? Do you intend to show yourself to us and not to the world?' Jesus replied: 'If anyone loves me he will keep my word, and my Father will love him, and we shall come to him and make our home with him. Those who do not love me do not keep my words. And my word is not my own: it is the word of the one who sent me. I have said these things to you while still with you; but the Advocate, the Holy Spirit, whom the Father will send in my name, will teach you everything and remind you of all I have said to you. Peace I bequeath to you, my own peace I give you, a peace the world cannot give, this is my gift to you. Do not let your hearts be troubled or afraid. You heard me say: I am going away, and shall return. If you loved me you would have been glad to know that I am going to the Father, for the Father is greater than I. I have told you this now before it happens, so that when it does happen you may believe. I shall not talk with you any longer, because the prince of this world is on his way. He has no power over me, but the world must be brought to know that I love the Father and that I am doing exactly what the Father told me. Come now, let us go.'

CHRIST THE LORD Jesus knows what is going to happen. He knows what will happen to him, what will happen to his disciples, and what will happen to the Church. But he not only knows what will happen, he is in charge of it. Therefore, when he says, "Do not let you hearts be troubled or afraid," we can trust him. He is the Lord; he is in control; he is watching out for us… In Christ, we have someone we can count on – absolutely.

Jesus bequeathed peace to his apostles. The battle of his Passion issued in the definitive victory over the "prince of this world," the devil, who rules by fear and intimidation and by providing a false sense of security. When Jesus commands a life, he brings peace. Peace to the ancient Jews was God's greatest gift. It was much more than a temporary feeling of contentment, like the feeling we get after a good meal. Peace implied the fullness of prosperity and fruitfulness, the hum of a life being lived to the max, like the hum of a healthy beehive. What greater gift could he have given? What does the human heart seek if not the deep joy of knowing that we are loved unconditionally, the strength and opportunity to love fully in return, the certainty that our lives have a meaning that no earthly power can take away, the invigoration of having a mission with eternal consequences? By coming to "dwell" in us, by sending us the Holy Spirit to be our guide, God wishes to imbue us with this peace. But we have to claim it and make it our own. We have to activate the faith and hope we have received, counteracting every disturbance with prayer and trust and overcoming all trouble and fear by turning to our Lord.

CHRIST THE TEACHER If Christ had not returned to the Father ("I am going to the Father"), he would have remained limited by time and space, as he was during his earthly life. But since he now dwells body and soul in heaven, he

941

can be present to each one of us at all times, through the Holy Spirit. The Church has long called the Holy Spirit the "sweet guest of the soul," as the ancient hymn puts it. He is the same Spirit that animated and animates Christ. When we were baptized, he came to dwell within us as well, to be our intimate friend, as if Christ climbed into our hearts to accompany us throughout the rest of our life's journey. The Holy Spirit is like our own personal trainer, but instead of honing our physique, he polishes our love, our holiness, our very hearts. Unfortunately, we often forget about him. He is polite; he knows he is only a guest, because even though he created us, he completely respects our freedom. And so he waits for us to listen to him, to ask him for guidance and strength. And if we listen, he will teach us, just as Christ taught his disciples during those three years when they walked together through the hills of Galilee and Judah.

Even though the Holy Spirit will be with us to remind us of Christ's lessons and to teach us more and more about the Kingdom, Christ wants to be sure to give us the most important lesson before he leaves. He tells us explicitly how to love him, how to live in communion with God, which is the meaning of human existence. If we love him, we will "keep his word," – i.e., we will follow his new commandment to love one another as he has loved us, and then the Father and the Son will come and take up their dwelling in our hearts. Do we want to live close to God? Here's the recipe… written by God himself.

CHRIST THE FRIEND *Christ: What I said to my apostles that night, I say to all of my followers: "I have told you this now before it happens, so that when it does happen you may believe." I explained everything to them – the betrayal, the arrest, the trial and condemnation, the scourging and mockery and crucifixion, and most importantly, my rising and ascension and the delivery of the Holy Spirit. When I told them these things, they didn't understand. Only as the events unfolded did they recognize them, and as they did, they were able to grasp their meaning. I am doing the same with you. You have the Gospels and the lives of my saints, and so you know that as you follow me you will face your own Gethsemanes and Calvaries, your own Resurrections and Pentecosts. You must pass through all that I passed through in order to grow to maturity in me. But I have told you this beforehand, so that whatever happens, you will find in me the comfort and light that will protect you from being troubled and afraid. You will never be caught off guard. I am always with you. You have believed in me and obeyed me, and I have made my home in your heart.*

CHRIST IN MY LIFE Blessed Trinity, you have taken up residence in my heart. How do you do that? How can my Creator dwell within me? But this is what love does. Wherever I go, you are with me. Whatever I do or say, you are with me. Whatever I look at or think about, you are there within me. I believe in you. Yet I have to ask: Why am I not more aware of you? Grant me that grace, Lord – teach me never to walk alone…

I believe in you, Lord, but help me to believe more fully. Help me to believe so completely that my life and yours become one. In all my activities, conversations, and relationships, I want to live and communicate the joy and peace that only you can give. Lord Jesus, I trust in you…

Mary, it was the Holy Spirit who overshadowed you and conceived Jesus in your womb. And how did he form Jesus in you? Through all the normal channels and processes, so subtly and quietly, from inside the depths of your being. Teach me to let the Holy Spirit teach and guide and form my Christian life. I want to know how, so that I can cooperate better. May Jesus be formed within me…

QUESTIONS FOR SMALL GROUP DISCUSSION

1. What struck you most in this passage? What did you notice that you hadn't noticed before?

2. How can we cultivate a deeper friendship with the Holy Spirit?

3. When have you experienced most palpably the peace that Jesus promises?

4. Jesus' promise of peace is repeated during every Mass right before we receive Holy Communion. Why do you think the Church puts his words in that particular place in the Liturgy?

Cf. Catechism of the Catholic Church,687-741 on the Holy Spirit; 227 on trust in God in all circumstances

THE GOSPEL OF JOHN CHAPTER 15

"O Lord Jesus, I surrender to you all my will. Let me be your lute. Touch any string you please, Always and forever let me make music in perfect harmony with your own. Yes, Lord, with no ifs, ands or buts, let your will be done in this family, for the father, for the children, for everything that concerns us, and especially let your will be done in me."

- St Jane de Chantal

285. BEARING FRUIT FOR CHRIST'S KINGDOM (JN 15:1-8)

"Others may have their wealth, may drink out of jeweled cups, be clad in silks, enjoy popular applause, find it impossible to exhaust their wealth by dissipating it in pleasures of all kinds, but our delight is to meditate on the Law of the Lord day and night…"

- St Jerome

John 15:1-8

'I am the true vine, and my Father is the vinedresser. Every branch in me that bears no fruit he cuts away, and every branch that does bear fruit he prunes to make it bear even more. You are pruned already, by means of the word that I have spoken to you. Make your home in me, as I make mine in you. As a branch cannot bear fruit all by itself, but must remain part of the vine, neither can you unless you remain in me. I am the vine, you are the branches. Whoever remains in me, with me in him, bears fruit in plenty; for cut off from me you can do nothing. Anyone who does not remain in me is like a branch that has been thrown away – he withers; these branches are collected and thrown on the fire, and they are burnt. If you remain in me and my words remain in you, you may ask what you will and you shall get it. It is to the glory of my Father that you should bear much fruit, and then you will be my disciples.'

CHRIST THE LORD The world's greatest leaders influence people from the outside in; their speech, their ideas, their example, their presence – they move us and motivate, they draw us and stir us. Christ, however, goes much deeper. He not only calls us from the outside, but he also unites himself to us so intimately that his very life flows through our veins. "I am the vine, you are the branches." Where does the vine stop and its branches begin? Their union is too complete to tell. The same sap gives life to the vine and to its branches. He is Lord from within, renewing hearts from the inside, as only God can do. Once again, Jesus Christ stands alone among great historical figures; not only does he excel over all others in their own game, but he plays in an entirely different league; he is a leader, but he is also the Lord.

CHRIST THE TEACHER Jesus tells us point blank what the Father wants. God wants us to "bear much fruit" and to "be [his] disciples." God wants our lives to show forth his goodness, to bring lost souls back into the fold, and to fill human society and culture with the justice and beauty they need to flourish. Our desire to do something with our lives is a gift from God; we are created in his image, and he is the Creator – we too yearn to build, to contribute, to make a difference that will last not only in this life, but into all eternity.

Bearing this fruit requires in the first place our own efforts to stay united to the vine, through prayer, the sacraments, and loving obedience to God's will. And it also requires our being pruned – the purification of our selfishness that comes through suffering and sacrifice. Love and sacrifice, as all the lives of the saints attest to, and as Christ himself exemplifies, keep the sap flowing. They yield the fruit we yearn for most: living a life that resounds with meaning and energy, a life that positively impacts others and exudes joy and enthusiasm, a life that changes this world for the better in as profound a way as Christ's own life did, and a life whose meaning and impact overflow into eternity. This is what God wants for us; this is why Jesus came to earth. Bearing such fruit makes life worth living; without it we are dry, dead branches good for nothing except the fire - pretty simple lesson, pretty dire consequences if we don't learn it well.

CHRIST THE FRIEND Christ goes on to tell us how to how to achieve this fruitfulness: "Remain in me... cut off from me you can do nothing." As long as we stay united to the vine, whatever apostolic activities we engage in will yield a harvest – even a small branch dangling near the ground will produce its fruits as long as it's united to the vine. Separated from Jesus Christ, no one can live in communion with God, the only source of lasting fruit. How much we need to learn how to pray and make this the center of our lives! This is Christ's constant refrain from the moment of his incarnation: *Come to me, learn from me, follow me... My heart yearns for you to make my friendship the highest value of your life, so that I can fill you with true peace, meaning, and joy – the kind that you long for but can never achieve on your own. The sacraments, the Church, prayer, the Bible – these are all extensions of my effort to stay intimately united with you, to guide you along the path of everlasting life, and to reveal to you the glories of my love. These were my final words before I went to death on the cross, my last lesson, and I really mean them: remain in me; stay close to me; do not forsake me; trust in me.*

CHRIST IN MY LIFE Lord, your very life flows through my veins. Why don't I think of this more? Why do I let myself act as if this world were all there is? I know that my life now is a training ground of love, a chance to exercise the virtues of faith, hope, and love that you have grafted into my soul, an opportunity to spread your Kingdom to those around me. In my fidelity to that mission is your pleasure; in it is my joy...

No one loves me more than you. No one has given me more than you – no one can. If I succeed on my own, the satisfaction is real, but it passes; I need another success to feel satisfied again. If I possess something nice, I enjoy it for a while, but then it gets old. You want me to enjoy fruit that will last, the undying fruits of the Spirit: "love, joy, peace, patience, kindness, goodness, gentleness, self-control" (Gal 5:22)...

Of all the people I know, how many are united to the vine of your friendship, Lord? Half? A little less, a little more? You are yearning for all of them to live close to you, so you can make their lives bear fruit, the kind they yearn for. So I ask you, why don't I feel a bigger burden to pray for them and to show them your love? Why am I satisfied in my comfort zone? Let the light of your heart illumine my heart…

QUESTIONS FOR SMALL GROUP REFLECTION

1. What struck you most in this passage? What did you notice that you hadn't noticed before?

2. Christ wants nothing more than to remain united to each of us in intimate friendship. This is his greatest desire. How can we measure if our greatest desire is the same?

3. What are some signs that we can look for in order to determine whether our lives are "bearing fruit" in the way that God desires?

4. What can we do to make sure that we always stay united to the vine? What do you think is the surest and most visible sign that we have cut ourselves off from the vine?

Cf. Catechism of the Catholic Church, 2558-2565 on the importance of a vital union between Christ and the Christian; 1382-1401 on the Eucharist as the efficacious sign of this communion of life with God in Christ; 1718-1724 on our desire for happiness from God's perspective; 1812-1829 on union with God through the theological virtues

286. YOU ARE MY FRIENDS (JN 15:9-17)

"He had no need of us in order to save us, but we can do nothing without him… So let us love one another as Christ loved us and gave himself for us."

- St Augustine

John 15:9-17

'As the Father has loved me, so I have loved you. Remain in my love. If you keep my commandments you will remain in my love, just as I have kept my Father's commandments and remain in his love. I have told you this so that my own joy may be in you and your joy be complete. This is my commandment: love one another, as I have loved you. A man can have no greater love than to lay down his life for his friends. You are my friends, if you do what I command you. I shall not call you servants any more, because a servant does not know his master's business; I call you friends, because I have made known to you everything I have learnt from my Father. You did not choose me, no, I chose you; and I commissioned you to go out and to bear fruit, fruit that will last; and then the Father will give you anything you ask him in my name. What I command you is to love one another.'

CHRIST THE LORD The moment is solemn. Jesus is at table with his intimate collaborators, his handpicked Twelve Apostles, and he knows that this is the last time they will be gathered in this way until they meet again in eternity.

Nothing is carelessly said. Everyone on their deathbed has their final words, what they want to leave as their legacy. Jesus explains that he has loved us, and that he longs for us to remain in his love, to stay in his friendship, so that we may experience the indescribable joy that flows from true love. And then he lays down his one commandment, the new commandment, the summary of all his teaching and of his entire life: "Love one another as I love you." The law of Christ, the law of Christ's Kingdom, the only eternal law, is the law of love. Christ is Lord, because he commands with authority. But he is Lord of love, in love, and because of love, and his "command" is a heartfelt invitation to follow his example.

We can think of this part of his discourse as his battle plan - indeed, he is on the verge of heading into battle, his final battle against evil and all the forces of darkness. And with the consummating sacrifice of his life he will give birth to his Church militant, the body of believers who will take that same battle to the ends of the earth and the far corners of human history and culture. The plan is simple and straightforward. It is all summed up in his single, final, definitive command: love one another as I have loved you. To fight for the Lord and his Kingdom is to fight to fulfill that command.

CHRIST THE TEACHER Jesus, God himself, teaches us the nature of love. Love is self-giving: the greater the self-giving, the greater the love. "A man can have no greater love than to lay down his life for his friends." When we put our lives at the service of others, when we live in order to give and not to take, when we are willing to suffer so that someone else can rejoice, then we may call ourselves his disciples.

Just to make sure we don't misunderstand this lesson, he illustrated it by his own suffering and death. He accepted mockery, humiliation, torture, rejection, injustice, misunderstanding, betrayal, and finally death, not because he was too weak to resist, but to show us what love really is: self-giving, self-forgetting generosity. Jesus Christ hanging on the cross, bearing the weight of our sins and the punishment these sins have earned, thinking not of himself but of the souls he came to save, even pleading for their forgiveness up until the very end – this is love. Far from warm fuzzies and dreamy emotions, the love of Christ – and therefore the love of the Christian – is a love that gives without ever counting the cost, a love that gives without ever asking for something in return, a love that gives and gives and gives, just like God. And the more it gives, the more it has; the more it loves, the better it loves. We learn to love by loving. When we learn this lesson of true love and self-giving, we tap into the inexhaustible source of energy and enthusiasm that is God himself.

CHRIST THE FRIEND *Mary: My child, Jesus has now told you the most important thing that is in his heart. He has looked into your eyes, he has chosen you, and he has revealed his soul to you. He has held nothing back. You know him. He has come to offer you his friendship. If you reciprocate, if you also bare your heart to him in prayer, heed his call to follow him, and fulfill his commands, then your life will bear "fruit that will last" and your "joy will be complete." It is his promise, and he keeps his promises. Following Jesus Christ is a matter of the heart, a personal response to a personal invitation. And since the heart is the core of your being, anything that touches your heart touches every aspect of your life. Jesus wants to abide in your heart so that his friendship can color every nook and cranny of your life. Let him in again, today, right now.*

CHRIST IN MY LIFE Lord Jesus, you have wished to be my friend. I have so many friends. Friendship seems so simple, so natural. Do you really want to live like that with me? Don't you want something more dramatic, more impressive, more historic? After all, you are the King of the universe. But no, you just want my friendship. And I want yours. It is all I want. Increase my faith, Lord, and teach me to walk always by your side…

You keep repeating the same lesson, Lord, that you want me to love as you have loved. Why do you keep insisting? Because I still haven't learned it. It's like when I was a kid and my coaches and teachers kept drilling the fundamentals. How many times I had to write out the alphabet! How many times I had to shoot a layup! The fundamentals of eternal life – help me get them right, so I can help others…

I am so grateful that you have made me your soldier. You didn't need me; you could have conquered without me. But you chose to include me, to make me your ambassador, to give me a mission, a responsibility, a field of action. Now I can show you that I love you, that I am thankful for the innumerable gifts you have given me. I can show it by giving myself wholly to the mission you have entrusted to me…

QUESTIONS FOR SMALL GROUP DISCUSSION

1. What struck you most in this passage? What did you notice that you hadn't noticed before?

2. What does "love one another as I have loved you" mean for us right here and now?

3. Why do you think Christ insisted so much on his followers obeying that commandment?

4. What has most helped your relationship with Christ grow towards the heartfelt friendship that he wants it to be?

Cf. Catechism of the Catholic Church, 1822-1829 on the law of charity; 1965-1974 on the "new commandment" of charity and the new law of the gospel; 2558 on the importance of a vital and personal relationship with God

287. HARD TIMES WILL COME (JN 15:18-27)

"Though our ancestors' institutions failed, public affairs are in tumult, and everything human is confused, the Catholic Church alone never vacillates, but instead looks confidently to the future."

- Pope Benedict XV

John 15:18-27

'If the world hates you, remember that it hated me before you. If you belonged to the world, the world would love you as its own; but because you do not belong to the world, because my choice withdrew you from the world, therefore the world hates you. Remember the words I said to you: A servant is not greater than his master. If they persecuted me, they will persecute you too; if they kept my word, they will keep yours as well. But it will be on my account that they will do all this, because they do not know the one who sent me. If I had not come, if I had not spoken to them, they would have been blameless; but as it is they have no excuse for their sin. Anyone who hates me hates my Father. If I had not performed such works among them as no one else has ever done, they would be blameless; but as it is, they have seen all this, and still they hate both me and my Father. But all this was only to fulfil the words written in their Law: They hated me for no reason. When the Advocate comes, whom I shall send to you from the Father, the Spirit of truth who issues from the Father, he will be my witness. And you too will be witnesses, because you have been with me from the outset.'

CHRIST THE LORD As Jesus draws his final discourse towards its conclusion, he returns to the themes that have been present throughout John's Gospel: he is the one who has been sent from the Father, he is one with the Father, and in spite of all the works he has done and signs he has given, many have still rejected him, and so they have also rejected the Father. But Jesus knows that God's power, wisdom, and love can take even such tragic rebellion and weave it into his providential plan of salvation, and so he invokes yet another Old Testament prophecy to explain the mystery, as if to say, simply, that God's plan includes and absorbs even the abuse of human freedom; he is the Lord.

Nevertheless, if we read between the lines, we can detect an air of sadness, a dose of regret. He quotes the Scripture almost to comfort himself, because his heart has been broken by their refusal to accept him. He tries to make an excuse for them, "If I had not come... If I had not performed such works..." but their rejection stands, and it pains him. It is the same sadness that colored the very beginning of John's Gospel, "He came to his own domain, and his own people did not accept him.... He was in the world... and the world did not know him" (John 1:11, 10). If we are to be true followers of the Lord, we need to remember that he is not a cold tyrant or a distant judge; his human heart beats for all his subjects – for those who obey as well as for those who rebel. If we truly love the Lord, ours will too.

CHRIST THE TEACHER Jesus is on the brink of his passion. The hatred and persecution that have long been simmering are about to boil over. He knows it's coming. But even in its very jaws, his mind stays focused on his apostles and on his mission. He comforts them now for the trials they will have later. He prepares them to accept his suffering as part of God's plan of salvation and also to accept the similar suffering that will come their way as part of that same plan. They too, if they faithfully follow the master's call in their life, will both win converts, as he did, and suffer persecution and the violence of hatred, just like him. Persecution will help show that they are authentic disciples of Christ, and it will give them a chance to show that their love and fidelity are authentic too. In this context, it is no wonder that throughout the centuries, saints have desired and prayed for persecutions; they wanted to follow Christ more closely.

The same applies to us and to Christians of all times and places. A fundamental division gives dramatic tension to human existence. This world is fallen and yet redeemed. We are sinners and yet still destined for glory. As long as the age of the Church lasts, this division will continue to erupt here and there in waves of hatred, persecution, and conflict. We cannot prevent it, and so we must be ready for it. We must decide ahead of time how we will react, following in the footsteps of Christ. Then we will be his witnesses, as he has chosen us to be – not only with our words, but with our lives and our deaths as well.

CHRIST THE FRIEND *Jesus: My choice withdrew you from the world. There was never a time when I wasn't thinking of you. I have watched over you since the moment of your conception, and I have loved you since before time began. I searched you out as you grew up, whispering in your heart and preparing you to hear my invitation in your life. I kept inviting you many times until you accepted. I am the one who chose you to be my companion, disciple, and ambassador. And I am the one who will give you the strength and light you need to persevere in this labor of faith and love. You must never think that everything depends on you. That is too much for you. You are my adjutant, my helper, my messenger. I will protect you. I will teach you* *and show you the way to go. You have committed your life to me, and now you belong to me, and so all your challenges and troubles are mine. You are my problem now; let me carry you.*

CHRIST IN MY LIFE Part of me is still mystified at why so many people who witnessed your presence and your miracles didn't accept you and believe in you. But another part of me isn't, because I can see in my own heart that same hard-heartedness. I know you and believe in you, and yet I still lash out at my neighbor, I still wound others with my tongue, and I still indulge my self-centeredness. With the mercy of your heart, soften my heart…

If I think of soldiers in wartime, it is impossible to picture them being surprised at having to engage in battle. That's what soldiers do; that's what war is. Then why am I surprised when I am tempted, when I am misunderstood or ridiculed for trying to advance your Kingdom? Part of me still resists thinking of history in terms of a battle. But it is: you are my general; my weapons are love, forgiveness, and truth…

Mary, why did Jesus choose me? Why did he choose you? Why does he even care about us at all? I know; it is because he is sheer goodness and doesn't want to live without me. He would rather be scourged, crowned with thorns, and crucified than live without me. Mother, teach me to know him, to love him, and to follow him…

QUESTIONS FOR SMALL GROUP DISCUSSION

1. What struck you most in this passage? What did you notice that you hadn't noticed before?

2. What more do you think Jesus could have done to convince his antagonists that he really was the Messiah?

3. In this passage Jesus speaks of the world as hating him and his disciples. It seems that the world is the enemy. But earlier in the Gospel, St John told us that "God so loved the world that he sent his only begotten Son…" (John 3:16). If the world is so evil, how can God love it so much?

4. What are the most common kinds of battles in the Christian life? What's the difference between accepting persecution when it comes and imprudently stirring it up?

Cf. Catechism of the Catholic Church, 402-409 on the Christian life as a hard battle; 1-3, 50, 279-281, 295-301 and 2559-2565 on God's taking the initiative in our lives

The Gospel of John CHAPTER 16

"The providence of our God and Savior in regard to man consists of his recall from the fall and his return to close communion with God from the estrangement caused by his

disobedience. This was the purpose of Christ's dwelling in the flesh, the pattern of his life described in the gospels, his sufferings, the cross, the burial, the resurrection; so that man could be saved, and could recover, through imitating Christ, the adoption of former times. So, for perfection of life it is necessary not only to imitate Christ, in the examples of gentleness, and humility, and patience which he gave us in his life, but also to imitate him in his death…"

- St Basil

288. AFTER THE COMING STORM (JN 16:1-15)

"It is better to be alone with God. His friendship will not fail me, nor his counsel, nor his love. In his strength, I will dare and dare and dare until I die."

- St Joan of Arc

John 16:1-15

'I have told you all this that your faith may not be shaken. They will expel you from the synagogues, and indeed the hour is coming when anyone who kills you will think he is doing a holy duty for God. They will do these things because they have never known either the Father or myself. But I have told you all this, so that when the time for it comes you may remember that I told you, but now I am going to the one who sent me. Not one of you has asked, Where are you going? Yet you are sad at heart because I have told you this. Still, I must tell you the truth: it is for your own good that I am going because unless I go, the Advocate will not come to you; but if I do go, I will send him to you. And when he comes, he will show the world how wrong it was, about sin, and about who was in the right, and about judgement: about sin: proved by their refusal to believe in me; about who was in the right: proved by my going to the Father and your seeing me no more; about judgement: proved by the prince of this world being already condemned.

'I still have many things to say to you but they would be too much for you now. But when the Spirit of truth comes he will lead you to the complete truth, since he will not be speaking as from himself but will say only what he has learnt; and he will tell you of the things to come. He will glorify me, since all he tells you will be taken from what is mine. Everything the Father has is mine; that is why I said: All he tells you will be taken from what is mine.'

CHRIST THE LORD Jesus knows that his mission will not come to an end after he returns to the Father – rather, it will just be the beginning. He established his Kingdom through his life, Passion, death and Resurrection, and he will spend the rest of history expanding it. The instrument of that expansion will be his Church, guided "to all truth" by the Holy Spirit. Jesus did not leave us a book; he left us the living Church, animated by the Holy Spirit, indestructible, guaranteed to last until he comes again at the end of time. (The Church, through the inspiration of the Holy Spirit, subsequently put together the world's best-selling book, the Bible.)

Christ is the only King whose Kingdom will have no end. Even now, through his Spirit he is here among us, guiding our hearts "to the complete truth." If ever we get bored with the faith, we can be sure that the faith is not to blame – rather, we will have stopped listening to the words of our Lord.

CHRIST THE TEACHER In words that can hardly sustain the meaning he hoists upon them, Jesus teaches us about the very structure of God. The Spirit can only speak what he hears from the Son, and everything the Son has he has received from the Father – each communicates the other. God is a total unity of persons, a community of love, of self-giving. Whatever one has, the others receive. There is no holding back, no hidden agendas, no manipulation – it's absolute generosity and unlimited self-donation. And, just think, we are created in his image. We are meant to interact with one another with that same generosity. This was the new commandment that Christ gave us during the Last Supper, that we "love one another" as he has loved us, which means to love as the Father has loved him. We can't grasp completely the mystery of the Trinity, but we can enter into it by loving, and loving is better than grasping anyway.

One of the Spirit's first jobs will be to vindicate Jesus, who was about to be wrongly condemned to death. In so doing, the Spirit will reveal to the world, all throughout history, the truth about sin, justice ("who was in the right"), and judgment. Through the enlightenment that comes at Pentecost, all will recognize that Jesus was not the sinner his accusers claimed him to be; rather, their rejection of him will be shown up as the sin of disbelief. At the same time, it will become clear that all Jesus had said about himself and his mission was right, and the criticisms of his antagonists were wrong. Finally, in the epoch of the Church, what seemed like Christ's defeat in the face of a false judgment will turn out to have been the definitive and lasting judgment that dethrones Satan – idolatry and demonic possession will roll back as the Church rolls forward.

In the light of the Holy Spirit, the truth about Jesus will shine without interruption, exposing evil and pushing back injustice in every generation and every nation. When we renew our faith in the truth of Jesus, we make that light shine brighter, and make reparation for those who still prefer the darkness.

953

CHRIST THE FRIEND Jesus knows what we need, and he offers it to us – he is always thinking about what we need. He told his apostles just enough on that first Holy Thursday so that their faith would endure the coming storm – both the storm of his passion and that of the persecutions they would face afterwards. And although he still had "many things to say," he knew that it "would be too much for them" then. And so he waited. How humble our God is to adjust himself to the paltry limitations of our fallen human nature! How glad we should be to have someone we can trust so completely! He is perfect wisdom, unlimited power, and undying love, and he puts himself at our service, paying attention to our needs just as a loving mother would. And what does he get out of it? Nothing but the joy of bringing us into his Kingdom – for some reason, he wants to enjoy our friendship from now through eternity, and he's willing to be very patient in order to do so.

How different the world would be if every Christian followed our Lord's example! Patience, kindness, determined love, and attention to the needs of those around us in all circumstances… a simple formula for a worldwide revolution, a moral coup d'état.

CHRIST IN MY LIFE I feel as if every sentence, every phrase you utter is overflowing with meaning that goes way beyond me. Your words are a waterfall of light, and they dazzle me. Dear Lord, take me by the hand and guide me. Every day, help me to understand just a little bit more about you and your Kingdom and how to follow you. This is all I desire, this is all I hope for. Teach me the way to go…

I want to lead those around me into the truth of your friendship, Lord, but how? You revealed yourself gradually to your disciples, before and after your Passion. You befriended them and lived with them. You spoke the truth, but above all you lived the truth. And you drew them closer and closer to you. Help me to do the same. Help me to love others with your love, so I will know exactly what to do…

Mary, you watched over the apostles, the fledgling Church, between Christ's Ascension and the coming of the Holy Spirit. You took care of the infant Church just as lovingly and energetically as you took care of the infant Jesus. I am still just a child, just a beginner in my journey of discipleship. Take care of me, too. My mind is so dark and weak and confused; my heart so scrawny. Mother, make me like Jesus…

QUESTIONS FOR SMALL GROUP DISCUSSION

1. What struck you most in this passage? What did you notice that you hadn't noticed before?

2. How can we make our faith more and more Christian – in other words, how can we cultivate a relationship with God the Father, God the Son, and God the Holy Spirit, not just with God "in general"?

3. One of the consequences of the doctrine of the Trinity is that love itself is the force behind the existence of the universe and the life of the Church. What impact should that truth have on our daily lives?

4. How can we live with a greater awareness that we are temples of the Blessed Trinity? How should the fact that others are, at very least potentially, also temples of the Trinity affect our interpersonal relationships?

Cf. Catechism of the Catholic Church, 238-260 on the Trinity; 50-67 on God's plan of "loving goodness"; 849-856 on the "missionary mandate" of the Church

289. IN CHRIST'S NAME (JN 16:16-33)

"There is nothing more beautiful than to be surprised by the gospel, by the encounter with Christ. There is nothing more beautiful than to know Him and to speak to others of our friendship with him."

- Pope Benedict XVI

John 16:16-33

'In a short time you will no longer see me, and then a short time later you will see me again.' Then some of his disciples said to one another, 'What does he mean, In a short time you will no longer see me, and then a short time later you will see me again and, I am going to the Father? What is this short time? We don't know what he means.' Jesus knew that they wanted to question him, so he said, 'You are asking one another what I meant by saying: In a short time you will no longer see me, and then a short time later you will see me again. I tell you most solemnly, you will be weeping and wailing while the world will rejoice; you will be sorrowful, but your sorrow will turn to joy. A woman in childbirth suffers, because her time has come; but when she has given birth to the child she forgets the suffering in her joy that a man has been born into the world. So it is with you: you are sad now, but I shall see you again, and your hearts will be full of joy, and that joy no one shall take from you. When that day comes, you will not ask me any questions. I tell you most solemnly, anything you ask for from the Father he will grant in my name. Until now you have not asked for anything in my name. Ask and you will receive, and so your joy will be complete.

'I have been telling you all this in metaphors, the hour is coming when I shall no longer speak to you in metaphors, but tell you about the Father in plain words.

When that day comes you will ask in my name; and I do not say that I shall pray to the Father for you, because the Father himself loves you for loving me and believing that I came from God. I came from the Father and have come into the world and now I leave the world to go to the Father.' His disciples said, 'Now you are speaking plainly and not using metaphors! Now we see that you know everything, and do not have to wait for questions to be put into words; because of this we believe that you came from God.' Jesus answered them: 'Do you believe at last? Listen; the time will come – in fact it has come already – when you will be scattered, each going his own way and leaving me alone. And yet I am not alone, because the Father is with me. I have told you all this so that you may find peace in me. In the world you will have trouble, but be brave: I have conquered the world.'

CHRIST THE LORD Christ's words during the Last Supper were spoken in intimacy. He was not aloof from his disciples, delivering a discourse from a lectern or distant podium. He was sitting beside them, eating with them. They could see every expression of his face, hear every inflection in his voice; they could feel the table move with the gestures of his hands. This is how he wishes to speak these words to us – intimately.

Part of the Christian mystery consists in Christ's decision to ascend into heaven after his Resurrection. In doing so, he inaugurated the era of the Church, to which the action of the Holy Spirit belongs in a special way. But Jesus is still involved. He sits at the right hand of the Father, meaning that he shares fully – both as the eternal Son *and as true man, in his human nature and with his human body* – in the divine splendor. He is the bridge that reestablishes communion between God and mankind. So whenever we address God in his name, our prayer shares the efficacy of his prayer – a perfect efficacy.

During the Last Supper, Jesus is overjoyed at this prospect. As the risen and ascended Lord, the fully accepted sacrifice of atonement, he will be able to unfurl his love in ways that he couldn't while he was still here on earth. He is looking forward to our being able to ask the Father for our needs and desires in his name: "Until now you have not asked for anything in my name. Ask and you will receive, and so your joy will be complete." Imagine how he spoke those words, "Ask and you will receive." Picture him spreading his arms wide in a sign of generosity, holding nothing back, his face eager and animated, his eyes glowing and shining and burning with anticipation. He is Lord not for himself, but for us. His Kingdom is our Kingdom, if only we have the childlike simplicity and faith to claim it.

CHRIST THE TEACHER Jesus teaches his apostles the true relationship between sorrow and joy. The fallen world has a distorted vision of this relationship. It considers them opposites; either you experience sorrow or you experience joy – all sorrow is to be avoided, and all joy is to be embraced. But precisely because the world is fallen, this vision is false. In a fallen world, the bad must be purged before the true good can be experienced. An abandoned and trampled garden has to be weeded, tilled, and cultivated before it can produce beautiful flowers and healthy fruit. An injured limb has to be operated on and rehabilitated before it returns to the vigor it is meant to have. Just so, to experience the life we were meant to experience, the life of grace and communion with God, requires the weeding and cultivating and healing of our minds and hearts. Every advance in the spiritual life is a new birth necessarily preceded by birth pangs. The apostles could only experience Christ's victory after going through the darkness of his apparent defeat.

The pattern of spiritual growth is always death to sin and self (the sorrow, the pain, and the purification of our fallen nature), making more and more room for life in Christ. Here on earth this purification can occur more efficiently and less painfully than in purgatory, because we are free to cooperate with it, as an athlete cooperates with his trainer. Any purification that remains to be done after death is completely passive, as a patient under the scalpel of a surgeon. In both cases, however, the goal remains the same. The more that self-love gives way to Christ-love, the more fully we will taste the peace and joy that no one can take away, because it flows from the One who has risen and who reigns forever: "In the world you will have trouble, but be brave: I have conquered the world."

CHRIST THE FRIEND *Mary: "I am not alone…" Jesus could say that, because he was always united to his Father through prayer and obedience. But he also wants you to be able to say that. He never wants you to have to feel the angst of loneliness, of not being known and loved by someone close at hand. Hell is eternal, unrelieved loneliness, because in hell there is no love. But you are never alone. He dwells in your heart, and he is always speaking with you, guiding you, and loving you. He has given you his presence in the Eucharist and his grace in all the other sacraments. He has extended his Incarnation through the living Church. He sends you the messengers of creation and art and beauty of every sort as gifts and reminders that he is always thinking of you and looking forward to welcoming you home to heaven. He has given you the Bible, the saints, and your vocation to spur you on to know and love him more and more. He even gave you me, his own Mother, so I can watch over you as closely as I watched over him. He wants to bring you life; he wants to bring you joy. Truly you can say, even when everyone else abandons you as everyone abandoned him, "I am not alone."*

CHRIST IN MY LIFE Teach me to pray, Lord. Teach me to pray in your name, to pray with faith, to pray unceasingly. Teach me to pray for the people you have entrusted to my care. You want to shower your graces down upon them, and you are just waiting for me to open up the faucet by my sincere, trusting prayers. In your name, Lord Jesus, I beg you to send the Father's blessing and the Spirit's grace into their hearts…

I am such a product of my times, Lord. I am a coke-machine Christian: I want to put the dollar in the slot, press a button, and have holiness pop right out. I still resist the cross. No more, Lord. You have promised that if I trust in you and follow you, all my sorrows will change into the kind of joy that nothing on earth can taint. I cannot say that I like to suffer, but I can say that I trust in you, Jesus…

I am never alone. You have made sure of that by giving me your friendship. I am sorry for being so closed in on myself at times. I spend most of my day living as if I were alone. In my heart I monologue with myself, while on the outside I bustle and chat. And where are you? I don't want to relegate you to a few minutes in the morning and a few at night. I want to live in your presence, because I know that's what you want…

QUESTIONS FOR SMALL GROUP DISCUSSION

1. What struck you most in this passage? What did you notice that you hadn't noticed before?

2. What can we do to become more and more aware of God's constant, active presence in our lives? What has helped you to become more aware?

3. Jesus seems to contradict the apostles' expression of faith when he tells them that they will be scattered during his passion. Does their scattering mean that they didn't really believe? If not, what did it mean?

4. What lessons have you learned from sorrow and difficulty in your life? What lessons have you learned from easy success?

Cf. Catechism of the Catholic Church, 2734-2741 on filial trust in our relationship with God; 2742-2745 on perseverance in prayer and fidelity; 571-573 on the suffering of Jesus; 30, 163, 301, 1804, 1829, 2015, and 2362 on the sources of joy in the Christian life

THE GOSPEL OF JOHN CHAPTER 17

"He said to me, 'My divine heart is so in love with people, and with you in particular, that it can no longer contain the flames of its ardent charity. It needs you to spread them. It must manifest itself to people and enrich them with the precious treasures that I will reveal to you. These treasures are the graces of salvation and sanctification,

necessary to rescue people from the abyss of perdition...' This divine heart was shown me on a throne of flames. It was more resplendent than the sun and transparent as crystal. The heart had its own adorable wound, and was surrounded by a crown of thorns, signifying the stings caused by our sins. And there was a cross above it."

- St Margaret Mary Alocoque

290. CASTING OUT THE DEVIL – FOREVER (JN 17:1-11)

"It is clear to me that if we wish to please God and to receive graces in abundance from him, it is God's will that these graces should come to us through the hands of Christ in his most holy humanity."

- St Theresa of Avila

John 17:1-11

'Father, the hour has come: glorify your Son so that your Son may glorify you; and, through the power over all mankind that you have given him, let him give eternal life to all those you have entrusted to him. And eternal life is this: to know you, the only true God, and Jesus Christ whom you have sent. I have glorified you on earth and finished the work that you gave me to do. Now, Father, it is time for you to glorify me with that glory I had with you before ever the world was. I have made your name known to the men you took from the world to give me. They were yours and you gave them to me, and they have kept your word. Now at last they know that all you have given me comes indeed from you; for I have given them the teaching you gave to me, and they have truly accepted this, that I came from you, and have believed that it was you who sent me. I pray for them; I am not praying for the world but for those you have given me, because they belong to you: all I have is yours and all you have is mine, and in them I am glorified. I am not in the world any longer, but they are in the world, and I am coming to you. Holy Father, keep those you have given me true to your name, so that they may be one like us.'

CHRIST THE LORD This is God speaking to God, Jesus the eternal Son praying to God the Father for you and me just moments before he begins the final act in his drama of the Incarnation. By sharing this prayer with us, he lets us in to the deepest recesses of his soul. What is on his heart? The Father's glory, the souls he came to save, the successful fulfillment of his life's mission – these things were always on his heart. This discourse is traditionally referred to as Christ's priestly prayer, since it contains an extended petition to God for the Church and the world and contains inexhaustible treasures. (And like him, the main function of a priest is to intercede for others before God.)

Jesus asserts once again that he has received "power over all mankind," – absolute authority, universal kingship. In the very next clause, he shows what kind of a King he is: "Let him give eternal life to all those you have entrusted to him." God's glory, as St Irenaeus puts it, consists in "man fully alive" *(Gloria Dei, vivens homo)*. Jesus Christ is a Lord completely at the service of his subjects, a King who exercises power not for selfish aggrandizement, but for the greater good of his subjects. Christ is the Leader par excellence and the model of all Christian leadership – and every Christian is called to be a leader, in one form or another.

CHRIST THE TEACHER Throughout his life and ministry, Jesus reiterated the lesson of unity. "Blessed are the peacemakers, for they will be called the children of God" (Matthew 5:9). "By this they will know you are my disciples, if you love one another" (John 13:35). One of the biblical names for the devil, *diabolus* (whence "diabolical"), means "divider." The devil sows division, anger, envy, hatred, suspicion, resentment, and confusion. Christ came "to destroy the works of the devil" (1 John 3:8), to bring unity back to the human family, the unity that mirrors the perfect unity within God himself, who is three persons and one God. It is on his heart even at this culminating moment before his Passion: "So that they may be one like us," he prays.

On a global level, his prayer has been answered; the Catholic Church has remained one in faith, one in worship, and one in organization through twenty long and difficult centuries. But on a personal level, attacks against unity have never ceased. Schisms and divisions litter the path of Christian history. Sterile criticism divides parishes and dioceses; it separates people from priests and priests from bishops. How this must pain the Sacred Heart of Jesus! Have we ourselves learned the lesson of unity? Do we know how to make peace? Or are we unsuspecting undercover agents of the devil, the "divider"?

As Christ raised his eyes to heaven and uttered these words, how much did the apostles understand? We can only guess. We can say with certainty, however, that the prayer before Christ's Passion must have often come to the apostles' minds later, when they were spreading the gospel throughout the world. Jesus had asked the Father to keep them "true to his name." In the face of persecution and martyrdom, how much comfort must they have derived from these words! His prayer applies equally to us, who have received the same vocation to holiness. Through the sacraments, we have inherited the apostles' mission, along with their union with Christ's heart. We belong to him, and he is faithful – we have nothing to fear.

CHRIST THE FRIEND The greatest joy of human existence is relationships of love. What would mansions and yachts, works of art and mountain cottages, sunrises and ocean voyages be without others to share them with? Love, in its various forms (parental, filial, spousal, friendship) can make the most mundane experiences into thrilling adventures, the simplest places into fairylands, the humblest activities into noble deeds. In this prayer, Jesus explains that heaven is nothing more than a perfect relationship of love. We will know God and Christ (and all the saints). We will spend eternity getting to know the One who can never be fully known. If the best of human friendships never grow old, how indescribable will be our eternal friendship with God, from whom all good things come!

Mary: My child, I never preached to the crowds, I never founded universities, I never wrote best sellers, I never established international apostolates, and yet Jesus made me Queen of the Universe. Why? Because his Kingdom isn't made up of flashy achievements. His Kingdom is the unbreakable and contagious bond of love for God and love for neighbor. And so he chooses as Queen his Mother, who had learned the lesson of love, who had learned through the grace of God to be a peacemaker, as all mothers must learn. Seek greatness, because you were created for greatness – no one else can know and love Jesus the way you can – but seek true greatness, and seek it in the only place it can be found, in the Kingdom of Christ, who loved you and gave himself up for you.

CHRIST IN MY LIFE Jesus, you only cared about fulfilling the Father's will and leading me to eternal life. You only cared about others. You didn't just call yourself a servant – you lived like a servant. Dear Lord, I want to live as you lived. But I need your help. Purify my heart. Teach me to forget myself, to give myself, to lose my life in your service, so that I will find the life you want me to have…

You spent your years of ministry casting out demons, healing, and preaching the good news to those who were in need. You finished your life by paying the price for our sins, by laying down your life as a bridge between us rebels and the God who loves us. Thank you, Lord. Teach me to be like that! Make my every word, decision, and action build up my neighbor and your Kingdom. Never let me sow division…

Help me think about heaven, Lord. You are leading me there. You went to prepare me a place there. What will it be like? You came to earth, lived, suffered, and died so that I would have the possibility of going there, of spending eternity with you there. Whatever I can imagine, you can outdo. Increase my hope, Lord, and draw many others to you through me…

QUESTIONS FOR SMALL GROUP REFLECTION

1. What struck you most in this passage? What did you notice that you hadn't noticed before?

2. Why do you think Christ would have spoken this prayer out loud to his disciples?

3. How can we be better agents of unity in the Church and in the world?

4. What effect has the promise of eternal life and the reality of heaven had on your life? What effect does Christ want it to have?

Cf. Catechism of the Catholic Church, 813-822 on the unity of the Church; 1023-1029 on heaven

291. TRUTH AND JOY (JN 17:12-19)

"But whenever we think of Christ, let us always bear in mind that love of his which drove him to bestow upon us so many gifts and graces."

- St Theresa of Avila

John 17:12-19

'While I was with them, I kept those you had given me true to your name. I have watched over them and not one is lost except the one who chose to be lost, and this was to fulfil the scriptures. But now I am coming to you and while still in the world I say these things to share my joy with them to the full. I passed your word on to them, and the world hated them, because they belong to the world no more than I belong to the world. I am not asking you to remove them from the world, but to protect them from the evil one. They do not belong to the world any more than I belong to the world. Consecrate them in the truth; your word is truth. As you sent me into the world, I have sent them into the world, and for their sake I consecrate myself so that they too may be consecrated in truth.'

CHRIST THE LORD Jesus Christ did not hoard his power. He did not reserve his greatness just for himself. He was indeed the Savior sent by God into the world, but he chose to carry out his saving mission through the ministry of his followers: "As you sent me into the world, I have sent them into the world." In the Liturgy, the Church puts this thought before our minds as the Easter season is drawing to a close. We have received its message of hope, of triumph, and of everlasting life; now our Lord is counting on us to broadcast that message throughout the world, by means of our words, our example, and our actions. He was sent, and he has in turn sent us.

A core principle of human leadership is delegation: good leaders know that they cannot do everything alone, so they find qualified people and divide the tasks among them. The case of Christ and his Church is analogous, except for one key difference. Jesus Christ delegates not because he is unable to run his

Kingdom without our assistance, but because he wants to give our lives eternal resonance by entrusting to us a mission that has real, everlasting consequences. He is the head who rules through the different members of his body, not because he has to, but because he wants to. In taking up the invitation to become his ambassadors, we come closer to him. We get to know him better, just as you always get to know people better when you work on a project together. We get to know ourselves better, and under his guidance we are able to develop all the qualities he has given us, qualities we may not even know we have (but he knows, since he gave them to us). The chance to work with Christ and for his Kingdom is one of his greatest gifts. It's how we become not just subjects of the Lord, but friends of the King.

CHRIST THE TEACHER The world gets bad press in this passage. Christ asserts that he does not belong to the world, and neither do his disciples, who have been "consecrated," which literally means "set apart," just as he has been. The world "hated" Christ and his followers, and yet it was that very world which Jesus came to save.

The "world" in this passage refers not to the created universe, which comes forth from God's hand as something "very good" (Genesis 1:31), but to the forces of human society that have been corrupted by sin, the tendency of many social and cultural norms to lure us away from the steep but liberating path of fidelity to Christ and his friendship. In this sense, the world is one of the Christian's traditional enemies; it is the kingdom of the devil as opposed to the Kingdom of God, the city of fallen man as opposed to the city of God. As St Augustine described them, the former is ruled by love for self to the point of despising God, while the latter is ruled by love for God to the point of self-sacrifice.

A Christian can never be completely at home in this world, never completely happy or comfortable. We are pilgrims traversing a dangerous route to heaven, soldiers marching from battle to battle in defense of our King. We must never be surprised at the challenges and opposition that we encounter; indeed, every obstacle should boost our hope, reminding us that just ahead we will find home.

CHRIST THE FRIEND Before he returned to his Father, Jesus prayed for his disciples. He prays that we may be consecrated in the truth, just as he is consecrated in the truth. He asks the Father to transplant our lives so that they may become rooted in the lasting, dependable, and rich soil of the truth. He is praying that we be given the grace to build our lives on the solid foundation of God's Word, so that when the storms come (the hatred of the world, the attacks of the evil one), we will stand strong.

What is the truth? What is the word of the Father? Pilate will soon ask the same question, and Jesus will give the definitive answer: he is the Truth; he is the Word. And when we look at him, what do we see? Love. Total self-giving and total concern for others, even to the point of self-annihilation on the cross. This is where Jesus wants us to root our lives – in love. And this consecration to the truth of love is the secret to lasting joy, to sharing in Christ's own joy: "I say these things to share my joy with them to the full."

Jesus: My child, I know what will fill your heart – love. I know what's at the bottom of your soul, because I created you. It is the need to love and be loved, to discover that another person is delighted that you exist, and to be glad in the existence of that other person. This is the deepest truth of your being, because I made you in my own image, and this is the deepest truth of my being. That night when I prayed for my Apostles to be consecrated in the truth, I was asking my Father to keep the flame of love alive forever in the heart of the Church, so that it can continuously spread love among all people, and so that it would eventually kindle that flame in your heart. I need to remind you that I am glad that you exist. Not because of what you can do for me, but just because you are. You don't need to earn my love; you just need to enjoy it. And if you do, you will be true to the mission I have given you, the same mission I have given to the whole Church: distributing the embrace of my love to every heart. Know that when I see you (which I always do), I smile, because I am pleased that you exist.

CHRIST IN MY LIFE You have sent me out, just as your Father sent you out. You have sent me into the lives of those around me, into this society and this culture, just as your Father sent you into the world. You want me to be true to your will, to love my neighbor as you have loved me, just as you were true to the Father's will. You have put your mission into my hands. Thank you, Lord! With you at my side, I have nothing to fear…

Why am I still surprised when things go wrong, when tragedy strikes, or when failure brings me to my knees? Why do I keep thinking earth should be heaven? O Lord, shine your light into my mind. Give me the mind and heart of a pilgrim, a soldier, a missionary. Remind me everyday that this life is a journey, a battle, and a mission. Remind me that with you in my heart I can travel and fight and work with joy and peace, no matter what…

Everything around me reminds me of your love. Every sunset is a gift flowing from your love. All the little pleasures of the day, all the beautiful memories of my life, all the hopes that fire my heart, all the goodness I receive from those who love me: all these remind me of your love. It all comes from you. You shine your love all around me, showering me with your light. Keep me aware of your goodness, Lord. Jesus, never let me forget your love...

QUESTIONS FOR SMALL GROUP DISCUSSION

1. What struck you most in this passage? What did you notice that you hadn't noticed before?

2. Theoretically, should it be possible to tell just from the way a Christian treats other people that he or she is a disciple of Christ?

3. How much is our concept of happiness dependent on having a good supply of the world's comforts and pleasures, and how much is it dependent upon knowing that we are following the narrow and hard path blazed by Jesus Christ? What should the ratio be like for a mature Christian?

4. What can we do to be more effective agents of unity in the Church, working for the fulfillment of Christ's prayer without compromising our adherence to the true Catholic faith?

Cf. Catechism of the Catholic Church, 813-822 on the mystery of the Church's unity; 405, 2015, 2516, 2725 on life as a spiritual battle; 164, 408, 1869 on the contrary influence of the "world"

292. ONE LOVE, ONE GLORY (JN 17:20-26)

"The whole Blessed Trinity dwells in us, the whole of that mystery which will be our vision in heaven. Let it be our cloister."

- Blessed Elizabeth of the Trinity

John 17:20-26

'I pray not only for these, but for those also who through their words will believe in me. May they all be one. Father, may they be one in us, as you are in me and I am in you, so that the world may believe it was you who sent me. I have given them the glory you gave to me, that they may be one as we are one. With me in them and you in me, may they be so completely one that the world will realise that it was you who sent me and that I have loved them as much as you loved me. Father, I want those you have given me to be with me where I am, so that they may always see the glory you have given me because you loved me before the foundation of the world. Father, Righteous One, the world has not known you, but I have known you, and these have known that you have sent me. I have made your name known to them and will continue to make it known, so that the love with which you loved me may be in them, and so that I may be in them.'

CHRIST THE LORD Christ's final words before his Passion, words which the Church puts before us each year during the Easter season, bubble up from the depths of the Trinitarian conversation. Jesus is addressing his Father; we are privy to God's interior dialogue – we can read into his mind and heart. We glimpse the love that exists in God, the love that links the Persons of the Trinity, the love that God is. This love is the theme of Christ's prayer. Love was the content of his New Commandment. Love, true, self-forgetful love, self-sacrificing love, was the lesson he left when he gave himself up to death on the cross.

One other thing is clear as well: Christ is speaking to the Father like one who knows him as well as we know our own fathers. It is as if a noble prince had gone into the countryside and befriended a band of peasants, then brought them into the palace and, in their presence, begged the King to grant them royal favor. He reminds the Father that he loved him "before the foundation of the world," that "the world has not known you, but I have known you," that they are "in" each other in an inexpressible way, that the Father's glory is his glory… And Jesus asks his Father to let these simple, peasant friends of his into this ineffable closeness, this eternal union. Christ is the only Son of the Father; he is the Lord. Thanks be to God he is our Lord!

CHRIST THE TEACHER By praying out loud, Christ teaches us how to pray. A Christian is another Christ, and so our prayers ought to follow the lines of his prayer. How does he pray? In an atmosphere of assurance that he is being heard by the Father. Whenever we pray, this must be our foundation: we are in conversation with God – with a real, personal God who cares about us more than we care about ourselves. The traditional acts of faith, hope, and love that Christians have long used as reference points in their prayer life are meant to activate this awareness, to enable us to enter into an intimate contact with the one we know loves us. What does Jesus pray for? For us and for all people to enter into the everlasting divine life – and for the Church, that all believers may be united among each other and in him. So too we must pray for the unity of Christians and for all men and women to come to know Christ, so that through him they can enter into the life of God as well. And how does he pray? With intimacy (note how often he says "Father"!) and with reverence, "Father, Righteous One." When we approach God, we should follow in his path, opening our hearts in utter confidence, but adoring him in utter humility.

CHRIST THE FRIEND On the night of that first Holy Thursday, Christ not only prayed for his Twelve Apostles, but he also prayed for those who "through their words will believe in me." In other words, he prayed for us. We have directly received faith through our parents, or perhaps through a friend or a priest, but ultimately, all Christians trace their lineage of faith back all the way to the Apostles, because they were Christ's original messengers. Even then, so long ago in the perspective of history, yet so recent from the perspective of love, Jesus had us in mind. He was thinking of each of us during every moment of his life. Each one of us, everyone who would come to believe in his name has a claim on his heart. If there's nothing else the gospel teaches us, no one can deny that it reveals God's personal love and concern for every human person. Only God's love can be like that, simultaneously intimate and global, personalized and universal, and only in God can we find ourselves so bathed in the purest of loves, with absolutely no strings attached.

Christ: I prayed for all of you to be one, to be united. This is life as I meant it to be: unity, charity, one heart, and one mind. Every sin causes division. Every sin hammers a wedge of discord. How I long for you to experience the joy of living in the unity and communion of true love! You were created for that. Learn from my example. Live in harmony with everyone, loving everyone as I have loved you. Put no conditions on your love, no limits. Guard your words. Speak only what will build up, never what divides. Find ways to knit hearts and lives together, to bridge gaps, to turn differences into mutual enrichment. Be of one heart and one mind – with me, with those closest to you, with those you work with, with those who are difficult to bear with. This is what it means to be my follower and to be created in the image of God.

CHRIST IN MY LIFE You have given me a glimpse of your own nature, of your relationship with the Father. I can't fully understand that, Lord. Why did you reveal it to me? You want to be known by me. You want me to enter into your friendship – even more, into your family. So I have to know the Father, the Son, and the Holy Spirit! I want to know you. The better I know you, the better I will be able to reflect your goodness in all I do…

You want me to pray well and often. It's something you want but can't get unless I give it to you. You have limited your omnipotence out of a desire for my friendship: only I can decide to give you my attention and my affection in prayer. Thank you for the gift of prayer, for this chance to show you that I love you and that I am grateful for all you have done for me. Teach me to speak to you intimately, simply, and honestly…

I believe in your personal, determined love for me. I believe that you were thinking of me during the Last Supper. I believe that you are always thinking of me. It pains me to think that I don't live with a keener, more constant awareness of this. I am always aware of what time it is, what the weather is like, who

I'm with – why can't I be more aware of this much more significant truth? Lord, increase my faith…

QUESTIONS FOR SMALL GROUP DISCUSSION

1. What struck you most in this passage? What did you notice that you hadn't noticed before?

2. Why do you think Christ prayed this prayer out loud? What does this prayer reveal about the Father?

3. What do you imagine the apostles were thinking as they listened to this prayer?

4. How, practically speaking, can we deepen our appreciation of God's personal love for each one of us?

Cf. Catechism of the Catholic Church, 232-260 on the relations between the three divine persons of the Trinity; 813-822 on the unity of the Church

THE GOSPEL OF JOHN CHAPTER 18

"Oh, the new and ineffable mystery! The Judge was judged. He who absolves from sin was bound. He was mocked who once framed the world. He was stretched upon the cross who stretched out the heavens. He was given up to the tomb who raises the dead. The powers were astonished, the angels wondered, the elements trembled, the whole created universe was shaken, the sun fled away… because it could not bear to look upon the crucified Lord."

- St Alexander of Alexandria

293. TRAITORS, TROOPS, AND TRIUMPHS (JN 18:1-11)

"God offers himself to us; there is no need to offer us more."

- St Augustine

John 18:1-11

After he had said all this Jesus left with his disciples and crossed the Kedron valley. There was a garden there, and he went into it with his disciples. Judas the traitor knew the place well, since Jesus had often met his disciples there, and he brought the cohort to this place together with a detachment of guards sent by the chief priests and the Pharisees, all with lanterns and torches and weapons. Knowing everything that was going to happen to him, Jesus then came forward and said, 'Who are you looking for?' They answered, 'Jesus the Nazarene'. He said, 'I am he'. Now Judas the traitor was standing among them. When Jesus said, 'I am he', they moved back and fell to the ground. He asked them a second time, 'Who are you looking for?' They said, 'Jesus the Nazarene'. 'I have told you that I am he' replied Jesus. 'If I am the one you are looking for, let these others go.' This was to fulfil the words he had spoken, 'Not one of those you gave me have I lost'. Simon Peter, who carried a sword, drew it and wounded the high priest's servant, cutting off his right ear. The servant's name was Malchus. Jesus said to Peter, 'Put your sword back in its scabbard; am I not to drink the cup that the Father has given me?'

CHRIST THE LORD St John gives us a more complete view of this encounter in the Garden of Gethsemane than the other Gospel writers. He skips over Jesus' agony and prayer and moves right on to the arrest. The night was bright, lit by a full moon – the Passover always took place during the first full moon of the spring equinox. John details the makeup of this dispatch. It includes a cohort and a detachment of Temple police, all of them armed. The Greek word translated cohort (*speira*) can refer to three different units of soldiers (during the Passover extra soldiers were always stationed in Jerusalem). It can either be a normal Roman cohort of six hundred men, or it can refer to a cohort of non-Roman auxiliary troops numbering twelve hundred men, or it can sometimes refer to a maniple of soldiers, which consisted of two hundred men. Any way we take it, even if St John is using the term loosely, the picture it paints shows the lone Jesus flanked by his frightened eleven Apostles courageously facing a small army.

The tough soldiers and Temple guards were made more confident by their own numbers, though perhaps irritated at being sent out in the cold late at night, and they certainly felt assured that they would soon have the famous rabbi under lock and key. But when they got to the spot and declared their purpose, it only took a word spoken by the Lord to push back the entire throng and knock them to the ground: "When Jesus said, 'I am he', they moved back and fell to the ground." Indomitable authority and power exuded from the Lord. Peter was so invigorated by this show of force that he brandished his own sword to join the attack. But Jesus wasn't going to conquer that way. Simply destroying his enemies was too easy. He wanted to convert them instead. And so, he freely 'drinks the cup" of suffering that his Father has prepared for him. All that follows throughout the Passion will display not the weakness of an inept Galilean rabbi, but the intrepid and unconquerable love of the Lord, always in control of himself and the situation surrounding him.

CHRIST THE TEACHER St John makes a point of explaining that Judas was right in the middle of this tragic encounter, even though in John's account Judas doesn't actually do anything. Each time he mentions his fellow apostle in this passage, St John calls him "Judas the traitor." This epithet contrasts starkly with how St John described Judas back in Chapter 6, as "one of the Twelve, who was to betray him." This small change illustrates a big lesson:

Our spiritual life, our friendship with Christ, is intricately connected to our moral life, the choices we make regarding right and wrong. Jesus is the Creator and Redeemer of the universe, so when we choose to act in accordance with his design for that universe (morally good choices), we deepen our friendship with him – or lay the groundwork for it if it does not yet exist. When we choose to act against his design (morally evil choices), we set ourselves up as rebels against him, which can hardly be a good thing for our friendship. Every individual moral choice, therefore, affects not only its particular situation, but also the kind of person we are and the kind of friend we can be to Christ. When we choose to lie, we become the kind of person who lies. When we choose to use other people as means to selfish ends, we become the kind of person who destroys and discards our fellow man.

Before Judas's betrayal, he is still one of the Twelve; he is a follower of Jesus, however imperfect he may be. After his betrayal, he has become a traitor. He is now the kind of person who is willing to climb the ladder of success by stepping on his friends. The drama of Judas's betrayal exemplifies, lucidly and tragically, the uniquely Christian vision of human dignity: the human person's every choice and action matter. People are not recycled bits and pieces of the universe inevitably making their way back to nothingness, as eastern mysticism and modern nihilism would have it. No, people are God's children, free to be faithful to this sublime vocation of glorifying God and living in communion with him or free to betray it. Every person is created with this indestructible core of dignity, because every person is created by God in God's image. Wherever we see a fellow human being, whether on the most mundane of subways or in the most exquisite of palaces, every single one of them bears in their soul this weight of eternal glory.

CHRIST THE FRIEND Modern existential philosophers criticize Christianity for being a religion of the weak. For them, gentle Jesus being overpowered by the cruelty of Roman might was a repellant display of feeble ineptitude. But they got it all wrong. Probably they hadn't read the Gospels, and certainly they hadn't read this passage. Jesus shows more strength and authority than anyone in history. He destroyed his enemies, not by annihilation but by turning them into his friends and disciples, and he did it by freely letting them do their worst to him, continuing to love them, and staying faithful to the truth of his mission all the same.

Jesus: You are used to hearing that I love you. But you still think of love in too limited a way. Think for a moment of the whole universe. Now think that I have given it all to you. Really, it is all yours, because when you receive me in Holy Communion, you receive the whole of my King-dom. Think for a moment of what you would be willing to do for someone you love. Think how hard it is sometimes to offer even the smallest sacrifice for their sake, especially when they show no appreciation. I offered the sacrifice of the cross for you, before you even knew me, let alone loved me. And I did it with total freedom. I didn't have to, I chose to, just because I can't bear the thought of spending eternity without you.

CHRIST IN MY LIFE   I wonder if I really believe in the power of love, Lord. You did. It was your one and only weapon, and with it you have established a Kingdom that has outlasted the world's mightiest empires. What about the battles I have to fight? My responsibilities, my relationships, my temptations – have I really learned to fight as you did? Am I wielding the sword of love? I think I need more lessons, Lord…

Father, when you look upon the world, you see the same people I see, but you see them differently. You see each one as your beloved child. When parents go to a school play, they see crowds of kids, but when they behold their own children something entirely different happens in their mind and heart. That's what you are like with each of us. Lord, teach me to see and love my neighbor as you do …

Lord Jesus, thank you for becoming my Savior. I am sorry that my heart is so hard, so insensitive. Soften it, Lord, so that I can truly appreciate all that you have done for me. Teach me to feel sincere sadness for my sins and the sins of everyone, but at the same time to feel the joy you want me to feel always, the deep joy of knowing that I am loved so purely, completely, personally…

QUESTIONS FOR SMALL GROUP DISCUSSION

1. What struck you most in this passage? What did you notice that you hadn't noticed before?

2. Why do you think St John made a point of telling us the name of the man whose ear Peter cut off with the sword?

3. Judas's betrayal is dramatic, but it is also possible to betray Jesus in subtler, more hidden ways. How are we tempted to betray him in our own life-situations?

4. Why do you think Jesus let loose his authority to the point of knocking the battalion to the ground, when he knew all along that he was going to let himself be arrested by those same men?

Cf. Catechism of the Catholic Church, 1730-1742 on morality and human freedom; 1749-1756 on the morality of human acts; 599-600 on Jesus' Passion as being ordained by the Father

294. THE POLITICAL TEMPTATION (JN 18:12-27)

"Behold, God the Father has sent down to earth as it were a bag filled with his mercy; a bag to be rent open in the passion so that our ransom which it concealed might be poured out; a small bag indeed, but full."

- St Bernard of Clairvaux

John 18:12-27

The cohort and its captain and the Jewish guards seized Jesus and bound him. They took him first to Annas, because Annas was the father-in-law of Caiaphas, who was high priest that year. It was Caiaphas who had suggested to the Jews, 'It is better for one man to die for the people'. Simon Peter, with another disciple, followed Jesus. This disciple, who was known to the high priest, went with Jesus into the high priest's palace, but Peter stayed outside the door. So the other disciple, the one known to the high priest, went out, spoke to the woman who was keeping the door and brought Peter in. The maid on duty at the door said to Peter, 'Aren't you another of that man's disciples?' He answered, 'I am not'. Now it was cold, and the servants and guards had lit a charcoal fire and were standing there warming themselves; so Peter stood there too, warming himself with the others. The high priest questioned Jesus about his disciples and his teaching. Jesus answered, 'I have spoken openly for all the world to hear; I have always taught in the synagogue and in the Temple where all the Jews meet together: I have said nothing in secret. But why ask me? Ask my hearers what I taught: they know what I said.' At these words, one of the guards standing by gave Jesus a slap in the face, saying, 'Is that the way to answer the high priest?' Jesus replied, 'If there is something wrong in what I said, point it out; but if there is no offence in it, why do you strike me?' Then Annas sent him, still bound, to Caiaphas the high priest. As Simon Peter stood there warming himself, someone said to him, 'Aren't you another of his disciples?' He denied it saying, 'I am not'. One of the high priest's servants, a relation of the man whose ear Peter had cut off, said, 'Didn't I see you in the garden with him?' Again Peter denied it; and at once a cock crew.

CHRIST THE LORD Power in the world often comes at a high cost. Those who are powerful constantly face the temptation to compromise their integrity in order to maintain their influence. Plenty of excuses can be found to justify such compromises: I can do more good if I stay in office, the good I do outweighs the evil, etc. When Jesus was brought before Annas, it was because the devil was presenting him with this temptation.

In those days, the high priest was both the highest authority in Israel and the closest collaborator with the Roman overlords. In previous eras, the office was held for life, but the Romans wanted to keep the high priests under control, so they imposed term limits, never letting one person get too powerful. Annas had been high priest during the years 6-15 AD. Since then, his four sons had each served as high priest, and the current holder of the office, Caiaphas, was his son-in-law. Clearly, Annas was the real power broker, the most influential of the Jewish leaders who continued pulling the strings behind a façade of propriety. He had recognized the threat posed by Jesus and was probably involved in the machinations against him. It is logical that he would have the Lord brought to him first. He wanted to gauge Christ's moral metal. If Jesus could be persuaded to join forces with Annas – if he could be corrupted – this would give yet more influence into his hands, most especially influence with the common people, something he didn't have. If not, and if Jesus truly were as influential as everyone said, he would have to be destroyed.

So Annas initiates talks with Jesus before sending him to any kind of an official trial, even before letting the others know that he has been successfully apprehended. And he questions him about his teachings. Jesus knew very well that it was against Jewish law to force a man to bear witness against himself – only third parties could speak evidence against a man on trial. If he were to answer Annas' questions, therefore, he would be breaking this law and putting himself on the side of Annas' corruption. It was the moment in which he could have compromised his integrity in order to protect his power. But Jesus' Kingdom is no earthly kingdom. He has no truck with evil. Knowing the mind of Annas, he merely reminds him of the law, perhaps hoping to stir the old conniver's conscience.

If all Christians – or even if half of all Christians – followed their Lord's example of unstinting integrity, the world might have more martyrs, but it would also have more justice.

CHRIST THE TEACHER Jesus teaches us how to respond to unreasonable blows. The guard who slapped the Lord after his response to Annas was acting unreasonably. Jesus had done nothing wrong; he had only reminded Annas of the law and refused to play his political game. But the guard saw a chance to demonstrate his loyalty to the powerful old man. He made a show of it, not because it was the morally right thing to do, but because it served his personal agenda. Many times in life we suffer similar blows. We are treated unfairly or uncharitably because others are out to use us as tools to satisfy their own passions and desires.

When the guard strikes the Lord, Jesus doesn't join the fray. He doesn't respond to an unreasonable blow by giving an unreasonable blow in return. He keeps his composure because, unlike the guard, he is not interested in satisfying self-centered desires; he is interested in fulfilling his mission and being faithful to the Father. Jesus will let his enemies drag him through the streets of Jerusalem, but not through the moral mud of impassioned physical or verbal fisticuffs. The more we can learn to seek first the Kingdom, as Jesus did, the freer we will be to parry wild thrusts of injustice with the sturdy two-edged sword of love and truth.

CHRIST THE FRIEND *Peter: After that night, for the rest of my life, people who didn't believe in Christ mocked me by imitating a cock crowing when I would walk into a room. At first it galled me. I always hated being made fun of. But as the years passed, I was glad of it. That night was the greatest night of my life. For the first time, I discovered that someone loved me, not because of what I could do for them or because I was so full of loveable traits, but simply because I was me. Jesus knew all along that I was too weak to follow him and fulfill my mission by leaning just on my own natural strength. But I didn't know it. I thought I could earn the honor he showed me by choosing me and inviting me to be his friend and build his Kingdom. How wrong I was! Who can earn honor from God? God is the one who confers honor. That night shattered once and for all the arrogance I had cultivated my whole life long. It taught me the most valuable lesson of all: when I am weak, then I am strong, because I have to lean on the strength of the Lord.*

CHRIST IN MY LIFE I am sorry for the times I cut corners on my conscience. My heart is still divided, Lord. I am your disciple, but I still seek the benefits of other kingdoms in addition to yours. I know that my life will never bear the fruit you and I both want it to bear until I seek first and uncompromisingly your Kingdom in all that I do. Purify my heart, Lord. Make me strong; give me courage…

I have so much trouble controlling my emotional reactions, Lord. I want to contemplate your composure, your inner strength, the balance and harmony and peace that flow from having your heart entirely engaged in your Father's will. I know that you can teach me to arrange the sail of my fidelity just right, so the wind of every emotion will drive me further into your Kingdom…

Why am I afraid of failing, Lord? You failed in the eyes of the world. Peter failed. The other apostles failed. Can my successes increase your love for me? Can my failures decrease it? The only reason I fear failure is because I value my own achievements too much. O Lord, what good are my achievements if they flow from fear and not from love? Teach me to love, Lord, to live from your love…

QUESTIONS FOR SMALL GROUP DISCUSSION

1. What struck you most in this passage? What did you notice that you hadn't noticed before?

2. Which do you think pained Christ's heart more, Peter's betrayal, Judas's betrayal, or Annas's connivance? Why?

3. Only Peter and the "other disciple" (tradition claims it was John, the author of this Gospel) followed Jesus from a distance to his trial. Where do you think the other apostles went after the arrest, and why do you think they didn't go with Peter and John?

4. In what situations are we most easily tempted to deny Jesus by word or action?

Cf. Catechism of the Catholic Church, 601-605 on God's love as shown in the Passion; 595-598 on the trial of Jesus; 1897-1904 on the proper understanding of political authority; 2465-2470 on the importance of honesty

295. TWO KINGS, TWO KINGDOMS (JN 18:28-40)

"Jesus responded to the questions of the Roman governor affirming that he was King, but not of this world. He did not come to dominate peoples and territories, but to free men from the slavery of sin and be reconciled with God."

- *Pope Benedict XVI*

John 18:28-40

They then led Jesus from the house of Caiaphas to the Praetorium. It was now morning. They did not go into the Praetorium themselves or they would be defiled and unable to eat. So Pilate came outside to them and said, 'What charge do you bring against this man?' They replied, 'If he were not a criminal, we should not be handing him over to you'. Pilate said, 'Take him yourselves, and try him by your own Law'. The Jews answered, 'We are not allowed to put a man to death'. This was to fulfil the words Jesus had spoken indicating the way he was going to die. So Pilate went back into the Praetorium and called Jesus to him, 'Are you the king of the Jews?' he asked. Jesus replied, 'Do you ask this of your own accord, or have others spoken to you about me?' Pilate answered, 'Am I a Jew? It is your own people and the chief priests who have handed you over to me: what have you done?' Jesus replied, 'Mine is not a kingdom of this world; if my kingdom were of this world, my men would have fought to prevent my being surrendered to the Jews. But my kingdom is not of this kind.' 'So you are a king then?' said Pilate. 'It is you who say it' answered Jesus. 'Yes, I am a king. I was born for this, I came into the world for this: to bear witness to the truth; and all who are on the side of truth listen to my voice.' 'Truth?' said Pilate 'What is that?'; and with that he went out again to the Jews and said, 'I find no case against him. But according to a custom of yours I should release one prisoner at the Passover; would you like me, then, to release the king of the Jews?' At this they shouted: 'Not this man,' they said 'but Barabbas'. Barabbas was a brigand.

CHRIST THE LORD As the liturgical year reaches its conclusion with the Solemnity of Christ the King, by presenting us with this passage the Church shows us the stark contrast between Christ's Kingdom and all other kingdoms. Pilate is the Roman Emperor's representative in Palestine. His career as procurator had been marked by violence and political blunders, by which he alienated the Jews he was supposed to be ruling. Though he recognized Jesus' innocence, he feared further conflict with the Jewish leaders, since that could cause them to denounce him to the emperor. Pilate is the typical earthly king, interested more in his personal career, prestige, and success than in what is true and right. Even when he finds himself face-to-face with the light of Truth itself, his own worldly ambitions blind him to it. We are sympathetic to him because we share his weakness.

Jesus, on the other hand, is fully identified with his Kingdom, the eternal Kingdom, established on the solid but hidden foundations of truth and divine love. His Kingdom is demanding but lasting. It involves obedience to the Father's will, even at times to the point of sacrificing one's earthly life. But it is the true Kingdom, the realm of meaning – deep, existential meaning – that abides. For the sake of this Kingdom, Jesus is willing to suffer rejection and injustice at the hands of an earthly king, because he knows that such a crime will only reveal more brilliantly the splendor of his Lordship. We are inspired by him because we know in our hearts that we are called to the same kind of nobility of spirit. We recognize that we cannot serve both Christ the King and the kings of this earth, and we are often torn between the two. Every such moment of decision (and there are plenty of them every day) presents us with a chance to renew our option for Christ, to confirm our citizenship in the Kingdom of God.

CHRIST THE TEACHER Pilate stands face-to-face with the Lord of the universe. They are having a conversation. No one can interrupt them. The cool morning air is refreshing. Pilate is agitated by the circumstances, but he is thinking clearly because it's still early in the day. Jesus is exhausted from the first twelve hours of his Passion, but his eyes glow with the love and determination that had led him to this hour. His love for Pilate is no less because of his tiredness. He came to earth in order to save Pilate's soul. Providence has brought them together. Jesus is eager to draw this Roman patrician close to his heart. All the conditions are right for Pilate to detect in Jesus the God for whom his heart longs. Yet he doesn't. He is in the same room with Jesus, speaking with him, but he remains unmoved. Why?

"Everyone who belongs to the truth listens to my voice." Here Jesus teaches us the secret to intimacy with God. Whoever lets himself be led by what is true will be drawn into communion with Christ and will hear and heed God's ceaseless invitations to follow him more closely. But being led by truth requires humility. It requires recognizing a higher authority than oneself: if I am obliged to discover, accept, and conform to what is objectively true (morally, physically, historically), then I am not autonomous, I am not the master of my universe, I am not God. That act of humility, which frees us from the enervating bonds of selfishness, is hard to make. Our fallen human nature tends towards pride, towards self-sufficiency, control, and dominance. To resist that tendency requires courage. It takes courage to obey the truth and expose oneself to the burning love of God. May he grant it to us all in abundance.

CHRIST THE FRIEND "Mine is not a Kingdom of this world." If it were, our friendship with Christ would be a lot easier than it sometimes is. He wants to lead us along the journey of life in this world towards our eternal home in heaven. Therefore, he often urges us to get up and move along when we are tired. He often asks us to take steep, demanding paths that we would prefer to avoid. But he knows the way, and he knows the destination. Like a true friend, he will never rest until we have reached the fullness of life – even if he has to put up with our complaining along the way.

Pilate: Many things confused me that day, but nothing confused me more than the crowd's choice to free Barabbas. Barabbas was a typical hotheaded revolutionary, a man who would kill or maim as easy as he would break a stick for the fire. But that Jesus was a noble man, a temperate man, a wise man. He had done nothing wrong. They were envious of him, that's all. But why did the crowd choose Barabbas? How could they not see that Jesus was a worthy man? I can say this now, but the fact is that I acquiesced to their choice; I made the same horrible mistake. If I had been in Jesus' place and he had been in my place, I know he never would have turned me over to that crowd. But he wasn't in my place; I was in my place. Why did I give in? Why didn't I stand my ground? I wish he hadn't brought up all that talk about the truth. That disconcerted me. No one believes in truth anymore – that went out of fashion long ago. But when he said the word, it rang in my ears like the single clap of a small silver bell, clear and penetrating. It is still ringing. I can't stop thinking about it. Why did I not listen to him? Why did I not trust him? Why did I not follow that voice that was speaking so clearly in me? Everything would be different if I had just done what I knew was right! Yet I know I can never undo what I did.

CHRIST IN MY LIFE Who is my king? Whom do I serve? I want to serve you, Lord, because you truly are the King. But I still tend so much to serve myself. I want people to do things my way – I want to have what I want, when I want it. I want my plans to work out exactly as I plan them. I guess all of this is natural, but you want to lead me to the supernatural realm. Renew my mind and heart, Lord; Thy will be done, not mine…

Every time I have followed your voice resounding in my conscience, I have experienced the peace and the satisfaction that comes from living in harmony with the truth. And every time I haven't, I writhe and agonize. And yet I still haven't learned, Lord. I still waffle. How do you put up with me? O Jesus, purify my heart, pour your love into my heart; with the courage of your heart, strengthen my heart…

Mary, I don't want to be like Pilate. Why am I such a reluctant disciple? I know Jesus; I have been given a share in his mission – what greater privilege could I desire? And yet, sometimes I look at it as if it were a burden. The spirit of self-centeredness and fascination with the trinkets of this world still pulls at me. Mary, teach me to be his faithful friend, his brave soldier. Mother most pure, pray for me…

QUESTIONS FOR SMALL GROUP DISCUSSION

1. What struck you most in this passage? What did you notice that you hadn't noticed before?

2. What do you think was in Christ's mind and heart during this interchange with Pilate? What do you think he was hoping for?

3. Pilate committed an injustice in order to protect his personal ambitions. In what ways are we tempted to do the same?

4. Christ tells Pilate that his Kingdom is "not of this world." Does this mean that our faith shouldn't affect our lives on earth? How should being a citizen of Christ's Kingdom affect our interaction with earthly realities? What exactly did Jesus mean by saying this?

Cf. Catechism of the Catholic Church, 668-682 on Christ's second coming and the last judgment; 595-598 on Jesus' trial; 2816-2827 on "Thy Kingdom Come, thy will be done…"

THE GOSPEL OF JOHN CHAPTER 19

"How great the cross! What blessings it holds! He who possesses it possesses a treasure. More noble, more precious than anything on earth, in fact and in name, it is indeed a

treasure, for in it and through it and for it all the riches of our salvation were stored away and restored to us. If there had been no cross, Christ would not have been cruci-fied. If there had been no cross, Life would not have been nailed to a tree. If he had not been nailed, the streams of everlasting life would not have welled from his side, blood and water, the cleansing of the world; the record of our sins would not have been cancelled, we would not have gained freedom, we would not have enjoyed the tree of life, paradise would not have been opened. If there had been no cross, death would not have been trodden under foot, the underworld would not have yielded up its spoils."

- St Andrew of Crete

296. A RELUCTANT SINNER AND A WILLING LAMB (JN 19:1-16)

"In the cross every apostle has gloried; by it every martyr has been crowned and every saint made holy."

- St Theodore the Studite

John 19:1-16

Pilate then had Jesus taken away and scourged; and after this, the soldiers twisted some thorns into a crown and put it on his head, and dressed him in a purple robe. They kept coming up to him and saying, 'Hail, king of the Jews!'; and they slapped him in the face. Pilate came outside again and said to them, 'Look, I am going to bring him out to you to let you see that I find no case'. Jesus then came out wearing the crown of thorns and the purple robe. Pilate said, 'Here is the man'. When they saw him the chief priests and the guards shouted, 'Crucify him! Crucify him!' Pilate said, 'Take him yourselves and crucify him: I can find no case against him'. 'We have a Law,' the Jews replied 'and according to that Law he ought to die, because he has claimed to be the Son of God.' When Pilate heard them say this his fears increased. Re-entering the Praetorium, he said to Jesus, 'Where do you come from?' But Jesus made no answer. Pilate then said to him, 'Are you refusing to speak to me? Surely you know I have power to release you and I have power to crucify you?' 'You would have no power over me' replied Jesus 'if it had not been given you from above; that is why the one who handed me over to you has the greater guilt.' From that moment Pilate was anxious to set him free, but the Jews shouted, 'If you set him free you are no friend of Caesar's; anyone who makes himself king is defying Caesar'. Hearing these words, Pilate had Jesus brought out, and seated himself on the chair of judgement at a place called the Pavement, in Hebrew Gabbatha. It was Passover Preparation Day, about the sixth hour. 'Here is your king' said Pilate to the Jews. 'Take him away, take him away!' they said. 'Crucify him!' 'Do you want me to crucify your king?' said Pilate. The chief priests answered, 'We have no king except Caesar.' So in the end Pilate handed him over to them to be crucified.

CHRIST THE LORD Those who insisted on crucifying Jesus revealed the reason behind their blindness in the very accusation they leveled against him: "Anyone who makes himself king is defying Caesar." This was the clincher. It convinced Pilate to betray his own conscience, because Pilate wanted nothing more that to stay in the emperor's good graces. If the Jewish leaders sent a report to Rome claiming that Pilate was neglecting to rein in rebels and usurpers, it could mean the end of Pilate's career. Pilate cared more about the passing kingdom of this world than his moral integrity, the ticket to eternal life. And so did the Jewish leaders who clamored for Christ's crucifixion. They too were so attached to their status and their desires for earthly pomp and success that they shut their eyes and ears to Jesus' message of a Kingdom of Heaven. They wanted God to provide a Messiah according to their own contaminated expectations; they refused to adjust and elevate those expectations in accordance with the Messiah God had sent.

Still today, among believers and unbelievers, Christ's message of a Kingdom of the heart and spirit, a Kingdom for which it is more than worthwhile to sacrifice earthly glamour and wealth, meets with stubborn resistance. We cling so much to our hopes for heaven on earth, to Caesar's power, prestige, and possessions, that we decline the Lord's unceasing invitation to leave behind everything and follow him. Like Pilate, we crucify Jesus to keep our jobs. And what fools we are when we do; Caesar went to dust long ago, but Christ reigns forever.

CHRIST THE TEACHER During the Last Supper, Jesus bequeathed his new commandment to his apostles, his Church, and the world: "This is my commandment: love one another, as I have loved you. No one can have greater love than to lay down his life for his friends" (John 15:12-13). Since that moment he has been engaged in showing what he meant. His whole Passion is the laying down of his life for his friends - for every human being ever created. By laying down his life in such a dramatic way, Jesus demonstrates with equal drama the great revelation of Christianity: "God is love" (1 Jn 4:16). This revelation brings hope to the human heart, which ever since original sin had doubted God's goodness and been reluctant or unable to trust him. Throughout all of pre-Calvary human history, God had been looking forward to the chance to make this definitive revelation of his love. He had been looking forward to offering himself as the saving sacrifice and thus winning back the trust of his beloved but estranged humanity. St John highlights this long-standing desire by telling us exactly when the condemnation of Jesus occurred: on the Passover Preparation Day, at the sixth hour.

The sixth hour (about noon) of Preparation Day was the hour when the Passover lambs began to be sacrificed. The lamb was bound, as Christ had been bound. It was taken to the center of the Temple, as Jesus was taken to the hill of Calvary. It was put on the altar, as Christ was nailed to the cross. It was slaughtered quickly and all its blood was drained away, just as Christ was to pour out all his blood, even to the point of letting them pierce his heart with a spear.

The Passover lamb commemorated the lambs that had been killed by the Israelites at the time of the original Passover, when Moses led the Jews out of Egypt. To convince Pharaoh to let his people go, God had sent a plague on the land, killing every firstborn son throughout Egypt. But instead of killing the Israelite children, God instructed every family to sacrifice a lamb and mark their doors with the lamb's blood. Thus, God killed the Passover lambs in order to save the lives and the freedom of his Chosen People. That Jesus' condemnation to death occurred at the very hour commemorating that ancient, ritual sacrifice is no coincidence. It finally reveals in brilliant fullness the heart of God. God, incarnate in Jesus Christ, takes upon himself the punishment due to fallen humanity; he dies for us, laying down his life for us in order that through faith in him we may enter into the fullness of life. With his words, with his life, and finally with his death, Jesus offers us the richest lesson in the history of the world: God is love, and love is the way to God.

CHRIST THE FRIEND *One of the soldiers: I was there that day. I watched it all happen. I watched the crowd and the Jewish leaders turn from calm and law-abiding docility to frenzied, violent hatred, as does everyone who tries to build their lives on selfish lies. I watched Pilate squirm like a cornered animal, desperately trying to have his cake and eat it too, until he caved in, just like everyone who puts personal ambition above duty and truth. I watched my fellow soldiers take ribald pleasure in humiliating and victimizing a man just like them, and I saw how it left them empty and disgusted with themselves, as sensual indulgence always does. But above all, I watched Jesus. The whole universe caved in on this man and he stood firm, not just physically, which was miraculous enough, but in his mind and his spirit. I have seen criminals go insane after scourging. I have seen fearless prisoners beg and whimper for mercy under the shadow of the cross. I have seen pagan kings prostrate themselves like sycophants at the feet of our Roman governors. But I have never seen a man withstand such a raging storm of malice with such inner strength and outward composure. No, "withstand" is not the right word. It was as if he were commanding that storm. It broke upon him because he wanted it to.*

The more I watched, the more it mesmerized me. And then he caught my eye. They were taking him away to pick up his cross. He passed beside me. He turned to look at me. I froze. I had never spoken to or laid eyes on him before that morning, but when he saw me, somehow, I knew that he knew my name. And his gaze addressed me in my conscience, where no one goes but me. It said, "Don't you know me? Don't you recognize me yet? I am the one you have been looking for, the one you can trust."

CHRIST IN MY LIFE I know you want me to be a saint, Lord; you created me for that. The restlessness I feel in my heart comes from my implacable need to live in an ever-deeper communion with you. But for some reason I keep trying to relieve it with man-made tranquilizers. O Lord, you know I believe in you. Make your will and your example more and more attractive to me, and the world's false promises will simply fade away…

Open my eyes, Lord; I want to see everything you want to show me. By your wounds I am healed. What does that mean? It means that each one of your countless wounds whispers to my heart the words I most long to hear and have the most trouble believing: "No matter what you do, I still love you." Every wound testifies to your love for me. Open my eyes, Lord; open my heart…

You embraced suffering. You were able to see your Father's will in everything that happened. Help me to do the same. Help me to live on the level of purpose, recognizing your providence in every event and relationship. Help me to walk in the light of your love, focused on my life's mission, spreading your love through my fidelity and prayer. Kindle in my heart the unquenchable fire that burns in yours…

QUESTIONS FOR SMALL GROUP DISCUSSION

1. What struck you most in this passage? What did you notice that you hadn't noticed before?

2. All the people around Jesus during his Passion reveal the state of their souls – what they really want – by their reaction to him. But what about Jesus, what does he want?

3. Jesus says that the sin of those who handed him over to Pilate is greater than Pilate's sin. Why do you think that is so?

4. What do you think Jesus means when he says that Pilate only has authority because it was given him from on high?

Cf. Catechism of the Catholic Church, 2771-2774 on bearing witness to the truth; 595-598 on the trial of Jesus; 608-614 on Jesus as the Lamb of God and the definitive sacrifice; 2234-2246 on the authorities of civil society and our duties towards them

297. A PARTING GIFT (JN 19:17-30)

"Mary has truly become the Mother of all believers. Men and women of every time and place have recourse to her motherly kindness and her virginal purity and grace, in all their needs and aspirations, their joys and sorrows, their moments of loneliness and their common endeavors."

- Pope Benedict XVI, Deus caritas est, 42

John 19:17-30

Then they took charge of Jesus, and carrying his own cross he went out of the city to the place of the skull or, as it was called in Hebrew, Golgotha, where they cruci-fied him with two others, one on either side with Jesus in the middle. Pilate wrote out a notice and had it fixed to the cross; it ran: 'Jesus the Nazarene, King of the Jews'. This notice was read by many of the Jews, because the place where Jesus was crucified was not far from the city, and the writing was in Hebrew, Latin and Greek. So the Jewish chief priests said to Pilate, 'You should not write King of the Jews, but This man said: I am King of the Jews'. Pilate answered, 'What I have written, I have written'. When the soldiers had finished crucifying Jesus they took his clothing and divided it into four shares, one for each soldier. His undergarment was seamless, woven in one piece from neck to hem; so they said to one another, 'Instead of tear-ing it, let's throw dice to decide who is to have it'. In this way the words of scripture were fulfilled: They shared out my clothing among them. They cast lots for my clothes. This is exactly what the soldiers did. Near the cross of Jesus stood his mother and his mother's sister, Mary the wife of Clopas, and Mary of Magdala. See-ing his mother and the disciple he loved standing near her, Jesus said to his mother, 'Woman, this is your son'. Then to the disciple he said, 'This is your mother'. And from that moment the disciple made a place for her in his home. After this, Jesus knew that everything had now been completed, and to fulfil the scripture perfectly he said: 'I am thirsty'. A jar-full of vinegar stood there, so putting a sponge soaked in the vinegar on a hyssop stick they held it up to his mouth. After Jesus had taken the vinegar he said, 'It is accomplished'; and bowing his head he gave up his spirit.

CHRIST THE LORD Even as Jesus' last drops of strength ebb away on the cross, he shows once again that he is the Lord of life and history. "To fulfill the scripture perfectly," St John tells us, Jesus said, "I am thirsty," and a sponge full of vinegar (the Greek word can also refer to cheap wine) was lifted up to his lips on a hyssop stick.

The flexible, willow-like wood of the hyssop plant was expressly designated for ritual purification in the Old Covenant. God had commanded his people to spread the blood of the Passover lambs on the lintels of their houses using a hyssop stick (Ex 12:22). He had commanded Israel to purify lepers and houses where leprosy has sprung up with sacrificial blood sprinkled by a hyssop stick (cf. Leviticus 14, Numbers 19). Moses had used a hyssop stick to distribute the sacrificial blood during the ceremony that established the Old Covenant at Sinai (Hebrews 9:19).

Is it only a coincidence that at the time when Jesus' blood is being poured out to purify the world itself from its sin, a hyssop stick is used to hold a sponge to his parched, cracked, and blood-stained lips? If it were, St John would not have made a point of identifying the type of wood. It was no coincidence. It is yet another sign, given for our sake, to convince us that the Crucified One is exactly who he claimed to be: the Son of God, the Word of Life and Redeemer of the world who governs and orders the universe in all its grandeur and in the tiniest details. Jesus Christ is Lord; nothing escapes his rule.

CHRIST THE TEACHER Jesus' final words were, "It is accomplished." It sums up what St John has repeated again and again throughout his Gospel: Jesus lived life focused on his mission. As his life draws to its close, he declares that that mission has been fulfilled. He had given himself completely – even to the point of sharing the very clothes on his back.

Jesus is the model for every Christian. He is also our Savior, Lord, brother, and companion, but he is still our model. And so, if he lived life focused on his mission, so should we. In this fallen world, the human family has forgotten who they are. They have come to think of themselves as autonomous mini-gods, instead of as God's stewards. In the original plan of Creation, the human family had been given the task of cultivating and protecting the Garden of Eden. We were created "to live in communion with God, in whom we find our happiness," as the Catechism reminds us (45). But that communion was never meant to be something passive. It is a relationship in which we glorify God through discovering his goodness in prayer and in action – as we do the work we were created to do, we become the saints we were created to be.

Jesus restores the possibility of that communion through reversing Adam's rebellious disobedience. He also points the way for us to partake of that restoration: by learning once again to see our lives as a mission. In this epoch of Redemption, the mission is not merely to cultivate and protect the garden, but to build the Kingdom of Christ, which we do the same way Jesus established it, seeking and fulfilling God's will: "I seek to do not my own will but the will of him who sent me" (Jn 5:30).

CHRIST THE FRIEND The beloved disciple mentioned in this passage is commonly considered to be the author himself, St John. Only he records Jesus' final will and testament, in which Jesus places his mother Mary under John's care and John under hers. St John was writing his Gospel later in life, when he was already an old man. For him to emphasize this detail means that it was significant not only for him personally, but for the whole Church. And indeed the Church has always considered this gesture of Jesus to be much more than a practical arrangement.

Jesus is on the verge of completing his earthly mission. As he does so, the mission of the Church (represented in a special way by the "beloved disciple," because the Church is Jesus' beloved) is just beginning. By explicitly transferring the care of the Church (the beloved disciple) to Mary's motherly attention and entrusting Mary to John in a filial way, Jesus extends Mary's mission. She had been the Mother of Christ, the head of the Church, and now she is to be the Mother of the whole body, the members of the Church. Christ had only one thing left to give as he breathed his last breath – his own Mother, and he didn't grudge us even that. Each follower of Christ, to enter fully into God's family and to have Christ as a true brother, has to follow John's example: "And from that moment the disciple made a place for her in his home."

Mary: I didn't choose to become Jesus' mother; that was God's choice. How could I have ever chosen for myself such an exalted role, when I always knew that I was only a blade of grass in the foothills beneath the mountain of God? Only God in his wisdom and goodness can give one of his creatures such a sublime mission. And though I didn't choose it, how much joy it gave me! Even the sorrow of his pain on Calvary filled me with a certain spiritual joy, because it allowed me to suffer too; it showed him in a new way that I would never leave him or doubt him. And I didn't choose to become your Mother either; that too was his choice. How could I have presumed to take upon myself such an exalted task, to be mother to a child born of water and the Holy Spirit? Only God in his goodness could give me such a joyful and worthy mission. And now I watch over you just as I watched over him; I accompany you just as I accompanied him; I love you just as I loved him. He made me Queen of Heaven so that I could be your refuge and solace.

CHRIST IN MY LIFE Nothing escapes your rule. Down to the tiny detail of a hyssop stick on Calvary, you govern every speck of the cosmos and every wrinkle of human history. You are the Lord. You are my Lord. Increase my faith, Lord. I want to rejoice in the peace of knowing you more deeply and trusting you more unconditionally…

For so many people, life is only a mystery, Lord. They don't know that it is a mission. They seek to refresh their souls at empty wells. Teach them about your

Kingdom! Call out to them so that they stop spiraling further down into sterile self-absorption! In you, Lord, life takes on the dimension of adventure that we all know it should take on. Ring out your message, Lord, louder and clearer...

Mary, how do you guide me? I don't see your face or hear your voice. But I know you are faithful to God's will, and it is his will for you to teach and nourish me as my mother in grace. How do you do it? You instruct me by your example: you stood at the foot of the cross, firm and faithful because your love was true and total. Teach me how to embrace fully the will of God, even when it means embracing the cross...

QUESTIONS FOR SMALL GROUP DISCUSSION

1. What struck you most in this passage? What did you notice that you hadn't noticed before?

2. Why do you think these three women were at the foot of Christ's cross while the other disciples kept their distance? Why do you think St John was the only one with them?

3. Why was St John so impressed by the exact fulfillment of the prophecy from Psalm 22:18, "They divide my garments among them and cast lots for my clothing"?

4. What do you think the expression on Jesus' face was as he uttered his last statement, "It is accomplished"? Was he grimacing, relieved, smiling, or something else?

Cf. Catechism of the Catholic Church, 599-605 on Christ's redemptive death in God's plan of salvation; 606-618 on Christ's self-offering to the Father for our sins and our participation in it; 487-507 on Mary's role in God's plan of salvation; 963-972 on Mary as Mother of the Church

298. A BITTER END AND A SWEET BEGINNING (JN 19:31-42)

"The Lord is the goal of human history, the focal point of the longings of history and of civilization, the center of the human race, the joy of every heart and the answer to all its yearnings."

- Gaudium et Spes, 48

John 19:31-42

It was Preparation Day, and to prevent the bodies remaining on the cross during the sabbath – since that sabbath was a day of special solemnity – the Jews asked Pilate to have the legs broken and the bodies taken away. Consequently the soldiers came and broke the legs of the first man who had been crucified with him and then of the other. When they came to Jesus, they found he was already dead, and so instead of breaking his legs one of the soldiers pierced his side with a lance; and immediately there came out blood and water. This is the evidence of one who saw it – trustworthy evidence, and he knows he speaks the truth – and he gives it so that you may believe as well. Because all this happened to fulfil the words of scripture: Not one bone of his will be broken; and again, in another place scripture says: They will look on the one whom they have pierced. After this, Joseph of Arimathaea, who was a disciple of Jesus – though a secret one because he was afraid of the Jews – asked Pilate to let him remove the body of Jesus. Pilate gave permission, so they came and took it away. Nicodemus came as well – the same one who had first come to Jesus at night-time – and he brought a mixture of myrrh and aloes, weighing about a hundred pounds. They took the body of Jesus and wrapped it with the spices in linen cloths, following the Jewish burial custom. At the place where he had been crucified there was a garden, and in this garden a new tomb in which no one had yet been buried. Since it was the Jewish Day of Preparation and the tomb was near at hand, they laid Jesus there.

CHRIST THE LORD Once again St John mentions that the details surrounding his death (no breaking of his bones, being pierced…) coincided with Scriptural prophecies. He notes that the day Christ died was Preparation Day. This was the day on which the Jews sacrificed their Passover lambs and prepared to begin the eight-day festival of Passover, commemorating their miraculous liberation from slavery in Egypt.

It is possible to misunderstand the meaning of these coincidences. Jesus, the Lamb of God, as St John the Baptist had called him back in Chapter 1 of this Gospel, didn't die on Preparation Day in order to associate himself with the past. Rather, the ancient events of the Passover had occurred and been commemorated in light of Christ's future sacrifice on Calvary. From God's perspective, Christ's self-immolation on the cross, the everlasting reversal of Adam's disobedience that brings salvation to the human race, was the fulcrum, the center – the very heart of human history. Everything that had come before was, in God's providence, leading up to it. All that has come after and is still to come flows from it. Jesus is not following a script; Jesus is the script that all history follows.

CHRIST THE TEACHER St John gives special emphasis to the blood and water that flowed out of Jesus' side when they pierced him with the lance to make sure he was dead. Why? He sees it as the fulfillment of the prophesy of Zechariah 12:10, "They will look on the one whom they have pierced," but considering that the details of his death fulfilled many other prophecies as well, that hardly merits the climactic testimony John gives us: "This is the evidence of the one who saw it… so that you may believe as well." Why is the flow of blood and water so important to John?

A dead body doesn't bleed. And yet, when they pierced Jesus' breast, blood and water flowed out. The scientists tell us that this may be explained by Jesus having died, literally, of a broken heart, instead of suffocation or loss of blood, as normally happened with crucifixion victims. If Jesus had died of suffocation, he most likely would not have had sufficient breath to utter the loud cry or prayer that preceded his death, nor the final words that John records. If he had died of blood loss, there most likely would not have been enough blood left inside the chambers of his heart to actually flow out when his heart was pierced with the lance. If Jesus' heart had simply broken to cause death, however, the blood in those chambers would have been mixed, as oil and water is mixed, with the watery fluid of the chest cavity around the heart, the pericardium. When the soldier pierced his side with the lance, he would have punctured the pericardium (a wider target than the heart itself), releasing the mixed liquid. This seems to go along with the timing of Jesus breathing his last breath, which happened right after he said, "It is accomplished," as if he willingly ended things at that moment, letting his divine love for sinful man burst his human heart. Maybe John knew these medical details and maybe he didn't.

The more obvious reason behind John's spotlighting the water and blood comes from the roles those two elements would take on in the life of the Church. The water of baptism was to become the gateway into sharing in Christ's death – dying to the ways of sin – and the blood of the Eucharist was to become the door to sharing in Christ's own life and thus becoming "children of God" (Jn 1:12). But that could only happen for those who believed in the Lord, the Word of God made flesh for our salvation, and that same blood and water flowing from Christ's heart was also an invitation to faith. For St John, they showed without any shadow of doubt that the Lord was true man, just as the new life in the Spirit that was to come through those sacraments showed without any doubt that the Lord was true God. In Christ's final gesture from the cross, the whole Gospel blazes forth and cries out to be believed.

CHRIST THE FRIEND *Joseph of Arimethea: I gave him my tomb – what irony! He was the one who had given me life and hope! He was the one who had loved me and let me taste the joy I had longed for all my life, and all I could do for him was supply a grave.*

That day something broke inside of me. Up until then, I had been so fearful of associating with him publicly. I was always watching my back, wondering what the other members of the Sanhedrin were saying. I was so cautious and tentative in coming to his defense! When he died – when we killed him, rather – all the convoluted excuses I had made for myself to justify that posturing and measuring and calculating just disintegrated. I wept. My entire soul collapsed. It was as if my old self died when I saw him die.

And then, in the midst of that collapse of my old self, I suddenly felt a change. I was freed.

Finally I was free from worrying about what the others said behind my back and how they might crimp my position and reputation. I didn't know what to do at first, there was such calm in my heart. I went and searched for Nicodemus. We looked at each other and we didn't need to say a word – I knew that the exact same thing had happened to him. And we went to Pilate without even a trace of fear. We took the Lord and buried him before sundown. There was such a sadness of loss in our hearts, but at the same time such a jubilation to finally be his true and undivided disciples, to finally bear witness to our love for him without hesitation. Why did we wait so long to trust him? We could have done so much more!

CHRIST IN MY LIFE You are the focal point of history, but are you the focal point of my life? I want to believe in you with a faith that gets brighter and stronger every day. I want to trust in you with total abandonment, like diving into the vast ocean. I want to love you with the simplicity and purity and humility of a young soldier in his first battle, of a bride on her wedding day, of a child in its mother's arms…

Thank you for the sacraments, Lord. They prove every day that your life and your death were for me. How could you have been thinking of me then? But I know you were. Your Church teaches that you were. You had me in mind. You eagerly laid down your life so that you could come and cleanse my soul in baptism and nourish it with the Eucharist. Teach me, Lord, to love my neighbor as you have loved me…

When my life comes to an end, what will my regrets be? That I didn't make enough money? That I didn't win enough awards? That I didn't pray enough? That I didn't follow my conscience more? That I didn't strive with all my heart, soul, mind, and strength to know, love, and imitate you? Give me wisdom, Lord. I want no more regrets. Life is too short. I want to invest all that I am in fulfilling your will…

QUESTIONS FOR SMALL GROUP DISCUSSION

1. What struck you most in this passage? What did you notice that you hadn't noticed before?

2. What can we do to find in our community those "secret disciples" of Christ who, like Joseph and Nicodemus, may need a boost in order to take that next step of faith to follow Christ more closely?

3. Why do you think St John didn't spend more time at this point of his Gospel criticizing those who condemned, tortured, and murdered Jesus? What lesson does his example of restraint have for us?

4. Jesus saved the world through self-sacrifice. What role should self-sacrifice have in our Christian lives? What should self-sacrifice look like in our life-situations?

Cf. Catechism of the Catholic Church, 1734, 2015, and 2340 on the role of self-sacrifice (ascesis) in the spiritual life; 1114-1126 on the sacraments in general and their relationship to Christ, the Church, and faith; 1213, 1322-1323 on the sacraments of baptism and the Eucharist in general; 624-628 on the significance of Christ's burial

THE GOSPEL OF JOHN CHAPTER 20

"Come then, all you nations of men defiled by sin, receive the forgiveness of sin. For it is I who am your forgiveness, the pasch of your salvation, the lamb slain for you; it is I who am your ransom, your life, your resurrection, your light, your salvation, your king. I am bringing you to the heights of heaven, I will show you the Father who is from all eternity, I will raise you up with my right hand."

- St Melito of Sardis

299. SON RISE (JN 20:1-10)

"So on Sunday we all come together. This is the first day, on which God transformed darkness and matter and made the world; the day on which Jesus Christ our Savior rose from the dead."

- St Justin Martyr

John 20:1-10

It was very early on the first day of the week and still dark, when Mary of Magdala came to the tomb. She saw that the stone had been moved away from the tomb and came running to Simon Peter and the other disciple, the one Jesus loved. 'They have taken the Lord out of the tomb' she said 'and we don't know where they have put him.' So Peter set out with the other disciple to go to the tomb. They ran together, but the other disciple, running faster than Peter, reached the tomb first; he bent down and saw the linen cloths lying on the ground, but did not go in. Simon Peter who was following now came up, went right into the tomb, saw the linen cloths on the ground, and also the cloth that had been over his head; this was not with the linen cloths but rolled up in a place by itself. Then the other disciple who had reached the tomb first also went in; he saw and he believed. Till this moment they had failed to understand the teaching of scripture, that he must rise from the dead. The disciples then went home again.

CHRIST THE LORD Easter Sunday, when the Liturgy presents this passage to the Church, brings Holy Week to its glorious climax. Indeed, this week, which ranks highest among the periods of the liturgical year, is made "holy" precisely by the Lord's resurrection. Imagine how a Good Friday without Easter Sunday would alter the Christian message: Jesus would be no more than another Socrates. His teaching would perhaps be remembered, but his outlandish claims to be the Messiah, the Son of God, and the Light of the World would be invalidated. The apostles would have remained passive and frightened, and the Church would never have come into existence. The Eucharist would be, at best, a mere myth, an empty ritual. The martyrs, virgins, and other saints who have flooded these last twenty centuries with such revolutionary holiness would have remained mere citizens of the earth…

Jesus Christ was Lord of heaven. By his resurrection, he has conquered this fallen world's reigning powers of death. Now he is Lord of heaven and earth; the kingdom of God is close at hand – among us, in fact, through the Church, which is the Risen Lord's body. There is only one Lord, Jesus Christ, crucified for our sins, risen for our redemption, and present through his Church. If now we embrace him there, he will make sure that we rise to embrace him forever in heaven.

CHRIST THE TEACHER St John's attention to detail is meaningful. He records how he himself ran to the empty tomb faster than St Peter, but waited for Peter to go in first. His reward: "he saw and believed" – faith. What could these minutiae have to teach us? Peter was the leader of the Twelve Apostles. Christ had dubbed him the rock upon which he would build his Church. At the Last Supper, he had commanded him to strengthen his brethren in the faith. Soon after his resurrection, he specially commissioned him to feed and tend his sheep. St John, the "beloved disciple," follows Peter into the empty tomb instead of rushing in ahead of him, and he receives the gift of faith; he comes to believe in the risen Lord.

The Church is not a conglomerate of individual believers all living out their own inspirations from the Holy Spirit. The Church is the unified Body of Christ and the organized people of God. It is the New Israel, and like the old Israel, it has a structure, and God has chosen to work through that structure. When we responsibly live out our membership in the Body of Christ, we stay in step with the Church, under the guidance of Peter's successor, the pope. We neither lag behind nor run too far ahead, and in that way Christ pours out upon us a strong and vibrant faith, just as he did for his beloved disciple, John.

CHRIST THE FRIEND He rose for us. He came to earth for us, he suffered for us, and he rose for us. Nothing in Christ was for himself. Nothing. He is all love, all self-giving, all obedience to the Father's will for the sake of our salvation. He rose so that we might rise with him. In his resurrection, we see what he is preparing for us. How eagerly he looks forward to that day when he will "wipe away every tear" (Revelation 7:17) from our eyes and welcome us into the fullness of life that is his eternal kingdom! The more faithful we are to him now, the more we will share in his glory when he raises us from the dead. Good friends fill our lives on earth with joy and comfort; only Christ can offer a joy that will keep growing forever.

Jesus: I know it's hard for you to feel the power and the joy of my resurrection. You still need to grow in your faith and humility to be able to feel it. But you don't need to feel it in order to believe in me. Think of my resurrection often. The more you turn the eyes of your heart towards it, the more its light will illumine and warm your heart, until your whole life is gradually bathed in its power and joy. And I have given you a reminder – the sunrise. Each day, the sun comes up and brings light to the world, just as I rose from the darkness of death in order to conquer it forever with the light of my life.

CHRIST IN MY LIFE I believe that you have risen from the dead, Lord, though I still tend to live as if this life were all there is – but you know that in my heart I am seeking your will and your kingdom. Help me to seek them as I ought. Why do I keep thinking that the broken chards of happiness that sparkle in this fallen world can have any meaning – for me or anyone – apart from a living friendship with you? …

Have mercy on your Church, Lord. In this day and age, it is so hard to trust in authority, even in your divinely established authority. But I want to. Teach me to discern your presence and your will in the words and indications of the pope, as all the saints have done. Teach me to see you in him, and to love you by serving the Church through obeying him. May I too become a saint…

I know that you lived your life for my sake, for my salvation, and for my instruction – and to comfort me, so that I never have to suffer alone. I want to live my life for your sake, building up your kingdom, obeying your will, making you known and loved by everyone around me. What else would be a worthy response to all that you have done for me? With the love of your heart, inflame my heart…

QUESTIONS FOR SMALL GROUP REFLECTION

1. What struck you most in this passage? What did you notice that you hadn't noticed before?

2. What might the emotional and intellectual reaction of the apostles and other disciples have been as they gradually began to understand that Jesus had risen from the dead?

3. Why would Christ have instituted a Church to mediate his saving grace, instead of just inspiring individuals directly?

4. If a non-believing acquaintance sincerely wanted to know why you believe that Jesus rose from the dead, what would you tell them?

Cf. Catechism of the Catholic Church, 880-887 on the role of the pope and bishops in the life of the Church; 651-655 on the meaning of Christ's Resurrection

300. TAKING THE JESUS RISK (JN 20:11-18)

"Our Lord was trodden underfoot by death, and in turn trod upon death as upon a road."

- *St Ephraem*

John 20:11-18

Meanwhile Mary stayed outside near the tomb, weeping. Then, still weeping, she stooped to look inside, and saw two angels in white sitting where the body of Jesus had been, one at the head, the other at the feet. They said, 'Woman, why are you weeping?' 'They have taken my Lord away' she replied 'and I don't know where they have put him.' As she said this she turned round and saw Jesus standing there, though she did not recognise him. Jesus said, 'Woman, why are you weeping? Who are you looking for?' Supposing him to be the gardener, she said, 'Sir, if you have taken him away, tell me where you have put him, and I will go and remove him'. Jesus said, 'Mary!' She knew him then and said to him in Hebrew, 'Rabbuni!' – which means Master. Jesus said to her, 'Do not cling to me, because I have not yet ascended to the Father. But go and find the brothers, and tell them: I am ascending to my Father and your Father, to my God and your God.' So Mary of Magdala went and told the disciples that she had seen the Lord and that he had said these things to her.

CHRIST THE LORD The first time Jesus speaks in the Gospel of John, he asks Peter and John a question: "What do you want?" In the Greek, his question to Mary Magdalene on the morning of his resurrection (here translated "Who are you looking for?") uses the same verb and the same pronoun. Only the case of the pronoun is different, turning the "what" of Chapter 1 into the "who" of Chapter 20. The verb has multiple shades of meaning, but most translations use "look for" or "seek" in both instances. The distinction between "want" and "seek" is subtle; you would never seek something that you don't want, and if you really do want something, you will naturally seek it out.

And so Jesus' question to Mary Magdalene, though he asks it after his Resurrection, brings us full circle, back to the beginning of the story. He asked the same question of his first followers as he did of Mary after the Resurrection: "What do you want? Who are you looking for?" It shows that Jesus always cares about the same thing – the state of our hearts. In the depth of our souls we decide the direction of our lives by deciding what we are going to look for. And this is what matters to Jesus. He is the Lord, the King, but he doesn't rule governments or boards of trustees – he rules hearts (and those in turn rule governments and boards of trustees). He asks us each day, in the inner sanctuary of our consciences, what we are looking for, what we desire, and what we want. If we truly want the fullness of life that he came to bring us, he will be able to give it to us, because we will be willing to take the risk of leaving behind the comfort of self-centeredness to launch out on the adventure of self-giving.

On the first Easter morning, Mary Magdalene might have thought that the risk she had taken wasn't panning out, but then the Lord appeared and ended her search. Trusting in Jesus Christ the Lord is a risk that always pans out.

CHRIST THE TEACHER Christ rose so that we too may someday rise. He conquered death so that we could look forward to everlasting life in the intense and indescribable excitement of heavenly fulfillment. In his post-resurrection appearances, he gives us clues about what that fullness of life will be like. One thing we notice right away is that his resurrected body, though a real body (St John will tell us later that the apostles can see and touch the wounds in his hands and side), has been somehow transformed. Mary Magdalene doesn't recognize him at first. He seems to appear and disappear at will and even pass through walls and doors.

Theologians call the resurrected body a "glorified body." A popular but mistaken idea among many Christians is that life in heaven is purely spiritual. After the last judgment, however, when we all have been raised ("Those who did good will rise again to life; and those who did evil, to condemnation" John 5:29), those who are welcomed into heaven will receive the fullness of life, which, for human beings, includes bodily existence. Just as Jesus and Mary are right now, at this very moment, physically present in heaven, so we will enjoy everlasting life not only with our souls but with glorified bodies. Much theological speculation has gone into describing the characteristics of our glorified state, but suffice it to say that it will be exempt from the physical sufferings and limitations of life on earth and will far surpass – very far – the physical delights of life on earth. It is something we should look forward to, something we should hope for, because it is something God wishes to give us.

CHRIST THE FRIEND Before Mary Magdalene was searching for Jesus, he was already watching over her. He lets her search, sorrowing, only so that the joy of their reunion will be that much more intense. It seems, in fact, that he wants to give her a chance to believe in the Resurrection before experiencing it. And so, the angels announce to her the Good News. But neither the daunting presence of the angels nor their remarkable announcement satisfied Mary. For her, nothing but the Lord himself, his very presence, would do. She turns away from them, because they can't give her that presence. But she perseveres in her search – asking the gardener for what the angels couldn't give. This perseverance moves the heart of Christ, and the first recorded appearance of the Resurrected Lord ensues.

Jesus came to earth in search of our love. So if we truly love him, and if we show it by seeking him in spite of obstacles and failures, how can he resist rewarding our desire? To experience the revolution of Christ in our lives, it is enough to want to do so – and to keep on wanting to.

Jesus: My child, while you are searching for me, I am already at your side. I never abandon you. Where can you hide from my love? Where can you flee from my presence? If you rise up on the wings of the dawn and set down across the farthest sea, my hand will still be guiding you, my strong arms will still be holding you fast. All that your heart seeks you will find in me. But you have to keep looking, because you're not ready to receive everything right away. If only you knew how much I long to fill every moment of your life with the light and warmth of my divine heart! I am always knocking at the door of your heart – my knocks give rise to your weeping and searching, just as they did with my faithful friend Mary Magdalene…

CHRIST IN MY LIFE What I am looking for? What do I want? You know, Lord. I want to follow you. I believe in you. My faith is puny and impure, but it's there. A myriad of other wants and desires swarm around my heart, and sometimes I let them get the upper hand, but even so, Lord, without you in my life, what direction, what hope could I possibly have? Keep me faithful to your will; never let me be separated from you…

Lord, increase my hope! You have revealed to me the truth about my final destiny. You have gone to prepare me a place in heaven. You want me to spend eternity in your company and in the company of all the saints. There the fullness of life that I have always longed for and have begun to taste here on earth will surpass my greatest longings. Lord, make these truths come to life for me…

Why do you let me weep and search? Why don't you show yourself to me always? Your ways are beyond me, Lord. But I know that they are wise. You are Wisdom and Goodness and Power and Love. It is enough for me to know you, to believe in you. That is already a gift far beyond what I deserve! O Lord, open my eyes to see your hand at work in all things, and strengthen my will to follow you more closely…

QUESTIONS FOR SMALL GROUP DISCUSSION

1. What struck you most in this passage? What did you notice that you hadn't noticed before?

2. When Jesus let Mary experience his presence, he didn't let her remain there long. Instead, he gave her a mission to share the good news with others. Why do you think Jesus did that (he could have gone himself to make the announcement), and how does this example apply to our lives?

3. Both the angels and Jesus ask Mary why she is weeping. Don't you think they should have known the reason? Why do you think they asked her that question?

4. Mary recognizes Jesus as soon as he says her name. Why do you think she did so at that point? What do you think this exchange teaches us about Christian prayer?

Cf. Catechism of the Catholic Church, 1718-1729 on our search for happiness; 631-658 on the nature and meaning of the Resurrection

301. THE CHURCH GETS GOING (JN 20:19-31)

"Christ who is God, supreme over all, has arranged to wash man clean of sin and to make our old nature new."

- St Hippolytus

John 20:19-31

In the evening of that same day, the first day of the week, the doors were closed in the room where the disciples were, for fear of the Jews. Jesus came and stood among them. He said to them, 'Peace be with you', and showed them his hands and his side. The disciples were filled with joy when they saw the Lord, and he said to them again, 'Peace be with you. 'As the Father sent me, so am I sending you.' After saying this he breathed on them and said: 'Receive the Holy Spirit. For those whose sins you forgive, they are forgiven; for those whose sins you retain, they are retained.' Thomas, called the Twin, who was one of the Twelve, was not with them when Jesus came. When the disciples said, 'We have seen the Lord', he answered, 'Unless I see the holes that the nails made in his hands and can put my finger into the holes they made, and unless I can put my hand into his side, I refuse to believe'. Eight days later the disciples were in the house again and Thomas was with them. The doors were closed, but Jesus came in and stood among them. 'Peace be with you' he said. Then he spoke to Thomas, 'Put your finger here; look, here are my hands. Give me your hand; put it into my side. Doubt no longer but believe.' Thomas replied, 'My Lord and my God!' Jesus said to him: 'You believe because you can see me. Happy are those who have not seen and yet believe.' There were many other signs that Jesus worked and the disciples saw, but they are not recorded in this book. These are recorded so that you may believe that Jesus is the Christ, the Son of God, and that believing this you may have life through his name.

CHRIST THE LORD We call St Thomas the Apostle "doubting Thomas"; we may be off the mark in doing so. Jesus did not ask the other apostles to believe in his resurrection without showing them the wounds in his hands and sides. Thomas was merely demanding his rights as an apostle when he demanded the same privilege. And none of the others responded to the risen Christ with a faith as complete and firm as Thomas': "My Lord and my God!" Thomas knew what this meant. He knew that if Christ has come back from the dead, then everything he said about himself, everything he claimed to be, was true. Jesus blessed him for his faith.

Our faith, and the faith of all Christians throughout the centuries, is built upon the solid foundation of the apostles' testimony to the risen Christ, a testimony validated by twenty uninterrupted centuries of Church life, of saints and martyrs, of sacraments, Liturgy, and a college of bishops that links us directly, even physically, to that little group of frightened apostles who encountered the Risen One. Blessed indeed are we who have believed: although we have not seen Christ in the flesh, we have seen, experienced, and benefited from the undeniable work of his Spirit. In times of darkness and doubt, we know where to look to recover the light.

At the beginning of creation, "the earth was a formless wasteland, and darkness covered the abyss, while a mighty wind swept over the waters." (Genesis 1:2) When God created man and woman, he "formed man out of the clay of the ground and blew into his nostrils the breath of life, and so man became a living being." The word for "wind" in Hebrew (and in Greek, the language of the New Testament) is the same as the word for "breath" and "Spirit." Thus, when St John points out the detail of Jesus breathing on the disciples as he gives them the gifts of the Holy Spirit and the commission to carry on his work of evangelization, he is calling to mind the "wind" and the "breathing" of the first creation. The Fathers of the Church understood this first post-Resurrection appearance to the apostles as the start of a new creation. Jesus has won the forgiveness of sin, which marred the first creation, and dubs his apostles messengers and distributors of this forgiveness. As they spread it throughout the world and build up the Church, all mankind is to be renewed, elevated to a more sublime intimacy with God. As St Paul put it, "So whoever is in Christ is a new creation: the old things have passed away; behold, new things have come" (2 Corinthians 5:17).

CHRIST THE TEACHER Jesus Christ is the only Savior, the only Mediator between sinful, fallen mankind and the one God who can give them eternal life. He achieved his mediation by his loving obedience to God's will even through humiliation, torture, and death on a cross. This obedience reversed the disobedience of Adam, and reestablished communion between God and men; it opened once again the flow of God's grace. In his first appearance to the confused group of apostles on the first Easter, he teaches us how he wants that flow of grace to irrigate the human family: through the ministry of the Church guided by the Twelve Apostles. He bequeathed his peace to them; he sent them on a mission just as his Father had sent him; he breathed his Spirit into them; he transferred to them his divine power of absolving from sin, the very thing that obstructs our communion with God. Do we wish to find Easter joy, won for us at such a terrible price? We need only dip into the flowing fountain of God's grace, which is his one, holy, catholic, and apostolic Church.

At the beginning of his Gospel, St Matthew told us why Jesus came among us: "He will save his people from their sins" (Matthew 1:21). In this first meeting with his apostles after his atoning sacrifice on the cross, Christ eagerly begins the fulfillment of that mission. His first post-resurrection deed is to "breathe" on the Twelve, inaugurating as it were a new creation (God had "breathed" into Adam's nostrils to give him life at the first creation), one that will rise up from the first creation that had been so disfigured by sin. And with that breath, he delegates to them his power to wipe sins away, to administer the forgiveness from sin that he won through his self-oblation on Calvary. Ever since, that ministry has been carried our through the sacrament of confession. How eager Christ was to grant this surpassing grace to his Church! How close it must be to his heart if it was one of the first things he did after coming back from the dead! If he cares about it that much, then so should we.

Often we look for extraordinary and emotional encounters with the Holy Spirit. Sometimes we think that unless we experience a special feeling or perceive a supernatural phenomenon, the Holy Spirit is not at work. Yet Jesus shows us that the primary mode of operation followed by the Holy Spirit is the same one he followed in his Incarnation: he turns normal realities into vehicles of grace. The Holy Spirit acts in our lives powerfully through the sacraments of the Church, through the preaching and teaching of the Church's ministers, and through our own prayer and reflection on the Scriptures. If we are ready to find the Holy Spirit in these ordinary channels that Christ has established, he will readily fill our lives with the extraordinary fruits of his action.

CHRIST THE FRIEND St John tells us why he wrote his Gospel: he wants us to believe in Jesus Christ, so that we may "have life through his name." Life. We cherish life, and yet we sense that there is more to it than the limited version we experience. Our hearts seem unsatisfied even by all that life offers us. We always want more. God made us like that. He made us thirsty for a happiness that only he can give, in order to make sure that we would seek him. Our life is a quest for Jesus Christ, a quest of which he is the author, the companion, and the end. He wants to give us what we most want; he asks only that we *believe* in him, that we trust and follow him.

Thomas: When Jesus turned to me and told me to touch his wounds, his eyes were merry. I had been stunned when he appeared, but then I felt ashamed when he made reference to my earlier comments. But his eyes were so bright, so inviting, that I stepped forward. He held out his hands, those same hands that had cured so many sick and crippled people, those strong, carpenter's hands that had multiplied the loaves and commanded the sea. He held them out to me. They were pierced through, but he was smiling. I looked at them. They were wounded hands; I held them, and I felt the wounds. Then he took my left hand and brought it to his side. He was really there. The Lord had returned – the same Lord. It was no ghost, no vision. It was the Lord, the Teacher. And I looked back into his eyes, and it was as if I had seen him for the first time. That's when I knew. I knew in an instant that it was true, that he was not simply a rabbi, a prophet, or a king. I knew that he was the Lord himself. The Lord himself had come to visit his people, to save them. I fell on my knees. I cried with joy. Emmanuel! Really, truly… The New Covenant had finally come.

CHRIST IN MY LIFE Why don't I trust you more? If you were to let me see the wounds in your hands and feet and sides, would that be any more evidence than you have already given me of your greatness, your goodness, your presence, and the transforming power of your love? Lord Jesus, I want you to be in the center of my life. You are God, and you know my name, and you call to me. I want to hear you, Lord…

How passionately I should love your Church! It is your chosen instrument for reaching out and touching each one of your beloved brothers and sisters everywhere in the world. How would I have found you if it were not for your Church? Bless your Church, Lord. Make it grow, make it flourish; fill it with saints. Teach me to be a joyful, faithful child of the Church. To build it up right here, right now…

I have tasted the life you have in store for me. I know the difference you have made in my life. I know that I need your grace, and I know where to find it and how to cooperate with it: by seeking out and fulfilling your will. But what about all the people in the world who don't know what a difference you can make, who don't know where to find the grace they thirst for? Make me a channel of your peace…

QUESTIONS FOR SMALL GROUP DISCUSSION

1. What struck you most in this passage? What did you notice that you hadn't noticed before?

2. Why do you think Christ waited until eight days after Easter Sunday to appear to Thomas?

3. St John puts Christ's conferral of peace on the apostles in the same sentence as "and he showed them his hands and his side." Do you see any connection between these two realities?

4. How would your faith change if Christ appeared to you physically, as he appeared to the apostles? What are the most meaningful signs God has already given to you personally that have made the most difference in your faith? How have you responded to those signs?

Cf. Catechism of the Catholic Church, 1076, 1086-1087 on the sacraments and the Church as the channels of God's saving grace; 731-741 on the meaning of Pentecost and the Holy Spirit's role in the Church; 694-701 on the Holy Spirit's individual action in each soul; 1849-1851 on the definition of sin; 1440-1449 on the sacraments of penance and reconciliation

THE GOSPEL OF JOHN CHAPTER 21

"Here, in Krakow, the beloved city of my predecessor John Paul II, no one is astonished by the words 'to build with Peter and on Peter.' For this reason I say to you: Do not be afraid to build your life on the Church and with the Church. You are all proud of the love you have for Peter and for the Church entrusted to him. Do not be fooled by those who want to play Christ against the Church. There is one foundation on which it is worthwhile to build a house. This foundation is Christ. There is only one rock on which it is worthwhile to place everything. This rock is the one to whom Christ said: 'You are Peter, and on this rock I will build my Church' (Matthew 16:18)… You know well the Rock of our times. Accordingly, do not forget: Neither that Peter who is watching our gathering from the window of God the Father, nor this Peter who is now standing in front of you, nor any successive Peter will ever be opposed to you or the building of a lasting house on the rock. Indeed, he will offer his heart and his hands to help you construct a life on Christ and with Christ."

- Pope Benedict XVI

302. FISHING FOR HUMILITY (JN 21:1-14)

"Consider, children, a Christian's treasure is not on earth, it is in heaven. Well then, our thoughts should turn to where our treasure is."

- St John Vianney

John 21:1-14

Later on, Jesus showed himself again to the disciples. It was by the Sea of Tiberias, and it happened like this: Simon Peter, Thomas called the Twin, Nathanael from Cana in Galilee, the sons of Zebedee and two more of his disciples were together. Simon Peter said, 'I'm going fishing'. They replied, 'We'll come with you'. They went out and got into the boat but caught nothing that night. It was light by now and there stood Jesus on the shore, though the disciples did not realise that it was Jesus. Jesus called out, 'Have you caught anything, friends?' And when they answered, 'No', he said, 'Throw the net out to starboard and you'll find something'. So they dropped the net, and there were so many fish that they could not haul it in. The disciple Jesus loved said to Peter, 'It is the Lord'. At these words 'It is the Lord', Simon Peter, who had practically nothing on, wrapped his cloak round him and jumped into the water. The other disciples came on in the boat, towing the net and the fish; they were only about a hundred yards from land. As soon as they came ashore they saw that there was some bread there, and a charcoal fire with fish cooking on it. Jesus said, 'Bring some of the fish you have just caught'. Simon Peter went aboard and dragged the net to the shore, full of big fish, one hundred and fifty-three of them; and in spite of there being so many the net was not broken. Jesus said to them, 'Come and have breakfast'. None of the disciples was bold enough to ask, 'Who are you?'; they knew quite well it was the Lord. Jesus then stepped forward, took the bread and gave it to them, and the same with the fish. This was the third time that Jesus showed himself to the disciples after rising from the dead.

CHRIST THE LORD Christ's authority is absolute. He is God's anointed, and he has risen from the dead: his Kingdom will stand forever. And yet, he shares that authority with others; he extends his Kingdom through the free collaboration of his followers. First among them is Peter. During his public ministry, the Lord repeatedly pointed out that Peter would have a unique role among the apostles and in Christ's Kingdom (e.g., Mt 16). This mysterious encounter on the shores of Lake Tiberias was a replay of Christ's original call to Peter three years earlier, when he also worked a miraculous catch of fish. The renewed encounter confirms Peter (and his successors, as the Church teaches us) as leader of this little band of Christians – a little band that would, through God's grace, rock the world. It was Peter whom Jesus was about to command to "feed his sheep," and it is through union with Peter and his successors, the popes, that we will be able to receive food for our own souls, as well as dish it out to others.

Peter dived into the water, even though the boats were close to shore and full of fish. The Lord has come looking for him again, and this time Peter has no objections, no comments of his own, no hesitations, and no fears. Jesus has finally won Peter's heart. Once so self-reliant and independent, so authoritative and in control, now Peter climbs onto the shore wet and bedraggled, overjoyed to kneel at Jesus' feet and embrace his Lord. Jesus had been patient with Peter, never giving up on him, and now his patience was paying off. Christ's love was now Peter's only nourishment, and so now he was ready to begin his career of fishing for men. His apprenticeship was over; the Lord was about to send him out.

CHRIST THE TEACHER Christ only asks for one thing from us: our trust. If we trust him, as the apostles did by throwing their nets over the starboard side, he will fill our nets. If we trust him, we will have everything we need to fulfill our life's mission, even a mission as grand as Peter's. During Christ's passion, Peter had wavered in his trust. Now Jesus gives him a chance to renew it. And Peter is ready to trust more, because has experienced his own weakness and so has grown in humility.

At the beginning of Peter's discipleship, he resisted the Lord's entreaty to throw out his net after a fishless night. Now, after the Resurrection, Peter voices no objection to the stranger's suggestion, even though Peter was an expert fisherman and the hour for catching fish had passed. But he is docile. He has grown in humility. Humility is the hardest but most necessary lesson that every Christian apostle has to learn. Many times, we wonder why God permits so many hardships and failures in our lives. Many times, he does so because it's the only way we will learn that we are limited, that we are not God. Substantial humility is the habitual and joyful awareness that we are utterly dependent on God for all things, from the most sublime to the most mundane. Jesus knew where the fish were; Peter didn't. Jesus still knows where the fish are; we don't. We need to trust in him and in the instruments he chooses to use – a confessor, a spiritual director, a superior in the apostolate. If we work hard doing all we can and then throw out our nets wherever Christ tells us to, he will surely never leave us empty-handed.

CHRIST THE FRIEND *Jesus: Begin again, as many times as necessary. With me, you can always begin again. The world doesn't let you do this. Other people often don't let you. With them, once you fail, it's over. But with me, you can always begin again. That morning on Lake Tiberias was just like a morning three years ago on the same lake. Both times they had spent* *the whole night working their nets and caught nothing. Both times I approached them – because they didn't know how to come to me. I told them to cast out their nets. And both times they pulled in a huge catch. Peter needed to begin again. How much this pleased me! Begin again: in your efforts to follow me, to be like me, to build my kingdom, in your attempts to repair broken relationships, to succeed where you have already failed, to form virtue where you have vice – in all these things you will need to begin again a thousand times. And though it may seem that you are starting from scratch each time, as it seemed to Peter, you're not. Each time you look at me, each time you hear my voice, each time you trust me after a failure, all the important virtues (humility, faith, hope, love) are stronger.*

If ever you feel discouraged when you should just be dusting yourself off and beginning again, I can guarantee that your discouragement doesn't come from me. I came not to condemn, but to save. My love for you doesn't depend on your impeccability – in fact, it doesn't depend on anything. My love for you is total, a waterfall that never stops flowing. You can always begin again.

CHRIST IN MY LIFE I believe in your Church, Lord, and in your vicar on earth, the pope. You have chosen to continue to walk with me through him. I wish I had more time to study all that he says, to keep up with his words and actions, to second them more completely in my own life and community. Show me how I can be more faithful to your vicar. Show me how I can love him as you want me to…

I have to be honest, Lord: humility is a mystery to me. I keep thinking I'm humble, mainly because I see so many people who are more arrogant or vain than I am, but then you remind me that I'm not really humble yet. Make me humble! Give me the docility I need so that I can give you a chance to fill my nets with hundreds of fish! Please do, Lord; all I long for is to be your faithful and fruitful apostle…

How can I help feeling discouraged? Lord, I will never give in to discouragement again. Maybe I can't help feeling the emotion, but when I do, you will remind me that it doesn't come from you, that with you I can always begin again, and that you can bring good even out of the worst failures, the worst evils. Thy will be done, Lord; I trust in you…

QUESTIONS FOR SMALL GROUP DISCUSSION

1. What struck you most in this passage? What did you notice that you hadn't noticed before?

2. Our adherence and obedience to the vicar of Christ reflects our dedication to Christ himself. How can we increase the former in order to intensify the latter?

3. Do you think Christ's hopes for us are being fulfilled? If not, why not?

4. What has helped you most in your efforts to grow in the crucial virtue of humility?

Cf. Catechism of the Catholic Church, 25, 49, 68 on the primacy of love in the Church's mission; 2559, 2631, 2713, 2546 on the role and nature of humility; 871-933 on the nature of the Church and the authority it has received from Christ

303. KEEP FOLLOWING ME (JN 21:15-25)

"What matters above all is to tend one's personal relationship with God, with that God who revealed himself to us in Christ."

- Pope Benedict XVI

John 21:15-25

After the meal Jesus said to Simon Peter, 'Simon son of John, do you love me more than these others do?' He answered, 'Yes Lord, you know I love you'. Jesus said to him, 'Feed my lambs'. A second time he said to him, 'Simon son of John, do you love me?' He replied, 'Yes, Lord, you know I love you'. Jesus said to him, 'Look after my sheep'. Then he said to him a third time, 'Simon son of John, do you love me?' Peter was upset that he asked him the third time, 'Do you love me?' and said, 'Lord, you know everything; you know I love you'. Jesus said to him, 'Feed my sheep. 'I tell you most solemnly, when you were young you put on your own belt and walked where you liked; but when you grow old you will stretch out your hands, and somebody else will put a belt round you and take you where you would rather not go.' In these words he indicated the kind of death by which Peter would give glory to God. After this he said, 'Follow me'. Peter turned and saw the disciple Jesus loved following them – the one who had leaned on his breast at the supper and had said to him, 'Lord, who is it that will betray you?' Seeing him, Peter said to Jesus, 'What about him, Lord?' Jesus answered, 'If I want him to stay behind till I come, what does it matter to you? You are to follow me.' The rumour then went out among the brothers that this disciple would not die. Yet Jesus had not said to Peter, 'He will not die', but, 'If I want him to stay behind till I come'. This disciple is the one who vouches for these things and has written them down, and we know that his testimony is true. There were many other things that Jesus did; if all were written down, the world itself, I suppose, would not hold all the books that would have to be written.

CHRIST THE LORD One of our most frequent and intense temptations is to try and control other people's lives. Like Peter in his relationship with John, we often let our laudable affection and interest in others override our humility. We cannot control other people's lives. Only Christ is Lord; only Christ governs hearts. The only heart we can govern is our own. Our task in life is to gradually train our own wild, rebellious hearts to run freely and fruitfully under the guidance of the Lord. That is more than enough to keep us busy. When it comes to other people, the most we can do is love them – but even that may not change them. Loving means treating them with respect, being attentive to their needs, seeking ways to make them happy, forgiving them without limit, refraining from judging and criticizing them, praying for them sincerely and continually, and encouraging them to pursue goodness by creating an environment where goodness is easier to pursue than selfishness – both by the power of our own example of seeking to follow Christ before all else and also, when the time is right, by our words. We can do no more. Only God can touch them more deeply.

Our relationships with others constitute one of the most difficult arenas in which to let the Lord be Lord. By not relinquishing our sense of control in this area, we heap huge quantities of fruitless frustration and needless suffering onto our already overburdened souls. By releasing this illusion of control, we find greater interior peace, finally get out of God's way, and please the heart of Christ immensely, because it shows that we trust him with what matters most – the ones we love. Every Christian should always keep these words of Jesus, with which St John concludes his Gospel, on the screensaver of their mind: "If I want him to stay behind till I come, what does it matter to you? You are to follow me."

CHRIST THE TEACHER This after-breakfast conversation between Peter and Jesus is a curious one. Peter had betrayed Jesus verbally three times the night before Good Friday. He is sorry for his infidelity, as he has shown clearly by his eagerness to be near the Lord during his post-resurrection appearances. Even so, Jesus gives him a chance to reverse his betrayals by verbally professing his love. Jesus wanted to give him this opportunity. Even though it makes Peter uncomfortable, Jesus knows that he needs it. The same dynamic is at work in the sacrament of confession. When we enter the confessional, we are already sorry for our sins (otherwise we wouldn't go), but Jesus knows that we need to express this in words to his chosen representative. Human beings are like that. We are not angels, who are pure spirits; we are incarnate spirits. Through all the sacraments, Jesus continues to come to us in the very same way he came to Peter on that cool spring morning at the shore of Lake Tiberias, where he served him a meal and then spoke with him heart-to-heart.

Another lesson is at work in this exchange, however. Peter may have been doubting whether after his failure he was still worthy of the mission Jesus had entrusted to him. He was called to be the visible head of the Church, the instrument of Church unity – a mission that Peter's successors, the popes, would continue to carry on until Christ's return in glory. In this conversation, Jesus reinstates Peter in this critical role. He commands him three times (just to make sure Peter won't have any doubts): "Feed my sheep." The context of this renewed commission, however, reinforces the lesson Peter had learned on Good Friday. The key to Peter's ability to resume his role and fulfill his mission will not be his natural capacities, however notable and apt they may be. Rather, what will enable him to stay faithful and succeed in his God-given task is his personal union with Jesus, his love for and dependence on Christ. "Peter, do you love me?" Jesus asks him, and on the heels of his profession of love, he commands him to lead the Church.

We all fall, as Peter did, and we all are subsequently approached by the Lord, who wishes to reinstate us in our place in the Church, to recommission us in our vocation. Christ's grace and our response of love, feeble and inconstant thought it may be, are more than sufficient for such a reinstatement and recommission – they are more than sufficient for everlasting success. We simply have to renew that response of love in prayer and then live it out by obeying his will.

CHRIST THE FRIEND "Follow me" are the last words that Christ speaks to Peter. How would he have said them? Would the tone have been harsh, commanding, military? Perhaps. But maybe it was warm, inviting, and excited. "Follow me, Peter! I have great things in store for you! Stick by my side; trust me; do whatever I ask of you, and you will come to share in my glory." The heart of Christ is full of hopes for each of us. First among them is his hope that we will stay close to him even if he leads us down difficult paths, which he will. Peter and all the other apostles except for John followed Christ down the path of martyrdom; every Christian must be led by the Lord "where we would rather not go" in one form or another. Otherwise, how could we prove our friendship, our loyalty, and our love? That's what Jesus wants – our friendship. This is the only reason he came to "dwell among us" – to be able to offer his friendship and ask for ours in return. And he asks for it every day by speaking those same words deep within our hearts in myriad ways, ways that only each one of us can hear, if we keep on listening: "Follow me."

John: We didn't see him again until the day he ascended into heaven, but we didn't need to. He had shown us everything. He had shown us that nothing we would ever do could lessen his love for us or increase it. He had shown us that he knew us through and through, and still he loved us, wanted to walk by our sides, and entrusted his Kingdom into our care.

Many times later in life I cast my nets and came up with nothing. Many times I told people about the Lord only to have them smirk and then belittle me. I was arrested, just as he had predicted. I was tortured and exiled because I refused to stop believing in his love and truth. Yes, there were many nights without a single catch. But there were also many mornings like that one on Lake Tiberias. He surprised me time and time again. Things I said or did without even thinking became occasions of conversion, moments of inspiration for people I didn't even know. Cities we visited almost by mistake became centers of thriving Christian communities – full nets. We made our plans and did our best, and always the Lord showed that his plans were bigger and that his grace would multiply our efforts. The longer I lived, the more confident I became in the power of his grace. He was always one step ahead of us, eager to show us his love. How I wish I could tell all his followers to simply trust him! He is the Lord and he is your Friend – why do you fear? Why do you hesitate? Why do you fret? Courage! Be brave, because you bear his name. Be patient, because the morning is coming. He is with you. He is calling to you from the shore of eternity, telling you to cast out your nets, preparing to welcome you home.

CHRIST IN MY LIFE You are the Lord. Everyone I love, everyone I care about, everyone I am afraid of – they are all under your Lordship. Nothing they do escapes your gaze, your justice, or your mercy. You are more interested in their salvation and happiness than I could ever be. O Lord! Grant me the peace that comes from trusting in you. You went to the cross to show that you deserve unshakable confidence…

You know everything Lord, so you know that I love you, even though I have failed you so many times, Lord. I get so wrapped up in secondary things. I go through my day and compromise my commitments, letting myself get swept into the self-seeking ways of the world. But you never fail to search me out, to feed me with your Word and your Eucharist. You are always faithful. Your grace is always there. Renew me again now, Lord, and accept my renewed profession of love…

If I try to imagine a more marvelous, wonderful, astonishing plan than the one you have given to my life, I can't. You, Creator, Redeemer, the all-powerful, all-knowing, all-loving God, have come into the mundane circumstances of my life, called out my name, and invited me to be your companion and your ambassador. And even that wasn't enough – you have even become my brother. Thank you, Lord…

QUESTIONS FOR SMALL GROUP DISCUSSION

1. What struck you most in this passage? What did you notice that you hadn't noticed before?

2. Why do you think John got up and followed Peter and Jesus while they were having their talk? Why do you think Peter asked about John's future? Why didn't Jesus give him an answer?

3. What do you think are some of the many things that Jesus did that were never recorded?

4. The first time Jesus asked Peter if he loved him "more than these others do." The second and third time he just asked him whether he loved him. Why the change?

Cf. Catechism of the Catholic Church, 1423-1433 on the sacrament of confession and the nature of ongoing conversion; 874-896 on the hierarchical constitution of the Church; 813-822 on the unity of the Church; 2015 on the necessity of the cross for spiritual growth

INDEX 1

UNITS LINKED TO PARTICULAR POINTS OF SPIRITUAL WORK

Note: Many units appear under more than one category.

EUCHARIST: 46, 47, 50, 67, 80, 82, 92, 109, 113, 114, 118, 139, 150, 155, 172, 173, 180, 210, 227, 236, 244, 255, 256, 257, 258, 259, 277, 284, 285, 298

FORGIVENESS/MERCY/REPENTANCE/CONFESSION: 1, 6, 16, 19, 22, 25, 26, 28, 38, 40, 49, 50, 57, 58, 61, 65, 66, 82, 85, 86, 88, 99, 100, 109, 116, 130, 131, 139, 142, 143, 166, 170, 171, 173, 175, 187, 198, 204, 205, 210, 213, 216, 229, 233, 241, 261, 263, 280, 294, 302, 303

HUMAN RESPECT/VANITY: 8, 13, 19, 22, 29, 31, 32, 34, 36, 42, 45, 53, 61, 62, 71, 72, 73, 78, 85, 87, 94, 95, 102, 110, 111, 112, 115, 123, 127, 130, 134, 144, 161, 163, 168, 169, 171, 175, 179, 180, 181, 188, 192, 193, 197, 201, 203, 204, 207, 213, 215, 221, 223, 224, 230, 231, 242, 245, 248, 250, 251, 254, 260, 263, 267, 276, 294, 295, 296, 298

HUMILITY/OBEDIENCE: 2, 4, 5, 6, 7, 8, 10, 11, 14, 16, 17, 19, 23, 25, 26, 27, 28, 29, 31, 36, 37, 38, 40, 41, 43, 45, 48, 49, 51, 54, 56, 58, 59, 60, 62, 65, 66, 67, 68, 70, 71, 72, 73, 78, 81, 83, 84, 86, 87, 88, 91, 93, 94, 95, 98, 99, 104, 105, 106, 108, 109, 115, 116, 119, 120, 121, 122, 123, 127, 130, 137, 138, 140, 141, 142, 144, 145, 147, 149, 151, 152, 153, 154, 157, 158, 159, 160, 161, 163, 165, 167, 169, 171, 172, 174, 175, 176, 177, 179, 180, 181, 183, 184, 186, 190, 191, 192, 196, 198, 200, 201, 203, 207, 209, 210, 211, 213, 214, 217, 218, 220, 226, 227, 228, 230, 231, 234, 240, 242, 243, 244, 246, 248, 251, 252, 253, 254, 255, 257, 259, 261, 265, 266, 267, 270, 272, 276, 277, 278, 279, 280, 282, 283, 285, 294, 295, 298, 302

LOVE FOR THE CHURCH AND THE POPE: 9, 10, 12, 30, 31, 43, 44, 46, 47, 52, 55, 57, 63, 64, 66, 74, 75, 81, 85, 87, 92, 96, 103, 109, 117, 118, 119, 125, 139, 148, 149, 150, 157, 162, 168, 185, 186, 187, 196, 198, 227, 228, 238, 239, 240, 242, 243, 245, 256, 264, 268, 269, 270, 271, 272, 285, 288, 290, 291, 292, 293, 297, 298, 299, 301, 303

MARY: 1, 2, 3, 4, 5, 41, 45, 84, 85, 86, 87, 88, 89, 91, 104, 110, 145, 146, 151, 152, 154, 155, 156, 157, 173, 177, 191, 230, 232, 234, 235, 244, 281, 283, 284, 286, 287, 288, 289, 290, 295, 297, 298

PATIENCE/FORTITUDE/PERSEVERANCE: 4, 11, 21, 23, 43, 45, 75, 76, 77, 80, 84, 85, 87, 88, 105, 106, 110, 111, 112, 119, 125, 31, 133, 135, 137, 140, 141, 144, 147, 149, 150, 161, 169, 171, 179, 181, 182, 183, 184, 185, 189, 193, 196, 198, 199, 203, 207, 211, 212, 217, 219, 224, 225, 230, 232, 233, 250, 251, 269, 275, 77, 287, 289, 293, 294, 300

POVERTY/DETACHMENT: 2, 9, 11, 14, 16, 17, 18, 42, 44, 56, 60, 66, 67, 76, 81, 86, 93, 95, 100, 105, 108, 120, 123, 126, 134, 135, 136, 137, 151, 154, 155, 156, 161, 167, 170, 184, 185, 186, 187, 194, 195, 196, 202, 203, 206, 207, 208, 214, 216, 220, 223, 232, 246, 259, 276, 279

PRAYER: 4, 9, 14, 15, 16, 20, 22, 23, 38, 46, 47, 49, 51, 54, 57, 81, 83, 90, 97, 98, 99, 105, 109, 114, 116, 117, 119, 121, 122, 128, 129, 140, 150, 152, 153, 154, 155, 161, 164, 165, 166, 176, 177, 182, 185, 188, 189, 210, 211, 212, 225, 228, 229, 243, 244, 245, 249, 260, 262, 273, 274, 276, 277, 283, 285, 286, 288, 289, 290, 291, 292, 297, 299, 300, 303

PURITY OF INTENTION/SPIRITUAL SIMPLICITY: 3, 6, 8, 11, 15, 17, 18, 19, 20, 21, 33, 34, 39, 45, 48, 61, 66, 71, 72, 76, 89, 101, 102, 104, 105, 110, 112, 115, 123, 127, 129, 130, 131, 134, 149, 152, 161, 162, 166, 169, 175, 186, 187, 188, 192, 195, 196, 201, 205, 207, 209, 221, 223, 231, 242, 245, 248, 250, 254, 260, 266, 267, 279, 294, 300, 302

PURITY/CHASTITY: 11, 13, 42, 59, 112, 115, 125, 132, 207, 222, 249, 263

SIN/TEMPTATION: 4, 8, 22, 24, 40, 66, 71, 84, 90, 93, 96, 98, 99, 124, 131, 137, 138, 142, 143, 144, 145, 158, 161, 166, 168, 171, 174, 175, 187, 190, 192, 198, 207, 208, 210, 213, 214, 217, 219, 225, 226, 229, 230, 232, 233, 239, 253, 259, 263, 265, 266, 267, 269, 270, 272, 276, 280, 281, 285, 290, 294, 295, 296

SINCERITY/HYPOCRISY/CONSCIENCE: 13, 15, 16, 19, 21, 40, 48, 51, 59, 61, 64, 65, 68, 71, 72, 73, 81, 84, 99, 100, 101, 102, 104, 112, 114, 115, 119, 130, 131, 134, 141, 142, 144, 166, 168, 187, 191, 192, 193, 199, 204, 207, 213, 219, 220, 221, 222, 223, 226, 231, 242, 245, 252, 261, 267, 269, 276

SUFFERING/SACRIFICE: 5, 8, 15, 18, 20, 22, 23, 24, 28, 32, 33, 34, 45, 49, 53, 55, 56, 64, 74, 75, 80, 82, 83, 84, 85, 87, 88, 89, 90, 96, 97, 98, 99, 100, 101, 105, 107, 108, 109, 113, 116, 117, 120, 121, 122, 124, 125, 126, 128, 135, 136, 137, 140, 141, 142, 144, 145, 147, 150, 156, 166, 167, 169, 173, 174, 177, 179, 181, 183, 184, 190, 197, 198, 199, 203, 211, 214, 215, 224, 225, 228, 229, 230, 232, 233, 236, 251, 260, 268, 269, 271, 273, 274, 275, 278, 285, 287, 288, 289, 291, 293, 294, 295, 296, 297, 298

VOCATION: 2, 8, 10, 11, 12, 17, 18, 23, 26, 30, 31, 36, 41, 43, 44, 45, 46, 53, 59, 60, 62, 67, 68, 78, 79, 91, 92, 94, 95, 97, 100, 103, 105, 108, 110, 111, 113, 120, 123, 125, 126, 131, 132, 133, 136, 139, 141, 143, 151, 156, 157, 158, 162, 163, 164, 165, 167, 168, 170, 174, 176, 177, 180, 181, 182, 183, 184, 185, 186, 187, 188, 189, 191, 193, 195, 196, 197, 200, 202, 203, 208, 209, 214, 219, 220, 224, 231, 232, 233, 235, 236, 237, 240, 241, 242, 243, 246, 250, 255, 258, 259, 260, 262, 264, 270, 278, 280, 281, 282, 285, 286, 287, 288, 291, 292, 295, 301, 302, 303

INDEX 2

UNITS CORRELATED TO THE LITURGICAL CALENDAR

Note: Since the meditation units were not designed specifically for the liturgy, the Gospel passages do not coincide perfectly. Some Gospel passages included in The Better Part never appear in the liturgy. In other cases, the passages used for one meditation unit may be spread over more than one liturgical day, or one liturgical reading may overlap more than one meditation unity.

The capital letters "A B C" refer to the three-year cycle of liturgical readings.

ADVENT

ADVENT	SUN			MON	TUE	WED	THU	FRI	SAT
	A	B	C						
ADVENT I	76	137	225	22	186	50	21	29	30
ADVENT II	6	93	158	166	56	37	36	36	54
ADVENT III	35	240	159	64	65	174	174	254	
ADVENT IV	1	151	152						
WEEKDAYS 17-24 Dec.	DEC 17 unit: 1			18 2	19 150	20 151	21-22 152	23-24 153	

CHRISTMAS

CHRISTMAS	VIGIL MASS ABC: 1	MIDNIGHT MASS ABC: 76	MASS AT DAWN ABC: 155	DAYTIME MASS ABC: 239	HOLY FMY A: 5; B: 156 C: 157	EPIPHANY (JAN 6 OR 2ND SUN AFTER XMAS) ABC: 3-4
	DEC 26 unit: 31	27 299	28 5	29-30 156		31 239
	JAN 1 (Mary Mother of God) ABC: 155			JAN 2: 240	JAN 3: 241	JAN 4: 242 JAN 5: 243
WEEKDAYS AFTER CHRISTMAS	JAN 6 (When Epiphany is celebrated on 2ND Sun. after Christmas): 94	JAN 7 (or Mon. after Epiphany): 9	JAN 8 (or Tues. after Epiphany): 113	JAN 9 (or Wed. after Epiphany): 114	JAN 10 (or Thu. after Epiphany): 162	JAN 11 (or Fri after Epiphany): 166 OR JAN. 12 (or Sat. after Epiphany): 248

LENT

LENT	SUN			MON	TUE	WED	THU	FRI	SAT
	A	B	C			Ash Wed 15	After A.W. 181	After A.W. 27	After A.W. 167
LENT I	8	94-5	161	79	16	191	20	13	14
LENT II	54	121	182	170	71	62	208	66	204-5
LENT III	249	245	198	163	58	13	190	133	213
LENT IV	268-9	246	204-5	251	252	253	254	260-1	262
LENT V	273-4	278	263	263	265	266	267	272	275
PALM SUN.	Palm Sunday (Procession) 63 129 218			Palm Sunday - Mass (Reading of the Passion): A: 81-90 B: 138-146 C: 226-234					
HOLY WK.	M: 276	T: 281		W: 81-2	Holy Th. (Last Supper Mass) ABC: 280	Good Friday ABC: 293-298		Holy Sat. (Easter Vigil) A B C 91 147 235	

EASTER

EASTER	SUN			MON	TUE	WED	THU	FRI	SAT
	A	B	C						
EASTER I	ABC: 299 (or 236)			90-91	300	236	248	302	
EASTER II	ABC: 301			246	246	247	248	255	256
EASTER III	236	236	302-3	256	256	257	257	258	259
EASTER IV	270	271	272	A: 271 B-C: 270	272	279	280	282	283
EASTER V	282	285	281	284	284	285	286	286	286-7
EASTER VI	283	286	284	287	288	288	289	289	289
ASCENSION	92	148	238						
EASTER VII	290	291	292	289	290	291	292	303	303
PENTECOST	ABC: 301								

ORDINARY TIME

ORDINARY TIME	SUN			MON	TUE	WED	THU	FRI	SAT
	A	B	C						
OT 1 (Baptism of Jesus)	7	94	159-60	95	96	97	98	99	100
OT 2	241	242	244	101	102	102	103	103	104
OT 3	9	95	149-50	104	104	105	106	106	107
OT 4	11	96	163	108	109	110	111	112	113
OT 5	12	97	165	114	115	115	116	117	118
OT 6	13	98	169	119	119	119	120	120	121
OT 7	14	99	170	122	123	124	124	125	125
OT 8	18	101	171	126	126	127	128	130	131
OT 9	21	102	172	131	132	132	133	133	134
TRINITY SUNDAY	247	92	288						
CORPUS CHRISTI	258	139	180						
SACRED HEART	37	298	204						
IMMACULATE HEART	155-157								
OT 10	26	104	173	11	12	13	13	13	13
OT 11	30	106	175	14	14	15	16	17	18
OT 12	33	107	181	19	20	21	21	22	22
OT 13	34	109	184	23	23	24	25	26	27
OT 14	37	110	185	28	28-9	30	31	32	33
OT 15	42	111	187	34	36	37	37	38	39
OT 16	43	113	188	41	41	42	42	42	43
OT 17	44	255	170	43	43	44	44	45	45
OT 18	46	256	194	46	47	49	52-3	53	55
OT 19	47	257	196	55	56	57	58-9	59	59
OT 20	49	258	197	60	60	61	67	70	71
OT 21	52	259	200	72	72	72	76	77	78
OT 22	53	115	201	162	164	164	165	167	168
OT 23	57	117	203	168	168-9	169	171	171	171
OT 24	58	120	204-5	172	173	174	175	176	176
OT 25	61	123	206	177	177	180	180	181	183
OT 26	65	124	208	183	184	184	185	186	186
OT 27	66	125	209	187	188	189	189	190	191

OT 28	67	126	210	191	192	192	192	193	193
OT 29	68	127	212	194	196	196	197	197	198
OT 30	70	128	213	199	199	200	200	201	201
OT 31	71	133	216	201	202	203	204	206	206-7
OT 32	77	134	222	209	209	210	211	211	212
OT 33	78	136	224	215	216	217-8	219	219	222
CHRIST THE KING (OT 34)	79	295	233	223	223-4	224	224-5	225	225

On the following Solemnities (S) and Feast Days (F), the Gospel readings proper to the celebration take precedence over normal weekday Gospel readings.

OTHER FEASTS & SOLEMNITIES

DATE	NAME	MEDITATION UNIT #
2 FEB	Presentation of the Lord (F)	156
22 FEB	Chair of St Peter, Apostle (F)	52
19 MAR	St Joseph, Husband of Mary (S)	1-2 or 157
25 MAR	Annunciation (S)	151
25 APR	St Mark, Evangelist (F)	148
3 MAY	Sts Philip & James, Apostles (F)	282-283
14 MAY	St Matthias, Apostle (F)	286
31 MAY	Visitation (F)	152
24 JUN	Birth of John the Baptist (S)	Vigil: 150; Day: 153
29 JUN	Sts Peter and Paul, Apostles (S)	Vigil: 303; Day: 52
3 JUL	St Thomas, Apostle (F)	301
25 JUL	St James, Apostle (F)	62
6 AUG	Transfiguration (F)	A: 54 B: 121 C: 182
10 AUG	St Lawrence (F)	278
15 AUG	Assumption (S)	Vigil: 191; Day: 152
24 AUG	St Bartholomew (F))	243
8 SEP	Birth of Mary (F)	1-2
14 SEP	Triumph of the Cross (F)	246-247
21 SEP	St Matthew, Apostle (F)	26
18 OCT	Luke, Evangelist (F)	185
28 OCT	Sts Simon &Jude, Apostles (F)	168
1 NOV	All Saints (S)	11
2 NOV	All Souls (S)	Mass1: 257; Mass2: 274; Mass3: 282
9 NOV	Dedication of St John Lateran Basilica (F)	249
30 NOV	St Andrew, Apostle (F)	10
8 DEC	Immaculate Conception (S)	151

For 17-31 DEC, see "Christmas" above

APPENDIX

BOOKS ON PRAYER AND THE SPIRITUAL LIFE

This Tremendous Lover, Eugene Boylan

The Secrets of the Interior Life, Luis Martinez

Difficulties in Mental Prayer, Eugene Boylan

Talking with God, Francois Fenelon

How to Pray Always, Raoul Plus

Spiritual Combat, Lorenzo Scupoli

Weeds among the Wheat, Thomas H Green, SJ

When the Well Runs Dry, Thomas H Green, SJ

Opening to God, Thomas H Green, SJ

A Vacation with the Lord, Thomas H Green, SJ

Darkness in the Marketplace, Thomas H Green, SJ

Prayer and Common Sense, Thomas H Green, SJ

Spiritual Progress, Thomas D. Williams, LC

INDEX OF MOSAICS

FROM THE BASILICA OF ST. PAUL OUTSIDE THE WALLS, ROME

AN ANGEL stands on the earth and writes with a golden sky in the background behind its wings. At its feet is an open book. This is the traditional symbol for St Matthew, author of the first Gospel. Matthew begins his Gospel with the genealogy of Jesus, which the humanized figure of the angel calls to mind. Throughout his Gospel he emphasizes Christ's fulfillment of the Old Testament prophecies, many of which were revealed by angels. (Unit 1)

THE RICHLY decorated imperial throne is empty except for the cross and some of the instruments of Christ's Passion: the crown of thorns, the three nails used to crucify him, the chalice from the Last Supper, and a royal purple cloak. The throne is empty because we are still waiting Christ's second coming, when he will take his place on the Judgment Seat. Until then, he rules the universe through the invincible power of his goodness and mercy, which was revealed through his suffering on behalf of sinners. (Units 89, 145, 234, 298)

THE RICHLY adorned marble altar stands firmly at the top of three short steps. It is draped with a royal blue and gold altar cloth. A cross rests on top of it, and the Book of the Gospels leans against the cross. Every altar is the meeting place between God and man: God descends (the cross, the sacrament of Christ's passion in the Eucharist, the revelation contained in the Scriptures), and we ascend, through the priest, who climbs the steps, celebrates the sacraments through which we worship and petition God, and proclaims God's Word in contemporary language. (Units 139, 280)

TWO DEER have come to drink from the water of four streams flowing from a rock upon which the Cross is planted. They gaze up at the cross. The deer, which run and jump through the woods so deftly, symbolize the thirsty soul. The four streams are the Gospels, which satisfy the yearning soul by revealing God's love in Christ, manifested most powerfully in his sacrifice on the rock of Calvary. They also call to mind God's Old Testament miracle of bringing water out of the rock during Israel's exodus in the desert. They also embody the four rivers of paradise as described in the book of Revelation, while the number four signifies universality by its correlation to the four points of the compass. (Units 188, 249)

A LION stands on a plateau high above the sea. An open book leans against the base of the plateau. This is the traditional image representing St Mark, whose Gospel begins with John the Baptist crying out in the wilderness and Christ experiencing temptation in the wilderness, where he was "with the wild beasts" (Mk 1:13). Mark's Gospel also emphasizes the theology of Christ's Kingdom, and in ancient times the lion was considered the king of beasts. The plateau above the ocean is the Christian faith, communicated through the Gospels, which raises us out of the chaos of the fallen world and gives strength and stability to our lives. (Unit 93)

AN EAGLE, perched on a rock in the sea, looks up into the sun. An open book leans against the rock. The eagle is the traditional symbol for St John the Evangelist. His Gospel soars to unique theological heights. One of the great themes of his Gospel is Christ as the Light of the World – it is said that eagles are the only birds that can look unblinkingly at the sun, the source of light. The rock is Christ. The ocean is often a symbol of the sinful world. We live in this fallen world, but by standing firmly on Christ we are able to see into the heavens. (Unit 239)

A SHIP in full sail plows the waters of the sea, surrounded on both sides by huge sea monsters. The ship is a traditional image of the Church, the Bark of Peter. The wind filling the sails and propelling the ship to the shore of heaven is the Holy Spirit. The sea symbolizes the chaos of this fallen world, and the monsters are the powers of evil that strain tirelessly but unavailingly to shipwreck the Church. Those same monsters, however, also symbolize the undying hope of the Resurrection, since it was out of the mouth of a great fish that the prophet Jonah was miraculously restored after three days. (Units 52, 148 289)

TWO BRILLIANTLY colored peacocks, perched on large rocks, drink from a fountain of fresh water that rises out of the salty sea and is topped with a cross. The rocks are the Church, founded on the rock of Peter. The peacock is the Christian, who looks just like everyone else on the outside, but underneath the ordinary appearances contains the life of grace, which beautifies the soul and which will spread forth its magnificence at the Resurrection. The cross is Christ, who through his sacrifice on Calvary has erected a purifying fountain in the midst of the sinful world: the sacraments. (Units 21, 175)

A BULL stands firmly on a plateau above the ocean. An open book leans against the foot of the plateau. This is the traditional symbol for St Luke, since his Gospel begins with Zechariah offering sacrifice in the Temple, and the bull is one of the common sacrificial animals. Throughout his Gospel, St Luke emphasizes Christ's mercy and forgiveness, his ministry of reconciling sinners with God. Such reconciliation is the heart of the Christian priesthood, also related in a special way to ceremonial sacrifice. The plateau above the ocean is the Christian faith, which raises us out of the chaos of the fallen world and gives strength and stability to our lives. (Unit 149)

THE CROSS, decorated with precious jewels that are linked together by a vine, surmounts the globe of the world. Christ's redeeming death is our precious jewel, our most valuable possession, since it alone gives us true hope. We possess it through the sacraments, which the Church, like a growing vine, has brought to all corners of the earth. Christ guides and governs human history, although the progress of his Kingdom is often hidden behind the appearances of suffering and injustice – the cross. We share in his victory and his everlasting Kingdom by following him along the way of the cross. The ancient prayer rings true: "Hail, O Cross, our only hope!" (Units 34, 120, 181, 285)